C.I.P.A. GUIDE TO THE PATENTS ACTS

AUSTRALIA
The Law Book Company Ltd.
Sydney : Melbourne : Brisbane : Perth

CANADA
The Carswell Company Ltd.
Toronto : Calgary : Vancouver : Ottawa

INDIA
N. M. Tripathi Private Ltd.
Bombay
and
Eastern Law House Private Ltd.
Calcutta and Delhi

M.P.P. House
Bangalore

ISRAEL
Steimatzky's Agency Ltd.
Jerusalem : Tel Aviv : Haifa

PAKISTAN
Pakistan Law House
Karachi

C.I.P.A. GUIDE TO THE PATENTS ACTS

TEXTS, COMMENTARY AND

NOTES ON PRACTICE

THIRD EDITION

THE CHARTERED INSTITUTE OF PATENT AGENTS

LONDON
SWEET & MAXWELL
1990

First Edition 1980
Second Edition 1984
Third Edition 1990

Published by
Sweet & Maxwell Ltd.
of South Quay Plaza, 183 Marsh Wall, London E14 9FT
Computerset by Promenade Graphics Ltd., Cheltenham
Printed and bound in Great Britain by Hartnolls Ltd, Bodmin

British Library Cataloguing in Publication Data
C.I.P.A. guide to the Patents Acts.—3rd ed.
1. Great Britain, Patents. Law
I. Chartered Institute of Patent Agents
344.1064'86
ISBN 0–421–39760–8

FOREWORD

It is a privilege to be able to welcome this new edition of the C.I.P.A. Guide, now entitled "The C.I.P.A. Guide to the Patents Acts".

Its origins were modest. When the Patents Act 1949 came into force, a commentary on it was published by The Chartered Institute of Patent Agents intended primarily to draw attention to the changes in the law made by the legislation. The success of that work led to something more ambitious: an entirely rewritten practical reference guide, through the sections of the Act and the Rules made thereunder, to patent law and practice. It was produced by a team of Fellows of the Institute (under the general direction of its Council). When the Patents Act 1977 came into operation, the present Guide to it and the still relevant earlier law was produced.

A detailed commentary on sections and rules was not seen originally as competing in any way with the existing legal texts. Yet the book has proved to be extremely popular not only with patent agents but also with lawyers and others. Whilst the major legal texts are indispensable for a broader, systematic analysis of the law, patent practitioners and others who are familiar with the underlying general legal principles of patent law will find this commentary on the statutory provisions and rules of greater practical relevance for many day to day matters. Features of the book which make it so useful include full discussion of the case law, excellent cross-referencing, wide-ranging references to periodical literature (including articles in the CIPA Journal which, sadly, are not often cited in the more traditional texts), clarity of exposition, and also references to European and United Kingdom Patent Office and other unreported decisions found only in the Science Reference and Information Service of the British Library.

Trainee patent agents embarking upon the Certificate course in Intellectual Property Law at Queen Mary College are required to have the Guide constantly with them. As they begin, so will they continue.

The C.I.P.A. Guide has become known as "the Black Book", perhaps to distinguish it from the earlier "Red" and "Blue" commentaries produced by the Chartered Institute on the 1949 Act. Whatever the colour of the skin, the body remains in excellent condition. The Chartered Institute of Patent Agents, and particularly those of its Members responsible for writing this work, are to be congratulated on their initiative, skill and industry. It is an important working tool for practitioners, academics and students. Although it is right up to date, incorporating the amendments introduced into the Patents Act 1977 by the Copyright, Designs and Patents Act 1988, patent law and practice is never static: the pace of development in national, European and international patent law will ensure that there will be many supplements and editions to come.

Gerald Dworkin

Herchel Smith Professor of Intellectual Property Law,
Centre for Commercial Law Studies,
Queen Mary College,
University of London.

PREFACE

THE First and Second Editions of this work were respectively published in 1980 and 1984 under the title *C.I.P.A. Guide to the Patents Act 1977*. The object has been to provide a detailed commentary by Members of the Chartered Institute of Patent Agents on that Act. As such these editions continued, and replaced, the similar commentaries which the Chartered Institute had previously published on the Patents Act 1949 under the title "Patent Law of the United Kingdom", the "Blue Book". The practice of issuing cumulative annual supplements has continued, the Fifth (and final) Supplement of the Second Edition of the C.I.P.A. Guide being published in March 1988. The origins and administration of the "Black Book" and of other publications prepared by The Chartered Institute of Patent Agents were described in detail in J. H. Dunlop's Presidential Address, (1982–83) 12 CIPA 99.

This Third Edition has been renamed as the *C.I.P.A. Guide to the Patents Acts*, though its distinctive black cover has been retained so that the book may continue to be familiarly known, and hopefully with affection, as "the Black Book". This change of title is in recognition that, while the principal statute governing the patent law of the United Kingdom remains the Patents Act 1977 ("the 1977 Act"), this Act has now been extensively amended, particularly by the Copyright, Designs and Patents Act 1988 ("the 1988 Act"), and also that the Patents Act 1949 ("the 1949 Act") continues to have considerable effect in relation to "existing patents", that is those dated prior to June 1, 1978, an effect which will continue at least until the last of these patents expires in 1998.

The basic format of the book remains largely unchanged from that of its previous editions. Thus, after an *Introduction* (to be found at p. lxxxvii) which describes the historical evolution of the patent law of the United Kingdom, the individual sections of the 1977 Act are each sequentially reprinted (as amended, if necessary), followed by: a reprinting of any current Patents Rule which predominantly applies to that section; a list of books and articles applicable to the section in question; and then detailed commentaries on the law and practice thereunder. One of the difficulties encountered when reading a section of the 1977 Act is to know whether there are other sections in the Act which may affect the meaning or scope of the section being read or the practice in relation thereto. To help overcome this difficulty, extensive cross-referencing to other sections and particular portions of the commentaries and Practice comments thereon has been used.

In this Edition, all deleted provisions of the 1977 Act are reprinted in italics within brackets, with new wording therein being shown in bold type. The new or prospective provisions of patent law introduced by specific sec-

vii

tions of the 1988 Act are reprinted following the italicised printing of the deleted sections of the 1977 Act which they replace. An innovation in this edition is to provide "para." numbers for the individual portions of the commentaries and to use these for cross-reference and index purposes.

A feature of the book continues to be the many references to decisions not, or not as yet, published in the specialist law reports, these being the official "Reports of Patent Cases" ("the RPC") and the Fleet Street Reports ("the FSR"), but available because of their deposit in the Science Reference and Information Service of the British Library at 25 Southampton Buildings, London WC1 and there filed in an "O/. . ." series and a "C/. . ." series, for decisions given in the Patent Office in the name of the Comptroller and decisions of the courts, respectively.

As previously, there are detailed Tables of Cases, Statutes, Statutory Instruments and Conventions cited in the text, together with a *Table of Amendments to the Patents Act 1977*, listing the legislation which has amended the 1977 Act from its original form.

The main commentary on the 1977 Act is followed (at para. 139.01) by a listing of the current Patents Rules and a table indicating their location in the preceding text and then by a number of Appendices. Thus, Appendix A follows the main text with a similar reprinting of the still effective sections of the 1949 Act and of the Patents Rules 1968 which remain applicable thereto, together with commentary thereon. Appendix B lists some provisions from former patent statutes which still have some effect. Then, Appendix C not only reprints the main provisions of the Treaty of Rome ("the TR") applicable to the existence and exercise of patent rights, but (newly) provides a basic commentary on these provisions; and this is followed (in Appendix D) by a new commentary on the EEC Block Exemption Regulations applicable to the licensing of intellectual property rights. Appendix E reprints relevant Rules of the Supreme Court, recognising that many patent agents may not have ready access to the full commentary thereon contained in The Supreme Court Practice ("the White Book"): here a wider selection of these Rules of Court has been reprinted than in the Second Edition. Provision is then made (in Appendices F and G) for reprinting of the Register of Patent Agents Rules and of the Examination Regulations for entry thereto but, as new versions of these will be required when the statutory changes made by the 1988 Act are brought into effect, this material is left to be presented in a Supplement.

As with the previous Editions, the Patents (Fees) Rules which specify the fees payable under the Patents Rules have not been reproduced because it is felt that the amounts of such fees are too transitory, but the fees payable from mid-1989 are set out in para. 144.02 as an indication of relative sizes of the various fees, see the note thereon at para. 144.01. However, the Forms which constitute Schedule 2 to the Patents Rules 1982 (as amended) are reprinted at paras. 141.01–141.58.

While decisions of the Appeal Boards of the European Patent Office ("the EPO") are referred to whenever it is thought that such might have a persuasive, or illustrative, effect on the interpretation of the Patents Acts and the Rules made thereunder, it is not the purpose of the present book to provide a detailed commentary on the European Patent Conventions, and practice thereunder. For such, the *European Patents Handbook ("EPH")* (also prepared by the Chartered Institute of Patent Agents, though published by Longman) should be consulted. Likewise, the present book does not provide a detailed commentary on the operation of the Patent Co-operation Treaty ("the PCT"), but the commentaries on sections 89, 89A and 89B of the 1977 Act are now of considerable length in order to provide a more detailed commentary on the entry of "international applications" (filed under the PCT) into "the UK national phase" as an alternative mode of seeking the grant of a patent under the 1977 Act commencing from an application filed under the PCT rather than one filed under the 1977 Act.

The *Implementing Regulations to the European Patent Convention*, the *Implementing Regulations to the Patent Cooperation Treaty*, and the *Guidelines for Examination in the European Patent Office*, are each amended from time to time. The up-to-date versions of these can be found in *EPH*.

To reduce the length of the book, and to facilitate its reading, many of the frequently used terms and expressions have been abbreviated in a manner which it is hoped is self-evident, at least once a basic familiarity with the work has been gained. However, a comprehensive *Table of Abbreviations* has been provided at p. lxxxiv.

As previously, the aim in preparing this book has been to provide patent agents, as well as other patent practitioners, with a comprehensive, and thoroughly up-to-date, exposition of United Kingdom patent law and practice. In particular, in this Third Edition, there has been extensive rewriting of the commentaries on: sections 3 (*Inventive step*); 37–43 (*Entitlement disputes and employee inventions*); 46 and 47 (*Licences of right*); 76 (*Amendment*); 89 (*International applications (UK)*); and 102 (*Representation before the Patent Office*).

It had been hoped to include in this book the revisions to the Patents Rules 1982 required to be made consequent on the bringing into force of Schedule 5 to the 1988 Act which will make many detailed changes to the Patents Act 1977. However, only part of that Schedule was made effective from August 1, 1989. Therefore, in order not to delay further publication of this Third Edition, the text of this book was revised to refer to "prospective' amendments to be made by those parts of the 1988 Act not yet effective, leaving the consequent revisions of the Rules to be dealt with in a future Supplement to the present "Main Work". It is hoped to produce such a Supplement shortly after the expected changes to the Rules do, eventually, take place.

Thus, in referring to the present work, the latest Supplement (the contents of which are also arranged under the same "para. numbers") should always be consulted because patent law, like any other branch of law, is continually in a state of flux with decisions issuing constantly both from the courts and from Patent Office hearing officers acting on behalf of, and in the name of, "the Comptroller".

This Third Edition has (like its predecessors) been prepared by a team of members of the Chartered Institute of Patent Agents entirely as a voluntary effort providing to others the benefit of their expertise and experience, or at least their fully considered views on the interpretation of the statutory provisions. The Chartered Institute wishes to take this opportunity of thanking this team which has consisted of: A. W. White (General Editor); J. W. Arthur; R. W. Beckham; J. L. Beton; M. Burnside; T. M. Cook; J. M. Davies; J. H. Dunlop; T. Z. Gold; M. G. Harman; K. Hodkinson; C. Jones; E. A. Kennington; P. L. Kolker; R. P. Lloyd; Monica Marshall; R. M. C. Nott; R. K. Percy; R. C. Petersen; and B. C. Reid. Thanks are also due to I. Inglis, Helen Jones and D. M. Waters for assistance, information and guidance, as well as to various staff of the Patent Office who have kindly responded to queries from time to time and provided assistance in other ways. Her Majesty's Stationery Office is also thanked for granting permission to reproduce the Patents Forms by photographic means. The Chartered Institute also wishes to acknowledge the help and encouragement afforded to them by the editorial staff of their publishers, Sweet & Maxwell Ltd., and by Professor Gerald Dworkin in the Foreword which he has graciously provided.

While care has been taken to avoid errors or omissions, it would be too much to hope that none exist. The Chartered Institute would welcome comments or corrections. These should be sent to the Editor, The C.I.P.A. Guide, The Chartered Institute of Patent Agents, Staple Inn Buildings, High Holborn, London WC1V 7PZ.

PUBLISHERS' NOTE

THE material in this book has been collected up to September 1, 1989, including [1989] RPC No. 16 and FSR, EIPR and CIPA for August 1989, with occasional later material.

In order to keep this work up to date, Supplements will be issued approximately annually. The first Supplement is published with this book, to deal with events during production.

CONTENTS

TABLE OF CASES

(References are to Para. numbers)

xxiii

xlv

TABLE OF CASES

1

TABLE OF STATUTES

References are to Para. numbers
Bold *type indicates a reprinted section*

Note. A subsection is only indexed for para. numbers relating to its section when the subsection number is featured in the para. heading.

lxiii

TABLE OF STATUTORY INSTRUMENTS

References are to Para. numbers
Bold *type indicates a reprinted section*

RULES OF THE SUPREME COURT

References are to Para. numbers
Bold *type indicates a reprinted Rule*

TABLE OF PATENT CONVENTIONS

References are to Para. numbers
Bold *type indicates a reprinted Provision*

EUROPEAN PATENT OFFICE GUIDELINES

References are to Para. numbers

TABLE OF ABBREVIATIONS

a.	Article (of a convention or treaty)
Act or Act [1977]	Patents Act 1977
Act [1949]	Patents Acts 1949–1961
AIIP	Australian Industrial and Intellectual Property
AIPL	Annual of Industrial Property Law
All ER	All England Law Reports
AOJP	Australian Official Journal of Patents
B. & Ald.	Barnewall & Alderson's Law Reports
B. & C.	Barnewall and Cresswell's Law Reports
Beav.	Beavan's Law Reports
Bus. Law Rev.	Business Law Review
CA	Court of Appeal
CB	Common Bench Reports
CCA	Court of Criminal Appeal
CCPA	United States Court of Customs and Patents Appeals
Ch.	Law Reports: Chancery Division
Ch. App.	Chancery Appeal Cases
C.I.P.A.	The Chartered Institute of Patent Agents
CIPA	Journal of the Chartered Institute of Patent Agents
CJJA	Civil Jurisdiction and Judgments Act 1982
CMLR	Common Market Law Reports
COPAC	Common Appeal Court
CPC	Community Patent Convention
CPCa.1	CPC, article 1
ECJ	European Court of Justice (in Luxembourg)
ECR	European Court Reports
EEC	European Economic Community
EIPR	European Intellectual Property Review
ELR	European Law Review
EPB	European Patent Bulletin
EPC	European Patent Convention
EPCa.1	EPC, article 1
EPCr.1	Implementing Regulations to EPC, rule 1
EPH	*European Patents Handbook*
EPI	European Patent Institute (Institute of Professional Representatives before the EPO)
EPO	European Patent Office
EPOAC	EPO Administrative Council
EPSF	*European Patents Source Finder*
E.R.	English Reports

FSR	Fleet Street Law Reports
GRUR	Gewerblicher Rechtsschutz und Urhebberrect
Guidelines	Guidelines for Examination in the EPO
HL	House of Lords
ICR	Industrial Cases Reports
IPB	Intellectual Property in Business
IPBB	Intellectual Property in Business Briefing
IRLR	Industrial Relations Law Reports
IIB	International Institute of Patents, The Hague
IIC	International Review of Industrial Property and Copyright
IPD	Intellectual Property Decisions
JBL	Journal of Business Law
JPOS	Journal of the Patent Office Society
KB	Law Reports: King's Bench Division
LQR	Law Quarterly Review
LR CP	Law Reports: Court of Common Pleas
LR Eq. Cas.	Law Reports: Equity Cases
LR HL	Law Reports: House of Lords
LR RP	Law Reports, Restrictive Practices
L.S. Gaz.	Law Society Gazette
Lloyd's Rep.	Lloyd's Law Reports
MLR	The Modern Law Review
NLJ	New Law Journal
NSWLR	New South Wales Law Reports
NZLR	New Zealand Law Reports
O.J.	Official Journal (Patents)
OJEC	Official Journal of the European Communities
OJEPO	Official Journal of the European Patent Office
Paris Convention	International Convention of the Protection of Industrial Property (1883)
PAT	Patents Appeal Tribunal
PC	Privy Council
PCT	Patent Cooperation Treaty
PCTa.1	PCT, article 1
PCTr.1	Regulations under the PCT, rule 1
PF 1/77	Patents Form No. 1/77 [1982 Rules]
PF No. 1	Patents Form No. 1 [1968 Rules]
Protocol on Recognition	Protocol on Recognition, annexed to EPC
QB	Law Reports: Queen's Bench Division
r.	rule or regulation
r.1 [1968]	Patents Rules 1968, rule 1
RPA	Register of Patent Agents
RPC	Reports of Patent Cases

RSC	Rules of the Supreme Court
Rules	Patents Rules 1982
SCA	Supreme Court Act 1981
S.I.	Statutory Instrument
SJ	Solicitors Journal
SLT	Scots Law Times
SR & O	Statutory Rules & Orders
SRIS	Science Reference and Information Service (of the British Library)
TRa.85	Treaty of Rome, article 85
Trans. Chart. Inst.	Transactions of the Chartered Institute of Patent Agents
UKAEA	United Kingdom Atomic Energy Authority
USPQ	United States Patents Quarterly
WIPO	World Intellectual Property Organisation
WLR	Weekly Law Reports
WPC	Webster's Patent Cases
1949 Act	Patents Acts 1949–1961
1977 Act	Patents Act 1977
1986 Act	Patents, Designs and Marks Act 1986
1988 Act	Copyright, Designs and Patents Act 1988

INTRODUCTION

THE HISTORICAL EVOLUTION OF
THE PATENT LAW OF THE UNITED KINGDOM

THE evolution of the patent law of the United Kingdom extends back over 350 years. Although the Statute of Monopolies of 1623 is usually cited as the earliest statute relating to patents, Letters Patent for inventions were granted well before that date. In the next two centuries following this Statute, while there were apparently changes in the practice with regard to Letters Patent for inventions there was little legislation, and it was not until the second half of the last century that the first major changes were introduced. The most important change was the comprehensive Patents, Designs and Trade Marks Act 1883 (46 & 46 Vict., c. 57) which set up the Patent Office for the reception of applications for Letters Patent and for the processing of such applications to grant.

Since then, the patent law has been modified from time to time to deal with difficulties or obscurities which have arisen in the course of practice or to amend the law in the light of new philosophies. The practice has usually been to institute a government committee to examine the law and to make recommendations, and then to introduce legislation, usually having regard to the committee recommendations. For example, the Fry Committee report was followed by the consolidating Act of 1907, the Sargant Committee report was followed by the Act of 1932, and the Swan Committee report by the consolidating Act of 1949.

Following this general pattern, the Government set up the Banks Committee in 1967, but the terms of reference of this Committee were somewhat different from those of the earlier committees, and extended to a more general consideration of the United Kingdom patent system, particularly in the light of the increasing need for international collaboration in patent matters and especially the intention of the United Kingdom Government to ratify the Strasbourg Convention on the unification of certain parts of substantive law on patents for invention signed in 1963 (Cmnd. 2362) and also the expected European Patent Convention. The Banks Committee reported in 1970 (Cmnd. 4407), but it was not until 1975 that a Green Paper was issued, setting out proposed changes in the patent law (ISBN 0 11 511639 7).

In the meantime, there had been international activity resulting in three major agreements which had a direct bearing on changes of law in the United Kingdom. In the 1960s consideration had been given to some form of international agreement by which the duplication of searching and examination that takes place when a series of corresponding applications are filed in a number of co-operation was drafted. The proposals were avoided, and a treaty of co-operation was drafted. The proposals were shelved but eventually revived and signed as the Patent Co-operation Treaty (Cmnd. 4530) in Washington in December 1970. The treaty provides for a co-ordinated search and examination of a single application, which is then transmitted to designated countries for further processing.

The second of these agreements was the European Patent Convention (Cmnd. 5656) which, like the Patent Co-operation Treaty, was directed to reducing the administrative work in cases where a number of corresponding applications were filed in different countries. The Convention was more ambitious than the Patent Co-operation Treaty, in that it provides for the European Patent Office, at which Office applications for patents are processed up to grant, to result in a European patent which, when granted, is given in each contracting State nominated initially by the applicant the same rights and effects as would be conferred by a national patent granted in that State. The European Patent Convention is a very complete document, and with its Implementing Regulations defines a virtually complete patent system, which includes for example its own definitions of novelty and inventive step. It follows, therefore, that an invention may be protected in the United Kingdom by virtue of a national application filed in the British Patent Office, or it may be protected by virtue of a European patent extended to the United Kingdom.

The third agreement affecting patents in the United Kingdom was the Community Patent Convention (Cmnd. 6553). This is aimed at providing one patent which covers the whole of the territory of the EEC: the Community Patent Convention closely follows on the European Patent Convention where appropriate, and the same standards of novelty, subject-matter and other matters are adopted. However, it has not yet (even after more than a decade) been brought into force. Nevertheless, there are presently signs of its revival and extensive amendments to the Community Patent Convention were agreed by the signature of a number of Protocols thereto in December 1985.

The Patents Act 1977 therefore provided for a new system of patent law to have effect within the United Kingdom, not only for applications filed at the United Kingdom Patent Office, but also for European patents (UK) granted under the European Patent Convention on applications filed at the European Patent Office, and for patents based on international applications filed under the Patent Co-operation Treaty and subsequently (after search, and perhaps after an advisory examination) being brought into a UK national phase with a view to being granted as patents under that Act. The Patents Act 1949 was, however, retained to govern some, but not all, aspects of patents (called "existing patents") which have resulted from applications filed before June 1, 1978, this being not only the "commencement date" for the 1977 Act but also the date on which the European Patent Convention and Patent Co-operation Treaty each came into effect.

The Strasbourg Convention was eventually ratified in 1980 and republished as Cmnd. 8002.

Not only did the Patents Act 1977 introduce a considerable number of changes in detail in domestic law, and add a group of sections dealing with European patents and patent applications, Community patents, and international applications for patents, but in fact made a radical change in the foundation for the new domestic law. Indeed the long title begins "An Act to establish a new law of patents . . .", and Part I of the Act (ss.1–76) is headed "New Domestic Law".

The Patents Act 1949 was based upon a number of major assumptions concerning the circumstances of domestic patent law. The basic assumption was that the power used to grant monopolies in respect of inventions was to be derived from the prerogative of the Crown. This had been the case since Tudor times. A consequence was that the Patent Office and the Comptroller, in receiving patent applications and granting patents, were acting as an administrative agency on behalf of the Crown.

This relationship between the Patent Office and the Crown was abolished by the 1977 Act. The power to grant a patent for an invention now lies directly with the Comptroller (s.18(4)), and the certificate of grant (Sched. 3 to the Patents Rules) contains no reference to the Crown so that the term "Letters Patent" only remains appropriate for still subsisting patents granted under the 1949 Act, *i.e.* for "existing patents".

Patents granted under the prerogative of the Crown were always, at common law, subject to adjudication by the High Court. The grounds of revocation were only gradually codified, but did become a code under section 32 of the Patents Act 1949. The consequence of this situation was, however, that the powers of the Patent Office to reject patent applications developed largely independently of the powers of the court and were separately prescribed in sections 7, 8 and 14 of the Patents Act 1949. In contrast, the Patents Act 1977 starts with a definition of patentability in sections 1 to 4, this definition being equally applicable to the activities of the Patent Office and of the court, and then section 72(1) adds some grounds of revocation which are not relevant prior to grant.

Finally, the right of a patentee under the 1949 Act to bring an action for infringement derived essentially from the words "make, use, exercise and vend" in the Letters Patent, and the law as to what acts of infringement were comprehended within these words was established case by case and was not codified in the 1949 Act. That Act only dealt with certain peripheral aspects of infringement actions. In contrast, the 1977 Act defines infringement in section 60.

To summarise, the Patents Act 1977 is, unlike the Patents Act 1949, a complete code of law relating to patents for inventions. The Act assumes the existence of the courts, the Patent Office and the Comptroller, and these institutions are embodied in the operation of the Act, but they are given powers which are different in kind, and different in foundation, from those they possessed previously. Thus, only when the wording of corresponding provisions in the 1949 and 1977 Acts is similar, and the underlying concept has not changed, are cases decided under the 1949 and former Acts authority for the interpretation of the 1977 Act. Nevertheless, the courts have tended to follow such previous decisions in relation to the concepts of obviousness, insufficiency and infringement. However, difficulty arises from the fact that, though the word "invention" is used frequently, there is no complete definition of its meaning in the Patents Act 1977.

It should also be commented, as a generality, that the Patents Act 1977, in its completely codifying approach, goes in considerably greater detail than did the Patents Act 1949 into questions of ownership of inventions and the right to be granted a patent, and also deals at length with the right of an employee-inventor to compensation from an employer.

As a result of the EPC and PCT (and in the future the CPC), there is a variety, if not a confusion, of routes by which inventions can be protected in the United Kingdom. With the obvious object of avoiding as far as possible an anomalous situation where patents for inventions in the United Kingdom could be judged by substantially different standards, the wording of the Patents Act 1977 was chosen in many respects to accord with the wording adopted for the European Patent Convention. It might have been thought that the Act could have gone further, in adopting more widely the wording of the European Patent Convention, but it was argued that the adoption in the United Kingdom statute of the European wording would not necessarily result in European patents and British national patents being judged by the same standards. The reason for this which was advanced is that the United Kingdom national law would be interpreted in accordance with British canons of interpretation, whereas the European law would be interpreted by the standards of the European courts. As is well known, there is a marked difference in these standards and one of the reasons for this Introduction is to point out to practitioners a very real danger in assuming that similar wording in the United Kingdom and European provisions will result in the same meaning.

Under United Kingdom standards of interpretation, the court takes the meaning of the words at their face value and is not concerned to modify that meaning to make it give effect to the intention of the legislation, see the article by T. C. Stancliffe ((1976–77) 6 CIPA 254) entitled "EPC, the new Patents Act and the Courts". Thus, if the terms of the legislation are clear and unambiguous, they must be given effect to, whether or not they carry out Her Majesty's treaty obligations, for the Sovereign power of the Queen in Parliament extends to breaking treaties. However, as Mr. Stancliffe also rightly points out, where there is a choice of meanings one of which is and one of which is not in agreement with an international convention, then it will be that which is in agreement with the convention which will be adopted. On the other hand, it is the practice of Continental courts generally to construe the law to give effect to the intention of the law and to consider themselves less bound by the precise wording adopted by the legislature.

The EPO has issued an elaborate publication, the *Guidelines for Examination*. These EPO Guidelines are referred to in this book because they constitute a carefully prepared opinion by EPO officials as to the interpretation of the EPC and EPC Rules, and are revised in accordance with decisions of the Appeal Boards of the EPO. They, therefore, throw light on possible interpretation of equivalent provisions of the United Kingdom Act and Rules. Nevertheless, these Guidelines are open to challenge and their status is clearly defined in the General Introduction thereto, see particularly para. 1.2 thereof. The *EPO Guidelines* are reprinted in *EPH*.

Various Official Notices relating to the Act and Rules have appeared in the Official Journal (Patents), published by the United Kingdom Patent Office ("the O.J."), and these are summarised or referred to in this book as appropriate.

The Copyright, Designs and Patents Act 1988 ("the 1988 Act") has made many amendments of detail to the 1977 Act, but many of these amendments remain to be brought into effect. Of greater importance, this Act has provisions which will fundamentally change the nature of representation of parties in proceedings in the Patent Office, and therefore in the status of patent agents. The 1988 Act has also provided enabling legislation to establish one or more Patents County Courts with the aim of providing an alternative (and hopefully cheaper, and more speedy) forum for the resolution of disputes relating to patents, particularly as regards actions for patent infringement and counterclaims for revocation which usually result therefrom. However, a new infra-structure must be constructed before this enabling legislation can be given effect.

The genesis of these changes is to be found in a Green Paper *"Intellectual Property Rights and Innovation"* by The Chief Scientific Adviser to the Cabinet Office (Cmnd. 9117, December 1983). This "Nicholson Report" appeared without warning and made a number of suggestions for streamlining the patent system, including recommendations: that "the Patent Office should become a separate statutory body"; that "the policy on intellectual property rights should aim to reduce the need for reliance on professional advice"; and that "the case for the monopoly right of representation held by patent agents should be reviewed". The first of these recommendations has not been adopted, perhaps because of practical difficulties as regards the judicial role of the Comptroller, though agency status is still being considered, see (1988–89) 18 CIPA 199. However, in July 1985, the other two were made the subject of an enquiry by the Office of Fair Trading, to which the Chartered Institute made a fully reasoned submission (published in November 1985 as a Supplement to

(1985–86) 15 CIPA OFT 1). Despite this, the resulting OFT Report
(*"Review of restrictions on the Patent Agents' profession"*), when published
in September 1986, contained as its principal recommendations, that there
should be a complete freedom on representation in proceedings before the
Patent Office, and that the criminal sanctions on use of the title "patent
agent" should be deleted from the Patents Act. The Government accepted
the first of these recommendations, but decided that the Register of Patent
Agents should be retained with a continued monopoly for the title "patent
agent" for persons entered therein.

Meanwhile, in April 1986, a White Paper (*"Intellectual Property and
Innovation"*, Cmnd. 9712) was published, the main purpose of which was
to pave the way for reform of the law of copyright and of that for the protection of industrial designs. However, it also recommended that patent
litigation should be removed from the purview of the courts and be adjudi-
cated exclusively by the Comptroller who should be given power to grant
injunctions. This proposal led to much criticism, though the Chartered
Institute and the Patent Office initially supported it, but the controversy
led to the establishment of an inter-professional working party under Sir
Derek Oulton of the Lord Chancellor's Office. In turn this led to the
"Oulton Report" which advocated the creation of a Patents County Court
as an alternative, rather than substitute, forum for patent litigation. This
proposal was accepted by the Government, and enabling provisions were
included in the Bill introduced into the House of Lords in November 1987
which (in November 1988) became the 1988 Act.

This Bill, besides reforming the law appertaining to copyright and
designs, and including provisions for removing the restrictions to the right
to represent others in proceedings in the Patent Office, also included (particularly in Schedule 5) a number of detailed amendments to the 1977 Act,
which greatly increased during the passage of the Bill through Parliament;
and the opportunity was also taken to enact legislation to mitigate the
effect of the automatic "licences of right" endorsement on "existing
patents" for medical products, which had resulted from Schedule 1 of the
1977 Act and which the pharmaceutical industry had been able to persuade
the Government was inimical to the national and public interest. These
last-mentioned provisions automatically came into force two months after
the Royal assent, but the remainder of the 1988 Act was left to be brought
into effect only after the issue of appropriate "Commencement Orders".

This Third Edition was therefore initially prepared on the basis that it
would be published only after the detailed changes made by Schedule 5 of
the 1988 Act had come into force, and the necessarily resulting revisions of
the Patents Rules had also been made. However, delays in the preparation
of these Rule revisions have left much of the changes to the 1977 Act set
out in Schedule 5 to the 1988 Act yet to be brought into effect. The
decision was therefore taken to proceed to publication on the basis of "prospective" amendments to the 1977 Act and, as yet unknown, revisions to

the Rules to be made when these amendments are given effect, as is expected during 1990. These matters are therefore left to be dealt with in a forthcoming Supplement to the present "Main Work", as also is the implementing secondary legislation for the statutory provisions governing representation before the Comptroller and the status of "patent agents", as well as that for the proposed new Patents County Courts.

Patents Act 1977 (c.37)

ARRANGEMENT OF SECTIONS

PART I

NEW DOMESTIC LAW

Copyright, Designs and Patents Act 1988 (c. 48)

ARRANGEMENT OF RELEVANT SECTIONS

PART V

PATENT AGENTS AND TRADE MARK AGENTS

Patent Agents

Supplementary

PART VI

PATENTS

Patents county courts

c

TABLE OF AMENDMENTS TO THE PATENTS ACT 1977

The Act has been amended by the following enactments:

Year	Enactment	Sections affected
1978	National Health Service (Scotland) Act (c.29) [Sched.16, para.48]	56
	Interpretation Act (c.30) [s.25(2); Sched.4, para. 7(2)]	41
	Patents Act 1977 (Isle of Man) Order (S.I. 1978 No.621)	22, 23, 41, 52, 58, 85, 88, 93, 107, 114, 130
1979	Perjury (NI) Order (S.I. 1979 No.1714) [Sched.1, para.28]	92
1980	Competition Act (c.21) [s.14]	51
	Magistrates' Courts Act (c.43) [s.32(2)]	22, 23, 84, 109, 114
1981	Supreme Court Act (c.54) [ss.6, 54(9), 62(1), 70(3), (4), Sched.7]	96, 97, Sched.3
	Armed Forces Act (c.55) [s.22]	42, 130
1982	Civil Aviation Act (c.16) [Sched.15, para.19]	60
	Oil and Gas (Enterprise) Act (c.23) [Sched.3, para.39]	132
	Criminal Justice Act (c.48) [ss.37, 46]	22, 23, 84, 109–112, 114
1985	Companies Consolidation (Consequent Provisions) Act (c.9) [s.30; Sched.2]	88, 114, 131
	Administration of Justice Act (c.61) [s.60]	84, 102, 114, 130, Sched. 5
1986	Patents, Designs and Marks Act (c.39) [ss.1, 2, 3, Scheds. 1, 2, 3]	19, 27, 32, 35, 123
1988	Copyright, Designs and Patents Act (c.37) [ss.295, 303, Scheds.5, 7, 8, see also ss.274–281, 285–293]	14, 15, 17, 18, 28, 28A, 37, 39, 43, 46, 49, 51, 53, 57, 57A, 58, 60, 64, 72–78, 80, 84, 85, 88, 89, 89A, 89B, 99A, 99B, 102, 104, 105, 114,

Year	Enactment	Sections affected
1988	Copyright, Designs and Patents Act—*cont.*	115, 118, 123, 125, 125A, 130, Sched. 5, paras. 1–3, 7, 8
1989	Design (Semiconductor Topographics) Regulations 1989 (S.I. 1989 No. 1100)	57

The amendments so made are in each case indicated in the reprinted sections in this work by new wording in bold type and deleted wording in italic type within brackets, or by an end note.

An Act to establish a new law of patents applicable to future patents and applications for patents; to amend the law of patents applicable to existing patents and applications for patents; to give effect to certain international conventions on patents; and for connected purposes.

[29th July 1977]

Be it enacted by the Queen's most Excellent Majesty, by and with the advice and consent of the Lords Spiritual and Temporal, and Commons, in this present Parliament assembled, and by the authority of the same as follows:—

PART I

NEW DOMESTIC LAW

SECTION 1   1.01

Patentable inventions

1.—(1) A patent may be granted for an invention in respect of which the following conditions are satisfied, that is to say—
  (*a*) the invention is new;
  (*b*) it involves an inventive step;
  (*c*) it is capable of industrial application;
  (*d*) the grant of a patent for it is not excluded by subsections (2) and (3) below;
and references in this Act to a patentable invention shall be construed accordingly.

(2) It is hereby declared that the following (among other things) are not inventions for the purposes of this Act, that is to say, anything which consists of—
  (*a*) a discovery, scientific theory or mathematical method;
  (*b*) a literary, dramatic, musical or artistic work or any other aesthetic creation whatsoever;
  (*c*) a scheme, rule or method for performing a mental act, playing a game or doing business, or a program for a computer;
  (*d*) the presentation of information;
but the foregoing provision shall prevent anything from being treated as an invention for the purposes of this Act only to the extent that a patent or application for a patent relates to that thing as such.

1

(3) A patent shall not be granted—

(*a*) for an invention the publication or exploitation of which would be generally expected to encourage offensive, immoral or anti-social behaviour;

(*b*) for any variety of animal or plant or any essentially biological process for the production of animals or plants, not being a microbiological process or the product of such a process;

(4) For the purposes of subsection (3) above behaviour shall not be regarded as offensive, immoral or anti-social only because it is prohibited by any law in force in the United Kingdom or any part of it.

(5) The Secretary of State may by order vary the provisions of subsection (2) above for the purpose of maintaining them in conformity with developments in science and technology; and no such order shall be made unless a draft of the order has been laid before, and approved by resolution of, each House of Parliament.

1.02   BOOKS

P. W. Grubb, "Patents in chemistry and biotechnology" (Clarendon Press, 1986);

Judith Curry, "The Patentability of genetically engineered plants and animals in the US and Europe" (Intellectual Property Ltd., 1987);

S. A. Bent, R. L. Schwab, D. G. Cronin and D. D. Jeffrey, "Intellectual property rights in biotechnology worldwide" (Stockton Press, New York, 1987).

1.03   ARTICLES—COMPUTER PROGRAMS

N. W. P. Wallace, "The patentability of software-related inventions", EPI-Information 3–1985, 32;

J. Appleton, "European Patent Convention: Article 52 and computer programs", [1985] EIPR 279;

J. Betten, "Patent protection for computer programs in Germany and the EPO", [1987] EIPR 10;

J. A. H. van Voorthuizen, "Patentability of computer programs and computer related inventions under the European Patent Convention", (1987) 18 IIC 627;

R. J. Hart, "Application of patents to computer technology—UK and the EPO harmonisation", [1989] EIPR 42.

1.04   ARTICLES—MICRO-ORGANISMS, PLANTS AND ANIMALS

R. S. Crespi, "Biotechnology and patents: Outstanding issues", [1983] EIPR 201;

R. S. Crespi, "Innovation in plant biotechnology: The legal options", [1986] EIPR 262;

International Bureau of WIPO, "Industrial property protection of biotechnological inventions", Industrial Property, June 1986, 253;

W. Lesser, "Anticipating UK plant variety patents", [1987] EIPR 172;

B. M. Roth, "Current problems in the protection of inventions in the field of plant biotechnology: A position paper", (1987) 18 IIC 41;

A. Heitz, "Intellectual property in new plant varieties and biotechnological inventions", [1988] EIPR 297;

R. Teschemacher, "The practice of the European Patent Office regarding the grant of patents for biotechnological inventions", (1988) 19 IIC 18;
R. S. Crespi, "Reflections on the *Genentech* decision", [1989] IPB 25;
R. Waite and N. Jones, "Biotechnological patents in Europe—The draft directive", [1989] EIPR 145;
S. Wright, "Patentability of plants and animals", (1988–89) 18 CIPA 323.

COMMENTARY ON SECTION 1

General   **1.05**

Section 1 is the first of the group of sections 1–6 directed to considerations of patentability. None of these have any applicability to "existing patents", the validity of which continues to be dealt with under the 1949 Act (Sched. 1, para. 1(2)).

Section 1 provides a definition of patentability which replaces the previous definition which had continued to adopt the wording of section 6 of the Statute of Monopolies 1623 (21 Jac. 1, c. 3) (reprinted in Appendix B at para. B01 and discussed at para. B02). The new definition displaces any residual element of Common Law in the application and grant of a patent and its revocation (*Genentech's Patent*, [1989] RPC 147 (CA)). The new definition conforms to that of EPCaa. 52 and 53 and articles 1 and 2 of the Strasbourg Convention (1963) (Cmnd. 8002). Subsection (5) gives the Secretary of State power, by positive resolution of each House of Parliament, to promulgate rules to vary the exceptive provisions of subsection (2) (*i.e.* matter excluded from being considered as a patentable invention corresponding to EPCa. 52(2)) "for the purpose of maintaining these exceptions in conformity with developments in science and technology". No such order has yet been made. Even if it were, there is no power to extend it to remove the specific exclusions to patentability listed in subsection (3), which correspond to EPCa. 53: nor could it override the specific exclusions to patentability to be found in section 4(2), corresponding to EPCa. 52(4), for which see paras. 4.05–4.08.

To ensure conformity with the EPC, subsections (1)–(4) are declared by section 130(7) to have been framed to have, as nearly as practicable, the same effects as the corresponding provisions of the EPC, CPC and PCT.

By section 91, judicial notice is to be taken of the EPC, CPC and PCT and of decisions of convention courts, see para. 91.03. Hence, both the United Kingdom Patent Office and the United Kingdom courts are under obligation to construe section 1, and indeed each of sections 1–6, as well as other sections to which section 130(7) applies, in a manner which will harmonise as far as possible with EPC decisions. Nevertheless, such decisions are only persuasive, not binding, authority (*Genentech's Patent, supra*), but it is noteworthy that, in *John Wyeth's and Schering's Applications* ([1986] RPC 545), a decision of the EPO Enlarged Board of Appeal was followed by the Patents Court despite the reservations of both the Patents Judges sitting *in banc*. It remains to be seen how appellate courts will view EPO decision; and, indeed, also the extent to which the EPO Boards of Appeal may temper their subsequent decisions if national appellate courts express disagreement with EPO precedents, for example as noted in para. 2.29.

The EPO Guidelines for Examination are referred to herein because, though only advisory in nature, they are put forward as giving a fully considered opinion on the interpretation of the EPC and the Rules made thereunder. Indeed the EPO itself recognises that these Guidelines are only "general instructions" intended to cover normal occurrences and has stated that there is a discretion for an EPO Examining Division to depart from a general directive in a particular case provided that the decision remains within the bounds defined by the EPC (*EPO Decision T 162/82, "Classifying areas/SIGMA".* [1987] 5 EPOR 375).

1.06 *Meaning of "invention"*

Although the meaning of the word "invention" is fundamental to the operation of much of the Act, there is no complete definition of "invention" and it appears to encompass anything "come upon" (from the latin—*invenire*) or "devised" (from s.7) by the inventor, but it must be something more than a mere discovery (*Genentech's Patent*, [1989] RPC 147 (CA)). Depending on the context, this refers to any such matter, whether specific or general, tangible or conceptual, and whether or not it fulfils the criteria of section 1 for a "patentable invention" as summarised in para. 1.07 *infra*.

It appears from the Act that, in circumstances where the "invention" has not yet been defined by claims, it can have whichever of these meanings suits the context in which it is used. Examples are where the invention has been made but an application, particularly one containing claims, has not yet been drawn up, see section 7(3) (*Definition of "inventor"*), section 15(1) (*Applications without claims*) and sections 39, 42(2) and 43(1), (2), (3) (*Rights in an employee's invention or when an invention was made*). Indeed, in relation to "entitlement" disputes, the word "invention" in sections 8, 12 and 37 means that which the alleged inventor thought he had invented in the light of the prior art of which he was then aware, see *Viziball's Application* ([1988] RPC 213) and para. 8.09.

Again, section 23(1)(*a*) refers to an application for the same invention on file at least six weeks before an application may be made abroad without written authority from the Comptroller; in this context, by long established practice, "invention" is used in a broad conceptual sense, especially as in many cases the earlier application is without claims. However, when the "invention" has been defined by claims, references in sections 14(2)(*b*) and (3), 15(1)(*c*) and 72(1)(*c*) to the description or disclosure of the invention appear to be primarily to specific and tangible aspects of it rather than to general and conceptual ones.

In contrast to this elastic, amorphous meaning of "invention", section 125(1) states that, unless the context otherwise requires, an invention for which an application has been made or a patent granted shall be taken to be that specified in a claim, as interpreted by the specification and any drawings, and this appears to refer to the extent of the invention as a logical definition in the general sense. The differing meaning of the word "invention" as used in various sections of the Act is further discussed in para. 125.08, see also *British United Shoe Machinery* v. *Fussell* ((1908) 25 RPC 631 at 651 (CA)) where four different meanings of the word were recognised. Section 125(2) indicates that more than one invention can be specified in a claim and section 125(3) states that the Protocol on Interpretation of EPCa. 69 applies for the purpose of section 125(1) as it applies to EPCa. 69. Section 125 is also declared by section 130(7) to have, as nearly as practicable, the same effects as the corresponding provisions of EPC. What these effects are, and their relation to the canons of construction applied to British patent claims under the previously applicable Common Law, is discussed more fully in paras. 125.11–125.13.

1.07 *Definition of "patentable invention" (subs. (1))*

The definition of a patentable invention, as for the purposes of the Act in subsection (1), is in terms of (*a*) novelty (as defined in s.2) (*b*) inventive step (as defined in s.3) (*c*) capability of industrial application (as defined in s.4), and (*d*) the express exclusions of subsections (2) and (3). The words "patentable invention" appear elsewhere in the Act, notably in section 72(1) wherein the first recited ground for revocation is that the invention is not a patentable invention, but also in section 21(1) in relation to observations made by third parties as to whether an invention is a patentable invention. The words are also implicit in "the requirements of this Act" in section 18(2) dealing with the substantive examination of an application. The term "patented invention," however, has the narrower meaning of an invention for which a patent is actually granted (s.130(1)). However, the term "patentable invention" involves a preliminary decision whether an "invention" as such is involved, see para. 1.08 *supra*.

In subsection (1)(*c*), the expression "capable of industrial application" is used whereas EPCa. 52(1) requires an invention to be "susceptible of industrial application". EPO Guideline C-II, 4.12 indicates that these expressions are synonymous. EPCa. 57 then states the expressions are satisfied if the invention is one which "can be made or used in any kind of industry including agriculture", and this expression is incorporated into the Act by section 4(1).

Matter excluded from patentability by not being regarded as "inventions" (subs. (2))   **1.08**

Subsection (2) declares that certain classes of matter are not inventions for the purposes of the Act (and therefore by subs. (1) not patentable), but the specified exclusions are subject to the important provisos that the alleged invention "consists of" the excluded things and that the exclusion is "only to the extent that a patent or a patent application relates to that thing as such". Subsection (2)(*a*), (*c*), (*d*) has wording which closely resembles that of EPCa. 52(*a*), (*c*), (*d*), but whereas EPCa. 52(2)(*b*) refers only to "aesthetic creations", subsection (2)(*b*) refers to "literary, dramatic, musical or artistic work or any other aesthetic creation whatsoever". These excluded categories have a common characteristic of *not* constituting or implying the use of technical methods to produce a concrete technical effect (*EPO Decision T* 366/87, "*Harmonic vibrations/STERNHEIMER*", [1989] 3 EPOR 131).

The applications of the excluded classes of matter are not themselves excluded. Thus, while subsection (2) prevents a discovery, scientific theory, mathematical method or computer program from validly being claimed as such, by virtue of the proviso to subsection (2) (corresponding to EPCa. 52(3)), a use or application thereof may be claimed if the other criteria for patentability are satisfied and the invention is not excluded from patent protection by some other provision of the Act, *e.g.* under subsection (3) or section 4(2), see paras. 1.14–1.16 and 4.05–4.08 respectively.

In *Merrill Lynch's Application* ([1988] RPC 1; OJEPO 1–2/1988, 61) the Patents Court construed the words "to the extent that" in subsection (2) as making the subsection applicable to cases where the invention includes one of the excluded categories of (*a*)–(*d*) but does not relate to such category *only*. However, the Patents Court indicated (as had the Comptroller) that, if some practical (technical) effect is achieved by a computer or machine operating according to instructions contained in a computer program, a claim directed to that practical effect would be patentable, *if* that effect were novel and unobvious. On this reasoning, the claims in issue were rejected. However, on further appeal ([1989] RPC 561 (CA)), it was held that the effect must be a technical one, which is not the case when the result of the invention is a business scheme unpatentable under subsection (2)(*c*), but matter excluded from patentability by section 1(2) could nevertheless contribute the required inventive step. This appeal decision, upholding the decisions below but on different reasoning, was stated to be in conformity with the view taken by the EPO, see para. 1.10 *infra*. Previously, this was not so, see *Genentech's Patent* ([1989] RPC 147 (CA)) where the correctness of the Patent Court's statements in *Merrill Lynch* was doubted by a majority of the Court of Appeal. Nevertheless, some difference between the view of the Court of Appeal in *Merrill Lynch* and that of the EPO can still be discerned, see para. 1.11 *infra*.

In the *Genentech* case, Purchas LJ held that claims (as construed according to s. 125 and the Protocol to EPCa. 69) which extend beyond what the inventor truly discovered are not to be regarded as "inventions" within the meaning of the Act, and therefore not patentable under subsection (2). Mustill LJ would have decided likewise, but felt that to do so would be invalidating the claims for undue breadth contrary to section 14(5)(*c*), which the whole Court of Appeal had held was not a ground of revocation under the Act, see para. 14.21. Dillon LJ, however, did not find the claims invalid under section 1(2), but he (and Mustill LJ) held the claims invalid for lack of inventive step, see para. 3.07. Thus, it would seem that, before proceeding to enquire whether a claim is to a "patentable invention" under subsection (1), it should be asked whether the claim is for an "invention" at all, within the meaning of subsection (2). This will not be so if the claim is in respect of a discovery as such, but (as the *Genentech* case makes clear) a patent claiming the practical application of a discovery does not relate to that discovery *as such*, and so is not excluded by subsection (2), even if that practical application might be obvious once the discovery had been made. A further test then to be overcome is whether, despite being for an invention, the claim is in respect of subject matter unpatentable under subsections (3) and (4). The *Genentech* case has been discussed: by R. S. Crespi ([1989] IPB 25) in relation to the patenting of inventions arising from recombinant DNA technology; by P. G. Cole (*Patent World*, January 1989, 31); and by J. P. Thurston ([1989] EIPR 66) more in relation to the objection of lack of invention of the *Genentech* claims.

1.09   —*Exclusion of abstract and non-technical matter*

EPO Guideline C-IV, 1.2(ii) states that an invention, to be patentable: must be of a "technical character" to the extent that it must relate to a technical field (EPCr. 27(1)(*b*)); it must be concerned with a technical problem (EPCr. 27(1)(*d*)); and it must have technical features in terms of which the matter for which protection is sought can be defined in the claims (EPCr. 29(1)). This requirement of "technical character" has apparently become decisive in determining whether or not an invention is excluded from patentability under EPCaa. 52(2)(4) and 53(*b*) (and therefore under subsections (2) and (3)(*b*)).

EPO Guideline C-IV, 2.1 notes further that the exclusions of EPCa. 52(2), corresponding to subsection (2), all have the character of being either abstract (discoveries, scientific theories) or non-technical (aesthetic creations or presentations of information), and that in contrast patentable inventions must be of both a concrete and a technical character. EPO Guidelines C-VI, 2.2 and 2.3 then analyse in depth the exclusions and what is required by "technical character", providing illustrative examples for each of the types of exclusion, see also *EPO Decision T* 366/87, "*Harmonic vibrations/STERNHEIMER*" ([1989] 3 EPOR 131) where the last integer in the claim was of a technical nature and this sufficed to confer patentability.

In *Merrill Lynch's Application* ([1989] RPC 561 (CA)) it was held, on different reasoning to that employed by the Patents Court ([1988] RPC 1; OJEPO 1–2/1988, 61), that a computer programmed to operate a business scheme is not patentable because the effect of that invention is one excluded from patentability under subsection (2)(*c*), see further para. 1.08 *supra*. Likewise, in the earlier case of *Good News Pty's Application* (SRIS O/190/83), claims were rejected as relating solely to a scheme or method of doing business. However, a method of distinguishing genuine from counterfeit articles by marking them according to a secret algorithm was found allowable in principle in *McNeight and Lawrence's Application* (SRIS O/66/85), though the EPO later rejected a somewhat similar claim, see *EPO Decision T* 51/84, "*Coded distinctive marks/STOCKBURGER*" (OJEPO 7/1986, 226; [1986] 5 EPOR 229) because the claims did not identify a technical means for carrying out the claimed procedural steps. Thus, it would appear that the EPO has also failed to take a consistent line on the interpretation of EPCa. 52(2), which corresponds to subsection (2), and therefore that further cases are needed to elucidate the ambit of these provisions.

It will be appreciated that, normally, the cases reported in relation to subsection (2) will concern applications which have been held to fail, rather than satisfy, the required criteria, at least at first instance. Examples of such cases include: *Simon's Application* (SRIS O/139/86 and C/6/87), for a scientific theory or literary work; *Price's Application* (SRIS O/105/84), relating to a trading stamp scheme for buying holidays, as a mere business scheme, the trading stamps themselves being aesthetic creations or, alternatively, a way of presenting information (as to which see para. 1.13 *infra*); and several inventions of a perpetual motion type, for example *Webb's Application* (SRIS O/84/88, *noted* IPD 11078).

In the EPO, a claim for a procedure for regulating traffic flow was rejected in *EPO Decision T* 16/85, *"Traffic regulation/CHRISTIAN FRANCERIES"* ([1988] 2 EPOR 65); and an application for a perpetual motion invention was rejected in *EPO Decision T* 5/86, *"Perpetual motion/NEWMAN"* ([1988] 5 EPOR 301), though on the ground of insufficiency of description, see para. 14.18.

Computer programs

—The EPO Guidelines   **1.10**

The extent of the exclusion from patentability under subsection (2)(*c*) of computer programs has been a matter of considerable debate and, after a period when the position being taken by the Patent Office appeared to be little different from that applied under the 1949 Act (for which see para. A101.07), a lead was eventually set by the EPO, after extensive discussion with interested circles, amending EPO Guidelines C-IV, 2.1–2.3 so that these dealt more fully with inventions involving the *use* of computer programs, see OJEPO 6/1985, 177. These amendments are discussed in the papers by N. W. P. Wallace and J. Appleton listed in para. 1.03 *supra*.

The revised EPO Guidelines now stress that patentability depends on technical effect and it is indicated that a program becomes technically meaningful only in combination with the computer it is intended to control. Thus claims will now, apparently, be accepted in the EPO when directed to a computer in combination with a defined program loaded in it, or to a method of operating the computer according to the program. Indeed, that has been specifically confirmed in *EPO Decision T* 208/84, *"Computer-related invention/VICOM"* (OJEPO 1/1978, 14; [1987] EPOR 66) where it was held that a claim directed to a technical process, which process is carried out under the control of a program (whether by way of hardware or software) cannot be regarded as relating to a computer program *as such*; and likewise that a claim which can be considered as directed to a computer set up in accordance with a specified program for controlling or carrying out a technical process cannot be regarded as relating to a computer program *as such*. However, provided the claim does include some technical means, it is then not one merely to a computer program *as such* (*EPO Decision T* 26/86, *"X-ray apparatus/ KOCH & STERZEL"*, OJEPO 1–2/1988, 19; [1988] 2 EPOR 72) wherein a request for the EPO Enlarged Board of Appeal to consider the *Vicom* decision was turned down. In the United Kingdom, however, the invention should have an effect which is not one specifically excluded from patentability, see para. 1.11 *infra*.

Also, a claim to a computer of known type set up to operate according to a new program cannot be regarded as lacking novelty as defined by EPCa. 54. The EPO practice is discussed further in the papers by J. Betten and R. J. Hart listed in para. 1.03 *supra*. For case comment on the *Vicom* case, see [1987] EIPR D-100.

1.11 *—Decisions of the Comptroller*

Although the Comptroller considered the EPO Guidelines in *Merrill Lynch's Application* ([1988] RPC 1; OJEPO 1–2/1988, 61), it was still held that, if the task performed by the computer is non-technical, for example a mathematical calculation or a business method, then the mere fact that it is being performed by a suitable machine, whether or not this involves a program, does not of itself provide a technical feature and so does not render the programmed computer patentable. On the appeal, the Patents Court endorsed the view of the EPO in the *Vicom* case (noted in para. 1.10 *supra*), but went further and stated that it is necessary to take into account whether the features not excluded by *(a)–(d)* were already known or obvious. A further application of similar nature was subsequently rejected by the Comptroller on similar reasoning (*Merrill Lynch's Application (No. 2)*, SRIS O/127/87). This reasoning was the subject of criticism in the paper by R. J. Hart listed in para. 1.03 *supra*, and also in *Genentech's Patent* ([1989] RPC 147 (CA)). Subsequently, an appeal, the first *Merrill Lynch* case was rejected ([1989] RPC 561 (CA)), but on reasoning consistent with part of that in the *Vicom* case, namely that the required technical result cannot confer patentability if this is something specifically excluded from patentability under subsection (2), in this case a business scheme excluded under subsection (2)(c). However, the extent to which the necessary novelty and inventive step can lie in the technical result still seems not completely resolved. In *Merrill Lynch*, decisions given under the 1949 Act were not considered helpful because of the change of law.

1.12 *Other protection for computers and computer programs*

As to copyright protection for computer programs, the 1988 Act continues the previously established principles, *viz.* that copyright resides in a computer program as if it were a literary work (s. 3(1) [1988]); that a version of the program in which it is converted into or out of a computer language or code, or into a different computer language or code, is a translation (and thereby an adaptation) of the program (s. 21(4) [1988]); and that storage of a work, such as a computer program, in any medium by electronic means (such as in a computer) involves reproduction of the work in material form (s. 17(2) [1988]). The 1988 Act also introduces (in s. 17(6) [1988]) the principle that the making of copies that "are transient or are incidental to some other use of the work" (as occurs when computer programs are run) is copying. However, neither the 1988 Act, nor section 1(2)(c) of the 1977 Act, defines the term "computer program". These provisions are broadly compatible with the Draft Directive on the legal protection of computer programs issued by the EC Commission, reprinted [1989] 2 CMLR 180. Attention is also drawn to the "topography right" under which the design of masking for a semiconductor product, a "mask work" or computer chip, is protected by a right akin to copyright. The protection was introduced, from November 7, 1987, by the Semiconductor Products (Protection of Topography) Regulations 1987 (S.I. 1987 No. 1497), now repealed and replaced by the Design Right (Semiconductor Topographies) Regulations 1989 (S.I. 1989 No. 1100). These Regulations now assimilate the topography right (now called a "right in a semiconductor topography") with the "design right" created under Part III [1988]. However, the Regulations create differences particularly between these two rights, for example in extending the topography right to designs created in a wider range of countries outside the EEC, and excluding the "licences of right" available in the last five years of the design right. These Regulations state that the right originates with the creator of the mask design, ("semiconductor topography"), but this becomes vested automatically in the employer of a creator who works under a contract of service, or, in preference thereto, in an

8

entity which commissioned the work from the creator or his employer. Like the "design right" created under the 1988 Act, the topography right has a duration of 10 years from its first commercial exploitation anywhere in the world, but expires 15 years after creation if not commercially exploited within that period.

Exclusion of presentation of information (subs. (2)(d))　　　　　　　　　　**1.13**

A claim to a magnetic tape cassette of conventional construction, but with one guide pole coloured to assist assembly, has been rejected as a mere presentation of information under subsection (2)(*d*) (*TDK Electronics' Application*, SRIS O/97/83). In *Kettle's Application* (SRIS O/41/86) an application for a vehicle licence plate with symbols denoting the month and year of first registration was refused as a mere presentation of information; and, likewise, in *Tusser's Application* (SRIS O/14/88) for a chart identifying the growth stages for a particular plant: here the method of use of the claim would only have been patentable if it had involved an inventive concept beyond the mere presentation of information. In *Price's Application* (SRIS O/105/84) trading stamps were regarded as unpatentable as either aesthetic creations or ways of presenting information. In *Thompson's Application* (SRIS O/50/89, *noted* IPD 12066) claims to a drinking vessel, characterised in displaying an informational message viewable through its base, were only allowed after addition of a structural feature which added novelty to the claim in addition to that novel informational feature.

Under the 1949 Act the Appeal Tribunal indicated that, while a patent could not be "sustained on the basis of novelty in information, for example artistic or literary content alone", a novel *method* of presenting information, or novel *article* by which information can be presented, ought to be patentable under section 101 [1949] (*Rhodes' Application*, [1973] RPC 243).

Applications previously rejected as in effect amounting to mere methods of presenting information, unpatentable under the test of "manner of new manufacture" in section 101 [1949], include: *Nelson's Application* ([1980] RPC 173) (instructional message presented as combination of visual, verbal and humorous forms); *Dixon's Application* ([1978] RPC 687) (invention relating to method and means of speech instruction); *Quigley's Application [Australia]* ([1977] FSR 373) (particular method of operating a plurality of steel production furnaces); *Kent and Thanet's Application* ([1968] RPC 318) (roulette wheel with double zero); *Stahl and Larsson's Application* ([1965] RPC 596) (method of recording passenger journeys); and *Lips' Application* ([1959] RPC 35) (claim to ship's propeller with novelty residing in formula for calculating its dimensions).

On the other hand, claims were allowed under section 101 [1949] where something more than the mere presentation of information was involved, as in: *Rhodes' Application* (*supra*) (speedometer indicating "impact speed"); *ITS Rubber's Application* ([1979] RPC 318) (blue ball for playing squash); and *Kessler's Application* ([1973] RPC 413) (folio device for recording patent renewal fees). Claims to a method of identifying diamonds from photographic records of their X-ray diffraction patterns (topograms) were allowed by the Court of Appeal in *De Beers' Application* ([1979] FSR 72), but a claim to the production of an index to a collection of topograms was not considered to involve a manner of manufacture. However, in *Thompson's Application* (*supra*), it was pointed out that, in the *Rhodes'* and *ITS Rubber* cases, there had been a functional effect in addition to the mere presentation of information.

The patentability of the presentation of information has also been considered, both under the 1949 and 1977 Acts, in connection with packaging for drugs, but this question is considered in the commentary on section 2, see para. 2.30, because of its inter-relation with the special provision of section 2(6).

1.14 *Specific exclusions from patentability despite being inventions (subs. (3))*

Subsection (3) corresponds to EPCa. 53(*a*), although not adopting the same wording, and states that patents shall not be granted for two specific classes of invention which would otherwise be patentable.

1.15 *—Exclusion on grounds of public policy (subss. (3)(a) and (4))*

Thus, subsection (3)(*a*) excludes from the class of patentable inventions those inventions the "publication or exploitation of which would be generally expected to encourage offensive, immoral or anti-social behaviour". By contrast EPCa. 53(*a*) refers to inventions which would be contrary to "*ordre public* or morality". The wording adopted in the Act can be taken as an attempt to render in English "*ordre public*", which in the past has resisted successful translation. EPCa. 53(*a*) is explained at Guidelines C-IV, 3.1–3.3. The purpose of these exclusions is to render unpatentable inventions likely to induce riot or public disorder or to lead to criminal or other generally offensive behaviour. The meaning of "generally expected" is undefined, and it is not clear whether it means by a majority of the public or merely "widely". EPO Guideline C-IV, 3.1 states that a fair test to apply is to consider whether it is probable that the general public would regard the invention as so abhorrent that the grant of patent rights would be inconceivable.

However, by subsection (4), an invention is not to be regarded as encouraging offensive, immoral or anti-social behaviour merely because it is prohibited by law in the United Kingdom. Moreover, the invention is presumably not unpatentable if only unobjectionable uses are mentioned in the specification. Nevertheless, the Comptroller has apparently suggested that, where a specification refers to a substance the use of which would be a contravention of the Carcinogenic Substances Regulations 1967 (S.I. 1967 No. 879), reference to such substance might be required to be deleted under subsection (3)(*a*), even though no objection would arise under subsection (4). If such use were an essential integer of the invention claimed, the Comptroller has apparently said that no patent could then be granted ((1979–80) 9 CIPA 256).

1.16 *—Exclusion for plant and animal varieties (subs. (3)(b))*

Subsection (3)(*b*) excludes from patentability any variety of animal or plant or any essentially biological process for their production, not being a microbiological process or the product of such a process. The corresponding EPCa. 53(*b*) (explained in EPO Guidelines C-VI, 3.4–3.5) is more direct in its wording, and states that the exclusion does not apply to microbiological processes or the products thereof. The exclusion of plant varieties from patent protection arises from the existence of plant breeders' rights in many EPC Member States as a result of their adherence to the 1964 International Convention for the Protection of New Varieties of Plants as revised in 1972 and 1978 (Cmnd. 9152): such rights are reviewed in the paper by A. Heitz, listed in para. 1.04 *supra*, and are discussed in para. 1.17 *infra*. However, on the basis of this Convention, the exclusion from patentability of animal varieties is illogical. The practice of the EPO regarding the patenting of biotechnological inventions was explained by R. Teschemacher in his paper listed in para. 1.04 *supra*, and the world-wide position was later reviewed by S. Wright in his paper likewise listed *supra*.

Thus, claims to micro-organisms *per se* and other products producible by biological techniques, such as cell lines, have been allowed, whether or not such microorganisms are naturally occurring, see the commentary on new section 125A where the patentability of microbiological inventions is particularly discussed at paras. 125A.06 and 125A.07, together with the difficulty of defining products of this type.

In *EPO Decision T* 49/83, "*Propagating material/CIBA-GEIGY*" (OJEPO 3/1984, 112) it was held by the EPO that no general exclusion of inventions in the sphere of animate nature can be inferred from the EPC and that the exclusion of patents for plant varieties was prompted by the availability of an alternative form of protection therefore, for which see para. 1.17 *infra*. Claims were then allowed to "Propagating material for cultivated plants treated with [X]" on the basis that the specified treatment was essentially a chemical one whereas the patentability exclusion corresponding to section 1(3)(*b*) relates to material produced by an essentially *biological* process.

In his later paper, listed in para. 1.04 *supra*, R. S. Crespi discussed the extent to which subsection (3)(*b*) may permit process and product claims relating to new plants and varieties thereof, noting the absence therein of the word "variety" in relation to process discoveries. These matters have also been discussed in the books by P. W. Grubb, Judith Curry and S. A. Bent *et al.*, listed in para. 1.02 *supra*. Each of these writers discusses the scope of plant and animal patents and the patentability of plant and animal genetic manipulation techniques with reference to the patenting of plant genes and other DNA molecules. In his paper, listed in para. 1.04 *supra*, W. Lesser also discussed further the possibility of plants being patentable in the United Kingdom and the further questions in relation to their validity and infringement which would then arise, see also the paper by S. Wright likewise so listed.

These commentators have taken the view that plants and animals, which have been altered by genetic manipulation, are not "varieties" within the meaning of the EPC and the Act, but rather representatives of a large family characterised by some novel gene, such as one imparting resistance to a herbicide. Here it may be noted that, in the USA, the patentability of a new strain of oyster was approved in principle, see S. A. Bent ((1987–1988) 17 CIPA 30), and US Patent No. 4,736,866 has issued for a mouse with particular chromosomal characteristics, but an EPO Examining Division rejected the corresponding "mouse" application (*noted* (1988–89) 18 CIPA 319), while recognising that in doing so it was drawing a distinction between the patentability of plants (if not a variety as such), for which see EP No. 122,791 of *Lubrizol Genetics* for "Plant gene expression", and the unpatentability of animals: see also the paper by S. Wright listed in para. 1.04 *supra*.

However, if patents for transgenic animals are eventually allowed, controversy seems certain to arise concerning the permissible breadth of claim for this type of invention. Other problems will arise, for example with patents for plant material whether such a patent could be enforced against those who obtain the patented transgenic material indirectly or dishonestly, but from the patentee; and whether the "exhaustion of rights" doctrine, for which see Appendix C at para. C15, would allow seed obtained from a crop to be re-used or used for the purpose of producing yet further modified plant material.

Parallel problems apply to animals into which new genes have been introduced "permanently", for example by micro-injection of the pronucleus of a fertilised egg with DNA material. In principle, such a technique could be used to harvest valuable proteins produced by the introduced gene, for example by milking the animal. The produce from such an animal would appear even more clearly to fall outside the patenting prohibition of subsection (3)(*b*): with the gene insertion being arguably microbiological in character. However, if the inserted gene has a "therapeutic" effect on the animal, further patenting problems will arise from the provisions of section 4(2), for which see paras. 4.05–4.08.

In its paper "COM (88) 496 final—Syn 159" ((1989) 20 IIC 55, *noted* [1988] EIPR

D–264) the European Commission has discussed the need for a uniform (and liberal) interpretation of the EPC to ensure the protection which it regards as appropriate for biotechnological inventions. This paper concludes with a Draft Council Directive on the legal protection of biotechnological inventions (OJEC 13.1.89, C 10/3; [1989] 1 CMLR 494; [1989] FSR 526). This paper is the subject of comment in the article by R. Waite and N. Jones listed in para. 1.04 *supra*, in which the Draft Directive is also reprinted. The Commission's paper states that the proposals of the Draft Directive are within the framework of the EPC, though this is doubtful as regards some of its proposals. The aim of the Draft Directive is to achieve harmonisation and a greater protection for biotechnological inventions, under both the EPC and national laws, by directing that the exclusions from patentability be narrowly construed, for example to permit patents for: all types of living matter, other than "plant and animal varieties", with that phrase being given a strictly limited meaning; processes in which human intervention consists in more than selecting an available biological material and letting it perform an inherent biological function under natural conditions; and material separated from a natural environment; as well as extending protection for a product with particular and essential genetic information to any product containing that information. It is thought that these proposals will require considerable refinement before they achieve a proper balance between promoting and inhibiting innovation; and that the implementation under British law of the Draft Directive would require at least detailed secondary legislation, but basis for this may exist by virtue of subsection (5). These proposals have also been discussed in a paper by P. Chua (*Patent World*, May 1989, 39), particularly in relation to the decision in *Genentech's Patent* ([1989] RPC 147 (CA)), and similarly discussed in an article ([1989] IPB 12).

1.17 *Plant breeders' rights*

Plant breeders' rights arise under the Plant Varieties and Seeds Act 1964 (c. 14) as amended, principally by the Plant Varieties Act 1983 (c. 17). The International Convention referred to in para. 1.16 *supra* provides that Member States "may" grant either a plant breeders' right or a patent, and that a Member State "whose national law admits of protection under both these forms may provide only one of them for one and the same botanical genus or species". This apparent exclusion of double protection has been the subject of much comment, see the papers by R. S. Crespi and by B. M. Roth each listed in para. 1.04 *supra* and the book by S. A. Bent *et al* listed in para. 1.02 *supra*. The Draft EEC Directive, as noted in para. 1.16 *supra*, proposes that this prohibition against dual protection should be strictly limited to plant and animal varieties as such.

A Guide to plant breeders' rights is available from the Plant Varieties Office, White House Lane, Huntingdon Road, Cambridge CB3 0LF (tel. 0223 277151). Since schemes are introduced for further plant species at the rate of about two per year, it is important to check with this Office whether plant breeders' rights exist, or are foreshadowed for a particular type of variety.

2.01

SECTION 2

Novelty

2.—(1) An invention shall be taken to be new if it does not form part of the state of the art.

(2) The state of the art in the case of an invention shall be taken to com-

prise all matter (whether a product, a process, information about either, or anything else) which has at any time before the priority date of the invention been made available to the public (whether in the United Kingdom or elsewhere) by written or oral description, by use or in any other way.

(3) The state of the art in the case of an invention to which an application for a patent or a patent relates shall be taken also to comprise matter contained in an application for another patent which was published on or after the priority date of that invention, if the following conditions are satisfied, that is to say—

(*a*) that matter was contained in the application for that other patent both as filed and as published; and

(*b*) the priority date of that matter is earlier than that of the invention.

(4) For the purposes of this section the disclosure of matter constituting an invention shall be disregarded in the case of a patent or an application for a patent if occurring later than the beginning of the period of six months immediately preceding the date of filing the application for a patent and either—

(*a*) the disclosure was due to, or made in consequence of, the matter having been obtained unlawfully or in breach of confidence by any person—

(i) from the inventor or from any other person to whom the matter was made available in confidence by the inventor or who obtained it from the inventor because he or the inventor believed that he was entitled to obtain it; or

(ii) from any other person to whom the matter was made available in confidence by any person mentioned in sub-paragraph (i) above or in this sub-paragraph or who obtained it from any person so mentioned because he or the person from whom he obtained it believed that he was entitled to obtain it;

(*b*) the disclosure was made in breach of confidence by any person who obtained the matter in confidence from the inventor or from any other person to whom it was made available, or who obtained it, from the inventor; or

(*c*) the disclosure was due to, or made in consequence of the inventor displaying the invention at an international exhibition and the applicant states, on filing the application, that the invention has been so displayed and also, within the prescribed period, files written evidence in support of the statement complying with any prescribed conditions.

(5) In this section references to the inventor include references to any proprietor of the invention for the time being.

(6) In the case of an invention consisting of a substance or composition for use in a method of treatment of the human or animal body by surgery or therapy or of diagnosis practised on the human or animal body, the fact that the substance or composition forms part of the state of the art shall not

prevent the invention from being taken to be new if the use of the substance or composition in any such method does not form part of the state of the art.

Relevant Rule

International exhibitions

2.02   **5.**—(1) An applicant for a patent who wishes the disclosure of matter constituting an invention to be disregarded in accordance with section 2(4)(*c*) shall, at the time of filing the application for the patent, inform the comptroller in writing that the invention has been displayed at an international exhibition.

(2) The applicant shall, within four months of filing the application, file a certificate, issued at the exhibition by the authority responsible for the exhibition, stating that the invention was in fact exhibited there. The certificate shall also state the opening date of the exhibition and, where the first disclosure of the invention did not take place on the opening date, the date of the first disclosure. The certificate shall be accompanied by an identification of the invention, duly authenticated by the authority.

(3) For the purposes of section 130(2) a statement may be published in the Journal that an exhibition described in the statement falls within the definition of international exhibition in subsection (1) of that section.

(4) In the case of an international application for a patent (UK), the application of this rule shall be subject to the provisions of rule 85(2A) below.

Notes. Sub-rule (4) was added by S.I. 1985 No. 1166 (r. 2). This will need amendment when rule 85(2A) is revised consequent upon the bringing into effect of new section 89A, for which see the latest Supplement to this Work *re.* para. 89A.02.

2.02A   Book

P. W. Grubb, "Patents in chemistry and biotechnology" (Clarendon Press, 1986).

2.03   Articles

B. C. Reid, "The right to work", [1982] EIPR 6;
B. C. Reid "Du Pont and I.C.I.: Chemical anticipation and prior patent specifications", [1982] EIPR 118;
A. W. White, "Patentability of medical treatment claims: The nimodipin cases", [1984] EIPR 380;
I. B. de Minvielle-Devaux, "The patenting of further medical indications", (1983–84) 13 CIPA 221;
A. W. White, "Patenting the second medical indication", [1985] EIPR 62;
J. Utermann, "Purpose-bound process claims for pharmaceuticals: Two solutions for the second indication", (1986) 17 IIC 41;
P. A. Chandler, "W. L. Gore & Associate, Inc. *v.* Kimal Scientific Products Ltd:

Premature dealing in inventions and its potential treatment under the Patents Act 1977", [1988] EIPR 221;

J. Jeffs, "Selection patents", [1988] EIPR 291;

J. C. H. Ellis, "Novelty in the EPO", (1988–89) 18 CIPA 3;

B. Hansen, "New problem of the second indication", (1988) 19 IIC 272;

G. S. A. Szabo, "Problems concerning novelty in the domain of selection inventions", (1989) 20 IIC 295;

M. F. Vivian, "Novelty and selection inventions", (1989) 20 IIC 303.

COMMENTARY ON SECTION 2

General **2.04**

Section 2 defines the concept of "novelty" to be applied under the Act. Like section 1 it is declared (by s. 130(7)) to have been framed to have, as nearly as practicable, the same effects as the corresponding provisions of the EPC, CPC and PCT, these provisions being EPCaa. 54, 55 and 89 and PCTrr. 33 and 64. Articles 4 and 6 of the Strasbourg Convention (1963) (Cmnd. 8002) are also relevant.

The definition of novelty is by reference to the (world-wide) state of the art (subs. (1)) which is defined in subsection (2), that definition being extended by subsection (3) to prior concurrent applications even though unpublished at the relevant date. Subsections (4)–(6) exempt certain limited circumstances from those which would otherwise be novelty-destroying under subsections (1)–(3).

It must be remembered that for validity a claim must possess, *inter alia*, both novelty under section 2 and inventive step under section 3. These are quite separate requirements, though (as will be seen) the boundary line between them is often indistinct. Nevertheless, the Comptroller has stated that there is nothing inconsistent in a finding that a claim lacks novelty, but would not be invalidated for obviousness (*Mita Industrial's Application*, SRIS O/125/85).

Novelty destroyed by the state of the art (subss. (1) and (2))

—The state of the art **2.05**

Subsection (1) defines "new" as not forming part of the state of the art and subsection (2) defines "state of the art" in terms calling for universal novelty. The Act contains no concession in respect of public trial such as that in section 51(3) [1959]. Novelty has to be absolute both as to the place and nature of the state of the art, which comprises all matter which, before the priority date of an invention, has been made available to the public anywhere and in any way. This is in sharp contrast to the position under previous United Kingdom patent statutes where the only relevant prior art was that available to the public within the United Kingdom. This principle of local, as compared to absolute, novelty is still applicable to "existing patents", for which see paras. A032.10–A032.12 in Appendix A.

There is no definition of "made available to the public" and the words are themselves used as the definition of "published" in section 130(1) (as they are also so used in the corresponding definition in s. 101 [1949]). The reference to inspection "at any place in the United Kingdom" in this definition does not affect the question of availability to the public under section 2, but the statement in the second part of the definition of section 130(1) that "a document shall be taken to be published if it can be inspected as of right at any place in the United Kingdom by members of the public, whether on payment of a fee or otherwise" (wording also found in the definition of "published" in s. 101 [1949]) would seem to suggest that, if these criteria are met, the question of "published" is to be beyond further argument. However, clearly a document may be held to be published even if it fails to meet these criteria. For further discussion of the meaning of "published" as determined under the previous statutes, see para. A101.10 in Appendix A.

It is also not clear if "made available to the public" implies something beyond a mere oral disclosure anywhere and in any way, but EPO Guideline C-IV, 5.2 follows the concept derived from *Humpherson v. Syer* ((1887) 4 RPC 403) as elaborated by *Bristol-Myers' Application* ([1969] RPC 146), and reviewed and applied in *Catnic v. Evans* ([1983] FSR 410): namely, that the state of the art includes anything which is in possession of any member of the public which he is free in law and equity to use as he pleases; and so he may disclose to others without any inhibiting fetter of confidence, whether express or implied. A literal application of this principle anywhere whatsoever in the world leads to a remarkable view of what is available to the public; nevertheless, the language in which the disclosure is made would seem to be irrelevant, provided that this is capable of being understood by the public (whether or not in the United Kingdom).

In *Genentech's Patent* ([1989] RPC 147 (CA)), it was stated that matter is not available to the public if it is merely known to one or two individual research workers pursuing their own experiments in private, the "public" being the community of research workers skilled in the art in general. In the context of the validity of a registered design, an inter-group communication not intended for, never communicated to, and never reaching, the public has been held not to have been made available to the public (*Sommer Allibert v. Flair Plastics*, [1987] RPC 599). In *James Industries' Patent* ([1987] RPC 235), following *Gallay's Application* ([1959] RPC 141), a letter had been written by the Patentees to the applicants for revocation at a time when it was held they were partners in a joint commercial venture. An obligation of confidence consequently ensued, despite the absence of an agreement between the parties, and the letter did not therefore form part of the state of the art. In *Codex v. Racal-Milgo* (SRIS C/135/81, *noted* IPD 4100) publication of an abstract of a thesis was held, under section 32(1) [1949], not to make the thesis itself available to the public in the absence of evidence that the offer of inspection of the thesis contained in the abstract was realistic.

A date of publication which appears on, or in connection with, a particular document is presumed to be the date on which its contents became available to the public. This presumption can only be rebutted by convincing evidence that the document did not in fact become available to the public on the date stated. Thus, in *Microsonics' Application* ([1984] RPC 29), a statement in the United States Patent Office Official Gazette that, though printing of certain patents had been delayed, the files thereof would be available from the official issue date was not overcome by affidavits merely reporting conversations with officials of the United States Patent Office which tended to contradict the official notice. The evidence submitted was not by persons who were personally qualified to testify on the point in issue, the statements presented being of a second-hand hearsay nature, and therefore were not admissible under the provisions of section 2 of the Civil Evidence Act 1968 (c. 64). This presumption was also applied in: *EPO Decision T 287/86*, "*Photoelectric densitometer/TOBIUS*" ([1989] 4 EPOR 214) in relation to a dated copyright notice appearing on a brochure; and in *EPO Decision T 381/87*, "*Publication/ RESEARCH CORP.*" ([1989] 3 EPOR 138), where it was held (on the balance of probabilities, which was considered sufficient) that a scientific paper had been made available to the public on its stated date of publication, it being considered immaterial whether or not any member of the public actually then knew that the paper was available or actually asked to see it. However, publication had not occurred on the stated date of submission of the paper for publication because, until actual publication, its contents were subject to an obligation of confidence.

16

—*The general test for lack of novelty* **2.06**

The test for lack of novelty (in contrast to what qualifies for inclusion in the state of the art) appears to be the same under the new law as under the old, with the possible exceptions of prior use (discussed in para. 2.17 *infra*) and of a non-enabling disclosure (discussed in paras. 2.18 and 2.20 *infra*). This test appears to have been authoritatively stated by Sachs L.J. in *General Tire* v. *Firestone* ([1972] RPC 457 at pp. 485–486) in the following terms:

"When the prior inventor's publication and the patentee's claim have respectively been construed by the court in the light of all properly admissible evidence as to technical matters, the meaning of words and expressions used in the art and so forth, the question whether the patentee's claim is new for the purposes of section 32(1)(e) [1949] falls to be decided as a question of fact. If the prior inventor's publication contains a clear description of, or clear instruction to do or make, something that would infringe the patentee's claim if carried out after the grant of the patentee's patent, the patentee's claim will have been shown to lack the necessary novelty, that is to say, it will have been anticipated. The prior inventor, however, and the patentee may have approached the same device from different starting points and may for this reason, or it may be for other reasons, have so described their devices that it cannot be immediately discerned from a reading of the language which they have respectively used that they have discovered in truth the same device; but if carrying out the directions contained in the prior inventor's publication will inevitably result in something being made or done which, if the patentee's patent were valid, would constitute an infringement of the patentee's claim, this circumstance demonstrates that the patentee's claim has in fact been anticipated.

If, on the other hand, the prior publication contains a direction which is capable of being carried out in a manner which would infringe the patentee's claim, but would be at least as likely to be carried out in a way which would not do so, the patentee's claim will not have been anticipated, although it may fail on the ground of obviousness. To anticipate the patentee's claim the prior publication must contain clear and unmistakeable directions to do what the patentee claims to have invented: *Flour Oxidizing Co. Ltd.* v. *Carr & Co. Ltd.* ((1908) 25 RPC 428 at p. 457, line 34, approved in *B.T.H. Co. Ltd.* v. *Metropolitan Vickers Electrical Co. Ltd.* (1928) 45 RPC 1 at p. 24, line 1). A signpost, however clear, upon the road to the patentee's invention will not suffice. The prior inventor must be clearly shown to have planted his flag at the precise destination before the patentee."

The *General Tire* approaches to novelty do not appear to be inconsistent with those of the EPO, see EPO Guidelines C-IV, 7 (and in particular C-IV, 7.2 and 7.5 discussed in para. 2.12 *infra*), though in some areas (notably those of selection inventions and the second medical use (respectively discussed in paras. 2.14–2.16 and 2.29 *infra*) there are differences of approach between the United Kingdom decisions and those given by the EPO. Another potential area of difference, discussed in paras. 2.18 and 2.20 *infra*, is that of the "enabling" disclosure and whether or not this is necessary in a prior art document for novelty to be destroyed thereby.

—*The "post infringement" or "right to work" test* **2.07**

The first part of the quoted *General Tire* definition is the "post-infringement" or "right to work" test: namely that which would infringe a patent would also anticipate that patent if unequivocally done, described or claimed before the priority date of that patent. Thus, a defendant who is conducting operations which were carried on before the priority date of the invention claimed can succeed either by a finding of lack of novelty (or obviousness) based on those prior operations or on a finding of non-infringement, see *Reymes-Cole* v. *Elite Hosiery* ([1964] RPC 255 and [1965] RPC 102 (CA)), where the former was held. Another example is *Gill* v. *Coutts* ((1896) 13 RPC 125) where the novelty-destroying prior user did not know the composition of the material he had been using. An extreme example of the post-infringement test was the casual, though novelty-destroying, disclosure in *Molins* v. *Industrial Machinery* ((1937) 54 RPC 94 and (1938) 55 RPC 31). *Per contra*, novelty may be held to reside merely because the claimed article is of a different type to that of the prior art. For example, in *Hickman* v. *Andrews* ([1983] RPC 147), the prior art was held not to describe a "workbench" though all the other features of the claim were described therein.

This "right to work" test was confirmed in *Bristol-Myers' (Johnson's) Application* ([1975] RPC 127 (HL)) wherein Lord Diplock stated (at p. 156) that a trader has a right to go on dealing by way of trade in any man-made substance in which he has dealt before even if he did not know what it was or how to make it, or even if he had not disclosed it to the public or given them the means to find out for themselves. The "right to work" test was also derived from the Statute of Monopolies by Lord Denning M.R. earlier in the same case ([1973] RPC 157 at pp. 164–166 (CA)).

The "post-infringement" test was also specifically upheld in *Windsurfing* v. *Tabur Marine* ([1985] RPC 59 (CA)) where it was stated:

"The notion behind anticipation is that it would be wrong to enable the patenteee to prevent a man from doing what he has lawfully done before the patent was granted."

The test was also applied, though not on the facts of the case upheld, in *Fairfax* v. *Filhol* ([1986] RPC 499). The "right to work" test is the subject of an article by B. C. Reid listed in para. 2.03 *supra*.

2.08   *—The requirement of "inevitable result"*

The second part of the *General Tire* definition for lack of novelty quoted in para. 2.06 *supra* is one of "inevitable result". The requirement of inevitability was first considered in *Fomento* v. *Mentmore* ([1956] RPC 87) and was more fully considered in *Letraset* v. *Rexel* ([1974] RPC 175 and [1976] RPC 51) and in *Letraset* v. *Dymo* ([1976] RPC 65), see also *Institute Français' Application* ([1972] RPC 364). It is submitted that the requirement of "inevitability" should not be applied blindly or unduly rigidly. Otherwise, conflict will arise with the "post-infringement" test discussed in para. 2.07 *supra*.

2.09   *—The "planting the flag" test*

The third part of the *General Tire* definition quoted in para. 2.06 *supra* is the test described therein as "planting the flag at the precise destination before the patentee". This requirement seems to override the first two parts of the general test with which it may sometimes be in conflict.

The "planting the flag" test was approved in *Du Pont's (Witsiepe's) Application* ([1982] FSR 303 (HL)) and it was also held not to have been fulfilled in *Bugges* v. *Herbon* ([1972] RPC 197 at p. 210). However, this type of test was held to be fulfilled in *Van der Lely* v. *Bamfords* ([1961] RPC 296 (CA) and [1963] RPC 61 (HL)) which involved the interpretation of a photograph by a man skilled in the art who could deduce therefrom features not explicitly disclosed therein.

A broader formulation of the test in the *Van der Lely* case was applied in *Dow Chemical* v. *Spence Bryson (No. 2)* ([1984] RPC 359 (CA)). Here it was stated that:

"A skilled technician, after considering [the cited document], would have been able to produce without anything more than ordinary workshop methods of trial and error a foam rubber which would have infringed claim 1 of the patent in suit. This satisfies the test for anticipation in *Van der Lely* v. *Bamfords* ([1963] RPC 61)."

Such an approach appears to combine the three parts of the *General Tire* test. Although it borders on the consideration of obviousness (which ought to be considered separately, now under s. 3), the difference remains that, in attacking novelty, it is not permissible to make a mosaic of separate items of prior art which were not (at the relevant date) part of the common general knowledge of a person skilled in the art.

In *Ward's Applications* ([1986] RPC 50) the Comptroller specifically applied, in relation to applications under the present Act, the *General Tire* test and held that the prior art must contain a clear and unmistakeable direction to do what was subsequently claimed, and then allowed the claims in suit.

—Mere novelty of purpose   **2.10**

Although a new use of an old article is patentable, the new use must normally be claimed as a new method of using the old article because novelty is not provided merely by specifying the purpose for which an old article is now intended (*Adhesive Dry Mounting* v. *Trapp*, (1910) 27 RPC 341), just as infringement of a claim to an article is not avoided by using that article for a purpose different from that envisaged by the patent. Nevertheless, in the special case of medical use (when the novel purpose cannot, by virtue of s. 4(2), be patented by a claim directed to a method of treatment of the human or animal body), the *Adhesive Dry Mounting* case has, in effect, been distinguished by *John Wyeth's and Schering's Applications* ([1983] RPC 545), discussed in para. 2.29 *infra* in relation to subsection (6), though having regard to the reservations expressed in that decision the intention was, apparently, to leave *Adhesive Dry Mounting* as good law in other areas. However, the EPO is considering this question further, see *EPO Decision T* 59/87, "*Friction reducing additive/MOBIL II*" (OJEPO 9/1988, 347; [1989] 2 EPOR 80) noted in para. 2.13 *infra*.

Previously, in *EPO Decision T* 231/85, "*Triazole derivatives/BASF*" (OJEPO 3/1989, 74; [1989] 5 EPOR 293), claims were allowed to "Use of X for controlling and preventing fungus growth" when X was already known for use as a growth promoter, the fact that the new use may need no technical realisation over the previously known use being regarded as irrelevant. In the United Kingdom claims to a "use" are generally required to be formulated as a claim to a method of doing something and then it is seen that, at least by traditional concepts, such a claim possesses only a novelty of purpose. Thus, at some stage, the *Adhesive Dry Mounting* decision may require re-appraisal in the light of developing treatment under the EPC.

—Construction of the prior art document   **2.11**

When considering novelty, it is important to read the prior art document as it would have been read as at its date of publication, without regard to the patent in suit or any other subsequent information (*Minnesota Mining* v. *Bondina*, [1973] RPC 491). It is, of course, possible that the person skilled in the art would not read the document in a different way at a later date, but that then is a question of obviousness, because at that date it may be that the person would then pay it no, or only scant, attention, see para. 3.13.

It is, however, possible to present evidence to show what a document conveyed at its date of publication to a person skilled in the art, see *Van der Lely* v. *Bamfords* ([1963] RPC 61 (HL)); but, where a document cited as a prior publication is susceptible of two possible interpretations, the onus of proof is on an applicant for revocation to establish that there truly is an anticipatory disclosure (*James Industries' Patent*, [1987] RPC 235). Perhaps, therefore, in *ex parte* proceedings, an applicant should be given the benefit of the doubt in such circumstances.

2.12 *—EPO Guidelines*

The concept of lack of novelty is discussed in EPO Guideline C-IV, 7. It is there pointed out that a mosaic must not be made of separate items of prior art unless, of course, the relevant documents are referenced to each other and would be read by the skilled person as one document. The EPO Guidelines also state that a disclosure takes away the novelty of any claimed subject matter, derivable directly and unambiguously from it, including any features implicit to a person skilled in the art in what is explicitly contained in it. A disclosure, however, does not include equivalents. Also, a generic disclosure does not usually take away the novelty of any specific example falling within it, though a specific disclosure does deprive of novelty a general claim embracing that disclosure: these aspects are discussed further in para. 2.16 *infra*.

In the case of a published document, the lack of novelty may be apparent from what is explicitly stated in the document itself. Alternatively, it may be implicit in that, in carrying out the teaching of the document, a skilled person would inevitably arrive at a result falling within the terms of the claim. The interpretation of a claim for these purposes should be such as to disregard non-distinctive characteristics such as statement of purpose (see Guidelines C-III, 4.8 and C-IV, 7.6). The usual interpretation rules apply, *i.e.* taking the normal grammatical meaning and giving the words their usual meaning in the relevant art unless another meaning is clearly intended (Guideline C-III, 4). In the case of a chemical compound there should, apparently, be an enabling disclosure so that it can be prepared and separated by the skilled person on the basis of knowledge generally available at the date of the document cited, a concept which is discussed more fully in para. 2.18 and 2.20 *infra*.

2.13 *—EPO decisions concerning lack of novelty*

The approach of the EPO to special areas of the law pertaining to novelty of patent claims is discussed: as to "selection inventions" in para. 2.16 *infra*; as to a non-enabling disclosure in paras. 2.18 and 2.20 *infra*; and as to discoveries of further medical uses of known substances in relation to subsection (6) in paras. 2.28 and 2.29 *infra*. Now here discussed are EPO decisions on more fundamental points, particularly the extent to which the inherent or implied teaching of a document is to be taken into account in addition to its explicit wording.

First, the EPO has held that, where a further functional attribute of an element of a device disclosed in a prior art document is immediately apparent to a person skilled in the art of reading that document, such attribute forms part of the state of the art with regard to that device (*EPO Decision T* 06/80, "*Intermediate layer for reflector*", OJEPO 10/1981, 434). Thus, this case has confirmed that lack of novelty may be implicit; it applies to what is both expressly and impliedly disclosed by a document to a reader skilled in the art.

Secondly, it is appropriate, in assessing novelty, to read the disclosure of one document together with that of another document cross-referenced therein (*EPO*

Decision T 153/85, *"Alternative claims/AMOCO CORPORATION"*, [1988] 2 EPOR 116), but not to combine a general statement contained in a prior art document with a specific statement which the skilled reader would not have read in combination therewith (*EPO Decision T* 291/85, *"Catalyst/BAYER"*, OJEPO 8/1988, 302; [1988] 6 EPOR 371). In other words a document must be read as a whole in relation to the invention described. Thus, where prior art is acknowledged in a priority document, the contents of that prior art cannot be relied upon to provide a basis for priority (*EPO Decision T* 85/87, *"Arthropodicidal compounds/CSIRO"*, [1989] 1 EPOR 24).

Similarly, in *EPO Decision T* 204/83 *"Venturi/CHARBONNAGES"* (OJEPO 10/1985, 310; [1986] 1 EPOR 1), it was held that features in a prior art drawing are part of the state of the art when a person skilled in the art is able to derive technical teaching from the drawing, but that dimensions obtained merely by measuring a diagrammatic representation in a prior patent specification do not form part of the art as no skilled person would rely upon dimensions so obtained. However, the EPO has since held that a publication cannot be removed from the state of the art, even if it contains foolish-looking instructions, and that the same applies to other publications irrespective of their geographical location or the alleged reputation of the periodical (*EPO Decision T* 48/85, *"Eimeria necatrix/NRDC"*, [1987] 3 EPOR 138).

In *EPO Decision T* 161/82, *"Electrical contact/AMP"* (OJEPO 11/1984, 551) it was stated that, where a disclosure in a prior art document could accidentally fall within the wording of a claim, a particularly careful comparison needs to be made between what can fairly be considered to fall within the wording of the claim and what is effectively shown in the document: the novelty of the claimed invention was then upheld over the alleged chance anticipation.

In *EPO Decision T* 205/83, *"Vinyl ester/crotonic acid copolymers/HOECHST"* (OJEPO 12/1985, 363; [1986] 2 EPOR 57) the Appeal Board disallowed a claim to a copolymer defined solely by a "product-by-process" claim on the basis that, if the product could only be defined by process, rather than structural, parameters, the onus is on the applicant to establish by evidence that modification of the stated process results in other products, for example by such other products having different properties; but reliance may not here be placed upon evidence showing differences in properties which cannot be due to different structural paramenters, for example in this case the absence of malodorous monomer impurities. Likewise, in *EPO Decision T* 248/85, *"Radiation Processing/BICC"* (OJEPO 8/1986, 261; [1986] 6 EPOR 311), a product-by-process claim was rejected on an admission that the product was *per se* indistinguishable from a product of the prior art and a process will not be new if the prior art discloses the same starting materials and reaction conditions because, then, identical products must inevitably result (*EPO Decision T* 302/86, *"Flavour concentrates/CPC"*, [1989] 2 EPOR 95). Also, a mere difference in wording is insufficient to establish novelty (*EPO Decision T* 114/86, *"Foam Plastic filter/ERIKKSON"*, OJEPO 11/1987, 485; [1988] 1 EPOR 25).

The EPO does not regard a document as inherently disclosing claimed parameters unless it is shown that these are inevitably obtained by following its disclosure (*EPO Decision T* 103/86, *"Phenylenediamine/DU PONT"*, [1987] 5 EPOR 265), thereby following United Kingdom law, see para. 2.08 *supra*.

While the EPO Guidelines C-III, 4.8 and C-IV, 7.6 generally adopt the British rule that there is no novelty in merely adding a statement of purpose (as discussed in para. 2.10 *supra*), this question has been referred to the Enlarged Board of Appeal (*EPO Decision T* 59/87, *"Friction reducing additive/MOBIL II"*, OJEPO 9/1988, 347; [1989] 2 EPOR 80) in the context of whether a claim to a compound X can be validated by limting it to "Use of X as a lubricating additive" in the face of a document which had described X as an oil additive for inhibiting rust formation, and apparently in view of varying jurisprudence in different EPC Contracting States.

2.14   *—Selection inventions*

The approach of the EPO to "selection inventions" is discussed in para. 2.16 *infra*, but these have long been regarded as patentable in the United Kingdom on the principles first clearly enunciated in *IG Farbenindustrie's Patents* ((1930) 47 RPC 289). These principles are discussed in the articles by J. Jeffs and M. F. Vivian each listed in para. 2.03 *supra*. They appear to be that a general disclosure is not to be regarded as a specific disclosure of everything embraced by the general disclosure, thereby permitting claims to protect further discoveries within (or selected from) the prior general disclosure without violating the requirement for novelty, always provided that the selected specific subject-matter involves an inventive step, usually demonstrated by some superiority in properties or effect of the selected class compared to that provided by the prior general disclosure or inherent therein, each as a matter of generality.

2.15   *—The Amoxycillin and Du Pont cases*

In *Beecham Group's (Amoxycillin) Application* ([1980] RPC 261) it was held, albeit under section 14 [1949], that an amended claim requiring a particular chemical compound to be comprised in "a pharmaceutical composition adapted for oral administration to human beings" was not anticipated by a prior disclosure which hinted at both the compound in question and the possibility of formulation of the disclosed compounds for oral administration. It was held that the cited document did not contain clear and specific directions to make up the particular composition as claimed in the amended claim. This case is further discussed as to inventive step in para. 3.19. In the corresponding case in New Zealand (*Beecham Group v. Bristol-Myers (Amoxycillin) (No. 2)* [*New Zealand*], [1980] 1 NZLR 192) the claim was to a compound in the form of an epimer. It was held (also in opposition proceedings) that this claim was not anticipated by a prior disclosure of a mixture containing the epimer as 50 per cent. thereof in the absence of specific instructions to make the pure epimer. The court here followed a similar decision in the United States (*Re May and Eddy*, (1978) 197 USPQ 601). However, on appeal the New Zealand Court of Appeal upheld the decision below, but regarded an unrestricted product claim as too wide in the circumstances and indicated that some amendment, for example as made in the United Kingdom, should be made (*Beecham Group's (Amoxycillin) Application* [*New Zealand*], [1982] FSR 181).

In *I.C.I.'s (Howe's) Application* ([1977] RPC 121) a claim to a class of resolved enantiomers was also found novel over a prior disclosure of these compounds where no reference was made to optical isomers. However, in Australia extension of term of a patent of addition was refused on a finding that its claims lacked novelty over, or were prior claimed by, the parent patent in a case which also involved the subsequent isolation and commercialisation of a particular isomer initially prepared as part of a mixture of isomers, (*ICI's Australian Patent Extensions* [1981] RPC 163). Claims to individual isomers have also been rejected by the EPO, see para. 2.16 *infra*.

In *Du Pont's (Witsiepe's) Application* ([1981] FSR 377 (CA) and [1982] FSR 303 (HL)) it was held (under section 14 [1949]) that a claim requiring the use of a glycol having four carbon atoms was not devoid of novelty though an earlier patent, dated some 30 years previously, had specified in the same process the generic use of a glycol having from one to ten carbon atoms, and the four carbon glycol had been specifically mentioned therein, though not in any example and only in the context of prior art discussed in its preamble. Both the Court of Appeal and House of Lords stated that the novelty of a claim is only destroyed by a clear disclosure and that a pointer is not sufficient, citing *General Tire* v. *Firestone* ([1972] RPC 457), as discussed on this point at para. 2.09 *supra*. It was thus held that there was no clear instruction in the prior document to use the specific glycol in question and the fact that this was mentioned by name in a list therein was an irrelevance. Thus, in a case involving prior published art where the later application exhibited a special advantage, the disclosure of a class was not a specific disclosure of each member thereof. In addition, both the Court of Appeal and House of Lords placed emphasis on the importance of a prior art chemical compound having previously been made and its properties ascertained before it could be regarded as "known" or "published", see also *Beecham* v. *Bristol SA* ([1978] RPC 521) and *Beecham Group's (Amoxycillin) Application (No. 2) [New Zealand] (supra)).

Thus the principle of selection inventions has been firmly upheld when special advantages for the selection material have been discovered; and it does not matter whether the original field was described by general formula or by enumeration of a list. It was also pointed out that the size of the group (or list) is irrelevant to the question of novelty, but it may be relevant to the question of obviousness, though this was not in issue in the *Du Pont* case.

The *Du Pont* decision would appear to be equally applicable to the question of novelty arising under section 2, but it can perhaps be seen as a case decided on special facts which has taken the law to its ultimate limit and is inconsistent with the approach adopted by the EPO to selection inventions, with the possible exception that in *Du Pont* part of the prior disclosure was contained in the acknowledged prior art, as noted *supra*. The implications of the statements in its judgments that a chemical compound is not deprived of novelty unless the prior art document states that it has been made and reports some of its properties has been considered by B. C. Reid ([1982] EIPR 118). This principle is still followed by the Comptroller under the Act, as it was under the 1949 Act in *Gyogyszeripari's Application* ([1958] RPC 51) and *SKF's Application* ([1968] RPC 415). However, it can produce results at variance with those from the EPO, which instead is concerned that the prior art document contains an "enabling disclosure", not in issue in the *Du Pont* case and as to which see paras. 2.18 and 2.20 *infra*. It should also be noted that, in the United States case of *In re. Sivaramakrishnan* ([1982] 213 USPQ 441 (CCPA)), with a similar fact situation to that in the *Du Pont* case, it was held that, as there is no legal requirement in United States law for a reference teaching to have been actually reduced to practice, there was lack of novelty.

—The EPO approach   **2.16**

The EPO approach to selection inventions is set out in EPO Guideline C-IV, 7.4 which states that a specific disclosure takes away the novelty of a generic claim embracing it. So far the EPO interprets "specific" as a mere matter of disclosure so that there is a clear divergence between the EPO and the unanimous view taken by all three United Kingdom courts in the *Du Pont* case (discussed in para. 2.15 *supra*) and also a divergence as regards the making and testing requirement stipulated by the appellate courts in that case, see para. 2.15 *supra*. The EPO view is perhaps closer to the approach to the novelty of selection inventions under German law, which was described and contrasted with the British view in the paper by G. S. A. Szabo listed in para. 2.03 *supra*. Nevertheless, the EPO has upheld selection inventions in a number of cases, for example in: *EPO Decision T* 01/80. *"Carbonless Copying Paper"* ([1982] RPC 321; OJEPO 7/1981, 206); *EPO Decision T* 198/84, *"Thiochloroformates/HOECHST"* (OJEPO 7/1985, 209); *EPO Decision T* 433/86, *"Modified Diisocyanates/ICI"* ([1988] 2 EPOR 97); and *EPO Decision T* 7/86, *"Xanthines/DRACO"* (OJEPO 10/1988, 381; [1989] 2 EPOR 65), see the paper by G. S. A. Szabo noted *supra*.

The most-often cited EPO decision concerning selection inventions is *EPO Decision T* 12/81 *"Diastereomers"* (OJEPO 8/1982, 296). Here the Appeal Board stated that the concept of novelty must not be given such a narrow interpretation that only what has already been described in terms is prejudicial to it: "the purpose of EPCa. 54(1) is to prevent the state of the art being patented again". In that decision it was stated that, while selection of the elements of a product from *two* lists (here of starting materials) avoids lack of novelty, where a starting material chosen from a list is combined with one of a number of listed processes, not only does the corresponding process lack novelty, but so also does the inevitably obtained end product. The actual decision in *"Diastereomers"* appears unsatisfactory because it does not comply with the "planting the flag" test discussed in para. 2.09 *supra*. However, the "selection from two lists" principle referred to in this case appears unexceptional and has been applied to find novelty when a selection was made from separate lists of substituents, see *EPO Decision T* 7/86, *"Xanthines/DRACO"* (*supra*) and *EPO Decision T* 61/85. *"Polyester crystallisation/ICI"* ([1988] 1 EPOR 20).

Much of the EPO jurisprudence in the area of selection has been developed in connection with attempts to patent a selection from a numerical range. Thus, in *EPO Decision T* 194/84, *"Thiochloroformates/HOECHST"* (*supra*), the principle was established that, for a sub-range selected from a broader range of numbers to be novel, the selected sub-range must be narrow and sufficiently far removed from the known range as illustrated by examples in the prior disclosure. On this basis, a claim which met these criteria was allowed. The sub-range claimed was novel by virtue of an effect which was demonstrated to occur only within the sub-range and was not merely a newly-discovered effect associated with the whole range. However, the stated criteria in this case were subsequently varied in *EPO Decision T* 7/86, *"Xanthines/Draco* (*supra*), so that the prior art should make "available", rather than merely "reveal the content" of, the invention's subject-matter to the skilled person in a technical teaching.

The earlier *EPO Decision T* 188/83, *"Vinyl acetate/FERNHOLZ"* (OJEPO 11/1984, 555), discussed in para. 2.20 *infra*, in which the earlier disclosure was held to be novelty-destroying, is consistent with this principle. In that case, it was also stated that the discovery of a previously unappreciated advantage in the claimed process does not provide novelty without the process having been modified. *EPO Decision T* 17/85, *"Filler/PLÜSS-STAUFFER"* (OJEPO 12/1986, 406; [1987] 2 EPOR 66) and *EPO Decision T* 124/87, *"Copolymers/Du Pont"* ([1989] 1 EPOR 33) were other numerical range cases in which the criteria formulated in *EPO Decision T* 194/84, *"Thiochloroformates/HOECHST"* (*supra*) were held not to have been met.

The latter decision was criticised by J. C. H. Ellis in his paper listed in para. 2.03 *supra*, where he points out that its finding, and by implication also many of the other EPO decisions concerning selection inventions, would not be expected under United Kingdom law after applying the *General Tire* tests discussed in paras. 2.06–2.09 *supra*. However, it may be that here the EPO failed to appreciate the distinction which it has drawn (for priority purposes) between an implied teaching and an obvious modification of express or implied teaching (see *EPO Decision T* 85/87, *"Arthropodicidal compounds/CSIRO"* ([1989] 1 EPOR 24). This distinction should also be applied to an invention of selection. Such is patentable even if it would fail the "could", but not the "would", test of what the skilled man was taught by the prior document could/should be done, see para. 3.40. Indeed, the "could/would" test was applied to the question of novelty of a selection in *EPO Decision T 7/86, "Xanthines/DRACO" (supra)*.

—Special considerations in cases of prior use   **2.17**

Under subsection 2 novelty is determined according to whether the invention has been *made available to the public* by written or oral description, by use or in any other way. Thus prior secret use no longer anticipates as it does for existing patents under s.32(1)(*l*) [1949]. Instead, the prior user acquires a prescriptive right to continue his former activity (see section 64 and the commentary thereon), but under the Act the patent is enforceable against third parties. However, section 64 does not apply unless the prior act would, if carried out after the patent grant, have been an act of infringement thereof, and hence the exceptions to infringement of "private and non-commercial use" (s. 60(5)(*a*)) and of "experimental use relating to the subject-matter of the invention (s. 60(5)(*b*)) cause difficulties, as discussed in para. 64.06. The distinction between public and secret prior use (under the Act, but in the context of s. 60) was discussed in *Monsanto* v. *Stauffer (No. 2)* ([1985] RPC 515).

Prior use must be distinctly pleaded, see RSC Ord. 104, rule 6(3) (reprinted in para. E104.6), and inspection must be given if the prior used apparatus, etc., is still in existence and in the possession of the party alleging invalidity, see RSC Ord. 104, rule 16(3) (reprinted in para. E104.16).

In *Dunlop's Application* ([1979] RPC 523) it was stated that proof of prior user is required only on the normal civil law standard of the "balance of probabilities". The test previously suggested in *Toyo's Application* ([1962] RPC 9) that prior use should be "strictly" (*i.e.* conclusively) proved was expressly disapproved. However, allegations of prior use based solely on recollection without corroborative documents are likely to be received with scepticism, see for example *Leggatt* v. *Hood* ((1949) 66 RPC 243 and (1951) 68 RPC 3 (CA)).

It is a matter of debate whether novelty is destroyed under the Act in the circumstances of *Bristol-Myers' (Johnson's) Application* ([1973] RPC 157; [1975] RPC 127) where a chemical compound was held to be the subject of prior public use, even though at the time the manufacturer who made and sold it was not aware that it had the nature specified in the attacked patent claim. P. R. Lambert ((1980–81 10 CIPA 246) suggests the decision would be different under the present section 2 on the basis that, following EPO Guideline D-V, 3.1 (*to qualify as prior use the public must have had access to the invention*), prior use that does not give means of knowledge to the public was abolished for the present Act. In his "Right to work" article listed in para. 2.03 *supra*, B. C. Reid, however, argues that it is inherent in the patent system that by prior use in public, the public acquires a right to work which cannot be taken away by a subsequent patent. The question has also been considered by Helen Jones ((1987–88) 17 CIPA 342) and by P. A. Chandler in his article listed in para. 2.03 *supra*.

The question is whether to destroy novelty the invention must be made available to the public in a manner giving them knowledge of it, or whether the post-infringement test of novelty referred to in para. 2.07 *supra* suffices. The answer awaits judicial evaluation, as discussed further in para. 2.18 *infra*. In the meantime, however, it seems that the "right to work" and "post-infringment" doctrines, being fundamental to the patent system, are very strong and in the absence of contrary decision of courts in other EPC countries are unlikely to be discarded. Also, in the

Bristol-Myers' case the claimed *product* had indeed been made available to the public, who had had the benefit of it.

The principle of the *Bristol-Myers'* case was followed in *Wheatley's Application* ([1985] RPC 91 (CA)) decided under the 1949 Act. Here, following a confidential demonstration of an article, an order for it was placed before the priority date but the article was (deliberately) only delivered thereafter. The claims were held anticipated even as to features not disclosed until possession of the article had passed, the confidential demonstration amounting to a "use", giving the word the broad meaning in ordinary English usage, and the element of confidentiality was removed by the acceptance of the offer for sale. Under the 1977 Act it would seem that the invention would thereby have been made available to the public, if not by use then, "in any other way". However, the EPO would not, apparently, regard the prior use in *Wheatley* as an enabling disclosure and accordingly would reject it as available prior art, see *EPO Decision T* 242/85, *"Reinforced channels/CHEMIE LINZ"* ([1988] 2 EPOR 77) where a prior use was discounted as novelty-destroying because this had not revealed to the public all of the features of the invention, though the claims were found to lack an inventive step.

In *Windsurfing* v. *Tabur Marine* ([1985] RPC 59 (CA)) a prior use construction was proved which had all the features of the claim except for a pair of arcuate booms. Though the booms in the prior art device were straight, they were also pliable and in use would have assumed an arcuate form. Since the device had been used and the tests of novelty and infringement were stated to be essentially the same, the prior use was held to be novelty-destroying under section 32(1)(*e*) [1949].

The question of the process by which a product has been made raises further problems: this was the issue in *Gore* v. *Kimal* ([1988] RPC 137) where it was held (under s.32(1)(*e*) [1949]) that public distribution of a product in the course of trade before the priority date constituted a prior use of the process claimed, irrespective of whether it would have been possible to ascertain from the product what process had been used and irrespective of whether the process took place in the United Kingdom or whether (as was the case) it took place abroad. It can be seen that, if the process claims had been upheld in these circumstances, importation of the product resulting therefrom would have been an infringement even though the same act had been done before the priority date. Thus, the "post-infringement" test discussed in para. 2.07 *supra* was, in effect, applied. For comment on this case, see P. A. Chandler ([1988] EIPR 221).

2.18   *—The "non-enabling" disclosure*

As noted in para. 2.12 *supra*, EPO Guideline C-IV, 7.3 refers to the need for a disclosure of a chemical compound to be one which is sufficient to enable the compound to be made by the skilled person if the compound is to be held to have been "made available to the public". The converse doctrine of the "non-enabling disclosure", originally (according to this Guideline) only to be applied in respect of disclosures of chemical compounds, seems to have been derived from the United States precedent case of *In re. Le Grice* ((1957) 133 USPQ 372), which has been more widely applied in subsequent cases in that country. In this case a plant patent claiming a rose variety was held not anticipated by a foreign-published catalogue from the patentee illustrating the same variety. This was because the information given in the catalogue did not enable the skilled artisan to be in possession of the invention. The doctrine of the "non-enabling disclosure" has so far been mostly applied by the EPO in the situation where the prior art document is a prior dated, but unpublished, patent application effective as prior art only under EPCa. 54(3) (corresponding to subsection (3)) and is therefore particularly discussed in relation thereto at para. 2.20 *infra*, but it has also been invoked in respect of a prior use, see para. 2.17 *supra*, and see the reformulation of *EPO Decision T* 198/84, "*Thiochloroformates/HOECHST*" (OJEPO 7/1985, 209) noted in para. 2.16 *supra*.

Whether the doctrine is part of English law appeared to be a debatable point, but it was upheld in *Genentech's [Human Growth Hormone] Patent* (SRIS C/64/89) though then applied only to a situation under section 2(3) (for which see below and para. 2.20 *infra*). The basis for this doctrine (even as applied in the USA) is *Hills* v. *Evans* ((1862) 31 L.J. Ch. 457; 4 De G.F. & J. 288; 44 E.R. 1195 (HL)), where Lord Westbury stated that:

> "the antecedent statement must be such that a person of ordinary knowledge of the subject would at once perceive, understand and be able practically to apply the discovery without the necessity of making further experiments and gaining further information before the invention can be made useful. If something remains to be ascertained which is necessary for the useful application of that discovery, that affords sufficient reason for another valid patent."

The first sentence of this quotation, with its reference to applying the discovery practically, has often been quoted with approval, see *Kaye* v. *Chubb* ((1887) 4 RPC 289 (CA); (1888) 5 RPC 641 (HL)); *Van der Lely* v. *Bamfords* ([1963] RPC 61 (HL), at p. 71); *Ransburg* v. *Aerostyle* ([1968] RPC 287 (HL), at p. 299) and *Genentech's [Human Growth Hormone] Patent* (*supra*). Nevertheless, it is submitted that Lord Westbury's statement is not in conflict with the "planting the flag" test subsequently enunciated, as discussed in para. 2.09 *supra*. Moreover, if reliance is to be placed upon Lord Westbury's quoted dictum, its second sentence should not be overlooked. This must surely mean that claims can only be valid over a non-enabling disclosure if they are expressly limited to the (inventive) means whereby the inventor has become enabled practically to apply the prior disclosure. In the *Genentech* decision (*supra*) it was held that, though the compound mentioned in the prior-dated application could have been made at the priority date of the invention in issue, the method of doing so was neither described therein nor a matter of common general knowledge: consequently, the compound was not prior disclosed for the purposes of section 2(3). However, attention is drawn to the words "information about either" which appear in section 2(2) as forming part of the state of the art made available to the public: these words do not appear to have been discussed in this *Genentech* case.

Also, the statement in *Hills* v. *Evans* (*supra*) was subsequently explained by Lord Westbury, in *Neilson* v. *Betts* ((1870–71) 5 LR HL 1 at 15) as having been made by him in the context of a claim to a chemical process. Both these decisions can therefore be seen as only involving a disclosure held insufficient to constitute an anticipation of a later claimed process.

Note that, a special situation arises where the novelty objection arises under subsection (3) from the contents of a prior-dated, but unpublished, patent application, because no inventive step is then required to distinguish the claim over that prior art. The artificiality of this provision is then likely to give rise to other abnormalities of patent law, see paras. 2.19–2.21 *infra* and 3.26.

Also, note that, particularly in cases of prior use (as discussed for example in para. 2.17 *supra*), if the doctrine of the non-enabling disclosure were to become adopted generally, then the "right to work" or "post-infringement" test for lack of novelty (as discussed in para. 2.07 *supra*) would often lead to a contrary conclusion, see for example *EPO Decision T* 242/85, "*Reinforced channels/CHEMIE LINZ*" ([1988] 2 EPOR 77) referred to in para. 2.17 *supra*. However, the author of the non-enabling disclosure may himself not be caught by the subsequent patent if he can rely upon rights granted by section 64 (for which see the commentary thereon), but this would only be so if that author had carried out his work within the United Kingdom. Other inequities arising from an application of the "non-enablement" doctrine were illustrated by M. F. Vivian in his paper listed in para. 2.03 *supra*.

Effect of prior concurrent application (subs. (3))

2.19 *—General*

Subsection (3) corresponds to EPCa. 54(3) and (4) and specifies that the state of the art also comprises the whole contents of (*i.e.* comprises all matter contained in) an earlier application published on or after the relevant priority date, provided that the matter concerned was contained in the earlier application both as filed and as published and provided it has an earlier priority date. The "earlier application" can be an application under the Act, a European application designating the United Kingdom (ss. 78, 79) or an International application designating the United Kingdom (ss. 89, 89A and 89B). The "whole contents" of an earlier application comprised as part of the state of the art by subsection (3) is, by section 3, relevant only to novelty and *not* to consideration of inventive step. An objection under subsection (3) can be raised by the Comptroller even after grant (s. 73(1)).

Objection cannot arise under subsection (3) in respect of matter contained in a priority document (for example one filed in the EPO in respect of an application for a European patent (UK)) where such matter does not appear in the published application. This is because such document is not "published", because this term as used in subsection (3) is defined as meaning published (or deemed to be published) under section 16 (see s.130(5)) and a priority document as such is not published in this sense, but merely laid open to public inspection (*Smith's Patent*, SRIS O/16/86).

The test of novelty applicable for the purposes of subsection (3) ought, prima facie, not to be any different from that under subsection (2) discussed in paras. 2.05–2.18 *supra*. Thus, anything disclosed in the relevant prior application must be taken into account under subsection (3), just as under subsection (2) (*Szucs' Application (No. 2)*, SRIS 0/34/89, *noted* IPD 12051). Novelty should, therefore, exist "if there is any difference between the invention and the known art", in accordance with EPO Guideline C-IV, 9.1. For this purpose the unpublished application will be deemed to have been published on the priority date of the later invention and its contents interpreted in the light of the then common general knowledge in the art, see *Genentech's [Human Growth Hormone] Patent* (SRIS C/64/89).

In *Upjohn's Application* (SRIS O/6/83), the Comptroller stated that "If the result of subtracting the substance of the prior disclosure from the disclosure of the application in suit is that there is nothing of practical utility left then the applicant's invention cannot be new". This suggests that the penumbra around the disclosure of the prior application is only patentable if that penumbra is sufficiently supported by the specification so that it can stand on its own as regards the requirements of the Act other than novelty (s. 2) and inventive step (s. 3). But, in *Etter's Application* (SRIS O/45/84), where the invention of a later claim was held not disclosed in an earlier specification, an argument that the difference between the two claims was a mere matter of information (unpatentable under s. 1(2)) was rejected as irrelevant, as also was an argument that the later claim was to a mere mechanical equivalent of the invention of the earlier application. It should also be borne in mind that the test of anticipation includes what would have been likely to have been done by a skilled technician working the prior art using ordinary workshop methods of trial and error, as in *Dow Chemical* v. *Spence Bryson (No. 2)* ([1984] RPC 359), see para. 2.09 *supra*.

The EPO has also held that, in order to mitigate the harshness of the "whole contents" approach and reduce the risk of "self-collision", a strict approach to lack of novelty arising from citations only available under EPCa. 54(3) should be adopted and, therefore, a prior specification does not comprise other features which are "equivalent" to the features according to the claims (*EPO Decision T* 167/84, *"Fuel injector valve/NISSAN"*, OJEPO 8/1987, 369; [1987] 6 EPOR 344), but this view is not in accord with decisions in other jurisdictions, see para. 2.21 *infra*, or indeed with the concept of novelty otherwise adopted by the EPO, see para. 2.13 *supra*.

The true effect of subsection (3) therefore still awaits authoritative judicial interpretation. The question is further complicated by the possible need to discount a prior application, the disclosure of which is insufficient to enable this to be reproduced by the skilled person, see para. 2.20 *infra*. Meanwhile, the Comptroller now takes the view that any citation under section 2 should be regarded as an enabling one until the applicant may satisfy him to the contrary, see *Toyama's Application* (SRIS C/69/89). Here the Patents Court granted extra time for the submission of experimental evidence of non-enablement on the appeal, but indicated that new evidence on appeal would in future be a rare concession, see para. 18.14.

—Enabling disclosure and subsection (3)   **2.20**

In the chemical field the EPO (following Guideline C-IV, 7.3) has held that a prior disclosure does not make an invention "available to the public" unless the disclosure is such as to enable its skilled reader to carry out what is described therein, there being a test of sufficiency for lack of novelty under EPCa. 54(2) (the equivalent of subsection (2)) which is the same as the test for sufficiency of a patent specification under EPCa. 83 (s. 14(3)). Although of application under subsection (2) (as discussed in para. 2.18 *supra*), this principle has largely arisen in cases under subsection (3) and its equivalent EPCa. 54(3), but for its relevance to cases of prior use, see para. 2.17 *supra*.

Thus, in *EPO Decision T* 206/83, *"Pyridine herbicides/ICI"* (OJEPO 1/1987, 5; [1986] 5 EPOR 232), claims were held not anticipated where the prior application citable under EPCa. 54(3) was held not to contain an enabling disclosure, because this had failed to indicate how the relevant starting materials for the chemical compounds listed and claimed therein could be prepared. The criteria applied by the Technical Board in so finding were that the prior art must be workable when read in the light of its reader's common general knowledge as evidenced by basic handbooks and textbooks, but that the contents of patent specifications (even if referenced in *Chemical Abstracts*) will not usually be regarded as part of that knowledge as such does not extend to information only obtainable after a comprehensive search.

In *Asahi's Kasei's Application* (O/32/88 *noted* IPD 11012 and SRIS C/103/88, *noted* IPD 11081), a case under subsection (3), the Comptroller refused to follow *EPO Decision T* 206/83, *"Pyridine herbicides/ICI"* (*supra*) and held that it was not necessary that the prior disclosure of a chemical compound be "enabling", but rather (following the decisions quoted in para. 2.15 *supra*) that the prior disclosure be sufficient to satisfy the skilled man that the compound had actually been made. On appeal, the Patents Court declined to express a preference between the "enabling disclosure" approach of the EPO and what was stated to be the established practice of the Comptroller that it is sufficient if the alleged anticipating disclosure indicate that the compound has been made and characterised as established under the 1949 Act in *Gyogyszeripari's Application* ([1958] RPC 51) and *SKF's Application* ([1968] RPC 415). However, in *Genentech's [Human Growth Hormone] Patent* (SRIS C/64/89), these two decisions were not followed, and *EPO Decision T* 206/83 was followed, on the basis that the doctrine of the "non-enabling disclosure" is part of British law, see para. 2.18 *supra*.

29

In the *Asahi* case, the Patents Court was able to dismiss the appeal on the basis that the relevant compound was claimed in the prior application citable under subsection (3) and that a claim to the compound was deemed by section 130(3) (which treats matter as disclosed if it is *either* claimed or disclosed in a priority application) to constitute a disclosure of that compound, the very nature of a claim making it unlikely that, in itself, such would be an enabling disclosure or to indicate whether or not it had been made. Such an approach, based on a definition for which there is no equivalent in the EPC (but which is derived from s.69(2) [1949] and its predecessor introduced in purported compliance with art. 4H of the Paris Convention), is unlikely to have wider application. Indeed, if applied to the facts in the "*Pyridine herbicides/ICI*" *decision*, that view would have given the opposite result in that case. The controversy may be resolved if the *Asahi* case is taken to the Court of Appeal, for which leave was granted.

2.21   *—Selection cases under subsection (3)*

Where a prior disclosure (whether specific or a class) is wholly embraced by a later class claim, there is no good reason not to apply the principle of *Molins* v. *Industrial Machinery* ((1937) 54 RPC 94 and (1938) 55 RPC 31), approved in *Du Pont's (Witsiepe's) Application* ([1982] FSR 303 (HL)) (noted respectively in paras. 2.06 and 2.15 *supra*) in which, if prior art falls within the relevant claim, there is lack of novelty whether or not the later application discloses advantages. Nevertheless, this could be overcome under the "prior claiming" test of the 1949 Act by a specific disclaimer of the prior specifically claimed subject matter because the question of obviousness over that unpublished disclosure of the prior application did not arise. The same holds true under subsection (3) and there therefore seems no reason why a section 2(3) objection should not be overcome by a claim of the "N-l" type, provided that what is left is described with sufficient particularity, see *Upjohn's Application* (SRIS O/6/83). However, in *Fruehof's Application* (SRIS O/185/83), it was held that objection under subsection (3) could not be overcome by insertion of a disclaimer to "all matter disclosed" in the prior application as the resulting scope of the claims would then be obscure, contrary to section 14(5), see para. 14.24.

The position may, however, be different in the EPO. Thus, in *EPO Decision T* 188/83, "*Vinyl acetate/FERNHOLZ*" (OJEPO 11/1984, 555), a Technical Board, in relation to a chemical production process previously described, refused to allow a claim of the "N-1"type containing a disclaimer to particular numerical ratios within the claimed general range of reactant ratios which had been disclosed in the prior art. The significance of this decision as regards the test for novelty is that the EPO Board of Appeal held the prior art here to be novelty-destroying, whereas the Examining Division had only rejected the claim for obviousness. Thus, the decision would probably have been the same even if the prior patent had not been published at the relevant date and had only been citable under EPCa. 54(3) (or under subsection (3)).

EPO Decision T 188/83 (*supra*) was, however, also an example of the much more difficult reverse case where the earlier disclosure is broader and the question is whether a narrower claim by way of "selection" can be granted thereover. This would normally be difficult as the earlier disclosure would have to be considered both as potentially novelty-destroying under section 2 and partially rendering the claimed matter obvious under section 3, such being overcome if there is no specific novelty-destroying disclosure (for which see paras. 2.14–2.16 *supra*), and whether the selected matter has unexpected advantages (for which see para. 3.13). But the presence of such advantages would, prima facie, not seem to be relevant under subsection (3) when inventive step under section 3 is not required to be present over the contents of the prior application.

In *Netherlands Patent Office Appeals Decision No. 14633* ([1981] FSR 356) it was held that, in judging the novelty of a later application under the Dutch equivalent of subsection (3), account must be taken not only of the literal text of the earlier application, but also of anything which an average person skilled in the art, interpreting what he had read, would have regarded as part of the earlier application. However, in that case, there was no advantage alleged for the species (specific numerical range of proportions of mixture components) over the genus of the earlier application (mixture of same components in broad range of proportions) and the applicant was given an opportunity to show that his claim implied more than an arbitrary selection.

This decision is discussed by R. P. Lloyd ((1981–82) 11 CIPA 44) who drew attention to a similar fact situation which occurred in *Miller's Patent* ((1940) 57 RPC 16) where patentability was denied under the 1907 Act. In reply, R. E. Perry ((1981–82) 11 CIPA 192) pointed out that, in the circumstances of these two cases, novelty exists when it can be seen that an invention has been made. *Du Pont's (Witsiepe's) Application* (discussed in para. 2.15 *supra*) is also important to show that *ex post facto* reasoning may not be employed in attempts to negate novelty of a good invention. Although a person practising the earlier invention in the *Du Pont* case *could* have done what was claimed by *Du Pont*, the test, for the purposes of lack of novelty under United Kingdom law, appears to be whether he *should* have done so, following *General Tire* v. *Firestone* quoted in para. 2.06 *supra*, see A. W. White ((1981–82) 11 CIPA 289). Nevertheless, it may be that the *General Tire* test for novelty is applicable only over prior published art and that the effect both of *Miller's Patent* and *Du Pont (Witsiepe's) Application* is that, in cases under subsection (3) where possible "selection" arises, to avoid lack of novelty the selected members cannot merely be the "same" in respect of properties, but must display a meaningful distinguishing property stated in, or at least inherent to the skilled person from, the later specification. It appears that German law gives the same result in view of the doctrine of "lack of inventive excess" which leads to lack of novelty ("*Cholin-Salicylat*" [1974] GRUR 324) the guiding principle of which is similar to the *Netherlands Decision* (*supra*). In that case it was also held that a selection from one list lacks novelty, but from two lists is novel, *i.e.* the position now adopted by the EPO for inventions of the "selection" type (see para. 2.16 *supra*). A further Dutch decision was discussed in another article by R. P. Lloyd ((1982–83) 12 CIPA 408): again the selected compounds were required to be shown to have a superior effect before an objection of implicit lack of novelty could be overcome.

—*Effect of a withdrawn, but published, application under subsection (3)*   **2.22**

Under subsection (3) an ordinary application under the Act obviously remains in the state of the art if it is withdrawn or refused after publication, because there is nothing in the Act to suggest otherwise. It would therefore be thought that a European application (or the UK designation) withdrawn after publication, or an international application withdrawn after entry into the United Kingdom phase, would likewise remain in the state of the art under subsection (3). However, the original form of section 78(5), when given its literal meaning (as it was held in *L'Oreal's Application*, [1986] RPC 19 should be done), led to the opposite result so that, if the European application (UK), or the United Kingdom designation of such an application, was withdrawn after publication, then that application ceased to have effect under subsection (3) despite the fact of that publication, a result which the judge characterised as bizarre. Accordingly, the effect of the *L'Oreal* decision is to be reversed by the 1988 Act which will (when it is brought into effect, for which see the note to para. 78.01) amend section 78(5) and introduce section 78(5A). As a result, it is to be provided that withdrawal, deemed withdrawal, or refusal of a European application (UK), or the United Kingdom designation thereof, will not affect the operation of subsection (3) so that the matter published in that application remains in the state of the art for such purpose, see also para. 78.07.

A similar result might have resulted from the original wording of section 89(8) (reprinted in para. 89.02) in respect of an international application (UK), but the prior art effect thereof is now to be made clear by the wording of the replacement section 89(2) (reprinted in para. 89.01), when read with section 89B(2) (reprinted in para. 89B.01) and section 89A(3)(*a*) (reprinted in para. 89A.01). If an international application (UK) does not, for any reason, enter the United Kingdom phase, it is never to form part of the state of the art for the purposes of subsection (3), whereas once such entry has occurred the prior art effect of the international application is to be preserved whatever happens to that application thereafter, see para. 89B.10 where it is pointed out that the position may be different if withdrawal of the international application occurred before sections 89, 89A and 89B in their present form were brought into effect.

Generally the form of the international application as first published, usually under the PCT (but occasionally under the Act when international publication then has no effect, see para. 89B.10), determines its prior art effect under subsection (3), irrespective of any amendment thereto. However, the position as to the prior art effect under subsection (3) is not at all clear where the international application is first published in a language other than English, French or German and/or where the international application is amended prior to publication in one of these languages.

Under section 79(2) an international application for a European patent (UK) (*i.e.* a "Euro-PCT" application (UK)) is deemed not to form part of the state of the art under subsection (3) until the European filing fee has been paid and a copy of the international application in English, French or German has been filed at the EPO. From that point new section 78(5) and (5A) will have effect, as described *supra*, so that any withdrawal, deemed withdrawal, or refusal thereafter will not affect the status of the Euro-PCT application (UK) as being part of the state of the art (under ss. 79(2) and new 78(5A)) for the purposes of subsection (3). However, see *supra* for doubts as to the form of the specification to be taken into account under subsection (3) when original publication occurs in a language other than English, French or German and/or where amendment is made prior to publication in one of these languages.

2.23   *—Proof of earlier date of citation under subsection (3)*

Whether matter contained in another application is to be considered as part of the state of the art under subsection (3) depends on whether the relevant matter in that application has an earlier priority date than the matter in conflict therewith. This question of priority date is discussed in the commentary on section 5. The importance of determining whether a citation under subsection (3) is truly entitled to its own declared priority date, and the conditions under which the "whole contents" effect of patent applications of prior date is to be taken into account, have also been discussed by C. Jones ((1980–81) 10 CIPA 11).

2.24   *—Effect of secret applications under subsection (3)*

If the publication of a patent application is prohibited under section 22, such an application has no effect under subsection (3) until it is eventually published. It will then have a "whole contents" effect as of its filing date and, if relevant, its priority date. However, if any matter is deleted under section 19, the deleted matter will not then have such an effect, and if the application as a whole is abandoned before publication it will have no whole contents effect. This leads to the following possibilities:

(i) a patent which is fully anticipated by a classified application may nevertheless remain valid in relation to that anticipation for the whole of its life if the classified application is never declassified and therefore is never published;

(ii) if declassification and publication were to occur within its life, the patent would be valid one day and invalid, with *ab initio* effect, the next day; or

(iii) the patent might be invalid retrospectively in the event that the declassification and publication occurs after expiry.

Excepted disclosures (subss. (4) and (5))

—General　　　　　　　　　　　　　　　　　　　　　　　　　　　　　　　**2.25**

Subsections (4) and (5) correspond to EPCa. 55. Subsection (4)(*a*) and (*b*) corresponding to EPCa. 55(1)(*a*), relate to unauthorised disclosure by "obtaining" and/ or breach of confidence from the inventor (or from the proprietor (subs. (5)). These provisions have a similarity to section 50(2) [1949] and cases in which these have been discussed may therefore be relevant, see *Tiefenbrun's Application* ([1979] FSR 97); *Ethyl Corp.'s Patent* ([1966] RPC 205) and *Chemithon's Patent* ([1966] RPC 365), see also para. A050.4. In the *Chemithon* case it seems to have been suggested that the court could in a suitable case restrain an applicant for revocation from relying on matters prejudicial to validity which had arisen as the result of a breach of confidence.

The provisions of subsections (4) and (5) should be relied upon only in those cases where no alternative exists as the exceptions which they provide are likely to be very limited in scope. In particular this is so because the six-month grace period under subsection (4) is reckoned back from the actual filing date of the application in suit *and not back from any claimed priority date, whether foreign or domestic.* Rule 111(5) (reprinted in para. 123.11) deals with the calculation of this grace-period in cases which involve excluded days under section 120 or rule 111(1).

—Disclosures in breach of confidence　　　　　　　　　　　　　　　　　**2.26**

It was indicated in *Microsonic's Application* ([1984] RPC 29) that it would not be possible to rely upon a breach of confidence to exempt a prior disclosure under subsection (4) unless evidence was provided which firmly established that, in all probability, a breach had occurred. In *EPO Decision T* 173/83 *"Antioxidant/ TELECOMMUNICATIONS"* (OJEPO 10/1987, 465; [1988] 3 EPOR 133) the EPO stated that there would be a disclosure in breach of confidence if a third party failed to honour a declaration of mutual trust linking him to the inventor, or if a third party acted in such a way as to cause harm to a person from whom he had received information which he was authorised to communicate to others, though in this case no breach of confidence was held to have occurred. A case where it has been held that prior disclosure was made by the applicants for the purpose of consultation and on the clear understanding that the disclosee would treat the information as confidential is *Riekie and Simpfendorfer* v. *McGrath* [*Australia*] ((1987) 7 IPR 120). M. G. Harman has raised some intriguing questions on the position when disclosure occurs in circumstances where any subsequent publication would be unlawful ((1986–87) 16 CIPA 369).

2.27   *—Disclosures at international exhibitions*

Subsection (4)(*c*) and rule 5 (under s. 130(2)), corresponding to EPCaa. 55(1)(*b*) and 55(2), concern disclosure at, or in consequence of display by the inventor (or proprietor (subs. (5)) at, an international exhibition. To take advantage of these provisions an applicant must so declare at the time of filing the application and provide an appropriate certificate within four months thereafter see para. *2.32 infra.*

The term "international exhibition" is defined in section 130(1) by reference to "the Convention on International Exhibitions". This term is also defined in section 130(1) as the convention signed in Paris on November 22, 1928 (which was last revised on November 30, 1972), as amended or supplemented by any protocol to that convention which is for the time being in force. Only very large international exhibitions can qualify (O.J. February 23, 1977). Further information on the requirements for an exhibition to qualify as an international exhibition within the definition of section 130(1) was given by A. C. Sergeant ((1985–86) 15 CIPA 319).

The words "in consequence of" exclude reliance on the provision where publication occurs in a catalogue of the exhibition which becomes available to the public *before* the opening of the exhibition (*Steel's Application*, [1958] RPC 411).

Relaxation of novelty-destroying rule in case of materials for use in medical indications

2.28   *—Patents for the first medical indication (subs. (6))*

Subsection (6) corresponds to, but is worded differently from, EPCa. 54(5); it is complementary to section 4(2) and (3) and allows a use-bound substance claim in respect of the first application of an otherwise known substance or composition "for use in a method of treatment of the human or animal body by surgery or therapy or of diagnosis practised on the human or animal body", such application itself being precluded from patentability by section 4(2). The meaning of the quoted words is discussed in paras. 4.05–4.08.

The EPO has now held that, provided the state of the art presents no restricting matter, the special form of claim permitted by EPCa. 54(5) (corresponding to subsection (6)) can be expressed broadly, *e.g.* as "Derivatives of formula X for use as an active pharmaceutical substance" (*EPO Decision T* 128/82, *"Pyrrolidine-Derivatives/HOFFMANN-LA ROCHE"*, OJEPO 4/1984, 164): EPO Guideline C-IV, 4.2 now reflects this. Also, the EPO has held that the special form of claim permitted by EPCa. 54(5) may be directed to a "substance" or to a "composition," and, consequently, that this type of claim may be used when the "composition" consists of two components present "as a combined preparation for simultaneous, separate or sequential use in therapy", that is as a kit-of-parts, the word "composition" being interpreted as including a "combination" or "aggregate" (*EPO Decision T* 09/81, *"Cytostatic Combination/ASTA"*, OJEPO 9/1983, 372). However, in *National Research Development Corp.'s Application* (SRIS O/117/85, *noted* IPD 9047), the Comptroller declined to permit a claim to a novel diagnostic use of a known diagnostic apparatus under subsection (6) holding this to be limited by its wording to "substances or compositions".

There is doubt as to when a use of a substance or composition in a method of treatment is to be taken to form part of the state of the art. It appears that the publication of laboratory tests results on animals might amount to such a disclosure when these tests establish a first medical or veterinary use. However, it seems that a mere paper allegation of a medical use (as contrasted with mere statements about pharmacological activity) in a patent specification relating to an invention which has nevertheless never been put into practice does amount to such a disclosure, and the substance or composition need not have actually been used for one of these purposes. The EPO disregards an alleged first indication if it is proved wrong or too general, for example a mere disclosure of the substance being "a medicament", see for example *EPO Decision T 7/86 "Xanthines/DRACO"* (OJEPO 10/1988, 381; [1989] 2 EPOR 65) where an exemplified compound of a class, stated as such to have a diuretic action, was not regarded as itself having been disclosed thereby for use in a therapeutic method.

Subsection (6) of itself provides no relaxation in the case of the second or subsequent medical and veterinary applications of the substance or composition. Thus, in *Sopharma's Application* ([1983] RPC 195), and in *Bayer's (Meyer's) Application*, ([1984] RPC 11, also reported as *"Hydropyridine (UK)"*, OJEPO 5/1984, 233), both approved by the Patents Court in *John Wyeth's and Schering's Applications* ([1985] RPC 545), subsection (6) was held to have the effect as if the end of it read " . . . shall not prevent the invention from being taken to be new if the use of the substance or composition in any [method of treatment of the human or animal body by surgery, therapy or of diagnosis practised on the human or animal body] does not form part of the state of the art". As explained in *John Wyeth's and Schering's Applications* (*supra*) the position would have been different had the word "any" been omitted in subsection (6).

However, as discussed in para. 2.29 *infra*, second and subsequent medical and veterinary applications can now be protected by means of the "Swiss form" of claim. It should also be noted that subsection (6) only applies if the substance or composition in question lacks novelty *per se*. In view of the difficulty of establishing this under the tests applied in the *General Tire* and *Du Pont* cases (discussed respectively at paras. 2.06–2.09 and in para. 2.15 *supra*); and, since bare novelty will often suffice because of an inventive step arising from the discovery of the previously unknown and unpredictable treatment provided by the new use for the previously known compound or substance, in many instances it may be possible to avoid questions of a second medical or veterinary use by appropriate drafting of claims to novel compositions as such, or as a novel selection from a class of known compositions.

According to EPO Guideline C-IV, 4.2 a claim to a substance or composition for use in a method of treatment or diagnosis is to be construed as restricted to the substance or composition when presented or packaged for the special use in contrast to the general position under EPO Guideline C-III, 4.8, for which see para. 2.10 *supra*. Such claims will then be infringed under section 60(1) by the sale of packaged medicaments bearing or containing indications for the new medicinal use. If the compound or substance is sold without such indication, infringement may nevertheless arise under section 60(2), subject to section 60(3), see paras. 60.14–60.16.

—Patents for the protection of the second (or further) medical indication   **2.29**

Subsection (6) only permits patent protection for the first medical or veterinary indication of a known substance, but it is convenient here to deal with possible ways of obtaining patent protection for inventions of the second (or further) medical indication, that is when a new therapeutic application has been discovered for a substance already described for use in some different type of therapy.

Under the former German law, the Federal Supreme Court, in *"Benzolsulfonyl-harnstoff"* ([1977] GRUR 652; (1978) 9 IIC 42) and *"Sytosterylglykoside"* ([1982] GRUR 548; (1983) 14 IIC 283), allowed claims of the form "Use of X in the treatment of disease Y" on the basis that it was the industrially applicable aspects of such a claim that would be asserted and that the protection they gave went beyond that of mere treatment. These decisions were further confirmed by the German

Supreme Court as being specifically in accordance with the EPC (*"Hydropyridine"* [*Germany*], OJEPO 1/1984, 26). The corresponding case in the EPO, together with seven similar cases, was referred to the EPO Enlarged Board of Appeal, see, *e.g. EPO Decision T* 17/81, *"Nimodipin/BAYER"* (OJEPO 7/1983, 266) and these cases, together with the German decisions, have been reviewed by A. W. White in his 1984 paper listed in para. 2.03 *supra*; they were also commented on by J. Pagenberg ((1984) 15 IIC 215). The EPO Enlarged Board eventually held (*EPO Decision Gr* 05/83, *"Second Medical Indication/EISAI"*, OJEPO 3/1985, 64), contrary to the decisions of the German Supreme Court, *supra*, that the "Use for medical treatment" form of claim could not, at least at present, be permitted under the EPC, thereby following the view previously expressed by the Comptroller in *Sopharma's Application* ([1983] RPC 185) and *Bayer's (Meyer's) Application*, ([1984] RPC 11 also reported as *"Hydropyridine (UK)"*, OJEPO 5/1984, 233). The Patents Court, in *John Wyeth's and Schering's Applications* ([1985] RPC 545) also expressed its agreement with the Comptroller's view and expressed the opinion that the German Supreme Court's *"Hydropyridine"* decision appeared to be based on earlier German national case law.

However, the EPO Enlarged Board in *EPO Decision Gr* 05/83 (*supra*) also stated that, having made a full study, "no intention to exclude second (and further) medical indications from patent protection can be deduced from the terms of the EPC or its legislative history". They then decided to permit claims directed to the use of a substance (or composition) for the manufacture of a medicament for a specified new and inventive therapeutic application. In doing so, the EPO Enlarged Board followed precedent set by the Swiss Patent Office (*"Second Medical Indication—Switzerland"*, OJEPO 11/1984, 581) and indicated that a claim in the form: "Use of X for the manufacture of a medicament for treatment of Y" should not be held to be deprived of novelty merely because some therapeutic use of the medicament was already known, stating that "It seems appropriate to take a special view of the concept of the 'state of the art' defined in EPCa. 54(2) (corresponding to subsection (2)), though only in the case of inventions which fall within the terms of the first sentence of EPCa. 52(4)" (corresponding to s. 4(2)). These decisions were reviewed by I. B. de Minvelle-Devaux and by A. W. White in their 1985 papers listed in para. 2.03 *supra*, and have led to the current form of EPO Guideline C-IV 4.2, see OJEPO 3/1985, 84, the paper by R. Teschemacher ((1988) 19 IIC 18), the book by P. W. Grubb listed in para. 2.02A *supra* and EPO Guideline C-IV, 4.3.

The Patents Court, sitting *en banc*, then specifically followed *EPO Decision Gr* 05/83 in *John Wyeth's and Schering's Applications* (*supra*). In doing so the Court indicated that the Swiss form of claim would have lacked novelty under the 1949 Act having regard to the decision in *Adhesive Dry Mounting* v. *Trapp* ((1910 27 RPC 341) (for which see para. 2.10 *supra*) and that, but for the EPO decision the better view under the 1977 Act would be that the Swiss form of claim lacked novelty. However, taking judicial notice (under s. 91(1)) of the EPO decision and acting in conformity with it, the Court held that, in the special circumstances of an inventive discovery which would not otherwise be patentable because of section 4(2), a claim in this form would not lack novelty. The EPO decision is the subject of a case comment ((1986) 17 IIC 111) and the scope and effect of this form of "purpose-bound process claim", or "utility-based use claim", is the subject of the papers by J. Utermann and B. Hansen listed in para. 2.03 *supra*. However, while in Sweden *EPO Decision Gr* 05/83 has been followed (*"Hydropyridine [Sweden]"*. (1988) 19 IIC 815), in the Netherlands *EPO Decision Gr* 05/83 has not been followed, see *"Second medical indication/NL"* (OJEPO 10/1988, 405) which held that such a claim did not meet the requirements of novelty and inventiveness.

EPO Decision Gr 05/83 (*supra*) would appear to alter the United Kingdom law of novelty as previously laid down in the *Adhesive Dry Mounting* decision (*supra*), though *ex facie* only in respect of inventions denied patentability by section 4(2). For example, the Comptroller declined to allow a claim limited to diagnostic apparatus to be worded in the "Swiss form" (*National Research Development Corp.'s Application*, SRIS O/117/85, *noted* IPD 9047) as an alternative to a claim held not to be permitted by subsection (6), as noted in para. 2.28 *supra*.

Nevertheless, it may be questioned whether, outside the special situation of the further medical indication, section 2 should operate, as did the law of novelty under the 1949 Act, to deny novelty to a claim where the sole statement of novelty is a mere indication of purpose for which the article or method is to be put, and indeed this is being questioned within the EPO, see the reference to *EPO Decision T 59/87*, "*Friction reducing additive/MOBIL II*" (OJEPO 9/1988, 347) in para. 2.13 *supra*.

Obviously, however, where mere novelty of purpose should come to be recognised as an essential element of novelty in a claim, as in the "Swiss form", that claim should not be held to be infringed unless the alleged infringing act embraces, or is intended to embrace, that purpose. It must also be recalled that, before *EPO Decision Gr 05/83* (*supra*) and *John Wyeth's and Schering's Applications* (*supra*), the Comptroller rejected a claim of the "for use in" type (*Du Pont (Buegge's) Application*, [1984] RPC 17) holding that there was a general objection to this type of claim except in the special circumstances covered by subsection (6) and section 4(3) (*i.e.* in the area of a discovery of a new and inventive medical indication). Clearly, these special conditions have been broadened by the later decisions, but to an extent which is not yet clear.

The EPO has tended, in applying *EPO Decision Gr 05/83* (*supra*) to grant patents by adopting a very narrow view of lack of novelty of claims presented in the "Swiss form". Thus, in *EPO Decision T 289/84*, "*3-Amino-pyrazoline derivatives/ WELLCOME*" ([1987] 2 EPOR 58), the prior description of a pharmaceutical composition for systemic application was held not to anticipate a composition "adapted for only topical, to the exclusion of oral and injectable, administration". The EPO has also held to be novel the same treatment for the same ailment, but applied to a new class of pigs (*EPO Decision T 19/86*, "*Pigs II/DUPHAR*", OJEPO 1–2/1989, 24; [1988] 1 EPOR 10).

—Patents for pharmaceutical packs   **2.30**

An alternative approach to attempting to protect medical uses of known compounds has been to try to claim a pack comprising a pharmaceutical preparation associated with instructions for its (new and inventive) manner of use on the basis that this should be regarded as an appropriate claim directed to section 60(2), and not as merely a disguised claim to a method of treatment. Nevertheless, the EPO has made it clear that pharmaceutical use claims are regarded as method claims and are, therefore, not apparently to be allowed (Guidelines C-III, 4.9 and C-IV, 4.2).

In *Bayer's (Meyer's) Application*, ([1984] RPC 11, also reported as "*Hydropyridine UK*" OJEPO 5/1984, 233), it was held (under the 1977 Act) that a claim to a package containing a known drug together with instructions for a new use could not be allowed because the inventive step set out in the claim resided in the information given in the instructions, and this was the mere presentation of information and accordingly not an invention under section 1(2)(*d*). This followed attempts to obtain such type of claim prior to the introduction of the EPC and the present Act, see: *Ciba-Geigy's (Dürr's) Applications* ([1977] RPC 83 (CA)); *Dow Corning's Application* ([1974] RPC 235 (PAT)); and *Wellcome Foundation's Australian Application* ([1981] FSR 72 (HC of Australia)).

However, a claim to a "pharmaceutical pack" has been accepted by the EPO in circumstances where one component has an interaction on the pharmaceutical effect of the other, even if the components are to be taken separately or sequentially rather than in combination (*EPO Decision T* 09/81, "*Cytostatic combination/ ASTA*", OJEPO 9/1983, 372). There is here an analogy with the claim allowed (under s. 101 [1949]) in *L'Oreal's Application* ([1970] RPC 656) to a two-pack product for permanent hair waving containing two known chemicals each to be used in a manner already known in themselves, in contrast to a card carrying two kinds of pill with printed instructions as to the order in which these should be taken, as in *Organon's Application* ([1970] RPC 574), where the two components were, in effect, held not to be interactive. For further discussion of the possibility of patenting a "pharmaceutical pack", see the note by I. B. de Minvielle-Devaux ((1983–84) 13 CIPA 120).

PRACTICE UNDER SECTION 2

2.31   *Avoiding self-collision with a related application*

In order to prevent self-collision under subsection (3) with subject matter contained in an earlier application of the same applicant, it may not be sufficient to delete the subject matter in question from the earlier application before this is published under section 16 as that application wil be published in the form as filed. As suggested in (1979–80) 9 CIPA 247, it would appear more prudent to file a divisional application on the earlier application before this is published under section 16. The divisional application can omit the offending subject matter and the original application can be abandoned before publication.

2.32   *Disclosures at international exhibitions*

As with section 51 [1949], the provisions of subsection (4)(*c*) concerning disclosure at an international exhibition before filing can be fatal to the validity of patents subsequently acquired, in some foreign countries, where a similar grace period based on Article 11 of the Paris Convention is not afforded.

The procedure when such exhibition has taken place is given in rule 5 (reprinted at para. 2.02). The Comptroller is informed in writing that the invention has been displayed at the exhibition at the time of filing the application for the patent. In accordance with rule 5(2), which corresponds to EPCr. 23, the applicant must file a certificate, issued at the exhibition by the authority responsible for the exhibition, stating that the invention was exhibited and the opening date of the exhibition and, if the invention was not disclosed on that date, the first date when it was disclosed. The certificate must be accompanied by an authenticated identification of the invention. No forms or fees are required for providing the information or to accompany the certificate. For the position where an international application is filed after an international exhibition, see rule 5(4) and para. 89A.30.

For examples of the certification of international exhibitions, see those referring to the Liverpool Garden Festival (O.J. May 31, 1984) and the World Exhibition of Achievements of Young Inventors at Plovdiv, Bulgaria (O.J. December 18, 1985).

3.01   **SECTION 3**

Inventive step

3. An invention shall be taken to involve an inventive step if it is not obvious to a person skilled in the art, having regard to any matter which forms part of the state of the art by virtue only of section 2(2) above (and disregarding section 2(3) above).

BOOK

3.02

J. Bochnovic, "The inventive step: Its evolution in Canada, the United Kingdom and the United States", IIC Studies, Vol. 5 (Max Planck Institute, Munich, 1982).

ARTICLES

3.03

S. Gratwick, "Having regard to what was known", (1972) 88 LQR 341;

A. W. White & J. C. Warden, "The British approach to obviousness", [1977] AIPL 447;

J. Pagenberg, "The evaluation of the 'Inventive step' in the European Patent System: More objective standards needed", [1978] 9 IIC 1 and 121;

P. G. Cole, "The amoxycillin case: A testing ground on the law of obviousness", [1979] EIPR 316;

P. G. Cole, "Obvious and lacking in inventive step", [1982] EIPR 102 and 142.

D. L. T. Cadman, "Inventive step in European patent law", (1982–83) 12 CIPA 274;

J. L. Beton, "Recent developments in the PCT and EPO", (1982–83) 12 CIPA 284;

J. M. Claydon, "The question of obviousness in the Windsurfing decision", [1985] EIPR 218;

R. Singer, "The case law of the EPO Boards of Appeal on inventive step (Article 56 (EPC)", (1985) 16 IIC 293 and 342;

S. Gratwick, " 'Having regard to what was known and used'—Revisited", (1986) 102 LQR 403;

G. S. A. Szabo, "The problem and solution approach to the inventive step", [1986] EIPR 293;

G. S. A. Szabo, "Questions on the problem and solution approach to the inventive step", (1986–87) 16 CIPA 351;

P. G. Cole, "Genentech loses battle in British patent war", *Patent World*, January 1989, 31;

J. P. Thurston, "The Commercial and legal impact of the Court of Appeal's decision in *Genentech* v. *Wellcome*", [1989] EIPR 66;

(Sir) Douglas Falconer, "The determination of subject matter protected by a patent in grant, infringement and revocation proceedings", (1989) 20 IIC 348.

COMMENTARY ON SECTION 3

General

3.04

Section 3 sets out the test of inventive step which section 1(1)(*b*) requires that an invention patentable under the Act must possess. This is a test of non-obviousness to the person skilled in the art having regard to the world-wide test of novelty defined by section 2(2) and discussed in paras. 2.05–2.18. However, the contents of applications of prior date, but unpublished at the priority date of the invention in question, are not to be taken into account in assessing obviousness, though such disclosures are potentially novelty-destroying under section 2(3), as discussed in paras. 2.19–2.24. As with the remainder of the group of sections 1–6, none of these sections applies to "existing patents"; for corresponding discussion of "obviousness" in relation thereto, see para. A032.13. For discussion of "priority date" see the commentary on section 5.

39

Section 3 corresponds to EPCa. 56 and is qualified by section 130(7) as being framed to have, as nearly as practicable, the same effect. This appears to require "inventive step" to be construed as "inventive activity" (*Genentech's Patent*, [1989] RPC 147 (CA)). PCTrr. 33 and 65 should also be noted. Section 3 also corresponds to Article 5 of the Strasbourg Convention (1963) (Cmnd. 8002).

However, though section 3 and EPCa. 56 are to be construed in conformity with each other, the route by which the EPO assesses obviousness is, *ex facie*, different from that traditionally adopted by British courts. The British attitude to assessment of obviousness is therefore first considered herein (in paras. 3.05–3.22 *infra*) quite separately from discussion of the assessment of inventive step by the EPO, which is considered in paras. 3.27 *et seq*. In between these separate treatments, paras. 3.23–3.25 attempt to show that the differences of approach may, conceptually, not be that much different, with a rationalisation of British cases analysed according to this approach being given in para. 3.25 *infra*. However, as will be seen, the traditional British approach has been essentially a pragmatic and practical one of considering each factual situation in isolation. Thus, in *Genentech's Patent* (*supra*), it was stressed that obviousness is a jury question to be assessed by the judge in the light of the totality of the facts before him, and that it is unsound to focus on the steps actually taken by the inventor, the history of the route by which he arrived at the invention not being material to the validity of the patent. On the other hand, the EPO attempts to reach its decisions by first formulating universal principles, particularly by analysing each invention in terms of "problem and solution", and then applying these principles to the factual situation before it.

In the context of the British law on obviousness, decisions of the Appeal Boards of the EPO are mainly of value for the principles developed thereby and because judicial notice of these decisions can be taken under section 91, though as yet there is little evidence of this being done. Also, the principles developed by the EPO may eventually come to be followed by the courts of the EPC Member States, including those of the United Kingdom, especially in view of the Judges Symposia (reports of which are published in *IIC*) which have been instituted for greater understanding of judicial methods used in the various Member States for determination of cases on aspects of patent law which the EPC indicates are to be harmonised in the individual national laws. The EPO decisions on obviousness are, therefore, reviewed herein by collecting them under representative headings, see paras. 3.27 *et seq*. The EPO decisions are, of course, of prime importance for examination and opposition proceedings within the EPO, but these are matters dealt with in *EPH* rather than herein. Many of the EPO decisions referred to in this Commentary are reprinted in Vol. 3 of *EPH* but, as these are reprinted therein in numerical order, no separate reference to *EPH* is given herein if a separate report has been published. Abstracts of the EPO decisions, together with a classified index, are also to be found in *EPSF*.

Also, if a Common Appeal Court (COPAC) should come to be instituted in relation to community patents (for which see para. 88.04), that court can be expected, as the EPO has done, to establish its own "European" or "Community" principles and not to follow the decisions of any particular Member State. It would not be surprising, therefore, if those COPAC principles were to follow those already established on a supra-national basis by the EPO.

Previous United Kingdom patent statutes did not include a definition of inventive step: section 32(1)(*f*) [1949] merely specifies that an (existing) patent can be revoked if the claimed invention "is obvious and does not involve any inventive step having regard to what was known or used, before the priority date of the claim, in the United Kingdom". In practice, no distinction was drawn between the concepts of "obvious" and "lacking in inventive step" (*Benmax* v. *Austin* (1955) 72 RPC 39 at p. 44–46 (HL)), and this would appear also to be so under the present

Act where inventive step is defined in terms of non-obviousness. The positive form of the definition is, however, noteworthy because it excludes other criteria, such as technical progress and inventive level as positive requirements of patentability.

Also, for the purpose of section 3, the state of the art is defined, as for the test of novelty under section 2, on a world-wide (rather than merely local United Kingdom) basis, as comprising "all matter (whether a product, a process, information about either, or anything else) which has at any time before the priority date of the invention been made available to the public (whether in the United Kingdom or elsewhere) by written or oral description, by use or in any other way" (s. 2(2)), except that prior-dated patent applications for United Kingdom patent protection which were not published at the priority date of the invention (as defined in s. 2(3)) are to be excluded from the "state of the art" for the purpose of section 3. The meaning of the "state of the art" is discussed in para. 3.17 *infra*.

The book by J. Bochnovic, listed in para. 3.02 *supra*, recounts the historial evolution of the concept of obviousness in English law and is a comparative study of that concept in relation also to Canadian and United States law. The article by J. Pagenberg, listed in para. 3.03 *supra*, describes and discusses the various subtests for presence, or absence, of inventive step which have been used particularly in the United States with the aim of improving the objectivity of the analysis of inventive step. The article by Sir Douglas Falconer (listed in para. 3.02 *supra*) contains a pithy account of the manner in which objections of lack of subject matter are dealt with respectively in grant, infringement and revocation proceedings under United Kingdom law, and practice.

Probable relationship to cases decided under the old law   **3.05**

The criteria for inventive step are, with marginal exceptions, the same under the Act as under the old law, other than the wider base of the state of the art against which the inventive step has to be assessed. It is, therefore, not surprising that cases decided under previous patent statutes continue to provide useful precedents though it must be understood that many decisions on inventive step are based upon facts rather than law and as such must therefore be applied as precedents with considerable caution. The principal difference is that, because the state of the art is not now geographically limited, the skilled person is probably also not limited to one resident in the United Kingdom.

A semantic difference that may well have no substance is that the old law was definite that the *whole* state of the art must be considered (*Olin Mathieson* v. *Biorex*, [1970] RPC 157; and *Beecham Group's (Amoxycillin) Application* ([1980] RPC 261), whereas section 3 refers to "*any* matter which forms *part* of the state of the art", see further para. 3.17 *infra*, but so far it has not been suggested that this effected a change in the law. Nevertheless, *Windsurfing* v. *Tabur Marine* ([1985] RPC 59 (CA)) (discussed in para. 3.09 *infra*) is a modern example where special attention was focused on individual items of prior art; and, in *Procter & Gamble* v. *Peaudouce* ([1989] FSR 180 (CA)), which purported to follow the *Windsurfing* decision, it was stated that the skilled but unimaginative addressee is to be assumed to have read carefully the literature, especially any relevant published patent specifications, though obviousness would then be assessed against the presumed knowledge of such a person, see para. 3.10 *infra*.

The British tests of obviousness

—The Cripps question   **3.06**

The main test of obviousness applied by British courts under the former patent statutes was generally to enquire, in the form of the *Cripps* question first formu-

41

lated in *Sharpe & Dohme* v. *Boots* ((1928) 45 RPC 153), *viz.* "Was it for all practical purposes obvious to any [skilled worker in the field covered], in the state of knowledge existing at the date of the patent, which consists of the literature then available to him and his general knowledge, that he *could* [make the invention claimed]?". In that case it was held that mere verification did not amount to invention and that would still seem to be a sound principle. However, in *Technograph* v. *Mills and Rockley* ([1969] RPC 395 (CA), *per* Harman L.J. at p. 404), the *Cripps* question was reformulated by replacing "could" with "*would* or *should*". Nevertheless, the *Cripps* question has the logical defect of being a circular definition and, in *Olin Mathieson* v. *Biorex* (*supra* at 187), it was reformulated as: "Would the notional research group at the relevant date, in the circumstances, . . . directly be led as a matter of course to try [the invention claimed] in the expectation that it might well produce [a useful desired result]."

3.07 —*The "obvious to try" test*

The form of Cripps question asked in the *Olin Mathieson* case ([1970] RPC 157) is a form of the "obvious to try" test more blatantly formulated in *Johns-Manville's Patent* ([1967] RPC 479 (CA)). Here it was held that a particular flocculating agent, recently made available on a commercial scale, "was well worth trying out in a generally known process in order to see whether it would have beneficial results"; and the second requirement of there being a reasonable expectation of a profitable result was stressed in *Akzo* v. *Du Pont* (SRIS C/43/88) where inventive step was upheld. Thus, this test should be applied with caution, and in *American Cyanamid* v. *Ethicon* ([1979] RPC 215) it was pointed out that a material could not be an obvious one to try if, at the relevant date, it was neither on the market nor had been suggested as having value. The "obvious to try" test failed on the facts in *Wavin* v. *Hepworth [Ireland]* ([1982] FSR 32), as it did in *Akzo* v. *Du Pont* (*supra*) where the Defendant, while considering improvements, had not thought of using the claimed process. The "obvious to try" test was specifically followed by the Patents Court under the 1977 Act in *PCUK Produit's Application* ([1984] RPC 487).

Also, in *Genentech's Patent* ([1987] RPC 553 and [1989] RPC 147 (CA)), claims to a product ("t-PA") made by recombinant DNA technology were revoked by the Court of Appeal partly because the existence of t-PA in a natural environment was part of the prior art and to attempt its preparation by such technology was an idea well worth trying out to see if it would have beneficial results as the useful properties of t-PA were known. The argument was supported by the fact that others had been working in parallel, though slightly later and in that the research work, though difficult and time-consuming, required no more than pertinacity, sound technique and trial and error, and such could not be regarded as characteristic of a patentable invention. *The Genentech* claims were also invalidated as based solely on a discovery unpatentable as such, see para. 1.08, and an analogy was drawn with a claim covering all solutions to a problem, *i.e.* to a known desideratum, as for example in *British United Shoe Machinery* v. *Collier (Simon)* ((1909) 26 RPC 21 and (1910) 27 RPC 567), where the invalid claim was for carrying out a known process "automatically". Indeed, the Comptroller has rejected an application in a similar fact situation to that in the *Genentech* case on the grounds that the claims were "either not novel or inventive or are not supported by the description" (*Schering Biotech's Application*, SRIS O/77/88). In *Genentech's Patent* (*supra*) the patent failed at first instance on this latter ground, but the Court of Appeal held that an objection under section 14(5) was one that could not, according to the law, be raised post-grant, see para. 72.20. The *Genentech* case, its factual background and commercial and legal significance have been analysed in the papers by P. G. Cole and J. P. Thurston listed in para. 3.03 *supra*.

In *Actagen's Application* (SRIS O/172/88), in finding it obvious to try the use in a genetic engineering method of a known probe in a forensic test by DNA analysis, the Comptroller alluded to the difficulty which an applicant has in trying to argue implied support in a specification for claims while at the same time trying to contend that their subject-matter was unobvious.

—The "lying in the road" test   **3.08**

It is doubtful, however, whether any particular verbal formula can be used in all cases (*per* Diplock L.J. in *Johns-Manville's Patent*, [1967] RPC 479), but *Philips' (Bosgra's) Application* ([1974] RPC 241) should be noted. This raised a question of obviousness of the use of a particular combination of emulsifying agents (often used to emulsify vaccines in the art) in connection with a known vaccine. Here it was stated that the *Olin Mathieson* decision (noted in para. 3.05 *supra*) put the test of obviousness far too high and far too favourably from the point of view of applicants for patents, saying:
> "Nothing would be more undesirable than that persons should be stopped from using materials which it is also established would lie readily to their hand, and would come to their mind as being likely materials to use . . . I think these (emulsifying) agents were obvious in this sense, indeed in the true sense of the word, that they were lying in the road, they were there for the research worker to use, and it is quite wrong that he should be stopped from using them."

Thus, this test is one of "*ob via*" or "lying in the road". Nevertheless, it must be remembered that the road itself must be one that the research worker would naturally choose to take.

This was not so in either *Beecham Group's (Amoxycillin) Application* ([1980] RPC 261) or *Du Pont's (Witsiepe's) Application* ([1982] FSR 303), each discussed more fully in para. 3.19 *infra*, but it was so according to Dillon L.J. in *Genentech's Patent* ([1989] RPC 147 (CA)), see para. 3.07 *supra*, even though the road there taken involved highly skilled work with no certainty of success.

—The "right to work" test   **3.09**

In *Windsurfing International* v. *Tabur Marine* ([1985] RPC 59 (CA)) the Court of Appeal stated that:
> "the philosophy behind paragraph (*f*) [of s.32 [1949]] . . . must, we think, take into account the same concept as anticipation, namely that it would be wrong to prevent a man from doing something which is merely an obvious extension of what he has been doing or of what was known in the art before the priority date of the patent granted";

and the Court of Appeal also indicated that members of the public, who clearly cannot be prevented from doing exactly that which they did before, cannot be prevented from doing that which is no more than the obvious variant of what they did before. For the "right to work" test in relation to the law of novelty, see para. 2.07. J. M. Claydon and S. Gratwick, in their respective 1985–86 papers listed in para. 3.03 *supra*, strongly criticise this view in the *Windsurfing* case because of the apparent unlikelihood, on the particular facts of that case, that the prior art constructions would in fact have been developed further, see also A. H. Duncan (EPI-Information 2–1988, 109). However, it is submitted that *Windsurfing* is a hard case liable to confuse the law, because over-wide claims were persisted in up to the Court of Appeal. A claim in that case restricted to a surfboard with a universally jointed mast, Bermuda rig and arcuate booms to keep the sails permanently taut might have succeeded, bu this was not the claim before the English courts. In Australia, a similar conclusion was reached (*Windsurfing International* v. *Petit* [*Australia*], [1984] 2 NSWLR 196), but in Canada a corresponding patent, though with differently worded claims, was upheld on appeal (*Windsurfing International* v. *Trilantic* [*Canada*], *noted* [1986] EIPR D-64 and see the paper by J. M. Claydon listed in para. 3.03 *infra*). It is interesting that, in the Canadian case, the independent author of the prior art publication, which had invalidated the corresponding patents in the United Kingdom and Australia, gave evidence for *Windsurfing* to the effect that he had not considered modifying his device in the manner which they had done. A corresponding patent was also upheld in the USA, mainly because of the commercial success which the invention had enjoyed (*Windsurfing International* v. *Fred Ostermann* [*USA*] ((1985) 227 USPO 927 and (1986) 228 USPQ 562).

The "right to work test" also prevailed in *Hallen* v. *Brabantia* ([1989] RPC 307) in circumstances where the invention had achieved considerable commercial success and others had not taken the same step as the inventors. Nevertheless, the court held that that step was one which it would be wrong to prevent the public from using, though sub-claims were upheld.

In similar manner, in *Dual Roofing's Application* (SRIS O/117/80, *noted* IPD 4064), the hearing officer stated that "It must be wrong to grant a monopoly which would have the effect of preventing the skilled worker from applying his normal technical expertise by any commercially available material": an appeal against the decision was dismissed (SRIS C/45/81). Likewise, in *Hoechst's Patent* (SRIS O/44/81, *noted* IPD 4081), the hearing officer stated "I conclude that, given what has been established concerning the state of the art before the priority date of the patent in suit, the skilled person intent on manufacturing an ERM would as a result of the routine selection of known materials, proportions and configurations, obtain an ERM falling within the scope of claim 1 of the patent in suit and I am not persuaded by the evidence that the particular combination claimed results in a product which possesses any special or unexpected advantage."

If a patent merely discloses known features then, even though there is a practical obstacle which has hitherto deterred people skilled in the art from combining those known features, yet, if to surmount the practical obstacles requires workshop trial and error and not any inventive step and the patent contains no teaching on how to surmount the obstacle, the patentee cannot escape the conclusion that the disclosures in his patent are obvious, see *Tetra Molectric* v. *Japan Imports* ([1976] RPC 54) and *Therm-a-Stor* v. *Weatherseal (No. 2)* ([1984] FSR 323).

The approach used in *Philips' (Bosgra's) Application*, and subsequently in *Genentech's Patent* ([1989] RPC 147 (CA)) (each *noted* in para. 3.08 *supra*) can also be seen in *Toppan Printing's Application* (SRIS C/72/82, *noted* IPD 7013) where (under s. 14 [1949]) it was said that "In suggesting a method of achieving the product [of the prior art] by a different route, the applicants have not found more than an alternative which the man skilled in the art would naturally have followed"; and likewise in *High Pressure Systems' Patent* (SRIS O/61/88) where the distinguishing feature over the prior art was one which would have readily occurred to the skilled person. Similarly, in *Hawker-Siddeley's Patent* (SRIS O/84/84; *noted* IPD 7096) the Comptroller held (under the 1949 Act) that the alleged invention was only a selection of an obvious alternative known to be available to those skilled in the art before the relevant date, and on this basis he held that the claim should be revoked, but an amendment was later allowed (SRIS O/24/87). However, the obvious alternative must be one that "would", not merely "could", be used, see para. 3.11 *infra*.

In *Van der Lely* v. *Ruston's Engineering* ([1985] RPC 461) Oliver L.J. stated that the starting point for consideration of obviousness is that of what it is the inventor claims to have invented; and that it is not sufficient to repel an attack of obviousness to demonstrate that what is now alleged to be an obvious solution was not the first solution that occurred to anyone. He then held that the claimed invention was obvious because it was something ascertainable simply as a result of workshop adjustment by trial and error by a technician in order to produce the best result.

However, in *Soc. Industrielle Lasaffre's Patent* (SRIS C/97/85) the Comptroller dismissed an allegation of obviousness (in proceedings under s. 33 [1949]) because there was no suggestion in the evidence that it had ever been thought or appreciated that it might be useful to work towards the claimed product, this decision being similar on this point to that in *American Cyanamid* v. *Berk Pharmaceuticals* ([1976] RPC 231): an appeal was dismissed (SRIS C/106/86, *noted* IPD 10037 (CA)).

—The test of doing the unexpected   **3.10**

This test may also be called the "inventive step test", and perhaps equates most closely to the test applied in the EPO, as discussed in paras. 3.25 *et seq. infra*, but nevertheless retains a significant degree of practicality. This test has most precisely been formulated in *Procter & Gamble* v. *Peaudouce* ([1989] FSR 180 (CA)) where the test was stated to be derived from *Windsurfing* v. *Tabur Marine* ([1985] RPC 59 (CA)), discussed in para. 3.09 *supra*. In *Procter & Gamble*, the Court of Appeal made the following points on the question of assessment of obviousness, at least under section 32(1)(*f*) [1949]:
  (1) Obviousness is a jury question;
  (2) The question is not to be assessed with hindsight;
  (3) It is to be answered objectively, irrespective of the actual knowledge of the inventor;
  (4) But the evidence of the inventor of the circumstances in which he made the invention may be highly relevant, as indicated in *SKM* v. *Wagner-Spraytech* ([1982] RPC 497); and
  (5) The question involves four steps, *viz.*
    (i) to identify the inventive concept in the patent;
    (ii) to assume the mantle of the skilled but unimaginative addressee, who must have imputed to him the common general knowledge of the art in question, and who must be assumed to have read carefully the literature, especially relevant published patent specifications;
    (iii) to identify what, if any, difference exists between matters known or used and the alleged invention; and
    (iv) to decide, without any knowledge of the alleged invention, whether these differences constitute steps which would have been obvious to the skilled man or whether they required any degree of invention.
If the inventor had to carry out lengthy experiments, this would tend to indicate non-obviousness. The claims, to a disposable diaper, were held to be non-obvious.

Also, in *Mutoh Industry's Applications* ([1984] RPC 35) the Patents Court, reversing the Comptroller, allowed claims to known drawing machines having magnetic bearings well-known in the bearing art on the basis that, following *Hickton's Patent Syndicate* v. *Patents and Machines* ((1909 26 RPC 339 (CA)), if it were not obvious to have the idea of doing a particular thing, the mere fact that the actual way of putting the idea into effect might not require invention does not mean that the result is not patentable. In the *Mutoh* cases it was held that the man skilled in the relevant art would not have considered seeking advice from outside that art, though if he had done so the solution may well have been suggested to him. Further, in *Ward's Applications* ([1986] RPC 50), the Comptroller held that the cited documents would not have led a skilled man to the arrangement specified in the claims and that a skilled man in the art would not have found a cited document published 23 years before the priority date to be relevant to the proposals of other documents. However, the *Mutoh* decision was distinguished in *ABT Hardware's Application* (SRIS O/36/87, *noted* IPD 10040) to find unpatentable an analogous use of available material, it being opined that the skilled man could have been expected to investigate the claimed solution and it being denied that this approach was one of *ex post facto* analysis see para. 3.12 *infra*: see also the practical nature of the British test of obviousness discussed in paras. 3.12–3.14 *infra*.

3.11   —*The application of the British tests in practice*

The traditional British tests of obviousness have been discussed in the articles by A. W. White and P. G. Cole, listed in para. 3.03 *supra*. P. G. Cole concludes the second part of his 1982 article with a check list of the various questions which he suggests should be asked in considering the question of obviousness under United Kingdom law. He makes the interesting observation that obviousness cases usually fall into one of two kinds: (a) cases involving mere collocations where each part works independently of the others and gives its own result, as contrasted with combinations, the claimed features of which produce a new result or function and so can be seen to solve the inventor's problem; and (b) factual obviousness where any advantageous effect would have been expected from the state of the art. Here the problem is often set by the art. The EPO "problem and solution" approach (discussed in paras. 3.23 and 3.27 *et seq. infra*) leads to similar results.

Nevertheless, it must be remembered that obviousness is now first judged by an examiner in *ex parte* examination, either under section 18 or in the examination of an application for a European patent in the EPO. In such an examination, the examiner necessarily has to try and assume the position of the man skilled in the art and therefore necessarily has to make somewhat hypothetical pronouncements on obviousness or unobviousness based upon his own perception of what the man skilled in the art would have thought at the relevant time. When matters are before a British court on an *inter partes* basis, the matter will, generally, be judged objectively on the basis of the rival evidence placed before it. The conventional British patent practice has then been to judge, *from this evidence*, what people *would*, not *could*, have done if faced with a particular problem at the priority date of the invention.

Study of this commentary on section 3 will therefore show two distinct lines of approach to the issue of obviousness: (a) the practical, or "would", test decided on an evidential basis; and (b) the perceived, or "could", or "thought likely that it would", test. It is not suggested that this dichotomy of thought process is a conscious one, and many would deny that it exists at all, but it is submitted that the second (perceived) test is one which is an inevitable consequence of an *ex parte* consideration of the question of obviousness. Also, the use of the second test is not confined to *ex parte* proceedings. It seems sometimes to be used by British courts, probably when the court has a gut reaction that it would be appropriate to use this test (supported as it is by authority) to achieve the result which it perceives to be fair in the particular circumstances of the case before it, see para. 3.17 *infra*.

Thus, it is extremely difficult to predict the outcome of an obviousness attack or objection. Suffice it to say that the British courts often, but not necessarily, will view the matter rather differently than a patent office examiner, to the advantage of the patent proprietor where the inventive step taken was only a small one as to size, but nevertheless one that actual evidence from contemporaneous events will show would not have been likely to be, or in fact was not, taken by others. During an *ex parte* examination an examiner may not feel himself able to accept such a contention, backed as it is then likely to be only by unsubstantiated assertions from the applicant.

The practical nature of the British tests of obviousness

—Limitation of powers under former statutes **3.12**

Prior to 1978 the question of obviousness was formulated and judged solely in the context of *inter partes* proceedings because, under the former patent statutes, the Patent Office examination stage did not extend to any consideration of inventive step at all, this (until the 1949 Act) being a question which the Comptroller was powerless to decide, even in opposition cases. Moreover, when under the 1949 Act the Comptroller became empowered to judge obviousness in *inter partes* opposition or belated opposition proceedings under section 14 or 33 [1949], the application or patent could only fail on this ground if it were held that the invention claimed was one which, at the priority date of the claim, is "obvious and *clearly* does not involve any inventive step"; and, furthermore, the Comptroller was required to uphold the claim in any case of doubt in order that the applicant/patentee could later have his day in court and defend his patent in a revocation action before the court should he so wish (*GEC's Applications*, [1964] RPC 453 (CA)). Thus, only in proceedings before the court was the ultimate test of obviousness applied, and decisions under the 1949 and 1907 Acts have to be considered in the light of these statutory provisions and practice: this consideration seems little understood in other European countries.

Thus, prior to the present Act of 1977, it was the firm United Kingdom practice only to judge, finally, the difficult question of obviousness in the light of evidence presented orally before the court where the deductions made, and opinions held, by persons skilled in the art, as well as their *actual* knowledge on the priority date, could be judged after their evidence had been tested by cross-examination, and with determinations by the Comptroller under section 14 or 33 [1949] being designed only to eliminate those patent claims which would have no chance whatever of being upheld in proceedings before the court.

—The question "If obvious, why was it not done before?" **3.13**

In *American Cyanamid* v. *Ethicon* ([1975] RPC 513 at pp. 517–518), the court remarked that the question of obviousness could often best be judged, either for or against, by the history of the matter and the question was asked: why, if the invention were obvious, did it take nine-and-a-half years before anyone tried the alleged prior art suggestion? Thus, it would seem that those seeking to invalidate a patent on the ground of alleged obviousness should have a credible answer to the question: if obvious, why was it not done before?

In *Lucas* v. *Gaedor* ([1978] RPC 297) it was stated that:

"The question of obviousness is probably best tested, if this be possible, by the guidance given by contemporaneous events . . . If an invention has resulted in the solution of a problem which has been troubling industry for years and achieves immediate success upon its introduction, then the suggestion after the event that the step was obvious inevitably rings a little hollow."

In that case an objection of obviousness was rejected because, on the evidence, it was held that there was an inability of other manufacturers to see, as the inventing company saw, that the claimed article was the answer to the production of an article which represented in substance a very substantial step forward. However, in the same case, three other patents were invalidated for obviousness on the ground that the inventions claimed each represented nothing more than techniques which the skilled worker would naturally use in the course of non-inventive development work. In one case four other companies, albeit abroad, had each independently arrived at the same solution and this also indicated its obviousness.

In *Dow Chemical* v. *Spence Bryson (No. 2)* ([1984] RPC 359 (CA)) obviousness was held to have been indicated by evidence that others had made the same discovery independently and, in doing so, had not used extensive research experimentation. That other workers were following the same objective was also influential in invalidating the patent in *Genentech's Patent* ([1989] RPC 147 (CA)). However, the fact that others reached the same solution, and applied for patent protection thereon, has been stated to be more an indication of inventiveness than obviousness (*Halcon* v. *BP Chemicals* (SRIS C/100/87) *noted* IPD 10072).

While, in *Hallen* v. *Brabantia* ([1989] RPC 307) there was, apparently, no answer to the question why, if obvious, was the invention not made by others; the "right to work test" (discussed in para. 3.09 *supra*) nevertheless prevailed for a finding of obviousness in respect of the main claim.

In *Fichera* v. *Flogates* ([1984] RPC 257 (CA)) the Court of Appeal approved the statement that the best guide when one is considering obviousness is to ask the question: What did people do?" Also relevant is what others have said about the invention. In *General Tire* v. *Firestone* ([1971] RPC 173 and [1972] RPC 457 (CA)) a scientist of the Defendant had written a book on the art and described the invention as a breakthrough! Then, in *Genentech's [Human Growth Hormone] Patent* (SRIS C/64/89), a textbook had described the inventors' experiment as a notable one. In each case inventivity was recognised. The practical nature of the test for obviousness, at least under the 1949 Act, is stressed by S. Gratwick in his 1986 paper listed in para. 3.03 *supra*, in which he provides trenchant criticism of the *Windsurfing* decision discussed in para. 3.09 *infra*.

It is submitted that the practical test of obviousness was well summed up by that respected United States patents judge, Judge G. S. Rich, when he said ((1978) 60 JPOS 271 at 288) that "the good patent gives the world something it did not truly have before, whereas the bad patent has the effect of trying to take away from the world something which it effectively already had".

3.14 *—Relevance of commercial success*

A court views with suspicion arguments based on prior art that an invention was obvious if, despite the prior art, the invention has been a commercial success (*British Westinghouse* v. *Braulik*, (1910) 27 RPC 209 at 230 (CA)). The following passage from *Parkes* v. *Cocker* ((1929) 46 RPC 241), is also often quoted:

"When it has been found that the problem had awaited solution for many years and that the device is in fact novel and superior to what had gone before and has been widely used and indeed in preference to alternative devices, it is practically impossible to say that there is not present that scintilla of invention necessary to support the patent",

see: *Rosedale* v. *Carlton* ([1960] RPC 59 (CA)); *Van der Lely* v. *Bamfords* ([1960] RPC 169 at p. 198 and [1963] RPC 61 (HL)); and *General Tire* v. *Firestone* ([1972] RPC 457 at p. 503). Nevertheless, such commercial success must truly be due to the invention claimed and not, for example, as the result of clever advertising, see *Wildey and White's* v. *Freeman* ((1931) 48 RPC 405). Also, in *Tetra Molectric* v. *Japan Imports* ([1976] RPC 541), claims were held obvious following a warning that one must be careful to judge commercial success not in respect of the plaintiff's own device, but in relation to a notional device embodying only the features of the claim in question, see also *Andrew Master Hones* v. *Cruikshank & Fairweather* ([1981] RPC 389 (CA)).

Of course commercial success may also have arisen because a new problem emerged and the claimed invention was the obvious way of solving this, or because of skilled advertising or some other extraneous cause. Thus, the present tendency is to look more closely into the causes of commercial success than hitherto. Nevertheless, there still remains the question: if obvious, why was it not done before, and the answer to this needs to be even more convincing if there has been commercial success, and only at the hands of the proprietor. In *Fichera* v. *Flogates* ([1983] FSR 198 and [1984] RPC 323 (CA)) a patent was upheld on this reasoning, see also *Hickman* v. *Andrews* ([1983] RPC 147) where the invention was found to have achieved outstanding commercial success and therefore the claims were valid. Here there was no answer to the question that, if the invention were an obvious one, surely the patented device would have been made before it was. However, in *Hallen* v. *Brabantia* ([1989] RPC 307), though there was no answer to this question, nevertheless, the "right to work test" (discussed in para. 3.09 *supra*) prevailed because the modification adopted by the inventor should remain free for others to adopt. The question whether unobviousness is illustrated by commercial success is not necessarily confined to national boundaries and, therefore, in *Unilever* v. *Gillette* ([1989] RPC 417), a pleading of foreign commercial success was allowed to remain as possibly, but not necessarily, relevant.

Where a party to proceedings before the Patents Court wishes to rely upon alleged commercial success to rebut a challenge of obviousness, it is now required that full particulars of such success be given in a formal answer to the pleading containing the obviousness allegation, see RSC Ord. 104, rule 6(5) reprinted in para. E104.6 and para. 3.51 *infra*. Thus, before pleading "commercial success", the implications for the discovery stage of litigation should be considered, because putting commercial success in issue will require disclosure of sensitive sales statistics and supporting papers, as well as documents which indicate the precise nature of the commercially successful product or process, and such may show that the success was due to an embodiment of a sub-claim rather than of the main claim, or be due to extraneous factors such as advertising: documents relating to such will then also become relevant at the discovery stage. Thus, even the Comptroller will order discovery of relevant documents related to exploitation of the invention by the proprietor, though this is likely to be more limited than would be ordered in proceedings before the court, see *John Guest's Patent* ([1987] RPC 259) and the discussion of this at para. 72.44.

Ex post facto analysis   **3.15**

Care must be taken not to construct an argument of obviousness based upon *ex post facto* analysis: hindsight is not to be confused with foresight. Such analysis "is unfair to inventors and not countenanced by English patent law" (*British Westinghouse* v. *Braulik*, (1910) 27 RPC 209, *per* Fletcher-Moulton L.J. at p. 230), a statement said to be as true in 1975 as it was in 1910 (*Hughes* v. *Ingersoll*, [1977] FSR 406). *Ex post facto* analysis was also considered in *Technograph* v. *Mills and Rockley* ([1972] PC 346 (HL)) where it was pointed out (*per* Lord Reid at p. 362) that inventive ingenuity can lie "in perceiving the final result which it is the object of the invention to achieve was attainable from the particular starting point and in selection of the particular combination of steps which would lead to that result."

In *Fichera* v. *Flogates* ([1984] RPC 257) the invention was held to be unobvious, though it "was plainly obvious to any one with the benefit of hindsight", because of the practical activities of experts in the field who had unsuccessfully been seeking to solve the same problems as the inventor. In *Intalite* v. *Cellular Ceilings (No. 2)* ([1987] RPC 537) the claimed invention was, at first sight, one obvious to the skilled worker to try, but after hearing the evidence the Patents Court was satisfied that the objection of obviousness was unsustainable. It was observed: "When skilled and inventive individuals, looking for improvements in the field, fail to arrive at the claimed construction it is impossible to suggest that it would have been obvious to the hypothetical skilled man". A similar case is *Fairfax* v. *Filhol* ([1986] RPC 499 (CA)) where the claimed idea had not been arrived at by several others, including "the most prolific inventor in the field", see also the discussion on *Windsurfing International* v. *Trilantic* [*Canada*] (*noted* [1986] EIPR D-64) in para. 3.09 *supra*.

The EPO takes the view that obviousness is to be judged over the closest prior art and denies that this approach results in an *ex post facto* analysis, see the 1987 paper by G. S. A. Szabo listed in para. 3.03 *supra*. For the opposite view, see the letter by A. W. White ([1986] EIPR 387).

3.16   *The person skilled in the art*

The teaching of the state of the art is to be judged through the eyes of a person skilled in the relevant art. In *Technograph* v. *Mills and Rockley* ([1972] RPC 346 (HL)) it was stated (*per* Lord Reid at p. 355) that:

"The hypothetical addressee is a skilled technician who is well acquainted with workshop technique and who has carefully read the relevant literature. He is supposed to have an unlimited capacity to assimilate the contents of, it may be, scores of specifications but to be incapable of a scintilla of invention. When dealing with obviousness, unlike novelty, it is permissible to make a mosaic out of relevant documents, but it must be a mosaic which can be put together by an unimaginative man with no inventive capacity."

However, in *General Tire* v. *Firestone* ([1972] RPC 457 at pp. 482–485), Sachs L.J. stated:

"If the art is one having a highly developed technology, the notional skilled reader to whom the document is addressed may not be a single person but a team, whose combined skills would normally be employed in that art in interpreting and carrying into effect instructions such as those that are contained in the document to be construed."

In *American Cyanamid* v. *Ethicon* ([1979] RPC 215), as in *Genentech's Patent* ([1989] RPC 147 (CA)), the man skilled in the art was also held to be a multi-disciplinary team rather than a single individual. The skilled man should, however, be credited with sufficient time and the best available equipment to carry out the work and, where the art requires intellectual jumps and ingenuity of approach, that person must have a degree of inventiveness, but ability to perform known techniques is not a criterion (*Genentech's Patent, supra*).

The question of inventive step has to be judged objectively by the person skilled in the art and the inventor may not actually be such a person, see *Wellcome Laboratories* v. *V.R. Laboratories* [*Australia*] ([1982] RPC 343), where there was a lengthy discussion on the questions of the state of mind of the inventor and the circumstances in which he came to make the alleged invention: the former is probably irrelevant, but the latter is not.

In *Genentech's Patent* (*supra*) it was argued that other workers in the art (who had reached the same goal) had had inventive capacity and should not, therefore, be equated with the man "skilled in the art", relying on *Valensi* v. *British Radio* ([1973] RPC 337). However, that case was referring to the concept of the skilled man in the context of the sufficiency of a specification and, in *Genentech*, the argument was rejected, with a difference of opinion whether the phrase "man skilled in the art" had the same meaning when considering the different concepts of obviousness and insufficiency. Anyhow, the argument was there held to have failed on the facts.

The state of the art

—*Meaning of the "state of the art"*   **3.17**

The traditional test of obviousness employed by British courts has been to evaluate this objectively, not subjectively, in the light of the whole state of the art. It is submitted that this remains the test under the Act despite the reference in section 3 to "any matter which forms part of the state of the art" because EPCaa. 54(2) and 56 (with which s. 3 is by s. 130(7) to be compatible) requires inventive step to be shown over the whole state of the art and not merely over that part of it which would be found by a diligent searcher. Thus the "state of the art" should be properly evaluated and obviousness considered over the stock of information which can truly be said to be "known" at the priority date, see *Technograph* v. *Mills and Rockley* ([1972] RPC 346 (HL)) and the first paper by S. Gratwick listed in para. 3.03 *supra*.

—*Obviousness over isolated prior art*   **3.18**

There has been a tendency to view with suspicion arguments of obviousness based upon an isolated example of prior art, particularly when there has been outstanding commercial success. The best example of this is probably that in *General Tire* v. *Firestone* ([1972] RPC 457 at pp. 500–506) where the prior art was obscurely located. In *Hickman* v. *Andrews* ([1983] RPC 147) a notional expert would not have found any of the cited prior art of assistance in solving the problem facing the inventor. An isolated instance of prior art is, therefore, likely to be downgraded in significance when it is thought by the court that this prior art document may have been taken out of its true context within the whole state of the art in order to construct the obviousness argument on an *ex post facto* analysis, see further para. 3.15 *supra*.

—*Invention by way of selection from the prior art*   **3.19**

There is a particular danger in judging obviousness over a pre-selected prior art document in the case of an invention of selection, where the inventive step may lie in the choice of a particular document as the starting point for further research and development which in itself is of a routine nature. On this point, see particularly the conflicting views of the majority and the dissenting judgment in *Beecham Group's (Amoxycillin) Application* ([1980] RPC 261) and the more detailed analysis of the technical facts in the corresponding case in New Zealand (*Beecham Group* v. *Bristol-Myers (Amoxicillin) (No. 2)* [*New Zealand*], [1980] 1 NZLR 192) and on appeal in that country (*Beecham Group's (Amoxycillin) Application* [*New Zealand*], [1982] FSR 181). In that New Zealand appeal the court noted that the search for medical advance is to be encouraged and that the pursuit of one of a number—perhaps many—obvious lines of research may produce a signal or particularly valuable discovery. To rule out such an approach automatically in the name of obviousness was held not to be in accord with a primary purpose of patent law. The New Zealand Court of Appeal was further of the opinion that the pursuit of an obvious line of research may be held to culminate in an invention which is not obvious and does involve an inventive step if a sufficiently distinctive advantage is discovered. The *Amoxycillin* case in the United Kingdom is the subject of explanation and comment in the 1979 article by P. G. Cole listed in para. 3.03 *supra*.

The House of Lords in *Du Pont's (Witsiepe's) Application* ([1982] FSR 303) quoted from the New Zealand *Amoxycillin* judgment with approval and pointed out that the obviousness of a selection invention was not determined solely by the size of the group from which the selection was made, even if this consisted of only two possibilities. The relevant question is whether it has been discovered that the selected material possesses a property, quality or use which could not have been predicted by anyone ordinarily skilled in the art in question. That discovery may then be an invention giving rise to a valid selection patent. The EPO, however, seems to take a different standpoint and looks, in order to recognise patentability, for a selection of a combination of elements, which can be taken from separate lists or groups in a single prior art document, and seems not to recognise novelty in a selection from a single list, see para. 3.45 *infra*.

Of course, in considering obviousness of an invention of selection, the "right to work" test discussed in para. 3.09 *supra* must be applied only in regard to the working of that which is *specifically* described or suggested in the prior art. Also, the result of the selection must be unpredictable, and not something that would be seen as obvious to try for some other purpose. Thus, merely making another substance of the same type for its expected purpose is not inventive (*Hybritech's Patent*, SRIS O/76/89, *noted* IPD 12040).

3.20 —*Obviousness judged over selected prior art*

Nevertheless, British courts have been known to hold claims invalid for obviousness over specific items of prior art, which do not appear to have been in the realm of common general knowledge and without apparent consideration of whether there might be a different picture if the prior art were considered as a whole. Thus, in *Allmanna Svenska* v. *Burntisland* ((1952) 69 RPC 63 (CA)), approved in *Martin* v. *Millwood* ([1956] RPC 125 (HL)), the Court of Appeal said:

"The matter of obviousness is to be judged by reference to the state of the art in the light of all that was previously known by persons versed in the art derived from experience of what was practically employed, as well as from the contents of previous writings, specifications, textbooks and other documents."

On this basis the Court of Appeal in 1982 refused to ignore a certain prior art document merely on the ground that it was old (*Jamesigns' Application*, [1983] RPC 68), decided under Section 14 [1949]. The *Allmanna Svenska* case was cited with approval in *Dow Chemical* v. *Spence Bryson (No. 2)* at first instance (SRIS C/158/82), later only partly reported and not on this point ([1982] FSR 598). In this case it was held that five patent specifications were part of the state of the art and, therefore, had to be considered under an attack of obviousness, though the allegations thereof were there rejected, but this attack succeeded on appeal ([1984] RPC 359 (CA)).

In *Windsurfing International* v. *Tabur Marine* ([1985] RPC 59 (CA)) the Court of Appeal held claims invalid, *inter alia*, over prior art which took the form of a prior use being a crude device constructed by a schoolboy, but it was held that the skilled adult applying his mind to the device would at once have seen that it should be modified into a structure within the scope of the claim as sought to be amended, see further para. 3.09 *supra*.

In *Dow Chemical's Application* (SRIS O/179/83) claims were disallowed to certain optical isomers of compounds already known in their racemic form. The novel isomers were stated to have advantageous properties compared with those known for the racemic forms. It was held, however, that the isomers had not been shown to possess a property of unexpected character and that the difference in properties was merely one of degree insufficient to support a selection patent. In *Shell Internationale's Application* (SRIS O/187/83) compounds which exhibited both optical and geometric isomerism were claimed in one of the four possible forms. The claims were rejected on the holding that there was no deterrent to optical resolution, it being predictable that one of the isomers would have superior properties to those of the racemic form. An argument that there was no economic incentive to carry out the final optical resolution of the separated geometric isomer was rejected as lacking sufficient supporting evidence, and it was stated that the advantages of the claimed isomers came only as a bonus and could not themselves confer inventiveness. A third case where claims to isomers were rejected was *Roussel-Uclaf's Application* (SRIS O/10/85; *noted* IPD 8028). Here it was stated that it is normal expectation that one isomer will have superior (pesticidal) activity. These three decisions indicate that claims to particular isomers are only likely to be accepted if the evidence of surprising superiority is quite startling and if there is strong evidence that the claimed isomer would not have been made during routine experimentation, compare here *Beecham Group's (Amoxycillin) Application* ([1980] RPC 261 (CA)) discussed in para. 3.19 *supra*.

In *Kim Production's Application* (SRIS O/143/85, *noted* IPD 9046) the Comptroller held that the notional skilled man concerned with the same problem as the alleged inventor, and having found the same citation [a United States patent specification] would have given it serious consideration, notwithstanding that it was published over 30 years previously: the application was refused.

However, the warning has been given that care needs to be taken when considering obviousness over a single document found by a diligent searcher, because he inevitably knows for what he is looking, see *ICI's (Pointer's) Application* ([1977] RPC 434 and *Moseley Rubber's Patent* (SRIS C/63/86).

The EPO also takes the view that obviousness is to be considered over the closest prior art, see para. 3.28 *infra*.

Mosaic of prior art   **3.21**

In *Allmanna Svenska* v. *Burntisland* ((1952) 69 RPC 63 (CA)) it was held obvious to consider substituting in a marine engine an electrodynamic coupling shown in one patent specification for a geared diesel drive shown in another specification. Thus the court here appeared to make a mosaic of two seemingly unconnected documents, but without giving clear reasons for so doing. The case is, therefore, an unsatisfactory precedent on this point, particularly as the court is normally wary of making a mosaic of documents in the absence of evidence that at least one of them was part of the stock of common general knowledge of the skilled person at the relevant date, or that the documents would for some other reason have been read together, *e.g.* because one contains a reference to the other. This caution of the court seems amply justified because the solution of a problem may well lie in the (inventive) notion that two apparently unconnected items of prior art should be considered together, just as it may in the selection of a particular document as the starting point for further research and development as discussed under the last preceding heading. It may have been, however, that in this case the Court of Appeal thought that the invention was a mere collocation, see para. 3.22 *infra*.

Collocations   **3.22**

A combination of known elements is different from a mere collocation thereof where each element performs its own function and there is no inter-relation between these elements giving rise to an unexpected synergistic effect, see *Williams* v. *Nye* ((1890) 7 RPC 62 (CA)). In the second part of his 1982 article listed in para. 3.03 *supra*, P. G. Cole argues that, where a claim is directed to a collocation of parts each known *per se*, no invention should be recognised unless there is a working relationship between the parts which provide a new function or result, see para. 3.09 *supra*. However, the "mere collocation" argument has rarely succeeded before the United Kingdom courts, see the first part of this article by P. G. Cole where he argues that it ought to be more favoured than it is.

In *International Paint Co.'s Application* ([1982] RPC 247), the doctrine of collocation was, however, described as an extremely sound and wholesome doctrine, but only to be applied "where the parts of an article each performs its own function and would do so even in the absence of the other parts." Nevertheless, the doctrine is not to be applied where all the parts "can do something together they could not do by themselves".

The problem and solution approach

3.23 —*The principles of this approach*

The Germanic approach to the consideration of obviousness has traditionally been to evaluate inventive step in terms of the formulation of a problem and the method(s) by which it is considered this could have been solved at the priority date. On such a type of analysis, the way in which an invention is arrived at can be dissected into three stages: (a) ascertaining the problem to be solved or difficulty to be overcome, including cases where the notional problem is how to arrive at a product having particular desirable properties; (b) choosing the technical principle to be applied (in non-empirical cases, since in chemical and biological empirical cases this often has no application); and then (c) choosing the particular means to be used, *i.e.* the solution of the problem. Unobviousness in any of these stages, or in a combination of them, will support an inventive step.

The EPO has increasingly adopted an "effects centred" problem and solution approach to obviousness, as contrasted with the Germanic problem and solution method which traditionally took no account of effects in the determination of inventive step, see the two articles by G. S. A. Szabo listed in para. 3.03 *supra*. This EPO approach is set out with clarity in *EPO Decision T* 31/84, "*Test device/ MILES*" ([1987] 1 EPOR 10; *abridged* OJEPO 11/1986, 369), see also *EPO Decision T* 01/80, "*Carbonless copying paper*" ([1982] RPC 321; OJEPO 7/1981, 206). However, the EPO insists on formulation of the problem over the closest prior art objectively determined, and then considers whether the solution claimed involved an inventive step over that art. This approach is to be contrasted with the view of S. Gratwick expounded in his 1986 paper listed in para. 3.03 *supra*. Previously the pros and cons of this approach had been debated in notes by S. J. Avery and A. W. White ((1984–85) 14 CIPA 166, 242, 405 and 407), see also T. I. M. Smith and N. Brook ((1985–86) 15 CIPA 23 and 24).

3.24 —*Adoption under British law*

The problem and solution approach to obviousness has rarely been adopted in explicit terms by British courts, but it can be seen to be reflected by the Cripps question (for which see para. 3.06 *supra*), particularly as explained in *Technograph* v. *Mills and Rockley* ([1972] RPC 346 (HL) at 353–356). Here, the Defendant argued that the problem of improving the tedious assembly of electrical circuits by wiring and soldering was easily solved by the application of common general knowledge to make a printed circuit by a series of workshop experiments. This contention was rejected by Lord Reid as based on a false analysis. Many workers in the field had tried, and failed, to find a satisfactory solution to this problem and it was not credible that this would have happened if the problem only needed workshop experiments to solve it. The analysis was an *ex post facto* one involving hindsight rejected as inadmissible in *British Westinghouse* v. *Braulik* ((1910) 27 RPC 209 (CA)), see para. 3.15 *supra*.

Lord Reid then stated that the question of obviousness was formerly left to a jury, but the real question is whether, at the relevant time, the invention would have been obvious to the unimaginative skilled technician. He pointed out that that which now seems obvious to anyone may at that date have been far from obvious to him; and that, in this case, he would have been faced with a large variety of different methods, none of which had proved commercially useful. "He would have had no assurance that any successful solution was possible, still less would he have known in what direction to look for it. He would be expected to try out all obvious modifications or combinations of these methods which seemed to him worth trying", provided that such would appear to him as giving any prospect of valuable results.

It can thus now be seen that the elements of Lord Reid's analysis in the *Technograph* case were: (1) the problem and solution framework to determine the issue to be decided; (2) a warning against *ex post facto* analysis; (3) consideration of the Cripps question to elucidate what is worth trying; and (4) assessment of what workers in the art actually did. Indeed, the obviousness approach to be adopted has more recently been set out in terms somewhat similar to this analysis, see *Procter & Gamble* v. *Peaudouce* ([1989] FSR 180 (CA)), as noted in para. 3.10 *supra*.

The problem and solution analysis of an obviousness objection can also be discerned in *Du Pont's (Witsiepe's) Application* ([1982] FSR 303 (HL)), discussed in para. 3.19 *supra* with reference to *Beecham Group's (Amoxycillin) Application* [*New Zealand*] ([1982] FSR 181). In each of these cases there was a finding of inventive step on the basis of a property, quality or use which could not have been predicted by the ordinary person skilled in the art in question, even if it was only a case of selecting from a list or from only two possibilities. Without it being expressed as such, these decisions can be seen as having applied an effects centred problem and solution approach directed to a problem based on an unexpected and surprising effect. The same approach had also previously been used by Buckley LJ. in *Beecham Group's (Amoxycillin) Application* ([1980] RPC 261 (CA)), likewise to find an inventive step present in the discovery that a particular chemical (amoxycillin) had a beneficial, but unpredictable, property which had resulted in huge commercial success. In his analysis, Buckley LJ. reviewed many of the cases referred to in paras. 3.05–3.20 *supra*. However, it should be noted that, if in the *Amoxycillin* cases there had been a recognised problem, perhaps one implied by the closest art, the result could have been different, see the dissenting judgment in the English case at [1980] RPC 298. It should also be noted that the problem in these cases was not just to make another penicillin, but a problem of obtaining one of high activity and blood absorption after oral administration.

A harsher line was, however, adopted in *Jamesigns' Application* ([1983] RPC 68 (CA)) where an invention was found obvious on the basis of a 1934 specification in the face of considerable commercial success. The solution to the problem facing the inventor was held to have been clearly pointed out with physical reasons for it in that specification. Although this can be seen as an application of an effects centred problem and solution method as applied by the EPO, the Court of Appeal did not employ "problem and solution" phraseology.

Sometimes, however, invention is recognised based upon the discovery of a new problem, rather than on an inventive solution of a known problem. If the formulation of the problem can be recognised as inventive, *i.e.* that the existence of the problem was itself unobvious, then it is immaterial whether the solution of that problem is or is not itself inventive. One such case, often cited, is *Hickton's Patent Syndicate* v. *Patents & Machine Improvements* ((1909) RPC 339 (CA)) where an inventive idea led to a special and new purpose for the means employed, *i.e.* a problem invention had arisen and its solution could be obvious without loss of invention, see para. 3.10 *supra*. Another is *Beecham Group's (Amoxycillin) Applications* (*supra*). Yet another is *Cleveland Graphite* v. *Glacier Metal* ((1950) 67 RPC

149 (HL)) which is only readily explicable on the basis that there was a new problem: to obtain hitherto unknown advantages in motor engine bearings. That that solution was obvious, but to make a thin-walled bearing by coin pressing was not decisive. Nor was the argument decisive that anyone *could* have made such bearings in that way. Thus, this was an early "*would* not *could*" case.

The classical case, however, that deals with a new problem is *Killick* v. *Pye* ([1958] RPC 366 (CA)). Here the Court of Appeal referred to the solution of a new problem of providing a sapphire stylus that could be used for playing both 78 rpm and the then fairly new long-playing records. The closest art was a 1907 patent specification showed a flat-bottomed steel stylus which addressed different problems. Moreover, the art then made no further mention of such a stylus, and led away and did not in any way indicate this as a natural variation to use. Most significantly, the Defendant failed to establish that a man skilled in the art *would*, at the date of the Plaintiff's patent, in the natural course of events, have been led to the claimed subject-matter.

As can be seen from the analysis of the EPO decisions contained in paras. 3.28 *et seq.*, the EPO Appeal Boards have adopted this "*would* not *could*" test and formulated it as an effects centred problem and solution approach. Indeed, in *EPO Decision T 142/84, "Inventive step/BRITAX"* (OJEPO 3/1987, 112); [1987] 3 EPOR 148), this approach was said to be entirely consistent with the decision in *Killick* v. *Pye* (*supra*), but before such a view is accepted uncritically it should be noted that, in *Killick*, the patent was upheld and that in *Britax* it was not.

3.25 *—Using this approach to rationalise the British decisions*

Using the problem and solution approach, many of the precedent British cases can, it is submitted, be seen to be decided according to the following principles. Firstly, the skilled person must have a problem to solve if the corresponding solution is to be held obvious. If the patentee's problem is a known or obvious one, "obvious to try" is a relevant consideration, provided that there was a reasonable prospect of some resulting success, but if the inventor's problem is part of the inventive step because it was unobvious to arrive at the inventor's achievement, "obvious to try" is irrelevant. Where the inventor's problem is known or obvious, the question is whether, at the priority date, the skilled person who is tackling that problem would have regarded any particular citation as giving him what he wanted, *i.e.* the solution provided by the claim in question (*BTH* v. *Metropolitan Vickers*, (1928) 45 RPC 1 (HL) at p. 23). The question is whether the citation deals with the same problem and suggests the same solution. This is not, however, the sole consideration since there is also the question of whether the relevant skilled person would have found the citation (*General Tire* v. *Firestone*, [1972] RPC 457 (CA)), or given it serious consideration (*Johns-Manville's Application*, [1967] 479) and *Electrochemie Ugines's Application*, ([1970] RPC 331).

However, if the problem was known to be important and took many years to be solved, this indication of long-felt want is usually decisive, see *Wood* v. *Gowshall*, (1937)) 54 RPC 37 (CA)); *Parkes* v. *Cocker* ((1929) 46 RPC 241), approved in *Non-Drip* v. *Strangers* ((1943) 60 RPC 135 (HL)); *Cleveland Graphite* v. *Glacier Metal* ((1950) 67 RPC 149 (HL)); and *Martin* v. *Millwood* ([1956] RPC 125 (HL)). This is particularly so if a large patent literature addressed the problem but failed to solve it, especially if the solution was simple (*Savage* v. *Harris*, (1896) 13 RPC 9); *Olin Mathieson* v. *Biorex* ([1970] RPC 157); *Parkes* v. *Cocker* (*supra*) and *Gillette* v. *Perma-Sharp* [*Scotland*] ([1966] FSR 284). If none of these factors can be found, the patent is likely to be revoked for lack of inventive step, sometimes called a lack of "subject-matter".

If the problem solved by the inventor was a known or obvious one, for instance where skilled persons did not even appreciate that there was a problem in cases of unfelt want, the patent is likely to be upheld (*Hickton's Patent Syndicate* v. *Patents & Machine Improvements* ((1909) RPC 339 (CA)), but such cases cause difficulties and their outcome is uncertain where the step taken from the prior art is but a small one in terms of structure or actions. It is to try and overcome such uncertainty that the EPO has developed its effects centred problem and solution approach to considerations of obviousness, as is discussed in paras. 3.27 *et seq*.

Effect of section 2(3) on test for obviousness   **3.26**

Because the contents of an unpublished application of prior date are effective only as novelty-destroying and are specifically excluded from the test of obviousness (s. 2(3)), it might have been thought that a broadening of the traditional, and purely factual, test of novelty would be inevitable to avoid the grant of patents for trivial variations from the subject matter of prior-dated specifications unpublished at the priority date of the later invention. Something like this occurred in Australia after the concept of obviousness in that country became limited to being considered only over the common general knowledge in the art, as was decided in *Minnesota Mining* v. *Beiersdorf [Australia]* ([1980] FSR 449), see for example *Windsurfing International* v. *Petit [Australia]* ([1984] 2 NSWLR 196). However, if this were to happen under the 1977 Act, the decision would still have to be one formulated as a lack of novelty: this point is, therefore, discussed further at paras. 2.19–2.24.

Nevertheless, it is to be noted that the EPO has stated that, in order to mitigate the harshness of the "whole contents" approach to the consideration of the impact of prior (but unpublished) applications, and reduce the risk of "self-collision" (where the earlier and later applications have a common origin), a strict approach to lack of novelty arising from the earlier application should be adopted (*EPO Decision T* 167/84, "*Fuel injector valve/NISSAN*", OJEPO 8/1987, 369; [1987] 6 EPOR 344). It is, therefore, suggested that an interpretation of section 2(3) is likely to be adopted in any particular case to grant a patent for an invention considered to be worthy of grant; and to refuse such, by a modification of the "strict" novelty test, when the difference between the claim in question and the description of the prior specification is seen to be of little or no importance. However, as yet, there appears to be little judicial consideration of how section 2(3), or the corresponding EPCa. 54(3), should be applied to specific cases.

EPO Guidelines   **3.27**

EPO Guidelines C-IV, 9 were formulated to assist EPO examiners in their consideration of the presence or lack of inventive step. At the commencement of the EPC the then President and Vice-President of the EPO stated ((1978) 9 IIC 297) that the proper standard of obviousness under the EPC should be broadly comparable with that then applied in the German Patent Office, but that the EPO Guidelines on obviousness were regarded as fully compatible with British case law. The Guidelines do not have the force of law, either in the EPO (see *EPO Decision T* 47/86, "*Alumina spinel/EXXON*", [1988] 6 EPOR 387) or in the United Kingdom, and it is not clear that section 130(7) requires them to be taken into consideration when considering the question of inventive step for applications filed under the Act.

Also the EPO Guidelines have been little quoted by the EPO Boards of Appeal, but it should be noted that EPO Guidelines C-IV, 9 indicate that: (1) "obvious" means that which does not go beyond the normal progress of technology (*cf*. the "lying in the road" test discussed in para. 3.08 *supra*); (2) mosaics are possible only when it is obvious and natural for the relevant skilled person to combine the documents in question (*cf.* para. 3.21 *supra*); and (3) there is a ban on analysis amounting to hindsight (*cf.* para. 3.15 *supra*). Nevertheless, the principles stated in these Guidelines are revised as necessary in order that they are kept in step with the Appeal Board decisions. Thus, they represent a convenient summary of the principles applied by the EPO. These Guidelines set out various sub-tests against which obviousness and unobviousness can be assessed. These are discussed in *EPH*. For further description and discussion of sub-tests of unobviousness that have been used (mainly in the United States), see the paper by J. Pagenberg listed in para. 3.03 *supra*.

EPO decisions

3.28   —*The EPO philosophy for assessment of inventive step*

Because decisions of the EPO Examining and Opposition Divisions, *i.e.* decisions in the EPO at first instance, are not reported and do not appear to be considered as authoritative, it is convenient herein to use the shorthand convention of referring to the decisions of the EPO Appeal Boards as those of the EPO itself, though by virtue of EPCa. 23, the Appeal Boards are nominally independent of the EPO.

In the decade since the EPO commenced operations, these Appeal Boards have often declared the desirability of developing a distinct "European" standard for the assessment of inventive step and have tried to do this by developing a philosophy according to which this assessment may be made by comparing the facts of the instant case against that philosophy. Indeed the EPO appears to take the view that the citation of precedent decisions is not normally helpful, it being more important to analyse the factual situation of a case against the principles which have been derived from that philosophy. This appears strange to British lawyers who are accustomed to distilling legal principles from the precedent decisions, rather than viewing those decisions as already decided according to some pre-ordained principle.

Since, however, the present Commentary is designed to comment on the patent law of the United Kingdom, decisions of the EPO on the assessment of inventive step (*i.e.* unobviousness) are reviewed herein by attempting to categorise these under various headings. A reader, faced with a particular fact situation, can then ascertain the attitude which the EPO can be expected to adopt. Also, the present commentary provides a note of precedent decisions which may possibly be cited as authority to a British tribunal as persuasive authority having regard to section 91. This requires EPO decisions to be taken note of in proceedings under the Patents Act 1977, though (as already noted in para. 3.04 *supra*) there is as yet little sign that English courts are prepared to be persuaded by EPO decisions on obviousness, see the attempt made to do so in *Genentech's Patent* ([1989] RPC 147 (CA)).

The EPO philosophy has been described and explained in the papers by D. L. T. Cadman, J. L. Beton, R. Singer and G. S. A. Szabo listed in para. 3.03 *supra*. While the initial view was that the standard of obviousness adopted by the EPO should be comparable with that previously prevailing in the German Patent Office (see (1978) 9 IIC 297), a desire to avoid undue rigidity can be discerned.

Nevertheless, the philosophy has become firmly founded in the view that a patentable invention must provide a solution to a problem, so that either that solution, or the problem, must itself have been unobvious at the priority date to the "man skilled in the art". That man must be presumed to know all the relevant art both in the field of the invention and in neighbouring fields. While the German doctrine of requiring an invention to have technical achievement, in addition to inventive step, is not be found in the EPC, nevertheless the EPO particularly looks for evidence of technical advantage provided by the invention as evidence of unobviousness (the problem, rather than its solution, then being regarded as unobvious), but provided that such advantage is of an unpredictable nature or degree, and is not one which arises inherently, and provided that it would not be obvious to come to the invention for some other reason, in which cases the invention will be seen as an inherently unpatentable "one way street" solution, as discussed in para. 3.48 *infra*.

However, it is impermissible to carry out an *ex post facto* assessment of inventive step. Instead, the position has been adopted, especially by the Chemical Board of Appeal, that the closest piece of prior art to the claimed invention must first be identified and then it is to be assessed whether an inventive step thereover can be recognised. It is said that, if this is so, then any other art must be less relevant (because it is not so close to the claimed invention) and therefore the patentability of the claim under EPCa. 56 has been substantiated. Surprisingly, this view does not appear to have been challenged by academic writers, even though the test substitutes an artificial problem for the one which actually faced the inventor and appears to give all prior art equal weight irrespective of its credibility to the man skilled in the art due to its age or the reputation of its author or circumstances or location of publication.

Also, the EPO does not regard its philosophy as impermissible *ex post facto* analysis even though identifying the closest art can only be done by hindsight. However, practitioners have to accept the law as it appears to be and, accordingly, hereafter, this Commentary attempts a factual synopsis of the EPO decisions on obviousness on the assumption that each case was correctly decided, though no tribunal should really be regarded as infallible.

The individual features of the above-summarised overlying view of the EPO on the interpretation of EPCa. 56 are, therefore, now considered separately in the remainder of this Commentary on section 3. In doing so, the question has been treated from the standpoint of the applicant who has to try and establish unobviousness. However, it should be appreciated that, when an examiner or opponent is trying to establish lack of inventive step, that person will be looking at the matter in a different light and, in particular, there appears to be a tendency for such a person to start by paying particular attention to whether the invention can be seen as a "one way street" solution to a known problem (for which see para. 3.48 *infra*), in which case any technical achievement of the invention will be seen as a bonus effect which does not assist patentability.

—The EPO standard for assessment of obviousness   **3.29**

Patents granted under the EPC are intended to have a sufficient standard to ensure that they are likely to be upheld by national courts (*EPO Decision T* 01/81, "*Thermoplastic sockets*," OJEPO 10/1981, 439) under a law which (by virtue of EPCa. 138) ought to be in harmony with EPCa. 56. However, circumstances have been recognised where the benefit of the doubt can be given to an applicant/patentee, *e.g.* where there is a conflict of evidence in opposition proceedings (*EPO Decision T* 209/85 "*Titanium catalyst/MATSUI*", [1987] 4 EPOR 235). On this point there is, perhaps, a realisation that a decision not to grant, or to revoke, a European patent is final, there being no further appeal from a decision of an EPO Appeal Board, save in exceptional circumstances by referral to the EPO Enlarged Board of Appeal.

Hindsight analysis is particularly condemned, with inventive step assessment being considered solely from the practical viewpoint of the person skilled in the art, see *EPO Decision T* 05/81, "*Production of hollow thermoplastic objects*" (OJEPO 7/1982, 249); and an application is not to be refused if those skilled in the art find the invention surprising, even if the claims are directed to a seemingly obvious situation (*EPO Decision T* 106/84, *"Packing machine/MICHAELSON"*, OJEPO 5/1985, 132).

The prior art to be considered

3.30 *—The extent of the relevant prior art*

While obviousness is to be judged in the light of "the state of the art" which comprises all knowledge available to the public as such, the EPO considers that particular attention has to be paid to that prior art which is seen to differ the least from the claimed invention, *i.e.* to "the closest art". For this, the person skilled in the art "must be presumed to study patent publications in the relevant patent classes with particular interest" (*EPO Decision T* 01/81, *"Thermoplastic sockets"*, OJEPO 10/1981, 439), and indeed to check all reports on material studies likely to be useful in solving the problem before him, unless these state explicitly that a particular material is unsuitable for his purpose (*EPO Decision T* 263/87, *"Garnet laser/ALLIED"*, [1988] 4 EPOR 243). Thus, *all* art has to be considered, even if relevant statements have not been emphasised therein (*EPO Decision T* 24/81, *"Metal refining/BASF"*, OJEPO 4/1983, 133).

That art may be in a parallel field to that of the invention because the skilled person is expected to be aware of developments in neighbouring arts, see *EPO Decision T* 32/81, *"Cleaning apparatus for conveyor belt"* (OJEPO 6/1982, 225); *EPO Decision T* 198/84, *"Thiochloroformates/HOECHST"* (OJEPO 7/1985, 209); and *EPO Decision T* 176/84 *"Pencil Sharpener/MöBIUS"* (OJEPO 2/1986, 50; [1986] 3 EPOR 177), but in *EPO Decision T* 57/84, *"Tolylfluanid/BAYER"* (OJEPO 5/1987, 177; [1987] 3 EPOR 131) the field of plant protection was considered too remote from that of wood preservation.

3.31 *—Age of the prior reference*

The age of the reference is immaterial (*EPO Decision T* 169/84, *"Endless power transmission belt/MITSUBOSHI"*, [1987] 3 EPOR 120), where a United States patent issued in 1893 was held to have been one which the skilled man should have looked for to see if the problem which he faced had already been solved in another technical field where the same problem had arisen. However, aged publications have been discounted where they have appeared to have played no part in the development of the art (*EPO Decision T* 10/83, Bexford's Application, noted IPD 6103; *EPO Decision T* 8/83, *"Paper Dyeing/BASF"*, [1986] 4 EPOR 186; *EPO Decision T* 95/87, *"Catalyst production/DYSON REFRACTORIES"*, [1988] 3 EPOR 171; and *EPO Decision T* 321/86, *"Display tube/PHILIPS"*, [1989] 4 EPOR 199).

3.32 *—Inherent disclosures*

Even features which are not explicitly described in the prior art, but which are inherent therein or implied thereby, are to be taken into consideration (*EPO Decisions T* 06/80, *"Intermediate layer for reflector"*, OJEPO 10/1981, 434).

3.33 *—Circumstances of publication*

The circumstances of publication, for example the location of a reference or the reputation of the publication, are normally considered irrelevant. Thus, even foolish-looking instructions are to be regarded as in the public domain (*EPO Decision T* 48/85, *"Eimeria necatrix/NRDC"*, [1987] 3 EPOR 138). However, a document must be read in its original language and as it would by a man skilled in the art: therefore, a rejection based on a mistranslation of a reference should be reversed as in *EPO Decision T* 106/86, *"Crepe fabric/VAL LESSINA"* ([1988] 6 EPOR 401). Also, an abstract and its parent document should be read together, with the parent disclosure being more credible in the case of inconsistency (*EPO Decision T* 77/87, *"Latex composition/ICI"*, [1989] 5 EPOR 246).

—Admissions of applicant   **3.34**

Where an applicant makes an admission as to the state of the art, this need not then be proved (*EPO Decision T* 04/83, *"Purification of sulphonic acids/EXXON"*, OJEPO 12/1983/ 498), but an erroneous acknowledgment of prior art will not be held against an applicant (*EPO Decision T* 22/83, *"Surface acoustic wave device/ FUJITSU"*, [1988] 4 EPOR 235).

Also, where an applicant makes an admission that a particular feature of his claim is not inventive, that feature will not be taken into consideration in assessing whether an inventive step is present (*EPO Decision T* 22/81, *"Ignition system/ LUCAS"*, OJEPO 6/1983, 226).

—Combination of references   **3.35**

Within the same field, it has been held permissible to combine references to deny an inventive step (*EPO Decision T* 183/84, *"Titanyl sulphate/BAYER"*, [1986] 4 EPOR 174), and even a third document has been combined with two others, though only for the purpose of identifying an element of the second reference (*EPO Decision T* 173/83, *"Antioxidant/TELECOMMUNICATIONS"*, OJEPO 10/1987, 465; [1988] 3 EPOR 133). However, a permissible combination (or mosaic) of documents only establishes prima facie obviousness and this can perhaps be overcome if the existence of unexpected technical advantage arising from the combination can be demonstrated (*EPO Decision T* 15/81, *"Eddy-current testing device"*, OJEPO 1/1982, 2; and *EPO Decision T* 271/84, *"Removal of hydrogen sulphide . . . /AIR PRODUCTS"*, OJEPO 9/1987, 405; [1987] 1 EPOR 23). For discussion of the need to demonstrate unexpected advantages to prove unobviousness, see paras. 3.46–3.48 *infra*.

However, it is inadmissible to combine unrelated, or conflicting, documents mosaically to deny inventive step (*EPO Decision T* 02/81, *"Methylenebis (phenyl isocyanate)"*, OJEPO 10/1984, 394), but (as this case shows) it is sometimes possible to combine documents to demonstrate a prejudice in the art against the making of the invention.

Indications of unobviousness in the prior art itself   **3.36**

Leaving aside (until paras. 3.46–3.48 *infra*) consideration of unobviousness being indicated by a showing of an unpredictable advantageous technical effect, there are cases where the prior art teaching itself indicates unobviousness. For example, the prior art may be shown to lead away from the invention, as in *EPO Decision T* 02/81, *"Methylenebis (phenyl isocyanate)"* (OJEPO 10/1982, 394); or a prior patent specification can indicate a prejudice against further development, though such normally requires some corroborative evidence, see *EPO Decision T* 19/81, *"Film coating"* (OJEPO 2/1982, 51). *Per contra*, a patent is to be denied if the claimed subject-matter is obvious for *any* purpose, even if an unexpected, advantageous, result is obtained therefrom (*EPO Decision T* 21/81, "*Electromagnetically operated switch*", OJEPO 1/1983, 15).

Also, a document can be discounted if it can be shown that a skilled man would take nothing from it (*EPO Decision T* 232/86, "*Electric fusion pipe fittings/ ESDAN*" ([1988] 2 EPOR 89), or where it can be shown that the invention was not obvious to an expert (*EPO Decision T* 271/84, "*Removal of hydrogen sulphide . . . / AIR PRODUCTS*". OJEPO 9/1987, 405; [1987] 1 EPOR 23).

There are also cases where an invention is prima facie obvious, but on more detailed analysis has been held not to be, see *EPO Decision T* 9/86, "*Polyamide-6/ BAYER*" (OJEPO 1–2/1988, 12; [1988] 2 EPOR 83), and the fact that a plurality of steps has been taken from the prior art to reach the invention may be a significant indicator of inventiveness (*EPO Decision T* 113/82, "*Recording apparatus/IBM*", OJEPO 1/1984, 10).

Inactive art *may* also be indicative of inventive step (*EPO Decision T* 109/82, "*Hearing aid/BOSCH*", OJEPO 10/1984, 473).

3.37 *Identification of problem to be solved by the invention*

The EPO requires each invention to solve a technical problem, see para. 3.28 *supra*. Indeed, this problem ought to be stated as such in the specification (EPCr. 27(1)(*d*)) though such statement is not a separate formal criterion for patentability (*EPO Decision T* 26/81, "*Containers/ICI*", OJEPO 6/1982, 211).

The problem must be properly stated so that inventive step may be assessed objectively (*EPO Decision T* 01/80, "*Carbonless copying paper*", [1982] RPC 321; OJEPO 7/1981, 206). Indeed, whether the preferred solution to the problem is inventive is also to be assessed objectively (*EPO Decision T* 24/81, "*Metal refining/ BASF*", OJEPO 4/1983, 133), but the whole matter must be looked at in a practical, and not abstract, manner without *ex post facto* reasoning. (*EPO Decision T* 05/81, "*Production of hollow thermoplastic objects*", OJEPO 7/1982, 249).

3.38 *Restatement and reformulation of the problem*

However, the problem need not be expressly described, at least in the application as filed (*EPO Decision T* 142/84, "*Inventive step/BRITAX*", OJEPO 1/1987, 112; [1987] 3 EPOR 148), and it is possible to reformulate the problem when more relevant prior art is brought to the attention of the applicant (*EPO Decision T* 13/84, "*Reformulation of the problem/SPERRY*", OJEPO 8/1986, 253; [1986] 6 EPOR 289), particularly when advantages over the reformulated problem can be demonstrated arising from small structural differences (*EPO Decision T* 44/85, "*Curable binder preparation/SHELL*", [1986] 5 EPOR 258). Even a lesser problem than that envisaged by the inventor can be accepted in an appropriate case (*EPO Decision T* 132/84, "*Tetramethylpiperidone/HÜLS*", [1986] 6 EPOR 303). A restatement of the problem to a more general level is also permissible (*EPO Decision T* 184/82, "*Poly (p-methylstyrene) articles/MOBIL*", OJEPO 6/1984, 261), or to a more exactly defined problem (*EPO Decision T* 162/86, "*Plasmid pSG2/ HOECHST*", OJEPO 12/1988, 452; [1989] 2 EPOR 107).

The problem need not be formulated in terms of matter disclosed in the specification, but once properly formulated (in the light of the closest art) the solution to the problem must not be an obvious one (*EPO Decision T* 229/85, "*Etching process/ SCHMID*", OJEPO 6/1987, 237; [1987] 5 EPOR 279). Also, in defining (objectively) the problem to be solved, it is impermissible partially to anticipate its solution (*EPO Decision T* 99/85, "*Diagnostic agent/Boehringer-Kodak*", OJEPO 9/1987 413; [1987] 6 EPOR 337).

Obvious and unobvious problems and solutions **3.39**

A so-called "problem invention" arises when the inventor perceives a hitherto unrecognised problem, even if this is then solved by an obvious solution thereto. In such circumstances an inventive step is recognised in the mere formulation of the problem, the solution of which has a surprising technical effect, see *EPO Decision T 2/83, "Simethicone tablet/RIDER"* (OJEPO 6/1984, 265). Thus, evidence of an advantageous, and unpredictable, technical effect often indicates the existence of inventive step (see paras. 3.46 and 3.47 *infra*) by creating a new and unobvious problem, it then being irrelevant whether the solution to that problem is an obvious or unobvious one.

However, it is always an obvious problem to seek the elimination of perceived deficiencies in a known article or process. Thus, where an advantageous effect is obtained merely from attempting to remove such deficiencies, this advantage is regarded as a mere "bonus effect" and therefore an unpatentable, "one-way street", solution to a known problem, see para. 3.48 *infra*. It then follows that evidence that there has been little activity in the art for a long time, coupled with evidence of the improvement of that article, is only indicative of inventive step if there had been during that time an urgent need to eliminate those deficiencies, see *EPO Decision T 109/82, "Hearing aid/BOSCH"* (OJEPO 10/1984, 473).

The unobviousness of the solution, rather than of the problem, is usually demonstrated by showing that the step taken by the inventor is one which others would have been unlikely to take, thereby rendering it irrelevant whether or not the problem solved by the solution (*i.e.* by the claimed product or process) was previously recognised (*i.e.* obvious) or previously unrecognised (*i.e.* unobvious). In such cases the purposes served by a known technical feature can be crucial to the assessment of inventive step, see *EPO Decision T 04/83, "Purification of sulphonic acids/EXXON"* (OJEPO 12/1983, 498), where it was held that the inventor had perceived that a procedure, known, but not previously used in the type of process being claimed, could be helpful, and that this was inventive in the absence of a pointer thereto in the prior art.

It has been stated that, if the problem differs significantly from the prior art, its solution is unlikely to be obvious (*EPO Decision T 39/82, "Light reflecting slats"*, OJEPO 11/1982, 419), but this case is perhaps now better seen as anyway involving an unobvious problem. Also, a solution is not obvious if it is contrary to previous experience (*EPO Decision T 19.86, "Pigs II/DUPHAR"*, OJEPO 1–2/1989, 24; [1988] 1 EPOR 10).

Assessment of the solution

—The "obvious to try" test in the EPO **3.40**

It is not sufficient that it is held obvious that the solution of the problem *could* be tried by the skilled person: it is necessary that it be considered that that solution *would* be so tried. This is the *"would* not *could"* test approved in *EPO Decision T 223/84, "Extraction of uranium/ALBRIGHT & WILSON"* ([1986] 2 EPOR 66), *EPO Decision T 255/85, "Antacid compositions/BEECHAM"* ([1987] 6 EPOR 351); and *EPO Decision T 392/86, "Catalyst/MOBIL"* ([1988] 3 EPOR 178).

Also, an inventive step can be recognised, even when it would have been obvious for an expert to have tried the claimed solution, if in fact he would not have tried this because he would not have expected to obtain a satisfactory result (*EPO Decision T 137/83, "Contaminant removal/DOW"* ([1987] 1 EPOR 15); or where there were many possibilities and the claimed solution was not the first choice (*EPO Decision T 274/87. "Cracking catalyst/PHILLIPS"*, [1989] 4 EPOR 207); or where the prior art is a speculative statement providing no real signpost towards the invention when read against the background of the whole state of the art (*EPO Decision T* 292/85, *"Polypeptide expression/GENENTECH I"*, OJEPO 7/1989, 275; [1989] 1 EPOR 1); or because there was an established trend in the art contrary to the further use of the idea in the field in question (*EPO Decision T* 253/85, *"Dry jet-wet spinning/AKZO"*, [1987] 4 EPOR 198); or where the properties of the envisaged product were foreseeable but this could not be made by known methods (*EPO Decision T* 219/83, *"Zeolites/BASF"*, OJEPO 7/1986, 211). However, in the last-mentioned case, it may be questioned whether the allowed claims ought to have been restricted to the inventive method used to achieve an objective of known desirability.

3.41 *—Probability of attainment of solution*

If the solution to the problem is one likely to be reached by others on the basis of trial and error, no inventive step is recognised (*EPO Decision T* 259/85, *"Two component polyurethane lacquer/WIEDERHOLD"*, [1988] 4 EPOR 209); and the fact that the solution was reached by trial and error does not make it unobvious. However, it may do so where *e.g.* trials are difficult to carry out, as in *EPO Decision T* 348/86, *"Cardiac defibrillator/MEDITRONIC"* ([1988] 3 EPOR 159), but did not in *EPO Decision T* 48/86, *"Ultrasonic transducer/TORAY"* ([1988] 3 EPOR 143). Also, an invention is not obvious if the search for a solution to the problem is a lottery as to whether success is achievable (*EPO Decision T* 122/84, *"Metallic paint coating/BASF"*, OJEPO 5/1987, 177; [1987] 4 EPOR 218).

3.42 *—Delay in reaching the solution*

Invention can be recognised if there is no adequate answer to the question: if obvious why was the solution not reached before? (*EPO Decision T* 165/85, *"Detection of redox reactions/BOEHRINGER MANNHEIM"*, [1987] 3 EPOR 125). However, the argument failed in *EPO Decision T* 265/84, *"Cobalt foils/ALLIED"* ([1987] 4 EPOR 193), where it was held the skilled person would have come to the apparatus claimed.

Also, the addition of a known feature to a known machine is inventive if this leads to a simpler design or improved performance *and* a solution to a long-standing problem (*EPO Decision T* 106/84, *"Packing Machine/MICHAELSON"*, OJEPO 5/1985, 132).

Although, at least under British law, it has been customary to plead commercial success as indicating that the invention was not obvious, because otherwise it would have appeared before in view of the commercial success achieved afterwards, the EPO seems to view any such evidence with suspicion, indicating that the commercial success may well be due to factors other than the intrinsic inventiveness of the solution to the problem which the art had faced, see *EPO Decision T* 270/84, *"Fusecord/ICI"* ([1987] 6 EPOR 357).

3.43 *Structural obviousness*

In the field of chemistry, the novelty of a compound is not enough for patentability. If the compound is a structure of a known type, inventive step will only be recognised if the new compound has a property not suggested by the prior art (*EPO Decision T* 20/83, *"Benzothiopyran derivatives/CIBA-GEIGY"*, OJEPO 10/1983, 419). This is because a structural difference has no value unless it give rise to a valuable property, effect or increase in an effect or increase in an effect (*EPO Decision*

T 22/82, *"Bis-epoxy ethers/BASF"*, OJEPO 9/1982, 341). However, the position is different if the product compound is not structurally obvious over the prior art: then no improvement over the prior art need be demonstrated provided that a problem (redefined if appropriate) has been solved, see *EPO Decision T* 162/86, *"Plasmid pSG2/HOECHST"* (OJEPO 12/1988, 452; [1989] 2 EPOR 107).

If a product is unpatentable as such, there remains the possibility of seeking protection for a particular (inventive) method of making it, see *EPO Decision T* 84/82, *"Chloral derivatives"* (OJEPO 11/1983, 451).

—Patentability of chemical intermediates   **3.44**

The patentability of chemical intermediates has been considered in a number of cases. To be patentable on the basis of the patentability of the final product, the intermediates must make a contribution to the structure of the final products, *e.g.* by displaying at least one of the features which differentiate the subsequent products from known compounds (*EPO Decision T* 372/86, *"Diphenyl ethers/ICI"*, [1988] 2 EPOR 93).

However, even then, a chemical intermediate may be held obvious when judged in relation to the prior art and here both "close to the intermediate" and "close to the product" art has to be considered (*EPO Decision T* 65/82, *"Cyclopropane/ BAYER"*, OJEPO 8/1983, 227). Nevertheless, an unexpected "process effect" will be recognised as conferring patentability on an intermediate compound (*EPO Decision T* 22/82, *"Bis-epoxy ethers/BASF"*, OJEPO 9/1982, 341), *e.g.* where the further processing is itself an inventive concept (*EPO Decision T* 163/84, *"Acetophenone derivatives/BAYER"*, OJEPO 7/1987, 301; [1987] 5 EPOR 284).

EPO attitude to selection inventions   **3.45**

A "selection invention" must first satisfy the criterion of novelty, for which see para. 2.16. Then, inventive step can be recognised provided that a surprising technical effect is demonstrated for the claimed product or process (for which see paras. 3.46–3.48 *infra*), so that an unpredictable solution is achieved to the known problem of improving already known products or processes (*EPO Decision T* 01/80, *"Carbonless copying paper"*, [1982] RPC 321; OJEPO 7/1981, 206). However, the evidence of surprising effect must be unique to the selection, so that selection of a sub-range from a larger range requires a "purposive", rather than arbitrary, selection of that sub-range which must be novel *per se* (*EPO Decision T* 198/84, *"Thiochloroformates/HOECHST"*, OJEPO 7/1985, 209). Also, the selection must not be of the most appropriate material for the required purpose, even if unexpected, advantageous results then arise, *i.e.* the selection itself must be an unobvious one (*EPO Decision T* 21/81, *"Electromagnetically operated switch"*, OJEPO 1/1983, 15), see also para. 3.48 *infra*.

Demonstration of advantages in support of inventive step

—Advantages must be unpredictable   **3.46**

As stated in paras. 3.23 and 3.28 *supra*, a seemingly obvious solution to a known problem can be regarded as inventive if that solution provides an unexpected improved result or advantageous technical effect, see *EPO Decision T* 270/84, *"Fusecord/ICI"* ([1987] 6 EPOR 357). This, of course, is not the case if the technical effect asserted is one that could itself have been predicted, see *EPO Decision T* 271/84, *"Removal of hydrogen sulphide . . . /AIR PRODUCTS"* (OJEPO 9/1987, 405; [1987] 1 EPOR 23; and *EPO Decision T* 229/84, *"Polyester polyols/ICI"* [1988] 4 EPOR 217). The technical effect can be the avoidance of a disadvantage, but that disadvantage must be one that would be expected otherwise to arise (*EPO Decision T* 49/85, "*Melt spinning/CYANAMID*", [1989] 4 EPOR 234).

However, a so-called "analogy process" becomes patentable if it leads to a novel and inventive result which is not derivable in an obvious manner from the state of the art (*EPO Decision T* 119/82, "*Gelation/EXXON*", OJEPO 5/1984, 217 and *EPO Decision T* 65/82, "*Cyclopropane/BAYER*", OJEPO 8/1983, 327). Nevertheless, the modifying feature, which provides the necessary novelty to the invention, must contribute causally to the improvement demonstrated (*EPO Decision T* 192/82, "*Moulding composition/BAYER*", OJEPO 9/1984, 415). Also, the advantage demonstrated must be a genuine one. Thus, no invention is involved in merely worsening the prior art, as when applying techniques previously disclosed for comparative purposes (*EPO Decision T* 155/85, "*Passivation of catalyst/PHILLIPS PETROLEUM*", OJEPO 3/1988, 87; [1988] 3 EPOR 164).

3.47   —*Advantages must be demonstrated*

If a technical effect is relied upon to establish inventive step, sufficient evidence of this is required (*EPO Decision T* 20/81, "*Shell/aryloxybenzaldehydes*", OJEPO 6/1982, 217). Indeed, this technical effect must be demonstrated, the EPO not considering mere allegations or assertions of such (*EPO Decision T* 124/84, "*Urea synthesis/UNIE VAN KUNSTMESTEFABRIEKEN*", [1986] 6 EPOR 297 and *EPO Decision T* 94/84, "*Paint layers/DUCO*", [1987] 1 EPOR 37).

At least the Chemical Appeals Board of the EPO requires, for recognition of patentability, an improved technical effect to be demonstrated by comparative tests normally carried out against the substance which it holds to represent the closest state of the art to the claimed product, that is that known compound which is deemed by the EPO to represent the closest similar structure to that of the claimed compound in a case of structural obviousness, for which see para. 3.43 *supra* (*EPO Decision T* 181/82, "*Spiro compounds/CIBA-GEIGY*", OJEPO 9/1984, 401). In *EPO Decision T* 164/83, "*Antihistamines/EISAI*" (OJEPO 4/1987, 149; [1987] 4 EPOR 205), this requirement was insisted upon despite a pleaded difficulty in carrying out such tests, even though results from comparative tests against a similar product which was commercially available were put forward, the commercially available compound not being accepted as the "closest art". However, a later case appears to have moved from that position, see *EPO Decision T* 274/87, "*Cracking catalyst/PHILLIPS*" ([1989] 4 EPOR 207).

While the required comparative tests must be carried out under *all* conditions likely to be encountered in practice, a technical effect is only required to be demonstrated in an overall manner (*EPO Decision T* 57/84, "*Tolylfluanid/BAYER*", OJEPO 5/1988, 177; [1987] 3 EPOR 131), and need not show advantages as regards other properties of prior art compounds provided that the latter are maintained at a reasonable level so that the improvement is not completely off-set by disadvantages in other respects (*EPO Decision T* 254/86, "*Yellow dyes/SUMITOMO*", OJEPO 4/1989, 115; [1989] 5 EPOR 257). The technical effect demonstrated can be quite small if it has a worthwhile commercial significance (*EPO Decision T* 38/84, "*Oxidation of toluene/STAMICARBON*", OJEPO 8/1984, 368). However, it cannot be demonstrated against a reference device for which no evidence is given that this was available to the public before the priority date (*EPO Decision T* 27/86, "*Poker vibrator/DYNAPAC*", [1989] 2 EPOR 100).

3.48   *Unpatentability of the "one-way street" solution*

Demonstration of a technical effect is irrelevant if the solution claimed to the existing technical problem represents the way forward which the skilled person would naturally adopt. This has become known as the "one-way street" solution, see *EPO Decision T* 192/82, *"Moulding composition/BAYER"* (OJEPO 9/1984, 415). It is a point of view now often put forward by an examiner, or opponent, as a prime consideration. It is based on the contention that an obvious solution to a known problem is not automatically inventive because it happens, unobviously to solve, in an unexpected way, some other problem, see *EPO Decision T* 69/83, *"Thermoplastic moulding compositions/BAYER"* (OJEPO 8/1984, 357). This is because an invention is unpatentable if it lacks an inventive step for whatever reason. However, a one-way street situation does not exist where there were alternative ways in which the skilled person might reasonably proceed (*EPO Decision T* 43/85, *"Film laminate production/MOBIL"*, [1987] 5 EPOR 272).

By the same line of reasoning, patentability is to be denied if the claimed subject-matter is obvious for *any* purpose, *e.g.* by a selection of the most appropriate material for the required purpose, even if unexpected, advantageous results then arise (*EPO Decision T* 21/81, *"Electromagnetically operated switch"*, OJEPO 1/1983, 15). Thus, optimisation of a known process is not inventive (*EPO Decision T* 36/82, *"Parabolic reflector antenna/CSELT"*, OJEPO 7/1983, 269): nor is a selection which represents a compromise in optimisation (*EPO Decision T* 263/86, *"Spectacle lens/ZEISS"*, [1988] 3 EPOR 150), nor can patentability be predicated on a technical effect that could be expected (*EPO Decision T* 229/84, *"Polyester polyols/ICI"* [1988] 4 EPOR 217).

Sometimes (and in the older cases), the "one-way street" solution has been described as a mere "bonus effect", *i.e.* an effect which arises automatically, even if unexpectedly, from an operation which it is itself obvious to perform or from a product which it is for some other reason obvious to make, see *EPO Decision T* 24/81, *"Metal refining/BASF"* (OJEPO 4/1983, 133). Thus, if an invention is obvious to try, *e.g.* because a solution to a similar problem was known in a neighbouring field, the fact that the solution automatically solves another part of the problem facing the inventor does not render the solution automatically inventive (*EPO Decision T* 286/84. *"Pressure-sensitive recording material/APPLETON PAPERS"*. [1987] 4 EPOR 212).

PRACTICE UNDER SECTION 3

Drafting of specification to assist argument of non-obviousness **3.49**

The way in which an invention is described and its advantages presented in the specification will often assist a subsequent contention of non-obviousness. However, care should be taken in acknowledging prior art in the body of the specification (which is required by the EPO, but not under British law and practice), in case that, by juxtaposition of statements, an unintended, erroneous inference is drawn by the reader by reading these statements as related to each other and consequently as an implied admission that invention is not intended to lie in the combination of those statements, or that one or more of those references is a representation of part of the common general knowledge of the person skilled in the art.

In the case of a selection invention, it is desirable and advantageous, though not apparently essential, for the advantage of the claimed selection to be specified in the specification. Thus, while a statement of advantage cannot be added to the specification after filing (because such an amendment is precluded by section 76), a statement of advantage may be submitted later for consideration by the examiner: such will then be placed in the open part of the file. The EPO adopts a similar position, see EPO Guidelines C-IV, 5.7a and 5.7b.

3.50 *Submission of evidence of unobviousness*

The submission of evidence, particularly of surprising technical effect or advantage, may often be useful in overcoming an objection of obviousness raised during the substantive examination under section 18. That evidence should be submitted to the Comptroller as it is unlikely to be permitted to be placed before the Patents Court for the first time on appeal, see *Wistar Institute's Application* ([1983] RPC 255) and para. 18.14.

3.51 *Pleading of commercial success*

In proceedings before the Patents Court a defence of commercial success to an allegation of obviousness now needs to be distinctly pleaded, see RSC Ord. 104, rule 6(5) (reprinted in para. E014.6) and the discussion in para. 3.14 *supra*. Such a pleading has the consequence of leading to distinct and detailed particularisation (see *John Deks* v. *Aztec Washer*, [1989] RPC 413) and thus of considerably expanding the scope of discovery, see para. 61.28. These factors may lead to such a plea being made less frequently than hitherto, if only to reduce the costs of the litigation.

4.01   **SECTION 4**

Industrial application

4.—(1) Subject to subsection (2) below, an invention shall be taken to be capable of industrial application if it can be made or used in any kind of industrial including agriculture.

(2) An invention of a method of treatment of the human or animal body by surgery or therapy or of diagnosis practised on the human or animal body shall not be taken to be capable of industrial application.

(3) Subsection (2) above shall not prevent a product consisting of a substance or composition being treated as capable of industrial application merely because it is invented for use in any such method.

4.02   ARTICLE

A. W. White, "Patentability of medical treatment: Wellcome Foundation's (Hitching's) Application", [1980] EIPR 364.

COMMENTARY ON SECTION 4

4.03 *General*

Section 4 is concerned with the definition of "industrial application" for the purposes of the definition of patentable invention under section 1(1)(*c*). It corresponds to EPCaa. 52(4) and 57 and must be considered in the light of section 130(7) to have as far as practicable the same effects as these corresponding EPC Articles. Industrial application is commented upon at length in EPO Guidelines C-IV, 4. As in section 1(1)(*c*), the expression "capable of" industrial application is used in subsection (1), whereas EPCa. 52(1) uses the phrase "susceptible of" industrial application. However, the EPO Guidelines (C-II, 4.12) suggest that these phrases are synonymous.

The section is not applied to "existing patents" which continue to be governed on this characteristic by the test of "manner of new manufacture", for which see paras. A101.06 and A101.08 in Appendix A.

Definition of "industrial application" (subs. (1))   **4.04**

As pointed out in para. 1.06 the Act does not define "invention" except that its extent is defined in section 125 as being in terms of the claims. To be patentable an invention has to be capable of industrial application, as defined in subsection (1), and must not fall into the excluded classes of subject matter indicated in section 1(2)–(4) and subsections (2) and (3). It is to be noted that these are separate requirements, and inventions excluded by section 1(2)–(4) are not rendered patentable even if they are capable of industrial application, see *EPO Decision T* 116/85, "*Pigs I/WELLCOME*" (OJEPO 1–2/1989, 13; [1988] 1 EPOR 1). On the other hand, although an invention must be capable of industrial application and the specification must indicate how (if it is not obvious) it is to be so applied, the claims may not need, apparently, to be restricted to industrial applications, see EPO Guideline C-IV, 4.5.

It is thought that "industry" should be interpreted in the broad sense as including any physical activity of "technical character", *i.e.* an activity which belongs to the useful or practical arts as distinct from the aesthetic or fine arts, see EPO Guideline C-IV, 4.1. Consequently, subsection (1) would seem to exclude from patentability few inventions which are not already excluded by section 1(2)–(4). One such excluded class would be articles or processes alleged to operate in a manner clearly contrary to well-established physical laws, for example, a perpetual motion machine. Thus, claims to an energy conservation device were rejected in *Paez's Application* (SRIS O/176/83) because its method of operation was regarded as being contrary to well-established natural laws, it being held that "made" in section 1(1)(*c*) embraces the operation of a device as well as its construction. The rejection was also based on a failure to comply with section 14(3), see para. 14.15. Also, applications for apparatus of the perpetual motion type were rejected in *Kershaw's Application* (SRIS O/23/86) and in *Renaut's Application* (SRIS O/25/86); and *Wilkinson's Application* (SRIS O/21/86) was rejected as being contrary to Newton's third law of motion.

Methods of testing would, however, appear to be patentable if the test is applicable to the improvement or control of a product, apparatus or process which is itself capable of industrial application, see EPO Guideline C-IV, 4.4.

It is to be observed that an invention in the ordinary sense which meets all the criteria except that it is not capable of industrial application, something associated with the person perhaps, is not patentable at all. It is not easy to think of such inventions; it seems clear that the expression, which derives from the Strasbourg Convention (1963) (Cmnd. 8002), was not intended to limit patentability, but to extend it and exclude the limitations which the test of "manner of manufacture" had imposed under section 101 [1949].

However, questions of infringement are not, apparently, to be considered in relation to patentability. For example, an attempt to limit a claim to "the supply or offer to supply" of a known resin for a novel purpose has been held not to be subject-matter which is capable of industrial application (*Du Pont's (Buegge's) Application,* [1984] RPC 17]: but this decision may come to be doubted, see paras. 2.10

and 2.29. This decision is also discussed in para. 14.24 in connection with section 14(5).

The words "capable of industrial application" do not appear to be capable of being used as a substitute for the "inutility" ground of objection to patentability arising under section 32(1)(g) [1949] (still applicable to existing patents, see paras. A032.14–A032.16 in Appendix A), because it is sufficient for the purposes of subsection (1) and of section 14(3) that the matter claimed can be made, though an objection of insufficiency may arise in these circumstances, see para. 14.18.

4.05 *Unpatentability of medical and veterinary treatment (subss. (2) and (3))*

Subsection (2) corresponds to EPCa. 52(4) and prejudges adversely the question of industrial applicability so far as concerns methods of treatment of the human and animal body by surgery or therapy, or of diagnosis practised on the human or animal body. Accordingly, "method of treatment" claims as such are, at least at present, not allowed, see *EPO Decision Gr* 05/83, "*Second Medical Indication/EISAI*" (OJEPO 3/1985, 64) adopted in the United Kingdom by *John Wyeth's and Schering's Applications* [1985] RPC 545), though "Use in treatment" claims are permitted in the German Federal Republic, see para. 2.29. This United Kingdom practice follows that adopted under the "manner of manufacture" test applicable under former statutes, though then applied only to treatment of the human body. Such practice was confirmed by *Upjohn's (Robert's) Application* ([1977] RPC 94) and by *Wellcome's (Hitching's) Application* [*New Zealand*] ([1983] FSR 593 reversing [1980] RPC 305). The development of this former practice was described and criticised by A. W. White in his paper listed in para. 4.02 *supra*.

However, the prohibition of subsection (2) is alleviated by subsection (3) which is complementary to section 2(6). These provisions taken together allow protection for the *first* application of a known substance or composition for the treatment of the human or animal body by surgery, by therapy or by diagnostic methods practiced on the human or animal body. They correspond to EPCa. 54(5) and are considered in para. 2.28 followed in para. 2.29 by discussion of the eventual acceptance (by drafting claims in a special "Swiss form") of some patent protection for inventions of the second (or further) medical indication, that is in respect of discoveries of new (and inventive) medicinal uses of substances already known to have some (other) pharmaceutical activity.

So far as the exclusion from patentability of methods of treatment or diagnosis is concerned it should be noted that only treatments of the human or animal body by surgery or therapy or diagnosis practised on the human or animal body are excluded. Other methods of a technical, rather than biological, character are not excluded, for example, treatment of animals to promote growth or non-therapeutic treatment of humans such as permanent waving of hair and methods of contraception. Moreover, a treatment or diagnostic method, to be excluded, must actually be carried out on the living animal or human body. The EPO Guidelines state that treatment of body tissues or fluids after removal from the body is not excluded (C-IV, 4.3), nor is the utilisation of test animals for test purposes in industry (C-IV, 4.4). However, the terms "surgery" and "therapy" have each been given a broad interpretation so as to expand the scope of the exclusion created by subsection (2), see paras. 4.06 and 4.07 *infra*.

Nevertheless, it appears that no significant change of practice was introduced by subsection (2) and, therefore, such cases as: *Schering's Application* ([1971] RPC 337), (method of contraception); *Bio-Digital Sciences Application* ([1973] RPC 668), (determination of which patients to treat); and *Joos* v. *Commissioner of Patents* [Australia] ([1973] RPC 59), (cosmetic treatment of nails and hair) should continue to be followed and patents granted as not falling within the prohibition of subsection (2). However, claims were rejected under the 1949 Act as not being in respect of a manner of manufacture for: a method of inducing abortion (*Upjohn's (Kirton's) Application*, [1976] RPC 324); removal of dental plaque from teeth (*Oral Health (Halstead's) Application*, [1977] RPC 612) and repair of teeth (*Lee Pharmaceutical's Application*, [1978] RPC 51). Patents for inventions of these types are also probably precluded by subsection (2) (as decided in the case of dental plaque removal, see para. 4.06 *infra*), unless "utility-based use" claims in the "Swiss form" can be drafted, for which see para. 2.29.

Decisions of the Comptroller and courts on the interpretation of subsections (2) and (3) are discussed in para. 4.06 *infra*. Decisions of the EPO on the corresponding EPCa. 52(4) are discussed in para. 4.07 *infra*, while para. 4.08 *infra* mentions decisions under EPCa. 52(4) in other jurisdictions.

—Decisions under the Act   **4.06**

In *Unilever's (Davis's)* Application ([1983] RPC 219) the Patents Court held that "therapy", as used in subsection (2), should be given its broader meaning of the medical treatment of disease rather than its narrower meaning of curative medical treatment because "surgery" is clearly not limited to curative surgery. On this basis subsection (2) was held to prevent the patenting of prophylactic treatments such as immunisation or vaccination, these being treatments of disease even though effected on healthy persons or animals because they are directed to the prevention of disease.

In *ICI's (Richardson) Application* ([1981] FSR 609), a claim to "A method of producing an anti-oestrogenic effect in warm-blooded animals, including man, but excluding any method of treatment of the animal or human body by therapy, which comprising administering [the compound]" was rejected as not relating to an invention within section 1(1)(*c*) because there was nothing left in the claim if effect were given to the exclusionary phrase. The specification described only the application of the compound for the treatment of breast cancer and infertility. The claim was also held to be indefinite and therefore objectionable under section 14(5).

In *ICI's Application* (SRIS O/73/82) a claim to a method of cleaning teeth for the removal of dental plaque from the teeth was rejected as a method of medical treatment, following *Oral Health's (Halstead's) Application* (1977) RPC 612).

In *Occidental Petroleum's Application* ((1985) 16 IIC 216; SRIS O/35/84, *noted* IPD 7070) it was concluded that, while "therapy" in subsection (2) covers curative and prophylactic treatment, the term "surgery" is not limited to therapeutic surgery, but includes any method of surgical treatment which need not necessarily involve making an incision into body tissue. On this basis, claims to embryonic transplantation were rejected.

In *Ciba-Geigy's Application* (SRIS O/30/85, *noted* IPD 8083) the Comptroller rejected claims to a method of treating intestinal helminths, such as tapeworms, on the basis that to rid a patient's body of such parasites should be regarded as "therapy". He refused to follow *Stafford-Miller's Applications* ([1984] FSR 268) because this case was decided under the 1949 Act, the criteria under the two statutes being different.

A method of purifying blood during renal dialysis was rejected in *Schultz's Application* (SRIS O/174/86, *noted* IPD 10003) as involving "therapy" because, like the administration of pain killers or insulin to diabetic persons, the method gives temporary alleviation of disease symptoms. This case also indicated that the phrase in subsection (2) "practised on the human or animal body" only qualifies the term "diagnosis" and not the terms "therapy" or "surgery", which therefore stand unqualified.

71

4.07 —*Decisions in the EPO*

The EPO has decided (*EPO Decision T* 81/84, "*Dysmenorrhoea/RORER*", OJEPO 6/1988, 202; [1988] 5 EPOR 297) that the concept of "therapy" should not be construed narrowly and that it is undesirable to distinguish between basic and symptomatic therapy, *i.e.* between healing or cure and mere relief, so that the relief of pain, discomfort or incapacity should each be considered as therapy or therapeutic use and, therefore, unpatentable under EPCa. 52(4). Accordingly, claims to the relief of discomfort of a human female attributed to menstruation were rejected.

The EPO also gave a broad meaning to the term "therapy" when, in *EPO Decision T* 19/86, "*Pigs II/DUPHAR*" (OJEPO 1–2/1989, 24; [1988] 1 EPOR 10), it followed the British decision in *Unilever's (Davis's) Application* ([1983] RPC 219), described in para. 4.06 *supra*, in holding that "therapy" embraces both curative and prophylactic treatment. Similarly, in *EPO Decision T* 116/85, "*Pigs I/WELLCOME*" (OJEPO 1–2/1989, 13; [1988] 1 EPOR 1), claims were rejected to a method of controlling ectoparasites on pigs by localised application to the pig body surface of a known pesticidal composition as being a method of therapeutic treatment, the EPO refusing to follow *Stafford-Millers Applications* ([1984] FSR 258), even though the treatment could be carried out on a large scale by farmers (an industrial activity), as this could not be distinguished from treatment by a veterinarian. An argument that the invention was patentable because it had industrial application under EPCa. 57 (corresponding to subsection (1)) failed because it was held that EPCa.57 could not override unpatentability under EPCa. 52(4) (corresponding to subsection (2)).

However, in *EPO Decision T* 385/86, "*Non-invasive measurement/BRUKER*" (OJEPO 8/1988, 308; [1988] 6 EPOR 357), the EPO Technical Board (reversing the Examining Division) held that EPCa. 52(4) should be interpreted narrowly "like all regulations governing exclusions" and therefore placed a restrictive interpretation on what constitutes a diagnostic method excluded from EPCa. 54(2) by holding patentable a non-invasive diagnostic method which did not provide results which enabled an immediate decision on medical treatment to be made. Here it was considered important that the patent would not hamper a physician in the exercise of his healing skills. Thus it appears that diagnostic methods are only excluded by EPCa. 52(4) if their results *as such* can be utilised in making a diagnosis, see also *EPO Decision T* 83/87, "*Diagnostic method/SIEMENS*" ([1988] 6 EPOR 365).

The principle that EPCa. 52(4) was only intended to permit physicians to be able fully to exercise their healing skills also formed the basis for *EPO Decision T* 245/87, "*Flow measurement/SIEMENS*" (OJEPO 5/1989, 171; [1989] 5 EPOR 241) where it was held that a method of measuring the flow of liquid particularly suitable for use in an implanted device for drug administration was patentable as it was a matter of apparatus design of no concern to the physician who used it and which left the physician completely free to exercise his skills. The same principle can be seen in *EPO Decision T* 58/87, "*Pigs III/SALMINEN*" ([1989] 3 EPOR 125) where "therapy" was defined as "covering any non-surgical treatment which is designed to cure, alleviate, remove or lessen the symptoms of, or prevent or reduce the possibility of contracting any malfunction of the animal body": a method of creating unpleasant conditions to prevent a sow lying upon and suffocating her litter was, therefore, held patentable, this not being regarded as a "treatment".

The EPO has allowed claims to cosmetic treatment, even where therapeutic activity is involved. Thus, in *EPO Decision T* 36/83, "*Thenoyl peroxide/ROUSSEL-UCLAF*" (OJEPO 9/1986, 295; [1987] 1 EPOR 1), claims were allowed in the same application to "X for its use in a method of therapeutic treatment [of acne] in humans or animals", and to "Use of X as a cosmetic product", X being a known compound. Also, in *EPO Decision T* 144/83, "*Appetite suppressant/DU PONT*"

(OJEPO 9/1986, 30; [1987] 1 EPOR 6), claims were allowed to a method of improving the bodily-appearance of a non-opiate-addicted mammal, comprising administering X in a total amount effective to achieve a cosmetically beneficial loss of body weight. This was so even though the active compound could also be used to treat obesity, it being held in both these cases that professional use of such an invention in a cosmetic salon is an industrial application in the sense of EPCa. 57. This case is the subject of comment by J. Pagenberg ((1987) 18 IIC 261).

The EPO has also been astute not to deprive an inventive claim of novelty by narrowly construing the prior art as relating only to injectable and oral compositions and then allowing claims limited to formulations adapted only for topical administration to the exclusion of oral and injectable administration. *(EPO Decision T 289/84, "3-Amino-pyrazoline derivatives/WELLCOME", [1987] 2 EPOR 58).*

—Other decisions under the EPC   **4.08**

The Swiss Supreme Court had held, under a statutory provision analogous to subsection (2) that a particular procedure for monitoring, recording and transmitting electro-cardiographic data from a patient is unpatentable as a method of diagnosis because the procedure has no purpose other than for the diagnosis and for the conclusions to be drawn therefrom by the physician (*AEK* v. *Federal Patent Office* [*Switzerland*], (1984) 15 IIC 82.

SECTION 5   5.01

Priority date

5.—(1) For the purposes of this Act the priority date of an invention to which an application for a patent relates and also of any matter (whether or not the same as the invention) contained in any such application is, except as provided by the following provisions of this Act, the date of filing the application.

(2) If in or in connection with an application for a patent (the application in suit) a declaration is made, whether by the applicant or any predecessor in title of his, complying with the relevant requirements of rules and specifying one or more earlier relevant applications for the purposes of this section made by the applicant or a predecessor in title of his and each having a date of filing during the period of twelve months immediately preceding the date of filing the application in suit, then—

(*a*) if an invention to which the application in suit relates is supported by matter disclosed in the earlier relevant application or applications, the priority date of that invention shall instead of being the date of filing the application in suit be the date of filing the relevant application in which that matter was disclosed or, if it was disclosed in more than one relevant application, the earliest of them;

(*b*) the priority date of any matter contained in the application in suit which was also disclosed in the earlier relevant application or applications shall be the date of filing the relevant application in which that matter was disclosed or, if it was disclosed in more than one relevant application, the earliest of them.

(3) Where an invention or other matter contained in the application in suit was also disclosed in two earlier relevant applications filed by the same applicant as in the case of the application in suit or a predecessor in title of his and the second of those relevant applications was specified in or in connection with the application in suit, the second of those relevant applications shall, so far as concerns that invention or matter, be disregarded unless–

(*a*) it was filed in or in respect of the same country as the first; and

(*b*) not later than the date of filing the second, the first (whether or not so specified) was unconditionally withdrawn, or was abandoned or refused, without—

(i) having been made available to the public (whether in the United Kingdom or elsewhere);

(ii) leaving any rights outstanding; and

(iii) having served to establish a priority date in relation to another application, wherever made.

(4) The foregoing provisions of this section shall apply for determining the priority date of an invention for which a patent has been granted as they apply for determining the priority date of an invention to which an application for that patent relates.

(5) In this section "relevant application" means any of the following applications which has a date of filing, namely—

(*a*) an application for a patent under this Act;

(*b*) an application in or for a convention country (specified under section 90 below) for protection in respect of an invention or an application which, in accordance with the law of a convention country or a treaty or international convention to which a convention country is a party, is equivalent to such an application.

RELEVANT RULE

Declaration of priority for the purposes of section 5

5.02   **6.**—(1) A declaration for the purposes of section 5 shall be made at the time of filing the application for a patent ("the application in suit") and shall state the date of filing of any application specified in the declaration and the country in or for which it was made.

(2) Subject to the provisions of rule 26 and paragraphs (3), (4) and (5) below, where the application in suit is for a patent under the Act, the applicant shall, within the period of 16 months after the declared priority date,

furnish to the Patent Office in respect of every application specified in the declaration—

  (a) its file number; and

  (b) except where paragraph (3) below has effect, a copy of that application duly certified by the authority with which it was filed or otherwise verified to the satisfaction of the comptroller.

(3) Where an application specified in the declaration is an application for a patent under the Act or an international application for a patent which is filed at the Patent Office—

  (a) if the application is filed under section 15(4), the applicant shall, at the time of filing the application, file—

    (i) a request that a copy of the application specified in the declaration be prepared for use in the Patent Office; and

    (ii) Patents Form No. 24/77 requesting the comptroller to certify the same; or

  (b) if the application is filed otherwise than under section 15(4), the applicant shall file that request and that form in compliance with any request made by the comptroller.

(4) Where the application in suit is an application for a European patent (UK) which, by virtue of section 81, is to be treated as an application for a patent under the Act, the requirements of paragraphs (1) and (2) above shall be treated as having been complied with to the extent that the requirements of rule 38(1) to (3) of the Implementing Regulations to the European Patent Convention have been fulfilled.

(5) Where the application in suit is an international application for a patent (UK) which is to be treated as an application for a patent under the Act, the requirements of paragraphs (1) and (2) above shall be treated as having been complied with to the extent that the requirements of rules 4.10(a) and (c) and 17.1(a) of the Regulations made under the Patent Co-operation Treaty have been fulfilled.

(6) Where a copy of an application is filed or treated as having been filed under paragraph (2)(b), (3), (4) or (5) above and that application is in a language other than English, a translation thereof into English verified to the satisfaction of the comptroller as corresponding to the original text shall be furnished to the Patent Office within the period of twenty-one months after the declared priority date:

Provided that, in the case of an international application in respect of which election of the United Kingdom has been effected under Article 31(4) of the Patent Co-operation Treaty prior to the expiration of the nineteenth month from the priority date as defined in Article 2(xi) of that Treaty, the period for furnishing the translation shall be the **thirty-one** [*twenty-six*] months after that priority date.

Note. The proviso to rule 6(6) was amended by the Patents (Amendment No. 2) Rules 1985 (S.I. 1985 No. 1166, r. 3).

COMMENTARY ON SECTION 5

5.03 *General*

Section 5 is concerned with the priority date of an "invention", whereas the corresponding section 5 [1949] defines the priority date of a "claim". Prima facie, the priority date of an invention contained in an application under the Act ("the application in suit") is the date of filing that application (subs. (1)). However, if a permitted priority date from an earlier "relevant application" is duly "declared" at the time of filing the application in suit; and, (*a*) if the invention to which the application in suit relates is "supported by matter disclosed" in the earlier relevant application, or (*b*) the matter contained in the application in suit is also contained in the earlier relevant application, then the date accorded to the claimed invention, or to the matter disclosed as the case may be, for the purpose of determining its priority in relation to prior art (including other applications of earlier priority under s. 2(3)), is deemed to be the date of the earlier relevant application, provided that this is within 12 months of the actual filing date of the application in suit (subs. (2)).

Subsection (3) deals with the position when there are two earlier relevant applications and provides for the second to be disregarded unless the first fulfils certain condition as to its prior withdrawal, abandonment or refusal. If these conditions are not met then, if the first application is dated more than 12 months before the application in suit, no priority earlier than its own filing date is accorded to the invention contained, or to the matter disclosed in both the application in suit and the first application.

Subsection (4) makes the provisions of the section equally applicable to applications and patents granted thereon, and subsection (5) defines the term "relevant application" by reference either (*a*) to an application filed under the Act, or (*b*) to one filed in a "convention country" (as defined in s. 90), including European and International applications.

The resolution of priority will often arise in the determination of conflicts between copending applications under section 2(3) as is discussed in paras. 2.17–2.24.

The procedure for making effective declarations of priority is regulated by rule 6, reprinted in para. 5.02 *supra* and discussed in paras. 5.19 and 5.20 *infra*; and section 128 provides a special transitional provision for deciding priority between applications filed under the Act and applications filed under the 1949 Act and patents granted thereon, see paras. 128.02 and 128.03.

Section 5 must also be read in conjunction with section 6 which has the object of providing some alleviation against invalidation where priority from an earlier relevant application is not itself effective and there has been some relevant intervening act, *i.e.* something published, or deemed to be published, or done, between the date of the earlier relevant application and the application in suit, see the commentary on section 6.

5.04 *Contrast with the test for claim priority under the 1949 Act*

Section 5 does not apply to "existing patents" (Sched. 2, para. 1(2)) to which section 5 [1949] remains applicable (Sched. 1, para. 1(2)), as discussed in paras. A005.2–A005.4. While section 5 [1977] and section 5 [1949] have a similar purpose, there are significant differences which are summarised here and discussed as appropriate more fully *infra*.

First, priority is now accorded to an invention claimed, or to matter contained, in a specification, whereas section 5 [1949] requires each claim to have a single priority date (*Thornhill's Application* [1962] RPC 199): now a claim may have a multiple priority for the individual inventions contained therein.

Secondly, whereas under section 5 [1949] the test for priority is whether the claim is "*fairly based* on the matter disclosed in the earlier application", now the test is whether the "invention to which the application in suit relates is *supported by matter* disclosed in the earlier relevant application" or whether the "matter disclosed in the application in suit is also *disclosed* in the earlier relevant application". The effect of this difference of wording is discussed in paras. 5.08–5.13 *infra*.

Thirdly, priority can now be claimed from an earlier, but different, application under the Act (subs. (5)(*a*)) so that the subject matter of an earlier application under the Act can be cognated with one filed in a convention country, the United Kingdom not itself being a "convention country" as that term is defined in section 90, see para. 90.02. The effect of this provision is also much the same as claiming priority from a provisional specification (now abolished as such) under the 1949 Act, but the later (complete) application now has a fresh number whereas under the 1949 Act a complete specification was filed in respect of the same application for which a provisional specification had earlier been filed.

Fourthly, if priority is incorrectly claimed (*i.e.* the 12 month period from the first application for protection of the invention is exceeded), the effect is now merely loss of priority, this now being the case also for existing patents, see para. A032.31.

Fifthly, because of the wording "supported by matter" in subsection (2)(*a*), to give rise to priority an earlier relevant application (unlike the position under the 1949 Act) may have to contain a disclosure which is sufficient for performance of that disclosure, sometimes described as a requirement for a disclosure to be "enabling". However, this point has not yet been definitively decided, at least under United Kingdom law, see paras. 5.09 and 5.12 *infra*. Whatever is the test on this point, it ought to apply also to priority on the basis of a disclosure under subsection (2)(*b*).

Sixthly, the rule from *Stauffer's Application* ([1977] RPC 33 (CA)) that a "convention application" (under s. 1(2)(*b*) [1949]) had to be in respect of an invention for which "protection had been sought", though in terms having a counterpart under present subsection (5)(*b*), may not have the same force in view of section 130(7). Nevertheless the "*Stauffer*" rule (as discussed in para. A005.03), is not unknown under the EPC when implicit disclosures are in issue, for which see paras. 5.13 and 5.14 *infra*. Also, priority may be refused if it is seen that the invention claimed is a further, or different, invention from that disclosed in the priority document, a mere mention of the subject matter being insufficient as "support", as was held (under the test of "fair basis") in *Coopers Animal Health* v. *Western Stock [Australia]* ([1988] 11 IPR 20).

The prima facie priority date (subs. 1)) and the onus of proof   **5.05**

Subsection (1) provides that, unless subsequent provisions of the Act provide otherwise, the priority date of an invention to which a patent application under the Act relates, or to any matter contained therein, is that of the filing date of that application, termed in section 5 "the application in suit". This is, therefore, the prima facie priority date. If any other (earlier) date is to be established, the onus for this should fall upon the applicant, see *International Paint Co.'s Application* ([1982] RPC 247) and *Stauffer's Application* ([1977] RPC 33 (CA)). However, when defending an application against another application, which forms part of the state of the art under section 2(3), the task of verifying that the relevant matter in that other application is *not* entitled to an earlier priority date falls upon the applicant defending his own application.

5.06 *According an earlier priority date (subs. (2))*

Under subsection (2), provided that a declaration of priority has been made as required by rule 6(1), as discussed in para. 5.18 *infra* (including the statement of the date and country of filing of the priority application), priority may be based on an earlier relevant application made by the applicant or his predecessors in title: (*a*) for an invention (*i.e.* as claimed in the whole or any part of a claim by virtue of s. 125), provided that this is supported by matter disclosed in the earlier relevant application; or (*b*) for any matter contained in the application, provided that this is disclosed in the earlier relevant application. In each case priority is based on the earliest relevant application if there is more than one, but is only accorded if this earliest date is within 12 months of the filing date of the application in suit. Otherwise, no priority is accorded unless the provisions of subsection (3) (discussed in para. 5.16 *infra*) are met. Note that, if an invention is not *supported* by matter disclosed in an earlier relevant application under subsection (2)(*a*), there may, nevertheless, be matter entitled to priority under subsection (2)(*b*) if this was *disclosed* in the earlier relevant application. The requirements of subsections (2)(*a*) and (*b*) would seem to be intended to correspond to EPCaa. 88(3) and (4), but EPCa. 88(3) refers to "elements" of the application in suit "which are included" in the priority application, and EPCa. 88(4) requires that priority may be accorded if "the documents of the previous application as a whole specifically disclose such elements".

It must also be noted that, for the purpose of section 5, the term "disclosed" is specifically defined in section 130(3) as meaning "claimed or disclosed (otherwise than by way of disclaimer or acknowledgment of prior art)" in a relevant application or specification of a patent granted thereon. This provision is similar to that previously applicable, see section 69(2) [1949] (reprinted in para. A069.1). In *Asahi Kasei's Application* (SRIS C/103/88, *noted* IPD 11081) the Patents Court interpreted "claimed" and "disclosed" disjunctively, holding that whether a disclosure must be an enabling one to afford priority need not be decided if the claims were supported by claims in the priority document.

Thus, the differences in wording between section 5(2), as defined by section 130(3), and EPCa. 83(3) and (4) may cause doubt whether the test for priority under British law is the same as that under the EPC, despite the reference to section 5 in the list of sections set out in section 130(7) as those "so framed as to have, as nearly as practicable, the same effects in the United Kingdom as the corresponding provisions of the EPC". This doubt is increased by the *Asahi* case (*supra*), see further paras. 5.09 and 5.12. It may also be noted that EPCa. 88(4) corresponds to article 4H of the Paris Convention and requires that "the documents of the previous application as a whole specifically disclose" the elements of the invention for which priority is claimed, but this is a difficult requirement to operate literally as discussed in paras. 5.14 and 5.15 *infra*.

Whether an abstract provided with the priority application is considered as part of the application is a matter of the national law of the country of the priority application. Under section 14(2)(*c*) the abstract is part of a United Kingdom application, but this is not so in the case of an application filed in the German Federal Republic as certified copies of applications therefrom make clear, but see section 14(7) and para. 14.29.

Section 125(2) makes it clear that a single claim can specify more than one invention and that different priorities may be claimed for different inventions. In contrast with the practice under the 1949 Act, it is therefore unnecessary under the 1977 Act to draft elaborate sets of claims to take into account multiple and partial priorities. It is now implicit that multiple priorities for a single claim are possible in general, see also EPCa. 88(2).

The necessity for a valid declaration of priority **5.07**

Rule 6 (reprinted at para. 5.02 *supra*) requires that to obtain a priority date earlier than the filing date of the application in suit, a priority declaration must be made at the time of filing the application in suit, though not now necessarily on PF 1/77 (r. 6(1)). The declaration must include the date of filing of the earlier application and the country in or for which it was made. There must also be furnished to the Patent Office details of the file number of the priority application and in most cases also a certified copy of it or equivalent conditions must be complied with (r. 6(2)–(5)), each within the time specified by the rules. These requirements are further discussed in paras. 5.19 and 5.20 *infra*. If the priority application is not in English, a verified translation thereof must be timely supplied (r. 6(6)), as discussed in para. 5.21 *infra*.

The term "declared priority date" relates to the priority date referred to in the priority declaration and is defined in rule 2 (reprinted at para. 123.04). In the case of an application filed under the Act, it means the date of filing of the earliest "relevant application" (as defined in subsection (5)), provided that this date has not been lost or abandoned and that the declaration therefor had not been withdrawn before the completion of preparations for publication of the application under section 16 (r. 2(*a*)). Alternatively, the declared priority date could arise: from a provisional specification filed under the 1949 Act and still extant on the "appointed day" (r. 2(*b*)); or from a declaration of priority filed in respect of an application for a European patent (UK) converted into an application under the Act under section 81(1) (r. 2(*c*)); or from a priority claimed for an International application for a patent (UK) entering the United Kingdom national phase under the PCT and present section 89(1) and (4) (to be replaced by s.89A(3)) and thereby becoming treated as an application under the Act, provided that such priority has not been lost or abandoned *under the provisions of the PCT* (r. 2(*d*)). The italicised words prevent a priority date of an international application being voluntarily abandoned after the application has entered the United Kingdom phase in order to post-date an application so that some required action could still be timely taken (*Daverio and Katz & Fogel's Applications*, SRIS O/102/85).

While the applicant for the application in suit must be the same as that for the priority application, or title must be derived therefrom (subs. (2)), there is no requirement under rule 6 to provide any proof of derivation of title to claim priority when the priority application is in another name. Presumably, it is thought that, unless there is derivation of title, the applicant under the Act will not be able to obtain the required certified copy of the priority application, but this does not necessary follow. If there were no assignment of at least the right to claim priority from the earlier application, it may be that any patent granted on the application in suit could be revoked under section 72(1)(*b*) because the patent was granted to a person not entitled to be granted the patent, for which see para. 72.17. Nevertheless, entitlement to apply and entitlement to claim priority are not necessarily the same so that a failure of entitlement to claim priority, but not to apply, may result only in a loss of priority by the false priority declaration merely being ignored.

Only when the requirements for a valid declaration of priority have been met can the declared priority for the application in suit be applied, *e.g.* for prior art purposes under section 2(3). The same applies to international applications (UK) under present section 89(1)(*a*) and (*c*) (to be replaced by s. 89B(1)(*b*)). However, for applications for European patents, if a priority document, not in English, French or German, was filed in due time at the EPO, but not its translation, the applicant loses his right of priority, but priority is apparently accorded for prior art purposes (EPO Guideline C–V, 3.3). Section 78(3)(*a*) may achieve the same result because it refers to a priority document that has been "made" in connection with the European application. However, subsection (2) requires that a declaration must comply with "the relevant requirements of rules". This seems to require that the conditions of rule 6(6), as well as those of sub-rule (2)(*b*), (3), (4) or (5) of rule 6, must be satisfied. If so then, despite the fact that section 5 is mentioned in section 130(7), there may be a different result with European applications, unless subsection (2) can be construed as not requiring rule 6(6) to be a relevant requirement before a priority date is accorded for the purpose of section 2(3). These questions were more fully considered in articles by C. Jones ((1980–81) 10 CIPA 11 and 383).

5.08   *Test of "supported by the matter disclosed"*

The test of "fair basis" under section 5 [1949] has been replaced by one of the invention being "supported by the matter disclosed" (subs. (2)(*a*)), or the matter "disclosed" (subs. (2)(*b*)) "in the relevant application". In so far as these phrases may differ, the present "support" test is certainly not less stringent than the "fair basis" test as discussed in para. A005.3. Indeed, it is almost certainly more rigid in respect of the required degree of disclosure, and perhaps also as regards "enablement" as discussed in para. 5.12 *infra*.

The phrase would seem to have the same meaning as the requirement in section 14(5)(*c*) that the "claims shall be supported by the description", for which see para. 14.25. Also apparently relevant are cases decided under section 76 (*Amendments not to result in "additional matter"*) as to whether an amendment would have the effect of matter being added to that contained in the specification as originally filed, for which see paras. 76.11–76.16. Furthermore, consideration has to be given to the test for lack of novelty contained in section 2(2) as to information previously "made" available to the public, as discussed in paras. 2.05–2.18; and to the reference in section 2(3) to matter "contained" in an application for another patent, as discussed in para. 2.19. As yet, there is no clear decision in the United Kingdom on the equivalence, or otherwise, of the tests of "sufficiency" and "disclosure" of "matter" in sections 2(2), 2(3), 5(2), 14(5)(*c*) and 76, but clearly the tests are related, if not identical. The question whether a disclosure for these purpose, as distinct from the purpose of the sufficiency of a specification under section 14(3) (for which see paras. 14.15–14.18) is a particularly difficult manifestation of the construction of these various provisions, as is discussed in more detail in para. 2.18.

5.09   *Decisions under the present section 5*

In *Asahi Kasei's Application* (SRIS O/32/88, *noted* IPD 11012 and SRIS C/103/88, *noted* IPD 11081) the Comptroller held that there is no requirement that, for satisfaction of section 5(2), the "matter disclosed in" an earlier application should be sufficient for its repetition, sufficiency being a matter to be judged solely under section 14(3). Here the (Japanese) priority document had a claim to a particular chemical compound though, apparently, without disclosure of how this could be obtained. The Comptroller held that, since the priority document indicated that the compound had been made, the test for priority under section 5(2) had been met, thereby giving rise to an objection under section 2(3), for which see para. 2.20. In reaching this decision, the Comptroller specifically refused to follow *EPO Decision T 206/83, "Pyridine Herbicides/ICI"* (OJEPO 1/1987. 5; [1986] 5 EPOR 232) discussed in para. 5.12 *infra*. However, on appeal, priority was accorded under section 130(3) because a corresponding claim in the priority document was held to be sufficient irrespective of the presence of further supporting or enabling disclosure, see para. 5.06 *supra*. Whether a prior document must contain an "enabling" disclosure for it to be effective to deny the novelty of a later claim is discussed in more detail in para. 2.18.

Some guidance of the meaning of "matter disclosed" may also be obtained from *Deyhle's Design Application* ([1982] RPC 526), a case relating to according convention priority to a design application.

If an earlier application mentioned in a declaration of priority does not support any invention or matter disclosed in the application in suit, the declaration may be nugatory, but it is not objectionable.

If priority should be lost, the possible alleviation of the position under section 6 should not be overlooked if there has been a "relevant intervening act", for which see the commentary on section 6.

Priority under the EPO Guidelines   **5.10**

EPO Guidelines C-V, 2.1–2.5 deal in some detail with priority under the EPC. For priority to be accorded to an earlier application, the elements of a claim must be included in the earlier application (EPCa. 88(3)). Alternatively if the elements do not appear in the claims of the earlier application, the documents of the earlier application as a whole must specifically disclose such elements (EPCa. 88(4)). Thus, EPCa. 88(3) and (4) are seen to resemble the provisions of subsection (2)(*a*) and (*b*) respectively, though different wording is used.

The EPO Guidelines point out that an element may be a feature disclosed, or it may be the combination of certain features, but in this connection it is not permitted to make a mosaic of priority documents unless, possibly, one priority document refers to the other (C-V 1.5). A claim to a detailed embodiment (*i.e.* to a species) is not supported by a general reference (*i.e.* a genus containing it), but exact correspondence is not required: it suffices that on a reasonable assessment there is in substance a disclosure of all the important features of the claim (C-V, 2.3). Originally, the Guideline C-V, 2.4 stated that a generic claim or a claim specifying an element in broad (*i.e.* generic) terms is supported by the disclosure of a specific example of it provided that the generalisation is obvious. However, it was realised by the EPO that, if the test for priority is not aligned with that for new matter and novelty, strange results are possible in the application of "whole contents" under section 2(3) when implicit disclosures are involved, as discussed in paras. 5.13 and 5.14 *infra*.

Relevant EPO decisions   **5.11**

Since the effect of section 130(7) is to require section 5 to be construed so as to have, as far as practicable, the same effects as the corresponding EPC provisions, EPO decisions on the interpretation of EPCaa. 87–89 should have a relevance to the interpretation of section 5, but see para. 5.06 *supra* for a contrary view. EPCa. 88(3) suggests that the priority right is accorded to a claim only to the extent that the prior application coincides with the content of the subsequent European application as filed. Thus, the only question to be examined is whether or not those features of the subsequent European application are included in the priority application. It appears to follow from this that the basic test for priority is the same as the test of whether an amendment to a European application satisfies the requirement of EPCa. 123(2), see EPO Guideline C-V, 2.4. This states that, for the priority date to be allowed, "the subject matter of the claim must be derivable directly and unambiguously from the disclosure of the invention in the priority document when account is taken of any features implicit to a person skilled in the art in what is expressly mentioned in the document". This, of course, is also the test for lack of novelty, see EPO Guidelines C-IV, 7.2 and C-VI, 5.4.

The point was explained further in *EPO Decision T* 201/83, *"Lead alloy/ SHELL"* (OJEPO 10/1984, 481), discussed in para. 76.22. Here it was posited that the test for compliance with EPCa. 123(2) is basically the same as the test for lack of novelty, *i.e.* the disclosures must effectively be the same so that no new matter has been generated by the amendment. The test for priority can then be seen to be a similar one, see para. 76.22.

However, the *"Lead alloy/SHELL"* decision should be contrasted with *EPO Decision T* 12/81, *"Diastereomers/BAYER"* (OJEPO 8/1982, 296) where it was held that a selection of elements of a product from two lists each of some length to form a new combination of elements can be regarded as new, whereas there is a lack of novelty if an allegedly new product is the inevitable result of a disclosed process applied to a starting material disclosed in the same document. This type of distinction between modified and inherent teaching should, therefore, also be drawn in a determination of priority under EPCa. 88, as it was in *EPO Decision T* 85/87, *"Arthropodicidal compounds/CSIRO"* ([1989] 1 EPOR 24) where a distinction was drawn between: a modification regarded as an obvious alternative to the literal disclosure, not giving rise to priority; and a modification inherently disclosed as part of the teaching of the priority document, which does provide basis for priority.

It can be seen from the foregoing that all EPO decisions bearing on permissible amendment or on novelty are also potentially relevant to the determination of priority date. Such decisions are discussed in paras. 2.13 and 76.19–76.23 respectively.

To be a "first application", in accordance with EPCa. 87(1), it is enough that the later application differs in the disclosure of subject matter in comparison to the earlier filed application.

The invention, or subject matter, of a previous application is considered (by the EPO) to be identical to that of a subsequent one if the essence of the two disclosures is the same, but the use of selected species from a previous general disclosure to give improved results is not an identical invention (*EPO Decision T* 184/84, *"Ferrite crystal/NGK INSULATOR"* ([1986] 4 EPOR 169), see also *EPO Decision T* 85/87 (*supra*). Also, an example not contained in the priority document is disregarded when considering that document as a potential anticipation under EPCa. 54(3) (s. 2(3)), see *EPO Decision T* 94/87, *"Radiation stabilisation/BECTON"* ([1989] 5 EPOR 264). This principle is further illustrated by *EPO Decision T* 61/85, *"Polyester crystallisation/ICI"* ([1988] 1 EPOR 20) where it was stated that "a generic disclosure in a priority document interpreted as covering two alternatives does not form a basis for the priority of a later specific disclosure of one of the two alternatives characterised by a quantitative result, unless this result would have been obtained inevitably from either of the two alternatives or is also expressly described". It may be noted that such a test is not dissimilar to the definitive rules for according priority laid down under the 1949 Act in *Mond Nickel's Application* ([1956] RPC 189) and *ICI's Patent* ([1960] RPC 223), for which see para. A005.3.

5.12 *The sufficiency requirement of a priority application*

A matter of some debate is whether, in contrast with section 5 [1949] (see *Ishihara Sangyo* v. *Dow Chemical* [1987] FSR 137 (CA)), the description in the priority document has to be sufficient under EPCa. 88 and/or section 5 [1977] to enable its disclosure to be repeated, *i.e.* if that disclosure is an "enabling" one. In *EPO Decision T* 206/83, *"Pyridine herbicides/ICI"* (OJEPO 1/1987, 5; [1986] 5 EPOR 232) it was held that a document does not effectively disclose a chemical compound even though it states the structure and the steps by which it is to be produced if the skilled person is unable to ascertain from the document, with the aid of his common general knowledge, how to obtain the required starting materials or intermediates. In other words, it was held that to destroy the novelty of a later claim, there must be an enabling prior disclosure. Thus, if novelty is equated to lack of priority, it can be deduced that, if a priority document would have no novelty-destroying effect had it been a prior publication, it cannot confer priority either. On this basis, it would seem that support for claims is the same for the purposes of priority and sufficient description, *i.e.* in view of EPCa. 88(3) and (4) it is a matter of sufficient disclosure (or disclosure and enablement). However, the Comptroller has specifically refused to follow the *"Pyridine herbicides/ICI"* decision, holding that sufficiency of disclosure is only relevant when the validity of a monopoly is in question under section 14(3) (*Asahi Kasei's Application*, SRIS 0/32/88, *noted* IPD 11012 and SRIS C/103/88, *noted* IPD 11081). However, on the appeal in that case, priority was accorded because section 130(3) was interpreted disjunctively, see paras. 5.06 and 5.09 *supra*.

Test of "disclosed in the earlier relevant application" (subs. (2)(b))   **5.13**

The test of subsection (2)(*b*) can be applied to any matter in an application in suit, whether such is claimed or not, and hence the test is available for use in a case of interlocking priorities to decide which claims, or parts of claims, have the earlier priority. This would suggest that the same test has to be applied to decide upon the novelty of the claims, or parts of claims, in the other contested application under section 2(3), but it may be that section 5(2) was drafted to allow for a possible distinction. However, in view of the EPO decisions discussed in para. 5.11 *supra*, the possibility that "supported by" is more generous to an applicant seeking to sustain priority than "disclosed in" seems unlikely.

Further problems caused by subsection (2) are discussed in paras. 5.14 and 5.15 *infra* in relation to conflicts based on implicit disclosures. By adopting a disclosure test equating to that applied in respect of lack of novelty, the EPO may have avoided these problems, but it remains to be seen whether the British courts will take a similar line, see para. 5.12 *supra*.

Support from implicit disclosure   **5.14**

With respect to a claim that is narrower than the disclosure in the earlier specification and is based on a feature not disclosed explicitly therein, but where no fresh inventive feature is involved, the same results may well now be obtained as under the 1949 Act, on the basis of a specific disclosure being held to be in substance implicit in the earlier documents. Examples of such cases were *BDH's Application* ([1964] RPC 237 at p. 244), *Glaxo's Application* ([1968] RPC 483), *CIBA's Patent* ([1971] FSR 616) and *Hoffmann-La Roche* v. *Commissioner [Australia]* ([1973] RPC 34).

However, in cases where a new feature imports an inventive step (*BDH's Application, supra*) or differentiates the claim from the prior art (*ICI's (Clark's) Application*, [1969] RPC 574), or results in an inventive combination not disclosed in the priority document (*Scherico's Application*, [1968] RPC 407), it will probably be held that there is no disclosure of the new feature in the priority document and priority will then be disallowed by analogy with the concept of "additional matter" in an impermissible amendment, as discussed in paras. 76.11–76.16. However, such would represent a departure from the effect of the case law under the 1949 Act, at least so far as concerns the *ICI* and *Scherico* cases. To minimise problems in according priority, it is advisable, therefore, to ensure that features upon which the case may ultimately rest are adequately and explicitly disclosed in the priority document. It will be appreciated that whether a case of this kind falls under the first or second set of cases discussed above is likely to depend very much on the facts, see further para. 2.12 where the concept of novelty being destroyed by an implicit disclosure is discussed in relation to EPO practice, and para. 76.13 on the question of impermissible amendment by adding to the implicit disclosure of a specification.

5.15   *Resolution of conflicts based on implicit disclosures*

Though EPCa. 88(4) refers to the conferring of priority only when the invention is claimed in the earlier application, or if the documents thereof "as a whole *specifically* disclose" the elements of the invention, nevertheless, it is thought that subsection (2) has to be construed to take account of implicit disclosures if there is not to be a different test in the application of section 2(3) to conflicting applications. It is clear from such cases as *Babcock and Wilcox's Application* ((1952) 69 RPC 224) and *Commercial Solvents' Application* ((1954) 71 RPC 143) that the problem of implied disclosure of an application has to be dealt with, because reliance on explicit disclosure only would often give an unfair result as it would have done in those two cases of "prior claiming" under the 1949 Act if the respective implied features and parameters had not been taken into account. Thus, as discussed in the commentary on section 2(3) at paras. 2.19 and 2.21, "disclosure" must in practice, include the implicit disclosure, see *EPO Decision T* 06/80, "*Intermediate layer for reflector*" (OJEPO 10/1981, 434). The direct and unambiguous derivability tests of Guideline C-IV, 7.2 were included to provide the necessary flexibility to the application of "whole contents" to questions of conflicting priorities, which in the United Kingdom are to be resolved under section 2(3) after a priority date has been accorded under section 5 (or s. 128 in case of conflict with an existing application or patent filed or granted under the 1949 Act).

Implicit disclosures may involve: the species of a disclosed genus, especially in mechanical cases where the species are immediately apparent to the skilled person; an implied genus derived from its species, as discussed in para. 5.11 *supra* with reference to EPO Guideline C-V, 2.4; implicit processes and intermediates in chemical cases; and implied features and parameters as indicated above. For example, an explicit disclosure of an end product in a senior party's priority document may arguably imply the intermediate necessary to make it (for the purposes of the novelty test on the basis of direct and unequivocal derivation (see C-IV, 7.2)) by a generally described process, but if the junior party's priority document states it explicitly and both parties attempt to claim it in their substantive applications, one of the following situations then seems to arise:

(a) The earlier implicit disclosure confers priority (despite the specific disclosure requirement of EPCa. 88(4)) and also prejudices novelty on the basis of C-IV, 7.2 (which must be the result under the Act if a novelty prejudicing disclosure is deemed also to be a disclosure for the purposes of subsection (2)(*b*); and the senior party wins the claim. This is equally the result if the senior party's priority document was published as a "relevant intervening act" under section 6 before the junior party's earliest date. This is much the most likely fact situation.

(b) Because of the generous approach to priority under the 1949 Act (discussed in para. A005.3), it is possible for an implicit disclosure to confer priority under section 5 while being insufficient to prejudice novelty under section 2, especially in view of the *General Tire* and *Du Pont (Witsiepe's)* cases discussed in paras. 2.06–2.09 and 2.15 respectively. This would give rise to the presence of "support" under subsection (5)(*a*) but no disclosure under subsection (2)(*b*). In these circumstances both parties would apparently obtain their claims and there would then be double patenting with each party able to prevent the other from exploiting his invention, though subject to section 64. This will also be the result if the senior party's priority document were published before the junior party's earliest date. Presumably the court would try and avoid such a result, but under the 1949 Act the court did not always perceive that this was the result of some of its prior claiming decisions, see paras. A032.03–A032.05.

(c) It is also possible that the implicit disclosure would be held insufficient to confer priority on the senior party's claim, perhaps under EPCa. 88(4), because there is no specific disclosure, but that that disclosure is nevertheless sufficient to prejudice novelty under section 2; the junior party would then win the contest. However, this possibility is apparently excluded by sub-section (2)(*b*) because a novelty-destroying disclosure can be expected always to be sufficient for conferring priority.

Thus, it is possible to analyse in some detail the effects of generic or implicit disclosures in a priority document, especially in relation to support or lack of it under subsection (2)(*a*) and disclosure or lack of it under subsection (2)(*b*). It is submitted that sensible results are obtained only when the priority document is treated as if it had been published at the priority date with respect to the same test for both novelty and priority. However, EPO Guideline C-V, 2.4 states that the test of prior disclosure is the same as that of whether an amendment satisfies the requirements of EPCa. 123(2) [as not adding matter to the application as filed], and therefore that the subject matter of the claim has to be derivable directly and unambiguously from the disclosure in the priority document when account is taken of any feature implicit to a person skilled in the art in addition to that expressly mentioned. This may, or may not, be the same test as that for lack of novelty, see para. 76.22. In *EPO Decision T* 85/87, "*Arthropodicidal compounds/CSIRO*" ([1989] 1 EPOR 24) a distinction was drawn between a disclosure implicit to the skilled man, which can give rise to priority; and one which is merely an obvious modification of that which is disclosed (explicitly or implicitly), which does not support priority, attention being drawn to cases cited in para. 2.16.

The EPO has also stated that, in order to mitigate the harshness of the "whole contents" approach and reduce the risk of "self-collision", a strict approach to lack of novelty arising from a citation only available under EPCa. 54(3) (corresponding to s.2(3)) should be adopted. This it then did by stating that a prior specification does not comprise other features which were only equivalent to the features according to the claims (*EPO Decision T* 167/84, "*Fuel injector valve/NISSAN*" (OJEPO 8/1987, 369; [1987] 6 EPOR 344), *i.e.* by using the same reasoning as later expounded in *EPO Decision T* 85/87 (*supra*). It would therefore seem that cases tend to be dealt with according to the particular circumstances prevailing and, certainly in respect of equivalent disclosures, a lenient attitude may be shown in a case of "self-collision". If so, this would be following the trend of decisions given under the different "fair basis" test, but directed to the same problem, as applied under section 5 [1949], see para. A005.3.

In *Asahi Kasei's Application* (SRIS O/32/88, *noted* IPD 11012 and SRIS C/103/88, *noted* IPD 11081), the Comptroller did interpret the provisions for lack of novelty and priority in a like manner, while refusing to accept that either disclosure need be "enabling" as the EPO apparently requires, see para. 2.18. On appeal, the Patents Court decided the case on an alternative basis, see para. 5.06 *supra*.

First convention filing and re-filing (subs. (3))   **5.16**

The effect of subsection (3) is that priority is only accorded if the relevant application was filed within the 12 month period prior to the application is suit, unless any earlier application had been withdrawn, abandoned or refused in the manner required by subsection (3)(*b*). Subsection (3) corresponds to EPCa. 87(4) and Paris Convention Article 4C(4). It does not apply to abandoned applications under the

1949 Act accompanied by provisional specifications that were not completed, although under section 127(4) these gave a right to priority if followed by a fresh application within 15 months.

Subsection (3) is in the negative form so that the second of two earlier relevant applications is to be disregarded unless filed in the same country as the first, and provided the first was unconditionally withdrawn, abandoned or refused for all purposes before filing the second; the corresponding EPCa 87(4) and Paris Convention Article 4C(4) (reprinted in para. A001.7) are in the positive form, and the second application is considered to be the first when the previous application was filed in the same country and was earlier abandoned for all purposes. Under subsection (3) the second earlier application will be disregarded for priority purposes if the application in suit contains matter common to both earlier applications, if the earlier applications were filed by the same applicant as the substantive application or by the predecessor in title and if the second earlier application is specified for priority purposes. However, the predecessor in title must be in respect of the title to make that application and does not include a predecessor of the applicant in respect of a different title, *e.g.* because this is derived from a different inventorship entity (*Genentech's [Human Growth Hormone] Patent*, SRIS C/64/89). Also, the second earlier application is disregarded only so far as concerns the invention or matter in the first earlier application, but this causes problems when the second earlier application broadens a specific disclosure in the first application into a generic disclosure. Priority from the second application may then be lost because it cannot be regarded as a "premier depôt" for the specific matter also contained within the generic claim. To overcome this it may be desirable to include a claim of the "N-1" type based solely on the second application.

EPCa 87(4) is not relevant to multiple earlier applications within the 12 month period; the intention was to enact Paris Convention Article 4C(4), concerned with the problem of alleviating the position of an applicant who is otherwise unable to replace an unsatisfactory first application without loss of priority (Bodenhausen, *Guide to the Paris Convention*, BIRPI (1968), p. 45).

Subsection (3) can apply to multiple earlier applications whether filed within the 12 months or not. Thus, if the first application was not abandoned for all purposes before filing the second application, whether or not it was specified for priority purposes in the substantive application, the second application is disregarded in so far as it concerns an invention or matter disclosed in the first application with the result that the first application also does not give priority if dated more than 12 months before the filing date of the application in suit (subs. (2)).

If the failure to declare priority, or to sustain such a declaration, results from an error or mistake, *e.g.* omission of the declaration of priority at the time of filing, or failure to supply details of its filing date or country of filing, or failure to supply any required certified copy or translation thereof within the prescribed time limit, priority is lost for all matter in the first application, see *Matsushita's Application* ([1983] RPC 105). This is consistent with subsection (2) requiring priority to be accorded only in respect of the earliest application when the matter in question was disclosed in more than one relevant earlier application. EPCa. 87(1) gives the same result when construed *a contrario* in the light of Paris Convention Articles 4A(1) and 4C(2) (see Bodenhausen, *supra*, p. 36, para. (3)). It confers priority only from the first application.

If the first application was filed before the 12 months and contains common subject-matter and was abandoned for all purposes, the second application is unaffected by it. If it was not abandoned for all purposes, whether or not it contains matter in common with the substantive application, the second application is not disregarded so far as concerns priority for the matter which is not in common but is otherwise disregarded. EPO Guideline C-V, 1.4 reaches the same conclusion. As noted above, the same effects arise under subsection (3) even when the first application was filed within the 12 months.

Particular care needs to be taken with claiming priority from a United States "continuation-in-part application". Priority is not claimable for features disclosed in these which were also present in the earlier United States application if the earlier application was filed more than 12 months before the application in suit, see *Karlgaard's Application* ([1966] RPC 553), the principle of which continues to apply.

"Relevant application" (subs. (5))   **5.17**

A "relevant application" (*i.e.* one from which priority may be claimed under subsection (2) for an application, or under subsection (4) for a patent, is either one filed under the Act (subs. (5)(*a*)) or one filed in a "convention country" (subs. (5)(*b*)), for the definition of which see section 90 and para. 90.02. The "relevant application" must be an "application for protection in respect of an invention" or an application equivalent thereto under the law of, or applicable in, such convention country. Thus priority cannot be claimed from an application filed in a country not recognised as a convention country under section 90, nor if the priority application is a design application, see *Agfa-Gevaert's Application* ([1982] RPC 441) where a priority claim from a German design application consisting only of drawings was refused. The EPO has decided likewise (*EPO Decision J* 15/80, OJEPO 7/1981, 213). The same would apply to an attempt to claim priority from a United Kingdom design application, not least because the United Kingdom is not a convention country within the meaning of section 90.

A "relevant application" can also be an application which is equivalent to an application in a convention country as a result of local law or a treaty or international convention, see EPCa. 66 and PCTa. 11(4). Thus a European or an international application is to be treated as equivalent to an application in a convention country whether the United Kingdom is designated therefor or not. The same result arises when the United Kingdom is designated, as a consequence of sections 78(1) and 80(1) whereby a European or international application is treated for the purposes of the Act as an application for a patent under the Act. Similar effects are envisaged in respect of EPC and PCT applications claiming priority from applications filed under an international convention (see EPCa. 87(2) and PCTr. 4.10(*a*)(iv)). These provisions follow from Paris Convention Article 4A (Lisbon and Stockholm Texts).

However, there is a danger that an originating European patent application might be held not to be capable of establishing a priority date in countries not a party to the EPC, particularly those countries which have not ratified the Stockholm text of the Paris Convention or whose ratification does not apply to Articles 1 to 12 thereof. The same is true of an originating PCT application.

The question whether an application is entitled to the status of "convention application" which arose under section 1(2) and (4) [1949], (for which see para. A001.01) cannot arise at all under the 1977 Act. Conflict of priorities between 1949 and 1977 Act applications and patents is dealt with in section 128, see paras. 128.02 and 128.03.

Subsection (5)(*b*) needs further explanation. The "application in or for a convention country . . . for protection of an invention" should, under the law of that country, be a regular national filing adequate to establish the date on which it was filed in the country concerned, whatever may be the outcome of the application (Paris Convention, Article 4A, and see also EPCa. 87(2) and (3)). In *Ishihara Sangyo* v. *Dow Chemical* ([1987] FSR 137 (CA)) it was held that, under section 5 [1949], an application duly filed in a convention country would give rise to a right of priority irrespective of its validity under its local law, unless the relevant priority application were not an application for a patent at all. Subsection (5) appears to be of like effect.

Practice under Section 5

5.18 *Claim drafting*

In view of the ease with which a limitation can be introduced into a claim without appreciation of the effect on the priority date, a set of claims should never be settled without being checked against the specification of the priority application(s) when such exist. This is particularly advisable on amendment to avoid anticipation.

When a broad claim is anticipated it may be possible by specific disclaimer, and without amendment to the claim, to retain a priority date which would be lost by a specific limitation in the claim.

When a specification contains more matter than a priority document, it is generally advisable to include one independent claim that is clearly entitled to the priority date. This is in view of the difficulties arising from the wording of section 125(2), see para. 125.21.

5.19 *Filing of declaration of priority*

Declarations of priority in connection with applications under the Act are dealt with by rule 6 (reprinted at para. 5.02 *supra*): they are made at the time of filing, usually (but not now necessarily) on PF 1/77. No extension of time can be granted if a declaration of priority is not made at this time (r. 110(2), reprinted in para. 123.10, referring to r. 6(1)). However, where the period expires on a day which is an excluded day under section 120, or where there is an interruption or subsequent dislocation in postal services within the United Kingdom (or an interruption in the normal operation of the Patent Office), certified in each case under rule 111(1), the declaration is effective if made on the first day following such excluded day (r. 111(3), (4)). There is also now provision (under r. 111(6), reprinted in para. 123.11) for the period for making this declaration to be extended, by discretion, when failure to file it is shown to be due to some failure or delay in the postal service *within the United Kingdom*, see para. 123.39. Also, it may be possible under section 117 to make a correction of a priority declaration if this is incomplete or inaccurate through error, see para. 117.10. The EPO has allowed a correction of this type when promptly requested, see para. 117.07 and *EPO Decision J* 04/82, *"Priority declaration/YOSHIDA"* (OJEPO 10/1982, 385).

5.20 *Filing of certified copy of priority application*

Certified copies must be filed within 16 months of the "declared priority date" (as defined in r. 2, reprinted at para. 123.04 and discussed in para. 5.07 *supra*), see rule 6(2), unless one of the special provisions of rules 6(3)–(5) applies. However an extension of one month is possible under rule 110(3), with its heavy fee, with further extension possible at the Comptroller's discretion, also on payment of heavy fees, under rules 110(3A) and (3C), for which see para. 123.33. If certified copies are physically unobtainable, the Comptroller cannot, apparently, invoke rule 101 (*Dispensation where something cannot be done*), but he may accept uncertified copies, verified by affidavit or statutory declaration, until identical certified ones become available.

In the case of an International application entering the United Kingdom phase under the PCT, a check should be made that the Patent Office has duly received from the International Bureau both a copy of the International application *and* a certified copy of the necessary priority application(s), as should have happened under PCTa. 20 and PCTrr. 17.2 and 47. If there has been a failure to file the priority document(s) with the International Bureau, it may be possible to rectify this mistake for the United Kingdom by filing the required certified copy or copies directly with the Patent Office, see *Matsushita's Application* ([1983] RPC 105).

If a required certified copy is not filed, but this is not noticed by the Patent Office and the application becomes published with a priority statement, this will be deleted under rule 100 when the error is discovered (*Brossman's Application*, [1983] RPC 109), unless a late filing under rules 110(3A) and (3C) should now be permitted.

If the priority application is one that was filed originally at the Patent Office, under rule 6(3)—when the application is a divisional application under section 15(4)—a certified copy as such is not required, but a photocopy of the priority document is to be prepared in the Patent Office, the applicant being required to file PF 24/77 for authentication of the same. Otherwise no certified copy of such an application is required unless the Comptroller so requires, when PF 24/77 must be filed as with a divisional application (r. 6(3)). The practice under rule 6(3)(*b*) is that a copy of an earlier application filed at the Patent Office is not required if this has been withdrawn and priority has not been claimed in respect of it in another application (O.J. June 1, 1978). A request by the Comptroller under rule 6(3)(*b*) is likely where, for instance, the priority application is one filed under the Act which, though perhaps abandoned, has served as priority for another application. A similar request could be made in the case of an international application (UK) if the International Bureau should fail to supply the priority document initially under PCTa. 20 and PCTrr. 17.2 and 47.

By section 78(3)(*a*) a declaration of priority made under EPCa. 88(1) and EPCr. 38 is treated as a declaration made under section 5(2). For further discussion of the requirements for certified copies of priority documents for applications under the Act, see para. 15.24 and (for divisional applications) para. 15.28.

Rule 6(4) and (5) makes special provision with regard to the supply of certified copies in the cases of a European application (UK) converted into an application under the Act (under s.81) and the entry of an international application (UK) into the national phase (under present s.89(1) and (3), to be replaced by s.89A(3)), for which see respectively paras. 81.12, 89A.15, 89A.26 and 89A.27.

Supply of translation of certified copy of priority application (r. 6(6))   **5.21**

Rule 6(6) deals with furnishing to the Patent Office translations of certified copies not in English. Thus must be done within 21 months of the declared priority date, unless Chapter II of PCT has been invoked when the period is 31 months. Again extensions of this period can be obtained under rules 110(3) and/or 110(3A) and (3C) as explained in para. 5.20 *supra*.

Declarations of priority and the supply of certified copies under PCTrr. 4.10(*a*) and (*c*) and 17(1)(*a*) apply for international applications but, while these should be provided automatically by the International Bureau (see para. 5.20 *supra*), a certified translation nevertheless is required to be filed under rule 6(6). It is all too easy to overlook this requirement, at least within the time limit imposed by rule 6(6), see paras. 89A.15, 89A.26 and 89A.27.

Like rule 113(1), reprinted in para. 123.12, which deals generally with the filing of translations of documents furnished to the Patent Office which are not in English, rule 6(6) requires that any translation furnished to the Office under that rule must be "verified to the satisfaction of the Comptroller". This requirement is discussed in para. 123.42 which also deals with the extent to which the formal parts of the priority document need to be translated.

5.22 *Obtaining of certified copies of the application as a priority document*

Where certified copies of a United Kingdom application are required to support claims to priority in foreign applications, application is made on PF 24/77 as described in para. 32.37.

6.01

SECTION 6

Disclosure of matter, etc., between earlier and later applications

6.—(1) It is hereby declared for the avoidance of doubt that where an application (the application in suit) is made for a patent and a declaration is made in accordance with section 5(2) above in or in connection with that application specifying an earlier relevant application, the application in suit and any patent granted in pursuance of it shall not be invalidated by reason only of relevant intervening acts.

(2) In this section—

"relevant application" has the same meaning as in section 5 above; and

"relevant intervening acts" means acts done in relation to matter disclosed in an earlier relevant application between the dates of the earlier relevant application and the application in suit, as for example, filing another application for the invention for which the earlier relevant application was made, making information available to the public about that invention or that matter or working that invention, but disregarding any application, or the disclosure to the public of matter contained in any application, which is itself to be disregarded for the purposes of section 5(3) above.

COMMENTARY ON SECTION 6

6.02 *General*

Section 6 is to the same intent as section 52 [1949] and is designed to protect an applicant against invalidity of his claims due to an "intervening act", of disclosure or use of the invention in the interval between the claimed date of the priority application and the filing date of the application in suit described in a priority application, the "intervening period". However, its actual effect is in some doubt, see para. 6.04 *infra*, but in any event the relevant intervening act could provide a right of use under section 64 to avoid infringement of a patent based on an application filed during the "intervening period".

Section 6 can only be operative when a declaration of priority has been made in accordance with section 5(2). It is not clear whether section 6 can apply when this declaration has been made but is invalid or inoperative because, for example, the requirements of rule 6(2)–(5) have not been met as to the supply of a certified copy (and, if necessary, a translation thereof) within the due time. Patent Office practice seems to be that priority is not then accorded (*Matsushita's Application*, [1983] RPC 105), but section 6 refers only to a priority having been "declared".

Operation of section 6 in practice   **6.03**

It will be noted that section 6 applies "in relation to matters disclosed in an earlier relevant application". In *International Paint Co.'s Application* ([1982] RPC 247) the word "described" in section 52 [1949] was held to have the same meaning as in section 5(2) [1949] and it would, therefore, seem likely that the same test for the "matter disclosed in the earlier relevant application" applies under section 6 as it does under section 5, for which see para. 5.08.

The corresponding section 52 [1949] was also discussed in *Ronson* v. *Lewis* ([1963] RPC 103) and applied in *Letraset* v. *Rexel* ([1976] RPC 51).

Relevant EPO decisions   **6.04**

Section 6 is qualified by section 130(7) and has therefore been framed to have, as nearly as practicable, the same effects as the corresponding EPC articles. However, the EPC has no direct counterpart to the wording of section 6, though the provisions of EPCa. 54 (*novelty*), EPCa. 88(2) (*multiple priority*), EPCa. 88(3) and (4) (*substantive priority*) and EPCa. 89 (*effect of priority*) ought to be construed in such a way that Article 4B of the Paris Convention is satisfied, because the preamble of the EPC states that the EPC is a special agreement within the meaning of Article 19 of the Paris Convention. However, the EPO has held that it is not directly bound by the Paris Convention as the European Patent Organisation is not a party to this, see *EPO Decision J* 15/80 (OJEPO 7/1981, 213). However, while the provisions of EPCaa. 87–89 and EPCr. 38 form a complete code of rules of law on the subject of priority rights, the provisions of the Paris Convention have generally been followed.

Nevertheless, there remains doubt whether section 6 is in accord with the EPC, even though section 130(7) requires the section to have the same effects as the EPC, as nearly as practicable. This doubt is not lessened by Article 4B of the Paris Convention because Bodenhausen (*Guide to the Paris Convention*, BIRPI 1968, pp. 41–42) makes it clear that protection is in respect to "acts accomplished in the priority application" with respect to *the invention, i.e.* the one disclosed in the priority application and not one that is obvious with respect to it. It seems, therefore, that reliance should not be placed on section 6 and that the old doctrine of "provisional protection" of section 52(1) [1949] is likewise not necessarily applicable for patents under the present Act. If a further development is made of an invention described in a priority application, a further priority application should, therefore, be filed in respect of it *and* intervening publication by the inventor or his assignee should, if possible, be avoided.

SECTION 7   **7.01**

Right to apply for and obtain a patent

7.—(1) Any person may make an application for a patent either alone or jointly with another.

(2) A patent for an invention may be granted—

(*a*) primarily to the inventor or joint inventors;

(*b*) in preference to the foregoing, to any person or persons who, by virtue of any enactment or rule of law, or any foreign law or treaty or international convention, or by virtue of an enforceable term of any agreement entered into with the inventor before the making of the invention, was or were at the time of the making of the invention entitled to the whole of the property in it (other than equitable interests) in the United Kingdom;

(*c*) in any event, to the successor or successors in title of any person or persons mentioned in paragraph (*a*) or (*b*) above or any person so mentioned and the successor or successors in title of another person so mentioned;

and to no other person.

(3) In this Act "inventor" in relation to an invention means the actual deviser of the invention and "joint inventor" shall be construed accordingly.

(4) Except so far as the contrary is established, a person who makes an application for a patent shall be taken to be the person who is entitled under subsection (2) above to be granted a patent and two or more persons who made an application jointly shall be taken to be the persons so entitled.

7.02   ARTICLE

R. P. Lloyd, "Inventorship amongst collaborators", (1979–80) 9 CIPA 16.

COMMENTARY ON SECTION 7

7.03   *General*

Section 7 concerns the identity of an applicant for a patent under the Act (subs. (1)), and of the person(s) entitled to be granted a patent (subs. (2)), including a European patent (UK) (s. 77(1)(*b*)), with a presumption of entitlement set out in subsection (4). The section is not referred to in section 130(7) as having the same effects as a corresponding EPC article.

The effect of the section is essentially different from that under the 1949 Act. This is a consequence of the change of the meaning of "inventor", now defined in subsection (3) and discussed in para. 7.07 *infra*, and the automatic ownership by an employer of certain inventions made by his employees, see section 39 and paras. 39.09–39.13.

7.04   *Who may apply for a patent (subs. (1))*

Subsection (1) states that any person may make an application for a patent. The subsection of itself does not call for the applicant as such to have any right in the invention, and subsection (4) states that the applicant is presumed to be entitled to the grant, except where the contrary is shown. It seems, from subsection (1) and section 15(1), that the application may be made by a person not entitled to the grant in the expectation that the patent will be granted eventually to the rightful owner.

Foreign unincorporated bodies are permitted to file patent applications on the assumption that they are capable of holding property in their own name under the laws of their country of origin. The Formalities Section at the Patent Office holds an extensive, though non-exhaustive, list of such bodies, the more common of which were listed in (1978–79) 8 CIPA 371. Formalities practice, however, goes little further than checking that the applicant is not merely a partnership and the onus is therefore on the applicant to ensure that his status is properly described and that the patent may properly be granted to him, see *Schwarzkopf's Application* ([1965] RPC 387).

Entitlement to grant of a patent (subs. (2))   **7.05**

Subsection (2) refers to the person(s) to whom the patent may be granted; it states that a patent may be granted: (*a*) "primarily" to the inventor(s); or (*b*) "in preference" to the inventor(s), to any person entitled to the whole of the property in the invention by virtue of law, convention or enforceable agreement made before the making of the invention. "Primarily" is likely to be taken as reflecting the traditional British view that the right to be granted a patent flows from the act of invention and not from the ownership of the invention. Such a view would be consistent with EPCa. 60. Then, "in preference" may be taken as meaning that the primary assumption is overridden when a legally enforceable right to the invention exists at the time when it is made, *e.g.* because the invention belongs to the inventor's employer by virtue of section 39(1).

The entitlement qualification for grant of the patent is the legal title to the patent property, ignoring equitable interests. This, apparently, admits a grant to be held in trust for an equitable owner, on which see para. 30.06 and an equitable title can be registered, see para. 32.19. Thus, the reference to "enactment or rule of law" in subsection (2)(*b*) presumably refers mainly to an employer owning the invention under the provisions of section 39(1), but preference over an inventor could also occur following the death of the inventor or the rightful applicant and a distribution of his estate, or with: a trustee in bankruptcy; a receiver appointed to administer a person's property under the Mental Health Act 1983 (c. 20); the custodian of enemy property in times of war; and, possibly, also a guardian of a person under the age of 18.

By subsection (2)(*c*) the successors in title to the persons primarily or in preference entitled to be granted a patent under subsection (2)(*a*) or (*b*) are also entitled to be granted a patent and are to be so entitled "in any event". However, an unenforceable assignment gives no rights under subsection (2)(*b*) or (*c*). Such an assignment is likely to be one made by an employee prior to the making of the invention and therefore unenforceable under section 42(2) if the assignment diminishes the employee's rights.

For procedure to change the applicant entity or entities, see para. 7.10 *infra*.

Importance of establishing entitlement prior to grant   **7.06**

Since a patent may be revoked under section 72(1)(*b*) on the ground that it was granted to a person who was not entitled to be granted that patent, presumably in accordance with section 7(2), see para. 7.09 *infra*, it is obviously of importance that the facts concerning entitlement should be correctly established before grant. Moreover, since by section 125 the invention for which a patent has been granted is to be taken as that specified in the claims of the patent, it is the claims of the patent as distinct from the claims of the application which have to be considered when there is any dispute as to entitlement after grant. However, entitlement is determined according to the alleged inventor's perception of what he has discovered, rather than what may turn out in the light of the prior art he has actually invented. In other words, validity considerations are not to be taken into account in assessing entitlement questions, see *Norris's Patent* ([1988] RPC 159) and *Viziball's Application* ([1988] RPC 213). Nevertheless, objection under section 72(1)(*b*) may arise if the patentee in respect of claims valid over the prior art does not derive title from a named inventor. Facilities exist for amendment or correction of the named inventor(s), see para. 7.10 *infra*.

The fact that an applicant has made an application for protection of the invention in a convention country does not in itself give to the applicant any right under subsection (2), as it did under section 1(2) [1949]. Nevertheless, in order to obtain a priority date under section 5(2), the applicant in the United Kingdom must be the same as, or be able to show title from, the applicant of the relevant application referred to in section 5(5), see section 5(2) and (3) discussed in para. 5.06.

The "time of making the invention" is referred to in subsection (2). In *Beecham* v. *Bristol SA* ([1978] RPC 521), the time of making of an invention of selection was considered to be the date when the necessary advantage was appreciated, see also *Du Pont's Patent* ([1961] RPC 336).

7.07 *Definition of "inventor" (subs. (3))*

"Inventor" is defined in section 130(1) as having the meaning given to it by section 7 and is defined in subsection (3) as the "actual deviser" of the invention. These words were used in section 16(2) [1949] where they were defined for the purposes of that section to exclude the first importer of an invention into the United Kingdom who was, nevertheless, regarded under the 1949 Act as an inventor for the purposes of making an application. This distinction is irrelevant to the 1977 Act and the first importer is no longer regarded as an inventor by virtue of "no other person" at the end of subsection (2). Thus, a patent agent may no longer (as under previous statutes) file an application in his own name as a "communication" from abroad on the basis of his being the first importer.

The statement in section 43(3) that, for the purposes of sections 39–42, a person is not an inventor if he merely contributes advice or other assistance in the making of the invention by another person, is believed to be in harmony with existing case law on inventorship, see, *e.g. Allen* v. *Rawson* ((1845) 1 CB 551; 135 E.R. 656), *Smith's Patent* ((1905) 22 RPC 57), and the article by R. P. Lloyd listed in para. 7.02 *supra*.

The inventor(s) has/have to be identified either on filing the application, see Section IV and Note 3 on PF 1/77 (reprinted at para. 141.01), or by the filing of a statement of inventorship on PF 7/77 (reprinted at para. 141.07) within a defined period thereafter, see paras. 13.05 and 13.06. The making of a change in the identified inventors is discussed in paras. 13.10 and 13.13.

7.08 *Entitlement to grant (subs. (4))*

Subsection (4) provides that, except in so far as the contrary is established, the applicant is entitled to grant of the patent. Thus, there is a rebuttable presumption that the person making the application under subsection (1) is entitled to have the patent granted to him under subsection (2). It was on the basis of this rebuttable presumption that the employee-referrer in *Peart's Patent* (SRIS O/209/87) was held to have failed to discharge the onus that was said to be upon him; the argument that, in an employer-employee entitlement dispute, the onus is reversed from the normal position under this subsection by the onus implied by section 39(2) (for which see para. 39.09) was apparently not put in that case. Joint applicants and grantees are provided for, as well as their rights *inter se* in the absence of an over-riding agreement, see section 36 and the commentary thereon. Entitlement to an international application may also be challenged under section 12(1).

Entitlement can be challenged before grant under section 8(1) and after grant under section 37(1). Although lack of entitlement is a ground of revocation, it is available only to the person duly found to have been properly entitled, see para. 7.09 *infra*.

Under EPCaa. 60, 61 and the Protocol to EPC on Recognition, and under CPCa. 27, entitlement is left as a matter for national law, see paras. 82.03–82.06. Entitlement to a European patent can be challenged before grant under section 12(1), subject to sections 82 and 83, see the commentaries thereon. Entitlement to an international application may also be challenged under section 12(1).

If the application is for a Community patent, however, section 86(4) will provide that section 12 shall not apply to it. Proceedings for entitlement to a Community patent before or after grant are to be governed by CPCa. 27, which is subject to CPCaa. 68–71.

Revocation after grant to non-entitled person   7.09

By section 72(1)(*b*) it is a ground of revocation that the patent was granted to a person who was not entitled to be granted that patent, *i.e.* was not a person entitled under section 7(2) to be granted the patent or a share thereof under section 36. This corresponds to EPCa. 138(1)(*c*) and CPCa. 57(1)(*e*). By section 72(2) this ground is available only to a person already found by the court under its general jurisdiction to grant a declaration, or the Comptroller under section 37, to be entitled to the patent or part of the matter comprised in it, and the ground is not available if the action before the court or the Comptroller was commenced more than two years after the patent was granted, unless the proprietor knew at the time of grant, or on transfer of the patent to him, that he was not entitled to it. Indeed, section 37(5) precludes the Comptroller from making an order under section 37 unless this condition is found to have been met, see *Peart's Patent* (SRIS O/209/87) where the Comptroller took the point on his own initiative. This time limit corresponds to CPCa. 27(3) and is reiterated in section 74(4). The meaning of "knew" in this context is discussed in para. 37.13. Other aspects of sections 72(1)(*b*) and 72(2) are discussed in paras. 72.17 and 74.05.

PRACTICE UNDER SECTION 7

Change of applicant   7.10

In summary, there are three routes available for addition or deletion of an applicant:
(1) By filing PF 11/77 under rule 35 (*Amendment of request for grant*), reprinted in para. 19.02 and discussed in para. 19.08: documentary support is not required, but this route can only be used before PF 7/77 has been filed.
(2) By filing PF 21/77 under rule 46 (*Application to register transaction, instrument or event under s. 33*), reprinted in para. 32.06 and discussed in paras. 32.25–32.31. Documentary support is required in the form of a certified copy or other evidence of the transaction, instrument or event giving rise to the need to change the applicant entity (r. 46(2)). This route can be used at any time prior to grant, and to change the registered proprietor after grant.
(3) By applying to make a correction to PF 1/77. This can be done either (a) by

filing PF 22/77 under rule 47 (*Request for correction of error in register or document filed in connection therewith*), reprinted in para. 32.07 and discussed in para. 32.32: a written explanation of the reasons for the request is required and evidence may be required to satisfy the Comptroller that there is an error which should be corrected in the manner requested; or (b) by filing PF 47/77 under rule 91 (*Correction of errors in patents and applications*), reprinted in para. 117.02 and discussed in para. 117.13: this is only possible where there is "an error of translation or transcription or a clerical error or mistake" to be corrected, see section 117(1). Unlike an application on PF 22/77, the Comptroller can require advertisement of the application and there is provision for opposition (rr. 91(3)(4)), see para. 117.14. An application for correction may be made at any time either before or after grant.

8.01

SECTION 8

Determination before grant of questions about entitlement to patents, etc.

8.—(1) At any time before a patent has been granted for an invention (whether or not an application has been made for it)—

    (*a*) any person may refer to the comptroller the question whether he is entitled to be granted (alone or with any other persons) a patent for that invention or has or would have any right in or under any patent so granted or any application for such a patent; or

    (*b*) any of two or more co-proprietors of an application for a patent for that invention may so refer the question whether any right in or under the application should be transferred or granted to any other person;

and the comptroller shall determine the question and may make such order as he thinks fit to give effect to the determination.

(2) Where a person refers a question relating to an invention under subsection (1)(*a*) above to the comptroller after an application for a patent for the invention has been filed and before a patent is granted in pursuance of the application, then, unless the application is refused or withdrawn before the reference is disposed of by the comptroller, the comptroller may, without prejudice to the generality of subsection (1) above and subject to subsection (6) below,—

    (*a*) order that the application shall proceed in the name of that person, either solely or jointly with that of any other applicant, instead of in the name of the applicant or any specified applicant;

    (*b*) where the reference was made by two or more persons, order that the application shall proceed in all their names jointly;

    (*c*) refuse to grant a patent in pursuance of the application or order the application to be amended so as to exclude any of the matter in respect of which the question was referred;

    (*d*) make an order transferring or granting any licence or other right in or under the application and give directions to any person for carrying out the provisions of any such order.

(3) Where a question is referred to the comptroller under subsection (1)(*a*) above and—

(*a*) the comptroller orders an application for a patent for the invention to which the question relates to be so amended;

(*b*) any such application is refused under subsection 2(*c*) above before the comptroller has disposed of the reference (whether the reference was made before or after the publication of the application); or

(*c*) any such application is refused under any other provision of this Act or is withdrawn before the comptroller has disposed of the reference, but after the publication of the application;

the comptroller may order that any person by whom the reference was made may within the prescribed period make a new application for a patent for the whole or part of any matter comprised in the earlier application or, as the case may be, for all or any of the matter excluded from the earlier application, subject in either case to section 76 below, and in either case that, if such a new application is made, it shall be treated as having been filed on the date of filing the earlier application.

(4) Where a person refers a question under subsection (1)(*b*) above relating to an application, any order under subsection (1) above may contain directions to any person for transferring or granting any right in or under the application.

(5) If any person to whom directions have been given under subsection (2)(*d*) or (4) above fails to do anything necessary for carrying out any such directions within 14 days after the date of the directions, the comptroller may, on application made to him by any person in whose favour or on whose reference the directions were given, authorise him to do that thing on behalf of the person to whom the directions were given.

(6) Where on a reference under this section it is alleged that, by virtue of any transaction, instrument or event relating to an invention or an application for a patent, any person other than the inventor or the applicant for the patent has become entitled to be granted (whether alone or with any other persons) a patent for the invention or has or would have any right in or under any patent so granted or any application for any such patent, an order shall not be made under subsection (2)(*a*), (*b*) or (*d*) above on the reference unless notice of the reference is given to the applicant and any such person, except any of them who is a party to the reference.

(7) If it appears to the comptroller on a reference of a question under this section that the question involves matters which would more properly be determined by the court, he may decline to deal with it and, without prejudice to the court's jurisdiction to determine any such question and make a declaration, or any declaratory jurisdiction of the court in Scotland, the court shall have jurisdiction to do so.

(8) No directions shall be given under this section so as to affect the

mutual rights or obligations of trustees or of the personal representatives of deceased persons, or their rights or obligations as such.

RELEVANT RULES

References under section 8(1)(a) or 12(1)(a)

8.02 **7.**—(1) A reference under section 8(1)(*a*) or 12(1)(*a*) shall be made on Patents Form No. 2/77 and shall be accompanied by a copy thereof and a statement in duplicate setting out fully the nature of the question, the facts upon which the person making the reference relies and the order or other relief which he is seeking.

(2) The comptroller shall send a copy of the reference and statement to—

(*a*) any person (other than the person referred to in paragraph (1) above) alleged in the reference to be entitled to be granted a patent for the invention;

(*b*) any person, not being a party to the reference, who is shown in the register as having a right in or under the patent; and

(*c*) where the application for the patent has not been published, any person who is an applicant for the patent or has given notice to the comptroller of a relevant transaction, instrument or event.

(3) If any person who is sent a copy of the reference and statement under paragraph (2) above wishes to oppose the making of the order or the granting of the relief sought, he ("the opponent") shall, within three months of the receipt of such copies, file in duplicate a counter-statement setting out fully the grounds of his opposition and the comptroller shall send a copy of the counter-statement to the person making the reference and to those recipients of the copy of the reference and statement who are not party to the counter-statement.

(4) The person making the reference or any such recipient may, within three months of the receipt of the copy of the counter-statement, file evidence in support of his case and shall send a copy of the evidence direct to the opponent.

(5) Within three months of the receipt of the copy of such evidence or, if no such evidence is filed, within three months of the expiration of the time within which it might have been filed, the opponent may file evidence in support of his case and shall send a copy of the evidence so filed to the person making the reference and those recipients; and within three months of the receipt of the copy of the opponent's evidence, that person or any of those recipients may file further evidence confined to matters strictly in reply and shall send a copy of it to the opponent.

(6) No further evidence shall be filed except by leave or direction of the comptroller.

(7) The comptroller may give such directions as he may think fit with regard to the subsequent procedure.

References by co-proprietors under section 8(1)(b) or 12(1)(b)

8.—(1) A reference under section 8(1)(*b*) or 12(1)(*b*) shall be made on **8.03** Patents Form No. 2/77 and shall be accompanied by a copy thereof and a statement in duplicate setting out fully the nature of the question, the facts relied upon by the co-proprietor making the reference and the order which he is seeking.

(2) The comptroller shall send a copy of the reference and statement to—

(*a*) each co-proprietor who is not a party to the reference and who has not otherwise indicated his consent to the making of the order sought (a "non-consenting co-proprietor"); and

(*b*) any person to whom it is alleged in the reference that any right in or under an application for a patent should be transferred or granted (an "alleged third party").

(3) Any person who receives a copy of the reference and statement and who wishes to oppose the order sought may, within three months of receipt of the copy, file a counter-statement in duplicate setting out fully the grounds of his opposition.

(4) The comptroller shall as appropriate send a copy of any counter-statement to—

(*a*) each co-proprietor who is party to the reference;

(*b*) any non-consenting co-proprietor; and

(*c*) any alleged third party.

(5) Any person who receives a copy of the counter-statement may, within three months of its receipt, file evidence in support of this case and shall send a copy of the evidence so filed to each of the other parties listed in paragraph (4) above.

(6) Any person who receives a copy of the evidence filed under paragraph (5) above may, within three months of its receipt, or, if no such evidence is filed, within three months of the expiration of the period within which it might have been filed, file evidence in support of his case and shall send a copy of the evidence so filed to each of the other parties listed in paragraph (4) above.

(7) Any person entitled to receive a copy of the evidence filed under paragraph (6) above may, within three months of its receipt, file further evidence confined to matters strictly in reply and shall as appropriate send a copy of the evidence so filed to the parties listed in paragraph (4) above.

(8) No further evidence shall be filed by either party except by leave or direction of the comptroller.

(9) The comptroller may give such directions as he may think fit with regard to the subsequent procedure.

Orders under section 8 or 12

8.04   **9.**—(1) Where an order is made under section 8 or section 12 that an application for a patent shall proceed in the name of one or more persons none of whom was an original applicant, the comptroller shall notify all original applicants and their licensees of whom he is aware of the making of the order.

(2) A person notified under paragraph (1) above may make a request under section 11(3) or under that section as applied by section 12(5)—

   (*a*) in the case of a request by the original applicant or any of the original applicants, within two months of being so notified; and

   (*b*) in the case of a request by a licensee, within four months of being so notified.

Prescribed period for new applications under section 8(3) or 12(6)

8.05   **10.** The prescribed period for the purposes of sections 8(3) and 12(6) shall be three months calculated from the day on which the time for appealing from an order made under either of those subsections expires without an appeal being brought or, where an appeal is brought, from the day on which it is finally disposed of.

Note. Rule 26 (reprinted at para. 15.05) and rules 33(3) and (4) and 34 (proviso) (reprinted at paras. 18.02 and 18.03 respectively) are also relevant to applications filed under sections 8(3), 12(6) and 37(4).

Authorisation under section 8(5)

8.06   **11.**—(1) An application under section 8(5) for authority to do anything on behalf of a person to whom directions have been given under section 8(2)(*d*) or (4) shall be made on Patents Form No. 3/77 and shall be accompanied by a copy thereof and a statement in duplicate setting out fully the facts upon which the applicant relies and the nature of the authorisation sought.

(2) The comptroller shall send a copy of the application and statement to the person alleged to have failed to comply with the directions.

(3) The comptroller may give such directions as he may think fit with regard to the subsequent procedure.

COMMENTARY ON SECTION 8

8.07   *General*

Section 8 introduced a new procedure by which any person claiming to have a right in an invention may make application to the Comptroller for him to resolve the matter and make an appropriate order. A claim under section 8 may be made at any time before grant of the patent, and even before the application is filed. A similar claim after grant may be made under section 37. However, an application under section 8 does not delay the prosecution of the application. If, as is often the case, grant of the patent occurs before the section 8 proceedings have been determined, section 9 causes these to be continued under section 37, for which see para. 37.08. Therefore, the present commentary deals mainly only with cases that have actually been decided under section 8, or which have involved some point of interpretation thereof: otherwise for relief under section 8, see para. 37.12.

Entitlement disputes can also be dealt with under section 12 (in respect of foreign, including international, patent applications) and, in preference to section 12, under section 82 (in respect of applications for a European patent).

Section 8 deals with two disparate questions, each of which may be referred to the Comptroller by a person whom it has become customary to call "the referrer". These questions are: (*a*) whether any person is entitled to be granted a patent or to have any right in or under it (subss. (1)(*a*), (2), (3), (5) and (6)) governed by rule 7 (reprinted at para. 8.02 *supra*); and (*b*) whether a right in or under an application of co-proprietors who cannot agree, should be transferred or granted to any other person (subs. (1)(*b*), (4) and (5)) governed by rule 8 (reprinted at para. 8.03 *supra*). The reference is notified to those known, or presumed, to be interested, including the applicant for the patent. It may then be contested by an opposition lodged under rule 7(3) or 8(3) by a person whom it is customary to call an "opponent", even if such be an applicant for the patent.

Question (*b*) arises out of section 36(3) which governs co-ownership of applications as well as of patents by virtue of section 36(7)(*a*). In *Pelling and Campbell's Application* (SRIS O/134/87), the question was raised whether the words "any other person" at the end of section 8(1)(*b*) have the narrow meaning of "any person other than the co-proprietor"; or the wider meaning of "any person other than the transferor or grantor", thereby allowing "the other person" to be a co-proprietor. No finding was made on the point as the dispute was resolved under section 10, see para. 10.04, but the amendment to be made to section 37(1) by the 1988 Act deals with the point for resolution of an objection post-grant. It is surprising that a corresponding amendment is not to be made likewise in sections 8(1) and 12(1) because sections 8(1), 12(1) and 37(1) each originally had closely similar wording.

Section 8 is not concerned directly with the correct declaration of inventorship. This is discussed in the commentary on section 13. Section 10 allows the Comptroller to decide between co-applicants as to how a patent application should be dealt with, and section 11 provides for directions consequent on a decision under section 8 (or 10) to order transfer of a right arising under the application.

There were no provisions in the 1949 Act corresponding to subsection (1)(*a*), but section 17(5) [1949] provided, in similar manner to present section 11, for the resolution of disputes between co-applicants. The general question of entitlement does, however, include that of "obtaining" which was a ground of opposition to grant under section 14(1)(*a*) [1949], and section 53 [1949] provided for a new application to be filed in such circumstances having the priority date of the application found to have been "obtained". A similar provision is retained in present subsection (3). "Obtaining" was also a ground of revocation under section 32(1)(*b*) [1949], see para. A032.08 and remains such under present section 72(1)(*b*), see para. 72.17.

Raising of questions of entitlement   **8.08**

A question of entitlement under section 8 may be referred to the Comptroller by the applicant himself or by any other person who believes himself to be entitled to a patent for the invention. The procedure is described in paras. 8.12–8.14 *infra*. The fact that a reference has been made is entered in the register under rule 44(4) (reprinted in para. 32.04). Proceedings under section 8 or under the other "entitlement" sections 12, 37 and 82), whether commenced by the employer or the employee, afford means for resolving any dispute there may be as to ownership of an invention under section 39, that is in respect of inventions made by persons mainly employed in the United Kingdom (s. 43(2)).

If entitlement is asserted based on some contractual obligation, the principles of contract law must be shown to have satisfied, *i.e.* there must have been an "offer", subsequently "accepted"; there must have been an intention for the parties to the agreement to create a legal relationship *inter se*; and the terms of the agreement made must be tolerably clear and free from ambiguity. Such a contract can be one made orally, but the existence and terms of such will be more difficult to prove. These criteria were held not to have been met in *James Industries' Patent* ([1987] RPC 235).

The onus of proof in section 8 proceedings is on the referrer (*Viziball's Application*, [1988] RPC 213), but see the comment in paras. 7.08 and 39.09 re. *Peart's Patent* (SRIS O/209/87). If there is a conflict of evidence which cannot be resolved, the referrer must fail (*Alsop's Application* SRIS O/120/84 and *Brockhouse's Patent (No. 2)*, SRIS O/100/85). However, conflicts should be tested by discovery of documents (for which see paras. 72.44 and 61.28–61.31 and cross-examination (for which see para. 72.40) (*Norris's Patent*, [1988] RPC 159). In *Amateur Athletic Association's Applications* (SRIS O/53/89) the referrer largely proved his case because of the more complete circuit diagram filed in his own application the following day, whereas the application-in-suit contained only outline details of this essential feature of the invention.

Notice of any reference under section 8 must be given to any person who it appears may be entitled to a share in the invention or any right in or under the patent (subs. (6)). To ensure this a caveat can be lodged by a potential claimant by filing PF 49/77 see para. 118.19.

Under subsection (7) (and likewise under ss. 12(2) and 37(8)) the Comptroller may refuse to deal with a question of entitlement if he considers this should more properly be determined by the court. Subsequent procedure is then governed by RSC Ord. 104, rule 17 (reprinted at para. E104.17) if reference is to the Patents Court, but because of the definition of "court" in section 130(1) reference could be to the relevant court of Scotland, Northern Ireland or the Isle of Man. In essence, if the Comptroller declines to deal with such a question, it is necessary for application to be made to the court, probably within 28 days. In England and Wales, the application will be made to the Patents Court and be made by originating summons seeking determination of the question originally referred to the Comptroller.

A referrer has no power to request the Comptroller to transfer the matter to the court for decision. This is to be decided by the Comptroller of his own motion (*Brockhouse's Patent*, [1985] RPC 332). Here it was decided: that there should be no transfer because inventorship proceedings under section 13 were also involved, and these could not be transferred; and that the availability of Legal Aid before the court, but not before the Comptroller, is not a matter relevant to the question of transfer.

The mere fact that questions of entitlement to a United Kingdom patent are raised is not conclusive as to whether the matter ought to be decided by the Comptroller. In *GAF Corp.* v. *Amchem* ([1975] 1 Lloyds Rep. 601) the Court of Appeal refused to allow an entitlement dispute which involved patent applications in several countries (including the United Kingdom) to be litigated in the English court, holding that the question was one which it would not be appropriate for the English court to decide having regard to the foreign residence of each of the parties, but see *Duijnstee* v. *Goderbauer* ([1985] FSR 221; [1985] 1 CMLR 220).

Any decision of the Comptroller under section 8 is subject to appeal to the Patents Court (s. 97(1)) and thereafter, with leave, to the Court of Appeal whether or not a question of law is involved (s. 97(3)). Proceedings under sections 8, 12 or 37 may also, if more convenient, take place in Scotland, see rule 108 (reprinted in para. 98.02 and discussed in para. 98.07); appeal would then be to the Court of Session (ss. 97(4) and (5)) see para. 97.11.

Nature of the invention to be considered under section 8   **8.09**

Because application under section 8 may be made even when no application for a patent has yet been filed, where there is such an application the form of any claims therein cannot determine the nature of the invention that has to be considered as to entitlement to its origin or ownership. Also, it has been held that prior art not known to the inventor(s) should not be taken into account in assessing entitlement to the invention which each inventor thought he had made and "invention" in the context of at least section 8 does not mean a "patentable invention" (*Viziball's Application*, [1988] RPC 213).

Relief under section 8—General   **8.10**

Under subsection (1) the Comptroller must determine the question referred to him and may make such order as he thinks fit to give effect to the determination. Without prejudice to the generality of this, subsection (2) gives the following specific remedies in relation to a subsisting application:
  (i) refusal of the application (s. 8(2)(c));
  (ii) amendment to exclude the matter in dispute (s. 8(2)(c);
  (iii) transfer of the application to the person or persons making the reference (s. 8(2)(a), (b));
  (iv) inclusion of the person making the reference alongside other applicants, with the exclusion of any specified applicant (s. 8(2)(a));
  (v) directions to grant a licence or other right in or under the application (s. 8(2)(d)).
The referrer may also be permitted to file a new (back-dated) application for the whole or part of the invention, see subsection (3) discussed in para. 8.11 *infra*; or the Comptroller may order a transfer or assignment of any right in the application to any other person (subs. (4)). For example, if the Comptroller decides that there should be a variation in entitlement, he may need to consider whether the rights of the apparently entitled parties are subordinated to one or more employers under the provisions of section 39(1). Thus, in *Inrad's Application* (SRIS O/164/88), where the parties to an entitlement dispute under section 8 were agreed that one of the four named inventors was not such, the Comptroller ordered: PF 7/77 to be endorsed with his decision; a correction slip to be issued for the specification; and publication of the order in the O.J. The proceedings were then adjourned for the remaining inventors to put forward proposals on proprietorship. Meanwhile the application could not be amended or abandoned.

If an order under any of heads (iii)–(v) above is to be made, notice of the reference must be given to any person not party to the reference who is alleged to be entitled to the patent or to have any right in or under it (subs. (6)) unless such notice had been given earlier in the section 8 proceedings. However, no directions are to be given under section 8 which would affect the mutual rights or obligations, or the rights and obligations as such, of trustees or of personal representatives of deceased persons (subs. (8)). Thus it seems that probate disputes should not be resolved under section 8.

However, in addition to the remedies provided by sections 8, 12, 37 and 82 in questions of entitlement, it would also appear possible to seek a declaration from the Comptroller that the referrer has an equitable interest in the application or patent as a result of some constructive trust having arisen, see *Kakkar* v. *Szelke* ([1989] FSR 225; [1989] 4 EPOR 184 (CA)). Also, if a patent application made by a person who is held to have been a wrongful applicant has been allowed to lapse, no order can be made under subsection (2), but a new application can be allowed to be filed under subsection (3), see *Jessamine Holdings' Application* (SRIS O/138/85) and para. 8.11 *infra*; or a declaration can be made under subsection (1), see *Szucs' Application* (SRIS O/4/86): for subsequent proceedings in the *Szucs'* case, see para. 37.11.

When an application is ordered to proceed with any new applicant under subsection (4), section 11 applies, see paras. 11.03–11.05.

When an order is made under subsections (2)(*d*) or (4) for a licence to be granted or an assignment made, subsection (5) applies. If there is non-compliance with such an order, any person in whose favour the order was made may apply to the Comptroller under rule 11 (reprinted at para. 8.06 *supra*) for authority to take the requisite action on behalf of the person ordered, see further at para. 8.13 *infra*.

8.11   —*Filing of new application*

If the original application is refused or amended by exclusion of the matter in dispute, subsection (3) (and similarly ss. 12(6) and 37(4)) allows the person who referred the question to file a new application for the relevant matter. This is accorded the filing date of the original application. No new matter can be added (s. 76(1)) and if such is added the application is now not to proceed until amended, see para. 76.07. Note, however, that any such "replacement" application has to comply with the Act and Rules within 18 months of its actual date of filing; or (if later) within four years and six months from the earliest declared priority date, or if none the filing date of the original application (r. 34 Proviso, reprinted in para. 18.03). Although there is no specific restriction against filing an application under sections 8(3), 12(6) or 37(4) with wider claims based on the same text, it should be noted that, in *X Ltd.'s Application* ([1982] FSR 143), an application with broader claims was held not to comply with section 53 [1949], see also para. 37.10.

Also, if the earlier application did not claim priority, there is no power to permit a replacement application under section 8(3) to claim priority. This has the result that, if the earlier application had prior-published the invention, a replacement application under section 8(3) will not be possible, see *Georgia Pacific's Application* ([1984] RPC 467). However, if the original application is allowed to lapse before determination of proceedings commenced under section 8, a replacement application can nevertheless be permitted (*Jessamine Holdings' Application*, SRIS O/138/85). Also, where a non-entitled application had been abandoned but had served as a priority document for a second application, a referrer has been allowed to file two replacement applications with the second claiming priority from the first (*Amateur Athletic Association's Applications*, SRIS O/53/89), it being here recognised that, while there is no specific power to allow a replacement application to claim priority, such has long been the settled practice with divisional applications with which there is an analogy. Moreover, only in this way could the referrer here be given any effective relief because the first non-entitled application had been filed one day before his own application and such was therefore prior art against him under section 2(3). Similar relief was granted in *Coin Control's Application* (SRIS O/95/89), though in each case with the new applications being limited to that part of the two earlier non-entitled applications which it was held the referrer had invented. Here the fact that the referrer had abandoned his own, later, applications did not affect the right to file replacement applications. For other instances where replacement applications have been allowed to be filed, see *Viziball's Application* ([1988] RPC 213) and *Miller and Law's Application* (SRIS O/46/87).

The applicant of the original application and his licensees, even if acting in good faith, have no rights under such a new application. This is in contrast to the position under section 11 where certain rights may be given in respect of the original application when this proceeds after having been transferred to a new applicant.

PRACTICE UNDER SECTION 8

Raising of questions under subsection (1)   **8.12**

Rule 7 (reprinted at para. 8.02 *supra*) is applicable to proceedings under sections 8(1)(*a*) or 12(1)(*a*) and rule 8 (reprinted at para. 8.03 *supra*) is applicable to proceedings under sections 8(1)(*b*) or 12(1)(*b*). The procedure under each rule is similar. In each case PF 2/77 (reprinted at para. 141.02) is initially filed in duplicate accompanied by a statement of case also in duplicate (rr. 7(1), 8(1)). As regards security for costs by an applicant not resident in the United Kingdom, see para. 107.05. The Comptroller sends a copy of PF 2/77 and the statement to the persons specified in rules 7(2) or 8(2), as the case may be, inviting opposition within three months, a period which is apparently extensible with discretion under section 110(1) (rr. 7(3)). Any opponent files his counterstatement in duplicate (rr. 7(3), 8(3)) and the Comptroller forwards a copy to each of the original recipients of the statement (rr. 7(3), 8(4)), but these documents are not apparently sent to others who may be thought to be affected by the proceedings, such as the inventor: compare rule 14(2)(*c*) (reprinted in para. 13.02) for inventorship disputes. Thereafter the parties file their evidence, in each case sending a copy to any other party to the proceedings (rr. 7(4)(5) and 8(5)–(7)). The persons receiving the counterstatement file their evidence first. Thereafter the opponent files his evidence and the recipients of the counter-statement can each file evidence "strictly in reply". Each period for submission of evidence is three months, which is extensible under the Comptroller's discretion under rule 110(1). This concludes the evidence stages (rr. 7(6) and 8(8)). The subsequent procedure is flexible (rr. 7(7) and 8(9)), but usually follows the general practice for contentious proceedings in the Patent Office, for which see paras. 72.32–72.52.

However, as noted in para. 8.07 *supra*, section 9 has the effect that most cases commenced under section 8 come to be decided under section 37. For Practice under section 37, see paras. 37.14–37.16. A parallel plea for revocation under section 72 may then also be appropriate. For the procedure where the Comptroller decides to refer the matter to the court, see para. 37.16.

Applications made under subsection (1), and the eventual outcome thereof, are now advertised in the Official Journal, see O.J. November 9, 1988 which published a complete back-list of such matters.

Orders made under sections 8 or 12   **8.13**

An order made under sections 8 or 12 that an application is to proceed in the name of someone else who was not the original applicant, the effect of that order and the procedure to be followed, particularly as regards subsequent proceedings, is governed by section 11 are discussed in para. 11.04: rule 9 (reprinted at para. 8.06 *supra*) then applies and a person so notified may make a request under section 11(3) or 12(5), see para. 11.05.

If there is non-compliance with an order under subsections (2)(*d*) or (4), an application for an order for substituted authority to act is made under rule 11(1) (reprinted in para. 8.06 *supra*) on PF 3/77 (reprinted in para. 141.03). PF 3/77 is filed in duplicate with a duplicate statement of case. A copy of PF 3/77 and the statement is sent to the person alleged to have failed to comply (r. 11(2)). Thereafter the procedure is flexible (r. 11(3)), but will usually follow that generally used in contentious proceedings before the Comptroller, for which see paras. 72.32–72.52.

8.14 *Filing of new application under section 8(3), 12(6) or 37(4)*

The procedure for filing a new application under sections 8(3), 12(6) or 37(4) is discussed in para. 15.22, this being generally similar to that for filing a divisional application under section 15(4), for which see paras. 15.13–15.21 and paras. 15.28–15.32. However, PF 1/77 must be filed and the filing fee paid not later than three months after the date of expiry of the term for appeal from the order under sections 8(3), 12(6) or 37(4), or after disposal of such appeal (rr. 10, 57), reprinted respectively at para. 8.05 *supra* and para. 37.05). This period is extensible at the Comptroller's discretion r. 110(1). The requirements of rule 26(1) and (2) (but not r. 26(3)) and of rule 33(3), (4) (reprinted respectively in paras. 15.05 and 18.02) must be complied with, and the application may also be placed in order for acceptance up to 18 months from the actual filing date (proviso to r. 34 reprinted in para. 18.03). The period under rule 26 (insofar as applied to r. 6(1)) is inextensible (r. 110(2)), but the other periods under rule 26 and the periods under rules 33(3), (4) and 34 can each be extended by one month under rule 110(3) by filing PF 50/77, and further on application under rule 110(3A) with discretion exercised under rule 110(3C).

9.01   **SECTION 9**

Determination after grant of questions referred before grant

9. If a question with respect to a patent or application is referred by any person to the comptroller under section 8 above, whether before or after the making of an application for the patent, and is not determined before the time when the application is first in order for a grant of a patent in pursuance of the application, that fact shall not prevent the grant of a patent, but on its grant that person shall be treated as having referred to the comptroller under section 37 below any question mentioned in that section which the comptroller thinks appropriate.

9.02   COMMENTARY ON SECTION 9

Section 9 sets out the procedure to be followed in those cases where a reference is made to the Comptroller under section 8 before a patent is granted, and the matter is not resolved by the time that the patent is granted. The grant of patent is not to be stayed, but thereafter the matter is to be treated as a reference under section 37. This has the effect that the majority of applications under section 8 are eventually resolved in proceedings continued under section 37, see the commentaries thereon and particularly paras. 8.07 and 37.08.

The procedure is different for an application for a European patent (including one designating the United Kingdom), where such a question is referred under section 12 rather than section 8. This is because proceedings in the EPO on an application for a European patent become suspended by virtue of EPCr. 13 until a decision has been given under section 12, though if the section 12 proceedings become protracted the EPO will resume the examination and even process the application to grant. Presumably, thereafter, declaratory relief would still be available.

SECTION 10

10.01

Handling of application by joint applicants

10. If any dispute arises between joint applicants for a patent whether or in what manner the application should be proceeded with, the comptroller may, on a request made by any of the parties, give such directions as he thinks fit for enabling the application to proceed in the name of one or more of the parties alone or for regulating the manner in which it shall be proceeded with, or for both those purposes, according as the case may require.

RELEVANT RULE

10.02

Request by joint application under section 10 or 12(4)

12.—(1) A request under section 10 or section 12(4) by a joint applicant shall be made on Patents Form No. 4/77 and shall be accompanied by a copy thereof and a statement in duplicate setting out fully the facts upon which he relies and the directions which he seeks.

(2) The comptroller shall send a copy of the request and statement to each other joint applicant who shall, if he wishes to oppose the request, within three months of the receipt of such copies, file in duplicate a counter-statement setting out fully the grounds of his opposition; and the comptroller shall send a copy of the counter-statement to the person making the request and to each other joint applicant who is not party to the counter-statement.

(3) The comptroller may give such directions as he may think fit with regard to the subsequent procedure.

COMMENTARY ON SECTION 10

General

10.03

Section 10 relates to the resolution of disputes between joint applicants as to their rights *inter se*. The section is substantially identical to section 17(5) [1949]. Disputes concerning entitlement to the whole of, or a share in, patent rights involving a non-applicant or non-patentee, are to be resolved under one of the "entitlement sections" 8, 12, 37 or 82, see para. 8.07.

It should be noted that any proceedings under section 10 must be terminated within the time limit set by rule 34 under sections 18(4) and 20(1) for compliance

107

with the Act and Rules, for which see para. 18.10. However, analogous proceedings after grant are open under section 37, but the proceedings do not automatically continue thereunder as do, by virtue of section 9, entitlement proceedings commenced under section 8. Disputes concerning inventorship are dealt with under section 13.

Because, by virtue of section 12(4), section 10 applies to disputes between joint applicants for a foreign, European or international application for a patent, the Comptroller is empowered to give directions for regulating the manner in which such application is to proceed.

Section 11 deals with the effects of directions given under section 10.

10.04   *Application of section 10 in practice*

In *Pelling and Campbell's Application* (SRIS O/134/87) the observation was made on behalf of the Comptroller that, under section 10, "the correct approach is for the Comptroller to seek to implement the overall purpose of the Act in the most equitable manner that he can". It was also here stated that the Comptroller will not make a pronouncement upon any alleged contract between applicants unless required to do so as part of his statutory duties. In this case one co-applicant C refused to bear any costs of the application. It was held that, if he wished to be treated as a full co-applicant, he should bear a fair share of the costs involved in obtaining the patent protection under which he seeks to shelter and, if he is not prepared to pay his fair share, he has no good cause to complain if his rights as co-applicant should be restricted. It was held that within three months C should assign his interest to the other co-applicant P and that P should then grant to C a free, non-assignable, non-revocable licence in similar terms to that produced under section 36, but excluding any right for C to grant sub-licences, and that P should agree to assign the application and any patent granted thereon to C in the event that P should relinquish his interest in it.

10.05   Practice under Section 10

The practice under section 10 (and also under s. 12(4)) is governed by rule 12 (reprinted at para. 10.02 *supra*). PF 4/77 (reprinted at para. 141.04) is filed in duplicate with a duplicate statement of case (r. 12(1)). A copy of PF 4/77 and the statement is then sent by the Comptroller to each other joint applicant inviting him to oppose within three months, a period which is extensible in the Comptroller's discretion under rule 110(1). Any opponent must within this period file a counter-statement in duplicate and the Comptroller sends a copy thereof to each other joint applicant (r. 12(2)). Thereafter the procedure is flexible (r. 12(3)), but usually follows that generally used in contentious proceedings before the Comptroller, for which see paras. 72.32–72.52.

Applications under section 10, and their eventual outcome, are now advertised in the O.J., see O.J. November 9, 1988 which published a complete back-list of such matters.

11.01   **SECTION 11**

Effect of transfer of application under section 8 or 10

11.—(1) Where an order is made or directions are given under section 8 or 10 above that an application for a patent shall proceed in the name of one or some of the original applicants (whether or not it is also to proceed in the name of some other person), any licences or other rights in or under the application shall, subject to the provisions of the order and any directions under either of those sections, continue in force and be treated as granted by the persons in whose name the application is to proceed.

(2) Where an order is made or directions are given under section 8 above that an application for a patent shall proceed in the name of one or more persons none of whom was an original applicant (on the ground that the original applicant or applicants was or were not entitled to be granted the patent), any licences or other rights in or under the application shall, subject to the provisions of the order and any directions under that section and subject to subsection (3) below, lapse on the registration of that person or those persons as the applicant or applicants or, where the application has not been published, on the making of the order.

(3) If before registration of a reference under section 8 above resulting in the making of any order mentioned in subsection (2) above—

(a) the original applicant or any of the applicants, acting in good faith, worked the invention in question in the United Kingdom or made effective and serious preparations to do so; or

(b) a licensee of the applicant, acting in good faith, worked the invention in the United Kingdom or made effective and serious preparations to do so;

that or those original applicant or applicants or the licensee shall, on making a request within the prescribed period to the person in whose name the application is to proceed, be entitled to be granted a licence (but not an exclusive licence) to continue working or, as the case may be, to work the invention.

(4) Any such licence shall be granted for a reasonable period and on reasonable terms.

(5) Where an order is made as mentioned in subsection (2) above, the person in whose name the application is to proceed or any person claiming that he is entitled to be granted any such licence may refer to the comptroller the question whether the latter is so entitled and whether any such period is or terms are reasonable, and the comptroller shall determine the question and may, if he considers it appropriate, order the grant of such a licence.

RELEVANT RULE

Referral to the comptroller under section 11(5)

13.—(1) Where, following the making of such an order as is mentioned in section 11(2), a question is referred to the comptroller under subsection (5) of section 11 or that subsection as applied by section 12(5) as to whether any person is entitled to be granted a licence or whether the period or   **11.02**

terms of a licence are reasonable, the reference shall be made on Patents Form No. 5/77 and shall be accompanied by a copy thereof and a statement in duplicate setting out fully the facts upon which the person making the reference relies and the terms of the licence which he is prepared to accept or grant.

(2) The comptroller shall send a copy of the reference and statement to every person in whose name the application is to proceed or, as the case may be, every person claiming to be entitled to be granted a licence, in either case not being the person who makes the reference, and if any recipient does not agree to grant or accept a licence for such period and upon such terms, he shall, within three months of their receipt, file a counter-statement in duplicate setting out fully the grounds of his objection and the comptroller shall send a copy of the counter-statement to the person making the reference.

(3) The comptroller may give such directions as he may think fit with regard to the subsequent procedure.

COMMENTARY ON SECTION 11

11.03 *General*

As a result of the operation of section 8 or 10 or (by virtue of section 12(4) and (5)) of section 12(1), it may occur that an application is transferred to different applicants while the application is still pending and yet there may be in existence at the time of the transfer a licence or mortgage granted by the original applicant; section 11 sets out the rights of the licensee or mortgagee in such circumstances.

The procedure adopted is governed by rules 9 and 13 (reprinted respectively at paras. 8.04 and 11.02 *supra*) and depends on whether or not the new applicants include at least one of the original applicants.

The provisions of section 11 are similar to those of section 38 for orders made after grant on the resolution of a dispute on entitlement under section 37. Rules 58 and 59, applicable under section 38, are analogous to rules 9 and 13 respectively.

11.04 *Effect of transfer of application under section 8 or 10*

If the Comptroller has ordered under section 8 or section 10 that there shall be a change of applicant, and if any of the original applicants remains as such, any licence or other right continues in force, subject to the provision of the order and any directions of the Comptroller (subs. (1)). Alternatively, if the application has been ordered to proceed in the name of a person or persons none of whom was an original applicant, as a result of a determination that none of the original applicants was entitled to be granted a patent, any licence or other right under the application lapses (subs. (2)).

However, in the circumstances of subsection (2), an original applicant or his licensee who, acting in good faith, had worked the invention in the United Kingdom or made serious and effective preparations to do so before the entitlement proceedings commenced is entitled to be granted a non-exclusive licence to continue to work or to work the invention for a reasonable period and on reasonable terms (subss. (3) and (4)). Subsections (3) and (4) are also applied to foreign, European and international applications for a patent by virtue of section 12(5). The terms "good faith" and "serious and effective preparations" also appear in section 28A(4) and 64(1) and are discussed particularly in paras. 28A.04 and 64.06. The term "non-exclusive licence" is defined in section 130(1) by reference to "exclusive licence". It would seem appropriate to construe "reasonable" both in relation to duration and to the terms as connoting an objective test as between willing, but arm's length, parties in the light of usages of the relevant industrial sector.

Result of making order under subsection (2) **11.05**

On the making of an order under subsection (2), the Comptroller notifies all original applicants and their licensees of whom he is aware, and a request for a licence must be made to the new proprietor within two months (four months if the request is by a former licensee) of the date of notification (r. 9). These periods are extensible at the Comptroller's discretion under rule 110(1).

Any dispute following the making of an order under section 11(2) may be referred to the Comptroller (subs. (5)), the procedure being prescribed by rule 13. Any licence granted as a result has effect as if it were a deed executed by all necessary parties, see section 108 and para. 108.02.

PRACTICE UNDER SECTION 11 **11.06**

A dispute to be commenced to the Comptroller under section 11(5) is commenced by filing PF 5/77 (reprinted at para. 141.05) in duplicate with a statement of case in duplicate. This must set out not only the facts relied on but also the terms of the licence which the applicant is prepared to accept or grant (r. 13(1)). The Comptroller sends a copy of the PF 5/77 and statement to each other applicant or prospective licensee, as the case may be, and invites opposition within three months, a period which is extensible at the Comptroller's discretion under rule 110(1). If the draft licence is not accepted and opposition is lodged, a counter-statement must be filed in duplicate within the opposition period and the Comptroller sends a copy of this to the applicant under rule 13 (r. 13(2)). Thereafter the procedure is flexible (r. 13(3)), but is likely to follow that generally used in contentious proceedings before the Comptroller, for which see paras. 72.32–72.52.

SECTION 12 **12.01**

Determination of questions about entitlement to foreign and convention patents, etc.

12.—(1) At any time before a patent is granted for an invention in pursuance of an application made under the law of any country other than the United Kingdom or under any treaty or international convention (whether or not that application has been made)—

> (*a*) any person may refer to the comptroller the question whether he is entitled to be granted (alone or with any other persons) any such patent for that invention or has or would have any right in or under any such patent or an application for such a patent; or
>
> (*b*) any of two or more co-proprietors of an application for such a patent for that invention may so refer the question whether any right in or under the application should be transferred or granted to any other person;

111

and the comptroller shall determine the question so far as he is able to and may make such order as he thinks fit to give effect to the determination.

(2) If it appears to the comptroller on a reference of a question under this section that the question involves matters which would more properly be determined by the Court, he may decline to deal with it and, without prejudice to the court's jurisdiction to determine any such question and make a declaration, or any declaratory jurisdiction of the court in Scotland, the court shall have jurisdiction to do so.

(3) Subsection (1) above, in its application to a European patent and an application for any such patent, shall have effect subject to section 82 below.

(4) Section 10 above, except so much of it as enables the comptroller to regulate the manner in which an application is to proceed, shall apply to disputes between joint applicants for any such patent as is mentioned in subsection (1) above as it applies to joint applicants for a patent under this Act.

(5) Section 11 above shall apply in relation to—

(*a*) any orders made under subsection (1) above and any directions given under section 10 above by virtue of subsection (4) above; and

(*b*) any orders made and directions given by the relevant convention court with respect to a question corresponding to any question which may be determined under subsection (1) above;

as it applies to orders made and directions given apart from this section under section 8 or 10 above.

(6) In the following cases, that is to say—

(*a*) where an application for a European patent (UK) is refused or withdrawn, or the designation of the United Kingdom in the application is withdrawn, after publication of the application but before a question relating to the right to the patent has been referred to the comptroller under subsection (1) above or before proceedings relating to that right have begun before the relevant convention court;

(*b*) where an application has been made for a European patent (UK) and on a reference under subsection (1) above or any such proceedings as are mentioned in paragraph (*a*) above the comptroller, the court or the relevant convention court determines by a final decision (whether before or after publication of the application) that a person other than the applicant has the right to the patent, but that person requests the European Patent Office that the application for the patent should be refused; or

(*c*) where an international application for a patent (UK) is withdrawn, or the designation of the United Kingdom in the application is withdrawn, whether before or after the making of any reference under subsection (1) above but after publication of the application;

the comptroller may order that any person (other than the applicant) appearing to him to be entitled to be granted a patent under this Act may within the prescribed period make an application for such a patent for the whole or part of any matter comprised in the earlier application (subject, however, to section 76 below) and that if the application for a patent under this Act is filed, it shall be treated as having been filed on the date of filing the earlier application.

(7) In this section—

    (*a*) references to a patent and an application for a patent include respectively references to protection in respect of an invention and an application which, in accordance with the law of any country other than the United Kingdom or any treaty or international convention, is equivalent to an application for a patent or for such protection; and

    (*b*) a decision shall be taken to be final for the purposes of this section when the time for appealing from it has expired without an appeal being brought or, where an appeal is brought, when it is finally disposed of.

RELEVANT RULES

        12.02

The rules relevant to section 12 are rules 7–13 reprinted at paras. 8.02–8.06, 10.02 and 11.02 respectively.

COMMENTARY ON SECTION 12

General

        12.03

Section 12 extends the provisions of section 8 from the resolution by the Comptroller of entitlement disputes relating to existing, or prospective, applications under the Act to existing, or prospective, applications filed under a foreign national law or a Treaty or International Convention, including applications claiming priority under the Paris Convention, and applications under the EPC and/or PCT. For this purpose, when section 12 applies, there is an extended meaning to be given to the terms "patent" and "application for patent" (subs. (7)(*a*)), though not so extended as under section 43(4) by virtue of the absence of the word "other" before "protection". Thus, the extension under subsection (7)(*a*) is likely to be confined to utility models and inventor's certificates.

Moreover, since subsection (1) expressly applies to entitlement disputes before any application has been filed, "invention" has to be given the broad meaning referred to in para. 8.09, see *Rawlplug's European Application* (SRIS O/145/88). However, in contrast to proceedings under section 8, there must presumably be some application in existence somewhere to bring section 12 into play, since otherwise the reference to "treaty or international convention" makes little sense. Indeed, perhaps section 12 requires that there already be in existence an application in or for the United Kingdom. Certainly, in practice, proceedings under section 12 are usually combined with proceedings commenced under section 8. As with section 8(1), for which see para. 8.07, it is surprising that section 12(1) likewise is not to be amended to maintain its wording in conformity with that of the corresponding amendment of section 37(1).

While section 11 concerns licences or mortgages following a reference under sections 8 or 10 in respect of a United Kingdom application, section 12 concerns similar circumstances arising in connection with an application filed or to be filed in a country other than the United Kingdom.

Subsection (1) is analogous to section 8(1) and subsection (2) to section 8(7). Disputes between joint applicants under subsection (1)(*b*) are dealt with as under section 10 (subs. (4)). Subsection (5) imports the effects of section 11 and applies these also to any orders made by "the relevant convention court", as defined in section 130(1) and discussed in para. 103.02. Subsection (6) provides that a new application can be allowed to be filed analogously to section 8(3). The commentaries on sections 8, 10 and 11 are, therefore, relevant and are to be applied *mutatis mutandis*, while rules 7–13 (reprinted as indicated in para. 12.02 *supra*) apply as appropriate. A non-United Kingdom resident making a reference under section 12 may be required to give security for costs, see para. 107.05.

However, the jurisdiction with regard to applications for European patents (UK) is subject to section 82 (subs. (3)), and section 12 will not extend to applications for Community patents, for which see the CPC, particularly CPCa. 70(2).

As under section 8, entitlement proceedings can take place in Scotland and can be referred to courts other than the Patents Court, see para. 8.08.

12.04 *Application of section 12 in practice*

The ECJ has held (*Duijnstee* v. *Goderbauer*, [1985] FSR 221; [1985] 1 CMLR 220) that Article 16(4) of Schedule 1 of the Civil Jurisdiction and Judgments Act 1982 (c. 27) (*Exclusive jurisdiction in proceedings concerned with registration or validity of patents, etc.*) has no applicability to questions of entitlement. Thus, within the EEC, only a single court should have jurisdiction in relation to an employer-employee dispute over ownership of corresponding patents in various countries in accordance with the provision of that Act (in force since January 1, 1987).

For proceedings which initially involved an application under section 12 in relation to an international and a European application, see *Kakkar* v. *Szelke* ([1989] FSR 225; [1989] 4 EPOR 184 (CA)). Here section 82(3) required that the proceedings under section 12 had to be struck out as regards the European application once this had become assigned to a Swedish company and, on appeal, that this was so even as regards a claim for a declaration that the applicant would hold the patents on a constructive trust for the referrers, see para. 82.06. The fact that the application also involved an international application does not appear to have been separately argued.

In *Norris's Patent* ([1988] RPC 159) an application under section 12 in respect of an application filed under the PCT was filed jointly with one under section 8 in respect of the corresponding United Kingdom application, subsequently granted. As noted in para. 37.12, the decision under sections 8 and 37 was one of joint entitlement to the patent. However, because no evidence was presented concerning foreign laws or procedures or the status of the foreign applications, no order was made on the section 12 application, though the decision would, presumably, act as a declaration of rights upon which foreign courts or patent offices could take cognizance if they felt this to be appropriate.

In *Rawlplug's European Application* (SRIS O/145/88) it was held that part of the invention claimed had been obtained from the referrer and that the subject matter of the application should be divided. This was achieved by an order to delete specified subject matter from the application, the Comptroller noting that the referrer should then be able (under EPCa. 61 and EPCr. 15) to file its own application for the subject matter, but limited to the matter arising from itself and excluding subject matter arising from the original applicant. In this division of subject matter it was stressed that no prior art had been taken into account. Such was a matter for the substantive examination of the applications.

When the proceedings concern entitlement to a European application, the tribunal must satisfy itself that it has jurisdiction under section 82 to decide the matter, even if the reference is not contested by the proprietor (*Bundy's European Application*, SRIS O/113/88).

New application under subsection (6)   **12.05**

Where the Comptroller decides under subsection (1) that a person other than the applicant is entitled to a patent, that person may file a new application under the Act which is treated as if it had been filed on the date of filing of an earlier application for a European patent (UK) or an international application (UK) that has been withdrawn, or refused, or in which the designation of the United Kingdom has been withdrawn after publication of the application (subs. (6)(*a*)). In the case of an application for a European application (UK), the withdrawal must have occurred before the initiation of entitlement proceedings, or after a final determination (as defined in subs. (7)(*b*)) of entitlement has been made by the Comptroller, court or relevant convention court (as defined in s. 130(1)) and the person entitled has requested the EPO to withdraw the application for a European patent or the designation of the United Kingdom therefrom (subs. (6)(*b*)). Note that, after the initiation of entitlement proceedings, an application for a European patent, or the designation of a country therein, cannot be withdrawn until the entitlement proceedings are concluded (EPCr. 14). A new application may likewise be filed if an international application is withdrawn, or the designation of the United Kingom therein is withdrawn (subs. (6)(*c*)). In the case of subsections (6)(*b*) or (*c*), a new application can be filed whether or not the withdrawn application has been published.

The new application under section 12(6) cannot contain new matter (s. 76(1)) and should be filed within three months from the date when the entitlement was finally disposed of on appeal, or from the last day for lodging an appeal if there was no appeal (r. 10). The commentary on the corresponding section 8(3), for which see para. 8.11, applies likewise to a new application under section 12(6), and see also para. 37.11 for the commentary on a new application allowed to be filed under section 37(4) following an entitlement decision given post-grant. The practice on the filing of any such new application is discussed in para. 8.14 and the other paragraphs referred to therein.

PRACTICE UNDER SECTION 12   **12.06**

Applications under subsections (1) and (4), and their eventual outcome, are now advertised in the O.J., see O.J. November 9, 1988 which published a complete back-list of such matters.

While proceedings under section 12 are pending on an application for a European patent, the EPO is required to stay their examination of the application, see EPCr. 13. However, the EPO may withdraw such stay if the section 12 proceedings become too prolonged, see *EPO Decision T* 146/82, "*Suspension of proceedings/ TAG*" (OJEPO 9/1985, 267).

SECTION 13   **13.01**

Mention of inventor

13.—(1) The inventor or joint inventors of an invention shall have a right to be mentioned as such in any patent granted for the invention and shall also have a right to be so mentioned if possible in any published application for a patent for the invention and, if not so mentioned, a right to be so mentioned in accordance with rules in a prescribed document.

(2) Unless he has already given the Patent Office the information hereinafter mentioned, an applicant for a patent shall within the prescribed period file with the Patent Office a statement—

(*a*) identifying the person or persons whom he believes to be the inventor or inventors; and

(*b*) where the applicant is not the sole inventor or the applicants are not the joint inventors, indicating the derivation of his or their right to be granted the patent;

and, if he fails to do so, the application shall be taken to be withdrawn.

(3) Where a person has been mentioned as sole or joint inventor in pursuance of this section, any other person who alleges that the former ought not to have been so mentioned may at any time apply to the comptroller for a certificate to that effect, and the comptroller may issue such a certificate; and if he does so, he shall accordingly rectify any undistributed copies of the patent and of any documents prescribed for the purposes of subsection (1) above.

Relevant Rules

Mention of inventor under section 13

13.02   **14.**—(1) An application to the comptroller under section 13(1) or (3) by any person who alleges—

(*a*) that he ought to have been mentioned as the inventor or joint inventor of an invention in any patent granted or published application for a patent for the invention; or

(*b*) that any person mentioned as sole or joint inventor in any patent granted or published application for the invention ought not to have been so mentioned,

shall be made on Patents Form No. 6/77 and shall be accompanied by a copy thereof and a statement in duplicate setting out fully the facts relied upon.

(2) The comptroller shall send a copy of an application and statement under section 13(2) to—

(*a*) every person registered as proprietor of, or applicant for, the patent (other than the applicant under section 13 himself);

(*b*) every person who has been identified in the patent application or a statement filed under section 13(2)(*a*) as being, or being believed to be, the inventor or joint inventor of the invention; and

(*c*) every other person whose interests the comptroller considers may be affected by the application.

(3) Any recipient of such a copy of an application and statement who wishes to oppose the application shall, within three months of its receipt,

file a counter-statement in duplicate setting out fully the grounds of his objection and the comptroller shall send a copy of the counter-statement to each of the persons described in this rule other than any person who is party to the counter-statement.

(4) The comptroller may give such directions as he may think fit with regard to the subsequent procedure.

(5) The document prescribed for the purposes of section 13(1) shall be an addendum or erratum slip.

Note. In sub-rule (2) the first reference to section 13(2) is wrong: it should have referred instead to "*this* application and statement".

Procedure where the applicant is not the inventor or sole inventor

15.—(1) Subject to the provisions of rules 26, 81(3), 82(3) and 85(3)(*a*)   **13.03**
below, if the applicant or applicants are not the inventor or inventors, a statement under section 13(2) identifying the inventor or inventors and, where required by section 13(2)(*b*), the derivation of the right of the applicant or applicants to be granted the patent shall be made on Patents Form No. 7/77, within the period of sixteen months after the declared priority date or, where there is no declared priority date, the date of filing the application.

(2) Where the applicant is not the sole inventor or the applicants are not the joint inventors of the invention the subject of the application and the application does not contain a declared priority date which relates to an earlier relevant application as defined in section 5(5)(*b*), a sufficient number of copies of Patents Form No. 7/77 shall be filed by the applicant or applicants within the said period to enable the comptroller to send one to each inventor who is not one of the applicants.

(3) Where the application is an application for a European patent (UK) which by virtue of section 81 is to be treated as an application for a patent under the Act, the requirements of paragraphs (1) and (2) above shall be treated as having been complied with to the extent that the requirements of rule 17 of the Implementing Regulations to the European Patent Convention have been fulfilled.

(4) Where the application is an international application for a patent (UK) which is to be treated as an application for a patent under the Act, the requirements of paragraphs (1) and (2) above shall be treated as having been complied with if the provisions of rules 4.1(*a*)(v) and 4.6 of the Regulations made under the Patent Co-operation Treaty have been complied with, whether or not there is any requirement that they have been complied with.

Notes. 1. Rule 15(4) was amended by the Patents (Amendment No. 2) Rules 1985 (S.I. 1985 No. 1166, r. 4).
2. For the revision of this rule consequent upon amendment of rule 85, to be made when the remainder of Sched. 5 [1988] is brought into effect, see the latest Supplement to this Work *re.* this para.

COMMENTARY ON SECTION 13

13.04 *General*

Section 13 concerns the right of an inventor to be named as such in the patent and to this extent is similar to section 16 [1949], though the wording is wholly different. Further, section 13 provides that the inventor shall have the right to be mentioned if possible in a published application or in a prescribed document. In this regard rule 44(2)(*b*) (reprinted in para. 32.17) provides for entry of declared inventorship in the register. For discussion of rule 44, see para. 32.17. Inventorship alone, without "entitlement" (for which see para. 7.05), for inventors who are not also employees, gives no right to an invention, other than the right to be named as inventor under section 13. Employee-inventors who are not entitled to the rights in their inventions have other rights in the circumstances set out in sections 40–43, see the commentaries on these sections. Entitlement to patent rights needs to be derived in some way from an inventor, see section 7(2), discussed in para. 7.05.

The definition of "inventor" is discussed in para. 7.07 in the light of cases mainly decided under the common law. Cases involving the application of section 39 (*Ownership of inventions made by employee inventors*) are also relevant, see paras. 39.09–39.13.

Section 13 is also a section where the meaning of "invention" is open to some doubt. This meaning is discussed in para. 1.06 and in para. 1.07 in the context of a "patentable invention", but until grant has occurred the term appears to relate to the concepts which persons are seen to have discovered irrespective of the novelty and inventiveness thereof, see para. 8.09. Where one inventor is wholly responsible for the full disclosure no difficulty is likely to arise, but where two or more inventors are concerned it appears that an application for mention as the, or an, inventor can be made in respect of a claim in any application or patent. Also, if the claims include an "omnibus" claim of the usual form, it is thought that the application for mention as a co-inventor may relate to subject matter described in the application, even though not otherwise specifically claimed.

13.05 *Declaration of inventorship (PF 7/77)*

Where the inventor is the applicant, or all the inventors with no other person are the applicants, the fact of inventorship is declared on the request (PF 1/77, reprinted at para. 141.01, see section IV and Note 3 therein). Where there is an inventor who is not an applicant, or an applicant who is not an inventor, a separate declaration of inventorship must normally be filed on PF 7/77 (reprinted at para. 141.07), see also rule 15 (reprinted at para. 13.03 *supra*), which is made under the authority of s. 123(2)(*i*)). The applicant must also state on PF 7/77 how he derives his right to be granted the patent (subs. (2)(*b*)), for example by assignment or operation of law. In the case of an application which does not claim priority under the International Convention (or equivalent provisions under the EPC or PCT) and which requires PF 7/77 to be filed, this form must be filed in a sufficient number of extra copies for the Comptroller to send one to each of the named inventors who is not also an applicant (r. 15(2)).

13.06 *Time for filing PF 7/77*

PF 7/77 must normally be filed within 16 months of the "declared priority date" (as defined in r. 2, reprinted at para. 123.04), or (where priority has not been claimed) within 16 months of the filing date of the application. It is thus possible to file an application to serve as a priority document without, at that stage, naming any inventor. The filing of a divisional application under section 15(4), or of a new or "replacement" application under sections 8(3), 12(6) or 37(4) after the end of the 16-month period, must be accompanied by PF 7/77 if such is required (r. 26, reprinted at para. 15.05). The 16-month period for complying with rule 15(1), or with rule 26(1), by the filing of PF 7/77 may be extended as of right by up to one month by filing PF 50/77 (r. 110(3)) and further on application under rule 110(3A) at the discretion of the Comptroller exercised under rule 110(3C), for which see para. 123.33. For the time limits for filing PF 7/77 in the case of a European application converted under section 81, and in the case of an international application, see para. 13.07 *infra*.

If PF 7/77 is not timely filed, the application is deemed to be withdrawn (subs. (2)). Failure to file PF 7/77 is not a "formal requirement" within the terms of section 17(2), see para. 17.07, so that the Patent Office has no obligation to draw attention to its absence and accordingly invite observations or amendment under section 17(3).

Inventor designation in international and European applications (UK) **13.07**

The procedure prescribed by rule 15 for designating inventorship is generally similar to that for a European application under EPCr. 17. Thus it is sufficient for EPCr. 17 to have been complied with in the EPO when a European application (UK) is converted into an application under the Act under section 81(3)(c), see also rule 15(3). However, if a European application (UK) is deemed to have been withdrawn because it has not been received in due time by the EPO, and EPCr. 17 has not been complied with, PF 7/77 will be required when the application is converted under section 81. In these circumstances, PF 7/77 must be filed within an inextensible two months of the request for conversion being made to the Comptroller either by the applicant or by some other patent office of a Member State, see rules 81(3) and 82(3) (reprinted in paras. 81.03 and 81.04 and discussed in para. 81.12). This period is extensible in the same way as indicated in para. 13.06 *supra*.

In an international application (UK), if the inventorship was correctly stated in the request, no declaration of inventorship is required under the Act (original s. 89(1)(c), s. 89B(1)(c), r. 15(4)). In these circumstances (and only in these circumstances) the applicant is not required by subsection (2)(b) to state how he derives his right to be granted the patent, but a question of entitlement can of course still be raised at any time under section 12(1)(a) (original s. 89(6) and s. 89B(4)), but subject to section 82, or under sections 8(1)(a) or 37(1)(a) as appropriate. If the inventors have not been named in the international application, PF 7/77 should be filed when the fee is paid for entering the United Kingdom phase, preferably by the filing of Form NP.1 as well as PF 7/77 (rr. 85(1) and 85(3)(a) reprinted in para. 89A.02 and discussed in para. 89A.28), where reference is made to the extensions of time that may be available for filing PF 7/77 under these rules.

Failure to effect timely filing of PF 7/77 **13.08**

In view of the introduction of rule 110(3A) and (3C), the cases discussed below are now of dubious assistance to applications filed since March 24, 1987, but are given here to illustrate the difficulties that may arise and arguments which failed under the previous form of the Rules.

In *Nippon Piston's Applications* ([1987] RPC 120) three applications were each filed claiming a Japanese priority, but PF 7/77 was only filed in respect of one of the applications: the other two applications were held to be deemed withdrawn under section 13(2). An attempt at correction of the single form filed, so that it would refer to all three applications, failed, partly because it was not clear that the information supplied on that form was sufficient as the assignment referred to thereon was found to have no specific mention of patent rights outside Japan. In this case it was noted that, unlike the position under section 1(2) [1949], the fact that the applicant is also the applicant for the priority application is not of itself sufficient as a statement of the right to make a United Kingdom application.

In *X's Application* (SRIS O/181/86) PF 7/77 was likewise not timely filed. An attempt to rectify this by contending that this form was not required because the missing information had been supplied to the Patent Office in another way failed on the facts. While the inventors' names were on the priority document, this was in the Japanese language and no translation was filed with the application. It was stated that: the Patent Office staff must have the information in a comprehensible form, they not being expected to have linguistic ability; and that, anyway, the inventors for the application might be different from those named in the priority document. Moreover, PF 7/77 must indicate the derivation of the right of the applicant to apply.

13.09 *Failure to file sufficient copies of PF 7/77*

The rules do not provide for the case where an applicant fails to file in due time the requisite number of copies of PF 7/77 to be sent to each non-applicant inventor. Strictly, failure to do this should result in loss of the application. Nevertheless, it is understood that, if PF 7/77 is filed in due time but with an insufficient number of copies, the Patent Office will often prepare the extra copies itself and merely admonish the agent; clearly this is an informal concession upon which reliance should not be placed.

13.10 *Amendment of inventorship entities*

The inventor cannot renounce his title as such under the Act, although in the case of a European patent (UK) a renunciation under EPCr. 18(3) is effective in keeping his name and address off the European register (EPCr. 91(1)(*g*)) and excluding the declaration of inventorship from inspection in the file (EPCr. 93(*c*)).

The Act provides means in subsection (1) for adding the name of an inventor and in subsection (3) for deleting the name of an inventor. The procedure in both instances is governed by rule 14 and is discussed in para. 13.13 *infra*. This procedure is more restrictive in some respects than the corresponding procedure under EPCr. 19. Under rule 14, an application to add a name can only be made by an inventor who seeks to have his name added, and cannot be made by the applicant or proprietor of the patent. Any person, however, may apply for the deletion of the name of an inventor.

The direct result of an application under subsections (1) or (3) is the issue of an addendum or erratum slip for the patent or published application showing the corrected inventorship (r. 14(5)) and (where appropriate) a certificate that a person formerly named as inventor should not have been so named (subs. (3)).

As an alternative to application under section 13 and rule 14, other procedures are available for "correction" of inventorship entities. If the statutory period for filing PF 7/77 has not expired, correction of the inventorship of an application may be made simply by filing a substitute PF 7/77. Otherwise, such correction may be effected under section 117 and rule 91(1) (*Correction of an error of translation or transcription or of clerical error or mistake*) by filing PF 47/77, for which see paras. 117.09, 117.10 and 117.13. It is also thought that such correction should be possible under section 34 and rule 47 (*Correction of error in document filed in connection with entry in the register*) by filing PF 22/77, see, para. 31.32. However, amendment under section 19 does not seem possible since PF 7/77 does not appear to be part of an "application", see section 14(2).

Reasons for proceedings under section 13   **13.11**

Proceedings under section 13 are not directly concerned with entitlement to the patent (for which, see the commentary on s. 8), though they may be used in parallel in which case the applications under the two sections should be heard at the same time (*Brockhouse's Patent*, [1985] RPC 332). Even in the absence of a question of entitlement, however, the possibility of compensation under section 40 gives employees a material reason to seek under section 13 a correct designation of inventorship. Here it may be noted that there is no time limit for making an application under section 13(1) and, if an omitted inventor can establish his claim to such, even many years after grant, he would appear to have an absolute right to be named as such, and then to claim compensation under section 40. This means that full records of inventorship should be maintained thoughout the life of the patent and, indeed, for one year thereafter in view of rule 60(2) (reprinted at para. 40.02).

PRACTICE UNDER SECTION 13

Filing of declaration of inventorship on PF 7/77   **13.12**

Naming the inventor is effected by filing PF 7/77 (reprinted at para. 141.07), which must normally be done within 16 months of the declared priority date or (where priority has not been claimed) the filing date of the application. It is not necessary to give either the full names or the nationality of an inventor, but the surname or family name of each inventor should be underlined, see Note on PF 7/77. This form can be signed by an agent and no signature by the inventor is required. Unless the applcation claims priority from a foreign application (or from an international or European application not designating the UK), PF 7/77 must be filed with a sufficient number of copies for the Comptroller to send one to each inventor who is not an applicant (r. 15(2), reprinted in para. 13.03 *supra*). It is understood that the Patent Office does not forward the copies of PF 7/77 to the inventors until after PF 9/77 has been filed for preliminary examination and search under section 17(1). The correctness of the information *e.g.* as to the name and address of the, or each, inventor in the "boxes" printed on the reverse of PF 7/77 is important because the Comptroller uses these "boxes" directly as address labels and will send a query to the agent if the postal services return a PF 7/77 which apparently bears an incorrect or out-of-date address.

PF 7/77 must indicate the derivation of the applicant's right to be granted the patent. That derivation should be stated in sufficient detail fully to identify the facts. While, in initial practice under the Act, such statements as, for example, "by assignment" (without details or date) or "by operation of law" (in cases where s. 39(1) applies) were accepted ((1979–80) 9 CIPA 34), such no longer satisfy the Comptroller and amplification will be required. Although a mere statement of employment is not sufficient because section 39(1) may not apply, phrases such as "by virtue of a contract of employment", or "by virtue of section 39(1)(*a*)", or "by virtue of section 39(1)(*b*)" will suffice in practice, as will "by virtue of an assignment" from the inventor(s) even without specifying the date or details of the assignment, O.J., November 23, 1983. Since that notice the Patent Office has also decided that an entry on PF 7/77 reading "by virtue of section 7(2)" is also an inadequate statement of the applicant's right to be granted the patent, it being necessary to identify whether the right to apply arises under section 7(2)(*b*) or 7(2)(*c*).

Thus, in *Nippon Piston's Applications* ([1987] RPC 120), two applications were refused for failure to comply with section 13(2)(*b*) because adequate identification of the applicant's right to apply had not been provided. However, in that case it was accepted that the requirement to identify the inventor(s) under section 13(2)(*a*) had been met by supplying a certified copy of the priority document which did name the inventor. Naturally, the applicant must always be in a position to substantiate his right to a patent, and the statement on PF 7/77, should this ever be disputed.

13.13   *Amendment of named inventor(s)*

In an application to add or delete an inventor under subsection (1) or (3) the onus of proof is on the applicant who seeks addition or deletion of an inventorship entity, see *Bond Knittings System's Patent* (SRIS O/125/86 and C/35/88) where an application failed on its facts. Such an application is made on PF 6/77, when the procedure is governed by rule 14 (reprinted at para. 13.02, *supra*). PF 6/77 (reprinted at para. 141.06) is filed in duplicate together with a statement in duplicate setting out fully the facts relied upon (r. 14(1)). The Comptroller sends a copy of the PF 6/77 and statement to all the hitherto identified inventors and to the proprietor (other than to the s. 13 applicant himself) and to any other person whose interests the Comptroller considers may be affected by the application (presumably including anyone who has filed a caveat for this purpose under rule 92(1)(*h*) (r. 14(2)). Opposition can be filed under rule 14(3) within three months, a period which can be extended by discretion under rule 110(1). Such an extension was granted in *Brockhouse's Patent* ([1985] RPC 332). Under rule 14(3) any opponent must within this time file a counter-statement in duplicate, setting out fully the grounds of his objection and the Comptroller sends a copy of this to each other person who received a copy of the PF 6/77 and to the section 13 applicant. Thereafter, the procedure is flexible (r. 14(4)), but will normally follow that generally used for contentious proceedings before the Comptroller, for which see paras. 72.32–72.52.

Applications under section 13, and their eventual outcome, are now advertised in the O.J., see O.J. November 1988, with a complete back-list published O.J. November 16, 1988.

14.01   **SECTION 14**

Making of application

14.—(1) Every application for a patent—
  (*a*) shall be made in the prescribed form and shall be filed at the Patent Office in the prescribed manner; and
  (*b*) shall be accompanied by the fee prescribed for the purposes of this subsection (hereafter in this Act referred to as the filing fee).
(2) Every application for a patent shall contain—
  (*a*) a request for the grant of a patent;
  (*b*) a specification containing a description of the invention, a claim or claims and any drawing referred to in the description or any claim; and
  (*c*) an abstract;
but the foregoing provision shall not prevent an application being initiated by documents complying with section 15(1) below.

(3) The specification of an application shall disclose the invention in a manner which is clear enough and complete enough for the invention to be performed by a person skilled in the art.

[(4) *Without prejudice to subsection (3) above, rules may prescribe the circumstances in which the specification of an application which requires for its performance the use of a micro–organism is to be treated for the purposes of this Act as complying with that subsection.*]

(5) The claim or claims shall—

(*a*) define the matter for which the applicant seeks protection;

(*b*) be clear and concise;

(*c*) be supported by the description; and

(*d*) relate to one invention or to a group of inventions which are so linked as to form a single inventive concept.

(6) Without prejudice to the generality of subsection (5)(*d*) above, rules may provide for treating two or more inventions as being so linked as to form a single inventive concept for the purposes of this Act.

(7) The purpose of the abstract is to give technical information and on publication it shall not form part of the state of the art by virtue of section 2(3) above, and the comptroller may determine whether the abstract adequately fulfils its purpose and, if it does not, may reframe it so that it does.

[(8) *Rules may require a person who has made an application for a patent for an invention which requires for its performance the use of a micro-organism not to impose or maintain in the prescribed circumstances any restrictions on the availability to the public of samples of the micro-organism and the uses to which they may be put, subject, however, to any prescribed exceptions, and rules may provide that in the event of a contravention of any provision included in the rules by virtue of this subsection the specification shall be treated for the purposes of this Act as not disclosing the invention in a manner required by subsection (3) above.*]

(9) An application for a patent may be withdrawn at any time before the patent is granted and any withdrawal of such an application may not be revoked.

Note. Subsections (4) and (8) were prospectively repealed by the 1988 Act (Sched. 8) to be replaced by new section 125A, see para. 125A.01. For the date of bringing these changes into effect, see the latest Supplement to this Work *re.* this para.

RELEVANT RULES

Applications for the grant of patents under sections 14 and 15

16.—(1) A request for the grant of a patent shall be made on Patents **14.02** Form No. 1/77.

(2) The specification contained in an application for a patent made under section 14 shall state the title of the invention and continue with the description and the claim or claims and drawings, if any, in that order.

(3) The title shall be short and indicate the matter to which the invention relates.

(4) The description shall include a list briefly describing the figures in the drawings, if any.

Drawings

14.03   **18.**—(1) Drawings forming part of an application for a patent made under section 14 shall be on sheets the usable surface area of which shall not exceed 26.2 cm by 17 cm. The sheets shall not contain frames round the usable or used surface. The minimum margins shall be as follows—

top	2.5 cm.
left side	2.5 cm.
right side	1.5 cm.
bottom	1.0 cm.

(2) Drawings shall be executed as follows—

(*a*) without colouring in durable, black, sufficiently dense and dark, uniformly thick and well-defined lines and strokes to permit satisfactory reproduction;

(*b*) cross-sections shall be indicated by hatching which does not impede the clear reading of the reference signs and leading lines;

(*c*) the scale of the drawings and the distinctness of their graphical execution shall be such that a photographic reproduction with a linear reduction in size to two-thirds would enable all details to be distinguished without difficulty. If, as an exception, the scale is given on a drawing, it shall be represented graphically;

(*d*) all numbers, letters, and reference signs, appearing on the drawings shall be simple and clear and brackets, circles and inverted commas shall not be used in association with numbers and letters;

(*e*) elements of the same figure shall be in proportion to each other, unless a difference in proportion is indispensable for the clarity of the figure;

(*f*) the height of the numbers and letters shall not be less than 0.32 cm and for the lettering of drawings, the Latin and, where customary, the Greek alphabets shall be used;

(*g*) the same sheet of drawings may contain several figures. Where figures drawn on two or more sheets are intended to form one whole figure, the figures on the several sheets shall be so arranged that the whole figure can be assembled without concealing any part of the partial figures. The different figures shall be arranged without wasting space, clearly separated from one another. The different figures shall be numbered consecutively in arabic numerals, independently of the numbering of the sheets;

(*h*) reference signs not mentioned in the description or claims shall not

124

appear in the drawings, and vice versa. The same features, when denoted by reference signs, shall, throughout the application, be denoted by the same signs;

(*i*) the drawings shall not contain textual matter, except, when required for the understanding of the drawings, a single word or words such as "water", "steam", "open", "closed", "section on AA", and, in the case of electric circuits and block schematic or flow sheet diagrams, a few short catchwords;

(*j*) the sheets of the drawings shall be numbered in accordance with rule 20(10) below.

(3) Flow sheets and diagrams shall be considered to be drawings for the purposes of these Rules.

The abstract

19.—(1) The abstract shall commence with a title for the invention. **14.04**

(2) The abstract shall contain a concise summary of the matter contained in the specification. The summary shall indicate the technical field to which the invention belongs and be drafted in a way which allows a clear understanding of the technical problem to which the invention relates, the gist of the solution to that problem through the invention and the principal use or uses of the invention. Where appropriate, the abstract shall also contain the chemical formula which, among those contained in the specification, best characterises the invention. It shall not contain statements on the alleged merits or value of the invention or on its speculative application.

(3) The abstract shall normally not contain more than 150 words.

(4) If the specification contains any drawings, the applicant shall indicate on Patents Form No. 1/77 the figure or, exceptionally, the figures of the drawings which he suggests should accompany the abstract when published. The comptroller may decide to publish one or more other figures if he considers that they better characterise the invention. Each main feature mentioned in the abstract and illustrated by a drawing shall be followed by the reference sign used in that drawing.

(5) The abstract shall be so drafted that it constitutes an efficient instrument for the purposes of searching in the particular technical field, in particular by making it possible to assess whether there is a need to consult the specification itself.

Size and presentation of documents

20.—(1) All documents other than drawings, making up an application **14.05** for a patent or replacing such documents, shall be in the English language.

(2) The specification, abstract and any replacement sheet thereof shall be filed in duplicate.

(3) All documents referred to in paragraph (1) above, including draw-

ings, shall be so presented as to permit of direct reproduction by photography, electrostatic processes, photo offset and micro-filming, in an unlimited number of copies. All sheets shall be free from cracks, creases and folds. Only one side of the sheet shall be used, except in the case of a request for the grant of a patent.

(4) All such documents and drawings shall be on A4 paper (29.7 cm. × 21 cm.) which shall be pliable, strong, white, smooth, matt and durable. Each sheet (other than drawings) shall be used with its short sides at the top and bottom (upright position).

(5) The request for the grant of a patent and the description, claims, drawings and abstract shall each commence on a new sheet. The sheets shall be connected in such a way that they can easily be turned over, separated and joined together again.

(6) Subject to rule 18(1), the minimum margins shall be as follows:

top	2 cm.
left side	2.5 cm.
right side	2 cm.
bottom	2 cm.

(7) The margins of the documents making up the application and of any replacement documents must be completely blank.

(8) In the application, except in the drawings—

(a) all sheets in the request shall be numbered consecutively; and

(b) all other sheets shall be numbered consecutively as a separate series,

and all such numbering shall be in arabic numerals placed at the top of the sheet, in the middle, but not in the top margin.

(9) [Revoked].

(10) All sheets of drawings contained in the application shall be numbered consecutively as a separate series. Such numbering shall be in arabic numerals placed at the top of the sheet, in the middle, but not in the top margin.

(11) Every document (other than drawings) referred to in paragraph (1) above shall be typed or printed in a dark, indelible colour in at least $1\frac{1}{2}$ line spacing and in characters of which the capital letters are not less than 0.21 cm high: Provided that Patents Form No. 1/77 may be completed in writing, and that graphic symbols and characters and chemical and mathematical formulae may be written or drawn, in a dark indelible colour.

(12) The request for the grant of a patent, the description, the claims and the abstract shall not contain drawings. The description, the claims and the abstract may contain chemical or mathematical formulae. The description and the abstract may contain tables. The claims may contain tables only if their subject-matter makes the use of tables desirable.

(13) In all documents referred to in paragraph (1) above, including drawings, units of weight and measures shall be expressed in terms of the metric

system. If a different system is used they shall also be expressed in terms of the metric system. Temperatures shall be expressed in degrees Celsius. For the other physical values, the units recognised in international practice shall be used, for mathematical formulae the symbols in general use, and for chemical formulae the symbols, atomic weights and molecular formulae in general use shall be employed. In general, use should be made of technical terms, signs and symbols generally accepted in the field in question.

(14) If a formula or symbol is used in the specification a copy thereof, prepared in the same manner as drawings, shall be furnished if the comptroller so directs.

(15) The terminology and the signs shall be consistent throughout the application.

(16) All documents referred to in paragraph (1) above, including drawings, shall be reasonably free from deletions and other alterations, overwritings and interlineations and shall, in any event, be legible.

Note. From June 1982 to March 1987 rule 20(9) required each fifth line of the specification to be numbered. This paragraph was revoked by the Patents (Amendment) Rules 1987 (S.I. 1987 No. 288, r. 1(4)). These Rules (r. 8) also deleted from rule 20(16) the words "free from" from before "other alterations. . . . "

Claims in different categories

22. Without prejudice to the generality of section 14(5)(*d*), an appli-   **14.06**
cation for a patent which includes—
   (*a*) in addition to an independent claim for a product, an independent
       claim for a process specially adapted for the manufacture of the product, and an independent claim for a use of the product; or
   (*b*) in addition to an independent claim for a process, an independent
       claim for an apparatus or means specifically designed for carrying
       out the process; or
   (*c*) in addition to an independent claim for a product, an independent
       claim for a process specially adapted for the manufacture of the product, and an independent claim for an apparatus or means specifically designed for carrying out the process,
shall be treated as relating to a group of inventions which are so linked as to form a single inventive concept.

ARTICLES   **14.07**

C. H. Greenstreet, "Alloy Patents", Trans. Chart. Inst., LXXVII (1958–59), C.119 and LXXVIII (1959–60), B.57;
H. I. Downes, "Novel chemical substances", Trans. Chart. Inst., LXXXVI (1967–68), C.11 and B.27;
P. R. B. Lawrence, "Chemical patents", (1972–73) 2 CIPA 385;
P. W. Grubb, "Omnibus claims", (1974–75) 4 CIPA 3;
B. Fisher, "Reference to co-pending patent applications", (1979–80) 9 CIPA 319;

R. S. Crespi, "Biotechnology and Patents", [1981] EIPR 134;
J. C. H. Ellis, "The Pedant's Revolt", (1982–83) 12 CIPA 2, see also (1982–83) 12 CIPA 116;
R. S. Crespi, "Biotechnology and patents: Outstanding issues", [1983] EIPR 201;
R. S. Crespi, "Biotechnology patents: A case of special pleading", [1985] EIPR 190:
P. Ford, "Functional claims", (1985) 16 IIC 325 and 358.

COMMENTARY ON SECTION 14

14.08 *General*

Section 14 lays down requirements as to the contents of a patent application; the minimum requirements to establish a filing date are prescribed by section 15(1). In section 14: subsections (1) and (2) provide for the form and contents of the documents making up an application; subsection (3) specifies the sufficiency requirements for a specification; subsection (5) specifies the requirements for the claims; subsection (6) provides for unity of invention; subsection (7) refers to the required abstract; and subsection (9) refers to withdrawal of an application. Repealed subsections (4) and (8) stipulated special requirements for the sufficiency of a specification in the case of inventions involving the use of micro-organisms. This subject is now dealt with in section 125A and rules made thereunder, see the commentary under section 125A.

Section 14 corresponds to EPCaa. 75(1), 78(1), (2)(part) and (3) and 82–85. The relevant EPC rules are EPCrr. 24, 26–33, 35, 36 and 47. Similar provisions can be found in PCTaa. 3–7 and 10 and PCTrr. 3–8, 10, 11, 13 and 32. Section 130(7) states that subsections (3) (*Adequate disclosure of the specification*), (5) (*Content of the claims*), and (6) (*Unity of invention*) are intended to have the same effect as the corresponding provision of EPC (*i.e.* EPCaa. 83, 84 and 82) or PCT (*i.e.* PCTaa. 5, 6 and PCTr. 13.1).

There is no provision in the Act for the grant of patents of addition as there was under former patent statutes, see section 26 [1949]. Entitlement to obtain a patent is discussed at paras. 7.05–7.08. Time limits for filing documents are discussed at paras. 17.13–17.15, and extensions of time limits under rule 110 are discussed in paras. 123.30–123.38.

14.09 *Filing of application (subss. (1) and (2))*

An application must be made in the prescribed manner (subs. (1)(*a*) introducing r. 16) and be accompanied by the filing fee (subs. (1)(*b*)). The "filing fee" is the fee prescribed for the purposes of section 14 (s. 130(1)), for which see paras. 123.05 and 144.01. Until the filing fee has been paid, a date of filing cannot be accorded (s. 15(1)(*d*)).

Subsection (2) specifies that an application for a patent shall contain: (*a*) a request for the grant of a patent (referred to in the rules as "the request"), (*b*) a specification, and (*c*) an abstract.

Rule 16 (reprinted at para. 14.02 *supra*) requires that the request in an application be made on PF 1/77 and that the specification must include: a short title; description; claims (which may be filed later, ss. 15(5)(*a*) and 25(1)); drawings (if any); and a list of drawings. However, it is not necessary to meet all of these requirements in order to establish a filing date under section 15, see paras. 15.06–15.08.

The Request (subs. (2)(a))

—General **14.10**

The request on PF 1/77 (reprinted at para. 141.01) calls for insertion of the title; name and address of each applicant, together with country (and, if relevant, state) of incorporation of the applicant when the latter is not a natural person; a statement relating to inventorship; name of appointed agent; address for service; declaration of priority; and details of any earlier application whose filing date is claimed under sections 8, 12, 15 or 37. Further, there is a check list and space for a suggestion for a figure of the drawings to accompany the abstract. PF 1/77 also requires signature by the applicant or his appointed agent.

PF 1/77 carries Notes concerning the completion of the form and its disposal. Since the Notes are included in Schedule 2 to the Rules, it would appear that PF 1/77 must be completed in accordance with these Notes unless the Comptroller consents to any modification (r. 4, reprinted at para. 123.06). The statement of inventorship should be included in the request if the applicant and the inventor are identical: otherwise a separate statement of inventorship on PF 7/77 (reprinted at para. 141.07) must be filed with a sufficient number of copies thereof for one copy to be sent to each non-applicant inventor unless the application claims a declared priority date from an earlier application (r. 15(2), reprinted at para. 13.03), see paras. 13.05–13.09.

Rule 90 (reprinted at para. 115.03, and discussed at paras. 102.21–102.22) does not require the filing of a written authorisation when any action is taken for the first time. Naming the appointed agent on the form commencing that action is sufficient and the address of the agent is then taken as the address for service, as required to be supplied by rule 30 (reprinted at para. 32.03 and discussed in para. 32.16). However, each form now carries a note drawing attention not only to rule 90 but also to rule 106 (*Directions as to furnishing of documents*, reprinted at para. 72.08 and discussed in para. 72.44) under which proof of authorisation can be required to be provided *ex post facto*. However, when an agent is newly appointed during the course of existing proceedings, a declaration of authorisation on PF 51/77 must be filed by the new agent. This should be filed, in duplicate, "on or before" the first occasion on which the newly appointed person acts as agent, but in practice a failure to do so will often result merely in a call for it from the Patent Office, see para. 102.22. Personal signature of the request by the applicant or authorised agent is not required, in contrast to practice before the EPO, see para. 102.21A.

—Claiming of priority **14.11**

When priority is being claimed under section 5(2), the declaration of priority must be made *at the time of filing the application* (r. 6(1), reprinted in para. 5.02) and provision is made for inclusion of this declaration in the request. The date of filing of the relevant application or of the earliest relevant application identified in such declaration is the "*declared priority date*" for the purposes of the rules, provided that such priority date has not been lost, or abandoned, or withdrawn before completion of preparations for publication (r. 2, reprinted at para. 123.04 and discussed in para. 5.07).

If the application claims an earlier filing date under the provisions of section 15(4) (*Divisional application*) or sections 8(3), 12(6) or 37(4) (*Order of the Comptroller following a dispute about entitlement*), then the number and filing date of the earlier application or patent must be given in section VIII on PF 1/77.

14.12 —*Title of the application*

The title of the application must be brief and indicate the subject of the invention (r. 16(3), reprinted in para. 14.04 *supra*). Failure to comply with rule 16(3), for example by the use of a wholly uninformative title such as "Electrical circuit" or "Chemical compound", could result in refusal of the application for failure to comply with section 14(1)(*a*): note that compliance with rule 16(3) is *not* regarded as a "formal requirement" under rule 31 for which time for compliance must be given under section 17(3), see para. 17.07, but presumably amendment to comply with rule 16(3) is permissible under section 18(3) or 19(1). The Patent Office has indicated that the title should not contain a fancy name, nor the word "patent", nor the abbreviation "etc". The provisions of PCTr. 4.3 and EPCr. 26(2)(*b*) are similar. The title of a specification advertised in the O.J. will, if necessary, be abbreviated to 158 characters (O.J. March 1, 1989).

The specification (subs. (2)(b))

14.13 —*General*

A description of the invention, a claim or claims and any drawing to which the description refers constitute the specification (subs. (2)(*b*)), the description beginning with the title (r. 16(2)). Subsection (2)(*b*) thus contrasts with EPCa. 78(1) and PCTa. 3(2) which do not refer to a specification as such.

The drawings must be filed with the description and as part of the specification. For the effect of missing or late-filed drawings, see section 15(2) and (3A), rule 23 (reprinted at para. 15.02) and para. 15.09. The requirements of subsection (2) are, therefore, not met by supplying the drawings as part of a priority document filed concurrently with the application (*U's Application*, SRIS O/147/84 and *VEB Kombinat Walzlager's Application*, [1987] RPC 405), but see *EPO Decision J 04/85, "Correction of drawings/ETAT FRANÇAIS"* (OJEPO 7/1986, 205; [1986] 6 EPOR 331) for a possible counter-argument.

An application need not contain claims in the specification at its date of filing (s.15(5)(*a*) and r. 25, reprinted at para. 15.04). It has been suggested that there are advantages with regard to the breadth of claims which may be filed in due course, and in the subsequent filing of a divisional application, if no claims are filed initially ((1984–85) 14 CIPA 369). However, failure to file claims initially may create uncertainty over the priority date of an invention which is subsequently claimed, though some assistance may be provided by article 4H of the Paris Convention.

A priority document is not part of the specification as such and, therefore, its contents do *not* form part of the contents of the application as originally filed for the purpose of support for a divisional application or for amendment without contravening section 76(1) or (2), but the priority document may, nevertheless, have evidentiary value, see *EPO Decision T 260/85, "Coaxial connector/AMP"* (OJEPO 4/1989, 105).

The specification must disclose the invention in a manner clear and complete enough for the invention to be performed by a person skilled in the art (subs. (3)). However, in contrast to the former patent statutes, there is now no express requirement that the specification must disclose the best method of performing the invention known to the applicant as was required by section 4(3) [1949]: note also PCTr. 51(*a*)(v), but this remains a most important requirement for patents in the United States and care therefore needs to be taken if the specification is also to be used for an application in that country. The "best method" requirement is discussed more fully in paras. A032.23–A032.26.

By "invention" is meant that which is specified in any claim (s. 125(1)) which is itself to be interpreted in accordance with the Protocol on the Interpretation of EPCa. 69 (s. 125(3)). Accordingly, it is useful to refer to the EPO Guidelines (see, *e.g.* C–II, 4.1, 4.6, 4.9 and 4.10) for guidance as to what matter should be included in the description.

Since the claims themselves form part of the specification, the content of the claims as well as that of any drawings (but not abstract) can apparently be taken into account when determining whether the requirement of subsection (3) has been met, see also *Proctor & Gamble's Application* ([1982] RPC 473).

—The description   **14.14**

The purpose of the description is twofold: first to disclose the invention clearly and completely (subs. (3)); and secondly to provide support for the claims (subs. (5)). The Act itself imposes no further requirements on the content of the description and the Rules merely impose the further requirement that the description shall include a list briefly describing the figures in drawings, if any (r. 16(4), reprinted in para. 14.02 *supra*). No mention is made either of the purpose of any drawings forming part of the specification, but any drawings filed may be used to interpret the claims (s.125(1), discussed in para. 125.11), and presumably may contribute to the fulfillment of the requirements of subsections (3) and (5)(*c*). In contrast to section 4(2) [1949], the Comptroller cannot require drawings to be furnished.

Current practice is to draft the description for patent specifications for the purposes of the Act in the same way as it was drafted under the 1949 Act, in the general belief that the requirements of subsections (3) and (5)(*c*) are not more onerous than those of section 4(3)(*a*) and (4) [1949], see also EPO Guideline C–II, 4.

The description must be preceded by the title (r. 16(2), reprinted in para. 14.02 *supra*) which should be the same as that given on PF 1/77, though the title appearing in the abstract (r. 19(1), reprinted in para. 14.04 *supra*) may be different. The title published in the O.J. under section 118(3)(*b*) and rule 95 is that of the abstract, see para. 14.29 *infra*.

It is usual for the description to begin with a summary or brief statement of the relevant state of the art, with specific references to relevant documents, such as prior patent specifications, where appropriate. If any prior United Kingdom application (or European or international application designating the UK) so quoted was published after the declared priority date of the application in suit so that such publication forms part of the state of the art under section 2(3) and is to be disregarded when considering whether the invention involves an inventive step, it is recommended that the description should draw attention to this fact, or at least to the date of publication of the prior specification (EPO Guideline C–II, 4.4). Following any discussion of the prior art, there may then appear an indication of its disadvantages or shortcomings which are overcome or avoided by the invention as claimed in the broadest claim or claims. The EPO sets great store in the invention being presented as a solution to a problem which faced the inventor, that problem being based on the closest prior art, see para. 3.28.

The specification should avoid disparaging statements, but if they are included they may be omitted by the Comptroller from the specification as published under section 16, see section 16(2) and para. 16.04.

Although not always required by the Comptroller, it is recommended that a statement of invention or "consistory clause" be included in the description in exact agreement with the, or each, independent claim. Such consistory clause helps to provide support for the claim, but it may also be necessary to provide some link or intermediate generalisations between the consistory clause and the particular embodiment or embodiments of the invention subsequently described, unless such link is self-evident. Otherwise the requirements of subsection (5), discussed in paras. 14.21–14.26 *infra*, may not be met.

As discussed more fully in para. 14.26 *infra*, there is no objection to the inclusion in the application of an "omnibus" claim directed to the particular embodiment(s) described, though the EPO does not allow such claims. The Comptroller will require a consistory clause when the description of those embodiments itself includes generalisations. The Patent Office (like the EPO) does not object to the inclusion in the description of a reference to one or more of the claims in order to avoid repetition. If a reference in the description to an identified claim should be objected to, it is thought that this could be replaced by wording conforming to the wording of that claim by way of amendment under sections 19, 27 or 75 without contravening section 76(2) or (3) (as to be amended).

Sufficiency of description (subs. (3))

14.15   *—General*

The description of the preferred embodiment or embodiments, as illustrated in the drawings (if any), must be clear enough and complete enough, taken in conjunction with any generalised description, to enable a person skilled in the art to perform the invention (subs. (3)). Failure to meet this requirement provides a ground for revocation under section 72(1)(*c*), the language of which is the same as that of subsection (3). This contrasts with the 1949 Act wherein the language of the first part of section 32(1)(*h*) [1949] differed from that of section 4(3)(*a*) [1949]. More important is the distinction between section 72(1)(*c*) [1977] and the first part of section 32(1)(*h*) [1949] in that the latter does not require the specification to *enable* a person skilled in the art to perform the invention. Accordingly, the person skilled in the art must have available not only the knowledge and skill, but also the materials to enable him to carry out the invention as claimed.

In *Genentech's Patent* ([1989] RPC 147 (CA)) sufficiency of the description was treated as referable to the claims, so that some claims would be invalid for insufficient description and others not. Statutory basis for this approach can perhaps be found in the definition of an invention in section 125(1), see para. 125.08.

The Patent Office considers that a specification which describes a device which functions contrary to an established natural law cannot satisfy subsection (3) unless it is established either that the law is wrong or that it does not apply to the device in issue (*Paez's Application*, SRIS O/176/83). However, if a claim is directed to the structure of the device without reference to its function, it could perhaps be argued (relying on s. 125(1)) that the specification sufficiently describes the invention if it enables the reader to construct a device falling within the claim.

The description should be clear and straightforward with avoidance of unnecessary technical jargon, but terms recognised in the art in question may be used and little-known terms may also be used, provided that they are adequately defined (EPO Guideline C–II, 4.14). Rule 20(14) requires: that units of weights and measures shall be expressed, at least in the alternative, in the metric system; that temperatures shall be given in degrees Celsius; and that customary mathematical and chemical symbols and formulae may be employed. As regards cross-references to patent applications which are unpublished at the date of filing, see para. 14.38 *infra*.

Where the description contains an opening statement setting out the essential features of the invention, the statement should be consistent with the definition of the invention as contained in the claims. Consequently, where it becomes necessary to restrict the scope of a claim to meet an objection of lack of novelty or of obviousness, it may also be necessary to amend the opening statement. However, where this is necessary, care should be taken to ensure that no matter is added contrary to section 76. Note that it will often be difficult to overcome an objection of insufficient description without adding subject matter contrary to section 76, though an objection under subsection (3) arising through lack of clarity, rather than incompleteness of the description, can perhaps be overcome by amendment without contravening that section.

Under section 16(2) the Comptroller has power to omit disparaging or offensive statements from the specification of a published application, see para. 16.04.

Special provisions apply for sufficiency of a specification for an invention involving an invention which requires for its performance the use of a micro-organism, see section 125A and the commentary thereon.

—Date at which sufficiency of the specification is required   **14.16**

Under the 1949 Act, it is sufficient that the specification discloses the invention clearly enough and completely enough as judged as of its date of publication, see *Illinois Tool Works* v. *Autobars* ([1974] RPC 337 at p. 369) and *Standard Brands' Patent (No. 2)* ([1981] RPC 499 at p. 530). However, under the 1977 Act, sufficiency of the description seems to be required to be met at the date of filing. This is because of the requirements of section 76 that thereafter no new matter can be added to the specification. Also, rule 17(1) (reprinted at para. 125A.02) requires the description of a micro-organism to be sufficient under section 125A at the date of filing. EPO Guideline C–II, 4.10 also assumes that the specification must be sufficient as of its date of filing. In conformity with this view, the Comptroller has held that a specification must at the time of filing put a reader in a position to follow its instructions with confidence that they are what the applicant intended (*Hulmes' Application*, SRIS O/176/86).

—Addressee as a person skilled in the art   **14.17**

Although the phrase "person skilled in the art" was not used in the 1949 Act or in previous Acts, the addressee of the specification has been so described in numerous decisions which are believed to be applicable also to the 1977 Act, and which have followed *Edison and Swan* v. *Holland* ((1889) 6 RPC 243). Such decisions include the cases of *Valensi* v. *British Radio* ([1973] RPC 337 at pp. 375 and 380), *Dual Manufacturing's Patent* ([1977] RPC 189 at p. 194). *Fuji Photo's (Kiritani's) Application* ([1978] RPC 413), *American Cyanamid* v. *Ethicon* ([1979] RPC 215 at p. 261) and *Standard Brands' Patent (No. 2)* ([1981] RPC 499 at p. 531). Thus, it seems that persons skilled in the art are "persons having a reasonably competent knowledge of what was known before on the subject to which his [the proprietor's] patent relates, and having reasonably competent skill in doing what was then known" within the meaning of *Edison* v. *Holland* (*supra* at p. 280). The specification must be construed as it would be understood by a person skilled in the art and, therefore, such a person should give evidence of the alleged insufficiency (*Fichera* v. *Flogates* [1983] FSR 198 and [1984] RPC 257 (CA)). It is irrelevant as to what the proprietor meant by the words he has used in his specification (*Osram Lamp* v. *Pope's Electric Lamp Co.* (1917) 34 RPC 369 at p. 391).

In drafting the specification it is essential to presume that the addressee, *i.e.* the person skilled in the art, is of no more than average knowledge and competence, for which see *Dual Manufacturing's Patent* (*supra*) and *Blendax-Werke's Application* [1980] RPC 491. Also, he must not be required to exercise any invention in carrying out the instructions given in the specification (*Valensi* v. *British Radio*, *supra* at p. 377). However, he may have to perform non-inventive experiments in order to discover how to obtain the desired result, and he may have to exercise individual judgment about the degree of adjustment of a feature (*Fichera* v. *Flogates, supra*), but it has been questioned whether the phrase "person skilled in the art" has the same meaning when applied to the consideration of obviousness, see para. 3.16. Similarly, an application is not insufficient merely because a feature essential for the operation of an invention is not explicitly disclosed (*EPO Decision T* 22/83, "*Surface acoustic wave device/FUJITSU*", [1988] 4 EPOR 234). However, the reader must not add anything of an inventive character (*EPO Decision T* 32/84, "*Redefining an invention . . . /COMMISSARIAT . . .*", OJEPO 1/1986, 9; [1986] 2 EPOR 94) and any required conditions must be apparent (*EPO Decision T* 219/85, "*Inadequate disclosure/HAKOUNE*", OJEPO 11/1986, 376; [1987] 1 EPOR 30), though each example need not be exactly repeatable provided the claimed process reliably leads to the desired product (*EPO Decision T* 281/86, "*Preprothaumatin/ UNILEVER*", OJEPO 6/1989, 202); ([1989] 6 EPOR 313).

The skilled reader may be presumed to have *access* to everything in the state of the art (EPO Guideline C–IV, 9.6) but, it is submitted, not *knowledge* of everything in the state of the art. Thus, specific references should be given to published documents of whose existence the average person skilled in the art cannot be presumed to be aware, the contents of which are deemed to be included in the specification; but, if specific prior art is to be relied upon to provide necessary details for working the invention, reference thereto should be included in the application as filed (*EPO Decision T* 165/88, "*Insufficient disclosure/IBM*", [1989] 3 EPOR 157).

The state of the art in the case of an invention is defined at section 2(2) as comprising all matter made available to the public. Accordingly, it seems that the word "art" as used in the expression "person skilled in the art" is to be construed narrowly, being the subject to which the invention relates, whereas the expression "state of the art" is to be construed as a broad expression meaning all knowledge and information. This view is supported by the reference in section 3 to "part of the state of the art".

The specification may be addressed to several persons skilled in respective arts (*Edison* v. *Holland, supra*; and *Osram* v. *Pope, supra*) or to a body of skilled persons (*American Cyanamid* v. *Ethicon, supra* at p. 245), see also EPO Guideline C–IV, 9.6).

14.18 —*Comparison with requirement of sufficiency under the 1949 Act*

Whilst pre-1977 Act decisions on "sufficiency" may be relevant to the meaning of "person skilled in the art", such decisions will not be generally or wholly applicable to sections 14(3) and 72(1)(c) because the provisions of the latter are in many ways different from those of section 32(1)(h)) [1949]. The applicant is no longer required to describe the best method known to him of performing the invention. However, it should be borne in mind that a sufficient description of some method of carrying the invention into effect is required, and the deliberate suppression of the best method, in order to prevent the invention being easily copied, is likely to lead to insufficiency, see *EPO Decision T* 219/85, "*Inadequate disclosure/HAKOUNE*", *supra.*

It was also often accepted under the 1949 Act that there was an overlap between "insufficiency", "inutility" and "false suggestion", of which the latter two have no obvious counterparts in the 1977 Act. Nevertheless, though the latter two grounds of invalidity under the 1949 Act are not explicitly expressed in the present Act, the Comptroller's decision in *Dukhovskoi's Applications* ([1985] RPC 8) suggests that the concept of "inutility" survives under the 1977 Act. In that decision, claims were rejected under both subsections (3) and (5)(b) when it was admitted, following refusal to permit a correction, that with the specification uncorrected the invention could not be performed as described: the correction was allowed on appeal, see para. 117.06. Also, in *Chinoin's Application* ([1986] RPC 39), a specification having a claim to all strains of a micro-organism genus, of which only one species was specifically described therein, was refused as not complying with subsection (3), see further para. 125A.11 on this case.

"False suggestion" may similarly survive under the 1977 Act as a failure to provide sufficient directions to perform the claimed invention, as was the case under the 1949 Act in *Zakarias' Patent* ([1956] RPC 254) and *Udylite's Application* ([1968] FSR 225). For relevant 1949 Act law, see the commentaries on section 32(1)(*g*) and (*j*) at paras. A032.14–A032.16 and A032.30–A032.33 respectively.

An unusual definition in a specification did not render a description insufficient or unfair under the 1949 Act, nor would it under the 1977 Act. However, the definition must not be lacking in clarity (*Warnant's Application* [1956] RPC 205), see also *Bell Aerospace's Application* ([1969] FSR 21) which serves to emphasise the need to distinguish between the different requirements of "disclosing" the invention (subs. (3)) and "defining" the matter to be protected (subs. (5)).

While an objection of insufficiency under subsection (3) should relate to the description, rather than the wording of the claims, the ground of objection previously available under section 32(1)(*i*) [1949] that the claims are not fairly based on the description is not, in terms, available because the ground for revocation under section 72(1)(*c*) is limited to the requirement of section 14(3) not being satisfied, see *Genentech's Patent* ([1989] RPC 147 (CA)). Nevertheless, it is possible under section 72(1)(*c*), to bring in objections that the claims are wider than the disclosure. This was done in *Genentech's Patent* (*supra*) and, under the 1949 Act, in *Eastman Kodak's Application* ([1970] RPC 548) by saying that the specification did not describe the invention clearly enough and completely enough to enable the invention to be performed. However, before the examiner this type of objection will usually be raised as one of failure to comply with subsection (5)(*c*) because the claim is not supported by the description. Further cases of this type (including the *Genentech* case) are discussed in para. 14.21 *infra*. The EPO has also rejected an application of the perpetual motion type on the basis of such insufficiency of description that "the person of average skill in the art would not be able to fill in the missing details from his own knowledge or following reasonable trial and error (*EPO Decision T 5/86, "Perpetual motion/NEWMAN"* ([1988] 5 EPOR 301). In other words, a broad claim will often require a description of several different embodiments (EPO Guideline C–II, 4.9). When the invention lies in the appreciation of the existence of a problem rather than in the means for solving the problem, the description of one embodiment may be sufficient (EPO Guideline C–II, 4.6).

For further comments on the "sufficiency" of the specification, see the commentary on section 72(1)(*c*) at paras. 72.18–72.24.

The drawings   **14.19**

Rule 18 (reprinted at para. 14.03 *supra*) sets out the requirements to be met by any drawings forming part of the application, the function of which is discussed in para. 14.14 *supra*. While drawings will almost always be useful in mechanical and electrical cases, they increase the risk that a patent application may endanger copyrights and design rights, see *infra*.

—Effect on copyright and design rights   **14.20**

In *Catnic* v. *Hill and Smith* ([1982] RPC 183) the Patents Court decision suggests that the act of filing a patent application implies the surrender of copyright in any drawings in the specification and of some related drawings from which the patent drawings are derived, see also *Rose Plastics* v. *William Beckett* ([1989] FSR 113). This point was left undecided by the Court of Appeal and House of Lords judgments in the *Catnic* case and the law, now to be applied to design rights rather than to copyrights, remains unclear. Courts in other jurisdictions have been reluctant to follow the *Catnic* decision on this point, see *Interlego* v. *Tyco [Hong Kong]* ([1987] FSR 409), and it should be appreciated that in *Catnic* the dimensions of the claimed article were derivable by the addressee so that the decision has been distinguished on this point, see *Gardex* v. *Serota* ([1986] RPC 623). For further discussion on this question, see para. 60.28.

The claims (subs. (5))

14.21   *—General*

The claims define the matter for which the applicant seeks protection (subs. (5)(*a*)), as was required by section 4(3) [1949]. The claims are to be interpreted in accordance with the Protocol to EPCa. 69 (s. 125(3)). For the function of claims, and hence the meaning of subsection (5)(*a*), see para. 125.08. Subsection (5) also requires that the claims be: (*b*) clear and concise; and (*c*) supported by the description; and (*d*) that they conform to the requirement for unity of invention, each discussed below. These latter provisions correspond to section 4(4) [1949].

Objections under section 14(5) can only be raised during the substantive examination so that, after grant, claims may not be held invalid on the former grounds of "ambiguity" and "not fairly based" (as under s.32(1)(*i*) [1949]) because these grounds are not among those listed in section 72(1), see *Genentech's Patent* ([1989] RPC 147 (CA), reversing the Patents Court, [1987] RPC 553). Here the Court of Appeal observed that, since objection under section 14(5) is not available after grant, the Patent Office ought to have clearly in mind during examination the undesirability of allowing claims the object of which was to cover a wide and unexplored field, or where there was no disclosure in the specification coterminous with the monopoly indicated in the claims. It was also observed that objection under section 14(5) could possibly arise if an attempt is made to amend a granted patent, on which see para. 27.13. In the *Genentech* case claims to a pure product ("t-pa") were held invalid by the Patents Court and the Court of Appeal but on different grounds. The existence of t-pa in a natural environment was already known and its synthesis (even though its structure was not yet known) was a desirable objective in view of its known properties, though that synthesis was a difficult one to achieve: the Court of Appeal found the claims to go beyond the specific method used and, therefore, invalid: for lack of inventive step, see para. 3.07; or as being for a mere discovery unpatentable under section 1(2)(*a*), see para. 1.08; or for insufficiency under section 14(3), see paras. 14.18 *supra* and 72.20.

The EPO has also stated that EPCa. 84 (which corresponds to s. 14(5)) is separate from the question of sufficiency under EPCa. 83 (which corresponds to s. 14(3)) and that objection under EPCa. 84 cannot be in issue in opposition proceedings before the EPO, see *EPO Decision T* 49/85, *"Eimeria necatrix/NRDC"* ([1987] 3 EPOR 138) and *EPO Decision T* 23/86, *"Computer controlled switch/NAIMER"* ([1987] 6 EPOR 383). Likewise, in *Smith's Patent* (SRIS O/16/86) the Comptroller stated he had no power to consider an objection under section 14(5)(*c*) during revocation proceedings.

The EPO has further stated that determination of the extent of protection is not a matter for the EPO, statements made by opponents and proprietors merely being noted (*EPO Decision T* 175/84, *"Combination claim/KABELMETAL"*, OJEPO

3/1989, 71; [1989] 4 EPOR 181). This attitude can lead to problems, see para. 125.06.

The Rules are silent as to the form of the claims, so that the so-called "characterising" form of claims and the presence of reference numerals in claims are neither required nor forbidden. "Omnibus" claims, referring back to the description or the drawings, are permitted. "Omnibus" claims are discussed further in para. 14.26 *infra*.

By contrast, the EPO will usually require each independent claim (but not dependant claims) to be divided into a preamble, setting forth the claimed features which are also shown in combination in the most relevant single item of prior art, and a second portion setting forth the novel claimed features, divided by "characterised in that" or "characterised by" (EPCr. 29(1), PCTr. 6.3(b)). The EPO will insist on reference numerals in the claims when they are required for an understanding of the claims (EPCr. 29(7)).

Under most circumstances "omnibus" claims are forbidden by EPCr. 29(6) and PCTr. 6.2(*a*), except possibly if such were "absolutely necessary" to obtain protection (*EPO Decision T* 150/82, *"Claim categories/IFF"*, OJEPO 7/1984, 309).

Likewise, product-by-process claims are only allowable if the product cannot be satisfactorily defined by reference to its composition, structure or some other testable parameter (*EPO Decision T* 150/82, *supra*), and will not be novel unless such products are distinguishable *per se* from products of the prior art (*EPO Decision T* 248/85, *"Radiation processing/BICC"*, OJEPO 8/1986, 261; [1986] 6 EPOR 311), but it is submitted that, under United Kingdom law, novelty can be conferred by a process feature included in a product claim. Further EPO decisions on product-by-process claims include: *EPO Decision T* 219/83, *"Zeolites/BASF"* (OJEPO 7/1986, 211; [1986] 5 EPOR 247); *EPO Decision T* 93/83, *"Ethylene polymers/ MONTEDISON"* ([1987] 3 EPOR 144); and *EPO Decision T* 205/83, *"Vinyl ester/ crotonic acid copolymers/HOECHST"* (OJEPO 12/95, 363; [1986] 2 EPOR 57, also discussed in para. 2.13).

Whilst EPCr. 29(7) indicates that the presence of reference numerals in a claim of a European patent does not limit the scope of the claim, there is no corresponding provision in the Act. In *EPO Decision T* 237/84, *"Reference signs/PHILIPS"* (OJEPO 7/1987, 309; [1987] 5 EPOR 310), the applicant was not permitted to delete reference numerals from the claims, but permission was given to insert a statement in the specification that the reference numerals were not to be regarded as limiting the extent of protection. Doubt was, however, expressed whether this would ever be so, at least in the United Kingdom, in the light of the analysis of the function of such signs given in *Philips Electronics' Patent* ([1987] RPC 244). In this, the Comptroller permitted amendment of a European patent (UK) to delete the reference numerals in the claims and to add a specific omnibus claim, holding (despite an opposition) that neither amendment involved addition of new matter nor claim broadening as the proposed omnibus claim was so worded as not to extend beyond the scope of the main claim of the patent. Also, as the authentic text of the European patent (UK) was English, deletions of the claim translations into French and German were also permitted since such translations served no useful purpose under national United Kingdom law. For further discussion on reference numerals in claims under the Act, see the article by J. C. H. Ellis listed *supra* and that by F. W. R. Leistikow ((1982–83) 12 CIPA 205).

Subsections (3), (5) and (6) are among those which are referred to in section

130(7) as being intended to have the same effect as the corresponding provisions of the EPC and the PCT. The corresponding provisions are contained in EPCaa. 83 and 84; EPCr. 30, PCTaa. 5 and 6 and PCTr. 13.

14.23   *—Types of claims*

Claims can be broadly divided into apparatus (or device) claims, process (or method) claims and product claims. Two or all three of these types of claims may be included in a single application, where appropriate, but see the discussion on "Unity of Invention" at para. 14.27.

An apparatus generally comprises a number of integers co-operating to produce a result. The apparatus may be claimed by specifying the integers, and normally the claim will be unclear unless the inter-relationships between the integers are also given. Where the apparatus is of a known type, it is generally not necessary to specify all the integers (EPO Guideline C–III, 4.4). In such a case, the apparatus may sometimes be claimed by specifying features of its operation. Where the invention resides in a new or modified integer (or integers) in a generally known type of apparatus, the claim may refer to the known type and then refer only to the new or modified integers.

A process may be directed to a single process step or to a series of such steps, not necessarily a process of manufacture, but the process must have industrial applicability (s. 1(1)(*c*)).

When the claim states that apparatus, or a product, or a method, is "for a" purpose, the claim is considered to be limited as to dimensions or as to type so as to be generally suitable for the stated purpose (and possibly for other purposes as well), but *not* limited to apparatus, etc. specifically limited or intended to be useful in, or as used in, such purpose, see *Adhesive Dry Mounting* v. *Trapp* ((1910) 27 RPC 341); *Raleigh* v. *Miller* ((1948) 65 RPC 141 (HL)) and EPO Guideline C–III, 4.8. However, an exception to this rule occurs when claiming an invention of a further medical indication for a known pharmaceutical product by a claim in the now permitted form of "A method of producing a medicament containing X for use in the treatment of Y", see *John Wyeth's and Schering's Applications* ([1985] RPC 545), discussed at para. 2.29.

A product claim is a claim to an article or substance and the invention in such a case may be defined by reference to features of the product or its use and/or features of its manufacture. On the history of claims to chemical products *per se* and the problems which these pose, see the paper by H. I. Downes, and for considerations of obviousness with respect thereto, and the fair basis therefor, see the paper by P. R. B. Lawrence, each listed in para. 14.07 *supra*.

Sometimes there is an overlap between these three types of claims. As noted, an apparatus claim may include limitations relating to its mode (or method) of operation; and a product claim may be in effect a product-by-process claim. A process claim may be limited to the use of a particular apparatus or may consist in the use of a particular article or substance. Note that product-by-process claims are permitted in the United Kingdom, but not normally by the EPO, see para. 14.22.

Special problems arise in claiming computer-related inventions, which may be refused under section 1(2)(*c*), or as not industrially applicable under sections 1(1)(*c*) and (4). These problems are discussed in paras. 1.08–1.11 in relation to *Merrill Lynch's Application* ([1989] RPC 561 (CA)) and *EPO Decision T* 208/84 *"Computer-related invention/VICOM"* (OJEPO 1/1987, 14; [1987] 2 EPOR 74), and see EPO Guidelines C-II, 4.2a and C-IV, 2.2 and 2.3.

—Claims to be clear and concise (subs. (5)(b))   **14.24**

It would seem that the requirement of subsection (5)(*b*), that the claims should be clear and concise, is effectively the same as the requirement of section 4(4) [1949] that they should be clear and succinct. Nevertheless, objections to "prolixity of language" in the claims are now less common and examiners seem to be more ready to allow several independent claims of progressively narrower scope. This is often an advantage to the applicant when he can use simpler language in his narrower claims.

A claim may, in appropriate circumstances, be a "functional" claim in the sense that it defines the invention by reference to the result to be achieved. However, in such a case the claim must mention those features which must be chosen to enable the result to be achieved and the description must explain to a person skilled in the art how to conduct tests (which must be routine and not themselves involve invention, see *Hughes* v. *Ingersoll*, [1977] FSR 406) in order to find out how to achieve the result and to know that the result has been achieved (*No-Fume* v. *Pitchford* (1935) 52 RPC 231.

The EPO appears to have adopted a similar approach, see EPO Guideline C–III, 4.7 and *EPO Decision T* 14/83, *"Vinylchloride resins/SUMITOMO"* (OJEPO 3/1984, 105); *EPO Decision T* 49/85, *"Eimeria necatrix"* ([1987] 3 EPOR 138); *EPO Decision T* 68/85 *"Synergistic herbicides/CIBA-GEIGY"* (OJEPO 6/1987, 228; [1987] 5 EPOR 302); and *EPO Decision T* 139/85, *"Pharmaceutical compositions/EFAMOL"* ([1987] 4 EPOR 229); and *EPO Decision T* 226/85, *"Stable bleaches/UNILEVER"* (OJEPO 9/1988, 336; [1989] 1 EPOR 18). Indeed, the EPO has stated that functional phrasing is proper where features cannot be defined more precisely without restricting the scope of the invention (*EPO Decision T* 292/85, *"Polypeptide expression/Genentech I"*, OJEPO 7/1989, 275; [1989] 1 EPOR 1), where it was held (perhaps in special circumstances): that the invention is sufficiently disclosed if at least one way is indicated to enable the skilled person to practise the invention; and that specific instructions for all component variables within the functional definition are not necessary. However, a claim will be rejected by the EPO under EPCa. 84 if it does not specify all features which are necessary for the technical problem with which that application is concerned to be solved (*EPO Decision T* 283/84, *"Ultra-violet emitters/ROHM"*, [1988] 1 EPOR 16), and though this objection is not available after grant, the question of clarity can have consequences for reproducibility under EPCa. 83 (corresponding to s. 14(3)) (*EPO Decision T* 226/85, *supra*).

Otherwise, the requirements for sufficiency of the functional type of claim are no different from those for other claims (*IBM's Application*, [1970] RPC 533), see also *Nestlé's Application* ([1970] RPC 84). Often the *No-Fume* functional type of claim defines some or all of the features of the claim by use of the phrase "the arrangement being such that".

However, in *Du Pont's (Buege's) Application* ([1984] RPC 17) a claim to a known resin limited by the phrase "for use in" was rejected, in accordance with precedents under the former law, as not clearly defining the invention as required by section 14(5)(*a*) and (*b*), because the phrase was a mere statement of intent. The provisions of sections 2(6) and 4(3) permitting this type of claim were held to apply only as a derogation from the general principle, see para. 2.29 where it is suggested that this decision may need reconsideration in the light of *John Wyeth's and Schering's Applications* ([1986] RPC 545) discussed therein.

In *Chevron Research's Patent* ([1975] FSR 1) the court remarked that "specifications are intended primarily to give practical information" and "should be drafted in such a way that a man skilled in the field in question should be able to understand the meaning of the words used"; and in *Mobil Oil's Application* ([1970] FSR 265) it was held that, although there may be cases (as in *Du Pont's Application*, (1952) 69 RPC 246) in which a chemical specification is insufficient without an example, there are many chemical cases which can be sufficiently described without examples.

A claim may contain a relative or imprecise term if its meaning is clear to the skilled addressee. Thus, in *British Thomson-Houston* v. *Corona* ((1922) 39 RPC 49 (HL)) claims referring to a "filament of large diameter" were upheld; as were claims referring to a "thin and flexible bearing liner" in *Cleveland Graphite* v. *Glacier Metal* ((1950) 67 RPC 149 (HL)). In *General Tire* v. *Firestone* ([1971] RPC 173) the main claim also contained a number of relative and imprecise terms. This first instance judgment (at pp. 229 and 230) is valuable in its exposition of the propriety (in a suitable case) of the use of such terms under English law. That judgment was upheld on appeal ([1972] RPC 457). In *Bugges* v. *Herbon* ([1972] RPC 197) the phrase "quick-breaking or unstable emulsion" was also held to be perfectly clear to the addressee of the specification.

However, it should be remembered that the scope of a claim should be determinable and that the use of vague and ill-defined terms in a claim may cause invalidity. In *Toyama's Application* (SRIS O/125/88) an attempt to overcome an objection under section 2(3) by a disclaimer to matter validly claimed in the cited application and having an earlier priority date was rejected as leaving the claims unclear contrary to section 14(5)(*b*).

Special considerations apply to inventions relating to alloys, the present and continuing practice being that established following the decision in the case of *Mond Nickel's Application* ((1948) 65 RPC 123). Following this decision, it is usual for alloy claims to specify the range of the respective proportions of each of the essential ingredients followed by a reference to incidental constituents and impurities whose ranges do not normally need to be specified, see the paper by C. H. Greenstreet listed in para. 14.07 *supra*.

The EPO has held that a claim to a mixture is not clear if the proportions stipulated for its constituents cannot add up to the requisite total (100 per cent. in the case of percentages) for each composition claimed (*EPO Decision T* 02/80, "*Polyamide Moulding Compositions*", OJEPO 10/1981, 431).

The EPO has also indicated that a claim which incorporates reference to an unpublished document would be objectionable as lacking clarity; however, there is no objection as such to a disclaimer within a claim provided that the claim as a whole is clear and concise (*EPO Decision T* 04/80, "*Bayer/Polyether Polyols*", OJEPO 4/1982, 149). Nevertheless, if a claim contains an exclusionary clause which is indefinite, the claim itself fails to meet the requirements of subsection (5), as also it does if its operative part is unsupported by the body of the specification (*ICI's (Richardson's) Application*, [1981] FSR 609).

A mere disclaimer to "all matter disclosed in" a prior concurrent application to overcome an objection under section 2(3) was refused in *Fruehauf Corp.'s Application* (SRIS O/185/83) as leaving the scope of the claims unclear contrary to section 14(5).

The EPO has allowed a claim to a chemical-type product which was defined by physical parameters (*EPO Decision T* 94/82, "*Gear crimped yarn/ICI*", OJEPO 2/1984, 75): it was, however, important that the parameters chosen were readily capable of being determined by analysis or measurement.

In *L. B. (Plastics)' Application* (SRIS O/90/86) the application contained a claim to "any novel subject matter" contained in the application. It was argued that this prevented an objection under section 76 of broadening the protection claimed, but it was held that the claim failed in this purpose, and that a reader was free with impunity to disregard it.

—Claims to be supported by description (subs. (5)(c)) **14.25**

Subsection (5)(c) requires that the claims be supported by the description. This requirement would seem to be similar to the test of "fair basis" as required under the former law by the second limb of section 32(1)(i) [1949] discussed in paras. A032.27–A032.29, see *Glatt's Application* ([1983] RPC 122). However, an objection under subsection (5)(c) may be one that can only be raised pre-grant, see para. 14.21 *supra*.

The Patent Office view is that classic precedents on the content of the claims are still relevant, although no longer binding except that obviousness must be taken into account. Such precedents include *Esau's Application* ((1932) 49 RPC 85) following which objection is raised against a claim which is speculative in that it embraces fields not yet explored by the applicant. In *Glatt's Application (supra)* it was observed, in rejecting a divisional application for failure to comply with section 14(5)(c), that it is not permissible to select certain features at will from the initial disclosure and otherwise rely on vague and inexplicit passages taken out of context; and that third parties should not have to face monopolies which were neither clearly sought nor founded by the inventor at the date of filing, but which were conceived later and claimed *post hoc*. In dismissing an appeal, the Patents Court held that the literal wording of the proposed claim covered something that was never within the contemplation of the inventor. In similar vein, in *Protoned BV's Application* ([1983] FSR 110), leave was refused pre-grant to change claim wording from "mechanical compression spring" to "mechanical spring," *inter alia*, because the specification would not support a claim broadened in this way. For further cases on the impermissibility of claims in divisional, or other back-dated, applications because of matter having been added thereto over the parent application as filed, see paras. 76.11–76.16.

The abstract is part of the application, but not part of the description. Therefore, it cannot provide support for the claims under subsection (5)(c), but can provide support for a divisional application without contravening section 76 (*Armco's Application*, SRIS O/84/85). By the same reasoning, it should be possible to amend the description by incorporating therein matter from the abstract, and thereby provide support for a claim.

—Omnibus claims **14.26**

"Omnibus" claims referring to the drawings are not forbidden by the Act or the Rules, though this is out of step with the Resolution on the Adjustment of National Patent Law contained in the CPC and the provisions of EPCr. 29(6). Such claims will probably be upheld in the United Kingdom, and even if they are ineffective they do not appear to do any harm. Therefore, it would normally be prudent to include a specific claim of this kind limited to any of the particular embodiments or examples given to illustrate the invention more generally described. However, such claims should be carefully drafted to avoid ambiguity, see the criticism in *Daikin Kogyo's (Shingu's)* Application ([1974] RPC 559 (CA)). Claims of the omnibus type were the only ones held valid and infringed in *Raleigh* v. *Miller* ((1948) 65 RPC 141 (HL)); *Surface Silos* v. *Beal* ([1959] RPC 331 and [1960] RPC 154); and *Rotocrop* v. *Genbourne* ([1982] FSR 241), see also *Deere* v. *McGregor* ([1965] RPC 461) and the article by P. W. Grubb listed in para. 14.07 above.

In *Philips Electronics' Patent* ([1987] R.P.C. 244) amendment of a European patent (U.K.) was permitted by adding an omnibus claim thereto, though this had been carefully worded so as not to extend beyond the scope of the remainder of the claims.

141

14.27 *Unity of invention (subs. (6))*

A plurality of independent claims can be incuded in a single application provided that they are directed to inventions linked to form a single inventive concept (subs. (6)). Rule 22 (reprinted at para. 14.06 *supra*) gives examples of process, apparatus and products which are linked by a single inventive concept, but these examples are not to be taken as exhaustive.

What constitutes a single invention is a question of fact, not law, and is commonly decided by the Comptroller (as he did previously under the 1949 Act) on the basis of practical considerations, including the size of the field of search. In a little-developed field the Comptroller may exercise discretion to allow claims which in a true sense may be said to be for different inventions, see *Celanese's Application* ((1952) 69 RPC 227), confirmed as applying to the present Act in *Nissan Chemical's Application* (SRIS O/42/83). However, where a group of inventions are linked by a common factor, mere novelty of the common factor may not itself avoid objection if the link it provides is obvious.

EPCa. 82 relates to unity of invention and this is considered in EPO Guidelines B–VII, 5 and C–III, 3 and 7. It seems to be important in the EPO whether the claims in question are directed to solutions of the same technical problem, see *EPO Decision W 07/86, "Lithium salts/MUCKTER"* ([1987] 3 EPOR 176) and *EPO Decision W 09/86, "Thromboxane antagonists/NRDC"* (OJEPO 10/87, 459; [1988] 1 EPOR 34) where more restrictive objections made by another PCT international searching authority appear to have been criticised. Thus, in the EPO, claims to a chemical intermediate may be included in a single application together with claims to a final product and with claims to a process for making this final product using such an intermediate (*EPO Decision T 57/82, "Bayer/Copolycarbonates"*, OJEPO 8/1982, 306), but a sufficiently close technical interrelation between the intermediate and final product must be evident (*EPO Decision T 110/82, "Benzyl esters/ Bayer"*, OJEPO 7/1983, 274); and, where the two subject matters are linked to form a general inventive concept, the claims to the intermediates can be of narrower scope (*EPO Decision T 35/87, "Hydroxy-pyrazoles/BASF"*, OJEPO 4/1988, 134). It has been suggested ((1985–86) 15 CIPA 162) that Patent Office examiners may now follow the slightly more liberal EPO practice as shown by *EPO Decision T 57/82, supra*, in view of the Patents Court decision in *John Wyeth's and Schering's Applications* ([1986] RPC 545) discussed in para. 2.29.

Where the Patent Office is of the opinion that there is lack of unity of invention, it is the subject matter of the first claim which forms the basis of the official search, see para. 17.10.

Section 26 expressly provides that objection cannot be raised in any proceeding that the claims of a patent lack unity of invention, see para. 26.03. In any case, such objection would apparently fall outside the scope of section 72(1)(*c*) assuming that this is limited in effect to a failure of the specification to comply with section 14(3).

14.28 *Micro-organisms*

The special requirements for sufficiency of a specification for an invention which requires for its performance the use of a micro-organism (formerly contained in subsections (4) and (8)) have been removed from section 14 and are now contained in new section 125A and are discussed in the commentary on that section.

14.29 *Abstract (subs. (7) and r. 19)*

Subsection (7) sets out the purpose of the abstract required by subsection (2)(*c*) and rule 19 (reprinted at para. 14.04 *supra*) sets out the requirements more explicitly. Subsection (7) specifies that the purpose of the abstract is to give technical information and apparently means that on publication it is not to form part of the state of the art against a later copending application under section 2(3). Rule 19 requires that the abstract should be a brief summary of the technical content of the description written in such a way as to facilitate searching. Reference characters denoting the most significant features shown in any drawing should be included in the abstract (r. 19(4)). Also, the abstract should normally have a maximum of 150 words (r. 19(3)). The abstract does not assist in defining the extent of the invention, see section 125(1).

If the abstract, including its title, is considered by the Comptroller to be unsatisfactory, he can reframe it, see subsection (7). There is no appeal from the Comptroller's decision as to the wording of the abstract (s. 97(1)). If the applicant suggests in the request one figure of the drawing to accompany the abstract, the Comptroller can choose another figure if he thinks it will be more suitable, see also PCTr. 11 and EPCr. 35.

Because it is a requirement that an abstract be filed (s. 15(5)), a failure to file within the prescribed period (for which see para. 15.10) anything which could be regarded as an abstract, *e.g.* merely a title or a totally inadequate form of words, will consequently result in the application being deemed withdrawn (O.J. August 28, 1978).

Although the abstract, reframed by the Comptroller if he wishes (s. 14(7)), is published under section 16 because it forms part of the application (s. 14(2)(*c*)), the abstract is not included in the document which is published under section 24(3) because the latter refers to the specification which does not include the abstract (s. 14(2)(*b*)).

The effect of the abstract on applications under the Act, and of applications for a European patent (UK), have been discussed by M. G. Harman ((1983–84) 13 CIPA 346). Since then, the Comptroller has agreed that the abstract forms part of the application by virtue of section 14(2)(*c*), and that it can be considered for the purposes of section 76 (*Armco's Application*, SRIS O/84/85), but the EPO has decided the opposite, holding that the abstract has only a documentation purpose and therefore that it cannot be used for the purposes of overcoming an objection under EPCa. 123(2) (*EPO Decision T* 246/86, "*Identification system/BULL*", OJEPO 6/1989, 199; [1989] 6 EPOR 344).

Documents and language   **14.30**

The documents making up the application must be in the format prescribed by rules 18 and 20 (reprinted at paras. 14.03 and 14.05 *supra* respectively), using A4 paper. Apart from the request and any statement of inventorship, they must be filed in duplicate; paper of foolscap size (8 inches by 13 inches) is not permissible, nor are large sheets permitted for the drawings. Some further details are mentioned *re* Practice at paras. 14.34–14.36 *infra*.

Rule 20(1)(*a*) requires that all documents, other than drawings, whether making up an application or replacing such documents, shall be in the English language: the requirement is not satisfied if only the replacement documents are in English. Foreign language documents are only acceptable if "accompanied by" a verified translation (r. 113(1), reprinted in para. 123.12). Accordingly, an attempt at filing in a foreign language failed (*Rohde and Schwarz's Application* [1980] RPC 155, the facts of which have been more fully described (1979–80) 9 CIPA 268). However, that case indicates that it may be possible to establish a priority date, as distinct from a filing date, by filing documents in a foreign language. The decision of the Hearing Officer also contains the general statement that the combined effect of sections 17(2) and (3) and rules 31(1) and former rule 20(1)(*a*) (now r. 20(1)) is that the Comptroller must allow a period of time to put the description into conformity with this requirement of the Rules. Presumably, such a statement has equal reference to any failure to meet any of the requirements of rule 20, except perhaps not those regarded as "formal requirements" by the terms of rule 31 (reprinted at para. 17.03 and discussed at para. 17.07).

14.31 *Withdrawal (subs. (9))*

An applicant may withdraw a patent application at any time before grant (subs. (9)). The date of grant for this purpose is the date of the letter to the applicant informing him of the grant of a patent under section 18(4), see para. 24.11. In contrast to practice under the 1949 Act, there is no possibility of reviving or securing restoration of a withdrawn application. In *General Motors' (Longhouse's) Application* ([1981] RPC 41), an attempt at restoration, on the grounds that a letter of withdrawal had been signed by someone other than the authorised agent, failed on a finding that the signatory had acted under an implied authority, see also *Moskovsky Nauchno-Isseldovatesky's Application* (SRIS O/5/88). Nevertheless, it was observed, *obiter*, by the Comptroller in *Tokan Kogyo's Application* ([1985] RPC 244) that, if an application has wrongly been treated by the Patent Office as having been withdrawn, the withdrawal might, and indeed should, be cancelled. This has in fact been done in a few instances, see para. 123.21. Also, if the application is withdrawn after its publication and if a dispute about entitlement to the grant of a patent on the application has been referred to the Comptroller under section 8(1), the Comptroller still has the power under section 8(3)(*c*) to allow a new application to be filed. This procedure contrasts with that under the EPC in which EPCr. 14 forbids withdrawal of an application for a European patent whilst proceedings concerning the entitlement to the grant are pending.

Practice under Section 14

14.31A *General*

In the following paragraphs the initial filing of an application is discussed. Matters which can be dealt with subsequently are discussed in the commentary on section 15, see particularly para. 15.10 (*Times for filing claims and abstract and for paying search fee*), as also is the claiming of priority (see para. 15.23) and the filing and content of divisional applications (see paras. 15.13–15.21 and 15.28 and 15.32).

14.32 *Filing of an application*

The Cashier's Department at the Patent Office prefers that application documents should be presented with the forms on which fees are to be paid at the top. Taking this factor into account, the preferred order of presentation of application documents is as follows:
(1) PF 1/77;
(2) PF 9/77;
(3) PF 10/77;
(4) description;
(5) claims;
(6) abstract;
(7) drawings;
(8) PF 7/77;
(9) priority document(s);

(10) translation(s); and
(11) other documents
((1978–79) 8 CIPA 410 and 509).

The surname or family name of an individual applicant on PF 1/77 (and on the other application form PF 40/77), and of each inventor on PF 7/77, should be underlined. It is not required (as it was formerly) to state the nationality of an applicant or inventor. However, when the applicant is a body corporate, the country and, if relevant, the state of incorporation must be stated below the company name and above the address. Note that, *e.g.* for United States and Australian corporations, the state of incorporation may be different from that given in its address. Space is also provided on PF 1/77 (reprinted at para. 141.01) for insertion of the applicant's ADP number where known.

As regards sections V and VI on PF 1/77 and notes 4 and 5 thereto, the Patent Office has pointed out that, where the authorised agent is employed "in house", the company name of his employer will not form part of the address for service unless it is entered in full in section VI of PF 1/77 (O.J. March 17, 1982).

The name of the Agent and the fact that he is a Chartered (or Registered) Patent Agent ought to be repeated in section VI of PF 1/77 if it is desired to ensure that this information appears on the front page of the printed specification. This is because rule 44(2)(g) specifies only the entering into the register (and hence in practice the inclusion in the printed specification) of the address for service, *i.e.* the data given in section VI, so that there is no guarantee that the data of section V will be entered in the register or published.

When an application is filed, the Patent Office transcribes the bibliographic data recorded on PF 1/77 and then issues a filing certificate identifying the application by a "file number". This is a seven digit figure of which the first two digits indicate the year and the other five digits the sequential number for applications filed in that year. Since the second half of 1988, a check digit has been added after a decimal point. This is determined according to the same algorithm used by the EPO, details of which were published O.J. November 23, 1988.

The agent should check this filing certificate for accuracy and particularly check if all papers intended to be filed with the PF 1/77 were duly filed, and should see that appropriate diary entries have been made for the dates by which other matters have to be dealt with. One difficulty here is the filing of PF 10/77 which is required six months after the publication of the application under section 16(1). However, since this should take place on or shortly after 18 months from the earliest declared priority date (as defined in r. 2, reprinted at para. 123.04), a preliminary diary entry can be made for this 18 month date.

The title   **14.33**

The original title appearing in the abstract may be of practical importance in conveying information to competitors, since it appears in the O.J. and the indexes in the SRIS. It should always be possible to devise a title which is reasonable, but yet does not disclose information which it is desired should not be published before the rest of the specification. Nevertheless, the use of a wholly uninformative title may jeopardise the application, see para. 14.12 *supra*.

Physical requirements

—General   **14.34**

The physical requirements as to the documents forming the application are prescribed by rule 18 (for *Drawings*), rule 19 (for the *Abstract*) and rule 20 (for *Docu-*

ments generally), see paras. 14.03–14.05 *supra*. The requirements are substantially the same (except for the numbers of copies required) as under EPCrr. 32 and 35; and are also the same as under PCTr. 11.

Briefly, all paper must be of international A4 size (r. 20(4)), and rule 20(11) requires that all documents (other than drawings and PF 1/77) referred to in rule 20(1) must be typed or printed in a dark indelible colour. It is understood that a carbon copy will be accepted provided that this can be regarded as "indelible". However, manuscript is unacceptable, except for PF 1/77 and on the drawings, for graphic symbols and characters, and for chemical and mathematical formulae, provided always that these are written in a dark indelible colour.

14.35 *—Form of documents*

The description, claims and abstract must each be filed in duplicate (r. 20(2)) and be typed (or printed) in at least one-and-a-half line spacing with a capital letter size of at least 0.21 centimetres and must each begin on a new sheet (r. 20(5) and (11)). The left-hand margin must be at least 2.5 centimetres and the other three margins must be at least 2.0 centimetres (r. 20(6)). The sheets of the description, the claims and the abstract are to be numbered consecutively in that order (O.J. May 4, 1978), but separately from the request and the drawings, and the sheets must be numbered at the top but below the top margin (r. 20(7)). Since March 1987 it has not been necessary to number every fifth line, as it was after June 1982, see *Note* to para. 14.05 *supra*. The margins must contain no markings whatsoever (r. 20(7)).

Rule 20(16) requires that all documents referred to in rule 20(1) (including drawings) shall be reasonably free from deletions and other alterations, overwritings and interlineations and in any event shall be legible. These requirements are often strictly interpreted in order that printed specifications can be provided by lithographic or electrostatic reproduction of the documents filed by the applicant (r. 20(3)). However, if any of these requirements are not met at the time of filing, the terms of rule 31(1) (reprinted in para. 17.03) make them "formal requirements" and an opportunity of amendment to comply with these requirements must be given, see paras. 17.07 and 17.17.

From April 1988 the "A-specification" has been published by electrostatic reproduction of the text provided by the applicant. For this purpose strict compliance with rule 20 is now required in time for publication of the specification under section 16 (O.J. March 30, 1988). Each application is therefore now examined shortly after filing for compliance with rule 20 and, if necessary, an official letter is issued setting out what is required. Further consequences of this change in the manner of printing the "A-specifications" are that copies of formulae, in accordance with rule 20(14), are no longer required unless specifically requested; and that some specifications were published by the new method after April 1988 with compliance with rule 20 having been waived for expediency (O.J. March 30, 1988). Previously, from 1984, strict compliance with rule 20 had not been required before publication under section 16 ((1983–84) 13 CIPA 355).

Also, pages of new or amended claims must now be self-explanatory and not rely on instructions in a covering letter, and should preferably be headed "Amendments to the claims". Such pages are checked for formal requirements prior to section 16 publication, but their contents are not otherwise examined until the substantive examination under section 18 (O.J. March 30, 1988).

A periodic notice in the O.J. (*e.g.* O.J. April 1, 1987) warns that, if the filed duplicate copy of the specification is indistinct, applicants are at risk that certified copies thereof, produced for claiming priority in other countries, may not there be found acceptable.

There is no prescribed introductory clause to the claims, but the claims should be headed as such in order that they can be quickly identified as purported claims. The EPO has ruled that the claims are not definitively identified by the heading used to introduce them, but by their inherent nature, see *EPO Decision J* 5/87, *"Number of claims incurring fees/PHILLIPS"* (OJEPO 7/1987, 295).

—Form of the drawings   **14.36**

The margin requirements for the drawings are different from those for other documents. The top and left-hand side margins must be at least 2.5 centimetres, the right-hand side margin at least 1.5 centimetres and the bottom margin at least 1.0 centimetres (r. 18(1)). The sheets of the drawings should be numbered with the sheet number and the number of sheets separated by a stroke. The sheet number may be placed towards the right-hand side of the sheet if there is no room in the middle. Figures of the drawings may be placed sideways on the sheet; it is suggested that the top of the figure in such case should be to the left of the sheet for consistency with EPCr. 32(2)(*h*) and PCTr. 11.13(*j*).

The drawings should be on strong paper, although the Patent Office apparently does not object to the use of light board. Electrostatically printed drawings may be accepted when the quality of the printing is exceptionally good.

Rule 18(2)(*i*) prescribes the instances where textual matter is allowed to appear in drawings and a notice (O.J. September 2, 1982) indicates that the use of catchwords in block, schematic or flow sheet diagrams is to be encouraged to avoid constant reference to the description while elucidating the meaning of drawings.

Other requirements with which the drawings must comply are clearly set out in rule 18 (reprinted at para. 14.03 *supra*).

Drawings filed with an application which is subsequently withdrawn may not be used as the formal drawings of another application, though one copy may be transferred as a part of a priority document, see para. 5.20.

—The abstract   **14.37**

The abstract should be headed "Abstract" for identification purposes and should commence with a title for the invention (r. 19(1) reprinted in para. 14.04 *supra*). This title does not need to be the same as that of the description. Although there is little incentive for practitioners to take special care in drafting the abstract (because it may be altered by the Examiner under subs. (7)), a genuine attempt to write a proper abstract must be made or otherwise there is the risk of the application being deemed withdrawn for failure to file an abstract within the prescribed period, see para. 14.29, *supra*. On unsatisfactory abstracts, see O.J. August 23, 1978.

Guidance on the preparation of abstracts is given in "General Guidelines for the Preparation of Abstracts of Patent Documents" published by WIPO and included in the pamphlet *"ICIREPAT Codes and Guidelines"* available from the Classification Section and from the SRIS. An adaptation of these guidelines for the purposes of the PCT has been reproduced in PCT Gazette 05/1978, at pp. 279–281.

Cross-references between applications   **14.38**

As discussed in the article by B. Fisher listed in para. 14.07 *supra*, it is unwise to rely, for sufficiency of disclosure, on the inclusion in the description of any reference to a document which is not available to the public at the time of filing. Such reference would be likely to be construed as not being a disclosure in the specification for the purpose of subsection (3). Any attempt to replace such reference by a reference to a published document or by corresponding description could invite objection either under new section 76(2) during the substantive examination under section 18 or under new section 76(3) if amendment is sought under section 75 during revocation proceedings under section 72.

Nevertheless, it is the practice of the Patent Office not to object to such references when the referenced document is an earlier filed or simultaneously filed application under the Act or under the EPC, provided that such earlier or simultaneously filed application is published no later than the date of publication of the application in suit. In such case, the publication number of the referenced application may be inserted during the substantive examination. In the case of a prior or simultaneously filed application under the Act, the filing number will be inserted by the Office, when the application in suit contains an identifying reference which also appears in the referenced application. Presumably, a reference to an earlier or simultaneously filed international application will be treated similarly to a reference to a European application, but possibly only when the international application was filed at the United Kingdom Patent Office as receiving office. Particular care needs to be taken in the case of specifications bearing mutual cross-references since, unless these have identical declared priority dates, the specification of the first published will necessarily contain a reference to a specification which is not at that time available to the public. Also, simultaneous publication of specifications having the same declared priority date cannot be guaranteed.

Most problems concerning cross-references between related documents can be avoided if a copy of the referenced document is filed with the application so that it becomes contained in the publicly available file of the application/patent from publication of the application under section 16.

14.39   *Withdrawal*

In view of the provisions of subsection (9) that any withdrawal of an application may not be revoked, only a clear and unqualified statement of withdrawal is regarded by the United Kingdom Patent Office as effective in this respect. Statements which fall short of this have no effect and the applications in question are treated as withdrawn or refused only when and if this becomes appropriate in due course. This is similar to practice in the EPO (*EPO Decision J* 11/80, OJEPO 5/1981, 141), though in *EPO Decision J* 06/86, "*Withdrawal/RIKER*" (OJEPO 4/1988, 124) the statement that "Applicant wishes to abandon the application" was held to be unambiguous in the absence of any circumstances suggesting that the statement be qualified. However, in *EPO Decision J* 11/87, "*Abandonment/DORIS*" (OJEPO 10/1988, 367; [1989] 1 EPOR 54, and in *EPO Decision J* 7/87, "*Abandonment/SCHWARZ ITALIA*" (OJEPO 11/1988, 422; [1989] 2 EPOR 91), statements that "the Applicant has decided to abandon" the application were held to be equivocal because it was not clear whether this was a statement of present action or of future intent. *Per contra*, in *EPO Decision J* 15/86, "*Withdrawal of application/AUSONIA*" (OJEPO 11/1988, 417; [1989] 3 EPOR 152), a statement of withdrawal, which contained a request for confirmation, and an enquiry on possible reimbursement of fees, was held to be a firm one.

Thus, if an application does comply with the requirements of the Acts and Rules, in the absence of a categorical statement of withdrawal, it will proceed in due course to grant (O.J. July 30, 1980). Accordingly, when withdrawing an application it would be prudent to request confirmation that the withdrawal is effective, see para. 14.31 *supra*. The Patent Office might follow the EPO practice in recognising a withdrawal before publication, which is stated to be in order to prevent publication, as effective only if publication can in fact be prevented, see para. 16.06.

A letter of withdrawal should normally state clearly whether the right to claim priority from the withdrawn application is being retained or surrendered. Presumably only in the latter case would the Comptroller be prepared to certify that the application was withdrawn or abandoned or refused on a given date without being open to public inspection and be incapable of being revived thereafter so that it has left no rights outstanding, such certificate being provided in order to show that the conditions required by Art. 4(C)4 of the Paris Convention have been met. thereby enabling a later application for the same subject matter to be used to claim priority under that Convention, see O.J. September 19, 1962.

SECTION 15

15.01

Date of filing application

15.—(1) The date of filing an application for a patent shall, subject to the following provisions of this Act, be taken to be the earliest date on which the following conditions are satisfied in relation to the application, that is to say—

(*a*) the documents filed at the Patent Office contain an indication that a patent is sought in pursuance of the application;

(*b*) those documents identify the applicant or applicants for the patent;

(*c*) those documents contain a description of the invention for which a patent is sought (whether or not the description complies with the other provisions of this Act and with any relevant rules); and

(*d*) the applicant pays the filing fee.

(2) If any drawing referred to in any such application is filed later than the date which by virtue of subsection (1) above is to be treated as the date of filing the application, but before the beginning of the preliminary examination of the application under section 17 below, the comptroller shall give the applicant an opportunity of requesting within the prescribed period that the date on which the drawing is filed shall be treated for the purposes of this Act as the date of filing the application, and—

(*a*) if the applicant makes any such request, the date of filing the drawing shall be so treated; but

(*b*) otherwise any reference to the drawing in the application shall be treated as omitted.

(3) If on the preliminary examination of an application under section 17 below it is found that any drawing referred to in the application has not been filed, then—

(*a*) if the drawing is subsequently filed within the prescribed period, the date on which it is filed shall be treated for the purposes of this Act as the date of filing the application; but

(*b*) otherwise any reference to the drawing in the application shall be treated as omitted.

(3A) Nothing in subsection (2) or (3) shall be construed as affecting the power of the comptroller under section 117(1) below to correct errors or mistakes with respect to the filing of drawings.

(4) Where, after an application for a patent has been filed and before the

149

patent is granted, a new application is filed by the original applicant or his successor in title in accordance with rules in respect of any part of the matter contained in the earlier application and the conditions mentioned in subsection (1) above are satisfied in relation to the new application (without the new application contravening section 76 below) the new application shall be treated as having, as its date of filing, the date of filing the earlier application.

(5) An application which has a date of filing by virtue of the foregoing provisions of this section shall be taken to be withdrawn at the end of the relevant prescribed period, unless before that end the applicant—

    (*a*) files at the Patent Office one or more claims for the purposes of the application and also the abstract; and

    (*b*) makes a request for a preliminary examination and search under the following provisions of this Act and pays the search fee.

Note. Subsection (3A) was prospectively added by the 1988 Act (Sched. 5, para. 2(1)), but to apply only to applications filed after its commencement (Sched. 5, para. 2(2)). For this, see the latest Supplement to this Work.

RELEVANT RULES

Late filed drawings

15.02   23. The period prescribed for the purposes of section 15(2) and (3) shall be one month calculated from the date on which the Patent Office sends out notification to the applicant that the drawing has been filed later than the date which is, by virtue of section 15(1), to be treated as the date of filing the application or, as the case may be, that it has not been filed.

New applications under section 15(4)

15.03   24.—(1) A new application which includes a request that it shall be treated as having as its date of filing the date of filing of an earlier application for a patent may be filed in accordance with section 15(4)—

    (*a*) in a case where the new application is filed after the earlier application has been amended in pursuance of section 18(3) so as to comply with the requirements of section 14(5)(*d*), within two months of such amendment; and

    (*b*) in a case which does not fall within sub-paragraph (*a*) above, at any time after filing of the earlier application, provided that where the new application is filed after the first report of the examiner under section 18 has been sent to the applicant—

        (i) if the report is made under section 18(3), the new application shall be filed before the end of the period specified for reply to that report, unless the comptroller agrees otherwise; and

        (ii) if the report is made under section 18(4), the new application

shall be filed within two months of that report being sent to the
applicant,
and in any event, any new application shall be made before the earlier
application has been refused, withdrawn or taken to be withdrawn and
before the expiration of the period prescribed for the purposes of section
20(1).

(2) Where possible, the description and drawings of the earlier application and the new application shall respectively relate only to the matter
for which protection is sought by that application. However, when it is
necessary for an application to describe the matter for which protection is
sought by another application, it shall include a reference by number to
that other application.

Period prescribed under section 15(5)(a) for filing claims and abstract

25.—(1) The period prescribed for the purposes of section 15(5)(*a*) shall **15.04**
be—
    (*a*) if the application contains no declared priority date, the period of
        twelve months calculated from its date of filing; or
    (*b*) if the application does contain a declared priority date, the last to
        expire of the period of twelve months calculated from the declared
        priority date and the period of one month calculated from the date
        of filing the application.

(2) Subject to the provisions of rules 80(2), 81(3), 82(3) and 85(3)(*a*)
below, the period prescribed for the purposes of sections 15(5)(*b*) and
17(1) shall be—
    (*a*) if the application contains no declared priority date, the period of
        twelve months calculated from its date of filing; or
    (*b*) if the application does contain a declared priority date, the period of
        twelve months calculated from the declared priority date.

(3) Where a new application is filed under section 8(3), 12(6), 15(4) or
37(4) after the end of the period prescribed in paragraph (1) or (2) above,
as the case may be, the period prescribed for the purposes of sections 15(5)
and 17(1) shall be the period which expires on the actual date of filing of
the new application.

(4) [*Revoked*]

Note. Rule 25(4) became spent and was revoked by the Patents (Amendment)
Rules 1987 (S.I. 1987 No. 288, r. 1(4)).

Extensions for new applications **15.05**

26.—(1) Where a new application is filed under section 8(3), 12(6), 15(4)
or 37(4) after the period of sixteen months prescribed in either rule 6 or
rule 15 above, then, subject to paragraph (3) below, the requirements of
those rules shall be complied with at the time of filing the new application.

(2) Where such a new application is filed after the period of twenty-one months prescribed in rule 6(6), then, subject to paragraph (3) below, the requirements of rule 6(6) shall be complied with in relation to the new application at the time of filing it.

(3) Where a new application is filed under section 15(4) after—

(*a*) the period of sixteen months prescribed in rule 6 or rule 15; or

(*b*) the period of twenty-one months prescribed in rule 6,

and that period has been extended in respect of the earlier application under rule 110(3) or (3C) below, the requirements of rule 6(2) and (3), rule 6(6) or rule 15, as the case may be, shall be complied with by the end of the extended period.

Note. Rule 26 is printed as amended by the Patents (Amendment) Rules 1987 (S.I. 1987 No. 288, r. 9).

COMMENTARY ON SECTION 15

15.06 *General*

This section and the relevant rules together: lay down the minimum requirements to establish a filing date; set out the procedures to be followed if the applicant omits to file drawings referred to in the description; set out the procedure for the filing of divisional applications; and provide for time limits for filing certain documents. The provisions of the EPC corresponding to those of section 15 and the rules thereunder are contained in EPCaa. 75(3), 76, 78(2) (part), 80, 90(3) and 91(6) and in EPCrr. 25, 26(2)(*e*) and 43. Some similar provisions are to be found in PCTaa. 11 and 14(2) and in PCTrr. 7, 14.1(*b*), 15.4(*a*), 16 and 20.2(*a*)(iii).

Date of filing

15.07 *—Definition*

By virtue of section 130(1), the "date of filing" (in relation to an application for a patent made under the Act) means the date of filing that application by virtue of section 15. This is not necessarily the actual date of filing because, under section 15(1), a date of filing is accorded only when, and as the date when, certain minimum requirements have been met, though subject to other provisions in the Act. Subsection (1) provides for such date of filing to be accorded to any patent application under the Act, howsoever initiated (*Antiphon's Application*, [1984] RPC 1).

The date of filing in the case of a divisional application is defined in subsection (4). Other relevant provisions of the Act relating to the date of filing are those concerning new applications under sections 8(3), 12(6) and 37(4). Although subsection (1) refers to "following provisions of this Act", it is not thought that there is any significance in the provisions set out in section 8(3) *preceding* section 15 in respect of the filing date accorded to an application permitted to be filed thereunder.

The date of filing of an application for a European Patent (UK) (which by definition (s. 130(1) and CPCa. 2(1)) must include a community patent) is defined in section 78(1), subject to section 78(3)(*c*) and discussed in para. 78.06, and the date of filing of a converted European application is defined in section 81(3)(*a*), discussed in para. 81.10.

The date of filing of an international application for a patent (UK) is now to be defined at section 89B(1)(*a*) and section 89(5), see paras. 89B.05 and 89.37 respectively.

The definition of subsection (1) is further subject to the operation of: rule 97 (*Service by post*), reprinted at para. 119.02 and discussed in para. 119.04; rule 98 (*Hours of Business*), reprinted at para. 120.02 and discussed in para. 120.04; rule 99 (*Excluded days*), reprinted at para. 120.03 and discussed in para. 120.05; and rule 111 (*Calculation of times or periods*), reprinted at para. 123.11 and discussed in paras. 123.38 and 123.39.

In particular the "date of filing" in the case of any other application, *i.e.* an application other than one for a United Kingdom patent, or a European patent (UK), or an international application (UK), is defined by section 130(1) to be the date which, under the laws of the country where the application was made in accordance of a treaty or convention to which that country is a party, is to be treated as the date of filing that application or is equivalent to the date of filing an application in that country (whatever the outcome of that application). This wording is not unlike that used in article 4A of the Paris Convention (Stockholm Text). It is to be noted that this definition includes the date of filing of applications under the EPC and PCT when the countries designated therein did *not* include the United Kingdom.

—Documents necessary to establish a date of filing   **15.08**

The provisions of subsection (1) differ from the corresponding provisions of EPCa. 80 and PCTa. 3(2) in that, in an application made under the Act, it is not necessary to include claims in order to establish a date of filing; this provision makes possible a facility equivalent to the filing of a provisional specification under the 1949 Act. Thus, while section 14(1) requires that an application be made in the prescribed manner, it is qualified by the last sentence of section 14(2) which states that the formal requirements are not to prevent an application being initiated by documents which comply with subsection (1), thus removing the need for claims in the above instance and also clearly envisaging the filing of an application with informal documents. However, an application cannot be accorded a filing date under section 15(1) unless it is accompanied on that day by the filing fee required by section 15(1)(*d*) (*Hydroacoustics' Application*, [1981] FSR 538), nor may the description be in a foreign language (*Rohde and Schwarz's Application*, [1980] RPC 155), see para. 14.30.

It would seem that any communication addressed to the Patent Office and meeting the requirements of subsection (1), will establish a filing date and, therefore, that the filing of PF 1/77 is not necessary to establish a date of filing under section 15(1). In taking advantage of this practice it may be necessary for further information or documents to accompany the application; for example, if priority is being claimed, the declaration of priority under section 5(2) must always be included with the application (r. 6(1), reprinted in para. 5.02) or, if disclosure of the invention at an international exhibition is to be disregarded, the Comptroller must be informed of the display of the invention at the time of filing of the application, see para. 2.32. With an invention which involves the use of a micro-organism, rule 17 must also have been complied with by the date of filing, see paras. 125A.16–125A.20. For further details of the minimum filing requirements, see para. 17.14.

In *Daini Seikosha's Application* (SRIS O/61/82; *noted* IPD 5035) an agent attempted to deal with possible deficiencies in a convention application by filing two separate, but consecutive, descriptions, one being that provided by the applicant and the other his own revision. Objection was taken by the Patent Office and, though no precise power could be found, the Patent Office, purporting to act within an inherent jurisdiction, gave the applicant one month to withdraw one or the other of the descriptions. A warning was also given to applicants of the risks they run if they delay filing their applications to a late date, which was stated not to be the purpose of the International Convention. This decision, and the alleged "inherent jurisdiction" assumed therein by the Comptroller has been criticised ((1982–83) 12 CIPA 17).

15.09 *Missing drawings (subss. (2), (3) and (3A))*

Under subsections (2) and (3) and rule 23 (reprinted at para. 15.02 *supra*), an applicant who omits to file a drawing to which the description refers has the option of either deleting the reference to the drawing from the description or belatedly filing the drawing (for which he has one month from the date the Patent Office issues the notification that the drawing is missing) and having the application post-dated to the date of filing the drawing. The one month period permitted by rule 23 is now extensible as of right for one month on filing PF 50/77 (r. 110(3)) and is further extensible at the Comptroller's discretion on filing PF 53/77 after prior application on PF 52/77 (r. 110(3A) and (3C)), see para. 123.33. This is the only circumstance in which an application under the Act may be post-dated, although the Act recognises the post-dating of applications for European patents (UK) (s. 78(3)(*c*)) and international applications for patents (UK), (s. 89(1)(*b*), to be replaced by s. 89B(1)(*a*)). There is no general facility for post-dating as there was under section 6(3) and (4) [1949].

Subsection (3A), to be added as indicated in the *Note* at the end of para. 15.01 *supra*, appears to allow missing drawings, omitted in error or by mistake, to be added to the application at a date later than its date of filing at the Comptroller's discretion under section 117(1), and without post-dating. When brought into effect, *Antiphon's Application* ([1984] RPC 1) will be over-ruled. Also, the significance will be reduced of the distinction between a missing drawing and an incorrect drawing which was made in *EPO Decision J* 19/80 (OJEPO 3/1981, 65; also reported as *Appeal Practice Decision No. 6*, [1981] RPC 277) and in *EPO Decision J* 01/82 (OJEPO 8/1982, 293).

Presumably, if discretion to correct under section 117(1) were refused, a missing drawing could then be added with post-dating under subsection (2) or (3), with extensions of time available under rule 110(3) and (3A) if necessary. Note that the option of post-dating only applies to the filing of missing drawings where this is due to error or mistake, and does not apply to the correction of mistakes in timely-filed drawings. Note also that for European applications, missing drawings can only be added with post-dating (*EPO Decision J* 01/82, *supra*).

However, since the drawings form part of the specification (s. 14(2)(*b*)), rule 91(2) (reprinted in para. 117.02) applies. It may be, therefore, that any correction under subsection (3A) must be one that is obvious and immediately evident, see para. 117.02. In *PPG Industries' Patent* ([1987] RPC 469) an obvious mistake was characterised (under s. 31 [1949]) as requiring that it should be evident to a reader of the uncorrected specification what the correction should be. Since the form of a drawing is often not discernible from a reading of the description in the absence of a drawing, the benefit when section 15(3A) is brought into effect may turn out to be small.

A drawing missing from the application, but present in an accompanying document such as a priority document, does not count as filed under subsections (2) and (3) (*VEB Kombinat Walzlager's Application*, [1987] RPC 405), because a priority document is not part of an "application" (*Mitsui Engineering's Application*, [1984] RPC 471).

If no drawing is filed in the circumstances specified in subsection (2)(*b*) or (3)(*b*) the references to the missing drawings are not deleted from the specification before publication under section 16, but a footnote is inserted on the front page to explain that the drawings themselves are omitted under section 15(2) or section 15(3). Presumably, a similar footnote will be printed when drawings are permitted to be filed late as described above.

Times for filing claims, abstract and for paying search fee (subs. (5)) **15.10**

Rule 25 (reprinted at para. 15.04 *supra*), despite its misleading title, deals with these three matters. Under subsection (5)(*a*) and rule 25(1), the claims and abstract, if not filed with the application, must be filed within 12 months after the filing date or, if priority is claimed, within 12 months after the declared priority date or one month after filing, whichever is later. The period prescribed by rule 25(2) under sections 15(5)(*b*) and 17(1) for payment of the search fee (which requires PF 9/77 to be filed, see para. 17.06) is 12 months after the filing date or, if priority is claimed, 12 months after the declared priority date.

An applicant is warned by a notice on the reverse of the certificate of filing that, if the request is not made within the terms specified, the application may be treated as withdrawn. The term "declared priority date" is defined in rule 2 (reprinted at para. 123.04 and discussed in para. 5.07).

It must be noted that the guarantee of a period of at least one month from the filing date under rule 25(1) applies only to the filing of the claims and abstract and does not apply to the filing of the search request and payment of the search fee under rule 25(2), but for extensions of time see para. 15.11 *infra*.

In the case of divisionals and other back-dated applications, the time limits are calculated using the effective (*i.e.* "parent") filing date. Therefore, rule 25(3) requires, for cases in which the application is filed after the deadline has expired, that the claims, abstract and search request (together with the fee for that request) must each be filed on (or possibly before) the filing date of the back-dated application. For further discussion of back-dated applications, see paras. 15.13–15.21 and under "Practice" at paras. 15.28–15.32.

When the claims are filed later than the filing date, this fact is indicated by a footnote on the front page of the specification when this is published under section 16.

Where an order is made under section 22(2) prohibiting publication of the application, the periods in which the search fee must be paid and the abstract and claims must be filed are not affected.

The rectification of informalities on filing (failure to comply with those requirements designated in the rules under section 17(2) as formal requirements) is dealt with under section 17(3) after the search fee has been paid under section 17(1), see para. 17.17.

Care should be taken that, should PF 9/77 be filed by an agent other than as specified on PF 1/77, PF 51/77 should be filed on or before PF 9/77: otherwise PF 9/77 may be held not to have been properly filed and the application therefore be deemed to have been withdrawn.

—Extensions of time for compliance with subsection (5) **15.11**

The period prescribed by rule 25(2) for requesting the preliminary examination and search and paying the search fee on PF 9/77 can be extended by one month as of right on filing PF 50/77 (r. 110(3)), and can be further extended at the Comptroller's discretion with PF 52/77 and PF 53/77 (r. 110(3A) and (3C)), see para. 123.33. This possibility of extension also applies to divisional applications under section 15(4) and new back-dated applications under sections 8(3), 12(6) and 37(4). Note that the extension fees are large compared to the search fee.

Rule 110(3A) allows a request for an extension on PF 52/77 to be filed after the expiry of the time limit to be extended. Thus the previous adverse decisions in *E's*

Applications ([1983] RPC 231 (HL), also reported less fully as *Energy Conversion's Applications* [1982] FSR 544; *P's Application* ([1983] RPC 269); and *Payne's Application* ([1985] RPC 193, see also the note by K. W. Nash in (1984–5) 14 CIPA 239), appear on this point to have been overruled.

The period for filing claims and the abstract, both under rule 25(1), and under rule 25(3) for back-dated applications under sections 15(4), 8(3), 12(6) and 37(4), may be extended under rule 110(1) without fee at the Comptroller's discretion. The Patent Office has indicated that such an extension can be obtained at least when PF 50/77 is filed to request extension of time for filing PF 9/77 ((1980–1) 10 CIPA 281).

15.12   *Applications filed initially under the EPC or PCT*

The conversion of European patent applications to United Kingdom patent applications is dealt with under section 81 and see EPCaa. 135 to 137. The treatment of international applications as United Kingdom patent applications is discussed under sections 89, 89A and 89B, see also PCTa. 25 and PCTr. 51; the prosecution of international applications for patents (UK) before the United Kingdom Patent Office is also discussed under section 89A, see the commentaries thereon, and see also PCTaa. 20, 22, 23, 26–28 and PCTrr. 47 and 52.

Divisional applications (subs. (4))

15.13   *—Time for filing*

The filing of a divisional application is governed by rule 24 (reprinted at para. 15.03 *supra*) and made under section 15(4), and is only permitted before the earlier application has been granted (s. 15(4)), refused, withdrawn or taken to be withdrawn and before the expiration of the period for acceptance under section 20(1). It has been held (*ITT's Application*, [1984] RPC 23) that, once the official letter under section 18(4) has issued indicating that a patent is to be granted, the administrative act of granting the patent has occurred. Section 24(1) purposely excludes from its effect the provisions of sections 1 to 24 and it is therefore then too late to file a divisional application under section 15(4) and rule 110(1) confers no discretionary power which would allow the requirements of section 15(4) to be varied, see also *Ogawa Chemical's Application*, ([1986] RPC 63). This is different from the position under the EPC where, in exceptional circumstances, a divisional application can be permitted to be filed, even after indication has been given under EPCr. 51(4) that the application will proceed to grant, see *EPO Decision T* 92/85, "*Belated division and amendment/WAVIN*" (OJEPO 10/1986, 352: [1986] 5 EPOR 281), though here division was refused.

Rule 24 also specifies that a divisional application can be filed as of right but only up to a deadline date which is calculated in one of three ways.

First, where an objection of lack of unity has been raised in an examiner's report (official letter) under section 18(3) in the substantive examination of the parent application, the deadline is two months after the filing of the amendment which overcomes the objection (r. 24(1)(*a*)). Note that the calculation is based on the actual filing date of the amendment, and not on the period set for response to the objection. Such right to file a divisional application will arise even if the Examiner's report raising a "plurality of invention" objection is not the first report under section 18(3), but it seems it should only arise once the objection is no longer challenged by the applicant.

Secondly, where no objection of lack of unity arises, but the first report of the examiner in the substantive examination of the parent application is made under section 18(3) (raising some other point or points), the deadline is the end of the period specified for reply to that examiner's report (r. 24(1)(*b*)(i)). Presumably, if a new period for response is specified, for example by the grant of an extension of time (for which see para. 18.07), such new period will also apply to the filing of a divisional application under rule 24(1)(*b*)(i).

Thirdly, if the first report on the substantive examination is one under section 18(4) that the application does comply with the requirements of the Act, the deadline is two months from the issuance of such report (r. 24(*b*)(ii)).

It appears that, in each case, the deadline can be extended at the Comptroller's discretion under rule 110(1) (*Secretary of State's Application*, SRIS O/188/84). Additionally, rule 24(1)(*b*)(i) gives the Comptroller power to agree to a late-filed divisional, but apparently only in the circumstances of that sub-paragraph. The exercise of discretion to permit such a divisional application to be filed belatedly is discussed in para. 15.30 *infra*.

The PCT does not provide for the filing of divisional applications on international applications, although PCTa. 17(3) and PTCr. 30 provide for additional searches and PCTa. 34(3) and PCTr. 68 provide for the examination of claims directed to several inventions. Division of international applications is left to national offices.

—Content of divisional applications   **15.14**

The request on a divisional application must include a claim to the filing date of the earlier application and must identify the latter by filing date and number but, by rule 24(2), the description and drawings of the earlier and divisional applications must, where possible, respectively relate only to the matter for which protection is sought.

The claim to divisional status must be made at the time of filing, and a substantive application cannot be converted to a divisional application after filing (*P's Application*, [1983] RPC 269). The priority claim must also be made at the time of filing (r. 110(2) as it applies to r. 26).

By section 76(1), any new matter contained in a divisional application must be removed by amendment if the application is to proceed, see para. 15.29 *infra*.

It had been confirmed that section 76 prevents the inclusion of *any* new matter in a divisional application under the Act (*Hydroacoustics' Application*, [1981] FSR 538) so that successive divisional applications with cascading priorities were not possible. However, the wording of section 76(1) is to be amended, see para. 76.01, in a manner designed to overcome the draconian effect of the *Hydroacoustics* decision. The position now will be that, while a divisional application containing new matter is allowed to be filed initially, this will not proceed unless (and until) it is amended so as to exclude the additional matter. It has been indicated ((1981–82) 11 CIPA 290) that the *Hydroacoustics* decision is interpreted by examiners to mean that the claim of the parent application may not be broadened without contravention of section 76, a view that would not seem to be supported by the requirement in section 76 limiting its application to the *disclosure* of additional matter. Nevertheless it will not normally be possible to obtain claims in a divisional application which are broader in scope than could have been obtained in the parent application. Attempts to broaden the claims of an application by filing a divisional application have failed on many occasions because it has been held that the claim broadening has resulted in the application disclosing matter extending beyond that disclosed in the earlier application, as filed, see para. 76.16. Because new section 76(2) refers to an "application", rather than to a "description", it would seem possible to claim in a divisional application matter disclosed only in the abstract of the parent application, because under section 14(2)(*c*) the abstract forms part of an application, see *Armco's Application* (SRIS O/84/85).

The *Hydroacoustics* decision (*supra*) formerly meant that inclusion of any new matter in an attempted divisional application led to the application being deemed not properly filed so that it could not be saved by amendment to remove the offending additional matter. The reworded section 76 now over-rules that decision on this point and makes it possible to amend a divisional application to cure the defect if it were to be held that the application as filed did contain new matter. Presumably, any necessary discretion would be given. Therefore, the previous practice, of filing divisional applications in exactly the same form as the initial form of the parent application and seeking to make amendments later, should no longer be necessary, but may still be desirable, see para. 15.29.

If a divisional application contains new matter by error or mistake, correction may also be possible under section 117 and reference could be made to the parent application for evidence that nothing other than the offered correction was intended. For further details, see para. 117.06.

Time limits for filing other documents on divisional applications

15.15   —*The applicable rules*

The time limits for filing documents on divisional applications, as discussed in paras. 15.16–15.21 *infra*, are governed by rules 6(3)(*a*), 25(3), 26, 33(3) and 33(4) and are complex. Times are computed from the "date of filing" of the parent application or from its "declared priority date", terms defined respectively in section 15(1) (discussed in para. 15.07 *supra*) and rule 2 (reprinted in para. 123.04 and discussed in para. 5.07). It should be noted that it is often necessary to comply with all the conditions at the time of filing the divisional application, and it is desirable to do this in any event.

15.16   —*Payment of search fee by filing PF 9/77*

If the divisional application is filed before the end of the period prescribed under rule 25(2) for filing the PF 9/77 and the search fee, for which see para. 15.10 *supra*, these are due by the end of that period. Note that the deemed (parent) filing date must be used in calculating the rule 25(2) period. If the divisional application is filed later, after the end of the rule 25(2) period, the PF 9/77 and the search fee are due on filing the divisional application (r. 25(3)). In either case, one month's extension can be obtained as of right under rule 110(3) with PF 50/77, and further extensions at the Comptroller's discretion under rule 110(3A) with PF 52/77 and PF 53/77, but heavy fees are then payable, see para. 123.33.

15.17   *Filing of claims and the abstract*

If the divisional application is filed before the end of the period prescribed under rule 25(1) for filing the claims and abstract, these are due by the end of that period. Note that the deemed (parent) filing date must be used in calculating the rule 25(1) period. If the divisional application is filed later, the claims and the abstract are due on filing (r. 25(3)). In either case, the period may be extended without fee at the Comptroller's discretion under rule 110(1), see para. 15.11 *supra*.

15.18   —*Payment of examination fee by filing PF 10/77*

If the divisional application is filed within two years of its declared priority date (or the parent filing date if no priority is claimed) then PF 10/77 and the examination fee are due at the end of the two year period (r. 33(3) and (4)). If the divisional application is filed later, they are due with that filing (r. 33(3) and (4)). Note that in some circumstances the due date for the divisional application may be before the due date for the parent application. In either case, one month's extension may be obtained as of right under rule 110(3) with PF 50/77, and further extensions may be obtained at the Comptroller's discretion under rule 110(3A) and (3C) with PF 52/77 and PF 53/77, but heavy fees are payable, see para. 123.33.

—Filing of inventorship statement on PF 7/77   **15.19**

If the divisional application is filed before the end of 16 months from the declared priority date (or the parent filing date if no priority is claimed), PF 7/77, if required, is due by the end of the 16 month period. If the divisional application is filed later, it is due on filing (r. 26(1)). If the corresponding period for the parent application has been extended under rule 110(3) with PF 50/77 or under rule 110(3A) and (3C) with PF 52/77 and PF 53/77, the period for the divisional application is automatically extended to the same date, provided that the divisional application is filed after the end of the 16 month period (r. 26(3)(*a*)). The automatic extension may perhaps only apply when the extension for the parent application has been obtained before the divisional application is filed, in view of the phrase "has been" in rule 26(3). In any case, one month's extension is available as of right under rule 110(1) with PF 50/77 and further extensions at the Comptroller's discretion under rule 110(3A) and (3C) with PF 52/77 and PF 53/77, but heavy fees are payable. It appears that the one month available with PF 50/77 can be added to the end of any automatic extension under rule 26(3).

—Filing of priority document   **15.20**

When priority is claimed, the requirements for the furnishing of convention documents depend on whether the basic (priority) application was filed at the United Kingdom Patent Office or abroad. Rule 6 (reprinted at para. 5.02) has sub-rules relating to the various circumstances which can occur.

When the basic application is a United Kingdom application, or an international application (whether or not the UK is designated) filed at the United Kingdom Patent Office as receiving office, rule 6(3)(*a*) applies (to the exclusion of rule 6(2)) for obtaining a certificate from the Comptroller so that PF 24/77 (reprinted at para. 141.24), even if this is filed before the expiry of the normal 16 month period, must be filed with the divisional application. The rules do not provide for the filing of a certified copy of the basic application in lieu of PF 24/77. It appears that PF 24/77 may be filed later at the Comptroller's discretion under rule 110(1), without an extension fee, because rule 6(3) is not listed in either rule 110(2) or (3). However, rule 26(3) (reprinted in para. 15.05) applies to rule 6(3) and requires this rule to be complied with within any extension period obtained under rule 110(3A) or (3C). From this, it appears that an automatic extension of the time for filing PF 24/77 is obtained when the 16 month period under rule 6(2) for the parent application has been extended under rule 110(3A) and (3C) and the divisional application is filed after the end of that 16 month period, even though rule 6(2) does not itself apply to divisional applications. For further comment on rule 26(3), see para. 15.19 *supra*.

When the basic application is *not* a United Kingdom application or an international application filed at the United Kingdom Patent Office as receiving office, rules 6(2), 6(6) and 26 apply. Accordingly, a certified copy of the basic application must be filed no later than 16 months from the declared priority date (r. 6(2)) or with the divisional application (r. 26(1)) when the latter is lodged after expiry of the 16 month period. Since rule 6(2) permits the copy of the basic application to be "otherwise verified to the satisfaction of the Comptroller", it is usual to file PF 24/77 in lieu of the certified copy, although it appears that the applicant has no absolute right to do so. When the divisional application has been filed after the end of the 16 month rule 6(2) period, the automatic extension provisions of rule 26(3) apply (by r. 26(3)(a)(i)). For further commentary on automatic extensions under rule 26(3), see para. 15.19 *supra*. The period for filing PF 24/77 or the certified copy can be extended by one month as of right under rule 110(3) with PF 50/77 and can be extended further at the Comptroller's discretion under rule 110(3A) and (3C) with PF 52/77 and PF 53/77, but heavy fees are payable, and this extension appears to be cumulative with any automatic extension under rule 26(3).

15.21 —*Verified translation of the priority document*

When the basic application is not in the English language, a verified translation must be filed no later than 21 months from the declared priority date (r. 6(6)) or with the divisional application when the latter is lodged later (r. 26(2)). In lieu of an original verified translation, it is usual for PF 24/77 filed to provide the certified copy of the basic application to refer also to a copy of the verified translation filed on the parent application.

By rule 26(3)(b), an extension of time for filing the verified translation on the parent application under rule 110(3) and/or (3A) and (3C) automatically extends the deadline on the divisional application to the same date, provided that the divisional application was filed within 21 months of the priority date. For further commentary on automatic extensions under rule 26(3), see para. 15.19 *supra*. In any case, one month's extension is available as of right under rule 110(3) with PF 50/77 and further extensions can be obtained at the Comptroller's discretion under rule 110(3A) and (3C) with PF 52/77 and PF 53/77, but heavy fees are payable, and this extension appears to be cumulative with any automatic extension under rule 26(3).

15.22 *New applications under sections 8(3), 12(6) and 37(4)*

The filing of new applications under section 8(3) (*Determination before grant of entitlement to patents, etc.*), section 12(6) (*Determination of questions of entitlement to foreign and convention patents, etc.*) and section 37(4) (*Determination of right to patent after grant*) is discussed in the commentaries on these sections and in relation to "Practice" in para. 8.14. Briefly, any such application must be filed within three months after the decision of the Comptroller or the Court under the relevant section has become final (rr. 10 and 57) and the filing date claimed for such application must be included on the request, together with the number of the relevant earlier application. The time limits for filing other documents are generally as for divisional applications as discussed in paras. 15.15–15.21 *supra*, but rules 26(3) (*Automatic extensions*) and 6(3)(a) (*PF 24/77 to be filed with the application even if less than 16 months from priority*) do not apply. Also, a certified copy of any priority document only needs to be filed if the Comptroller so requests (r. 6(3)(b)).

PRACTICE UNDER SECTION 15

15.23 *Filing of initial application*

Applicants wishing to make an initial filing in the United Kingdom corresponding to the former provisional application under the 1949 Act in order to secure a priority date at minimum expense, may file without claims or abstract. The description should disclose the invention in a manner to enable the invention to be performed by a person skilled in the art and to support the ultimate claims (for which see paras. 14.15 and 14.25), and also to provide an adequate basis to establish a priority date for a later application in other countries. At any time within 12 months following the filing date, the applicant can add claims to that application, or he can file another application in the United Kingdom claiming priority from the earlier application, or he can file an application for a European patent or an international application designating *inter alia* the United Kingdom and claiming priority from the earlier United Kingdom application.

The 12 month period for filing the claims and the abstract and for paying the search fee specified in rule 25(1) is extensible under rule 110(3) and/or (3A) and (3C) (see para. 15.11 *supra*), but the 12 month period for filing a new application claiming priority is laid down in section 5(2) and is inextensible. If a new United Kingdom, European or international application is filed, additional matter can be included and multiple priorities can be claimed. It is possible to claim priorities from an earlier United Kingdom application and an earlier foreign application jointly. The documents of an initial filing can be informal, and formal replacements are never needed if the initial filing serves solely as a priority basis. However, care should be taken that the documents are clear enough to enable legible certified copies to be obtained.

For the procedure for filing documents after normal hours of opening of the Patent Office, see para. 120.06.

Priority   **15.24**

There is no obligation to withdraw an earlier United Kingdom application which has served to establish a priority date for a later United Kingdom application, an application for a European patent (UK) or an international application for a patent (UK). For example, if the earlier application discloses several inventions, the application can be pursued for protection of one of those inventions and the later United Kingdom application or the European or international application can be pursued, possibly with additional matter, in respect of another of those inventions. Section 18(5) gives the Comptroller power to prevent two patents being granted in the United Kingdom to the same person for the same invention and a United Kingdom patent will normally be revoked on the Comptroller's own initiative under section 73(2) if a European patent (UK) is granted to the same patentee for the same invention, see para. 73.06. If, however, the application has served its intended purpose solely of establishing priority, the Office prefers its specific withdrawal, once the second application claiming priority has been filed, in order to avoid duplicate publication, see para. 16.09.

Since the term of a patent is reckoned from the date of filing (s. 25), the filing of a second application claiming priority from a first application results in a later expiry of the patent and a later date for the payment of the first renewal fee. However, the period prescribed by section 16 for publication is reckoned from the "declared priority date" (defined in r. 2, reprinted at para. 123.04), and publication is therefore not delayed by filing a second application claiming priority from the first. The period prescribed by rule 34 (reprinted at para. 18.03) for complying with the requirements of the Act and Rules is also calculated from the "declared priority date", and is therefore not affected by filing a second application claiming priority from the first.

An international application or a European patent application can itself serve as a "relevant application" within the meaning of section 5(5) to establish a priority date in respect of a later application under the Act. When claiming priority from a prior European or international application, it would seem to be necessary to name at least one of the countries designated in the prior application (see Note 6 to PF

1/77 (reprinted at para. 141.01) and see also section VII of EPO Form 1001; OJEPO, 11/1981, 505).

When a United Kingdom application, other than a divisional application, claims priority from an earlier United Kingdom application or international application filed at the United Kingdom Patent Office as receiving office, PF 24/77 does not need to be filed unless called for (r. 6(3)(*b*), reprinted in para. 5.02). If the application from which priority is claimed becomes withdrawn or is deemed to be withdrawn, one copy of that application may be transferred to the file of the later application, there to serve as the priority document. If the applicant proceeds with the earlier application as well as the later application, then the Office will request the filing of PF 24/77.

15.25   *Disclosure at international exhibition prior to filing*

If the earlier United Kingdom application is accompanied by a statement under section 2(4)(*c*) that the invention was displayed at an international exhibition (*i.e.* one certified as such by notice in the O.J. (r. 5(3)), a later application will not be protected against the disclosure at such exhibition unless the later application is filed also within six months of the exhibition and is also accompanied by a similar statement, for otherwise the disclosure at the exhibition becomes part of the state of the art in respect of the later application. Further, it is to be noted that EPCa. 55, which relates to non-prejudicial disclosures and similarly discounts disclosure at an international exhibition, applies only where the European application is filed within six months of the exhibition, and does not apply where the national application on which priority is based is filed within six months but the European application is not. If an embodiment of an invention patentably different from that disclosed in an earlier patent application for the invention is displayed at an international exhibition, it is advisable for any later application which is filed claiming priority from the earlier application to be filed within six months after such display and for this to be accompanied by a statement as to such display as under section 2(4)(*c*). For further discussion relating to prior display at an international exhibition, see para. 2.27.

15.26   *Cross-references*

As to cross-references between corresponding applications, see para. 14.38.

15.27   *Missing drawings*

The late filing of drawings missed out from the original filing is discussed in para. 15.09 *supra*. Para. 117.06 is also relevant to the addition of drawings omitted by mistake.

Divisional applications

15.28   *—Documents required for filing*

The requirements of rules 6(3)(*a*), 25(3), 26, 33(3) and 33(4) relating to the filing of divisional applications under section 15(4) and the extensions possible under rule 110(1) and rule 110(3) are complicated and have been discussed in paras. 15.15–15.21. It is safest for any divisional application to be accompanied by the claims and abstract, by PF 9/77, PF 10/77 and PF 7/77 (if the inventor is not the applicant) and also by PF 24/77, together with a request to the Office to make a copy of the priority document to be certified (if priority is being claimed). PF 24/77 should identify the priority documents by reference to their filing numbers particularly when more than one priority is claimed on the parent application. Each basic application from which priority is claimed attracts a separate fee on PF 24/77.

The Office prefers that a deposit account order form "Sales 3" should accompany PF 24/77. If form "Sales 3" does not accompany PF 24/77 or if the applicant or his appointed agent does not hold a deposit account at the Patent Office, the Office will telephone the applicant or his agent and ask for form "Sales 3" or payment by cash or cheque to cover the cost of making the necessary copy of the priority document.

It is *always* necessary to file PF 9/77 and pay the search fee on a divisional application in the first instance. It is suggested that, when appropriate, remission under rule 102(1)(*c*) (reprinted at para. 123.09 and discussed in para. 123.25) of the search fee paid on a divisional application should be requested when filing the divisional application.

If the request for a divisional application (PF 1/77) names an agent different from that on the original PF 1/77, it would seem prudent, in view of the terms of rule 90(2), also to file PF 51/77, see para. 102.22.

—Content of divisional application   **15.29**

In view of the amendment of section 76 (discussed in para. 15.14 *supra*), it should no longer be necessary to ensure that a divisional application as filed contains only the claims of the parent application and no added wording. However, it will still be useful to file the divisional application with a description identical to that originally filed in the parent application, and to include the original claims of the parent application, in order to ensure that all the matter of the parent application is available to support claims in the divisional application. On the possibility of adding matter from the abstract of the parent application, see para. 15.14 *supra*.

Section 76, as amended, seems to allow claims to the invention of the divisional application to be presented as claims 1 *et seq.* when the divisional application is filed, even if these claims did not appear in the parent application. Placing the new claims first should ensure that the search report is directed to the invention of the divisional application as, where there is non-unity of the invention, these claims are those searched initially, see para. 17.10. Doing this may have increased importance in view of the impending addition of new subsections 17(8) and 18(1A), discussed in paras. 17.10 and 18.08 respectively.

In view of rule 24(2), the description of the divisional application will normally need to be amended to differ from that of the parent application, and drawings not relevant to the invention of the divisional application may have to be cancelled. Complementary amendments may be required in the parent application. It is normal to insert cross-references to the other in each of the parent and divisional applications, regardless of whether these are strictly necessary under rule 24(2).

The new procedure for examining for new matter is not yet known. However, it is assumed that the first examination report under section 18 will either confirm the divisional status of the application or raise an objection of additional matter, either as a preliminary point or in a letter raising other points as well. Where an objection is raised, amendment to remove the additional matter will be possible under section 18(3). Any view expressed in the first examination report must be regarded as provisional, and it is always possible for an examiner to raise an objection on the basis of additional matter at any time before grant under section 18(4). What constitutes added matter is discussed in paras. 76.09–76.14. The Comptroller also appears to take into account the public interest in deciding whether the claims of a divisional application find adequate support in the accompanying description, see *Glatt's Application* ([1983] RPC 122).

In view of the provisions of section 72(1)(*d*), if the applicant becomes aware of any new matter in a divisional application or a patent granted thereon, voluntary application to amend the specification to delete the offending matter should be made under section 19(1), 27(1) or 75 as appropriate.

15.30   —*Time for filing divisional application*

The time for filing a divisional application is prescribed by rule 24. For the calculation of the deadline, and the possibilities for extension, see para. 15.13 *supra*. Where an objection of plurality of invention arises in a preliminary report under section 18(3), it is understood that the period set for response thereto will not be less than four months, thereby giving a period of up to six months within which a divisional application can be filed following the objection.

If a plurality objection raised by the examiner is not agreed with, it can be contested in arguments filed in reply to the examination report. If no amendment to remove the objection is made, then apparently the period set by rule 24(1)(*a*) does not expire but, if the objection is withdrawn, the right to file a divisional application (if still desired) is apparently extinguished. In this case, a voluntary divisional application would have to be filed under rule 24(1)(*b*)(i) and would need the Comptroller's agreement. If the objection is maintained, the right to file a divisional application under rule 24(1)(*a*) appears to continue. If the objection is contested, but an amendment to comply with it is provisionally made as an alternative plea, any divisional application should be filed within two months of the amendment, unless an extension is requested under rule 110(1). However, one should be ready to file a divisional application immediately if the time extension is refused.

Both extensions of the prescribed period under rule 110(1) and the filing of a divisional application outside the prescribed period under rule 24(1)(*b*)(i) require the Comptroller's discretion. It is therefore necessary in these circumstances to make written submissions in support of the request for the exercise of favourable discretion. Matters which may be taken into account by the Office before deciding whether to allow the divisional application to be filed late include: the reasons why the applicant did not file within the time limit; whether the applicant unduly delayed filing the divisional application, once he became aware of the circumstances which led to his decision to seek to file a divisional; whether the applicant would be unfairly prejudiced if the divisional application is not filed; whether the public will be unfairly prejudiced if the divisional application is filed; and whether it would unduly disrupt the Office routine if the divisional application is filed, on account of the four-and-a-half year period (r. 34) for putting the application in order.

It is now clear from a line of cases that there is no presumption of discretion in the applicant's favour. It is necessary to show some good reason for needing to file the divisional application. It is not sufficient merely that the applicant desires it or sees the possibility of a commercial advantage (*N's Application*, SRIS O/140/87). It must be shown that the applicant acted with due diligence and that it was not reasonable to expect the applicant to have decided on the need to file the divisional application within the period allowed as of right under rule 24(1) (*Penwalt's Application*, SRIS O/72/82, *noted* IPD 5049; *Sony's Application*, SRIS O/184/84; *Secretary of State's Application*, SRIS O/188/84; and *Kiwi Coder's Application*, [1986] RPC 106).

It is expected that discretion will normally be exercised favourably if newly-discovered prior art destroys the patentability of a unifying claim, if only because it would be possible to disclose the prior art to the examiner, amend under section 18(3) following an objection to the unpatentable claim so as to leave a lack of unity, and file a divisional application as of right under rule 24(1)(*a*) following a subsequent plurality objection. However, note that in *Kiwi Coder's Application* (*supra*) the contention that recently-discovered prior art had occasioned the need to file the divisional application was rejected. When a divisional application is sought to cover a newly-discovered potential infringement, the Comptroller may have to weigh the legitimate interest of the applicant against the public interest of allowing a third party to assume that he is free to do a certain act described but not claimed in a pending application once the period prescribed by rule 24(1) has expired.

It also seems that there is nothing to prevent a divisional application from being filed on an earlier divisional application and it is understood that such has been allowed. The EPO also apparently allows a divisional application to be further divided (EPI Info. 1–1988, 18). Such procedure could be useful if the period prescribed under rule 24(1) for filing further divisionals on the parent application has expired, but such period has not yet expired in relation to an existing divisional application. This could mean that it would be possible to file an indefinite number of divisional applications in succession right up to the end of the section 20 acceptance period permitted by rule 34, but presumably the Patent Office would resist this.

—Prosecution of divisional application   **15.31**

When prosecuting a divisional application, particularly in the last six months of the period permitted by section 20 for placing the application in order for acceptance, it is prudent to endorse correspondence prominently with the words "DIVISIONAL: URGENT". This is in order that the examiner is alerted that the expiry of the acceptance period will occur before the date which the serial number of the application would itself suggest ((1981–82) 11 CIPA 295 and, *e.g.* O.J., April 20, 1988).

If a divisional application is filed for an invention for which a search report has been drawn up on the parent application, the search fee paid on the divisional application may be refunded under rule 102(1)(*c*), see paras. 17.11 and 123.25.

If the divisional application is filed very late in its acceptance period under rule 34, the Patent Office may have practical difficulties in providing timely publication of the "A-specification" under section 16, but may allow inspection of the file if this is administratively possible, see para. 118.20.

It is understood that the Patent Office indicates on the file of a parent application if a divisional application has been filed thereon, but past practice in this regard has not been uniform.

It is further understood that a divisional application will not be found to be formally in order for acceptance until the parent application is likewise in order and *vice versa*. Thus, the parent and all divisional applications therefrom are likely to proceed to grant on or about the same date.

—Applicant for divisional application   **15.32**

It is a requirement of section 15(4) that a divisional application be filed by the original applicant of the parent application or his successor in title. Where more than one applicant is named in the parent application, the divisional application may be in the name or names of fewer than all those applicants; this may especially be the case where the applicants are also the inventors. Where the relationship between the applicants in the parent and divisional applications is not self-evident and no explanation is submitted with the application, the Office will query the relationship and the application will not be permitted to proceed as a divisional if it is found that there has not been compliance with the requirements of section 15(4).

Where one applicant from more than one in the parent application is the applicant in the divisional application, his name may be removed from the applicants in the parent application on filing PF 11/77 (reprinted at para. 141.11) requesting the change together with evidence showing that he has no interest in, or right to, the invention of the parent application.

16.01

SECTION 16

Publication of application

16.—(1) Subject to section 22 below, where an application has a date of filing, then, as soon as possible after the end of the prescribed period, the comptroller shall, unless the application is withdrawn or refused before preparations for its publication have been completed by the Patent Office, publish it as filed (including not only the original claims but also any amendments of those claims and new claims subsisting immediately before the completion of those preparations) and he may, if so requested by the applicant, publish it as aforesaid during that period, and in either event shall advertise the fact and date of its publication in the journal.

(2) The comptroller may omit from the specification of a published application for a patent any matter—

(*a*) which in his opinion disparages any person in a way likely to damage him, or

(*b*) the publication or exploitation of which would in his opinion be generally expected to encourage offensive, immoral or anti-social behaviour.

Relevant Rules

Period for publication of application

16.02   27. The period prescribed for the purposes of section 16 shall be the period of eighteen months calculated from the declared priority date or, where there is no declared priority date, the date of filing the application.

Completion of preparations for publication

16.03   **28.** [*Revoked*]

Note Rule 28 was revoked by the Patents (Amendment) Rules 1987 (S.I., 1987 No. 288, r. 1(4)).

Commentary on Section 16

16.04   *General*

Section 16 provides for the publication of an application after a prescribed period and references in the Act to an application being "published" are references to its being published under section 16 (s. 130(5)). This gives rise to the "A-specifica-tion", that is the printed specification having a new "Publication Number" with the suffix "A", see para. 16.08. Although the practice of laying certain applications open to public inspection prior to acceptance was at one time followed under British practice, there was no corresponding provision in the 1949 Act. By rule 27 the prescribed period is 18 months from the declared priority date, or where there is no declared priority date, from the filing date. A warning that automatic publi-cation will take place at that time if the application is not withdrawn, or deemed to be withdrawn, before preparations for its publication are complete is given on the reverse of the certificate of filing issued by the Patent Office.

Section 16 is not one of the sections specified in section 130(7) as being intended to have the same effect as the corresponding provisions of EPC or PCT, but there are similar provisions in EPCa. 93 and EPCrr. 34, 48, 49 and 50(1) and in PCTaa. 21 and 29 and PCTrr. 9.1 and 48.

The "application" to be published is defined by section 14(2). This will include the claims as originally filed and also any amendments thereto made before com-pletion of the preparations for publication. The date on which preparations for publication are completed is a matter of fact to be determined objectively and on a case-by-case basis (*Intera's Application*, [1986] RPC 459 (CA)), but for the current practice see para. 16.06 *infra*.

Under subsection (2) the Comptroller has power to omit from the published spe-cification any matter which he considers disparaging or offensive and there is no appeal from a decision on this point (s. 97(1)). The specification will not be pub-lished if the application is withdrawn before the completion of the preparations for publication, on which see para. 16.06 *infra*.

The applicant may request publication earlier than 18 months after the declared priority date or the filing date, as the case may be, provided that the claims and the abstract have been filed and the search fee has been paid. Such requests should only be made for good reason and then by letter marked "Request for accelerated publi-cation", see O.J., July 13, 1989 and para. 24.05.

Upon publication, an entry is created in the register of patents maintained under section 32, see para. 32.15. By rule 44(2) (reprinted in para. 32.04), this entry then records: (*a*) the name and address of the applicant(s); (*b*) the name and address of the person(s) stated by the applicant(s) to be believed to be the inventor(s); (*c*) the title of the invention; (*d*) the date of filing and the file number of the application; (*e*) the date of filing and the country and filing number of any application from which priority has been claimed under section 5(2) (and formerly also s. 127(4)); (*f*) the date of publication of the application; and (*g*) the address for service of the applicant(s) (for which see para. 32.16). For subsequent entries in the register, see rule 44(3) and (4) (reprinted in para. 32.04) and paras. 24.09 and 32.17. There is no obligation to record the fact that a divisional application has been filed, but this is sometimes done.

Extent of publication under section 16   **16.05**

The search under section 17(5) is carried out before the application is published under section 16(1) and a list of documents cited in the search report is included on the front sheet of the published specification. The Patent Office endeavours to issue the search report within 15 months of the declared priority date or within nine months of the filing date if there is no declared priority date, provided that PF 9/77 and the claims have already been filed. If, for any reason, the issue of the search report is delayed, publication under section 16 is also delayed. This contrasts with the provisions of EPCa. 93 under which the search report and the abstract are either published as an annex to the description and claims and any drawings, or are separately published later if they are not ready by the time the technical preparations for the publication of the description, etc., have been completed. PCTr. 48.2(*g*) has a similar provision.

The publication of the application is advertised in the O.J. (subs. (1)). The date of advertised publication is important as it defines the start of the term of six months prescribed by rule 33(2) (reprinted in para. 18.02) for applying for the substantive examination under section 18. This is the only procedural period which is not referable to the date of filing or declared priority date and it therefore necessitates a separate entry to be made in the progress diary which should be maintained for each application to ensure that all required procedures are timely carried out: otherwise there is great risk that the application will become deemed to have been withdrawn, with revival only possible after paying heavy fees for extension of time under rules 110(3), (3A) and (3C), see para. 123.33.

Normally, printed copies of the "A-specification" (the first printing) will be made available on the advertised publication day but, if not, publication is still deemed to have taken place on that day. Any amendments made to the description are not included in this first printing though presumably obvious clerical errors which have been corrected under section 117 should be included.

The form of the claims immediately before publication is important in determining the rights arising on publication in accordance with section 69(2) and (3) (*Infringement of rights conferred by publication of application*).

An application on which, for security reasons, directions prohibiting publication have been imposed under section 22(2) will not be published until such directions have been revoked under section 22(5)(*e*).

References throughout the Act to an application for a patent being published are defined (by section 130(5)) as references to the application being published under section 16, *i.e.* the first printing. By section 78(3)(*d*), an application for a European patent (UK) published under EPCa. 93 is deemed to be published under section 16, see para. 78.06. Likewise, by section 89(1)(*a*) (to be replaced by s. 89B(2)), an international application for a patent (UK) published under PCTa. 21 is deemed to be published under section 16, but only if the international application has subsequently entered the United Kingdom phase, and subject to the provisions of section 89(7), (to be replaced by s. 89B(3)), see para. 89B.11.

Under section 118(1), after publication of an application, all documents relating to it and information specified in rule 92(1) (reprinted in para. 118.04), subject to certain exclusions specified in rule 93(5) (reprinted in para. 118.05), are available or open to inspection. Further, under section 118(4) any person threatened with a future infringement action on an application can have sight of the file before publication.

For further details of publication of specifications, see para. 123.45.

When a divisional application is filed 13 months or less before the expiry of the section 20 period for bringing the application into compliance with the Act and Rules, it was the practice of the Patent Office not to publish the application under the provisions of section 16 ((1983–84) 13 CIPA 16), though there appears no legal basis for such publication being avoided. However, it is understood that this practice changed during 1984. While the file of a divisional application ought to be open to public inspection under section 118(5), it is understood that administrative arrangements may make this difficult. Also it should be noted that the file of the parent application does not necessarily contain any indication that a divisional application has been filed thereon, though it is understood that such marking has now been adopted. The prejudice arising from late publication of a divisional application, even after the rule 34 period has expired, to those with an interest in lodging observations under section 21, and a possible consequence of this, has been the subject of comment ((1984–85) 14 CIPA 446).

Amendment or withdrawal before publication **16.06**

No amendments may be made to the description or claims before the search report has been received. Nevertheless, the Patent Office will receive amendments to the specification before publication under section 16, but these are then treated as effectively filed only upon the issuance of the search report ((1978–79) 8 CIPA 504). This is because of rule 36 (reprinted at para. 19.03), the effect and validity of which was the subject of comment by C. Jones ((1978–79) 8 CIPA 178).

Rule 28, which formerly purported to give the Comptroller absolute power to determine when preparations for publication should be regarded as complete, was revoked, as noted in para. 16.03, *supra*, following *Intera's Application* ([1986] RPC 459), in which the Court of Appeal held, over-ruling *Pierce Chemical's Application* ([1980] RPC 232), that rule 28 was *ultra vires* the terms of section 16 and that the time when preparations for publication of the specification have been completed by the Patent Office (according to s. 16(1)) has to be determined objectively on a case-by-case basis, this probably being the time when the print-out of the computer data and the specification have been allocated to one of the printing contractors and these are ready to be sent to, or collected by, him from the Printing Branch of the Office at St. Mary Cray. Accordingly, it was held that, up to that time, the applicant is entitled to withdraw or amend the application, but thereafter the Comptroller has no discretion. Thus, in *Peabody International's Application* ([1986] RPC 521), following and adopting the view of the Court of Appeal in the *Intera* decision, that date had already been reached, and indeed the printer had already collected the papers: withdrawal of the application was therefore not permitted. It was also stated that, from the present wording of section 16(1), the same cut-off date applies both for withdrawal and for inclusion of amendments in the published specification.

The date when preparations for publication are complete is, therefore, now determined on a case-by-case basis, at a date not earlier than $15\frac{1}{2}$ months after the declared priority date (or, if none, the filing date), unless a request for early publication has been made (O.J. March 30, 1978 and April 9, 1986). In a letter giving the intended publication date, the applicant is now advised that preparations for publication will shortly be complete, but not before one week after the date of the letter and that no further notice of this completion will be given. In view of the short period between this letter and the start of the printing operation, applicants are asked when filing, on or after 15 months from the priority or filing date, amended claims for inclusion in the published specification, or a notification of withdrawal intended to prevent publication, to mark such a letter, prominently in red "URGENT—SECTION 16 PUBLICATION IMMINENT" (O.J. April 5, 1989), see also para. 14.39.

PRACTICE UNDER SECTION 16

Form of publication **16.07**

The front page of the "A-specification" published under section 16 contains the bibliographic information defined in rule 95(*a*)–(*d*) (reprinted at para. 118.07), that is: the filing date and filing number; the name of the applicant; the filing date, the filing number and country of the basic application (if a declaration of priority has been filed); and the title. In addition, the front page contains: the address of the applicant; the name of the inventor; the name and address of the appointed agent, if any; a list of the documents cited in the search report under section 17(5); the international classification; the abstract; and possibly one or more figures of any drawings. If a statement that the invention was exhibited at an international exhibition has been filed, this information also appears on the front page of the printed specification. Footnotes indicate if the claims and/or drawings were filed after the date of filing, but no indication is given whether any matter has been divided out into a separate application. The various items of bibliographic data are linked to the numbers of the ICIREPAT code, for which see the INID standard code of WIPO, as explained OJEPO 10/1988, 395, see also para. 123.45.

Originally, both the "A-specification" and the re-published specification when a patent is granted (the "B-specification") were printed in letterpress. However, this is no longer so and both specifications are now published by reproduction of the documents filed by or on behalf of the applicant. Thus, printing errors are now avoided. Where a specification has been published in type-set form, it should be remembered that this may contain printing errors and that the authentic text is not the printed form but that held on the Patent Office file.

The front pages of the "A-specifications" are also published separately as a convenient means of publishing the abstracts, though this publication occurs a little later than the publication of the "A-specifications" themselves. These front pages are collected together in accordance with the Patent Office classification codes and made available as published collections of classified abstracts which continue the practice under the former statutes of publishing classified abridgments of patent specifications. Consolidated file lists are also published listing under each classification mark the specifications indexed thereunder. Regular orders can be placed for these in designated classification groups.

In error the abstracts of applications due for publication September 3, 1986 were mailed with the O.J. of August 27, 1986 thereby causing their premature publication ((1986–87) 16 CIPA 28, O.J. May 28, 1987).

16.08 *Numbering of published specifications*

The application as published under section 16 is allotted a seven digit serial number in a series beginning with 2,000,001, followed by the letter A. This number should be used for ordering copies of the printed specification, but the application filing number should be used for all correspondence concerning prosecution up to grant (O.J. November 1, 1978), see also para. 123.45.

Under section 118(3)(*b*) the bibliographic information defined in rule 95 (reprinted at para. 118.02) may be published before the publication date of the application. In fact it is published in the O.J. about five weeks after the date of filing and is entered in a card index in the SRIS. A register is also maintained by the SRIS, which is compiled on an informal basis from entries in the O.J. In this is entered in due course the Publication Number of the application or when notice of its withdrawal is published in the O.J. This register also lists European and international applications which claim priority from an application under the Act, this information being gleaned by the SRIS from the EPB for published European, and the International Bulletin for published international applications. This informal register therefore acts as a most useful concordance between the different numbers allotted by the Patent Office to an application (i) on its filing and (ii) on its publication under section 16, and may also serve to indicate that an initial application under the Act is being continued via the EPC and/or PCT routes, possibly to obtain protection in the United Kingdom as well as in other countries.

16.09 *Withdrawal of application before publication*

To avoid publication the application can be withdrawn, but this must be done before completion of the preparations for publication, see para. 16.06 *supra*. It is, therefore, useful to state that "withdrawal is in order to prevent publication" if this is the case, see para. 14.39.

The Patent Office desires to avoid publication of applications filed solely to establish priority. When this is done the Office welcomes formal withdrawal when the second application claiming priority therefrom is filed. Alternatively, the priority application can be allowed to become abandoned by deliberate failure to file claims and/or an abstract. However, there remains doubt whether an application once it has been withdrawn could still be claimed to be an "earlier relevant application" for the purposes of section 5(2), see (1979–80) 9 CIPA 133.

SECTION 17

17.01

Preliminary examination and search

17.—(1) Where an application for a patent has a date of filing and is not withdrawn, and before the end of the prescribed period—

    (*a*) a request is made by the applicant to the Patent Office in the prescribed form for a preliminary examination and a search, and

    (*b*) the prescribed fee is paid for the examination and search (the search fee);

the comptroller shall refer the application to an examiner for a preliminary examination and search, except that he shall not refer the application for a search until it includes one or more claims.

(2) On a preliminary examination of an application the examiner shall determine whether the application complies with those requirements of this Act and the rules which are designated by the rules as formal requirements for the purposes of this Act and shall report his determination to the comptroller.

(3) If it is reported to the comptroller under subsection (2) above that not all the formal requirements are complied with, he shall give the applicant an opportunity to make observations on the report and to amend the application within a specified period (subject to section 15(5) above) so as to comply with those requirements (subject, however, to section 76 below) and if the applicant fails to do so the comptroller may refuse the application.

(4) Subject to subsections (5) and (6) below, on a search requested under this section, the examiner shall make such investigation as in his opinion is reasonably practicable and necessary for him to identify the documents which he thinks will be needed to decide, on a substantive examination under section 18 below, whether the invention for which a patent is sought is new and involves an inventive step.

(5) On any such search the examiner shall determine whether or not the search would serve any useful purpose on the application as for the time being constituted and—

    (*a*) if he determines that it would serve such a purpose in relation to the whole or part of the application, he shall proceed to conduct the search so far as it would serve such a purpose and shall report on the results of the search to the comptroller; and

(b) if he determines that the search would not serve such a purpose in relation to the whole or part of the application, he shall report accordingly to the comptroller;

and in either event the applicant shall be informed of the examiner's report.

(6) If it appears to the examiner, either before or on conducting a search under this section, that an application relates to two or more inventions, but that they are not so linked as to form a single inventive concept, he shall initially only conduct a search in relation to the first invention specified in the claims of the application, but may proceed to conduct a search in relation to another invention so specified if the applicant pays the search fee in respect of the application so far as it relates to that other invention.

(7) After a search has been requested under this section for an application the comptroller may at any time refer the application to an examiner for a supplementary search, and **subsections (4) and (5)** [*subsection (4)*] above shall apply in relation to a supplementary search as **they apply** [*it applies*] in relation to any other search under this section.

(8) A reference for a supplementary search in consequence of—

(a) an amendment of the application made by the applicant under section 18(3) or 19(1) below, or

(b) a correction of the application, or of a document filed in connection with the application, under section 117 below,

shall be made only on payment of the prescribed fee, unless the comptroller directs otherwise.

Note. Subsection (7) was prospectively amended, and subsection (8) prospectively added, by the 1988 Act (Sched. 5, para. 3). For the commencement of these provisions, see the latest Supplement to this Work.

RELEVANT RULES

Preliminary examination under section 17

17.02 **29.**—(1) A request under section 17(1)(*a*) for a preliminary examination and search shall be made on Patents Form No. 9/77.

(2) On a preliminary examination the examiner shall determine, not only whether the application ("the application in suit") complies with those requirements of the Act and these Rules which are designated by rule 31 as formal requirements for the purposes of the Act, but also whether the requirements of rules 6(1) and (2) and 15(1) and the provisions of section 15(3) have been complied with.

(3) Where the preliminary examination reveals that an earlier relevant application declared for the purposes of section 5 has been stated in the application in suit to have a date of filing more than twelve months before

the date of filing of the application in suit, the Patent Office shall notify the applicant that the earlier relevant application will be disregarded unless, within one month, he supplies the Patent Office with a corrected date, being one which falls within those twelve months.

Formal requirements

31.—(1) The requirements of rules 16(1), 18(1) and (2) (other than those   **17.03**
contained in paragraph (2)(*h*) of that rule), 20 (other than those contained in the last sentence of paragraph (12) or paragraph (13) or (15) of that rule) and 30 shall be formal requirements for the purposes of the Act.
(2) Where the application is—
 (*a*) an application for a European (UK); or
 (*b*) an international application for a patent (UK)
which by virtue of section 81 or 89, as the case may be, is to be treated as an application for a patent under the Act, the said requirements of rules 16(1), 18(1) and (2) and 20 shall be treated as having been complied with to the extent that the requirements of the corresponding provisions of the Implementing Regulations to the European Patent Convention or, as the case may be, of the Regulations made under the Patent Co-operation Treaty, have been fulfilled.

Note. For the amendment of this rule, to be made when the remainder of Sched. 5 [1988], and/or section 281(5) [1988] (as regards r. 30), is brought into effect, see the latest Supplement to this Work *re.* the present para.

Searches under section 17(6)

32.—(1) Where an examiner conducts a search under section 17(6) in   **17.04**
relation to the first only of two or more inventions specified in the claims of an application, the Patent Office shall notify the applicant of that fact.
(2) If the applicant desires a search to be conducted under section 17(6) in relation to a second or subsequent invention specified in the claims, he shall, before the expiry of the period specified for the making of observations on the report made under section 18(3), request the Patent Office on Patents Form No. 9/77 to conduct such a search and pay the search fee for each invention in respect of which the search is to be made.

COMMENTARY ON SECTION 17

General   **17.05**

Under the Act, examination of patent applications is effected in two distinct stages: a first stage under section 17 involving (*a*) a search and (*b*) a preliminary examination; and a second stage under section 18 which involves a substantive examination. The second stage is not commenced until a search report has been issued under section 17 and the necessary examination fee prescribed by subsection

18(1) has been paid. Sections 17 and 18 are not included in section 130(7) and so are not specified as having been intended to have the same meanings as the corresponding sections of EPC and PCT, but similar provisions exist in EPCaa. 90(1), 91(1) to (3) and 92 and in EPCrr. 39 to 42 and 44 to 46, and in PCTaa. 14, 15, 17 and 18 and PCTrr. 26 to 30, 33, 37, 38, 40 and 43.

Preliminary examinations (subss. (1)–(3))

17.06 *—Scope and definitions*

The request for preliminary examination is made by filing PF 9/77 (reprinted at para. 141.09) on which the search fee is paid, see para. 144.02. Rule 29 (reprinted at para. 17.02 *supra*) governs that filing and the subsequent procedure. If the request is not made within the period prescribed by section 15(5)(*b*) and rule 25(2) made thereunder, the application is deemed to be withdrawn (s. 15(5)). The prescribed period is normally 12 months from filing or the declared priority date whichever is the earlier, see para. 15.10.

In the preliminary examination the examiner must determine whether the application complies with the formal and certain other requirements as prescribed in rules 6(1) and (2) (and, where necessary, rr. 6(3), (4) or (5)), 15(1) and (3) and 31). These rules are reprinted in paras. 5.02, 13.03 and 17.03 respectively. From rule 29(3) it is clear that the preliminary examination must extend to ascertaining whether any earlier application from which priority is sought, is dated more than 12 months before the filing date.

Section 130(1) defines the terms "search fee" and "formal requirements" by reference to section 17(1) and (2) respectively. The latter term is further defined by rule 31 made under section 17(2) and this rule sets out the requirements which are specifically designated as "formal requirements" for the purposes of the preliminary examination conducted under these subsections. The "search fee", according to subsection (1)(*b*), is the prescribed fee for the preliminary examination as well as the search. The search fee is prescribed as being the fee payable on PF 9/77, see paras. 122.05 and 144.01. However, the Schedule to the Patents (Fees) Rules does not specifically name the "search fee" as such (contrast the naming of the "filing fee" in relation to PF 1/77).

17.07 *—Meeting of formal requirements (r. 31)*

Rule 31 is reprinted in para. 17.03 *supra*. The formal requirements specified therein relate to: the request (*i.e.* PF 1/77) (r. 16(1)); the requirements as to drawings (r. 18); the requirements as to other documents (r. 20); and the furnishing of an address for service (r. 30). These rules are reprinted in paras. 14.02, 14.03, 14.05 and 32.03 respectively. The location of an address for service is discussed in para. 32.16.

However, failure to comply with rule 17 is not a formal requirement so that (unlike the position under the EPC, see *EPO Decisions J* O8/87 and *J* O9/87, "*Submitting culture deposit information/IDAHO*" ([1989] 3 EPOR 170), no attention need be drawn during the preliminary examination to a failure to provide the accession number of a deposited micro-organism under the present form of rule 17(2), as to which see para. 125A.11. Also, consistency of use of reference numerals (rr. 18(2)(*h*) and 20(15)) and use of metric units (r. 20(13)) are not "formal requirements", and any objections to non-conformity with these requirements are raised in the substantive examination under section 18.

By subsection (3), the Comptroller is required to give the applicant an opportunity to amend the application by filing replacement documents within a specified period if it does not comply with the formal requirements, subject to compliance with the period prescribed by rule 25(1) concerning the filing of the claims and the abstract, see paras. 15.10 and 15.11.

By rule 29(2), the preliminary examination also extends to the requirements concerning: the declaration of priority under rule 6(1): the certified copy of the basic application under rule 6(2) or PF 24/77 under rule 6(3); the statement of inventorship under rule 15(1) or EPCr. 17; and the drawings under section 15(3). However, these are not "formal requirements" within the definition of rule 31. Therefore, subsections (2) and (3) do not apply to them. There is, therefore, no need for the Comptroller to check whether the requirements of rules 6(2) (*Provision of certified copy of priority document*) and 15(1) (*Provision of statement of inventorship on PF 7/77*) have been complied with before the ends of the prescribed periods (*Mitsui Engineering's Application*, [1984] RPC 471; *X's Application*, SRIS O/181/86), or indeed that of rule 6(6) (*Provision of certified translation of priority document*) either. In practice, if these requirements have not been met at the time of carrying out the preliminary examination, the Office may send a reminder, but is not obliged so to do.

The formal and other requirements checked in the preliminary examination are in effect those with which the application must comply to enable the specification (including any drawings) to be printed and to enable the determination of the contents of the frontsheet of the "A-specification" to be published under section 16 for which see particularly para. 14.35. Failure to file replacement documents complying with the formal requirements within the specified term may result in the application being refused, see para. 17.16 *infra*.

—Declaration of priority   **17.08**

If during the preliminary examination (or during the substantive examination under s. 18) it is noted that a declaration of priority made under section 5 contains irregularities or deficiencies which cannot be rectified or are not rectified within the prescribed or specified periods, the claim to priority will be lost, see also paras. 5.07 and 5.19. The Act and the Rules contain no explicit provisions corresponding to that part of EPCa. 91(3) relating to the right of priority.

The requirement of rule 6(6) that a verified translation of the certified copy of the basic application be filed within 21 months of the declared priority date when priority is claimed and the basic application is not in English, is not one of the requirements mentioned in rule 29(2), presumably because such verified translation need not be filed until after publication under section 16, at least in normal circumstances. Although the Patent Office may remind applicants if it is noted that a verified translation is required, but has not been filed at the time the preliminary examination is carried out, there is no obligation upon it to do so, see para. 17.07 *supra*.

The periods prescribed by: rules 6(2)(*b*) (for filing a certified copy of a priority document), rule 6(6) for filing any necessary translation thereof), and rule 15(1), (for filing a statement of inventorship on PF 7/77) may each be extended under rule 110(3) and/or (3A) and (3C) upon payment of a heavy fee, while the period for filing the claims and abstract under rule 25(1) can be extended under rule 110(1), see respectively paras. 5.20, 5.21, 13.12 and 15.11. Note that an extension under rule 110(3) is only obtainable if PF 50/77 is filed within the one month period obtainable under rule 110(3) (*Konishiroku's Application*, SRIS O/16/83, followed in *Aisin Seiki's Application*, [1984] RPC 191), but an additional extension under rules

110(3A) and (3C) can now be obtained with the Comptroller's discretion if the one month extension period under r. 110(3) is insufficient, see para. 123.33.

17.09   *The search (subss. (4)–(7))*

The search will not be commenced until the application includes one or more claims; see subsection (1). By subsection (4) the purpose of the search is to identify documents which the examiner thinks will be needed to enable a decision to be made as to whether the invention is new in accordance with section 2, and whether it involves an inventive step in accordance with section 3. Two copies of the search report are sent to the applicant, but the Act and Rules contain no provision for a copy of the references to be sent to the applicant: *cf.* EPCa. 92(2). The Patent Office endeavours to issue the search report within 15 months of the declared priority date in order that publication under section 16 will not be delayed, or within nine months of the filing date if priority has not been claimed, provided that the claims and PF 9/77 have already been filed. Occasionally, search reports issue within a few weeks after filing an application with claims and PF 9/77 but without claim to priority (M. Dean, (1980–81) 10 CIPA 485).

By subsection (5), the search is conducted only in so far as it will serve a useful purpose. Accordingly, the search examiner confines his search to material which is relevant to novelty and inventive step in relation to the invention as presented at the time of the search.

If the search examiner decides that a search would serve no useful purpose, the applicant is notified under subsection (5)(*b*) by a letter containing the examiner's report to this effect, and the applicant may amend his application after receipt of such report (r. 36(2), reprinted in para. 19.03). In *Hulmes' Application* (SRIS O/176/86) an explanation was given of the steps taken by the Patent Office when an application is filed apparently without professional assistance. In that case the application was rejected for insufficient disclosure as originally filed: no search could be performed and the fee paid on PF 9/77 was certified for refund, see also *Poon's Application* (SRIS O/51/89) for a similar case where the Applicant insisted on a hearing. When amendments are made to the claims which will enable the examiner to conduct the search, the search will be carried out before publication under section 16 if the amendments are received in time. Otherwise the search is deferred until after publication.

17.10   *Search against further inventions and supplementary search (r. 32)*

If the examiner conducting the search considers that the claims are directed to two or more inventions not so linked to form a single inventive step, he is required by subsection (6) to conduct the search against the first-claimed invention. Rule 32 (reprinted at para. 17.04 *supra*) then requires that the examiner must notify the applicant of the fact that he has done so. Under rule 32(2), the applicant may request a search under subsection (6) against any further claimed invention, provided that he makes such request on PF 9/77, identifies on that form the claims to be searched, and pays a further search fee, all within the period specified for reply to the first official report under section 18(3) on the substantive examination.

A supplementary search may be carried out at any time, see subsection (7). Use is made of this provision to enable the search to be up-dated during the substantive examination of the application under section 18 to include recently published United Kingdom, European and international applications and to extend the field of search in the event that the examiner finds the search report to be inadequate to enable him to make a decision under section 18(4) as to patentability of the invention.

Newly added subsection (8) will, when brought into effect, allow the Comptroller to require a fee for a supplementary search if the need for such a search arises from an amendment under section 18(3) or 19(1) or from a correction under section 117. The situation will arise typically when an amendment to remove a lack of unity leaves the application containing claims to an unsearched invention. It is assumed that the Patent Office will use this power to avoid examining an invention for which a search fee has not been paid under subsections (1), (6) or (8). This resembles the EPO's attitude as set out in the EPO Guidelines C–III, 7.10–7.12 and C–IV, 3.2, but is not identical since in the United Kingdom it will be possible to pay a fee under subsection (8) in cases where the rule 32(2) period for paying a further fee under subsection (6) has passed. It may also be noted that subsection (8) appears to provide the Comptroller with a discretion whether to demand a fee for every supplementary search.

Under new subsection 18(1A), if a fee is required under section 17(8), substantive examination will not proceed until the fee is paid or the application is amended to render the supplementary search unnecessary. If neither the fee is paid nor the application amended, the Comptroller will be entitled to refuse the application, see para. 18.08. Presumably, there will be first the opportunity to contend that a supplementary search is unnecessary even without amending the application.

Refund of search fee   **17.11**

Provision for refund of the search fee in certain specified circumstances is provided for by rule 102 (reprinted at para. 123.09 and discussed at para. 123.25).

If it is successfully argued during substantive examination under section 18 that the inventions of claims against which separate search reports have been drawn up under subsection (6) or (8) do involve the same inventive concept, the search fee paid on the second PF 9/77 may be refunded by way of rectification of an irregularity in procedure (r. 100) (reprinted at para. 123.07), see para. 123.21, despite the wording of rule 102.

If a divisional application is filed for an invention for which a search report was drawn up under subsection (6) on the parent application, the search fee paid on the divisional application may be refunded (r. 102(1)(c)), see para. 17.18 *infra*.

Under rule 102(1)(b), when an international search report has already been established on an international application which has commenced its national phase before the United Kingdom Office, all or a part of the United Kingdom search fee may be refunded, see para. 89A.33.

If an application is irrevocably withdrawn after the search fee has been paid, but before the search has issued, the search fee may be refunded (O.J. July 16, 1980).

There is apparently no rule which would enable the Comptroller to refund all or part of the search fee paid on an application claiming priority from an earlier United Kingdom application on which a search report for the same invention has already issued, see para. 123.25.

Furnishing of translations of cited documents   **17.12**

If an international or European search report refers to documents not in English, the applicant may be directed to furnish a translation of such documents within two months of the date of such direction (r. 113(3)). The Comptroller has a discretionary power to extend this two month period (r. 110(1)).

PRACTICE UNDER SECTION 17

Time limits

17.13 *—General*

For convenience, set out below are the various formal requirements and the periods, if any, allowed under the Act and the Rules for amending or supplementing the application documents in the event of non-compliance. In practice, an official report that the application does not comply with formal requirements will specify a period within which amendments and deficiencies may be corrected, subject to the overall periods prescribed. The specified period will usually be either one month from the date of the report or 15 months from the declared priority date or from the filing date if there is no declared priority date. If the preliminary examination reveals that a declaration of priority contained in the request specifies a filing date for the earlier application more than 12 months before the filing date of the application in question, there is a prescribed period of one month from the date of the examiner's report in which to substitute a correct filing date within that 12 month period or otherwise the priority date is lost (r. 29(3)). This one month period is extensible at the Comptroller's discretion under rule 110(1).

17.14 *—Minimum requirements on filing*

The minimum requirements on filing to obtain a filing date, as specified in section 15(1), are: an indication that a patent is being sought; an identification of the applicant; a description of the invention; the payment of the filing fee. If priority is being claimed a declaration of priority is required also, under section 5(2), giving the date and the country of the first filing. If the invention involves the use of a micro-organism not generally available to the public at the time of filing, section 125A(2) and (3) and rule 17 require that a culture of the micro-organism must be deposited in a culture collection and this made available to the public as specified in that rule, see para. 125A.17. If the invention was displayed at an international exhibition a statement to that effect must be provided under section 2(4)(c), see para. 2.32.

17.15 *—Requirements which can be met after filing*

Within two months after the filing date, rule 17(2) (reprinted in para. 125A.02) requires that, if the invention involves the use of a micro-organism not available to the public at the time of filing, information must be given identifying the culture collection in which the culture of the micro-organism is deposited, the date of deposit and the accession number of the deposit. This two month period is extensible as of right by one month by filing PF 50/77 with its heavy fee (r. 110(3)), and further extensible at the Comptroller's discretion with PF 52/77 and PF 53/77, again with heavy fees (r. 110(3A) and (3C)), see para. 123.33.

Within four months after the filing date, if the application includes a statement to the effect that the invention was displayed at an international exhibition, rule 5(2) requires that a certificate by the exhibition authority, giving the exhibition dates and date of disclosure of the invention, be supplied. This period is extensible at the Comptroller's discretion under rule 110(1), see para. 2.32.

Within 12 months after the declared priority date, or within 12 months after the filing date (if no declared priority date), section 15(5)(b) and 17(1) require PF 9/77 (*Request for preliminary examination and search*) to be filed accompanied by the search fee. This 12 month period is extensible by one month as of right with PF

50/77 (r. 110(3)) and further extensible at the Comptroller's discretion with PF 52/77 and PF 53/77 (r. 110(3A) and (3C)), see paras. 15.10 and 15.11.

Within 12 months after the declared priority date, or one month after the filing date (whichever is later), or within 12 months after the filing date (if no declared priority date), section 15(5)(*a*) requires the filing of a claim or claims, and the abstract. This period is extensible at the Comptroller's discretion under rule 110(1). One month's extension will be granted when PF 50/77 has been filed to extend by one month the period for filing PF 9/77, see paras. 15.10 and 15.11.

Within 16 months after the declared priority date, or within 16 months after the filing date (if there is no declared priority date), a statement of the inventorship on PF 7/77 is required under section 13(2) (if not included in the request) giving the name and address of the inventor or each inventor, and the manner in which the applicant derives the right to grant the patent. This 16 month period for filing PF 7/77 is extensible by one month by filing PF 50/77 (r. 110(3)) and further extensible at the Comptroller's discretion with PF 52/77 and PF 53/77 (r. 110(3A) and (3C)), see para. 13.12.

Within 16 months after the declared priority date, when priority is being claimed, the filing number of the first filing is required; and a certified copy of the first filing must be filed (except when the first filing is at the United Kingdom Patent Office) (r. 6(2)). This 16 month period is also extensible by one month by filing PF 50/77 and further extensible at the Comptroller's discretion with PF 52/77 and PF 53/77 (r. 110(3A) and (3C), see para. 5.20.

Within 21 months after the declared priority date, if priority is being claimed and the certified copy of the first filing is not in English, an English translation of the certified copy must be filed (r. 6(6)). This period is likewise extensible by one month by filing PF 50/77 and further extensible at the Comptroller's discretion with PF 52/77 and PF 53/77 (r. 110 (3A) and (3C)), see para. 5.21.

While failure to comply with the requirements of filing a priority declaration (r. 6(1)), a copy of a priority application (r. 6(2) and PF 7/77 (rr. 15(1) and (3)) are each now pointed out under rule 29(2) in the preliminary examination report, there is still an obligation upon the applicant (making r. 100 inapplicable) to meet these requirements within the time specified in the rules therefor, or as extended under rule 110 in the case of compliance with rules 6(2) and 15(1) (*Nippon Piston's Applications*, [1987] RPC 120).

Subsequent procedure is covered in the commentary on section 18 *infra*.

For the applicable time limits in the case of a divisional application or a new application under sections 8(3), 12(6) or 37(4), see paras. 15.15–15.22.

—Comparison with practice under EPC   **17.16**

Practice under the EPC differs from the practice under the Act in that EPCa. 80 requires that at least one claim and the designation of at least one contracting state should accompany the application in order to establish a filing date, and in that EPCa. 78(2) permits the filing fee and the search fee to be paid up to one month after the filing date. The designation fee is payable under EPCa. 79 within 12 months after the filing date if priority is not claimed, or within 12 months after the priority date or one month after the filing date, whichever is later, if priority is claimed. The corresponding provisions for an international application are covered in PCTa. 11 and PCTrr. 14–16.

Preliminary examination   **17.17**

The preliminary examination is commenced as soon as PF 9/77 has been filed. The application is referred to a formalities officer who not only checks whether the application conforms with the formal requirements recited in rule 31 (reprinted at para. 17.03 *supra*) but also whether the requirements concerning any claim to convention priority have been met (r. 6(1) and (2) reprinted in para. 5.02) and whether the application complies with the requirements concerning the naming of the inventor (r. 15(1) reprinted in para. 13.03).

Although the Patent Office may draw attention to any seemingly missing documents as part of the preliminary examination under subsection (2), it is under no obligation to do so. Therefore, rule 100 will not apply to any omission to give such a reminder (*Mitsui Engineering's Application*, [1984] RPC 471), see further para. 17.15 *supra*. Also, no reminder is sent for international applications when they enter the national phase as section 17(2) does not then apply (*Application des Gaz's Application*, [1987] RPC 279).

The normal practice is for the formalities officer to specify a term of 15 months from the declared priority date, or from the filing date if there is no declared priority date, in which the applicant may file replacement documents complying with the rules. If the formalities officer's report issues late, it will usually specify a one month term for response. Since the response period is not specified in the Act or prescribed in the rules, it is open to extension by a new period for response being specified. However, the applicant should not expect extensions to be granted as a matter of course, since they would lead to delay in publication under section 16, see para. 18.15.

If the applicant fails to file satisfactory replacement documents within the specified period, the Comptroller may refuse the application (subs. (3)). Accordingly, when the response term has not been met, a letter is sent to the applicant saying that the application will be refused if satisfactory documents are not filed within a further specified term of at least 14 days. If an application is refused for failure to meet a formal requirement, an appeal may be lodged (s. 97(1)).

If the preliminary examination reveals that a drawing is missing, the application may be post-dated, see para. 15.09.

When the application is an international application which has entered the United Kingdom phase (s. 89) (to be replaced by s. 89A), or a European application which has been converted into a United Kingdom application (s. 81), then a check for compliance with the requirements of rule 31 (1) is not made (r. 31(2) and (3)).

When priority is claimed, the preliminary examination includes a check on compliance with rule 6(1). The file number of the basic application may be inserted at any time up to expiry of the 16 month term for filing the certified copy, but the date and country of filing of the basic application must be given at the time of filing the application, though not necessarily on PF 1/77 (r. 6(1)). If the given date of filing of the basic application is more than 12 months before the filing date of the application in suit, the special provisions of rule 29(3) apply, whereby a term of one month (extensible under r. 110(1) at the Comptroller's discretion) is prescribed for giving a corrected filing date. Otherwise any discrepancy between the date of filing as given in the application in suit and the certified copy may be corrected in the course of the preliminary examination.

The preliminary examination will usually be commenced before expiry of the term of 16 months specified in rules 6(2) and 15(1) and, in the event that a certified copy of the basic application or PF 7/77 are required and have not been filed, the applicant will be reminded of this 16 month term. If the basic application is not in English and a verified translation has not been filed, the applicant will also be reminded of the 21 month term prescribed in rule 6(6), although this is not a procedural step which is required by rule 29 to be checked on the preliminary examination under section 17(3) and the application will normally be published before the verified translation need be filed. Such reminders may be contained in a letter objecting to non-compliance with formal requirements or in the letter which accompanies the search report under subsection (4).

If PF 7/77 is required and has not been filed within 16 months of the declared priority date, or from the filing date if there is no declared priority date, or within any extension under rule 110(3) or (3A), the application is deemed withdrawn (s. 13(2)) and the application will not be published.

If priority is claimed from an application abroad and a certified copy is not filed within 16 months of the declared priority date, or (together with PF 50/77) within 17 months of this date, priority will be lost and this will result in the loss of the declared priority date (or in a later declared priority date) and a re-calculation of all those time limits which were calculated from the declared priority date. When priority is claimed from a United Kingdom application, no certified copy of the basic application is required, but PF 24/77 must be filed if requested by the Comptroller (r. 6(3)(*b*)), see para. 5.20.

Special considerations apply in the case of divisional applications under section 15(4), see paras. 5.15–5.21, and in the case of applications under sections 8(3), 12(6) and 37(4), see paras. 15.22 and 8.14.

The search   **17.18**

No limit is placed by subsection (4) on the field and extent of the search. In practice, the area of search, at least for the time being, is similar to that under the 1949 Act, *i.e.* concentrated on United Kingdom patent specifications published since 1925, but the search files are being extended to include United States patent specifications, and European and international patent applications as they are published are added to the search files. The search will include United Kingdom specifications, European patent applications and international applications published up to the date of the search and may include recent specifications from the United States. The search may also now include reference to on-line databases. If so, the search results therefrom are reported in standard abbreviated form, as explained O.J. August 9, 1989. However, the specifications of European and international patent applications are no longer, in general, being classified according to the highly developed United Kingdom patent classification system, see O.J. August 31, 1989.

Supplementary searches   **17.19**

If the examiner considers that the claims are directed to two or more inventions not so linked as to form a single inventive concept, he is required under subsection (6) to conduct the search against the first-claimed invention and to inform the applicant to this effect under rule 32(1), and the applicant should choose the subject of claim 1 accordingly, see *Hollister's Application* ([1983] RPC 10). The search report will identify those claims which the examiner considers are not directed to the first invention and against which he has not conducted a search. Under rule 32(2) the applicant will then be permitted to request a further search against such claims and pay the additional search fee. Although the applicant has up to the end of the period specified for response to the first report on the substantive examination under section 18(2) in which to do this, the earlier the request is made the more time will be left in which to file a divisional application if the further search is favourable. If it is established during the substantive examination under section 18(2) that the examiner's decision that the claims are not directed to a single invention or inventive concept is wrong, the additional search fee paid on the further search may be refunded by way of rectification of an irregularity in procedure under rule 100, see para. 123.21.

A further search under subsection (6) may only be requested where the examiner has reported that some claims define a further invention. A further search under subsection (6) should not be requested in respect of new or amended claims nor in respect of original claims on which the examiner has not so reported. A separate PF 9/77 is required in respect of each such further invention for which a search is required (O.J. October 17, 1979). Requests on PF 9/77 for further searches under subsection (6) should not be filed until the initial search report under subsection (5) has been issued, and then only if the examiner has reported under subsection (1) or section 18(3) that the application relates to a plurality of inventions (O.J. July 30, 1980).

If the first search report of the examiner indicates that the search has not been completed, but it is unclear therefrom whether a non-unity objection arises or not, it is suggested that the examiner be asked to clarify whether objection is being raised under subsection (6) because, if it is, the time for requesting further searches under rule 32(2) may expire without it being appreciated that rule 32(1) has been applied by the examiner.

New subsection (8) only comes into play when the applicant amends or corrects the specification. Presumably, if a fee is required for a supplementary search under subsection (8), an official letter will be issued notifying the applicant of this fact. It should be possible to contest the need for the supplementary search, and if such a contest is successful after the fee has been paid it should be possible to obtain a refund of the fee under rule 100.

The amendment to subsection (7), to make subsection (5) apply to it also, requires a search report to be issued following any supplementary search.

The Note on PF 9/77 (reprinted in para. 141.09) indicates that, where an additional search is requested, the area for that search should be fully identified on that form by reference to the claims to be searched. If this is not done, the further search will be carried out on the second invention in the previous search report, as the Note on PF 9/77 makes clear. For a discussion on the nature of a search report issued on a divisional application, see para. 15.29.

If a divisional application is filed for an invention on which a search report has already been drawn up upon the parent application, the search fee paid on the divisional application may be refunded on request (r. 102(1)), see para. 123.25. However, it is always necessary to pay the search fee on the divisional application in the first instance to enable the preliminary examination to take place, see para. 15.28.

For a discussion on the timing of the filing of divisional applications following a report under subsection (6), see paras. 18.13, 15.13 and 15.30.

17.20   *Amendment after the search*

Once the applicant has received the search report, he may voluntarily amend his application. Voluntary amendment is discussed in para. 19.05.

Amendments made to the description before the publication under section 16 are not included in the printed "A-specification", but any amendments to the claims and/or any additional claims, filed before the preparations for publication are complete, will be printed together with the claims as originally filed.

Whilst there is no obligation on the applicant to offer any amendment upon receipt of the search report, it is relevant to early amendment of the claims that the rights arising under sections 55 and 69 on publication of the application refer to the claims as they were immediately before completion of the preparations for publication of the application under section 16.

SECTION 18

18.01

Substantive examination and grant or refusal of patent

18.—(1) Where the conditions imposed by section 17(1) above for the comptroller to refer an application to an examiner for a preliminary examination and search are satisfied and at the time of the request under that subsection or within the prescribed period—

(*a*) a request is made by the applicant to the Patent Office in the prescribed form for a substantive examination; and

(*b*) the prescribed fee is paid for the examination;

the comptroller shall refer the application to an examiner for a substantive examination; and if no such request is made or the prescribed fee is not paid within that period, the application shall be treated as having been withdrawn at the end of that period.

(1A) If the examiner forms the view that a supplementary search under section 17 above is required for which a fee is payable, he shall inform the comptroller, who may decide that the substantive examination should not proceed until the fee is paid; and if he so decides, then unless within such period as he may allow—

(a) the fee is paid, or

(b) the application is amended so as to render the supplementary search unnecessary,

he may refuse the application.

(2) On a substantive examination of an application the examiner shall investigate, to such extent as he considers necessary in view of any examination and search carried out under section 17 above, whether the application complies with the requirements of this Act and the rules and shall determine that question and report his determination to the comptroller.

(3) If the examiner reports that any of those requirements are not complied with, the comptroller shall give the applicant an opportunity within a specified period to make observations on the report and to amend the application so as to comply with those requirements (subject, however, to section 76 below) and if the applicant fails to satisfy the comptroller that those requirements are complied with, or to amend the application so as to comply with them, the comptroller may refuse the application.

(4) If the examiner reports that the application, whether as originally filed or as amended in pursuance of section 17 above, this section or section 19 below, complies with those requirements at any time before the end of the prescribed period, the comptroller shall notify the applicant of that fact and, subject to subsection (5) and sections 19 and 22 below and on payment within the prescribed period of any fee prescribed for the grant, grant him a patent.

(5) Where two or more applications for a patent for the same invention having the same priority date are filed by the same applicant or his succes-

183

sor in title, the comptroller may on that ground refuse to grant a patent in pursuance of more than one of the applications.

Note. Subsection (1A) was prospectively added by the 1988 Act (Sched. 5, para. 4). For its commencement, see the latest Supplement to this Work.

RELEVANT RULES

Request for substantive examination under section 18

18.02 **33.**—(1) A request for a substantive examination of an application for a patent shall be made on Patents Form No. 10/77.

(2) Subject to the provisions of rules 83(1), 85(3)(*b*) and paragraphs (3) and (4) below, the request shall be made and the fee for the examination paid within six months of the date of publication of the application in accordance with section 16.

(3) Where an application is subject to directions under section 22(2) or (2), the request shall be made and the fee paid within two years of the declared priority date or, where there is no declared priority date, from the date of filing the application except in the case of new application made under sections 8(3), 12(6) or 15(4) after the expiry of the said two years, when the request shall be made and the fee paid at the time of filing the new application.

(4) Where a new application is filed under sections 8(3), 12(6), 15(4) or 37(4) then—

(*a*) if the new application is filed within two years calculated from the declared priority date or, where there is no declared priority date, from the date treated as its date of filing, the request shall be made and the fee for the examination paid within those two years; and

(*b*) if the new application is filed after the expiration of those two years, the request shall be made and the fee for the examination paid at the time of filing the new application.

Note. For the revised form of this rule when new section 89A is brought into effect with the consequent amendment of rule 85, see the latest Supplement to this Work *re.* this para.

Period for putting application in order

18.03 **34.**—Subject to the provisions of rules 83(3) and 85(3)(*c*) below, for the purposes of sections 18(4) and 20(1), the period within which an application for a patent shall comply with the Act and these Rules shall be the four years and six months calculated from its declared priority date, or where there is no priority date, from the date of filing of the application:

Provided that, in the case of an application made under section 8(3), 12(6), or 37(4), the period shall be the four years and six months calculated from the declared priority date or, where there is no declared priority date, from the date of filing of the earlier application, or the eighteen months calculated from its actual date of filing, whichever expires the later.

Notes. 1. The period specified in this rule was three years and six months prior to September 1, 1980.

2. For the revised form of this rule when new section 89A is brought into effect with the consequent amendment of rule 85, see the latest Supplement to this Work *re.* this para. It is also possible that some extension of the acceptance period will be provided in the case of late-filed observations under section 21, for which see para. 21.05.

COMMENTARY ON SECTION 18

General   **18.04**

The first stage of examination procedure is the search and preliminary examination as set out in section 17.

The second stage is the substantive examination prescribed by subsections (1) and (2). Subsection (1A), when brought into effect, will deal with the possible suspension of the substantive examination when a fee is required for a supplementary search under section 17 until appropriate action is taken, for which see para. 17.10. Subsections (3)–(5) deal with refusal, amendment and grant of the application as the result of the examination. There are corresponding provisions in EPCaa. 94, 96 and 97 and EPCrr. 51 and 52, but section 18 is not one of the sections specified in section 130(7) as being intended to have the same effect as the corresponding provisions of EPC. The international preliminary examination under Chapter II of the PCT is a substantive examination, but results only in an international preliminary examination report, which a national office can regard as advisory rather than determinative of patentability.

Rule 33 (reprinted at para. 18.02 *supra*) governs the method and time for filing the request for substantive examination, and rule 34 (reprinted at para. 18.03 *supra*) governs the period within which the substantive examination under the Act is to be completed.

Request for substantive examination (subs. (1))   **18.05**

By rule 33(1) a request for substantive examination is made by filing PF 10/77 (reprinted at para. 141.10) with its prescribed fee (referred to in this commentary as the "examination fee"), the relative amount of which is indicated in para. 144.01. Under subsection (1) and rule 33(2) such request must be made and the examination fee paid within six months from the date of publication of the first printing of the application under section 16, see para. 16.05. This period may be extended by one month by filing PF 50/77 and paying a heavy fee (r. 110(3)), and may be further or alternatively extended at the Comptroller's discretion with PF 52/77 and PF 53/77 which also bear heavy fees (r. 110(3A) and (3C)). This is to be compared to the analogous provision for requesting substantive examination under the EPC or PCT. Thus, under EPCa. 94(2), a six month period is allowed for requesting examination of a European patent application reckoned from the date of mention of the publication of the novelty report in the EPB; and under PCTaa. 39 and 40 the demand of the competent International Preliminary Examination Authority for an international preliminary examination of an international patent application is unlikely to be useful unless made within 19 months from the priority date.

Under rule 33(3) the period for paying the examination fee on an application of which publication under section 16 is prohibited by a direction under section 22(2) is two years from the declared priority date or, if there is no declared priority date, from the filing date.

In the case of a divisional application filed under section 15(4), or a new application filed under sections 8(3), 12(6) or 37(4) following entitlement proceedings, PF 10/77 must be filed and the examination fee must be paid no later than two years from the declared priority date, or from the filing date if there is no declared priority date, or when lodging the divisional or other new application (r. 33(4)), see para. 15.18. This period is extensible by one month by filing PF 50/77 and further extensible (with discretion) under rule 110(3A) and (3C) with PF 52/77 and PF 53/77.

For payment of the examination fee in the case of a converted European application, see para. 81.13 in relation to rule 83(1) (reprinted in para. 81.03). The provisions laid down for international applications for which the United Kingdom has been designated under PCTa. 4 are considered in para. 89A.25 in relation to the present form of rule 85(3)(*b*) (reprinted at para. 89A.02).

By subsection (1) failure to request examination and pay the examination fee within the aforesaid prescribed period, or the one month extension period obtainable as of right under rule 110(3) by filing PF 50/77, will result in the application being deemed to have been withdrawn at the end of this period, unless that period can be further or alternatively extended with the Comptroller's discretion under rules 110(3A) and (3C), discussed at para. 123.33.

18.06   *Refund of the examination fee*

If an application is irrevocably withdrawn after the examination fee has been paid, but before the first examination report has issued, the examination fee may be refunded (O.J. July 16, 1980).

Where an international application enters national processing before the United Kingdom Patent Office, and an international preliminary examination has already been carried out by the United Kingdom Patent Office, a sum equal to the fee for international preliminary examination will be refunded under rule 102(2) (reprinted in para. 123.09) (O.J. December 29, 1983). However, if international preliminary examination has been carried out elsewhere, *e.g.* by the EPO, the circumstances fall outside both rules 102(1)(*b*) and 102(2) so that no refund is then made, see paras. 89A.33 and 123.25.

18.07   *Substantive examination (subss. (2) and (3))*

The purpose of the substantive examination under subsection (2) is to determine whether the application complies with the requirements of the Act and the Rules, other than the formal requirements which are dealt with in the preliminary examination under section 17. In the event of non-compliance, the Comptroller is required by subsection (3) to give the applicant an opportunity to make observations and amendments within a specified period, but new matter must not be added, see new section 76(2).

Under rule 36(3) (reprinted in para. 19.03 *supra*) the applicant may once amend the application of his own volition when reply is made to the examiner's report, or within two months of the report if the first report is one under subsection (4) that the application complies with the requirements of the Act, see para. 19.05.

The period set for response under section 18(3) is specified by the Comptroller and may therefore be extended by exercise of his discretion. Because the section 18(3) period is not specified in the Act or prescribed by the rules, the provisions of rule 110 do not apply. Extension of the period prescribed in rule 36(3) for filing a voluntary amendment can be obtained at the Comptroller's discretion under rule 110(1), but it is suggested that it is better to file PF 11/77 (reprinted at para. 14.11) and request the Comptroller's discretion under rule 36(4), see para. 19.05.

Before the Comptroller's discretion is exercised adversely under section 18(3) (for which see paras. 18.14 and 18.15 *infra*), or under rules 36(4) or 110(1), an opportunity of a hearing must be granted, see para. 101.04. If the decision of the hearing officer is adverse to the applicant, section 97(1) provides for appeal to the Patents Court with further appeal (both on facts and the law), with leave, to the Court of Appeal. Though section 97(5) provides for further appeals in Scotland, rule 108 (reprinted at para. 98.02) does not provide for hearings of the Comptroller under section 18 to be held in Scotland.

During substantive examination the examiner may raise any objection arising under the Act or rules, including formal requirements. Thus, an application can be rejected under subsection (3) at any time (even before PF 10/77 is filed for substantive examination) if the Comptroller holds, after a hearing if requested, that the specification is such that it cannot be brought into compliance with the Act and Rules, for example because it describes a device which can only function in a manner contrary to established natural laws (*Paez's Application*, SRIS O/176/83; *Simon's Application*, SRIS O/139/86 and C/6/87; and *Rohde and Schwarz's Application*, [1980] RPC 155).

In *Microsonics' Application* ([1984] RPC 29) it was doubted whether, despite the use of the word "may" in the final words of section 18(3), the Comptroller had any real discretion not to refuse an application once he had held that an objection to grant existed.

The principal object of the substantive examination is to determine whether the invention claimed is patentable according to section 1(1) having regard to the search report made under section 17 and any prior art acknowledged as such in the description. The Comptroller is being given power to call for a supplementary search and a fee therefor, see the proposed amendment to section 17(7) and new subsections 17(8) and 18(1) discussed in para. 18.08 *infra*. Reference should be made to the commentaries on sections 1–4 for discussions of novelty, inventive step, industrial applicability and exclusions from patentability. The substantive examination will also decide whether the description satisfies section 14(3) (*Sufficiency of the description*) and whether the claims satisfy section 14(5) (*Succinctness, supported by the description and unity of invention*). It may be noted that the Act contains nothing corresponding to section 9 [1949] (*Insertion of reference in case of potential infringement*), described at para. A009.5.

Supplementary searches (subs. (1A))   **18.08**

When subsection (1A) is brought into effect, if the examiner decides that a correction or amendment has resulted in the need for a supplementary search, a fee will normally become payable (s. 17(8)), see para. 17.10. In this case, it will be possible to suspend the substantive examination under new subsection (1A) until the fee has been paid (and also presumably until the supplementary search has been carried out) or until the application is amended to remove the need for the supplementary search. Note that, if examination is suspended and then the supplementary search fee is not paid, and the specification is not amended to remove the need for the supplementary search, the application may be refused. However, it would appear that the Comptroller could exercise his discretion on this and, therefore, the applicant ought to be provided with an opportunity of contending (if desired at a hearing held under s. 101, with the possibility of appeal under s. 97(1)) that no supplementary search is necessary even without amendment, see further paras. 17.10 and 17.19.

18.09   *Grant of the patent (subs. (4))*

After the examiner has reported under subsection (4) that the application complies with the Act and Rules then (save for subs. (5) and s. 22) the application will proceed to the grant of a patent and the applicant is notified accordingly. That notification is to the effect that a period of two months is allowed for: either possible filing of a divisional application under rule 24(1)(*b*)(ii) and/or voluntary amendment under rule 36(3) at the discretion of the applicant, if the notification is the *first* report of the examiner; or for seeking leave to make such filing under rule 24(1)(*b*)(i), or amendment under rule 36(4), where objection under section 18(3) has previously issued: rules 24 and 36 are reprinted at paras. 15.03 and 19.03 respectively. Only after this two months period does the grant under section 18(4) actually occur. However, once this notification of compliance with the Act and Rules has been given, third party objections under section 21 are no longer accepted, see para. 21.05. Also, if expedited grant is desired, the opportunities provided by rules 24 and 36 can each be waived. The application will then proceed to grant without delay (O.J. November 9, 1988).

After the end of this two months period, the applicant is notified that a patent has been granted and that notice of the grant will be published in the O.J. on a specified date, several weeks later. The Act contains no equivalent to section 102(1) [1949] which preserved the Royal prerogative to refuse the grant. The grant under subsection (4) terminates the possibility of any further proceedings under sections 1–23. In particular, it becomes no longer possible to withdraw the application under section 14(9) or amend the application under section 19. The grant, though made when the aforesaid notification of grant is given to the applicant, does not actually take effect until the notice of the grant has been published in the O.J. under section 24(1), see para. 24.11.

A similar situation arises on the grant of a European patent. The decision to grant a European patent under EPCa. 97(2) terminates the application procedure, though the European patent does not take effect until the grant is mentioned in the EPB (EPCa. 97(4)). A difference between the United Kingdom and European procedures is that a European application (or a country designation) may be withdrawn right up to the date of publication of the mention of the grant. This is important if it is preferred to have a national, rather than a European, patent for any particular country. Otherwise, if a European patent (UK) is actually granted where a corresponding patent has already been granted under the Act, that patent is likely to be automatically revoked, see para. 73.05.

Once a notice under section 18(4) has been issued, the Comptroller has held that he has no power to withdraw it, for example: to allow the filing of a divisional application under section 15(4) outside the two month period allowed therefor by rule 24(1)(*b*)(ii) in the case of the notice being the first report from the examiner; or for consideration of an amendment, the request for which cannot then be filed until section 27 is effective after notice of the grant has been published in the O.J. (*ITT's Application*, [1984] RPC 23).

No form or fee for securing grant has been prescribed under subsection (4). The certificate of grant and its effect are discussed in para. 24.06.

There is no provision in the Act for opposition, as was provided by section 14 [1949], because grant is mandatory once the examiner has reported under subsection (4) that the application complies with the requirements of the Act and the

Rules, but an application for revocation under section 72 may be made to the Comptroller at any time after grant.

Time for complying with Act and Rules   **18.10**

The period prescribed under sections 18(4) and 20(1) for meeting the requirements of the Act and Rules, equivalent to placing an application "in order" under the 1949 Act, is four and a half years from the declared priority date or, if there is no declared priority date, from the application date. The consequent deadline date is not altered if a priority date is lost or withdrawn after preparations for publication under section 16 are completed (r. 2(*a*), reprinted at para. 123.04). Under rule 34 (reprinted at para. 18.03 *infra*) the same period applies to a divisional application filed under section 15(4) and to applications subject to a secrecy order under section 22(1), but in the case of an application filed under sections 8(3), 12(6) or 37(4) (by a person deemed entitled) the period is 18 months from the actual filing date, if that period expires later. The period within which the application is to be placed in order is extensible by one month under rule 110(3) by filing PF 50/77 and is further or alternatively extensible at the Comptroller's discretion with PF 52/77 and PF 53/77 (r. 110(3A) and (3C)), but heavy fees are payable. PF 50/77 or PF 52/77, as the case may be, can be filed during the extension period, but if this is not done the application is deemed to have been withdrawn at the end of the normal period prescribed by rule 34 (*P's Application*, [1983] RPC 269), but under rule 110(3A) it should be possible to obtain a retrospective extension of the rule 34 period even if PF 52/77 is not filed until after that period has expired, see para. 123.33.

If an appeal to the Patents Court is pending, the time for placing the application in order may be extended by the Court, or (if the period for lodging an appeal has not expired, but an appeal has not been lodged) the time for placing the application in order extends to the end of such appeal period or any extension thereof (s. 20(2)). Furthermore, when secrecy directions under section 22(1) are revoked, the Comptroller may extend the time for doing anything, including placing the application in order for grant (s. 22(5)(*e*)).

Corresponding identical patents (subs. (5))   **18.11**

Under subsection (5) two patents may not be granted to the same person in respect of the same invention. In *International Business Machine's (Barclay and Bigar's) Application* ([1983] RPC 283) a second application was refused under subsection (5) despite the argument that in it the subject matter was defined more precisely than in the first application which had employed a functional definition. The Hearing Officer held that refusal was mandatory unless the situation giving rise to the objection was overcome and that this would not occur by surrender of the patent on the first application because such would not amount to revocation of its grant, see para. 29.03.

Similarly, if a proprietor of a United Kingdom patent obtains a European patent (UK) for the same invention and having the same priority date, the Comptroller will, probably, revoke the United Kingdom patent on his own initiative under section 73(2), see para. 73.05.

It is not clear what action the Comptroller could take under subsection (5) should different (though perhaps connected) persons claim the same invention with the same priority date.

PRACTICE UNDER SECTION 18

18.12   *Request for substantive examination*

If the application is to be further prosecuted, the request for examination must be made and the fee paid within six months after the publication of the application under section 16. Examination is requested by filing PF 10/77 (reprinted at para. 141.10). Under rule 36(2), reprinted in para. 19.03, amendments may be made to the application when PF 10/77 is filed. The period for filing PF 10/77 is extensible by one month by filing PF 50/77 and is further or alternatively extensible at the Comptroller's discretion with PF 52/77 and PF 53/77, see para. 123.33.

The application is then referred to an examiner for investigation under section 18(2). Contrary to procedure before the EPO, where the search division is based at The Hague and the examining divisions are in Munich, the usual practice in the Patent Office is for the search and substantive examiners to be one and the same person. At present, the Patent Office takes up cases for substantive examination within each classification heading in order of priority (or filing date if there is no declared priority date). The date of filing of PF 10/77 does not affect this order ((1980–81) 10 CIPA 195). This means that no substantive examination takes place until at least six months has elapsed from publication under section 16.

The Comptroller is prepared to accept a request for accelerated substantive examination, but if such request is made before publication of the application, it should be made clear whether accelerated publication (for which see para. 16.04) is also requested, see *e.g.* O.J. April 5, 1989, and also para. 24.05.

Before an applicant needs to request substantive examination and pay the examination fee, he will have available the search report issued under section 17(5)(*b*), and any written observations already made to the Comptroller under section 21(1). The applicant will usually have at least six months in which to come to a decision as to whether to pay the examination fee, since he should receive a copy of the search report before the date of publication under section 16 which starts the six month period for filing PF 10/77. The applicant can allow the application to lapse merely by failing to pay the examination fee; the search fee will not then be refundable. If the applicant desires that the application should not be published, the application must be formally withdrawn before preparations for publication are complete, see paras. 16.06 and 16.09.

It is understood that the fee paid on PF 10/77 can be refunded if the application is withdrawn before the examiner has commenced work on the substantive examination.

It is important to preserve the filing receipt after filing PF 10/77. Should is subsequently be asserted that the form was not filed in due time, so that the application is stated to be treated as withdrawn, the onus of proof that discretion for a further extension under rules 110(3A) and (3C) should be exercised, or that there has been a default on the part of the Patent Office thereby permitting rule 100 to be invoked, will lie on the applicant and this filing receipt can be crucial evidence, see *SRM Hydromeckanik's Application* (SRIS O/14/83); as also can entries on the fee sheet lodged at the Patent Office (*Aoki's Application*, [1987] RPC 133). In *Sanyo's Application* (SRIS O/31/88) the records kept by the Patent Office of fee sheets filed and of receipts issued were explained.

In *BOC's Application* (SRIS O/113/86, *noted* IPD 9072), PF 10/77 was filed bearing the number of another application on which another PF 10/77 had been filed. Correction was refused as no PF 10/77 had been filed in respect of the application before it was deemed to be withdrawn, and thereafter correction was not possible, following *Paez's Application* ([1985] RPC 455). However, each of these cases was decided at a time when no discretionary extension of the rule 34 period was obtainable, as is now possible under rule 110(3A) and (3C).

It is possible to pay the examination fee before publication, but there appears to be no advantage in so doing. Where actual infringement is taking place, the Comptroller will give sympathetic consideration to expedited examination, see para. 24.05.

Plurality of inventions   **18.13**

If the search examiner considers that the claims are directed to more than one invention and has so indicated in his search report under section 17(6), a "plurality of inventions" objection under section 14(5)(*d*) can be expected in the first report on the substantive examination under subsection (3). Occasionally, the substantive examiner will direct his examination to the first-claimed invention and will call for the claims to the other invention(s) to be cancelled, giving a six month term for reply. Usually, however, the examiner will call for the claims to be limited to a single invention before he will commence his full examination and will set a four month period for initial response, thereby giving a total time of six months within which divisional applications can be filed following the objection, if use is made of the full four month term set and the two month period which then follows (r. 24(1)(*a*)). In exceptional circumstances, the Comptroller may grant an extension to the specified term for response to his first report (see below), thereby effectively also extending the period in which a divisional application may be filed in respect of the claims to be cancelled.

The temptation to amend the claims voluntarily before the first substantive examination report has been issued, for the purpose of forestalling a "plurality of inventions" objection, should be avoided, unless a divisional application is filed at the same time. If the first substantive examination report should be a favourable one under subsection (4), there would then only be a two month period under rule 24(1)(*b*)(ii) for filing any divisional applications and the only possible discretionary power the Comptroller would have to allow the divisional application to be filed later would be under rule 110(1).

The filing of divisional applications under section 15(4) is extensively discussed in paras. 15.15–15.21 and, in relation to "Practice", in paras. 15.28–15.32.

Substantive examination

—Filing of response   **18.14**

During the substantive examination, preliminary objection may be raised that the claims are not clear and concise (s. 14(5)(*b*)) and/or are not supported by the description (s. 14(5)(*a*)). The main purpose of the substantive examination, however, is to determine whether the invention claimed is novel (s. 2) in relation to the state of the art as represented by the documents cited in the search report established under section 17(4) and any supplementary search conducted under section 17(7); and whether it involves an inventive step (s. 3) having regard to the state of the art. The examiner will also check that the invention claimed is not one for which the grant of a patent is expressly excluded (s. 1(2) and (3)) and that the invention is capable of industrial application (s. 4). For these matters see the commentaries on sections 1–4 and 14.

In replying to an examination report, the applicant may amend the description and claims to meet the objections claimed and/or he may present a reasoned argument in defence of his application. In particular, if the examiner has objected that the invention claimed in any claim is obvious, it is necessary, if this claim is maintained, to refute the examiner's objection. Although it is, apparently, incumbent on the examiner, in all but the most obvious cases, to construct an argument, it is not uncommon for a first examination report simply to allege that the invention claimed is not novel and/or does not involve an inventive step. It may therefore be sufficient to argue that no such argument has been constructed to which proper response can be made, but obviously it will generally be prudent to go somewhat further than this.

If an applicant thinks that his case against rejection, for example on an objection of obviousness, would be strengthened by the introduction of evidence, it is up to him to seek to introduce evidence. If he chooses not to do so, the Patents Court has stated (*Wistar Institute's Application*, [1983] RPC 255 and *Toyama's Application*, SRIS C/69/89) that it is unlikely he will be allowed to introduce such evidence on appeal, unless it should be evidence of the character which is normally admitted on appeal, for which see para. 97.16. However, such evidence was admitted on appeal in *PCUK's Produits' Application* ([1984] RPC 482), though here the Patent Office hearing had taken place near the end of the section 18(4) period.

Care should be taken to file a response to all points in the examination report under section 18(3), even if only to refute the objection as one that is not soundly based. If a response is considered not to be, or to be less than, a genuine attempt to meet the objections raised, or at least advance the prosecution of the application, the application may be refused, as it was in *General Electric's Application* (SRIS O/94/89). Refusal will also occur if no response is filed within the time set (*Incom's Application,* SRIS O/39/83, *noted* IPD 6015), though in both cases subject to the applicant being given an opportunity to be heard, see para. 101.04.

Although they are not binding upon the Comptroller, decisions of the EPO, and especially those of its Appeal Boards, and the EPO Guidelines (all reprinted in *EPH*) are taken note of by examiners, and may be persuasive. It is often worth citing these in a response to a substantive examination report if they are relevant to a point being made therein.

Where objections are raised during substantive examination, six months will normally be permitted for reply to a first action, four months to a second action and two months to subsequent actions. However, less time may be set if the overall time for putting the application in order has already been severely eroded.

18.15   —*Extension of time for response*

In *Jaskowski's Application* ([1981] RPC 197) the Comptroller pointed out that discretion to grant an extension of time for response under section 18(3) should only be exercised where there is "some adequate reason for exercising that discretion which is peculiar to the particular applicant or application in suit". In that case the patent agent found himself without instructions, despite repeated reminders to his client. In these circumstances, it was held that there was nothing advanced which could be regarded as an adequate reason for extending the specified period and an extension of time, and hence the application itself, was refused. Following that decision the Patent Office wrote to the Chartered Institute stating that:

"In general we would expect to grant extensions only by reason of unforeseen incidents such as illness, personal accident, disruption or destruction caused by fire, natural disasters, political upheavals and the like. So far as interruptions of and dislocations in the postal service in the United Kingdom are concerned, sufficient protection to applicants may be afforded by rr. 97 and 111: *ad hoc* (but not endemic) postal interruptions and dislocations may, however, justify an extension. An isolated slip in office procedure by the applicant, his agent or his servants may be a good ground. Voluntary absences from base by applicants and agents on holiday or business would not normally warrant an extension; on the other hand, really exceptional complexity of subject-matter or of objections raised, or difficulty of communication between applicant and agent, also the necessity of adducing technical evidence and abnormal pressure in the agent's office (the applicant having given his instructions as to the response in good time) might do so".

In *Lintott's Application* (SRIS O/66/82, *noted* IPD 5077), the Hearing Officer refused a further extension requested on the ground that an action was expected on a corresponding United States application and the applicant would withdraw the United Kingdom application if the United States action were to be adverse.

In *Fibre Optic's Application* (SRIS O/156/85) the Comptroller stated that the reason why the applicant did not, or could not, respond within the unextended period should be considered in the exercise of discretion, and in particular the extent to which the burden placed on the applicant exceeded the norm. The applicant "must be seen to have acted reasonably vis-à-vis the public". An extension was refused as it appeared that the need arose mainly because the applicant had decided to abandon the application and then had changed his mind.

Note that discretion still exists to grant an extension even if the period set for reply has passed, as the application continues to exist (unless withdrawn) until it is refused. However, in *Nauchno-Proizvodstvennoe's Application* (SRIS O/65/82, *noted* IPD 5038) it was pointed out that requests for extension should be made while time still remained available for dealing with the objections. It is not to be presumed that extension will be granted. In this case the absence of an inventor on a business trip of uncertain length and the patent agent's absence from his office were each held to be inadequate reasons.

Where rule 100 was successfully invoked because an official letter had not been received by the applicant, due to use of an incorrect address, the section 18(4) period was extended to allow time for response (*Opatowski's Application*, SRIS O/74/88), but the hint was given that the application would be refused if that response did not put the application entirely in order for grant.

Examination procedure   **18.16**

If no response is filed within the prescribed period, the application becomes dormant. It is only treated as refused at the expiry of the four and a half year period prescribed by section 20(1). There thus remains the possibility of filing a belated response simultaneously with a request for extension of the period for reply to the report under subsection (3) in the inherent discretion of the Comptroller thereunder. If the rule 34 period has already expired, or is about to expire, a simultaneous request under rule 110(3A) for extension of that period should also be made by filing PF 52/77.

—Procedure during substantive examination   **18.17**

Usually an informal interview or telephone discussion can be held with the examiner. This will normally lead to the preparation of an official minute, a copy of which will be sent to the applicant. The minute becomes part of the official file. If the applicant disagrees with any part of the minute, he may register his disapproval in a letter which is also placed in the open part of the file. The applicant or his agent attending a personal interview may be asked to sign the minute.

The fact that application documents are not returned to the applicant or his agent for amendment to meet objections made in the examination necessitates that all apparent errors or suggested amendments are listed *in extenso* in the official letter. The reasons for retaining these documents in the Office are set out in a note in (1980) 10 CIPA 256. This note contains the suggestion that applicants may care to file a third copy of the specification under rule 93(5)(*c*) (reprinted in para. 118.05) with the request that this be returned to the sender with any annotations made thereon which the examiner thinks appropriate, but it is not clear whether the Patent Office is prepared to operate in this way. Occasionally an examiner will append to an official letter photocopies of pages indicating suggested amendments or infelicitous language or grammar.

Although subsection (5) does not apply to concurrent applications under the Act and under the EPC for the same invention (but see s. 73(2)), the examiner will often mention the existence of any conflicting application for a European patent (UK) of which he is aware. If the application under the Act is desired to give rise to a patent, it will then be necessary to abandon at least the United Kingdom designation for any such corresponding application for a European patent (UK) before the notice of its grant is published in the EPB: otherwise the patent under the Act is likely eventually to be revoked, see para. 73.06.

18.18 *—Amendments*

Any amendments made to the description and claims should normally be effected by filing substitute pages in duplicate. The need for clean pages arises because the specification of the granted patent is now produced by reproduction from any documents filed by the applicant. In practice, examiners will sometimes make very minor amendments by hand on request. However, retyped pages which have not been amended are not now accepted because these would require checking by the examiner (O.J. November 23, 1988).

Similarly, if any amendments are made to the drawings, replacement sheets of drawings will generally need to be filed in duplicate. In a few exceptional cases when the amendment to the drawings is very minor, the examiner may, at his discretion, make the amendments himself, since there is no rule forbidding manuscript amendments to the drawings. If an examiner is requested to make an amendment to the drawings, it is prudent to file further copies of the drawings "as filed" together with a copy showing the desired amendment in red and an offer to furnish substitute formal sheets of drawings, if required.

18.19 *—Miscellaneous*

It is important to remember that, if priority is dropped after the preparations for the publication of the application have been completed, the declared priority date still remains valid for the purpose of calculating time limits (see r. 2(1), reprinted at para. 123.04), particularly the four and a half year period for complying with requirements under rule 34 (reprinted at para. 18.03 *supra*).

There is no limit on the number of official reports which may be issued within the period set by rule 34 for placing the application in compliance with the Act and Rules.

Where a communication is filed after the issue of the examiner's report under subsection (4) that the application complies with the requirements of the Act and the Rules, the Patent Office will need to give such communication urgent attention. Consequently a request has been made that any such communication should be marked "URGENT" in a bold and prominent manner (O.J. August 18, 1982).

Grant **18.20**

The date of grant for the purposes of the provisions of sections 1–24(1) is the date of the letter sent to the applicant notifying him that a patent has been granted (O.J. September 2, 1982), the specification of the patent is then republished under the same serial number as the application as published, but followed by the letter B. This "B-specification" is published on the date of publication of the notice of grant in the O.J., this being the relevant date for the purposes of section 25 onwards, see para. 24.11. In *Ogawa Chemical's Applications* ([1986] RPC 63) the Comptroller explained the practice of the Office with regard to the issuing of the notice of grant under section 24(1). If the examiner reports the application to be in order when he makes his first substantive examination, the applicant is so notified and informed that he may file voluntary amendments under rule 36(3) and divisional applications under section 15(4) within a two month period: the notice of grant is then issued at the end of that period. However, when the application is found to be in order for grant after an acceptable response to an objection under section 18(3), the administrative act of grant under section 24(1) occurs automatically two months after the date of notification to the applicant that the application is in order. Once the administrative act of grant has taken place, further amendment under section 19, and the filing of divisional applications under section 15(4), is precluded.

Examination may be re-opened under section 73 after publication of the notice of grant, but the extent to which examination may be re-opened is very limited.

SECTION 19 **19.01**

General power to amend application before grant

19.—(1) At any time before a patent is granted in pursuance of an application the applicant may, in accordance with the prescribed conditions and subject to section 76 below, amend the application of his own volition.

(2) The comptroller may without application being made to him for the purpose, amend the specification and abstract contained in an application for a patent so as to acknowledge a registered trade mark **or registered service mark**.

Note. Subsection (2) was effectively amended, as indicated, by the 1986 Act (s. 2(3) and Sched. 2, para. 1(2)(*e*)).

RELEVANT RULES

Amendment of request for grant

35. An application for amendment of the request for the grant of a **19.02** patent shall be made on Patents Form No. 11/77.

Amendment of application before grant

36.—(1) Before being informed under section 17(5) of the examiner's **19.03** report, the applicant may not amend the description, claims or drawings contained in his application, except where so required by the comptroller.

(2) After being informed under section 17(5) of the examiner's report and before the first report of the examiner under section 18 is sent to the applicant, the applicant may, of his own volition, amend the description, claims or drawings of the application.

(3) After the applicant has been sent the first report of the examiner under section 18, in addition to his right under section 18(3) to amend the application so as to comply with the requirements of the Act and these Rules, the applicant may, of his own volition, amend once the description, claims or drawings of the application provided that, if the examiner's first report is made under section 18(3), the amendment shall be filed at the same time as the applicant replies to that report, or, if the examiner's first report is made under section 18(4), the amendment shall be filed within two months of that report being sent to the applicant.

(4) Any further amendment to the description, claims or drawings which the applicant desires to make of his own volition may only be made with the consent of the comptroller following the filing of Patents Form No. 11/77.

(5) An application may not be amended by the applicant of his own volition except as provided in paragraphs (1) to (4) above.

COMMENTARY ON SECTION 19

19.04 *General*

Section 19 concerns amendment of an application at the volition of the applicant (subs. (1)); and by the Comptroller to acknowledge in the specification or abstract a registered trade mark or registered service mark (subs. (2)). Amendment of a European Patent application is covered by EPCa. 123 and EPCr. 86, and of an international application by PCTaa. 19 and 34(2)(*b*) and PCTrr. 46, 66.1 and 66.3–66.5.

Amendment after grant is dealt with under sections 27 and 75, and (at the initiative of the Comptroller) under section 73. For amendment prior to publication of the application under section 16, see para. 16.06.

For an amendment to the request (PF 1/77), rule 35 (reprinted at para. 19.02) applies, requiring the use of PF 11/77 (reprinted at para. 141.11), whereas for a voluntary amendment of any other part of the application, *i.e.* of the description, drawings, claims or abstract, prior to substantive examination, no form (or fee) is prescribed, see para. 19.05 *infra*.

19.05 *Amendments to the specification*

Although subsection (1) states that the applicant may, of his own volition, amend the application at any time before grant, this generality is restricted by the presence of the words "in accordance with the prescribed conditions". Rule 36 (reprinted at para. 19.03 *supra*) then provides that an applicant may not amend the description, claims or drawing, unless so required by the Comptroller, before the search report under section 17(5) is issued (r. 36(1)). After the issuance of this report, but before the issuance of the first report of the substantive examination under section 18, the description, claims and drawings may be amended (more than once, if desired) at the applicant's own volition. Again, no form (or fee) is required for amendment at this stage (r. 36(2)).

Amendments *to the claims* which are received by the Patent Office before the preparations for publication under section 16 are complete (for which see para. 16.06) will appear in the "A-specification", together with the claims as originally filed. If PF 9/77 was filed sufficiently early, the letter forwarding the search report now states that the preparations for publication of the application under section 16 will not be completed within four weeks from the date of the letter. This gives a short time within which amendments may be submitted to be included within the application as published. This practice may have arisen because, in *Intera's Application* ([1986] RPC 459 (CA)), it was observed that, as section 16(1) expressly contemplates the feasability of last-minute amendments of an application before publication, it must be assumed that this was not intended to give rise to serious practical difficulties.

When an application for voluntary amendments to the specification is filed before the search report issues, the Patent Office holds the application and treats it as effectively filed upon the issuance of the search report ((1979–80) 9 CIPA 504). This is because of rule 36(1). Nevertheless, it is understood that the examiner will take the proposed amendments into consideration on an informal basis. The subject of voluntary amendment and the effect and validity of rule 36 is the subject of a paper by C. Jones ((1978–79) 8 CIPA 178). However, rule 36 does not apply to corrections allowed under section 117 and therefore these can be treated differently.

During substantive examination under section 18(2) and (3) the applicant has the right (under s. 18(3)) to amend the description, claims and drawings in response to the examiner's report on the substantive examination with the object of meeting the requirements of the Act, see para. 18.07; and, in addition, when the report has been issued the applicant has a right under rule 36(3) to amend the description, claims and drawings, only once, at his own volition without payment of a fee. However, this voluntary amendment must be filed at the same time as the applicant replies to the section 18(2) report. Alternatively, if the examiner's first report is made under section 18(4), that is that the requirements for grant have been met, then the voluntary amendment must be filed within two months of the report (r. 36(3)).

After a response to the first official report on the substantive examination has been lodged, under rule 36(4) voluntary amendments may be made only with the consent of the Comptroller. Such consent should be sought in an accompanying letter and the amendment request must now be made on PF 11/77 (reprinted at para. 141.11).

The right to amend under section 19 is lost with effect from the date of a letter sent to the applicant notifying him that grant under section 18(4) has occurred, see para. 24.11. But, as explained therein, amendment under section 27 is not possible until notice of the grant has been published in the O.J. under section 24(1), that is until after the grant has taken effect under section 25(1).

Limitations on allowable amendments   **19.06**

The allowability of amendment under section 19 is fettered by the provisions of new section 76(2) according to which no amendment to the specification is to be allowed if this "results in the application disclosing additional matter", which appears to mean "matter extending beyond that disclosed in the application as filed", see para. 76.09. Similar wording has been interpreted as a severe restriction on possible amendments and the changed wording of section 76 may have little effect in this regard, as is discussed in paras. 76.11–76.14. Breach of the terms of section 76(2) provides a ground of revocation of the patent under section 72(1)(*d*), see paras. 72.25 and 72.26.

A voluntary amendment under section 19 made within the periods prescribed at rule 36(2) and (3) does not entail exercise of the Comptroller's discretion. In particular, any amendment to the claims filed before preparations for publication under section 16 have been completed for the purpose of inclusion in the "A-specification" is not examined for allowability prior to the substantive examination under section 18. It is not clear whether any amended or new claim which contains additional matter and therefore contravenes section 76(2) may be taken into account for the purposes of sections 55(5)(*b*) and 69(2)(*b*).

Under the Act more restraints are imposed on voluntary amendment than was the case under the 1949 Act, where the applicant was afforded considerable latitude in the timing and extent of amendments which could be made voluntarily. The major difference in the practices under the two Acts is that whereas under the 1949 Act an amendment once allowed was not (in the absence of fraud) open to subsequent dispute, under the Act not only is the amendment open to dispute but can become a ground of invalidity under section 72(1)(*d*). A further difference is that an application cannot be post-dated to the date of filing the amendment, as was possible under section 6(4) and (5) [1949].

Neither rule 36 nor section 76(2) applies to corrections under section 117 and therefore these can be treated differently, see para. 117.08.

Amendment of documents other than the specification

19.07 *—General*

Section 19 concerns amendment to an application, for which rule 35 (reprinted in para. 19.02 *supra*) covers amendment of the request (PF 1/77), and rule 36 (reprinted at para. 19.03 *supra*) covers amendment of the description, claims and drawings. Thus an application on PF 11/77 under rule 35 to amend PF 1/77 is not fettered by any prescribed conditions and may be lodged at any time before issue of the letter notifying grant of the patent under section 18(4). Amendment of the abstract at any time also seems possible.

19.08 *—Change of applicant*

Prior to the filing of the statement of inventorship on PF 7/77, an applicant may be added or deleted by filing an application on PF 11/77 (reprinted at para. 141.11) to amend PF 1/77. The reasons for the amendment must be given on PF 11/77, but no evidence is required. When PF 7/77 is subsequently filed, the statement of the right to the grant thereon must be consistent with such reasons. Instead of PF 11/77, PF 21/77 (reprinted at para. 141.21) may be filed to record a change of ownership, but then evidence in support of the request to change the applicant (*e.g.* an assignment) must also be filed, see para. 32.19. To change the applicant once PF 7/77 has been filed, PF 21/77 must be filed. The practice for filing PF 21/77 is discussed in paras. 32.25–32.31. However, an alteration in a name or address, not involving a change in applicant entity, is made under rule 45 on PF 20/77, see paras. 32.19 and 32.24.

19.09 *—Change in designated inventorship*

If the statutory period for filing the statement of inventorship on PF 7/77 has not expired a new PF 7/77 can be simply substituted for that originally filed, see para.

13.10. Otherwise, PF 7/77 can be corrected by filing PF 47/77 under section 117 and rule 91(1), see para. 117.13. For the correction of an error of translation or transcription, clerical error or mistake as the case may be, see para. 117.06. Correction of PF 7/77 under section 19 would not seem possible because this only permits amendment "of an application" and PF 7/77 is not part of an application, see para. 14.09.

Acknowledgment of registered trade mark or service mark (subs. (2))   **19.10**

Subsection (2), as now effectively amended (see *Note* to para. 19.01 *supra*), gives the Comptroller power for himself to insert in the specification and abstract an acknowledgment that a trade (or service) mark is a registered trade (or service) mark. There is no corresponding rule, and the subsection does not, apparently, require the Comptroller to give notice to the applicant that the reference is being made. While subsection (1) is expressed in discretionary terms, under which an applicant would have a right under section 101 to be heard before a decision is made with appeal possible under section 97(1), the Comptroller has held, under the somewhat similar wording of section 73(2), that in fact he has no discretion once the wording of the provision is found to have been met, see para. 73.06.

While the Patent Office may insert an acknowledgement of a registered trade (or service) mark before publication of the application under section 16, the usual practice is for the applicant to be invited to insert such an acknowledgment during substantive examination.

The subsection refers merely to a registered trade (or service) mark and not to a mark registered in the United Kingdom. There is no definition of "trade mark" (or "service mark") in section 130(1) so that it would appear that the Comptroller has power unilaterally to make a reference to registration, even where the applicant uses a trade mark to identify a product obtained abroad under that trade mark and there is no evidence that the material obtainable under the registered trade mark (*i.e.* in the United Kingdom) is the same product.

PRACTICE UNDER SECTION 19

Amendment of description, claims or drawings   **19.11**

Any request to amend the description, claims or drawings of an application must be accompanied by replacement documents prepared in accordance with rules 16, 18 and 20. In order to comply with rule 20(16), it is usually necessary to file replacement sheets whenever amendment is made, but very minor amendments can be inserted in manuscript without contravening this rule. Because publication under section 16 now takes place by reproduction of the specification in the form supplied by the applicant, instead of in letterpress type as previously, pages of new or amended claims should be self-explanatory and should preferably be headed "Amendments to the claims" (O.J. February 24, 1988).

It is also understood that, when a request for amendment is filed after issue of a favourable examination report under section 18(4), and within the two month period permitted therefor by rule 36(3), it is the practice of the Patent Office both to acknowledge receipt of the request and also to indicate whether or not the requested amendments have been found acceptable.

Amendment of the request (PF 1/77)   **19.12**

Where it is desired to record that a change of applicant before publication under section 16 has taken place, application should be made on PF 11/77 (reprinted at para. 141.11) under rule 35 (reprinted at para. 19.02 *supra*). Proof of the change should be supplied and the initial entry in the register, which is only made after publication under section 16 (r. 44(1)), will then record the new name. If this is done before preparations for publication of the application have been completed, the "A-specification" will show the new name. The Patent Office prefers that an application to record an alteration in the proprietor's name is not made after preparations for publication have been completed and before publication (for which see para. 16.06), whereafter such application should be made on PF 20/77 under rule 45, see paras. 32.19 and 32.24.

20.01

SECTION 20

Failure of application

20.—(1) If it is not determined that an application for a patent complies before the end of the prescribed period with all the requirements of this Act and the rules, the application shall be treated as having been refused by the comptroller at the end of that period, and section 97 below shall apply accordingly.

(2) If at the end of that period an appeal to the court is pending in respect of the application or the time within which such an appeal could be brought has not expired, that period—

(*a*) where such an appeal is pending, or is brought within the said time or before the expiration of any extension of that time granted (in the case of a first extension) on an application made within that time or (in the case of a subsequent extension) on an application made before the expiration of the last previous extension, shall be extended until such date as the court may determine;

(*b*) where no such appeal is pending or is so brought, shall continue until the end of the said time or, if any extension of that time is so granted, until the expiration of the extension or last extension so granteed.

Commentary on Section 20

20.02　*General*

Section 20 provides for the refusal of an application which is not brought into a condition in compliance with the Act and Rules within the period prescribed by rule 34 (reprinted in para. 18.03) and extends that period when an appeal is lodged. It is not a section specified in section 130(7) as having the same effect as the corresponding provision of EPC; no period is prescribed for placing a European application in order.

Subsection (1) complements section 18(3). Section 18(3) does not mention the prescribed period for compliance with the Act and Rules, but empowers the Comptroller to issue a decision of refusal at any time. Subsection (1) provides for an application to be treated as refused (no decision of refusal need be issued) if it does not comply with the Act and Rules within the prescribed period, *i.e.* that specified in rule 34.

Period for acceptance   **20.03**

Because sections 18(4) and 20(1) do not specify the period in which the application is to be brought into compliance, the period for compliance can be altered when circumstances warrant without a change in the Act. Both the period for complying with the Act and Rules, and the possibility of extending it under rule 110, are discussed in para. 18.10.

Appeal from refusal   **20.04**

Under subsection (1) an application is to be treated as having been refused by the Comptroller if it is not in compliance with the requirements within the due period. The refusal is therefore a decision taken by the Comptroller and as such is subject to appeal under section 97(1). Further appeal from an initial decision of the Patents Court under section 20 (whether on fact or law) can be taken, with leave, to the Court of Appeal under section 97(3).

—Time for appeal   **20.05**

An appeal against refusal of an application may be brought within six weeks of the decision (RSC Ord. 104, r. 19(2), reprinted in para. E104.19). Thus, if a decision of refusal is issued under section 18(3), the period for bringing the appeal is six weeks from the date of the decision. If section 20(1) applies, because by the end of the rule 34 period there has been no determination on compliance with the Act and Rules, the application is treated as having been refused "at the end of that period", which suggests that there is a notional decision of refusal at the end of the rule 34 period. However, the rule 34 period is automatically extended by subsection (2) to the end of the appeal period. The effective date of a decision cannot be the same as the date of the end of a six-week appeal period from that decision. Therefore it is suggested that the effective date of the deemed decision of refusal, when subsection (1) applies, is the end of the rule 34 period, or the end of any extension to that period obtained under rule 110(3) or (3A), but ignoring any extension under subsection (2). This would be consistent with the decision in *P's Application*, ([1983] RPC 269).

Since an extension to the rule 34 period may be applied for under rule 110(3A) after the end of the period, it would be possible to obtain an effective post-dating of the date of the deemed decision under subsection (1) by means of such an extension, and thus post-date the deadline for filing an appeal. In such a case, the Comptroller might refuse discretion under rule 110(3A), but under section 97 that refusal would itself be subject to appeal.

—Effect of appeal   **20.06**

If an appeal is duly lodged, the four-and-a-half year period for acceptance may be extended to a date specified by the court (subs. (2)). It is customary for the Patents Court to grant an extension of time sufficient in the circumstances to permit the application to be placed in compliance with the Act and Rules in accordance with the decision of the Court, but a request for such an extension should be made immediately after the decision is given.

Effect of failing to comply with Act and Rules within prescribed period **20.07**

The words in subsection (1) "at the end of that period" mean that if the requirements of the Act and Rules have not been complied with, the application is treated as having been refused at the end of the period specified by rule 34 (as extended under rule 110 if appropriate). Thus in *P's Application* ([1983] RPC 269), decided before rule 110(3A) was introduced, it was held that if PF 50/77 was not filed within one month of the end of the acceptance period, the application is treated as having been refused when the filing of PF 50/77 first became due.

Since an extension of any length of time may be obtained retroactively under rule 110(3A), it should always be possible to revive an application which has passed the normal acceptance period, if the Comptroller is prepared to exercise his discretion. This would reverse the previous position, before the introduction of rule 110(3A), in which an application could not be saved after the end of the acceptance period even if the failure to place the application in good order was due to an irregularity in the Patent Office, as there was no longer an application to which rule 100 could be applied. The decision in *Farmitalia's Application* (SRIS O/88/87) suggests that the section 20(1) period for complying with the Act and Rules will be extended in appropriate circumstances.

When an application is deemed to be withdrawn because the examiner regards the statutory requirements as not being met in due time, the possibility exists of arguing that the examiner's objections were not justified so that in fact those requirements had been met. Such an argument succeeded in *Akebono Brake's Application* (SRIS O/2/85) and similarly in *Coal Industry's Application* ([1986] RPC 57). In each case rule 100 was then invoked to rectify the register, see para. 123.22.

PRACTICE UNDER SECTION 20

20.08 *Correspondence towards end of rule 34 period*

While the Patent Office gives precedence to dealing with applications nearing the end of the permitted acceptance period, it does so by reference to the application numbers. This method of operation does not work for divisional applications, or for international applications which have entered the United Kingdom phase (s. 89, to be replaced by s. 89A), or European applications which have been converted to United Kingdom applications (s. 81), the application numbers of which do not relate to priority dates in any predetermined way. The Patent Office, therefore, requests that correspondence on divisional applications or the like be endorsed prominently at the head of the text with words, such as "DIVISIONAL URGENT" (O.J. August 18, 1982). Also, when less than six months of the period prescribed by section 20 remains, the Office makes the plea frequently in the O.J. that correspondence should be marked "URGENT" in a bold an prominent manner, see, *e.g.* O.J. April 5, 1989.

Because of problems which arise when applications are recorded in the register as having been withdrawn and it is later found that an official letter under section 18(3) or a response thereto had gone astray, with the result that the register is rectified under rule 100 (for which see para. 123.21), the Patent Office (since January 1986) has issued shortly before the end of the four-and-a-half-year period provided under section 20 and rule 34 a letter forewarning of the intention to treat as having been refused an application on which a report under section 18(3) has been issued and a response thereto is overdue (O.J. January 15, 1986). When such response is overdue, other than as the result of some default or omission by the Patent Office, the applicant will still need to seek discretion for an extension of time under section 18(3) in order that that a response is permitted to be filed outside the time set therefor in the report, see para. 18.15. Any such request should likewise be prominently marked "URGENT" in view of the short time that will then remain under rule 34.

Appeals against refusal   **20.09**

The lodging of an appeal against a decision refusing the application, or because it has not been brought into compliance with the Act and Rules before the end of the rule 34 period, is governed by section 97(1) and RSC Ord. 104, r. 19, see para. 97.12. The Comptroller will normally be represented by counsel on the hearing of the appeal and will ask for his costs if the appeal is unsuccessful, see para. 97.24. If the appeal decision results in patentable subject matter being found, or conceded, to exist in the application, it will often be necessary to seek an extension of time under subsection (2) from the Court, and a specific request therefor should be made to the Court immediately following the handing down of its decision.

SECTION 21   **21.01**

Observations by third party on patentability

21.—(1) Where an application for a patent has been published but a patent has not been granted to the applicant, any other person may make observations in writing to the comptroller on the question whether the invention is a patentable invention, stating reasons for the observations, and the comptroller shall consider the observations in accordance with rules.

(2) It is hereby declared that a person does not become a party to any proceedings under this Act before the comptroller by reason only that he makes observations under this section.

RELEVANT RULE

Observations on patentability under section 21

37.—(1) The comptroller shall send to the applicant a copy of any obser-   **21.02**
vations on patentability which he receives under section 21 in connection with an application.

(2) If the applicant has not already been notified under section 18(4) that the application complies with the requirements of the Act and these Rules, the observations shall be referred to the examiner conducting a substantive examination of the application under section 18, who shall consider and comment upon them as he thinks fit in his report under that section.

COMMENTARY ON SECTION 21

General   **21.03**

Section 21 introduces a procedure by which any person may make observations formally bringing to the notice of the Comptroller material affecting the patentability of an invention, at any time after publication and before grant. The section is

203

governed by rule 37 (reprinted at para. 21.02 *supra*) and corresponds to EPCa. 115; there is no equivalent PCT article. The section has some resemblance to section 15 [1949], but differs therefrom in that action can be taken under section 21 before the substantive examination has been carried out in most cases.

21.04 *Nature of permitted observations*

The observations to be submitted are those which concern the patentability of the invention. The Comptroller is not required to consider observations which relate to other matters, such as the right to be granted a patent under section 7 or matters which may be raised in revocation proceedings under section 72, *e.g.* the adequacy of the disclosure under section 14(3) or the wording and content of the claims under section 14(5). The Comptroller is obliged to consider the observations under section 21 so far as they relate to patentability, *i.e.* to the definition of patentable invention in section 1(1). Also, in view of the decision in *Genentech's Patent* ([1989] RPC 147 (CA)), it is submitted that the examiner should take into account observations submitted alleging non-compliance of the claims with section 14(5)(*a*), (*b*) or (*c*) because, otherwise, such non-compliance cannot, according to that decision, be raised as such post-grant (except possibly on a question of amendment), though over-broad claims may well fail on other grounds as was held in the *Genentech* case, see paras. 1.08, 3.07 and 14.18. Once PF 10/77 has been filed, and so long as the application is not already notified as in compliance with requirements, the observations must be referred to the examiner under rule 37(2). An acknowledgement is issued but, by subsection (2), the person making the observations is expressed not to be a party to any proceedings. Therefore, no estoppel can arise against him in relation to the observations.

21.05 *Time for making observations*

Observations under subsection (1) may be filed at any time before grant, but the Patent Office will not consider these if they are filed after the Patent Office has notified the applicant, under section 18(4), that the application complies with the requirements of the Act and Rules. It should be noted that this notification is *not necessarily* the letter relating to the administrative date of grant, for which see para. 24.11, but will, if issued, be an earlier letter giving the applicant a period of two months during which he could: (a) file a divisional application under rule 24(1)(*b*)(ii), if that sub-rule applies, or otherwise seek leave to do so under rule 24(1)(*b*)(i); and/or file a voluntary amendment under rule 36(3), if that sub-rule applies, or seek leave to do so under rule 36(4). It is understood that late-filed observations are simply placed on the public file where they can be inspected under section 118: in any event, they are reported to the applicant under rule 37(1).

However, if an observation under section 21 is received by the examiner before the section 18(4) notification has been dispatched, he is obliged to consider it and raise any apparent objection to patentability with the applicant. The applicant will then be required to deal with the objection within whatever time remains of the section 20 acceptance period (*Secretary of State for Defence's Application*, SRIS O/177/83). Nevertheless, the hardship imposed on an applicant by a late-filed observation under section 21 is now mitigated by rule 110(3A), which allows the Comptroller discretion to extend the section 20 period beyond the one month extension automatically available under rule 110(3), see para. 123.33. It is also possible that some revision of rule 34 may take place to provide for an automatic extension of the acceptance period in such circumstances, see *Note* to para. 18.03.

There is no bar to any person who files observations under section 21 from making the same observations in subsequent revocation proceedings under section 72 because no estoppel is created as noted in para. 21.04 *supra*. There is also no restriction on a person making repeated observations under section 21.

PRACTICE UNDER SECTION 21   **21.06**

By rule 37(1), a copy of any observations filed under section 21 has to be sent to the applicant, whether or not a request for substantive examination under section 18(1) has yet been filed. Although there is no express right to comment on these observations, it may be assumed he could do so during that examination. The examiner may himself comment on the observations in a report under section 18(3), in which case the applicant in his own interest ought to reply, as otherwise the application may be refused (s. 18(3)). If the examiner considers that there is no substance in the observations he need make no reference to them.

All observations submitted under section 21 should be placed on the public file 14 days after submission, see rule 93 reprinted at para. 118.05 and discussed in paras. 118.12 and 118.16. Obvious problems arise where observations are made which may be defamatory of the applicant. To make such observations knowingly could amount to professional misconduct by a Chartered Patent Agent. Nevertheless, the Comptroller would seem to have no power to refuse to communicate defamatory statements to the applicant, though the applicant could presumably request, under rule 94(1), that such statements should not appear on the public file, see further para. 118.16.

Since official letters and replies thereto are in the public file of an application after section 16 publication, it is possible for an interested third party to monitor the progress of an application by repeated file inspection, and file observations under section 21 whenever and as often as desired.

Apparently, the Patent Office will accept section 21 observations which are submitted anonymously ((1984–5) 14 CIPA 13). In this way an applicant could submit observations on his own application.

SECTION 22

Information prejudicial to defence of realm or safety of public

22.—(1) Where an application for a patent is filed in the Patent Office   **22.01**
(whether under this Act or any treaty or international convention to which the United Kingdom is a party and whether before or after the appointed day) and it appears to the comptroller that the application contains information of a description notified to him by the Secretary of State as being information the publication of which might be prejudicial to the defence of the realm, the comptroller may give directions prohibiting or restricting the publication of that information or its communication to any specified person or description of persons.

(2) If it appears to the comptroller that any application so filed contains information the publication of which might be prejudicial to the safety of the public, he may give directions prohibiting or restricting the publication

of that information or its communication to any specified person or description of persons until the end of a period not exceeding three months from the end of the period prescribed for the purposes of section 16 above.

(3) While directions are in force under this section with respect to an application—

    (a) if the application is made under this Act, it may proceed to the stage where it is in order for the grant of a patent, but it shall not be published and that information shall not be so communicated and no patent shall be granted in pursuance of the application;

    (b) if it is an application for a European patent, it shall not be sent to the European Patent Office; and

    (c) if it is an international application for a patent, a copy of it shall not be sent to the International Bureau or any international searching authority appointed under the Patent Co-operation Treaty.

(4) Subsection (3)(b) above shall not prevent the comptroller from sending the European Patent Office any information which it is his duty to send that office under the European Patent Convention.

(5) Where the comptroller gives directions under this section with respect to any application, he shall give notice of the application and of the directions to the Secretary of State, and the following provisions shall then have effect:—

    (a) the Secretary of State shall, on receipt of the notice, consider whether the publication of the application or the publication or communication of the information in question would be prejudicial to the defence of the realm or the safety of the public;

    (b) if the Secretary of State determines under paragraph (a) above that the publication of the application or the publication or communication of that information would be prejudicial to the safety of the public, he shall notify the comptroller who shall continue his directions under subsection (2) above until they are revoked under paragraph (e) below;

    (c) if the Secretary of State determines under paragraph (a) above that the publication of the application or the publication or communication of that information would be prejudicial to the defence of the realm or the safety of the public, he shall (unless a notice under paragraph (d) below has previously been given by the Secretary of State to the comptroller) reconsider that question during the period of nine months from the date of filing the application and at least once in every subsequent period of twelve months;

    (d) if on consideration of an application at any time it appears to the Secretary of State that the publication of the application or the publication or communication of the information contained in it would not, or would no longer, be prejudicial to the defence of the realm or the safety of the public, he shall give notice to the comptroller to that effect; and (*e*) on receipt of such notice the comptroller shall revoke the directions and may, subject to such conditions (if any) as he thinks fit, extend the time for doing anything required or authorised to be done by or under this Act in connection with the application, whether or not that time has previously expired.

(6) The Secretary of State may do the following for the purpose of enabling him to decide the question referred to in subsection (5)(*c*) above—

(*a*) where the application contains information relating to the production or use of atomic energy or research into matters connected with such production or use, he may at any time do one or both of the following, that is to say, inspect and authorise the United Kingdom Atomic Energy Authority to inspect the application and any documents sent to the comptroller in connection with it; and

(*b*) in any other case, he may at any time after (or, with the applicant's consent, before) the end of the period prescribed for the purposes of section 16 above inspect the application and any such documents;

and where that Authority are authorised under paragraph (*a*) above they shall as soon as practicable report on their inspection to the Secretary of State.

(7) Where directions have been given under this section in respect of an application for a patent for an invention and, before the directions are revoked, the prescribed period expires and the application is brought in order for the grant of a patent, then—

(*a*) if while the directions are in force the invention is worked by (or with the written authorisation of or to the order of) a government department, the provisions of sections 55 to 59 below shall apply as if—

(i) the working were use made by section 55;

(ii) the application had been published at the end of that period; and

(iii) a patent had been granted for the invention at the time the application is brought in order for the grant of a patent (taking the terms of the patent to be those of the application as it stood at the time it was so brought in order); and

(*b*) if it appears to the Secretary of State that the applicant for the patent has suffered hardship by reason of the continuance in force of the directions, the Secretary of State may, with the consent of the Treasury, make such payment (if any) by way of compensation to the applicant as appears to the Secretary of State and the Treasury to be reasonable having regard to the inventive merit and utility of the invention, the purpose for which it is designed and any other relevant circumstances.

(8) Where a patent is granted in pursuance of an application in respect of which directions have been given under this section, no renewal fees shall

be payable in respect of any period during which those directions were in force.

(9) A person who fails to comply with any direction under this section shall be liable—

(a) on summary conviction, to a fine not exceeding **the prescribed sum** [*£1,000*]; or

(b) on conviction on indictment [**on information in the Isle of Man**], to imprisonment for a term not exceeding two years or a fine, or both.

Note. The amendment to subsection (9)(*a*) was effected by the Magistrates' Courts Act 1980 (c. 43, s. 32(2)); and that to subsection (9)(*b*) was effected by S.I. 1978 No. 621.

COMMENTARY ON SECTION 22

22.02 *General*

Section 22, which should be read in conjunction with section 23 and which together replaced section 18 [1949], takes account of the EPC and PCT, in neither of which are there any corresponding provisions. It covers not only matters relating to defence purposes as previously, but also extends to matters of public safety.

Secrecy orders under section 18 [1949] (or s. 12 of the Atomic Energy Act 1946 (c. 80)) remain in force (Sched. 4, para. 5) despite the repeal of these provisions in Schedule 6, but the special provisions for compensation under section 12(4) of that Atomic Energy Act in respect of expense and work in connection with an atomic energy invention appear to have lapsed (Sched. 6). Section 22 applies to "existing" patents and applications (Sched. 2, para. 1(2)).

22.03 *Power to give secrecy directions (subss. (1) and (2))*

By subsections (1) and (2) the Comptroller is empowered to give directions (often called "secrecy" or "prohibition" orders) if the application contains information of a description having relevance for the defence of the realm (subs. (1)) or for the safety of the public (subs. (2)). The directions given will prohibit or restrict publication of information concerning the application and the information contained therein, and will also restrict the filing of corresponding applications in other countries, see section 23(1)(*b*). The description by which the defence relevance is decided by the Comptroller is as notifed to him by the Secretary of State. However, where prohibition is imposed on grounds of public safety, the directions given cannot endure longer than three months after the normal period prescribed for publication of the application, *i.e.* not longer than 18 months after the declared priority date (subs. (2)) unless the prohibition is explicitly extended under subsection (5)(*b*) and (*e*).

By the Interpretation Act 1978 (c. 30, Sched. 1), the term "Secretary of State" as used in any statute, means "one of Her Majesty's Principal Secretaries of State". Throughout section 22 he is (generally speaking) the Secretary of State for Defence, whereas elsewhere in the Act he is the Secretary of State for Trade and Industry, see para. 130.04.

No claim against the Secretary of State in respect of the exercise of powers under section 22 would seem to be possible by virtue of Schedule 5, para. 1, and possibly also by virtue of section 116(*b*). Nor is it possible to appeal from any decision of the Comptroller under subsections (1) and (2) (s. 97(1)(*c*)).

208

Patent Office procedure while directions are in force (subss. (3) and (4))   **22.04**

By subsections (3) and (4), while directions under subsections (1) or (2) are in force, the normal examination procedure is to be followed. But if the application is for a European patent it must not be sent to the EPO (EPCa.77 so permitting); and, if it is an international application, it must not be forwarded to WIPO or the searching authority (PCTr. 22(1)(*a*) so permitting). By section 118(3)(*a*), information concerning an application for a European patent may be sent to the EPO by the Comptroller but only if it is his duty so to do. EPCa. 77 would seem to remove this duty once directions have been given under section 22(1), but this is not necessarily so when the directions are given under subsection (2) as such may perhaps not be regarded as given "in the interests of the State".

Notice of directions to Secretary of State (subss. (5) and (6))   **22.05**

The Comptroller is required to give notice of his action under subsections (1) or (2) to the Secretary of State who must then consider whether the directions should be maintained (subs. (5)(*a*)). If so, they are continued (subs. (5)(*b*)) until revoked under subsection (5)(*a*). At the time the original directions are given the Secretary of State has no right to examine the documents of the application. He may only do so after the end of the period normally allowed for publication, unless the consent of the applicant to earlier inspection is obtained. However, if the application concerns atomic energy there is a right under subsection (4) to inspect it at any time; and the UKAEA may be authorised to make an inspection on which a report is to be made to the Secretary of State (subs. (6)(*a*)). Provision for this inspection is made in section 118(3) by way of exception to the general rule that the contents of applications shall not be accessible to third parties before publication.

If the directions are to be maintained, a notification from the Secretary of State to the Comptroller is necessary where the relevance is for the safety of the public because of the time limit in subsection (2). Whilst directions continue to be maintained the matter must be reconsidered by the Secretary of State during a period of nine months following the date of application and at least once in every subsequent period of 12 months (subs. (5)(*c*)). On a secrecy order being lifted by the Secretary of State under subsection (5)(*d*), the Comptroller is empowered to grant any necessary extension of time (subs. (5)(*e*)).

Effect of application during continuance of directions (sub. (7))   **22.06**

So long as directions are in force the patent will not be granted, but if the application has been brought in order for grant and the invention is used for the services of the Crown, that use is to be treated as though the patent had been granted and the provisions of sections 55–59 are to apply (subs. (7)(*a*)). Where the secrecy direction is considered by the Secretary of State to have caused hardship, a payment by way of compensation can be made (subs. (7)(*b*)). This payment is to be one considered "reasonable" by the Secretary of State and the Treasury having regard to the "inventive merit" of the invention (rather than its "novelty" as under s.18(3)(*b*) [1949]) as well as its "utility" and "the purpose for which it is designed and any other relevant circumstances".

Renewal fees during continuance of directions (subs. (8))   **22.07**

Renewal fees are not required in respect of a patent granted on an application which has been the subject of directions for the period during which the directions were in force (subs. (8)). Once a prohibition order has been lifted, any renewal fee falling due between the date of rescission and grant of the patent must be paid within three months of the grant, see para. 2.11 *infra*.

22.08 *Penalties (subs. (9))*

The offence under subsection (9) is one triable either way, *i.e.* by summary conviction in a magistrates' court or on indictment before the Crown Court. The maximum penalty in the former case, the "prescribed sum", is now equated with the fine of the "statutory maximum" (Criminal Justice Act 1982, c. 48, s.74). This can be increased by order (Magistrates' Courts Act 1980, c. 43, s.143) and is now "£2,000" (Criminal Penalties, Etc. (Increase) Order 1984 (S.I. 1984 No. 447, Sched. 1, para. 4). There is no maximum fine on an indictment, except that the penalty imposed must not be excessive in the circumstances, see para. 109.02. For offences by companies, see section 113 and para. 113.02.

PRACTICE UNDER SECTION 22

22.09 *Procedure on imposition, and effect, of secrecy order*

It is understood to be the normal practice that, when a secrecy order is imposed before or within six weeks after filing an application, no details of that application appear either in the O.J. or in the SRIS card index of applications. However, if the secrecy order is lifted during the five-year period in which that card index is maintained, a card is then inserted therein, but no entry is made in the Journal.

When drafting applications it is desirable not to include a cross-reference to another application which has attracted, or is likely to attract, a secrecy order because the existence of that cross-reference will then require both applications to be treated likewise. Also, when registering assignments, separate documentation should be used for any applications subject to a secrecy order as "it is a basic security requirement that there should be no reference in potentially open documents to the application numbers, titles or contents of cases subject to section 22 direction" ((1985–86) 15 CIPA 215).

When a secrecy order is imposed, the Patent Office invites the applicant to agree to early inspection of the application. Agreement is advisable since the secrecy order is unlikely to be lifted until an inspection has been made. It is acceptable to the Patent Office that agreement is given over the signature of the appointed agent.

Although a secrecy order imposes a blanket prohibition against disclosure of the information in the application, it is always possible to seek permission for disclosure to specified persons and such permission may be given by the Comptroller in appropriate cases subject to conditions regarding transmittal of documents and procedures to prevent unauthorised disclosure.

Even if the imposition of a secrecy order is anticipated, it is undesirable that the specification and drawings included in the application should bear markings to indicate the classified nature of the subject matter. Such markings become an embarrassment if and when the secrecy order is lifted.

Where a secrecy order is imposed on an application for a European patent filed at the United Kingdom Patent Office, it has happened that the order was not lifted soon enough for the application to be received by the EPO in due time, this being 14 months from the priority date (EPCr. 77(5)). If this happens, the applicant's only recourse is to convert the European application into individual national applications under section 81(1) and EPCa. 135, see *EPO Decision J 03/80* ([1980] RPC 381, OJEPO 4/1980, 92). It is understood that the government departments concerned now have a procedure which should prevent this situation occurring in other than genuine cases.

The Patent Office has ceased the practice of sending to applicants each year a notification that the reconsideration required by section 22(5)(c) has been undertaken. However, it is open to applicants to enquire at any time about whether the secrecy order could be revoked.

Avoidance of secrecy orders on subsequent applications   **22.10**

When a secrecy order is revoked on an application which may later serve as a priority document, it is often the practice of the Patent Office to inform the applicant that a secrecy order may reasonably be expected on any subsequent application claiming priority therefrom, but that this may be avoided if a letter is written to the Security Section at the Patent Office stating whether changes have been made compared with the earlier application and, where this is so, supplying a copy of the later application together with any drawings showing where these changes occur. These documents are retained in the Security Section and therefore do not at any time become open to public inspection. Likewise, correspondence with the Security Section on other matters, *e.g.* seeking permission to file corresponding applications in certain foreign countries, is not placed on that part of the file which becomes open to public inspection. The legal basis for this is not clear from the wording of rule 93 (reprinted in para. 118.05).

Renewal fees   **22.11**

As regards subsection (8), no renewal fee is payable for the remainder of the year in which the secrecy order was revoked. The basis is that, under rule 39(1) (reprinted in para. 25.02), a renewal fee is prescribed to be paid prior to the year in which it is to be effective.

When a secrecy order is revoked prior to grant, but after a date three months before the expiration of the fourth year of the patent, the renewal fee is due within three months from the date on which the patent is granted (proviso to r. 39(1)). Since this rule is made under section 25(3), which is a "following provision" as referred to in section 25(1), this date of grant will be the date on which the notice of grant is published in the Journal under section 25(1) and not the administrative date of grant referred to in section 24(1), see para. 24.11. Should a prohibition order be lifted in any year after the fourth, and the anniversary of the filing date falls between the date of rescission of the prohibition order and the date of grant, the renewal fee for the year starting with that anniversary is likewise payable within three months of publication of the notice of grant (r. 39(1)).

Withdrawal of secret application   **22.12**

Under sections 16(1) and 22(3)(a) it is possible to withdraw an application while still under a secrecy order (and even perhaps a little later) and thereby avoid publication even though the period prescribed by section 16(1) has expired. Section 13(2) [1949] is to be amended to give the same effect to applications filed under the 1949 Act, see para. A013.2.

Effect of other statutes

—Official Secrets Act   **22.13**

It should be borne in mind that, if any invention is in fact of a military nature, then the transmission of information about it is governed not only by section 22, but also by the Official Secrets Act 1911 (c. 28) and 1920 (c. 75). In particular, section 1A thereof (inserted by s. 9 of the 1920 Act) reads:

"If any person having in his possession or control any sketch, plan, model, article, note, document or information which relates to munitions of war, communicates it directly or indirectly to any foreign power, or in any other manner prejudicial to the safety or interests of the State, that person shall be guilty of a misdemeanour".

Section 9 also inserted the following definition in section 12 of the 1911 Act:

"The expression 'munitions of war' includes the whole or any part of any ship, submarine, aircraft, tank or similar engine, arms and ammunition, torpedo or mine, intended or adapted for use in war, and any other article, material, or device, whether actual or proposed, intended for such use".

Not dissimilar in some respects is the practice for the implementation of article 16 of the Euratom Treaty (Cmnd. 4865) to which the United Kingdom is now a party. If the Patent Office regards the subject matter of an application as being specifically nuclear in nature, whether or not requiring the imposition of a secrecy order, the applicant will be notified at an early stage after filing and invited to agree to disclosure of the contents of the specification to the Euratom Commission. Failing such agreement, the Commission is informed by the Patent Office of the existence of the application and in the event that the Commission calls for the contents to be disclosed the applicant's agreement will be sought by the Patent Office a second time. Should agreement again not be forthcoming, a compulsory disclosure is required "within eighteen months of the date on which the application was filed". Since publication at that time is now the norm, except where secrecy orders have been imposed, there is less purpose in this requirement which in present times therefore seems unlikely to arise.

22.14 *Export of Goods (Control) Order*

The Export of Goods (Control) Order 1987 (S.I. 1987 No. 2070), made under the Import, Export and Customs Powers (Defence) Act 1939 (2 & 3 Geo. 6, c. 69), specifies categories of goods which it is unlawful to export to certain countries. This Order applies export restrictions to, *inter alia*, "technological documents (other than documents generally available to the public), the information contained in which relates to goods and processes" as defined in relation to export to a specified list of countries which, in respect of such documents, is presently limited to countries of the COMECON, or "Eastern bloc", group. However, applications for patents (as well as for other forms of protection for innovations, including registered designs), and documents necessary to enable such applications to be filed or made or pursued, relating to any goods specified in Groups 1 to 3 of Part II of Schedule 1 to that Order, or to any goods or processes specified in group 4 of Part II of Schedule 1 to the Order, are exempt (S.I. 1987 No. 2070, article 2(xiii)). These exemptions replace the general licence granted February 17, 1984 under a previous form of the order.

The list of goods and processes categorised in the 1987 Order is extensive and complex and the Order should be consulted for details. It should also be noted that the categories of prohibited goods, and though less likely also the list of countries specified in relation thereto, is liable to change without prior notice, as also may the terms of the aforesaid general licence. Thus, the position on amendments to the Order should also be checked in relation to any particular goods. General advice on the operation of the Export of Goods (Control) Order can be obtained by inquiry to Dept. OT 2/3c, Room 323, Department of Trade and Industry, 1 Victoria Street, London SW1H 0ET, Tel. 071–215 5731.

SECTION 23

Restrictions on applications abroad by United Kingdom residents

23.—(1) Subject to the following provisions of this section, no person 23.01
resident in the United Kingdom shall, without written authority granted by
the comptroller, file or cause to be filed outside the United Kingdom an
application for a patent for an invention unless—

(*a*) an application for a patent for the same invention has been filed in
the Patent Office (whether before, on or after the appointed day)
not less than six weeks before the application outside the United
Kingdom; and

(*b*) either no directions have been given under section 22 above in relation to the application in the United Kingdom or all such directions
have been revoked.

(2) Subsection (1) above does not apply to an application for a patent for
an invention for which an application for a patent has first been filed
(whether before or after the appointed day) in a country outside the
United Kingdom by a person resident outside the United Kingdom.

(3) A person who files or causes to be filed an application for the grant of
a patent in contravention of this section shall be liable—

(*a*) on summary conviction, to a fine not exceeding **the prescribed sum**
[*£1,000*]; or

(*b*) on conviction on indictment [**on information in the Isle of Man**], to
imprisonment for a term not exceeding two years or a fine, or both.

(4) In this section—

(*a*) any reference to an application for a patent includes a reference to
an application for other protection for an invention;

(*b*) any reference to either kind of application is a reference to an application under this Act, under the law of any country other than the
United Kingdom or under any treaty or international convention to
which the United Kingdom is a party.

Note. The amendment to subsection (3)(*a*) was effected by the Magistrates' Courts
Act 1980 (c. 43, s.32(2)); and that to subsection (3)(*b*) was effected by S.I. 1978
No. 621.

ARTICLES 23.02

Letters on "Patent Office Practice under sections 22 and 23" have been published
as follows:— (1979–80) 9 CIPA 187, 417, 537 and 539; (1980–81) 10 CIPA 27; and
(1987–88) 17 CIPA 15 and 90.

COMMENTARY ON SECTION 23

General 23.03

The EPC and PCT contain no corresponding provisions to section 23, though
EPCaa. 75 and 77 refer to national security requirements, as does PCTr. 22(1)(*a*).

Section 23 is specifically applied to applications made before, on or after the appointed day, June 1, 1978 (see, *e.g.* the parenthesised passages in subss. (1)(*a*) and (2)) and also applied to "existing" patents and applications (Sched. 2, para. 1(2)).

23.04 *General purpose of section*

The general purpose of section 23 is to provide for official review of a United Kingdom patent application before a United Kingdom "resident" can apply for a foreign patent or cause such an application to be filed. Unless subsection (2) applies (for which see para. 23.05 *infra*), the filing of any application outside the United Kingdom by a United Kingdom resident, or where such a resident "causes" such filing, is prohibited unless the permission of the Comptroller has been obtained, or unless at least six weeks have elapsed since the filing of an application for the same invention in the United Kingdom and during that time no directions have been given by the Comptroller or any that have been given have been revoked.

The word "resident" has not in this context been judicially construed. The word has, of course, often been construed in the context of taxation law, but this may raise different considerations. Giving the word a common sense interpretation, an employee of a United Kingdom company who works for an associated company abroad for several months may well be regarded as having ceased during that period to be a person resident in the United Kingdom. Conversely, if a person normally resident abroad makes an invention while in the United Kingdom and thereupon files an application abroad giving a postal address in the United Kingdom and later files a convention application in the United Kingdom, an explanation may be called for by the Patent Office.

23.05 *Definitions applicable to section 23 (subs. (4))*

By subsection (4), an application for a patent is defined by subsection (4)(*a*) to include an application for any "other protection of an invention"; and by subsection (4)(*b*) either kind of application is to be taken as comprising applications abroad or under any treaty or convention to which the United Kingdom is a party. The generality is wide and would seem to extend to applications for design or utility model protection if such an application can be said to be one for "protection of an invention".

23.06 *Exceptions to applicability of subsection (1) (subs. (2))*

By subsection (2), the restrictions on filing abroad do not apply in respect of an invention for which an application for protection has first been filed abroad by a person resident abroad. In the common case, therefore, in which a United Kingdom company has rights abroad in respect of an invention made by an associated company overseas, and receives a copy of a patent application made by the associated company, there is no need to obtain permission or to wait six weeks before any corresponding application is made in a territory in which the United Kingdom company has such rights.

23.07 *Penalties (subs. (3))*

The penalties specified in subsection (3) correspond to those in section 22(9), for which see para. 22.08. Section 113 explains where the liability shall be placed in the case of offences committed by bodies corporate, see para. 113.02.

The words used in subsection (1) are "files or causes to be filed" and these appear to be wide enough to include the patent agent who sends instructions abroad.

PRACTICE UNDER SECTION 23

Obtaining leave to file application abroad   **23.08**

To avoid contravention of section 23, any inventor normally resident in the United Kingdom, and travelling abroad from the United Kingdom for short periods, should be advised never to file a foreign application while he is abroad.

Because a secrecy order can be imposed on an application claiming priority from an earlier application, even when the earlier application has not been so treated, difficulties can arise if foreign applications are being made at the same time. The letters in CIPA listed in para. 23.02 *supra* refer to these difficulties and suggest how these may be minimised. Clearance under subsection (1) may be sought, and is usually obtainable quite quickly, by personal application to the Security Section of the Patent Office. This clearance is facilitated by identifying the priority application and marking any additional matter to be included in the new application. Where application for security clearance for permitted foreign filing is made by post, it is desirable to mark the envelope "For the urgent attention of Security Section, Room 331". Otherwise, delays have been known to occur.

As mentioned in para. 22.10, it is often the practice of the Patent Office, when revoking a secrecy order on an application not claiming priority, to advise the applicant to seek security clearance before filing foreign applications, preferably with marked documents as already described for showing any additional matter. As also noted in para. 22.10, such marked documents are retained by the Security Section and, therefore, do not at any time become open to public inspection.

Filing application abroad while secrecy order is in force   **23.09**

While a secrecy order under section 22 is in force on a United Kingdom application, the filing abroad of corresponding patent applications is not impossible. Arrangements exist between the United Kingdom and many other countries, notably those in the North Atlantic Treaty Organisation, for the mutual safeguarding of patent applications subject to secrecy orders. For filing in these countries the permission of the Patent Office should be sought. Under the NATO arrangements (see "Agreement for the Mutual Safeguarding of Inventions relating to Defence and for which Applications for Patents have been made" (Cmnd. 1595: Cmnd. 2167 provides implementing procedures)), it appears to be a precondition for the permission to be granted that an application covering the invention shall have been filed in the United Kingdom. Similar arrangements also exist with a few non-NATO countries.

It is recommended that, if advantage is being taken of the reciprocal filing arrangements discussed *supra* in order to secure protection abroad for an invention in respect of which a prohibition order under section 22 is in force, an approach should be made to the Security Section at the Patent Office for a permit under section 23 as soon as the proposed filing programme is known. A minimum period of 10 weeks before the desired filing date is suggested. Documents for foreign filing of an application subject to a prohibition order should be received by the Ministry of Defence at the address given on the Patent Office permit at least seven weeks before the desired filing date for the German Federal Republic, and four weeks for elsewhere.

If the suggested minimum periods cannot be adhered to, it is suggested that an applicant wanting protection in Europe may wish to consider filing an application for a European patent with the Security Section at the Patent Office, designating the EPC Member States for which a permit has been given, and pointing out that the requested European application should be made subject to a prohibition order under section 22. Such an application will not be forwarded to the EPO and, eventually, a notice of withdrawal will be issued by the EPO under EPCa. 77(5). The application may then be converted to national applications under EPCa. 135; and, for the United Kingdom, under section 81(1)(*b*) by filing PF 41/77 within three months of the date of notice of withdrawal, for which see paras. 81.08 and 81.11. However, no conversion procedure exists for international applications filed under the PCT.

23.10 *Secrecy conditions for foreign-originating applications*

It is understood that a secrecy order under section 22 will normally only be imposed on an application from abroad if the country of origin is one with which the United Kingdom has a reciprocol arrangement, for which see para. 23.09 *supra*, the authorities of that country having requested that such an order be imposed on the equivalent case filed in the country of origin and subject there to a secrecy order. An applicant wishing to file such an application in the United Kingdom should seek approval from his domestic authorities who will give instructions and make arrangements for the transmission of documents for filing through secure channels to the British agent nominated to receive them and act for the foreign applicant in the filing and prosecution of an application under the Act. If the nominated agent cannot be cleared to receive the documents, applicants will be asked to nominate an alternative agent.

For cases filed in this way, the Ministry of Defence does issue guidance to agents on his handling of such cases in the United Kingdom and his continuing correspondence with the foreign applicant or his associates. So far as dealings with the United Kingdom Patent Office are concerned, these will be as for similar domestic cases, except that a copy of the application is automatically made available to the appropriate United Kingdom authority for information purposes.

Whilst, in theory, there is nothing to prevent a foreign applicant filing a European application and requesting the imposition of a secrecy order—provided that the authorities in the country of origin were prepared to permit this—there would be considerable practical difficulties in the conversion procedure under EPCa. 135 once the notice under EPCa. 77(5) had been received. Filing from abroad an international application under the PCT under security would seem a pointless exercise. Further guidance on matters raised in this paragraph can be obtained from the Security Section of the Patent Office.

24.01

SECTION 24

Publication and certificate of grant

24.—(1) As soon as practicable after a patent has been granted under this Act the comptroller shall publish in the journal a notice that it has been granted.

(2) The comptroller shall, as soon as practicable after he publishes a notice under subsection (1) above, send the proprietor of the patent a certificate in the prescribed form that the patent has been granted to the proprietor.

(3) The comptroller shall, at the same time as he publishes a notice under subsection (1) above in relation to a patent publish the specification of the patent, the names of the proprietor and (if different) the inventor and any other matters constituting or relating to the patent which in the comptroller's opinion it is desirable to publish.

RELEVANT RULE

Certificate of grant

38. A certificate that a patent has been granted shall be in the form set   **24.02**
out in Schedule 3 to these Rules.

PATENTS RULES 1982—SCHEDULE 3   *Rule 38*   **24.03**

FORM OF CERTIFICATE OF GRANT OF PATENT

In accordance with section 24(2) of the Patents Act 1977, it is hereby certified that a patent having the specification No. [   ] has been granted to [   ] in respect of an invention disclosed in an application for that patent having a date of filing of [   ] being an invention for [   ]

Dated this [   ] day of [   ] 19

Comptroller-General of Patents,
Designs and Trade Marks

COMMENTARY ON SECTION 24

General   **24.04**

Section 24 concerns the notification and publication of grant of patents under the Act. The provisions differ substantially from those of the 1949 Act. In particular, patents are no longer granted under seal and the royal prerogative. This makes it inappropriate to refer to patents granted under the present Act as "Letters Patent" and the Act carefully avoids the use of the term "patentee," replacing this with "proprietor".

Under section 101 [1949] the term "patent" is defined as meaning "Letters Patent for an invention" and the term "patentee" as meaning "the person or persons for the time being entered on the register of patents as grantee or proprietor of the patent". These definitions remain applicable in relation to "existing patents", that is those in respect of which complete specifications were filed under the 1949 Act before the "appointed day" (June 1, 1978). The term "patent" as used in the Act only includes an "existing patent" in relation to those provisions which are listed in Schedule 2, para. 1(2) (Sched. 2, para. 2(*d*)).

217

For the terms of life of "patents" and "existing patents", see paras. 25.06 and 25.10 respectively.

24.05   *Notification of grant (subs. 1(1))*

Subsection (1) requires the Comptroller, as soon as practicable after the patent has been granted, to publish in the O.J. a notice to that effect. While section 20 requires an application to be brought in order for grant within a prescribed period, the Act is silent on exactly when the patent shall be granted. Prima facie it should be when the requirements of section 18(4) have been met. For the meaning of the term "date of the patent", see para. 24.11 *infra*.

The Comptroller will give sympathetic consideration to granting patents "out of turn" where the applicant can show he is suffering "real and substantial hardship", for example, where actual infringement is taking place, especially if by importation, see *e.g.* O.J. July 13, 1988. However, mere fear of possible infringement or desire to expedite licensing negotiations would probably not be sufficient reason ((1980–81) 10 CIPA 492). Where expedition is refused it might still be possible to seek judicial review under RSC Ord. 53 (for which see para. E053.1) to require the Comptroller to perform his statutory duty, though it is not clear that the Comptroller has any duty to carry out examination unusually expeditiously.

24.06   *Issue of Certificate of Grant (subs. (2))*

Subsection (2) requires the Comptroller to send a Certificate of Grant to the proprietor as soon as practicable after notification of grant in the O.J. By rule 38 (reprinted in para. 24.02 *supra*), this Certificate is in the form set out in Schedule 3 of the Rules (reprinted in para. 24.03 *supra*). The simplistic and stark wording of this is to be contrasted with the wording of the Grant of Letters Patent which issued under the 1949 Act, see para. A021.3, but the difference arises because the rights now arising from the patent grant are set out in the statute itself, whereas previously these rights were determined by the application of the Common Law to the wording of the Grant document in relation to the alleged infringing act.

The Certificate of Grant has no legal force under United Kingdom law and, apparently for this reason, it is understood that the Patent Office refuses to issue a duplicate if a certificate is lost or destroyed, as can be done in the case of a lost Letters Patent document under section 80 [1949]. This can be troublesome if a certified copy of the certificate is required to support registration of the patent in another country, as is apparently a requirement in Singapore. In such circumstances the Patent Office will provide an explanatory letter, but this may not be sufficient evidence to obtain registration of the patent abroad. The EPO will not apparently issue a certified copy of a European patent (UK), but will issue a "duplicate patent certificate" to the proprietor or his authorised agent ((1984–85) 14 CIPA 111).

24.07   *Publication of patent specification (subs. (3))*

At the same time as he publishes the notification of grant in the O.J. under subsection (1), the Comptroller is required by subsection (3) to publish the specification of the granted patent, the name(s) of the proprietor(s) and inventor(s) and any other matters concerning the patent which he considers desirable. This publication is made under the same number as that given to the application when published under section 16, but with the suffix "B" instead of the former suffix "A", see further para. 24.12 *infra*.

As from October 19, 1983 the "B" specification has been printed by photographic reproduction of the specification on file. For applications already pending when rule 20 was revised on June 14, 1982, the applicant was given the opportunity of submitting a retyped text for printing, but when this was done the retyped text was not checked (O.J. August 24, 1983 and ((1982–83) 12 CIPA 467). Such specifications bear a note that the text may not be authentic and it should be noted that the authentic version of the specification of the granted patent is that on file in the Patent Office. It would, therefore, always be prudent to check a patent specification published in letterpress form against the authentic version on the Patent Office file, and to use a certified copy of that version in any subsequent proceedings on the patent. That should not be necessary now that the "B specification" is a direct reproduction of that authentic text.

The authentic text of the patent specification can be inspected, and copies obtained, as from the date when the notice of grant is published in the O.J., see para. 118.20.

European patents (UK)   **24.08**

Under section 77 a European patent (UK) is, as from notice of grant appearing in the EPB, to be treated as though it were published in the O.J. on that date for the purposes of Parts I and III of the Act. The corresponding provisions of EPC are EPCa. 97 relating to grant and publication, and EPCa. 98 relating to publication procedure.

Despite the wording of subsection (3), European patents (UK) are not published as such by the United Kingdom Patent Office, see para. 77.09 where there is discussed the propriety of this and the problem which arises on amendment of such a patent.

PRACTICE UNDER SECTION 24

Entries in the register   **24.09**

When an application proceeds to grant, further entries are made in the register already established for the specification when the application was published under section 16. At that time the entries set out in rule 44(2) (reprinted in para. 32.04) are entered, see para. 16.04. By rule 44(3) (reprinted in the same para.) these further entries are the date when the patent is granted (for which see para. 24.11 *infra*); and the name and address of the person(s) to whom the patent is granted, and the address for service, each if different from the entries for these items of data which were made on publication under section 16.

Entries in the O.J.   **24.10**

The O.J. containing notice of grant of a patent also includes its subject matter classification according to the current United Kingdom Classification Key (which may be different from that for the specification as published under s. 16). However, until May 11, 1988 the O.J. carried no index of granted patents as it does for notices of publication of applications under section 16. From that date the O.J. has listed: (a) in numerical order the patents, the notification of grant of which is being published, together with bibliographic data; (b) a "subject matter index" listing classification codes; and (c) a name index of proprietor(s) and inventor(s) with cross-references there between, each list being headed with an explanatory note illustrating typical wording of such an entry. Inventorship details were added to these entries from March 1, 1989 (O.J. February 15, 1989).

European patents (UK) granted under EPCa. 97 are listed in the O.J. some weeks after notice of their grant has appeared in the EPB, but only the patent number, publication number and name of proprietor are listed in such O.J. entries.

24.11   *Date of grant*

There are actually two dates of grant of a patent, see O.J. September 2, 1982. For the purposes of those sections of the Act preceding section 24(1), *i.e.* for administrative and pre-grant purposes, the date of grant is that of the date of issue of the letter notifying the applicant that a patent has been granted and informing him of the date (several weeks ahead) when notification will appear in the O.J. After that date no withdrawal of the application under section 14(9), no divisional application under section 15(4), nor any further amendment under section 19 is admitted, see *ITT's Application* ([1984] RPC 23) and *Ogawa Chemical's Application* ([1986] RPC 63). However, for the purposes of the "following" sections of the Act, the date of grant is that of the O.J. in which notice of grant is published (s. 25(1)), and it is this date which is entered in the register under rule 44(3)(*c*) as the date of grant. Only thereafter can amendment be sought under sections 27 and 75. Thus, there is a short time between the date of the letter and the publication in the O.J. during which amendment of a patent cannot be requested. Also, any assignment executed after the date when notice of grant is given to the applicant and before the publication of the notice of grant in the O.J. is treated as an assignment of an application, rather than of a patent, as sections 30 and 31 are provisions which "follow" section 24, see, *e.g.* O.J. April 5, 1989.

The two dates of grant could cause confusion in determining the period within which a granted patent may be registered in those countries where patent protection is secured by registration of the United Kingdom patent within a specified time, particularly as some of the Patent Ordinances provide for computing the time from the date of "grant" of the patent (see (1981–82) 11 CIPA 414 and (1982–83) 12 CIPA 25), but it is understood that some territories (*e.g.* Antigua, Belize, Jersey and Hong Kong) have amended their Ordinances specifically to define the date of grant as the date of the O.J. publication. Nevertheless, the prudent practitioner will compute the time from the earlier of the two dates. However, it can be argued that, as "patent" is defined in section 130(1) (which is a "following" provision of the Act), the latter date is controlling.

24.12   *Specification of granted patent*

It is the practice of the Patent Office to attach to the Certificate of Grant a copy of the specification of the granted patent, but this does not include the abstract as this does not form part of the patent (s. 125(1)). The specification bears the same number as that published under section 16, preceded by the letters "GB" and followed by the letter "B". The requirements of rule 20(16) are designed to facilitate the publication of this "B-specification" by reproduction of the file copy of the accepted specification in the form in which it has been accepted. The "other matters" published are presently the bibliographic data published under section 16, replaced as appropriate, and likewise presented on a front sheet. This is annotated according to the ICIREPAT code, for which see para. 123.45. It appears that the Comptroller has a wide discretion in respect of the publication of indexes, classified file lists and other information retrieval tools. This has been the subject of adverse comment ((1978–79) 8 CIPA 287), see para. 123.46.

SECTION 25   25.01

Term of patent

25.—(1) A patent granted under this Act shall be treated for the purposes of the following provisions of this Act as having been granted, and shall take effect, on the date on which notice of its grant is published in the journal and, subject to subsection (3) below, shall continue in force until the end of the period of 20 years beginning with the date of filing the application for the patent or with such other date as may be prescribed.

(2) A rule prescribing any such other date under this section shall not be made unless a draft of the rule has been laid before, and approved by resolution of, each House of Parliament.

(3) A patent shall cease to have effect at the end of the period prescribed for the payment of any renewal fee if it is not paid within that period.

(4) If during the period of six months immediately following the end of the prescribed period the renewal fee and any prescribed additional fee are paid, the patent shall be treated for the purposes of this Act as if it had never expired, and accordingly—

(*a*) anything done under or in relation to it during that further period shall be valid;

(*b*) an act which would constitute an infringement of it if it had not expired shall constitute such an infringement; and

(*c*) an act which would constitute the use of the patented invention for the services of the Crown if the patent had not expired shall constitute that use.

(5) Rules shall include provision requiring the comptroller to notify the registered proprietor of a patent that a renewal fee has not been received from him in the Patent Office before the end of the prescribed period and before the framing of the notification.

RELEVANT RULES

Renewal fees

39.—(1) If is is desired to keep a patent in force for a further year after   25.02
the expiration of the fourth or any succeeding year from the date of filing an application for that patent as determined in accordance with section 15, Patents Form No. 12/77, in respect of the next succeeding year, accompanied by the prescribed renewal fee for that year, shall be filed in the three months before the expiration of the fourth or succeeding year, as the case may be:

Provided that, where a patent is granted in the three months before the expiration of the fourth or any succeeding year as so determined or at any time thereafter, except in the case of a European patent (UK), Patents

Form No. 12/77 in respect of the fifth or succeeding year may be filed not more than three months before the expiration of the fourth or relevant succeeding year but before the expiration of three months from the date on which the patent is granted.

(2) If it is desired, at the expiration of the fourth or any succeeding year from the date of filing an application for a European patent (UK) as determined in accordance with Article 80 of the European Patent Convention and provided that mention of the grant of the patent is or has been published in the European Patent Bulletin, to keep the patent in force, Patents Form No. 12/77, accompanied by the prescribed renewal fee, shall be filed in the three months before the expiration of that year:

Provided that, where any renewal fee is due within two months after the date of the publication in the European Patent Bulletin of the mention of the grant of the patent, that renewal fee may be paid within those two months.

(3) On receipt of the prescribed renewal fee accompanied by Patents Form No. 12/77 duly completed, the comptroller shall issue a certificate of payment on the appropriate portion of that form.

(4) Where the period for payment of a renewal fee pursuant to paragraph (1) or (2) above has expired, the comptroller shall, not later than six weeks after the last date for payment under that paragraph and if the fee still remains unpaid, send to the proprietor of the patent a notice reminding him that payment is overdue and of the consequences of non-payment.

(5) The notice shall be sent to the address in the United Kingdom specified for that purpose by the proprietor of the patent when last paying a renewal fee in respect of the patent or, if no such address was specified, to the relevant address for service entered in the register.

(6) A request for extension of the period for payment of any renewal fee shall be made on Patents Form No. 13/77.

Note. The wording of this rule is rather tortuous and it is thought it may soon be revised. Therefore, the latest Supplement to this Work should be consulted *re.* this para. In particular it is thought that sub-rule (5) will be amended to provide for a renewal reminder to be sent on request to an address other than that specified on the last-filed PF 12/77; and that PF 12/77 and PF 13/77 will be combined.

Notification of lapsed patent

25.03   **42.** Where a patent has ceased to have effect because a renewal fee has not been paid within the period prescribed in rule 39(1) or (2) above and the extended period specified in section 25(4) has expired without the renewal fee and prescribed additional fee having been paid, the comptroller shall, within six weeks after the expiration of the extended period, notify the proprietor of the patent of the fact and draw his attention to the provisions of section 28.

ARTICLE **25.04**

A. W. White, "Transitional Provisions of the U.K. Patents Act 1977", [1983] EIPR 5.

COMMENTARY ON SECTION 25

General **25.05**

Section 25 deals with the term of patents granted under the Act (also European Patents (UK)) and with the payment of renewal fees. Subsections (3)–(5) also apply to "existing" patents (Sched. 2, para. 1(2)), but subject to provision discussed separately in para. 25.10 *infra*.

Grant and term of patent (subss. (1) and (2)) **25.06**

Subsection (1) provides that, for the purposes of subsequent provisions of the Act, a patent is to be regarded as having been granted and as taking effect on the date on which notice of grant is published in the O.J., see para. 24.11. The term of the patent is 20 years from and including the date of filing. This date is defined in section 130(1) as that specified in section 15 in the case of an application made under the Act, *i.e.* the date when the minimum requirements have been met or are treated as having been met, *e.g.* in the case of a divisional application, see para. 15.07. In the case of any other application, *i.e.* one filed under the EPC or PCT, it is the date treated as the date of filing of that application in accordance with the relevant convention or treaty, whatever the outcome of that application in relation to other countries.

Subsection (1) further provides for the term of the patent running from some other date to be prescribed by rule, but subject to affirmative resolution by both Houses of Parliament pursuant to subsection (2). These provisions would, if activated, make it possible for the term of a patent to run not from the date of filing but from the declared priority date should this be required by any revised convention to which the United Kingdom should become a party (see H.L.Deb. Vol. 379, ser. 28, col. 1469 (February 15, 1977)). Presumably, such a rule could also be made to extend the term of patents generally to meet special circumstances, *e.g.* war. However, there is no specific provision for extension of term as in earlier legislation.

EPCa. 63(1) similarly provides for a 20 year term for European patents running from the date of application. EPCa. 63(2) provides a Contracting State with the right to extend European patents on the same terms as national patents in the case of war or similar emergency conditions; section 77(1) incorporates these provisions into the terms of section 25.

Renewal fees (subs. (3)) **25.07**

Subsection (3) provides that a patent shall lapse if a renewal fee is not paid within the prescribed period. Under rule 39(1) (reprinted in para. 123.10) this period is the three months preceding the end of the fourth and each succeeding year after the date of filing and includes the anniversary of this date. This three month limit is not extensible (r. 110(2)): it is therefore not possible to pay more than one year's fee at a time in order to avoid paying increased fees. It is not, however, clear what action the Patent Office will take if a fee is paid too early. For late payment under subsection (4), see para. 25.08 *infra*.

Under the present proviso to rule 39(1), when grant has not taken place by a date three months before expiration of the fourth year, the appropriate fee(s) are to be paid within three months of grant, again not extensible (r. 110(2)).

In the case of a European patent (UK), rule 39(2) requires that the renewal fee shall be paid within the three months preceding the expiry of the fourth or subsequent year from the date of filing, provided that mention of grant thereof has been published in the EPB. However, if the fee is due within two months after the date of notice of grant in the EPB, the fee may be paid within those two months. Each of these periods is also inextensible (r. 110(2)). For a note on the renewal of European patents (UK), see *e.g.* O.J. April 27, 1988.

25.08 *Late payment of renewal fees (subs. (4))*

Under subsection (4) a renewal fee can be paid with an additional extension fee during the six months following the end of the normal period for payment: this period is inextensible (r. 110(2)). This extension period appears in the Act itself because subsection (4) enacts the requirement under Article 5bis of the Paris International Convention.

Where fees are increased during this extension period, the old scale applies to the renewal fee itself, but the new scale will apply to any extension fee paid after the date of change of the fee scales. Although subsection (3) states that a patent ceases to have effect if a renewal fee is not paid within the prescribed period, subsection (4) also makes it clear that, if the fee and the extension fee are paid within six months, the patent will be treated as if it had not lapsed. If the fee is not then paid, the patent is deemed to have lapsed at the end of the normal period for payment subject, however, to possible restoration under section 28, see *Daido Kogyo's Patent* ([1984] RPC 97). Also, when a renewal fee has been paid within the extension period, relief in respect of Crown use or infringement during that period may be refused (ss. 58(5) and 62(2)).

Accordingly, it is not safe to treat a patent as having lapsed until six months after the due date for payment of a renewal fee, and even then an application for restoration is possible during the permitted period therefor (for which see para. 28.05), though continuing rights will arise for acts commenced during that period, see para. 28A.04.

25.09 *Reminders (subs. (5))*

Pursuant to subsection (5) and rule 39(4) (reprinted in para. 25.02 *supra*) the Comptroller is required to send the proprietor a reminder not later than six weeks after the expiry of the normal date for payment pointing out the consequences of non-payment. The reminder is sent to the address in the United Kingdom specified by the proprietor when last paying a renewal fee or (failing any such address) to the address for service entered in the register (r. 39(5) reprinted in para. 25.02 *supra*). At present there is no provision whereby the Comptroller can accede to a request for the reminder to be sent elsewhere, for example after an assignment, but see *Note* to para. 25.02. Similarly, under rule 42 (reprinted at para. 25.03 *supra*), when the renewal fee has been paid within the extended period provided by subsection (4), a further reminder is to be sent not later than six weeks after the expiry of the six month extension period drawing attention to the provisions of section 28 (*Restoration*). This reminder is sent to the address for service entered in the register. If no address for service has been entered in the register, which may particularly be the case with a European patent (UK), the Comptroller is unable to send the required reminders (*Deforeit's Patent*, [1986] RPC 142). The address for service may now be within the United Kingdom (including the Isle of Man) or elsewhere within the European Community, see para. 32.16.

Existing patents   **25.10**

Section 22(1)–(3) [1949] remains in force in relation to existing patents, but with considerable effective revision of section 22(3) [1949] (*"Term of patent"*) made by Schedule 1, paras. 3 and 4 (reprinted in para. 133.01). However, the present subsections (3)–(5) apply to the payment of renewal fees thereon (Sched. 2, para. 1(2)), with rule 39(1) modified by reference to "the date of the patent" rather than the date of filing (unrepealed r. 124(4) [1978], reprinted in para. 127.04). The effect of the transitional provisions of the Act on the renewal of existing patents is discussed in the article by A. W. White listed in para. 25.04 *supra*, and is summarised below.

"Old existing patents"—patents granted under the 1949 Act and bearing dates 11 years or more before June 1, 1978, *i.e.* with a complete specification dated on or before June 1, 1967 and including patents of addition to such patents—retained the maximum term of 16 years under the 1949 Act, but could have been made the subject of extension of term up to a maximum of four years (Sched. 1, para. 3(1)(*a*) and 3(3)). However, these provisions are now spent and all "old existing patents", even those extended, have expired. The term "old existing patent" is therefore now obsolete.

"New existing patents"—patents which on June 1, 1978 had more than five years of their term still to run, *viz.* with a complete specification dated after June 1, 1967, and including patents granted on applications made under the 1949 Act but prosecution of which continued after June 1, 1978—have had their term automatically extended to 20 years (Sched. 1, para. 3(1)(*b*) and 4(1)). However, this extension of term of those "existing patents" which still subsist is subject to the conditions set out in Schedule 1, para. 4, *viz.*:

(a) Renewal fees must be paid under section 25(3)–(5) (para. 4(1)(*a*));
(b) The patent may only be renewed by or with the consent of the patentee (para. 4(1)(*b*)); it is not clear, however, whether the Patent Office requires the explicit consent of the patentee;
(c) Any licence which was in force before June 1, 1978 and which remains in force at the end of the original 16 year term continues, but on a non-exclusive basis (para. 4(2)(*a*));
(d) The holder of any such licence is not required to make any further payment in respect of any licence extended under (c) above, notwithstanding the terms of such licence (para. 4(2)(*b*));
(e) Such patents are treated as endorsed "licences of right" under section 35 [1949] as from the end of the original 16 year term (para. 4(2)(*c*)), though now subject to the possible exclusion of licences for pharmaceutical or pesticidal uses of patented products (new para. 4A, discussed in paras. 47.10–47.14);
(f) Government Departments, and persons authorised thereby, who used the invention before June 1, 1978 have the right to continue to do so free of any payment to the patentee (para. 4(3)); and
(g) The court is given broad powers to relieve or apportion loss or liability between persons who are affected by the extension of such a patent (paras. 4(4) and 4(5)).

Apart from a considerable number of proceedings for settlement of licence terms in relation to the deemed "licences of right" endorsement on existing patents, for which see para. 25.11 *infra*, the remaining provisions of Schedule 1, paragraph 4 appear as yet to have led to only one decision. Here it was held (in proceedings to settle a licence of right) that paragraph 4(2)(*b*) only applies if the licence is in force at the end of the 16th year (*Bergwerksverband's Patent*, SRIS O/58/89, *noted* IPD 12065): here the licence had not only been terminated, but had been renegotiated to run afresh from June 1, 1978, and this also probably took the licence outside the scope of paragraph 4(2)(*a*).

25.11   *Deemed endorsement of existing patents "licences of right"*

Schedule 1, para. 4(2)(*c*) now deems all existing patents to be endorsed "licences of right" at the end of the sixteenth year of their term as if this had occurred under section 35 [1949], itself repealed under Schedule 6. This endorsement is deemed to occur by operation of law so that the Letters Patent document does not itself become endorsed, as section 35 [1949] itself required. However, once so deemed endorsed, the patent becomes governed as to the effect of such endorsement by section 46 (*Allen & Hanburys* v. *Generics* ([1986] RPC 203 (HL), *per* Lord Diplock). A periodic notice in the O.J., *e.g.* that of January 27, 1988, explains this and reminds proprietors that, under section 46(3)(*d*), only half the normal renewal fees are payable in respect of such patents for the seventeenth to twentieth years of their terms, unless PF 58/77 has been filed as noted *infra*.

This deemed endorsement has given rise to many heavily contested applications under section 46(3)(*c*) for settlement of the terms of licences of right which have become available thereunder, particularly under patents for medicinal products, see paras. 46.07–46.27.

However, Schedule 1, para. 4A (added by s. 293 of the 1988 Act, and reprinted in para. 133.01) provides that such a "licence of right" endorsement can, in effect, be limited to exclude certain uses of a patented product, in particular pharmaceutical and other prescribed uses thereof, if the proprietor files an appropriate declaration under rule 67A inserted by the Patents (Amendment) Rules 1988 (S.I. 1988 No. 2089, reprinted at para. 47.06) by filing PF 58/77 (reprinted at para. 141.58), for which see para. 47.19, but renewal fees payable after the filing of such a declaration must then be paid in full. These provisions are discussed more fully in paras. 47.10–47.14.

Schedule 1, para. 4B (also added by the 1988 Act, s. 294, and reprinted in para. 133.01) provides that any application for settlement of the terms of a licence of right on an existing patent deemed endorsed "licences of right" under Schedule 1, para. 4(2)(*c*) is ineffective if made before the beginning of the sixteenth year of the term of the patent. This provision is discussed in para. 46.12.

PRACTICE UNDER SECTION 25

25.12   *Payment of renewal fees*

Renewal fees are paid on PF 12/77 (reprinted at para. 141.12), the fees being those specified in Schedule 1 to the Rules, see paras. 144.01 and 144.02. However, where a patent is subject to "licences of right" (or in the case of a new existing patent is deemed to be so endorsed after its sixteenth year), only one half of the specified renewal fee is payable (s. 46(3)(*d*)). The date on which the renewal fee actually falls due, *i.e.* the anniversary of the date of filing of the application upon which the patent was granted, must be shown on PF 12/77, and a portion of this form constitutes the certificate of payment required by rule 39(3) to be sent by the Comptroller. This certificate should be completed. The Patent Office will then date it, detach this portion and return it to the address given on the form. If there is no address given, the dated portion is sent to the address for service entered in the register. This return address given on PF 12/77 need not be in the United Kingdom, but note that the returned portion will be sent by surface mail and that a reminder will not be sent to an address outside the United Kingdom.

The additional fee for late payment within the six month extension period provided by subsection (4) is made on PF 13/77 (reprinted at para. 141.13), the fee again being as specified in Schedule 1 to the Rules. This fee for late payment is not subject to reduction if the patent is subject to "licences of right".

Both PF 12/77 and PF 13/77 (which may become combined, see *Note* to para. 25.02) may be filed in the name of any person, and there is no need to show any relationship to, or authorisation by, the proprietor, but note that "existing" patents can only be renewed after their sixteenth year by or with the consent of the proprietor (Sched. 1, para. 4(1)(*b*)).

Since June 14, 1982 no entry has been made in the register of payment of a renewal or extension fee. A request for information as to the date of payment of a renewal fee can be made on PF 23/77 (reprinted at para. 141.23), see rule 48 (reprinted at para. 118.02). No additional fee is required for this if the register or file is also inspected, see para. 118.20.

Patents which have ceased through non-payment of renewal fees, and also patents which have expired through the effluxion of time, are listed in the O.J.

If a patent has lapsed by failure to pay a fee and the next year's fee is tendered, this is authorised for refund, but the former practice of giving prompt warning to the payer is no longer followed and, as a result, the proprietor may become aware of that lapsing too late to seek restoration, see *Borg-Warner's Patent* ([1986] RPC 137) where rule 100 was not permitted to be invoked to extend the time limit under section 28(1), itself inextensible under rule 110(2) (see para. 28.06).

Reminders

—By general notice   **25.13**

The notice of grant issued by the Patent Office specifically draws attention to the responsibility of the proprietor to arrange for payment of renewal fees, and advises him to check if any renewal fee is due at the time of grant or in the near future, and to set up a suitable reminder system. A Note on the back of the Certificate of Grant reads:

> The proprietor is responsible for ensuring that effective renewal arrangements are set up and maintained and that fees are paid on time. He should not await any communication from the Patent Office before paying fees: an official reminder sent to the last recorded address for service six weeks after the anniversary of the date of the patent is intended to alert the proprietor to possible failure of his renewal arrangements.

A notice is also published periodically in the O.J. (*e.g.* July 14, 1982) reminding proprietors of their responsibility for timely payment of renewal fees to the Patent Office in respect of United Kingdom patents. A further periodic notice (*e.g.* O.J. July 19, 1989) refers in detail to the renewal of European patents (UK) and the need to supply an address for service in respect thereof, see para. 32.22. A further notice was published by the EPO (OJEPO 9/1984, 445); see also para. 77.14 for an individual notice now given by the EPO in its notice of intention to grant the patent.

European patent applications require the payment of renewal fees two years after filing and then annually until the year of notice of grant appearing in the EPB. For guidance on the payment of renewal fees on European patent applications, see OJEPO, 4/1980, 101.

25.14   —*By statutory notice*

The requirement to issue reminders of non-payment of a renewal fee (r. 39(4)), and of lapsing of the patent (r. 42) have been discussed in para. 25.09 *supra*. Although these reminders are issued six weeks and six months after the due payment date respectively, they are not intended to be a back-up to a renewal reminder system operated by the proprietor or his agent. However, the Patents Court has accepted the argument that a proprietor (albeit an individual) is entitled to set up a system for payment of these fees which relies on these official notices reminding him of the need to pay renewal fees, see *Ling's Patent* and *Wilson and Pearce's Patent* ([1981] RPC 85) discussed in para. 28.09.

25.15   *Legal obligations of agents in respect of statutory notices*

The legal implications of the professional obligations accepted by a patent agent in relation to receipt of reminder notices because his address is entered in the register as the official address for service in respect of a patent is the subject of advice and comment in (1979–80) 9 CIPA 504 and (1980–81) 10 CIPA 30. The attitude of the Patent Office with regard to alteration of the address for service has been set out in a letter to the Institute ((1980–81) 10 CIPA 255). This states that "There can, of course, be no question of deletion of an address for service without substitution of another". However, while this may have been the attitude of the Office, the question of renunciation of a recorded address for service is a matter of contract between the proprietor and his agent and it is understood that the Comptroller now accepts this, but nevertheless the renounced address for service will not be removed from the register until another is substituted therefor.

Particular care needs to be taken by a joint proprietor or a licensee who does not have the responsibility for paying renewal fees to check that the fee has been paid, *e.g.* by filing PF 23/77 at the date the fee is due. It is dangerous to rely on the caveat system ((1981–82) 11 CIPA 254).

26.01   **SECTION 26**

Patent not to be impugned for lack of unity

26. No person may in any proceeding object to a patent or to an amendment of a specification of a patent on the ground that the claims contained in the specification of the patent, as they stand or, as the case may be, as proposed to be amended, relate—

   (*a*) to more than one invention, or
   (*b*) to a group of inventions which are not so linked as to form a single inventive concept.

COMMENTARY ON SECTION 26

26.02   *General*

Section 26 concerns unity of invention and corresponds generally to section 21(4) [1949] which continues to apply to existing patents (Sched. 1, para. 1(2)).

26.03   *Objection to lack of unity*

While section 14(5)(*d*) requires that the claims of a specification must relate to one invention or a single inventive concept, section 26 provides that no person can in any proceedings object to a patent on the ground that the claims do not comply with that requirement. This provision goes beyond section 21(4) [1949] in making it clear that objection to a proposed amendment under sections 27, 75 or 76 similarly cannot be based on the ground that the amendment would result in lack of unity, for example as occurred under the 1949 Act in *North Western Gas Board's Application* ([1972] RPC 597). Presumably the same would apply to a correction under section 117. In any event, a patent granted under the Act can only be revoked on the specific grounds listed in section 72(1), but see *Genentech's Patent* ([1989] RPC 147 (CA)) discussed in para. 72.20.

There is no corresponding provision in the EPC, but EPCa. 82 corresponds to section 14(5)(*d*), while the comprehensive grounds of opposition specified in EPCa. 100 (to which s. 72(1) corresponds) do not include lack of unity.

The question of unity of invention is more fully dealt with in para. 14.27.

SECTION 27

27.01

General power to amend specification after grant

27.—(1) Subject to the following provisions of this section and to section 76 below, the comptroller may, on an application made by the proprietor of a patent, allow the specification of the patent to be amended subject to such conditions, if any, as he thinks fit.

(2) No such amendment shall be allowed under this section where there are pending before the court or the comptroller proceedings in which the validity of the patent may be put in issue.

(3) An amendment of a specification of a patent under this section shall have effect and be deemed always to have had effect from the grant of the patent.

(4) The comptroller may, without an application being made to him for the purpose, amend the specification of a patent so as to acknowledge a registered trade-mark **or registered service mark**.

(5) A person may give notice to the comptroller of his opposition to an application under this section by the proprietor of a patent, and if he does so the comptroller shall notify the proprietor and consider the opposition in deciding whether to grant the application.

Note. Subsection (4) was effectively amended, as indicated, by the 1986 Act (s. 2(3) and Sched. 2, para. 1(2)(*e*)).

RELEVANT RULE

Amendment of specification after grant

27.02

40.—(1) An application to the comptroller for leave to amend the specification of a patent shall be made on Patents Form No. 14/77 and shall be advertised by publication of the application and the nature of the proposed amendment in the Journal and in such other manner, if any, as the comptroller may direct.

(2) Any person wishing to oppose the application to amend shall, within three months from the date of the advertisement in the Journal, give notice to the comptroller on Patents Form No. 15/77.

(3) Such notice shall be accompanied by a copy thereof and be supported by a statement in duplicate setting out fully the facts upon which the opponent relies and the relief which he seeks. The comptroller shall send a copy of the notice and of the statement to the applicant.

(4) Within three months of the receipt of such copies, the applicant shall, if he wishes to continue with the application, file a counter-statement in duplicate setting out fully the grounds upon which the opposition is resisted; and the comptroller shall send a copy of the counter-statement to the opponent.

(5) The comptroller may give such directions as he may think fit with regard to the subsequent procedure.

(6) Unless the comptroller otherwise directs, an application to amend the specification of a patent shall be accompanied by a copy of the printed specification, clearly showing in red ink the amendment sought.

(7) Where leave to amend a specification is given, the applicant shall, if the comptroller so requires, and within a time to be fixed by him, file a new specification as amended, which shall be prepared in accordance with rules 16, 18, and 20 above.

COMMENTARY ON SECTION 27

27.03 *General*

Section 27 provides a general power for the Comptroller to amend a specification after grant. Amendment before grant is governed by section 19 and amendment during contested proceedings before either the court or the Comptroller, in which validity is in issue, is governed by section 75. Amendment may also be allowed under section 73, see para. 73.04. "Amendment" is, however, not to be confused with "correction" which is provided for by section 117, see the commentary thereon. Section 27 does not extend to "existing patents" (Sched. 2, para. 1(2) read with the definition of "patent" in s. 130(1)). For such patents, sections 29–31 [1949] remain applicable (Sched. 1, para. 1(2)), see the commentaries thereon in Appendix A. The section does, however, apply to the amendment by the Comptroller of European patents (UK) after the grant thereof, see section 77(1), though such a patent can also be amended during opposition proceedings commenced in the EPO under EPCa. 99 within nine months of the date of notification of grant of the European patent in the EPB.

Since a licence granted under a patent may contain a covenant prohibiting the proprietor from amending the specification without the consent of the licensee, care should be taken to check whether any such licence exists before an application to amend is made.

27.04 *Power to permit amendment (subs. (1))*

Subsection (1) empowers the Comptroller to permit amendments to be made to the specification of a patent after grant. The use of "may" indicates a continuation of the general discretionary power concerning amendments which previously prevailed under United Kingdom patent law and which is discussed in paras. 27.05–27.07 *infra*. The power to permit amendment is also subject to the severe restraints imposed by new section 76(3), see paras. 76.08–76.18. While section 27 has some similarity with section 29 [1949], the restraints imposed are different and more stringent. EPCa. 123 corresponds in substance to sections 27 and 76, but these two sections are not specifically referred to in section 130(7) as having been intended to have the same effect as the corresponding EPC provisions.

No application to amend under section 27 may be made prior to the date when notice of grant has been published in the O.J. (s. 25(1)), whereas an application to amend under section 19 is precluded once grant has administratively taken place, by issue of the administrative notice of grant under section 18(4). Thus, there is a short period during which an application for amendment cannot be filed, see para. 24.11.

If an amendment is made under section 27 which contravenes section 76(3), a basis for revocation arises under section 72(1)(*d*) or (*e*), see paras. 72.25 and 72.26. An application for revocation may be made on these grounds whether or not the applicant for revocation opposed the application to amend.

When proceedings are pending, whether before the court or the Comptroller, in which validity *may be* put in issue, amendment can only be effected under section 75 as this is prohibited under section 27 by subsection (2), see para. 27.09 *infra*.

Discretion

—Duty of full disclosure   **27.05**

Whether amendment is sought from the court or from the Comptroller, it has long been a feature of United Kingdom patent practice that permitting amendment involves an exercise of discretion, see *V.D. Ltd.* v. *Boston* ((1935) 52 RPC 303 at 331) and *Mullard* v. *British Belmont* ((1939) 56 RPC 1 at 21 (C.A.)). As a consequence, an applicant for amendment must be prepared to demonstrate to the tribunal (*i.e.* to the court or Comptroller) that at all times he has acted, in relation to the patent and the proposed amendment, with the utmost good faith, *i.e. uberrimae fidei*; and he has a duty to put the whole story before the tribunal in an acceptable manner, see *Schwank's Patent* ([1958] RPC 53); *Clevite Corp.'s Patent* ([1966] RPC 199); *Du Pont's (Robert's) Patent* ([1972] RPC 545); *SCM's Application* ([1979] RPC 341); *Chevron Research's Patent* ([1980] RPC 580); and *Therm-a-Stor* v. *Weatherseal (No. 2)* ([1984] FSR 323 (CA)). The Comptroller at least regards this philosophy as unchanged under the 1977 Act, see *Waddington's Application* ([1986] RPC 158) and particularly *Smith Kline & French's (Bavin's) Patent (No. 2)* (SRIS C/49/89) where the cases were reviewed and the principles governing the exercise of discretion to allow amendment were set out.

Therefore, in accordance with the equitable maxim that "He who seeks Equity must come with clean hands", full explanatory evidence should be given, for example to explain if the amendment is sought in order that an alleged infringement should more clearly fall within the amended claims (*Therm-a-Stor* v. *Weatherseal (No. 2), supra*) and *Osterman's Patent* ([1985] RPC 579). This is especially so if it is to be contended that a false suggestion was unintentional (*Parry-Husband's Application*, [1965] RPC 382), or when a mistake is sought to be corrected, see *Heberlein's Application* ([1971] FSR 373) and *SCM's Application* (*supra*).

In all such circumstances, it may well be inadvisable for a proprietor to resist a request for discovery, or to claim any privilege for documents for which such could be claimed, see *Smith Kline & French's (Bavin's) Patent (No. 2)* (*supra*) and C. P. Tootal ((1984–85) 14 CIPA 362). Thus, in *Medlicott's Patent* (SRIS O/148/84, *noted*

IPD 8108), the patentee expressly declined to give sworn evidence that he had previously been unaware of the prior art, though he had made an unsworn denial of this: the amendment was refused because the patentee had not discharged his duty of putting the whole story forward, as required by *Chevron (supra)*. Also, in *Smith Kline & French's (Bavin's) Patent (No. 2) (supra)* the failure to present evidence from British patent agents and a lawyer who had been involved was the subject of adverse comment with discretion to allow amendment being refused; and in *Johnson Matthey's Patent* (SRIS O/6/86), the Comptroller indicated that an applicant who chooses to remain behind a wall of silence cannot expect discretion to be exercised in his favour when questions of prior knowledge, delay, covetous claiming, etc. arise. Also, in *Beumer (Bernhard) Maschinenfabrik's Patent (No. 2)* (SRIS O/87/85), the Comptroller refused to allow an amendment application to proceed until evidence had been filed indicating why discretion should be exercised to permit amendment.

In *PPG's Industries Patent* (SRIS O/119/85 and C/116/85; *noted* [1985] EIPR D–212), had the amendment been allowable as a matter of law, discretion to permit it would have been refused by the Comptroller where the proposed amendment would have left the claim open to an objection of disunity of invention and, by the Patents Court because the specification should not set puzzles for its readers and because the proposed amendment was a broadening one to cure an alleged obvious mistake but the broadened scope would not have been subjected to search by the examiner. In dismissing a further appeal the Court of Appeal declined to comment on these views ([1987] RPC 469).

Cases involving specific discretionary considerations are discussed in paras. 27.06 and 27.07 *infra*. Those involving issues of law arising only under the 1949 Act are discussed in para. A031.15.

27.06   *Undue delay*

Discretion to permit amendment may be denied once a proprietor appreciates the need to seek amendment but there is then an unreasonable delay before he does so (*Chrome-Alloying* v. *Metal Diffusions*, [1962] RPC 33); or where, having filed an application in court proceedings which did not attract an opposition, there was delay in bringing the application before the court for decision until some years after the amendment had been advertised in the O.J. (*ICI* v. *Darenas*, SRIS C/155/82); or where the Patentee decided on a policy of inaction in the face of conflicting reports from British patent agents on the necessity for amendment (*Smith Kline & French's (Bavin's) Patent (No. 2)*, SRIS C/49/89). However, mere delay is not sufficient to justify refusal of the exercise of discretion (*Unilever's Patent*, SRIS O/21/84, *noted* IPD 7087). Thus, delay is more likely to be excused when no person is likely to have been prejudiced by the continuing existence of invalid claims, but this argument failed on the facts in the *Smith Kline* case (*supra*); and, in all cases, the *bona fides* of the applicant and his conduct remain important. The amendments in both the *Unilever* and *Smith Kline* cases were refused. Likewise, amendment was refused in *Autoliv Development's Patent* ([1988] RPC 425) where the Patentee had threatened infringement proceedings before seeking amendment, despite already having been informed of the prior publication which led to the amendment application.

In *Western Electric* v. *Racal-Milgo* ([1981] RPC 253), amendment was refused after the need to amend had been apparent to the patentees for seven years and meanwhile infringement proceedings had been commenced. However, by contrast, in *Diamond Controls* v. *Fisher-Karpack* (SRIS C/14/81, *noted* IPD 4003), amendment was allowed although there had also been delay of seven years and infringement proceedings had likewise been commenced, but here the patent agent had forgotten to draw the attention of the patentee to the desirability of applying for amendment so that the delay was not the fault of the patentee. Likewise, where the patentee has genuinely believed his claims to be supportable, delay in applying to amend may well be excused (*Bristol-Myers* v. *Manon*, [1973] RPC 836; and *Matbro* v. *Michigan*, [1973] RPC 823). Also, in *Codex* v. *Racal-Milgo* (SRIS C/135/81, *noted* IPD 4100 and (SRIS C/77/83, *noted* IPD 6025) correction of errors was allowed because these were self-evident and presented no real difficulty to the reader.

Questions of discretion were considered in *Lucas* v. *Gaedor* ([1978] RPC 297). In permitting amendment to the use of one particular material which gave the advantage promised by the specification, the court observed that "Today a patentee seeking to amend is given considerable latitude to amend purely by way of disclaimer". The court noted with sympathy that "An inventor is at some disadvantage when he comes to frame his claim . . . and if the claim is [initially] too narrowly drawn others will be able to borrow the concept or idea without entering the forbidden territory". Yet, when faced in an action with all the prior art that the defendants can find, "the patentee not infrequently sees how his claim might be strengthened without damage to his claim on infringement and he seeks to amend". Nevertheless, the court would have refused leave (had the amendment otherwise been permissible) to introduce a further limitation into the claim based on a feature referred to only incidentally in the body of the specification, on the ground that to do so at a late stage could have prejudiced the defendants.

Lack of good faith and covetous claiming   **27.07**

Amendment will be refused where it is shown that the proprietor ought to have been aware at the time of filing his application that his claims were not valid (*Armco's Application*, [1969] FSR 33), unless the original claim wording can be explained as genuinely unintentional (*Parry-Husband's Application*, [1965] RPC 382). Amendment will also be refused where the prior art which has prompted the amendment application came to the attention of the proprietor some years before amendment was sought, as in *Unilever's Patent* (SRIS O/21/84, *noted* IPD 7087) and *Norsea's Patent* (SRIS O/9/86), in each of which the relevant prior art had been cited against a corresponding foreign application some years previously, see also *Autoliv Development's Patent* ([1988] RPC 425) where the claims were covetous and the Patentee, in seeking amendment, had failed to state that it had been informed of the prior publication and, thereafter, had threatened infringement proceedings.

It is, therefore, submitted that there is a lack of good faith in any case where a proprietor has put forward broader claims than those to which he knows, or ought to know from the knowledge which he has, cannot be maintained. Such conduct gives rise to allegations of covetous claiming and, if proved, discretion to amend will then not be exercised. Thus, in *Donaldson's Patent* ([1986] RPC 1), amendment was refused for covetous claiming on a finding that the Patentee had knowingly and deliberately obtained claims which did not include the feature regarded as the invention and therefore were claims of unjustified breadth, but it is not necessary that the proprietor should have known that he was not legally entitled to the claims, nor that he must have known that the claims which he sought, and maintained, were invalid.

However, it has been stated that amendment should not be refused on the ground that the original claims were covetously broad unless it is proved (as in *Donaldson, supra*) that the proprietor had knowingly and deliberately obtained claims of unjustified breadth (*ICI's (Whyte's) Patent*, [1978] RPC 11), though in a case of covetous claiming clear evidence from the proprietor as to his intention and actions would seem to be desirable, if not essential.

In *Borden's Patent* (SRIS O/160/86, *noted* IPD 9116) the original claims were held not to be invalid and, in that circumstance, it was held that the objections to the exercise of discretion for making the amendments requested need not be considered.

27.08   *Amendment subject to conditions*

Subsection (1) appears to give the Comptroller unlimited power to permit amendment subject to such conditions as he thinks fit. However, in doing so, the Comptroller must only consider whether the amendments as such are allowable and may not pay any regard to the merits of the invention. Thus, in *Autoliv Development's Patent* ([1988] RPC 425) the Comptroller found that the granted claims were covetous and that there had been undue delay in seeking amendment but, as the invention was meritorious, it ought not to be made available to the public royalty free. He therefore permitted amendment subject to the condition that a "licence of right" entry were first entered in the register. On appeal, this approach was condemned and the amendments were disallowed.

27.09   *Inapplicability of section 27 (subs. (2))*

By subsection (2) no amendment is to be allowed by the Comptroller where there are pending before the court or the Comptroller any proceedings in which the validity of the patent *may be* (not are) put in issue, herein called "validity proceedings". Application must then be made, if at all, under section 75. Thus, sections 27 and 75 create complementary, but mutually exclusive, jurisdictions, see *Lever Bros.' Patent* ((1955) 72 RPC 198) decided under the 1949 Act where the division of jurisdiction is between proceedings before the Comptroller (to which s. 29 [1949] applies) and proceedings before the court (to which s. 30 [1949] applies). Thus, whether section 27 or section 75 is to apply would seem to depend upon the nature of any pending proceedings, not whether validity has already been put in issue therein. Indeed, amendment under either section could be precluded if proceedings are pending in which validity *could be*, but *is* not, challenged, see para. 75.09. Section 74 recites the "validity proceedings" when section 27(2) is to apply. These are: section 61 (*Infringement of patent*); section 69 (*Infringement of application*); section 70 (*Threats*); section 71 (*Declaration of non-infringement*); section 72 (*Revocation*); and section 58 (*Crown user compensation*). No other proceedings are relevant (s. 74(2)).

If the application to amend under section 27 is presented to the Comptroller prior to the commencement of any "validity proceedings" as mentioned in section 74 (whether before the court or the Comptroller), but such proceedings are commenced subsequently, it appears that the Comptroller must stay the proceedings under section 27. This is different from the position under the corresponding provisions of sections 29 and 30 [1949] where the Comptroller has a discretion to continue with a first-filed application under section 29 [1949] if he wishes. The question when the "validity proceedings" are deemed to be "pending" is considered in para. 75.04, but that question is now relevant to the *termination* of the section 74 proceedings, whereas for the proviso to section 29(1) [1949] the question relates to the *commencement* of the amendment proceedings under section 29.

Thus, in *Wilkinson Sword Warner-Lambert* (SRIS C/124/87), proceedings under section 27 were already in being when application was made to the court for a declaration of non-infringement (under s. 71) and for revocation (under s. 72). In these circumstances subsection (2) would seem to have required a stay of the proceedings before the Comptroller. However, the proprietor sought a stay of the court proceedings pending resolution by the Comptroller of the amendment application, but the court refused a stay, indicating that the amendment proceedings should be re-commenced before the court under section 75. Subsequently, the court allowed the amendment and found the amended patent valid, but not infringed (SRIS C/35/88).

Effect of amendment (subs. (3))   **27.10**

By subsection (3) it is declared that where a patent has been amended, the amendment is considered to have had effect from the grant of the patent. This would suggest that, if an invalid patent is infringed and the invalid patent is subsequently amended into valid form, still infringed, infringement can be considered to have taken place during the time when the claim was in invalid form; and, conversely, if a patent is not infringed after amendment, there will have been no infringement at any time. Section 31(2) [1949] is probably of similar effect, but there has been no re-enactment of the provision therein that the amendment "shall not be called in question except on the ground of fraud". Instead, any amendment is now specifically subject to challenge under section 72(1)(*d*) and (*e*), for which see paras. 72.25 and 72.26. At that time comparison of the amended and unamended specifications will clearly be admissible, as it was under the proviso to section 31(2) [1949], discussed in para. A031.06.

Amendment may have an effect on an award of damages for infringement prior to amendment. Thus, section 62(3) (discussed in para. 62.05) states that where a patent has been amended, no damages are to be awarded in respect of infringements committed before the decision allowing amendment, unless the specification as published was drafted in good faith and with reasonable skill and knowledge. Section 58(6) applies similar restrictions to Crown user compensation.

Acknowledgements of registered trade marks or service mark (subs. (4))   **27.11**

Subsection (4) empowers the Comptroller to amend a patent of his own volition to make reference to a registered trade mark, or now a registered service mark (see *Note* to para. 27.01), in the same way as he is able to amend a patent application under section 19(2). The matter is discussed in para. 19.10, as also is the question of a reference in a specification to a foreign trade or service mark. There would seem to be no good reason to exclude the provisions of section 101 from operation under sections 19(2) or 27(4). The Comptroller should, therefore, give notice to the proprietor of his intention to amend to insert a reference to a registered trade (or service) mark and to give him a chance to be heard before he takes a definite decision on the matter, see para. 19.10 and the commentary on section 101.

Opposition to application to amend a patent (subs. (5))   **27.12**

Subsection (5) provides for opposition to amendment. Such proceedings are governed by rule 40 (reprinted at para. 27.02 *supra*) and require the filing of PF 15/77 (reprinted at para. 141.15) and a statement of case. The opposition period is three months (r. 40(2)): which is inextensible (r. 110(2)).

An opponent does not have to show an interest in the patent before he is entitled to oppose (*Braun AG's Application*, [1981] RPC 355), it being in the public interest that anyone who has evidence which might cast doubt on the *bona fides* of the applicant's application to amend should be entitled to oppose. Accordingly, in *Sanders Associates' Patent* (SRIS O/89/81, *noted* IPD 4128) the Comptroller permitted a

235

patent agent to oppose an application to amend as nominee for an undisclosed principal. Although this ruling was challenged on the ground that opposition to the application to amend had to be accompanied by a statement setting out fully the facts upon which the opponent relies (see rr. 40(3), 78(2) and 91(5)), the hearing officer declined to decide such a question as it called into question whether the rules were *ultra vires* the Act, thereby following *Dirks' Applications* ([1960] RPC 1). However, the EPO has taken the view that a professional representative acting as such may not oppose the grant of a European patent, see *EPO Decision T* 10/82, "*Opposition: admissibility/BAYER*" (OJEPO 10/1983, 407). A clear distinction is here seen to have been drawn between an opponent acting on his own behalf and one acting as agent for an undisclosed principal, the latter being unacceptable to the EPO, especially where the agent is a professional representative. Indeed, this was so much so that amendment of the opposition to name the true opponent was subsequently not permitted ("*Opposition: admissibility/BAYER II*", OJEPO 2/1986, 56; [1986] 3 EPOR 154).

27.13   *Grounds of opposition*

By analogy with the practice which developed under section 29 [1949], the common grounds of opposition are likely to be:
(1) that the amendment does not meet the requirements of new section 76(3) (for which, see paras. 76.08–76.18);
(2) that the amendments should not be allowed in the exercise of discretion (for which see the discussion at paras. 27.05–27.07 *supra*); and
(3) that the amendments would still leave the patent invalid.
On this last point, it now seems clear that an opponent is not permitted to raise a general attack on validity, but is limited to arguments which can be based on the documents already before the Comptroller and where the invalidity can be established without real controversy, for example as to arguments of ambiguity and insufficiency under section 14(3). Thus, in *Great Lakes' Patent* ([1971] RPC 117), allegations of anticipation and obviousness, said not to be cured by the amendment, were struck out, but that decision was partially distinguished in *Hauni-Werke's Application* ([1976] RPC 328). Here an opponent was allowed to plead that the unamended claim was covetous in that an attempt had been made to claim all solutions to the problem rather than limit the claims to the actual contribution made. This pleading was distinguished from one of obviousness, but any evidence adduced in support was required to be limited to the allegations of covetousness and not to extend to the broader issue of obviousness.

Subsequently, in *General Electric's Amendment Application* ([1984] RPC 311), the Comptroller discussed, as a matter of principle, the extent to which an opponent to amendment could raise objections of invalidity. It was held that, in such an opposition, the public interest requires the Comptroller to consider evidence directed to the question of covetousness and that any charges of misconduct by a patentee must likewise be considered since such go to the question of the exercise of discretion, as discussed in paras. 27.05–27.07 *supra*. However, as was made clear in *Donaldson's Patent* ([1986] RPC 1), decided under the 1949 Act, objections of obviousness, as distinct from covetousness, should not be considered in amendment proceedings. In *Borden's Patent* (SRIS O/160/86, *noted* IPD 9116) it was indicated that the amended claim ought, at least prima facie, to be distinguished from the prior art as regards novelty and obviousness, but in that case the unamended claims were held already to be distinguished from the cited art.

In *Bucher-Guyer's Patent* (SRIS O/167/87) an opponent was not permitted to contend that the proposed amendment would only add an obvious feature to the claim, or leave it clearly anticipated by some further prior art, but was permitted to contend that the amendment did not cure the defect which the proprietor had indicated it was his intention that the requested amendment should cure. Likewise, in *Smith Kline & French's [Bavin's] Patent* ([1988] RPC 224), a clear distinction was drawn between an opponent raising a new ground of invalidity (not generally raisable) and of contending that the amendments offered will not cure the invalidity which the proprietor has himself indicated in his statement of case may exist. The latter can be raised because the Comptroller is entitled to refuse discretion to amend if he considers, on the basis of the documents put before him by the proprietor, that the proposed claims are clearly invalid: it is therefore considered proper to allow an opponent to assist the Comptroller with evidence and argument directed to this point. In *Minister of Agriculture's Patent* (SRIS O/15/89, *noted* IPD 12027 and C/70/89) the opposition statement was allowed to be amended to raise this type of plea, but the opponent was not permitted to base its arguments of invalidity upon additional documents. Here the Patents Court pointed out that the Patentee was seeking an indulgence and that an opponent should not be denied an opportunity of raising matters, unless injustice would thereby be caused.

In *Genentech's Patent* ([1989] RPC 147 (CA)), Dillon L.J. observed that an application to amend a granted claim could let in the objection that the claim did not comply with section 14(5). If correct, this view means that an amendment application could result in re-opening the substantive examination for patentability. However, it is supported by *EPO Decision T* 301.87, *"Alpha-interferons/BIOGEN"* (*unreported*) though that decision was given under a specific provision (EPCa. 102(3)) which has no precise counterpart in the Act.

If an opponent attacks the conduct of the proprietor, the proprietor was allowed under the 1949 Act to terminate the proceedings by surrendering his patent (*Upjohn's (Beal's) Patent*, [1973] RPC 77), but see now para. 29.06.

PRACTICE UNDER SECTION 27

Procedure for applying to amend a patent   **27.14**

Amendment under section 27 is governed by rule 40 (reprinted at para. 27.02 *supra*). The application to amend is made on PF 14/77 (reprinted at para. 141.14) and is accompanied by a copy of the printed specification showing the proposed amendments in red ink (r. 40(1)(b)). In view of the similarities between rule 40 and rules 90–93 and 95 [1968], it is presumed that the procedure under section 27 generally follows that previously used under section 29 [1949].

Thus the printed specification should show in red only the actual amendments sought; it is, therefore, unnecessary and undesirable for a partly amended passage to be completely re-presented in red. If a whole block of text is to be inserted or re-presented, this may be given in black encircled in red. If further or different amendments are submitted at a later date then these should be incorporated in a further copy of the printed specification. However, if the further amendment is of a simple nature, it may be submitted in a letter for incorporation by the examiner on the original amended printed copy using ink of a different colour ((1975–76) 5 CIPA 261).

An opposition statement which pleads delay and covetous claiming must detail "the date and circumstances under which the patentee had knowledge of the prior art and the alleged action or inaction which gives rise to a contention of improper conduct should be stated" (*Minister of Agriculture's Patent* (SRIS O/15/89, *noted* IPD 12027 and C/70/89).

Oppositions to amend filed under subsection (5), and the outcome thereof, are now published in the O.J., see O.J. November 9, 1988. A complete back-list of such matters was published, O.J. November 16, 1988.

27.15 *Amendment of European patent (U.K.)*

If the patent to be amended is a European patent (UK) of which the specification is in the French or German language, it is understood that the amendment should be formally requested to the text in that language, but at the same time there should be filed a verified translation into English of the specification and of the proposed amendment (r. 113(1)). The amendment proceedings will then be conducted using the English translation and, if the amendment accepted differs in any way from that originally sought, the applicant will be required to provide a verified translation into the original language of the specification in accordance with rule 113(5). (Rule 113 is reprinted at para. 123.12). The amendment is now advertised in the O.J. only in the official language of the specification, but the English translation of the proposed amendment may be inspected without payment, see for example that advertised in the O.J. October 8, 1986.

27.16 *Statement of reasons for amendment*

As stated in para. 27.05 *supra*, the whole question of amendment is one of inherent discretion. Therefore, the reasons for amendment need to be given *uberrimae fidei* and the prior art sought to be distinguished has to be identified, see *Clevite Corp.'s Patent* ([1966] RPC 199) and *Warnant's Application* ([1956] RPC 205).

In *Waddington's Application* ([1986] RPC 158) the Comptroller decided that it is not sufficient to state on PF 14/77 that amendment is "by way of voluntary amendment as a result of prior art which has come to the applicant's attention". The Comptroller requires that such prior art should be identified, basing this requirement on the provisions of rule 106 (reprinted at para. 72.08) under which the Comptroller has power to call for documents to be produced to him, see para. 72.44.

27.17 *Advertisement of amendment*

The existence of an application to amend is advertised in the O.J. immediately it is filed and prior to its examination, but without specifying the proposed amendments themselves. These can then be inspected at the Patent Office. The amendments are advertised only when they have been found acceptable by the Comptroller, whereupon they are open to opposition. If as a result of an opposition the amendments are materially changed they are then advertised again, but otherwise not.

An exception to the procedure arises if the applicant for amendment and the Comptroller have not reached agreement on the permissibility of the amendments and the applicant has asked for a hearing; the Comptroller then advertises the proposed amendments to ascertain if there is any opposition before he proceeds with the hearing. The advertisement indicates that the advertised amendments have not yet been approved.

The advertisement for opposition appears in the O.J. and the Comptroller only rarely exercises his power (r. 40(1)) to require any other advertisement.

27.18 *Procedure on opposition*

After the advertisement in the O.J., notice of opposition to the amendment may be lodged on PF 15/77 (reprinted at para. 141.15) within an inextensible three month period from the date of the advertisement (rr. 40(2) and 110(2)). PF 15/77 is filed in duplicate and must be supported by a statement of case also in duplicate

(r. 40(3)). This statement can be filed within 14 days of the PF 15/77 (s. 107, reprinted at para. 72.09). Security for costs will be required from a non-United Kingdom resident opponent (s. 107(4)). The applicant should respond with a counter-statement, also filed in duplicate within three months (r. 40(4)), a period which could be extended under rule 110(1). The subsequent procedure is flexible (r. 40(5)), but is likely to follow that in any other contested proceedings before the Comptroller, see paras. 72.32–72.52.

If the application is one for amendment of a European patent (UK) which is in the French or German language, it is understood that opposition proceedings will, nevertheless, be conducted in English and, if the amendment finally allowed differs in any way from the version advertised, a translation into French or German, as the case may be, will be required (r. 113(5)).

Procedure when amendment is allowed **27.19**

If leave to amend is given, the proprietor is likely to be required to file, within a time specified, a copy of the amended specification prepared in accordance with rules 16, 18 and 20 (r. 40(7)). The amended specification may then be reprinted or, if the amendments are short, an amendment slip is printed for attachment to printed copies of the specification thereafter sold. The amendment slip is also attached to the copy of the specification in the SRIS collection. Since March 24, 1976 specifications reprinted after amendment under the 1949 Act have had their numbers preceded by the letter "B". However, under the 1977 Act, granted patents are published as "B-specifications". Amended "B-specifications" are, therefore, designated as "C-specifications", see O.J. April 7, 1983. For the presentation of bibliographic data and the INID codes used therewith, see para. 123.45.

After amendment, copies of the specification before amendment can still be obtained from the Patent Office Sales Branch, but only on special application on which it is advisable to state very firmly that the amended specification is *not* required. Since July 1977 it has been the practice of the Office to overstamp the front page of a printed specification when at the time of sale an application to amend it is pending. When the application to amend has been concluded, it has also been the practice for a notice to this effect to be attached to specifications where these are sold before a printed amendment slip or a reprinted specification becomes available ((1976–77) 6 CIPA 585).

SECTION 28 28.01

Restoration of lapsed patents

28.—(1) Where a patent has ceased to have effect by reason of a failure to pay any renewal fee [*within the prescribed period*], an application for the restoration of the patent may be made to the comptroller **within the prescribed period** [*under this section within one year from the date on which the patent ceased to have effect*].

(1A) Rules prescribing that period may contain such transitional provisions and savings as appear to the Secretary of State to be necessary or expedient.

(2) An application under this section may be made by the person who was the proprietor of the patent or by any other person who would have been entitled to the patent if it had not ceased to have effect; and where the

patent was held by two or more persons jointly, the application may, with the leave of the comptroller, be made by one or more of them without joining the others.

(2A) Notice of the application shall be published by the comptroller in the prescribed manner.

(3) If the comptroller is satisfied that—

(*a*) the proprietor of the patent took reasonable care to see that any renewal fee was paid within the prescribed period or that that fee and any prescribed additional fee were paid within the six months immediately following the end of that period, [*and*

(*b*) *those fees were not so paid because of circumstances beyond his control,*]

the comptroller shall by order restore the patent on payment of any unpaid renewal fee and any prescribed additional fee.

(4) An order under this section may be made subject to such conditions as the comptroller thinks fit (including a condition requiring compliance with any provisions of the rules relating to registration which have not been complied with), and if the proprietor of the patent does not comply with any condition of such an order the comptroller may revoke the order and give such directions consequential on the revocation as he thinks fit.

[*(5) Where an order is made under this section and, between the end of the period of six months beginning with the date when the patent concerned ceased to have effect and the date of the application under this section,—*

(*a*) *a person continued to do or did again an act which would have constituted an infringement of the patent if it had not expired and which he first did before the end of that period, that act shall constitute such an infringement; or*

(*b*) *a person began in good faith to do an act which would constitute an infringement of the patent if it had been in force or made in good faith effective and serious preparations to do such an act, he shall, after the order comes into force, have the rights conferred by subsection (6) below.*

(*6) Any such person shall have the right—*

(*a*) *to continue to do or, as the case may be, to do that act himself; and*

(*b*) *if it was done or preparations had been made to do it in the course of a business, to assign the right to do it or to transmit that right on his death or, in the case of a body corporate on its dissolution, to any person who acquires that part of the business in the course of which the act was done or preparations had been made to do it, or to authorise it to be done by any partners of his for the time being in that business;*

and the doing of that act by virtue of this subsection shall not amount to an infringement of the patent concerned.

(7) The rights mentioned in subsection (6) above shall not include the right to grant a licence to any person to do an act so mentioned.

(8) Where a patented product is disposed of by any person to another in exercise of a right conferred by subsection (6) above, that other and any other person claiming through him shall be entitled to deal with the product in the same way as if it had been disposed of by a sole registered proprietor.

(9) Subsections (5) to (7) above shall apply in relation to an act which would constitute the use of a patented invention for the services of the Crown if the patent had been in force as they apply in relation to an act which would constitute an infringement of the patent if it had been in force, and subsection (8) above shall apply accordingly to the disposal of a patented product in the exercise of a right conferred by subsection (6) above as applied by the foregoing provision.]

Note. The amendments noted were prospectively made by the 1988 Act (Sched. 5, para. 6 and Sched. 8). Para. 6(4) of this Schedule further provides that the amendment to subsection (3) is not to apply to a patent which had ceased to have effect in accordance with section 25(3) *(failure to renew within prescribed period)* and in respect of which the period referred to in section 25(4) *(six months' grace period for renewal)* had expired before commencement of the amendment of section 28. Also, subsections (5)–(9) were prospectively repealed by Schedule 8 [1988] to be replaced by new section 28A (Sched. 5, para. 7 [1988]). For the commencement of all these amendments, see the latest Supplement to this Work *re.* this para.

RELEVANT RULE

41.—(1) An application under section 28 shall be made on Patents Form No. 16/77 and shall be supported by evidence in support of the statements made in that application.   **28.02**

(2) If, upon consideration of the evidence, the comptroller is not satisfied that a case for an order under section 28 has been made out, he shall notify the applicant accordingly and, unless within one month the applicant requests to be heard in the matter, the comptroller shall refuse the application.

(3) If the applicant requests a hearing within the time allowed, the comptroller shall, after giving the applicant an opportunity of being heard, determine whether the application shall be allowed or refused.

(4) If the comptroller decides to allow the application, he shall notify the applicant accordingly and require him to file Patents Form No. 17/77, together with Patents Form No. 12/77, duly completed, and the amount of the unpaid renewal fee, upon receipt of which the comptroller shall order the restoration of the patent and advertise the fact in the Journal.

Notes. 1. From 1978 until the Patents (Amendment No. 4) Rules 1980 (S.I. 1980 No. 1783, r. 2(*k*)), rule 41(2) contained the words "prima facie" before the word "case".

2. This rule will need considerable amendment when the amendments to section 28 are brought into effect, for which see para. 28.01 *supra.* The new form of rule 41 will stipulate: the length of the new "prescribed period"; transitional provisions; and a requirement for advertisement of a restoration application in the O.J. in

accordance with new subsection (2A). The latest Supplement to this Work *re.* this para. should therefore be consulted.

28.03   Article

J. V. Gowshall, "Re-establishment of rights before the European Patent Office: Article 122 EPC", (1988–89) 18 CIPA 182.

Commentary on Section 28

28.04 *General*

Section 28 is concerned with the restoration of patents which have lapsed by failure to pay a renewal fee within the prescribed period. It applies to patents granted under the 1977 Act and to "existing patents" (Sched. 2, para. 1(2)). A comprehensive notice of the need to pay renewal fees is periodically published in the O.J., as noted in para. 25.13. The section does not require the Comptroller to exercise a discretion: he must restore the patent if the conditions of subsection (3) have been fulfilled (*Textron's Patent*, [1988] RPC 177). Originally subsections (5)–(9) provided for third party rights upon a patent being restored under the section, but the subject matter of these provisions is to be transferred to a new section 28A (see *Note* to para. 28.01) and is therefore now dealt with in the commentary thereon *infra*.

In the EPC restoration after failure to pay a renewal fee in due time is dealt with under the general provision of EPCa. 122 for restitution of rights, for which see the article by J. V. Gowshall listed in para. 28.03 *supra*. However, section 77(1) applies section 28 to European patents (UK). Section 28 has some similarity to section 27 [1949], but the period during which restoration may be sought was reduced in the original form of section 28 from three years to one year; there is now no provision for opposition; and the conditions for restoration are different and in practice much more stringent, the emphasis being now on providing adequate protection of the public who may have relied upon the lapse of the patent (*Dynamics Research's Patent*, [1980] RPC 179).

28.05 *Amendments to section 28*

The amendments to subsection (1), noted at the end of para. 28.01 will, from their commencement, change the period within which restoration of a lapsed patent can be sought from one year to a period prescribed by rule. However, a rule made under new subsection (1A) is likely to provide that the amendment shall have no effect on patents which had ceased to have effect before the date of commencement of the amendments to the section.

The amendment to subsection (3) will remove the previous second requirement for restoration to be permitted, namely that the fees have not been paid due to circumstances outside the proprietor's control. It arose following the decision in *Textron's Patent* ([1988] RPC 177 (CA)) that restoration should be refused on this ground even though it was held that the proprietor had taken reasonable care to see that the renewal fee was duly paid as required by subsection (3)(*a*). Of intrinsic interest is that, after the 1988 Act had been enacted, the *Textron* decision was reversed ([1989] RPC 441 (HL)). However, the deletion of subsection (3)(*b*) is to have no effect on patents which, before commencement of the amending provision in the 1988 Act (on which, see *Note* to para. 28.01 *supra*), had entered the effective period for requesting restoration, *i.e.* after the patent had ceased to have effect (on an anniversary of its filing date) and after the six months' grace period therefrom (allowed under s. 25(4)), had also expired.

The provisions of subsections (5)–(9) are to be replaced by new section 28A, as explained in the *Note* to para. 28.01 *supra* and in paras. 28A.01 *et seq. infra*.

Application for restoration (subs. (1))   **28.06**

Thus, under the present subsection (1), an application for restoration must be filed within a period of 12 months after the date when the patent ceased to have effect, *i.e.* from the end of the normal period for payment of a renewal fee (s. 25(3)), see *Daido Kokyo's Patent* ([1984] RPC 97). However, during the first six months of that period, the renewal fee may be paid as of right, with fine for late payment, under section 25(4), see para. 25.08, and such late renewal should always prove cheaper than attempted restoration under section 28.

When the amendments to the section are given effect, and rule 41 is amended consequently (for which, see the latest Supplement to this Work), this 12 months' period will be replaced by "the prescribed period". This is expected to be a somewhat longer period because 12 months has been shown to be too short for detection of an inadvertent failure to pay a renewal fee and many hard cases have resulted with the present limited period where the patent has been lost due to no fault of the applicant himself.

The 12 months', or the prescribed, period within which restoration is to be requested is inextensible (r. 110(2), reprinted in para. 123.10). However, when lapsing has occurred as the result of "error, default or omission" of the Patent Office, it may be possible to pay the renewal fee out of time by invoking rule 100 (for which see para. 123.20). This apparently happened in the *Daido Kogyo* case after there had been a late issue of a renewal reminder. But there is no failure by the Comptroller to carry out his statutory duty (to issue renewal and lapsing notices under rules 39(4) and 42, for which see para. 25.14) where no address for service has been provided by the proprietor, as happened in *Deforeit's Patent* ([1986] RPC 142). In *Dynamics Research's Patent* ([1980] RPC 179), it was argued, but unsuccessfully, that an application to pay a renewal fee made within the permitted period could itself be a sufficient act to be regarded as an application for restoration.

Applicant for restoration (subs. (2))   **28.07**

By subsection (2) the application may be made by the proprietor of the patent or by a person who would have been entitled to the patent had it not ceased to have effect and, where a patent is held by two or more persons jointly, the Comptroller may permit one or more of them to apply without joining the others.

The proprietor is the person whose name is at the relevant time entered in the register, or someone who is owner of the rights in respect of the patent at the due time (*Border's Patent*, SRIS O/157/79) and that "someone" can be a person who either owns a right to the invention or is a prospective owner thereof, whether or not a claim to such right has been entered in the register (*Whiteside's Patent*, SRIS O/44/84). However, in *Triten Corp.'s Patent* (SRIS O/65/88), the lack of an assignment complying with the formalities required by section 30(6) (for which see para. 30.07) precluded the assignee from relying upon his alleged reasonable care after the patent should have been assigned to him and subsequently effected, retrospectively. The reference in subsection (2) to "any other person" would also seem to include someone to whom the patent might have been assigned after the date of, but in ignorance of, the lapsing of the patent.

Grounds for restoration (subs. (3))

28.08   *—General*

Under revised subsection (3) the Comptroller will now be required only to satisfy himself that the proprietor took reasonable care to ensure that the renewal fee was paid within the prescribed period (or that the renewal fee and any extension fee were paid within the six months extension period), the further requirement that the fee or fees were not paid because of circumstances beyond the proprietor's control having been abolished, see para. 28.05 *supra*. This remaining requirement has, however, been strictly interpreted as is illustrated by the cases mentioned in para. 28.09 *infra*. If the Comptroller is so satisfied, he is required to issue an order restoring the patent on payment of the unpaid renewal fee and any prescribed additional fee, see para. 28.15 *infra*, but there is a partial loss of the rights conferred by the patent, see section 28A and the commentary thereon.

There is no provision for opposing an application for restoration as there was under section 27 [1949]. Appeal from the Comptroller's decision lies to the Patents Court (s. 97(1)).

28.09   *—Lack of reasonable care*

In the decided cases, it has been stated that reasonable care requires a system affording greater safeguards than are, for example, present for meeting everyday accounts (*Convex's Patent*, [1980] RPC 437), and that the primary source of guidance is the wording of subsection (3) itself, particularly as section 28 is not listed in section 130(7), rather than in decisions of the EPO decided on particular facts (*Reiss Engineering's Patent*, SRIS O/180/86, *noted* IPD 10017). Thus, on several occasions, the EPO has been prepared to allow re-establishment of rights lost as the result of an isolated procedural mistake, see *EPO Decisions J* 02/86 and *J* 03/86, "*Isolated mistake/restitutio/MOTOROLO*" (OJEPO 8/1987, 362; [1987] 6 EPOR 394); *EPO Decision T* 27/86, "*Poker vibrator/DYNAPAC MARTIN*" ([1987] 3 EPOR 179); and *EPO Decision T* 137/86, "*Re-establishment of rights/THORN EMI*" ([1987] 3 EPOR 183).

In contrast, the Comptroller and the Patents Court have interpreted subsection (3) restrictively and often refused restoration because some way has been perceived in which the proprietor could have taken further steps and, having failed to do so, it has been held that he has not taken "reasonable care" to see that the renewal fee was paid within the prescribed period.

However, in *Textron's Patent* ([1989] RPC 441 (HL)), (reversing [1988] RPC 177 (CA)), it was held that a proprietor should not be held responsible for a failure of junior staff to obey appropriate instructions because this is a circumstance beyond the control of the proprietor. Although this decision was given under the now to be repealed subsection (3)(*b*), the principle can be seen to apply equally under the retained subsection (3)(*a*) because a proprietor will have taken reasonable care if he has laid down proper instructions for his employees to follow, as was accepted was so in the *Textron* case. Nevertheless, as was recognised by Lord Oliver in that case, the situation could be different when the failure to renew arises from the default of a more senior employee who can be seen as the directing mind of the company as regards patent renewals. This was later the position in *British Broadcasting's Patent* (SRIS O/49/89) where restoration was, accordingly, refused.

Prior to the *Textron* decision, the following circumstances have been held to involve a lack of reasonable care:

    (a) Delegating responsibility for paying the renewal fee to inexperienced staff (*Hadjiyannakis' Patent*, SRIS O/53/81, *noted* IPD 4083; and *Goldsmith and*

Pratt's Patent, SRIS O/67/81, *noted* IPD 4077 and SRIS C/71/83, *noted* IPD 6016); or a failure by staff to carry out instructions timely given (*Tekdata's Application*, [1985] R.P.C. 201), but these cases may now be decided differently having regard to the *Textron* decision, though not where there was a failure properly to instruct staff, see the warning in *Albright & Wilson's Patent* (SRIS O/109/80);

(b) failing to set up an appropriate reminder system (*Francis' Patent*, SRIS O/154/82, *noted* IPD 5091; *Warwick's Patent*, SRIS O/150/82; and *Soc. Minerva's Patent*, SRIS O/55/82); or failing to follow up reminder notices which had been received (*Goldsmith and Pratt's Patent, supra; Barnes-Hide's Patent*, SRIS O/53/82, *noted* IPD 5034);

(c) cutting oneself off from the receipt of the statutory reminders sent out by the Patent Office (*Convex's Patent, supra*), for example by a failure to file an address for service so that these reminders could not be dispatched (*Deforeit's Patent*, [1986] RPC 142); or (for a corporate patent department) relying on the overdue reminders and failing to instruct agents handling assigned patents of standing instructions to renew in the absence of instructions to let the patent lapse (*Sony's Patent*, SRIS O/176/88, *noted* IPD 12025); or by failing to notify the appointed agent of the proprietor's change of address (*Nakamura's Patent*, SRIS O/121/84);

(d) entrusting renewal to a licensee (*Lichenstein's Patent*, SRIS O/152/83, *noted* IPD 6138 and SRIS C/34/84, *noted* IPD 7083), or to a co-proprietor (*Ho and Wang's Patent*, SRIS O/152/87);

(e) designing deficiently a record system so that it failed to take account of unusual situations: *Halcon's Patent* (SRIS O/94/85), where a computer had not been programmed to deal with a date of grant close to the renewal date; or failing to enter an assigned patent in the renewal list (*Davchem's Patent*, SRIS O/111/86, *noted* IPD 9073);

(f) overlooking renewal in circumstances of change of ownership (*Reiss Engineering's Patent, supra; Dytap Revetements' Patent*, SRIS O/76/87; and *Triten Corp.'s Patent, supra*); and

(g) overlooking the interest of a licensee (*Cement and Concrete Association's Patent*, [1984] RPC 131).

However, more leniency has been shown, and restoration permitted, where an individual has entrusted his affairs to an inexperienced solicitor who failed to pass on the Letters Patent document with its warning of the need to pay renewal fees and to take action on official reminders (*Frazer's Patent*, [1981] RPC 53); and where individual proprietors decided to rely upon the Patent Office reminders which were not received (*Ling's Patent and Wilson and Pearce's Patent*, [1981] RPC 85). In each of these cases it was held that the proprietor had set up a system reasonable in his circumstances and, in *Frazer*, that the normal rule that a principal stands in the shoes of his agent does not apply under section 28(3), as has now been endorsed by the *Textron* decision (*supra*). However, a more sophisticated proprietor is expected to set up his own reminder system (*Soc. Minerva's Patent, supra*). The decision in *Frazer* is to be contrasted with the EPO practice which requires that a professional representative must show the due care required of a proprietor, a care which was not displayed when a task requiring professional expertise was delegated to an unqualified assistant (*EPO Decision J* 05/80, OJEPO 9/1981, 343).

Three cases may be noted wherein, though a finding of reasonable care was made under subsection (3)(*a*), restoration was nevertheless refused because of a failure to meet the now repealed criterion of subsection (3)(*b*) that the circumstances were not beyond the proprietor's control. These were: *Crompton Parkinson's Patent* (SRIS O/108/81, *noted* IPD 4127), where reasonable care was only found on appeal (SRIS C/58/84, *noted* IPD 7128), in which there had been a failure by a junior employee whom it had been reasonable for the employer to trust, though this decision would now appear to be over-ruled by the allowance of the appeal in similar circumstances in *Textron's Patent (supra)*; and *Sabateur Designs' Patent* (SRIS O/34/86), where the foreign agent had misappropriated the funds entrusted to him for the purpose, it here being noted that the patent agent had not been instructed to renew the patent in the absence of receiving instructions.

In *Albright & Wilson's Patent (supra)*, restoration was also allowed because not only had there been a failure by a junior employee, but this had been compounded by a failure of a back-up system as well.

For further instances where restoration was refused, on a finding of circumstances not beyond the proprietor's control rather than on a lack of reasonable care, see para. 28.10 *infra*. As noted therein, it is probable that in some of these cases restoration could alternatively have been refused under subsection (3)(*a*), and some might now be decided differently in the light of the *Textron* decision (*supra*).

28.10 *Circumstances beyond proprietor's control*

Because there will no longer the need to prove also that failure to pay the renewal fee was beyond the control of the proprietor, see para. 28.05, this repealed criterion is not discussed in detail. However, decisions given under repealed subsection (3)(*b*) are summarised here because it is possible that, in similar circumstances, restoration will still be refused by a finding of lack of reasonable care by the proprietor.

Thus, restoration was refused under repealed subsection (3)(*b*) in the following circumstances:

  (*a*) failing to make alternative arrangements to cope with known ill-health of the proprietor's accounts clerk (*Francis' Patent, noted* in para. 28.09 *supra*);

  (*b*) failing to borrow money to pay the renewal fee (*Winventive's Patent*, SRIS C/55/83, *noted* IPD 6034), a shortage of funds being no basis for restoration (*Edwards' Patent*, SRIS O/76/80, *noted* IPD 3103 and *Warwick's Patent, noted* in para. 28.09 *supra*;

  (*c*) a duly appointed officer taking a deliberate decision not to renew the patent (*Cement and Concrete Association's Patent, noted* para. 28.09 *supra*);

  (*d*) an important employee failing to enter details of the patent in the records (*GNB Inc.'s Patent*, SRIS O/76/86); or the sending of the responsible person to other duties without re-allocation of his duty to monitor official reminders (*Corning Glassworks' Patent*, SRIS O/4/87; and

  (*e*) failing to note at an earlier date that lapsing had occurred (*Crompton Parkinson's Patent, noted* in para. 28.09 *supra*); or failing to check records (*Borg-Warner's Patent*, [1986] R.P.C. 137).

28.11 *Conditions for restoration (subs. (4))*

Under subsection (4) the Comptroller has power to impose upon the order restoring the patent such conditions as he sees fit, including compliance with any requirement of the rules relating to registration which have not been complied with. If the proprietor does not comply with any such conditions, the Comptroller may revoke the restoration order and give any consequential directions as he sees fit.

In *Daido Kogyo's Patent* ([1984] RPC 97 (CA)) a special condition was imposed on restoration by making the patent subject to the provisions of subsection (6) up to the date when notice of the application for restoration was actually entered on the register because of a delay in so doing.

The Comptroller has adopted a policy of imposing similar conditions to those specified in subsection (6) when allowing revival of an application which has apparently lapsed, for example when rule 100 is successfully invoked, see para. 123.22; when granting an extension of time under rule 110(3C) having the effect of reviving an application, see para. 123.33; and when excusing a failure to request examination, as in *Elf Union's Application* (SRIS O/96/81, *noted* IPD 5011).

PRACTICE UNDER SECTION 28

Filing application for restoration   **28.12**

An application for restoration is made on PF 16/77 (reprinted at para. 141.16) and the procedure is governed by rule 41 (reprinted at para. 28.02 *supra*). The reasons for the application must be given (see PF 16/77) and these must be supported by evidence (r. 41(1)) which should be filed within 14 days of PF 16/77 (r. 107 (reprinted at para. 72.09)). Although filing without undue delay is not a specific requirement, as it was under section 27(1) [1949], the filing of PF 16/77 should not be delayed while evidence is prepared, if only to reduce any period of intervening rights, see para. 28.12 *supra*. If evidence is not filed with PF 16/77, it is understood that the practice is to issue an official letter requiring evidence to be filed within a stated term, usually 14 days, or an extension to be requested by the exercise of discretion under rule 110(1), see (1982–83) 12 CIPA 504.

The Comptroller has pointed out that, because there is no provision for opposition to restoration, there is a need for full comprehensive evidence from all those personally involved who are available to give evidence, supported, where possible, by contemporary documents (*Arcan Eastern's Patent*, SRIS O/140/179). Moreover, further evidence will normally not be admitted for consideration on appeal, see *Winventive's Patent* (SRIS C/55/83, *noted* IPD 6034), and RSC Ord. 104, rule 19(14) (reprinted in para. E104.19 and discussed in para. 97.16).

Determination of the restoration application   **28.13**

Under rule 41(2) the Comptroller considers the stated reasons and supporting evidence (which is no longer required merely to support the application "prima facie", see *Note* to para. 28.02 *supra*); and, if he is not satisfied that a case for restoration has been made out, he notifies the applicant accordingly and will refuse the restoration order unless the applicant asks for a hearing within one month. This period is extensible under rule 110(1). Under rule 41(3) the Comptroller will then decide the case after a hearing which will be by way of appeal against the decision under rule 41(2); additional evidence will be admitted at this stage only with difficulty, see para. 28.12 *supra*.

Allowance or refusal of restoration   **28.14**

If the application is successful the applicant is required to file PF 12/77 and PF 17/77 (reprinted at paras. 141.12 and 141.17 respectively) with the appropriate unpaid renewal and prescribed additional fees.

Applications for restoration, orders for restoration, and applications not proceeded with, are advertised in the O.J. (as now required by subs. (2A) as a consequence of *Daido Kogyo's Patent*, [1984] RPC 97), and are entered in the register.

SECTION 28A

Effect of order for restoration of patent

28A.—(1) The effect of an order for the restoration of a patent is as follows.

(2) Anything done under or in relation to the patent during the period between expiry and restoration shall be treated as valid.

(3) Anything done during that period which would have constituted an infringement if the patent had not expired shall be treated as an infringement—

(*a*) if done at a time when it was possible for the patent to be renewed under section 25(4), or

(*b*) if it was a continuation or repetition of an earlier infringing act.

(4) If after it was no longer possible for the patent to be so renewed, and before publication of notice of the application for restoration, a person—

(*a*) began in good faith to do an act which would have constituted an infringement of the patent if it had not expired, or

(*b*) made in good faith effective and serious preparations to do such an act,

he has the right to continue to do the act or, as the case may be, to do the act, notwithstanding the restoration of the patent; but this right does not extend to granting a licence to another person to do the act.

(5) If the act was done, or the preparations were made, in the course of a business, the person entitled to the right conferred by subsection (4) may—

(*a*) authorise the doing of that act by any partners of his for the time being in that business, and

(*b*) assign that right, or transmit it on death (or in the case of a body corporate on its dissolution), to any person who acquires that part of the business in the course of which the act was done or the preparations were made.

(6) Where a product is disposed of to another in exercise of the rights conferred by subsection (4) or (5), that other and any person claiming through him may deal with the product in the same way as if it had been disposed of by the registered proprietor of the patent.

(7) The above provisions apply in relation to the use of a patent for the services of the Crown as they apply in relation to infringement of the patent.

Note. Section 28A was prospectively inserted by Schedule 5, paragraph 7 [1988] to replace section 28(5)–(9). For its commencement, see the latest Supplement to this Work.

COMMENTARY ON SECTION 28A

Origin of the section   **28A.02**

Subsections 28(5)–(9) are to be replaced by section 28A, with consequential amendments in sections 60(6)(*b*), 77(5), 78(6) and 80(4) (Sched. 5, para. 8 [1988]), and an analogous substitution of a new section 64 (Sched. 5, para. 17 [1988]). These amendments reflect, and arise from, the changes in the provisions for restoration of registered designs by the addition of new sections 8A and 8B to the Registered Designs Act (12, 13 & 14 Geo. 6, c. 88) (effected by s. 269 [1988]). Section 28A will provide a simplified version of the rights that are accorded to third parties upon patent restoration, but it appears that there will be little significant change. The new section will not apply to patents for which the grace period for late renewal under section 25(4) had already expired prior to commencement of the new section, for which see the latest Supplement to this Work *re.* para. 28A.01 *supra*. For such patents the former section 28(5)–(9) will remain applicable. However, the following commentary has been prepared on the basis that the new section will take effect from about the time of publication of this Work.

General   **28A.03**

A patent "expires" on an anniversary of its filing date if the renewal fee for the following year has not by then been paid (s. 25(3)). However, if that renewal fee (together with an additional fee for late payment) is paid within the permissible following six months, the patent is deemed not to have expired at the earlier anniversary date (s. 25(4)), see para. 25.08. Section 28A provides for automatic rights to be accorded to a third party if that party has reasonably relied upon the patent having ceased to have effect, when the patent is later restored. These rights are in addition to any order made under section 28(4) imposing special conditions upon restoration, for which see para. 28.11.

The section deals with acts of a third party carried out during the period between its expiry (that is after the anniversary date) and the date when an order for restoration of the patent is made. In this commentary this period is called the "restoration period", but it has three parts: (1) the period during which the patent could have been renewed under section 25(4), which a potential user should have appreciated; (2) the period from that date up to the date when notice of a restoration application is published in the O.J. under section 28(2A), during which a third party could reasonably take the view that the patent had lapsed; and (3) the period from that date up to the date when the order for restoration is made, during which a user should have appreciated that he was at risk of the patent being re-established. The section therefore treats differently acts commenced and/or continued during each part of the restoration period. Similar third party rights have on occasions been imposed as a condition for permitting re-establishment (under r. 100) of a published application after its apparent deemed abandonment, see para. 123.22, and this is also customary when a time limit is extended with discretion exercised under rule 110(3C), see para. 123.33.

Synopsis of the provisions of section 28A   **28A.04**

An order for restoration (made under s. 28) has automatic effect to impose the third party rights set out in section 28A (subs. (1)). Firstly, "anything" done during the restoration period under or in relation to the patent is treated as valid (subs.

(2)). This provision therefore provides validity to assignments and licences executed during this period.

Then, anything done which would have constituted an infringement if the patent had been extant is treated as an infringement if done either (*a*) during the first part of the restoration period, or (*b*) is a continuation or repetition of an "earlier infringing act" (subs. (3)). The quoted words from subsection (3)(*b*) appear apt to include acts commenced not only before the patent lapsed, but also acts which were commenced during the first part of the restoration period and seemingly caused to be infringing acts by virtue of subsection (3)(*a*). Thus, contrary to the previous position, acts carried out during the restoration period can be regarded as infringing acts, if these continue acts commenced certainly before the date of lapsing and, probably, also those initially carried out during the first part of the restoration period, that is when restoration of the patent was automatically possible.

Otherwise, third party rights are provided, but only in respect of acts "begun", or serious and effective preparations made to do so, during the second part of the restoration period (subs. (4)). However, no relief is granted in respect of acts begun during the first or the third part of the restoration period because, in each of these periods, the user had constructive notice either that the patent might be renewed or that an application for restoration of the patent was under consideration by the Comptroller.

The acts which give rise to third party rights must be acts carried out "in good faith", so that for example acts carried out in knowledge that the proprietor is considering making a restoration application would appear to be excluded. The act must be an actual one which would, if the patent had been alive, have been an infringing one; *or* must constitute "effective and serious preparations" to do such an act. However, rights are only accorded in respect of acts not previously done, or seriously and effectively considered, during the period prior to expiry of the first part of the restoration period. It is thought that the word "began" (in subs. (4)) should apply equally to both "continuations" and "repetitions" (as these words are used in subsection (3)(*b*)) of an otherwise now infringing act. Thus, it is thought that no rights are acquired in respect of acts either continued or repeated during the second part of the restoration period, if these acts had been initially carried out (or seriously and effectively contemplated) before then, because these are regarded as actual infringements (by virtue of subs. (3)) and, therefore, in any event would not be acts carried out "in good faith". However, the position is not clear, particularly when the first act was carried out during the first part of the restoration period and later acts are repetitions, rather than continuations, of that act.

28A.05   *Nature of third party rights*

The person (which can of course be a corporate entity) which carried out the required act (for which see para. 28A.04 *supra*) then acquires the right to "continue" to do an act *begun* during the second part of the restoration period, or to do the act for which effective and serious preparations had *then* been made, notwithstanding the subsequent restoration of the patent. The right will operate as a defence to an action for infringement.

However, the right is a personal one to the doer and therefore he may not pass on that right by way of granting a licence (subs. (4)). Nevertheless, if the act was done, or preparations made "in the course of a business", the person acquiring the right under subsection (4) may authorise partners in a firm with him to do that act (subs. (5)(*a*)), or assign that right (or transmit it on death, or dissolution in the case of a body corporate), provided that this is done as part of the acquisition of "that part of the business" in the course of which the necessary act, or the preparations therefor, were done (subs. (5)(*b*)). Also, the rights conferred by subsections (4) and (5) extend to any subsequent dealing by another with a product disposed of according to those rights (subs. 6)); and the provisions of these subsections (4)–(6) apply *mutatis mutandis* to acts of Crown user (subs. (7)), for which see sections 55–59.

Scope of third party rights 28A.06

The scope of the third party rights accorded by the section is unclear and awaits judicial evaluation. In particular, it is unclear whether the right to "continue to do *the act*" permits any change in the nature, or extent, of that act, and whether the continuity must be without interruption. However, it is not thought that this phrase would in practice be construed so literally as to preclude *any* change in that act whatsoever, or not to permit resumption of an act which has begun but then discontinued temporarily, but rather would be given a purposive construction. Thus, it is not seen that "continue" in subsection (4) should be limited to a "continuation", as that word is used in subsection (3)(*b*), but rather that "continue" in subsection (4) embraces acts of repetition also. However, the meanings of "began" and "continue" in subsection (4) are not clear.

The same difficulties arise with the right to continue a prior secret use under section 64, as is discussed in para. 64.05, and see *Astra* v. *Pharmaceutical* ([1957] RPC 16) and *Rotocrop* v. *Genbourne* ([1982] FSR 241). Further doubts surround the question of whether the level, as well as the character, of the "infringing" acts is restricted by the section, for example as to use of an infringing component in a particular machine or activity; and exactly what is meant by "effective and serious preparations".

Also, a person who has relied upon the lapsing of the patent, but who has not taken such steps as bring subsection (4) into play, is in a vulnerable position. This was considered (under the former provisions) in *Dynamics Research's Patent* ([1980] RPC 179) where it was indicated that, if appropriate, steps could be taken to safeguard interests which ought to be safeguarded. Presumably the Patents Court had in mind that restoration could be made subject to a special condition under section 28(4) which would provide third party rights additional to those provided automatically by section 28A(4). This was done in *Daido Kogyo's Patent* ([1984] RPC 97) where the third part of the restoration period was added to the second because the making of the restoration application had not been advertised under the then prevailing provisions (now to be altered by the addition of s. 28(2A)).

Of course, in circumstances where section 28A(4) cannot be relied upon to accord, or accord fully, the required rights, some steps should, if possible, be taken to bring the facts before the Comptroller before the order for restoration is made, as thereafter the imposition of a special condition under section 28(4) would not seem possible, for example, leave could be sought to intervene in the restoration application under section 28, but the Comptroller may perhaps not permit such an intervention as no provision is now made for formal opposition to an application for restoration, as was the position under section 27 [1949].

In any event, subsection (4) (as likewise s. 64) would appear to give no relief where the act in question was timely begun but outside the United Kingdom, though in the case of acts done elsewhere in the EEC it is possible that in such circumstances the statute is *ultra vires* TRa. 30, and not saved by TRa. 36 for similar reasons to those which applied in *Allen & Hanburys* v. *Generics (Case 434/85)* ([1988] 1 CMLR 701; [1988] FSR 312 (ECJ)), discussed in para. 46.21.

29.01   SECTION 29

Surrender of patents

29.—(1) The proprietor of a patent may at any time by notice given to the comptroller offer to surrender his patent.

(2) A person may give notice to the comptroller of his opposition to the surrender of a patent under this section, and if he does so the comptroller shall notify the proprietor of the patent and determine the question.

(3) If the comptroller is satisfied that the patent may properly be surrendered, he may accept the offer and, as from the date which notice of his acceptance is published in the journal, the patent shall cease to have effect, but no action for infringement shall lie in respect of any act done before that date and no right to compensation shall accrue for any use of the patented invention before that date for the services of the Crown.

RELEVANT RULE

Surrender of patents

29.02   **43.**—(1) A notice of an offer by a proprietor of a patent under section 29 to surrender his patent shall be given on Patents Form No. 18/77 and shall be advertised by the comptroller in the Journal.

(2) At any time within three months from the advertisement any person may give notice of opposition to the surrender to the comptroller on Patents Form No. 19/77.

(3) Such notice shall be accompanied by a copy thereof and be supported by a statement in duplicate setting out fully the facts upon which the opponent relies and the relief which he seeks. The comptroller shall send a copy of the notice and of the statement to the proprietor of the patent.

(4) Within three months of the receipt of such copies, the proprietor of the patent shall, if he wishes to continue with the surrender, file a counter-statement in duplicate setting out fully the grounds upon which the opposition is resisted; and the comptroller shall send a copy of the counter-statement to the opponent.

(5) The comptroller may give such directions as he may think fit with regard to the subsequent procedure.

COMMENTARY ON SECTION 29

29.03   General

Section 29 provides for the surrender of a patent and corresponds to section 34 [1949], but with certain changes, particularly in the provisions of subsection (3). Section 29 applies to "existing patents" (Sched. 2, para. 1(2)). There is no directly corresponding provision in the EPC, but section 29 applies equally to European patents (UK) by virtue of section 77(1).

Offer to surrender (subs. (1))   **29.04**

Under subsection (1) a proprietor may at any time give notice to the Comptroller
of an offer to surrender his patent. By rule 43(1) (reprinted in para. 29.02 *supra*)
the offer is advertised in the O.J.

Opposition to surrender (subs. (2))   **29.05**

Subsection (2) affords any person the opportunity to oppose surrender within a
three month period from the date of advertisement in the O.J. under rule 43(1)
(r. 43(2)): this period is inextensible (r. 110(2), reprinted in para. 123.10). The use
of similar wording in section 72 (*Revocation*) suggests that no *locus standi* is
required to oppose, see also *Braun AG's Application* ([1981] RPC 355) and
para. 27.12. No doubt the most likely opponent would be a licensee or a person
seeking revocation in order that the patent may be deemed never to have had any
effect. Subsection (2) requires the Comptroller to notify the proprietor of any
opposition.

Acceptance of offer to surrender (subs. (3))   **29.06**

Subsection (3) provides that, if the Comptroller is satisfied that the patent may
properly be surrendered, he can accept the offer and the patent ceases to have
effect from the date the acceptance is advertised in the O.J.

No action for infringement and no claim in respect of Crown use lies in respect of
any act done before the date of the advertisement of the acceptance of the offer to
surrender. However, the patent is not revoked as it would have been under the
1949 Act and therefore the surrender is only *ex nunc*. Thus, for any other purpose,
the patent continues to have effect up to that date, *e.g.* licence royalties paid cannot
be reclaimed and the operation of section 73 cannot be avoided by surrender of the
United Kingdom part of a European patent, see para. 73.00 and *International Business Machine's (Barclay and Bigar's) Patent* ([1983] RPC 283).

If a proprietor desires that the effect of this patent should be surrendered *ex tunc*,
rather than *ex nunc*, it may be possible for him to apply for revocation of his own
patent under section 72, see para. 72.15. A European patent will also be revoked
for all its designated countries if, during opposition proceedings thereon in the
EPO under EPCa. 99, the proprietor disapproves the text of the patent (*EPO
Decision T* 186/84, "*Revocation at proprietor's request/BASF*", OJEPO 3/1986, 79;
[1986] 3 EPOR 165).

An offer to surrender does not therefore automatically terminate revocation proceedings and if the surrender offer is made during revocation proceedings before
the Comptroller, the Comptroller's practice is first to reach a decision on the, *ex
tunc*, revocation before considering the offer to surrender which would only operate *ex nunc*, see *Murray's Patent* (SRIS O/73/86, *noted* IPD 9096); *Don Valley's
Patent* (SRIS O/166/86); and *Kelsey-Hayes' Patent* (SRIS O/14/87). In *Wellworth's
Patent* (SRIS O/119/81) the Comptroller treated the revocation action as uncontested, assumed the truth of every statement by the applicant for revocation, and as
a result decided to revoke the patent and consequently to take no further action on
the offer to surrender. Thus, a proprietor can no longer evade a finding of invalidity
by offering to surrender his patent as he could under the 1949 Act, though it is
understood that the Comptroller is prepared to accept an offer to surrender when
this is made during revocation proceedings before the court. This would seem to
leave the application for revocation theoretically in being and possibly effective
should damages for infringement be claimable for acts carried out before the date
of surrender.

Practice under Section 29

29.07 *Making an offer of surrender*

An offer to surrender is made on PF 18/77 (reprinted at para. 141.18). This requires no fee but must contain a statement of the reasons for the offer and a declaration that there is no pending action for infringement or revocation before the court (though not before the Comptroller). If there is any such pending action the declaration must be deleted and full particulars of such action provided in writing to the Comptroller. It would be sensible for these particulars to contain consents to the surrender by all parties to that action and for the consent to indicate how the matter of costs in the court proceedings is to be dealt with.

29.08 *Opposing surrender*

Any notice of opposition is made on PF 19/77 (reprinted at para. 141.19) and must be lodged within an inextensible period of three months from the advertisement of the offer in the O.J. (r. 43(2), reprinted in para. 29.02 *supra* and r. 110(2) reprinted in para. 123.10). PF 19/77 must be filed in duplicate and supported within 14 days (r. 107, reprinted at para. 72.09) by a statement of the facts relied on by the opponent and the relief sought, also filed in duplicate. An opponent not resident in the United Kingdom is likely to be required to give security for costs, see para. 107.05.

Copies of the PF 19/77 and statement are sent by the Comptroller to the proprietor (r. 43(3)) who, if he wishes to contest the opposition, must similarly within three months (extensible under r. 110(1)) file a counter-statement (r. 43(4)). Subsequent procedure is as directed by the Comptroller (r. 43(5)), but is likely to follow that generally applicable to contentious proceedings before the Comptroller, for which see paras. 72.32–72.52. Appeal lies to the Patents Court (s. 97(1)).

Oppositions filed under subsection (2), and the eventual outcome thereof, are now advertised in the O.J., see O.J. November 9, 1988: a complete back-list of such matters was published O.J. November 16, 1988.

SECTION 30

Nature of, and transactions in, patents and applications for patents

30.01   **30.**—(1) Any patent or application for a patent is personal property (without being a thing in action), and any patent or any such application and rights in or under it may be transferred, created or granted in accordance with subsections (2) to (7) below.

(2) Subject to section 36(3) below, any patent or any such application, or any right in it, may be assigned or mortgaged.

(3) Any patent or any such application or right shall vest by operation of law in the same way as any other personal property and may be vested by an assent of personal representatives.

(4) Subject to section 36(3) below, a licence may be granted under any patent or any such application for working the invention which is the subject of the patent or the application; and—

    (*a*) to the extent that the licence so provides, a sub-licence may be granted under any such licence and any such licence or sub-licence may be assigned or mortgaged; and

(*b*) any such licence or sub-licence shall vest by operation of law in the same way as any other personal property and may be vested by an assent of personal representatives.

(5) Subsections (2) to (4) above shall have effect subject to the following provisions of this Act.

(6) Any of the following transactions, that is to say—

(*a*) any assignment or mortgage of a patent or any such application, or any right in a patent or any such application;

(*b*) any assent relating to any patent or any such application or right;

shall be void unless it is in writing and is signed by or on behalf of the parties to the transaction (or, in the case of an assent or other transaction by a personal representative, by or on behalf of the personal representative) or in the case of a body corporate is so signed or is under the seal of that body.

(7) An assignment of a patent or any such application or a share in it, and an exclusive licence granted under any patent or any such application, may confer on the assignee or licensee the right of the assignor or licensor to bring proceedings by virtue of section 61 or 69 below for a previous infringement or to bring proceedings under section 58 below for a previous act.

Books 30.02

Gallafent, Eastaway and Dauppe, *Intellectual Property Law and Taxation*, (Longmans, 3rd ed., 1989).

Articles 30.03

J. Douglas and A. Shipwright, "A review of United Kingdom taxation of royalties", [1986] EIPR 48;

D. Latham and N. Frome, "Securing lendings to high-technology companies", [1987] EIPR 367;

A. W. White and N. J. Flower, "Stamp duty on intellectual property conveyances", (1986–87) 16 CIPA 348.

Commentary on Section 30

General 30.04

Section 30 defines the nature of patents and patent applications as property and prescribes how such property rights may be transferred or licensed. It applies also to "existing patents" (Sched. 2, para. 1(2)), and to European patents (UK) and applications therefor (ss. 77(1), 78(2)). It does not extend to Scotland where the provisions of section 31 apply (s. 31(1)). A "right" in a patent or application includes an interest in it, and reference to a right in a patent includes reference to a share in it (s. 130(1)). The registration of transactions, instruments or events affecting rights in or under patents and applications is dealt with by section 32, see para. 32.19; for the procedure of registration see paras. 32.25–32.31. Subsections (2) to (4) are subject to subsequent provisions in the Act. In particular, the non-registration of transfers and licences of patent rights has adverse effects arising under section 33, regarding priority of registration, see para. 33.04, and under section 68, regarding remedies for infringement, see para. 68.03.

There is no definition in the Act of the "proprietor" of a patent. (The term "patentee" used in the 1949 Act is strictly not appropriate to a patent under the 1977 Act which is not granted under seal, but is commonly used.) The wording of section 68 indicates that a person becomes the proprietor by virtue of a transaction, instrument or event and not by virtue of its registration. In decisions under section 28 (*Border's Patent*, SRIS O/157/79, and *Whiteside's Patent*, SRIS O/44/84), the proprietor has been held to be the owner of the rights in respect of the patent at the time and not necessarily the person whose name is registered as such under section 32.

Patents are personal property, and subsection (1) reverses the position at common law under which "existing patents" were regarded as choses (or things) in action. For that reason the formerly granted "Letters Patent" could not be seized in execution of a writ of *fieri facias* (*British Mutoscope* v. *Homer*, (1901) 18 RPC 177), but this may now be possible. Whether "existing patents" remain choses in action is obscure.

30.05 *Vesting by operation of law*

A patent or application, or any right in or under it, vests by operation of law in the same way as any other personal property (subs. (3)) on the death or bankruptcy of the proprietor, as also does a licence (subs. (4)(*b*)). A personal representative must sign a written assent (subs. (6)(*b*)). Where the patent vests in the Crown as *bona vacantia*, the patent does not disappear by merger and, if the proprietor held the patent as trustee for some other person, the court may make an appropriate vesting order (*Dutton's Patent*, (1923) 40 RPC 84).

30.06 *Transfer of rights*

Where there are joint proprietors, section 36(3) requires all of them to consent to any assignment or mortgage of a patent or grant of a licence under it, see para. 36.05.

A "mortgage" includes a charge for securing money or money's worth (s. 130(1)), and the grant of charges or other forms of mortgage over intellectual property rights is discussed by D. Latham and N. Frome in the article listed *supra*. A covenant by the proprietor of a patent to pay certain profits or royalties may take effect as a charge and bind a legal assignee of the patent having notice of the covenant (*Dansk Rekylriffel Syndikat* v. *Snell*, (1908) 25 RPC 421). A mortgagee does not have the powers of a proprietor (*Van Gelder Apsimon* v. *Sowerby Bridge Flour*, (1890) 7 RPC 208 (CA)).

A licence generally passes no proprietary interest and only makes lawful what would otherwise have been unlawful (*Allen & Hanburys* v. *Generics*, [1986] RPC 203 (HL) *per* Lord Diplock). However, an exclusive licensee has an interest sufficient to prevent an assignee of the patent from granting further licences under the order of a foreign court (*British Nylon Spinners* v. *ICI*, (1954) 71 RPC 327) and by section 67 may sue for infringement in his own name, see para. 67.04.

A licence may be void, or unenforceable, in whole or in part, if it is a term in a contract of employment contrary to section 42(2), see para. 42.03, or if it contains a provision contrary to section 44, see paras. 44.05–44.08, or if it is contrary to the Restrictive Trade Practices Act 1976 (c. 34), see para. 44.13, or if it contains a provision contrary to TRaa. 85 or 86, see paras. C11, C12, C17 and C18 in Appendix C and the EEC Block Exemption Regulations discussed in Appendix D.

The terms of the instrument determine whether an assignee or exclusive licensee can bring proceedings for previous acts of infringement or Crown use (subs. (7)), and whether a licence can be assigned or mortgaged or whether a sub-licence can be granted (subs. 4(*a*)). Thus, a licence confers no right to grant a sub-licence unless this is so stated or can be inferred from the other terms of the licence. A licensee having no right to sub-license may exercise his powers through an agent, but not by an independent contractor (*Dixon* v. *London Small Arms*, (1876) 1 App. Cas. 632 (HL); *Allen & Hanburys' (Salbutamol) Patent*, [1987] RPC 327 (CA)).

An equitable assignee of a patent (*i.e.* a person to whom the proprietor has agreed to assign it or an assignee whose assignment has not been registered under section 32(2)(*b*)) may sue for infringement and obtain an interlocutory injunction, but before either damages or a perpetual injunction can be obtained, the legal proprietor must be added as a co-plaintiff or the equitable assignment must be converted into a legal assignment by registration (*Bowden's Patent Syndicate* v. *Smith*, (1904) 21 RPC 438; *Performing Right Society* v. *London Theatre of Varieties*, [1924] AC 1 (HL); and *Pfizer* v. *Jiwa [Hong Kong]*, [1988] RPC 15).

"Existing patents" may be assigned for part of the United Kingdom under section 22(1) [1949] (Sched. 1, para. 1(2)), but this is probably not possible for patents and applications under the 1977 Act. So far as European patent applications are concerned, the difference in wording in EPCaa. 71 and 73 with regard to transfer on the one hand and licensing on the other indicates that assignment for part of a contracting state is not possible.

Execution of documents (subs. (6))   **30.07**

An assignment or mortgage, or an assent by other than a personal representative, must be signed by or on behalf of *both* parties (subs. (6)(*a*)); otherwise it is merely equitable and subject to adverse registration under section 33, though it will still have equitable effect as between the parties and can be registered, see *Kakkar* v. *Szelke* ([1989] FSR 225; [1989] 4 EPOR 184 (CA)) and *EPO Decision J* 19/87, "*Assignment/BURR-BROWN*" ([1988] 5 EPOR 350), and also para. 32.19. In *Triten Corp.'s Patent* (SRIS O/65/88) an assignment instrument, which had validly been created retrospectively under a foreign law, was disregarded (for the purpose of permitting the assignee to rely upon it in restoration proceedings under section 28) because the document failed to comply with section 30(6). From a decision under EPCa. 71 it appears that the instrument may consist of two documents each signed by one of the parties which are then exchanged between them (*EPO Decision J* 18/84, "*Register of European Patents—Entries in*", OJEPO 6/87, 215; [1987] 5 EPOR 321). A seal is not required, except perhaps for an assignment or mortgage of an "existing patent" which should prudently be executed as a deed (because the patent itself was granted under seal).

A licence is not a transaction governed by subsection (6) and the licensor may give it under hand, by word of mouth (*Crossley* v. *Dixon*, (1863) 10 HLC 293 (HL)) or by implication, see *Morton-Norwich* v. *Intercen* ([1981] FSR 337). Also, the licensor may be estopped, by acquiescence or by some inconsistent act (*e.g.* sale of means for putting the invention into effect), from denying the existence of a licence.

An agreement to assign, mortgage or license a patent need not be in writing and, subject to section 42(2) in the case of a contract of employment, as discussed in para. 42.03, may be enforced by an order for specific performance.

PRACTICE UNDER SECTION 30

30.08 *Documentation*

There is no need to prepare a separate document omitting information, *e.g.* financial terms, which the parties wish to keep off the public record; appropriate extracts of the instrument are sufficient for registration under section 32, see paras. 32.25 and 32.31.

Any number of patents and applications may be assigned by the same instrument, but an application subject to a secrecy order under section 22 should be dealt with separately so that no reference to it is made in a document open to public inspection, see para. 22.09.

Where an instrument relates also to patents in other countries or to other intellectual property (*e.g.* trade marks and/or designs) requiring registration, separate documents should be prepared for each type of registrable right in each country so that a single document exists for each register in which it is to be recorded. Although such a document can be a confirmation of an assignment already executed in some more comprehensive document, this is bad practice: in some countries the comprehensive document may have to be produced and perhaps translated.

An assignment of an application should prudently refer to the assignment of "all right, title and interest" in that application *and in any patent granted on the application*, so as to avoid difficulty or ambiguity when registering the instrument subsequently. Note that an assignment executed after issue of the notice of grant to the applicant, but before such notice has been published in the O.J., is treated as an assignment of an application, see para. 24.11.

An assignment or exclusive licence should take advantage of subsection (7) by including a provision conferring rights to bring proceedings for previous acts of infringement or Crown use.

30.09 *Liability of assignor*

There is no implied covenant for validity when a patent is assigned (*Hall* v. *Conder* (1857) 26 LJCP 138 (Ex.Ch.)). Unless the instrument states otherwise, however, an assignment by a proprietor "as beneficial owner" automatically includes certain other covenants in favour of the assignee, including covenants of title to convey the property free of encumbrance and capable of being held and enjoyed by the assignee (Law of Property Act 1925 (15 Geo. 5, c. 20), s. 76; Sched. 2, part 1). Care is therefore needed in the wording where a licence already exists or where there is a possibility of infringement of some other patent by use of the invention. Liability may be excluded contractually in the transfer of a right or interest in a patent, etc., by way of exception to the provisions of the Unfair Contract Terms Act (c. 50) (s. 1(2), Sched. 1, para. 1(*c*)), see also para. 102.24.

30.10 *Transfer of rights by companies*

On the dissolution of a corporate proprietor its patents (and other intellectual property rights) vest in the Crown as *bona vacantia* (Companies Act 1985 (c. 6), s. 654). A purchaser from the liquidator should, therefore, take care to obtain an actual legal assignment before the company is dissolved.

A charge on a patent, or on a licence under a patent (or indeed on any intellectual property right), which belongs to a limited company is void against creditors and the liquidator unless it is registered at the Companies Registration Office at which the company is registered (Companies Act 1985 (c. 6), ss. 395, 396(1)(*j*), and 396(3A), as amended by the 1988 Act (Sched. 7, para. 31), and s. 410, as similarly amended by the same provision: for companies registered in Scotland, see para. 31.04). For companies registered in Northern Ireland, see article 403 of the Companies (Northern Ireland) Order (S.I. 1986 No. 1032 (N.I. 6)), likewise amended by the 1988 Act (Sched. 7, para. 35)). For the purpose of registration of such a charge under the Companies Act 1985, Companies Form M395, together with the instrument itself, must be received for registration by the Companies Registration Office within 21 days of the date of the charge, and the Registrar of Companies has no discretion to accept papers which are late or incomplete. It is often prudent also to enter notice of such a charge in the register of patents as a mortgage, see paras. 32.19 and 32.29.

Maintenance and prosecution   **30.11**

An assignee of a patent or application ought to ensure that any required procedure for maintaining the patent or prosecuting the application is carried out in due time. It may be prudent to call for official receipts for documents purportedly filed or to make independent enquiry of the Patent Office rather than rely merely on assurances from the assignor or his patent agent, see *Thermo Technic's Application* ([1985] RPC 109).

Stamp duty   **30.12**

This topic is summarised in the paper by A. W. White and N. J. Flower listed in para. 30.03 *supra*. A document for the conveyance or transfer of property on sale is liable to *ad valorem* stamp duty (currently at one per cent., increasing in steps of 50p up to £5.00 duty and thereafter in steps of £1.00) on the stated amount of the consideration (Finance Act 1963 (c. 25), s. 55 as amended by Finance Act 1984 (c. 43), s. 109), except as mentioned below. Such a document unless duly stamped cannot be registered under section 32, see para. 32.30, and cannot be received by a court in the United Kingdom. No enquiry is made as to the correctness of the amount of consideration stated in the document, but to mis-state the amount for the purpose of fraud is a criminal offence and could render the assignment unenforceable, see *Saunders* v. *Edwards* ([1987] 2 All ER 651) and T. Z. Gold ((1988–89) 18 CIPA 20). An agreement to assign a patent, if it is to be relied upon, must be stamped *ad valorem* (Stamp Act 1891 (54 & 55 Vict., c. 39), s. 59), but duty paid on the agreement does not have to be paid again when the assignment is executed. An exclusive licence in which the grant of exclusive rights is irrevocable must be stamped, but this is not necessary in the usual case where the licence provides for termination or conversion into a non-exclusive licence in certain circumstances, *e.g.* for breach by the licensee.

If the document is not stamped within 30 days after its date, the penalty for late stamping is a doubling of the duty plus a fine of £10 (Stamp Act 1891 (54 & 55 Vict., c. 39), s. 15(2)), although this is usually mitigated where failure to stamp is shown to have been unintentional. The need for execution by the assignee after the date stated in the document has been accepted as a satisfactory explanation.

If part of the consideration is for foreign property, this is probably not justiciable in the United Kingdom and should be dealt with in a separate document: stamp duty then need be paid only on the transfer of the United Kingdom property and not on the whole, but a certificate of value cannot be included, see *infra*. If a document is executed *wholly* abroad, however, stamp duty is levied only on the proportion of the consideration attributable to the United Kingdom property (Stamp Act

1891, (54 & 55 Vict., c. 39), s. 14(4)), and separate documents are not required, but there should then be an apportionment of the consideration for the United Kingdom transfer(s) in the instrument itself, see note by R. E. Perry ((1987–88) 17 CIPA 120).

Patents, copyrights, designs, design rights, trade marks and service marks, as well as "goodwill", are all property for this purpose but know-how is not, and stamp duty is not levied on any part of the total consideration specifically stated to be for the transfer of know-how.

If the total consideration for the transaction (or the series of related transactions) does not exceed a certain limit (at present £30,000), no stamp duty is payable if the document "contains a statement certifying that the transaction effected by the instrument does not form part of a larger transaction or series of transactions in respect of which the amount or value, or aggregate amount or value, of the consideration exceeds [£30,000]" (Finance Act 1958 (6 & 7 Eliz. 2, c. 56), s. 34(4)). This wording may not be varied, and the "consideration" here is regarded as the total price paid for the transactions, even if partly in respect of foreign property or of know-how (L.S.Gaz. July 4, 1979, p. 671), but the value of "goods, wares and merchandise" is left out of account.

Ad valorem duty is not payable on dispositions between companies which are members of the same group or on amalgamation or reconstruction. However, if a certificate of value cannot be given, it may sometimes be cheaper to pay *ad valorem* duty than prove the relationship between the parties. The Patent Office will first require formal adjudication that the instrument is not subject to stamp duty on this basis.

Likewise if there is doubt as to the amount of stamp duty payable, the document can be submitted to the Controller of Stamps for adjudication. It is desirable to avoid this if possible where the value of patent property may be in question, because the cost of valuing an intellectual property right to the satisfaction of the Controller of Stamps is often much greater than the stamp duty found to be payable.

No stamp duty will be payable on transfers of Community patents and applications therefor when the CPC is implemented, see section 126 and para. 126.02.

30.13 *Value added tax*

Where the owner of intellectual property rights is registered for VAT purposes, which is usually the case unless he is resident abroad, VAT is normally payable on royalties for the use or sale of his rights. He should therefore see that licences and other agreements provide for any VAT payable to be paid to him in addition to the agreed consideration, and he should supply a VAT invoice or receipt.

30.14 *Income and corporation tax*

The taxation in the United Kingdom of payments made and received in respect of patent licences and assignments is now governed by sections 520–533 of the Income and Corporation Taxes Act 1988 (c. 1). A payment made for purchase of patent rights can be written off as a capital allowance by 25 per cent. per year on a reducing balance basis. For further information on the taxation aspects of intellectual property, see the book by Gallafent, Eastaway and Dauppe and the article by J. Douglas & A. Shipwright, listed respectively in paras. 30.02 and 30.03 *supra*.

SECTION 31 31.01

Nature of, and transactions in, patents and applications for patents in Scotland

31.—(1) Section 30 above shall not extend to Scotland, but instead the following provisions of this section shall apply there.

(2) Any patent or application for a patent, and any right in or under any patent or any such application, is incorporeal moveable property, and the provisions of the following subsections and of section 36(3) below shall apply to any grant of licences, assignations and securities in relation to such property.

(3) Any patent or any such application, or any right in it, may be assigned and security may be granted over a patent or any such application or right.

(4) A licence may be granted, under any patent or any application for a patent, for working the invention which is the subject of the patent or the application.

(5) To the extent that any licence granted under subsection (4) above so provides, a sub-licence may be granted under any such licence and any such licence or sub-licence may be assigned and security may be granted over it.

(6) Any assignation or grant of security under this section may be carried out only by writing probative or holograph of the parties to the transaction.

(7) An assignation of a patent or application for a patent or a share in it, and an exclusive licence granted under any patent or any such application, may confer on the assignee or licensee the right of the assignor or licensor to bring proceedings by virtue of section 61 or 69 below for a previous infringement or to bring proceedings under section 58 below for a previous act.

ARTICLE 31.02

J. McLean, "Security over intellectual property: A Scottish perspective", [1988] EIPR 115.

COMMENTARY ON SECTION 31

General 31.03

Section 31 provides for Scotland similar provisions on the nature of, and transactions in, patents and applications as apply elsewhere under section 30, but modified so as to conform with Scots legal practice and terminology. Like section 30, section 31 applies also to "existing patents" (Sched. 2, para. 1(2)), to European patents (UK) (s. 77(1)), and to European applications (UK) (s. 78(2)).

31.04 *Nature of patents and patent rights under Scots law (subss. (2)–(5))*

Whereas, under section 30(1), patents under English law are "personal property (without being a thing in action)", under Scots law "any patent, application for a patent, and any grant in or under any patent or any such application" (herein called "a patent right") is "incorporeal moveable property". Both sections, therefore, seem to accept that the *situs* of a patent right is *not* where the register which records its existence is kept.

The differences between sections 30 and 31 appear generally linguistic and not substantive, except in relation to the grant of security over a patent, discussed in para. 31.04 *infra*; and the required manner of execution of instruments of transfer under Scots law, discussed in paras. 31.06 and 31.07 *infra*.

Thus, subsections (2)–(5) correspond generally to sections 30(2)–(4) in relation to: "assignations" (corresponding to "assignments" under English law); the grant of licences and (if permitted by the terms of the head licence) also of sub-licences; and the "grant of security" (corresponding to "mortgages", but not "charges", under English law). These subsections provide the necessary power for such transfers and grants to be valid if they took place under Scots law. Also such transfers and grants are, as under section 30, subject to the terms of section 36 in the case of patent rights that are held in joint names.

The commentaries under section 30 and 32–36, therefore, generally apply to transactions, instruments and events occurring under Scots law, and therefore under section 31.

As regards registration of a grant of security made by a company with its registered office in Scotland, section 410 of the Companies Act 1985 (c. 10) applies instead of sections 395 and 396(1)(j) thereof. However, a grant of security under Scots law can only be effected by an absolute assignation *ex facie*, with a "back letter" for re-transfer on redemption, or by an assignation-in-security, that is an assignation expressed in its text to be "in security", see the article by J. McLean, listed in para. 31.02 *supra*. The required registration procedure, without which a grant of security will be ineffective under Scots law, is discussed in para. 30.10.

31.05 *Applicability of section 31*

The main question to consider, as between sections 30 and 31, is which section applies to a particular transaction, instrument or event. It is suggested in "The Conflict of Laws" (J. C. H. Morris, Stevens, 3rd. Ed., 1986) that the leading case of *Republica de Guatamala* v. *Nunez* ([1927] 1 KB 669) leads to the conclusion, in the case of assignments of intangible moveable property, that the formal validity of the transfer instrument is governed by the law of the place where the transfer was made, though the instrument will also be valid if its execution complies with the formalities prescribed by its "proper law" (*i.e.* the law with which the instrument has its closest connection); and that the "proper law" of the contract will also govern any question of the capacity of the assignor and the essential validity of the assignment.

This would seem to suggest that section 31 (rather than s. 30) will govern any transfer or licence of a patent right which takes place under Scots law, for example in the case of the distribution of the estate of a person who died domiciled in Scotland. Nevertheless, whenever it is intended that section 31 should apply, the instrument of transfer or grant should expressly state that this is governed by Scots law.

Assignations and grants of security under Scots law (subss. (6) and (7))

—Manner of execution   **31.06**

Section 31(6) requires that execution of the assignation (transfer instrument), or grant of security (mortgage) which must also be by an assignation (see para. 31.04 *supra*), be "carried out by writing probative or holograph of the parties to the transaction". This provision (like s. 30(6), see para. 30.07) does *not* extend the grant of a patent licence. "Probative" means, in the case of an individual, that it is signed by the party in the presence of *two* witnesses who also sign, adding their occupations and addresses. These witnesses should have no interest in the instrument or be related to the signatory. In the case of a company, it means formal execution under seal. "Holograph" means, in the case of an individual, that a typewritten document can be formally executed by the grantor writing in his own hand immediately above his signature "Adopted as Holograph", and then signing it. Under Scots law, a document which is either written wholly in the hand of an individual signing it, or which is "Adopted as Holograph" has the same effect as a "probative" deed. While a partnership may adopt a typewritten deed "as holograph" with the firm's signature being applied above these words in the usual way, a company cannot execute an instrument in this way.

Thus, a patent assignation, or grant of security, to be made, or accepted, by a company under Scots law *must* be executed under seal. This is not necessary for a company executing this type of instrument under English Law (except in relation to an "existing patent"), see para. 30.07.

—Dual execution of transfer and security instruments   **31.07**

The Second Edition of this work stated that section 31 differed from section 30 in not requiring dual execution of transfer instruments of patent rights by both transferor and transferee. It was also stated that it was understood that the Patent Office accepts for registration instruments of transfer of patent rights signed by only the transferor if the transfer instrument has been executed in Scotland. However, since both sections 30(6) and 31(6) refer, in relation to such instruments, to "the *parties* to the transaction", it would seem the better practice for such instruments to be subjected to dual execution, whether this takes place under section 30 or 31.

Transfer of rights of action (subs. (7))   **31.08**

Subsection (7) corresponds to section 30(7) and permits an assignation of patent rights, or the grant of an exclusive licence thereunder, to pass therewith rights of action in relation to pre-assignation or -licence events, whether these rights be under sections 69 or 70 for infringement or under section 58 for compensation for Crown use, see para. 30.06.

SECTION 32 [Substituted]

Register of patents, etc.

32.—(1) The comptroller shall maintain the register of patents, which **32.01**
shall comply with rules made by virtue of this section and shall be kept in
accordance with such rules.

(2) Without prejudice to any other provision of this Act or rules, rules

may make provision with respect to the following matters, including provision imposing requirements as to any of those matters—

(a) the registration of patents and of published applications for patents;

(b) the registration of transactions, instruments or events affecting rights in or under patents and applications;

(c) the furnishing to the comptroller of any prescribed documents or description of documents in connection with any matter which is required to be registered;

(d) the correction of errors in the register and in any documents filed at the Patents Office in connection with registration; and

(e) the publication and advertisement of anything done under this Act or rules in relation to the register.

(3) Notwithstanding anything in subsection (2)(b) above, no notice of any trust, whether express, implied or constructive, shall be entered in the register and the comptroller shall not be affected by any such notice.

(4) The register need not be kept in documentary form.

(5) Subject to rules, the public shall have a right to inspect the register at the Patent Office at all convenient times.

(6) Any person who applies for a certified copy of an entry in the register or a certified extract from the register shall be entitled to obtain such a copy or extract on payment of a fee prescribed in relation to certified copies and extracts; and rules may provide that any person who applies for an uncertified copy or extract shall be entitled to such a copy or extract on payment of a fee prescribed in relation to uncertified copies and extracts.

(7) Applications under subsection (6) above or rules made by virtue of that subsection shall be made in such manner as may be prescribed.

(8) In relation to any portion of the register kept otherwise than in documentary form—

(a) the right of inspection conferred by subsection (5) above is a right to inspect the material on the register; and

(b) the right to a copy or extract conferred by subsection (6) above or rules is a right to a copy or extract in a form in which it can be taken away and in which it is visible and legible.

(9) Subject to subsection (12) below, the register shall be prima facie evidence of anything required or authorised by this Act or rules to be registered and in Scotland shall be sufficient evidence of any such thing.

(10) A certificate purporting to be signed by the comptroller and certifying that any entry which he is authorised by this Act or rules to make has or has not been made, or that any other thing which he is so authorised to do has or has not been done, shall be prima facie evidence, and in Scotland shall be sufficient evidence, of the matters so certified.

(11) Each of the following, that is to say—

(a) a copy of an entry in the register or an extract from the register which is supplied under subsection (6) above;

(b) a copy of any document kept in the Patent Office or an extract from any such document, any specification of a patent or any application for a patent which has been published,

which purports to be a certified copy or a certified extract shall, subject to subsection (12) below, be admitted in evidence without further proof and without production of any original; and in Scotland such evidence shall be sufficient evidence.

(12) In the application of this section to England and Wales nothing in it shall be taken as detracting from section 69 or 70 of the Police and Criminal Evidence Act 1984 or any provision made by virtue of either of them.

(13) In this section "certified copy" and "certified extract" mean a copy and extract certified by the comptroller and sealed with the seal of the Patent Office.

(14) In this Act, except so far as the context otherwise requires—
"register", as a noun, means the register of patents;
"register", as a verb, means, in relation to anything, to register or register particulars, or enter notice, of that thing in the register and, in relation to a person, means to enter his name in the register;
and cognate expressions shall be construed according.".

Note. Section 32, as reprinted above, has been substituted for the original form of section 32 by the 1986 Act (s. 1 and Sched. 1, para. 4), which Act also prospectively repealed section 35 (by s. 3 and Sched. 3, Part 1). These provisions took effect from January 1, 1989 (Patents, Designs and Marks Act 1986 (Commencement No. 2) Order, S.I. 1988 No. 1824), and for the Isle of Man from April 1, 1989 (S.I. 1989 No. 493).

SECTION 32 [Repealed]   **32.02**

Before its substitution, as indicated in para. 32.01 (*supra*), section 32 was in the form:

[32.—(1) There shall continue to be a register kept at the Patent Office and known as the register of patents which shall comply with rules made by virtue of this section and shall be kept in accordance with such rules; and in this Act, except so far as the context otherwise requires—
"register", as a noun, means the register of patents;
"register", as a verb, means, in relation to anything, to register or register particulars, or enter notice, of that thing in the register and, in relation to a person, means to enter his name in the register;
and cognate expressions shall be construed accordingly.

(2) Without prejudice to any other provision of this Act or rules, rules may make provision with respect to the following matters, including provision imposing requirements as to any of those matters, that is to say—
(a) the registration of patents and of published applications for patents;
(b) the registration of transactions, instruments or events affecting rights in or under patents and applications;
(c) the furnishing to the comptroller of any prescribed documents or des-

265

cription of documents in connection with any matter which is required to be registered;

(d) *the correction of errors in the register and in any documents filed at the Patent Office in connection with registration;*

(e) *making the register or entries or reproductions of entries in it available for inspection by the public;*

(f) *supplying certified copies of any such entries or reproductions to persons requiring them; and*

(g) *the publication and advertisement of anything done under this Act or rules in relation to the register.*

(3) Notwithstanding anything in subsection (2)(b) above, no notice of any trust, whether express, implied or constructive, shall be entered in the register and the comptroller shall not be affected by any such notice.]

RELEVANT RULES

Address for service

32.03   **30.** Every person concerned in any proceedings to which these Rules relate and every proprietor of a patent shall furnish to the comptroller an address for service in the United Kingdom and that address may be treated for all the purposes connected with such proceedings or patent as the address of the person concerned in the proceedings or the proprietor of the patent.

Note. Rule 30 is likely to become amended when section 281(5) [1988] is brought into effect permitting an address for service also to be situated elsewhere in the EEC, as discussed in para. 32.16 *infra.* For the possible revision of rule 30, see therefore the latest Supplement to this Work *re.* the present para.

Entries in the register

32.04   **44.**—(1) No entry shall be made in the register in respect of any application for a patent before the application has been published in accordance with section 16.

(2) Upon such publication, the comptroller shall cause to be entered in the register—

(a) the name and address of the applicant or applicants;

(b) the name and address of the person or persons stated by the applicant or applicants to be believed to be the inventor or inventors;

(c) the title of the invention;

(d) the date of filing and the file number of the application for the patent;

(e) the date of filing and the file number of any application declared for the purposes of section 5(2) or 127(4) and the country in or for which the application was made;

(f) the date on which the application was published;

(g) the address for service of the applicant or applicants.

(3) The comptroller shall also cause to be entered in the register—

(a) the date of filing of the request for substantive examination;

(b) the date on which the application is refused, withdrawn or deemed to be withdrawn;

(c) the date on which the patent is granted;

(d) the name and address of the person or persons to whom the patent is granted if different to the entries made in accordance with paragraph (2)(a) above;

(e) the address for service if different to the entry made in accordance with paragraph 2(g) above;

(f) notice of any transaction, instrument or event referred to in section 33(3).

(4) The comptroller may at any time enter in the register such other particulars as he may think fit.

Request for alteration to names and addresses

45.—(1) A request by the proprietor of a patent or an applicant for a patent for the alteration of a name, address or address for service entered in the register in respect of his patent or application shall be made on Patents Form No. 20/77.   **32.05**

(2) Before acting on a request to alter a name, the comptroller may require such proof of the alteration as he thinks fit.

(3) If the comptroller is satisfied that the request should be allowed, he shall cause the register to be altered accordingly.

Registrations under section 33

46.—(1) An application to register, or to give notice to the comptroller of, any transaction, instrument or event to which section 33 applies shall be made on Patents Form No. 21/77.   **32.06**

(2) Unless the comptroller otherwise directs, an application under paragraph (1) above shall be accompanied by a certified copy of any document which establishes the transaction, instrument or event or by an official document verifying it or by such extracts from any such document as suffice to establish it.

Request for correction of error

47.—(1) A request for the correction of an error in the register or in any document filed at the Patent Office in connection with registration shall be made on Patents Form No. 22/77.   **32.07**

(2) The comptroller may call for such written explanation of the reasons

for the request or evidence in support of it as he may require in order to satisfy himself that there is an error and, upon being so satisfied, shall make such correction as may be agreed between the proprietor of the patent or applicant and the comptroller.

Advertisement in relation to register

32.08   **50.** The comptroller may arrange for the publication and advertisement of such things done under the Act or these Rules in relation to the register as he may think fit.

Entries relating to sections 8(1), 12(1) and 37(1)

32.09   **51.** On the reference to the comptroller of a question under sections 8(1), 12(1) or 37(1), he shall, subject to rule 44(1) above, cause an entry to be made in the register of the fact and of such other information relating to the reference as he may think fit.

32.10   **52.**—(1) Upon request made on Patents Form No. 24/77 and payment of the appropriate fee, but subject to paragraph (3) below, the comptroller shall supply—
   (*a*) a certified copy or certified extract falling within section 32(11);
   (*b*) a copy of an entry in or an extract from the register or a copy of or an extract from anything referred to in section 32(11)(*b*), certified by the impression of a rubber stamp;
   (*c*) a certificate for the purposes of section 32(10).
   (2) Upon request made on Patents Form No. 23/77 and payment of the appropriate fee, but subject to paragraph (3) below, the comptroller shall supply an uncertified copy of an entry in or an uncertified extract from the register or an uncertified copy of or an uncertified extract from anything referred to in section 32(11)(*b*).
   (3) The restrictions on making documents available for inspection contained in rule 93(5) shall apply equally to the supply by the comptroller under this rule of copies of or extracts from such documents or requests for information as are referred to in rule 93(5) and nothing in this rule shall be construed as imposing upon the comptroller the duty of supplying copies of or extracts from any documents filed with or sent to or by the Patent Office before 1st June 1978.

Note. Rule 52 was substituted by the Patents (Amendment) Rules 1988 (S.I. 1988 No. 2089, r. 2).

Order or direction by court

32.11   **53.** Where any order or direction has been made or given by the court—
   (*a*) transferring a patent or application or any right in or under it to any person;

(*b*) that an application should proceed in the name of any person;

(*c*) allowing the proprietor of a patent to amend the specification; or

(*d*) revoking a patent;

the person in whose favour the order is made or the direction is given shall file Patents Form No. 25/77, accompanied by an office copy of such order or direction, and thereupon the specification shall be amended or the register rectified or altered, as the case may be.

Entries in the register

79.—(1) Upon publication of an application for a European patent (UK) under Article 93 of the European Patent Convention, the comptroller shall cause to be entered in the register a copy of every entry which, at the date of such publication, has been made in the Register of European Patents kept under Article 127 of that Convention in respect of that application.   **32.12**

(2) The comptroller shall also cause to be entered in the register in respect of an application for a European patent (UK) which has been published under Article 93 of the Convention copies of any entry made in the Register of European Patents following such publication, provided that an application to that effect is made to the comptroller on Patents Form No. 39/77, accompanied by a copy of the relevant entry in the Register duly certified to the satisfaction of the comptroller.

Application to and Orders at Court [under existing patents]   **32.13**

150 [1968]. Where any Order has been made by the Court under the Act revoking a patent or extending the term of a patent, or allowing a patentee to amend his specification, or affecting the validity or proprietorship of a patent or any rights thereunder, the person in whose favour such order has been made shall file Patent Form No. 69 accompanied by an office copy of such order, and thereupon the specification shall be amended or the register rectified or altered as the case may be.

PATENTS (COMPANIES RE-REGISTRATION) RULES 1982   **32.14**
(S.I. 1982 No. 297)

1. These Rules may be cited as the Patents (Companies Re-registration) Rules 1982 and shall come into operation on April 5, 1982.

2. Where a body corporate has re-registered under the Companies Act 1980 with the same name as that with which it was registered immediately before the re-registration save for the substitution as, or the inclusion as, the last part of the name (in either upper or lower case of letters and with or without punctuation marks) of—

(*a*) the words "public limited company" or their equivalent in Welsh; or

(*b*) the abbreviation "p.l.c." or its equivalent in Welsh,

then references to the name of the body corporate in any application to the comptroller, in the register and in any other record kept at, or any document issued by, the Patent Office and relating to patents shall be treated on and after the date of such re-registration as references to the name with which the body corporate is so re-registered.

COMMENTARY ON SECTION 32

32.15 *General*

Section 32 continues the register of patents kept under previous statutes, the word "register" now being defined in subsection (14). It applies to applications as well as patents and also to "existing patents" (Sched. 2, para. 1(2)) and to European patents (UK) and applications therefor (ss. 77(1), 78(2)). However, entries relating to European applications are best dealt with directly in the Register of European Patents at the EPO (see EPH, 2nd ed., Chapters 17, 58.10 and 58.19) because no separate register of applications for European patents (UK) is kept, see para. 32.18 *infra*.

Subsection (2) gives power to make rules relating to the register without prejudice to the general power given by section 123(1), and rules 44–47 and 49–51, as well as rule 79 (see s. 78(4)), are to be regarded as made under it.

No entry is made in the register before publication of an application (r. 44(1)), though notice may be given to the Comptroller for the purpose of section 33(1)(*b*) which will afterwards be registered under rule 44(3)*f*), see para. 33.04.

An entry regarding licences of right may be made under section 46(1), see para. 46.06, or section 48(1)(*b*), see para. 48.15, or under section 51, see para. 51.07.

Falsification of the register is a criminal offence under section 109, see para. 109.02.

32.15A *The register as evidence*

Subsection (4)–(14) effectively replace the former section 35 now repealed, see *Note* to para. 32.01 *supra*. Subsection (4) allows for the register to be kept in a non-documentary, *e.g.* computerised, form and it need no longer be kept "at the Patent Office". Indeed, apart from patents granted under former statutes, the register became computerised from November 8, 1989 for patents and applications then in force, see (1988–89) 18 CIPA 122 and O.J. November 8, 1989. Subsection (5) provides a right of inspection of the register and subsection (6) provides for obtaining extracts in accordance with rules made under subsection (7). Subsection (8) provides for inspection of a computerised entry and obtaining an extract thereof. The necessary rules are provided by rule 49 (reprinted at para. 118.03), discussed in paras. 118.12 and 118.20.

Subsections (9)–(13) provide for copies of entries from the register, certified by the Comptroller under seal (subs. (13)), to be received in legal proceedings as "prima facie" (in Scotland, "sufficient") evidence of the extracted entry, though with a saving for the evidential requirements for computer records in criminal proceedings. These matters are discussed further in paras. 32.36–32.38 *infra*.

32.16 *Address for service (r. 30)*

Rule 30 requires an address for service to be furnished for all applications and patents. No form or fee is prescribed, but see para. 32.22 *infra*. An address for ser-

270

vice is registered irrespective of how, or by whom, it is furnished. At present the address can only be in the United Kingdom (or the Isle or Man under s. 132(2)), but (by virtue of section 281(5) [1988]) the address for service required under a revised rule 30 is likely to become one in any Member State of the European Communities (or in the Isle of Man). However, an address in the Channel Islands should remain unacceptable because these are not Member States. For the revision of rule 30, see the latest Supplement to this Work *re*. this para.

An address for service is not deleted from the register without substitution of another, see para. 32.23 *infra*. However, legal obligations flowing from a recorded address for service, *e.g.* under the Supply of Goods and Services Act 1982 (c. 29), can be renounced as a matter of contract between the proprietor and his agent, and the Patent Office may then be informed accordingly.

While the address for service is clearly the address to which the Comptroller can send communications to meet his obligations under the Act and Rules, it is not clear whether this address has a wider status, *e.g.* for service of a petition to the court of revocation, or of an appeal by an applicant for revocation against a decision of the Comptroller, where the proprietor is resident outside the jurisdiction of the court and leave of the court might otherwise be needed (under RSC Ord. 11) for service out of the jurisdiction.

Entries made automatically (r. 44)   **32.17**

When an application is published under section 16, or an international application for a patent (UK) satisfies the conditions of section 89(4) (to be replaced by s. 89A(3), see paras. 89A.07–89A.12), all the items listed in rule 44(2) (reprinted at para. 32.04 *supra*) are then entered in the register, including the country, date of filing and file number of any application from which priority is claimed under section 5(2). Subsequently, entry is made under rule 44(3) of the date of requesting substantive examination under section 18(1) and the date on which the application is granted (the publication of notice of grant in the O.J. under s. 24(1)) or the date on which it is refused, withdrawn or deemed to be withdrawn. Entry is made under rule 51 (reprinted at para. 32.10 *supra*) of any reference to the Comptroller of a question about entitlement under section 8, 12, or 37, see para. 37.14).

Under rule 44(4), giving a general discretion to enter in the register other particulars, entries are customarily made in respect of such "events" as restoration, surrender, amendment, correction and revocation of the patent, and of the grant of any licence of right under section 46(1) or compulsory licence under section 48 or 51 and (if notice thereof is given) of the grant by the court of a certificate of contested validity under section 65. Entries are normally made when such events have actually occurred, but sometimes an entry is made to indicate the filing of an application therefor. For example entries are now made in respect of all applications for restoration, even if submitted out of time or apparently unarguable (*Daido Kogyo's Patent*, [1984] RPC 97).

No entry has been made since June 14, 1982 of the nationality of any person, but the names and addresses of applicants, and of persons named as inventors, are recorded (r. 44(2)(*a*) and (*b*)).

Payment of a renewal fee under rule 39 has not been recorded in the register since June 14, 1982, but information is available under rule 48 (reprinted at para. 118.02) by filing PF 23/77 (reprinted at para. 141.23), see para. 118.20.

Register of European patents   **32.18**

On the publication (under EPCa. 93) of an application for a European patent (UK), the entries in the Register of European Patents are treated as forming part of the register under the Act under rule 79(1) (reprinted at para. 32.13 *supra*) by access to the European register. The Comptroller is not obliged to update the register under the Act automatically between publication of an application for a European patent (UK) and its grant, but this happens in practice through access to the European register. Thus, the Comptroller does not accept PF 39/77 for recording an assignment of an application for a European patent (UK), which form is therefore redundant, but he requires the assignment to be registered in the EPO, see para. 78.09. A separate register of European patents (UK) is, however, created upon the publication by the EPO of its notice of grant. Copies of entries made in the European register after grant of a European patent (UK) are not entered automatically in the United Kingdom register but only if requested under rule 79(2).

32.19 *Transactions, instruments and events (rr. 45 and 46)*

Alterations to names and/or addresses of proprietors and applicants, as distinct from changes in ownership, are made under rule 45 (reprinted at para. 32.05), see para. 32.24 *infra*. However, where the names of United Kingdom public limited companies were required by statute to be altered, the Patents (Companies Re-registration) Rules 1982 (S.I. 1982 No. 297), reprinted at para. 32.14 *supra*, deem the former name to be treated as the new name without formal application for alteration. A notice to this effect is entered upon any certified copy of a register entry where the proprietor is a United Kingdom limited company. However, these Re-registration Rules have no effect in relation to foreign patents or on entries on the Register of European Patents maintained at the EPO.

Subsection (2)(*b*) and rule 46 (reprinted at para. 32.06 *supra*) provide for registration of any transaction, instrument or event of the kind listed in section 33(3). The procedure is discussed at paras. 32.25–32.31. Assignments and other changes in proprietorship, mortgages and licences fall into this category and are discussed generally under section 30 at paras. 30.06–30.08. The effect of registration is considered under section 33 at para. 33.04. Notification may be made before publication under section 16, and the register entry is then made under rule 44(3)(*f*) when the register entry is created. Entries can be registered after expiry or lapse of the patent (*Davchem's Patent*, SRIS O/111/86, *noted* IPD 9073), as it may still be involved in proceedings for infringement under section 61, or compensation for Crown use under section 58, or an application by an inventor for compensation under section 40.

Damages or an account of profits are not awarded to an assignee or exclusive licensee for the period between the date of the instrument and the date of registration unless the entry is made less than six months after the date of the instrument or can be shown to have been made as soon as practicable (s. 68, discussed at para. 68.03).

Although subsection (3) prohibits entry of notice of a simple trust, an equitable interest can be registered if it is of such a nature that specific performance could be enforced to affect the proprietorship of the patent, whether by creating a trust or otherwise (*Stewart* v. *Casey*, (1892) 9 RPC 9 (CA)), applied in *Kakkar* v. *Szelke* ([1989] FSR 225; [1989] 4 EPOR 184 (CA)), see also *EPO Decision J* 19/87, "*Assignment/BURR-BROWN*" ([1988] 5 EPOR 350). A letter to the Comptroller relating to an equitable right or claim is open to inspection on the public file under rule 93(1) (reprinted in para. 118.05, see also para. 118.12), even if the letter itself gives no legal or equitable right and could not be registered (as in *Fletcher's Patent*, (1893) 10 RPC 252). It is not yet clear whether the presence of information concerning an equitable interest, such as a trust, in the file open to public inspection, but not entered in the register, gives constructive notice of that equitable interest sufficient to defeat a claim under the general rule of equity by a subsequent purchaser that he was a *bona fide* purchaser without notice of the equitable interest and therefore took what he purchased free of that interest, see para. 33.03.

Legal proceedings   **32.20**

There is no obligation to notify the Comptroller of the commencement of legal proceedings relating to a patent. A court order or direction resulting from proceedings should be transmitted to the Patent Office under rule 53 (reprinted at para. 32.11), or, in the case of an order made under the 1949 Act in respect of an "existing patent", under rule 150 [1968] (reprinted at para. 32.12 *supra*), by the party in whose favour it is given, see para. 32.29 *infra*, but there is no sanction for non-compliance. Thus, a court order for revocation could remain unrecorded and therefore not generally known to the public. No entry is made where an action is settled and proceedings are stayed or discontinued without formal order.

Correction of errors   **32.21**

Correction of errors in the register or any document filed in connection with registration is provided for by subsection (2)(*d*) and rule 47 (reprinted at para. 32.07), see para. 32.32. In the case of an "existing patent" clerical errors in the register can be corrected alternatively under section 76 [1949], see para. A76.11. Under this provision, but not under rule 47, the Comptroller may make such a correction of his own motion. Where an error has occurred in the register attributable wholly or in part to an error, default or omission on the part of the Patent Office, correction can be made under rule 100 (reprinted at para. 123.07), as was done, *e.g.* in *Coal Industry's Application* ([1986] RPC 57).
The register may be rectified by the court under section 34, see commentary thereon.

Register entries as prima facie evidence   **32.21A**

The term "prima facie evidence" in subsections (9) and (10) means evidence which, if not balanced or outweighed by other evidence, is sufficient to establish a particular contention. Subsections (11) and (13) allow certified copies sealed with the seal of the Patent Office to be admitted in evidence without need to produce the original or rely on section 9 of the Civil Evidence Act 1968 (c. 64). Subsection (12) provides that nothing in the section detracts from sections 69 and 70 of the Police and Criminal Evidence Act 1984 (c. 60): these relate to computer records in criminal proceedings and the need to show that the computer was functioning satisfactorily and under proper control.
Certificates are signed by an authorised officer of the Patent Office under unrepealed section 62(3) of the Patents and Designs Act 1907 (7 Edw. 7, c. 29, reprinted in para. B03). A certificate which refers to a limited company contains extended reference to the Patents (Companies Re-registration) Rules 1982 (S.I. 1982 No. 297), reprinted at para. 32.14 *supra*, as a reminder that the entry may be deemed to be an entry referring to a "public limited company", or "plc", without specific entry to this effect having been made in the register, see para. 32.19 *supra*.
Unrepealed section 64 of the Patents and Designs Act 1907 (reprinted at para. B07) provides generally that impressions of the seal of the Patent Office shall be judicially noted and admitted in evidence.
For inspection of the register and of documents filed at the Patent Office and caveats for entries or prospective entries in the register, see paras. 32.33–32.35 *infra* and paras. 118.19 and 118.20.

Practice under Section 32

32.22 *Furnishing address for service*

The need to satisfy the requirement under rule 30 (discussed in para. 32.16 *supra*) for an address for service (which probably can be anywhere within the EEC, see para. 32.16 *supra*) arises mainly with international applications for a patent (UK) and European patents (UK). In an application made under the Act the address for service is contained in the request for grant filed under rule 16(1) (see para. 14.10). For an international application it may conveniently be furnished on Form NP.1 (reprinted at para. 143.01) when the national fee is paid (for which, see para. 89A.18). Alternatively, PF 51/77 (reprinted at para. 141.51) can be used, though this is not a prescribed use of this form, see (1984–85) 14 CIPA 155 and O.J. December 2, 1987.

For a European patent (UK) the professional representative responsible for the application in the EPO has no standing (*Deforeit's Patent*, [1986] RPC 142), and an address for service must be furnished if the proprietor is to receive notice under rules 39(4) and 42 of the non-payment of the next renewal fee, see para. 25.09. The ways in which the address for service for a European Patent (UK) can be conveniently supplied are discussed in para. 77.13.

Payment of a renewal fee under rule 39 giving an address on PF 12/77 for dispatching the receipt will, if this is within the United Kingdom (or the Isle of Man), be treated as the address for service under rule 30 to which a reminder in the subsequent year will be sent under rule 39(4), see para. 25.14. Presumably this practice will also apply if the address for service is situated in some other Member State of the European Communities, see para. 32.16 *supra*.

The Patent Office treats the lack of an address for service as a formal objection and sends a single letter (not necessarily by air mail) to the foreign proprietor (not to his EPO representative) drawing attention to the requirement.

32.23 *Alteration of address for service*

Filing of PF 20/77 (reprinted at para. 141.20) is required to alter an address for service recorded in the register (r. 45(1)), but no extra fee is required if the change is made on the PF 20/77 used to alter the name or address of the proprietor or applicant. Appointment of a new agent under rule 90(2) on PF 51/77 (reprinted at para. 141.51), as discussed in para. 102.22, only alters the address for service for the proceedings specified on PF 51/77. Where an "address for service" stated on any other patents form differs from the address for service entered on the register, the register is likewise not altered and the address on the form is treated as an address for service for those proceedings only, see, *e.g.* O.J. July 19, 1989.

32.24 *Alteration of name or address of proprietor*

A request under rule 45 (reprinted at para. 32.05) by the proprietor or applicant to alter his name and/or address (and/or his address for service) on the register is made by filing PF 20/77 (reprinted at para. 141.20), but in practice notification that a recorded name or address is not correct is not ignored by the Patent Office. Evidence must be furnished of a change of name, such as:

for a United Kingdom company: certificate from the Registrar of Companies;

for a United States company: certificate from the Secretary of State of the state of incorporation;

for a German company: appropriately certified extract from the commercial register;

for a French company: copy of the formal announcement of change of name in "Petits Affiches". In general, an official announcement in a government gazette of the change of name is sufficient for the purpose. A verified English translation must accompany any document in a foreign language (r. 113(1), discussed in para. 123.41).

PF 20/77 may be filed by an agent in his own name, though under rule 106 (reprinted at para. 72.08 and discussed at para. 72.44) the Comptroller can require him to establish his authority to do so. A single PF 20/77 may be used to effect the same change for a number of patents and applications listed in an annexed schedule, but the fee is then the appropriate multiple of the fee for a single case.

Registration of transactions, instruments and events

—General   **32.25**

An application under rule 46 (reprinted at para. 32.06 *supra*) to register or notify a transaction, instrument or event is made on PF 21/77 (reprinted at para. 141.21) and must be accompanied by sufficient documentation to establish the position. The original document is not required; a copy certified by someone who has verified it against the original or an earlier certified copy suffices, and relevant certified extracts may be provided where disclosure of the entire document is not desired. The certification may be in the form "I certify that this is a true copy of [an extract of] . . . ".

A verified English translation must be supplied of any document in a foreign language (r. 113(1)) and, if the translator works from the original, he may provide a combined certification and translation, see paras. 123.41 and 123.42.

—Inter-company transfers   **32.26**

Where company A assigns rights to company B and is then dissolved, and B subsequently changes its name to A, the latter is a different legal entity and the name of the old A should not be allowed to remain as the registered proprietor. Both the assignment and the subsequent change of name should be recorded under rules 46 and 45, using PF 21/77 and PF 20/77 respectively.

Where a United States company A merges with company B and then changes its name to C, the Patent Office requires a certificate by the Secretary of State of the state of incorporation to the effect that the merger has taken place. This is regarded solely as an alteration of name to be recorded under rule 45 using PF 20/77 only.

If a German company is converted without liquidation, but is dissolved by the conversion, a notarially certified copy of the resolution for conversion and officially certified copies of entries in the commercial registers of both previous and subsequent owners are required.

—Transmission on death or insolvency   **32.27**

On death of an individual, the original or an office copy of the grant of probate or letters of administration is required. Where the grant is in respect of a will containing a gift of the patent or application, and the personal representative has not been registered as the proprietor, the Patent Office will register the beneficiary under the will (if supplied with a certified copy) without requiring an assent. Until the grant is extracted from the Probate Registry the Patent Office regards no person as authorised to act in respect of a pending application; extensions of time are granted under rule 110(1) (discussed at para. 123.35), but even in the absence of formal authority it may be important to file any necessary documents under the rules specified in rule 110(2) and (3) where extensions or further extensions are not available.

The Patent Office (Assignments Branch) should be consulted for its requirements in cases such as insolvency, receivership or the appointment of an administrator, or in any unusual or complex matter.

32.28   *—Execution of documents*

The requirements for execution of assignments, etc. by the parties are discussed at para. 30.07 and (under Scots law) at paras. 31.06 and 31.07. Where several copies of a document were produced simultaneously on "no carbon required" paper, one of the lower copies bearing the signature in blue print was accepted for registration by the EPO as the "original" under EPCa. 72 and EPCr. 20(1) (*EPO Decision J* 18/84, "*Register of European Patents—Entries in*", OJEPO 6/87, 215; [1987] 5 EPOR 321).

32.29   *—Filing request for registration*

The application for registration may be made by, or on behalf of, any of the parties but is normally filed by the beneficiary (assignee, licensee, mortgagee, etc.) to protect his interest. Under rule 106 (reprinted at para. 72.06, discussed at para. 72.44), the Comptroller can require a person filing PF 21/77 to establish his authority to do so. The fact that PF 21/77 has been filed is entered immediately in the register and, though the requested entry may not be made for some time, it is effectively back-dated under section 33(4). If the instrument to be recorded is a mortgage given by a United Kingdom registered company, to be effective it must also be registered as a charge at the Companies Registration Office, see para. 30.10.

Where the devolution of title or rights arises in the same manner for more than one patent and/or application, a single PF 21/77 should be filed with an annexed schedule listing them: a reduced fee is then payable for all cases beyond the first, see para. 144.02. However, if two transactions (*e.g.* successive assignments) are to be recorded on the same patent or application, there is no reduction in fee and the Patent Office prefers the filing of a separate PF 21/77 for each.

Where the event is an order or direction by the court (s. 33(3)(*e*)), entry in the register need not be applied for under rule 46. An office copy of the court order or direction should be filed at the Patent Office with PF 25/77 (reprinted at para. 141.25) under rule 53, or, in the case of an order under the 1949 Act in respect of an "existing patent", with PF No. 69 (reprinted at para. A138) under rule 150 [1968] (reprinted at para. 32.12 *supra*); no fee is payable in either case.

32.30   *—Comptroller's requirements*

Before he will effect registration, the Comptroller must be satisfied that documents have been duly stamped (Stamp Act 1891 (54 & 55 Vict., c. 39) s. 17); stamp duty is discussed at para. 30.12.

Where there are joint proprietors, the Comptroller also requires to be satisfied that section 36(3) has been complied with, see para. 36.05.

Otherwise, if a document for registration appears to be in order, the circumstances under which it was entered into are not considered. Challenge to its validity must then be by legal proceedings, presumably by an application for rectification of the register under section 34. The court may, where appropriate, grant an injunction restraining any disposal or licensing of specified patents pending resolution of disputed ownership (*Landi den Hertog* v. *Sea Bird* [1975] FSR 502).

—*Documents placed on public file*   **32.31**

The documents supplied for registration are placed on the patent file and become a matter of public record under rule 93(1), see para. 118.12. If the original, or an additional copy, is furnished the Patent Office endorses this as having been registered and returns it. A document sent to the Patent Office with a statement that it is supplied merely for inspection and return is not placed at all on the public file (r. 93(5)(*c*), discussed in para. 118.16). In order to prevent other terms in an instrument becoming open to public inspection, only extracts of the relevant parts should be supplied for registration.

Correction of errors in register or documents   **32.32**

A request for correction is made under rule 47 (reprinted at para. 32.07 *supra*) on PF 22/77 (reprinted at para. 141.22). If the error is in a document filed in connection with registration, a copy of the document should be provided and the desired correction should be shown on a further copy or set out on the PF 22/77. If the error is not self-evident, or the person filing PF 22/77 is not obviously entitled to request correction, the Comptroller is likely to call for supporting evidence under rule 106 (reprinted at para. 72.08, discussed at para. 72.44). If the error is one which arose in the Patent Office, correction can be requested under rule 100 (reprinted at para. 123.07).
Correction of a clerical error in the register relating to an "existing patent" can alternatively be requested under section 76 [1949] and rule 129 [1968] (reprinted at para. A76.02) on PF No. 64 (reprinted at para. A135), see para. A76.11.

Inspection of register and documents   **32.33**

Inspection of the register is requested on PF 23/77 (reprinted at para. 141.23). This form may be filed by anyone and does not itself become open to public inspection under rule 93(1), see rule 93(5)(*e*) (reprinted in para. 118.05). An address must be given but apparently does not have to be in the United Kingdom. The request includes inspection of the public file under rule 93(1), see para. 118.20. Uncertified copies of, or extracts from, the register and publicly available documents can be ordered on the same form but a separate fee is payable (and also a copying charge, best arranged by supplying a Form "Sales 3" with PF 23/77). Information as to whether a renewal fee has been paid under rule 39 (reprinted at para. 25.02) can also be requested on PF 23/77 without additional fee. On occasion the register has erroneously indicated that a patent has lapsed, and in an important case it is prudent to ask for the Comptroller's certificate that the patent has lapsed rather than rely on inspection of the register. However, it is not clear whether the Comptroller would be liable for loss arising if he issued such a certificate in error of the true position.
If a certificate or copy certified by the Comptroller under section 32(6) is required, it must be requested on PF 24/77 (reprinted at para. 141.24) and not on PF 23/77, see rule 52(1) and (2) (reprinted in para. 32.10 *supra*) and para. 35.36 *infra*.
For further information on inspection of the register and files open to public inspection, see paras. 118.12–118.18.
The SRIS maintains an alphabetical card index of assignees of applications and patents to supplement the name indexes of applicants. Facilities also exist at SRIS for obtaining information from the Register of European Patents.

32.34   *Inspection of Register of European Patents*

The Register of European Patents may be inspected with regard to an application for a European patent (UK) by filing PF 23/77 at the United Kingdom Patent Office; a current extract of the European register is supplied in the form of a computer printout. The European register may also be accessed directly by computer link or (without charge) by telephone enquiry during normal office hours to the EPO information desk at Munich (010.49.89.2399.4538) or The Hague (010.31.70.90.67.89) (OJEPO 5/87, 197). The EP publication number should be quoted if possible, though the application number may be used.

32.35   *Caveats*

A caveat may be filed under section 118(1) and rule 92(1), as discussed more fully in para. 118.19. Application is made on PF 49/77 (reprinted at para. 141.49) for information to be given when an entry is made in the register or an application is made for the making of an entry. If such a caveat is filed in respect of an application to register an assignment or licence, registration is suspended for a short time to give the caveator an opportunity to prevent registration, *e.g.* by seeking an injunction from the court. In a proper case registration may be stayed to await the outcome of legal proceedings, see para. 32.30 *supra*.

32.36   *Certificate from Comptroller*

Rule 52(2) (reprinted in para. 32.10 *supra*) requires PF 24/77 (reprinted at para. 141.24) to be filed to obtain any certificate of the Comptroller. The person filing the form must be duly authorised if it is filed in respect of a document not yet open to public inspection, but anyone may obtain a certified copy of the register or of any document open to public inspection under rule 93(1) (reprinted at para. 118.05). The wording on PF 24/77 suggests that the address for despatch of the certificate need not be in the United Kingdom.

The person making the request on PF 24/77 must state whether he has any special requirements, such as the need for patent register extracts or details of renewal payments made, and the number and type of certificates required divided as between those authenticated by a rubber stamp impression and those for which the certificates are to be signed and sealed. A separate fee is charged for each certificate required. There is a higher fee for a certificate sealed with the seal of the Patent Office (whether or not attached to documents), see para. 144.02. The copying charge for documents to be certified is best arranged by supplying with PF 24/77 a Form "Sales 3" for payment from a deposit account. Otherwise cash can be paid on collection.

A request can be made for a certified copy of a specification indicating that a correction or amendment has been made and the date when it was requested and/or allowed. This may be important in registering a granted United Kingdom patent abroad. Where certification of a printed specification is required, the Patent Office supplies the printed copy if requested, subject to payment (*e.g.* by supplying Form "Sales 3"), but it is quicker to file the necessary copy with the PF 24/77.

To obtain a certified copy of the letters patent grant of an "existing patent", the original must be produced to the Patent Office for copying and verification ((1974–75) 4 CIPA 356).

32.37   *Certification of priority documents*

Certified copies of United Kingdom applications for use as priority documents under the Paris Convention must be ordered on PF 24/77 (reprinted at para. 141.24). A Form "Sales 3" should preferably be supplied for payment from a deposit account to cover the cost of copying, but it is possible to pay cash on collection of the certificates.

If a certified copy is required urgently, this should be stated prominently on PF 24/77, preferably in red ink.

The countries for which the copies are required should be specified, and the Patent Office (Office Copy Section) then provides certification appropriate for each. For example, a copy of PF 7/77 is automatically included in a certified copy for the United States; and, where legalisation is necessary, the certificate bears the manuscript signature of the Comptroller which can be authenticated by the Foreign Office before this is legalised by the appropriate consulate.

It is recommended that PF 24/77 itself should simply state the number of certificates required, with the countries being listed on an accompanying Form "Sales 3", as this (unlike PF 24/77) will not be placed on the file. When PF 24/77 becomes open to public inspection under rule 93(1) (reprinted at para. 118.05), it will not then reveal the countries for which priority documents have been requested.

Where a withdrawn application under the Act serves as a priority document for a later application under rule 6(3)(b) (reprinted at para. 5.02), a single request on PF 24/77 suffices for a certified copy of both applications, and likewise for a certified copy of provisional and complete specifications of an "existing patent" (O.J. April 1, 1987).

If an earlier United Kingdom application was withdrawn without being open to public inspection and leaving no rights outstanding, the Comptroller will certify accordingly in the terms of Art. 4C(4) of the Paris Convention (O.J. September 19, 1962).

Copies of provisional specifications   **32.38**

Copies of provisional specifications filed under the 1949 Act, whether or not required to be certified, should be requested by application to the Public Search Room of the Patent Office and not to its Sales Branch. If no certificate is required, PF 24/77 need not be filed, but payment must be made in advance or by means of Form "Sales 3" from a deposit account.

SECTION 33

Effect of registration, etc., on rights in patents

33.—(1) Any person who claims to have acquired the property in a   **33.01**
patent or application for a patent by virtue of any transaction, instrument
or event to which this section applies shall be entitled as against any other
person who claims to have acquired that property by virtue of an earlier
transaction, instrument or event to which this section applies if, at the time
of the later transaction, instrument or event—

(a) the earlier transaction, instrument or event was not registered, or

(b) in the case of any application which has not been published, notice
of the earlier transaction, instrument or event had not been given to
the comptroller, and

(c) in any case, the person claiming under the later transaction, instrument or event, did not know of the earlier transaction, instrument
or event.

279

(2) Subsection (1) above shall apply equally to the case where any person claims to have acquired any right in or under a patent or application for a patent, by virtue of a transaction, instrument or event to which this section applies, and that right is incompatible with any such right acquired by virtue of an earlier transaction, instrument or event to which this section applies.

(3) This section applies to the following transactions, instruments and events:—

(*a*) the assignment or assignation of a patent or application for a patent, or a right in it;

(*b*) the mortgage of a patent or application or the granting of security over it;

(*c*) the grant, assignment or assignation of a licence or sub-licence, or mortgage of a licence or sub-licence, under a patent or application;

(*d*) the death of the proprietor or one of the proprietors of any such patent or application or any person having a right in or under a patent or application and the vesting by an assent of personal representatives of a patent, application or any such right; and

(*e*) any order or directions of a court or other competent authority—

(i) transferring a patent or application or any right in or under it to any person; or

(ii) that an application should proceed in the name of any person;

and in either case the event by virtue of which the court or authority had power to make any such order or give any such directions.

(4) Where an application for the registration of a transaction, instrument or event has been made, but the transaction, instrument or event has not been registered, then, for the purposes of subsection (1)(*a*) above, registration of the application shall be treated as registration of the transaction, instrument of event.

ARTICLE

33.02   A. K. Lewis "Dealings with U.K. Patents and Know-How", [1979] EIPR 217.

COMMENTARY ON SECTION 33

33.03   *General*

Section 33 deals with the effect of entries in the register of patents concerning rights in patents. It applies to applications as well as patents and also to "existing patents" (Sched. 2, para. 1(2)) and European patents (UK) and applications therefor (ss. 77(1) 78(2)). It applies to the transactions, instruments and events listed in subsection (3): these affect title to a patent or application and are considered generally under section 30, particularly at para. 30.06.

Priority by registration or notice (subss. (1) and (2))   **33.04**

Subsections (1) and (2) provide that a person who acquires the property in, or a right in or under, a patent or application is not affected by an earlier transaction, instrument or event if he did not know of it at the time of his own acquisition *and* if at that time it had not been registered or (if the application had not yet been published under s. 16) notified to the Comptroller under section 32, see para. 32.19. The degree of "knowledge" is discussed in para. 33.05 *infra* and the importance of the section is discussed in the article by A. K. Lewis, listed in para. 33.02 *supra*. Subsection (4) provides that for this purpose registration is backdated to the date of application for the entry to be made in the register. The later transaction, instrument or event need not itself be registered.

Knowledge   **33.05**

Knowledge of the earlier transaction, instrument or event deprives a person of the benefit of subsections (1) and (2) even if it is not definite or complete. It is not clear whether subsection (1)(*c*) requires actual knowledge, or whether constructive or imputed knowledge would suffice, see para. 32.19.

In *Morey's Patent*, ((1858) 25 Beav. 581: 53 E.R. 759), where a patentee had assigned half the patent to A and afterwards assigned the whole to B by a deed reciting that he had already granted a "licence" to A, and B's assignment was registered first, the court held that B had constructive notice of A's rights and ordered an entry to be made in the register that the "licence" referred to in B's assignment was the subsequently registered assignment to A. More generally, proof of knowledge on the part of a person can be based on evidence that he "had deliberately shut his eyes to the obvious or refrained from inquiry because he suspected the truth but did not wish to have his suspicion confirmed" (*Westminster City Council* v. *Croyalgrange*, [1986] 2 All ER 353; [1986] 1 WLR 674 (HL) *per* Lord Bridge). Whether this imposes an obligation to inspect the file of the patent as well as its register entry remains to be decided, see para. 32.19.

Decided cases   **33.06**

There appears to have been no decision as yet under section 33, but its effect was inconclusively discussed in *BICC* v. *Burndy* ([1985] RPC 273 (CA)).

PRACTICE UNDER SECTION 33

General   **33.07**

Registration of any transaction, instrument or event to which section 33 applies is governed by rule 46 and is dealt with under section 32 at paras. 32.25–32.31.

Desirability of registration and inspection of register and file   **33.08**

Registration is obviously desirable to prevent the proprietor or former proprietor purporting to grant incompatible rights in future. In the absence of registration, rights to monetary relief for infringement may be lost, see section 68. Where there is doubt as to registrability of a claim to have an interest in or under a patent or application, the application on PF 21/77 should be accompanied by a letter to the Comptroller setting out the claim, see para. 32.19. A third party who inspects the file, or who deliberately refrains from such inquiry, may then be fixed with knowledge of the claim and may be unable to rely on subsections (2) and (3) even if no entry is made in the register, see paras. 32.19 and 33.05.

Conversely a person seeking to rely on the protection of subsection (2) or (3) should inspect the public file under rule 93(1) at the same time as the register. A single request on PF 23/77 suffices for both.

SECTION 34

Rectification of register

34.01   **34.**—(1) The court may, on the application of any person aggrieved, order the register to be rectified by the making, or the variation or deletion, of any entry in it.

(2) In proceedings under this section the court may determine any question which it may be necessary or expedient to decide in connection with the rectification of the register.

(3) Rules of court may provide for the notification of any application under this section to the comptroller and for his appearance on the application and for giving effect to any order of the court on the application.

COMMENTARY ON SECTION 34

34.02   *General*

Section 34 provides for rectification by the court. It applies also to "existing patents" (Sched. 2, para. 1(2)). The section provides a remedy for wrongful refusal by the Comptroller to register a transaction, instrument or event under section 32, as discussed in para. 32.19; and also a remedy in respect of an entry in the register which should not have been made. As indicated in para. 32.32, errors in the register can be corrected by direct application to the Comptroller under rule 47 or rule 100, or (in the case of an "existing patent") under section 76 [1949].

It is uncertain whether a patent granted by the Comptroller *ultra vires, e.g.* because a time limit was not met which the Comptroller had no power to excuse (see *E's Applications,* [1983] RPC 231 (HL)), is a nullity and thus subject to rectification of the register; if the grant is merely voidable and not void, section 72(1) specifies the only grounds upon which it can be revoked, see para. 72.12.

It is not usual to apply for rectification of the register in revocation proceedings. Thus, the Comptroller need not be notified, but the practice is not necessarily sound, see para. 61.09. A court order for revocation should, however, be communicated to the Patent Office as if it were a court order for rectification.

34.03   *Forum for rectification*

Application for rectification of the register under section 34 must be made to the court. The "court" is defined in section 130, and, despite the fact that the register is kept in England (or Wales), the courts of Scotland, Northern Ireland and the Isle of Man appear also to have jurisdiction in addition to the Patents Court, see para. 96.24. The Civil Jurisdiction and Judgments Act 1982 (c. 27, by s. 17,

Sched. 5, para. 2 and Sched. 8, para. 4(2)), appears specifically to exclude provision for exclusive jurisdiction of any one court of the United Kingdom (excluding for this purpose the Isle of Man).

Applicant for rectification   **34.04**

An applicant for rectification under section 34 must be a "person aggrieved" (subs. (1)). This may be a person who has some proprietary interest in the patent in question, as in *Manning's Patent* ((1903) 20 RPC 74) where the purchaser of a share of a patent was held to be a person aggrieved by the entry of an assignment of a share purporting to have been made by someone who in fact was a bankrupt. However, the proprietor himself is not a "person aggrieved"; thus under analogous provisions in Ireland a patentee failed to rectify the register to delete a priority date claimed for his patent (*Beecham Group's Irish Application [Ireland]*, [1983] FSR 355).

Effect of rectification   **34.05**

A court order for rectification is given effect by serving a copy on the Comptroller, normally under rule 53, see para. 32.20. Rectification will not be ordered if the entry in the register, although incorrect when proceedings began, is no longer incorrect at the date of the hearing (*Manning's Patent, supra*).

PRACTICE UNDER SECTION 34

Procedure before the Patents Court   **34.06**

RSC Ord. 104, rule 22 (reprinted at para. E104.22) prescribes the practice to be followed on any application for rectification of the register made to the Patents Court. Application is made by originating motion, except in proceedings for a vesting order under section 51 of the Trustee Act 1925 (15 & 16 Geo. 5, c. 19) where it is made by originating summons. The applicant must forthwith serve a copy on the Comptroller (subs. (3) and RSC Ord. 104, r. 22(2)). The Comptroller then usually indicates (via the Treasury Solicitor) whether he wishes to appear and be heard. This generally depends on whether there is any other respondent to the application. If the Comptroller does appear, his costs become an issue in the proceedings as with any other party.

Proceedings by originating motion need not come before the judge for directions as to the conduct of the proceedings where the parties have agreed the pre-trial directions which should be given. These may be obtained from an associate of the Chancery Division in chambers (subject to his discretion to require the application to be made in court) by counsel or solicitors who represent all parties or represent any party and produce consents signed by those representing all other parties (*Practice Direction (Chancery Division: Motions Procedure)*, [1980] FSR 590, para. 9, applied to applications for rectification of the register of patents by *Practice Direction*, [1985] 1 All ER 192). Often such directions include provision for evidence to be given by affidavit with liberty to cross-examine the witnesses. The directions may include liberty to apply to the master if any further directions are required. The associate gives the necessary direction for setting the matter down in the appropriate list for hearing when the agreed pre-trial procedures have been completed.

34.07   *Effecting rectification of the register*

Rectification will follow automatically from a decision of the court when an office copy of the court order is transmitted to the Patent Office under rule 53, see para. 32.29. An order for revocation of the patent should be treated as an order for rectification of the register.

SECTION 35 [Repealed]

Evidence of register, documents, etc.

35.01   *[35.—(1) The register shall be prima facie evidence of anything required or authorised by this Act or rules to be registered and in Scotland shall be admissible and sufficient evidence of any such thing.*

(2) A certificate purporting to be signed by the comptroller and certifying that any entry which he is authorised by this Act or rules to make has or has not been made, or that any other thing which he is so authorised to do has or has not been done, shall be prima facie evidence, and in Scotland shall be admissible and sufficient evidence, of the matters so certified.

(3) Each of the following, that is to say—

(a) a copy of any entry in the register or of any document kept in the Patent Office, any specification of a patent or any application for a patent which has been published;

(b) a document reproducing in legible form an entry made in the register otherwise than in legible form; or

(c) an extract from the register or of any document mentioned in paragraph (a) or (b) above;

purporting to be certified by the comptroller and to be sealed with the seal of the Patent Office shall be admitted in evidence without further proof and without production of the original, and in Scotland such evidence shall be sufficient evidence.]

Note. Section 35 was repealed by the 1986 Act (s. 3 and Sched. 3) with effect from January 1, 1989 (Patents, Designs and Marks Act 1986 (Commencement No. 2) Order 1988, S.I. 1988 No. 1824). At the same time the provisions of this section were re-enacted in modified form in section 32(4)–(13). These provisions are discussed in paras. 32.15A, 32.21A and 32.36–32.38.

SECTION 36

Co-ownership of patents and applications for patents

36.01   **36.**—(1) Where a patent is granted to two or more persons, each of them shall, subject to any agreement to the contrary, be entitled to an equal undivided share in the patent.

(2) Where two or more persons are proprietors of a patent, then, subject to the provisions or this section and subject to any agreement to the contrary—

(*a*) each of them shall be entitled, by himself or his agents, to do in respect of the invention concerned, for his own benefit and without the consent of or the need to account to the other or others, any act which would apart from this subsection and section 55 below, amount to an infringement of the patent concerned; and

(*b*) any such act shall not amount to an infringement of the patent concerned.

(3) Subject to the provisions of sections 8 and 12 above and section 37 below and to any agreement for the time being in force, where two or more persons are proprietors of a patent one of them shall not without the consent of the other or others grant a licence under the patent or assign or mortgage a share in the patent or in Scotland cause or permit security to be granted over it.

(4) Subject to the provisions of those sections, where two or more persons are proprietors of a patent, anyone else may supply one of those persons with the means, relating to an essential element of the invention, for putting the invention into effect, and the supply of those means by virtue of this subsection shall not amount to an infringement of the patent.

(5) Where a patented product is disposed of by any of two or more proprietors to any person, that person and any other person claiming through him shall be entitled to deal with the product in the same way as if it had been disposed of by a sole registered proprietor.

(6) Nothing in subsection (1) or (2) above shall affect the mutual rights or obligations of trustees or of the personal representatives of a deceased person, or their rights or obligations as such.

(7) The foregoing provisions of this section shall have effect in relation to an application for a patent which is filed as they have in effect in relation to a patent and—

(*a*) references to a patent and a patent being granted shall accordingly include references respectively to any such application and to the application being filed; and

(*b*) the reference in subsection (5) above to a patented product shall be construed accordingly.

COMMENTARY ON SECTION 36

General   **36.02**

Section 36, in the absence of agreement to the contrary, defines the respective rights and obligations of co-owners of patents (except those who have become co-owners as trustees or personal representatives, see subs. (6)), and it also protects those who purchase patented articles from a co-owner or supply a co-owner with means for means for putting the patented invention into effect. Section 36 applies also to applications (subs. (7)) as well as to "existing patents" (Sched. 2, para. 1(2)) and to European patents (UK) and applications therefor (ss. 77(1), 78(2)).

Disputes between co-owners can be resolved by proceedings under section 37 or, in the case of an "existing patent", under unrepealed section 55 [1949] (discussed in para. A055.4).

36.03   *Prima facie entitlement of co-owners to equal undivided shares in patent*

Co-ownership of property generally may be as joint tenants, where the survivor acquires ownership of the whole automatically, or as tenants in common, where ownership of a deceased owner's share devolves on his personal representatives; and the share of a company which is dissolved becomes vested in the Crown as *bona vacantia*. The wording of subsection (1) provides that, unless otherwise agreed, two or more persons to whom a patent is granted hold it as tenants in common in equal shares. An allegation by a co-owner that he had a greater share was rejected on the evidence in *Florey's Patent* ([1962] RPC 186).

Trustees *inter se* hold property as joint tenants, and subsection (6) preserves their position in this respect. The existence of a possible constructive trust of ownership was in issue in *Kakker* v. *Szelke* ([1989] FSR 225; [1989] 4 EPOR 184 (CA)). For the registrability of equitable interests of this type, see para. 32.19.

Where joint proprietors acquire their interest after grant, the instrument by which they do so normally indicates whether they hold the property as tenants in common (and, if so, in what shares) or as joint tenants. The former is usual, and is implied in a business relationship or where the co-owners contribute unequally to the cost.

36.04   *Rights and freedom of each co-owner (subss. (2), (4) and (5))*

Subsection (2) provides that, unless they have agreed otherwise (and subject to the position of trustees or personal representatives under sub. (6)), none of the co-owners is accountable to the others for any act which would be an infringement of the patent. This excludes acts of Crown use, however, so that compensation under sections 55(4) and 57A (discussed at paras. 55.11, 57A.02–57A.07 and 58.05) is due to all the co-owners if one of them is authorised to use the invention for the services of the Crown (*Patchett's Patent*, [1963] RPC 90).

Subsections (4) and (5) save a supplier to one co-owner from being an indirect infringer under section 60(2) (discussed at para. 60.15) and also protect persons acquiring a patented product from one co-owner only. The protection extends to acts done before grant of the patent, see subsection (7)(*b*). "Patented product" is defined in s. 130(1) (discussed in para. 60.11). It includes a product to which a patented process has been applied, as well as the "products" of section 60(1)(*a*) and (*c*).

The rights of free use of the invention provided by subsection (2) are confined (unless otherwise agreed) to the co-owner and his agents. They extend neither to a sub-contractor nor to a partner of the co-owner, and he cannot form a company to exploit the invention on his behalf (*Howard & Bullough* v *Tweedales & Smalley*, (1895) 12 RPC 519).

36.05   *Rights not exercisable by co-owners individually without consent (sub. (3))*

Except where so directed by an order made in entitlement proceedings (see section 37(1)(*b*), discussed at para. 37.12) or (for an "existing patent") under section 55 [1949] (as discussed at para. A055.4), one co-owner cannot license the patent, or assign or mortgage his share in it, without the consent of all the others (subs. (3)). This prohibition is expressly reserved in sections 30(2) and (4) and 31(2). The consent given by other co-owners for the purpose of over-riding subsection (3) need not be in writing, but written evidence of it is required if the licence, assignment or mortgage is to be registered under section 32, see para. 32.30.

Rights against infringers   **36.06**

Each co-owner has the rights of the proprietor as regards infringement of the patent (section 66(1)), and one co-owner may sue for infringement, or claim compensation for Crown use, without joining the others as plaintiffs, as in *Turner* v. *Bowman* ((1925) 42 RPC 29) where the co-owner had exceeded his authority to act. In such circumstances another co-owner may himself be sued for infringement. In any case, other co-owners must be made parties to the proceedings, if only as nominal defendants, see sections 66(2) and 58(13), discussed at paras. 66.02 and 58.07, so that at least they have notice thereof.

PRACTICE UNDER SECTION 36   **36.07**

Section 36 provides only a basic framework of the rights and obligations of co-owners: this is often unsatisfactory in practice. Co-ownerhip should, therefore, only be entered into with an agreement between the co-owners which clearly defines the rights and obligations of each. The provisions of subsections (2) and (3) can be overriden by agreement (*Young* v. *Wilson*, (1955) 72 RPC 351), and this may be particularly important where one co-owner has facilities to work the invention himself but another can only do so by licensing a third party. An agreement between co-owners should indicate whether co-ownership is as tenants in common or joint tenants, see para. 36.03 *supra*, and it should define the responsibility for paying renewal fees, suing infringers and resisting revocation or compulsory licensing. The agreement should also state how any money which may be received from the patent by way of assignment, licensing, damages or compensation for Crown use is to be shared.

The possible dangers of failing to comply with obligations in a co-ownership agreement are illustrated by *BICC* v. *Burndy* ([1985] RPC 273 (CA)), where one party had failed to reimburse the other for renewal fees and was saved from having to relinguish its share in the patents only by the court exercising its discretion in equity against forfeiture.

SECTION 37   **37.01**

Determination of right of patent after grant

37.—(1) After a patent has been granted for an invention any person having or claiming a proprietary interest in or under the patent may refer to the comptroller the question—

(*a*) **who is or are the true proprietor or proprietors of the patent,**

(*b*) **whether the patent should have been granted to the person or persons to whom it was granted, or**

(*c*) **whether any right in or under the patent should be transferred or granted to any other person or persons;**

and the comptroller shall determine the question and make such order as he thinks fit to give effect to the determination.

[(**1**) *After a patent has been granted for an invention—*

(a) *any person may refer to the comptroller the question whether he is the true proprietor of the patent or whether the patent should have been granted to him (in either case alone or jointly with any other persons) or whether the patent or any right in or under it should be transferred to him (alone or jointly with any other persons); and*

(b) *any of two or more persons registered as joint proprietors of the patent may refer to the comptroller the question whether any right in or under the patent should be transferred or granted to any other person;*

and the comptroller shall determine the question and make such order as he thinks fit to give effect to the determination.]

(2) Without prejudice to the generality of subsection (1) above, an order under that subsection may contain provision—

(*a*) directing that the person by whom the reference is made under that subsection shall be included (whether or not to the exclusion of any other person) among the persons registered as proprietors of the patent;

(*b*) directing the registration of a transaction, instrument or event by virtue of which that person has acquired any right in or under the patent;

(*c*) granting any licence or other right in or under the patent;

(*d*) directing the proprietor of the patent or any person having any right in or under the patent to do anything specified in the order as necessary to carry out the other provisions of the order.

(3) If any person to whom directions have been given under subsection (2)(*d*) above fails to do anything necessary for carrying out any such directions within 14 days after the date of the order containing the directions, the comptroller may on application made to him by any person in whose favour or on whose reference the order containing the directions was made, authorise him to do that thing on behalf of the person to whom the directions were given.

(4) Where the comptroller finds on a reference under **this section** [*subsection (1)(a) above*] that the patent was granted to a person not entitled to be granted that patent (whether alone or with other persons) and on an application made under section 72 below makes an order on that ground for the conditional or unconditional revocation of the patent, the comptroller may order that the person by whom the application was made or his successor in title may, subject to section 76 below, make a new application for a patent—

(*a*) in the case of unconditional revocation, for the whole of the matter comprised in the specification of that patent; and

(*b*) in the case of conditional revocation, for the matter which in the opinion of the comptroller should be excluded from that specification by amendment under section 75 below;

and where such a new application is made, it shall be treated as having been filed on the date of filing the application for the patent to which the reference relates.

(5) On any such reference no order shall be made under this section transferring the patent to which the reference relates on the ground that the patent was granted to a person not so entitled, and no order shall be made under subsection (4) above on that ground, if the reference was made after the end of the period of two years beginning with the date of the grant, unless it is shown that any person registered as a proprietor of the patent knew at the time of the grant or, as the case may be, of the transfer of the patent to him that he was not entitled to the patent.

(6) An order under this section shall not be so made as to affect the mutual rights or obligations of trustees or of the personal representatives of a deceased person, or their rights or obligations as such.

(7) Where a question is referred to the comptroller under **this section** [*subsection (1)(a) above*] an order shall not be made by virtue of subsection (2) or under subsection (4) above on the reference unless notice of the reference is given to all persons registered as proprietor of the patent or as having a right in or under the patent, except those who are parties to the reference.

(8) If it appears to the comptroller on a reference under **this section** [*subsection (1) above*] that the question referred to him would more properly be determined by the court, he may decline to deal with it and, without prejudice to the court's jurisdiction to determine any such question and make a declaration, or any declaratory jurisdiction of the court in Scotland, the court shall have jurisdiction to do so.

(9) The court shall not in the exercise of any such declaratory jurisdiction determine a question whether a patent was granted to a person not entitled to be granted the patent if the proceedings in which the jurisdiction is invoked were commenced after the end of the period of two years beginning with the date of the grant of the patent, unless it is shown that any person registered as a proprietor of the patent knew at the time of the grant or, as the case may be, of the transfer of the patent to him that he was not entitled to the patent.

Note. Subsection (1) was prospectively replaced, with consequential amendment of subsections (4), (7) and (8), by the 1988 Act (Sched. 5, para. 9). For commencement of this amendment, see the latest Supplement to this Work *re.* this para.

RELEVANT RULES

Reference of question to the comptroller under section 37(1)(a)

54.—(1) A reference under section 37(1)(a) shall be made on Patents   **37.02**
Form No. 2/77 and shall be accompanied by a copy thereof and a statement in duplicate setting out fully the nature of the question, the facts upon which the person making the reference relies and the order which he is seeking.

(2) The comptroller shall send a copy of the reference and statement to every person who is not a party to the reference who is shown on the register as having any right in or under the patent. If any such person wishes to oppose the making of the order sought, he shall, within three months of the receipt of such copies, file in duplicate a counter-statement setting out fully the grounds of his opposition and the comptroller shall send a copy of the counter-statement to the person making the reference and to those recipients of the copy of the reference and statement who are not party to the counter-statement.

(3) The person making the reference or such recipients may, within three months of the receipt of the copy of the counter-statement, file evidence in support of his case and shall send a copy of the evidence to any person opposing the making of the order sought.

(4) Within three months of the receipt of the copy of such evidence or, if no such evidence is filed, within three months of the expiration of the time within which it might have been filed, any such person may file evidence in support of his case and shall send a copy of that evidence to the person making the reference and such recipients; and within three months of the receipt of the copy of that evidence, the person making the reference or any such recipient may file further evidence confined to matters strictly in reply and shall a copy of it to any such person.

(5) No further evidence shall be filed by either party except by leave or direction of the comptroller.

(6) The comptroller may give such directions as he may think fit with regard to the subsequent procedure.

Note. This rule will require some amendment when the amendments to section 37 are brought into effect, for which see para. 37.01 *supra.* The latest Supplement to this Work *re.* this para. should therefore be consulted.

Reference by joint proprietors under section 37(1)(b)

37.03   **55.**—(1) A reference under section 37(1)(*b*) shall be made on Patents Form No. 2/77 and shall be accompanied by a copy thereof and a statement in duplicate setting out fully the nature of the question, the facts relied upon by the co-proprietor making the reference and the order which he is seeking.

(2) The comptroller shall send a copy of the reference and statement to each of the co-proprietors other than those who are party to the making of the reference or have indicated their consent to the making of the order sought and if any recipient of the copies wishes to oppose the order sought, he shall, within three months of their receipt, file a counter-statement in duplicate setting out fully the grounds of his opposition and the comptroller shall send a copy of the counter-statement to each of the co-proprietors who are party to the reference and to all other co-proprietors who have not indicated that they consent to the making of the order sought.

(3) Any co-proprietor who is party to the reference or has not indicated such consent may, within three months of the receipt of the copy of the counter-statement, file evidence in support of his case and shall send a copy of the evidence to the opposing co-proprietor.

(4) Within three months of the receipt of the copy of such evidence or, if no such evidence is filed, within three months of the expiration of the time within which it might have been filed, the opposing co-proprietor may file evidence in support of his case and shall send a copy of that evidence to each co-proprietor who is party to the reference or has not indicated such consent and, within three months of the receipt of the copy of that evidence, any such person may file further evidence confined to matters strictly in reply and shall send a copy of it to the opposing co-proprietor.

(5) No further evidence shall be filed by either party except by leave or direction of the comptroller.

(6) The comptroller may give such directions as he may think fit with regard to the subsequent procedure.

Note. The *Note* to para. 37.02 *supra* applies likewise to rule 55.

Application under section 37(3)

56.—(1) An application under section 37(3) for authority to do anything **37.04** on behalf of a person to whom directions have been given under section 37(2)(*d*) shall be made on Patents Form No. 3/77 and shall be accompanied by a copy thereof and a statement setting out fully the facts upon which the applicant relies and the nature of the authorisation sought.

(2) The comptroller shall send a copy of the application and statement to the person alleged to have failed to comply with the directions.

(3) The comptroller may give such directions as he may think fit with regard to the subsequent procedure.

Time limit for new application

57. Where the comptroller orders that a new application may be made **37.05** under section 37(4), it shall be made within three months calculated from the day on which the time for appealing from that order expires without an appeal being brought or, where an appeal is brought, from the day on which it is finally disposed of.

Note to Relevant Rules **37.06**

For applications filed under section 37(4), rule 26 (reprinted at para. 15.05), rule 33(4) (reprinted in para. 18.02), and the proviso to rule 34 (reprinted in para. 18.03) are also relevant.

ARTICLE **37.07**

M. G. Harman, "Disputed entitlement to patent", (1986–87) 16 CIPA 274.

COMMENTARY ON SECTION 37

37.08 *General*

Subsections (1)–(7) provide for the determination by the Comptroller of questions of entitlement to granted patents which have been referred to him under section 37. Because section 9 provides that entitlement proceedings initiated under section 8, but not determined before the application has proceeded to grant, are then to be continued under section 37, this section tends in practice to govern the determination of most entitlement disputes and the relief available thereunder, but see section 12 for such proceedings concerning foreign applications (including European and international applications, as limited by section 82 in the case of European applications).

Section 37 applies also to granted European patents (UK), but it does not apply to "existing patents" (Sched. 2, para. 1(2)). Section 55 [1949] continues to apply to disputes between co-owners of such patents (for which see the commentary thereon in Appendix A). Also, if an "existing patent" can be shown to have been granted to a person having no entitlement thereto, a ground of revocation ensues under section 32(1)(*b*) [1949], for which see para. A032.08.

The courts have a concurrent jurisdiction, see para. 37.09 *infra*, and proceedings under the section can be heard in Scotland (r. 1088, reprinted at para. 98.02 and discussed in para. 98.07).

Any decision of the Comptroller under the section is appealable to the Patents Court (s. 97(1)), or (if heard in Scotland) to the Court of Session (s. 97(4)), and thereafter, with leave, to the Court of Appeal or to the Inner House of the Court of Session, whether or not a question of law is involved (s. 97(3) and (5)).

A decision under the section that a patent has been granted to a person not entitled under the Act to be granted the patent, or a share thereof, can lead to its revocation under section 72(1)(*b*). However, section 72(2) makes entitlement proceedings (either under s. 37, or in declaratory proceedings before the court) a prerequisite to an application for revocation under section 72(1)(*b*) and such application can only be brought by a person who is successful in these proceedings, see *Dolphin Showers* v. *Farmiloe* ([1989] FSR 1). This case also decided that this prohibition against revocation could, in effect, be overcome by putting validity of the patent in issue under section 74(1), if necessary by taking advantage of section 74(5), but then only by a person alleging that the patent should, on the facts as they existed at the date of grant, have been granted to him, a post-grant assignment being ineffective for this purpose.

Subsection (1) was prospectively amended by the 1988 Act (see note to para. 37.01 *supra*) as a consequence of the parallel amendment to be made to section 72(1)(*b*) which has failed to provide adequately for a situation involving joint inventors and/or proprietors, where only some of those so named properly give rise to entitlement to grant. This situation had arisen, but was avoided, in *Pelling and Campbell's Application* (SRIS O/134/87). It is surprising, however, that sections 8(1) and 12(1) are not to be amended similarly to subsection (1), in view of their original similar wording, but one explanation could be that these two sections concern entitlement disputes determined pre-grant, rather than post-grant.

37.09 *Scope of section 37*

Section 37 complements sections 8 and 12 which relate to entitlement proceedings before grant. In its original form, subsection (1) provided (like ss. 8(1) and 12(1)) for two circumstances, *viz.* (*a*) where the person referring the matter to the

Comptroller ("the referrer") seeks to have the patent, or any right in or under it, transferred to him, alone or jointly with others; or (*b*) where any of two or more proprietors seek to have a right in or under the patent transferred or granted to some other person.

In its new form, subsection (1) will be cast more in the form of types of question referred to the Comptroller for determination, the first two corresponding to (*a*), and the third to (*b*), above. These questions can be posed by any person "having or claiming a property right in or under the patent" and this "referrer" may seek determination of questions as to: (*a*) who is or are the true proprietor(s) of the patent; or (*b*) whether the patent should have been granted to the person(s) to whom it was granted; or (*c*) whether any right in or under the patent should be transferred or granted to any other person(s). The Comptroller's primary duty is, therefore, to determine these questions and to declare accordingly. He may "make such order as he thinks fit" to give effect to that determination.

It must, however, be realised that, while a referrer may show that he is an inventor of (part of) the subject matter claimed, so that the person(s) granted the patent may not have (full) entitlement thereto, the referrer['s own rights may be subjugated to those of his employer at the time the invention was made having regard to the provisions of section 39. Thus, in *Hopkins' Application* (SRIS O/83/88), a referrer was held to be entitled to be named as a co-inventor, but whether the resulting co-proprietorship should be to the referrer or to his employer was left to be decided after further submissions. Also, the provisions of section 36 (*Co-ownership of patents*) need to be borne in mind, see the commentary thereon.

Subsection (2) sets out four particular types of relief which the Comptroller is, *inter alia*, empowered to grant. These are orders: (*a*) that the referrer should become a proprietor of the patent, perhaps to the exclusion of (all) others; (*b*) directing the registration of a transaction, instrument or event by which the referred has acquired a right in or under the patent; (*c*) directing the grant of a licence or other right in or under the patent; and (*d*) directing any person having any right in or under the patent to perform the directions of the order. This last-named power is supported by subsection (3) which permits the Comptroller to authorise the beneficiary of the order to perform the required act on behalf of a person who has been directed, but has failed to do so. The procedure is governed by rule 56 and is discussed in para. 37.14 *infra*.

Subsection (4), like sections 8(3) and 12(6), provides for a referrer, in certain circumstances, to be permitted to file a replacement application in respect of matter found to have been improperly granted to another: this is discussed further in para. 37.11 *infra*.

Where an order is made for the transfer of proprietor of the patent, section 38 comes into play with respect to licences already granted under the patent and to persons who, in good faith, had made "effective and serious" preparations to work the patent, see the commentary thereon. Also, if any order is to be made under subsection (2) or (4), all persons who are named in the register as having an interest in or under the patent, if not already parties to the proceedings, are to be notified by the Comptroller (subs. (7)). Further, no order is to be made under the section which affects the mutual rights and obligations of trustees or of personal representatives (subs. (6)). This suggests that probate disputes are not to be decided by the Comptroller.

Subsection (5) imposes a time limit on the powers of the Comptroller under the section, and a similar time bar is imposed on the court by subsection (9). This may have the effect of severely limiting the relief which can be granted in cases of improper grant due to a wrongful claim to entitlement and is discussed in para. 37.13 *infra*.

The power of the Comptroller under the section does not, however, include the provision of a priority date which was not claimed at the date of filing the application. Thus, in a case where it was alleged that an earlier application had been filed in contravention of rights and an application to revoke the patent was pending, the Comptroller refused to allow the later application to proceed because of anticipation by publication of a foreign specification corresponding to the allegedly improper application, and held that there was no power to overcome this by effective back-dating of the application (*Georgia Pacific's Application*, [1984] RPC 468). However, where the referrer was held entitled to file a replacement application for an application which had been abandoned, but which had served as a priority document for a second application, the referrer was allowed to file also a replacement application for the second application so that this could claim priority from the first replacement application (*Amateur Athletic Association's Applications*, SRIS O/53/89; and *Coin Control's Application*, SRIS O/95/89).

37.10 *Powers of the court to determine entitlement disputes*

Section 37 does not exclude application to the court for a declaration or other relief concerning ownership of a patent or application for which it has relevant jurisdiction, and the Comptroller may decline to deal with a question referred to him under subsection (1) and consequently require reference thereof to the court (subs. (8)). Whether he does so is, however, a matter to be decided by the Comptroller of his own motion (*Brockhouse's Patent*, [1985] RPC 322), see para. 8.08.

The section imposes two statutory limitations on the jurisdiction of a court. Firstly, subsection (9) imposes a time bar for exercising its declaratory jurisdiction, see para. 37.13. Secondly, for entitlement issues which involve a foreign element, the court may not have, or may decline to exercise, jurisdiction if the question is one more appropriate to be dealt with by a foreign court, see *GAF Corp.* v. *Amchem* ([1975] 1 Lloyds Rep. 601). This is particularly so if the Civil Jurisdiction and Judgments Act 1982 (c. 27) (in force in the United Kingdom since January 1, 1987 and now for all EEC Member States other than Denmark, Greece, Portugal and Spain) should apply. Under this Act, a defendant, unless an exception applies, has to be sued in a court of his domicile in the sense of habitual residence. One such exception is to provide exclusive jurisdiction to a national court in proceedings concerned with validity or registration of patents (Sched. 1, art. 16(4)). However, it has been held that this provision has no applicability to questions of patent entitlement (*Duijnstee* v. *Goderbauer (Case 288/82)*, [1985] FSR 221; [1985] 1 CMLR 220 (ECJ)).

The "court" for such purposes is one defined in section 130(1) and is not necessarily the Patents Court: other courts, including courts in Scotland, Northern Ireland and the Isle of Man, have a concurrent jurisdiction, see para. 96.14, provided that there is an appropriate connection of at least one of the parties with such jurisdiction, this now also being regulated by the above-mentioned 1982 Act.

Normally, reference from the Comptroller under subsection (8) would be to the Patents Court, for which see para. 37.16 *infra*. However, if the Comptroller should think it appropriate, the question(s) arising under subsection (1) could be referred to another defined court, for which see para. 96.14; alternatively, the Comptroller could simply decline to deal with the question, leaving the referrer to seek relief from the court of his choice.

While the court has an inherent jurisdiction to grant relief by way of a declaration of rights, the powers of the court otherwise to deal with wrongly claimed entitlement are not clear. On general principles, it is thought that the court could grant any relief of the types specifically available to the Comptroller under subsection (2), but presumably the court would not have power to permit filing of a replacement application under subsection (4). In particular, there would seem to be no reason in principle why the court should not hold that a patent is held on some form of trust for the benefit of one or more others, see *Kakkar* v. *Szelke* ([1989] FSR 225 (CA)).

Filing of replacement application after order for revocation (subs. (4))   **37.11**

Under subsection (4), if the Comptroller finds that the patent was granted to a person not entitled to it (or to all of it), then the person or persons found by the Comptroller to be entitled to the patent can make an application under section 72(1)(*b*) to revoke the patent (or part of it), though only after the decision on entitlement has been made by the Comptroller or the court (s. 72(2)(*a*)). If the Comptroller than makes an order for conditional or unconditional revocation of the patent, he may permit the person or persons making the revocation application to make a new application for a patent, which will be treated as having been made on the same date as the original patent application (subs. (4)).

The proviso to rule 34 (reprinted in para. 18.03) requires any such replacement application to be treated as refused if it does not comply with the Act and Rules within four years and six months from the declared priority date, or (if none) the date of filing, of the original application upon which the (partially) revoked patent was granted, or within 18 months from the actual date of filing of the replacement application, whichever period expires the later. Thus, normally, the 18 month limit from the actual filing date will apply for placing the replacement application in compliance with the Act and Rules under section 20(1). However, this period may be too short, see *Robert Bion's Patent* (SRIS O/66/86, *noted* IPD 9068). Applications under the provision were permitted (in proceedings commenced under s. 8) in *Jessamine Holdings' Patent* (SRIS O/138/85), *Viziball's Application* (SRIS O/23/87) and *Miller and Low's Application* (SRIS O/4/86).

Any replacement application filed under subsection (4) cannot proceed if it contains any additional matter over that contained in the original, improperly filed, application, see section 76(1) discussed in paras. 76.06 and 76.09. However, the section is not listed in section 76 and hence there is no direct prohibition against the claims of the replacement application extending the protection conferred by the (improperly granted) patent. Because subsection (4), therefore, in effect by-passes the general prohibition against permissible amendments extending the scope of a granted patent, the Comptroller has indicated that relief under the subsection should only be considered if no other satisfactory order can be found (*Szucs' Application (No. 2)*, SRIS O/27/88); and in *X Ltd.'s Application* ([1982] FSR 143), broadening was not allowed under the analogous section 53 [1949] even though not directly prohibited by the 1949 Act.

In any case, because the Comptroller has power under subsection (2)(*a*) to add or exclude proprietors, it is not evident in what circumstances it may be desirable or necessary to adopt the procedure of subsection (4) to revoke the patent as a whole and then permit a new application to be made, though the procedure is clearly appropriate when a person is held to be entitled to part only of the patent. Such a situation was dealt with in *Szucs' Application* (SRIS O/4/86 and O/27/88) discussed in para. 37.12 *infra*.

Section 72(1)(*b*) is discussed in para. 7.09 as well as in para. 72.17. As section 72(2)(*a*) states that an application for revocation on the ground specified in section 72(1)(*b*), which is the ground relevant to section 37, can be made only by a person who "has been found" by the Comptroller to be entitled to the patent or a part of it on a reference to him of a matter under section 37, it would appear that the procedure first requires the reference to be made to the Comptroller under section 37, or to the court under its inherent jurisdiction, for the question of entitlement to be determined, and then to make the application for revocation under section

72(1)(*b*). It is not clear whether at that juncture the Comptroller will issue the order which he is required to make, under subsection (1), to give effect to his determination of the matter, or whether he will indicate to the person or persons referring the matter to him that, subject to the outcome of an application under section 72(1)(*b*), he will issue an appropriate order giving effect to the proceedings under both sections. However, if all the relevant persons have been parties to the section 37 proceedings, or their equivalent before the court, the revocation proceedings under section 72(1)(*b*) can only be a formality because the doctrine of *res judicata* would prevent the entitlement question from being relitigated in the revocation proceedings and, accordingly, the proprietor would appear not to be competent to oppose the application for revocation.

37.12   *Relief granted under section 37*

It must first be noted that, to establish entitlement to relief under section 37, the onus of proof, as in proceedings under sections 8 and 12, lies firmly with the referrer. Several cases have failed on a conflict of evidence because the referrer was then held to have failed to establish a case for relief. For examples of such cases, see para. 8.08.

In *James Industries' Patent* ([1987] RPC 235) and *Hook's Patent* (SRIS O/70/87) applications under section 37 were combined with applications under section 72 so that, if the referrer failed to establish entitlement, the patent might nevertheless not be an obstacle to his commercial activities. In the *James* case both applications failed, the entitlement proceedings because the referrer failed to establish an unconditional acceptance of an oral offer of an agreement between the parties for sharing of patent rights; but in *Hook's* case the plea for the revocation succeeded after a finding under section 37 that the proprietor was entitled only to part ownership because his employer had provided other persons to assist him in developing his personal invention. Also, in *Norris's Patent* ([1980] RPC 159), though the referrer failed to establish that he was entitled to the patent in substitution of the original applicant/proprietor, he was held to have contributed to a significant aspect of the claimed invention and therefore entitled to become a co-proprietor of the patent which had by then been granted. Subsequently, the referrer claimed that the original applicant's share should be assigned to their then common employer (*Norris's Patent (No. 2)*, SRIS O/179/88) and it was held no issue estoppel excluded such a claim as the original proceedings had only concerned the referrer's own entitlement.

In *Robert Bion's Patent* (SRIS O/66/86, *noted* IPD 9068) two features of claim 1 were held to have been respectively invented by employees of different companies then collaborating with each other. The non-applicant company was ordered to become a co-proprietor under subsection (2)(*a*). Had the collaborative development been that of a sub-claim, it would appear that a licence to the referrer would have been ordered under subsection (2)(*c*).

In *Szucs' Application* (SRIS O/4/86) a declaration was made (under s. 8(1)) that certain defined subject matter had been invented during the course of the applicant's former employment and that, accordingly, that subject matter belonged to his former employer. The section 8 proceedings were then continued under section 37 with the request that the employer should become sole proprietor under subsection (2)(*a*), or become a licensee under subsection (2)(*c*), possible relief under subsection (4) being rejected for the reason explained in para. 37.11 *supra*. Sole proprietorship was rejected and co-proprietorship was held to be unattractive, and it was decided that the patent should remain in the sole ownership of the inventor, but that that former employer should be granted a free licence under the patent.

In *Rosin Engineering's Patent* (SRIS O/9/89, *noted* IPD 12023) the referrer was held to have failed to make out its claim to proprietorship. However, because the Patentee may have acknowledged that the referrer had some right under the patent, the referrer was given an opportunity to file further evidence as to whether such right established an equitable entitlement to a licence under the patent.

From the similarity of the wording of section 36(1) and section 54(1) [1949], it would appear that the decision in *Florey's Patent* ([1962] RPC 186) would still be relevant. In that case the Comptroller ordered that one of the proprietors should join in the sale of the patent desired by the others and it was held that the order could not be inconsistent with section 54 [1949], and that each proprietor should share equally in the proceeds of the sale.

Time bar for orders under section 37 (subss. (5) and (9))   **37.13**

Subsection (5) corresponds to CPCa. 27 and imposes a time limit of two years from grant on a reference to the Comptroller under section 37 for an order transferring the patent in suit on the ground that it was granted to a person not entitled thereto. Subsection (9) was presumably intended to impose the same time limit on the court's exercise of its declaratory jurisdiction, but the provision may be limited by the phrase "declaratory jurisdiction" which refers back to subsection (8) where that phrase is used with reference only to proceedings referred by the Comptroller to the court in Scotland. However, the better view is surely that this phrase is used in subsection (9) in its general sense of referring to the inherent jurisdiction to grant declaratory relief of any "court" within the meaning defined therefor by section 130(1), for which see para. 96.14 and para. 37.10 *supra*.

This time bar is mirrored in sections 72(2)(*b*) and 74(4)(*b*) which provide respectively that revocation and challenge to validity, each under section 72(1)(*b*), is only to be entertained if entitlement proceedings (under s. 37 or before the court under its inherent jurisdiction) have been brought within two years from the grant of the patent, unless it is shown that any registered proprietor "knew" at the date of grant that he was not entitled to be granted the patent. However, section 74(5) does permit entitlement proceedings to be raised outside this time limit for the purpose of putting validity in issue, though apparently not for the purpose of seeking revocation, if the court or Comptroller "thinks it just to do so", see para. 74.05. This two year limit appears to arise from CPCa. 27, but that refers only to a bar on raising questions of entitlement and the prohibitions of sections 72(2)(*b*) and 74(4)(*b*) are not to be found, as such, in either the EPC or CPC, see EPCa. 138(1)(*e*) and CPCa. 57(1)(*e*). This may explain the presence of section 74(5) in the Act. Nevertheless it is not clear that section 74(5) can be invoked to commence entitlement proceedings after the two year period.

It is also not clear what is meant by "knew". In particular, clarification is awaited as to whether the test is subjective or objective. Thus, despite *Peart's Patent (infra)*, it is still unclear whether a proprietor can be "fixed" with the appropriate knowledge by the prospective referrer making an allegation of proprietorship entitlement, and what the effect is where such an allegation is dismissed by the proprietor without investigation and/or without taking legal advice.

In *Peart's Patent* (SRIS O/209/87) an application under section 37 to transfer ownership of the patent was refused on other grounds but the Comptroller stated that anyway he would have refused it as being made more than two years after its grant. He said that knowledge by the proprietor that the referrer was disputing proprietorship was not sufficient to excuse the lapse of more than two years, and that the onus was on the referrer to establish that the proprietor knew that he was not entitled to the grant, but did not elaborate on the degree of knowledge that the referrer would need to establish. The evidential mountain that a referrer must climb may thus be a high one, but it is submitted that the public interest is clearly that patents improperly granted should be capable of being challenged in order to render them ineffective. Consequently, it is thought, at least under section 74(5), there should be no fetter in practice on a challenge to validity for lack of entitlement to grant because, otherwise, the provisions of sections 37(5) and (9), 72(2)(*b*) and 74(4)(*b*) would, conceptually at least, appear to be *ultra vires* the Treaty of Rome, see the discussion on "no challenge" clauses in patent licence agreements in Appendix D at para. D23.

For additional discussion on the effect of the two year limit on proceedings under section 37 and the meaning of "knew" in sections 37(5) and (9), 72(2)(*b*) and 74(4)(*b*), see the article by M. G. Harman listed in para. 37.07 *supra* and paras. 72.17 and 74.05. Also, the suggestion has been made ((1980–81) 10 CIPA 254) that it may be possible to circumvent this time bar by application under section 34 to rectify the register rather than seek relief for wrongful entitlement under sections 37, 72 and/or 74.

Perhaps a better way round the time bar, in appropriate circumstances, would be to contend that the patent is held by its legal owner on a constructive trust for the referrer-beneficiary, who may then apply to the court: (*a*) to terminate the trust; (*b*) to order the trustee to assign the patent to the equitable owner, the beneficiary; and (*c*) to order the trustee to account to the beneficiary for the profits that have accrued from the trust. If viable, this procedure would seem to have a considerable added advantage over filing a new application under section 37(4). Thus, it would avoid the problem involved in suing the grantee-trustee for infringement: since the original patent would (under s. 72(1)(*b*)) be revoked, and revoked *ab initio*, the owner of the *new* patent would seem to be disabled from suing the original patentee for infringement in respect of acts committed before its grant, and (under s. 69) for damages in respect of acts committed after publication of the *new* application.

Neither section 37 nor the rules set any time limit for filing the application for revocation consequent on a finding under section 37, but under rule 54(6) (reprinted in para. 37.02 *supra*) the Comptroller has a general discretion with regard to the procedure subsequent to formal filing of evidence in the matter referred to him, and therefore has power to impose a time limit.

Practice under Section 37

37.14 *Proceedings under section 37 before the Comptroller*

The powers and duties of the Comptroller under section 37 to determine questions of entitlement to a patent, and to issue an order to give effect to his decision, are closely parallel to his powers and duties under section 8 in connection with a United Kingdom application and under section 12 in connection with an application in a foreign country. A reference to the Comptroller under any of these sections is made on PF 2/77 (reprinted at para. 141.02), and the procedure applicable under section 37 under rules 54 and 55 (reprinted respectively at paras. 37.02 and 37.03 *supra*) is analogous to that under these sections, rule 54 corresponding to rule 7 (applicable under ss. 8(1)(*a*) and 12(1)(*a*)) and rule 55 corresponding to rule 8 (applicable under ss. 8(1)(*b*) and 12(1)(*b*)). Likewise, an applicant not residing in the United Kingdom may be required to give security for costs (s. 107(4)).

In each case the reference on PF 2/77 is accompanied by a statement and copies are sent to relevant parties. If the person notified wishes, he may oppose the making of the order sought by filing a counter-statement. There is no formal entry of opposition, no prescribed form and no fee. Periods of three months are allowed to the parties for the filing of evidence, and subsequent procedure is at the discretion of the Comptroller. The procedure is considered in rather more detail in para. 8.12.

If a person to whom directions have been given fails to carry them out within 14 days of the order, the Comptroller can be requested on PF 3/77 (reprinted at para. 141.03) to authorise the person in whose favour the order was made to do anything necessary himself (ss. 8(5), 37(3)). The procedure is set out in rule 56 (reprinted at para. 37.04 *supra*). This is similar to rule 11 for the corresponding request under section 8, see para. 8.13.

Notice of the making of a reference under any of sections 8(1), 12(1) or 37(1) is entered in the register with such other information relating to the reference as the Comptroller thinks fit, though subject to rule 44 (*i.e.* not before the application is published under section 16), see rule 51 (reprinted at para. 32.10). Applications under subsection (1), and the eventual outcome thereof, are now also advertised in the O.J., see O.J. November 1988: a complete back-list of such applications was published O.J. November 16, 1988.

Filing of replacement application under subsection (4)   **37.15**

Where a replacement application is permitted to be filed under subsection (4), for which see para. 37.11, rule 57 (reprinted at para. 37.05 *supra*) requires this to be filed within three months calculated from the day on which the time for appealing the order under section 37 expires, or if appeal is brought from the day when that appeal is finally disposed of. Under section 29(1), and the proviso to rule 34 (reprinted in para. 18.03), any such application has to be placed in compliance with the Act and Rules within 18 months from its actual date of filing, unless the normal period of four years and six months from the declared priority date (or, if none, the deemed date of filing) should expire later. Nevertheless, if an appeal to the court has been brought before the end of this acceptance period, such period can be extended at the court's discretion under section 20(2)(*a*).

In any case, it is necessary to file with any such application the requests for search (on PF 9/77) and examination (on PF 10/77) as well as ensuring that an abstract and the claims have been filed. Copies of the inventorship statement (on PF 7/77), the priority document(s) and any necessary verified translations thereof must, in practice, also be filed with the application, see para. 15.22, or within such extended times as the Rules may permit, for which see paras. 15.15–15.21.

Procedure before the court in entitlement proceedings   **37.16**

If the Comptroller refers a question under the section to the court under subsection (8), then a person entitled to do so, *i.e.* a party to the proceedings before the Comptroller (assuming a reference to the English High Court is chosen) is required by RSC Ord. 104, rule 17 (reprinted at para. E104.17) to bring the proceedings before the Patents Court by originating summons within 28 days of the Comptroller's decision. However, presumably, proceedings for a declaration may be commenced before the court at any time under its inherent jurisdiction, but the relief available may then be curtailed, see para. 37.10 *supra*.

Any application for the rectification of the register (as a possible alternative method of proceeding, as suggested in para. 37.13 *supra*) would (if brought before the Patents Court) be brought by originating motion under RSC Ord. 104, rule 22 (reprinted at para. E104.22), while an application for revocation (brought before the Patents Court) is brought by petition under RSC Ord. 104, rule 4 (reprinted at para. E104.04).

38.01   SECTION 38

Effect of transfer of patent under section 37

38.—(1) Where an order is made under section 37 above that a patent shall be transferred from any person or persons (the old proprietor or proprietors) to one or more persons (whether or not including an old proprietor), then, except in a case falling within subsection (2) below, any licences or other rights granted or created by the old proprietor or proprietors shall, subject to section 33 above and to the provisions of the order, continue in force and be treated as granted by the person or persons to whom the patent is ordered to be transferred (the new proprietor or proprietors).

(2) Where an order is so made that a patent shall be transferred from the old proprietor or proprietors to one or more persons none of whom was an old proprietor (on the ground that the patent was granted to a person not entitled to be granted the patent), any licences or other rights in or under the patent shall, subject to the provisions of the order and subsection (3) below, lapse on the registration of that person or those persons as the new proprietor or proprietors of the patent.

(3) Where an order is so made that a patent shall be transferred as mentioned in subsection (2) above or that a person other than an old proprietor may make a new application for a patent and before the reference of the question under that section resulting in the making of any such order is registered, the old proprietor or proprietors or a licensee of the patent, acting in good faith, worked the invention in question in the United Kingdom or made effective and serious preparations to do so, the old proprietor or proprietors or the licensee shall, on making a request to the new proprietor or proprietors within the prescribed period, be entitled to be granted a licence (but not an exclusive licence) to continue working or, as the case may be, to work the invention, so far as it is the subject of the new application.

(4) Any such licence shall be granted for a reasonable period and on reasonable terms.

(5) The new proprietor or proprietors of the patent or any person claiming that he is entitled to be granted any such lience may refer to the comptroller the question whether that person is so entitled and whether any such period is or terms are reasonable, and the comptroller shall determine the question and may, if he considers it appropriate, order the grant of such a licence.

RELEVANT RULES

Request under section 38(3)

58.—(1) Where an order is made under section 37 that a patent shall be **38.02**
transferred to one or more persons none of whom was an old proprietor of
it or that a person other than an old proprietor may make a new application
for a patent, a request under section 38(3) for the grant of a licence to continue working or, as the case may be, to work the invention shall, in the
case of any of the old proprietors, be made within two months, and in the
case of a licensee, four months, of his being notified by the comptroller of
the making of the order.
(2) Where such an order is made, the comptroller shall notify the old
proprietor or proprietors, and their licensees of whom he is aware, of the
making of the order.

Reference to comptroller under section 38(5)

59.—(1) Where a question is referred to the comptroller under section **38.03**
38(5) as to whether any person is entitled to be granted a licence or
whether the period or terms of a licence are reasonable, the reference shall
be made on Patents Form No. 5/77 and shall be accompanied by a copy
thereof and a statement in duplicate setting out fully the fact upon which
the person making the reference relies and the terms of the licence which
he is prepared to accept or grant.
(2) The comptroller shall send a copy of the reference and statement to
the new proprietor or proprietors and every person claiming to be entitled
to be granted a licence, in either case not being the person who makes the
reference, and if any recipient does not agree to grant or accept a licence
for such period and upon such terms, he shall, within three months of their
receipt, file a counter-statement in duplicate setting out fully the grounds
of his objection and the comptroller shall send a copy of the counter-
statement to the person making the reference.
(3) The comptroller may give such directions as he may think fit with
regard to the subsequent procedure.

COMMENTARY ON SECTION 38 **38.04**

Section 38 is the counterpart of section 11; section 11 deals with licences and other
rights where the Comptroller has made an order changing the proprietorship of an
application and section 38 deals correspondingly with such matters where an order
has been made under section 37 changing the proprietorship of a patent.
Where an order has been made under section 37 affecting proprietorship, the
position with respect to any licences or other rights depends upon whether or not
the new proprietor(s) include the old proprietor(s) or any of them.
Subsection (1) deals with the case where the new proprietor(s) include the, or at
least one of the, old proprietor(s); in this case any existing licences or other rights

will continue in force, and will be treated as having been granted by the new proprietor(s).

Subsection (2) deals with the case where the new proprietors do not include the old proprietors or any of them; in this case any licences or rights cease as from the date of registration of the new proprietors. However, in these circumstances, under subsection (3), as under sections 11(3) and (4), an old proprietor or his licensee who, acting in good faith, had worked the invention in the United Kingdom or made effective and serious preparations to do so before the entitlement proceedings commenced is entitled, on request to the new proprietors, to be granted a non-exclusive licence to continue to work or to work the invention for a reasonable period and on reasonable terms (ss. 38(3), (4)); these provisions of section 38 also apply to a patent resulting from a new application filed under section 37(4). The terms "good faith" and "effective and serious preparations" also arise in sections 28A(4) and 64(1) and are discussed particularly in paras. 28A.05 and 64.05.

Under subsection (5) the new proprietor or the person making the request can refer to the Comptroller the question of whether or not the request is justified, and the Comptroller can then decide the matter, including the terms of the licence, and may order the grant of a licence. No time limit is set for the making of the reference. If, as a result of a reference under section 8, 12 or 37, an employer-owned patent resulting from an employee's invention were transferred to a third party who is not a person connected with the employer, the employee's rights to compensation under section 40 would be lost, see para. 41.05. However, it would seem that an order to transfer ownership would not be retroactive and thus such an employee could rely on any right to compensation which had accrued up to the date of the order for transfer.

38.05   Practice under Section 38

Any request under subsection (3) by an old proprietor or a licensee thereof must be made within the period prescribed by rule 58 (reprinted at para. 38.02 *supra*), that is within two months from the date of the order if made by an old proprietor and four months if made by a former licensee. These periods are, however, extensible at the Comptroller's discretion under rule 110(1), for which see para. 123.35. Since the request is to be made directly to the new proprietor, no form is specified for the request. Nor is it required that the Comptroller be notified of the request, though it may be prudent to do so, but the request would then become of public record on the file of the patent. Rule 58 is analogous to rule 9 (reprinted at para. 8.04 and discussed in para. 11.04).

Any reference to the Comptroller, either by the new proprietor or the person seeking a licence, is to be made on PF 5/77 (reprinted at para. 141.05) under rule 59 (reprinted at para. 38.03 *supra*). This rule is analogous to rule 13 (reprinted at para. 11.02 and discussed in para. 11.06).

39.01   SECTION 39

Right to employees' inventions

39.—(1) Notwithstanding anything in any rule of law, an invention made by an employee shall, as between him and his employer, be taken to belong to his employer for the purposes of this Act and all other purposes if—

   (*a*) it was made in the course of the normal duties of the employer or in the course of duties falling outside his normal duties, but specifically assigned to him, and the circumstances in either case were such that an invention might reasonably be expected to result from the carrying out of his duties; or

(b) the invention was made in the course of the duties of the employee and, at the time of making the invention, because of the nature of his duties and the particular responsibilities arising from the nature of his duties he had a special obligation to further the interests of the employer's undertaking.

(2) Any other invention made by an employee shall, as between him and his employer, be taken for those purposes to belong to the employee.

(3) Where by virtue of this section an invention belongs, as between him and his employer, to an employee, nothing done—

(a) by or on behalf of the employee or any person claiming under him for the purposes of pursuing an application for a patent, or

(b) by any person for the purpose of performing or working the invention,

shall be taken to infringe any copyright or design right to which, as between him and his employer, his employer is entitled in any model or document relating to the invention.

Note. Subsection (3) was prospectively added by the 1988 Act (Sched. 5, para. 11(1)). For commencement of this new provision, see the latest Supplement to this Work *re.* this para.

BOOKS   39.02

J. Phillips, "Employees' Inventions, a Comparative Study" (Fernsway Publications, 1981);
J. Phillips and M. J. Hoolahan, "Employees' Inventions in the United Kingdom" (ESC Publishing Ltd., 1982).

ARTICLES   39.03

W. R. Cornish, "Employee inventions: The new United Kingdom patent law", [1978] EIPR 4;
R. P. Lloyd, "Inventorship amongst collaborators", (1979–80) 9 CIPA 16;
D. C. L. Perkins and P. A. Molyneaux, "Rights of employee inventors in the United Kingdom under the Patents Act 1977", [1979] AIPL 353;
M. J. Hoolahan, "Employees' inventions: The practical implications: Ownership and compensation: UK Patents Act 1977", [1979] EIPR 140;
B. C. Reid, "Employee inventions under the Patents Act 1977", [1979] JBL 350;
B. Bercusson, "The contract of employment and contracting out: The UK Patents Act 1977", [1980] EIPR 257;
H. Davis-Ferid, "The employed inventor under United Kingdom and German Law", [1981] EIPR 102.
K. Hodkinson, "Employee inventions and designs: Ownership, claims and compensation; and Managing employee inventions", *The Company Lawyer*, (1986) Vol. 2, 146 and 183.

COMMENTARY ON SECTION 39

39.04   *General scope of provisions for "Employees' Inventions" (ss. 39–43)*

Section 39 is the first of a group of sections (ss. 39–43) headed "Employees' Inventions": which defines a self-contained code for determining ownership of an "invention" (s. 39); which regulates circumstances in which it would be "just" for an employer of such an "employee" to make payments, curiously termed "compensation", to that employee for the benefit which the employer has derived from a "patent" which has been granted for an "invention" made by the "employee" (s. 40); which lays down guidelines for determining the quantum of such compensation (s. 41); which renders unenforceable certain clauses in contracts of employment widely used before 1978 (s. 42); and limits the applicability of this group of sections to inventions made on or after June 1, 1978 and by persons "mainly employed" in the United Kingdom (including the Isle of Man). Some of the words in quotation marks in the preceding sentence are defined in section 43 (which is, in effect, a mini-interpretation section for ss. 39–42) and in section 130(1). These all receive discussion below and in the commentaries on the following sections 40–43.

39.05   *General scope of section 39*

Section 39 is a provision of substantive, rather than procedural, law. It has effect in relation to the settlement of entitlement disputes under section 8, 12, 37 or 82; and to the question of "compensation" under section 40. In all these matters it must first be decided who is the "inventor", a question on which the Act gives very little guidance, see para. 7.07 and the article by R. P. Lloyd listed in para. 39.03 *supra*. Section 39 then settles the question of ownership of inventions made by persons who are "employees", as between an employee and his "employer", provided that the invention was made by a person "mainly employed" in the United Kingdom (s. 43(2), as discussed in para. 43.03.

However, section 39 has no effect upon the ownership of inventions made before June 1, 1978 (s. 43(1)) and is therefore entirely inapplicable to "existing patents". The resolution of employee/employer disputes in relation to such patents continues to be determined under section 56 [1949], see paras. A056.03–A056–10. There are no provisions in the EPC, CPC or PCT relating to ownership of patent rights in inventions made by employees. These remain to be determined by individual national laws, generally (it is believed) applicable only to persons normally employed in the country in question. By the same token, section 39 relates to the ownership of patent rights anywhere in the world resulting from an invention made by a person who, at the time of making the invention (as to which, see para. 7.07), was "mainly employed" in the United Kingdom (see para. 43.03).

Section 39 also has no applicability to inventions made by non-employees. The disposition of patent rights arising from inventions made by such persons, however, remains subject to possible contractual obligations, for example in the case of research work commissioned from a non-employee. A contract between an employer and a third party concerning the disposition of patent rights of employee inventions can have no effect on patent rights which belong to an employee under subsection (1). That contract may then become incapable of fulfilment, the consequences of which will depend upon the default provisions therein and the doctrine of frustration in the law of contract.

Meaning of "invention" in sections 39–43   **39.06**

"Invention" (as used in s. 39) is a term clearly wider than "patentable (or patented) invention", but is not defined: sections 1, 125 and 130, *inter alia*, deal only with inventions for which a patent under the Act has been applied for or granted. In *Viziball's Application* ([1989] RPC 213) it was held that "invention", as used in section 8, encompasses unpatentable subject-matter, whether because already known or because expressly excluded from the ambit of the Act (*e.g.* by ss. 1(2), 1(3) or 4(2)). Indeed, it is submitted that, for the purposes of section 39, it is immaterial whether a patent application has been filed or not. In this context, the phrase in the introductory part of subsection (1) "for . . . all other purposes" is noteworthy. Furthermore, the reference in section 43(4) to "other protection" supports this view, particularly now that this provision has been amended specifically to relate also to section 39, see paras. 39.14 and 43.05.

This wide meaning of "invention" may well encompass many "suggestions" submitted by employees under company suggestion schemes. Care should, therefore, be taken to ensure that any rules of such schemes purporting to regulate the ownership of the submitted suggestions remain in harmony with the provisions of section 39. The effect of section 42(2) may also need to be considered, see para. 42.03.

Meaning of "employee" for sections 39–43   **39.07**

"Employee" is defined for the purposes of the Act in section 130(1) by reference to a contract of employment, a definition closely similar to that in section 153 of the Employment Protection (Consolidation) Act 1978 (c. 44), but this definition was extended by the Armed Forces Act 1981 (c. 55), by amendment of section 42(4) and 130(1) by adding the words thereto "or a person who serves (or served) in the naval, military or air forces of the Crown" (see paras. 42.01 and 130.01), thereby equating members of the armed forces to employees [of the Crown] for the purposes of sections 39–43.

Also, the 1988 Act defines "employee", though for the purposes of copyright and design law only, as referring to employment "under a contract of service or of apprenticeship" (ss. 176 [1988] and 263(1) [1988]), thereby raising a doubt as to the position of apprentices under the present Act.

The status of the inventor as employee   **39.08**

In most cases, the status of the inventor as employee is not in doubt, but difficult problems can arise with regard to directors (*Parsons* v. *Parsons*, [1979] FSR 25), consultants, and the increasing number of "home workers". In such cases one must first determine if there is a contract at all, and then, if so, whether the contract is one "of service" or "for services". The question is one of law, rather than fact (*Davies* v. *Presbyterian Church of Wales*, [1986] 1 WLR 323; [1986] IRLR 194 (HL)).

An equity-holding partner in a firm is an employer of its staff and cannot therefore be said to be himself employed by it, but the ownership of shares in a company, even by a majority shareholder, is irrelevant as the company is an entity quite separate from its members (*Salomon* v. *Salomon & Co. Ltd.* ([1897] AC 22 (HL)).

Given the crucial difference in treatment of employees for tax and national insurance purposes, as well as for entitlement to social security benefits and employment protection rights (*e.g.* as regards redundancy, unfair dismissal, health and safety provisions, protection of pay when the employer becomes insolvent, etc.), a huge body of case law on the point has built up in labour law. To summarise it here is beyond the scope of this commentary, but in one of the leading cases (*O'Kelly* v. *Trusthouse Forte*, [1984] QB 90; [1983] 3 All ER 456; [1983] IRLR 240 (CA)) it was said that, in order to determine employee status, all aspects of the relationship must be considered and no single factor is in itself decisive. One such factor is the label the parties themselves put on the relationship (*Narich Property* v. *Comm. of Pay-Roll Tax*, [1984] ICR 285 (PC), following *Massey* v. *Crown Life Insurance*, [1978] 1 WLR 676; [1978] 2 All ER 576; [1978] IRLR 31 (CA)). No single test is adequate in all circumstances, *e.g.* not the older "control" or master-and-servant test, but currently courts favour the so-called "economic reality" (or "mixed") test. In its simplest form, one simply asks whether the person doing the work is in business on his own account or not; and whether there are mutual obligations between the alleged employer and alleged employee.

Cases in which it was held that that a creator was *not* an employee at the relevant time are: *Coffey's Registered Designs*, ([1982] FSR 227), where the designer was at the time only a partner in an informal partnership under no trust obligation thereto or to a company incorporated only subsequently; and *Gleave's Application* (SRIS O/22/88), where a referrer (in s. 37 proceedings) failed to prove that the patent proprietor was an employee at the relevant time and where it appeared that the alleged employer company had not then been incorporated.

Ownership of employee inventions by an employer

39.09 —*The basic rule*

The introductory phrase of subsection (1) simply sweeps away any rule evolved under the common law before June 1, 1978 (*Harris's Patent*, [1985] RPC 19). This renders precedents decided under the common law of dubious assistance.

Although the question of onus of proof under section 39 is not free from doubt, the better view is that an employee will own his invention by virtue of subsection (2) *unless* his employer can prove that the situation under either part of subsection (1)(*a*) or under subsection (1)(*b*) exists in fact. However, in entitlement proceedings under section 8, 12, 37 or 82, the Comptroller holds the view that the onus is on the referrer to prove his contentions. This view, based on section 7(4), is open to the criticism that it overlooks the effect of section 39(2). It is submitted that the better view, supported by *Harris's Patent* (*supra*), is that, when section 39 is under consideration, the onus should be on the employer to show that the facts correspond to one of the situations in section 39(1).

The fact situation can be proved under subsection (1)(*a*) either by reference to the employee's "normal duties" or to other duties "specifically assigned to him", whereas subsection (1)(*b*) provides a third gateway through which an employer can claim rights by reference to the employee's "particular responsibilities" and an ensuing "special obligation", though still provided that the invention was made within the scope of the duties of that employee.

Subsections (1) and (2) are mutually exclusive as between employer and employee. It is submitted that this overrides the Comptroller's discretionary powers under sections 8 and 37 to grant a patent to joint proprietors where these would be employer and employee and confirms the position under the 1949 Act, decided in *Patchett* v. *Sterling* ((1955) 72 RPC 50 (HL)). However, in *Szucs' Application (No. 2)* (SRIS O/27/88) (decided under s. 37) ownership was awarded to the employee, but with a free licence under the patent to the employer. The Comptroller stated that joint proprietorship was unattractive, but did not suggest that the law precluded this.

For each of the three gateways of subsection (1) a two-stage enquiry is required, the first stage being broadly common to each of these, *viz.* the establishment of the actual duties of the employee. The second stage is then: (in both parts of subs. (1)(*a*)) consideration of the circumstances in which the invention was made; and (in subs. (1)(*b*)) consideration of the particular responsibilities and obligations of the employee. As *Harris* (*supra*) shows, the Comptroller or court will not be satisfied with job titles but will "lift the veil" to establish the detailed facts.

These facts will often show that a person, though an employee, engages in a number of activities at different times. Not all those activities may be "duties" of employment at all. For example, the position of University lecturers is particularly obscure in relation to their research activities if they are engaged primarily to teach, with spare time allowed for research, but no obligation to carry it out.

In *Peart's Patent* (SRIS O/209/87) the Comptroller did not accept an argument that conception of an invention outside working hours fell outside the scope of an employee's duties. However, this decision is open to the criticism that, having accepted that the invention was not made in the course of the referrer's normal or specifically assigned duties for the purposes of subsection (1)(*a*), it was overlooked that, for the purposes of subsection (1)(*b*) also, it must first be shown that the invention was made in the course of the duties of the employee, before proceeding to focus on the "special obligations", *i.e.* more than the general duty of fidelity.

—*The employee's "normal duties"*   **39.10**

In *Harris* (*supra*) the "normal duties" of an employee were defined as the actual duties which he was employed to do. Thus, an employee's "normal duties" will be those defined by his contract of employment, including additional terms which may be implied, *e.g.* the duty of good faith, terms which are incorporated from collective agreements between employers and trade unions, from custom and practice, and from ancillary documents such as pre-employment correspondence, engagement letters, Handbooks, Works Rules, notices on noticeboards, etc. In *Harris* (*supra*) it was held never to have been part of the duties of the employee to turn his mind to solving technical problems.

Harris also settled the controversy over the scope of the implied term of an employee's duty of good faith, sometimes referred to as the duty of fidelity: it is co-extensive with, and does not go beyond, contractual duties. In this, *Harris* followed *United Sterling* v. *Felton and Mannion* ([974] RPC 162) in which it was stated that the duty of fidelity expires at the moment the contract of employment terminates, though there is a continuing obligation not to disclose the employer's confidential information (*Faccenda Chicken* v. *Fowler*, [1986] FSR 29 (CA)). It should be noted, however, that contractual duties may be implied rather than expressed (*Attorney-General* v. *Guardian Newspapers (No. 2)*, [1989] 2 FSR 181; [1988] 3 All ER 545, the "Spycatcher" case).

—*Duties specifically assigned to employee*   **39.11**

For a discussion of an employee's duties falling outside of his normal duties, but specifically assigned to him, see the article by B, Bercusson listed in para. 39.03 *supra*. Given that it is an implied term of a contract of employment that an employee must obey lawful orders, and that an order to carry out duties outside the contract is a breach of that contract and is thus unlawful (unless an employee agrees and there is consideration to support the consensual variation), an employee who carries out specifically assigned duties under protest and reserving his position may not be caught by subsection (1)(*b*); and see para. 39.13A *infra*.

39.12   —*Performance of normal or specifically assigned duties*

The second stage of enquiry under subsection (1)(*a*) is concerned with whether the performance of the duties, as established in the first stage, is expected to result in an invention. Again, *Harris* (*supra*) has settled that the words "an invention" have a narrower meaning than "any invention", but are wider in scope than "the invention the subject of the dispute". But it is still unclear *whose* expectations are decisive, the employer's or the employee's, and whether the time of the expectation is the date of commencement of the duties in question or the date when the invention is made.

It is arguable that subsection (1)(*a*) achieves the same result as reached by 1977 under the common law, albeit by a different route. Thus, in *Electrolux* v. *Hudson* ([1977] FSR 312), a clause in a contract of employment under which the employer claimed ownership of an employee's invention was declared void as being wider than required to protect the employer's legitimate interest and therefore against public policy and in restraint of trade, in effect for not being confined to inventions flowing naturally from the performance of the employee's duties. On this basis former precedents may still have some persuasive value.

39.13   —*Employees with special obligations*

Subsection (1)(*b*) provides the third gateway whereby an employer can establish ownership of an invention made by an employee. The invention must still be one made "in the course of the duties of the employee". Then, in addition, the employee must be one who, at the relevant time, had a special obligation to the employer, arising from the nature of his duties and responsibilities, to further the interest of the employer's undertaking. The omission of "normal" in the reference to "duties" is no doubt deliberate and in contrast with subsection (1)(*a*). Subsection (1)(*b*) clearly covers employees in senior management whose duties are not so closely definable as to make "normal" meaningful in relation thereto. Thus, in *Peart's Patent* (SRIS O/209/87), a works manager was held not to have discharged the onus on him to show that he did not have an obligation which extended to an invention he made at a time when he had been instructed not to involve himself in research and development matters. However, just how far down in the hierarchy of a given organisation one can go before an employee will cease to be covered by subsection (1)(*b*), irrespective of his inventions being covered by subsection (1)(*a*), will always be a difficult question.

39.13A   *Employee holding invention on constructive trust for employer*

Where it is established that the employee is entitled to the benefit of an invention held on trust for him by the employer, the common law of constructive trusts will come into force, as discussed in the book by J. Phillips and M. J. Hoolahan listed in para. 39.02 *supra*. In such a trust the employee not only takes the benefit, but also the liabilities, of the resulting trusts (*Triplex* v. *Scorah*, (1938) 55 RPC 21). The employee is then entitled to compensation for any expenditure he may have incurred in developing and protecting the invention, as was required in *Hindmarch and Horner's Application* (SRIS O/158/80, *noted* IPD 3147). In the case where an employer solicits the aid and services of an employee beyond the scope of his normal duties without any "consideration" or promise of remuneration subsequent to his performance of the requested services, the employee may have a quasi-contractual remedy of *quantum meruit* to recover the value of those services from the employer.

Application of section 39 to particular cases   **39.14**

The application of the principles set out in section 39(1) to particular facts usually arise in proceedings under section 8, 12, 37 or 82 (*Determination of entitlement to patent ownership*). Decisions on these are therefore discussed mainly in the commentary on section 37 at para. 37.12, but see also para. 8.10.

Decisions under the former law   **39.15**

Precedents decided under the former common law principles should be treated with considerable caution. This is partly due to the inconsistency of pre–1978 cases such as *British Syphon* v. *Homewood* ([1956] RPC 225 and 330) and *Selz's Application* ((1954) 71 RPC 158 (PAT)); and partly because these cases were generally concerned to determine, as a first step, whether the invention was made "in the course of employment", for example as in *Hindmarch and Horner's Application* (SRIS O/158/80, *noted* IPD 3147, decided under s. 56 [1949]). It is submitted that this phrase had a wider meaning than the "duties of an employee".

The phrase "in the course of employment" has also been the subject of interpretation in numerous labour law cases involving, *e.g.* employers' vicarious liability for their employees' acts. It is closely bound up with the concept of authorisation, express or implied, for a given act.

Determination of inventor ownership disputes   **39.16**

An inventorship dispute can arise under section 13 (*Mention of inventor*) or under section 8, 12, 37 or 82 (*Determination of question of entitlement*). Employee-employer ownership disputes on "existing patents" are resolved under section 56 [1949]. The procedure for resolving such disputes is discussed in the commentaries on these sections.

Settlement of disputes by employers   **39.17**

Employers will naturally seek to settle inventorship disputes with, or between, their employees by informal and internal procedures. If this is to be done, it is important that the procedures used by the employer should be fair, not too lengthy, and generally comply with rules of natural justice. Failure to treat an employee reasonably is a breach of an implied term of every contract of employment which entitles an employee (with a qualifying period of service, currently of two years) to resign and claim compensation for unfair *constructive* dismissal under section 57(1)(*c*) of the Employment Protection (Consolidation) Act 1978 (c. 44), see in general *Western Excavating* v. *Sharp* ([1978] QB 761; [1978] 1 All ER 713 (CA)) and a dictum in *Courtaulds Northern Textiles* v. *Andrew* ([1979] IRLR 84), *viz.* that it is an implied term of the employment contract that employers should not "without reasonable and proper cause conduct themselves in a manner calculated or likely to destroy or seriously damage the relationship of confidence and trust between the parties".

Contrast with employer ownership of copyrights and design rights created during   **39.18**
employment

Sections 11(2) [1988] and 215(3) [1988] have respective effect to pass first ownership of copyrights and design rights created by an employee "in the course of his employment" automatically to the employer, subject in the latter case only to the prior right of one who commissioned the making of the design. A topography right is treated in the same way as a design right, except that here the statutory provision

309

may be varied by a written agreement (Design Right (Semiconductor Topographies) Regulations 1989 (S.I. 1989 No. 1100, rr. 2, 5). First ownership of registered designs is also now governed as for a design right (Registered Designs Act 1949 (c. 88), s. 2(1B) as inserted by s. 267 [1988] and as reprinted in Sched. 4, para. 2(1B) [1988]). If, as is submitted, this phrase is wider in scope than the combined effect of the three gateways of section 39(1), then decisions in relation to these other types of intellectual property rights will have no direct effect on the interpretation of section 39.

However, this dichotomy between employees' rights in different species of intellectual property will often arise from the same, or closely associated, acts leading to a position where, even though an employee may own patent rights because his employer is unable to establish any of the criteria of subsection (1), nevertheless the employer may own associated copyrights, designs rights, registered designs, etc. because these have been created by the same employee "in the course of his employment".

39.19 *Employees' freedom under associated copyrights and designs rights (subs. (3))*

To alleviate the position set out in para. 39.18, subsection (3) is to be added, and an amendment made to section 43(4), by the 1988 Act (Sched. 5, para. 11). Under new subsection (3), where by virtue of subsection (2) an invention belongs to an employee, rather than to his employer, then nothing done by or on behalf of the employee, or his successor in title, for the purpose of prosecuting an application for a patent, or by any person for the purpose of performing or working the invention, "shall be taken to infringe any copyright or design right" in "any model or document" to which the employer is entitled, rather than the employee.

Thus, the employer will not be able to use these other intellectual property rights to prevent the employee from obtaining patents on his own invention. Also, new subsection (3)(*b*) is presumably intended to provide a defence in any action for infringement of any copyright or design right (though curiously not in respect of a registered design) arising from a model or document to which the employer is entitled. However, this provision may not be as wide as it seems at first sight. It is clearly intended to apply to copyrights of which the employee in question is the author (designer) but, as regards documents or models created by his colleagues, the resulting copyright or design right may not perhaps be a right "between him [the employee] and the employer".

The amendment to section 43(4) will have the effect that any reference to "patent" in section 39 will extend to a "patent or other protection" granted whether under the law of the United Kingdom or otherwise. This provision is discussed further in para. 43.05. However, in its application to section 39(3) (the word "patent" not appearing otherwise in s. 39), it is difficult to see how United Kingdom law can effectively provide a defence to an action brought in another country for infringement of an intellectual property right in that country, unless perhaps a United Kingdom court would grant an injunction against the employer to prevent him seeking to assert his foreign "protection" contrary to section 39(3)(*b*), as extended by section 43(4). Also, because copyrights (and design rights) are not "granted", the provision may be ineffective anyway, see para. 43.05.

PRACTICE UNDER SECTION 39

39.20 *Keeping of records*

In establishing whether section 39(1) applies to an invention made by an employee, it becomes very clear that much depends on the circumstances in which an invention was made. In the interest of both employer and employee it is most desirable to set out in writing the employee's normal duties and whether he has any special duties or obligations, and to record the assignment of any new duties and to record: (a) any duties specifically assigned; (b) the employee's consent to such assignment; and (c) the consideration therefor.

It must be a question of fact whether an employee might reasonably be expected to make inventions in carrying out of his duties. An attempt can be made to deal with this point in his contract of service, but in cases of doubt past experience of the employer as to whether a particular class of employee (*e.g.* a sales engineer) has made, or been expected to make, inventions as a result of carrying out his normal duties might be relevant in determining ownership of the invention.

In the interests of certainty it may be desirable, before a patent application is filed, that an employee-inventor be asked to sign a declaration as to the ownership of the invention. In any event, personnel records of inventors should be maintained for at least one year after the patent has ceased to have effect, see rule 60(2) reprinted at para. 40.02. There is also the possibility that an attempt may be made to claim inventorship many years after the application was filed, see para. 13.11. The papers by K. Hodkinson, listed in para. 39.03 *supra*, contain useful hints on the keeping of records of employee inventions, the handling of ownership claims, and the management of employee inventions. Specimen documentation is provided at the end of his second paper.

SECTION 40   40.01

Compensation of employees for certain inventions

40.—(1) Where it appears to the court or the comptroller on an application made by an employee within the prescribed period that the employee has made an invention belonging to the employer for which a patent has been granted, that the patent is (having regard among other things to the size and nature of the employer's undertaking) of outstanding benefit to the employer and that by reason of those facts it is just that the employee should be awarded compensation to be paid by the employer, the court or the comptroller may award him such compensation of an amount determined under section 41 below.

(2) Where it appears to the court or the comptroller on an application made by an employee within the prescribed period that—

(*a*) a patent has been granted for an invention made by and belonging to the employee;

(*b*) his rights in the invention, or in any patent or application for a patent for the invention, have since the appointed day been assigned to the employer or an exclusive licence under the patent or application has since the appointed day been granted to the employer:

(*c*) the benefit derived by the employee from the contract of assignment, assignation or grant or any ancillary contract ("the relevant contract") is inadequate in relation to the benefit derived by the employer from the patent; and

311

(*d*) by reason of those facts it is just that the employee should be awarded compensation to be paid by the employer in addition to the benefit derived from the relevant contract:

the court of the comptroller may award him such compensation of an amount determined under section 41 below.

(3) Subsections (1) and (2) above shall not apply to the invention of an employee where a relevant collective agreement provides for the payment of compensation in respect of inventions of the same description as that invention to employees of the same description as that employee.

(4) Subsection (2) above shall have effect notwithstanding anything in the relevant contract or any agreement applicable to the invention (other than any such collective agreement).

(5) If it appears to the comptroller on an application under this section that the application involves matters which would more properly be determined by the court, he may decline to deal with it.

(6) In this section—

"the prescribed period", in relation to proceedings before the court, means the period prescribed by rules of court, and

"relevant collective agreement" means a collective agreement within the meaning of the Trade Union and Labour Relations Act 1974 [c. 52], made by or on behalf of a trade union to which the employee belongs, and by the employer or an employers' association to which the employer belongs which is in force at the time of the making of the invention.

(7) References in this section to an invention belonging to an employer or employee are references to it so belonging as between the employer and the employee.

RELEVANT RULE

Application under section 40 for compensation

40.02   **60.**—(1) An application to the comptroller under section 40 for an award of compensation shall be made on Patents Form No. 26/77 and shall be accompanied by a copy thereof and a statement in duplicate setting out fully the facts relied upon.

(2) The prescribed period for the purposes of section 40(1) and (2) shall, in relation to proceedings before the comptroller, be that period which begins when the relevant patent is granted and which expires one year after it has ceased to have effect:

Provided that, where a patent has ceased to have effect by reason of a failure to pay any renewal fee within the period prescribed for the payment thereof and an application for restoration is made to the comptroller under section 28, the said period shall—

(*a*) if restoration is ordered, continue as if the patent had remained continuously in effect; or (*b*) if restoration is refused, be treated as expiring one year after the patent ceased to have effect or six months after the refusal, whichever is the later.

(3) The comptroller shall send a copy of the application and statement to the employer who, if he wishes to contest the application, shall within three months of receiving them, file a counter-statement in duplicate setting out fully the grounds on which he disputes the employee's right to the relief sought, and the comptroller shall send a copy of the counter-statement to the employee.

(4) The employee may, within three months of the receipt of the copy of the counter-statement, file evidence in support of his case and shall send a copy of the evidence to the employer.

(5) Within three months of the receipt of the copy of the employee's evidence or, if the employee does not file any evidence, within three months of the expiration of the time within which the employee's evidence might have been filed, the employer may file evidence in support of his case and shall send a copy of the evidence to the employee; and within three months of the receipt of the copy of the employer's evidence, the employee may file evidence confined to matters strictly in reply and shall send a copy of that evidence to the employer.

(6) No further evidence shall be filed by either party except by leave or direction of the comptroller.

(7) The comptroller may give such directions as he may think fit with regard to subsequent procedure.

BOOKS AND ARTICLES **40.03**

For books and relevant articles, see paras. 39.02 and 39.03.

COMMENTARY ON SECTION 40

General **40.04**

Section 40 is the second of the group of sections, 39–43, relating to inventions made by employees. There is no corresponding provision in EPC, CPC or PCT.

Section 40 is concerned with an employee-inventor making a claim for "compensation" from his employer. It has two limbs relating respectively to employer-owned patented inventions (subs. (1)), and patented inventions originally owned by the employee but assigned or exclusively licensed to the employer (subs. (2)). Under either limb an award of compensation is based on three prerequisites. Firstly, the invention must be one for which a "patent" has been granted. Secondly, the ownership of the invention must already have been determined in accordance with section 39. Finally, in all the circumstances, it must be "just" to make an award in favour of the employee. Compensation is to be assessed under either head in relation to the benefit which the employer (including persons "connected with him, see s. 41(1) and (2)) derives from the "patent" (in the extended sense to be defined by s. 43(4), see para. 43.05).

40.05 *When a compensation award may not be "just"*

The circumstances in which it may not be just for the employee to receive compensation would, presumably, concern some form of inequitable conduct, *e.g.* misuse of confidential information or other acts inconsistent with the employee's general duty of fidelity and honesty. For the position of fiduciaries, see *Boardman* v. *Phipps* ([1967] AC 46 (HL)); and generally *Bell* v. *Lever Bros.* ([1932] AC 161 (HL)). Since both subsections (1) and (2) use the word "may", the making of an award is discretionary and the maxim of Equity applies: He who comes into equity must come with clean hands.

40.06 *Determination of amount of compensation*

The amount of compensation payable under section 40 is to be determined according to the principles set out in section 41. Section 40 does not apply to patents granted on inventions made before June 1, 1978 (s. 43(1)), nor where the inventor was not mainly employed, or attached to employment, in the United Kingdom (s. 43(2)). However, section 40 does extend to joint inventors (s. 43(3)) and to foreign patents and "other protection" (s. 43(4)), see further para. 43.05. How far, if at all, section 40 is applicable to copyrights, design rights and designs remains to be seen. For the time when an invention is made, see para. 7.06.

Section 43(7) requires that "benefit" means benefit in money or money's worth. For the definition of "employee", see para. 39.07. However, doubt may arise as to who is the employer, for the purposes of section 40, where the employer is a company which is a subsidiary, associate or service company of a larger corporation. Also, the effect of section 41(1) and (2), with regard to benefit obtained by an employer from persons "connected" with him, has to be borne in mind, see para. 41.05.

In section 130(1), the definition of "employer" is given as "in relation to an employee, means the person by whom the employee is or was employed". This excludes from consideration any benefit derived from the patent by an assignee or licensee, unless such is a "connected person", see para. 41.05. However, where the employee's business is transferred to another entity as a going concern, the Transfer of Undertakings (Protection of Employment) Regulations 1981 (S.I. 1981 No. 1794), by regulation 5 thereof, provide that all the transferor's rights, powers, duties and liabilities under, or in connection with, a contract of employment of a person who immediately before the transfer was employed by the transferor are transferred with the undertaking. This regulation has been interpreted in a purposive manner, in accordance with the EEC "Business Transfer Directive" (No. 77/187) and subsequent decisions of the ECJ on the effect thereof, so as to include an employee whose employment contract was terminated, in a way automatically rendered unfair by the Regulations, by the transferring employer in contemplation of the subsequent transfer of the undertaking (*Litster* v. *Forth Dry Dock Engineering*, [1989] 2 CMLR 194; [1989] 2 WLR 634; [1989] 1 All ER 1134 (HL)). Thus, in such circumstances, it would appear that the new employer will assume the responsibilities which the former employer had under section 40 and is not to be regarded as a mere assignee, but rather as a "continuing" employer.

40.07 *Time for making application for compensation*

An application under section 40 can be made either to the Comptroller or to the court and must be made within a prescribed period which is that from grant of the patent to one year after it has ceased to have effect, or six months after my application for restoration under section 28 has been refused (r. 60(2); subsection (6) and RSC, Ord. 104, r. 18(1), reprinted in para. E104.18. The period under rule 60(2) is inextensible (r. 110(2)), but the court may have more latitude to accept an application made out of time.

An employee will not necessarily know when an employer decides not to renew a patent and so may be unaware when the prescribed final period starts to run. Thus, he would be well-advised to file the appropriate "caveat" on PF 49/77 at the Patent Office, and to take similar precautions (if available) in respect of corresponding foreign patents. Equally, he might wish to file a further PF 49/77 to be informed of any assignments or licences recorded at the Patent Office in the register of patents. The filing of caveats is explained in para. 118.19.

By virtue of section 22(7), where an application under a secrecy order is placed in order for grant, it is treated as if a patent had been granted thereon. Thus, employee-inventors of such applications are not disabled from making an application for compensation under section 40.

Forum for seeking an award of compensation   **40.08**

The choice of forum may be influenced by the availability of Legal Aid in the Patents Court and (probably) in the Patents County Courts when these are set up under section 287 [1988] to financially qualifying (ex-)employees, though the low maximum limits for income and disposable capital before Legal Aid can be granted for civil litigation are likely to deprive most litigants of Legal Aid for section 40 proceedings. However, though in theory available in court proceedings, Legal Aid is *not* available in Patent Office proceedings (Legal Aid Act 1988 (c. 34), s.14 and Sched. 2, Part I). Also, the provisions of section 106 may have a bearing on the choice of forum as, under that section, the court *shall* have regard to the financial position of the parties in determining an award of costs (or, in Scotland, expenses), see para. 106.02.

Patent belonging to the employer (subs. (1))

—Basis of compensation   **40.09**

By subsection (1) an employee is entitled to compensation in respect of an invention which he has made, which belongs to his employer under section 39(1) as between the employer and employee (subs. (7)), and for which a patent has been granted, but only if the patent has provided a benefit to the employer which is "outstanding" having regard (among other things) to the size and nature of the employer's undertaking, and it is "just" to do so. Such compensation is to be determined according to the guidelines set out in section 41(1) and (4), see para. 41.06.

—Meaning of "patent of outstanding benefit"   **40.10**

It is to be observed that it is the *patent*, and not the invention, from which the outstanding benefit to the employer has to derive. Usually, of course, the patent will confer benefit by protecting sales of a product or by way of licence or assignment income. Indeed, in *Elliott Brothers' Patent*, (SRIS O/47/89, *noted* IPD 12047) the Comptroller held that, where an employer-patentee secures a monetary benefit from selling goods protected by a patent, there is a rebuttable presumption that at least a part of that benefit has derived from the existence of that patent, the onus being on the employer to show that the benefit was unconnected with the patent. However, a patent which is not exploited, but which blocks competitors, may also be of benefit,

315

even though the quantum of it will be difficult to assess. The recommendation of the Government Green Paper ("Intellectual Property Rights and Innovation", Cmnd. 9117, December 1983), that employee inventors should be given the right to take title in their inventions which are not being exploited by their employer, has not been adopted. However, if the invention is being inadequately exploited, there is the possibility for the employee-inventor to obtain a compulsory licence under section 48.

The meaning of "outstanding" is unclear. The only guidelines in the section recognise that a given size of benefit will signify more to a small employer than to a giant multi-national corporation. The reference to the nature of the employer's undertaking is also unclear. In *Elliott Brothers' Patent*, (*supra*) it was said that, for a benefit to be "outstanding", it must be something out of the ordinary and not such as would be expected to arise from the performance of the employee's contractual duties. As for the "nature" of the employer's undertaking, it was considered relevant to examine whether the invention belonged to the main field of the employer's operations. In the actual case, while there was evidence of substantial benefit arising to a medium-sized company at least in part from the patent, there was also evidence of comparable benefit from the sale of a similar, but unpatented, product, and accordingly the employee-applicant was held not to have discharged the burden of proving that the benefit from the patent was "outstanding", which burden was upon him.

Until further precedents, including court decisions, are established, a degree of caution remains necessary. It is here observed that there has in recent years been a marked tendency in both the civil and criminal courts to resist construing ordinary words in too technical a manner (insofar as they have not become terms of art). Rather, they are to be construed according to their natural meaning, in the way a jury would construe them. Lord Diplock's famous phrase "purposive construction" in *Catnic* v. *Hill and Smith* ([1982] RPC 183 (HL)) is an aspect of that tendency. It would seem likely, therefore, that the courts will look on "outstanding" as a normative word and will take a fairly broad and robust view of its meaning.

It is not apparent that the Comptroller or the court when considering an application for compensation need have any regard to the validity of the patent except in so far as validity has an effect on the benefit derived from the patent. Thus, a patent which had attracted licence fees during much of its term before being held invalid would no doubt be considered to have given benefit. Equally, a patent of merit and originality in a field where the employer had a dominating position for other reasons, so that that patent of itself contributed little to the benefit of the employer, might not qualify for an award. The reference to the patent, and the limitation of the period in which an application for compensation can be made, substantially confines consideration to benefits obtained from the patent during its subsistence.

40.11   *—Post-invention employer-employee agreements*

Since subsection (4) only refers to subsection (2), it would seem possible for an employer to make an agreement with an employee-inventor *after* he has made an invention which belongs to the employer under section 39(1) and which includes conditions excluding the employee making a claim under section 40(1). It would seem that such agreement would be binding so as to exclude operation of section 40(1), even if "outstanding benefit" to the employer results, despite the fact that in this way the object of the statute might be frustrated, see also para. 42.03. Alternatively, the court might declare such an agreement void as being contrary to public policy, but such agreement could be beneficial to the inventor as giving him additional reward even though the patent turned out not to be of outstanding benefit to the employer. However, subsection (4) prevents a contract of this type from being enforceable in the case of an invention belonging to the employee under section 39(2), in which case the compensation provisions of subsection (2) cannot be excluded.

Patent assigned to the employer (subs. (2)) **40.12**

Subsection (2) relates to the situation where an employee has made his invention which belongs to him under section 39(2) as between him and his employer (subs. (7)), which he has "patented" in the sense of section 43(4), and the employee has made over to the employer all rights under the patent, by way of assignment or exclusive licence, and it appears subsequently that the benefit obtained by the employee from the contract was inadequate having regard to the benefit to the employer from the patent, see para. 40.04. Thus sole and non-exclusive licences are excluded from consideration. Any such assignment or exclusive licence must be one made after the making of the invention because agreements made before an invention is made, *e.g.* an agreement to assign future inventions to the employer, are not enforceable (s. 42(2)). Where there has been such a valid assignment or exclusive licence, the employee may also apply for compensation. Any such application is to be determined according to the principles set out in section 41, particularly sections 41(1) and (5), see paras. 41.06 and 41.07. The application must be made within the same (prescribed) period as applies under subsection (1), see para. 40.07.

For subsection (2) to be operative, the employee must have made over to his employer (presumably to whosoever was the employer at the time of making the invention) "his rights" under the patent. Such handing over can be by assignment or exclusive licence. The term "exclusive licence" is defined in section 130(1) and means a licence from the proprietor conferring on the licensee, or on him and persons authorised by him, to the exclusion of all other persons (including the proprietor), any right in respect of the invention to which the patent relates. This term is discussed more fully in para. 67.03. Although an "exclusive licence" as such can be in respect of "any right" under the patent, for the purpose of section 40(2) it may be argued that an exclusive licence must pass all "his rights" under the patent so that an exclusive licence which is limited territorially, or to part of the invention, or to some kind of act only, may be insufficient to permit compensation to be claimed under section 40(2).

Collective trade union agreements (subs. (3)) **40.13**

Under subsection (3) an employee is, apparently, precluded from making a claim under subsections (1) or (2) if, at the time of making the invention, he belonged to a trade union which has negotiated a "relevant collective agreement" (as defined in subs. (6) by reference to the Trade Union and Labour Relations Act 1974 (c. 52), "TULRA", for which see *infra*) which provides for payment of compensation in respect of inventions of the same description to employees of the same description as the employee. An employee who does not belong the the relevant trade union is free to make a claim under subsection (1) or (2). The agreement has to be in force and the employee has to have been a member of the trade union concerned at the time of making the invention; an employee who subsequently leaves such a union would, presumably, still be bound by the collective agreement and not able to make a claim for compensation.

"Collective agreement" is defined in section 30(1) of TULRA as "any agreement or arrangement made by or on behalf of one or more trade unions and one or more employers or employer's associations and relating to one or more of the matters included in section 29(1)" of that Act. These matters do not refer to inventions as such, but reward for the making of inventions could be included under the head of "terms and conditions of employment" under section 29(1)(*a*) of that Act. Few such collective agreements are believed to exist, but the articles by K. Hodkinson, listed in para. 39.03, include two examples. It is noteworthy that collective agreements are not normally legally enforceable. Thus, under TULRA (s. 18), collective agreements are not intended to have legal effect unless the parties expressly so provide: yet they may override statute.

40.14 *Procedure, hearing, costs and appeals*

Applications under section 40 may be made either to the Comptroller (under r. 60(1)) or to the court (under RSC, Ord. 104 r. 18, reprinted at para. E104.18), see paras. 40.16 and 40.17 respectively. However, under subsection (5) the Comptroller may decline to deal with an application if it involves matters more properly dealt with by the court and application to the Patents Court is then made within 28 days (RSC, Ord. 104 r. 17(*b*), reprinted in para. E104.17). In England and Wales, the court will be the Patents Court (RSC, Ord. 104, r. 2, reprinted at para. E104.2), but the definition of "court" in section 130(1) enables applications to be made to the appropriate courts in Scotland, Northern Ireland or the Isle of Man, and if the proprietor is domiciled in these parts of the United Kingdom any application to the court under section 40 may have to be made to the court of that part of the United Kingdom having regard to the Civil Jurisdiction and Judgments Act 1982 (c. 27).

It can be expected that application will normally be made to the Comptroller because of the reduced expense, but see the comments relating to Legal Aid in para. 40.07 *supra*. The Comptroller can appoint advisers to assist him in assessing compensation; and in the debates on the Patents Bill indication was given that the Comptroller would often wish to appoint advisers in section 40 proceedings, see the commentary on section 123(2)(*g*) at para. 123.29. The Comptroller can hear proceedings in Scotland (but not apparently in Northern Ireland) and again it was indicated during the passage of the Patents Bill that this would be done whenever convenient, see commentary on section 123(2)(*f*) at para. 123.28. During these debates, concern was also expressed at the prospect of an inventor having to face heavy legal costs in contesting proceedings before the court, particularly on appeal. Consequently, section 106 provides the court with broad powers (whether in initial proceedings or on appeal from the Comptroller) to make special awards of costs in section 40 proceedings taking into account the relevant circumstances, particularly the financial position of the parties, see para. 106.02. The question of the availability of Legal Aid for section 40 proceedings is discussed in para. 106.02. Costs in proceedings before the Comptroller are dealt with in paras. 107.03 and 107.04.

Any decision of the Comptroller under section 40 is subject to appeal to the Patents Court (s. 97(1)) and thereafter, with leave, to the Court of Appeal whether or not a question of law is involved (s. 97(3)). If proceedings take place in Scotland, any appeal would be to the Court of Session (s. 97(4) and (5)).

40.15 *Taxation of compensation*

Compensation under section 40 may be a lump sum, periodical payments or both (s. 41(6)) and the employee should seek that compensation be paid to him in a manner which minimises his liability to tax on the sum received. The method by which taxation of compensation obtained under section 40 may be assessed may also seriously affect the net payment obtained. This subject has been briefly considered by N. Eastaway (NLJ, April, 1981, p. 375) and is more fully dealt with in "*Intellectual Property Law and Taxation*" by Gallafent, Eastaway and Dauppe

(Longmans, 3rd. Ed., 1989). It is understood that the Inland Revenue take the view that compensation arising under section 40(1) will be taxable under Schedule E (PAYE), whereas that under section 40(2) is taxable under Schedule D. *Ex gratia* payments made in lieu of compensation under section 40 may also be taxable in the same way. The Inland Revenue position is discussed in (1982–83) 12 CIPA 501.

Practice under Section 40

Application to the Comptroller   **40.16**

The procedure is governed by rule 60 (reprinted at para. 40.02, *supra*). Application is made by an employee on PF 26/77 (reprinted at para. 141.26), filed in duplicate with a statement (also in duplicate) setting out fully the facts relied upon (r. 60(1)). If foreign patents are contended to have contributed to, or be the cause of, the outstanding benefit claimed to have been derived by the employer (as is permissible under s. 43(4)), these patents should be identified in the statement of case (*Elliott Brothers' Patent*, SRIS O/47/89, *noted* IPD 12047). Application can be made at any time after grant of the patent, but not later than one year after the patent has ceased to have effect, or six months after refusal of any application for restoration (r. 60(2)). This period is inextensible (r. 110(2)). The Comptroller sends a copy of the PF 26/77 and statement to the proprietor inviting him, if he wishes to contest the application, to file a counter statement within three months (r. 60(3)), a period which is extensible with discretion under rule 110(1). The Comptroller then sends a copy of the counter-statement to the employee inviting the submission of evidence within a further three months (r. 60(4)). Thereafter the employer filed evidence also within a further three months and the employee also then files evidence which is strictly in reply thereto (r. 60(5), in each case the party filing evidence sending a copy thereof to the other party. All the periods for filing evidence are extensible on discretion exercised under rule 110(1). No further evidence can be filed, except with leave or direction of the Comptroller (r. 60(6)). Thereafter the Comptroller may give such directions as he thinks fit (r. 60(7)). A hearing must be offered (s. 101) and the procedure is likely to follow that generally used in contentious proceedings before the Comptroller, for which see paras. 72.32–72.52.

In proceedings before the Comptroller under sections 40(1), 40(2) or 41(8), no documents filed at the Patent Office become open to public inspection unless the Comptroller otherwise directs (r. 93(5)(*d*), reprinted in para. 118.05), but the existence of the proceedings is now advertised in the O.J., see O.J. November 9 and 16, 1988. M. J. Hoolahan has pointed out ((1985–86) 15 CIPA 121) that it is, apparently, not the practice of the Comptroller to direct that any such inspection of documents filed in these proceedings should take place and that this rule creates a difficulty in following the progress of applications already made under section 40 to the Comptroller. However, this rule does not prevent the publication of decisions given under the section after a hearing held in public (*Ibstock Building Products' Patent*, SRIS O/65/88).

In the *Ibstock* case requests for extensive discovery of documents and financial data from the patent proprietor had been requested and conceded (SRIS O/1/89). As a result, as the preliminary hearing noted above indicates, the proceedings may take several years to resolve. On the other hand, without extensive discovery and the submission of financial data, it will usually be very difficult for the employee to discharge the burden of proving that the benefit of the patent has been "outstanding", as happened in *Elliott Brothers' Patent* (*supra*).

40.17 *Application to the court*

An application to the Patents Court is made by originating summons within the same period as under rule 60(2) (RSC, Ord. 104, r. 18(1), reprinted in para. E104.18). The initial hearing is one for the giving of directions as to future procedure, including directions as to the manner of presentation of "accounts of expenditure and receipts relating to the claim" (Ord. 104, r. 18(2)) and for providing "reasonable facilities for inspecting and taking extracts from the books of account by which the defendant proposes to verify such accounts" (Ord. 104, r. 18(3)). In the usual case it can be expected that the giving of evidence by affidavit will be ordered, but in proceedings before the court cross-examination of witnesses cannot be avoided if requested. As regards cost in section 40 proceedings, see para. 106.02.

If the proceedings are taken to the court by way of appeal from a decision of the Comptroller the procedure is governed by RSC, Ord. 104, r. 19 (reprinted at para. E104.19) and the appeal will be by way of re-hearing on the evidence before the Comptroller, see paras. 97.20–97.23.

41.01

SECTION 41

Amount of compensation

41.—(1) An award of compensation to an employee under section 40(1) or (2) above in relation to a patent for an invention shall be such as will secure for the employee a fair share (having regard to all the circumstances) of the benefit which the employer has derived, or may reasonably be expected to derive, from the patent or from the assignment, assignation or grant to a person connected with the employer of the property or any right in the invention or the property in, or any right in order or under, an application for that patent.

(2) For the purposes of subsection (1) above the amount of any benefit derived or expected to be derived by an employer from the assignment, assignation or grant of—

(*a*) the property in, or any such right in or under, a patent for the invention or an application of such a patent; or

(*b*) the property or any right in the invention;

to a person connected with him shall be taken to be the amount which could reasonably be expected to be so derived by the employer if that person had not been connected with him.

(3) Where the Crown or a Research Council in its capacity as employer assigns or grants the property in, or any right in or under, an invention, patent or application for a patent to a body having among its functions that of developing or exploiting inventions resulting from public research and does so for no consideration or only a nominal consideration, any benefit derived from the invention, patent or application by that body shall be treated for the purposes of the foregoing provisions of this section as so derived by the Crown or, as the case may be, Research Council.

In this subsection "Research Council" means a body which is a Research Council for the purposes of the Science and Technology Act 1965 [c. 4].

(4) In determining the fair share of the benefit to be secured for an employee in respect of a patent for an invention which has always belonged to an employer, the court or the comptroller shall, among other things, take the following matters into account, that is to say—

(a) the nature of the employee's duties, his remuneration and the other advantages he derives or has derived from his employment or has derived in relation to the invention under this Act;

(b) the effort and skill which the employee has devoted to making the invention;

(c) the effort and skill which any other person has devoted to making the invention jointly with the employee concerned, and the advice and other assistance contributed by any other employee who is not a joint inventor of the invention; and

(d) the contribution made by the employer to the making, developing and working of the invention of the provision of advice, facilities and other assistance, by the provision of opportunities and by his managerial and commercial skill and activities.

(5) In determining the fair share of the benefit to be secured for an employee in respect of a patent for an invention which originally belonged to him, the court or the comptroller shall, among other things, take the following matters into account, that is to say—

(a) any conditions in a licence or licences granted under this Act or otherwise in respect of the invention or the patent;

(b) the extent to which the invention was made jointly by the employee with any other person; and

(c) the contribution made by the employer to the making, developing and working of the invention as mentioned in subsection (4)(d) above.

(6) Any order for the payment of compensation under section 40 above may be an order for the payment of a lump sum or for periodical payment, or both.

(7) Without prejudice to section 12[32] of the Interpretation Act 1978 [1889] (which provides that a statutory power may in general be exercised from time to time), the refusal of the court or the comptroller to make any such order on an application made by an employee under section 40 above shall not prevent a further application being made under that section by him or any successor in title of his.

(8) Where the court or the comptroller has made any such order, the court or he may on the application of either the employer or the employee vary or discharge it or suspend any provision of the order and revive any provision so suspended, and section 40(5) above shall apply to the application as it applies to an application under that section.

(9) In England and Wales any sums awarded by the comptroller under

section 40 above shall, if a county court so orders, be recoverable by execution issued from the county court or otherwise as if they were payable under an order of that court.

(10) In Scotland an order made under section 40 above by the comptroller for the payment of any sums may be enforced in like manner as a recorded decree arbitral.

(11) In Northern Ireland an order made under section 40 above by the comptroller for the payment of any sums may be enforced as if it were a money judgment.

(12) In the Isle of Man an order made under section 40 above by the Comptroller for the payment of any sums may be enforced in like manner as an execution issued out of court.

Note. Amendment to subsection (7) was effected by the Interpretation Act 1978 (c. 30, s. 25(2)); and to subsection (12) by S.I. 1978 No. 621.

RELEVANT RULE

Application under section 41(8) to vary, etc., awards of compensation

41.02   **61.**—(1) Where an award of compensation has been to an employee under section 40(1) or (2), an application under section 41(8) to vary, discharge, suspend or revive any provision of the order shall be made on Patents Form No. 27/77 and shall be accompanied by a copy thereof and a statement setting out fully the facts relied upon and the relief which is sought.

(2) Thereafter the provisions of rule 60(3) to (7) shall apply to an application made under section 41(8) by an employee as they apply to an application referred to in that rule and to an application made under section 41(8) by an employer as if references in those sub-rules to the employee were references to the employer and references to the employer were references to the employee.

41.03   ARTICLE

A. N. Devereux, "Compensation and awards to employee inventors", (1985–6) 15 CIPA 47.

COMMENTARY ON SECTION 41

41.04   *General*

Section 41 is the third of the group of sections 39–43 which relates to employee inventors, and deals with the basis on which compensation under either sections 40(1) or (2) is to be computed.

The phrase in subsection (1) "may reasonably be expected to derive" makes it clear that, at the time when a determination of the amount of compensation is made, not only the employer's past benefit, but also his future benefit, will be taken into account. The test of future benefit seems to be an objective one and not the employer's subjective evaluation.

Connected persons   **41.05**

The phrase "person connected with" the employer occurs in both subsections (1) and (2). By subsection (2), where an employer assigns or licences the invention or the patent to a person connected with him, the benefit obtained is that benefit which would have been obtained by a transaction at arm's length. From this it would appear that, if the employer assigns the patent to an unconnected person by an arm's length transaction, the benefits to be attributed to the employer from the patent will thereupon be frozen as the benefits enjoyed before assignment together with the consideration obtained therefor. Equally, where an employer licenses the patent to a third party at arm's length for a royalty, and the licensee derives a large benefit from the agreement, the employee will not be able to claim any share of that benefit and his claim will be limited to the royalty receipts of his employer.

The definition of "connected person" now contained in section 839 of the Income and Corporation Taxes Act 1988 (c. 1) which is to be applied (s. 43(8), as amended), refers to persons related by marriage or ascent or lineal descent, to trustees and beneficiaries, and to partnerships (and relatives of partners). It also defines companies as being connected if the same person (or group of persons) has control of each company, or if one company controls the other company; and persons acting together to secure or exercise control of a company are treated in relation to that company as being connected with one another. The word "control" is itself now defined in section 416 of the same Act. By this, a person has control of a company if he is able or entitled to exercise or secure direct or indirect control over the company's affairs, particularly if he possesses or is entitled to acquire the greater part of the issued share capital or voting power of the company or be entitled on a distribution or winding up of the company to the greater part of its income or assets. Again the definition embraces trustees and nominees in relation to such a person.

Fair awards (subss. (1), (4) and (5))   **41.06**

Subsection (1) sets out the worthy principle that the award (whether under ss. 40(1) or (2)) is to be "fair" having regard to all the circumstances, but includes no definition of the word "fair". The subsection in practice seems likely to result in much debate, but to afford little assistance.

Subsections (4) and (5) set out factors which have to be taken into account when arriving at a decision as to what is a fair award. Subsection (4) applies to a claim under section 40(1), in respect of an invention owned by the employer, when account is to be taken of: the employee's duties; his remuneration and other advantages he derived from the invention; his skill and the contributory skill of others; and the contribution to the invention by the employer. Subsection (5) applies to a claim under section 40(2), in respect of an invention owned by the employee, when account is to be taken of: the conditions of any licences granted under the invention or patent; the contribution by any other joint inventor; and the contribution made by the employer. But despite these general directions there remains the problem of "fair".

An award which would be fair considered in relation to the remuneration of the inventor might be very different in absolute value from an award in the same circumstances which was fair in relation to the benefit to the employer. At this stage it would not be helpful to speculate on the practice which may develop; the court and the Comptroller are not to be envied in their difficult task.

A. N. Devereux, in the article listed in para. 41.03 *supra*, has suggested that the Crown Awards Scheme, under which Crown employees have in the past been rewarded for their inventive contributions, may provide, by analogy, a method of assessing compensation for employee inventors under section 40. The words "among other things" which appear in both subsections (4) and (5) indicate that the factors listed are not to be taken as exhaustive. "Developing" occurs both in subsections (4)(*d*) and (5)(*c*). Whilst this word could mean developing the first germ of an idea to the stage where it is a feasible, or at least a patentable, proposition, it seems more likely that it means developing the invention to the stage of producibility and marketability because of the way the word is sandwiched between "making" and "working", implying a chronological sequence.

The use of the word "shall" before "among other things" may mean that the matters stated in subsection (4) are to be considered in a case arising under subsection (5) (*Invention belonging to employee, with compensation claimed under s.40(2)*); and that, vice versa, the matters listed in subsection (5) are to be considered in a case arising under subsection (4) (*Invention belonging to employer, with compensation claimed under section 40(1)*). However, this literal interpretation may well be tempered by the *ejusdem generis* rule which would confine the matters to be considered in each case to those of the same ilk as those specifically listed in the respective subsections. Clearly the words import a degree of liberality into the provisions, but to an extent which is obscure.

41.07   *Payment of compensation (subs. (6))*

By subsection (6) payment can be a lump sum or a periodical payment or both. Any order made may subsequently be varied, discharged, suspended or revived (subs. (8)) by application made by either employee or employer to the Comptroller or court as under section 40, see para. 41.11 *infra*.

41.08   *Crown and Research Councils (subs. (3))*

Subsection (3) refers to the circumstances where the employer is the Crown or a Research Council (as defined in the Science and Technology Act 1965 (c. 4, s.1) and the patent or any right thereunder is assigned to a body devoted to exploitation. Benefit to such a body is to be treated as benefit obtained by the Crown or Research Council. Subsection (3) is specifically aimed at patents, etc., assigned to the National Research Development Corporation, now the British Technology Group.

41.09   *Unsuccessful applications (subs. (7))*

By subsection (7), where an employee makes an unsuccessful application under section 40, he (or his successors in title after death) can make a further application under that section. It is not clear whether "a further" application means one further or includes more than one. The provisions of the Limitation Act 1980 (c. 58) do not appear to affect the position since the exploitation of a patent is a continuing event and rule 60(2) (reprinted in para. 41.02) sets a wide period within which applications for compensation may be made.

41.10   *Procedure*

A foreseeable difficulty in applying section 41 to proceedings under section 40 is the fact that in the majority of cases the applicant for an award of compensation will not be in possession of the information on which to base his case so that, if the application is to be justly considered, it will be necessary for the employer to produce, voluntarily or by order for discovery, the details of his benefit derived from the patent. In this connection it should be noted that the provisions of RSC, Ord. 104, rr. 8(2) and (3) (reprinted in para. E104.8) make provision for disclosure and verification of financial information and books of account of the employer. No doubt the Comptroller would make similar directions under rule 106, for which see para. 72.44. The situation is not parallel with opposed applications for extension of term of patent under the 1949 Act, for there the onus lay on the patentee to produce the information to support his own case. Where no such information is available, or is incompletely available (and the relevant period may extend over most of the term of the patent) no doubt the court or Comptroller will resort to educated estimation.

PRACTICE UNDER SECTION 41   **41.11**

An application to vary, discharge, suspend or revive an award of compensation to an employee under section 40 may be made under subsection (8). As with an application under section 40, the application can be made to the Comptroller or to the court as under section 40(5). Application to the Comptroller is made under rule 61 (reprinted at para. 41.02) by filing PF 27/77 (reprinted at para. 141.27) in duplicate and a statement (also in duplicate) setting out fully the facts relied upon and the relief sought (r. 61(1)). Thereafter the procedure laid down in rules 60(3)–(7) is to apply with amendment of references to employee and employer interchanged as appropriate (r. 61(2)), for which procedure see Practice under section 40 at paras. 40.16 and 40.17.

Presumably, in any application to the Patents Court the procedure of RSC, Ord. 104, rr. 17(*b*) and 18 (reprinted at paras. E104.17 and E104.18) would apply, though this is not explicitly stated therein.

SECTION 42   **42.01**

Enforceability of contracts relating to employees' inventions

42.—(1) This section applies to any contract (whenever made) relating to inventions made by an employee, being a contract entered into by him—

  (*a*) with the employer (alone or with another); or

  (*b*) with some other person at the request of the employer or in pursuance of the employee's contract of employment.

(2) Any term in a contract to which this section applies which diminishes the employee's rights in inventions of any description made by him after the appointed day and the date of the contract, or in or under patents for those inventions or applications for such patents, shall be unenforceable against him to the extent that it diminishes his rights in an invention of that description so made, or in or under a patent for such an invention or an application for any such patent.

(3) Subsection (2) above shall not be construed as derogating from any duty of confidentiality owed to his employer by an employee by virtue of any rule of law or otherwise.

325

(4) This section applies to any arrangement made with a Crown employee by or on behalf of the Crown as his employer as it applies to any contract made between an employee and an employer other than the Crown, and for the purposes of this section "Crown employee" means a person employed under or for the purposes of a government department or any officer or body exercising on behalf of the Crown functions conferred by any enactment **or a person serving in the navy, military or air forces of the Crown.**

Note. Amendment was effected by the Armed Forces Act 1981 (c. 55, s. 22).

COMMENTARY ON SECTION 42

42.02 *General*

Section 42 relates to contracts between an employer and an employee, whether made before or after the Act came into force, and provides that no contract is enforceable to the extent that it diminishes the "rights" of an employee in any invention that he may make after the appointed day, June 1, 1978, and after the date of the contract. The section applies also to any contract between an employee and a third party made at the request of the employer, or in pursuance of the employee's contract of employment. Under subsection (2) a contract which diminishes the employee's "rights" is unenforceable to the extent that it does so, see *infra.* "Rights", in relation to any patent or application, is defined (in s. 130(1)) as including an "interest" therein. "Right", in relation to an invention, is not mentioned in section 130(1), but would presumably include an "interest" in the invention.

The difficulty is that neither "right", nor "interest", is capable of precise definition. Jurisprudentially, many different classifications exist, *e.g.* legal rights and moral rights; rights and duties (obligations); rights *in personam* and rights *in rem*; personal rights and proprietary rights; legal rights and equitable rights, etc. A basis of right is interest, but not every interest is protected by a legal right. In relation to property, both "interest" and "right" appear to converge into a connection a person has with a thing entitling him to make a claim in respect thereof. Elsewhere in the Act there are references, *inter alia*, to the right to apply for and obtain a patent (s. 7); any right in or under a patent or application (ss. 8, 10, 12, 37, 38, 82 and 86); a right to be mentioned as inventor (s. 13); "continuing rights" under restored patents and applications (ss. 28A, 77(5) and 78(6)); personal property rights (ss. 30, 31, 33); rights of third parties in respect of Crown use (s. 57); the right to receive payment for Crown use (s. 58, referring to s. 55(4) which itself does not use the term "right"; the right to bring proceedings for infringement (ss. 67, 69); rights of appeal; the right to continued use (s. 64); and right of audience (s. 102). In many instances the Act uses "entitlement" in preference to "right". From this survey one may conclude that "right", for the purposes of section 42(2), is capable of bearing a meaning wider than rights of mere ownership as, for example, arising under section 39. Further discussion awaits judicial construction of subsection (2) in relation to particular fact situations.

42.03 *Unenforceability of contracts with employees (subs. (2))*

Under subsection (2) a contract is unenforceable only to the extent that it diminishes the employee's rights: the remainder of the contract will therefore remain enforceable provided the unenforceable provisions are severable from the remainder of the contract.

For a detailed discussion on the complex rules of severability (the "blue pencil" rule), see standard textbooks on the law of contract, but the following brief comments may assist. Courts will not add, or alter, words to reframe the clause (*Greer* v. *Sketchley*, [1979] FSR 197 (CA)). Their attitude to severance is more rigorous in relation to service contracts, than to, *e.g.* contracts for sales, see *Attwood* v. *Lamont* ([1920] 3 KB 571) and *Mason* v. *Provident Clothing* ([1913] AC 724 at p. 745). An important consideration is whether the provision in the clause goes to substantially the whole, or only to part, of the consideration. If it is merely subsidiary to the main purpose of the contract, severance may be possible; *e.g.* a clause in a service contract purporting to oust the jurisdiction of the courts.

It appears irrelevant that severance of void parts of a contract results in a total transformation of the economic balance of interest between the parties, see *Chemidus Wavin* v. *Soc. pour la Transformation* ([1977] FSR 19 and 181) where certain clauses were excised as contrary to TRa. 85.

Under subsection (2), not only are clauses purporting to regulate ownership of the employee's *future* inventions void, but so also are the frequently encountered clauses requiring employees to give their employers a first refusal or option on their inventions.

An area of controversy concerns the frequently occurring clause in contracts of employment requiring an employee to disclose his inventions to his employer. If under section 39 the invention belongs to the employee, does this clause diminish the employee's "rights in inventions . . . made by him"? Given the possibly wide interpretation of "rights" (see para. 42.02 *supra*), it probably does; but how can an employer claim *his* rights in the invention if he is not made aware of the existence of the invention? Anyway, as long as the clause is not central to the contract it will probably be severable. Including a "severability" clause in the contract may also assist. In any event, employers requiring such disclosure should bear in mind the need to maintain the confidentiality of the employee's submission pending determination of its ownership. Reference should also be made to para. 39.17 concerning the possibility of a claim for unfair constructive dismissal by failure to treat an employee reasonably.

The commentary on section 40 at para. 40.11 suggests that it may be possible for an employer to make a binding agreement with an employee which could over-ride the provisions of section 40(1), though not those of section 40(2). In similar vein, J. Phillips has commented ([1980] EIPR 347) that if the "rights" referred to in section 42(2) do not also include benefit of compensation under section 40(1), much of section 42 could be rendered ineffective.

The impact of subsection (2) on company suggestion schemes needs to be considered carefully in the light of comments in para. 39.06.

Duty of confidentiality (subs. (3))   **42.04**

Subsection (3) provides that subsection (2) is not to operate to derogate from any duty of confidentiality which an employee may have to his employer. It will be advisable to spell out this duty of confidentiality in future conditions of employment. If an invention belongs to an employee he has the right to apply for a patent for it, but care must be taken not to disclose in the specification matter which is confidential to his employer. Presumably an employer could obtain an injunction against an employee disclosing such confidential information, for example in a patent application made under section 39(2).

The Court of Appeal, in *Faccenda Chicken* v. *Fowler* ([1986] FSR 29) reviewed the general principles governing the law of confidence, and stated that in every case the starting point is the contract of employment. If the contract contains no express terms protecting confidential information, the implied term of the duty of confidence, itself a facet of the implied duty of good faith, must be considered. The scope of this duty after termination of employment is more restricted than during it, but a limited duty will survive if the degree of confidentiality is high enough. The distinction between confidential information and information which forms part of an employee's stock in trade formulated in *Printers & Finishers* v. *Holloway* ([1965] RPC 239) was affirmed. The following factors were held to assist in the determination whether a particular item of information falls within the implied duty of confidence: (i) the nature of the employment and status of the employee; (ii) the nature of the information; (iii) whether the employer expressly indicated to the employee that the information was confidential; and (iv) the severability of the confidential information from non-confidential information. The court also said that an express restrictive covenant to protect information is valid only if that information is properly "confidential".

Clearly, an employee-owned invention making use of employer-owned confidential information leads to an impasse under section 42(3). It is interesting to speculate whether the employer could obtain an injunction against the Patent Office to prevent publication under section 16 of an application filed by the employee for such an invention, but see *Rex Co.* v. *Muirhead and Comptroller-General* ((1927) 44 RPC 38).

42.05   *Crown and Government employees (subs. (4))*

Subsection (4) confirms that section 42 applies to employees of the Crown. Section 22 of the Armed Forces Act 1981 (c. 55) states that "The Patents Act 1977 shall have effect and be deemed always to have had effect with the following amendments (being amendments to secure that members of the Armed Forces are 'employees' for the purposes of that Act)" and then adds the words shown in bold type at the end of subsection (4). This amendment appears to have been made to remove any possible doubt that members of the armed forces are "Crown employees" for the purposes of the Act. A similar amendment has been made in the definition of "employee" in section 130(1), see para. 39.07. The definition of "Crown Employee" in subsection (4) differs from the definition of "employee' in section 130(1) in that the latter includes persons who have left the armed forces, whereas the former is confined to persons currently employed in the armed forces.

43.01   **SECTION 43**

Supplementary

43.—(1) Sections 39 to 42 above shall not apply to an invention made before the appointed day.

(2) Sections 39 to 42 above shall not apply to an invention made by an employee unless at the time he made the invention one of the following conditions was satisified in his case, that is to say—

    (*a*) he was mainly employed in the United Kingdom; or

    (*b*) he was not mainly employed anywhere or his place of employment could not be determined, but his employer had a place of business in the United Kingdom to which the employee was attached, whether or not he was also attached elsewhere.

(3) In sections 39 to 42 above and this section, except so far as the context otherwise requires, references to the making of an invention by an employee are references to his making it alone or jointly with any other persons, but do not include references to his merely contributing advice or other assistance in the making of an invention by another employee.

(4) Any reference in sections **39** [*40*] to 42 above to a patent and to a patent being granted are respectively references to a patent or other protection and its being granted whether under the law of the United Kingdom or the law in force in any other country or under any treaty or international convention.

(5) For the purposes of sections 40 and 41 above the benefit derived or expected to be derived by an employer from a patent shall, where he dies before any award is made under section 40 above in respect of the patent, include any benefit derived or expected to be derived from the patent by his personal representatives or by any person in whom it was vested by their assent.

(6) Where an employee dies before an award is made under section 40 above in respect of a patented invention made by him, his personal representatives or their successors in title may exercise his right to make or proceed with an application for compensation under subsection (1) or (2) of that section.

(7) In sections 40 and 41 above and this section "benefit" means benefit in money or money's worth.

(8) Section **839** [*533*] of the Income and Corporation Taxes Act **1988** [c. 1] [*1970*] (definition of connected persons) shall apply for determining for the purposes of section 41(2) above whether one person is connected with another as it applies for determining that question for the purposes of the Tax Acts.

Note. Subsection (4) was prospectively amended by the 1988 Act (Sched. 5, para. 11(2). For the commencement of this amendment, see the latest Supplement to this Work *re.* this para. Subsection (8) was effectively amended, as indicated, by Sched. 30, para. 21(3) of the Income and Corporation Taxes Act 1988 (c. 1).

COMMENTARY ON SECTION 43

General   **43.02**

Section 43 is the last of the group of sections 39–43 relating to the rights of employees in inventions which they make and sets out a number of supplementary provisions which affect the operation of the other sections.

Subsection (1) provides that sections 39–42 apply only to inventions made on or after June 1, 1978. For the time of making an invention, see para. 7.06.

Employee's place of employment (subs. (2))   **43.03**

Subsection (2) limits the operation of sections 39–42 to an invention made by an employee who at the time was mainly employed in the United Kingdom, or by an employee whose main place of employment is indeterminate, but the employer has a place of business in the United Kingdom to which the employee was attached. Its wording closely echoes the wording of section 141 of the Employment Protection (Consolidation) Act 1978 (c. 44) under which there is considerable case law. Factors to be considered under the so-called "base test" evolved by the courts include: the *express* terms of the contract of employment as to the location of the employer's headquarters; where the employee's private *residence* is or is expected to be; where, and in what *currency*, he is paid; and whether he is subject to *national insurance* contributions in the United Kingdom (*Wilson* v. *Maynard Shipbuilding*, [1978] QB 665; [1978] 2 All ER 78 (CA)). In *Janata Bank* v. *Ahmed* ([1981] IRLR 457; [1981] ICR 791 (CA)) there was a warning about encrusting the test with legal technicalities and a "broad brush" approach was urged.

The Employment Protection (Offshore Employment) Order 1976 (S.I. 1976 No. 1766, as amended by S.I. 1981 No. 208) extended employment protection to British Territorial Waters and to designated waters of the Continental Shelf so as to cover employees on off-shore oil and gas exploration and production installations. The present Act extends to acts occurring at these locations, see section 132(3) and (4), discussed in para. 132.06.

The Isle of Man is also part of the United Kingdom for the purposes of the Patents Act, see section 132(2) and S.I. 1978 No. 621, discussed in para. 132.05.

43.04 *Joint inventions (subs. (3))*

Subsection (3) provides that sections 39–42 relate to joint inventions and joint inventors as they relate to a sole invention and inventor, but excludes from joint inventorship any person whose contribution is merely by way of advice or assistance. No doubt subsection (3) is intended to minimise disputes as to inventorship which often arise where inventions are made in large research organisations or by a research team, but in the absence of definitions of "advice" and "assistance" the operation of the subsection, or the assistance it gives in resolving questions of joint inventorship, is difficult to foresee, see also the discussion on the definition of "inventor" in para. 7.07.

43.05 *Extension to other forms of protection (subs. (4))*

Subsection (4) extends the scope of sections 39–42 to include other forms of protection and to protection in other countries; and benefit under a United States' patent was in issue in *Elliott Brothers' Patent* (SRIS O/47/89, *noted* IPD 12047). There is no indication of whether "other protection" is intended to cover only closely similar forms of protection, such as petty patents, which exist for the protection of patentable or near-patentable inventions, or whether a broader view is to be taken so that these sections apply also to, for example, registered designs, which may or may not involve "inventions" in the broad sense of section 39 and which are "granted"; and copyright, design and topography rights, each of which again may or may not embody an "invention", but which in United Kingdom law are not "granted" and which, moreover, are not necessarily new and do not necessarily involve an inventive step. In any event, copyright is "granted" in certain foreign jurisdictions, *e.g.* in the United States. By definition, a registrable trade mark may include an invented word, but whether for the purpose of section 43 a registered trade mark thereby can be considered to be an invention in respect of which protection is "granted", as distinct from registered, is not clear. It may or may not be relevant that some invented trade marks have proved to be of great commercial value, not less than that of many patents. That the broader view should be preferred is supported by the contrast with 12(7)(*a*) where the word "other" before "protection" is omitted, see para. 12.03.

It may be argued that the essential test is whether an "invention" receives "protection" under the law and that protection confers such benefit on the employer that the employee should receive "a fair share (having regard to all the circumstances)", see section 41(1) discussed in para. 41.06. If that is correct, then confidential information may also be covered by the words "other protection". Otherwise, the anomalous situation could arise that an employee-inventor is unable to claim compensation in respect of inventions belonging to, or acquired by, an employer who decides to keep the invention secret and to whom the protection of the law of confidentiality may well afford considerable benefit. It may also be noted in this connection that section 64 confers potentially very valuable rights which, moreover, are (within certain limits) assignable for valuable consideration.

With regard to protection outside of the United Kingdom, in *Elliott Brothers' Patent* (*supra*), it was said that the application on PF 26/77 should explicitly identify the foreign patent(s) in respect of which it is made, and that it is insufficient to rely on the implication that *e.g.* foreign equivalents of a specified United Kingdom patent are automatically included in the claim by virtue of section 43(4).

The prospective amendment to subsection (4) extending its scope to refer also to section 39 follows the introduction of section 39(3) by the 1988 Act, and is discussed in para. 39.19. It is there noted that this extension may be less effective than its intended purpose. That purpose is to extend the defence provided under section 39(3) to an employee-inventor who owns patent rights arising from his invention under section 39(2) in respect of copyrights and design rights owned by his employer so that the employee (and his licensees) may practise that invention without infringement of other forms of protection, both in the United Kingdom and abroad whether these other forms of protection arise from the employee's own efforts or those of his colleagues. This extension may not be as effective as intended because: (i) the other forms of protection may not have been "granted", see *supra*; and (ii) United Kingdom law cannot provide an effective defence to litigation brought abroad under a foreign law.

Deceased employer (subs. (5))   **43.06**

Subsection (5) provides that, where an employer has died, account shall be taken for the purposes of sections 40 and 41 of any benefit derived from the patent by his personal representatives or any person in whom it has been vested with the assent of the personal representatives. Section 40 requires claims to be made to the "employer" who is the person by whom the employee is or was employed (s. 130). This seems to suggest that, when the patent becomes vested in another, the employee still looks for compensation to whoever was the employer at the time of making the invention, see also section 41(2) and para. 40.06. However, when the employer dies, subsection (5) provides for benefit enjoyed by the personal representatives, or by a person in whom the patent becomes vested with their assent, to be included in the benefit of the "employer" as such, just as if these were all "connected persons", see subsection (8) and para. 41.05. Nevertheless, it would seem that a claim may have to be made against the deceased employer's personal representatives and such persons may need to make provision for possible compensation claims before completing their distribution of the employer's estates. Should the employer go into liquidation or be wound up, the employee will probably have to make his claim without delay since at a later date there may be no assets left against which he could enforce a claim for compensation under section 40(1).

43.07   *Deceased employee (subs. (6))*

Subsection (6) provides that where an employee has died his personal representatives or their successors may make a claim under section 40(1) or (2) on behalf of his estate.

43.08   *Meaning of "benefit" (subs. (7))*

Subsection (7) defines "benefit" as benefit in "money or money's worth". "Money's worth" probably means any benefit which is capable of being assessed in monetary terms and when this term has been used in other statutes it has been given a broad meaning. For example, it includes a purchase at more than the full value of a property (*Attorney-General* v. *Lethbridge*, [1970] AC 19 (HL)), and also a purchase for a nominal consideration (*Midland Bank Trust* v. *Green (No. 2)*, [1981] 1 All ER 153; [1981] 2 WLR 28 (HL)), but does not include a consideration represented by a mere rearrangement of assets already held (*Attorney-General* v. *Smith-Marriott*, [1899] 2 QB 595). Thus, it perhaps excludes the type of benefit which is incapable of having a value assigned to it, such as an increase in the goodwill of the employer's business. Also, promotion of an employee in recognition that he made a meritorious invention may be irrelevant to "benefit", except insofar as this results in a direct or indirect increase of income.

Over periods of high inflation the award will no doubt have regard to the changed value of money, but it seems doubtful if an award can include a separate element of interest.

In the context of intellectual property, the phrase "money or money's worth" also appears in section 263(1) [1988] in the definition of a "commission" which can create first ownership of a design right according to section 215(3) [1988]; and, likewise, in relation to the first ownership of a commissioned registered design in section 2(1A) of the Registered Designs Act 1949 (c. 88), as inserted by section 267 [1988] and reprinted as Schedule 4, paragraph 2(1A) [1988]. Any cases decided under these provisions may therefore be of particular assistance in the interpretation of the present subsection (7).

43.09   *Connected persons (subs. (8))*

Subsection (8) now has the effect that connections between companies, for the purposes of section 41(2), are as defined in section 839 of the Income and Corporations Taxes Act 1988 (c. 1). This definition is discussed in para. 41.05.

SECTION 44

Avoidance of certain restrictive conditions

44.01   **44.**—(1) Subject to the provisions of this section, any condition or term of a contract for the supply of a patented product or of a licence to work a patented invention, or of a contract relating to any such supply or licence, shall be void in so far as it purports—

> (*a*) in the case of a contract for supply, to require the person supplied to acquire from the supplier, or his nominee, or prohibit him from acquiring from any specified person, or from acquiring except from

the supplier or his nominee, anything other than the patented product;

(*b*) in the case of a licence to work a patented invention, to require the
licensee to acquire from the licensor or his nominee, or prohibit him
from acquiring from any specified person, or from acquiring except
from the licensor or his nominee, anything other than the product
which is the patented invention or (if it is a process) other than any
product obtained directly by means of the process or to which the
process has been applied;

(*c*) in either case, to prohibit the person supplied or licensee from using
articles (whether patented products or not) which are not supplied
by, or any patented process which does not belong to, the supplier
or licensor, or his nominee, or to restrict the right of the person supplied or licensee to use any such articles or process.

(2) Subsection (1) above applies to contracts and licences whether made
or granted before or after the appointed day, but not to those made or
granted before 1st January 1950.

(3) In proceedings against any person for infringement of a patent it shall
be a defence to prove that at the time of the infringement there was in force
a contract relating to the patent made by or with the consent of the plaintiff
or pursuer or a licence under the patent granted by him or with his consent
and containing in either case a condition or term void by virtue of this
section.

(4) A condition or term of a contract or licence shall not be void by
virtue of this section if—

(*a*) at the time of the making of the contract or granting of the licence
the supplier or licensor was willing to supply the product, or grant a
licence to work the invention, as the case may be, to the person supplied or licensee, on reasonable terms specified in the contract or
licence and without any such condition or term as is mentioned in
subsection (1) above; and

(*b*) the person supplied or licensee is entitled under the contract or
licence to relieve himself of his liability to observe the condition or
term on giving to the other party three months' notice in writing and
subject to payment to that other party of such compensation (being
in the case of a contract to supply, a lump sum or rent for the residue of the term of the contract and, in the case of a licence, a royalty
for the residue of the term of the licence) as may be determined by
an arbitrator or arbiter appointed by the Secretary of State.

(5) If in any proceeding it is alleged that any condition or term of a contract or licence is void by virtue of this section it shall lie on the supplier or
licensor to prove the matters set out in paragraph (*a*) of subsection (4)
above.

(6) A condition or term of a contract or licence shall not be void by virtue of this section by reason that it prohibits any person from selling goods

other than those supplied by a specific person or, in the case of a contract for the hiring of or licence to use a patented product, that it reserves to the bailor (or, in Scotland, hirer) or licensor, or his nominee, the right to supply such new parts of the patented product as may be required to put or keep it in repair.

44.02   Books

R. Merkin and K. Williams, "Competition law: Antitrust policy in the United Kingdom and the EEC", (Sweet & Maxwell, 1984);
R. Whish, "Competition law", (Butterworths, 1985);
N. Green, "Commercial agreements and competition law: Practice and procedure in the UK and EEC" (Graham and Trotman, 1986).

Note. For books on competition law of the EEC, see also para. C09.

44.03   Articles

A. K. Lewis, "Dealings with patents and know how", [1979] EIPR 217;
N. J. Byrne, "Patent tying arrangements and Article 85", [1980] EIPR 141;
M. Burnside, "Licensing and tie-in clauses", (1987–88) 17 CIPA 237.

Commentary on Section 44

44.04   *General*

Section 44 applies to "existing patents" (Sched. 2, para. 1(2)), and concerns supply contracts or licences which impose certain restrictive conditions on the licensee in relation to the supply or use of patented and unpatented articles or materials, or prohibit the use of any patented process (but not apparently an unpatented process, see subs. (1)(c)). It renders void certain provisions in contracts and provides for several additional consequences. Because section 44 is regarded as a highly penal provision, it is to be construed strictly, see *Fichera* v. *Flogates* ([1984] RPC 257 (CA)). Other cases usefully to be studied on the construction of the section are: *Tool Metal* v. *Tungsten Electric* ((1955) 72 RPC 209 (HL)) and *Hunter's Patent [Ireland]* ([1965] RPC 416).

Apart from changes in wording, there appears to be little, if any, change in the scope of the section over that of the previous section 57 [1949]. The article of A. K. Lewis discussed these differences, and that of N. J. Byrne, (each listed in para. 44.03 *supra*) described the history of the section and related its provisions to those of TRa. 85.

There are no corresponding provisions in the EPC, PCT or CPC, but the decisions of the European Commission make it clear that licence agreements or assignments which include such restrictive conditions will be considered to offend against TRa. 85 if they also affect trade between Member States. Such an effect is rather readily implied: see for example *Re Case 126/80) Vacuum Interrupters' Agreement (No. 2)* ([1981] FSR 469; [1981] 2 CMLR 217); *Salonia* v. *Poidamani* ([1981] ECR 745; [1982] 1 CMLR 64 (ECJ)); and *Vaessen* v. *Morris* ([1979] 1 CMLR 511; [1979] FSR 259). The Articles of the Treaty of Rome which are relevant to patent licence and assignment agreements are reprinted and discussed in Appendix C. The Block Exemption Regulations which increasingly govern the permissibility of various types of provisions in such agreements are reprinted and discussed in Appendix D. On the importance of these matters, and for reference to other relevant United Kingdom legislation, see paras. 44.10–44.17, particularly para. 44.11, *infra*.

The void conditions (subss. (1) and (2))   **44.05**

Subsection (1) provides that any condition or term of a contract for, or relating to, the supply of a patented product or a licence to work a patented invention shall be void in so far as it purports to impose restraints on the acquisition of anything other than the patented product or the product of the patented process. The references in the corresponding section 57 [1949] to "sale or lease" and "article" are replaced in section 44 by "supply" and "product". The terms now used would appear to be not less comprehensive and consistent with similar changes in other sections of the Act. The definition in section 130(1) of "patented product" could leave the meaning of "product" in subsection (1)(*b*) in doubt, see paras. 55.04 and 60.11.

The unenforceable restriction specified in subsection (1)(*a*) is one by which a supplier stipulates or prohibits the acquisition by the person supplied by anything other than the patented product. Subsection (1)(*b*) recites a corresponding restriction applied to a licence, and subsection (1)(*c*) forbids any limitation of the use of an article supplied by, or of a patented process owned by, anyone other than the supplier or licensor or his nominee. There is no stipulation that the void condition or term must be in writing so that a condition in an oral contract can probably be pleaded, but see para. 30.07.

The provisions and affect of section 44 were extensively discussed in *Fichera* v. *Flogates* ([1984] RPC 257 (CA)). It was there held: (1) that a sales agency is not an agreement for the supply of goods: (2) that subsection (1) applies only to terms and conditions which are enforceable by an action for damages for breach of contract; (3) that the subsection does not extend to provisions in an agreement which looks only to future possibilities; and (4) that the term "patented product", as used in the contract, could not extend to components outside the scope of the claims.

Nevertheless, section 44 does not contain any public interest saving provision, as for example where a patentee wishes to impose a tie-in clause on the grounds of safety which he can demonstrate to be justified. M. Burnside (in his article listed in para. 44.03 *supra*) suggests that this makes British law more strict than EEC law, but see the discussion on *Eurofix and Bauco* v. *Hilti* (OJEC 11.3.88, L65/19; *abridged* [1988] FSR 473) in para. C17.

Subsection (2) provides that subsection (1) applies to contracts and licences back to January 1, 1950, which was the date the 1949 Act came into operation, although it might be argued that contracts actually dated on the "appointed day" (June 1, 1978) are excluded.

Consequences of void conditions in patent licences (subs. (3))   **44.06**

Subsection (3) retains the very important provision that the existence, at the time of an infringement (not at the time of the action for infringement), of any condition void by section 44 provides for any person, not only the parties to a contract or licence, a defence to infringement proceedings under the relevant patent. The defence is available notwithstanding that the plaintiff patentee or exclusive licensee is not a party to the contract provided that this was made with his (the plaintiff's) consent.

44.07   *Avoidance of void condition (subss. (4) and (5))*

Subsection (4) provides that in certain circumstances a condition or term of a contract or licence falling within subsection (1)(*a*), (*b*) or (*c*) shall not be void if the supplier or licensor at the time the contract was made was willing to make alternative conditions or terms available which were reasonable and without the offending restrictions (subs. (4)(*a*); *and also if* the purchaser or licensee is entitled under the contract or licence to relieve himself of liability to observe the offending condition or term (subs. (4)(*b*)). But, by subsection (5), the supplier or licensor has the onus of proving these matters as set out in subsection (4)(*a*).

44.08   *Acceptable condition (subs. (6))*

By subsection (6) an agreement containing a clause which merely forbids a person from selling goods (whether patented or not), other than those supplied by the licensor, is not void under section 44. Likewise, subsection (6) permits a contract for hire or use of a patented product to reserve to the supplier the right to supply "such new parts of the patented product as may be required to put or keep it in repair". This provision covers the replacement of worn, as well as damaged, parts (*Fichera* v. *Flogates*, [1984] RPC 257 (CA)).

44.09   *Covenant to use best endeavours*

In *Transfield* v. *Arlo [Australia]* ([1981] RPC 141 (HC of Australia)) a provision corresponding to the second part of section 44(1)(*a*) was considered. It was held, following *Tool Metal* v. *Tungsten Electric* ([1955] 72 RPC 209 (HL)) that a covenant to use best endeavours to exploit an invention did not require exclusive use of that invention and, therefore, the covenant was not a prohibition against use of other articles so that it was not a void condition under the provisions. This decision was followed in *Fichera* v. *Flogates* ([1983] FSR 198 and [1984] RPC 257 (CA)) where it was stated that a covenant to use best endeavours to promote sales was not objectionable in itself. Also in that case, a licence condition that the customer might only use the device if all the necessary components for operation were supplied by or through the patentee was held not to contravene section 44 because, unless the components were so supplied, then no licence to use them was given. Furthermore, subsection (6) was held to apply.

Other relevant legislation

44.10   *—General*

For general discussion on other legislation which places restrictions on the freedom to license intellectual property rights as the parties might wish, and for the terms and conditions which are allowable in agreements for such licences (or assignments), see the books listed in para. 44.02 *supra*. The more important points arising from this other domestic United Kingdom legislation which may affect the terms of patent licences are discussed in paras. 44.11–44.17 *infra*.

44.11   *—European competition law*

Often of much greater importance are the requirements of European competition law arising from TRa. 85 (reprinted in para. CO5), as discussed in paras. C11–C14, and the Block Exemption Regulations for patent and know-how agreements reprinted and discussed in Appendix D. Indeed, it can well be argued that, in the great majority of situations encountered in practice, European law is of paramount importance and the effect of domestic British law is relatively insignificant.

—Settlement of litigation   **44.12**

Nor should European competition law be ignored in concluding a litigation settlement. This is because an agreement to settle litigation may be an agreement or arrangement within TRa. 85(1), see *Oy Airam* v. *Osram* ([1982] 3 CMLR 614; [1983] FSR 108), a case relating to trade mark use. Indeed, any settlement of litigation which has the potential effect of decreasing competition may well be in violation of TRa. 85. Nevertheless, if the settlement should eliminate, or at least reduce greatly, restraints on competition and the free circulation of goods flowing from the previous conflicting rights under existing national laws, an agreement may be held not to have the object or effect of preventing, restricting or distorting competition to an appreciable extent within the EEC and, then, negative clearance under TRa. 85(1), or exemption under TRa. 85(3), may be given, see *Penney's Trade Mark,* [1978] FSR 385; [1978] 2 CMLR 100, and *Bayer and Sülhöfer's Agreement* (OJEC 27.9.88, L 281/17, *noted* [1989] EIPR D–14, (1989) 20 IIC 127 and *The Times,* October 11, 1988).

—The Restrictive Trade Practices Act 1976   **44.13**

In addition to the restrictions on patent licence terms levied by section 44, and those arising from the Treaty of Rome, as referred to above, it is necessary also to consider the restrictive trade practices legislation, now to be found mainly in the Restrictive Trade Practices Act 1976 ["the RTPA"] (c. 34), but also in the Resale Prices Act 1976 (c. 53) discussed in para. 44.14 *infra.*

The RTPA subjects to registration with the Director General of Fair Trading any restrictive agreement as to goods (s. 6) or services (s. 11) or any information agreement as to goods (s. 7) or services (s. 12). The Director then refers any such agreement to the Restrictive Trade Practices Court. If that Court finds the agreement to be contrary to the public interest, it is declared void in respect of those restrictions or information provisions (s. 2(1)). However, certain agreements are exempt from the provisions of the RTPA (s. 28), these being elaborated in Schedule 3 of that Act. The following provisions of that Schedule are here briefly noted: the exclusion of exclusive dealing arrangements between two persons, neither of whom is a trade association (para. 2); the exclusion of agreements for the exchange of know-how and information between two persons, neither of whom is a trade association (para. 3); the exclusion of agreements for the use of trade or service marks (para. 4 as amended as to service marks by s. 2(3) and Sched. 2, para. 8 of the 1986 Act): the exclusion of licences and assignments of patents and registered designs which do not contain any other provisions otherwise registrable and which are not a patent or design "pooling agreement", *i.e.* an agreement involving more than two persons (para. 5); and the exclusion of agreements as to goods exported from, or manufactured outside, the United Kingdom.

While the RTPA exempts from registration under that Act agreements of various types, for example patent licence agreements involving only two parties, the decision in *Automatic Telephone* v. *Registrar* ((1965) LR 5 RP 135) suggests that an agreement is not exempt from such registration just because it is a licence of this type. This is because investigation may show that the agreement made goes beyond a patent licence as such. Nevertheless, an agreement only becomes registrable if it constitutes a restraint against trade and it has been indicated (*Ravenseft* v. *Director General,* [1977] 1 All ER 47) that the grant of a qualified licence is not a restriction against freedom because, without the licence, no freedom would exist to operate lawfully in the field excluded by the qualification. While Merkin and Williams, at p. 297 of their book listed in para. 44.02 *supra,* suggest that the *Ravenseft* case was wrongly decided, Green, at p. 88 of his book listed likewise states that the Office of Fair Trading regards it of general applicability to proprietary rights so that the grant of any intellectual property licence does not constitute the supply of a service within the meaning of the legislation. However, the *Ravenseft* principle will not apply when it is the licensee who agrees to restrictions upon his freedom, for example in relation to grant-back provisions on his improvement inventions.

If there is doubt about the registrability of an agreement under the RTPA, a copy can be submitted to the Office of Fair Trading with a request for confirmation that the agreement is not one registrable under the Act. If this submission is accepted the agreement will then be returned.

It should be noted that, once accepted for registration under the RTPA, the agreement becomes open to public inspection at the Office of Fair Trading under section 23(4) of the RTPA. The Director General of Fair Trading has only limited powers to keep such an agreement off the public register, see RTPA (s. 23(3)).

44.14 —*The Resale Prices Act 1976*

The Resale Prices Act 1976 (c. 53) makes unlawful collective agreements restricting the supply of goods and, by section 9, makes void any term or condition in a contract or agreement between supplier and dealer which may have the effect of establishing a minimum resale price for goods, even if such goods are "patented articles or articles made by a patented process" (s. 10(1)). Moreover, any term void by section 9 is of no effect for the purpose of limiting the right to dispose of that article without infringement of a patent, design or of plant breeders rights (s. 10(2) and (4), as amended by Schedule 7, para. 19 [1988]) to include also "design rights" which, (by S.I. 1989 No. 1100) include rights in semiconductor topographies). Nevertheless, the validity of terms and conditions in licences or assignments of patents, etc., which may regulate the price at which articles produced or processed by the licensee or assignee may be sold by him, are not affected (s. 10(3)). Thus, *resale* price maintenance agreements are prohibited, but agreements for sales by a direct licensee or assignee are not affected by the Resale Prices Act 1976, but such agreements have to be checked for legality (and therefore effectiveness) under section 44 and, of greater importance, against the provisions of TRa. 85 (reprinted at para. C05), as discussed in paras. C11–C14 and in Appendix D.

44.15 —*The Unfair Contract Terms Act 1977*

The Unfair Contract Terms Act 1977 (c. 50) generally renders void conditions in contracts which are deemed to be unfair, often because of a perceived inequality in bargaining power between the contract parties, for example as will often be the case with contracts entered into by a domestic consumer. However, this Act does not void clauses in a patent licence agreement which have the effect of excluding the proprietor (or head licensee in the case of a sub-licence) from liability resulting from his negligence or breach of contract or from any indemnity in respect thereof. This is because Schedule 1 of this Act excludes the operation of sections 2–4 thereof to "any contract so far as it relates to the creation or transfer of a right or interest in any patent . . . or other intellectual property, or relates to the termination of any such right or interest", see also para. 102.24.

—Contracts for the sale of goods   **44.16**

Contracts for the sale of goods can, of course, include an implied patent licence for use and re-sale of the purchased (patented) product and such a licence will normally be implied. Under the Common Law, the right of re-sale could be prevented by a specific notice given to the purchaser of a patented product before or at the time of sale (*Betts* v. *Willmott*, (1871) LR 6 Ch. App. 239 at 245; and *National Phonograph Company of Australia* v. *Menck*, [1911] AC 336 at 349 (PC)). However, any attempt to impose such a restriction now would probably be ineffective under the "exhaustion of rights" doctrine discussed in para. C15 or otherwise be impermissible under TRa. 85, see *Soc. de Vente de Ciments* v. *Kerpen* ([1985] 1 CMLR 551, *noted* [1985] FSR 281).

In any event, in a contract for the sale of goods, there are normally implied warranties that the seller has an unencumbered right to sell the goods (Sale of Goods Act 1979 ["the SGA"] (c. 54, s. 12(1) and (2)(*a*)), and that the buyer will have quiet enjoyment of the goods (SGA, s. 12(2)(*b*)), and that the goods will be of merchantable quality (SGA, s. 14(2)). Thus, if the goods, or their intended use, should be covered by a patent, or become so covered in the future, liability may fall upon the seller for breach of such warranties, as happened in *Niblett* v. *Confectioners' Materials* ([1921] 3 KB 387), where goods were supplied bearing an infringing trade mark and all three warranties were held to have been broken, and in *Microbeads* v. *Vinhurst* ([1976] RPC 19) where, after delivery of the goods, a third party patent was published covering them and the warranty of "quiet enjoyment" was held breached.

Liability under section 12 of the SGA cannot be excluded by a term of the contract (Unfair Contract Terms Act 1977 ["the UCTA"] (c. 50, s. 6(1)), but the warranties under section 12(1) and (2) of the SGA do not apply if the seller indicates, expressly or by inference, that he is transferring only such title as he, or a third person, may have (SGA, s. 12(3)), and that all charges and encumbrances known to the seller but not to the buyer have been disclosed to the buyer before the sale contract is made (SGA, s. 12(4)). Thus, it could be prudent for a seller to include in his standard conditions of sale a statement that, while he is not aware of any patent (or other intellectual property right) which may be infringed by the possession or intended use of the goods being sold, (except as may be disclosed in sales literature already handed to the buyer), the sale is made on the basis that no licence is granted with the sale of the goods other than in respect of patents (and other intellectual property rights) owned by the seller or an associated company thereof. Liability under section 14 of the SGA can, however, be excluded if the exclusion clause is "reasonable" in the circumstances (UCTA, s. 6(2)).

Severability of void conditions from patent licence agreements   **44.17**

A court is not required to sever a void condition from a contract leaving the remainder to be enforced, unless there is a specific clause in the contract for severance of conditions which may be held to be void, or unless the governing statute which causes the condition to be a void one indicates that the agreement should be construed by omission of the void clause, as for example in section 42(2) which only requires a "term" of the contract to be unenforceable. In any case the void clause must be capable of being severed from the remainder of the agreement, for example by mere excision (as in the "blue pencil" test). For a case where severance was not possible, see *Hansen* v. *Magnavox* ([1977] RPC 301 (CA)). However, if the void condition is capable of severance, then it appears that the court will strive to do so rather than deprive the agreement of any validity whatever, and this so even if the severance of the void parts totally transforms the economic balance of interest of the parties as in *Chemidus Wavin* v. *Soc. pour la Transformation* ([1977] FSR 19 and 181).

PRACTICE UNDER SECTION 44

44.18 *Pleading a defence under section 44*

An allegation in an infringement action that there was at the time of the alleged infringement in being a contract containing a condition void under section 44 should be a positively pleaded defence, for example in the terms of subs. (3), see RSC Ord. 104, r. 5(3) reprinted in para. E104.5. Such a defence requires a formal reply, even if only by way of denial.

44.19 *Avoidance of effect of section 44*

Persons invited to advise on the terms of an agreement should always remember section 44 and, if there is any requirement in the agreement that is itself contrary to section 44(1), make sure that the effect of subsection (1) is avoided under subsection (4) by including in the agreement an appropriate alternative provision of a (royalty-bearing) licence conforming with subsection 4(1)(*a*), including reciting this fully in the agreement, as well as a provision satisfying subsection (4)(*b*) by which the licensee may give the required three months' notice in writing to operate in future under the alternative (non-restrictive) condition, see para. 44.07 *supra*.

Those advising on patent licence agreements should also check the proposed terms of an agreement against the requirements needed to avoid conflict with TRa. 85 (as discussed in Appendix D), as well as for compliance with other domestic British legislation (as discussed in paras. 44.13–44.16 *supra*).

44.20 *Label licensing*

"Label licensing" is a device that may be useful when goods are sold for use in a patented process since it would appear that a statement on a label that the sale carries a licence with it to use the goods sold therewith (but no other goods) in the patented method cannot be contrary to section 44. However, in *Hunter's Patent* [*Ireland*] ([1965] RPC 416), supply of a machine, without a licence to use it, together with the application of a label licence to materials sold by the patentee for use with the machine, were collectively transactions construed as a restriction on use of rival materials under legislation corresponding to section 57 [1949] so that the restriction on use of the unpatented machine was unlawful. Had the label licence scheme stood on its own, *i.e.* if the patentee had not supplied an unpatented machine but only articles for use in the patented method, the requirements of section 44(1) would not appear to have been breached. Thus a "label" licensing scheme is best used in connection with a patented method, as distinct from a licence to use an unpatented machine, see also para. 44.16.

SECTION 45

45.01 **Determination of parts of certain contracts**

45.—(1) Any contract for the supply of a patented product or licence to work a patented invention, or contract relating to any such supply or licence, may at any time after the patent or all the patents by which the product or invention was protected at the time of the making of the contract or granting of the licence has or have ceased to be in force, and notwithstanding anything to the contrary in the contract or licence or in any other contract, be determined, to the extent (and only to the extent) that the contract or licence relates to the product or invention, by either party on giving three months' notice in writing to the other party.

(2) In subsection (1) above "patented product" and "patented invention" include respectively a product and an invention which is the subject of an application for a patent, and that subsection shall apply in relation to a patent by which any such product or invention was protected and which was granted after the time of the making of the contract or granting of the licence in question, on an application which had been filed before that time, as it applies to a patent in force at that time.

(3) If, on an application under this subsection made by either party to a contract or licence falling within subsection (1) above, the court is satisfied that, in consequence of the patent or patents concerned ceasing to be in force, it would be unjust to require the applicant to continue to comply with all the terms and conditions of the contract or licence, it may make such order varying those terms or conditions as, having regard to all the circumstances of the case, it thinks just as between the parties.

(4) Without prejudice to any other right of recovery, nothing in subsection (1) above shall be taken to entitle any person to recover property bailed under a hire-purchase agreement (within the meaning of the Consumer Credit Act 1974 [c. 39]).

(5) The foregoing provisions of this section apply to contracts and licences whether made before or after the appointed day.

(6) The provisions of this section shall be without prejudice to any rule of law relating to the frustration of contracts and any right of determining a contract or licence exercisable apart from this section.

COMMENTARY ON SECTION 45

General **45.02**

Section 45 provides for the termination, on three months' notice in writing by either party, of patent licences or of contracts to supply patented products following the cessation, from any cause, of relevant patents. It applies to "existing patents" (Sched. 2, para. 1(2)). The section is similar in substance to section 58 [1949], but there are significant differences.

Alternatives to use of section 45 **45.03**

By subsection (6) other legal rights concerning the frustration of contracts or any right of determination of a contract or licence are not affected by an action taken under section 45. Thus, the provisions of the section are wholly additional to any other remedies existing under the law of contract, as indeed they are to treating the agreement as void for its failure to comply with European competition law.

Thus, for a licensee seeking grounds for terminating a licence, the provisions of section 45 can be supplemented or replaced by arguments based on the possible invalidity of the licence because it falls within TRa. 85(1) without exemption being possible under TRa. 85(3). Here the provisions of the Block Exemption Regulations on patent and know-how licensing discussed in Appendix D should be taken into account, particularly the condemnatory provision of Article 3(2) of Regulations No. 2349/84 and 556/89 concerning payment of royalties after expiry of a licensed patent, see also paras. D09 and D23. Unlike section 45, this Article 3(2) deals also with the concomitant licensing of know-how, but to avoid this Article it is sufficient if a licence can be terminated at yearly intervals after patent expiry. Thus, in this respect, section 45 may provide a more favourable termination right to the licensee than does the Patent Licence Block Exemption Regulation. However, under this Article 3(2), no provision for termination need be provided so long as *still secret* know-how continues to be used by the licensee, and here section 45 is probably to like effect, as termination under section 45 may leave the licensee with no right to continue using still secret know-how, see also *Ottung* v. *Klee (Case No. 320/87, unreported judgment of May 12, 1989* (ECJ)).

45.04 *Determination of certain contracts (subss. (1) and (2))*

Subsection (1) appears to cover most acts which would, unless licensed, be regarded as working an invention. Thus it refers to "supply" and "patented product" whereas the 1949 Act referred respectively to "sale or lease" and "patented article". However, the termination provisions of the section relate only to the "patented product or invention" and this could leave in force other provisions of the contract or licence or result in the licensee being disenabled to use still secret know-how, as indicated in para. 45.03 *supra*. For the severability of contract terms, see para. 44.17.

The terms "patented product" and "patented invention" are specially defined in subsection (2) for the purposes of section 45 so that patent applications pending at the date of the contract or licence are treated as patents. Otherwise, the term "patented product" is discussed in paras. 55.04 and 60.11; and the term "patented invention" is discussed in para. 125.08.

There was some doubt whether section 58 [1949] could be effective to terminate a contract or licence entirely, but this doubt is now removed in that subsection (1) limits the extent to which a contract or licence may be determined and the new provisions apply, by subsection (5), to contracts and licences irrespective of when these were made.

The Chartered Institute has expressed the view that the words "product or invention" in the penultimate line of subsection (1) are sufficiently wide as to allow, for example, the supplier of a washing machine on a hire-purchase contract to determine that agreement if *any* patent on that machine should expire ((1985–86) 15 CIPA 283), but see para. 45.05 *infra*.

45.05 *Variation of offending contract (subss. (3) and (4))*

Under subsection (3), for which there was no equivalent under the 1949 Act, on application to the court by either party, the court can order variation of unjust terms or conditions after cessation of the relevant patent or patents.

The question sometimes raised as to the effect of cessation of one or several, but not all, patents included in a contract or licence should be answered by reference to the fact that, under subsections (1) and (2), as well as under section 58(1) [1949], only a patent "by which the product or invention ["article or process" in the 1949 Act] was protected" can be relevant. If any particular product or invention is no longer protected, there is a right to terminate to the extent that that product or invention is concerned.

By subsection (4), there is provision to prevent subsection (1) being used to recover property subject to a hire-purchase agreement as defined in the Consumer Credit Act 1974 (c. 39), but this statute would not prevent a hirer from determining such an agreement, for example as envisaged in para. 45.04 *supra*.

Case commentaries   **45.06**

In *Advance Industries* v. *Frankfurther* ([1958] RPC 392), a licensing agreement under a single United Kingdom and several foreign patents was construed as being determinable under section 58 [1949] so far only as concerned the United Kingdom patent on the expiry of that patent. It was held that the section did not apply to foreign patent monopolies and presumably this would also be the case with respect to section 45. The court was not asked to consider the question of severability of the contractual terms as between the United Kingdom patent and the foreign patents.

However, in *Hansen* v. *Magnovox* ([1977] RPC 301 (CA)), the agreement related to both United Kingdom and foreign patents, but the royalty provisions, particularly one for a minimum payment, were complex and the manner in which the agreement would terminate as the various patents expired was obscure. The terms of the agreement were held to be so interlinked that they could not be severed. In these circumstances Lord Denning M.R. held that section 58 [1949] could not be used to terminate the contract, whereas Bridge L.J. held that it could, but in doing so the agreement was terminated even as to the existing foreign patents. Ormrod L.J. construed the contract in a different manner. Thus, though the appeal was allowed, as a precedent the effect of the decision is obscure.

Under section 58 [1949] the licensee's licence to improvements (even his own) can perhaps be determined after expiry of the patents initially included in the licence, as happened in *National Broach* v. *Churchill* ([1967] RPC 99 (HL)) when a licence was terminated on proper notice. Presumably, such a situation would now be dealt with more equitably under subsection (3). However, in *Regina Glass* v. *Schuller* ([1972] RPC 229 (CA)), terminability of an improvement patent was indicated to depend on the wording of the agreement. In this case the licensee was held to have a continuing licence under an improvement patent after the main patents, and the agreement itself, had expired; and indeed not only on a then royalty-free, but also exclusive, basis. An allied point, even though not directly arising on section 58 [1949], was what royalty should be paid when one patent expires and another remains in force. In *Bristol* v. *Fomento* ([1961] RPC 222) sub-licensees contended in vain that they should not be required to pay royalty under an expired patent. Subsections (1) and (3) would now, presumably, provide a remedy for the sub-licensees.

Post-termination royalties   **45.07**

Whatever the effect of section 45, any attempt to collect royalties for use of an expired patent, at least when calculated on sales taking place after termination, is likely to be held to be contrary to TRa. 85(1), unless such royalties are paid in respect of know-how that remains secret (*Cartoux* v. *Terrapin*, [1981] 1 CMLR 182). Any agreement to such an effect is now likely to render at least the licensor liable to a fine from the European Commission, see *Windsurfing International* v. *E.C. Commission (Case 193/83)* ([1986] ECR 643; [1986] 3 CMLR 489; [1988] FSR 139 referred to in para. C18.

PRACTICE UNDER SECTION 45

45.08 *Referring matter to the court under subsection (3)*

For the procedure for applying to the court under section 45(3), see RSC Ord. 104, r. 21(1)(*b*) reprinted in para. E104.21. The application is brought by originating motion with at least 10 clear days notice between the serving of notice of the motion and the initial hearing. This will be a hearing for directions for the further conduct of the proceedings including directions for serving particulars of the claim, the manner in which evidence should be given (probably by affidavit with liberty to cross-examine), and the date for the full hearing.

45.09 *Preparation and scrutiny of draft licence agreements*

As pointed out in para. 44.11, the effect of the Treaty of Rome on permissible conditions in a patent licence agreement may be considerable and reference on this point should be made to Appendix D. In practice, the statutory provisions of United Kingdom law may be less significant, but the provisions of sections 44 and 45, as well as the other domestic British legislation discussed in paras. 44.13–44.16 should not be overlooked.

46.01
SECTION 46

Patentee's application for entry in register that licences are available as of right

46.—(1) At any time after the grant of a patent its proprietor may apply to the comptroller for an entry to be made in the register to the effect that licences under the patent are to be available as of right.

(2) Where such an application is made, the comptroller shall give notice of the application to any person registered as having a right in or under the patent and, if satisfied that the proprietor of the patent is not precluded by contract from granting licences under the patent, shall make that entry.

(3) Where such an entry is made in respect of a patent—

(*a*) any person shall, at any time after the entry is made, be entitled as of right to a licence under the patent on such terms as may be settled by agreement or, in default of agreement, by the comptroller on the application of the proprietor of the patent or the person requiring the licence;

(*b*) the comptroller may, on the application of the holder of any licence granted under the patent before the entry was made, order the licence to be exchanged for a licence of right on terms so settled;

(*c*) if in proceedings for infringement of the patent (otherwise than by the importation of any article **from a country which is not a member State of the European Economic Community**) the defendant or defender undertakes to take a licence on such terms, no injunction or interdict shall be granted against him and the amount (if any) recoverable against him by way of damages shall not exceed double the amount which would have been payable by him as licence if such a licence on those terms had been granted before the earliest infringement;

(*d*) the renewal fee payable in respect of the patent after the date of the entry shall be half the fee which would be payable if the entry had not been made.

(3A) An undertaking under subsection (3)(c) above may be given at any time before final order in the proceedings, without any admission of liability.

(4) The licensee under a licence of right may (unless, in the case of a licence the terms of which are settled by agreement, the licence otherwise expressly provides) request the proprietor of the patent to take proceedings to prevent any infringement of the patent; and if the proprietor refuses or neglects to do so within two months after being so requested, the licensee may institute proceedings for the infringement in his own name as if he were proprietor, making the proprietor a defendant or defender.

(5) A proprietor so added as defendant or defender shall not be liable for any costs or expenses unless he enters an appearance and takes part in the proceedings.

Note. Section 46 was amended by Schedule 5, paragraph 12 of the 1988 Act with formal effect from August 1, 1989 (S.I. 1989 No. 816).

RELEVANT RULES

Application under section 46(1) for entry in the register

62.—(1) An application under section 46(1) shall be made on Patents   **46.02** Form No. 28/77.

(2) Every entry made in the register consequent upon such an application shall be published in the Journal and in such other manner (if any) as the comptroller thinks necessary.

Application under section 46(3) for licence of right

63.—(1) An application under section 46(3)(*a*) or (*b*) shall be made on   **46.03** Patents Form No. 29/77 and shall be accompanied by a copy thereof and a statement in duplicate setting out fully the facts upon which the applicant relies and the terms of the licence which he is prepared to accept or grant.

(2) The comptroller shall send a copy of the application and statement to the proprietor of the patent or, as the case may be, the person requiring a licence, who, if he does not agree to the terms set out in the statement, shall, within three months of the receipt of such copies, file a counterstatement in duplicate setting out fully the grounds of his objection and the comptroller shall send a copy of the counter-statement direct to the applicant.

(3) The comptroller may give such directions as he may think fit with regard to the subsequent procedure.

Note. It is thought that at the next general revision of the Rules, the opportunity may be taken to effect some change in the procedure under rule 63 for settlement of the terms of a licence of right in the light of the Comptroller's experience of the operation of the present rule which may have enabled patentees to delay the outcome of the proceedings. The latest Supplement of this Work *re.* this para. should therefore be consulted.

46.04   ARTICLES

A. Firth, "Licences of right: 'New existing patents' under the Patents Act 1977", [1986] EIPR 168;

M. Hills, "Compulsory licences of right", (1987–88) 17 CIPA 134;

J. Turner, "Allen & Hanburys v. Generics: Acte claire—and wrong", [1988] EIPR 186.

COMMENTARY ON SECTION 46

46.05 *General*

Section 46 concerns the practice of permitting a proprietor to make available as of right licences under his patent, thereby reducing by half the renewal fees payable to maintain the patent in force. It applies also to "existing patents" (Sched. 2, para. 1(2)), but only for applications for endorsements made on or after June 1, 1978. Endorsements requested before that date continue to be dealt with under the repealed section 35 [1949] (Sched. 4, para. 8(1)), see para. A035.3. Also a "new existing patent" after its sixteenth year is to be treated as if endorsed "licences of right" under section 35 [1949] (Sched. 1, para. (4)(2)(*c*)), see para. 25.11. Because such deemed endorsement occurs as the result of operation of the present Act and did not occur before June 1, 1978, the present section 46 (and not the repealed s. 35 [1949]) applies for the settlement of the terms of licences of right thereunder (*Allen & Hanburys* v. *Generics*, [1986] RPC 203 (HL)). There are no special provisions for existing patents which are patents of addition and, therefore, these become subject to separate deemed endorsements and separate licences have to be sought thereunder.

The procedure for voluntarily according "licences of right" status to a patent under section 46 is closely similar to that which prevailed under section 35 [1949], except that the concept of endorsement of the patent with the words "licences of right" is replaced in the Act by that of making an appropriate entry in the register, a change necessary due to the absence of a Letters Patent document in the present form of patent grant.

The entry in the register is one that licences under the patent are "available as of right" (subs. (1)). An application for such an entry is notified by the Comptroller to any registered licensee or other person entered in the register as having an interest in or under the patent (subs. (2)), for example a mortgagee or chargee.

The consequences of such an entry (or deemed entry in the case of a new existing patent) are set out in subsection (3), *viz.* (*a*) an entitlement to a licence on terms to be settled by the Comptroller if not otherwise agreed; (*b*) an order by the Comptroller for an existing licence under the patent to be exchanged for a new one on terms settled by the Comptroller in absence of agreement (as discussed in paras. 46.07–46.27 *infra*); (*c*) a potential limitation in infringement proceedings on the grant of an injunction and on an award of damages; and (*d*) reducing by half the renewal fees payable on the patent (as discussed in para. 46.28 *infra*). A licensee under a licence of right also has the right to call for infringement proceedings to be instituted under the patent, or otherwise to take such action himself (subs. (4)), without the patentee taking an active part in those proceedings (subs. (5)), each also discussed in para. 46.28 *infra*.

An appeal lies from any decision of the Comptroller (s. 97(1)), but with further appeal to the Court of Appeal only on a point of law and with leave (s. 97(3)). It would not appear that a proprietor or putative licensee domiciled in Scotland can require proceedings to be held in Scotland, see section 123(2)(*f*) and para. 98.07.

Under section 35 [1949] and its predecessors there was only one reported case (*Cassou's Patent*, [1971] RPC 91), but with the deemed endorsement of new existing patents commencing in 1982 many cases have since arisen in which the terms of licences of right have come to be settled, often in fiercely contested proceedings, leading to a plethora of decisions many of which can now be seen to have had transient effect as they have been overtaken by later decisions, particularly where these have been decided on appeal. These cases are reviewed in paras. 46.14–46.27 *infra*, but now perhaps have a diminished importance because, from January 15, 1989, it became possible to cancel the deemed endorsement of an existing patent in so far as this claims a "medical product" (s. 293 [1988] and rule 67A, discussed in paras. 47.10–47.14). The way in which the law developed in this area can be partly seen from the papers by A. Firth and M. Hills listed in para. 46.04 *supra*.

Nevertheless, the cases decided under section 46(3)(*a*) may come to be of importance for a different reason. This is because the concept of "licences of right" has been applied to the new design right (under s. 237 [1988]), as well as to copyrights existing prior to August 1, 1989 from a date five years thereafter (Sched. 1, para. 19(2) [1988], and S.I. 1989 No. 816). It would not be surprising if cases decided under section 46(3)(*a*) did not have at least some precedent effect under these sections of the 1988 Act.

As a consequence of the cases decided after 1982 under subsection (3)(*a*), subsection (3)(*c*) came to be amended and subsection (3A) added by the 1988 Act, as discussed in para. 46.21 *infra*.

Application to make "licences of right" entry in the register (subss. (1) and (2))   **46.06**

Under subsection (1) an application by the proprietor of the patent for an entry to be made in the register can be made at any time after grant. Application is under rule 62, reprinted in para. 46.02 *supra* and discussed in para. 46.29 *infra*. It is not clear what procedure would be followed if the grant took place under section 9 at a time when a question of entitlement under section 8 was unresolved, and an application is made by the proprietor under section 46 before the pending matter is decided under section 37. The application for an entry is not advertised, but the Comptroller is required by subsection (2) to give notice to any person registered as having a right in or under the patent and, if he is satisfied that the proprietor is not precluded by contract from granting licences, he must make the entry. After an entry has been made in the register, a notice is published in the O.J.

Settling terms of licence of right (subs. (3)(a) and (b))

—The basic procedure   **46.07**

Subsection (3)(*a*) states that, after the register entry has been made (which includes a deemed endorsement of an existing patent at the end of its 16th year, see

347

para. 46.05 *supra*), *any* person is "entitled as of right to a licence under the patent". This means that the procedure can be invoked by any person intending to take a licence, even if only as an insurance against infringement and even if the patentee would not have willingly negotiated the terms with him (*Du Pont's (Blades') Patent*, [1988] RPC 479). Thus, the proceedings under section 46(3)(*a*) are essentially different from those under section 48, since in the latter there is in issue whether a licence should be ordered at all, while under the former only the terms of the licence are in issue, see *Halcon's Patent* ([1989] RPC 1).

The terms of the "licence of right" are to be settled by agreement or, in default thereof, by the Comptroller on application by either the proprietor or the prospective licensee. The procedure for this is governed by rule 63 (reprinted in para. 46.03 *supra*, and discussed in para. 46.30 *infra*). Curiously, the Comptroller does not seem to have the power to order the grant of a licence himself as he can do under section 48, see section 108 and para. 108.02. Subsection (3)(*b*) provides for an existing licensee also to apply to have his license exchanged for one settled under subsection (3)(*a*). The procedure is the same as for the settlement of terms of a new licence under subsection (3)(*a*)).

Rule 63(1) provides that the party making the application for settlement of terms of a licence of right should file a statement "setting out fully the facts upon which the application relies and the terms of the licence which he is prepared to accept or grant". Rule 63(2) provides for opposition to that application. Normally the application will be made by a prospectively licensee, with the patentee entering that opposition by filing a counter-statement setting out his objection. Often the patentee will feel it prudent to put forward with such counter-statement the form of licence which he would not contest further.

In *Kaken Pharmaceutical's Patent* (SRIS O/40/89, *noted* IPD 12048) the existing exclusive licensee under the patent sought to intervene in the settlement proceedings, but the Comptroller held he had no power to permit this: and, even if he had such power, intervention was not necessary on the facts because the licensee worked the invention by importation and its development expenditure had been to establish the market rather than develop the invention as such.

46.08   *—Comptroller only settles terms in dispute*

The Comptroller is required to "settle" the terms of a licence. Accordingly, the Comptroller only gives a decision on licence terms which are in dispute between the parties. Thus, if during proceedings under subsection (3)(*a*) or (*b*) the parties reach an understanding as to the terms which patentee would no longer contest, then there is nothing left for the Comptroller to settle and, in these circumstances, the Comptroller feels obliged to make an order that a licence should be granted in the terms no longer in contention, see *ICI's Patent* [Generics' Application] (SRIS O/128/86). Here a royalty equivalent to 47 per cent. of the Patentee's selling price was voluntarily accepted by each of two licencees, see *Smith Kline & French's Patents [Generics' Application]* (SRIS C/12/89, *noted* IPD 12036) and *Smith Kline & French's Patents [Harris's Application]* (SRIS C/22/89). In the *ICI* case it was indicated that, had the Comptroller been required to give a decision on the hearing which had already taken place, he would have been unlikely to have settled the licence on these terms.

The reason why it has been customary to request the Comptroller to make a formal order for the grant of a licence on terms which the patentee indicates he would not appeal, though without implying *consent* thereto, is so that the licence can be seen as one granted against the wishes of the patentee, in order possibly to take advantage of the decision in *Pharmon* v. *Hoechst (Case 19/84)* ([1985] ECR 2281; [1985] 2 CMLR 775; [1986] FSR 108 (ECJ)) in which it was held that the EEC doctrine of "exhaustion of rights" in relation to importation of a patented product from elsewhere within the EEC (other than from Spain or Portugal) would not apply in the case of a licence which the patentee was compelled to grant, see para. C15. However, it is not clear that a licence of right arising under section 46(3)(*a*) or (*b*) is to be equated with a compulsory licence ordered under section 48, see the remarks of Lord Diplock in *Allen & Hanburys* v. *Generics* ([1986] RPC 203 (HL)).

Also, where a patentee was not prepared to offer his witnesses for cross-examination, he felt constrained to accept the licensee's offered royalty of 5 per cent. of the licensee's selling price, though originally the patentee had sought a 30 per cent. royalty on this basis, see *Hilti's Patent* [*Structural Fastening's Application*] (SRIS O/65/86, *noted* IPD 9069).

—Other limitations on power of Comptroller   **46.09**

The Comptroller takes the view that subsection (3) does not give him the power to review an existing licence (*Diamond Shamrock's Patent*, [1987] RPC 91), but the applicant can apply for a licence additional to his existing licence (as was done in that case) or seek exchange of that licence for a new one under subsection (3)(*b*).

The Comptroller also has no power to settle terms on an interim basis when the applicant is prepared to accept the patentee's terms if these could be varied should an application by another lead to settlement of more favourable terms (*ICI's Patent* [*Harris's Application*], SRIS O/59/86 and C/82/86, *noted* IPD 9070).

It also seems doubtful whether the Comptroller has power to grant a licence under any intellectual property right other than the patent which is the specific subject of the proceedings. Certainly, there is no such power in respect of a patent not yet subject to the "licence of right" provisions; and it is not seen that the position should be any different as regards any associated copyrights, because the licensee is not obliged to copy the precise form of the patentee's own product. However, whether there is a freedom to copy the drawings in a patent specification is a matter of some controversy, see para. 60.28. Also, in *Eurofix and Bauco* v. *Hilti* (OJEC 11.3.88, L. 65/19), *Hilti*, under pressure from the E.C. Commission, gave an undertaking that it would not enforce its copyrights against those who had obtained licences of right under its patents.

—The basic principles for settlement of terms of licence of right   **46.10**

The basic principles upon which the terms of a licence of right are to be settled are those which, notionally, would be agreed between a willing licensor and willing licensee (*Allen & Hanburys* v. *Generics*, [1986] RPC 203 (HL)), even though in many cases this concept is wholly artificial because the patentee would not, of his free will, have been prepared to grant any licence to the entity seeking the licence of right. That case also decided that the licence terms should not compensate the patentee for loss of manufacturing profit, following *Patchett's Patent* ([1967] RPC 237 (CA)). It further decided that the terms of a licence of right are essentially a matter for the Comptroller's discretion, with the power to impose any terms thought appropriate to restrict the acts of the applicant which, in the absence of a licence, would be an infringement of the patent and terms consequent thereon, though the Comptroller is not able to impose any positive obligation on the patentee. However, for limitations on the powers of the Comptroller as to certain licence conditions, see para. 46.09 *supra*.

Nevertheless, the Comptroller's discretion must be exercised judicially so that, if the Comptroller misdirects himself, the decision may be varied on appeal (*Ciba-Geigy's Patent* [*FMC Corp.'s Application*], [1986] RPC 403). Moreover, since an

349

appeal from the Comptroller involves a rehearing of the case, an appellate court is, anyway, entitled to exercise a fresh discretion (*Allen & Hanbury's (Salbutamol) Patent*, [1987] RPC 327 (CA)), see para. 97.07.

The four years extension of an existing patent is not to be regarded as a windfall for the patentee (*Purac's Patent*, SRIS O/64/85): indeed a meritorious patentee might have looked forward to an extension of five years under section 23 [1949] (*Smith Kline & French's Patents [Generics' Application]*, SRIS C/12/89, noted IPD 12036) or even 10 years in an exceptional case (s. 23(1) [1949]). In *Bergwerksverband's Patent* (SRIS O/58/89, noted IPD 12065) the applicant sought a royalty-free licence on the ground that he had held a licence on the Commencement Day (June 1, 1978) so that Schedule 1, paragraph 4(2)(*b*) should apply. However, this was held not so: firstly, the licence had been terminated prior to the application for the licence of right, and it was held that this paragraph 4(2)(*b*) only applies to subsisting licences; and, secondly, the licence had been renegotiated to start afresh from June 1, 1978 so that the parties had not contemplated a royalty-free position after the 16th year.

Because the licence is one to be granted as "of right", the suitability of the applicant to hold a licence is an irrelevant factor in proceedings under subsection (3)(*a*) (*Suspa-Federungstechnik's Patent*. SRIS O/113/85, noted IPD 8084).

The Comptroller has also held that the patent is to be assumed to be valid (*Schering's Patent (No. 2)*, SRIS O/128/87 and C/91/87; and *Holywell Mining's Patent*, SRIS O/47/88), but this seems unrealistic if the terms are to be settled on a willing licensor/willing licensee basis where the probability of invalidity will often be an important negotiating factor.

46.11   —*Lack of preconditions for settlement of terms*

It is *not* a pre-condition to an application under subsection (3)(*a*) that negotiations for a voluntary licence should first have been concluded. A potential licensee may make his application suggesting terms he thinks appropriate. If these are not acceptable, application under the subsection may then be filed (*Eli Lilly's Patent*, SRIS O/5/86). Indeed the applicant may even file his application without prior approach to the patentee, because it is always open to a patentee to accept the terms offered in the statement of case and, if he opposes the application by filing a counterstatement, there is then the necessary default of agreement, see *Roussel-Uclaf's (Clemence & Le Martret's) Patent*, [1987] RPC 109).

46.12   —*Time for seeking settlement of terms*

A licence of right cannot take effect until its terms have been agreed or settled by the Comptroller (*Allen & Hanburys* v. *Generics*, [1986] RPC 203 (HL)) and, accordingly, the Comptroller normally states explicitly that the licence which he orders shall take effect from the date of his decision. An application for settlement of terms can, however, be filed in advance of the deemed endorsement of an existing patent so that it may come into effect at an early date (*Allen & Hanburys* v. *Generics, supra*). After that decision, the Comptroller decided administratively to accept applications under subsection (3)(*a*) (or (*b*)) from the end of the 15th year of an existing patent (see *Eli Lilly's Patent [Second Preliminary Decision]*, SRIS O/56/89, noted IPD 12081), and this became a statutory rule from January 15, 1989 (Sched. 1, para. 4B, inserted by s. 294 [1988]) and made effective by s. 305(2) [1988]).

46.13   —*Multiple applications under the same patent*

Where there are multiple applications for licences under the same patent, the Comptroller has stated that all should be licensed on the same terms (*ICI's Patent*

[*Harris's Application*], SRIS O/59/86 and C/82/86 and *Ciba-Geigy's Patent* [*Portman's Application*], SRIS O/159/86). However, this statement should be accepted only as a guide because each licence has to be settled on the basis of the evidence before the deciding tribunal. Nevertheless, where royalty rates have been separately calculated in different applications under the same patent, the conclusion has generally been the same in each case, see *Bayer's Patent* [*Nifedipine*] [*Generics' Application*] (SRIS O/49/86, *noted* IPD 9050) and *Bayer's Patents* [*Nifedipine*] [*Harris's Application*] (SRIS O/8/88, *noted* IPD 10110); and also *Smith Kline & French's Patents* [*Generics' Application*] (SRIS C/12/89, *noted* IPD 12036) and *Smith Kline & French's Patents* [*Harris's Application*] (SRIS C/22/89).

However, terms imposed to deal with a particular corporate structure of one applicant, *e.g.* to permit sub-licensing to an associated company, will not necessarily be included in another licence under the same patent (*Hilti's Patent* [*Bauco's Application*] (SRIS O/170/86), though on appeal the sub-licence provision was deleted on the facts of the case ([1988] RPC 51).

Assessment of royalty terms

—*The basic criterion*   **46.14**

No guidance is given in section 46 itself as to the criteria on which the applicable royalty terms should be settled. However, besides the inchoate willing licensor/willing licensee approach mentioned in para. 46.10 *supra*, in *Allen & Hanburys* v. *Generics* ([1986] RPC 203 (HL)), Lord Diplock found guidance in the criteria set out in section 50 because section 53(4) requires section 46 to be applied to a "licence of right" endorsement imposed under either section 48 or 51.

Thus, the principle of section 50(1)(*b*), that the patentee should receive "reasonable remuneration having regard to the nature of the invention", assumes importance; and, in *Allen & Hanburys' (Salbutamol) Patent* ([1987] RPC 327 (CA)), considerable emphasis was placed on the principles enunciated in *Geigy's Patent* ([1964] RPC 391) for the settlement of terms for a compulsory licence on a medicinal patent under section 41 [1949], and these principles have been applied, to some extent, in many of the cases settled under the present subsection (3)(*a*), as discussed in para. 46.16 *infra*. Nevertheless, those principles are not entirely apposite in the present context because section 41 [1949] required that, in settling the terms of a licence on a patent for food or medicine, the Comptroller "should endeavour to secure that food, medicines and surgical and curative devices should be available to the public at the lowest prices consistent with the patentees' deriving a reasonable advantage from their patent rights" (s. 41(2) [1949]), as noted in *Smith Kline & French's Patents* [*Generics' Application*] (SRIS C/12/89, *noted* IPD 12036) and this sentiment is not contained in section 50.

—*The different approaches*   **46.14**

Three distinct approaches to the assessment of an appropriate royalty rate have been applied. These are: (1) an accounting assessment of the value of the patent to the patentee *as such* (*i.e.* manufacturing profits earned by the patentee having to be disregarded, at least so long as the majority decision in *Allen & Hanburys (Salbutamol) Patent*, ([1987] RPC 327 (CA) remains controlling on the point), such assessment usually being conducted in accordance with the principles determined in *Geigy's Patent* ([1964] RPC 391), this method being discussed in para. 46.16 *infra*; (2) a comparison approach, *e.g.* against other licences granted by the patentee, or accepted by the licensee, where the circumstances can be seen to be comparable, and/or a comparison with decisions in licence of right or compulsory licence determinations concerning inventions of corresponding nature, as discussed in para. 46.17 *infra*; and (3) a profit-sharing approach between the licensor and licensee, or a consideration of what the licensee can afford to pay, as discussed in para. 46.18 *infra*.

It has become customary that, where there is sufficient evidence, each of these methods of assessment should be used, each result then serving as a cross-check against the other, with a final assessment then being made at a sort of average of the rates derived from the different approaches applied, see in particular *Smith Kline & French's Patents [Generics' Application]* (SRIS C/12/89, *noted* IPD 12036).

46.16   —*The section 41 [1949] calculations*

In *Geigy's Patent* ([1964] RPC 391) it was laid down that royalty rates for a compulsory licence under a patent relating to food, medicine or a surgical or curative device under section 41 [1949] should be assessed by an accounting exercise consisting of separately calculating three elements, *viz.* (1) a figure for recovery of the patentee's research and development costs; (2) a figure for the recoupment of the promotional expenditure incurred by the patentee in creating and maintaining a market for the patented product; and (3) a reward by an appropriate profit margin. This approach has been used in many cases under section 46(3)(*a*), see particularly the appeal decisions in *Allen & Hanburys' (Salbutamol) Patent* [1987] RPC 437 (CA)), where it was held that this calculation was appropriate in order to estimate the patentee's "reasonable remuneration having regard to the nature of the invention" (as required by s. 50(1)(*b*)); and those in *Syntex's Patent* ([1986] RPC 585); and *Smith Kline & French's Patents [Generics' Application]* (SRIS C/12/89, *noted* IPD 12036).

While the Comptroller has taken the view in several cases that this approach "consistently overstates" the appropriate royalty (see *e.g. Ciba-Geigy's Patent [Agan's Application]*, SRIS O/85/86) and accordingly tended to discount the result of the calculation by up to 40 per cent., that view would now seem discredited in view of the above-mentioned appeal decisions, and especially in view of the *Smith Kline & French* decision (*supra*) where it was pointed out (as noted more fully in para. 46.14, *supra*) that section 41 [1949] required consideration to be given to making medicines, etc., available at a low price, a criterion missing from section 50 and anyway inconsistent with a licence granted by a willing licensor (as noted in the *Smith Kline & French* decision, *supra*). Nevertheless the section 41 approach is to be regarded as illustrative, rather than determinative, see the *Salbutamol* decision (at p. 360) and the *Syntex* decision (at p. 599).

In the first, R & D expenditure, element it has been customary, as in *Geigy's case* (*supra*), to assess that element as the percentage corresponding to the percentage of the patentee's current world-wide expenditure on research and development as a percentage of its current world-wide sales of products which are "the fruits of that research". Each of these figures is usually taken over a period of the latest three years for which figures are available, and in each case limiting the figures broadly to the class of business within which the patent in suit falls, *e.g.* where a patent is in the prescription pharmaceutical field and the patentee has activities in other fields, the calculations are carried out only in relation to R & D expenditure and sales figures in the prescription pharmaceutical field. The delimitation of this field can lead to controversy but, because it is customary to exclude expenditure on development of new formulations of existing products, sales figures attributable to inventive formulations of known products should also be excluded (*Smith Kline & French's Patents, supra*).

The second, promotional, element is normally calculated as the costs incurred by the patentee in promoting the patented product, expressed as a percentage of its sales thereof, the calculation being divided up into an annual cost of maintaining the market and an initial cost in creating that market, the latter being averaged over the remaining life of the patent after the first marketing of the patented product, for details of which see the *Geigy* case (*supra*).

In that case, as well as in another section 41 [1949] case (*Hoffman-La Roche's Patent*, [1973] RPC 601 at 625), the promotional element was then reduced on the basis that some of the promotion would have been of the brand name used by the patentee to identify its product, rather than for that product as such. Following that principle, it became the standard practice for the Comptroller under section 46(3)(*a*) to discount the calculated promotional element by 40 per cent. However, in *Smith Kline & French* (*supra*), the Patents Court accepted the argument that (at least in the case before it where the drug was of an entirely new type) the patentees had created the whole market for the patented product and that, therefore, there should be no discounting of the calculated figure.

The third, profit, element was assessed in the *Geigy* case (*supra*) as an uplift of 22.5 per cent. of the sum of the research and promotional expenditure elements, but under section 46(3)(*a*) the Comptroller has consistently refused to allow more than a 20 per cent. uplift as a so-called traditional figure for a return on capital in the current economic climate. However, in *Smith Kline & French* (*supra*), the Patents Court accepted the contention that the patentees were entitled to a profit contribution corresponding to the current level of profitability of the business division of the Patentee responsible for marketing the patented product, this being the difference between the operating profits and costs of that Division, with the expenditure of that Division on research, development and promotion being taken into account as part of its operating costs, giving in that case a profit uplift of 43 per cent. to the sum of the R & D and promotional expenditure elements.

—By considering "comparables"   **46.17**

The "comparables" approach is best seen in relation to inventions which the patentee himself exploits only by licensing, when the licence of right will be settled on terms providing him with an equivalent royalty (*Upjohn's and Takeda's Patents (No. 2)*, SRIS O/161/87, *noted* IPD 10091); and where the invention is not seen to involve a high degree of innovation, for example with an unremarkable mechanical development. Here there is a tendency for the Comptroller at least to start from the position that the standard rate of royalty applicable to licensing of a mechanical invention is at 5 per cent. of the licensee's selling price, this being the rate settled in *Cassou's Patent* ([1971] RPC 91), decided under section 35 [1949]), and in some of the compulsory licence cases decided under section 37 [1949]. Thus, this royalty rate was settled in: *Purac's Patent* (SRIS O/64/85) relating to water treatment; in *Ashland Oil's Patent* (SRIS O/35/86 and C/24/87, *noted* [1987] EIPR D–53) for a foundry binder; and in *Robert Abraham's Patent* (SRIS O/186/87, *noted* IPD 10112) for a machine for moulding cement slabs. Such rate was also expressed in *Cyprane's Patent* (SRIS O/108/88, *noted* IPD 11061) to be customary for a mechanical invention.

A patentee must then seek to justify a higher rate of royalty based upon special factors, *e.g.* as for: the 7 per cent. royalty settled in *Suspa-Federungstechnik's Patent* (SRIS O/113/85, *noted* IPD 8084) for a washing machine leg; and the like royalty in *Holywell Mining's Patent* (SRIS O/47/88) because of the grant of limited sub-licensing rights; and especially the 15 per cent. royalty settled in *Shiley's Patent* ([1988] RPC 97) for a heart valve prosthesis because of the specialist manufacturing requirements of the product and the efforts made to establish the specialist market for it. In *Vendking Industrial's Patent* (SRIS O/23/88) the royalty for a brewing mechanism of a hot beverage vending machine was likewise initially calculated at 5 per cent. of the patentee's price for the machine, but then adjusted to allow for: (a) the lower price expected to be charged by the licensee; and (b) the enhanced value which the machine would have from the incorporation of the invention therein, resulting in a settled royalty equivalent to 4 per cent. of the Patentee's price. In *Bergwerksverband's Patent* (SRIS O/58/89, *noted* IPD 12065) the royalty was settled as that applicable at the time the applicant had terminated the licence it previously held under the patent.

From the outset it was accepted that patents for pharmaceutical products would justify a higher royalty and, in *Allen & Hanburys (Salbutamol) Patent* ([1987] RPC 327 (CA)) and *Syntex's Patent* ([1986] RPC 525), royalties were each settled by the Patents Court at 27–28 per cent. of the patentee's selling price, though the *Salbutamol* royalty was reduced to 23.6 per cent. by the Court of Appeal. Shortly after this decision, the Comptroller settled royalties in respect of five pharmaceutical products at rates within the range corresponding to 23–27.4 per cent. of the patentee's selling price, see: *Eli Lilly's Patent (No. 2)* (SRIS O/69/87); *Pfizer's Patent* (SRIS O/78/87, *noted* IPD 10058); *AB Hassle's Patent* (SRIS O/79/87); *Frosst's Patent* (SRIS O/84/87, *noted* IPD 10059); and *Merck's Patent* (SRIS O/85/87), but in *Eli Lilly* the rate settled by the Comptroller was increased on appeal to the equivalent of 30 per cent. of the Patentee's selling price (*Eli Lilly's Patent (No. 4)*. SRIS C/33/89) because others had voluntarily accepted a royalty at this level.

In *Pfizer's Patent* (*supra*) a comparison was made of the royalty on a cost per patient day against that settled for a drug of similar utility in *Syntex's Patent* (*supra*).

Consequently, the Comptroller tended to take the view that the royalty for a pharmaceutical product would vary between about 25–28 per cent. of the patentee's selling price according to his perception of the medical value of the product in question. Thus, on this basis, he settled the royalty in *Smith Kline & French's Patents [Generics' Application]* (SRIS O/46/88), and in the parallel case of *Smith Kline & French's Patents [Harris's Application]* (SRIS O/63/88) each at a value equivalent to 28 per cent. of the Patentee's selling price, but in *Upjohn's and Takeda's Patents (No. 2)* (*supra*) at only 24 per cent., the drug here being judged to be in the lower range of medical value. However, on the appeals on the two *Smith Kline* cases (SRIS C/12/89, *noted* IPD 12036 and C/22/89 respectively) this approach was criticised and the royalty was raised to a value equivalent to 45 per cent. of that selling price because this was shown to be justified by each of the three basic approaches to royalty assessment described broadly in para. 46.15 *supra*. In particular, it was noted that each of these applicants had accepted royalty terms on a patent judged to relate also to a drug of pioneering importance at a rate corresponding to 47 per cent. of the patentee's selling price for that product (for which see para. 46.08 *supra*) and had, apparently, been able to market that drug profitably despite payment of such a royalty.

Meanwhile, the Comptroller has been asked to settle royalties in advance of hearings and on the basis of little filed evidence. In these circumstances a "comparables" approach has necessarily been adopted, with regard being particularly paid to terms settled in other applications by the same applicant, see *Farmitalia's Patent* (SRIS O/159/88) and *Science Union's Patent (No. 2)* (SRIS O/181/88, *noted* IPD 12002), where royalties for pharmaceutical products were respectively settled at 25 and 30.5 per cent. of the Patentees' selling prices.

Rates of royalty voluntarily accepted under the patent in suit by others have also been held in other cases to be a firm guide as to the appropriate royalty, see particularly *Syntex's Patent* (*supra*) and *Eli Lilly's Patent (No. 2)* (*supra*). In *Smith (T.J.) & Nephew's Patent (No. 2)* (SRIS O/126/87 and C/21/88) a lump sum paid by a voluntary licensee under the patent was taken into account but converted into a percentage factor, a lump sum royalty not being deemed appropriate for a licence of right; and in *Kaken Pharmaceutical's Patent* (SRIS O/40/89, *noted* IPD 12048), the Comptroller ordered production of the exclusive licence already in existence under the patent so that the terms thereof could be taken into consideration.

It is here convenient to note the levels of royalty rates which have been awarded for inventions not having either the character of a mere mechanical invention, nor the sophistication of a pharmaceutical product involving highly speculative research with successful products having to pay for the many abortive research avenues necessarily explored, and the high cost of obtaining regulatory approval under the Medicines Act 1968 (c. 67). Thus, for example, where regulatory approval is necessary before marketing can commence, but where (as with agrochemical products) it is thought research is less costly or speculative than with pharmaceutical products, royalty rates have been settled at rates intermediate between those assessed for pharmaceutical products and those for inventions of a general mechanical nature. For example, royalty rates were settled: at 7.2 per cent. for an anaesthetic inhalation apparatus in *Cyprane's Patent* (*supra*); at 12.7–14 per cent. for herbicides in *Schering's Patent (No. 2)* (SRIS O/128/87 and C/91/87), in *Schering Agrochemicals' Patent* (SRIS O/115/88), and in *Ciba-Geigy's Patent* [*Agan's Application*] (SRIS O/85/86); at 11.25 per cent. for an adhesive wound dressing in *Smith (T.J.) & Nephew's Patent (No. 2)* (SRIS O/126/87 and C/21/88); at 15 per cent. for a heart valve prosthesis in *Shiley's Patent* (*supra*); and at 25 per cent. for an allergen test material, though it should be noted that these rates are not uniformly based, some being based on the selling price of the patentee and some on that of the licensee.

The "comparables" approach has also, perforce, been adopted by the Comptroller when he is asked to settle a royalty rate with little or no evidence placed before him. In such a case, average values for the three elements of the section 41 [1949] calculations (considered in para. 46.16 *supra*), as decided in cases held to be comparable, have been taken, see *Procter & Gamble's Patent* (SRIS O/88/88) and *Farmitalia's Patent* (*supra*).

Because of the availability of the "comparables" approach, each party to proceedings under section 46(3)(*a*) proceedings can now be expected to be required to disclose licence agreements already entered into which the other party is able to contend are prima facie to be considered as granted, or taken, in comparable circumstances. Such disclosure will be either by normal discovery (as in *Smith (T.J.) & Nephew's Patent*, SRIS O/120/86, *noted* IPD 9083) or upon requirement by the Comptroller under rule 106 (as in *Smith Kline & French's Cimetidine Patents*, [1988] RPC 148) when the documents become available as evidence whether or not relied upon by either party), for which see para. 72.44. However, all such disclosures will normally be treated as confidential documents under rule 94, and sometimes with special provisions limiting disclosure to legal advisers of the receiving party, for which see para. 72.44A. Also, a licence granted by a patentee in special circumstances will not necessarily be regarded as a comparable licence to that to be granted in the proceedings under section 46(3)(*a*), see for example *Smith Kline & French's Patents* [*Harris's Application*] (*supra*).

—By considering the profits available   **46.18**

While it is not a relevant consideration whether the licensee can trade profitably at the royalty rate settled, one method that has been used for the assessment of an appropriate royalty is to consider the profits likely to be earned by the licensee and then to consider sharing these in some proportion between the licensee and the patentee. This method has been used less often than the other methods of assessment considered in paras. 46.16 and 46.17 *supra*, because often there is no available evidence, or at least no reliable evidence, as to the price at which the licensee will sell the patented product or of the level of profits likely to be achieved by the licensee. Also, in *Allen & Hanburys' (Salbutamol) Patent* ([1987] RPC 327 (CA)), it was indicated that the licensee should only receive an equitable share of the profit available if it sold the product at the same price as the patentee, which is rarely the case.

Nevertheless, this approach was adopted in the following cases at the stated percentage of the estimated profit to go to the patentee: *Diamond Shamrock's Patent* ([1987] RPC 91) at 25 per cent.; *Schering's Patent (No. 2)* (SRIS O/128/87 and C/91/87) at 30 per cent.; *Tanabe's Patent* (SRIS O/140/86) at 50 per cent.; and *Ciba-Geigy's Patent [Agan's Application]* (SRIS O/85/86) at 55 per cent.

A modification of the profit-sharing approach was adopted in *Smith Kline & French's Patents [Generics' Application]* (SRIS C/12/89, *noted* IPD 12036) where the average profit level of the applicant, as a return on investment (rather than on sales) was estimated based upon its activities thought to consist largely of selling drugs on a generic basis often under licences obtained after similar proceedings under section 46(3)(*a*). When this profit margin was deducted from the level of profit which the Patentee calculated the Licensee could be expected to make, a profit of 43 per cent. on the Patentee's wholesale price was calculated to be achievable and it was noted that this was comparable to the Patentee's own level of operating profit: accordingly, the 43 per cent. figure represented a royalty which the Patents Court thought was affordable by the licensee.

46.19 *—Basis on which royalty rate is to be paid*

While the calculations are normally carried out first to derive a royalty rate expressed as a percentage of the patentee's own selling price, it is recognised that this should then be modified to account for the presumed lower selling price of the licensee, particularly with pharmaceutical products where the licensee sells the drug on a generic, rather than brand name, basis at a considerably lower level than the patentee's price. Thus, in cases decided under section 41 [1949] it was customary to apply an uplift factor in converting the settled royalty from one based on the patentee's price to one based on the price of the licensee, and that approach was followed in some of the early cases decided under section 46(3)(*a*).

However, in *Allen & Hanburys' (Salbutamol) Patent* ([1987] RPC 327 (CA)) and in *Syntex's Patent* ([1986] RPC 585), it was considered appropriate to convert the percentage figure to a fixed sum per unit weight of the product supplied, calculated on the patentee's wholesale selling price. This method has, since these decisions, become the normal method of expressing the settled royalty, see: *Upjohn's Patents (No. 4)* (SRIS C/70/88, reversing the Comptroller's decision on this point in *Upjohn's and Takeda's Patents (No. 2)*, SRIS O/161/87, *noted* IPD 10091); and *Smith Kline & French's Patents [Generics' Application]* (SRIS C/12/89, *noted* IPD 12036). Indeed, in that case, it was held appropriate to apply the fixed rate to hospital sales whereas these had been excluded from the fixed unit price in the appealed decision of the Comptroller (SRIS O/46/88), there being no basis for fixing a different royalty for hospital sales.

However, a royalty will be expressed on the licensee's selling price if the parties so agree, as in *Farmitalia's Patent* (SRIS O/159/88), or where the Comptroller has no evidence enabling him to calculate the royalty on any other basis, as in *Procter & Gamble's Patent* (SRIS O/88/88).

Also, the parties may expressly agree on some other basis which they deem to be more convenient, as in *Diamond Shamrock's Patent* ([1987] RPC 91), where the patent was for a coated electrode and the royalty was based on the area of that coating.

Occasionally, though not usually, the royalty terms settled on a fixed unit price basis have included a provision for indexation of this figure in accordance with some published price index, see *Shiley's Patent* ([1988] RPC 97).

—Miscellaneous points on royalty terms   **46.20**

Where the same patentee holds two patents for which a joint licence of right can be (and is) sought, a patentee must provide evidence for the royalty split between the two patents if that is desired (*Smith Kline & French's Cimetidine Patents*, [1988] RPC 148), though eventually in that case the royalty was set as a total figure for the two patents in issue (*Smith Kline & French's Patents [Generics Application]*, SRIS O/46/88 and C/12/89, *noted* IPD 12036). An alternative is to grant a royalty-free licence under the second patent, especially if this is a patent of addition. Another example of licences granted under multiple patents is *Upjohn's Patents (No. 3)* (SRIS O/176/87). However, where multiple patents are involved which are held by different proprietors, separate licences have to be granted and separate royalty rates computed: an example of such is *Upjohn's and Takeda's Patents* (SRIS C/49/87).

Security for royalty was ordered in *Shiley's Patent* ([1988] RPC 97), where the applicant was resident abroad, this to be effective throughout the life of the patent, and also in *Pharmacia's* (SRIS O/47/87) where the applicant was a newly-formed company with few apparent assets. Also, in this latter case, a minimum royalty provision was included in case of undue price cutting by the licensee, but this should be regarded as an unusual case.

While, normally, royalties are payable on sale or delivery of the patented product, or use of the patented process, in *Holywell Mining's Patent* (SRIS O/47/88) royalties were ordered to be paid on the placing of orders by the licensee, since it wished only to exploit the patent by having the patented product made for it, this being regarded as a sub-licensing activity, normally not permitted in a licence of right, see para. 46.25 *infra*. Also, in *Shiley's Patent* (*supra*), a provision was inserted in the licence for royalties to be paid on stocks of the patented product held in the United Kingdom at the expiry of the licence.

When royalties have been increased on appeal, the Patents Court has ordered an additional royalty to be paid, within a short defined period, on disposals made between the date of the original order and that of the appeal decision, this corresponding to the difference between the two settled rates (*Eli Lilly's Patent (No. 4)*, SRIS C/33/89, *noted* IPD 12050; and *Smith Kline & French's Patents [Generics' and Harris's Applications]*, (SRIS C/48/89): in neither case did the licensee present evidence that the additional royalty could not be afforded by it. In *Cyprane's Patent* (SRIS O/108/88) the parties jointly asked the Comptroller to take into account sales made after deemed endorsement, and therefore to be considered as patent infringements, by fixing an average unit rate of royalty. This was done by assessing infringing sales at twice the royalty rate settled for the licence of right, *i.e.* at the maximum figure permitted by section 46(3)(*c*) discussed in para. 46.28 *infra*.

Attempts by applicants to have clauses of the "most favoured nation" type included have invariably been rejected, see: *Diamond Shamrock's Patent* ([1987] RPC 91); *Allen & Hanburys' (Labetelol) Patent* (SRIS O/175/85, *noted* IPD 8082 and C/42/86); *Bayer's Patent [Nifedipine] [Generics' Application]* (SRIS O/49/86); and *Tanabe's Patent* (SRIS O/140/86)

Other terms of settled licences

46.21 —*Prohibitions on importation*

Prior to the decision in *Allen & Hanburys* v. *Generics (Case No. 434/85)* ([1988] 1 CMLR 701; [1988] FSR 312 (ECJ)), settled licence terms would, on request, include a prohibition on importation of the patented product, if the patentee himself manufactured that product within the United Kingdom, see *Ciba-Geigy's Patent [FMC's Application]* ([1986] RPC 403) and *Allen & Hanbury's (Salbutamol) Patent* ([1987] RPC 327, where the Court of Appeal declined to vary the decision of the Patents Court on this point in relation to importation from elsewhere within the EEC), but not if there was no local manufacture by the patentee, see *Bayer's Patent [Nifedipine] [Generics' Application]* (SRIS O/49/86) and (*Tanabe's Patent* (SRIS O/140/86), or if the patentee has voluntarily granted a licence for importation as in *Smith (T.J.) & Nephew's Patent (No. 2)* (SRIS O/126/87 and C/21/88).

However, the ECJ decision in the *Allen & Hanburys'* case ruled it to be contrary to EEC law to discriminate in a licence of right between manufacturers in the United Kingdom and those elsewhere within the EEC. Consequently, after that decision and on request, the Comptroller varied the terms of licences which he had previously settled with an import prohibition so as to limit this to a prohibition against importation only from outside the EEC; and subsection (3)(*c*) was eventually amended (by Sched. 5, para. 12 [1988]) so that, in infringement proceedings on a patent subject to a "licences of right" provision, an injunction can now only be imposed (if the infringer undertakes to take a licence on settled terms) in respect of importation "otherwise than from another member State of the EEC".

A prohibition against importation from outside the EEC is still, however, permissible and is imposed upon request if the patentee himself manufactures within the United Kingdom, but not otherwise (*Bergwerksverband's Patent* (SRIS O/58/89, *noted* IPD 12065). Since the basis for the import prohibition derives from section 50(1)(*c*), which was not amended by the 1988 Act, and under this section in the grant of compulsory licences the interests of any person working an invention within the United Kingdom are not to be unfairly prejudiced, working by the patentee elsewhere within the EEC does not itself provide basis for an import prohibition.

Thus, in *Smith Kline & French's Patents [Generics' Application]* (SRIS C/12/89, *noted* IPD 12036), importation of the raw material was permitted because the Patentee itself imported this from Ireland, but an import ban was imposed in respect of formulated pharmaceutical compositions which the Patentee did manufacture in the United Kingdom, the patent containing a specific claim to such compositions. However, previously, the Comptroller had refused to recognise a conversion of timolol to its commercial form, timolol maleate, as a sufficient activity within the United Kingdom to merit an import prohibition (*Frosst's Patent*, SRIS O/84/87, *noted* IPD 10059).

The *Smith Kline & French* decision (*supra*) did, however, impose a complete ban on imports of the patented products (whether raw material or as formulated compositions) from Spain and Portugal because of special provisions in the Treaties of Accession of Spain and Portugal in relation to patented pharmaceutical products exported from those countries (for which see para. C15). Thus, these two countries were treated as outside the EEC for the present purpose, even though those special provisions only relate to the doctrine of exhaustion of rights (see para. C15) and despite the fact that amended section (46)(3)(*c*) (not then in force) would now prohibit the imposition of an injunction against such importation.

In *Pfizer's Patent* (SRIS O/78/87, *noted* IPD 10058) the Comptroller deemed it irrelevant whether the proposed act of importation would apparently involve an act of infringement of a parallel patent in the country of manufacture. However, subsequently, in *Smith Kline & French's Patents [Generics' Application]* (SRIS C/12/89, *noted* IPD 12036) the granted licence specifically did not extend to the importation of material manufactured in infringement of a parallel patent.

—Export prohibitions **46.22**

Since export of a patented product involves an act of infringement by disposal of that product within the terms of section 60(1)(*a*), acts of export can be prohibited by the settled terms of a licence of right (*Smith Kline & French's Patents [Generics's Application]* (SRIS C/12/89, *noted* IPD 12036), but (as in that case) export is only likely to be prohibited to countries where parallel patents subsist and not otherwise, see also: *Allen & Hanbury's (Salbutamol) Patent* ([1987] RPC 327 (CA)); *Bayer's Patent [Nifedipine] [Generic's Application]* (SRIS O/49/86); and *Tanabe's Patent* (SRIS O/140/86), in the last mentioned of which it was stated that "where a licensee infringes a foreign patent it should not be necessary to institute proceedings abroad but he should have a cause for action under the licence in the United Kingdom".

In *Diamond Shamrock's Patent* ([1987] RPC 91) a licence to export was explicity granted at the same rate or royalty as for use of the invention within the United Kingdom, for which see para. 46.19 *supra*.

—Marketing controls on licensee **46.23**

A contractual restriction against "passing off" the licensee's product as that of the patentee has been rejected (*Syntex's Patent*, [1986] RPC 585), the patentee being left to his remedy by an action therefor. Also rejected has been a requirement that the licensee should *not* indicate that his product has been licensed or approved by the patentee (*Hilti's Patent*, [1988] RPC 51). However, in *Holywell Mining's Patent* (SRIS O/47/88) where sub-licensing rights were granted to permit the licensee (*British Coal*) to have the product made for it, employees of the licensee were required to be warned that the product had *not* been made by the Patentee.

In another case, the patentee has requested, and been granted, a term that the licensee should indicate that his product *is* sold "under a licence of right" giving the patent number but not the name of the patentee; and in this case licence terms were included restricting the licensee from unfairly comparing his product against that sold by the Patentee in the United Kingdom (*Shiley's Patent*, SRIS O/95/86, *noted* IPD 9082 and [1988] RPC 97).

Quality control provisions are also not usually imposed, because the market place is thought to be the most effective control as to quality, see *Suspa-Federungstechnik's Patent* (SRIS O/113/85, *noted* IPD 8084), where it was noted that the Patentee anyway had no proprietary rights over the component which the licensee sought to supply, this being an unpatented spring leg for a patented washing machine. However, such a term was ordered in *Hilti's Patent* (*supra*), to take account of the public interest in avoiding faulty magazines for dangerous nail guns.

—Licence for unpatented components **46.24**

In *Suspa-Federungstechnik's Patent* (SRIS O/115/85, *noted* IPD 8084) the patent claimed a washing machine having a particular, but not novel, spring leg. The applicant sought a licence to sell only the leg. This was not granted because such sale would be an infringement under section 60(2) and because the Patentee itself exploited the patent in this way. However, in *Monsanto's Patent* (SRIS O/45/88), a compulsory licence under section 48 was refused for supply of an unpatented solvent for use in a particular application because section 49(1) specifically provides for licences to be granted to customers, see para. 49.02.

46.25   —*Sub-contracting, sub-licensing and assignment of the licence*

The licence ordered to be granted is one personal to the applicant. Provisions against assignment, or for termination in the event of a take-over situation, may therefore be included (*Allen & Hanburys' (Salbutamol) Patent*, [1987] RPC 237 (CA); *Syntex's Patent*, [1986] RPC 585; and *Diamond Shamrock's Patent*, [1987] RPC 91). Although sub-licensing can be permitted (*Hilti's Patent*, [1988] RPC 51), this is often refused, as in that case and also in *Allen & Hanburys' (Salbutamol) Patent* (*supra*).

In the *Salbutamol* case sub-contracting of manufacture by the licensee was not permitted, because the patent had a claim to pharmaceutical compositions containing the patented product and this claim would have been infringed by the manufacturing operation intended to be sub-contracted, so that this operation required a sub-licence rather than an agency agreement; and likewise in *Eli Lilly's Patent (No. 2)* (SRIS O/69/87).

In *Holywell Mining's Patent* (SRIS O/47/88) the applicant (*British Coal*) sought only a licence to have the patented apparatus manufactured for it as the result of a tender offer: this was permitted, but subject to the Patentee being given notice of the terms of the successful tender and the identity of that tenderer.

The question of permitting sub-licensing can, however, be avoided by making the prospective sub-licensee a co-applicant and therefore a joint licensee, *e.g.* as in *Tanabe's Patent* (O/140/86), where a specified subsidiary company was joined as co-applicant and, in effect, granted a separate licence.

While there is nothing in the Act against the applicant for a licence being a foreign entity, such will often need to operate the licence by operations at least akin to sub-licensing. In *Ciba-Geigy's Patent [Agan's Application]* (SRIS O/85/86) this was overcome by adding a United Kingdom company as joint applicant. In *Shiley's Patent* ([1988] RPC 97) it was agreed that the foreign applicant should operate only through a distributor previously identified as such to the Patentee, but the foreign licensee had to provide a bank guarantee to secure royalty payments, see para. 46.20 *supra*.

46.26   —*Termination of licence by patentee*

As is normal in patent licence agreements, provisions have been included in licences of right settled by the Comptroller for termination of the licence on breach of the terms of the licence, *e.g.* by the non-payment of due royalties. Customarily a period for rectification of such a breach is stipulated before termination takes effect, and in *Hilti's Patent* ([1988] RPC 51) 30 days' notice was deemed sufficient for this purpose.

The Comptroller can also, reasonably, include a term in the licence that this should terminate if validity of the patent is challenged by the licensee (*Du Pont's (Blades') Patent*, [1988] RPC 479; and *Schering Agrochemicals' Patent*, SRIS O/115/88). In the *Du Pont* case the prospective licensee was already challenging the validity of the patent in a pending appeal against a finding of validity in infringement proceedings. It was held that, while the applicant could have the terms of a licence of right settled, if such a clause were included the licensee would then immediately have to elect whether to continue with its appeal in the validity proceedings or to exercise the licence, but the position would now seem to be different with the introduction of subsection (3A), see para. 46.28 *infra*.

—Other non-royalty licence terms **46.27**

Because, under section 46(4), a licensee of right may himself ensure that infringement proceedings are brought under the patent against another, the settled licence will not impose a requirement on the patentee that he should institute such proceedings himself (*Bayer's Patent [Nifedipine] [Generics' Application]*, SRIS O/49/86).

Effect of "licences of right" register entry (subss. (3)(c) and (d), (4) and (5)) **46.28**

The decision in *Allen & Hanburys* v. *Generics' (Case 434/85)* ([1988] 1 CMLR 701; [1988] FSR 312 (ECJ)) held that the effect of TRa. 30 is such that importers of a patented product from elsewhere within the EEC cannot be treated differently from domestic manufacturers of that product, for case comment on which see the article by J. Turner listed in para. 46.05 *supra*. Accordingly, subsection (3)(*c*) then could no longer be given its literal meaning, and it was formally amended (by Sched. 5, para. 12 [1988]) to bring (from August 1, 1989) its wording into accord with this declaratory decision.

Under subsection (3)(*c*) (as amended) in any proceedings for infringement, except where the infringement takes place by importation, from outside the EEC, the defendant (defender in Scotland) can avoid an injunction (interdict in Scotland) by undertaking to take a licence on terms as settled under subsection (3)(*a*); and, if he does so, his damages are not to exceed double the amount which would have been payable if the licence had been granted before the actual infringement.

In *Cyprane's Patent* (SRIS O/108/88, *noted* IPD 11061) the Comptroller was asked by the parties to assess the royalty that should be paid in respect of infringing activities which had taken place before the licence of right was granted. The Comptroller saw no reason why such damages should be less than twice the rate settled for the licence of right, but it should be noted that subsection (3)(*c*) specifies a maximum limit in this regard and not a norm.

The introduction (from August 1, 1989) of subsection (3A) (by Sched. 5, para. 12(3) [1988]) has made it clear that a defendant in infringement proceedings under a patent which becomes subject to the "licences of right" provisions may take advantages of the provisions of subsection (3)(*c*) while continuing to contend that no licence is needed, either because of no infringement of the patent or because of its invalidity. Previously, there was doubt about this, see *Upjohn's Patents (No. 2)* (SRIS O/102/87); *Du Pont's (Blades') Patent* ([1988] RPC 479) and *Du Pont* v. *Enka (No. 2)* ([1988] RPC 497). Indeed, there is no reason why a person who thinks he may possibly infringe a patent should not seek a licence (either as a licence of right, as in *Du Pont's (Blades') Patent (supra)*; or as a compulsory licence, as in *Halcon's Patent* ([1988] RPC 1) as an insurance policy in case his contentions of non-infringement and/or invalidity should not succeed. However, under section 48, there is an issue whether a licence should be granted at all, whereas in proceedings under section 46(3)(*a*) only the terms of the licence which must eventually be granted are in issue.

To take advantage of subsection (3)(*c*), it would appear necessary for a defendant actually to give an undertaking to the court; and the terms of a licence of right do not apply until such has actually been granted (*Du Pont* v. *Enka (No. 2), supra*). In that case an injunction imposed in infringement proceedings was lifted from the date the patent became subject to the licence of right provisions, but note that the importation in that case was from another EEC Member State, and subsection (3)(*c*) prior to its amendment had already then been held to be incompatible with the Treaty of Rome as regards importation from elsewhere within the EEC, see *supra*.

The limitation on damages also contained in subsection (3)(*c*) would not seem to affect an account of profits instead of damages, see *Codex* v. *Racal-Milgo* (SRIS C/77/83, *noted* IPD 6025). It is also not seen that this provision should affect the grant of an injunction in respect of infringement of some other intellectual property right, for example of copyright in engineering drawings, which continues to be enforceable under Schedule 1, paragraph 19 [1988], for which see para. 46.09 *supra*.

Under subsection (3)(*d*) only half renewal fees are to be paid after the date when the register entry has been made or is deemed to have been made. It should be noted that making the register entry after the due date for renewal and then paying the renewal fee with fine for late payment does *not* enable a half renewal fee to be paid, this arising from the phrase "would be payable", see para. 46.29 *infra*.

Subsection (4) provides for a licensee of right to call for the proprietor to take proceedings for infringement of the patent (unless the licence expressly provides otherwise) and, if the proprietor refuses or neglects to do so, for the licensee himself to become the plaintiff, making the proprietor a nominal defendant (defender in Scotland), though when this is done no costs (expenses in Scotland) are to be awarded against the proprietor unless he enters an appearance in the proceedings (subs. (5)). It is not, however, clear what remedies a plaintiff who is only a nonexclusive licensee can seek other than an injunction, in view of the terms of sections 61 and 67.

PRACTICE UNDER SECTION 46

46.29   *Making of entry in the register*

The procedure on application to make the entry is covered by rule 62 (reprinted at para. 46.02 *supra*). The application is made on PF 28/77 (reprinted at para. 141.28) on which a statement has to be made to the effect that the proprietor is not precluded by contract from granting licences. There is no longer a requirement that evidence verifying this shall be filed: no doubt the Comptroller would call for evidence if he were in any doubt on the point. However, it would appear that the required declaration may only apply to licences that are recorded in the register, see *Fabran's Patent* (SRIS O/103/88) decided under section 36 [1949].

If a renewal fee is to be accepted at the half rate, it is not enough simply to file the application for an entry in the register before the date on which the fee is due. At least 10 working days should be allowed for the entry to be made before the renewal date, otherwise, the full renewal fee will be payable (O.J. July 13, 1983).

In addition to the publication of the register entry in the O.J., rule 62(2) provides for such publication thereof as the Comptroller thinks necessary. This is in order to bring the entry to the notice of manufacturers, but in practice no use is made by the Comptroller of this provision.

PF 28/77 contains a tear-off slip to be stamped by the Patent Office and returned to the address given thereon when the relevant entry has been made in the register. That address need not be the address for service entered in the register, but it must be one within the EEC (or Isle of Man).

46.30   *Application for settlement of licence terms*

The procedure on application for settlement of the terms of a licence of right under subsection (3)(*a*) or (*b*) is set out in rule 63 (reprinted at para. 46.03 *supra*). The application is made on PF 29/77 (reprinted at para. 141.29) and must be accompanied by a statement setting out the facts on which the applicant relies and the terms of a licence which the applicant would be prepared to grant or accept, each filed in duplicate. In the case of an existing patent not yet subject to a licence of right endorsement or entry, an application under subsection (3)(*a*) or (*b*) may be made in advance of the deemed endorsement at the end of the 16th year of the term of such patent, but any such application is ineffective if made before the beginning of that year (Sched. 1, para. 4B, as inserted by s. 294 [1988]) and the Patent Office will take no action on any such application and refund the fee (O.J. December 14, 1988).

The Comptroller sends a copy of the PF 29/77 and the statement to the proprietor or the person seeking the licence, as the case may be, who may file a counter-statement within three months setting out fully the grounds of the objection. The application is also listed in the O.J., see O.J. December 10, 1986: retroactive lists were published in this and subsequent issues. The subsequent procedure is at the discretion of the Comptroller, but normally follows that generally used in *inter partes* proceedings before the Comptroller, for which see paras. 72.32–72.52, except that the periods within which evidence is required to be filed are usually fixed at two (rather than three) months, with the Comptroller reluctant to grant extensions (unless the other party consents thereto) in order that the grant of a licence shall not be unduly delayed, on which see *Allen & Hanburys* v. *Generics* ([1986] RPC 203 (HL)). Where procedural disputes delay any of the stages for filing the counter-statement or evidence, the Comptroller has exercised his discretion to impose a shorter time limit, see: *Roussel-Uclaf's Patent [Second Preliminary Decision]* (SRIS O/114/87); *Science Union's Patent* (SRIS O/185/87, *noted* IPD 10102); *Du Pont's Patent* (SRIS O/210/87); and *American Cyanamid's Patent* (SRIS O/80/88).

A hearing date is fixed (sometimes even before the conclusion of the evidence stages, as in *Roussel-Uclaf's Patent [Third Preliminary Decision]*, SRIS O/115/87), so that the hearing will follow closely the conclusion of the evidence stages. It is customary for the form of licence settled by the Comptroller to be appended to his written decision and for this to state that the licence takes effect from the date of that decision.

The position where the settled licence terms are varied on appeal is discussed in para. 46.20 *supra*.

It should be noted that it is the applicant under rule 63 who proposes the terms of the licence he requests. It may, therefore, be advantageous for the proprietor to make an application before the putative licensee. However, while a prospective licensee under subsection (3)(*a*) or (*b*) may file his application under rule 63 without prior discussions, or even approach, to the patentee (for which see para. 46.11 *supra*), it may be more difficult for a patentee to establish the "default of agreement" required under subsection (3)(*a*). Also, a licence granted on an existing patent deemed to be endorsed under section 35 [1949] may be regarded as a compulsory, rather than a voluntary, licence so far as concerns parallel imports under EEC law, but perhaps only if the terms of the licence have been settled other than at the request of the patentee, for the reason explained in para. 46.08 *supra*.

—*Sufficiency of statement of case under rule 63*   **46.31**

From the time of *Rousel-Uclaf's (Clemence & Le Martret's) Patent* ([1987] RPC 109 and [1989] RPC 405) there have been several challenges to the sufficiency of the original statement filed by the applicant with consequent delay while the Comptroller has ruled on the challenge, sometimes with further delay arising from a lodging of an appeal thereon. However, the Comptroller is then likely to set a shortened term for filing the counter-statement, see para. 46.30 *supra*. Also, the Comptroller should only intervene when the statement of case is manifestly inadequate, but the applicant will not be permitted to go outside its ambit without amending that pleading (*Smith Kline & French's Cimetidine Patents*, [1988] RPC 148).

The statement must indicate the royalty sought to be paid and the basis on which this is to be calculated (*Upjohn's Patents*, SRIS O/40/87, *noted* IPD 10056). The statement should also include the principles upon which the applicant has arrived at the royalty figure which he has put forward as appropriate, but he need not go into the question of costs and profits (*Roussel-Uclaf's (Clemence & Le Martret's Patent, supra*), nor need he set out details of his projected purchase and selling prices (*Roussel-Uclaf's Patent [Second Preliminary Decision]*, SRIS O/114/87), though in *Smith Kline & French's Cimetidine Patents* (*supra*) details of the proposed selling price were ordered to be given so that an appropriate uplift could be calculated if the royalty were to become based on the licensee's selling price, for which see para. 46.19 *supra*. However, this is not necessary if the royalty contentions are based only on comparability with other licences granted for products of a similar nature (for which see para. 46.17 *supra*), see *Sandoz's Patent* (SRIS O/89/89).

In *Roussel-Uclaf's (Clemence & Le Martret's) Patent* (*supra*) it was indicated that an applicant should state whether he intends to manufacture the patented product or have it manufactured for him; and, if the latter, to indicate the intended source and in particular the applicant's intentions as regards its importation, and likewise in *Rhône-Poulenc's (Ketoprofen) Patent* ([1989] RPC 570). However, there is no need to specify a route of manufacture (*Smith Kline & French's Cimetidine Patents, supra*). In *Science Union's Patent* (SRIS O/185/87, *noted* IPD 10102) details of proposed sub-contractors were given, though the question whether such should be joined in as co-applicants (for which see para. 46.25 *supra*) was left until after the evidence had been considered.

In *Roussel-Uclaf's (Clemence & Le Martret's) Patent* (*supra*) the Comptroller also indicated that the applicant should state whether he intends to export the product; the form of product to be sold by him; and the types of customers intended. This decision was followed in *Rhône-Poulenc's Patent (No. 2)* (SRIS O/48/89) despite the intervening judgment of the Patents Court in the *Smith Kline & French* case (*supra*), see also *Eli Lilly's Patent [Second Preliminary Decision]* (SRIS O/56/89, *noted* IPD 12081), but was later not required in *Sandoz's Patent* (*supra*).

Where, as in *Hoffman-La Roche's Patent* (SRIS O/50/88), the nature of the patented drug seems to make it unlikely that the licensee will be able to obtain a licence under the Medicines Act 1968 (c. 67) before the patent expires, the putative licensee has been required to amplify his statement of case by indicating whether such a licence has been obtained and, if not, whether application therefor had been made and, if so, when this was likely to be obtained.

46.32   —*Striking out of application under subsection (3)(a)*

There have also been attempts by patentees to have applications under subsection (3)(*a*) struck out on various grounds, but none appears to have succeeded. In *Roussel-Uclaf's (Clemence & Le Martret's) Patent* ([1989] RPC 405) the Comptroller agreed that he had the power to do this if he were satisfied that the application was scandalous, frivolous, vexatious or an abuse of process, as the court would do under RSC Ord. 18, rule 19 (reprinted at para. E018.9). This view was endorsed by the Patents Court in *Rhône-Poulenc's (Ketoprofen) Patent* ([1989] RPC 570). However, neither case fell into this category: in *American Cyanamid's Patent* (SRIS O/80/88) it was stated that the fact that the applicants had made many similar applications should be seen as prudent, rather than frivolous. In none of these cases had the Patentee established that the applicant would be unable to obtain the necessary regulatory marketing approval before the patent expired: and earlier, in the *Rhône-Poulenc* case, see (SRIS O/121/88), some of the proposed activities of the licensee were shown not to require such approval. In *Eli Lilly's Patent (No. 3)* (SRIS O/116/88) it was stated that an untrue statement in the statement of case would not justify striking out the application, at least not in the absence of a showing that such was intended to deceive.

—Confidential disclosure during proceedings under subsection (3)(a)   **46.33**

The evidence filed in relation to applications for settlement of the terms of a licence of right often includes commercially sensitive financial and commercial information, disclosure of which would be valuable to competitors as well as to the other party to the settlement proceedings. Accordingly, the Comptroller is generally, but not necessarily, prepared to issue an order under rule 94(1) that documents containing such information be treated as confidential (as discussed in para. 118.17). However, the Patents Court has indicated that justification must be provided for departure from the norm of making the documents available to the public, see *Diamond Shamrock's Patent* ([1987] RPC 91). Subsequent to this decision a notice on the practice which the Comptroller adopts was issued (O.J. May 28, 1987).

In *Vidal's Patent* (SRIS O/24/89) the Patentee requested an order that the royalty rate it sought should not be disclosed, nor made use of outside the proceedings by the putative licensee, on the ground that such would jeopardise the Patentee in exploiting the patent in a competitive tender situation. The Comptroller doubted if he had any power to make such an order, but anyway here found such unjustified: the royalty rate settled might be quite different from that sought by the Patentee.

Where possible, the parties are expected to provide duplicate documents for the public file of the patent in which the confidential passages have been masked out so that as much of the document as possible may be open to public inspection. This had already been done in the *Vidal* case (*supra*).

The order for confidentiality may, and often does, go beyond the terms of rule 94(1), which concerns only documents which would otherwise be open to inspection in the patent file under section 118. Thus, it is commonplace for distribution of documents containing particularly sensitive information to be restricted to the parties' legal advisers, but these can be in-house patent agents as discussed in para. 72.44A. Where confidential information has been provided in evidence, or where a witness is cross-examined about such, the Comptroller is often prepared to sit *in camera*, though this is much less likely in appeal proceedings before the court. Nevertheless, even then, counsel and the judge are often prepared to take steps such that the sensitive information is not disclosed orally during the proceedings. Similar care is usually taken over the wording of decisions and judgments and, if appropriate, confidential financial data may be presented in an appendix which it is ordered should not become open to public inspection, as happened in *Geigy's Patent* ([1964] RPC 391) and *Smith Kline & French's Patent* ([1965] FSR 98), each decided under section 41 [1949].

As noted in para. 46.17 *supra*, either the patentee or the putative licensee may be ordered to produce licence agreements voluntarily entered into since these may be relevant to the determination of royalty terms on the "comparables" approach. When this is done, a confidentiality order can be expected to be made.

However, where "without prejudice" discussions have taken place between the parties prior to the application under subsection (3)(a), though reference may be made in the statement and evidence to the existence of such discussions, the terms offered therein should *not* be disclosed in the absence of agreement; and, if this is done, the details may be ordered to be removed, as happened in *King Instruments' Patent* (SRIS O/124/88).

47.01   SECTION 47

Cancellation of entry made under section 46

47.—(1) At any time after an entry has been made under section 46
above in respect of a patent, the proprietor of the patent may apply to the
comptroller for cancellation of the entry.

(2) Where such a application is made and the balance paid of all renewal
fees which would have been payable if the entry had not been made, the
comptroller may cancel the entry, if satisfied that there is no existing
licence under the patent or that all licensees under the patent consent to
the application.

(3) Within the prescribed period after an entry has been made under section 46 above in respect of a patent, any person who claims that the proprietor of the patent is, and was at the time of the entry, precluded by a
contract in which the claimant is interested from granting licences under
the patent may apply to the comptroller for cancellation of the entry.

(4) Where the comptroller is satisfied, on an application under subsection (3) above, that the proprietor of the patent is and was so precluded,
he shall cancel the entry; and the proprietor shall then be liable to pay,
within a period specified by the comptroller, a sum equal to the balance of
all renewal fees which would have been payable if the entry had not been
made, and the patent shall cease to have effect at the expiration of that
period if that sum is not so paid.

(5) Where an entry is cancelled under this section, the rights and liabilities of the proprietor of the patent shall afterwards be the same as if the
entry had not been made.

(6) Where an application has been made under this section, then—

  (*a*) in the case of an application under subsection (1) above, any per-
       son, and

  (*b*) in the case of an application under subsection (3) above, the pro-
       prietor of the patent,

may within the prescribed period give notice to the comptroller of opposition to the cancellation; and the comptroller shall, in considering the
application, determine whether the opposition is justified.

RELEVANT RULES

Application by proprietor under section 47(1) for the cancellation of entry

47.02   **64.** An application under section 47(1) shall be made on Patents Form
No. 30/77 and shall be accompanied by Patents Form No. 12/77 and fees to
the amount of the balance of all renewal fees which would have been payable if the entry had not been made.

Application under section 47(3)

65.—(1) An application under section 47(3) shall be made on Patents **47.03**
Form No. 31/77 within three months after the making of the relevant entry
and shall be accompanied by a copy of the application and supported by a
statement in duplicate setting out fully the nature of the claimant's interest
and the facts upon which he relies.

(2) The comptroller shall send a copy of the application and statement to
the proprietor of the patent.

Procedure on receipt of application made under section 47

66.—(1) Every application under section 47(1) or (3) shall be advertised **47.04**
in the Journal and the period within which notice of opposition to the cancellation of an entry may be given under section 47(6) shall be three
months after the advertisement.

(2) Such a notice shall be given on Patents Form No. 32/77 and shall be
accompanied by a copy thereof and supported by a statement in duplicate
setting out fully the facts upon which the opponent relies.

(3) The comptroller shall send a copy of the notice and statement to the
applicant for cancellation of the entry who, if he desires to proceed with
the application, shall, within three months of the receipt of such copies, file
a counter-statement in duplicate setting out fully the grounds on which the
opposition is contested and the comptroller shall send a copy of the counter-statement to the opponent.

(4) The comptroller may give such directions as he may think fit with
regard to the subsequent procedure.

Procedure after cancellation of entry pursuant to section 47(3)

67. Where the comptroller cancels an entry in the register pursuant to **47.05**
section 47(3), he shall inform the proprietor of the patent who shall, within
such period as the comptroller specifies, file Patents Form No. 12/77,
accompanied by fees to the amount of the balance of all renewal fees which
would have been payable if the entry had not been made.

Declaration under paragraph 4A of Schedule 1

67A.—(1) A declaration under paragraph 4A of Schedule 1 to the **47.06**
Patents Act 1977 shall be made on Patents Form No. 58/77.

(2) The comptroller shall cause to be entered in the register notice of any
declaration filed under the said paragraph 4A and the entry in the register
shall be published in the Journal and in such other manner (if any) as the
comptroller thinks necessary.

Note. Rule 67A (as well as PF 58/77, reprinted at para. 141.58) was added by the

Patents (Amendment) Rules 1988 (S.I. 1988 No. 2089, r. 3) and took effect from January 15, 1989.

Commentary on Section 47

47.07 *General*

Section 47 concerns the cancellation of entries which have been made in the register in accordance with the provisions of section 46. The section applies to the cancellation of "Licences of Right" entries made in the register in respect of "existing patents" (Sched. 2, para. 1(2)), provided that such entries were made under section 46. This proviso prevents the use of the provisions of section 47 to cancel the deemed "Licence of Right" endorsement of an existing patent (*Bayer's Patent*, SRIS C/56/85), but Schedule 4, paragraph 8 provides a saving provision for endorsements made on existing patents before June 1, 1978 enabling such to be cancelled under repealed section 36 [1949], see para. A036.6 and *Glaverbel's Patent* ([1987] RPC 73 (CA)). However, this transitional provision cannot be used in respect of existing patents because these only received a deemed endorsement (under Schedule 1, paragraph 4(*c*)) after that date. Also, in *Glaverbel's Patent (No. 2)* (SRIS O/1/88), the Comptroller took the view that, once a deemed endorsement of an existing patent had taken place, it would then not be possible to cancel retroactively a pre-existing voluntary endorsement.

Nevertheless, under a special provision (s. 293 [1988]), the deemed endorsement on existing patents relating to *certain types* of invention became effectively cancellable as from January 15, 1989 (s. 305(2) [1988]). This is discussed in paras. 47.10–47.14 *infra*.

47.08 *Application for cancellation (subss. (1)–(5))*

By subsection (1) application for cancellation of the entry can be made at any time by the proprietor and, by subsection (2), if the unpaid half fees are paid and the Comptroller is satisfied that there are no licensees under the patent, or if there are that they consent to the cancellation, the entry will be cancelled. Rule 64 (reprinted in para. 47.02 *supra*) applies as discussed in para. 47.15 *infra*.

Subsection (3) gives to an interested person the right to apply to cancel an entry made under section 46 where it is claimed by the applicant for cancellation that the proprietor is, and was at the time of making the entry, precluded by a contract in which the applicant has an interest from granting licences under the patent. Rule 65 (reprinted at para. 47.03 *supra*, and discussed in para. 47.16 *infra*) governs the procedure. This sets a time limit of three months from the date of the register entry for the cancellation application to be filed and this period is inextensible (r. 110(2)), reprinted in para. 123.10).

By subsection (4), if the application under subsection (3) to cancel is successful and the entry is cancelled, the proprietor must pay the unpaid half renewal fees, failing which the patent lapses at the end of a period specified by the Comptroller under rule 67 (reprinted at para. 47.05 *supra*).

When an entry has been cancelled, the rights and liabilities of the proprietor after cancellation are the same as if the entry had not been made (subs. (5)).

As with section 46, patents of addition fall to be treated as individual patents and so register entries (or deemed endorsements on those patents of addition to which s. 293 [1988] applies) have to be separately cancelled.

368

Opposition to cancellation (subs. (6))   **47.09**

Subsection (6) provides for opposition under either subsection (1) or (3). Where the application for cancellation is made under subsection (1), any person can oppose the cancellation: but when the application is made under subsection (3) only the proprietor can oppose. The opposition period is three months from the date of the O.J. in which the application to cancel is advertised (r. 66) and is inextensible (r. 110(2)). A foreign opponent can be expected to be asked to supply security for costs under section 107(4)(*c*), see para. 107.05.

An opponent does not have to show an interest, in contrast to the position under section 36 [1949], on which see *Glaverbel's Patent* ([1987] RPC 73 (CA)). In that case the Comptroller took the view that validity of the patent should not be called into question in proceedings for a cancellation of a "licences of right" endorsement.

In *Serenyi's Patent* ((1938) 55 RPC 228) it was held that an opposition to cancellation of a "licences of right" endorsement should not be treated as if it were an application for a compulsory licence. Cancellation was allowed in that instance as being in the best interests of the public.

Exception from section 46 for existing patents for certain uses of patented products (Sched. 1, para. 4A)

—Relevant dates for patents affected by the exception (para. 4A(6)(a))   **47.10**

From January 15, 1989, *i.e.* two months after the Royal Assent to the 1988 Act (s. 305(2) [1988]), it has been possible for patentees of *certain* existing patents to file, under rule 67A (reprinted at para. 47.06 *supra*), a declaration (on PF 58/77, reprinted at para. 141.58) that the deemed "licences of right" endorsement of such patents under Schedule 1, paragraph 4(2)(*c*) should *not* extend to a use which is excepted by or under Schedule 1, paragraph 4A (reprinted in para. 133.01). The patents in question are those which on that date had not passed the end of their 15th year (sub-para. (6)(*a*)), *i.e.* patents for which their complete specification is dated on or after January 15, 1974 up to May 31, 1978.

—Subject matter scope of the exception (sub-paras. 4A(1)–(4))   **47.11**

The filing of a declaration on PF 58/77 is only possible for patents "for an invention which is a product" (sub-para. (1)): the definition of "patented product" in section 130(1) is presumably here applicable, for which see para. 60.11. Such declaration only initially led to the exception of "pharmaceutical uses" of that product, this term being defined as a "use as a 'medicinal product' within the meaning of the Medicines Act 1968" (c. 67), or the doing of any other act mentioned in section 60(1)(*a*) "with a view to such use" (sub-para. (2)), such use being then termed "an excepted use", the scope of which is to be determined at the beginning of the 16th year of the patent (sub-para. (4)). By virtue of the Patents (Licences of Right) (Exception of Pesticidal Uses) Order 1989 (S.I. 1989 No. 1202, reprinted at para. 133.01A), the "excepted uses" of a patented product have (since August 14, 1989) been extended to include also "pesticidal uses" of such a product.

Thus, for a "product" invention only, "pharmaceutical uses" (*i.e.* uses as a medicinal product) and "pesticidal uses" (together with any other act mentioned in s. 60(1)(*a*) "with a view to such use") now become excepted from the "licence of right" provisions applied to "existing patents" at the end of their 16th year upon the filing of a declaration on PF 58/77, but otherwise the filing of such declaration has no effect.

By section 130 of the Medicines Act 1968 (as amended by the Animal Health and Welfare Act 1984, c. 40, s.13(2), Sched. 2, paras. 3(7)–(10) and Sched. 3) a "medicinal product" is at present a substance or article (not being an instrument, apparatus or appliance) for use by administration to humans or animals for a "medical purpose." Such "purpose" may be: for "treating or preventing disease"; "diagnosing disease or ascertaining the existence, degree or extent of a physiological condition"; "contraception"; "inducing anaesthesia"; or "otherwise preventing or interfering with the normal operation of a physiological function". A medicated animal feedstuff may also be treated as a medical product by order of the Agriculture Ministers (Medicines Act, s. 130(3A), inserted by the aforesaid 1984 Act), but no such order has yet been made. However, dental fillings, bandages and non-medicated surgical dressings are excluded, as are other substances as may be specified by order (Medicines Act, s. 130(5)). The meaning of "pharmaceutical use" and the scope of section 130 of the Medicines Act has been discussed by R. H. Burnett-Hall ((1988–89) 18 CIPA 154).

The term "pesticidal use" for present purposes is defined in S.I. 1989 No. 1202 (*supra*) in terms closely similar to the definition of the same term contained in the Control of Pesticides Regulations 1986 (S.I. 1986 No. 1510), read in conjunction with certain conditions in the Food and Environment Protection Act 1985 (c. 48). As can be seen from para. 133.O1A, this definition of "pesticidal use" is extremely complex, containing as it does sub-terms defined by reference to other statutory provisions and exceptions (and exceptions to exceptions) to some of the defined sub-terms.

There is no overlap between "pharmaceutical uses" and "pesticidal uses" as the latter are defined as excluding "substances whose use or sale within the United Kingdom is controlled" under the Medicines Act 1968 (c. 67) (for which see *supra*), as well as those likewise "controlled" under: the Agriculture Act 1970 (c. 40, Part IV) (*i.e.* fertilizers and feeding stuffs); the Food Act 1984 (c. 30) and the Food and Drugs (Scotland) Act 1956 (c. 30) (*i.e.* food); or the Cosmetics Products (Safety) Regulations 1984 (S.I. 1984 No. 1260) (*i.e.* cosmetics). However, these exclusions cause obscurity because the "control" under at least some of these enactments is limited to a requirement which permits use or sale of a particular product provided that such is labelled in a prescribed manner. It should also be noted that the Exception of Pesticidal Uses Order is self-standing so that any amendment of the Control of Pesticides Order would not affect the definitions contained in S.I. 1989 No. 1202 unless this latter Order were likewise amended.

47.12   —*When declaration for exception may not be filed (sub-paras. 4A(5) and (6))*

While the filing of PF 58/77 may be made at any time after the patent has passed the end of its 15th year (no further time limits having been specified, though provision for such was made) (sub-para. (5)), such declaration may *not* be filed if there is at the date of filing an existing licence for any description of excepted use of the product, *or* if there is then an outstanding application under section 46(3)(*a*) or (*b*) for the settlement by the Comptroller of the terms of a licence for any description of excepted use of that product, *and* such licence took, or is to take, effect at or after the end of the 16th year of the patent (sub-para. (6)). Here it is to be noted that, under Schedule 1, para. 4B (reprinted in para. 133.01), an application for a licence of right is now ineffective if made before the beginning of the 16th year of the patent, so that a patentee normally has up to one year within which he can file PF 58/77 before this can be frustrated by the filing of an application for the settlement by the Comptroller of the terms of a licence of right. However, this is not so when further "excepted uses" are prescribed under sub-paragraph (3) as happened with the extension to "pesticidal uses" from August 14, 1989 by an Order made without warning just one month before its commencement. Where the patentee has granted a licence under the patent, which licence could be implied as is often the case with intra-group corporate licences, the final words of sub-para. (6) will not prevent the filing of PF 58/77 because such licence, whether express or implied, is likely to have been in existence before the beginning of the 16th year of the patent, thereby avoiding the provisions of the sub-paragraph. Presumably, if PF 58/77 is filed in circumstances which fall within the scope of the prohibition of sub-para. (6), that filing would be regarded as a nullity.

—Effect of filing declaration of excepted use (sub-para. 4A(7))　　　　**47.13**

The effect of filing PF 58/77 is: (*a*) that section 46(3)(*c*) does not apply in infringement proceedings in respect of the excepted use of the patented product; and (*b*) that section 46(3)(*d*) also does not apply so that, from the time PF 58/77 is filed, full renewal fees under the patent then become payable (sub-para. (7)). However, if PF 58/77 is filed when there is no "excepted use" under the patent, its only effect is that the patentee has then to pay full renewal fees, see para. 47.14 *infra*.

—Effect of Schedule 1, paragraph 4A in practice　　　　**47.14**

Clearly, any patentee who has a patent which he believes is in respect of a product having a pharmaceutical or pesticidal use (for which see para. 47.11 *supra*) should file PF 58/77, probably during the 15th year of the patent: thereafter such filing may be frustrated by the filing of an application for settlement of the terms of a licence of right under Schedule 1 paragraph 4B. Note that the filing of PF 58/77 causes full renewal fees thereafter to be payable. It is not clear whether a patentee could subsequently voluntarily enter a "licences of right" entry in the register under section 46(1) (for which see para. 46.08), whereupon only half renewal fees would once again become payable (s. 46(3)(*d*)).

However, the filing of PF 58/77 does *not* make section 46(3)(*c*) completely ineffective in respect of the patent. First, the declaration made on PF 58/77 may be a nullity under the circumstances discussed in para. 47.12 *supra*; or, secondly, because the patent is held not to be one "for an invention which is a product" (para. 4A(1)). Thirdly, the settlement of terms of a licence of right is only precluded in respect of the "excepted use" of such product. Accordingly, the patent remains subject to licences of right where the product also claims a process, as well as in respect of uses of the patented product which fall outside the definitions of "pharmaceutical use", (as set out in para. 4A(2)), reprinted in para. 133.01) and the definition of "pesticidal use" contained in S.I. 1989 No. 1202 (reprinted in para. 133.01A), each as discussed in para. 47.11 *supra*. However, where there is a "pharmaceutical" or "pesticidal" use, the exception applies to acts of making, disposing of, offering to dispose of, and importing the product for such a purpose (para. 4A(2)(*b*)).

All this will make exceedingly difficult the drafting of a licence of right for the non-excepted uses of a patented product. While it is tempting to limit such licence to "the preparation of the product" and "uses thereof which are other than those excluded under the terms of Schedule 1, paragraph 4A (including S.I. 1989 No. 1202)", a licence so worded may only postpone a dispute to an action brought by the patentee for infringement for alleged working outside the terms of the licence possessed by the defendant. It is even conceivable that the licence agreement could be regarded as void because of the uncertainty of its terms.

PRACTICE UNDER SECTION 47

47.15 *Application under subsection (1) by proprietor for cancellation of entry under section 46*

An application by the proprietor under section 47(1) for cancellation of the entry "licences of right" in the register is made on PF 30/77 (reprinted at para. 141.30) under rule 64 (reprinted at para. 47.02 *supra*). This form includes a declaration that there is no existing licence under the patent or that all licensees consent to the application. This declaration is in lieu of evidence verifying one or the other situation which was formerly required, and it appears that the declaration only applies to licences which are recorded in the register, see *Fabran's Patent* (SRIS O/103/38) decided under section 36 [1949] and rule 104 [1968] (reprinted at para. A036.2). The application must be accompanied by PF 12/77 and the unpaid half renewal fees. PF 30/77 contains a confirmation slip which the Comptroller uses to inform the applicant of the cancellation of the "licences of right" entry. This need not be completed for return to the address for service entered in the register, for the location of which see para. 32.16.

47.16 *Application under subsection (3) by interested party for cancellation of entry under section 46*

With regard to applying under subsection (3) for cancellation of an entry in the register under section 46, it is to be observed that the Comptroller is not required under rule 62(2) to correlate the date of making of an entry under section 46(2) and the date of the O.J. advertising that entry, and that the three month period in rule 65 (which is inextensible under r. 110(2)) for an interested party to object to the entry in the register runs from date of the entry and not necessarily from the date of the O.J.

Application under subsection (3) for the cancellation of an endorsement made under section 46 is made on PF 31/77 (reprinted at para. 141.31) under rule 65 (reprinted at para. 47.03 *supra*) within the prescribed inextensible period of three months from the date of the entry, supported by a statement setting out the facts on which the applicant relies, all in duplicate. The statement need not be filed with PF 31/77, but must be filed within 14 days thereof (r. 107, reprinted at para. 72.09).

By rule 65(2) the Comptroller sends a copy of the application and statement to the proprietor and invites the filing of a counter-statement within three months, a period which can be extended by discretion exercised under rule 110(1). Thereafter, the procedure is flexible, but the procedure will follow that generally employed in contentious proceedings before the Comptroller, for which see paras. 72.32–72.52.

47.17 *Opposition to cancellation of "licences of right" entry*

Rule 66 (reprinted at para. 47.04 *supra*) governs opposition to a cancellation application whether made under subsection (1) or (3). By rule 66(1) all such applications are advertised in the O.J. Opposition thereto may then be filed on PF 32/77 (reprinted at para. 141.32) within three months (inextensible under r. 110(2)) of the advertisement of the application for cancellation of an entry under section 46, supported by a statement of facts filed within 14 days of filing PF 32/77 (r. 107), reprinted at para. 72.09), both PF 32/77 and the statement being filed in duplicate.

Copies of the form and statement are sent by the Comptroller to the applicant for cancellation inviting the filing of a counter-statement within three months, which period can be extended by discretion under rule 110(1). Thereafter the procedure is at the discretion of the Comptroller, but again will follow that generally employed, as discussed in paras. 72.32–72.52. Any party can require to be heard (s. 101) and appeal will lie to the Patents Court (s. 97(1)), but only thereafter to the Court of Appeal on a point of law and with leave (s. 97(3)).

Effecting the cancellation of "licences of right" entry   **47.18**

By rule 67 (reprinted at para. 47.05 *supra*), if the Comptroller cancels an entry on an application made under subsection (3), he will inform the proprietor and set a period within which the proprietor must file PF 12/77 to pay the unpaid half renewal fees, failing which the patent lapses at the end of the period allowed.

Filing of declarations under Schedule 1, paragraph 4A   **47.19**

A declaration under Schedule 1, paragraph 4A is made under rule 67A (reprinted at para. 47.06 *supra*) on PF 58/77 (reprinted at para. 141.58). No fee is required on the filing of this form. The permitted and recommended timing for the filing of PF 58/77 are discussed respectively in paras. 47.12 and 47.14 *supra*. Details of declarations filed have been advertised in the O.J. from February 15, 1989 where those filed on the first permitted day of January 15, 1989 were listed.

SECTION 48   48.01

Compulsory licences

48.—(1) At any time after the expiration of three years, or of such other period as may be prescribed, from the date of the grant of a patent, any person may apply to the comptroller on one or more of the grounds specified in subsection (3) below—

(*a*) for a licence under the patent,

(*b*) for an entry to be made in the register to the effect that the licences under the patent are to be available as of right, or

(*c*) where the applicant is a government department, for the grant to any person specified in the application of a licence under the patent.

(2) A rule prescribing any such other period under subsection (1) above shall not be made unless a draft of the rule has been laid before, and approved by resolution of, each House of Parliament.

(3) The grounds are:—

(*a*) where the patented invention is capable of being commercially worked in the United Kingdom, that it is not being so worked or is not being so worked to the fullest extent that is reasonably practicable;

(*b*) where the patented invention is a product, that a demand for the product in the United Kingdom—

(i) is not being met on reasonable terms, or

(ii) is being met to a substantial extent by importation;

(c) where the patented invention is capable of being commercially worked in the United Kingdom, that it is being prevented or hindered from being so worked—

    (i) where the invention is a product, by the importation of the product,

    (ii) where the invention is a process, by the importation of a product obtained directly by means of the process or to which the process has been applied;

(d) that by reason of the refusal of the proprietor of the patent to grant a licence or licences on reasonable terms—

    (i) a market for the export of any patented product made in the United Kingdom is not being supplied or,

    (ii) the working or efficient working in the United Kingdom of any other patented invention which makes a substantial contribution to the art is prevented or hindered, or

    (iii) the establishment or development of commercial or industrial activities in the United Kingdom is unfairly prejudiced;

(e) that by reason of conditions imposed by the proprietor of the patent on the grant of licences under the patent, or on the disposal or use of the patented product or on the use of the patented process, the manufacture, use or disposal of materials not protected by the patent, or the establishment or development of commercial or industrial activities in the United Kingdom, is unfairly prejudiced.

(4) Subject to the provisions of subsections (5) to (7) below, if he is satisfied that any of those grounds are established, the comptroller may—

(a) where the application is under subsection (1)(a) above, order the grant of a licence to the applicant on such terms as the comptroller thinks fit;

(b) where the application is under subsection (1)(b) above, make such an entry as is there mentioned;

(c) where the application is under subsection (1)(c) above, order the grant of a licence to the person specified in the application on such terms as the comptroller thinks fit.

(5) Where the application is made on the ground that the patented invention is not being commercially worked in the United Kingdom or is not being so worked to the fullest extent that is reasonably practicable, and it appears to the comptroller that the time which has elapsed since the publication in the journal of a notice of the grant of the patent has for any reason been insufficient to enable the invention to be so worked, he may by order adjourn the application for such period as will in his opinion give sufficient time for the invention to be so worked.

(6) No entry shall be made in the register under this section on the ground mentioned in subsection (3)(d)(i) above, and any licence granted under this section on that ground shall contain such provisions as appear to

the comptroller to be expedient for restricting the countries in which any product concerned may be disposed of or used by the licensee.

(7) No order or entry shall be made under this section in respect of a patent (the patent concerned) on the ground mentioned in subsection (3)(*d*)(ii) above unless the comptroller is satisfied that the proprietor of the patent for the other invention is able and willing to grant to the proprietor of the patent concerned and his licensees a licence under the patent for the other invention on reasonable terms.

(8) An application may be made under this section in respect of a patent notwithstanding that the applicant is already the holder of a licence under the patent; and no person shall be estopped or barred from alleging any of the matters specified in subsection (3) above by reason of any admission made by him, whether in such a licence or otherwise, or by reason of his having accepted such a licence.

Note. The word "fit" in subsection 4(*c*) was omitted from the initial Queens Printer's copy of the Act, see O.J. March 8, 1978.

RELEVANT RULES

Application under section 48(1) for compulsory licence

68.—An application under section 48(1) shall be made on Patents Form No. 33/77 and shall be accompanied by a statement of the facts upon which the applicant relies and evidence verifying the statement. **48.02**

Procedure on receipt of application under section 51

70.—(1) If upon consideration of the evidence submitted with Patents Form No. 33/77 or 34/77, the comptroller is not satisfied that a prima facie case has been made out for the making of an order or entry, he shall notify the applicant accordingly, and unless, within one month of such notification, the applicant requests to be heard in the matter, the comptroller shall refuse the application. **48.03**

(2) Where the applicant requests a hearing within the time allowed, the comptroller, after giving the applicant an opportunity of being heard, shall determine whether the application may proceed or whether it shall be refused.

(3) If upon consideration of the evidence the comptroller is satisfied that a prima facie case has been made out for the making of an order or entry, or if, after hearing the applicant, he so determines, he shall direct that the application shall be advertised in the Journal and shall send a copy of the application, the statement and the evidence filed in support thereof to the proprietor of the patent and any other person shown on the register as having any right in or under the patent.

48.04   Article

W. V. Higgs, "Compulsory Licences," Trans.Chart.Inst., LXXIII (1954–55), C.65.

Commentary on Section 48

48.05   *General*

Section 48 is the first of a group of sections (ss. 48–54) which concern the granting of compulsory licences where there has been abuse of the monopoly rights. These sections apply also to "existing patents" (Sched. 2, para. 1(2)). When the CPC is in force, CPCaa. 46–48 (providing for compulsory licences under Community patents) will be given effect in the United Kingdom by section 86. By CPCa. 47(4) compulsory licences include licences granted in the public interest.

Section 48 is in many ways similar to section 37 [1949] and it can be assumed that much of the earlier case law continues to apply. However, see para. 48.08 *infra* as regards working by way of importation from elsewhere in the EEC. The historical evolution of section 37 [1949], and the early cases, are discussed in the paper by W. V. Higgs listed in para. 48.04 *supra*.

48.06   *When application can be made, by whom and for what (subss. (1) and (2))*

By subsection (1) an application can be made by any person (who need not show an interest as was required under s. 37 [1949]) to the Comptroller at any time after the expiration of three years from grant of the patent, that is from the date of publication of the grant in the O.J., see para. 24.11. Application may be made on the grounds set out in subsection (3) for a licence (subs. (1)(*a*)), or for an entry in the register that licences are to be available as of right (subs. (1)(*b*)), or, if the applicant is a government department, for the grant of a licence to any person specified in the application (subs. (1)(*c*)). The period of three years could be modified by rule, but only by affirmative resolution passed by each House of Parliament (subs. (2)). Subsection (1) corresponds, in effect, to the combination of sections 37(1) and 40(1) [1949].

48.07   *Grounds for application (subs. (3))*

The grounds available to the applicant in support of the application are limited to those set out in subsection (3)(*a*) to (*e*). They are, in principle, that there has been what used to be called an "abuse of monopoly rights". However, these words are not used in the section, and the emphasis is rather that there should be the fullest practical use of a patented invention and that patent rights should be exercised without prejudice to the development of industry. Section 37 [1949] had as its object the encouragement of manufacture rather than mere selling (*Co-operative Union's Applications*, (1933) 50 RPC 161) and presumably this still applies. It may be noted that there is no positive requirement in the Act that a patentee should work his invention or exercise his patent rights in any particular way, but if he embarks on any action or inaction as specified in subsection (3) he opens himself to an application under the section.

The grounds of subsection (3)(*a*)–(*e*) are respectively considered in paras. 48.09–48.13 *infra*, but these grounds overlap in that often it will be appropriate, on the same facts, to rely on a plurality of the grounds. Decisions under the Act are therefore reviewed generally in para. 48.14 *infra*.

An application for a compulsory licence can proceed even if the applicant does not admit, or indeed is contesting, that the actions for which he seeks a licence would infringe the patent, such being an alternative type of plea in case infringement proceedings should succeed against him, or in case the applicant has not yet decided whether to work the patent, see *Halcon's Patent* ([1989] RPC 1). In fact the patent here was held to be not infringed (*Halcon v. BP Chemicals*, SRIS C/100/87, *noted* IPD 10072).

The ECJ has decided that the "exhaustion of rights" doctrine, under which parallel imports of a patented article may not be prevented when that article has first been put on the market within the EEC by the proprietor or with his consent (as discussed in para. C15), does not apply where the first marketing within the EEC took place under a compulsory licence, because this was not with the "consent" of the proprietor (*Pharmon v. Hoechst*, [1986] FSR 108, for case comment on which see D. Guy [1986] EIPR 252). However, whether a "licence of right" granted on an existing patent compulsorily endorsed is subject to the exhaustion of rights doctrine is not clear, see para. 46.08.

—*Effect of EEC law on these grounds*   **48.08**

In *Extrude Hone's Patent* ([1982] RPC 361) the argument was rejected that subsection (3)(*b*)(ii) contravenes the Treaty of Rome and that the provisions of this Treaty meant that importation from an EEC country should be equated with working within the United Kingdom. The Comptroller held that it was unlikely that the Act would have been worded contrary to the provisions of the Treaty and he declined to refer the matter to the ECJ. However, in view of the decision in *Allen & Hanburys v. Generics (Case 434/85)* ([1988] FSR 312; [1988] 1 CMLR 701 (ECJ), discussed in paras. 46.21 and C13), which has led to the amendment of section 46(3) (see para. 46.01), the correctness of this view must be in doubt. Indeed, it is understood that the E.C. Commission regards at least some of the provisions of section 48 as being contrary to TRa. 30, and not saved by TRa. 36, for the same reason as applied in the *Allen & Hanburys* case. The main reason for this view is that references to working (or lack of it) merely within the United Kingdom, as distinct from the EEC as a whole, is seen to act as a disguised restriction on trade between EEC Member States. This view can be doubted, both because of section 53(5), for which see para. 53.06, and because the foreign EEC working may not be on a scale sufficient to correct the failure to work the invention within the United Kingdom.

—*Insufficient domestic working (subs. (3)(a))*   **48.09**

Ground (*a*) is that the patent is not being adequately worked in the United Kingdom while being capable of being commercially worked in the United Kingdom. This ground is the same as that in section 37(2) [1949] and the observations on what is meant by the "fullest extent" of working found in *Kamborian's Patent* ([1961] RPC 403) presumably still apply.

"Commercially worked" has been given a plain meaning and held to be satisfied by "straight-forward manufacture of goods for the purposes of trade" (*Enviro-Spray's Patents*, [1986] RPC 147). Here the proprietor's argument that the invention had been imperfectly developed for commercial working was rejected, partly because the invention was being worked abroad and so was "capable of being commercially worked in the United Kingdom". In any event the words "in the United Kingdom" may now need to be qualified by the words "or elsewhere within the EEC" for the reason given in para. 48.08. However, neither a mere statement of potential interest, nor the maintenance of the patent, is sufficient to prove a capability of commercial working (*Monsanto's Patent (No. 2)*, SRIS O/91/89).

48.10 —*Failure to meet demand for patented product (subs. (3)(b))*

Ground (*b*) is that the patented invention is a product and the demand for it is not being adequately met on reasonable terms or is being met by importation. Again, "importation" may now need to be qualified as in amended section 46(3)(*c*) as meaning importation from other than an EEC Member State, see para. 48.08 *supra*.

The corresponding ground in section 37(2)(*b*) [1949] referred to the "patented article". It is not clear whether this change was for the purpose only of consistency, or whether any change of meaning was intended. "Patented product" is defined in section 130(1) as a product which is a patented invention, but this still leaves doubt as to the meaning of "product". There are numerous references in the Act to a product or patented product (*e.g.* in ss. 2, 4, 36, 44, 45, 60, 61, 62 and 64), and in these sections a product would appear to be anything which has been made, without reference to the manner in which it has been made: that is, an article. However, "article" is used in some sections (*e.g.* in ss. 46, 110, 111 and 122) where the use of "product" might have been equally appropriate. It would seem that the intended meaning of "product" comprehends both the result of a process of manufacture and any article covered by a patent, not necessarily identified by its manner of manufacture. The definition of "patented product" is discussed further in paras. 55.05 and 60.11, and the definition of "patented invention" is discussed in para. 125.08.

The significance of the reference to "a demand" in section 37(2)(*b*) [1949] was said to be obscure: under the 1907–46 Acts the expression was "the demand" and it was then established that the demand referred to was the public demand and not that of an individual person or company (*Robin Electric Lamp's Petition*, (1915) 32 RPC 202). Whether the wording of the 1949 Act changed this is unclear. However, it was evident that, though the demand in one particular field might be fully satisfied, an application could be made under the 1949 Act in respect of an unsatisfied demand in another field, and presumably this remains the law.

48.11 —*Commercial working hindered by importation (subs. (3)(c))*

Ground (*c*) is that the commercial working of the invention in the United Kingdom is being hindered by importation: where the invention is a product, by the importation of the product; and where the invention is a process, by the importation of the product of the process. As with grounds (*a*) and (*b*), the meaning of "imported" is now likely to be held to mean "importation, other than from another EEC Member State", for the reasons explained in para. 48.08 *supra*.

The wording of subsection 3(*c*) differs from that of section 37(2)(*c*) [1949] which referred merely to the importation of the patented article, and to this extent the ground has been broadened.

48.12 —*Refusal to grant licence on reasonable terms (subs. (3)(d))*

Ground (*d*) is that, by reason of the refusal of the proprietor to grant a licence on reasonable terms, (i) an export market is not being supplied, or (ii) the working of another substantial invention is prevented or hindered, or (iii) the establishment of commercial or industrial activities in the United Kingdom is unfairly prejudiced. It is more uncertain whether the literal wording of this ground is affected by EEC law than is the case with grounds (*a*)–(*c*), for which see para. 48.08 *supra*.

Ground (*d*) is in the same terms as section 37(2)(*d*) [1949] and cases decided thereunder will presumably still apply. Under that provision it appeared that, before an application could succeed, there must have been a concrete refusal by the patentee to grant a reasonable licence (*Loewe Radio's Application*, (1929) 46 RPC 479). Moreover, an insistence by the patentee that the licence must be a bulk licence including other patents may not constitute such a refusal (*Brownie Wireless' Application*, (1929) 46 RPC 457), and nor (in *Monsanto's Patent (No. 2)*, SRIS O/91/89) was an offer of a world-wide licence for a lump sum payment of $1 m. Since section 37(2)(*d*) [1949] referred only to the patentee, it did not apply where an exclusive licensee refused to grant a licence (*Colbourne Engineering's Application*, (1955) 72 RPC 169). That would still appear to be the case under the present wording.

In *Penn Engineering's Patent* ([1973] RPC 233), in which there had been no manufacture in the United Kingdom and accordingly section 37(2)(*a*) [1949] was satisfied, a licence including power to export was granted. A contention by the patentee that such a licence should not be granted unless a case was made out that there was an unsupplied export market was dismissed, the Patents Appeal Tribunal holding that section 37(2)(*d*)(i) [1949] applied only to cases in which an export market for goods made in the United Kingdom was not being satisfied, thus partly overruling the *Brownie Wireless* case (*supra*).

Section 37(2)(*d*)(ii) [1949] was applicable only where the invention which was being prevented or hindered was both patented and had made a "substantial contribution to the art". This had, of course, to be assessed on the evidence, but it had the effect of protecting the patentee against claims for compulsory licences by third parties merely with minor advances to their credit. Again, the same position would appear to obtain under the present wording.

The phrase "development of commercial or industrial activities" in section 37(2)(*d*)(iii) [1949] was held to include an increase in the size of a business (*Kamborian's Patent*) (*supra*).

—*Prejudice due to imposed licence conditions (subs. (3)(e))*　　　　　　**48.13**

Ground (*e*) is that, by reason of conditions imposed by the proprietor on the grant of licences under the patent, or on the disposal or use of the patented product or process, the manufacture or use or disposal of materials not protected by the patent or the establishment or development of commercial or industrial activities in the United Kingdom is unfairly prejudiced. The position as to the possible effect of EEC law on this wording would appear to be the same as that under ground (*d*), see paras. 48.08 and 48.12 *supra*.

The wording of ground (*e*) resembles that used in section 37(2)(*e*) [1949] but the present provision refers to "disposal" of the product or materials, instead of "sale" thereof as in the 1949 Act. This change is consistent with the new definition of infringement in section 60.

The applicant has the onus of proving the necessary "unfair prejudice". This must be more than showing a mere wish to exploit the patent, or relying on a statement of advantage contained in the patent (*Monsanto's Patent (No. 2)*, SRIS O/91/89).

Cases decided under the 1977 Act　　　　　　**48.14**

Very few applications have been made under the present section.

In *Extrude Hone's Patent* ([1982] R.P.C. 361) a compulsory licence at 7 per cent. royalty was granted under the provisions of paras. (*a*), (*b*)(ii), (*d*)(i) and (*d*)(iii) of subsection (3), but an undertaking was required from the prospective licensee that it would manufacture in the United Kingdom. The argument was rejected that subsection (3)(*b*)(ii) contravened the Treaty of Rome and that the provisions of this Treaty meant that importation from an EEC or associated EEC country should be equated with working in the United Kingdom. The Comptroller held that it was unlikely that the Act would have been worded contrary to the provisions of that Treaty, and he declined to refer the question to the ECJ under TRa. 177. Moreover, reliance on CPCaa. 47 and 82 was rejected because the CPC had not yet been ratified and its provisions were therefore not binding. However, the decision on these points may need reconsideration in the light of *Allen & Hanburys* v. *Generics* (*Case 434/85*) ([1988] FSR 312; [1988] 1 CMLR 701 (ECJ)), on which see paras. 46.21 and C13. A licence to export was ordered, following *Penn Engineering's Patent* ([1973] RPC 233), despite the existence of an exclusive licence which precluded the patentee himself from granting such a licence. The *Extrude Hone* decision was entirely upheld on appeal following which a further decision was given by the Comptroller ([1984] FSR 105) setting out the full terms of the licence which he granted. Following *Geigy's Patent* ([1966] RPC 250), the date of the licence was set as the date when its terms were before the Comptroller and settled by him.

In *Montgomerie Reid's Application* (SRIS O/145/83) the only real dispute on the grant of a compulsory licence concerned the rate of royalty. The invention was a particular mechanism for a forklift truck and the expert evidence on the two sides led to widely disparate views on the appropriate royalty. It was held that the royalty must be one which the applicant was capable of bearing, even if the patentee was entitled to reasonable remuneration (s. 50(1)(*b*)), and that this should be determined as that which would be negotiated between a willing licensor and a willing licensee. The conclusion was that the royalty should be based on 5 per cent. of the value of the mechanism which was seen "as close to the lower end of the general range for invention in the mechanical field". However, as this mechanism was not sold separately, it was then estimated that the mechanism contributed 20 per cent. to the price of the truck and, accordingly, the royalty was fixed at "1 per cent. of the full ex-works selling price of each truck falling within the claims of the patent". A further case under the Act is *Enviro-Spray's Patents* ([1986] RPC 147) mentioned in para. 48.09 *supra*.

48.15   *When ground for licence is established (subss. (4)–(7))*

Where the Comptroller is satisfied that one or more of the cited grounds is established, he may, by subsection (4), grant the licence or make the entry sought, subject to the provisions of subsections (5)–(7). Thus, the Comptroller may: allow more time for the commercial exploitation to be carried out (subs. (5)); may specify countries in which licensed products can be disposed of (subs. (6)); and (in respect of an application under subs. (3)(*d*)(ii)) he must be satisfied that the proprietor of the other patent is able and willing to grant to the proprietor of the patent concerned and his licensees a licence under his patent on reasonable terms (subs. (7)). Subsections (5)–(7) are closely similar to the provisos in section 37(3) [1949].

Under subsection (5) the Comptroller must consider whether the time which has elapsed since the date of publication of grant of the patent has been insufficient to enable the patented invention to have been worked in compliance with subsection 3(*a*). The grant of relief is discretionary, as indicated by the word "may" in subsection (4); and the Comptroller must exercise his powers in accordance with the general directions given to him in section 50, for which see the commentary thereon. Under the 1949 Act, a patentee could not rely on proviso (*a*) to section 37(3) [1949] if the time elapsed had been sufficient to work the invention abroad and the demand in this country had been satisfied by importation (*Fette's Patent*, [1961] RPC 396). Presumably the situation is the same under subsection (5).

The proviso in subsection (6) is that a licence granted on the ground of neglect of exploitation of an export market may restrict the disposal or use by the licensee to such territories as the Comptroller thinks fit. An entry in the register "licences of right" cannot be made on this ground.

Where an entry "licences of right" is ordered to be made in the register, the provisions of sections 46–47 thereafter have effect with regard to that entry (s. 53(4)).

Application by licensee (subs. (8))   **48.16**

Subsection (8) provides that an application under section 48 can be made by a licensee under the patent, who is not to be estopped by any terms in his licence or otherwise from raising any of the grounds specified in the section. Subsection (8) is in the same terms as section 37(4) [1949] and it is to be read in conjunction with section 49(2).

Hearing and Appeal   **48.17**

A hearing must be held if requested before a decision is given by the Comptroller (s. 101). Appeal from the Comptroller's decision lies to the Patents Court (s. 97(1)) with further appeal to the Court of Appeal only on a point of law and with leave (s. 97(3)). There is no provision for proceedings to be held in Scotland, see para. 98.07.

Relevant provisions in other sections   **48.18**

Licences granted under section 48 are subject to certain provisions set out in sections 49 and 50 and are to have effect as from the date of the Comptroller's order and as if made by deed by the proprietor, see section 108 and para. 108.02.

When an entry is made in the register, by section 49(4) any licence granted on an application under section 48 is subject to the operation of section 46(4) and (5); that is that the licensee has power to institute infringement proceedings if, on request, the proprietor fails to do so, see para. 46.28. Section 50 sets out the general objects and principles which the Comptroller has to consider in exercising his powers under section 48.

Opposition to the grant of a compulsory licence can be filed under section 52(1) by the proprietor of the patent concerned and special provisions then apply *re* possible reference of the matter to arbitration and for appearance on the hearing of any appeal, see paras. 52.06 and 52.05 respectively. If the proprietor does not lodge opposition under section 52(1) to the compulsory licence application, he is precluded from being heard on the settlement of the terms of the licence if the Comptroller decides that one should be granted, see *Ultimatte Corp.'s Patent* (SRIS SRL O/1/84, *noted* IPD 6141) and para. 52.04.

There are further provisions with regard to the granting of licences of right in sections 53 and 54. Section 53 concerns: (1) possible operation of the CPC under section 86; (2) reports of the Monopolies and Mergers Commission; (3) entries in the register irrespective of any contract, with such entry having the same effect as an entry under section 46; and (4) the effect of any entry under sections 48–51 has to be consistent with international agreements. Section 54 provides for certain cases where an invention is being worked abroad. For further discussion on these points, see the commentaries on sections 53 and 54.

There is no longer any provision for revocation of a patent where an order for compulsory licence fails to cure the abuse of monopoly, as existed under repealed section 42 [1949].

PRACTICE UNDER SECTION 48

48.19 *General procedure*

The procedure for an application for a compulsory licence under section 48 is set out in rules 68 and 70 (reprinted at paras. 48.02 and 48.03 *supra*). An application for a licence under section 48(1) must be made on PF 33/77 (reprinted at para. 141.33), and be accompanied by a statement of the facts on which the applicant relies and evidence verifying the statement (r. 68). By rule 70, if the Comptroller is not satisfied that a prima facie case has been made out, the applicant is notified. If the applicant wishes to proceed he must within one month of the notification request a hearing. When (after the hearing, if necessary) the Comptroller is satisfied that the application can proceed, the application is advertised in the O.J. and copies of the documents sent to the proprietor and any other person shown on the register as having an interest in the patent. There are no provisions for further procedure in the absence of opposition under section 52. If such opposition is filed, the procedure is as set out in rule 71 (reprinted in para. 52.02 and discussed in para. 52.07).

Under the 1949 Act, it was clear, from *Fette's Patent* ([1961] RPC 396) and *Kamborian's Patent* ([1961] RPC 403), that the Comptroller would consider all facts relevant to the case and hence evidence filed had to be of the fullest possible nature. It is thought that this still applies. However, if an applicant is wholly unable to support his contention of non-working of the invention by evidence, he has no case and the application should be dismissed and not proceed to discovery on the point (*Richco Plastic's Patent*, SRIS O/22/89, *noted* IPD 12037).

The period of one month within which an applicant who fails to establish a prima facie case can request a hearing can apparently be extended at the Comptroller's discretion under rule 110(1). The retention of the words "prima facie" in rule 70(1) is now to be contrasted with the absence of these words from rule 41(2) for an application for restoration under section 28, see para. 28.13.

Once proceedings under section 48 have commenced the Comptroller has ruled that they should continue unless there is good reason to postpone them, but it is not open to the applicant merely to request adjournment, especially if the opponent (here an exclusive licensee) has objected to this (*Montgomerie Reid's Application*, SRIS O/198/92, *noted* IPD 5112).

Because most applications for a compulsory licence under section 48 are opposed by the patentee under section 52, further matters of procedure are considered in relation to Practice under that section, see paras. 52.07–52.09.

49.01   **SECTION 49**

Provisions about licences under section 48

49.—(1) Where the comptroller is satisfied, on an application made under section 48 above in respect of a patent, that the manufacture, use or disposal of materials not protected by the patent is unfairly prejudiced by reason of conditions imposed by the proprietor of the patent on the grant of licences under the patent, or on the disposal or use of the patented product or the use of the patented process, he may (subject to the provisions of that section) order the grant of licences under the patent to such customers of the applicant as he thinks fit as well as to the applicant.

(2) Where an application under section 48 above is made in respect of a patent by a person who holds a licence under the patent, the comptroller—

(*a*) may, if he orders the grant of a licence to the applicant, order the existing licence to be cancelled, or

(*b*) may, instead of ordering the grant of a licence to the applicant, order the existing licence to be amended.

[*(3) Where, on an application under section 48 above in respect of a patent, the comptroller orders the grant of a licence, he may direct that the licence shall operate—*

(a) to deprive the proprietor of the patent of any right he has to work the invention concerned or grant licences under the patent;

(b) to revoke all existing licences granted under the patent.]

(4) Section 46(4) and (5) above shall apply to a licence granted in pursuance of an order under section 48 above and to a licence granted by virtue of an entry under that section as it applies to a licence granted by virtue of an entry under section 46 above.

Note. Subsection (3) was repealed by the 1988 Act (Sched. 5 para. 13 and Sched. 8) with effect from August 1, 1989 (S.I. 1989 No. 816).

COMMENTARY ON SECTION 49

General   **49.02**

Section 49 gives to the Comptroller power to grant licences to customers of an applicant under section 48 or to the applicant himself who successfully establishes the ground that the use or disposal of materials not covered by the patent is unfairly prejudiced by the action of the proprietor of the patent in regard to the granting of licences. Thus, where an applicant under section 48(3)(*e*) is successful, the Comptroller can order the granting of a licence to the applicant or his customers, as the Comptroller sees fit, subject to the other provisions of section 48. The section is in terms similar to those of section 38 [1949].

Because section 49(1) provides for licences to be granted to customers of the applicant for a licence, it was held in *Monsanto's Patent* (SRIS O/45/88) that the applicant should not be granted a licence permitting it to sell unpatented solvent with the right to pass therewith a licence to customers to use this in manufacturing the patented product. It was stated that the customers would need to be named in the compulsory licence application or be a party to it. The fact that the supply of the solvent would be an act of infringement of the patent under section 60(2) or (3) does not mean that this is part of the protection conferred by the patent (as referred to in s. 125(1)). For a contrary decision on the terms of a "licence of right" under section 46, see *Suspa-Federungstechnik's Patent* (SRIS O/113/85, *noted* IPD 8084).

In *Monsanto's Patent (No. 2)* (SRIS O/91/89) the applicant sought a licence for a named potential customer, but the application was refused (under s. 50(2)(*b*)) because the Comptroller was not satisfied that this customer would work the invention if the licence were granted.

Subsection (2) refers to the case where an application is made under section 48(8) and where the applicant is already a licensee under the patent. It empowers the Comptroller to cancel the existing licence when making a new licence (para. (*a*)), or to amend the existing licence (para. (*b*)).

Subsection (3) was deleted by the 1988 Act. It had provided for the possibility of the Comptroller ordering a compulsory licence to be exclusive, even of the patentee, but operation of the provision appears never to have been seriously considered and its existence was an embarrassment to the Government in resisting the implementation of similar provisions by some developing nations.

Subsection (4) provides that section 46(4) and (5), which gives a licensee who has obtained a "licence of right" the power to sue for infringement, shall apply to a licensee under a compulsory licence granted under section 48. For further discussion, see para. 46.28.

An appeal lies under section 49 as it does under section 48 and likewise an order for a licence under section 49 operates as a deed (s. 108), see paras. 48.17 and 48.18.

49.03 *Effect of treaty obligations*

Sections 49 is governed by the over-riding provisions of section 53 and therefore, by virtue of section 53(5), no compulsory licence can be granted which would offend the provisions of TRa. 85, or of the EPC or (when in force) the CPC. This would appear to prevent any compulsory licence from prohibiting importation from another EEC Member State, see paras. 46.21 and C13. For discussion on section 53(5), see para. 53.06.

50.01   **SECTION 50**

Exercise of powers on applications under section 48

50.—(1) The powers of the comptroller on an application under section 48 above in respect of a patent shall be exercised with a view to securing the following general purposes:—

(*a*) that inventions which can be worked on a commercial scale in the United Kingdom and which should in the public interest be so worked shall be worked there without undue delay and to the fullest extent that is reasonably practicable;

(*b*) that the inventor or other person beneficially entitled to a patent shall receive reasonable remuneration having regard to the nature of the invention;

(*c*) that the interests of any person for the time being working or developing an invention in the United Kingdom under the protection of a patent shall not be unfairly prejudiced.

(2) Subject to subsection (1) above, the comptroller shall, in determining whether to make an order or entry in pursuance of such an application, take account of the following matters, that is to say—

(*a*) the nature of the invention, the time which has elapsed since the publication in the journal of a notice of the grant of the patent and the measures already taken by the proprietor of the patent or any licensee to make full use of the invention;

(*b*) the ability of any person to whom a licence would be granted under the order concerned to work the invention to the public advantage; and

(*c*) the risks to be undertaken by that person in providing capital and working the invention if the application for an order is granted,

but shall not be required to take account of matters subsequent to the making of the application.

COMMENTARY ON SECTION 50

General   **50.02**

Section 50 sets out the objects and principles which are to be considered by the Comptroller when settling the terms of a licence granted under section 48. The section is in terms which are almost the same as those of section 38 [1949] and gives the Comptroller very wide powers of discretion in reaching a decision.

Just as the terms of section 50 have been held relevant to the terms upon which a "licence of right" should be settled by the Comptroller under section 46 (*Allen & Hanburys* v. *Generics*, [1986] RPC 203 (HL)), so the decisions given under section 46 on such "settlement" applications should have relevance to the application of section 50 to the grant of compulsory licences under section 48.

Grant of compulsory licences (subs. (1))   **50.03**

Subsection (1) sets out the general purposes of, or objects which underlie, the compulsory licence provisions in the Act, namely: that inventions which can be worked in the United Kingdom should be worked promptly and fully, where such working is in the public interest (para. (*a*)); that the inventor or beneficial owner shall be reasonably remunerated (para. (*b*)); and that the interests of anyone working or developing an invention in the United Kingdom under the protection of a patent shall not be unfairly prejudiced.

In *Montgomerie Reid's Application* (SRIS O/145/83) it was held that the royalty for a compulsory licence under section 48 should be one which would be negotiated between a willing licensor and a willing licensee; and that it should be such that the applicant would be able to bear it, even if section 50(1)(*b*) requires the proprietor to receive "reasonable remuneration".

Subsection (1)(*a*) might appear to imply, by the words "which should in the public interest be so worked", that (notwithstanding s. 48) there may be circumstances in which, for instance, it would be sufficient for a patented article to be imported. However, subsections (1) and (2) were each considered in *Extrude Hone's Patent* [1982] RPC 361). It was here pointed out that subsection (1)(*a*) amounts to a clear preference of United Kingdom manufacture over foreign manufacture and this was held not to be contrary to the principles of the EEC. However, this remark now needs to be questioned, see para. 48.08.

Subsection (1)(*c*) makes no reference (as does s. 48(3)(*d*)(ii)) to the invention which is hindered making a substantial contribution to the art, though section 48 is perhaps dominant in this respect. However, this subsection (1)(*c*) may be intended to be wider in scope, and may have the effect of instructing the Comptroller not to prejudice the interests of the proprietor of the patent in question or of his licensees.

385

50.04 *Principles for grant of compulsory licences (subs. (2))*

Subsection (2) sets out the matters, or principles, upon which the Comptroller is to exercise his power to grant compulsory licences and fix the terms thereof. It requires the Comptroller in coming to a decision to take account of: the nature of the invention, the time which has elapsed since grant, and the action of the proprietor or licensee in developing full use of the invention (para. (*a*)); the ability of the intending licensee to work the invention to the public advantage (para. (*b*)); and the risks to be taken by that person in providing capital and working the invention (para. (*c*)). Account need not be taken of matters subsequent to the filing of the application.

In subsection (2)(*a*) the reference to the time which has elapsed since publication of the notice of grant indicates, in the light of the fact that an application can be made under section 48 at any time after three years from grant, that the Comptroller is empowered to give the proprietor further time. The corresponding provision, section 39(2)(*a*) [1949], was considered in *Hamson's Application* ([1958] RPC 88).

In *Enviro-Spray's Patents* ([1986] RPC 147) a licence was refused because the applicant had not demonstrated to the Comptroller's satisfaction (as required by subs. (2)(*b*)) that he was capable of working satisfactorily a licence found to be justified under section 48(3)(*a*). It was pointed out that an applicant for a compulsory licence had an obligation to explain as far as possible what he expected to do and put the Comptroller in a position where he can form some estimate of the licensee's likelihood of achieving that aim; and terms, which would effectively defer a decision on whether or not to grant a licence, could not form part of a licence granted under sections 48 and 50.

In *Monsanto's Patent (No. 2)* (SRIS O/91/89) a licence was refused partly because the Comptroller was not satisfied that the proposed licensee would work the patent, see para. 49.03 further on this case.

In *Halcon's Patent* ([1989] RPC 1) the applicant was permitted to attack the validity of the patent as the extent to which the claimed process represented a major advance would be a factor in settling an appropriate royalty.

The final words of subsection (2) are to the effect that the Comptroller need not take into account any action by the proprietor subsequent to the application under section 48, which means that a proprietor who remedies his errors after such an application may not thereby be protected. These words were noted in *Halcon's Patent* (*supra*) with regard to a refusal to order discovery of a licence agreement offered to the applicant after the making of the application. However, the wording of the subsection is permissive, and merely relieves the Comptroller of being "required" to take this into account. In such an event subsection (1)(*c*) might nevertheless be relevant.

51.01   **SECTION 51** *[Substituted]*

Powers exercisable in consequence of report of Monopolies and Mergers Commission

51.—(1) Where a report of the Monopolies and Mergers Commission has been laid before Parliament containing conclusions to the effect—

  (a) on a monopoly reference, that a monopoly situation exists and facts found by the Commission operate or may be expected to operate against the public interest,

(b) on a merger reference, that a merger situation qualifying for investigation has been created and the creation of the situation, or particular elements in or consequences of it specified in the report, operate or may be expected to operate against the public interest,

(c) on a competition reference, that a person was engaged in an anticompetitive practice which operated or may be expected to operate against the public interest, or

(d) on a reference under section 11 of the Competition Act 1980 (reference of public bodies and certain other persons), that a person is pursuing a course of conduct which operates against the public interest,

the appropriate Minister or Ministers may apply to the comptroller to take action under this section.

(2) Before making an application the appropriate Minister or Ministers shall publish, in such manner as he or they think appropriate, a notice describing the nature of the proposed application and shall consider any representations which may be made within 30 days of such publication by persons whose interests appear to him or them to be affected.

(3) If on an application under this section it appears to the comptroller that the matters specified in the Commission's report as being those which in the Commission's opinion operate, or operated or may be expected to operate, against the public interest include—

(a) conditions in licences granted under a patent by its proprietor restricting the use of the invention by the licensee or the right of the proprietor to grant other licences, or

(b) a refusal by the proprietor of a patent to grant licences on reasonable terms

he may by order cancel or modify any such condition or may, instead or in addition, make an entry in the register to the effect that licences under the patent are to be available as of right.

(4) In this section "the appropriate Minister or Ministers" means the Minister or Ministers to whom the report of the Commission was made.

Note. The present section 51 was substituted for the former section (reprinted at para. 51.02 *infra*) by the 1988 Act (Sched. 5, para. 14), with effect from August 1, 1989 (S.I. 1989 No. 816).

SECTION 51 *[Repealed]*   51.02

[Application by Crown in cases of monopoly or merger

51.—(1) Where on a reference under section 50 or 51 of the Fair Trading Act 1973 (the 1973 Act) a report of the Monopolies and Mergers Commission (the Commission) as laid before Parliament, contains conclusions to the effect—

(a) that a monopoly situation (within the meaning of the 1973 Act) exists in relation to a description of goods which consist of or include

patented products or in relation to a description of services in which a patented product or process is used, and

(b) that facts found by the Commission in pursuance of their investigations under section 49 of the 1973 Act operate, or may be expected to operate, against the public interest,

the appropriate Minister or Ministers may, subject to subsection (3) below, apply to the comptroller for relief under subsection (4) below in respect of the patent.

(2) Where, on a reference under section 64 or 75 of the 1973 Act, a report of the Commission, as laid before Parliament, contains conclusions to the effect—

(a) that a merger situation qualifying for investigation has been created;

(b) that one of the elements which constitute the creation of that situation is that the condition specified in section 64(2) or (3) of the 1973 Act prevails (or does so to a greater extent) in respect of a description of goods which consist of or include patented products or in respect of a description of services in which a patented product or process is used; and

(c) that the creation of that situation, or particular elements in or consequences of it specified in the report, operate, or may be expected to operate, against the public interest,

the Secretary of State may, subject to subsection (3) below, apply to the comptroller for relief under subsection (5) below in respect of the patent.

(2A) Where,

(a) on a reference under section 5 of the Competition Act 1980, a report of the Commission, as laid before Parliament, contains conclusions to the effect that—

    (i) any person was engaged in an anti-competitive practice in relation to a description of goods which consist of or include patented products or in relation to a description of services in which a patented product or process is used, and

    (ii) that practice operated or might be expected to operate against the public interest; or

(b) on a reference under section 11 of the Act, such a report contains conclusions to the effect that—

    (i) any person is pursuing a course of conduct in relation to such a description of goods or services, and

    (ii) that course of conduct operates against the public interest,

the appropriate Minister or Ministers may, subject to subsection (3) below, apply to the Comptroller for relief under subsection (5A) below in respect of the patent.

(3) Before making an application under subsections (1) or (2) above, the appropriate Minister or Ministers shall publish, in such manner as he or they think appropriate, a notice describing the nature of the proposed application, and shall consider any representations which, within the period of

thirty days from the date of publication of the notice, may be made to him or them by persons whose interests appear to the appropriate Minister or Ministers to be likely to be affected by the proposed application.

(4) If on an application under subsection (1) above it appears to the comptroller that the facts specified in the Commission's report as being those which, in the Commission's opinion, operate or may be expected to operate against the public interest include—

> *(a) any conditions in a licence or licences granted under the patent by its proprietor restricting the use of the invention concerned by the licensee or the right of the proprietor to grant other licences under the patent, or*

> *(b) a refusal by the proprietor to grant licences under the patent on reasonable terms,*

the comptroller may by order cancel or modify any such condition or may, instead or in addition, make an entry in the register to the effect that licences under the patent are to be available as of right.

(5) If on an application under subsection (2) above it appears to the comptroller that the particular matters indicated in the Commission's report as being those which, in the Commission's opinion, operate or may be expected to operate against the public interst (whether those matters are so indicated in pursuance of a requirement imposed under section 69(4) or 75(3) of the 1973 Act or otherwise) include any such condition or refusal as is mentioned in paragraph (a) or (b) or* subsection (4) above, the comptroller may by order cancel or modify any such condition or may, instead or in addition, make an entry in the register to the effect that licences under the patent are to be available as of right.

(5A) If on an application under subsection (2A) above it appears to the Comptroller that the practice or course of conduct in question involved or involves the imposition of any such condition as is mentioned in paragraph (a) of subsection (4) above or such a refusal as is mentioned in paragraph (b) of that subsection, the Comptroller may by order cancel or modify any such condition or may, instead or in addition, make an entry in the register to the effect that licences under the patent are to be available as of right.

(6) In this section "the appropriate Minister or Ministers," in relation to a report of the Commission, means the Minister or Ministers to whom the report is made.]

Notes. Subsections (2A) and (5A) were added by the Competition Act 1980 (c. 21, s. 14).

* Presumably "or" here should have read "of."

RELEVANT RULE

Application by Crown under section 51

69.—An application under section 51(1) for an order or entry under section 51(3) shall be made on Patents Form No. 34/77 and shall be accompa- **51.03**

nied by a statement of the facts upon which the applicant relies and evidence verifying the statement.

Notes. Rule 69 was amended by S.I. 1989 No. 1116 (r. 2). Rule 70 (reprinted at para. 48.03) is also relevant.

COMMENTARY ON SECTION 51

51.04 *General*

Section 51 concerns the right of a government department to apply for a licence under a patent, or seek an entry in the register that licences are obtainable as of right, in each case when a report of the Monopolies and Mergers Commission ("the MMC") has been laid before Parliament. It applies also to "existing patents" (Sched. 2, para. 1(2)).

The wording of the section was totally revised (though not amended in substance) by the 1988 Act, see para. 51.01. The result is to consolidate the previous wording which had been augmented by amendments made by the Competition Act 1980 (c. 21 s. 14), see para. 51.02. In addition to the powers given to a Minister under the section, a government department can, alternatively, make an application for a licence to be granted to a specified person under section 48(1)(*c*), or more generally under section 48(1)(*a*) or (*b*), for the remedies specified therein.

While, under section 90 of the Fair Trading Act 1973 (c. 41), a Minister has a general power to declare things unlawful if found contrary to the public interest, and to prohibit the carrying out of existing agreements, he is not permitted thereby to restrict the doing of anything for restraining infringement of a United Kingdom patent, *e.g.* to restrain a patentee from seeking an injunction in respect thereof, nor can he restrict a person from attaching conditions to a patent licence (s. 90(5)). These effects can, instead, be achieved by action taken under the present section.

The powers of section 51 have now been augmented by the 1988 Act by enacting therein provisions similar to those of section 51 in respect of other forms of intellectual property, *viz.* for registered designs (by s. 270, inserting a new section 11A in the Registered Designs Act 1949 (12, 13 & 14 Geo. 6, c. 88), see Sched. 4, para. 11A [1988]); for design rights (by s. 238 [1988]) and for copyrights (by s. 144 [1988]). These increased powers were presumably provided because it was thought that such did not previously exist, see the MMC Reports on the Ford Motor Company (Cmnd. 9437) (*noted Re. Ford's Replacement Parts*, [1986] FSR 147) and on the British Broadcasting Corporation (Cmnd. 9614).

51.05 *Relevant conclusions of the Monopolies and Mergers Commission (subs. (1))*

Subsection (1) now operates when a report of the MMC has been laid before Parliament containing conclusions which arise from a reference to the MMC of one of the following types: (*a*) a "monopoly reference", that is one defined in section 5(1)(*a*) of the Fair Trading Act 1973 (c. 41) ("the FTA") in relation to a "monopoly situation" relating to the supply of goods (s. 6(1) FTA), or to the supply of services (s. 7(1) FTA), or in relation to exports (s. 8, FTA); (*b*) a "merger reference", that is one defined in section 5(1)(*b*) or (*c*) of the FTA as relating to a newspaper merger (under s. 59 FTA) or another merger (under s. 64 FTA); (*c*) a "competition reference," that is one under section 5 of the Competition Act 1980 (c. 21); or (*d*) a reference under section 11 of the Competition Act that a person is pursuing a course of conduct which operates against the public interest. The offending conclusions which arise from any such reference are that a situation, practice or course of conduct exists which "operates against the public interest".

390

Procedure under section 51   **51.06**

When a MMC report containing a conclusion as indicated in para. 51.05 *supra* has been laid before Parliament, the relevant "Minister or Ministers" (*i.e.* the Minister or Ministers to whom the MMC report is made (subs. (4)) may propose taking action under the section, but before so doing an appropriate notice of intention has to be published, in such manner as the Minister(s) think appropriate, and 30 days allowed for representations to be made by any person "whose interests appear to be affected" (subs. (2)), *e.g.* by the patentee or a licensee under the patent. The Minister(s) must consider any representations so made, and presumably are not precluded from considering late-filed representations. Thereafter, the Minister(s) may make application to the Comptroller for him to take action under the section. An application can also be made to the Comptroller for exercise by him of similar powers in respect of other forms of intellectual property, see para. 51.04 *supra*.

Any application under section 51 is made by the Minister(s) in question under rule 69 (reprinted at para. 51.03 *supra*) using PF 34/77 (reprinted at para. 141.34), as discussed in para. 51.08 *infra*. Rule 70 (reprinted at para. 48.03), permitting opposition to the application, then applies, see para. 48.19.

Powers of the Comptroller (subs. (3))   **51.07**

On application duly made to him by a Minister under subsections (1) and (2), the practice for which is discussed in para. 51.08 *infra*, the Comptroller may order the cancellation or modification of any conditions in licences granted under the patent (and/or other forms of intellectual property) which either restrict the use of the invention by the licensee or the right of the proprietor to grant other licences (subs. (3)(*a*)), if such condition has been found by the MMC to operate, in its opinion, against the public interest. Surprisingly, the provisions of section 108 (*Order to take effect as licence under deed*) do not appear to extend to a licence granted or modified by order under section 51.

Alternatively, the Comptroller may order a "licence of right" entry to be made in the register in respect of the patent(s) in issue (subs. (3)(*b*)). In this case, any person may then seek a licence under the patent which the Comptroller will settle, if necessary, under section 46(3)(*a*), for which see paras. 46.07–46.27, which the patentee and/or licensees will be able to oppose even if they had previously made representations to the Minister(s) under subsection (2).

Analogous powers to those of section 51 for patents now exist for registered designs, design rights and copyrights, as noted in para. 51.04 *supra*.

PRACTICE UNDER SECTION 51   **51.08**

Rule 69 (reprinted at para. 51.03 *supra*) requires that an application under section 51 is to be made on PF 34/77 (reprinted at para. 141.34) and is to be accompanied by a statement of the facts on which the applicant relies and evidence verifying the statement. The procedure is thereafter as set out in rule 70 (reprinted at para. 48.03) and is the same as with an application under section 48, see para. 48.19.

By section 52 opposition to the application can be filed, the procedure then being as set out in rule 71, for which see paras. 52.07–52.09.

In proceedings under section 51 statements contained in an MMC report are prima facie evidence thereof, see section 53(2) and para. 53.04.

52.01   **SECTION 52**

Opposition, appeal and arbitration

52.—(1) The proprietor of the patent concerned or any other person wishing to oppose an application under sections 48 to 51 above may, in accordance with rules, give to the comptroller notice of opposition; and the comptroller shall consider the opposition in deciding whether to grant the application.

(2) Where an appeal is brought from an order made by the comptroller in pursuance of an application under sections 48 to 51 above or from a decision of his to make an entry in the register in pursuance of such an application or from a refusal of his to make such an order or entry, the Attorney General, **Attorney General for the Isle of Man,** Lord Advocate or Attorney General for Northern Ireland, or such other counsel as any of them may appoint, shall be entitled to appear and be heard.

(3) Where an application under sections 48 to 51 above is opposed under subsection (1) above, and either—

(*a*) the parties consent, or

(*b*) the proceedings require a prolonged examination of documents or any scientific or local investigation which cannot in the opinion of the comptroller conveniently be made before him,

the comptroller may at any time order the whole proceedings, or any question or issue of fact arising in them, to be referred to an arbitrator or arbiter agreed on by the parties or, in default of agreement, appointed by the comptroller.

(4) Where the whole proceedings are so referred, section 21 of the Arbitration Act 1950 [14 Geo. 6, c. 27] or, as the case may be, section 22 of the Arbitration Act (Northern Ireland) 1937 [1 Edw. 8 & 1 Geo. 6, c. 8, N.I.] (statement of cases by arbitrators) shall not apply to the arbitration; but unless the parties otherwise agree before the award of the arbitrator or arbiter is made an appeal shall lie from the award to the court.

(5) Where a question or issue of fact is so referred, the arbitrator or arbiter shall report his findings to the comptroller.

Note. Subsection (2) was amended by S.I. 1978 No. 621.

RELEVANT RULE

Opposition under section 52(1)

52.02   **71.**—(1) The time within which notice of opposition under section 52(1) may be given shall be three months after the advertisement of the application in accordance with rule 70 above.

(2) Such notice shall be given on Patents Form No. 35/77 and shall be accompanied by a copy thereof and supported by a statement in duplicate

setting out fully the facts upon which the opponent relies and evidence in duplicate verifying the statement.

(3) The comptroller shall send a copy of the notice, the statement and the evidence to the applicant who, if he desires to proceed with his application, shall within three months of the receipt of such copies, file evidence in duplicate confined to matters strictly in reply and the comptroller shall send a copy thereof to the opponent.

(4) No further evidence shall be filed by either party except by leave or direction of the comptroller.

(5) The comptroller may give such directions as he may think fit with regard to the subsequent procedure.

COMMENTARY ON SECTION 52

General   52.03

Section 52 permits opposition by a proprietor or any other person wishing to oppose an application under any of sections 48–51. Such other person could be an existing licensee under the patent. The section brings together provisions which in the 1949 Act were separated in different sections as follows: subsection (1) is analogous to section 43(3) [1949]; subsection (2) is analogous to sections 36(8), 44(1) and 44(2) [1949]; and subsections (3)–(5) are analogous to section 44(3)–(5) 1949].

Opposition to compulsory licence application (subs. (1))   52.04

Subsection (1) gives the patent proprietor or "any other person" the right to oppose any application under sections 48–51 and requires the Comptroller to consider the opposition in deciding whether to grant that application. A foreign opponent can be expected to be requested to give security for costs, see section 107(4)(*c*) and para. 107.05.

It is imperative that the proprietor lodge opposition under subsection (1) if he wishes to be heard on the terms of any licence which the Comptroller may decide should be granted on an application under section 48, which otherwise will be decided in *ex parte* proceedings (*Ultimatte Corp.'s Patent*, SRIS O/1/84, *noted* IPD 6141). However, by agreement in that case, and because the Comptroller is entitled to consider any material information obtained from whatever source, the proprietor was permitted to make submissions in writing on the terms of the licence to be granted, but with consideration of these restricted to *ex parte* proceedings held in his absence, see also *Zanetti-Streccia's Patent* ([1973] RPC 227) discussed in para. 52.08 *infra*.

Appeals under sections 48–51 (subs. (2))   52.05

Subsection (2) refers to appeal, and gives to the Attorney-General (or his equivalent in other parts of the United Kingdom) the right to appear, or to be represented by counsel, and be heard, in any appeal on an application under sections 48–51, irrespective of whether the application was opposed. It seems that there is no such right of audience in the initial proceedings before the Comptroller. Where the Attorney-General, etc., does so appear on such an appeal, there is precedent for him being permitted to call evidence should he so wish, see *Hoffman-La Roche* v.

393

Bamford [*New Zealand*] ([1976] RPC 346) decided under the corresponding enactment in New Zealand.

Any appeal lies to the Patents Court under section 97(1) and further to the Court of Appeal, but only if a point of law is involved and with leave (s. 97(3)). There is no provision for the proceedings to take place in Scotland, see section 123(2)(*f*).

52.06   *Arbitration (subss. (3)–(5))*

By subsection (3), if the parties agree, or the proceedings become protracted, the Comptroller can refer the matter to an agreed or appointed arbitrator (arbiter in Scotland), the reference to which suggests the possibility of arbitration proceedings in Scotland despite section 123(2)(*f*), see para. 52.05 *supra*.

Subsection (4) states that section 21 of the Arbitration Act 1950 (14 Geo. 6, c. 27), or the corresponding section 22 of the Arbitration Act (Northern Ireland) 1937 (1 Edw. 8 & 1 Geo. 6, c. 8; N.I.), will not apply, and that instead (unless there is prior agreement) the decision of the arbitrator is subject to appeal to the court. However, this is now the normal rule in an arbitration, section 21 of the 1950 Act having been repealed and replaced by the Arbitration Act 1979 (c. 42). By subsection (5) the arbitrator reports his finding to the Comptroller. Presumably, where the Comptroller does not refer the *whole* proceedings to an arbitrator (or arbiter), the proceedings will eventually return to the Comptroller for decision taking into account the questions decided, or facts found, in the arbitration. No use of these provisions has become apparent.

PRACTICE UNDER SECTION 52

52.07   *Procedure on opposition*

The procedure on opposition is governed by rule 71 (reprinted at para. 52.03 *supra*). The period for opposition is three months from the advertisement of the application in the O.J. and this period is inextensible (r. 110(2), reprinted in para. 123.10). The opposition is filed on PF 35/77 (reprinted at para. 141.35) and is required to be supported by a statement of the facts on which the opponent relies and evidence verifying the facts, all in duplicate. The statement and evidence may be filed within 14 days of the PF 35/77 (r. 107, reprinted at para. 72.09), though the periods under rule 107 (for filing the statement), and under rule 71(2) (for filing the evidence), are each extensible at the Comptroller's discretion under rule 110(1).

Thus, the initial proceedings differ from the norm for opposition proceedings before the Comptroller in that the opponent is required to file his evidence with the opposition statement and there is no counter-statement to this by which the issues in contention come to be defined. This is because the applicant will have already filed his evidence when applying for the compulsory licence under rule 68 (reprinted at para. 48.02), and the Comptroller has already been satisfied (under r. 70, reprinted at para. 48.03) that the applicant has made out a prima facie case before opposition to the application is invited, see para. 48.19.

Copies of the statement and evidence filed by the opponent are sent by the Comptroller to the applicant who, if he desires to proceed with the application must file (within three months) evidence strictly confined to matters in reply, so that new supporting evidence cannot be filed by the applicant at this stage. This period is extensible by discretion exercised under rule 110(1) (reprinted in para. 123.10). Further evidence can only be filed by leave or direction of the Comptroller. The subsequent procedure is flexible, but will follow that generally used in contentious proceedings, for which see paras. 72.32–72.52.

In *Halcon's Patent* ([1989] RPC 1) the proceedings were stayed until pending infringement proceedings (and subsequently an appeal thereon) were completed so that it could first be determined whether the applicant's activities did infringe the patent and whether this was valid.

Discovery during opposition proceedings under section 52   **52.08**

The practice of the Comptroller concerning discovery in contentious proceedings before him is discussed in para. 72.44, and para. 72.44A discusses the restrictions which have been imposed in particular cases, not only to protect the confidentiality of commercially sensitive information put forward in the proceedings by means of orders under rule 94 (for which see para. 118.17), but also orders made for limiting disclosure of specified documents to legal advisers of the other party, and sometimes other specified persons on conditions designed to secure the secrecy, and provide protection against potential misuse, of the information contained in those documents.

Often such orders have been made in proceedings for the settlement of terms of a "licence of right" under section 46(3)(*a*) (for which see paras. 46.07–46.27), or in oppositions under the present section. On the latter ground, the cases include: *Heathway Machine's Compulsory Licence Application* (SRIS O/111/80), which was a preliminary to *Extrude Hone's Patent* ([1982] RPC 361 and [1984] FSR 105), discussed in para. 48.14, concerning discovery of a licence agreement between the patentee and the applicant; *Geigy's Patent* ([1964] RPC 391) and *Smith, Kline & French's Patent* ([1965] RPC 98), each of which concerned accountancy evidence filed on behalf of the patentee in proceedings under section 31 [1949]; and *Halcon's Patent* (SRIS O/118/86, *noted* IPD 9081), which concerned an assessment of costs and profitability which was presumed had been made by the applicant for a compulsory licence, but other requests for discovery were here left for determination after the pending infringement proceedings had been completed, see [1989] RPC 1).

Appeals   **52.09**

In *Zanetti-Streccia's Patent* ([1973] RPC 227) the patentee failed, as the result of a muddle, to enter opposition under section 43(3) [1949] to the grant of a compulsory licence, and when the licence was granted he appealed under section 44 [1949]. Since section 44 [1949] did not speak of an appeal from an opposition but an appeal from an order of the Comptroller, it was held that the patentee had *locus* to enter appeal if he could make a complaint about anything appearing on the face of the order made by the Comptroller. Subsection (2) also refers to an appeal brought from an order of the Comptroller and the general provisions for appeal in section 97 would not appear to alter the law, in this respect at least, from that prevailing under the 1949 Act. The main ground of the appeal in the *Zanetti* case was that negotiations for the grant of a voluntary licence to another company, which had begun after the application for the compulsory licence, were known to the Comptroller and should have prevented him from ordering a compulsory licence. The Patents Appeal Tribunal, noting that section 39 [1949] concludes by observing that the Comptroller should not be required to take account of matters subsequent to the making of the application, declined to interfere with the Comptroller's discretion and dismissed the appeal. The same provision is now to be found in subsection (2).

53.01   **SECTION 53**

Compulsory licences; supplementary provisions

53.—(1) Without prejudice to section 86 below (by virtue of which the Community Patent Convention has effect in the United Kingdom), sections 48 to 51 above shall have effect subject to any provision of that convention relating to the grant of compulsory licences for lack or insufficiency of exploitation as that provision applies by virtue of that section.

(2) In any proceedings on an application made **under section 48 above in respect of a patent** [*in relation to a patent under sections 48 to 51 above*], any statement with respect to any activity in relation to the patented invention, or with respect to the grant or refusal of licences under the patent, contained in a report of the Monopolies and Mergers Commission laid before Parliament under Part VII of the Fair Trading Act 1973 [c. 41] **or section 17 of the Competition Act 1980 [c. 21]** shall be prima facie evidence of the matters stated, and in Scotland shall be sufficient evidence of those matters.

(3) The comptroller may make an entry in the register under sections 48 to 51 above notwithstanding any contract which would have precluded the entry on the application of the proprietor of the patent under section 46 above.

(4) An entry made in the register under sections 48 to 51 above shall for all purposes have the same effect as an entry made under section 46 above.

(5) No order or entry shall be made in pursuance of an application under sections 48 to 51 above which would be at variance with any treaty or international convention to which the United Kingdom is a party.

Notes. Subsection (1) has not been brought into force (see para. 132.08). The amendments to subsection (2) were made by the 1988 Act (Sched. 5, para. 15) with effect from August 1, 1989 (S.I. 1989 No. 816).

COMMENTARY ON SECTION 53

53.02   *General*

Section 53 contains certain supplementary provisions relating to compulsory licences arising from sections 48–51, but subsection (1) has not been brought into force.

53.03   *Compulsory licences under the CPC (subs. (1))*

Subsection (1) is not yet in force because the CPC is not yet in force. It concerns the operation of sections 48–51 in relation to the CPC. Section 86 would give effect to the CPC in the United Kingdom and require that all rights, obligations, restrictions, etc., of the CPC are to have legal effects in the United Kingdom. The CPC contains provisions with regard to compulsory licences in CPCaa. 46–48. CPCa. 46(1) provides that national law relating to compulsory licences shall apply to Community patents. CPCa. 47 provides that a compulsory licence may not be granted in respect of a Community patent on the ground of lack or insufficiency of exploitation if the product covered by the patent, which is manufactured in a Contracting State, is put on the market in the territory of any other Contracting State, in sufficient quantity to satisfy needs in the territory of that other Contracting State, except for licences granted in the public interest.

Reports of Monopolies and Mergers Commission (subs. (2))   **53.04**

Subsection (2) is the same as section 46(6) [1949] and states that in respect of proceedings under sections 48–51, a statement of facts concerning a patent in a report of the Monopolies and Mergers Commission is to be taken as prima facie evidence of those facts. This means that these facts are to be presumed to be true unless a challenger is able to disprove them, the onus being upon him to do so. The term "prima facie evidence" is discussed in para. 32.21A. The subsection is most likely to be of relevance in proceedings under section 51.

Entries in the register (subss. (3) and (4))   **53.05**

Subsection (3) gives the Comptroller power to make an entry in the register under sections 48–51, notwithstanding any contract which would have precluded the entry on an application by the proprietor under section 46. Such an entry would be one stating that "licences of right" are available under the patent (s. 46(1)). Subsection (4) states that an entry under sections 48–51 is to have the same effect as an entry under section 46. These provisions correspond to those of section 45(2) [1949]. Thus, if the Comptroller makes a "licence of right" entry as the result of an application for a compulsory licence under section 48 (or in proceedings instituted by a Minister under s. 51), thereafter any person can take advantage of that entry and obtain a licence with its terms settled, in default of agreement between the parties, by the Comptroller under section 46(3)(*a*). The proceedings for such settlement are discussed in paras. 46.07–46.27 with the relevant practice discussed in paras. 46.30–46.33.

Conformity with treaties and international conventions (subs. (5))   **53.06**

Subsection (5) is the same as section 45(3) [1949] and prohibits the making of any order or entry which would be at variance with any international agreement to which the United Kingdom is a party. Such agreement could be the Paris Convention, EPC, CPC, PCT or the Treaty of Rome. Thus subsection (5) makes these conventions self-executing to some extent as regards provisions for compulsory licences.

For possible conflict between some of the provisions of section 48 with the Treaty of Rome, see para. 48.08.

SECTION 54   54.01

Special provisions where patented invention is being worked abroad

54.—(1) Her Majesty may by Order in Council provide that the comptroller may not (otherwise than for purposes of the public interest) make an order or entry in respect of a patent in pursuance of an application under sections 48–51 above if the invention concerned is being commercially worked in any relevant country specified in the Order and demand in the United Kingdom for any patented product resulting from that working is being met by importation from that country.

(2) In subsection (1) above "relevant country" means a country other than a member state whose law in the opinion of Her Majesty in Council incorporates or will incorporate provisions treating the working of an invention in, and importation from, the United Kingdom in a similar way to that in which the Order in Council would (if made) treat the working of an invention in, and importation from, that country.

54.02   Commentary on Section 54

Section 54 was a new provision. It contemplates reciprocal arrangements between the United Kingdom and non-EEC countries regarding the working of patents.

Subsection (1) provides that, by Order in Council to that effect, the Comptroller may not grant a compulsory licence under sections 48–51 if the invention in question is being worked in a foreign country named in the Order, and the demand in the United Kingdom is being met by importation from that country; by subsection (2) the country named is a country where a reciprocal right exists or will exist, "other than a member state". A "member state" is defined in the European Communities Act 1972 (c. 68) and means a member of the EEC. In effect, section 54 enables extension by reciprocal arrangement to countries other than EEC countries an arrangement similar to that which CPCa. 47 would provide if it were in force. As for the position concerning working in a Member State, see para. 48.08, and section 53(5) discussed in para. 53.06.

No order under section 54 has yet been made and it is, therefore, at present of no effect, but see para. 48.08. If it were, it would be applicable to "existing patents" (Sched. 2, para. 1(2)).

55.01   **SECTION 55**

Use of patented inventions for services of the Crown

55.—(1) Notwithstanding anything in this Act, any government department and any person authorised in writing by a government department may, for the services of the Crown and in accordance with this section, do any of the following acts in the United Kingdom in relation to a patented invention without the consent of the proprietor of the patent, that is to say—

(a) where the invention is a product, may—
    (i) make use, import or keep the product, or sell or offer to sell it where to do so would be incidental or ancillary to making, using, importing or keeping it; or
    (ii) in any event, sell or offer to sell it for foreign defence purposes or for the production or supply of specified drugs and medicines, or dispose or offer to dispose of it (otherwise than by selling it) for any purpose whatever;

398

(*b*) where the invention is a process, may use it or do in relation to any product obtained directly by means of the process anything mentioned in paragraph (*a*) above;

(*c*) without prejudice to the foregoing, where the invention or any product obtained directly by means of the invention is a specified drug or medicine, may sell or offer to sell the drug or medicine;

(*d*) may supply or offer to supply to any person any of the means, relating to an essential element of the invention, for putting the invention into effect;

(*e*) may dispose or offer to dispose of anything which was made, used, imported or kept in the exercise of the powers conferred by this section and which is no longer required for the purpose for which it was made, used, imported or kept (as the case may be),

and anything done by virtue of this subsection shall not amount to an infringement of the patent concerned.

(2) Any act done in relation to an invention by virtue of this section is in the following provisions of this section referred to as use of the invention; and "use", in relation to an invention, in sections 56 to 58 below shall be construed accordingly.

(3) So far as the invention has before its priority date been duly recorded by or tried by or on behalf of a government department or the United Kingdom Atomic Energy Authority otherwise than in consequence of a relevant communication made in confidence, any use of the invention by virtue of this section may be made free of any royalty or other payment to the proprietor.

(4) So far as the invention has not been so recorded or tried, any use of it made by virtue of this section at any time either—

(*a*) after the publication of the application for the patent for the invention; or

(*b*) without prejudice to paragraph (*a*) above, in consequence of a relevant communication made after the priority date of the invention otherwise than in confidence;

shall be made on such terms as may be agreed either before or after the use by the government department and the proprietor of the patent with the approval of the Treasury or as may in default of agreement be determined by the court on a reference under section 58 below.

(5) Where an invention is used by virtue of this section at any time after publication of an application for a patent for the invention but before such a patent is granted, and the terms for its use agreed or determined as mentioned in subsection (4) above include terms as to payment for the use, then (notwithstanding anything in those terms) any such payment shall be recoverable only—

(*a*) after such a patent is granted; and

(*b*) if (apart from this section) the use would, if the patent had been granted on the date of the publication of the application, have infringed not only the patent but also the claims (as interpreted by the description and any drawings referred to in the description or claims) in the form in which they were contained in the application immediately before the preparations for its publication were completed by the Patent Office.

(6) The authority of a government department in respect of an invention may be given under this section either before or after the patent is granted and either before or after the use in respect of which the authority is given is made, and may be given to any person whether or not he is authorised directly or indirectly by the proprietor of the patent to do anything in relation to the invention.

(7) Where any use of an invention is made by or with the authority of a government department under this section, then, unless it appears to the department that it would be contrary to the public interest to do so, the department shall notify the proprietor of the patent as soon as practicable after the second of the following events, that is to say, the use is begun and the patent is granted, and furnish him with such information as to the extent of the use as he may from time to time require.

(8) A person acquiring anything disposed of in the exercise of powers conferred by this section, and any person claiming through him, may deal with it in the same manner as if the patent were held on behalf of the Crown.

(9) In this section "relevant communication", in relation to an invention, means a communication of the invention directly or indirectly by the proprietor of the patent or any person from whom he derives title.

(10) Subsection (4) above is without prejudice to any rule of law relating to the confidentiality of information.

(11) In the application of this section to Northern Ireland, the reference in subsection (4) above to the Treasury shall, where the government department referred to in that subsection is a department of the Government of Northern Ireland, be construed as a reference to the Department of Finance in Northern Ireland.

COMMENTARY ON SECTION 55

55.02 *General*

Section 55 is the first of a group of sections, sections 55 to 59, which concern the use by the Crown of patented inventions, including those of European Patents (UK). When the CPC comes into force, CPCa. 46(4) should be broad enough to cover Crown use of Community patents.

Subsection (4) provides for compensation for Crown use to be paid to the patent proprietor, see para. 55.11 *infra*. Section 57(4) provides for that compensation to be paid to a third party in certain circumstances, see para. 57.05. Moreover, new section 57A now provides for additional compensation to be paid under either of sections 55 or 57 for loss of manufacturing profit due to Crown use of a patented product or patented process, see the commentary thereon. In all such cases, if the question of compensation payment, or the quantum thereof, cannot be settled between a claimant and the relevant government department, the dispute can be referred to the court under section 58, see the commentary thereon.

Section 59 contains special provisions for extended Crown use of inventions during a declared period of emergency, see the commentary thereon.

Other legislation covering Crown use of intellectual property is to be found as follows:–

(a) for registered designs, in section 12 and Schedule 1 of the Registered Designs Act 1949 (12, 13 & 14 Geo. 6, c. 85), as amended by the 1988 Act, and re-presented in Schedule 4 [1988];

(b) for unregistered design rights, in sections 240–244 [1988]; and

(c) for all forms of intellectual property, in the Defence Contracts Act 1958 (6 & 7 Eliz. 2, c. 38), reprinted (as amended) in Appendix B at paras. B10–B17 with commentary at para. B18.

The term "design right" also includes rights in a "semiconductor topography" (Design Right (Semiconductor Topographies) Regulations 1989, S.I. 1989 No. 1100).

In contrast to the position for patents and registered designs, and unless section 57 applies, Crown use of the unregistered design right is limited to use for the National Health Service and for home and foreign defence purposes. The Defence Contracts Act is restricted to "defence" and relates to technical information in the possession of a contractor or proposed contractor, which is subject to a restriction agreement with a third party or the use of which for the contract purpose is subject to copyright. The Defence Contracts Act could, therefore, presumably be used to authorise use of software for defence purposes. A short commentary on the Defence Contracts Act appears in Appendix B at para. B18. Authorisations for Crown user under the unregistered design right and the Defence Contracts Act should be given by Ministers, whereas for patents and registered designs (under the 1977 Act and the Registered Designs Act 1949) authorisations for Crown user may be given by civil servants.

Principles of Crown use   55.03

The principle is maintained by sections 55–59 that the Crown, or its agents (*i.e.* government departments or persons authorised in writing by a government department), have the right to use patented inventions, without the consent of the proprietor of the patent, for the services of the Crown in the United Kingdom (including the Isle of Man). The word "agents" is used here not in a legal sense but as a convenient word to embrace the bodies specified. The armed forces are direct servants of the Crown and it has been put beyond doubt that the term "Crown employees" includes members of the armed forces, see the Armed Forces Act 1981 (c. 55, s. 22) which amended the definition of "employee" in section 130(1).

However, it should be noted that the term "government department" is not defined in the Act and it can sometimes be a matter of some difficulty to discover the status of a public body. The point was discussed in *Pfizer* v. *Minister of Health* ([1965] RPC. 261 (HL)). In general, a nationalised industry is not a government department; neither (since 1961) is the Post Office, save for a transitional provision (Post Office Act 1969, c. 48, Sched. 10, paras. 8 and 18). In recent years it has become customary to include in legislation setting up new public bodies under statute a definition disclaiming Crown status for that body. Therefore, in the case of public corporations set up under statute, that statute (as possibly amended) should be checked for any provision defining the status of that corporation *vis-à-vis* the Crown. An example is the British Telecommunications Act 1981 (c. 38), see Schedule 5, paragraphs 9 and 19 thereof for saving transitional provisions.

401

The possibility that the Crown can be an infringer of a patent is covered by section 129 and by section 3 of the Crown Proceedings Act 1947 (c. 44) for both of which see para. 129.02.

Thus, the right to sue the Crown for patent infringement under section 60 is subject to the exclusion of Crown use to the substantial extent permitted by section 55. Subject, however, to these limitations, it is otherwise possible to bring action against the Crown for infringement by Crown servants or agents, including government departments, for example in respect of any sales not provided for by subsection (1).

Since Crown use of inventions within the terms of section 55 is not regarded as any act of infringement, there are certain consequences. For example, the definition of infringement included in section 60 does not apply, and the extent to which a patent is used by the Crown is to be judged by section 55 only. Thus, the acts specified in section 60(5) as excluded from infringement (private, experimental use, and use on ships and aircraft) will not be excluded from Crown use if they are with Crown authority, but will be excluded from infringement if they are not with Crown authority. By section 60(6)(a) the right under section 60(2) to supply means relating to an essential element of the invention to a person entitled to use is extended to a person entitled by virtue of section 55, see also para. 55.07 *infra*.

Various of the provisions relating to infringement in section 60 are made applicable to Crown use by specific recital in section 58, but otherwise the reliefs available to a proprietor of a patent in a case of infringement, such as injunction and recovery of damages, or an account of profits, are not available as against the Crown in respect of the use of the invention by the Crown. However, subsection (4) provides for compensation to be paid for use of the patented invention by the Crown and, in some circumstances, compensation for loss of manufacturing profit can now also be awarded, under the new section 57A, see paras. 55.11 and 57A.02–57A.07.

The definitions in section 130(1) of "services of the Crown" and "use for the services of the Crown" refer to the meanings given in section 56(2), see para. 56.03.

55.04   *Acts for Services of the Crown (subs. (1))*

Subsection (1) lists the acts which are permitted to be done "for the services of the Crown." All such acts are "Crown use" for the purposes of sections 55(4)–(11) and 56–58, see subsection (2).

55.05   *—Where the invention is a product (subs. (1)(a))*

In subsection (1), paragraph (a)(i) provides that, where the invention is a product, the Crown may make, use, import or keep the product or, incidentally thereto, sell or offer the product for sale; and paragraph (a)(ii) comprehends the right to sell such a product for foreign defence purposes, or for the production or supply of specified drugs or medicines, or to dispose of the product otherwise than by selling. Use of the invention for "foreign defence purposes" is defined in section 56(3) and is discussed in para. 56.04.

Although the term "patented product" is defined in section 130(1), the term "product" alone covers other than the product of a patented process and appears to mean any article or substance which can be made by, or which results from, a process. Indeed, it has been held that the word "product" is a perfectly general one apt to describe any article (*Therm-a-Stor* v. *Weatherseal*, [1981] FSR 579 (CA)), see also para. 60.11. It therefore seems clear that all patented inventions are to be classed as either a product or a process. In *Pfizer* v. *Minister of Health* ([1965] RPC

261 (HL)), it was held that the right to authorise import must include the right of sale to the government department concerned.

—Where the invention is a process or a specified drug or medicine   **55.06**
(subs. (1)(b) and (c))

By paragraph (*b*), if the invention is a process, the Crown has similar rights in relation to the process or the product of the process, and by paragraph (*c*) the Crown specifically has the right to sell or offer to sell the invention where it, or the product obtained therefrom, is a specified drug or medicine; "specified drugs and medicines" are defined in section 56(4). Paragraphs (*a*), (*b*) and (*c*) thus give to the Crown wide powers in relation to drugs and medicines for Crown use, including use for the National Health Service, and for other services where the Secretary of State has specified that the use of such drugs or medicines is required in accordance with section 56(4). It would appear, however, that the Crown has the right to sell surgical or curative devices (not being drugs or medicines as such) only where such selling is incidental or ancillary to their making, using, importing or keeping for the services of the Crown.

—Supply of contributory means (subs. (1)(d))   **55.07**

By paragraph (*d*) the rights of Crown user extend to the supply of, or an offer to supply, the means relating to an essential element of the invention, for putting the invention into effect. This paragraph reflects the provisions for contributory infringement in section 60(2) and (3), but it is not in the same terms as section 60(2) because, in order that the powers of the Crown should have appropriate breadth, there was no need for the same measure of qualification. Having regard to section 60(6)(*a*) which has the effect of permitting supply to a person entitled under the present section, the provisions of this paragraph will cover the possibility that the supply is to be made abroad and therefore to a person not entitled under section 55, for example where spare parts are required for original equipment made available for foreign defence purposes.

—Disposals by Crown (subs. (1)(e))   **55.08**

By paragraph (*e*) the Crown can dispose of, or offer to dispose of, anything which has been made or obtained by virtue of the section and which is no longer required for its intended purpose. However, no claim can be made for Crown use of a patented invention unless that use falls within the definition of section 55. Thus, it seems that, where an act is done by the Crown with the consent of the proprietor, a claim for Crown user compensation under subsection (4) should not arise.

—Use of micro-organisms   **55.09**

Besides the rights of the Crown specified in paragraphs (*a*) to (*e*) of subsection (1), the Crown also has the right under the proviso to rule 17(2)(*b*) (reprinted at para. 125A.02) to obtain, without the undertaking otherwise required, a sample of a micro-organism deposited in a culture collection for the purpose of Crown use of a patent, the specification of which refers to such a deposited culture.

Prior recordal of invention (subs. (3))   **55.10**

The Crown is given under subsection (3) the right to use, free of royalty or payment, any invention which has been duly recorded or tried by or for a Government department or the United Kingdom Atomic Energy Authority, provided that the recordal or trial takes place before the priority date of the invention and otherwise than as the result of a "relevant communication" made in confidence; "relevant communication" is defined in subsection (9) as being a communication directly or indirectly from the proprietor.

Research and development work of a purely commercial nature carried out by the United Kingdom Atomic Energy Authority, funded by industry, will not constitute a prior record for the purposes of subsection (3). It can be expected that this exception will apply to other establishments in future.

Some ambiguities are encountered in practice and it is not clear how wide an interpretation should be put on the words "so far as . . . duly recorded", that is whether this last expression gives to the Crown the right to use only that which has been "duly recorded" or whether it gives to the Crown the right to use anything which falls within a claim which covers that which has been "duly recorded". It is understood that government departments, perhaps not unnaturally, adopt the latter view, though this would not seem to be supported by a literal meaning of the provision.

Where dispute as to such matters has arisen, various issues of law have been formulated for decision by the court under subsections (3)–(5) (*Hughes Aircraft's Patent*, SRIS C/145/83, *noted* IPD 7019), but leave was not granted here for these to be decided as preliminary points and it appears that the case was settled before trial.

55.11   *Compensation (subs. (4))*

Subsection 4 provides that, where an invention has not been so duly recorded, the proprietor of the patent can make a claim in respect of its use after publication of the application or at any time after the priority date as a result of a communication otherwise than in confidence; use is on terms as agreed, or as settled by the Court. A co-proprietor may claim compensation, but any payment therefor is, apparently, to be paid to all the co-proprietors jointly, see *Patchett's Patent* ([1963] RPC 90) and para. 36.34.

The terms will normally be on a willing licensor/willing licensee basis, not taking into account loss of manufacturing profit, as determined in *Patchett's Patent* ([1967] RPC 237 (CA)). However, if the proprietor, or an exclusive licensee, was in a position to supply the product, or use the process concerned, loss of manufacturing profit can now be compensated under new section 57A. The terms are to be agreed by the Treasury or, by subsection (11), by the Department of Finance for Northern Ireland if appropriate. Subsection (10) provides that subsection (4) is subject to the rule of law concerning confidentiality, and appears to preserve any right which may exist to proceed on the basis of breach of confidence.

A limitation is imposed by section 5 of the Atomic Energy Authority (Weapons Group) Act 1973 (c. 4) (as amended by Sched. 5, para. 6) to the effect that, in respect of patents owned by the United Kingdom Atomic Energy Authority and appertaining on April 1, 1973 to the Weapons Group, which previously was part of the Authority, any remuneration for Crown use is to be determined by the Secretary of State for Defence and not by the court.

The taxation of sums received by way of compensation for Crown use under the former sections 46–49 [1949] was equated with the taxation of sums in respect of patent licences under provisions now re-enacted in sections 520–533 of the Income and Corporation Taxes Act 1988 (c. 1), see particularly section 533(4) thereof. This Act contains no similar express provision concerning sums received by way of compensation for Crown use under sections 55–59 of the present Act, and the basis of taxation of these is, therefore, somewhat obscure, though it is understood that

H.M. Inspectors of Taxes assume that the previous regime continues. It would, of course, be strange if compensation payments for Crown use now fell to be treated differently from those received under the 1949 Act, especially since the said section 533(4) refers also to equivalent foreign legislation: it is possible that section 17(2)(*a*) of the Interpretation Act 1978 (c. 30) has the effect of extending section 533(4) to cover similar sums received under the present Act.

Use before grant (subs. (5))   55.12

In respect of Crown use of an invention after publication but before grant, the Crown is placed under subsection (5) in a position equivalent to an infringer under section 69(2). There is in section 58(10) an equivalent of section 69(3) (*Reasonable expectation of grant as affecting relief*).

Retrospective authorisation (subs. (6))   55.13

Retrospective authorisation of use for the Crown is permitted by subsection (6). A slight doubt persists on whether a joint proprietor may alone be authorised, but the reference to "any person" appears to cover the point, see *Patchett's Patent* ([1963] RPC 90 and [1967] RPC 77 and 237).

In *Jacques Dory* v. *Stratford Health Authority* (SRIS C/22/88) the Ministry of Defence, acting for the Crown gave retrospective authorisation for use of a patented medical apparatus in the National Health Service after proceedings for infringement had been commenced. The court then held that the proceedings should be struck out as involving no cause of action.

Notification to proprietor (subs. (7))   55.14

Information on the extent of Crown use is to be given to the proprietor under subsection (7), but only after grant of the patent and if not precluded on grounds of public interest, a term presumably wider than national security.

Rights on acquisition (subs. (8))   55.15

Subsection (8) gives to a person acquiring anything disposed of in accordance with the section a continuing right of use. The position may obtain anyway under the EEC "exhaustion of rights" doctrine, for which see para. C15 in Appendix C.

Position in Northern Ireland and the Isle of Man   55.16

In the applicability of the section to Northern Ireland, the term "government department" includes "a Department of the Government of Northern Ireland" (s. 131(*b*)) and reference to "the Crown" includes "the Crown in the right of Her Majesty's Government in Northern Ireland" (s. 131(*c*)).

There is no special provision defining a "government department" as regards the Isle of Man. The application of section 55 thereto therefore seems to raise an intriguing constitutional question.

PRACTICE UNDER SECTION 55   55.17

Many contracts issued by government departments have standard conditions which require a contractor to notify the relevant authority if he is aware of relevant intellectual property rights thought to be necessary for performing the contract, and to refer any claim arising.

Where a contact name and address is not given in a contract, compensation claims for Crown use, and enquiries in relation thereto, can be addressed to the Ministry of Defence, Director of Patents A, Room 2131, Empress State Building, Lillie Road, London SW6 1TR.

56.01

SECTION 56

Interpretation, etc., of provisions about Crown use

56.—(1) Any reference in section 55 above to a patented invention, in relation to any time, is a reference to an invention for which a patent has before that time been, or is subsequently, granted.

(2) In this Act, except so far as the context otherwise requires, "the services of the Crown" includes—

(a) the supply of anything for foreign defence purposes;

(b) the production or supply of specified drugs and medicines; and

(c) such purposes relating to the production or use of atomic energy or research into matters connected therewith as the Secretary of State thinks necessary or expedient;

and "use for the Services of the Crown" shall be construed accordingly.

(3) In section 55(1)(a) above and subsection (2)(a) above, references to a sale or supply of anything for foreign defence purposes are references to a sale or supply of the thing—

(a) to the government of any country outside the United Kingdom, in pursuance of an agreement or arrangement between Her Majesty's Government in the United Kingdom and the government of that country, where the thing is required for the defence of that country or of any other country whose government is party to any agreement or arrangement with Her Majesty's Government in respect of defence matters; or

(b) to the United Nations, or to the government of any country belonging to that organisation, in pursuance of an agreement or arrangement between Her Majesty's Government and that organisation or government, where the thing is required for any armed forces operating in pursuance of a resolution of that organisation or any organ of that organisation.

(4) For the purposes of section 55(1)(a) and (c) above and subsection (2)(b) above, specified drugs and medicines are drugs and medicines which are both—

(a) required for the provision of pharmaceutical services, general medical services or general dental services, that is to say, services of those respective kinds under Part II of the National Health Service Act 1977 [c. 49], **Part II of the National Health Service (Scotland) Act 1978** [c. 29] [*Part IV of the National Health Service (Scotland)*

Act 1947] or the corresponding provisions of the law in force in Northern Ireland or the Isle of Man, and
(*b*) specified for the purposes of this subsection in regulations made by the Secretary of State.

Note. Subsection (4) was amended by the National Health Service (Scotland) Act 1978 (c. 29, Sched. 16, para. 48).

COMMENTARY ON SECTION 56

General **56.02**

This section needs to be read in conjunction with the Defence Contracts Act 1958 (c. 38) (as amended by Schedule 5, para. 4), reprinted in Appendix B at paras. B10–B17. Any dispute under that Act is to be referred to the Patents Court (Sched. 5, para. 4), see RSC, Ord. 104, r. 2(1) reprinted in para. E104.2.

Definitions of "patented invention" and "services of the Crown" (subss. (1) and (2)) **56.03**

By subsection (1) reference to a patented invention in section 55 is to include reference to an invention which is patented at the relevant date or is subsequently patented.
By subsection (2)(*a*) the "services of the Crown" includes the supply of anything for foreign defence purposes which is defined in subsection (3), see para. 56.04 *infra*. Similarly, the production or supply of specified drugs and medicines included by virtue of subsection (2)(*b*) is defined in subsection (4), see para. 56.05 *infra*.
A further inclusion is made by subsection (2)(*c*) of such purposes relating to the production or use of atomic energy or research into matters connected therewith as the Secretary of State may consider necessary or expedient. It is possible that the Secretary of State will not now apply this provision to research and development work of a purely commercial nature carried out by the United Kingdom Atomic Energy Authority or other governmental establishments and funded by industry, see para. 55.10. Thus, those seeking to place research contracts with such establishments may wish to check the position before entering into such a contract. Presumably, for the purpose of subsection (2)(*c*), the Secretary of State will be the Minister for Defence; and, for the purpose of subsection (4), he will be the Minister for Health.

Foreign defence purposes (subs. (3)) **56.04**

By subsection (3)(*a*) use for foreign defence purposes includes sale or supply to a foreign government, in pursuance of an agreement or arrangement with that country, of anything for the defence of that country or any other country party to a defence agreement or arrangement with the Government. "Arrangement" covers "Memoranda" and "Understandings" and like documents which are often used as vehicles for putting into effect collaboration between governments.
Subsection (3)(*b*), relating to use in connection with United Nations resolutions, falls under the head of use for foreign defence purposes, but distinction is made between things required for defence in paragraph (*a*) and things required for "any armed forces" in paragraph (*b*).

56.05 *"Specified" drugs and medicines (subs. (4))*

The "specified drugs and medicines" referred to in section 56(2)(*b*) are defined in subsection (4)(*a*) as drugs and medicines required for the services set up under Part II of the National Health Service Act 1977 (c. 49) and the corresponding legislation for Scotland, Northern Ireland and the Isle of Man; and by subs. (4)(*b*), which are so specified in regulations made by the Secretary of State, presumably the Secretary for Health. Drugs and medicines for the National Health Service, *e.g.* for use in the hospital services, are not required to be "specified" as this supply falls under section 55(1)(*a*). The supply of surgical or curative devices, and ameliorating devices such as hearing aids, by implication appears to be confined within the limits of section 55(1)(*a*).

57.01   SECTION 57

Rights of third parties in respect of Crown use

57.—(1) In relation to—

(*a*) any use made for the services of the Crown of an invention by a government department, or a person authorised by a government department, by virtue of section 55 above, or

(*b*) anything done for the services of the Crown to the order of a government department by the proprietor of a patent in respect of a patented invention or by the proprietor of an application in respect of an invention for which an application for a patent has been filed and is still pending,

the provisions of any licence, assignment, assignation or agreement to which this subsection applies shall be of no effect so far as those provisions restrict or regulate the working of the invention, or the use of any model, document or information relating to it, or provide for the making of payments in respect of, or calculated by reference to, such working or use; and the reproduction or publication of any model or document in connection with the said working or use shall not be deemed to be an infringement of any copyright **or design right** subsisting in the model or document.

(2) Subsection (1) above applies to a licence, assignment, assignation or agreement which is made, whether before or after the appointed day, between (on the one hand) any person who is a proprietor of or an applicant for the patent, or anyone who derives title from any such person or from whom such person derives title, and (on the other hand) any person whatever other than a government department.

(3) Where an exclusive licence granted otherwise than for royalties or other benefits determined by reference to the working of the invention is in force under the patent or application concerned then—

(*a*) in relation to anything done in respect of the invention which, but for the provisions of this section and section 55 above, would constitute an infringement of the rights of the licensee, subsection (4) of

408

that section shall have effect as if for the reference to the proprietor of the patent there were substituted a reference to the licensee; and

(*b*) in relation to anything done in respect of the invention by the licensee by virtue of an authority given under that section, that section shall have effect as if the said subsection (4) were omitted.

(4) Subject to the provisions of subsection (3) above, where the patent, or the right to the grant of the patent, has been assigned to the proprietor of the patent or application in consideration of royalties or other benefits determined by reference to the working of the invention, then—

(*a*) in relation to any use of the invention by virtue of section 55 above, subsection (4) of that section shall have effect as if the reference to the proprietor of the patent included a reference to the assignor, and any sum payable by virtue of that subsection shall be divided between the proprietor of the patent or application and the assignor in such proportion as may be agreed on by them or as may in default of agreement be determined by the court on a reference under section 58 below; and

(*b*) in relation to any act done in respect of the invention for the services of the Crown by the proprietor of the patent or application to the order of a government department, section 55(4) above shall have effect as if that act were use made by virtue of an authority given under that section.

(5) Where section 55(4) above applies to any use of an invention and a person holds an exclusive licence under the patent or application concerned (other than such a licence as is mentioned in subsection (3) above) authorising him to work the invention, then subsections (7) and (8) below shall apply.

(6) In those subsections "the section 55(4)" payment means such payment (if any) as the proprietor of the patent or application and the department agree under section 55 above, or the court determines under section 58 below, should be made by the department to the proprietor in respect of the use of the invention.

(7) The licensee shall be entitled to recover from the proprietor of the patent or application such part (if any) of the section 55(4) payment as may be agreed on by them or as may in default of agreement be determined by the court under section 58 below to be just having regard to any expenditure incurred by the licensee—

(*a*) in developing the invention, or

(*b*) in making payments of the proprietor in consideration of the licence, other than royalties or other payments determined by reference to the use of the invention.

(8) Any agreement by the proprietor of the patent or application and the department under section 55(4) above as to the amount of the section 55(4) payment shall be of no effect unless the licensee consents to the agreement; and any determination by the court under section 55(4) above as to the

amount of that payment shall be of no effect unless the licensee has been informed of the reference to the court and is given an opportunity to be heard.

(9) Where any models, documents or information relating to an invention are used in connection with any use of the invention which falls within subsection (1)(*a*) above, or with anything done in respect of the invention which falls within subsection (1)(*b*) above, subsection (4) of section 55 above shall (whether or not it applies to any such use of the invention) apply to the use of the models, documents or information as if for the reference in it to the proprietor of the patent there were substituted a reference to the person entitled to the benefit of any provision of an agreement which is rendered inoperative by this section in relation to that use; and in section 58 below the references to terms for the use of an invention shall be construed accordingly.

(10) Nothing in this section shall be construed as authorising the disclosure to a government department or any other person of any model, document or information to the use of which this section applies in contravention of any such licence, assignment, assignation or agreement as is mentioned in this section.

Note. Subsection (1) was amended as to "design right" by the 1988 Act (Sched. 7, para. 20). The term "design right" includes rights in a "semiconductor topography" (Design Right (Semiconductor Topographies) Regulations, S.I. 1989 No. 1100).

COMMENTARY ON SECTION 57

57.02 *General*

This section concerns the rights of third parties in respect of Crown use. The language is involved and the interpretation is not free from difficulty. The extent of application to "existing patents" is covered by Schedule 4, para. 2.

57.03 *Position under licences or assignments (subss. (1) and (2))*

Any Crown use is not to be subject under subsection (1) to any restraint by virtue of any existing licence or agreement between the proprietor and any third party. Typically, a licensee of the proprietor may by authorisation under section 55 be discharged from certain obligations under the licence for the purposes of the Crown use.

Subsection (1) refers to items, such as models and documents, which might have been passed by a patentee to, typically, a licensee in connection with a patent agreement. The provision enables the Crown, in placing a contract with such a person, to set aside an agreement which, through its terms or by the existence of copyright or unregistered design right (including rights in a "semiconductor topography", see *Note* to para. 57.01 *supra*), could inhibit that party from fulfilling a contract which the Crown may wish to place therewith, the copyright and design right thereby being overridden. In addition, subsection (1) enables the Crown to set aside any royalty or other payment otherwise required by such an agreement. When payments under a licence are set aside, settlement with the proprietor of the patent concerned is made by way of compensation under section 55(4); and, if the licensee is an exclusive licensee, that person can now claim, under new section 57A, for loss of his manufacturing profit.

The words "any person whatever" in subsection (2) would apparently include a joint patentee, whose position under the 1949 Act was considered in *Patchett's Patent* ([1963] RPC 90 and [1967] RPC 77 and 237).

Exclusive licences (subs. (3))   57.04

Subsection (3) puts, in the same position as the proprietor, an exclusive licensee who has acquired his right for a lump sum or for some other consideration not based on use. The term "exclusive licensee" is defined in section 130(1) and discussed in para. 67.03.

Assignments for royalty (subs. (4))   57.05

Where the patent has been assigned for a consideration based on use, subsection (4) provides that the assignor shall be treated in some respects as if he were a joint proprietor. Sums payable in respect of Crown use are to be divided between the assignor and the proprietor. However, if the latter himself is a contractor, it would appear equitable that payments under section 55(4) should be paid to the assignor, as the latter could now presumably have made a claim under section 57A if he had not been awarded the contract in question. Section 57(1)(*b*) makes clear that such a proprietor may be required to supply articles for Crown use, but it seems unlikely that he would then be entitled to compensation under section 55(4). However any "dispute" between a proprietor-contractor and the Crown can be referred to the court under section 58.

Entitlement of certain exclusive licensees (subss. (5)–(8))   57.06

Subsection (5), in conjunction with subsections (7) and (8) to which it refers, provides for a royalty-paying exclusive licensee to have a right to an agreed or settled portion of the payment by the Crown for the use of the invention, defined in subsection (6) as "the section 55(4)" payment; and for the consent of such an exclusive licensee to be necessary for any agreement between the Crown and the proprietor as to payment for the use of the invention. In the event of the payment being settled by the court the exclusive licensee must be informed, and he has then the right to be heard.

Use of documents, models and information (subss. (9) and (10))   57.07

Subsection (9) replaced, in the same terms, section 1(2) of the Defence Contracts Act 1958 (c. 38). It concerns the position of parties to an agreement rendered inoperative by virtue of section 57. The subsection provides that there is a right of claim in respect of use of models, documents and information where an agreement is ineffective by virtue of section 57.

Subsection (10) replaced, in the same terms, section 1(3) of the same Act and precludes disclosure of matter in breach of an agreement with which the section is concerned. The provisions of the Defence Contracts Act are reprinted in Appendix B at paras. B10–B17. These cover use for "defence" purposes of technical information in the possession of contractors, or potential contractors, who are subject to restrictions imposed by agreements or copyrights, see para. B18. Access to other relevant intellectual property rights has now been provided by the 1988 Act, see para. 55.02.

57A.01   **SECTION 57A**

Compensation for loss of profit

57A—(1) Where use is made of an invention for the services of the Crown, the government department concerned shall pay—
(a) to the proprietor of the patent, or
(b) if there is an exclusive licence in force in respect of the patent, to the exclusive licensee,
compensation for any loss resulting from his not being awarded a contract to supply the patented product or, as the case may be, to perform the patented process or supply a thing made by means of the patented process.

(2) Compensation is payable only to the extent that such a contract could have been fulfilled from his existing manufacturing or other capacity; but is payable notwithstanding the existence of circumstances rendering him ineligible for the award of such a contract.

(3) In determining the loss, regard shall be had to the profit which would have been made on such a contract and to the extent to which any manufacturing or other capacity was under-used.

(4) No compensation is payable in respect of any failure to secure contracts to supply the patented product or, as the case may be, to perform the patented process or supply a thing made by means of the patented process, otherwise than for the services of the Crown.

(5) The amount payable shall, if not agreed between the proprietor or licensee and the government department concerned with the approval of the Treasury, be determined by the court on a reference under section 58, and is in addition to any amount payable under section 55 or 57.

(6) In this section "the government department concerned", in relation to any use of an invention for the services of the Crown, means the government department by whom or on whose authority the use was made.

(7) In the application of this section to Northern Ireland, the reference in subsection (5) above to the Treasury shall, where the government department concerned is a department of the Government of Northern Ireland, be construed as a reference to the Department of Finance and Personnel.

Note. Section 57A was inserted into the Act by the 1988 Act (Sched. 5, para. 16) with effect from August 1, 1989 (S.I. 1989 No. 816), and is subject to sub-para. (4) of that paragraph, reprinted in para. 57A.02 *infra.*

Commentary on Section 57A

57A.02   *General*

Section 57A was introduced by the 1988 Act and provides for compensation in respect of loss that a manufacturing patentee or licensee incurs as a result of not being awarded a contract which, but for the exercise of powers under section 55, he might reasonably have expected to have received. Compensation under this head is additional to compensation payable to a patentee under section 55(4) or to a third party under section 57(4) (subs. (5)). In some cases this additional compensation could increase very markedly the compensation payable for Crown use of a patented invention, and the section has the effect of overruling in part the decision in *Patchett's Patent* ([1967] RPC 237 (CA)). In the absence of agreement, a claimant or the relevant government department may, by subsection (5), refer the question of compensation, or its quantum, under the section to the court under amended section 58, for which see the commentary thereon. The new section applies to "existing patents" by virtue of Schedule 4, para. 2.

Schedule 5, paragraph 16(4) [1988] states:

"The above amendments apply in relation to any use of an invention for the services of the Crown after the commencement of this section, even if the terms for such use were settled before commencement."

The "commencement date" for this provision was August 1, 1989, see para. 57A.01 *supra*.

The 1988 Act has made similar provision in the case of registered designs (by adding para. 2A to Sched. 1 of the Registered Designs Act 1949 (12, 13 & 14 Geo. 6, c. 88), re-presented in Sched. 4 [1988], Sched. 1, para. 2A thereto), and in the case of unregistered design rights by section 243 [1988].

Entitlement to compensation under section 57A (subs. (1))   **57A.03**

By subsection (1), compensation is payable either to the patentee or, if there is an exclusive licensee for the patent, to the exclusive licensee. Compensation is not payable to a non-exclusive licensee under either of sections 55 or 57A.

"Use" in subsection (1) is defined in section 55(2) and the section applies to Crown use after August 1, 1989 even if terms were settled before that date, see para. 57A.02 *supra*.

Extent of compensation (subs. (2))   **57A.04**

Under subsection (2), compensation is only payable to a person to the extent that the contract for the Crown use could have been fulfilled by him from his existing manufacturing capacity. The first part of subsection (2) suggests that only circumstances outside the direct control of the claimant are intended to make the section applicable. Thus, for example, inadequate quality control systems may exclude an otherwise valid claim under the section, at least to the extent that the circumstances extended over a particular period of time; and, in the case of repeat orders, the circumstances will apparently need to be judged in relation to each contract. However, under the second part of the subsection, compensation is payable if circumstances outside the control of the claimant (*e.g.* security, public policy, etc.) render him ineligible for the contract.

It is clear, therefore, that in determining eligibility, consideration will have to be given to the ability of the claimant to have met the requirements of the contract in terms of specification, delivery time and quality. It appears that any refusal to pay compensation under section 57A can be referred to the court under section 58, though subsection (5) is silent on the point. It is by no means clear how eligibility for compensation could be established in the face of a decision from a government department that the potential contractor could not have met the order in question.

413

57A.05   *Quantum of compensation (subs. (3))*

Under subsection (3), regard is to be had to the profit which would have been made on such a contract and to the extent to which manufacturing or other capacity was under-used. Presumably, a government department will take the view that "profit" should be determined by the conventional rules applied by government departments for determining profit under government contracts. Whether the court would take the same view is more problematical. If a claimant is due to make payments to a third party under a licence or other agreement relating to the patent, "profit" should be determined after deduction of such payments. Compensation to that other party, if he is entitled, will then be determined under sections 55 and 57A and will take the place of royalty.

57A.06   *Exclusions (subs. (4))*

Subsection (4) makes clear that the section applies only to failure to secure contracts for "the services of the Crown", as that term has been construed in relation to section 55, for which see para. 55.03. Loss sustained through failure to secure other contracts continues to be dealt with, if at all, as acts of infringement under section 60.

Compensation under section 57A will not be payable if the Crown can establish that the patent in question is not valid, or (by analogy with section 62) that any valid claims do not cover the matter in issue. This stems from the fact that compensation is only payable in respect of a "patented product" or "patented process". However, there might still be a claim under the equivalent design right provision contained in section 243 [1988] if a design right can be shown to be involved in the contract.

57A.07   *Other points (subss. (5)–(7))*

The arrangements in subsection (5) for approval by the Treasury, and settlement of disputes by the court under a reference under section 58, are similar to those provided for in section 55(4) for compensation under section 55, but subsection (5) makes it clear that compensation under section 57A is additional to any other compensation payable to the proprietor under section 55 or to a third party under section 57.

Subsection (6) provides a special definition of a "government department" for the purposes of the section, *viz.* that which gave the authority for Crown use under section 55.

Subsection (7) mirrors section 55(11) and the position in Northern Ireland, and the Isle of Man, is therefore the same as that under section 55, for which see para. 55.16.

57A.08   Practice under Section 57A

Section 57A is unlike any previous provision relating to Crown use. However, cases decided under section 50 may be relevant. For example, in *Enviro-Spray's Patents* ([1986] RPC 47), an applicant for a compulsory licence was not able to demonstrate satisfactorily that he was capable of working the invention. Subsection (2) makes it clear that applicants for compensation under section 57A cannot be successful unless they had the ability and capacity to have fulfilled the order in question, though it is not clear whether the onus lies to establish an eligibility or an ineligibility. The words "only to the extent that" suggest the latter, see para. 57A.04 *supra*.

Applications for compensation should be addressed in writing to the Department concerned, but in the case of the Ministry of Defence it is appropriate to write to the Director of Patents A at the address given in para. 55.17. That person can also be contacted on any query arising under the section.

SECTION 58   58.01

References of disputes as to Crown use

58.—(1) Any dispute as to—
  (*a*) **the exercise by a government department, or a person authorised by a government department, of the powers conferred by section 55 above,**
  (*b*) **terms for the use of an invention for the services of the Crown under that section,**
  (*c*) **the right of any person to receive any part of a payment made in pursuance of subsection (4) of that section, or**
  (*d*) **the right of any person to receive a payment under section 57A,**
may be referred to the court by either party to the dispute after a patent has been granted for the invention.

[(1) *Any dispute as to the exercise by a government department or a person authorised by a government department of the powers conferred by section 55 above, or as to terms for the use of an invention for the services of the Crown thereunder, or as to the right of any person to receive any part of a payment made or agreed to be made in pursuance of subsection (4) of that section, may be referred to the court by either party to the dispute after a patent has been granted for the invention.*]

(2) If in such proceedings any question arises whether an invention has been recorded or tried as mentioned in section 55 above, and the disclosure of any document recording the invention, or of any evidence of the trial thereof, would in the opinion of the department be prejudicial to the public interest, the disclosure may be made confidentially to counsel for the other party or to an independent expert mutually agreed upon.

(3) In determining under this section any dispute between a government department and any person as to the terms for the use of an invention for the services of the Crown, the court shall have regard—
  (*a*) to any benefit or compensation which that person or any person from whom he derives title may have received or may be entitled to receive directly or indirectly from any government department in respect of the invention in question;
  (*b*) to whether that person or any person from whom he derives title has in the court's opinion without reasonable cause failed to comply with a request of the department to use the invention for the services of the Crown on reasonable terms.

(4) In determining whether or not to grant any relief under **subsection**

415

(1)(a), (b) or **(c)** above [*this section*] and the nature and extent of the relief granted the court shall, subject to the following provisions of this section, apply the principles applied by the court immediately before the appointed day to the granting of relief under section 48 of the 1949 Act.

(5) On a reference under this section the court may refuse to grant relief by way of compensation in respect of the use of an invention for the services of the Crown during any further period specified under section 25(4) above, but before the payment of the renewal fee and any additional fee prescribed for the purposes of that section.

(6) Where an amendment of the specification of a patent has been allowed under any of the provisions of this Act, the court shall not grant relief by way of compensation under this section in respect of any such use before the decision to allow the amendment unless the court is satisfied that the specification of the patent as published was framed in good faith and with reasonable skill and knowledge.

(7) If the validity of a patent is put in issue in proceedings under this section and it is found that the patent is only partially valid, the court may, subject to subsection (8) below, grant relief to the proprietor of the patent in respect of that part of the patent which is found to be valid and to have been used for the services of the Crown.

(8) Where in any such proceedings it is found that a patent is only partially valid, the court shall not grant relief by way of compensation, costs or expenses except where the proprietor of the patent proves that the specification of the patent was framed in good faith and with reasonable skill and knowledge, and in that event the court may grant relief in respect of that part of the patent which is valid and has been so used, subject to the discretion of the court as to costs and expenses and as to the date from which compensation should be awarded.

(9) As a condition of any such relief the court may direct that the specification of the patent shall be amended to its satisfaction upon an application made for that purpose under section 75 below, and an application may be so made accordingly, whether or not all other issues in the proceedings have been determined.

(10) In considering the amount of any compensation for the use of an invention for the services of the Crown after publication of an application for a patent for the invention and before such a patent is granted, the court shall consider whether or not it would have been reasonable to expect, from a consideration of the application as published under section 16 above, that a patent would be granted conferring on the proprietor of the patent protection for an act of the same description as that found to constitute that use, and if the court finds that it would not have been reasonable, it shall reduce the compensation to such amount as it thinks just.

(11) Where by virtue of a transaction, instrument or event to which section 33 above applies a person becomes the proprietor or one of the proprietors or an exclusive licensee of a patent (the new proprietor or

licensee) and a government department or a person authorised by a government department subsequently makes use under section 55 above of the patented invention, the new proprietor or licensee shall not be entitled to any compensation under section 55(4) above (as it stands or as modified by section 57(3) above), **or to any compensation under section 57A above** in respect of a subsequent use of the invention before the transaction, instrument or event is registered unless—

 (*a*) the transaction, instrument or event is registered within the period of six months beginning with its date; or

 (*b*) the court is satisfied that it was not practicable to register the transaction, instrument or event before the end of that period and that it was registered as soon as practicable thereafter.

(12) In any proceedings under this section the court may at any time order the whole proceedings or any question or issue of fact arising in them to be referred, on such terms as the court may direct, to a Circuit judge discharging the functions of an official referee or an arbitrator in England and Wales, **the Isle of Man** or Northern Ireland, or to an arbiter in Scotland; and references to the court in the foregoing provisions of this section shall be construed accordingly.

(13) One of two or more joint proprietors of a patent or application for a patent may without the concurrence of the others refer a dispute to the court under this section, but shall not do so unless the others are made parties to the proceedings; but any of the others made a defendant or defender shall not be liable for any costs or expenses unless he enters an appearance and takes part in the proceedings.

Note. The replacement of subsection (1) and the amendment of subsections (4) and (11) were made by the 1988 Act (Sched. 5, para. 16(2) and (3)) with effect from August 1, 1989 (S.I. 1989 No. 816). These amendments are subject to the transitional provision of para. 16(4), reprinted in para. 57A.02. The amendment to subsection (12) was effected by S.I. 1978 No. 621.

COMMENTARY ON SECTION 58

General   **58.02**

Section 58 specifies the procedure to be followed if a dispute arises as to the use, or the terms of use, by the Crown of a patented invention, or the entitlement to payment therefor under sections 55(4), 57(4) or 57A. It applies to "existing patents by virtue of Sched. 4, para. 2". The Crown cannot prevent a "dispute" being referred to a court under section 58, even apparently in matters concerning use by a proprietor-contractor. *Patchett's Patent* ([1963] RPC 90 and [1967] RPC 77 & 237) is relevant to the position of co-proprietors.

The provision formerly present in section 48(2) [1949] that, in the event of a dispute being brought before the court, the Crown can put the validity of the patent in issue, is now to be found in section 74(1)(*e*). Thus, as formerly, a proprietor wishing to have a dispute resolved by the court must face the possibility of the expense of full validity proceedings. If validity is put in issue then section 75(1) operates, and the court may allow the specification to be amended.

A referral under section 58 may be made to any court as defined in section 130(1) (as amended), for discussion of which see para. 96.14. However, it is to be expected that proceedings under the section will normally be commenced in the High Court, when they will come before the Patents Court under RSC Ord. 104, r. 21 (reprinted at para. E104.21). The Patents Court is also required to hear any dispute arising under the Defence Contracts Act 1958 (c. 38) (reprinted in Appendix B at paras. B10–B17), see RSC 104, rule 2(1) (reprinted in para. E104.2). On the possible jurisdiction of Patents County Courts in relation to section 58, see para. 58.06 *infra* and para. 96.17.

58.03 *Reference of disputes (subs. (1))*

Subsection (1) was amended by the 1988 Act to provide for disputes under the new section 57A, but no longer providing for settlement of disputes as to payments agreed, or determined, but not paid. If a dispute arises as to the exercise by a government department of its rights under section 55, or the terms of use of an invention, or as to a division of payments, or as to compensation under section 57A, either party may refer the matter to the court provided that a patent has been granted.

In theory, it may not be easy to determine at what stage of negotiations a dispute can be said to have arisen, but the difficulty can be circumvented if one party desires to put the matter before the court.

58.04 *Disclosure of prior recordal of invention (subs. (2))*

In the case of a dispute as to prior recordal of an invention with reference to section 55(3), subsection (2) provides for counsel or an agreed expert to examine confidential prior records.

58.05 *Determination of relief (subss. (3)–(11))*

Under subsection 3(*a*) the court must have regard to any benefit or compensation the claimant may have received from a government department in respect of the invention when settling payment.

Subsection 3(*b*) provides that the court is to have regard also to whether the claimant has failed to comply with a request to use the patent for the Crown use on reasonable terms, but the provision gives no indication of the way in which the court is to relate the failure to offer reasonable terms to the payment made.

Subsection (4) provides that in determining whether or not to grant relief, the court is to adopt principles the same as those adopted before the appointed day in granting relief under section 48 [1949]. The wording is similar to that adopted in section 61(6), concerning relief in respect of infringement. The direct effect of the provision is not clear. Few cases reached the court under section 48 [1949] and principles can scarcely be said to have developed, except possibly the "willing licensor and willing licensee" of *Patchett's Patent* ([1969] RPC 237 at 252), but the effect of this case has been considerably changed by the introduction of section 57A.

The later subsections of section 58 make Crown use of patented inventions subject to certain provisions which apply in the case of infringement of a patent, such as those referred to in section 62 of the Act, but which would not otherwise apply to Crown use since, by section 55, Crown use is not infringement.

Thus, subsection (5) gives to Crown use the same dispensation as arises with an infringement committed in the six months allowed for belated renewal of a patent as is provided in section 62(2), but section 25(4)(*c*) provides that use in the further period allowed is to be taken as Crown use for the purpose of section 55(4).

418

Similarly, subsection (6) concerns the case where the patent in question has been amended; the proprietor must show that the specification as published was framed in good faith and with reasonable skill and knowledge. The subsection parallels section 62(3) concerning infringement.

Subsections (7) and (8) deal with a similar situation with regard to a partially valid patent. Section 63 provides that where a partially valid patent is infringed, relief may be granted if the specification was framed in good faith and with reasonable skill and knowledge, and subsections (7) and (8) similarly provide for relief in respect of Crown use in such circumstances. Likewise, in subsection (9) the court can call for amendment of a partially valid specification, as under section 63(3) with an infringement action.

Subsection (10) applies to Crown use of a patent before grant, a condition similar to that which applies to infringement under section 69(3): it must be reasonable to expect that the patent would be granted on the basis of the application as published covering the use, and if not the court has power to vary the compensation.

Subsection (11) provides that where a patent is the subject of an event warranting registration under section 33, the right to claim compensation for Crown use is diminished in the same way as are the rights to relief for infringement is diminished by section 68: the event must be registered within six months, or as soon as may be, or the right for compensation for use thereafter until registration is forfeited.

The commentaries on the above-mentioned provisions are therefore also relevant to the consideration of points arising under section 58.

Reference to a Circuit judge (subs. (12))   **58.06**

Subsection (12) permits the court to refer part or whole of the dispute to a circuit judge acting as an arbitrator or the equivalent in parts of the United Kingdom other than England and Wales. It is possible that similar powers will also be provided for a referral of proceedings, or certain questions arising thereunder, to a Patents County Court, the jurisdiction of which is discussed in para. 96.17.

Joint proprietors (subs. (13))   **58.07**

Subsection (13) requires that, as in infringement proceedings by section 66(2), where there are joint proprietors of a patent concerned in dispute all must be joined as parties to the matter, but if joined as a defendant any joint proprietor will not be liable for costs if he does not appear.

SECTION 59   **59.01**

Special provisions as to Crown use during emergency

59.—(1) During any period of emergency within the meaning of this section the powers exercisable in relation to an invention by a government department or a person authorised by a government department under section 55 above include power to use the invention for any purpose which appears to the department necessary or expedient—

(*a*) for the efficient prosecution of any war in which Her Majesty may be engaged;

(*b*) for the maintenance of supplies and services essential to the life of the community;

419

(*c*) for securing a sufficiency of supplies and services essential to the well-being of the community;

(*d*) for promoting the productivity of industry, commerce and agriculture;

(*e*) for fostering and directing exports and reducing imports, or imports of any classes, from all or any countries and for redressing the balance of trade;

(*f*) generally for ensuring that the whole resources of the community are available for use, and are used, in a manner best calculated to serve the interests of the community; or

(*g*) for assisting the relief of suffering and the restoration and distribution of essential supplies and services in any country or territory outside the United Kingdom which is in grave distress as the result of war;

and any reference in this Act to the services of the Crown shall, as respects any period of emergency, include a reference to those purposes.

(2) In this section the use of an invention includes, in addition to any act constituting such use by virtue of section 55 above, any act which would, apart from that section and this section, amount to an infringement of the patent concerned or, as the case may be, give rise to a right under section 69 below to bring proceedings in respect of the application concerned, and any reference in this Act to "use for the services of the Crown" shall, as respects any period of emergency, be construed accordingly.

(3) In this section "period of emergency" means any period beginning with such date as may be declared by Order in Council to be the commencement, and ending with such date as may be so declared to be the termination, of a period of emergency for the purposes of this section.

(4) A draft of an Order under this section shall not be submitted to Her Majesty unless it has been laid before, and approved by resolution of, each House of Parliament.

COMMENTARY ON SECTION 59

59.02 *General*

Section 59 only has effect during a period for which a "declaration of emergency" has been made. Subsection (3) provides that a period of emergency is one declared so to be by an Order in Council; by subsection (4) the draft of such an order must be approved by both Houses of Parliament. Since the 1977 Act came into force no such declaration has been made: the South Atlantic conflict in 1982 did not lead to the declaration of an emergency for the purposes of this section.

59.03 *Extension of powers*

Section 59 provides wider powers during a declared emergency for use by the Crown of inventions. It applies to "existing patents" by virtue of Schedule 4, para. 2. Subsection (1) refers alone to "use" which, in subsection (2), is defined as

including that which constitutes Crown use as defined by section 55 and also anything which, but for section 55, would be an infringement of the patent and anything which would fall within section 69.

However, the provisions or section 59 are limited to patents. Similar rights exist
for registered designs and unregistered design rights respectively under the Registered Designs Act 1949 (s. 88) (Sched. 1, para. 4, as amended by the 1988 Act
(Sched. 3, para. 37(4) and (5)), and re-presented in Sched. 4 [1988] (Sched. 4,
para. 4 thereof), and section 244 [1988]. "Topography rights" are now included
within the concept of "design rights", see para. 55.02. Whilst there appears to be
no corresponding emergency provisions, apart from those of section 57(1), in relation to copyrights, no doubt the Defence Contracts Act 1958 (c. 38), reprinted in
Appendix B at paras. B10–B17, would be used in appropriate circumstances.

The definition in section 130(1) of "services of the Crown" and of "use for the
services of the Crown" for the purposes of section 59 are those in section 59 itself,
see section 130(1).

War-time legislation   **59.04**

On the outbreak of any war, it is likely that further legislation would be enacted
for confiscation of enemy-owned intellectual property rights, *e.g.* as was done
under the Trading with the Enemy Act 1939 (2 & 3 Geo. 6, c. 89); and also for the
taking of even wider powers in relation to the ordering of compulsory licences. Section 2 of the Patents, Designs, Copyright and Trade Marks (Emergency) Act 1939
(2 & 3 Geo. 6, c. 107, which was amended: by the 1986 Act (Sched. 2, para. 7), to
refer also to "service marks"; and by the 1988 Act (Sched. 6, para. 3) to refer to
"design rights") provides powers which can be exercised in a time of war for the
compulsory licensing of any patent, registered design, trade or service mark, design
right, or copyright in which an "enemy or enemy subject" has an interest. The term
"design right" also includes rights in a "semiconductor topography" (Design Right
(Semiconductor Topographies) Regulations 1989, S.I. 1989 No. 1100). This 1939
Act is further noted in Appendix B at para. B09.

SECTION 60   60.01

Meaning of infringement

60.—(1) Subject to the provisions of this section, a person infringes a
patent for an invention if, but only if, while the patent is in force, he does
any of the following things in the United Kingdom in relation to the invention without the consent of the proprietor of the patent, that is to say—

(*a*) where the invention is a product, he makes, disposes of, offers to
dispose of, uses or imports the product or keeps it whether for disposal or otherwise;

(*b*) where the invention is a process, he uses the process or he offers it
for use in the United Kingdom when he knows, or it is obvious to a
reasonable person in the circumstances, that its use there without
the consent of the proprietor would be an infringement of the
patent;

(*c*) where the invention is a process, he disposes of, offers to dispose of, uses or imports any product obtained directly by means of that process or keeps any such product whether for disposal or otherwise.

(2) Subject to the following provisions of this section, a person (other than the proprietor of the patent) also infringes a patent for an invention if, while the patent is in force and without the consent of the proprietor, he supplies or offers to supply in the United Kingdom a person other than a licensee or other person entitled to work the invention with any of the means, relating to an essential element of the invention, for putting the invention into effect when he knows, or it is obvious to a reasonable person in the circumstances, that those means are suitable for putting, and are intended to put, the invention into effect in the United Kingdom.

(3) Subsection (2) above shall not apply to the supply or offer of a staple commercial product unless the supply or the offer is made for the purpose of inducing the person supplied or, as the case may be, the person to whom the offer is made to do an act which constitutes an infringement of the patent by virtue of subsection (1) above.

(4) Without prejudice to section 86 below, subsection (1) and (2) above shall not apply to any act which, under any provision of the Community Patent Convention relating to the exhaustion of the rights of the proprietor of a patent, as that provision applies by virtue of that section, cannot be prevented by the proprietor of the patent.

(5) An act which, apart from this subsection, would constitute an infringement of a patent for an invention shall not do so if—

(a) it is done privately and for purposes which are not commercial;

(b) it is done for experimental purposes relating to the subject-matter of the invention;

(c) it consists of the extemporaneous preparation in a pharmacy of a medicine for an individual in accordance with a prescription given by a registered medical or dental practitioner or consists of dealing with a medicine so prepared;

(d) it consists of the use, exclusively for the needs of a relevant ship, of a product or process in the body of such a ship or in its machinery, tackle, apparatus or other accessories, in a case where the ship has temporarily or accidentally entered the internal or territorial waters of the United Kingdom;

(e) it consists of the use of a product or process in the body or operation of a relevant aircraft, hovercraft or vehicle which has temporarily or accidentally entered or is crossing the United Kingdom (including the air space above it and its territorial waters) or the use of accessories for such a relevant aircraft, hovercraft or vehicle;

(f) it consists of the use of an exempted aircraft which has lawfully entered or is lawfully crossing the United Kingdom as aforesaid or of the importation into the United Kingdom, or the use or storage there, of any part or accessory for such an aircraft.

(6) For the purposes of subsection (2) above a person who does an act in

relation to an invention which is prevented only by virtue of paragraph (*a*), (*b*), or (*c*) of subsection (5) above from constituting an infringement of a patent for the invention shall not be treated as a person entitled to work the invention, but—

(*a*) the reference in that subsection to a person entitled to work an invention includes a reference to a person so entitled by virtue of section 55 above, and

(*b*) a person who by virtue of section **28A(4) or (5)** [*28(6)*] above or section 64 below is entitled to do an act in relation to the invention without it constituting such an infringement shall, so far as concerns that act, be treated as a person entitled to work the invention.

(7) In this section—

"relevant ship" and "relevant aircraft, hovercraft or vehicle" mean respectively a ship and an aircraft, hovercraft or vehicle registered in, or belonging to, any country, other than the United Kingdom, which is a party to the Convention for the Protection of Industrial Property signed at Paris on 20th March 1883; and "exempted aircraft" means an aircraft to which section **89** [*53*] of the Civil Aviation Act **1982** [*1949*] [c. 16] aircraft exempted from seizure in respect of patent claims) applies.

Notes. Subsection (4) has not been brought into force (see para. 132.04). Subsection (6) was prospectively amended by the 1988 Act (Sched. 5, para. 8); and subsection (7) was amended by the Civil Aviation Act 1982 (c. 16, Sched. 15, para. 19). For the commencement of the amendment to subsection (6), see the latest Supplement to this Work *re.* this para.

ARTICLES 60.02

M. Vitoria, "Contributory Infringement", [1979] EIPR 91;

M. Howe, "Infringing Goods and the Warehouseman", [1979] EIPR 287;

I. C. Baillie, "Contributory Infringement in the United States", (1980–81) 10 CIPA 56;

M. G. Harman, "Contributory Infringement", (1981–82) 11 CIPA 2;

R. J. Hart, "Computer Software: Contributory Infringement", (1981–82) 11 CIPA 131;

J. Handel, "*Merck* v. *Stephar*: Patentee's rights bow to EEC principles", [1982] EIPR 26;

J. Turner, "*Dow Chemical* v. *Spence Bryson*: 'Contributory infringement' under the old law", [1983] EIPR 131;

M. Howe, "The White Horse case: Whisky as an 'instrument of deception' ", [1984] EIPR 262;

D. Gladwell, "The exhaustion of intellectual property rights", [1986] EIPR 366;

C. T. Harding, "Will the bride altar an exhaustion rite?", (1987–88) 17 CIPA 306.

COMMENTARY ON SECTION 60

General 60.03

Section 60 codifies the substantive law of infringement. The old law of infringement, founded in the Common Law and the terms of the Letters Patent grant, has now largely given way to the new code, as explained in para. 60.05 *infra*. Accordingly, the former law is not dealt with separately herein except in so far as may be necessary for an understanding of the present provisions.

In section 60, subsection (1) defines the tort of substantive (or direct) infringement, while subsections (2) and (3) have brought contributory (or indirect) infringement into the scope of infringing acts by defining a new aspect of the tort of patent infringement. Subsection (4) is not yet in force because it deals with exhaustion of rights under a Community patent. However, because exhaustion of rights is an existing doctrine under EEC law which overrides the provisions of United Kingdom law, this doctrine is discussed in para. 60.17 *infra*. Subsections (5)–(7) exempt or limit certain acts which might otherwise be patent infringement under subsections (1)–(3).

The "extent of invention" protected by a patent is defined in section 125 and questions of infringement which depend on the scope of the patent, in the sense of the technical extent of the protection which it confers, are therefore dealt with in the commentary on that section. Accordingly, the present commentary deals only with liability under the law of torts for infringement of a patent, now made a statutory tort. In particular, it deals with the types of acts which are considered as infringing or which are exempted therefrom as the case may be.

It must be remembered that Crown use (for which see sections 55–59 and the commentaries thereon) is permitted use and is therefore not infringement under section 60. Moreover, the following sections 61–71 deal with limitations restricting the tort in certain circumstances. Thus: sections 61–63 and 65 relate to procedure and remedies (including restrictions therein); section 64 provides a right of continuing user to persons who worked, or planned to work, the patented invention before its priority date; sections 66–68 specify the persons who can bring actions for infringement under section 60; section 69 relates to rights arising from published pending applications; section 70 makes certain threats of infringement actionable as a separate, but related, tort; and section 71 relates to declarations of non-infringement. These matters are discussed in the respective commentaries on these sections.

60.04   *Historical background*

The statutory tort of patent infringement created by section 60 replaces the common law tort of infringement. The source of the present infringement code is European international law and not domestic law. The "Resolution on the Adjustment of National Patent Law" (reprinted in *EPH* (2nd. ed.) at § 67.6) annexed to the CPC and effective upon signature of CPC, *i.e.* before ratification, obliges the EEC Member States to bring their laws into conformity, as far as practicable, with corresponding provisions of the EPC, CPC and PCT. Section 60 is intended to bring the national law into conformity with CPCaa. 29–32 and is specified in section 130(7) as a section which has been so framed as to have, as nearly as practicable, the same effects in the United Kingdom as the corresponding provisions of (in this case) the CPC have in the territories to which that Convention is intended to apply. Until the CPC comes into force the courts may find themselves in the difficult position of trying to conform to the Convention without the benefit of any authoritative rulings on its interpretation from the Court of Justice of the European Communities. This will no doubt be done by the traditional British method of construing the terms of the statute and assuming that this does in fact conform to the CPC, though the provisions of the CPC will be looked at to resolve any uncertainty, as was done in *Smith, Kline & French* v. *Harbottle* ([1980] RPC 363).

Application of section 60 **60.05**

Section 60 is based on the provisions of the CPC and applies to infringement of patents granted under the Act (s. 130(1)), to European patents (UK) (s. 77(1)), and to "existing patents," *i.e.* those granted under the 1949 Act (unless the act of infringement was one which started before June 1, 1978 and continued thereafter (Sched. 4, para. 3(3), see para. 136.04). It has displaced any residual element of Common Law in the protection of the monopoly against infringement (*Genentech's Patent*, [1989] RPC 147 (CA)). Section 60 also applies to the rights arising from published applications under section 69, for which see the commentary thereon. However, when the CPC is in force, infringement of a Community patent is to be determined solely in accordance with the provisions of the CPC (s. 86), though section 60 is still likely to be followed because section 130(7) requires section 60 to be interpreted in accordance with the EPC and CPC.

For a discussion on related tortious acts, see para. 60.25 *infra*.

Territorial scope of infringement **60.06**

Section 60 is only applicable if an act of infringement takes place in the United Kingdom. For the purposes of the Act the "United Kingdom" includes the Isle of Man (s. 132(2), for which see para. 132.05), and the territorial waters of the United Kingdom (s. 132(3), for which see para. 132.06). Also, as discussed in para. 132.06, section 132(4) (as amended) extends the operation of the Act to acts done "in an area designated by Order under section 1(7) of the Continental Shelf Act 1964 [c. 29] or specified under section 22(5) of the Oil and Gas (Enterprise) Act 1982 [c. 23]".

In *Kalman* v. *PCL Packaging* ([1982] FSR 406) the word "disposal" was construed as requiring a disposal of property within the jurisdiction so that, where property in goods passed abroad under an f.o.b. contract, there was no infringement by the vendor. However, there may be liability if the vendor retains any lien on the goods while in transit to the United Kingdom, see *Morton-Norwich* v. *Intercen* ([1978] RPC 501). In the *Kalman* case it was also held that an "offer to dispose of goods" requires both the offer and the subsequent disposal to take place within the United Kingdom for such to constitute infringement under section 60.

It is possible that the restrictive effect of the *Kalman* case could be overcome by a broader construction of the word "supply" ((1983–84) 13 CIPA 105); and, in *Electric Furnace Co.* v. *Selas* ([1987] RPC 23 (CA)), leave was given to serve proceedings out of the jurisdiction against a foreign defendant who had designed and supplied the second defendant in the United Kingdom with a furnace, the use of which was alleged to infringe a method claim, it being sufficient that the remedy in damages might be more advantageous against the foreign defendant either in scope or in enforceability, and in any event an account of profits (for which see para. 61.15) could be claimed against both defendants if they were joint tortfeasors (for which see para. 60.25). However, there must be some act within the United Kingdom (*Def Lepp Music* v. *Stuart-Brown*, [1986] RPC 273).

In *Puschner* v. *Tom Parker (Scotland)* ([1989] RPC 430) the existence of a joint marketing agreement between a foreign supplier and his domestic customer, under which the foreign supplier supplied sales and promotional literature and helped to train the sales staff of his customer, was held sufficient to establish the necessary "common design" for the supplier to be sued as a joint tortfeasor. Likewise, a defendant's foreign parent company can be joined as a co-defendant if the patentee has a good arguable case that the two companies have acted in concert pursuant to a common design resulting in infringement (*Unilever* v. *Gillette*, [1989] RPC 583 (CA)). In both these cases mere supply of goods from abroad, even with technical back-up support from the supplier, would not in itself have established a common design for United Kingdom sales; and, in the *Unilever* case, the parent-subsidiary relationship was not in itself sufficient. In *Mars* v. *Azkoyen* (SRIS C/57/89, *noted* IPD 12079) the claimed apparatus required a setting-up operation which was carried out by the parent company in Spain. This was sufficient for an interlocutory injunction to be imposed if adequate security for damages was not forthcoming from the defendants.

60.07 *Authorised use of invention*

Infringement only occurs if the act in question has taken place without the consent of the proprietor of the patent (subss. (1) and (2)). "Proprietor" is not directly defined in the Act but its meaning is evident from sections 30 and 31. The proprietor is prima facie the person entered as such in the register. From section 30(6) it appears that consent, as distinct from assent, need not be in writing, see para. 30.07. Consequently, the consent of the proprietor to the alleged act may be express (as in the case of a formal written or a provable oral licence) or implied from the acts or conduct of the proprietor or a licensee thereof, whose licence may itself be implied. For example, it is well established that an implied licence to use or re-sell a patented product arises in the case of an ordinary sale of the product (*Betts* v. *Willmott*, (1871) LR 6 Ch.App. 239) and it should be noted that such implied licence can also arise in the case of the supply of essential means for putting the invention into effect under subsection (2).

For infringement of a patent where there are joint proprietors, see paras. 36.06 and 66.02.

60.08 *Implied licence to repair*

An example of implied authorised use of an invention arises from the licence which is implied to a purchaser of a patented article that he may repair and maintain that article. For a modern successful plea of implied licence to repair, both under patent and copyrights, see *Solar Thompson* v. *Barton* ([1977] RPC 537). However, such a licence to repair does not extend to renewing a patented article under the guise of repair (*Sirdar Rubber* v. *Wallington Weston*, (1907) 24 RPC 539 (HL)). Nor does it, apparently, extend to open offers for sale of spare parts in relation to patented articles (*British Leyland* v. *Armstrong*, [1986] RPC 279 (HL)), where a distinction appears to have been drawn between the implied licence to repair arising under true monopoly rights, such as patents (and presumably also registered designs), and those arising from copyright. In the latter, but not the former, case the intellectual property rights may not be invoked to prevent a purchaser of an article from keeping it in good repair by procuring the spare part from another: otherwise there would be a derogation from the grant implied upon sale of the article.

The cases on implied right to repair were reviewed in *Dellareed* v. *Delkin* ([1988] FSR 329). Here it was held that an implied licence to modify a purchased product is no wider than the implied licence to repair it. The Defendant had therefore broken a previous undertaking not to modify the patented apparatus because it had, in effect, changed that apparatus into a new article.

60.09 *Laches, acquiescence and estoppel*

If a proprietor delays unduly in bringing an action, or makes a representation that he does not propse to do so, and the defendant has acted upon that representation, the proprietor may be held to be estopped from bringing an action at all, even if the limitation period (for which see para. 60.27 *infra*) has not expired. One basis for this is for the court to hold that the proprietor has impliedly consented to the defendant's acts, or that it would be unconscionable in equity to allow the plaintiff to enforce his rights, see the passing off case of *Habib Bank Ltd. v. Habib Bank AG* ([1982] RPC 1 (CA)). For further examples see the copyright cases of *Hoover v. Hulme* ([1982] FSR 565) and *Redwood Music v. Chappell* ([1982] RPC 109). However, in *Dellareed v. Delkin* ([1988] FSR 329) a plea of acquiesence was not upheld, though the Plaintiff had delayed for a year after its initial complaint before sending a "letter before action", it being held that the Defendant should have realised that the Plaintiff intended to proceed; and failure to take action in respect of one act of infringement does not preclude proceedings in respect of later infringing acts (*Raychem v. Thermon*, [1989] RPC 423). Also, in *Mars v. Azkoyen* (SRIS C/57/89, *noted* IPD 12079), a failure to sue under a corresponding Spanish patent did not preclude later action in the United Kingdom.

It may also here be noted that, where proceedings have been brought against one tortfeasor and have failed, further proceedings can be brought against others involved in the same alleged acts of infringement provided that there was no privity of interest between the different defendants (*Gleeson v. Wippell*, [1977] FSR 301). There is no estoppel unless the two proceedings involve identity of parties and identity of subject matter and there has been a final judgment in the first proceedings (*Carl-Zeiss-Stifftung v. Rayner and Keeler (No. 2)*, [1967] RPC 497).

In *Harrison v. Project & Design* ([1987] RPC 151 (CA)) the Defendant was held, in an enquiry into damages, to be estopped from putting forward arguments of non-infringement which could have been raised at the trial of the issue of liability.

For circumstances in which there may be an estoppel to a challenge to validity, see para. 74.04.

Infringement of an amended patent   **60.10**

Where the patent in suit has been amended, section 75(3) provides that the amended specification is deemed to have had effect from the grant of the patent, so that, if an infringement of the patent has taken place and the patent is then amended so that infringement no longer occurs, the infringement before amendment will be nullified and will be deemed not to have taken place. However, the position may be different with "existing patents" because section 75 does not apply thereto (Sched. 2, para. 1(2) and Sched. 4, para. 3(2)). To recover damages on an amended patent, the patentee must satisfy the court that the specification was framed in good faith and with reasonable skill and knowledge (s. 62(3), discussed in para. 62.05).

Substantive (or direct) infringement (subs. (1))

—Scope of subsection (1)   **60.11**

Subsection (1) corresponds to CPCa. 29 and classifies infringing acts according to whether the invention is: (*a*) a product; (*b*) a process; or (*c*) the product of a process.

The terms "product" and "process" are not defined as such in the Act, but "patented product" is defined in section 130(1) as "a product which is a patented invention or, in relation to a patented process, a product obtained directly by means of the process or to which the process has been applied". Mention must also be made here of section 100 which, where a patent is granted for a process for making a *new* product, places the onus on the defendant to prove that such product has *not* been made by the process patented, the legal presumption being that it has been so made, see the commentary on section 100. Thus, the definition of "patented product" extends beyond that of a product which is the subject of a *per se* claim to certain products of a patented process. First, a product obtained directly by means of a patented process is deemed to be a patented product and this seems to be in accordance with section 100; and, secondly, a product to which a patented process "has been applied" is also deemed to be a patented product. Thus, where a substance or article is treated according to a patented process, the substance or article after such treatment is also deemed to be a patented product even if, *qua* product, it has not been altered by the treatment. For example, if the patented process is one for moving an article from one location to another, the article after having been so moved could be regarded for the purposes of the Act as a "patented product".

Each type of infringement must be the subject of a separate pleading if relief for such infringement is to be obtained (*Serota* v. *Gardex*, [1984] RPC 317).

60.12   *—Infringement of product invention (subs. (1)(a))*

Subsection (1)(*a*) deals with infringement of a product invention and, differing in some respects from CPCa. 29, it specifies that, when the invention is a product, infringement occurs in the acts of making, disposing of, offering to dispose of, using or importing the product or keeping it whether for disposal or otherwise. In CPCa. 29 importing and stocking of the product are prohibited only for the purposes of making, offering, putting on the market or using the product. In *Smith, Kline & French* v. *Harbottle* ([1980] RPC 363) "keeping" was construed in conformity with CPCa. 29 so that the mere activities of a warehouseman did not infringe the patent, see article by M. Howe listed in para. 60.02 *supra*.

Nevertheless, under the 1949 Act, it was held that any possession of infringing goods for the purposes of trade, and from which a profit to the alleged infringer had resulted, was to be regarded as an infringement of the patentee's rights (*Hoffmann-La Roche* v. *Harris Pharmaceuticals*, [1977] FSR 200). Importation with subsequent re-export was also held to infringe under the common law rules (*Smith, Kline* v. *DDSA*, [1978] FSR 109) on the basis that this was a trading transaction carried out in the United Kingdom from which the defendants had derived profit, it being immaterial that the patentee had not suffered any loss thereby.

It must also be noted that, since *Norwich Pharmacal* v. *Commissioners of Customs & Excise* ([1974] RPC 101 (HL)), an action is possible merely to obtain the identity of other infringers when that identity is known to the defendant, even though the defendant may himself not be an infringer as was held in that case. However, in such a case, the proprietor will have to bear the costs of the action, but he can recoup these as a head of damage in a subsequent infringement action against a person identified as a result of the first action, see para. 61.14.

The principle of the *Norwich Pharmacal* case has been extended to require a defendant in interlocutory proceedings to disclose the identity of the foreign source from whom the patented product had been imported (*Smith, Kline and French* v. *Global Pharmaceutics*, [1986] RPC 394).

While "dispose of" is obviously broader than "vend" (as under the former test of infringement), *e.g.* as covering a gift, it should be remembered that the mere inclusion of an article in a price list, or its exposure in a shop window, is not necessarily an offer to dispose of it: it may be merely an "invitation to treat", that is a willingness to consider sale if a suitable offer is made, see the copyright case of *Norgren* v. *Technomarketing* (*The Times*, March 3, 1983). However, a *quia timet* injunction would doubtless be obtainable in such circumstances to restrain a threat to infringe.

—Infringement of process invention (subs. (1)(b) and (c))   **60.13**

Subsection (1)(*b*) deals with infringement of a process invention and specifies as an infringement use of the process or offering such process for use. In the case of an offer for use it must be obvious to a reasonable person that the use will infringe.

In *Furr* v. *Truline* ([1985] FSR 553), where the Defendant was directing purchasers to use certain articles in a way which was not the way of the method claim of the patent (even on the Plaintiff's construction of that claim, which the court did not accept), it was held that the Defendant could not be said to have offered a process for use as required by section 60(1)(*b*) as it clearly did not intend that the articles should be used in the claimed way.

Where a method claim is alleged to be infringed by importation of the product of that method, a positive case of infringement must be shown, at least if an interlocutory injunction is to be granted (*Jakob Schlaepfer* v. *Frankle*, SRIS C/9/88).

Subsection (1)(*c*) clarifies the law as the protection afforded to the product of a process invention. The provision corresponds to CPCa. 29(*c*) and EPCa. 64(2). For infringement the product must have been obtained directly by means of the patented process. As noted above, section 100 provides for reversal of the burden of proof when the product is "new". It is not apparent that infringement extends under subsection (1)(*c*) to an article when made by a patented apparatus but this may be arguable, see R. F. Haslam ((1982–83) 12 CIPA 319).

Contributory (or indirect) infringement under subsection (2)

—Historical derivation   **60.14**

A classic contributory infringement situation arose in *Innes* v. *Short* ((1898) 15 RPC 449) where an injunction was granted to restrain the sale of packets of powdered zinc bearing instructions for the use thereof in the patented method (of preventing corrosion in water boilers). The correctness of this decision as a finding of patent infringement was doubted, though it could nowadays be justified as arising from an act of joint tortfeasorship (for which see para. 60.25 *infra*), but such is now to be considered as an act of infringement by virtue of CPCa. 30, the wording of which appears to have been derived from United States law (35 USC 271), see the paper by I. C. Baillie listed in para. 60.02 *supra*. Various aspects of the law of contributory infringement have also been discussed in the articles by M. Vitoria, M. G. Harman, R. J. Hart and J. Turner also there listed.

—Scope of subsection (2)   **60.15**

Subsection (2) corresponds to CPCa. 30(1). It permits action to be brought against any person who supplies or offers to suply any of the means, relating to an essential element of the invention, for putting the invention into effect. It has always proved difficult to define contributory infringement and establish a distinction between the rights of the inventor and those of the public. Subsections (2) and (3) reflect this difficulty and many doubts must remain on the scope of these provisions until a body of case law is established, but United States cases may be of assistance in view of the provenance of the provision, see para. 60.14 *supra*.

A major difficulty lies in the scope of the phrase "means relating to an essential element. . . . ". It would be reasonable to suppose that "means" was intended to imply a tangible and physical means for implementing a function, and not, for example, an intellectual means, such as an instructional manual or a magazine article or even mere know-how, or the grant of a licence as has certainly been contended. "Essential" is also difficult to define in this context; it could have the meaning of necessary, or it could mean necessary to the exclusion of any alternative, or it could mean that it relates to an element of the invention as claimed without which the invention would be imcomplete. "Means" includes a staple commercial product, though such a product is excluded in certain circumstances by subsection (3), for which see para. 60.16 *infra*.

By subsection (2) the infringer who supplies or offers to supply within the United Kingdom must know, or be taken to know, that the "means" in question are suitable for the infringing purpose and there must be an intention to infringe in the United Kingdom: note the double territorial requirement. However, proof of substantive infringement under subsection (1) does not seem necessary. In *Furr* v. *Truline* ([1985] FSR 553) it was held, in refusing an interlocutory injunction, that the defendant had not intended its articles to be used in the claimed manner and that it would not have been obvious to a reasonable person that the articles were intended to be used in that manner, as required by subsection (2).

The act of applying for a product licence under the Medicines Act 1968 (c. 67) is not itself an infringing act under subsection (2); and, even if such application had to include test data, such data may have been generated abroad and so would not be infringement under subsection (1) (*Upjohn* v. *Thomas Kerfoot*, [1988] FSR 1).

For a case where contributory infringement was held to have occurred, see *Rhône-Poulenc* v. *Dikloride Herbicides [Malaysia]* ([1988] FSR 282) where the Plaintiff proved, on the balance of probabilities, that the Defendant's composition was designed to be used in the same manner as the Plaintiff's product was used, *i.e.* according to the patented method.

The wording of subsections (1) and (2) also leaves doubt as to some aspects of acts which may perhaps be regarded as contributing to infringement. Thus, while the supply of a patented apparatus in dismantled form for use in the United Kingdom is clearly an infringement under subsection (2), the position is not clear where the dismantled apparatus is for export. Export of less than a complete apparatus does not fall within either subsections (1) or (2), but against this must be considered the interpretation to be given to the extent of the claim in accordance with section 125, see the commentary thereon.

The supply of an essential part knowingly, for repair of an infringing apparatus will be an infringement under subsection (2), but if the apparatus is not an infringing apparatus the question of infringement by repair will depend upon the extent of any implied licence to use the invention (for which see para. 60.08 *supra*), or the conditions of sale. It is explicit in subsection (2) that, if the person who is supplied (or to whom the offer of supply is made) is a licensee or other person entitled to work the invention, no action for contributory infringement will lie; but, as noted in para. 60.08 *supra*, there appears to be no such defence when spare parts are made as such and offered on the open market.

60.16   —*Involving supply of a staple product (subs. (3))*

Subsection (3) corresponds to CPCa. 30(2) and provides that the doctrine of contributory infringement defined in subsection (2) shall not apply to the supply or offer of a staple commercial product *unless* the supply or offer is made for the purpose of inducing a substantive infringement under subection (1). The expression "staple commercial product" is not defined, but a parallel law in the United States (for which see the article by I. C. Baillie listed in para. 60.02, *supra*), and other usages, suggest a definition of a generally-available raw product or commodity of commerce suitable for uses of which at least some are non-infringing. Thus, in the United States, a toothpaste containing potassium nitrate has been held not to be a staple article of commerce merely because toothpaste and potassium nitrate, individually, were such (*Hodosh* v. *Block Drug* [*USA*], *noted* [1988] EIPR D-115).

It would therefore appear that, in order to be liable for the supply of a staple commercial substance or article, a defendant has, in effect, to be a joint tortfeaser, for which see para. 60.25.

Exhaustion of rights (subs. (4))   **60.17**

Subsection (4) (which is not yet in force) corresponds to CPCa. 81 and would provide that, once a product patented in a Community patent has been lawfully put on the market in one of the Member States, the patent shall not extend to that product in any of the other States of the Community *unless* there are grounds under Community law which justify the extension to such acts of the rights conferred by the patent. Subsection (4) is to be without prejudice to section 86, but neither provision will be given effect in the United Kingdom until the CPC is ratified by all the signatory States.

However, it can be questioned whether subsection (4) is needed because the doctrine of the exhaustion of rights is now well established under Community law as a result of decisions under TRaa. 30 (and 36) and 85 (reprinted in Appendix C at paras. C02, C04 and C05 respectively) and discussed in paras. C15 and C16. See also the papers by J. Handel and C. T. Harding listed in para. 60.02 *supra*.

The historical development of the separate doctrines of restriction of a licence by notice, express or implied, and of the exhaustion of rights upon first sale of a patented product, and the consequent absence of an over-riding rule of general applicability to control the course of patented articles placed in the stream of commerce, are the subject of the paper by D. Gladwell listed in para. 60.02 *supra*. The doctrine of notice was in issue in *Christian Salvesen* v. *Odfejeld Drilling* [*Scotland*] ([1985] RPC 569), see para. 68.02.

In *Dellareed* v. *Delkin* ([1988] FSR 329) the Defendant contended that there was no infringement in modifying the patented apparatus sold by the Plaintiff because of the exhaustion of rights doctrine as set out in subsection (4) and CPCa. 32 (it apparently not being noted that neither of these provisions was then in force). However, the court held that this doctrine did not apply because the Defendant had sold an article essentially different from that which the Plaintiff had put on the market, the Defendant having so modified this as to produce a new article.

Acts exempted from infringement (subs. (5))   **60.18**

Subsection (5), which corresponds to CPCa. 31, exempts certain acts from infringement, but subsection (6) prevents persons who are exempted from infringement under (*a*), (*b*) or (*c*) of subsection (5) from relying upon this exemption to avoid contributory infringement under subsection (2). Because section 60 was enacted to bring United Kingdom law into line with, *inter alia*, the CPC, decisions under the Common Law concerning phrases such as "reasonable trial or experiment" are no longer of assistance (*Monsanto* v. *Stauffer (No. 2)*, [1985] RPC 515 (CA)), see para. 60.20 *infra*.

—Private and non-commercial acts (subs. (5)(a))   **60.19**

Under subsection (5)(*a*) acts which are both private and non-commercial are exempt, though a person who supplies or offers to supply a private, non-commercial user may nevertheless be liable for substantive infringement under subsection (1) and for contributory infringement under subsection (2). If the acts have a dual purpose, one non-commercial (for example, for the purpose of testing the validity of some other patent), and the other leading to valuable commercial information, the exemption may not apply (*Smith Kline & French* v. *Evans Medical*, [1989] FSR 513).

60.20 —*Acts done for experimental purposes (subs. (5)(b))*

Subsection (5)(*b*) excludes experimental purposes provided that these relate to the subject-matter of the invention. There is no definition of experimental, but in conformity with CPCa. 31(*b*), "experimental purposes" contemplated in this provision (in contrast to that of subs. (5)(*a*)) may have a commercial end in view (*Monsanto* v. *Stauffer (No. 2)*, [1985] RPC 515 (CA)). Here, it was held that trials carried out in order to discover something unknown, or to test an hypothesis, or even in order to find out whether something which is known to work in specific conditions would work in different conditions, can fairly be regarded as experiments, but trials carried out in order to demonstrate to a third party (such as a regulatory body) that a product works as its maker claims, are not to be regarded as acts done for "experimental purposes".

Here it was also stated that experiments could be carried out for the purposes of the litigation on the basis of an order made under what is now RSC Ord. 104, rule 14 (reprinted at para. E104.14), but in *Smith Kline & French* v. *Evans Medical* ([1989] FSR 513) it was held that experiments for the purposes of litigation are only exempted under this provision if these relate to the subject matter of the patent alleged to be infringed, so that experiments performed for the purpose of invalidating some other patent may not be covered by subsection (5)(*b*).

The purchaser of an infringing product for experimental purposes appears (under subs. (5)(*b*)) to escape infringement, but not the supplier. The difficulties which arise under these provisions when the supplier is outside of the United Kingdom are the subject of comment by M. J. Butler ((1982–83) 12 CIPA 317), and see para. 60.06 *supra*. It is also doubtful if a supplier of a product which is then used experimentally is excused by the provisions: such supply is not itself an act done for experimental purposes.

60.21 —*Extemporaneous pharmaceutical preparations (subs. (5)(c))*

Subsection (5)(*c*) excludes the extemporaneous pharmaceutical preparation of medicine to a prescription by a registered medical practitioner or dentist. "Extemporaneous" is not defined, but may be taken as meaning as and when required, so that medicines made available in advance of a specific need therefor arising are probably not exempt. It would appear that veterinary preparations are in any event not exempted by the provision as such would not be provided by a "medical or dental practitioner", at least practising as such.

60.22 —*Acts done on transiently visiting ships, aircraft, etc. (subs. (5)(d)–(f))*

Subsection (5)(*d*), (*e*) and (*f*) refers to use of inventions on ships, aircraft, etc., and corresponds broadly to section 70 [1949]. Hovercraft are specifically mentioned in paragraph (*e*) and "ship" and "vehicle" are used rather than "vessel" and "land vehicle" in CPCa. 31, the 1949 Act and the Stockholm revision of the Paris Convention of 1883. Subsection (5)(*d*) relates to "relevant" ships, aircraft, hovercraft and vehicles, these being those from countries (other than the UK) which are members of the Paris Convention (note: *not* the countries which are designated by section 90 as "convention countries" for other purposes of the Act), while subsection

(5)(*e*) relates to "exempted" aircraft which are defined in subsection (7) (as amended) by reference to the Civil Aviation Act 1982 (c. 16). Under section 89 of that Act, foreign aircraft coming temporarily into the United Kingdom (and spare parts and equipment for such aircraft) are exempted from claims of patent infringement. This provision gives effect to the Chicago Convention, but Schedule 12 of this 1982 Act also extends section 89 thereof to patent claims against aircraft not protected under that Convention. The precise definition of exempted aircraft is in fact based upon Orders in Council designating specified countries. The Order presently effective for this purpose is The Aircraft (Exemption from Seizure on Patent Claims) Order 1977 (S.I. 1977 No. 829) made under section 53 of the Civil Aviation Act 1949 (12, 13 & 14 Geo. 6, c. 6), now repealed by the aforesaid section 89 of the eponymous 1982 Act, but with previous Orders made thereunder given continuing effect.

The provisions of subsection (5)(*d*), (*e*) and (*f*) are subject to the transitional provisions of Schedule 4, paras. 9(2) and 18(3) which give continuing effect to Orders in Council which designated "convention countries" for the purposes of section 70 [1949].

Entitlement of persons to work the invention (subs. (6)) **60.23**

Although subsections (5)(*a*)–(*c*) exempt certain acts from being considered as ones of patent infringement, associated contributory acts of the type covered by subsection (2) (rather than by subsection (1)) are, by subsection (6), not exempted.

In *Monsanto* v. *Stauffer (No. 2)* ([1985] RPC 515 (CA)) the Patents Court accepted the Plaintiff's argument that the supply of the patented product would have been an infringement under subsection (2), notwithstanding that the activities of the person supplied were exempted under subsection (5)(*b*), but the Court of Appeal declined to express an opinion on the point though it indicated there was force in the argument. Thus, the immunity of a user under subsection (5)(*a*)–(*c*) seems not to exonerate the supplier of that user of means relating to an essential element of the invention.

However, besides persons entitled to work a patented invention under the provisions of subsection (5), others so entitled include those carrying out acts authorised by the Crown under section 55. Also to be entitled to work the invention are persons who have acquired rights under section 28A(4) or (5) (or presumably under their predecessor provision), or under section 64, that is both an interim or planned user of an invention forming the subject of a restored patent (*i.e.* one who will meet the requirements of section 28A(4) and whose subsequent acts are deemed not to amount to infringement if they fall within section 28A(5), for which see paras. 28A.03–28A.06) and a person whose activities before the priority date give him the right to work the invention by virtue of section 64 (for which see paras. 64.04–64.07), but in all cases only so far as concerns the permitted infringing act.

The Crown also has the right to dispose of, or use, articles forfeited under the laws relating to customs and excise, see section 122, but otherwise proceedings for patent infringement against the Crown can lie, see para. 129.02.

Terms of full licence to work the invention **60.24**

Under the 1949 Act, the acts reserved to the patentee by the wording of the Letters Patent grant were those of "making, using, exercising and vending" the invention. It was therefore customary to draft licence agreements in those terms, or some of them, if the licence was to be restricted. Having regard to the extension of the concept of infringement by subsections (2) and (3), the specific exemptions from infringement of subsections (5)–(7) and the exclusion of rights exhausted under Community law and of Crown use by section 55, it has become more difficult to define the terms of a full licence. If a licensee wishes to ensure that his licence under the patent is total, he should perhaps ask that the grant clause of the licence gives him the right "to work in any manner whatsoever the invention protected by the patent or to carry out any act (except possibly one of sub-licensing) which would otherwise be regarded as an infringement of the patent under section 60 of the Patents Act 1977".

60.25 *Related acts giving rise to joint tortfeasorship*

A proprietor is concerned, if he can, to preserve the monopoly in the invention afforded by the patent by stopping unlicensed use of the invention and/or obtaining compensation for such use. Prospective users must also be discouraged or prevented. The relative importance of each of these aims will depend on the commercial situation, but proceedings for claims for patent infringement under section 60(1) and/or (2) will usually be the principal courses of action leading to the types of relief set out in section 61, for which see the commentary thereon. However, action can also be taken against a defendant for inducing or procuring infringement of an intellectual property right because it has been held (*CBS Songs* v. *Amstrad*, [1988] RPC 567 (HL)) that a defendant who procures a breach of a right (in that case copyrights) is liable jointly and severally with the actual infringer for the damages suffered by the plaintiff as a result of the acts of infringement. In such circumstances the procurer, or inducer, is a joint infringer (tortfeasor) on the basis that he intends and procures and shares a common design that infringement shall take place. This principle applies to patent rights (*Gillette* v. *Unilever*, [1989] RPC 583 (CA)).

But, in *CBS Songs* v. *Amstrad* (*supra*) the House of Lords held, contrary to the previous suggestion in *Belegging* v. *Witten* ([1979] FSR 59 (CA)), that there is no *separate* tort of inducing, inciting, or persuading someone to commit an act of infringement of an intellectual property right, and that "generally speaking, inducement, incitement, or persuasion to infringe must be by a defendant to an individual infringer and must identifiably procure a particular infringement in order to make defendant liable as a joint infringer". In this case, once a twin tape copier had been sold, *Amstrad* had no control over, or interest in, its use and therefore had no control over any copying which a purchaser might carry out in infringement of a plaintiff's copyright. A clear distinction is therefore to be drawn between "facilitating" and "inducing" infringement. For example, *Kalman* v. *PCL Packaging* ([1982] FSR 406) involved only "facilitating" patent infringement; and in *Dow Chemical* v. *Spence Bryson (No. 2)* ([1982] FSR 598) "procuring" was held to have occurred, though such procuring must occur within the jurisdiction (*Dow Chemical* v. *Spence Bryson*, [1982] FSR 397). For case comment on *CBS Songs* v. *Amstrad* (*supra*), see I. Purvis ([1988] EIPR 345).

In *Rotocrop* v. *Genbourne* ([1982] FSR 241) a defendant manuacturer who made and sold (under the 1949 Act) compost bins which, when assembled, would infringe a patent, together with assembly instructions, was held liable with its customers, though under the present Act such a manufacturer would appear to be directly liable for infringement under subsection (2). In that case, as in *Innes* v. *Short* ((1898) 15 RPC 449) where the defendant sold powdered zinc with specific instructions to the purchaser to infringe a process patent, the vendor and the purchaser had a common design to carry out an infringing act and both decisions can now be seen as ones of joint tortfeasorship.

In such cases relief can be claimed against either or both of the joint tortfeasors, even as regards a defendant out of the jurisdiction who trades with, but not in, the

United Kingdom, see *Morton-Norwich* v. *Intercen* ([1978] RPC 501) and also *Electric Furnace Co.* v. *Selas* ([1987] RPC 23 (CA)), as well as other cases noted in para. 60.06 *supra*.

In *North Western Trailer* v. *Itel* (*The Times*, December 19, 1979; SRIS HC/PC/41/79) an interlocutory injunction was granted against a German manufacturer who sold goods (collapsible shipping containers) to a United States corporation knowing that the goods would then be sold or leased to persons who would inevitably bring them into the United Kingdom where they would infringe a patent. It was held that there was sufficient common design to make the German manufacturer, the United States buyer and the lessee shipping line each a joint tortfeasor as soon as an infringement actually occurred. The balance of convenience was in favour of granting an injunction unless the parties could agree on a method of preventing importation pending trial. Such importation would not be exempted under section 60(5)(*d*) or (*e*).

Liability of directors   60.26

In *Evans* v. *Spritebrand* ([1985] FSR 267) the Court of Appeal indicated (in a copyright case) that a director should be in no more favourable position than an employee who would be liable for tortious acts which he carries out personally. Thus, a director will be personally liable for acts of patent infringement carried out by his company if the director has personally participated in the carrying out of the infringing act, though the Court of Appeal indicated that "where there is no knowing, deliberate wilful quality in the participation the court may naturally be more reluctant to hold the director personally liable", see also *Besson* v. *Fulleton* ([1986] FSR 319). The principle of participating in a common design rendering each participant a joint tortfeasor separately liable for any unlawful activity involved in that design, as discussed in para. 60.25 *supra*, therefore seems to apply to the liability of a director for patent infringement committed by his company.

Liability under the Sale of Goods Act   60.27

It should be noted that liability can also arise under the Sale of Goods Act 1979 (c. 54, s. 12(1), (2)(*b*) and 14(2)) ["the SGA"] where a purchaser of goods finds himself unable to use these goods because of the existence of a third-party patent, see *Niblett* v. *Confectioners' Materials* ([1921] 3 KB 387). This can be so even apparently where the patent only issues some time after the sale has taken place, see *Microbeads* v. *Vinhurst* ([1976] RPC 19 (CA)), liability then arising from breaches of a seller's implied warranties of his right to sell the goods (imposed by SGA, s. 12(1)) and/or of the buyer's right of quiet enjoyment of the goods (imposed by SGA, s. 12(2)(*b*)) and/or of the seller's implied warranty that the goods are of merchantable quality (imposed by SGA, s. 14(2)), unless these warranties have validly been excluded or avoided by the terms of the contract, as to which see section 6 of the Unfair Contract Terms Act 1977 (c. 50), and para. 44.16: see also para. 61.14.

Expiry of the patent   60.28

Actions for infringement may be brought before the English court within six years of the act complained of (Limitation Act 1980 (c. 58), s. 2). After that an action would be statute-barred so that damages (or an account of profits) are not claimable for more than six years before the date of the writ, even in the case of an "existing patent" when opposition proceedings had delayed grant of the patent and so issue of the writ (*Sevcon* v. *Lucas*, [1986] RPC 609 (HL)), for comment on whch see [1987] EIPR 115. Thus, in *Serota* v. *Gardex* ([1984] RPC 317 (CA)), the pleadings were not permitted to be amended to allege also infringement in respect of unmodified articles sold more than six years prior to the application for amendment when the action had originally been brought alleging infringement solely by a later-modified article. However, the limitation period does not run if there has been concealed fraud, see *Morton-Norwich* v. *Intercen and United Chemicals*, [1981] FSR 337).

In Scotland limitation would appear to arise if only five years elapse without proceedings being commenced or an acknowledgment of liability being given by the defender (Prescriptions and Limitations (Scotland) Act 1973 ((c. 52), s. 6), but various ancillary provisions of this Act may alter the limitation period in Scotland in particular cases.

However, despite the expiry of the patent, a proprietor may continue to have some residual rights. For example, if he has built up a reputation for producing the patented article in a distinctive get-up, he may be able to restrain imitation of that get-up, see *Hoffman-La Roche* v. *DDSA* ([1969] FSR 410) and *Industrie Diensten* v. *Beele* (*Case 6/81*) ([1982] ECR 707; [1982] 3 CMLR 102; [1983] FSR 119 (ECJ)), though a registered trade mark for the patented product may become invalid two years after the patent has expired if there is then no reasonable alternative name for the product (Trade Marks Act 1938 (c. 22), s. 15).

It should not be assumed that copyright in the drawings of the patent specification has necessarily lapsed with the patent. Although Whitford J. so held at first instance in *Catnic* v. *Hill & Smith* ([1982] RPC 183), that decision was based on a concession by counsel which was withdrawn on appeal citing *Werner Motors* v. *Gamage* ((1904) 21 RPC 621). The appeal courts made no ruling on the point in the *Catnic* case. Falconer J. also did not decide the point in *Gardex* v. *Serota* ([1986] RPC 623) where the drawings in the patent specification and the drawings alleged to have been copied were not "substantially identical", but in *Rose Plastics* v. *William Beckett* ([1989] FSR 113) Whitford J. reiterated the view he had expressed in the *Catnic* case, though he explicitly refrained from comment on the question whether his view extended beyond drawings not substantially different from those in the patent specification. However, courts in New Zealand have twice firmly refused to hold that copyright is abandoned on filing a patent application (*Dennison* v. *Prestige Toys* [*New Zealand*], noted [1981] EIPR D-62; and *Wham-O Manufacturing* v. *Lincoln Industries* [*New Zealand*], [1982] RPC 281), the latter case explicitly following the *Werner Motors* case which concerned a registered design; see also *Interlego* v. *Tyco* [*Hong Kong*] ([1987] FSR 409) for a decision of the Hong Kong Court of Appeal. The Irish Supreme Court also refused to follow Whitford J.'s view in the *Catnic* case, see *House of Spring Gardens* v. *Point Blank* ([1985] FSR 327). An Australian court has similarly declined to follow Whitford J. (*Ogden* v. *Kis* [*Australia*], [1983] FSR 619), but in Canada Whitford J.'s view has apparently prevailed (*Rucker* v. *Gavel's Vulcanising* [*Canada*], noted [1986] EIPR D-32).

61.01

SECTION 61

Proceedings for infringement of patent

61.—(1) Subject to the following provisions of this Part of this Act, civil proceedings may be brought in the court by the proprietor of a patent in respect of any act alleged to infringe the patent and (without prejudice to any other jurisdiction of the court) in those proceedings a claim may be made—

(a) for an injunction or interdict restraining the defendant or defender from any apprehended act of infringement;

(b) for an order for him to deliver up or destroy any patented product in relation to which the patent is infringed or any article in which that product is inextricably comprised;

(d) for damages in respect of the infringement;

(d) for an account of the profits derived by him from the infringement;

(e) for a declaration or declarator that the patent is valid and has been infringed by him.

(2) The court shall not, in respect of the same infringement, both award the proprietor of a patent damages and order that he shall be given an account of the profits.

(3) The proprietor of a patent and any other person may by agreement with each other refer to the comptroller the question whether that other person has infringed the patent and on the reference the proprietor of the patent may make any claim mentioned in subsection (1)(c) or (e) above.

(4) Except so far as the context requires, in the following provisions of this Act—

(a) any reference to proceedings for infringement and the bringing of such proceedings includes a reference to a reference under subsection (3) above and the making of such a reference;

(b) any reference to a plaintiff or pursuer includes a reference to the proprietor of the patent; and

(c) any reference to a defendant or defender includes a reference to any other party to the reference.

(5) If it appears to the comptroller on a reference under subsection (3) above that the question referred to him would more properly be determined by the court, he may decline to deal with it and the court shall have jurisdiction to determine the question as if the reference were proceedings brought in the court.

(6) Subject to the following provisions of this Part of this Act, in determining whether or not to grant any kind of relief claimed under this section and the extent of the relief granted the court or the comptroller shall apply the principles applied by the court in relation to that kind of relief immediately before the appointed day.

RELEVANT RULES

Procedure on reference to comptroller under section 61(3)

72.—(1) Where a reference is made to the comptroller under section 61(3), the parties thereto shall make it on Patents Form No. 36/77, accompanied by a joint statement giving full particulars of the matters which are in dispute and of those on which they are in agreement.   **61.02**

(2) The procedure set out in this rule shall apply unless the only matter

stated in the reference to be in dispute is the validity of any patent or part of a patent.

(3) The party to the dispute who is the proprietor of the patent or an exclusive licensee of the patent (such party being referred to in this and the next following rule as the plaintiff) shall within fourteen days of making the reference file a statement in duplicate giving full particulars of his case on the matters in dispute.

(4) The comptroller shall send a copy of the plaintiff's statement to the other party to the dispute (referred to in this and the next following rule as the defendant), who shall, within three months after receipt thereof, file a counter-statement in duplicate setting out fully the grounds on which he contests the plaintiff's case and the comptroller shall send a copy of the counter-statement to the plaintiff.

(5) If the defendant alleges in his counter-statement that the patent or any part of it alleged by the plaintiff to have been infringed is not valid, the plaintiff shall, within three months after receipt of the counter-statement, file a further statement in duplicate setting out fully the grounds on which he contests the defendant's allegation; and the comptroller shall send a copy of the further statement to the defendant.

(6) Subject to such directions as the comptroller may give, the plaintiff may, within three months after the receipt of the counter-statement, or, if he has filed a further statement under paragraph (5) above, within three months thereof, file evidence in support of his case and shall send a copy thereof direct to the defendant.

(7) Within three months of the receipt of the copy of the plaintiff's evidence or, if the plaintiff does not file any evidence, within three months of the expiration of the time within which such evidence might have been filed, the defendant may file evidence in support of his case and shall send a copy of it to the plaintiff; and, within three months of the receipt of the copy of the defendant's evidence, the plaintiff may file further evidence confined to matters strictly in reply and shall send a copy of it direct to the defendant.

(8) No further evidence shall be filed by either party except by leave or direction of the comptroller.

(9) The Comptroller may give such directions as he may think fit with regard to the subsequent procedure.

Procedure where validity of patent in dispute

61.03 **73.**—(1) Where the only matter stated in a reference made under section 61(3) to be in dispute is the validity of any patent or part of a patent, the procedure set out in this rule shall apply.

(2) The defendant shall, within fourteen days of making the reference, file a statement in duplicate giving full particulars of the grounds on which he alleges that the patent or part of the patent is invalid.

(3) The comptroller shall send a copy of the defendant's statement to the plaintiff, who shall, within three months after the receipt thereof, file a counter-statement in duplicate giving full particulars of the grounds on which he contests the defendant's allegations, and the comptroller shall send a copy of it to the defendant.

(4) Subject to such directions as the comptroller may think fit to give, the defendant may, within three months of the receipt of the copy of the plaintiff's counter-statement, file evidence in support of his case, and shall send a copy of it to the plaintiff.

(5) Within three months of the receipt of the copy of the defendant's evidence or, if the defendant does not file any evidence, within three months of the expiration of the time within which such evidence might have been filed, the plaintiff may file evidence in support of his case and shall send a copy of it to the defendant; and, within three months of the receipt of the copy of the plaintiff's evidence, the defendant may file further evidence confined to matters strictly in reply and shall send a copy of it to the plaintiff.

(6) No further evidence shall be filed by either party except by leave or direction of the comptroller.

(7) The comptroller may give such directions as he may think fit with regard to the subsequent procedure.

BOOK   61.04

R. N. Ough, "The Mareva injunction and Anton Piller Order" (Butterworths, 1987);
M. S. W. Hoyle, "The *Mareva* injunction and related orders" (Lloyd's of London, 2nd. ed., 1989).

ARTICLES   61.05

J. G. Marshall, "The European Court", (1974–75) 4 CIPA 125;
B. C. Reid, "Agents in court", (1980–81) 10 CIPA 222;
P. A. Chandler, "Parasitic damages and patent infringement", [1984] EIPR 155;
J. Adams, "*Anton Piller*" orders, An introduction", [1985] EIPR 292;
C. Tritton and G. Tritton, "The Brussels Convention and intellectual property", [1987] EIPR 349;
M. Burnside and A. Burnside, "Patent litigation under the Judgments Convention", *Patent World*, March 1988, 18;
M. Hoyle, "Interlocutory injunctions in intellectual property disputes", [1988] EIPR 112;
P. Prescott, "*Improver Corp.* v. *Remington Consumer Products Ltd.*", [1989] EIPR 259.

COMMENTARY ON SECTION 61

General   61.06

Section 61 defines the relief obtainable as the result of a finding of infringement under section 60 (or in the case of infringement pre-grant under s. 69), and lays down the basis for the procedure for infringement proceedings. The section applies to "existing patents" (Sched. 4, para. 3(2)). The procedure for infringement actions is discussed *re*. Practice in paras. 61.21–61.38 *infra*.

Section 61 provides (by subs. (1)) for infringement proceedings to be brought before "the court" as that term is defined, for which see para. 61.07 *infra* (subs. (1)). Also, by agreement between the proprietor and the alleged infringer, infringement may be determined by the Comptroller (subs. (3), though little use has been made of this facility, see further para. 61.19 *infra*. In such proceedings the Comptroller can refer the case to the court for decision (subs. (5)).

There is also now power for courts in other EEC countries (except those in Portugal or Spain) to determine infringement disputes in relation to acts carried out in the United Kingdom because Art. 5(3) of the Brussels Convention of 1968 (which is enacted into British law by the Civil Jurisdiction and Judgments Act 1982 (c. 27, Sched. 1, Art. 5(3)) provides that, in matters relating to tort, a person domiciled in a Contracting State may be sued either in his country of domicile or in the courts of the place where the harmful event occurred. Indeed, where parallel actions are brought in another Contracting State, a United Kingdom court may be required to cede jurisdiction to a foreign court, and may choose to do so where related actions are involved, see para. 61.25 *infra*.

Proceedings cannot be commenced under section 61 (or under s. 69) until notice of the patent grant has been officially published, see para. 24.11, and for European patents (UK) see para. 77.09. An exclusive licensee under the patent, or the published application, has the same rights as a proprietor (ss. 67 and 69). For the meaning of "proprietor", see para. 60.07 and the commentary on section 68; and for the meaning of "patent", see para. 60.05.

Unlike section 60, however, section 61 would apply also to a Community patent (CPCaa. 36, 74, 79), but the original proposal (CPCa. 76) that, in an infringement action relating to a Community patent, it would not be possible to dispute validity, other than as a defence (s. 74(1)(*a*)), has been varied and it is now envisaged that the CPC should be amended before it comes into effect. Thus, it is now proposed that infringement proceedings under a Community patent will first be brought before a national court designated as a "Community Patent Court". Such a court is to have a power, when trying an infringement action on a Community patent, to consider a counterclaim for its revocation, but subject to appeal which will fall to be decided by a "Common Appeal Court ("COPAC"), a court which is to be created on a supra-national basis, see para. 87.03 and the articles by C. Wadlow ([1986] ELR 295) and K. Bruckhausen ((1987) 18 IIC 682).

61.07   *The forum for infringement proceedings*

"Court", for the purposes of the Act, is defined (s. 130(1)). In England and Wales at present it means "the High Court", but the term will also include proceedings before a Patents County Court when sections 287–292 [1988] are brought into force, for which see paras. 96.17–96.23. In Scotland, Northern Ireland and the Isle of Man "court" means the local equivalent of the High Court in England and Wales, as defined in section 130(1) (as amended), see para. 96.24 which also discusses the effect of the Civil Jurisdiction and Judgments Act 1982 (c. 27) where the case has an intra-United Kingdom or an intra-EEC dimension. Infringement proceedings in England and Wales are, by the Rules of Court, assigned to the Patents Court constituted as part of the Chancery Division of the High Court, see para. 96.15. For the position in Scotland, Northern Ireland and the Isle of Man, see paras. 98.05, 131.03 and 132.05 respectively.

Appeals **61.08**

The normal procedure for appeals from the "court" apply to patent infringement proceedings. Thus, there is an appeal as of right to the Court of Appeal from decisions of the High Court (as there will also, in due course, be from decisions of Patents County Courts); and then, with leave, to the House of Lords. The position in Northern Ireland is similar, initial appeal being to the Court of Appeal in Northern Ireland. In Scotland, appeal lies from the Outer House of the Court of Session to the Inner House thereof and then, with leave, to the House of Lords. In the Isle of Man, the final appeal would be to the Judicial Committee of the Privy Council.

An appeal from a decision of the Comptroller under subsection (3) lies as of right to the Patents Court, but then only to the Court of Appeal with leave (s. 97(3)(*a*), see para. 97.06, and for appeals if the Comptroller hears proceedings in Scotland see para. 97.11.

Defence of invalidity **61.09**

While the validity of the patent in suit may always be put in issue as a defence to proceedings under section 60 (s. 74(1)(*a*)), the right to counterclaim for revocation of the patent sued upon, previously specified under section 61 [1949] (and still applicable to "existing patents", Sched. 1, para. 1(2)) has not been re-enacted. Consequently and strictly speaking, to secure revocation, as distinct from merely pleading invalidity (since an invalid patent cannot be infringed, see *Pittevil* v. *Brackelberg* ((1932) 49 RPC 23)), a cross-petition or application under section 72 should be lodged when the patent in suit is one granted under the Act, but in such cases the former practice of seeking revocation in a counterclaim seems not to have been questioned by the Patents Court.

The defence of invalidity is not available when the action is for breach of a contractual undertaking not to infringe (*Van der Lely* v. *Maulden Engineering*, [1984] FSR 157), see also section 74(1).

Relief **61.10**

The plaintiff may claim the reliefs set out in paragraphs (*a*) to (*e*) of subsection (1). These are discussed separately in paras. 61.11–61.16 *infra*, but include (*a*) granting an injunction (interdict in Scotland) against the defendant (defender in Scotland), (*b*) an order for delivery up or destruction of infringing articles or products, (*c*) damages, (*d*) an account of profits, and (*e*) a certificate of contested validity. Subsection (2) makes damages and an account of profits alternative remedies, but in proceedings before the Comptroller (under subs. (3)) relief is limited to (*c*) and (*e*) above. By subsection (6), in determining relief, the court or Comptroller is to apply the same principles as before June 1, 1978 so that there was then no change in the law. In addition the successful party will normally be entitled to an award of costs, for which see para. 61.18.

Relief by injunction (subs. (1)(a))

—Interlocutory injunctions **61.11**

An interlocutory injunction is one granted pending full trial. Delay in applying can result in this discretionary relief being refused. If granted an interlocutory injunction, the plaintiff must give a "cross-undertaking" to the court to pay the defendant damages if he is unsuccessful at full trial. Prior to *American Cyanamid* v.

Ethicon ([1975] RPC 513 (HL)), the plaintiff had to show a prima facie case, both as to infringement and validity, but in that case the principles (which now apply generally to interloctury injunctions in all types of litigation) were redefined so that the court would not find itself prejudging the issues to be contested at full trial or becoming involved in factual issues of considerable complexity.

Accordingly, the present position is that a plaintiff must show that he has an "arguable" case. In patent actions this hurdle is one which is often readily overcome. First, only a strong attack of invalidity based on points not hitherto considered by a tribunal is likely to outweigh the arguable case arising from the grant of the patent following examination, see *Nat Shipping* v. *Dobson Park* (SRIS C/11/86) and *Ultraseal* v. *Space Seal* (SRIS C/53/88, *noted* IPD 11033) even when the European patent (UK) is under opposition in the EPO (*Improver Corp.* v. *Innovations*, SRIS C/16/88, *noted* IPD 11002). Secondly, as to infringement, the Protocol to EPCa. 69 can be prayed in aid to show an arguable case of infringement, as in *Improver Crop.* v. *Remington* ([1989] RPC 69 (CA)), but not so in *Jakob Schlaepfer* v. *Frankle* (SRIS C/9/88). However, a patentee does not have an arguable case if proceedings to amend the patent are pending as the court could not then adjudicate on a contempt motion for breach of the injunction (*Mölnlycke* v. *Procter & Gamble*, SRIS C/60/89, *noted* IPD 12092).

The *Cyanamid* decision then requires the court to consider the "balance of convenience", that is to consider whether the plaintiff will be adequately compensated in damages if successful at full trial but denied an injunction meanwhile; and, likewise, whether the defendant will be adequately compensated under the cross-undertaking if a pre-trial injunction is imposed and he is successful at full trial. The "balance of convenience" has been stated to be a "balance of the risk of doing an injustice," see *Fleming Fabrications* v. *Albion Cylinders* ([1989] RPC 47 (CA)), applying *Allen* v. *Jambo* ([1980] 1 WLR 1253) and *Cayne* v. *Global Natural Resources* ([1984] 1 All ER 225 (CA)).

If the court finds the balance of convenience evenly divided, it is directed by the *Cyanamid* decision to maintain the *status quo ante bellum*, *i.e.* to maintain the commercial situation which existed immediately prior to the commencement of the proceedings. Only if the court is then still able to decide between the parties, is it permitted by the "*Cyanamid*" rules to consider the relative merits of the case. Indeed these rules were formulated because an application for an interlocutory injunction is normally decided only upon affidavit evidence, in which there is a relaxation of the rule against "hearsay" evidence, and without the benefit of discovery and cross-examination. It is therefore not practicable for a court to reach more than a tentative conclusion on the merits of the case.

Nevertheless, a judge would be less than human if his judgment on the balance of convenience were not (covertly) influenced by his perception of those merits, and accordingly the merits are inevitably canvassed to some extent in the evidence for and against the grant of an injunction; and an injunction is likely to be refused, for one reason or another, if the court thinks that the plaintiff is likely to lose at full trial, for example as in *Newsweek* v. *BBC*, [1979] RPC 441). Conversely, an interlocutory injunction is more likely to be granted if the court has doubt whether the defendant has a genuine intention of defending the main action, for example because he is reluctant to reveal his defence (*Smith (T.J.) & Nephew* v. *3M United Kingdom*, [1983] RPC 92). Also, if the interlocutory proceedings are likely to determine the whole proceedings because neither party would have an interest in full trial, it has been held appropriate to consider the merits, see *Associated Newspapers* v. *News Group Newspapers* ([1986] RPC 515). For the operation of these principles in practice, see the Case Comment at [1986] EIPR D-143 on *Reckitt & Colman* v. *Borden* ([1987] FSR 228 (CA)) and the papers by M. Hoyle and P. Prescott each listed in para. 61.05 *supra*.

Each party, therefore, seeks to show that without, or with, an injunction it is likely to suffer damage which is unquantifiable because, if damages are an adequate remedy and the defendant has the ability to pay these, no injunction should normally be granted (*Garden Cottage Foods* v. *Milk Marketing Board*, [1983] 3 CMLR 13; [1982] 2 All ER 770; *noted* [1984] FSR 23 (HL) and *Polaroid* v. *Kodak*, [1977] RPC 379). Thus, if the plaintiff has granted a licence on a royalty basis, damages for infringement are likely to be calculated on a like basis and, hence, such will normally preclude the grant of an interlocutory injunction if the defendant has the ability to pay such sums, see *Zaidener* v. *Barrisdale* ([1968] RPC 489), *Smith (T.J.) and Nephew* v. *Vygon* (SRIS C/28/85) and *General Electric* v. *GTE Valeron* (SRIS C/45/85, *noted* [1985] EIPR D-212). Likewise, damages will be calculated on a royalty basis where the patentee has only exploited his invention by importation and will then be more readily calculable (*Mölnlyckle* v. *Procter & Gamble, supra*).

Arguments which have successfully been used to show that the plaintiff's pre-trial loss will be unquantifiable are: if the defendant establishes a bridgehead or springboard position in the market, as in the *Cyanamid* case itself, and see: *Corruplast* v. *Harrison* ([1978] RPC 761); *Netlon* v. *Bridport-Gundry* ([1979] FSR 530); and *Monsanto* v. *Stauffer* ([1984] FSR 574), particularly where such might cause price erosion (*Smith, Kline & French* v. *Global Pharmaceutics* (SRIS C/167/83, *noted* IPD 6125, there being no appeal on ths point, see [1986] RPC 394); where there will be an adverse effect on the plaintiff's research programme (as also in the *Netlon* case); where the plaintiff is in the process of establishing a market for the patented article, see the *Netlon* case also, and *E.A.R. Corp.* v. *Protector Safety Products* [1980] FSR 574); and where there is a difficulty of estimating lost sales, particularly where continued infringement would lead to a snowball effect with other infringers appearing. Although the "snowball" argument did not succeed in *Condor International* v. *Hibbing* ([1984] FSR 312), it has since been increasingly successful, see *Hallen* v. *Brabantia* (SRIS C/70/87, *noted* [1988] EIPR D-17; IPD 10069); *Improver Corp.* v. *Innovations* (*supra*); *Ultraseal* v. *Space Seal* (*supra*); *ICI* v. *Montedison* (SRIS C/75/88, *noted* IPD 11047); *Fleming Fabrications* v. *Albion Cylinders* (*supra*); *Helitune* v. *Stewart-Hughes* (SRIS C/94/88); *Neotronics* v. *Anglo-Nordic* (SRIS C/96/88, *noted* IPD 11046) and *Improver Corp.* v. *Remington* (*supra*). A further factor in the *Neotronics* case was that the product was predicted to have only a short market life.

A reason for not granting an interlocutory injunction is, however, if third parties such as the defendant's licensees (not protected by the cross-undertaking) would be prejudiced (*Standard Telephones* v. *Plessey*, SRIS C/171/82).

Where there is a doubt whether a defendant has the financial resources to pay damages after full trial, an interlocutory injunction has been avoided by the defendant paying a proportion of its sales revenue from the alleged infringing activities into a trust account, for example one held jointly by the respective solicitors, see *Vernon* v. *Universal Pulp* ([1980] FSR 179) and *Brupat* v. *Sandford Marine* ([1983] RPC 61 (CA)) or provide security for damages in some other way (*Mars* v. *Azkoyen*, SRIS C/57/89, *noted* IPD 12079).

Analogously, an impecunious, or a foreign, plaintiff may be required to provide security to back his cross-undertaking in damages, see *Pellow* v. *Hunters Leather-craft* (SRIS C/24/81, *noted* IPD 4034) and *Pall Corp.* v. *Owens* (SRIS C/29/86, *noted* IPD 9035); and particularly *Improver Corp.* v. *Remington (No. 2)* (SRIS C/1/89, *noted* IPD 11048 and C/19/89, *noted* IPD 12067), where a bank guarantee for £5.5m. was eventually required. However, a probability that the plaintiff would not be able to meet a liability under his cross-undertaking is not the end of the road, particularly where its financial position owes much to persons connected with the defendant, see *Fleming Fabrications* v. *Albion Cylinders* (*supra*).

Finally, it should be noted that the grant of any injunction is a discretionary remedy. Accordingly, it has been indicated that no injunction should issue to prevent a life-saving drug, different from that marketed by the patentee, from being available to the public (*Roussel-Uclaf* v. *Searle*, [1977] RPC 125).

If an interlocutory injunction is granted, this will normally be in specific terms, since an injunction in terms of a prohibition on infringing the patent would require a full trial to determine whether such had been breached, see *Staver* v. *Digitext* ([1985] FSR 512) and *Video Arts* v. *Paget Industries* ([1988] FSR 501), but for a more robust view, see *Spectravest* v. *Aperknit* (SRIS C/77/87).

There are also special forms of interlocutory relief of an injunctionary nature. These are: the *Anton Piller* Order, discussed in para. 61.27 *infra*; the *Mareva* injunction, for freezing the assets of a defendant; and the writ *ne exeat regno*, to restrain a defendant from leaving the jurisdiction of the court. The two last-mentioned of these are not often required in patent litigation and are therefore considered outside the scope of this Work, but see the books by R. N. Ough and M. S. W. Hoyle each listed in para. 61.04 *supra*.

61.12   *—Injunction after trial*

An injunction is always a discretionary remedy of the court and may therefore be refused in an appropriate case, the court having hinted that *Roussel-Uclaf* v. *Searle* ([1977] FSR 125, discussed in para. 61.11 *supra*) might have been such a case, see also para. 62.05. Of course, no injunction can be granted once the patent has expired (*Monsanto* v. *Stauffer* [*South Africa*], [1988] FSR 57) and any injunction then in force automatically lapses.

At the end of the substantive trial in *American Cyanamid* v. *Ethicon* ([1979] RPC 215), the interlocutory injunction granted in 1975 was ordered to be continued during the prosecution of an appeal by the defendant against findings of infringement and validity on the ground that thereby the plaintiff's cross-undertaking in damages would be continued. However, in *Rotocrop* v. *Genbourne* ([1982] FSR 241) the court, following *Bugges* v. *Herbon* ([1972] RPC 197 at 214), stayed an injunction upon undertakings to keep an account of sales and to pay 10 per cent. of the sale price into a special account and to serve promptly a notice of appeal.

It is possible for an injunction to be granted which is intended to have extra-territorial effect by restraining acts carried out abroad which are likely to lead to infringing acts within the United Kingdom, see the passing-off case of *Dunhill (Alfred)* v. *Sunoptic* ([1979] FSR 337) and also *North Western Trailer* v. *Itel* (*The Times*, December 19, 1979; SRIS HC/PC/41/79).

61.13   *Relief by delivery up or destruction (subs. (1)(b))*

Relief by an order for delivery up or destruction of infringing goods still in the possession of the defendant is ancillary to relief by injunction, and therefore is, likewise, a discretionary remedy and cannot be granted once the patent has expired (*Monsanto* v. *Stauffer* [*South Africa*], [1988] FSR 57).

In *Codex* v. *Racal-Milgo (No. 3)* ([1984] FSR 87) it was held not sufficient for compliance with an order for delivery up or destruction of infringing apparatus merely to dismantle it without either handing the parts removed to the plaintiff or destroying the same upon oath, but it was sufficient to deliver up or destroy the elements in the apparatus which caused the act of infringement. The court commented that requests for an order of this nature should perhaps be more specific than had been the custom. However, in *Spectravest* v. *Aperknit* (SRIS C/77/87) the Order was too specific as only covering articles in the possession of the Defendant at the date of the Order and not articles coming into its possession subsequently.

In *Smith Kline & French* v. *Harbottle* ([1980] RPC 363), D was ordered to deliver up for destruction supplies of a patented drug which they had consigned at the request of H by air for delivery to H, but which at the time were in the hands of British Airways as warehouseman, the warehousing being a non-infringing act, see para. 60.12.

Relief by damages (subs. (1)(c))   **61.14**

In proceedings for patent infringement it is customary first to seek a decision on liability and an order for an enquiry to be held into the damages suffered. The quantum of damages is then assessed in separate proceedings, usually based on affidavit evidence with further discovery, see *Catnic* v. *Hill & Smith (No. 2)* ([1983] FSR 512). This enquiry is available as of right to a successful plaintiff if he has an arguable case of loss suffered (*McDonald's Hamburgers* v. *Burgerking*, [1987] FSR 112). In infringement proceedings brought before the Comptroller, an award of damages is the main relief available, see subsection (3).

There is little authority on the assessment of damages for patent infringement except that damages are compensatory and not punitive. Damages must result from the infringing acts and not merely be caused by them, see the *Catnic* case (*supra*) where parasitic damages were disallowed, as criticised in the paper by P. A. Chandler listed in para. 61.05 *supra*. Thus, damages calculated on the loss of profit by the proprietor can only be awarded if the court is satisfied that, if infringement had not occurred, the proprietor would himself have had the business of the infringing acts, see the *Catnic* case (*supra*). Otherwise, as also illustrated in the *Catnic* case, damages are likely to be assessed on the basis of a royalty for the infringing use. This will especially be the case where the proprietor has shown himself willing to license others to use his invention, such royalty then being applied to the infringing acts (*General Tire* v. *Firestone* [1975] RPC 203 (CA) and [1976] RPC 197 (HL)); and in *Harrison* v. *Project & Design (No. 2)* (SRIS C/53/85) damages were assessed on a royalty basis, at 3 per cent. of the invoiced price, largely because serious negotiations at such a figure had taken place. The case contains some observations on the calculation of interest on such damages. The appeal ([1987] RPC 151 (CA)) concerned only the question whether the previous finding of infringement ([1978] FSR 81) could be re-opened on the enquiry into damages. It was held that the previous findings were *res judicata*. When such royalty rate is inapplicable, some guidance may be gained from the principles for assessment of damages in cases where the damage is largely unquantifiable, for example as is the position in cases of misuse of confidential information, see *Talbot* v. *General Television [Australia]* ([1981] RPC 1).

In *Smith Kline & French* v. *Doncaster Pharmaceuticals* ([1989] FSR 401) liquidated damages were claimed without an enquiry in a case involving importation without licence from Spain of a patented product produced there by the proprietor's associated company. It was contended that the measure of damages was the difference in price between the Spanish and United Kingdom prices for the proprietor's product, but this argument was rejected in favour of the difference between the Spanish and French (or Belgian) prices of the proprietor, presumably on the basis that importation from those EEC countries wuld not be an infringing act in view of the EEC doctrine of "exhaustion of rights", not yet applicable to products sold initially in Spain, see para. C16.

Where a patented article is resold, the resale is a separate act of infringement and damages (or on account of profits) can be claimed from the second vendor even when damages have already been obtained from the initial vendor (*Catnic* v. *Evans* [1983] FSR 410).

Interest on damages (on a simple interest basis) is usually awarded (though strictly this is at the discretion of the court) in respect of the whole or part of the period between each act of infringement and the date of the assessment (Supreme Court Act 1981 (c. 54), section 35A as inserted by section 15 and Schedule 1 of the Administration of Justice Act 1982 (c. 53)), see *Catnic* v. *Hill & Smith (No. 2)*, *supra* and also *General Tire* v. *Firestone* (*supra*) and *Fablaine* v. *Leygill (No. 2)* ([1982] FSR 427), the latter two cases arising under the previous enactment relating to interest on an award of damages. However, in the *Catnic* v. *Hill & Smith* case, interest was not allowed as a head of damage suffered for the bank financing which was required in the absence of profits from exploitation of the patent by the patentee.

Exemplary damages will not apparently ever be awarded for patent infringement even when the infringer has cynically made profits greater than the loss suffered by the patent proprietor (*Catnic* v. *Hill & Smith (No. 2)*, *supra*), but an account of profits (for which see para. 61.15 *infra*) may be appropriate.

In *Morton-Norwich* v. *Intercen and United Chemicals* ([1981] FSR 337) damages were awarded for acts of infringement committed more than six years before the issue of the writ because there had been "concealed fraud" which extended the normal six year period for claiming relief under the Limitation Acts (see now Limitation Act 1980 (c. 58), s. 2). Damages were here also held to include the cost of proceedings previously brought (*Norwich Pharmacal* v. *Commissioners for Customs and Excise* [1974] RPC 101) in order to discover the identity of the infringers (for which see para. 60.12), such costs being a foreseeable consequence of the tort committed by the defendants. The court also held here that the exclusive licensees under the patent were entitled to compensatory damages in the usual way and indicated that, if these were calculated on a royalty basis, in the circumstances these might be of the order of 20 per cent.

A person who incurs costs in defending a patent infringement action, particularly if he is required to pay damages or an account of profits therein, may be able to recover his loss if his act of infringement resulted from an innocent purchase of goods by him. By section 12(2) of the Sale of Goods Act 1979 (c. 54), there is in any sale of goods an implied warranty that the buyer will enjoy quiet possession of those goods except as to any charge or encumbrance on the goods disclosed or known to the buyer. That warranty may not be excluded by the terms of a contract governed by English law (Unfair Contract Terms Act 1977 (c. 50), section 6(1) as amended by Sale of Goods Act 1979, Schedule 2, para. 19(*a*)). Authority for this proposiion is to be found in *Microbeads* v. *Vinhurst* ([1976] RPC 19), though that case was decided under former statutory provisions, see also *Niblett* v. *Confectioners' Materials* ([1921] 3 KB 387 (CA)) and para. 60.27.

Also, where there is more than one possible defendant in respect of the same act of infringement, then any defendant who pays damages can bring action for a contribution from the other joint tortfeasors under the Civil Liability (Contribution) Act 1978 (c. 47).

61.15 *Relief by account of profits (subs. (1)(d))*

The remedy of an account of profits is one which was not available for patent infringement between 1919 and 1950 but, being an equitable remedy, its grant is (as with injunctory relief) strictly speaking a matter for the discretion of the court. In any event, an account has rarely been requested in preference to an award of damages under subsection (1)(*c*), both not being possible (subs. (2)). This is because of the difficulties in computation, see *Siddell* v. *Vickers* ((1892) 9 RPC 152) and the possibility that the computation would show that the defendant suffered a financial loss on its activities. However, an account may have to be requested when the infringing activities have not caused the proprietor any financial loss. The distinction between damages (the loss suffered by the plaintiff) and an account of profits (the profits made by the infringer) is illustrated by the trade mark case of *Colbeam Palmer* v. *Stock [Australia]* ([1972] RPC 303).

In computing an infringer's profits, it may be that the infringer is entitled to a liberal allowance in respect of skill and labour expended in arriving at the infringing article provided that he had acted without dishonest intent, see the remarks in relation to copyright infringement in *Redwood Music* v. *Chappell* ([1982] RPC 109). Also, as was observed in a passing-off case (*My Kinda Town* v. *Soll,* ([1983] RPC 15 (CA)) in taking an account the master should seek by reasonable approximation, rather than mathematical exactness, to ensure that neither party will have that which justly belongs to the other. Subsequently (when the finding of passing off was reversed, [1983] RPC 407 (CA)), it was observed (at p. 432) that the account that had been ordered appeared "to be one that is virtually impossible to take", thereby emphasising the importance of the careful formulation of an order of this kind. It is also noted that a much more restrictive attitude to allowable deductions from gross profits has apparently been adopted in Canada (*Teledyne* v. *Lido Industrial [Canada]*, *noted* [1983] EIPR D-116).

In *Codex* v. *Racal-Milgo* (SRIS C/135/81) the argument appears to have been accepted that, if the proprietor seeks an account of profits rather than damages, he need not lead evidence that the specification of the patent as published was framed in good faith and with reasonable skill and knowledge, see paras. 62.05 and 63.03.

When an account of profits is taken, only acts of infringement up to the point where the profit was made are condoned thereby, so that subsequent acts of infringement involving the patented product are not apparently franked by the account taken (*Codex* v. *Racal-Milgo (No. 3)*, [1984] FSR 87). Where there are multiple defendants, the plaintiff can apparently make a different election as between damages and an account for each defendant (*Electric Furnace Co.* v. *Selas*, [1987] RPC 23).

Declaration of validity and infringement (subs. (1)(e))   **61.16**

When action under section 60 is successful, a declaration (declarator in Scotland) that the patent has been found valid and infringed is given as a matter of course, but the declaration has only formal effect. It is usual to request that the declaration contain a certificate of contested validity under section 65(1), for the effect of which see para. 65.04 and such declaration will also be granted as a matter of course unless the defendant merely contested infringement and accepted that the patent was valid for the purpose of the proceedings against him. A declaration under subsection (1)(*e*) is also available in proceedings before the Comptroller under subsection (3).

Eurodefences   **61.17**

It has been indicated that, where the conduct of the plaintiff has involved breach of the Treaty of Rome, particularly of TRaa. 85 or 86 (reprinted in Appendix C at paras. C05 and C06), he *may* become disentitled to relief (*Aero-Zipp* v. *YKK*, [1974] RPC 625) and *Application des Gaz* v. *Falks Veritas*, [1975] RPC 421). No such defence has yet succeeded in a case involving intellectual property, and in *Minnesota Mining* v. *Geerpres* ([1974] RPC 35) such an alleged defence did not prevent an interlocutory injunction but, where there is a counterclaim alleging a breach of TRa. 85 or 86, a defendant may be able to secure an injunction against the plaintiff (*Garden Cottage Foods* v. *Milk Marketing Board*, [1983] 3 CMLR 43; [1983] 2 All ER 770, *noted* [1984] FSR 23 (HL)). However, it is not a breach of the Treaty of Rome merely to enforce an intellectual property right which the law provides, see *Keurkoop* v. *Nancy Keen (Case 114/81)* ([1982] ECR 2853; [1982]

2 CMLR 47; [1983] FSR 387 (ECJ)); *Thetford* v. *Fiamma (Case 35/87)* ([1988] 3 CMLR 549; [1989] FSR 57 (ECJ)); and para. C18.

Nevertheless, the Court of Appeal has allowed pleadings of breach of TRa. 85 to remain in order to provide for possible eventual appeal to the ECJ in Luxembourg under TRa. 177 (reprinted at para. C07 and discussed in para. C10), see *British Leyland* v. *TI Silencers* ([1981] FSR 213); *Dymond* v. *Britton* ([1976] FSR 330); *Hagen* v. *Moretti* ([1980] FSR 517 and *Lansing Bagnall* v. *Buccaneer* ([1984] FSR 241), but not unless there is a nexus between the alleged activities of the plaintiff and the alleged breach of a dominant position under TRa. 86, see *Ransburg-Gema* v. *Electrostatic Plant Systems* ([1989] 2 CMLR 712). In the *British Leyland* case the pleaded Eurodefence was the alleged existence of licensing arrangements contrary to TRa. 85, whereas the *Aero-Zipp*, and *Application des Gaz* and *Lansing Bagnall* cases concerned alleged abuse of a dominant position contrary to TRa. 86. Here it may be noted that in the *United Brands* decision ([1976] 1 CMLR D.28; [1976] FSR 204) the European Commission condemned, as being contrary to TRa. 86: contractual provisions for restricting resale of purchased goods; refusal to supply goods to certain persons; and the charging of dissimilar, or unfair, prices for equivalent transactions. Indeed, any unfair commercial practice on the part of a dominant enterprise intended to eliminate, discipline or deter small companies is potentially an abuse of marketing power and contrary to TRa. 86 (*Engineering and Chemical Supplies* v. *AKZO*, [1986] 3 CMLR 273), for case comment on which see [1987] EIPR 86. TRa. 86 is discussed further in Appendix C at paras. C.17 and C.18.

61.18 *Costs*

Under the English legal system the successful party in civil litigation is normally entitled to recover costs from the party.

Costs are now normally awarded on the "standard" basis as defined by RSC Ord. 62, rule 12 (reprinted at para. E062.12). This provides for allowance of "a reasonable amount in respect of all costs reasonably incurred", but with any doubts whether costs were "reasonably incurred" or were "reasonable" to be resolved in favour of the paying party. This leads to an incomplete recovery of costs actually incurred and there is no allowance for the executive time incurred by a litigating party. Also, in proceedings for infringement or revocation, costs may still *only* be awarded to the extent that the court certifies that the pleaded particulars of objections were proven or were reasonable and proper, see RSC Ord. 62, App. 2, part VII, para. 4(3) (reprinted in para. E062A2.3). In *Harrison* v. *Project & Design (No. 2)* (SRIS C/2/87, *noted* [1987] RPC 151 (CA)) costs were awarded to a successful defendant out of the Legal Aid Fund.

Where a defendant to an infringement action seeks to amend his defence to allege a new ground of invalidty, the plaintiff is given a period of time within which he can elect to discontinue the action. If he does so, the normal order as to costs sometimes called an "*Earth closet*" order from the case in which it was originally devised) is that the defendant has his costs up to the date of serving the original defence, but the plaintiff has his costs thereafter up to the date of discontinuing the action (*See* v. *Scott-Paine*, (1933) 50 RPC 56, approved in *Williamson* v. *Moldline*, [1986] RPC 556 (CA)). It is incumbent on a defendant to put forward complete particulars of objection at a reasonably early date in the proceedings and the usual order will only be departed from where the new defence could not, by reasonable diligence, have been discovered earlier, even where there is a late allegation of prior use (*Gill* v. *Chipman*, [1987] RPC 209).

Costs may only be recovered in respect of actual or threatened litigation and, where experiments are carried out by a corporate litigant itself, only a reasonable sum for the actual and direct costs of the work undertaken will be awarded (*Nossen's Patent*, [1969] 1 All ER 775).

In *Smith, Kline & French* v. *Harbottle* ([1980] RPC 363) there was an interesting discussion on the award of costs when the action for infringement succeeded against two defendants, one of whom had made payment into court before trial (which can be a useful way of limiting liability for future costs in the action) but had failed against a further defendant.

Interest is now payable on costs from the date when the trial order is made rather than from the date when the order on taxation of costs is made (*Hunt* v. *Douglas*, [1988] 3 All ER 823; [1988] 3 WLR 975 (HL)).

Proceedings before the Comptroller (subs. (3))   **61.19**

Infringement proceedings can be held before the Comptroller under subsection (3) and all references in the Act to "infringement proceedings" include proceedings under this subsection (subs. (4)(*a*)). However, such proceedings can only take place with the consent of the parties and relief is limited to damages and a declaration under subsection (1)(*c*) and (*e*) respectively, but a declaration of non-infringement can be sought unilaterally under section 71 and this may have a similar effect, see *Hawker-Siddeley* v. *Real Time* ([1983] RPC 395), though the reversal of the burden of proof may be a serious obstacle to use of section 71, see para. 71.04. Proceedings before the Comptroller cannot be started if there are already any proceedings before the court involving the patent in question, unless the court gives leave, see section 74(7) discussed in para. 74.06. While an injunction cannot be granted by the Comptroller, a decision on infringement by the Comptroller will probably create an issue estoppel and, as a consequence, court proceedings against continuing infringement by the same party could lead to an injunction under summary procedure. However, a defendant could still challenge validity as for this no estoppel is created by the Comptroller's decision in view of section 72(5), see para. 72.28, but he could then be faced with a certificate of contested validity under section 65, see para. 65.04.

The apparent advantages of cheapness and expedition of proceedings under subsection (3) have not led to any cases under the present Act. There were only two cases under the analogous section 67 [1949], one of which was reported (*Central Electricity* v. *Chamberlain*, [1958] RPC 21). Some economies are possible, including representation by the patent agent alone and the presentation of evidence more succinctly to a technically qualified tribunal, but these are offset because the Comptroller can only grant damages and cannot grant an injunction, nor order delivery up, nor order an account of profits. Under subsection (4)(*a*) and section 62(1), ignorance of the patent can be pleaded as affecting the relief granted by the Comptroller.

When Patents County Courts are introduced (for which see para. 61.20 *infra*), it seems likely that subsection (3) will remain unused, but it is noted that in *Multifarm* v. *Whitmarley* ([1956] RPC 143 (CA) and [1957] RPC 260 (HL)) the Court of Appeal regretted that the parties had not availed themselves of the procedure under section 67 [1949] to determine whether the defendants were in contempt of an injunction previously imposed when they had introduced a modified device.

The procedure under subsection (3) is set out in rule 72 (reprinted at para. 61.02 *supra*). Reference is made on PF 36/77 (reprinted at para. 141.36) accompanied by a joint statement setting out points of agreement and disagreement (including the question of costs and any security therefor), followed by statements by the proprietor and a further statement by the other party. If validity is impugned, the proprietor can file a further statement. Evidence can be filed. Subsequent proceedings are at the discretion of the Comptroller. If validity only is in dispute, rule 73 (reprinted at para. 61.03 *supra*) applies and a slightly abridged procedure is adopted. Rules 103–107 (reprinted at paras. 72.05–72.69 and discussed at paras. 72.40–72.46) regulate the giving of evidence and invest the Comptroller with the powers of a judge of the High Court (other than the power to punish summarily for contempt of court) in relation to the giving of evidence, the attendance of witnesses and the discovery and production of documents. By rule 109 (reprinted at para. 72.10) the Comptroller may appoint an adviser to assist him in the proceedings and these may take place in Scotland (r. 108 reprinted at para. 98.02). As to relief, subsection (6) also applies.

The Comptroller may decline to deal with the matter and refer it to the court (subs. (5)), and the court may then determine the matter, see RSC Ord. 104, r. 17 (reprinted at para. E104.17).

If the Comptroller finds the patent invalid, the defendant can then apparently apply under section 72(1) for revocation. Presumably an application for revocation under section 72 could run concurrently with the section 61 proceedings before the Comptroller, just as the two issues of infringement and validity are usually dealt with together in proceedings before the court. A determination by the Comptroller, or on appeal from the Comptroller, that the defendant's act is or is not an infringement will apparently bind the parties in subsequent proceedings based upon similar facts.

The application of the Arbitration Act 1950 to subsection (3) proceedings is specifically excluded by section 130(8). Under section 97 the decision of the Comptroller is subject to appeal to the Patents Court and thence, with leave, to the Court of Appeal. If the proceedings before the Comptroller are held in Scotland, the corresponding appellate courts are the Outer House and the Inner House of the Court of Session (s. 97(4) and (5)).

Costs in proceedings before the Comptroller are considered in paras. 107.03 and 107.04.

61.20   *Infringement proceedings in a Patents County Court*

The 1988 Act (by ss. 287–292 [1988]) has provided skeleton primary legislation for the creation of one or more Patents County Courts to operate generally under the provisions of the County Courts Act 1984 (c. 28). It is hoped that these will enable patent litigation to be carried out more cheaply and simply, and hopefully more expeditiously also. Sections 287–292 [1988] are reprinted at paras. 96.06–96.11 and discussed in paras. 96.17–96.23. These provisions have yet to be brought into effect. When they are, they will no doubt be supplemented by special rules of procedure adding to and varying the normal County Court Rules, for which see the "County Court Practice" (the "Green Book").

PRACTICE UNDER SECTION 61

61.21   *General*

The basic essentials of court procedure in patent actions brought before the Patents Court, and the pre-trial procedures that are there available to a litigant, have been explained in the paper by B. C. Reid listed in para. 61.05 *supra*. This procedure is governed by the Rules of the Supreme Court (RSC). For special rules in court actions for patent infringement, see RSC Ord. 104, reprinted in Appendix E at paras. E104.01–E104.22. The present rules 9–14 of RSC Ord. 104 (reprinted at paras. E104.9–E104.14) arise from revisions made in 1986. These revisions effected major changes in procedure from that described in the *Reid* article. Thus, requests for admissions (r. 10); discovery of documents (r. 11); experiments (r. 12); and prior identification of expert witnesses whom it is intended to call to give oral evidence (r. 13) are now required to be dealt with before the issue of the summons for directions (r. 14). Rule 14 sets out nine matters upon which the judge hearing such a summons may make specific orders and it is clearly intended that in a normal action each of these matters should be dealt with in pre-trial procedure, thereby (hopefully) shortening the trial and removing much of the element of surprise on one party of evidence given at the trial by the other. The procedure is also intended to facilitate the use of affidavit evidence and prior submission of experts' written reports. Also, the Chancery Division now generally requires an exchange of witness statements of all oral evidence which a party intends to lead at trial (*Practice Direction (Chancery: Summons for Directions) No. 1 of 1989*, [1989] FSR 400, see also RSC Ord. 38 r. 2A reprinted at para. E038.2A), and there is no reason why a different rule should apply to the Patents Court, this being part of the Chancery Division. Rules 10–14 apply equally to the hearing of a petition for revocation as they do to an action for patent infringement. Where the parties are agreed as to the order they wish the Court to make, the order can be made without attendance, but for patent actions the draft minutes of order should be signed by counsel for all parties (*Practice Direction No. 4 of 1977*, [1977] 1 WLR 421). A specimen form of Order on a Summons for Directions in a patent action was suggested in a Practice Direction ([1974] RPC 1). This is reprinted at para. E104.14A, but requires modification to adapt it to the revised rules.

If the patentee desires to amend the patent in the course of infringement proceedings, the amendment must be sought in separate, though concurrent, proceedings brought under section 75, for which see para. 75.11. However, where proceedings are brought under a European patent (UK) which is, or becomes, subject to opposition in the EPO under EPCa. 99, the infringement proceedings will, apparently, continue on the patent as granted until an order for its amendment (or revocation) should finally come to be made by the EPO, which order then becomes binding on the United Kingdom court, see para. 77.11.

The Court can be assisted by a scientific adviser, see para. 96.25. It can also refer any question of fact or opinion to the Patent Office for inquiry and report, see section 99A and the commentary thereon. Where a European patent (UK) is in issue, a technical opinion can also be requested from the EPO (EPCa. 25), for which see EPO Guidelines E-XII.

For proceedings before the Comptroller under subsection (3) and rules 72 and 73 the practice will generally follow that normally adopted in *inter partes* proceedings before the Comptroller, as is discussed in paras. 72.32–72.52. The time limits specified in rules 72 and 73 can apparently be extended by the discretion of the Comptroller exercised under rule 110(1).

Pleadings   **61.22**

There is an increasing tendency to require greater particularisation of pleadings. Nevertheless, pleadings should be limited to a statement of material facts and to a setting out of the issues of law involved in the proceedings. These should be particularised so that the other party knows the case it has to meet. Proof of the facts is a matter of evidence to be left to the trial, as also are the conclusions to be drawn therefrom. In *Nolek Systems* v. *Analytical Instruments* ([1984] RPC 556), which raised the sufficiency of pleadings of particulars of infringement, it was stated that the role of pleadings is to inform the other party of the case he has to meet and hence, as a defendant manufacturer must know what he is doing, the extent of information on the nature of the alleged infringing act which he needs may not be as extensive as might be needed by an importer. Nevertheless, "people should be,

451

at the earliest possible stage, as frank as they conceivably could be". However, where possible a party should serve his counter-pleading and only then seek further particularisation of the case he has to meet (*Intel* v. *General Instrument* (SRIS C/15/89, *noted* IPD 12053).

Pleadings may include such pleas that: the patent is invalid (usually accompanied by a counterclaim for revocation under s. 72); that infringement is denied; that the alleged acts did not take place within the jurisdiction; or that these acts were authorised, or deemed to be so, by the proprietor. Existence of an agreement contrary to section 44 may be pleaded, as also can that the plaintiff is disentitled to relief because of breaches of the Treaty of Rome, for which see para. 61.17 *supra*. The effect of such a pleading may lead to a reference to the ECJ, for which see para. C10.

RSC Order 104, rule 6 (reprinted at para. E104.6) requires that allegations of prior user must be specifically pleaded and in some detail (r. 6(3)); as also (in the case of an "existing patent") must allegations of inutility (r. 6(4)); and if commercial success is to be relied upon to rebut an allegation of obviousness, such must also be distinctly pleaded (r. 6(5)): this last-mentioned requirement, which was introduced in 1986, has ramifications both as regards particularisation of the pleading and as to discovery, see paras. 3.51and 61.28 *infra*.

An action can also be statute-barred if it is not commenced during the permitted period, see para. 60.28.

61.23 *Striking out of pleadings*

A motion to strike out a pleading is possible under RSC Ord. 18, rule 19 (reprinted at para. E018.19), for example if it can be demonstrated, from the papers in the case, that a pleading is frivolous, vexatious, or otherwise an abuse of process of the court. Such a plea, however, will only succeed in the clearest of cases. Examples of such cases are: *Upjohn* v. *Thomas Kerfoot* ([1988] FSR 1) where the Plaintiff was unable to demonstrate any potentially infringing act carried out in the United Kingdom; and *Desoto* v. *Lankro and Coates* (SRIS C/14/88, *noted* IPD 10104 and SRIS C/6/89, *noted* IPD 12029 (CA)), where the court rejected the Plaintiff's broad interpretation of the claims and therefore held that there could be no infringement by the activities of the Defendants. A similar ruling was given by the Patents Court in *Improver Corp.* v. *Remington*, but the striking out was reversed on appeal ([1989] RPC 69 (CA)) because meanwhile a German court had held the same claim in the common European patent infringed by the same device and so the issue of infringement was no longer a clear one. Likewise, both in *Unilever* v. *Schöller Lebensmittel* ([1988] FSR 596) and *Southco* v. *Dzus Fastener* ([1989] RPC 82), the Patents Court held that the proper construction of the claims might be influenced by expert evidence so that striking out would seldom be right for a determination of patent actions, even though the court itself apparently thought in each case that there was no infringement as alleged.

However, a plaintiff must be able to plead an arguable case. This is particularly so where leave of the court has first to be obtained for service of the proceedings outside the jurisdiction upon a foreign defendant. Such requires a mere assertion from a patent agent that there is infringement. Consequently, in *Raychem* v. *Thermon* ([1989] RPC 423), service was set aside because, in seeking leave, there had not been supplied sufficient particulars and details for the court and the Defendant to understand the facts and matters upon the claim was alleged to be made.

The Comptroller has also held that a case wholly unsupported by evidence is no case at all and should therefore be dismissed and not proceed to discovery which might enable a case to be founded (*Richco Plastic's Patent*. SRIS O/22/89, *noted* IPD 12037).

Striking out the pleadings in an action is also the sanction when there is undue delay in proceeding with an action before the court. However, the court will not normally strike out an action unless a defendant can show that otherwise he will suffer undue prejudice or a fair trial made impossible (*Birkett* v. *James*, [1978] AC 297 (HL)) and *Department of Transport* v. *Smaller* ([1989] 1 All ER 897).

Thus, if the patent remains alive and infringement continues, the court is likely to conclude that there is little point in striking out an action for undue delay because a new action could nevertheless be started for the continuing infringement. Possible prejudice would perhaps be that substantial damages might be saved if some of the liability would become statute-barred if a new action had to be commenced. For an action that was struck out for inordinate delay, see *Horstmann Gear* v. *Smiths Industries* ([1979] FSR 461 and [1980] FSR 131) discussed by E. Swinbank ((1980–81) 10 CIPA 422). However, in *Matbro* v. *Massey-Ferguson* (SRIS C/66/82) striking out was refused on findings that the delay was not inordinate and was explained by sporadic negotiations, and that the defendants had suffered insufficient prejudice by the delay.

Hearing of a preliminary point   **61.24**

While there is power for the Patents Court to order the hearing of a preliminary point, the court is reluctant so to order and is only likely to do so where the point will be decisive if decided one way and would not lead to increased delay and costs, but a special order as to costs may eventually be appropriate (*Sankyo* v. *Merck*, SRIS C/128/88). On this basis, a preliminary hearing was refused in *Masi* v. *Color-oll* ([1986] RPC 483), but in *Gore* v. *Kimal* (SRIS C/90/87) a pure point of law was in issue (see para. A032.11) and trial of a preliminary point was ordered which led to the revocation of the patent, see [1988] RPC 137.

In *General Foam* v. *Ryburn Foam* ([1979] FSR 477) the defendants were granted leave to have the issue of claim construction tried as a preliminary point. In doing so they undertook to abandon certain arguments of invalidity if it were held that the claims had the narrower construction for which they contended.

Application to stay proceedings   **61.25**

While the court has power to stay proceedings, it is generally reluctant so to order, see *Chemithon's Patent* ([1966] RPC 365).

In *Western Electric* v. *Racal-Milgo* ([1979] RPC 501) the defendants applied to stay the proceedings pending determination of issues raised in litigation in the United States under a corresponding patent. The stay was refused because the delay would prejudice the plaintiffs. In the United States the defendant's associate was seeking an injunction to prevent the plaintiffs from continuing with the United Kingdom action on the grounds of anti-trust offences, patent misuse and breach of a consent decree. It was held that, until a United States court might actually grant such an injunction, the United Kingdom action should continue. Although the United Kingdom and United States patents might seemingly correspond, the issues in the two proceedings would not be the same. Whether circumstances existed which might cause the United States court to grant such an injunction was a wholly domestic matter of United States public policy which should be decided in the United States. A case where a United States court has refused a similar injunction on the ground that the validities of the United States and United Kingdom patents are judged by separate and distinct legal standards is *Cryomedics* v. *Frigitonics* ((1978) 196 USPQ 526).

Under the Civil Jurisdiction and Judgments Act 1982 [the "CJJA"] (c. 27, Sched. 1, art. 21), enacting the terms of the Brussels Convention of 1968 (for further information on which see paras. 88.04 and 96.24, *EPH* and the papers listed in para. 88.03), a United Kingdom court is obliged to order a stay of proceedings when proceedings involving the same cause of action are brought in a different Contracting State (*i.e.* at present any EEC State, other than Portugal or Spain). It remains to be seen whether infringement proceedings in different EEC States against the same product under parallel patents, particularly where these have a common origin as a European patent, are regarded as "the same cause of action". In any case, a court has an option (under Art. 22 of this Convention, see CJJA, Sched. 1, art. 22) to stay proceedings where "related actions" are pending in different Contracting States. Neither of these provisions appears yet to have been invoked by a United Kingdom court in relation to proceedings for patent infringement. Note, however, that proceedings concerning the registration (*i.e.* grant) or validity of a United Kingdom patent can *only* be conducted in the United Kingdom (CJJA, Sched. 1, Art. 16(4)). The possibility of a court in another EEC State determining infringement proceedings under a United Kingdom patent is also mentioned in para. 61.06 *supra*.

The court has refused to stay infringement proceedings commenced before an opposition to a European patent was lodged in the EPO, holding that the EPO is not a forum for the issue of infringement, or even for some of the possible grounds of revocation (compare EPCaa. 100 and 138) and, even if it were a forum, the *forum conveniens* for resolution of the dispute was the English court where infringement and validity could be dealt with together and that to await the result of the EPO proceedings might mean a delay of four to five years (*Amersham International* v. *Corning Limited*, [1987] RPC 53; OJEPO 12/1987, 558). A similar decision was given in *Pall Corp* v. *Commercial Hydraulics* ([1988] FSR 274 and SRIS C/80/89 (CA)), particularly because, again, there was an issue of infringement to be resolved and especially because the Defendant was not prepared to accept that the EPO decision should be binding upon him, see also *Improver Corp.* v. *Innovations* (SRIS C/16/88, *noted* IPD 11002) where the EPO opposition had been started before the infringement proceedings but where the court thought the opposition would fail. It does not, however, appear to have been appreciated in these cases that a decision in the EPO would either revoke the patent or act as an issue estoppel against the defendant/opponent, see para. 72.28.

61.26 *Transfer of proceedings*

Within the United Kingdom, the Patents Court is not the only forum for patent infringement proceedings, see para. 61.07 *supra*. The jurisdiction of the Sottish courts is discussed at para. 98.05, particularly in the light of the provisions of the Civil Jurisdiction and Judgments Act 1982 (c. 27), discussed as to intra-United Kingdom jurisdiction in para. 96.24. As there indicated, these provisions may cause a case started in one part of the United Kingdom to be transferred to a court in some other part.

When the Patents County Court system comes into effect, there will also be the question of transfer of proceedings between the Patents Court and a Patents County Court and *vice versa*. This is discussed in para. 96.19 with reference to the provisions governing such transfer contained in section 289 [1988] (reprinted in para. 96.08).

When a "Eurodefence" is put forward (for which see para. 61.17 *supra*), there may be a transfer of proceedings to the European Court of Justice in Luxembourg under TRa. 177 (reprinted in Appendix C at para. C07) for an opinion on EEC law to be given by the ECJ, see para. C10.

The Anton Piller Order   **61.27**

Where the court can be persuaded, *ex parte*, that there is a grave danger that vital evidence may be destroyed if the party concerned is forewarned, the court can order that solicitors be authorised to enter the party's premises and remove or take copies of documents of specified categories in order that evidence may be preserved. This Order is known as an *Anton Piller* Order following its approval in *Anton Piller* v. *Manufacturing Processes* ([1976] RPC 719 (CA)) and *EMI* v. *Sarwar* ([1977] FSR 146). Such an Order normally includes an interlocutory injunction and, therefore, the plaintiff must give a cross-undertaking in damages and a foreign plaintiff may be required to provide security for this, see para. 61.11 *supra*.

The practice is summarised in the paper by J. Adams listed in para. 61.05 *supra*. The precautions which must be followed in applying for and executing an *Anton Piller* Order are noted in *Columbia Pictures* v. *Robinson* ([1986] FSR 367), for case comment on which see [1986] EIPR 187. The steps that should be taken in executing such an Order are also summarised in *Booker McConnell* v. *Plascow* ([1985] RPC 425). The Order must be meticulously executed (*AB* v. *CDE*, [1982] RPC 509) and in the presence of a solicitor. If there is delay in seeking the Order, it will subsequently be discharged with resulting penalty in costs (*Burroughs Machines* v. *Computer Instruments*, SRIS C/87/86).

An *Anton Piller* Order may be granted against a foreign resident defendant, but that defendant should first be given an opportunity to challenge the jurisdiction of the court (*Altertex* v. *Advanced Data Communications*, [1986] FSR 21). It can also be granted against a representative defendant (*EMI Records* v. *Kudhail*, [1985] FSR 36 (CA)) and can then be enforced against any other defendant, even if the identity of the defendant is not known, in order to confiscate from him any alleged infringing articles. Such an order has been termed "The roving *Anton Piller* Order", see P. Prescott ([1986] EIPR 58). The possibility of effecting abroad a *Saisie Description* under French law for the purpose of obtaining evidence for use in the United Kingdom has been suggested by G. W. White ((1987–88) 16 CIPA 137).

Because an *Anton Piller* Order is inevitably made *ex parte*, there is an obligation upon the plaintiff to disclose to the court *all* material facts even those adverse to the plaintiff (*Thermax* v. *Schott*, [1981] FSR 289). These facts include whether the plaintiff has the funds to meet the cross-undertaking in damages which has to be given. It also includes facts which become available after the Order was made but before it was executed (*O'Regan* v. *Iambic Productions*, *noted Financial Times*, August 2, 1989; *The Independent*, August 11, 1989). It is important to appreciate that an *Anton Piller* Order is granted at the extremity of the powers of the court and that, after 10–12 years of liberal practice, there is an increasing emphasis that such an Order is only justified when there is a paramount need to prevent a denial of justice which could not be met by an order for delivery up or preservation of the documents. Thus, the court has to be "satisfied by evidence that there is a strong probability that, if the Order is not made *ex parte*, the defendant will destroy evidence or otherwise pervert the course of justice" (*Swedac* v. *Magnet & Southerns*, [1989] FSR 243). Nevertheless, few applications for such an Order fail in practice, but the Order may be discharged, even after its execution, if the defendant shows that the Order was improperly obtained, for example because incomplete or false information was given to the judge, or if the Order was improperly executed, but the Court has a discretion not to discharge the Order or it could grant a final injunction (*Brink's-Mat* v. *Elcombe*, [1989] FSR 211 (CA)). Where the Order is discharged the plaintiff will often be required to pay costs on an enhanced basis and, probably, damages, even aggregated damages, on his cross-undertaking. This happened in *Columbia Pictures* v. *Robinson* (*supra*). An improperly executed Order can also lead to a prohibition on the use of evidence obtained thereby. (*Guess? Inc.*

v. *Lee Seck Mon* [*Hong Kong*], [1987] FSR 125) and even return of all notes made and documents taken on the execution of the Order (*VDU Installations* v. *Integrated Computer Services*, SRIS C/93/88). In *Wardle Fabrics* v. *Myristis* ([1984] FSR 263) it was pointed out that failure to comply with an *Anton Piller* Order is a contempt of court, even if the Order is subsequently discharged.

In *Columbia Pictures* v. *Robinson* (*supra*) it was laid down: that the Order must not extend beyond the minimum extent necessary to achieve its purpose; that a detailed record of material taken must be made; that all documents taken must be returned to their owners after necessary copying with retention by the *defendant's* solicitors in case of ownership dispute; that no material should be taken unless clearly covered by the terms of the Order; and that the supporting evidence should err on the side of excessive disclosure with relevance to be decided by the judge, not by the plaintiff's solicitors. Other decisions of similar effects are the *Wardle Fabrics* case (*supra*); *Jeffrey Rogers Knitwear* v. *Vinola* ([1985] FSR 186); *Booker McConnell* v. *Plascow* (*supra*; and *Piver* v. *S & J Perfume* ([1987] FSR 159). Goods seized must be returned after photographs or samples have been taken (*Dormeuil Freres* v. *Nicolian*, [1989] FSR 256).

In *International Electronics* v. *Weigh Data* ([1980] FSR 423) an *Anton Piller* Order was made in relation to evidence of alleged prior use of the invention by the patentee itself. This Order was made just before the trial and produced documents indicating forgery by a witness.

An example of a detailed *Anton Piller* Order indicating what can be obtained from it, and the safeguards which are built into it by the Court to protect the party against whom it is made, is set out, in relation to alleged breach of copyright, in *Gates* v. *Swift* ([1982] FSR 339), see also the book by R. N. Ough listed in para. 61.04 *supra*. On execution of an *Anton Piller* Order made in a dispute concerning intellectual property, a witness cannot claim privilege against self-incrimination, see para. 61.32 *infra*.

61.28 *Discovery*

The general procedure of discovery during the course of litigation in the High Court is discussed in paras. 104.06–104.09 together with the question of privilege against discovery. In patent infringement proceedings discovery is governed by RSC Ord. 104 rule 11 (reprinted at para. E104.11). Below are mentioned the more important of the cases which have in recent years considerably broadened the scope of permitted discovery in patent litigation, and the restrictions on use of the documents disclosed as a result of discovery. Initial discovery is in the hands of the party having the document and the ordering of further discovery is entirely a matter within the discretion of the court. Para. 72.44 discusses discovery in proceedings before the Comptroller, as well as the Comptroller's power to require production of documents to him under rule 106 (reprinted at para. 72.08).

The general rule is that any document in the custody, possession or power of a litigant should be disclosed to the other party if its contents are relevant to any issue in the proceedings, unless privilege for that document can be claimed. However, discovery cannot be used as a fishing exercise when there is no supporting evidence for the case put forward, see para. 61.23 *supra*.

For the purposes of discovery a document is relevant if its contents *may* enable the other party to advance its case or damage the case of the discovering party on any issue that exists between the parties having regard to the state of the pleadings. Such documents must be preserved. In *Rockwell* v. *Barrus* ([1968] 2 All ER 98) it was pointed out that solicitors must take positive steps to ensure that their clients appreciate at an early stage of the litigation, promptly after writ issue, not only the duty of discovery and its width but also the importance of not destroying documents which might possibly have to be disclosed. This burden extends to taking steps to ensure that in any corporate organisation knowledge of this burden is passed on to any who may be affected by it. In an inquiry into damages in a copyright action (*Infabrics* v. *Jaytex* [*Damages*], [1985] FSR 75) the court referred to the *Rockwell* case and admonished the Defendant for having destroyed after the start of the action, invoices and similar documents which ought to have been discovered during the damages inquiry. It would be dangerous to assume that some more punitive action will not be taken in a future case. The extent of the obligation to provide full discovery in actions involving intellectual property is well illustrated by *Format Communications* v. *ITT* ([1983] FSR 473) where the precedent cases are reviewed.

If commercial success is an issue in the action, not only must such be distinctly pleaded with particularisation (see *John Deks* v. *Aztec Washer*, [1989] RPC 413) and (para. 61.22 *supra*), but discovery of relevant documents must be given (*3M United Kingdom* v. *Angus*, (SRIS C/133/83). However, here reference was made to the sensible practice of the parties agreeing that audited summary statements should replace the primary accounting records. Frequently, before and for the purposes of the trial, the parties agree such summaries.

The limitation of discovery to documents relevant to the *pleaded* issues has been thought not to require a patentee to disclose documents which might give rise to further, as yet unpleaded, contentions of invalidity (*Belegging* v. Whitten, [1979] FSR 59). However, the practice was challenged, but not decided, in *Intel* v. *General Instruments* (SRIS C/15/89, *noted* IPD 12053), relying on the principle that interrogatories as to the existence of such documents are apparently allowable (*Edison & Swan* v. *Holland*, (1888) 5 RPC 213 (CA)).

In *Halcon* v. *Shell (Discovery No. 2)* ([1979] RPC 459) discovery of documents was ordered concerning: (a) research and development in the course of which the invention was made, because this would assist the court in deciding whether an inventive step, or little more than routine work, was involved; (b) experimental work which might show that the patentee had failed in trying to use a certain type of catalyst falling within the scope of protection which, if so, would not be without relevance to the issue of insufficiency (albeit under the 1949 Act); and (c) papers relating to the filing and prosecution of the patent, including the files of the patent agents, because the specification and claims differed from those of the basic United States patent. Items (a) and (c) represented a change in practice because hitherto it had been considered that the way in which the alleged invention was made was irrelevant and the application and prosecution papers have generally been protected from discovery, for example in *Poseidon* v. *Cerosa* ([1975] FSR 122) where it was held that these papers would not disclose any matter that would be relevant to the issues to be determined. The *Halcon* decision has also been followed in *SKM* v. *Wagner Spraytech* ([1982] RPC 497 (CA)) where it was held that the inventor's notes would be of help either offensively or defensively to the Defendant's case in several aspects and, therefore, these should be discovered even though such would lead to delay, expense and a substantial addition to the documentation of the case.

The relevance of evidence to the question of obviousness was considered at some length in *Wellcome Foundation* v. *VR Laboratories* [*Australia*] ([1982] RPC 343 (HC of Australia)). The conclusion was that evidence of research and experiments (if any) of a patentee leading up to his claimed invention is generally admissible though not always likely to be helpful. Nevertheless, because documents are discoverable if it can be said that they may fairly lead to a train of inquiry which would help to establish the case of the party seeking discovery, discovery was ordered of documents relating to research and development and to experimental work on the claimed invention but, unlike the order in *American Cyanamid* v. *Ethicon* ([1978] RPC 647), was limited to such work carried out before the priority date of the patent.

457

Now that a defence of commercial success to an allegation of invalidity due to lack of inventive step has to be distinctly pleaded (see para. 3.14), the consequence of making such a plea is that the scope of discovery will be greatly broadened to include commercially sensitive documents relating to sales data and market research information.

In *Aluma Systems* v. *Hunnebeck* ([1982] FSR 239) it was held that discovery ought to be given of all documents which would be relied upon in support of a plea of invalidity based on common general knowledge in the art and that the opposite party should not be taken by surprise by reliance on a document of this character of which no notice had been given.

The extent of discovery was further broadened by *Vickers* v. *Horsell Graphics* ([1988] RPC 421). Here the Plaintiff was ordered to produce all documents "which show or tend to show the teaching of [a prior art patent] to a man skilled in the art". Discovery was also ordered of documents which show or tend to show whether a feature of the claims can be determined to be satisfied. It was recognised that these orders would involve discovery of papers from the files of applications for corresponding foreign patents but opinions expressed, or experiments conducted, in connection with such applications, though unlikely to be conclusive, were relevant because they would assist the Defendant by disclosing the line which the Plaintiff might take in defence to an invalidity objection and the approach to the issue of infringement.

It is possible that discovery may be granted in a proper case directed to the issue of the quantum of damages even though this only strictly arises after the substantive trial of whether any infringement has occurred (*Hazeltine Corp* v. *BBC* ([1979] FSR 523)). However, in this case the discovery application was refused as burdensome to the plaintiffs and of no substantial benefit to the defendants.

Where there is a possibility of a defence to infringement based on a licence, express or implied, to supply replacement parts for a machine purchased by another from the proprietor of the patent, early discovery of the purchase contract in question may be ordered by the court (*General Electric* v. *Turbine Blading* [1980] FSR 510).

However, a party can only be ordered to produce documents which are in its custody, possession or power. Accordingly, discovery was refused in respect of documents concerned with the method of preparation used abroad for an imported alleged infringing product where the Defendant did not have any such documents and had no power under the licence from his foreign supplier to call upon him to provide these (*Unilever* v. *Gillette*, [1988] RPC 416).

61.29   *Limitation of discovery*

The court has power to order a restriction on discovery when this is likely to be injurious to one party with little prospect of it being of material service to the other at the hearing (*Carver* v. *Pinto Leite*, (1871) 7 Ch.App. 90). On this basis, discovery of names of customers has been refused when the action was initially one to determine liability for, rather than the quantum of, damages and the rights of the plaintiff to recover damages from the defendant appeared to be safeguarded (*Sega* v. *Alca Electronics*, SRIS C/108/82, *noted* IPD 7008 (CA)). Also, in *Smith Kline and French* v. *Doncaster Pharmaceuticals* ([1989] FSR 401), the court refused to order disclosure of names of customers in a case where the proprietor's damages had already been calculated. In *British Leyland* v. *Wyatt Interpart* ([1979] FSR 39), the court reduced a pleading of abuse of a dominant position contrary to TRa. 86 to a narrowly formulated issue and thereby reduced the scope of discovery.

Application for further discovery   **61.30**

Bristol-Myers' Australian Application [*Australia*] ([1980] FSR 533) illustrates the procedure that can be adopted when it is suspected that discovery given in a patent action may not be complete. Normally an affidavit of discovery is deemed conclusive, but this decision shows that a further affidavit may be ordered:
  (1) where the applicant for further discovery can identify specific documents, or a class of documents, which the pleadings, documents already discovered or other facts known to him, indicate once existed and were likely to have been in the custody, power or control of the discovering party;
  (2) where documents may exist in the hands of independent persons who had been commissioned by the discovering party to carry out relevant experimental work, in each case the court having "reasonable ground for being fairly certain" that there are other relevant documents which ought to have been disclosed; and
  (3) where the court has a "degree of certainty that the affiant of the discovery affidavit has had a mistaken view of the issues in the case so that he may have misconceived the nature of the documents that ought to have been discovered as relevant to a pleaded issue.
However, a court will not sanction further discovery if it is satisfied that the request is a fishing expedition to elicit support for a pleading not itself so far supported by more than a mere suspicion: there must be an opportunity for a party to apply to have the offending pleading struck out as having no proper basis (*RHM Foods* v. *Bovril*, [1983] RPC 275). Likewise, discovery of documents relating to corresponding foreign applications was refused when this would serve no useful purpose in relation to a plea of lack of fair basis under section 32(1)(*i*) [1949] (*Schering Agrochemicals* v. *ABM Chemicals*, [1987] RPC 185). The decision in *Avery* v. *Ashworth* ((1915) 32 RPC 560 (CA)) also prevents discovery being requested of papers from parallel actions which have been settled. This is because discovery is limited to issues which are already supported by a pleading, see *Intalite* v. *Cellular Ceilings (No. 1)* ([1987] RPC 532).

Limitation on use of documents produced on discovery   **61.31**

Documents produced to the other party as the result of the discovery process may not be used by that other party save for the purposes of that litigation and therefore they should be treated as confidential (*Alterskye* v. *Scott*, [1948] 1 All ER 469); and *Home Office* v. *Harman*, [1983] AC 280; [1982] 1 All ER 532 (HL)), though the Rules of Court now relax this rule after the contents of the documents have been disclosed in open court (RSC Ord. 24, r. 14A, reprinted at para. E024.14A), and this includes any papers read privately by the judge (*Derby* v. *Weldon*, *noted The Times*, October 20, 1988). In particular the documents may not be used in proceedings on corresponding patents in other countries where similar discovery could not be obtained under the law of that country (*Halcon* v. *Shell (Discovery)*, [1979] RPC 97), but see *Bayer* v. *Winter (No. 2)* ([1986] FSR 357) for a possible contrary case. In any event, it is possible to seek the leave of the court to make use of documents disclosed in discovery in one action for use in another action, though this will probably only be granted where the same tortious actions are involved, see *Crest Homes* v. *Marks* ([1987] 1 AC 829; [1987] 2 All ER 1074 (HL)); or where the two litigations are essentially linked as in *Wilden Pump* v. *Fusfield* [*Discovery*] ([1985] FSR 581); or where it is a matter of mere convenience without prejudice to the other party, as in *Jacques Dory* v. *Richard Wolf (No. 2)* (SRIS C/38/89). However, leave is unlikely where the parties are different, even if the information has already been given in open court, as in *CBS Songs* v. *Amstrad* ([1987] RPC 417).

Leave to use documents produced in discovery in other proceedings should be sought from the court, preferably the court seized of these other proceedings, whenever there is doubt, but leave does not appear to be necessary where an order has previously been made particularly for the purpose of identifying such persons, see *VDU Installations* v. *Integrated Computer Systems* (SRIS C/93/88), following *Sony* v. *Anand* ([1981] FSR 398).

Where discovery involves production of documents which disclose technical or financial information which would be of commercial value to the other party and would not otherwise be available to it, the court may, if it is satisfied that the restrictions automatically applied by *Alterskye* v. *Scott* (*supra*) would not adequately protect the discovering party, make a special order restricting the persons to whom the document may be shown or the use that may be made of it, see *Warner-Lambert* v. *Glaxo* ([1975] RPC 354) and other cases discussed in para. 72.44A.

61.32 *Removal of privilege against self-incrimination*

Normally a party can claim privilege against any disclosure which might incriminate it of committing a criminal offence but, in proceedings related to intellectual property, section 72 of the Supreme Court Act 1981 (c. 54) (over-ruling *Rank Film* v. *Video Information*, [1981] FSR 363 (HL)) provides that the privilege against self-incrimination cannot be invoked in such proceedings, though no statement or admission made as a result is admissable in criminal proceedings for any related offence, see the article by Shelley Lane ([1981] EIPR 300). Indeed, the privilege appears to be entirely destroyed in relation to proceedings brought to prevent an apprehended infringement of intellectual property rights of any apprehended passing off, see *Universal Studios* v. *Hubbard* ([1984] RPC 43 (CA)), even if criminal proceedings are already in being; and in contempt proceedings (*Crest Homes* v. *Marks*, [1987] 1 AC 829; [1987] 2 All ER 1074 (HL)). The question is, however, one of discretion and an order for disclosure should be made unless it would result in injustice (as distinct from disadvantage). Disclosure of the names of potential witnesses is disadvantage, not injustice (*Charles of the Ritz* v. *Jury*, [1986] FSR 14). While the Supreme Court Act extends only to England and Wales, similar provisions for Scotland and Northern Ireland appear respectively in: the Law Reform (Miscellaneous Provisions) (Scotland) Act 1985 (c. 72, s. 15); and in the Judicature (Northern Ireland) Act 1978 (c. 23, s. 94A), as inserted by the Administration of Justice Act 1982 (c. 53, Sched. 8, para. 11). In each of these provisions "intellectual property" is now defined as "any patent, trade mark, service mark, copyright, registered design, design right, technical or commercial information or other intellectual property", this definition having been amended by: section 2(2) [1986] and Schedule 2, paragraph 1(2)(*h*) [1986] and by Schedule 7, paragraphs. 25, 28 and 32 [1988]. The term "design right" includes rights in a "semiconductor topography" (S.I. 1989 No. 1100).

61.33 *Inspection*

As part of the pre-trial procedure it is possible to obtain an order for inspection of the defendant's premises. However, such is not obtainable on mere suspicion that infringement may be taking place: a prima facie case must first be established, see *British Xylonite* v. *Fibrenyle* ([1959] RPC 252) and *Wahl* v. *Bühler-Miag* ([1979] FSR 183). Nevertheless, in a suitable case, inspection of an alleged infringing process can be carried out even before service of an adequate statement of claim

(*Unilever* v. *Pearce*, [1985] FSR 475). Here the inspection was in confidence and the Plaintiff's representatives were required to supply to the Defendant a report of its inspection, a patent agent employed by the Plaintiffs being permitted to attend in his professional capacity. For discussion on restriction of disclosure of confidential information in circumstances of restricted disclosure, see para. 72.44A.

If a defendant alleges prior use he must not only plead specific details thereof (see RSC Ord. 104 r. 6(3), reprinted in para. E104.6, and para. 61.22 *supra*), but he must permit inspection of the prior user apparatus, etc., if such be still in his possession (RSC Ord. 104, r. 16(3), reprinted in para. E104.16).

Admissions and interrogatories   **61.34**

RSC Ord. 27 (for which see paras. E027.1–E027.4) permits a party to litigation to serve upon the other a "Notice to admit facts". If admissions are not made as so requested, which the court eventually decides ought reasonably to have been made, a penalty in costs may ensue. Such notices are thought to be particularly important in patent proceedings, see RSC Ord. 104, rule 10 (reprinted at para. E104.10).

A further possible aspect of pre-trial procedure is an order to answer interrogatories. These are written questions submitted by one party to be answered by a responsible officer of the other party. However, interrogatories can only be administered with the leave of the court (RSC Ord. 26, r. 1, reprinted at para. E026.1) and such will only be given if the interrogatories are regarded as necessary for disposing fairly of the action and will not be ordered as part of a fishing exercise. Thus, it has been held that a plaintiff is entitled to interrogate a defendant as to facts which tend to support the plaintiff's case or imperil the defendant's case, but not as to facts which support the defendant's case, see the copyright case of *Rockwell* v. *Serck* [*Interrogatories*] ([1988] FSR 187).

Experiments   **61.35**

Experiments, the results of which are to be given in evidence, will normally be required to be repeated in the presence of representatives of the other party if a request therefor is made, see RSC Ord. 104, rule 12 (reprinted at para. E104.12) and the specimen *Summons for Directions* reprinted at para. E104.14A. The court will be reluctant to make an Order which excludes particular persons from observing that repetition, see *Gore* v. *Kimmal* (SRIS C/51/83, *noted* IPD 6023).

In *Roussel-Uclaf* v. *ICI*, ([1989] RPC 59 (CA)) experiments, which involved the repetition by the Plaintiff's expert witness of the Defendant's secret process disclosed to him (and to the Plaintiff's legal advisers) under a strict order of confidentiality (for which see para. 72.44A), were ordered to be conducted within the jurisdiction of the court in order that the court could be in a position to impose sanctions if any breach of the confidentiality order should occur.

An order for experiments can contain a direction that the party performing the experiment should give details of the facts which he claims to be able to establish thereby (*Van der Lely* v. *Watweare*, [1982] FSR 122). In this case it was also observed that the party need only give a reasonable account of facts which he says the experiment establishes and, if it later comes to his attention, without prejudice or detriment to the other party, that the experiments he has done do establish some other facts, then he will of course be at liberty to seek an application to amend the notice of experiments and such an application ought to be received with the greatest judicial sympathy.

61.36 *Evidence*

No evidence can be given unless it relates to an issue on the pleadings, see RSC Ord. 104, rule 16 (reprinted at para. E104.16). This may preclude the presentation of evidence of commercial success of the invention if such has not been pleaded as required by RSC Ord. 104, rule 6(5) (reprinted in para. E014.6). Also, if opinion evidence by an expert is to be offered, prior notice of the name(s) thereof must be given before the Summons for Directions (RSC Ord. 104, r. 13, reprinted at para. E104.13). The court can then order a pre-trial exchange of expert's reports. There are indications that the Patent's Court may increasingly require this in a move towards a greater use of a partly written, rather than an almost wholly oral, procedure.

Though the rules of court permit the parties to agree that evidence in chief shall be presented in affidavit form with liberty to call a witness for examination on his affidavit, this mode of giving evidence is unusual in infringement and validity proceedings, though it is the normal style in interlocutory proceedings, in amendment proceedings and in an enquiry as to damages. Otherwise, evidence for each party is given orally in court with, at least hitherto, little opportunity for the other party to the litigation to have foreknowledge of the type of evidence that may be given or who the witnesses giving it may be. However, the Civil Evidence Acts 1968 (c. 64) and 1972 (c. 30) allow a party to put in written statements as evidence, see RSC Ord. 38, rule 2 (reprinted at para. E038.2). Such statements must usually be served within 21 days of the Action being set down for trial, unless the court otherwise grants leave. Note on this point that a case is normally "set down" for trial some considerable time before the trial takes place. Such statements are usually from persons abroad or others whom it is impracticable to call. However, in *Genentech's Patent* (SRIS C/66/87), leave was given to put in evidence at the trial "all statements contained in the documents disclosed by the defendants on discovery". Nevertheless, a witness, even if an expert, may not give his opinion on a matter which the court has to decide, *e.g.* on whether a patent claim is infringed or invalid. On these points, see the article by W. L. Hayhurst ((1982–83) 12 CIPA 191) and the cases cited therein.

Since the making in 1986 of new rule 2A under RSC Order 38 (reprinted at para. E038.2A), it has been increasingly common for orders to be made (often on the hearing of the Summons for Directions) requiring a party to serve on the other, by a specified pre-trial date, written statements of the oral evidence which it intends to lead at the trial on specified issues, with such statements admissable at the trial if the witness does not then appear. However, such statements are not (unless expressly so stated) to be treated as notices under the Civil Evidence Acts (for which see *supra*). If the ordered service does not take place, the party in default can only adduce evidence on the issue in question with the leave of the court. With this procedure, the element of surprise in the evidence to be presented at trial should become much reduced. Also, the form of Order on the Summons for Directions (for which see para. E104.14A) contains (in para. 12) provision for prior notice to be given by a party wishing to rely at the trial upon any "model, apparatus, drawing, photograph or cinematographic film". In *H & R Johnson Tiles* v. *Candy Tiles* ([1985] FSR 253) a party was forbidden to rely at trial on certain photographs where such notice was only served a few days prior to trial.

61.37 *Security for costs*

The court can order a foreign plaintiff; or (under the Companies Act 1985, c. 6, s. 726(1)), a corporate plaintiff who may be unable to pay the defendant's costs, to give security for costs in any litigation which he chooses to bring in the English courts. If the security ordered is not produced within the time set, the action can be dismissed, see *Speed Up Holdings* v. *Gough* ([1986] FSR 330). It is nowadays customary to give security by way of a bank guarantee, or by an indemnity given by a local company with adequate assets to meet a likely award of costs. An application for security from a corporate plaintiff failed in *Spark Tee* v. *Sarclad* (SRIS C/11/89), it not being established that the Plaintiff would be unable to meet an award of costs against it.

In *Meijer* v. *Taylor* ([1981] FSR 279) an argument that security for costs should not be ordered in the case of an action for patent infringement by a plaintiff from another EEC country was rejected and the giving of security was ordered, there being no special circumstances for departing from the normal rule. Security for costs was also ordered in *Compagnie Française de Television* v. *Thorn* ([1981] FSR 306). Then, in *Mom Marcy* v. *Surinstyle* (SRIS C/21/87) it was argued, unsuccessfully, that an EEC plaintiff should not be required to provide security for costs because the Brussels Convention of 1968 (enacted into British law by the Civil Jurisdiction and Judgments Act 1982 (c. 27)) would make a court order to pay costs directly enforceable in the plaintiff's own country. However, this Convention is one of the factors to be taken into account and, in *Porzelack KG* v. *Porzelack (UK)* ([1987] FSR 353), security was not ordered for this reason and also because it was not certain that the defendants would be awarded costs even if successful. For comment on these two cases, see [1987] EIPR D-54. Also, since a plaintiff of United Kingdom residence is not normally required to provide security for costs, it is possible that the first above-mentioned argument might now succeed on the rationale of the decision in *Allen & Hanburys (Case 434/85)* ([1988] 1 CMLR 701; [1988] FSR 312 (ECJ)), for which see Appendix C at para. C15.

Procedure at trial   **61.38**

In cases of technical complexity it is customary to place a scientific "primer" before the court, agreed between the parties as far as possible but otherwise indicating the rival contentions, for example as to the meaning of scientific nomenclature, see *Olin Mathieson* v. *Biorex* ([1970] RPC 157). A further case where a primer was produced was *Akzo* v. *Du Pont* (SRIS C/43/88).

For the appointment of a scientific adviser to assist the court, see para. 96.25 and RSC Ord. 104, rule 15 (reprinted at para. E104.15).

A court can sit *in camera* and routinely does so in applications for an *Anton Piller* Order. However, otherwise good cause must be shown for this, as in *Akzo* v. *Du Pont* (*supra*) where evidence on the chemical process used by the Defendant was heard in closed court. For restrictions on disclosure of information to the parties themselves or to their legal advisers, see para. 72.44A.

SECTION 62   **62.01**

Restrictions on recovery of damages for infringement

62.—(1) In proceedings for infringement of a patent damages shall not be awarded, and no order shall be made for an account of profits, against a defendant or defender who proves that at the date of the infringement he was not aware, and had no reasonable grounds for supposing, that the patent existed; and a person shall not be taken to have been so aware or to have had reasonable grounds for so supposing by reason only of the application to a product of the word "patented", or any word or words expressing or implying that a patent has been obtained for the product, unless the number of the patent accompanied the word or words in question.

(2) In proceedings for infringement of a patent the court or the comptroller may, if it or he thinks fit, refuse to award any damages or make any such order in respect of an infringement committed during any further period specified under section 25(4) above, but before the payment of the renewal fee and any additional fee prescribed for the purposes of that subsection.

(3) Where an amendment of the specification of a patent has been allowed under any of the provisions of this Act, no damages shall be awarded in proceedings for an infringement of the patent committed before the decision to allow the amendment unless the court or the comptroller is satisfied that the specification of the patent as published was framed in good faith and with reasonable skill and knowledge.

COMMENTARY ON SECTION 62

62.02   *General*

Section 62 is closely similar to section 59 [1949] and concerns relief from damages in the diverse circumstances set out in its three subsections. The section applies to "existing patents" (Sched. 4, para. 3(2)).

62.03   *Innocent infringement (subs. (1))*

By subsection (1) an award of damages, or an order for an account of profits, cannot be made against an innocent infringer, that is against a person who proves (and the onus is upon him so to do) that "at the date of the infringement he was not aware, and had no reasonable grounds for supposing, that the patent existed". Marking with the word "patented" is insufficient unless the patent number is included in the marking. The onus would appear to be a heavy one, see *Lancer v. Henley Forklift* ([1975] RPC 307) and *Benmax v. Austin* ((1953) 70 RPC 143 and 284). False marking is dealt with by section 110, see the commentary thereon. By section 69(1), the operation of subsection (1) applies equally to proceedings for infringement of the rights conferred by publication of an application. Ignorance of the patent may be raised in infringement proceedings before the court (or the Comptroller in proceedings under s. 61(3), see s. 61(4)).

However, subsection (1) has no application where an infringer is unaware that his actions amount to infringement: subsection (1) only concerns his ignorance of the *existence* of the patent. Ignorance of the former kind can be quite common when use is made of a proprietory product, the composition of which is not known to the user.

62.04   *Lost rights after restoration or late renewal (subs. (2))*

Subsection (2) gives the court or the Comptroller discretionary power to refuse to award damages, or make an order for an account of profits, in respect of an infringement committed between the end of the period prescribed under section 25(3) for payment of a renewal fee and the payment of the fee within the following six months prescribed by section 25(4). For loss of rights prior to restoration, see section 28A and the commentary thereon.

Damages after amendment (subs. (3))   **62.05**

Subsection (3) refers to the case where the specification of the patent has previously been amended. For the position where a previously unamended patent is found infringed but only partially valid, see section 63 and the commentary thereon. Under subsection (3) damages (but not apparently an account of profits) can be refused to the proprietor in respect of infringements committed before amendment, unless the court or Comptroller is satisfied that the patent specification as published, was framed in good faith and with reasonable skill and knowledge. The requirement under subsection (3) to show that a specification was originally framed with reasonable skill and knowledge is discussed more fully in para. 63.03. The onus of proof is placed on the proprietor, who will probably need to offer testimony by the patent draftsman, see para. 63.03. However such proof can be avoided if the proprietor elects for an account of profits rather than damages (*Codex* v. *Racal-Milgo*, [1983] RPC 369).

The corresponding section 59(3) [1949] refers to amendment "allowed under the provisions of this Act". Because amendment of an existing patent continues to take place under the 1949 Act, it may be that section 59 [1949] continues to apply to existing patents under Schedule 1, para. 1(2), though the point is probably pedantic in view of the similarity between section 59(3) [1949] and section 62(3) [1949]. However, it may be noted that the 1977 Act does not contain the provision of section 31(2) [1949] permitting challenge of an amendment shown to have been obtained by fraud.

Section 62 does not re-enact section 59(4) [1949] stating that section 59 [1949] did not prevent the court from granting an injunction. This must, of cousre, still be so since the grant of an injunction is always within the inherent jurisdiction of the court. Nevertheless, the deletion of section 59(4) [1949] may suggest that in appropriate cases the court could refuse to grant an injunction so that operations could continue, for example where heavy capital expenditure had been incurred in erecting plant to operate a patented process when at the time there was ignorance of the existence of the patent.

SECTION 63   63.01

Relief for infringement of partially valid patent

63.—(1) If the validity of a patent is put in issue in proceedings for infringement of the patent and it is found that the patent is only partially valid, the court or the comptroller may, subject to subsection (2) below, grant relief in respect of that part of the patent which is found to be valid and infringed.

(2) Where in any such proceedings it is found that a patent is only partially valid, the court or the comptroller shall not grant relief by way of damages, costs or expenses, except where the plaintiff or pursuer proves that the specification for the patent was framed in good faith and with reasonable skill and knowledge, and in that event the court or the comptroller may grant relief in respect of that part of the patent which is valid

and infringed, subject to the discretion of the court or the comptroller as to costs or expenses and as to the date from which damages should be reckoned.

(3) As a condition of relief under this section the court or the comptroller may direct that the specification of the patent shall be amended to its or his satisfaction upon an application made for that purpose under section 75 below, and an application may be so made accordingly, whether or not all other issues in the proceedings have been determined.

COMMENTARY ON SECTION 63

63.02 *General*

Section 63 concerns the relief to be granted in respect of a partially valid patent and applies to "existing patents" (Sched. 4, para. 3(2)). The section is closely similar to section 62 [1949] and provides (in analogous manner to the case where the patent had previously been amended, for which see s. 62 and the commentary thereon) that relief by way of damages and costs (expenses in Scotland) may be granted in respect of the valid part of the patent (subs. (1)), but only (according to subs. (2)) where the plaintiff (pursuer in Scotland) proves (and the onus is upon him so to do) that the specification was framed in good faith and with reasonable skill and knowledge.

Amendment of the patent may be required as a condition for relief under the section (subs. (3)); and, in *Hallen* v. *Brabantia* ([1989] RPC 307), the question of relief on a patent found infringed but only partially valid was adjourned for the Plaintiff to offer evidence that the specification had been drafted in good faith and with reasonable skill and knowledge. The responsible patent agent then gave evidence and the court held (SRIS C/40/89) that the specification had been framed honestly to obtain a monopoly to which the agent felt the applicant was entitled on the facts known to him. The criterion of reasonable skill and knowledge was also satisfied when the reasonable person was someone with reasonable skill in drafting patent specifications and a knowledge of patent law and practice. The Plaintiff was then held entitled to full damages, the Defendant having received legal advice that he was at risk and there being no special circumstances. In this case it was also held that, because a claim is now a bundle of notional claims (if necessary having different priority dates, see s. 125(2) and para. 125.21), a claim dependent on an invalid claim is not itself invalid prior to amendment so that relief can be granted thereon without amendment first being required.

Section 62 [1949] referred to relief on any claim found valid despite other claims being held invalid. The present section refers to a "partially valid patent". Thus, it may no longer be sufficient to obtain an interlocutory injunction to sue only on some claims and argue that the validity of claims not sued upon is irrelevant, as was done in *Hoffmann-La Roche* v. *DDSA* ([1965] RPC 503).

The validity of the patent may only arise in the types of proceedings specified in section 74, on the grounds given in section 72, or in the case mentioned in section 77(3) where, after proceedings for infringment of a European patent have been commenced before the court or the Comptroller but have not finally been disposed of, it is established in proceedings before the EPO that the patent is only partially valid.

Section 63 applies in proceedings before the Comptroller under section 61(3) (s. 61(4)), but section 63 is not referred to in section 69(1) and, therefore, does not apply to rights conferred by publication of an application.

Effect of section 63   **63.03**

Subsection (2) does not, apparently, affect the grant of an injunction, or an account of profits (see *Codex* v. *Racal-Milgo*, [1983] RPC 369). Both are discretionary remedies, see paras. 61.12 and 61.15, so that, for example, an injunction could be refused where there had been a lack of good faith.

It is usual to offer as a witness the agent who drafted the specification, see *Page* v. *Brent Toy Products* ((1950) 67 RPC 4) and *Hallen* v. *Brabantia* (SRIS C/40/89), but this is not essential (*Lucas* v. *Gaedor*, [1978] RPC 297). There is lack of reasonable skill and knowledge where the patent agent departed in a material (and erroneous) respect from the instruction of the applicant (*Ronson* v. *Lewis*, [1963] RPC 103). The question of good faith and reasonable skill and knowledge should normally be considered at the same hearing as an application to amend the patent (*Kahn (David)* v. *Conway Stewart*, [1974] RPC 279; and *Hallen* v. *Brabantia*, *supra*). These cases also show some of the factual circumstances in which a plea of lack of good faith, etc., has failed, but it succeeded in *Ronson* v. *Lewis* (*supra*).

Direction of amendment as condition of relief on partially valid patent (subs. (3))   **63.04**

Subsection (3) corresponds to section 62(3) [1949]. It provides that the court (or the Comptroller in proceedings under s. 61(3), see s. 61(4)) in addition to having a discretion as to costs and damages, may impose as a condition for the granting of relief under section 63 a direction that the patent be amended. A similar condition can be imposed under section 72(4) when, in an application for revocation, the patent is found only partially invalid, see para. 72.27. Under the 1949 Act, a distinction was drawn, in allowing amendment of a specification found only partially valid, between mere excision of claims (permitted) and more extreme amendment (disallowed), see para. 75.06. Amendment may be made subject to conditions, see para. 75.07. If discretion for amendment of a patent is refused (for an example of which see *Autoliv Development's Patent*, [1988] RPC 425), it would appear that no relief could then be granted under such a patent. In *Hallen* v. *Brabantia* (SRIS C/40/89) the order for amendment was stayed pending the disposition of the Patentee's appeal against the decision of partial invalidity ([1989] RPC 307).

SECTION 64 [Prospectively substituted]   **64.01**

Right to continue use begun before priority date

64.—(1) Where a patent is granted for an invention, a person who in the United Kingdom before the priority date of the invention—

    (*a*) **does in good faith an act which would constitute an infringement of the patent if it were in force, or**

    (*b*) **makes in good faith effective and serious preparations to do such an act,**

has the right to continue to do the act or, as the case may be, to do the act, notwithstanding the grant of the patent; but this right does not extend to granting a licence to another person to do the act.

(2) If the act was done, or the preparations were made, in the course of a business, the person entitled to the right conferred by subsection (1) may—

467

(*a*) authorise the doing of that act by any partners of his for the time being in that business, and

(*b*) assign that right, or transmit it on death (or in the case of a body corporate on its dissolution), to any person who acquires that part of the business in the course of which the act was done or the preparations were made.

(3) Where a product is disposed of to another in exercise of the rights conferred by subsection (1) or (2), that other and any person claiming through him may deal with the product in the same way as if it had been disposed of by the registered proprietor of the patent.

Note. Section 64 was prospectively substituted by Schedule 5 paragraph 17 [1988]. For the commencement of the substituted section, see the latest Supplement to this Work *re.* this para.

64.02   SECTION 64 [Prospectively replaced]

Before its substitution, as indicated in the preceding para., section 64 was in the form:

[**64.**—(1) *Where a patent is granted for an invention, a person who in the United Kingdom before the priority date of the invention does in good faith an act which would constitute an infringement of the patent if it were in force, or makes in good faith effective and serious preparations to do such an act, shall have the rights conferred by subsection (2) below.*

(2) *Any such person shall have the right—*

(*a*) *to continue to do or, as the case may be, to do that act himself; and*

(*b*) *if it was done or preparations had been made to do it in the course of a business, to assign the right to do it or to transmit that right on his death or, in the case of a body corporate on its dissolution, to any person who acquires that part of the business in the course of which the act was done or preparations had been made to do it, or to authorise it to be done by any partners of his for the time being in that business;*

and the doing of that act by virtue of this subsection shall not amount to an infringement of the patent concerned.

(3) *The rights mentioned in subsection (2) above shall not include the right to grant a licence to any person to do an act so mentioned.*

(4) *Where a patented product is disposed of by any person to another in exercise of a right conferred by subsection (2) above, that other and any person claiming through him shall be entitled to deal with the product in the same way as if it had been disposed of by a sole registered proprietor.*]

64.03   ARTICLES

A. W. White, "Transitional provisions of the UK Patents Act", [1983] EIPR 5; Helen Jones, "Made available", (1985–86) 15 CIPA 342.

COMMENTARY ON SECTION 64

General **64.04**

Section 64 establishes the rights of a person to continue to carry out acts which were first done before the priority date of a patent, and which would be infringements if the patent were in force.

An important application of the section is to give rights in respect of secret prior use. Unlike the practice under section 32(1)(*l*) [1949], and in harmony with EPC, secret prior use is not a ground of invalidity under the 1977 Act. By section 2(1) an invention is new if it does not form part of the prior art, defined in section 2(2) as all matter which has been made available to the public, thus excluding secret use. Under section 64, though any such use does not invalidate the patent, continuation of the use is permitted as a matter of right, though on a personal basis only. The effect and scope of the section are discussed in the paper by Helen Jones listed in para. 64.03 *supra*.

The present wording of the section (substituted as indicated in the note to para. 64.01 *supra*) is clearer than that of the original provision, but probably does not affect its scope. The revision to be made was a consequence of the like prospective revision of section 28, introducing a new section 28A dealing with personal rights which arise after a restoration of a patent. Clearly, the two sections are interrelated in that each provides for a third party right detracting from the monopoly right of the patent in certain circumstances. For present purposes the new wording is presumed already to be in effect, but for its commencement see the latest Supplement to this Work *re.* this para.

Scope of the section **64.05**

The prior acts (defined in subs. (1)) which give rise to rights (as defined in subss. (2) and (3)) must have been carried out in good faith, and are acts: (*a*) which, if the patent had been in force, would be an infringement thereof; or (*b*) were acts of preparation therefor which were effective and serious. The need for good faith presumably excludes use based on information obtained from the patenteee, or another, without consent. Good faith is not defined in the 1977 Act but it is an expression of wide legal application. "Effective" and "serious" in relation to preparations are also not defined, but the words are also used in section 28A(4)(*b*) in respect of acts giving rights under a restored patent, see para. 28A.06.

In many cases, where acts done before the priority date of a patent are done in a manner which makes them part of the state of the art, those acts will provide a basis of invalidity of the patent, but even in such cases the existence of the statutory right affords a direct and indisputable defence to any allegations of infringements by later acts. When such later acts are merely repetitions of the prior act; it matters not whether the acts are secret or not. The right of continued use is personal and can be assigned (or transmitted on death or dissolution) only in the circumstances set out in subsection (2)(*b*) and cannot be licensed because of the final words of subsection (1), though (by subs. (3)) disposal of a product carries with it an implied licence for further dealings in that product. This provision is analogous to the doctrine of "exhaustion of rights", under which the patentee cannot prevent further dealings in respect of a product resulting from the invention first put on the market, within the EEC, by him or his licensee, see Appendix C at para. C15.

Subsections (2) and (3) are to be in the same terms as section 28A(5) and (6) respectively, which relate to third party rights arising on the restoration of patents and are discussed in paras. 28A.03–28A.06. There is no obvious reason why the two sets of provisions should not be construed in the same way.

It appears likely that a difficulty which will occur in practice under section 64 is the question of how far an act done after the priority date of the patent is the same as the act done before that date; as to this there is no guide in the section or in section 28A, but see para. 28A.05. It would be an absurdity to limit the right of continuation to that which was in all respects identical with the act done before the priority date, so that some variation at least must be envisaged, but the degree of variation is indefinite. Possibly the act might be the operation of a process or apparatus, or the "disposal" of a product, but this is speculation, and see also the paper by Helen Jones listed in para. 64.03 *supra*.

A difficulty also arises with the right to "continue" to do an act, and to what extent, if any, the right extends to repeat an act after an interval of time. Again, it might be absurd in practical terms to limit the right to continuation only, and to extinguish the right if there is any cessation of the act, but there is no guide as to whether it was the intention of the legislature to treat such cases liberally or not. Past decisions on the meaning of continuity may not therefore be relevant. The question whether an act is a "continuing" one has been considered under the transitional provisions (of Sched. 4, para. 3) in relation to section 60 (*Infringement*), see *Rotocrop* v. *Genbourne* ([1982] FSR 241).

64.06 *No prior use right arises from act which would not be "infringement"*

It is important to note that section 64 only provides rights where the prior act, actual or contemplated, would have been an act of "infringement" if the patent had been in force. Thus, prior acts of Crown use, or preparations therefor, under section 55 do not give rise to third party rights under the section as such would not be acts of "infringement, see para. 55.03.

Also excluded are acts which fall within the exclusions to infringement set out in section 60(5)–(7), for which see paras. 60.18–60.23. A particular problem arises here in connection with acts which were "done privately and for purposes which are not commercial" (excluded by s. 60(5)(*a*) and discussed in para. 60.19); or which were "done for experimental purposes", which section 60(5)(*b*) only excludes if such purposes related "to the subject-matter of the invention" (as discussed in para. 60.20). However, even if the acts carried out before the priority date were not (by virtue of these provisions) themselves to be considered as "infringing" ones, they could still be regarded as "serious and effective preparations" to do an infringing act. Mere experiment in the hope of obtaining some result which could then be exploited commercially would not, it is submitted, amount to "effective" preparations to do an "infringing" (commercial) act. Indeed "effective preparations" seems to suggest a settled intention to do an act already proven to have commercial potential.

64.07 *Application to "existing patents"*

As discussed in the article by A. W. White listed in para. 64.03 *supra*, it is not exactly clear what effect (if any) section 64 has in relation to "existing patents". By Schedule 4, para. 3(2), subsections 60–71 are to apply to acts of infringement taking place after June 1, 1978. However, where such an act is one that was also carried out before the priority date of the patent claim, it will usually rank as prior public or secret user invalidating the patent under section 32(1)(*e*) or (*l*) [1949] and there will be no infringement of the patent since no invalid patent can be infringed (*Pittevil* v. *Brackelberg*, (1932) 49 RPC 23). In such a situation section 64 may have no effect; nevertheless the defendant will usually be protected by the invalidity of the patent if the circumstances were such as would bring section 64 into play in respect of a patent granted under the Act. As indicated in para. 64.06 *supra*, section 64 can have no applicability if the prior act was one which is excluded from consideration as an act of infringement by the terms of section 60(5), or because it constitutes Crown use under section 55, though here the prior act will probably not be sufficient to invalidate the existing patent having regard to the terms of sections 32(1)(*l*) and 32(2)(*a*), (*b*) and (*c*) [1949]. Consequently, a defendant who can only prove a prior act of such a nature would probably find himself with no defence either of invalidity or under section 64.

However, even more difficult is the case where the prior act was not carried out but the defendant made "in good faith effective and serious preparations to do such an act", *i.e.* an act of infringement. Clearly, if the defendant's prior act had been of the type contemplated in section 32(2)(*c*) [1949], this would not be an act carried out in good faith and then again section 64 would provide no protection to a defendant, but in other cases it may be argued that section 64 does provide protection to a defendant, but only provided that the defendant proves that prior to the priority date the preparations he had made were to do an act of infringement, *i.e.* something not excluded by section 60(5) or an act of Crown user.

Even then, against that position, there can be put the argument that the Act cannot, in the absence of clear words (and certainly the words of Sched. 4, para. 3(2) are far from clear in relation to their applicability to s. 64) be interpreted to take away an accrued right; that is the right to an injunction which clearly existed prior to June 1, 1978 because Schedule 4, para. 3(2) has no effect in relation to alleged acts of infringement committed before that date. While in *Therm-a-Stor* v. *Weatherseal* ([1981] FSR 579 (CA)) it was the Court of Appeal stated that paragraph 3(2) plainly seeks to apply the specified sections to any question which arises as to acts done after the appointed day and which are alleged to be infringements of the patent, it was also said then that the paragraph will be "subject to any modifications which would be inappropriate or inapplicable having regard to the inescapable fact that what has to be dealt with is an infringement of a 1949 Act patent".

The subject of "accrued right" in relation to the transitional provisions of the Act is discussed further in para. 127.09.

SECTION 65

65.01

Certificate of contested validity of patent

65.—(1) If in any proceedings before the court or the comptroller the validity of a patent to any extent is contested and that patent is found by the court or the comptroller to be wholly or partially valid, the court or the comptroller may certify the finding and the fact that the validity of the patent was so contested.

(2) Where a certificate is granted under this section, then, if in any subsequent proceedings before the court or the comptroller for infringement of the patent concerned or for revocation of the patent a final order or judgment or interlocutor is made or given in favour of the party relying on the validity of the patent as found in the earlier proceedings, that party shall, unless the court or the comptroller otherwise directs, be entitled to his costs or expenses as between solicitor and own client (other than the costs or expenses of any appeal in the subsequent proceedings).

COMMENTARY ON SECTION 65

65.02   *General*

Section 65 provides for the grant of a certificate of contested validity (subs. (1)) and specifies the effect of such a certificate (subs. (2)). The section is broader than the corresponding section 64 [1949] (see para. 65.03 *infra*), but does not apply to revocation proceedings brought against existing patents under section 33 [1949] (as amended), see para. 65.05 *infra*.

65.03   *Grant of certificate of contested validity (subs. (1))*

Section 65 is broader than section 64 [1949] in that the certificate may now be granted by the Comptroller as well as by the court. The grant of the certificate is discretionary, but may be given in any proceedings in which validity of the patent was contested and found wholly or partially valid. The certificate may be qualified by reference to the grounds, or to particular claims, upon which the validity was contested. The mere fact that validity was in issue is not sufficient since the certificate is granted in respect of *contested* validity. Thus, where validity was conceded during the course of a trial, but after full argument and evidence, a certificate of validity was granted (by a Scottish court) even though no decision on validity was required to be given (*Brupat* v. *Smith*, [1985] FSR 156). However, the Patents Court has refused, in its discretion, to grant such a certificate where an application for revocation failed (*Moseley Rubber's Patent*, SRIS C/67/86).

The required contest may take place in the context of any of the proceedings listed in section 74(1).

65.04   *Effect of certificate of contested validity (subs. (2))*

Subsection (2) provides that, if a proprietor successfully relies upon the finding of validity made in earlier proceedings in which a certificate of contested validity was given, he shall (unless it is specifically directed otherwise) be entitled to his costs (expenses in Scotland) "as between solicitor and own client" on final order at first instance in the subsequent proceedings, though not on any appeal therefrom. The quoted words are no longer used as such, costs now being awarded on either the "standard basis" (for which see paras. E062.3 and E062.12) or on the "indemnity basis" (for which see RSC Ord. 62, r. 15, reprinted at para. E062.15). Thus, presumably, following a certificate under section 65, costs will now be awarded on the indemnity basis as this is used on taxation of a solicitor's bill to his own client.

A certificate of contested validity is a powerful deterrent and its availability now from an unsuccessful revocation application brought before the Comptroller under section 72 may make these proceedings less attractive than they would otherwise be, though no formal estoppel arises as regards the issues raised in that application, see section 72(5). There is also incentive for a proprietor to bring initial proceedings against an infringer of little financial substance in the hope that his challenge to validity will not be so strongly pressed as other infringers may do, but nevertheless sufficient to obtain a certificate of contested validity effective as a deterrent against more formidable defendants. It should here be noted that such initial infringement action could well take place before the Comptroller under section 61(3) where the advantage of obtaining a certificate under section 65 for future use in proceedings against others may outweigh the disadvantage of proceedings under that provision, for which see para. 61.19.

Application of section 65 to "existing patents"   **65.05**

In *Canon K.K.'s Patent* ([1982] RPC 549) the Patents Court held that section 65 has no applicability to "existing patents" because Schedule 4, para. 3(2) applies only to acts of "infringement", whereas section 65 refers to "proceedings" and section 65 is not listed in Schedule 2, para. 1(2) so that the term "patent" is limited by section 130(1) to one granted under the Act. Consequently, there is no power to grant a certificate of contested validity in revocation proceedings under section 33 [1949] (as amended). For "existing patents," section 64 [1949] continues to have effect (Sched. 1, para. 1(2)), but under that provision only the court may grant the certificate and, as noted above, the effect thereof is limited to an entitlement to costs "as between solicitor and client", though that term no longer applies so that, presumably, costs would now also be awarded on the indemnity basis following a certificate under section 64 [1949].

PRACTICE UNDER SECTION 65   **65.06**

When the court grants a certificate of contested validity an office copy of the court order should be filed at the Patent Office. Notice thereof will then be published in the O.J. (*e.g.* as in O.J. August 2, 1989).

SECTION 66   **66.01**

Proceedings for infringement by a co-owner

66.—(1) In the application of section 60 above to a patent of which there are two or more joint proprietors the reference to the proprietor shall be construed—

(*a*) in relation to any act, as a reference to that proprietor or those proprietors who, by virtue of section 36 above or any agreement referred to in that section, is or are entitled to do that act without its amounting to an infringement; and

(*b*) in relation to any consent, as a reference to that proprietor or those proprietors who, by virtue of section 36 above or any such agreement, is or are the proper person or persons to give the requisite consent.

(2) One of two or more joint proprietors of a patent may without the concurrence of the others being proceedings in respect of an act alleged to infringe the patent, but shall not do so unless the others are made parties to the proceedings; but any of the others made a defendant or defender shall not be liable for any costs or expenses unless he enters an appearance and takes part in the proceedings.

COMMENTARY ON SECTION 66   **66.02**

Section 66 defines the position of joint proprietors in relation to infringement proceedings. It applies to "existing patents" (Sched. 4, para. 3(2)). The section complements the provisions of section 36 which defines the rights, *inter se*, of patent co-owners, see the commentary thereon.

By subsection (1) a reference in section 60 to a proprietor in respect of a patent of which there are two or more proprietors is to be taken as meaning, in the absence of agreement to the contrary, the proprietor or proprietors who by section 36 would be entitled to do the appropriate act or give the appropriate consent to the use of the patent. Although the provision is new in terms, it is not apparent that any difficulties are likely to occur in practice.

Subsection (2) gives a joint proprietor a statutory right by himself to bring infringement proceedings provided that the other proprietors are made parties to the proceedings, at least as nominal defendants; they are not then liable for costs (expenses in Scotland) if they do not enter an appearance. Previously a similar practice obtained, see *Turner* v. *Bowman* ((1925) 42 RPC 29). The object of this provision is to ensure that all co-owners of a patent are given notice of infringement proceedings brought by any one of them.

67.01

SECTION 67

Proceedings for infringement by exclusive licensee

67.—(1) Subject to the provisions of this section, the holder of an exclusive licence under a patent shall have the same right as the proprietor of the patent to bring proceedings in respect of any infringement of the patent committed after the date of the licence; and references to the proprietor of the patent in the provisions of this Act relating to infringement shall be construed accordingly.

(2) In awarding damages or granting any other relief in any such proceedings the court or the comptroller shall take into consideration any loss suffered or likely to be suffered by the exclusive licensee as such as a result of the infringement, or, as the case may be, the profits derived from the infringement, so far as it constitutes an infringement of the rights of the exclusive licensee as such.

(3) In any proceedings taken by an exclusive licensee by virtue of this section the proprietor of the patent shall be made a party to the proceedings, but if made a defendant or defender shall not be liable for any costs or expenses unless he enters an appearance and takes part in the proceedings.

Commentary on Section 67

67.02   *General*

Section 67 gives the holder of an exclusive licence the same power as the proprietor of the patent to sue for infringement occurring after the date of the licence, and the word "proprietor" throughout the Act is to be construed (in relation to infringement) accordingly (subs. (1)). The exclusive licensee may then be awarded damages (or an account of profits) for infringement of his rights as exclusive licensee (subs. (2)). The proprietor is to be made a party to the proceedings, at least as a nominal defendant; he is not, however, liable for costs (expenses in Scotland) if he does not put in an appearance (subs. (3)).

The section is closely similar to section 63 [1949] and applies to "existing patents" (Sched. 4, para. 3(2)).

Definition of "exclusive licence" **67.03**

"Exclusive licence" is defined in section 130(1) and means a licence to the exclusion of all others, including the proprietor of the patent (or the applicant where the licence is granted under a pending application) of "any right" in respect of the invention to which that patent or application relates. The words "any right" appear to be very wide. Presumably, a licence comes within the definition if it confers the sole right to manufacture but not the sole right to use a patented invention, or the sole right to make and sell some but not all of the articles covered by the claims. It also seems that a licence limited territorially, *e.g.* one conferring all the rights in respect of Scotland, is within the definition. Several exclusive licences can be granted under one patent, see *Courtauld's Application* ([1956] RPC 208).

Rights of exclusive licensee to sue for infringement **67.04**

It is sufficient to enable a licensee to become a plaintiff in an infringement action if he is the possessor of any exclusive right under the patent, and, once a plaintiff, he can probably recover damages for any loss suffered according to the usual principles (*Morton-Norwich* v. *Intercen and United Chemicals*, [1981] FSR 337). Whether such an exclusive right is possessed may be a mixed question of fact and law; in that case the licence was held to be partly written and partly oral.

A licence is not "exclusive" within the definition unless it excludes the proprietor himself. Thus, the holder of a sole, rather than exclusive, licence is not entitled to sue for patent infringement. In (*PCUK* v. *Diamond Shamrock* ([1981] FSR 427) it appears to have been accepted that an exclusive licensee can sue if he can establish only an informal *de facto* licence which is exclusive to him as against all others, including the proprietor of the patent. However, see now the effect of section 68 on an exclusive licensee whose licence had not been registered.

An exclusive licensee's entitlement to sue does not depend upon registration of the licence, though non-registration may entail forfeiture of damages or an account of profits between the date of the licence and the date of ultimate registration, see section 68 and the commentary thereon. However, the exclusive licence should exist prior to the issue of the writ (*Procter & Gamble* v. *Peaudouce*, [1989] FSR 180 (CA)).

Under section 67 the power of the exclusive licensee to sue is limited to action in respect of infringement after the date of the licence, but sections 30(7) and 31(7) permit an exclusive licence to confer on the licensee the right of the licensor to bring proceedings under sections 61 or 69 for a previous infringement or under section 58 for a previous act of Crown use.

SECTION 68   68.01

Effect of non-registration on infringement proceedings

68. Where by virtue of a transaction, instrument or event to which section 33 above applies a person becomes the proprietor or one of the proprietors or an exclusive licensee of a patent and the patent is subsequently infringed, the court or the comptroller shall not award him damages or order that he be given an account of the profits in respect of such a subsequent infringement occurring before the transaction, instrument or event is registered unless—

(a) the transaction, instrument or event is registered within the period of six months beginning with its date; or

(b) the court or the comptroller is satisfied that it was not practicable to register the transaction, instrument or event before the end of that period and that it was registered as soon as practicable thereafter.

COMMENTARY ON SECTION 68

68.02 *General*

Section 68 relates to the effect of a proprietor or licensee failing to register his title. Under previous patent statutes there was a widespread failure to record changes of title and the granting of rights. Section 68 now imposes penalties which make it very desirable for registration to be effected. These penalties appear to be mandatory, unless the proprietor or exclusive licensee can prove there are exceptional circumstances justifying delayed registration. The section applies to "existing patents" (Sched. 4, para. 3(2)).

Section 68 relates to registration that could have been made under section 33 of any transaction, instrument or event that creates a new proprietor, whether sole or joint, or an exclusive licensee of a patent application. However, section 68 concerns only the effect of non-registration. In *Christian Salvesen* v. *Odefejld Drilling Scotland*] ([1985] RPC 569) a registered exclusive licensee for Scotland was refused an interim interdict because he had failed to aver that the alleged infringer had had notice of the restriction on use in Scotland of patented apparatus which the purchaser had bought from the head licensor.

68.03 *Effect of non-registration of assignment or licence*

The penalty for non-registration of an assignment or licence is that the court (or the Comptroller in proceedings under s. 61(3), see s. 61(4)) shall not award damages (or order an account of profits) in respect of infringements committed during the period in which the title remained unregistered, unless registration is effected within six months, or otherwise as soon as possible. Also, the penalty attaches to the person in default and not to the patent. There is thus now every persuasion for a person who becomes a proprietor or exclusive licensee of a patent or a patent application to apply for registration within six months of the date of the transaction, instrument or event by virtue of which he becomes entitled.

For the registration of an assignment or licence under an application for a European patent (UK), see para. 32.18. Once a European patent (UK) has been granted, any assignment or licence in respect thereof is required to be registered at the Patent Office under section 33, see para. 32.19. The priority of conflicting assignments and/or licences is governed by section 33 and is discussed in the commentary thereon.

69.01   **SECTION 69**

Infringement of rights conferred by publication of application

69.—(1) Where an application for a patent for an invention is published, then, subject to subsections (2) and (3) below, the applicant shall have, as from the publication and until the grant of the patent, the same right as he would have had, if the patent had been granted on the date of the publication of the application, to bring proceedings in the court or before the comptroller for damages in respect of any act which would have infringed the patent; and (subject to subsections (2) and (3) below) references in sections 60 to 62 and 66 to 68 above to a patent and the proprietor of a patent shall be respectively construed as including references to any such application and the applicant, and references to a patent being in force, being granted, being valid or existing shall be construed accordingly.

(2) The applicant shall be entitled to bring proceedings by virtue of this section in respect of any act only—

(*a*) after the patent has been granted; and

(*b*) if the act would, if the patent had been granted on the date of the publication of the application, have infringed not only the patent, but also the claims (as interpreted by the description and any drawings referred to in the description or claims) in the form in which they were contained in the application immediately before the preparations for its publication were completed by the Patent Office.

(3) Section 62(2) and (3) above shall not apply to an infringement of the rights conferred by this section, but in considering the amount of any damages for such an infringement, the court or the comptroller shall consider whether or not it would have been reasonable to expect, from a consideration of the application as published under section 16 above, that a patent would be granted conferring on the proprietor of the patent protection from an act of the same description as that found to infringe those rights, and if the court or the comptroller finds that it would not have been reasonable, it or he shall reduce the damages to such an amount as it or he thinks just.

COMMENTARY ON SECTION 69

General   **69.02**

Section 69 departs fundamentally from the principles previously followed by giving a proprietor the right to recover damages in respect of infringements committed before substantive examination has been completed and grant has occurred. The section is one of those declared by section 130(7) to have been so framed as to have, as nearly as practicable, the same effects in the United Kingdom as the corresponding provisions of the EPC, CPC and PCT have in the territories to which these Conventions apply. These corresponding provisions are EPCa. 67, CPCa. 34 and PCTa. 29.

Applicability of section 69   **69.03**

Section 69 is only applicable to "applications". However "applications" includes applications for European patents (UK) (s. 78(1)) and international applications (UK) (s. 89(1)) and international applications for a European patent (UK) ("Euro-PCT applications") (s. 79(1)), but provided that such applications have been "published" in the manner prescribed by the respective provision. These provisions are:

for European applications, section 78(3)(*d*), discussed in para. 78.03; for international applications, section 89B(3), discussed in para. 89B.11; and for Euro-PCT applications, section 79(3), discussed in para. 79.04. Infringement of an application for a Community patent will be treated in accordance with the CPC (s. 86).

69.04 *Rights conferred by section 69 (subs. (1))*

The right conferred by subsection (1) applies to the period between publication of an application and grant of the patent. Under section 16 and rule 27 an application is published about 18 months from the declared priority date, or from the date of filing if no priority is claimed. The date of grant for the purposes of section 69 is the date of publication of grant in the O.J. (s. 25(1)) and not the date when grant administratively takes place under section 24(1), see para. 24.11.

The right to bring proceedings for damages under subsection (1) is equated with that of the proprietor of the patent as if the patent had been granted on the publication date of the application, but subject to subsections (2) and (3) as explained below. Thus sections 60–62 (other than s. 62(2) and (3), see subs. (3)) and 66–68 are applied to applications as if they were patents. The proceedings themselves will be under section 61 and may therefore be before a "court" (for which see para. 61.07); or (under s. 61(3)) before the Comptroller (s. 61(4)), but in that case section 74(7) prevents proceedings being started if there are already any proceedings before the court, unless the court gives leave, see para. 74.06.

69.05 *Limitation on rights conferred (subss. (2) and (3))*

Under subsection (2)(*a*) the right to bring proceedings under section 69(1) can only be exercised after the patent has in fact been granted. By virtue of subsection (2)(*b*) the plaintiff must satisfy a double test by proving infringement of the patent and of the latest version of the claims appearing in the application as published. In both cases the question of infringement is governed by section 60, but irrespective of the validity of the published claims. Thus a plaintiff should succeed if an act infringes a broad, invalid claim of his application and a narrower but valid claim of his patent, but in such circumstances the damages may be reduced under subsection (3). However, if the applicant should be able to broaden his claim during prosecution over that as originally published (which anyway is unlikely, see para. 76.16), the test of subsection (2)(*b*) will not be satisfied in respect of the broadened scope.

The decision in *Sevcon* v. *Lucas* ([1986] RPC 609 (HL)), though decided under the 1949 Act, would appear to apply, by analogy, to restrict actions for infringement of a published application to acts of infringement which occurred within six years before the date of issue of the writ, even though the right to issue that writ only commences from the later date of grant.

Under subsection (3) damages may be reduced if it would not have been reasonable to expect, from a consideration of the published application, that the ultimate patent would be infringed. The presence in the published application of an untenably broad main claim is unlikely to avail the defendant who unreasonably disregards another claim which is valid and infringed. It is thus important to file an application with a set of claims of differing scope in order that the application may contain at least one claim that is both valid and infringed.

Although damages under section 69 are not claimable until the patent has been granted, it seems that interest on such damages could be awarded from the date of the infringing act, see para. 61.14. Note, however, that in *General Tire* v. *Firestone* ([1976] RPC 197) interest on pre-grant damages under the 1949 Act was refused, in the court's discretion.

The exclusion from section 69 of sections 63–65 calls for no explanation since these sections are inappropriate. The absence from section 69 of reference to section 70 (*Threats*) and the fact that the defence provided by section 70(2) does not apparently extend to threats uttered during the application stage is curious, as discussed further in para. 70.03.

SECTION 70   70.01

Remedy for groundless threats of infringement proceedings

70.—(1) Where a person (whether or not the proprietor of, or entitled to any right in, a patent) by circulars, advertisements or otherwise threatens another person with proceedings for any infringement of a patent, a person aggrieved by the threats (whether or not he is the person to whom the threats are made) may, subject to subsection (4) below, bring proceedings in the court against the person making the threats, claiming any relief mentioned in subsection (3) below.

(2) In any such proceedings the plaintiff or pursuer shall, if he proves that the threats were so made and satisfies the court that he is a person aggrieved by them, be entitled to the relief claimed unless—

(*a*) the defendant or defender proves that the acts in respect of which proceedings were threatened constitute or, if done, would constitute an infringement of a patent; and

(*b*) the patent alleged to be infringed is not shown by the plaintiff or pursuer to be invalid in a relevant respect.

(3) The said relief is—

(*a*) a declaration or declarator to the effect that the threats are unjustifiable;

(*b*) an injunction or interdict against the continuance of the threats; and

(*c*) damages in respect of any loss which the plaintiff or pursuer has sustained by the threats.

(4) Proceedings may not be brought under this section for a threat to bring proceedings for an infringement alleged to consist of making or importing a product for disposal or of using a process.

(5) It is hereby declared that a mere notification of the existence of a patent does not constitute a threat of proceedings within the meaning of this section.

COMMENTARY ON SECTION 70

General   70.02

Section 70 concerns groundless (*i.e.* unjustifiable) threats of action for infringement of a patent. While similar to section 65 [1949], new subsection (4) added a further limitation on the scope of the section to that now continued in subsection (5). The section applies to "existing patents" (Sched. 4, para. 3(2)), as decided in *Therm-a-Stor* v. *Weatherseal* ([1981] FSR 579 (CA)), as well as to European patents (UK) (s. 77(1)(*b*)).

Section 70 provides that, where any person makes a threat of action for infringement against any other person, which if challenged he cannot justify, anyone aggrieved can bring action to restrain the further issue of such threats, and seek damages unless an exemption applies under subsection (4) or (5), as discussed in paras. 70.08 and 70.09 *infra*. A similar provision exists in relation to threats of infringement of a registered design (Registered Designs Act 1949 (c. 88, s. 26) and also for the new unregistered design right (s. 253 [1988]), but there is no corresponding provision in relation to infringement of other intellectual property rights such as trade marks or copyright. In the absence of the same, an action for wrongful interference with contractual relations, following a threat of proceedings for infringement of copyright, has been struck out as disclosing no cause of action (*Granby* v. *Interlego*, [1984] RPC 209), but see *Jaybeam* v. *Abru Aluminium* ([1976] RPC 308) in para. 70.09 *infra*. However, threats made under a patent in respect of primary infringement (*i.e.* an infringement of patent by manufacture or importation) are not now actionable, see para. 70.08 *infra*.

While the section can, apparently, be avoided by issuing a writ, even if this has not at the time been served: because, if proceedings have been commenced, they can scarcely be threatened, if the "threat" is made to the already-named defendant the courts have been prepared to restrain the issue of a writ where such could be regarded as harassment rather than legitimate, especially if allegations of infringement are insufficiently particularised (as in *Landi den Hartog* v. *Sea Bird*, [1976] FSR 489); or if separate writs have been issued against customers of an existing defendant (as in *Jacey* v. *Norton & Wright*, [1977] FSR 475), but see *Revlon* v. *Cripps & Lee* ([1980] FSR 85 at 98) for a contrary case.

70.03 *Threats made in relation to pending applications*

By section 69 the publication of an application before grant may give rise to a right of action for infringement, though that right can only be enforced after grant. If a threat is issued in respect of such an application, it may be taken to be an implied threat under the patent to be granted and so fall within the ambit of section 70. The absence from section 69 of reference to section 70, and the fact that the defence provided by subsection (2) does not apparently extend to threats uttered during the application stage, may mean that a threat issued in respect of a pending application is incapable of justification: see *Continental Linen* v. *Kenpet* [*South Africa*] (*noted* [1987] EIPR D–87), where it was held that an actionable threat arises even if the threat is only of proceedings which will be brought once the patent is granted and that justification (for which see para. 70.06 *infra*) can only be established by proof of infringement of an existing right.

70.04 *What constitutes a threat (subs. (1))*

To be actionable, a threat must be by "circulars, advertisements or otherwise", but in the Scottish case of *Speedcranes* v. *Thomson* ([1978] RPC 221) the word "otherwise" was given a broad meaning and not construed *ejusdem generis* with the words "circulars and advertisements". However, as that case decided, a general warning not directed to anyone in particular is not an actionable threat; and, as decided in *Alpi* v. *Wright* ([1972] RPC 125), where an advertisement that an infringement action had been commenced was considered, a plaintiff must satisfy the court that a warning finger was pointed against the products of some other specified person, though an actionable threat need not be made directly to the alleged infringer.

In *Continental Linen* v. *Kenpet* [*South Africa*] (*noted* [1987] EIPR D–87) it was held that the test whether or not a letter constitutes a threat is an objective one to be decided regardless of how the addressee read it or what the sender intended. So too in *C & P Development* v. *Sisabro* ((1953) 70 RPC 277) where it was held that certain letters amounted to actionable threats since the "language used had been such as would convey to a reasonable man that there was an intention to bring proceedings for infringement of patent".

In *Bristol-Myers* v. *Manon* ([1973] RPC 836) it was held to be an actionable threat to tell a retailer that a writ would be issued against the manufacturer, though not the retailer, of alleged infringing goods.

Even if a statement is not an actionable threat, it may nevertheless be actionable as a malicious falsehood. In *Mentmore* v. *Fomento* ((1955) 72 RPC 12 and 157) the patent had been held by the Court of Appeal in other proceedings to be valid and infringed, but the injunction was stayed pending an appeal to the House of Lords. In that case a representative told a buyer of a large store that an injunction had been granted but did not say that the operation of the order had been suspended.

Contempt of court   **70.05**

In making any public comment on active legal proceedings, care must be taken not to commit a contempt of court. This will occur if the comment is one tending to interfere with the course of justice in particular legal proceedings regardless of intent to do so (Contempt of Court Act 1981 (c. 49, s. 1). Nevertheless, it is permissible to make a factual statement that litigation is in process, particularly to warn the trade of the existence of that ligitation, see *Carl-Zeiss-Stiftung* v. *Rayner and Keeler* ([1961] RPC 1) and *Easipower* v. *Gordon Moore* ([1963] RPC 8) as examples in intellectual property disputes. However, care must be taken that such statements are entirely accurate both in what they state and what they imply. Thus, pending judgment, the comment should *not* state, explicitly or by inference, that the patent is valid or infringed since these are questions yet to be determined by the court, see also *Mentmore* v. *Fomento* (discussed in para. 70.04 *supra*). For cases of contempt in relation to a patent action, where a patentee tried to arouse public indignation against the alleged infringer, see *Michigan* v. *Mathew* ([1966] RPC 47) and where the defendant's solicitor wrote a tendentious letter to the press under a pseudonym commenting on the litigation, see *Daw* v. *Eley* ((1868) LR 7 Eq.Cas. 49).

Justification (subs. (2))   **70.06**

The heading to section 70 refers, as did that of section 65 [1949], to "groundless" threats of proceedings, but the section does not itself use the word "groundless" and subsection (3) refers to threats that are unjustifiable. "Unjustifiable" means that infringement of a valid claim is not ultimately established. Thus, it is the practice in an infringement action where threats of infringement proceedings have been uttered for the defendant to counterclaim to restrain threats and especially to claim damages if the infringement action is unsuccessful. In such an action, relief is granted to the defendant unless the plaintiff shows that the acts complained of are infringements, and the defendant is unable to prove that the relevant claims are invalid.

Justification has been held not to be available as a defence to a threat issued in respect of a pending application (see para. 70.03 *supra*); and the allegation of justification has been held insufficient to prevent the grant of an interlocutory injunction to restrain threats (see para. 70.07 *infra*).

481

70.07 *Relief (subs. (3))*

The relief may be a declaration that the threats are unjustified, an injunction to restrain further threats, and damages.

The statement in subsection (2) that the plaintiff is entitled to certain relief including an injunction does not override the discretion of the court, see *Benmax* v. *Austin* ((1953) 70 RPC 143 and 284) and *Tudor Accessories* v. *Somers* ([1960] RPC 215. Thus where a plaintiff is not inconvenienced by the threat and treats his right of action as a weapon in a dispute relating to a contract between the parties, an injunction may be refused.

The importance of applying for an interlocutory injunction to restrain unjustified threats should not be overlooked. Such an injunction can be granted even if infringement proceedings have already been started (*H.V.E.* v. *Cufflin*, [1964] RPC 149 and *Cerosa* v. *Poseidon*, [1973] RPC 882). While it is established that an interlocutory injunction will not be imposed in respect of threatened publication of a defamatory statement if the defendant asserts he proposes to plead the defence of justification thereto, that principle has been held to be inapplicable to threats of patent infringement proceedings (*Johnson Electric* v. *Mabuchi*, [1986] FSR 280).

70.08 *Exclusion of threats made to primary infringers (subs. (4))*

Subsection (4), new in the 1977 Act, excludes action for a threat where the threat is to a primary infringer; that is, it is made in respect of making or importing a product for disposal or using a process. It excludes the threat rather than the person threatened, so that a letter threatening proceedings for primary infringement would appear to be excluded regardless of whether the recipient was a primary infringer or not, for example, if the person threatened is a manufacturing agent. Thus, in *Therm-a-Stor* v. *Weatherseal* ([1981] FSR 579 (CA)) it was held that subsection (4) is not confined to threats against a primary infringer, but appeared to enable any person (whether a patent proprietor or not) to threaten infringement proceedings with impunity under either section 60(1) or (2) when the alleged infringement is the making of a product for disposal. Accordingly, threats against persons who supplied the defendants with products for use according to the invention claimed could not properly be made the subject of a threats action under section 70. Examples where subsection (4) has been held not to apply are *Neild* v. *Rockley* ([1986] FSR 3), where the threat related to acts of sale; and *Johnson Electric* v. *Mabuchi* ([1986] FSR 280), where a threat against *use* of electric motors was not a threat made in respect of manufacture or use of a process and, hence, was not protected under subsection (4). Where subsection (4) prevents action under the section, it may nevertheless be possible to seek a declaration from the court that the threats made were unjustified, see *Leco Instruments* v. *Land Pyrometers* ([1982] RPC 133).

70.09 *Mere notification of patent existence is not a threat (subs. (5))*

Subsection (5) follows the former practice that mere notification of the existence of the patent is deemed not to be a threat.

Despite the provision of subsection (5), a notification of the existence of a patent may constitute an actionable threat if the notification is given in such a context that a threat is seen to be intended. For example, in a design cae (*Jaybeam* v. *Abru Aluminium*, [1976] RPC 308), the notification of design registration was included at the end of a letter clearly threatening proceedings for infringement of copyright. An injunction against repetition was granted on the basis that, in the context of the threatening letter, reference to the design registration was not a mere notification, see also the Scottish case of *Speedcranes* v. *Thomson* ([1978] RPC 221). In *Reymes-Cole* v. *Elite Hosiery* ([1964] RPC 255 and [1965] RPC 102) a letter notifying the existence of patents, but stating that a number of firms were infringing and that action was being taken against some of them, was held to be an actionable threat. *Quarae*: would a letter of notification, which also directed attention to section 70(5), be regarded as an actionable threat?

Advice to laymen   **70.10**

Because a threat can be made orally, there is frequently a need to give a warning to prevent salesmen referring to patents, and in particular to pending applications (see para. 70.03 *infra*). Laymen also need to be told that advertisements may render them liable to an action under the section. When litigation is pending, care also needs to be taken against committing a contempt of court (see para. 70.05 *supra*), and there is also the danger of uttering a malicious falsehood if reports of litigation are not entirely accurate, see para. 70.04 *supra*.

Although it might be thought that, if infringement or validity is contested and the whole matter is ultimately decided in court, it is immaterial whether this is done in a direct infringement action or a threats action, it must be remembered that the right to open and close in court (much prized by the Bar) belongs to the plaintiff, even if there is a counterclaim alleging infringement (thereby justifying the threat) and a counterclaim to the counterclaim alleging invalidity of the patent (thereby rebutting the justification).

PRACTICE UNDER SECTION 70   **70.11**

Actions to restrain threats are often brought as part of a counterclaim to an action for infringement. Procedure in such cases will be governed by RSC Ord. 104, rules 5–16 (reprinted in paras. E104.50–E104.16) and is described in paras. 61.21–61.38. Where the party threatened wishes to take the initiative, it may institute proceedings by Writ, or by Originating Summons pursuant to RSC Ord. 15, rule 16 (reprinted at para. E15.16). The defendant to such proceedings will usually put forward the defence of justification (see para. 70.06 *supra*) and serve a counterclaim in the proceedings alleging infringement, in which case subsequent procedure will likewise be governed by RSC Ord. 104, rules 5–16. A counterclaim to that counterclaim alleging that the patent is invalid (and therefore cannot be infringed), optionally praying for its revocation, will then be possible.

SECTION 71   **71.01**

Declaration or declarator as to non-infringement

71.—(1) Without prejudice to the court's jurisdiction to make a declaration or declarator apart from this section, a declaration or declarator that an act does not, or a proposed act would not, constitute an infringement of a patent may be made by the court or the comptroller in proceedings between the person doing or proposing to do the act and the proprietor of the patent, notwithstanding that no assertion to the contrary has been made by the proprietor, if it is shown—

(a) that that person has applied in writing to the proprietor for a written acknowledgment to the effect of the declaration or declarator claimed, and has furnished him with full particulars in writing of the act in question; and

(b) that the proprietor has refused or failed to give any such acknowledgment.

(2) Subject to section 72(5) below, a declaration made by the comptroller under this section shall have the same effect as a declaration or declarator by the court.

RELEVANT RULE

Procedure on application under section 71

71.02   **74.**—(1) An application to the comptroller under section 71 for a declaration that an act does not, or a proposed act would not, constitute an infringement of a patent shall be made on Patents Form No. 37/77 and shall be accompanied by a copy thereof and a statement in duplicate, setting out fully the facts upon which the applicant relies as showing that sub-paragraphs (a) and (b) of section 71(1) have been complied with and the relief which he seeks.

(2) The comptroller shall send a copy of the statement to the proprietor of the patent who shall, if he wishes to contest the application, within three months after receipt of the copy of the statement, file a counter-statement in duplicate setting out fully the grounds on which he contests the applicant's case; and the comptroller shall send a copy thereof to the applicant.

(3) Subject to such directions as the comptroller may think fit to give, the applicant may, within three months of his receipt of the copy of the counter-statement, file evidence in support of his application and shall send a copy thereof to the proprietor of the patent.

(4) Within three months of the receipt of the copy of the applicant's evidence or, if the applicant does not file any evidence, within three months of the expiration of the time within which such evidence might have been filed, the proprietor of the patent may file evidence in support of his case and shall send a copy of that evidence to the applicant; and, within three months of the receipt of the copy of the proprietor's evidence, the applicant may file further evidence confined to matters strictly in reply and shall send a copy of it to the proprietor.

(5) No further evidence shall be filed by either party except by leave or direction of the comptroller.

(6) The comptroller may give such directions as he may think fit with regard to the subsequent procedure.

484

COMMENTARY ON SECTION 71

General   **71.03**

Section 71 concerns applications to the court or the Comptroller for a declaration of non-infringement. In contrast to section 66 [1949], jurisdiction is now given to the Comptroller and validity can be challenged at the same time. On the basis of Schedule 4, para. 3(2), the section applies fully to "existing patents": see *Reckitt & Colman* v. *Biorex* ([1985] FSR 94) approving *Martinez's Patent* ([1983] RPC 307). It also applies to European patents (UK) by virtue of section 77(1)(*b*), but section 71 does not permit a declaration to be sought before the patent is granted (*Acme Signs* v. *Edwards*, SRIS C/89/87, *noted* IPD 10071).

A decision from the Comptroller under section 71 can be appealed to the Patents Court, but further appeal is only possible with leave and on a point of law (s. 97(3)). Decisions of the court under the section are appealable as of right to the Court of Appeal and further, with leave, to the House of Lords.

An application under section 71 can only be made by a person doing or proposing to do the act in respect of which the declaration of non-infringement is sought. The application can be in respect of a committed or proposed act. The applicant must first write to the proprietor for the declaration giving *full* particulars in writing of the act in question (subs. (1)(*a*)). An application is made to the Comptroller or court in default of acknowledgment of non-infringement (subs. (1)(*b*)). However, the proposed applicant need only wait a short time for an acknowledgment before filing his application as the patentee can then choose not to contest the application (*MMD Designs' Patent*, [1989] RPC 131).

Costs are now borne in the normal way, and not wholly by the applicant as under section 66 [1949]. Section 71 does not refer (as did s. 66 [1949]) to proceedings involving an exclusive licensee.

Effect of declaration   **71.04**

A declaration by the Comptroller has the same effect as one made by the court (subs. (2)), that is it sets up an estoppel between the parties preventing them from re-litigating the same issue subsequently. Thus, a declaration of non-infringement could be conclusive if action is later brought under section 60 in respect of the same alleged act. However, dismissal of an application for a declaration is not necessarily to be equated with a positive finding that infringement does exist. For this reason it would seem inappropriate for dismissal of an application under section 71 normally to be accompanied by a positive finding of infringement. Rather the decision ought to be merely a finding that the case for a declaration of non-infringement is not proven, see *Hirst's Application* ((1954) RPC 251). However, no estoppel will arise in relation to the issue of validity when this is raised before the Comptroller during proceedings under section 71 because such are exempted therefrom by section 72(5). For further discussion on questions of estoppel, see para. 72.28.

It should be noted that, in the absence of a concurrent application for revocation under section 72, a finding of invalidity in proceedings under section 71 does not itself lead to revocation, and that relief under section 71 is limited to the grant of a declaration in negative form, see *Zeigler's Patent* (SRIS O/64/87).

Required description of the alleged non-infringement   **71.05**

It is important, in complying with the requirements of subsection (1)(*a*), that the applicant should give precise and complete information in relation to the article, process, etc., alleged not to infringe, because no declaration can be granted if there is any doubt that no article, etc., corresponding to the description before the court or Comptroller could infringe the patent, see *Mallory Metallurgical* v. *Black Sivalls* ([1977] RPC 321) and *Plasticisers* v. *Pixdane* ([1978] FSR 595). However, the provision is satisfied by providing a sample of the alleged non-infringing article, provided that its inspection by competent persons will make clear all aspects of the device material to the question of infringement (*Acme Signs* v. *Edwards*, SRIS C/89/87, *noted* IPD 10071). Also, a description to be read in conjunction with a detailed drawing will suffice (*MMD Design's Patent*. [1989] RPC 131). Further, it is not necessary (at least at the pleading stage) to take into account whether the described apparatus might infringe as the result of wear or deliberate adjustment (*Bonas Machine's Patent*, SRIS O/25/89, *noted* IPD 12039).

It should be appreciated that, to obtain a declaration under section 71, the applicant bears the onus of proving non-infringement: the so-called presumption of innocence has no application in such a situation, see the copyright case of *Amstrad* v. *British Phonographic Society* ([1986] FSR 159). Thus, an applicant under section 71 assumes a burden of proof which would fall upon the patentee if the action were one brought against him for infringement, as was pointed out in *Zeigler's Patent* (SRIS O/64/87), but a point emerging directly from the evidence can be taken into consideration even if not raised by the applicant (*MMD Designs' Patent. supra*).

71.06 *Use of section 71 in practice*

The changes introduced in section 71 have made the use of the procedure, especially before the Comptroller, more attractive than previously. The section now affords a way of putting the validity of a patent to the test in a "squeeze" situation where the proprietor may seek to put forward a broad interpretation of his claims in order to have the declaration of non-infringement denied, but in doing so expose the patent to objections of invalidity that would perhaps not otherwise arise.

The section is also useful when an alleged infringer has changed the alleged infringement and wishes to ensure that a modification will not amount to infringement, and hence perhaps a contempt of court if an injunction has been or were to be granted on the first device: see *Filhol* v. *Fairfax* (SRIS C/143/86, *noted* IPD 9091), where an injunction had already been granted; and *Rodi & Wienenberger* v. *Showell* ([1966] RPC 441), where the application for a declaration in respect of a modification of the alleged infringement was heard at the same time as the infringement action.

71.07 *Concurrent proceedings*

Proceedings under section 71 cannot be started before the Comptroller if there are *any* proceedings involving the patent before the court, unless the court gives leave, see section 74(7) discussed at para. 74.06. Where proceedings under section 71 had already been commenced before the Comptroller and infringement proceedings were then commenced before the court against the section 71 applicant, the court has been prepared to stay the proceedings before it, see *Hawker Siddeley* v. *Real Time* ([1983] RPC 395 and for subsequent proceedings SRIS O/84/84, *noted* IPD 7096 and SRIS O/24/87).

In *Wilkinson Sword* v. *Warner-Lambert* (SRIS C/124/87) proceedings for amendment were already pending before the Comptroller when proceedings were commenced before the court for a declaration under section 71 and for revocation under section 72. The court refused to stay the proceedings before it and indicated that the amendment proceedings should be recommenced before the court under section 75. Subsequently, the court allowed the amendments and found the patent valid, but not infringed (SRIS C/35/88).

For further discussion on concurrent proceedings, see para. 72.30.

PRACTICE UNDER SECTION 71

Procedure before the Comptroller **71.08**

Procedure on application to the Comptroller is set out in rule 74 (reprinted para. 71.02 *supra*). Application is made on PF 37/77 (reprinted at para. 141.37) and is accompanied by a statement of the facts. A copy of the statement is sent to the proprietor who may contest the application by filing a counter-statement within three months; there is no prescribed form and no fee. The parties are given periods of three months in which to file evidence. The procedure thereafter is at the discretion of the Comptroller, but follows that generally adopted in *inter partes* matters before the Comptroller, see paras. 72.32–72.52. The time limits specified in rule 74 can each, apparently, be extended by the discretion of the Comptroller exercised under rule 110(1).

If the application for a declaration is opposed by the patentee, as will usually be the case, and the patentee files a counter-statement which can be interpreted as a positive allegation that infringement is involved, the counter-statement should explain the basis of the argument, but need not specify any particular construction of the claims (*Woolard's Patent*, [1989] RPC 141), where the Patentee's first attempt at amplification of his counter-statement was held to be unsatisfactory (SRIS O/13/89).

Procedure before the court **71.09**

RSC Ord. 104 contains no special provision in relation to section 71. The procedure is therefore that of RSC Ord. 15, r. 16 (reprinted at para. E015.16) and the proceedings may be commenced by writ or originating summons, in each case requesting that the court make a declaration. A form of Order making such a declaration is given in *Flexheat* v. *Bolser* ([1966] RPC 374).

Where a proprietor is domiciled within the EEC, service of proceedings upon him abroad without leave of the court is permitted in matters relating to the validity of patents by RSC Ord. 11, rule 1(2)(*a*)(ii) and the Civil Jurisdiction and Judgments Act 1981 (c. 27, Sched. 1, art. 16). Where a proprietor is domiciled outside the EEC, it appears not possible to serve a writ or originating summons for a declaration of non-infringement on that proprietor at an address outside the jurisdiction of the court, because this is not a case where leave is not required pursuant to RSC Order 11 and equally it does not fall within the provisions of Ord. 11, rule 1 which sets out when leave can be granted for service of proceedings out of the jurisdiction. In such circumstances, it is submitted that service should be effected on the address for service entered in the register of patents under rule 30, discussed in para. 32.16. If that address were in Scotland, Northern Ireland or the Isle of Man, it is not clear whether the English court would have jurisdiction to entertain an action brought under section 71 if the patentee were resident outside England and Wales. However, if an address for service is permitted elsewhere in the EEC (after s. 281(5) [1988] has been brought into effect, for which see para. 32.03), service of proceedings at that address would still seem possible under the Civil Jurisdiction and Judgments Act 1982 (c. 27, Sched. 1, Art. 5) and RSC Ord. 11 (*not* reprinted in Appendix E).

72.01   SECTION 72

Power to revoke patents on application

72.—(1) Subject to the following provision of this Act, the court or the comptroller may on the application of any person by order revoke a patent for an invention on (but only on) any of the following grounds, that is to say—

(*a*) the invention is not a patentable invention;

(*b*) the patent was granted to a person who was not [*the only person*] entitled [*under section 7(2) above*] to be granted that patent [*or to two or more persons who were not the only persons so entitled*];

(*c*) the specification of the patent does not disclose the invention clearly enough and completely enough for it to be performed by a person skilled in the art;

(*d*) the matter disclosed in the specification of the patent extends beyond that disclosed in the application for the patent, as filed, or, if the patent was granted on a new application filed under section 8(3), 12 or 37(4) above or as mentioned in section 15(4) above, in the earlier application, as filed;

(*e*) the protection conferred by the patent has been extended by an amendment which should not have been allowed.

(2) An application for the revocation of a patent on the ground mentioned in subsection (1)(*b*) above—

(*a*) may only be made a person found by the court in an action for a declaration or declarator, or found by the court or the comptroller on a reference under section 37 above, to be entitled to be granted that patent or to be granted a patent for part of the matter comprised in the specification of the patent sought to be revoked; and

(*b*) may not be made if that action was commenced or that reference was made after the end of the period of two years beginning with the date of the grant of the patent sought to be revoked, unless it is shown that any person registered as a proprietor of the patent knew at the time of the grant or of the transfer of the patent to him that he was not entitled to the patent.

[(3) *Rules under section 14(4) and (8) above shall, with any necessary modifications, apply for the purposes of subsection (1)(c) above, as they apply for the purposes of section 14(3) above.*]

(4) An order under this section may be an order for the unconditional revocation of the patent or, where the court or the comptroller determines that one of the grounds mentioned in subsection (1) above has been established, but only so as to invalidate the patent to a limited extent, an order that the patent should be revoked unless within a specified time the specification is amended under section 75 below to the satisfaction of the court or the comptroller, as the case may be.

(5) A decision of the comptroller or on the appeal from the comptroller shall not estop any party to civil proceedings in which infringement of a patent is in issue from alleging invalidity of the patent on any of the grounds referred to in subsection (1) above, whether or not any of the issues involved were decided in the said decision.

(6) Where the comptroller refuses to grant an application made to him by any person under this section, no application (otherwise than by way of appeal or by way of putting validity in issue in proceedings for infringement) may be made to the court by that person under this section in relation to the patent concerned, without the leave of the court.

(7) Where the comptroller has not disposed of an application made to him under this section, the applicant may not apply to the court under this section in respect of the patent concerned unless either—

(*a*) the proprietor of the patent agrees that the applicant may so apply, or

(*b*) the comptroller certifies in writing that it appears to him that the question whether the patent should be revoked is one which would more properly be determined by the court.

Note. The 1988 Act (by Sched. 5, para. 18) prospectively amended subsection (1)(*b*); and (by Sched. 8) prospectively repealed subsection (3). For the commencement of these changes, see the latest Supplement to this Work *re.* this para.

RELEVANT RULES

Form of statements, counter-statements and evidence

21. Any statement, counter-statement or evidence filed at the Patent Office shall, unless the comptroller otherwise directs, comply with the requirements of rule 20(1) and (4) and, except that both sides of the sheet may be used in the case of statutory declarations and affidavits, with the requirements of rule 20(3). **72.02**

Procedure on application for revocation under section 72

75.—(1) An application to the comptroller for the revocation of a patent shall be made on Patents Form No. 38/77 and shall be accompanied by a copy thereof and a statement in duplicate setting out fully the grounds of revocation, the facts upon which the application relies and the relief which he seeks. **72.03**

(2) The comptroller shall send a copy of the application and statement to the proprietor of the patent.

(3) Within three months of the receipt of such copies, the proprietor of the patent shall, if he wishes to contest the application, file a counter-statement in duplicate setting out fully the grounds upon which the application is contested; and the comptroller shall send a copy of the counter-statement to the applicant.

(4) The applicant may, within three months of the receipt of the copy of the counter-statement, file evidence in support of his case and shall send a copy of the evidence to the proprietor.

(5) Within three months of the receipt of the copy of the applicant's evidence or, if the applicant does not file any evidence, within three months of the expiration of the time within which such evidence might have been filed, the proprietor of the patent may file evidence in support of his case and shall send a copy of that evidence to the applicant; and, within three months of the receipt of the copy of the proprietor's evidence, the applicant may file further evidence confined to matters strictly in reply and shall send a copy of it to the proprietor.

(6) No further evidence shall be filed by either party except by leave or direction of the comptroller.

(7) The comptroller may give such directions as he may think fit with regard to the subsequent procedure.

Award of costs

72.04   **76.** If, in proceedings before the comptroller under section 72, the proprietor of the patent offers to surrender it under section 29, the comptroller shall, in deciding whether costs should be awarded to the applicant for revocation, consider whether proceedings might have been avoided if the applicant had given reasonable notice to the proprietor before the application was filed.

Evidence

72.05   **103.**—(1) Where under these Rules evidence may be filed, it shall be by statutory declaration or affidavit.

(2) The comptroller may if he thinks fit in any particular case take oral evidence in lieu of or in addition to such evidence and shall allow any witness to be cross-examined on his affidavit or declaration, unless he directs otherwise.

(3) In England and Wales, the comptroller shall, in relation to the giving of evidence (including evidence on oath), the attendance of witnesses and the discovery and production of documents, have all the powers of a judge of the High Court, other than the power to punish summarily for contempt of court.

(4) In Scotland, the comptroller shall, in relation to the giving of evidence (including evidence on oath), have all the powers which a Lord Ordinary of the Court of Session has in an action before him, other than the power to punish summarily for contempt of court, and, in relation to the attendance of witnesses and the recovery and production of documents, have all the powers of the Court of Session.

Statutory declarations and affidavits

104. Any statutory declaration or affidavit filed under the Act or these **72.06** Rules shall be made and subscribed as follows—
  (*a*) in the United Kingdom, before any justice of the peace, or any commissioner or other officer authorised by law in any part of the United Kingdom to administer an oath for the purpose of any legal proceedings;
  (*b*) in any other part of Her Majesty's dominions, or in any state or territory which is a protectorate or protected state for the purposes of the British Nationality [Act] 1948 [11 & 12 Geo. 6, c. 56] or in the Republic of Ireland, before any court, judge, justice of the peace, or any officer authorised by law to administer an oath there for the purpose of any legal proceedings; and
  (*c*) elsewhere, before a British Minister, or person exercising the functions of a British Minister, or a Consul, Vice-Consul, or other person exercising the functions of British Consul, or before a notary public, or before a judge or magistrate.

Note. The reference to the British Nationality Act 1948 (11 & 12 Geo. 6, c. 56) should now be read as one to the British Nationality Act 1981 (c. 61).

Admission of documents

105. Any document purporting to have affixed, impressed or subscribed **72.07** thereto or thereon the seal or signature of any person authorised by the last foregoing rule to take a declaration, in testimony that the declaration was made and subscribed before him, may be admitted by the comptroller without proof of the genuineness of the seal or signature or of the official character of the person or his authority to take the declaration.

Directions as to furnishing of documents, etc.

106. At any stage of any proceedings before the comptroller he may **72.08** direct that such documents, information or evidence as he may require shall be furnished within such period as he may fix.

Supporting statements or evidence

107.—(1) Where, by virtue of any of the rules mentioned in paragraph **72.09** (2) of this rule, any notice or application is required to be supported by a statement or evidence, such statement or evidence shall be filed on, or within fourteen days after, the date on which the notice is given or the application is made.
  (2) The rules referred to in paragraph (1) above are rules 40(3), 41(1), 43(3), 65(1), 66(2), 71(2) and 91(5).

Appointment of advisers

72.10   109. The comptroller may appoint an adviser to assist him in any proceedings before the comptroller and shall settle the question or instructions to be submitted or given to such adviser.

Copies of documents

72.11   112. Where a document, other than a published United Kingdom specification or application, is referred to in any reference, notice, statement, counter-statement or evidence required by the Act or these Rules to be filed at the Patent Office or sent to the comptroller, copies of the document shall be furnished to the Patent Office within the same period as the reference, notice, statement, counter-statement or evidence in which they are first referred to may be filed and in the following number—

    (*a*) where the document in which they were so referred to had to be filed or sent in duplicate or the original document had to be accompanied by a copy thereof, in duplicate; and

    (*b*) in all other cases, one:

Provided that where a copy of any evidence is required by the Act or these Rules to be sent direct to any person, a copy of any document referred to in that document shall also be sent direct to that person.

COMMENTARY ON SECTION 72

72.12   *General*

Section 72 is an important section and relates to the revocation of patents. It sets out in subsection (1) the *only* grounds on which a patent can be declared invalid (and therefore on which the patent can be revoked) either by the court or by the Comptroller, apart from the special provisions of section 73 and, perhaps, subject to rectification of the register under section 34. The terms of section 72 are reiterated in section 74(3). Thus, in conjunction with section 74 which specifies the only *proceedings* in which validity can be put in issue, there is now a concise and comprehensive statement of the manner and nature of proceedings in which validity can be contested. The grounds of revocation are those specified in (*a*)–(*e*) of subsection (1) and correspond to the provisions of EPCaa. 138 and 139 which specify the only grounds upon which a European patent may be revoked under the law of an EPC Contracting State. These grounds are discussed individually in paras. 72.16–72.25 *infra*. The absence of specific reference to non-compliance of the claims with section 14(5) is discussed in para. 72.20 *infra*.

Subsection (2) qualifies subsection (1)(*b*) as to who may make an application under this provision and when; and the effect of subsection (1)(*c*) is now extended, in the case of inventions relating to micro-organisms by section 125A(4) which replaced repealed subsection (3). Subsection (4) provides for unconditional revocation unless the specification can be validated by amendment under section 75. Subsection (5) provides that proceedings before the Comptroller result in no estoppel in subsequent proceedings in which validity of the patent may be put in issue, but an unsuccessful applicant for revocation is thereafter restricted in bringing evocation proceedings before the court (subs. (6)). Subsection (7) restricts appli-cation to the court by an applicant already proceeding before the Comptroller unless the proprietor so agrees; and also provides that the Comptroller may certify hat the question of revocation before him is one that ought more properly to be letermined by the court.

Section 72 not only corresponds to EPCaa. 138 and 139, but also to CPCa. 57. EPCa. 100, which specifies the only grounds upon which opposition to the grant of a European patent may be lodged in the EPO under EPCa. 99, differs from these provisions in excluding therefrom questions of entitlement which can be raised under subsection (1)(*b*), as well as the ground of revocation under subsection (1)(*e*) which only relates to events occurring post-grant. Subsections (1) and (2) are referred to in section 130(7) as having been intended to have the same effect as the corresponding provisions of EPC, PCT and CPC. However, any decision of revo-cation, or partial revocation, made by the EPO as a result of opposition proceed-ings before it under EPCa. 99, has automatic effect by virtue of section 77(4) and 4A), see para. 77.11.

Section 72 is *not* applicable to "existing patents", the revocation of which is governed by sections 32 and 33 [1949] (as amended), for which see the commentar-es thereon in Appendix A.

Under section 18(4), once the examination of an application is complete and the examiner reports that the application is in compliance with the requirements, the patent is in due course granted. There is no provision for pre-grant opposition as here was under section 14 [1949]. In its place (and with similar effect to amended ections 32 and 33 [1949] for existing patents), section 72 provides for an appli-cation to revoke the patent to be made either to the Comptroller or to the court at any time after grant has taken place.

Section 72 is therefore complementary to section 33 [1949] (as amended) in giv-ng to the Comptroller almost the full powers of the court with regard to revo-cation. This is quite different from the position before June 1, 1978 when the powers of the Comptroller as regards revocation were much more limited, see paras. A032.01 and A033.01. Because revocation proceedings are typical, and intended to be the most common of the various types of contested proceedings which take place before the Comptroller, the discussion on Practice in paras. 72.32–72.52 *infra* deals generally with all *inter partes* disputes before the Comptroller, points of difference for proceedings under other sections being noted *e* Practice under the respective sections.

Forum for revocation   **72.13**

Besides bringing action under section 72 before the Comptroller, the definition of "court" in section 130(1) (as amended) permits applications for revocation to be brought before the Patents Court, and will also permit application for this purpose to be brought before a Patents County Court when the legislation therefor is brought into effect (see para. 96.14); or to the Court of Session in Scotland (see para. 98.06); or to the respective High Courts in Northern Ireland or the Isle of Man (see paras. 131.03 and 132.05 respectively). The wording of the Civil Jurisdic-tion and Judgments Act 1982 (c. 27) ["the CJJA"], as discussed on this point in para. 96.24, is consistent with the wording of the 1977 Act in giving no single court in the United Kingdom exclusive jurisdiction in the matter of revocation, though his has the apparent effect that each court permitted to revoke a patent may do so or the whole of the United Kingdom (including the Isle of Man).

While, under the CJJA, the courts of the United Kingdom now have power to consider questions of infringement of patents of other Contracting States to the Brussels Convention on Jurisdiction and the Enforcement of Judgments, that is at present in respect of all EEC states other than Portugal and Spain (as discussed in para. 61.06), that Convention (by Article VD of the Protocol annexed thereto and incorporated into the CJJA by Sched. 1 thereof) provides that the courts of each of the Contracting States who are members of the EPC are to have exclusive jurisdiction, regardless of domicile, in proceedings concerned with the registration and validity of any European patent granted for that State, other than a Community patent granted under the CPC.

Any court dealing with an application for revocation of a European patent is entitled to seek a technical opinion from the EPO under EPCa. 25, the procedure for which is governed by EPO Guidelines E-XII. Also, in any proceeding under the Act, the Patent Office may now be able to be asked to inquire into, and report on, any question of fact or opinion. This may be done by the Patents Court (under s. 99A, discussed in paras. 99A.02–99A.04), or in Scotland by the Court of Session (under s. 99B, discussed in para. 99B.02), or by a Patents County Court (under s. 279(3) [1988], reprinted in para. 96.10 and discussed in para. 96.12), each from such time as these provisions may be brought into effect, for which see the latest Supplement to this Work re. paras. 99A.01, 99B.01 and 96.10 respectively. Presumably similar powers will be conferred by secondary legislation upon the relevant courts of Northern Ireland and the Isle of Man should the need therefor arise.

Proceedings before the Comptroller take the form of the usual judicial process and, therefore, the provisions of the Arbitration Act 1950 (c. 27) are made inapplicable, see para. 130.12.

In revocation proceedings before the Comptroller, it is possible to hold a hearing in Scotland (r. 108, reprinted at para. 98.02 and discussed in para. 98.07). There is no corresponding provision for Northern Ireland, see para. 131.04.

72.14 *Appeals*

Applications made to any of the tribunals entitled to hear applications for revocation are subject to appeal in the normal way, that is as of right to the respective courts of appeal and then, with leave, to the House of Lords (Privy Council for the Isle of Man). There is the possibility of a leapfrog appeal directly from the Patents Court to the House of Lords under the Administration of Justice Act 1969 (c. 58, ss. 12, 13). This, and appeals from decision of the Comptroller, are dealt with in the commentary on section 97 which governs all appeals from the Comptroller.

Revocation is automatic when the time for any further appeal has expired. Thereafter no application to amend can be entertained (*Kyowa's Application*, [1969] RPC 259).

72.15 *Who may apply to revoke and when*

An important difference between the present Act and former statutes is that it is no longer necessary for the applicant for revocation to show a *locus standi*; any person can now apply for revocation, except on the ground of non-entitlement (s. 72(1)(*b*)), see para. 712.17 *infra*. This freedom appears to go further than the position in the EPO where, in *EPO Decision T* 10/82, *"Opposition: admissibility/BAYER"* (OJEPO 10/1983, 407), the EPO rejected an application for opposition from an ooponent acting as agent for an undisclosed principal. "Any person" may extend to the proprietor himself, as has been permitted in oppositions before the EPO under EPCa. 99 (*EPO Decision Gr* 01/84, *"Opposition by proprietor/MOBIL OIL"*, OJEPO 10/1985, 299; [1986] 1 EPOR 39), where a proprietor wished to amend his European patent during the opposition period in order to avoid separate amendment applications under the separate national patents. A further reason for making such an application could be to surrender the patent *ex tunc*, rather than *ex nunc* as is the case when surrender is made under section 29, see para. 29.06.

Section 72 applies to a patent granted under the Act or to a European patent (UK) (s. 77), either of which may have been obtained by the PCT route (ss. 89 and 79 respectively). However, section 72 does not apply to Community patents (s. 86(4)). An application under section 72 can be made at any time after notice of grant has been published in the O.J. under section 25(1), even after the patent has lapsed or expired and, if a European patent (UK), even after it has already been opposed in the EPO, though on this point see para. 72.30 *infra*. Neither the lapsing nor surrender of a patent is sufficient to terminate revocation proceedings and these continue (normally undefended) in such circumstances (*Ritzerfeld's Patent*, SRIS 0/102/81).

Grounds of revocation

—Invention is not a patentable invention (subs. (1)(a))   **72.16**

Ground (*a*) of subsection (1) is that the invention is "not a patentable invention." This refers back to the definition of patentable invention in section 1 and the concomitant definitions of sections 2–4, and subject further to possible exclusion under section 1(2) or (3) and to the definitions of sections 5 and 6 as to priority. The ground corresponds to EPCaa. 100(*a*) and 138(1)(*a*) and to CPCa. 57(1)(*a*). The effect and extent of this ground of revocation is discussed in the commentaries on these sections.

—Patent granted to person not entitled thereto (subss. (1)(b) and (2))   **72.17**

Ground (*b*) of subsection (1) is that the patent was granted to some person who was not entitled thereto. It corresponds to EPCa. 138(1)(*e*) and CPCa. 57(*e*). As originally worded, subsection (1)(*b*) was limited in its application to a person who was not entitled to the patent "under section 7(2)", for which see para. 7.05. However, this original wording was defective as not dealing adequately with issues involving co-inventors and/or co-proprietors. This deficiency is to be corrected by amendment of subsection (1)(*b*) by the 1988 Act (Sched. 5, para. 18, as noted in para. 72.01) and section 37(1) is to be amended at the same time, though curiously like amendments to those for section 37(1) were not made to the corresponding sections 8(1) and 12(1).

By subsection (2) this ground is only available to an applicant who has already been found by the court or the Comptroller (in the case of the Comptroller as the result of a reference under section 37, which by virtue of s. 9 will include proceedings commenced before grant under s. 8) to be entitled to the patent or part of the matter comprised in it. Also the ground is not available if the action before the court or Comptroller was commenced more than two years after the patent was granted, unless the proprietor knew at the time of grant (or on transfer of the patent to him) that he was not entitled to it. These restrictions reflect those of CPCa. 27(3) and CPCaa. 56(1) and they are reiterated in section 74(4), but there is a possibility of alleviation of this two year period under section 74(5). Also, even if revocation cannot be sought under subsection (1)(*b*) because the conditions of subsection (2) are not met, there remains the possibility of putting validity in issue under section 74(1), see *Dolphin Showers* v. *Farmiloe*, ([1989] FSR 1) and para. 74.05.

The question of entitlement is to be determined as at the date of grant so that a post-grant assignment does not alter the position as regards the original grantee

(*Dolphin Showers* v. *Farmiloe, supra*). Entitlement is more fully dealt with in para. 7.08. Challenge to entitlement is considered mainly in paras. 37.10–37.13, but see also the commentaries on sections 8, 12 and 82 for entitlement questions arising thereunder. The effect of section 74(4) and (5) is discussed in para. 74.05. It is not clear what is meant by "knew" and particularly whether knowledge of an allegation of non-entitlement made before grant is sufficient. However, the meaning can scarcely be absolute because such would involve a conclusion of law that the grantee was not entitled, thereby making the provision otiose, see further para. 37.08.

Insufficient description (subs. (1)(c))

72.18   —*General*

Ground (c) of subsection (1) is that the specification "does not disclose the invention clearly enough and completely enough for it to be performed by a person skilled in the art". It corresponds to EPCaa. 100(*b*), 138(1)(*b*) and CPCa. 57(1)(*b*). Subsection (1)(*c*) adopts the wording of section 14(3), and of EPCa. 83, PCTa. 5 and the Strasbourg Convention (1963), article 8(2).

The special sufficiency requirements for microbiological inventions, presently set out in rule 17 made under section 14(4) and applied to revocation under subsection (1)(*c*) by subsection (3), are to be transferred to revised rule 17 made under new section 125A (with continued application under s. 72(1)(*c*) by s. 125A(4)), see paras. 125A.01 *et seq*. For the commencement of this change, see the latest Supplement to this Work *re*. para. 72.01.

The question of sufficiency in relation to subsection (1)(*c*) is discussed more fully in paras. 14.15–14.18. Because a specification cannot be validly amended after its filing date in a manner which would result in it disclosing "additional matter" (as discussed in paras. 76.09–76.15), it would appear that a specification must be "sufficient", in regard to the subject matter covered by the scope of its claims, as of its filing date, see further para. 14.16. Thus, the claims, as granted, determine "the invention" and this needs sufficient supporting disclosure at the date of grant but, as that disclosure must not contain any matter not as filed, the supporting disclosure eventually required to support the granted claims must be present *ab initio* if the patent is not to be invalid on one ground or another.

72.19   —*Meaning of "insufficiency" under the Act*

The requirement of sufficiency, to enable the patented invention to be put into practice by others, has been a requirement in British law for many years and a substantial case law has been built up in cases decided under sections 14(1)(*g*) and 32(1)(*h*) [1949] in regard to the requirement of section 4(3)(*a*) [1949] that the specification "particularly describe the invention and the method by which it is to be performed". However, caution suggests that the test under the 1977 Act may be different. One reason for this is that there are fewer grounds of revocation set out in section 72 [1977] than in section 32 [1949] and thus the ground of subsection (1)(*c*) is likely to be used as a basis for objections not previously considered as questions of sufficiency. To summarise, section 72(1) contains no ground explicitly corresponding to any of the following grounds, or parts of grounds, in section 32(1) [1949]: (*g*) *inutility*; (*h*) *invention not fairly described*; (*i*) *scope of claim not clear, or claim not fairly based on disclosure*; (*j*) *false suggestion*; or (*k*) *contrary to law*. In general, it is prudent to consider sections 14(3) and 72(1)(*c*) objectively and not to regard them too closely as equivalent to the requirements of sufficiency under the

1949 Act, but see para. 14.18 for suggestions as to how and why these objections available under section 32 [1949] may perhaps be brought within the ambit of section 72(1)(c).

—Insufficiency under subsection (1)(c) and lack of fair basis under section 14(5)(c)   **72.20**

Objection under subsection (1)(c) is limited to insufficiency of the specification under section 14(3) (or in the case of microbiological inventions with rules to be made under new s. 125A, as discussed in the commentary on that section). Therefore, objection that the claims do not comply with section 14(5) is not specified as a ground of revocation, as was firmly held in *Genentech's Patent* ([1989] RPC 147 (CA)). This is because the EPC envisaged that breadth of claims would be decided by the granting authority under EPCa. 84, to which section 14(5) corresponds. It is thought that objections to undue breadth of claim under section 14(5)(c) can be made a ground for revocation under subsection (1)(c) on the basis that the specification, as regards particular aspects of the invention claimed, does not sufficiently describe how this aspect of the invention is to be performed, as was held in the *Genentech* case. On this ground it may be thought that the test under section 14(5)(c) is the obverse of that under section 14(3). However, it seems likely that cases could exist where the specification discloses the invention specified in a claim sufficiently for it to be performed and yet the claim is broader than is equitable in view of the contribution to the art made by the description. That gives rise to great difficulties as shown in the *Genentech* case (*supra*), where the patent was held invalid on various alternative grounds by different members of the Court of Appeal, see paras. 1.08, 3.07 and 14.18. It was held under the 1949 Act that objections of ambiguity and indefiniteness of claiming could not be raised under the guise of insufficiency (*Proctor & Gamble's Application*, [1982] RPC 473 and *Dual Manufacturing's Patent*, [1977] RPC 189) and this principle could apply under subsection (1)(c) in view of the emphasis therein on the performance of the invention. However, the EPO has hinted that, if there is an inconsistency between the scope of the specification and the apparent scope of the claims, this may lead to the claims being given a restricted meaning in order to rationalise the pre-grant decision of conformity with EPCa. 84 (*EPO Decision T* 406/86, "*Trichloroethylene/WACKER*", OJEPO 7/1989, 302; [1989] 6 EPOR 338).

—Insufficiency and EPO Guidelines   **72.21**

The EPO Guidelines also contain some general remarks on sufficiency and, in Guideline D–III, 5, it is suggested that objection may lie where the claims are so broadly worded that the description in the specification does not sufficiently disclose the subject matter within the meaning of EPCa. 100(b). The Guidelines are based on the principle intended from section 125 that the specification is sufficient if there is an adequate description to enable the skilled person to put into effect the invention claimed, see Guidelines C–II, 4 (particularly C–II, 4.1 and 4.9), and also D–V, 4 in relation to oppositions. In particular, the Guidelines suggest that the objection of insufficiency may arise when an embodiment of the invention fails to give the effects stated in the specification, see: Guidelines C–II, 4.11 when alleged results are unrepeatable or not reliably repeatable; D–V, 4.3 on burden of proof when unrepeatability has been alleged; and D–V, 4.4.1 on requirements in opposition to amend to remove embodiments (and amend correspondingly any relevant claims), that are not capable of being performed or do not achieve the desired technical result. This is the objection of inutility as it was understood under section 32(1)(g) [1949] and it therefore seems possible that an objection of this nature could be raised under subsection (1)(c) on which see further para. 14.18.

72.22   *—Insufficiency and disclosure of the best method of performing the invention*

It is particularly relevant to a consideration of subsection (1)(*c*) that it is no longer necessary that the applicant should disclose the best method known to him of carrying the invention into effect. Accordingly, it is not necessary for the specification to disclose the details of that form of execution of the invention which gives the best results, though the objection may lie if the results stated cannot be obtained by following the method disclosed, see (*EPO Decision T* 219/85, *"Inadequate disclosure/HAKOUNE"* (OJEPO 11/1986, 376; [1987] 1 EPOR 30) where the applicant admitted that he had not included necessary directions in the specification in order to prevent the invention from being copied.

In the *"Report of Working Party I"* of the Intergovernmental Conference for Setting up of a European System for the Grant of Patents, Luxembourg April 20–29, 1971, at p. 71, there is a passage which suggests that a requirement of suffiency is that the specification should be clear as to what the invention is and give enough information to enable a person skilled in the particular art to perform the invention without having to exercise further inventive ingenuity. If this is the test to be adopted, it would seem that the failure to point out the best of many alternatives, or the best of many alternative sources of supply of a component of the invention, will not invalidate, since the selection requires only trial and error and not invention.

A reason for the omission of this requirement from British law is that it is not required under the EPC, and a European application nominating the United Kingdom will lead to a British patent with the same criteria as one obtained directly. It is to be observed, however, that if a PCT application designating the United Kingdom is filed and the best method is not disclosed, although this may not damage the British patent it may render invalid the patent obtained in some other designated country which requires it under its own law. Moreover failure to disclose the best method may damage a claim to priority, especially in the United States.

72.23   *—Patents relating to micro-organisms*

Section 125A is to provide for special rules in relation to the sufficient description of inventions relating to the use of micro-organisms. Rule 17 is such a rule and, by section 125A(4), non-compliance with the requirements of this rule also provides a ground of revocation under subsection (1)(*c*). These prospectively changed requirements are dealt with in the commentary of section 125A, particularly in paras. 125A.09 and 125A.11.

72.24   *—Addressee of the specification*

The specification is to be sufficient to the person skilled in the art, *i.e.* the addressee of the specification. Such a person is described in the EPO Guidelines (C–IV, 9·6) as a person or team, fully equipped and fully aware of the state of the art. For further comment on "the person skilled in the art", see para. 3.16.

Impermissible amendments (subss. (1)(d) and (e))

72.25   *—General*

Grounds (*d*) and (*e*) of subsection (1) represent grounds of invalidity which were new as such in the 1977 Act.

Subsection (1)(*d*) has the effect of imposing an absolute bar on the ability of a proprietor validly to make any amendment after filing which results in the specification disclosing "additional matter" over that contained in it at its date, or deemed date, of filing, *i.e.* subject matter to an application. There is a corresponding ground in EPCaa. 100(*c*) and 138(1)(*c*) and in CPCa. 57(1)(*c*). The presence of added matter, extending beyond that previously disclosed, whether in a specification as originally filed or in a divisional specification under section 15(4) or a new specification filed by the true proprietor in entitlement cases under sections 8(3), 12 or 37(4), is a ground of revocation; section 76 forbids adding new matter in such cases and in amendments under sections 17(3), 18(3), 19(1), 27(1), 73 and 75 and, if any such amendment is made or permitted, a ground of revocation arises under section 72(1)(*d*). There is a slight difference in language between sections 72(1)(*d*) and 76 ("matter . . . beyond that disclosed") and EPCa. 123(2) ("matter that extends beyond the content"), but these can be assumed to have the same effect. The prohibition against the introduction of "added matter" contained in section 76 is discussed in detail in paras. 76.09–76.16.

Ground (*e*) of subsection (1) is complementary to that of ground (*d*). There is a corresponding ground in EPCa 138(1)(*d*) and in CPCa. 57(1)(*d*). Whereas ground (*d*) prohibits any extension of the "disclosure" of a specification, ground (*e*) prohibits any amendment which "extends the protection conferred by the patent". Such an amendment can only arise from post-grant proceedings under any of sections 27(1), 73 or 75, or during opposition proceedings before the EPO under EPCa. 99 (see s. 77(4) and para. 17.11), *i.e.* as the result of an amendment which offends under new section 76(3)(*b*), for which see para. 76.17. This is because, until grant has occurred, the "extent of protection" is not determined. Therefore, amendments to extend the scope of existing claims can in principle, be made during prosecution under sections 17(3), 18(3) and 19(1), but provided that the amendment does not involve added matter, see new section 76(2). However, any such amendment is rarely allowed, see para. 76.16.

Objections under grounds (*d*) and (*e*) can be raised by an applicant for revocation whether or not he was a party to the amendment proceedings.

While ground (*e*) refers to "amendment", ground (*d*) does not. Thus, because correction (of a self-evident mistake in the specification) under section 117 does not appear to be regarded as an amendment (see para. 117.08), it may be that any impermissible correction under section 117 would be a ground for revocation under subsection (1)(*d*) if it added new matter, but not under subsection (1)(*e*) if it extended the scope of protection. However, as (under r. 91(4), discussed in para. 117.06) a specification can only be corrected if the correction is self-evident, it can surely be argued that the effective content of the specification and the effective scope of protection is not varied by a permissible correction having regard particularly to section 125.

—Effect of subsection (1)(d) and (e) in practice   **72.26**

Where revocation is established under subsection (1)(*d*) and (*e*) it can be argued that the invalidity of the patent should be total, rather than limited, and consequently that subsection (4) is inapplicable with the result that a correcting amendment under section 75 would then be precluded. However, the view that a finding of invalidity under subsection (1)(*d*) or (*e*) may have fatal effect was not followed by either the Comptroller or the Patents Court in *Harding's Patent* ([1988] RPC 515), discussed in para. 76.17, and the possibility of avoiding revocation by amendment seems implicit from the wording of EPCa. 102(3), though neither subsection (4) nor section 75 are mentioned in section 130(7). The fact that subsections 72(1) and (2) are specified in section 130(7), while section 76 with which these subsections are linked is not so specified, is discussed in para. 76.19.

Also, it is difficult to see how either of grounds (*d*) or (*e*) could normally be applied because amendment (whether pre-grant or post-grant) is always an exercise of discretion which would not normally be permitted unless the tribunal were satisfied that there was no violation of the restrictions imposed by section 76, and a proprietor is presumably entitled to defend an allegation under subsection (1)(*d*) or (*e*) on the basis that he has a finding in his favour that there has been no improper amendment. By analogy with section 31(2) [1949], which provides that any amendment made (to an existing patent) "shall not be called in question except on the ground of fraud" it may be that grounds (*d*) and (*e*), which were inserted in the Act to conform with EPC principles, would only be applied if the applicant for revocation could show that the amendments made were obtained either as the result of fraudulent conduct or at least by a failure to disclose to the tribunal some relevant fact then known to the applicant or proprietor. Certainly, to succeed under subsection (1)(*d*) or (*e*) there would appear to be a heavy onus on the applicant for revocation.

In *Smith's Patent* (SRIS O/16/86), objections were raised, during revocation proceedings before the Comptroller, under both subsections (1)(*d*) and (*e*). It was held that the objections only had to be considered in the light of section 76: these were then dismissed on the facts of the case. An objection under subsection (1)(*d*) was also rejected in *Genentech's Patent* ([1987] RPC 553 and [1989] RPC 147 (CA)) where a mistake in the specification as filed, subsequently amended but apparently not in a manner wholly correcting the previous mistake, was held to be only a minor irritant to the reader. This suggests that, for an objection to be upheld under subsection (1)(*d*) or (*e*), the amendment must be one of significance with the unamended specification misleading the reader in a material respect. In *Harding's Patent* (*supra*), the court held that an amendment contrary to subsection (1)(*d*) had been made, but remitted the case to the Comptroller for the consideration of a possible validating amendment.

Of course these two particular grounds of revocation are inapplicable if there has been no amendment to the specification since the date of filing or (in the case of subsection (1)(*e*)) to the claims since grant. However, the making of any amendment gives rise to a potential attack under these grounds, though the indications are that, while such contentions will often be raised, they are unlikely to succeed in the absence of a showing that the tribunal previously allowing the amendment had in some way been misled.

Objection under subsection (*d*) or (*e*) can act as a squeeze argument. Thus, in *Hindmarch's Patent* (SRIS O/31/89, *noted* IPD 12049), the Patentee successfully defended an objection of having added matter by showing that the added matter was implicit in the specification. However, as such, it was also implicit in the prior art and the claims were then invalidated in the light of the prior art as so construed.

72.27   *Partial revocation (subs. (4))*

Subsection (4) provides for an order by the court or the Comptroller for unconditional revocation of the patent, but if the patent is invalid to a limited extent there may be an order for revocation unless the specification is satisfactorily amended under section 75 within the time specified. There is a similar provision in section 63(3) where, in the course of infringement proceedings, the patent is found only partially valid. In the past, as discussed in para. 75.06, the courts have drawn a distinction, in exercising discretion to permit amendment, between mere excision of invalid claims and more extensive amendment when the patentee had chosen to support his claims and appeal unfavourable decisions.

An order of revocation, or partial revocation, of a European patent (UK) made by the EPO as the result of opposition proceedings brought under EPCa. 99 is to have automatic effect in the United Kingdom under section 77(4) or (4A), see para. 77.11.

Estoppel (subss. (5) and (6))   **72.28**

Subsection (5) provides that, where a decision has been given on validity by the Comptroller, or on appeal from the Comptroller, a party to civil proceedings can again raise the issue of validity. Section 74 specifies the types of proceedings in which validity can be challenged, so that the proceedings in which subsection (5) can be invoked are those under sections 58, 61, 69, 70, 71 or 72, with the position under section 73 being unclear in the absence of reference thereto in section 74. However, findings of the EPO in an opposition to a European patent (UK) under EPCa. 99 may well give rise to an issue estoppel between the parties because subsection (5) only applies to a decision of the Comptroller or an appeal therefrom, see *Amersham International* v. *Corning Limited* ([1987] RPC 53 at 60; OJEPO 12/1987, 558) where the point appears to have been appreciated and conceded.

As a result of subsection (5), a proprietor may be called upon to defend revocation proceedings under section 72, which may prove to be lengthy and expensive, and, if successful in defending validity, may still find that if infringement proceedings are later instituted he may yet again be called upon to defend an attack on validity on the same grounds as before, and, as subsection (5) refers to "any person", possibly against the same person. If the proprietor succeeds in obtaining a certificate of contested validity under section 65 (for which see para. 65.03), the matter of costs will to some extent be alleviated. On the other hand, if the proprietor is unsuccessful in proceedings under section 72, the patent is wholly or partly revoked. The proprietor finds at least some respite in subsection (6) which provides that an unsuccessful applicant for revocation before the Comptroller may not make a similar application to the court without leave of the court, see also para. 72.31 *infra*.

Referral to the court (subs. (7))   **72.29**

Subsection (7) also precludes an applicant for revocation before the Comptroller from aplying for revocation to the court under the same patent while his application is still pending, unless the proprietor of the patent agrees (subs. (7)(*a*)). Under subsection (7)(*b*) the Comptroller may at any time during section 72 proceedings before him certify in writing that the question whether the patent should be revoked is one which would, in his opinion, be more properly determined by the court. The proceedings before the Comptroller then effectively terminate and the applicant for revocation, if he wishes to proceed, is required to commence proceedings before the court within 28 days, see RSC Ord. 104, r. 17(*c*) reprinted at para. E104.17.

Concurrent proceedings   **72.30**

Without the leave of the court, revocation proceedings before the Comptroller under section 72 cannot be instituted if *any* proceedings involving the patent are already before the court, see section 74(7) discussed in para. 74.06. In a case where proceedings under section 72 (as well as for a declaration of non-infringement under s. 71) had already been commenced before the Comptroller and the proprietor subsequently started infringement proceedings before the court against the applicant for revocation, the court stayed the court proceedings on a plea by the applicant for revocation that he could not afford to defend the court action and was prepared to abide by the Comptroller's decision (*Hawker Siddeley* v. *Real Time*, [1983] RPC 295). However, this decision was distinguished in *Gen Set* v. *Mosarc* ([1985] FSR 302) where: the court proceedings were commenced first; both parties could afford High Court costs, which were unlikely greatly to exceed those in the Patent Office; and where the court felt that a determination of the dispute by the court was likely to be reached more quickly than by an application for revocation brought before the Comptroller.

The Patents Court has firmly taken the view that, despite the existence of a pending opposition in the EPO to a European patent (UK), its validity is a matter for the national court so that proceedings should not be stayed pending determination of the opposition (*Amersham International* v. *Corning Limited*, [1987] RPC 53; OJEPO 12/1987, 558), see also *Pall Corp.* v. *Commercial Hydraulics* ([1988] FSR 274 and SRIS C/80/89 (CA)): nor should the existence of the opposition prevent the imposition of an interlocutory injunction (*Improver Corp.* v. *Innovations*, SRIS C/16/88, *noted* IPD 11002).

When two proceedings become co-pending before the Comptroller (for example an application for amendment under s. 27 and one for revocation under s. 72), the Comptroller apparently has power to decide which of the proceedings should be heard first (*Gibbons' Patent*, [1957] RPC 155).

72.31 *Effect of previous proceedings before the Comptroller or EPO*

Had the provisions of subsection (5) not been inserted, an unsuccessful applicant for revocation before the Comptroller, hindered perhaps by failure to request (or obtain) full discovery or cross-examination of witnesses before the Comptroller, could have found himself unable to contest validity when subsequently sued for infringement because at least an issue estoppel would likely have been held against him on the principles as laid down in *Carl-Zeiss-Stiftung* v. *Rayner and Keeler (No. 2)* ([1967] RPC 497 (HL)) namely that an estoppel will arise from proceedings which have previously taken place between the same parties (or their privies) involving the same issue and which have led to a final determination of that issue. *Bristol-Myers* v. *Beecham [Israel]* ([1978] FSR 553) was a case which concerned the possible application of issue estoppel to patent proceedings where an issue of validity had perhaps previously been litigated (although in another country). However, in that case, no estoppel was held because the previous proceedings were not a final determination of the issue. On the question whether an estoppel could arise where the previous litigation involved two separate grounds of invalidity, only one of which pertained in the subsequent proceedings, the Israel Supreme Court was equally divided and so no decision was given on this particular point which may therefore be considered open. However, in the *Carl Zeiss* case, Lord Reid pointed out that estoppels from foreign judgments should be applied with considerable caution.

Thus, questions of issue estoppel can arise where corresponding patents have been litigated elsewhere between the same parties. Whereas, normally, an allegation of issue estoppel could be resisted on the ground that the issues (validity of patents to be dealt with under different laws) are not the same, this argument did not find favour in the Israel case (*supra*) and, anyway, is one difficult to sustain in the case of patents granted in EPC countries, perhaps centrally, and in any event under laws which are intended to have been harmonised and to be given similar effect by reason of the Strasbourg Convention on Harmonisation (1963) and the EPC. Certainly such estoppels will arise under a Community patent granted under CPC because such would be a unitary patent and it appears will also arise from failure of an opposition in the EPO against a European patent (U.K.), see para. 72.28 *infra*. Certainly subsection (5) will not protect an opponent who has been unsuccessful under EPCa. 99, but there will nevertheless be no estoppel if the EPO decision to uphold the patent is regarded not as a final one but one on the grounds raised therein only, and then perhaps only on the material then put before the EPO. While the basis of estoppel is that it is in the public interest that there should be an end to litigation, it is also in the public interest that invalid monopolies should not be perpetuated lest they affect some other member of the public. Another argument against an estoppel from EPO opposition proceedings may be based on the provisions of the Brussels Convention referred to in para. 72.13 *infra*.

PRACTICE UNDER SECTION 72

General **72.32**

Because applications for revocation made to the court are normally filed as counterclaims to actions for infringement, cases involving procedure before the court are mainly discussed *re* Practice under section 61 at paras. 61.21–61.38. The relevant rules of court are those of RSC Ord. 104, rr. 4–16 reprinted at paras. E104.04–E104.16. Separate petitions would appear to be necessary when more than one patent is sought to be revoked. Where the proprietor is outside the jurisdiction, service of a petition for revocation by the court may be subject to the same problems as are discussed in para. 71.09.

Accordingly, unless otherwise stated, the practice considered hereunder applies only to proceedings before the Comptroller. Such practice applies, in principle, to all contested (*i.e. inter partes*) proceedings heard by the Comptroller and, therefore, the remarks hereunder apply generally to such proceedings and not only to applications for revocation made to the Comptroller under section 72. Individual variations from this general procedure for particular proceedings are discussed *re. Practice under the sections pertaining thereto.

The following rules are generally relevant, not only to applications for revocation under section 72, but for all *inter partes* proceedings before the Comptroller. Any variations from the general position for particular proceedings is noted in the commentaries on these proceedings.

Rule	Subject of rule	Reprinted at para.	Relevant commentary at para.
21	(Form of statement, counter-statement and evidence)	72.02	72.37
88	(Comptroller's discretionary powers)	101.02	101.08
89	(Hearings in public)	101.03	101.07
90	(Powers of agent)	115.02	115.03
91	(Correction)	117.02	117.14
94	(Confidential documents)	118.06	118.21
100	(Correction of irregularities)	123.07	123.20
101	(Dispensation by Comptroller)	123.08	123.23
103	(Evidence)	72.05	72.40
104	(Statutory declarations and affidavits)	72.06	72.41
105	(Admission of documents)	72.07	72.41
106	(Directions as to furnishing of documents, etc.)	72.08	72.44
107	(Supporting statements or evidence)	72.09	72.34

Rule	Subject of rule	Reprinted at para.	Relevant commentary at para.
109	(Appointment of advisers)	72.10	72.49
110	(Alteration of time limits)	123.10	123.30
112	(Copies of documents)	72.11	72.37
113	(Translations)	123.12	123.41

Note. Rule 107 is relevant for certain *inter partes* proceedings, though not for applications for revocation.

In all proceedings before the Comptroller an address for service must be given in accordance with rule 30, normally on the form by which a party enters the proceedings in question. Rule 30 is discussed in para. 32.16 where it is pointed out that the address given may be changed so that it need no longer be within the United Kingdom, though it would have to be within the EEC.

72.33 *General procedure in applications for revocation made to the Comptroller*

The specific procedure for revocation proceedings before the Comptroller is specifically governed by rules 75 and 76, reprinted respectively at paras. 72.03 and 72.04 *infra*. The application is made by filing PF 38/77 (reprinted at para. 141.38) accompanied by a statement of case (complying in form with r. 21, reprinted at para. 72.02, and filed in duplicate) (r. 75(1)). Rule 107 does not apply under rule 75 so that in the case of an application for revocation the statement must accompany the form (but with some proceedings, where there is a more rigid time limit for filing the initiating form, rule 107 permits the filing of the accompanying statement (or evidence) within 14 days after the filing of the form constituting the notice initiating the proceedings, see para. 72.34 (*infra*). The statement of case (discussed more fully in para. 72.37 *infra*) should set out fully the grounds of revocation, the facts relied upon and the relief sought (r. 75(1)).

If the application is formally in order, the Comptroller sends the duplicate form and statement to the proprietor (r. 75(2)) and invites him to file, within three months if he wishes to contest the application, a counter-statement (also complying with r. 21 and in duplicate, and discussed more fully in para. 72.39 *infra*) setting out fully the grounds upon which the application is contested: the duplicate copy is then sent by the Comptroller to the applicant at the notified address for service, usually that of the appointed agent (r. 75(3)). The application is also noted in the O.J., see para. 123.27, as also, eventually, is the result.

Successive periods each of three months are provided for the submission of evidence (in each case complying with r. 21), with the applicant for revocation filing his evidence in chief first, the proprietor then filing his evidence (which should include both his evidence in chief and that in reply to the applicant for revocation), and finally the applicant for revocation filing further evidence strictly in reply to that of the proprietor (rr. 75(4), (5)). Thereafter, no further evidence can be filed except with leave of the Comptroller (r. 75(6)). For an example of inadmissible reply evidence, see *Ford Motors' (Nastas') Application* ([1968] RPC 220). Late-filed evidence will be admitted if it is "both relevant and decisive" (*Rohm and Haans' Application* [1966] FSR 403), and when amendments are put forward which change the situation (*Reuter's Application* [1973] RPC 83).

In each case the evidence (attested as required by r. 104, reprinted at para. 72.06) is filed at the Patent Office (together with original exhibits thereto) and the party filing the same supplies a copy directly to the other party or his agent.

Where exhibits cannot be copied, they can be inspected at the Patent Office. Each of the three month periods is extensible by discretion exercised under rule 110(1), for which see para. 123.35.

Thereafter the procedure is flexible (r. 75(7)), but the application will eventually proceed to a hearing under section 101, for procedure at which, and publication of the ensuing decision, see paras. 101.09–101.12.

Time limits and extensions of time   **72.34**

In the case of certain proceedings (though not those under s. 72), rule 107 (reprinted at para. 72.09) provides a 14 day grace period after the necessary form to initiate the proceedings has been filed within which the required statement (and evidence) may be filed. These proceedings are those under the following rules:

40(3) (Opposition to amendment under s. 27);
41(1) (Opposition to restoration);
43(3) (Opposition to surrender);
65(1) (Opposition to "Licence of right" entry);
66(2) (Opposition to cancellation of "Licence of right" entry);
71(2) (Opposition to grant of compulsory licence);
78(2) (Opposition to amendment under s. 75); and
91(5) (Opposition to application for correction).

When the initiating application by way of opposition (including an application for revocation) is filed, the Comptroller normally sends a copy of such papers as have been initially filed to the proprietor or otherwise as required by the relevant rule. At that time it is stated whether the application for revocation (or otherwise as the case may be) is prima facie in order. The time for filing a counter-statement (or taking other action) does not begin until the formal requirements (r. 75(1) in the case of a revocation application) have been met, and such documents and translations as required by rules 112 and 113 (reprinted respectively at paras. 72.11 and 123.12) have been supplied. The proprietor (or other relevant person) is then notified that if he wishes to contest the application, a counter-statement (or notice of opposition) should be filed within the prescribed period, normally three months.

Extensions of time for filing a counter-statement, or subsequently for the filing of evidence, are obtainable under rule 110(1) (reprinted in para. 123.10 and discussed in para. 123.35). The consent of the other party or parties should first be sought and preferably accompany the request, which should reach the Patent Office before the term expires, though extension is still possible thereafter, see section 123(3A). If consent is refused, the Comptroller may still grant an extension with or without a hearing. Any party can, however, require a hearing, see para. 101.04.

The form of request which is preferred by the Patent Office is a letter as follows: "We ask for an extension of time of . . . for filing the . . . in these proceedings. The reason is that . . .

Yours faithfully
Agents for the Patentee
(or Applicant for Revocation)
We agree to the extension requested above.
Agents for the Applicant for Revocation
(or Patentee)

A note on the practice under the 1949 Act was pubished in the O.J. May 29, 1969 and is believed to remain generally applicable after necessary adaptation to the present statute and rules.

An appeal lies to the Patents Court from any decision of the Comptroller regarding an application for extension of time, but because such would be an appeal on a procedural matter, it would be necessary to lodge the notice of appeal at the Chancery Chambers within 14 days of the decision, see para. 97.12. However, the Patents Court will normally not disturb an exercise of discretion by the Comptroller, though see para. 99.02. Also, an extension could be refused entirely, with the appellant then being out of time, if the Patents Court were to think that an appeal had only been brought to gain time beyond that contemplated by the rule or deliberately in order to delay the proceedings.

72.35 *Acting through an agent*

Normally an applicant for revocation will act through an agent who will file PF 38/77 giving his own address as that for service. Although no authorisation is required to be filed (r. 90(1)), an agent should first satisfy himself that he has in fact been duly authorised to apply for revocation. As discussed in para. 115.03, the Comptroller can require to be satisfied that such authorisation does exist; here it should be noted that an existing general authorisation may not be broad enough to provide authority for proceedings against a third party patent or application, also as discussed in para. 115.03.

72.36 *Prior notice and security for costs*

If the proprietor is given no previous notice of the intention to apply for revocation, the applicant for revocation may be denied an award of costs if the proprietor offers to surrender his patent under section 29 (r. 76, reprinted at para. 72.04).

When an applicant for revocation neither resides nor carries on business in the United Kingdom, security for costs may be required to be given (s. 107(4)(*b*)), and likewise as regards any persons in entitlement proceedings under section 8, 12 or 37 (s. 107(4)(*a*)) or by an opponent under section 27(5), 29(2), 47(6) or 52(1) (s. 107(4)(*c*)). The procedure and amount of security required is discussed in para. 107.05.

72.37 *Statement of case*

This must comply with the requirements of rule 21 (reprinted at para. 72.02 *infra*, which in turn requires compliance with r. 20(1), (3) and (4), for which see para. 14.05). The statement should also set out fully the grounds of revocation, the facts relied on and the relief sought (r. 75(1)). All relevant documents to be relied upon should be fully cited and preferably be given a label such as the name of the inventor or author in question, see *Du Pont's (Dahlstrom and Bunting's) Patent* ([1976] RPC 177 at 195 (CA)) and (1975–76) 15 CIPA 269. An indication should be given as to which claims are attacked and on which grounds, see *Benz's Application* ([1958] RPC 78), and copies thereof (except for United Kingdom published patent specifications) should be supplied (r. 112, reprinted at para. 72.11) together with a verified translation of any cited document which is not in English (r. 113(1) reprinted in para. 123.12 and discussed in para. 123.41), all in duplicate.

Rule 112 is couched in more mandatory terms than the former rule (r. 44(1) [1968], reprinted at para. A033.08) because the former discretion to waive the requirement to supply copy documents is no longer explicitly stated in rule 112. Thus, care should be taken not to cite documents unnecessarily, especially if in a foreign language, because copies of such must then be made available to the other party (even if not available to the public as such), together with any necessary translation. Any instance of alleged prior use should be fully particularised, see

Gibbons' Patent ([1957] RPC 155). On the sufficiency of the statement, see further RSC Ord. 104, r. 6 (reprinted at para. E104.6), the principles of which can be expected to be followed if objection to its sufficiency is taken, either by the Comptroller or the other party. Indeed, a wholly speculative case may be dismissed *in limine* because "a case wholly unsupported by evidence is in reality no case at all" (*Richco Plastic's Parent*, SRIS O/22/89, *noted* IPD 12037), though this *dictum* is more likely to apply to other proceedings before the Comptroller rather than ones for revocation, the *Richco* case being a speculative application for a compulsory licence, see para. 48.19.

In *Powerscreen* v. *Finlay* ([1979] FSR 108) the court indicated that, in an appropriate case, it would be proper to require an applicant for revocation to make a statement identifying which features of apparatus disclosed in a publication were to be considered as corresponding to the features of the claim under attack for alleged anticipation or obviousness.

Amendment of a statement of case, or the filing of a supplementary statement, may be allowed in the exercise of the Comptroller's discretion and the counter-statement may then be amended or a supplementary counter-statement filed. The question of allowing amendment is essentially a question of discretion to be exercised in the public interest, bearing in mind: (a) whether the application to add new grounds has been made diligently; (b) the relevance of those grounds; (c) the current length of the proceedings; and (d) whether the delay which amendment would cause would be unjust to the patentee or against the public interest (*Owens-Corning's Patent*, [1972] RPC 684). In this case, which has been followed in *Rockwool International's Patent* (SRIS O/27/89, *noted* IPD 12038) the former Patents Appeal Tribunal stated (in proceedings under s. 33 [1949]) that the Patent Office is under an obligation to pay attention in proceedings to any new document which may be brought to their attention in one way or another; and, in *Rockwool*, the Comptroller stated that new grounds ought to be admitted if they arise as a direct response to an unforeseeable aspect of the patentee's case, unless there are overriding considerations. The Comptroller and the court may make an independent investigation in any case in which this may appear useful (*Warnant's Application*, [1956] RPC 205). However, it could be that the public interest would be sufficiently satisfied by reference to the new document becoming recorded in the patent file, even if there were no determination whether it prejudiced the validity of the patent.

Multiple applications   72.38

If more than one application for revocation becomes co-pending, the proceedings are quite separate from each other, though a joint hearing can be requested if two cases are ready for hearing at about the same time. The various applicants for revocation should make arrangements to keep themselves informed of events occurring in the parallel applications for revocation. In particular, different parties relying on the same foreign language document are advised to check the accuracy of the translation provided by another applicant for revocation because a conflict may weaken their own case.

Counter-statement   72.39

The counter-statement must also comply with the formal requirements of rule 21, *i.e.* with the formal requirements of rule 20(1), (3) and (4) (reprinted in para. 14.05); it should fully set out the grounds upon which the application is contested. Thus the counter-statement should correspond to a defence to an action before the court. Any allegation not specifically denied is likely to be taken to be admitted. However, a mere denial of allegations made by the applicant for revocation has been held to be sufficient, see *Marshall's Application* ([1969] RPC 83). Nevertheless, any positive defence to be relied upon should be properly pleaded (*Du Pont's (Werner's) Application*, [1975] FSR 193), see also *Woollard's Patent* ([1989] RPC 141) supporting the proposition that a party making a positive allegation (in this case in contesting an application for a declaration of non-infringement on the ground that there would be infringement) should explain the basis for his allegation.

Where the fact whether a particular document was ever made available to the addressee of the attacked specification and, if so, at what date, is desired to be resisted, a specific denial should be made, thereby requiring the applicant for revocation to prove the facts of publication as part of his evidence, see *Benz's Application* ([1958] RPC 78): availability to the public will otherwise be assumed. If the fact of publication is denied, informal proof (for example, a letter from a librarian) can be supplied and the other party asked to consider making a formal admission.

A failure to file a counter-statement will mean that the application for revocation is undefended; see *Fontaine's Patent* ([1959] RPC 72) and *Curtis' Patent* ([1965] FSR 59) in each of which there was an inability to take action. The Comptroller may then revoke the patent or he may proceed to decide the matter, as he will also do if the patent is allowed to lapse or is surrendered, see *Ritzerfeld's Patent*, SRIS O/102/81.

Evidence

72.40   *—Form of evidence*

The mode of providing evidence in proceedings before the Comptroller is generally governed by rule 103 (reprinted at para. 72.05). Rule 103(1) provides that evidence is to be by way of statutory declaration or affidavit. For the mode of attesting such evidence, see para. 72.41 *infra*. Although evidence before the Comptroller need not comply with requirements for the court, by rule 21 it must comply as to form with rules 20(1), (3) and (4) (reprinted at para. 72.05), that is presented on A4 paper and capable of reproduction in an unlimited number of copies, though such evidence may be printed on both sides of the sheet. Although rule 20(1) requires presentation in English, presumably evidence in a foreign language is permitted if accompanied by a satisfactory translation, probably a sworn one in this case.

A statutory declaration should be in the form:

"I, A.B., of . . . do solemnly and sincerely declare that. . . . And I make this solemn declaration conscientiously believing the same to be true, and by virtue of the provisions of the Statutory Declarations Act 1835."

An affidavit should be in the form:

"I, A.B., of . . . make oath [or affirm] and say as follows: . . . ".

Each of these types of written evidence should be headed with reference to the proceedings for which it is to be made and conclude with the signature of the declarant/affiant followed by a jurat reading:—

Declared/Sworn [Affirmed] at . . .

this . . . day of . . . 198.

before me

and the qualification of the attesting officer should be stated, *e.g.* as "A solicitor entitled to administer oaths". The affidavit/declaration would appear to be void if the attesting officer is a solicitor to any of the parties or if he has an interest in the proceedings for which it is made (Commissioners for Oaths Act, 1889 (52 & 53 Vict., c. 10, s. 1(3)), see also RSC Ord. 41, rule 8 (reprinted at para. E041.8).

Exhibits to evidence may be lodged at the Patent Office. If possible a copy should be supplied to the other party. Otherwise, the exhibits may be inspected at the Patent Office and borrowed with the consent of the agent who lodged them.

Although evidence presented to the Comptroller need not comply with the rules of court, it is possible that it may subsequently be needed on appeal to the Patents Court and later to the Court of Appeal. Difficulties could then arise if the more detailed requirements of RSC Ord. 41, rr. 1 and 11 (reprinted at paras. E041.1 and E041.11) in relation to affidavits and exhibits thereto have not been met. A note ([1980] FSR 118) and a more complete *Practice Direction* ([1983] 1 WLR 922; [1983] 3 All ER 33) give details, the salient points of the latter being reprinted at para. E041.11A. Original affidavits filed in the Patent Office may be used on appeal to the Patents Court under the term of RSC Ord. 41, rule 10 (reprinted at para. E041.10). A copy of an affidavit used in court proceedings does not satisfy the requirements of rule 103 (*Taylor's Patent*, [1970] RPC 108).

The fee payable on making an affidavit, statutory declaration or affirmation is now £3.50, with an additional £1.00 for each exhibit thereto, inclusive of any value added tax (Commissioners for Oaths (Fees) (No. 2) Order, S.I. 1988 No. 998).

—Attestation of evidence **72.41**

Rule 104 (reprinted at para. 72.06 *infra*) prescribes the form of attestation for declarations and affidavits, while rule 105 (reprinted at para. 72.07 *infra*) dispenses with the need for authentication of the seal or signature of the person making the declaration or swearing the affidavit. An affidavit is on oath and subject to the penalties for a false oath. Under the Solicitors Act 1974 (c. 47, s. 81), an affidavit or declaration can be attested in the United Kingdom by any practising solicitor (other than one having an interest in the proceedings). Outside the United Kingdom, the most convenient procedure is to arrange attestation by a notary public or authorised consular office (r. 104(*b*) and (*c*)). Where evidence is attested in a part of the Commonwealth outside England and Wales, proof of the seal or signature of the attesting person is not required, but elsewhere verification of the attesting signature is required, see RSC Ord. 41, rule 12 (reprinted at para. E041.12).

—Powers of the Comptroller concerning evidence **72.42**

Rule 103(2) provides for oral evidence, in addition to or in lieu of, the normal written form of evidence. It also provides that the Comptroller "*shall* allow any witness to be cross-examined on his affidavit or declaration, unless he directs otherwise" (emphasis added).

The powers of the Comptroller under a rule 103(3) and (4) would now seem to extend to the possible ordering of a party to answer (on oath) approved interrogatories, because this is a power possessed by the court in relation to the giving of evidence, see RSC Ord. 26, rule 1 (reprinted at para. E026.1). Indeed this seemed possible under rule 141 [1968], see *Fuji Photo's Patent* ([1974] RPC 639), but the Comptroller is generally reluctant to exercise all the powers of the court in relation to the giving of evidence, etc., even when he is empowered to do so.

Rule 103(3) and (4) gives the Comptroller no power to punish summarily for contempt of court. It should be noted that under rule 103(3) and (4) the Comptroller, or the court acting for him could, presumably, issue a subpoena against a reluctant witness. However, there is no power whereby a subpoena can be issued against a witness who is resident outside the jurisdiction specified in rules 103(3) and (4). The principles which should be considered when cross-examination of a witness is resisted were extensively discussed in the case of *Beecham Group* v. *Bristol-Myers (No. 2)* [*New Zealand*] ([1979] 2 NZLR 629). In *Loewy's Application* ((1952) 69 RPC 3) it was argued that a declaration by a declarant who failed to attend for cross-examination, though summoned, should not be received or read, but the Comptroller received it in the exercise of his discretion.

A failure to challenge testimony by cross-examination can be relevant (*Laguerre's Patent*, [1971] RPC 384 (CA) and *Technic's Application*, [1973] RPC 383 at 406 (CA)). Otherwise, on a conflict of written evidence, the application for revocation should fail (*General Electric's (Cox's) Patent*, [1977] RPC 421).

In *Sainsbury's Application* ([1981] FSR 406) the Court of Appeal was informed that it was not the practice of the patent bar to cross-examine deponents in Patent Office proceedings. In refusing leave to cross-examine a witness on appeal to the Patents Court, the Court of Appeal stated: "If that be the practice, it is one which is a bad practice, because if there is good reason for wanting to cross-examine a deponent, then the proper time to do this is before the superintending examiner and not on appeal to the Patents Court". A failure by the parties to request cross-examination (as well as discovery) was also criticised in *Norris's Patent* ([1988] RPC 159).

Although the Comptroller has no power to issue an injunction, under rule 103(3) he can restrain a party from using before him any evidence which is shown to be subject to legal privilege, see *Sonic Tapes' Patent* ([1987] RPC 251).

On the possible admission of further evidence on appeal, see para. 97.16.

In proceedings under sections 48–51, a statement made in a report of the Monopolies and Mergers Commission in respect to any activity in relation to a patented invention is to be taken as prima facie evidence and does not require any supporting declaration or affidavit (s. 53(2)).

72.43   —*Evidence of a hearsay nature*

Section 2 of the Civil Evidence Act 1968 (c. 64) permits a statement made, whether orally or in a document or otherwise, to be admitted as evidence of any fact stated therein, provided that direct oral evidence of that fact by the maker of the statement would itself be admissible, and subject to due notice of the intention to rely upon such a statement being given to others involved in the proceedings. Section 1 of the Civil Evidence Act 1972 (c. 30) extends this provision to evidence of opinion subject to the same limitations. However, the proviso precludes the giving of evidence of a second-hand hearsay nature under those sections, though other provisions of the 1968 Act permit second-hand hearsay evidence when it is contained in documentary or computer records. The provisions of these two Acts do not apply to proceedings to which the strict rules of evidence do not apply (1968 Act, s. 18; 1972 Act, s. 5) and proceedings before the Comptroller may be proceedings of this type (*Miller* v. *Minister of Housing*, [1969] RPC 91). However, the principles of the 1968 and 1972 Acts are likely to be applied in proceedings before the Comptroller, particularly to exclude hearsay evidence which is other than that given first hand, see *Microsonics' Application* ([1984] RPC 29) where some of the evidence presented would not have been admitted in the court even if it had been given orally.

In *Genentech's Patent* (SRIS C/66/87) the Court gave the Plaintiffs leave, under the Civil Evidence Acts, to give in evidence at the trial "all statements contained in the documents disclosed by the Defendants on discovery".

—Discovery and power to require production of documents **72.44**

Rule 103(3) and (4) gives the Comptroller the powers of the relevant court to order discovery. This topic is mainly discussed, in relation to court proceedings, in paras. 61.28–61.32. However, rule 106 gives the Comptroller a more extensive, and entirely general, power to require production of documents and to set terms within which they are to be furnished. This supplements the powers of discovery and production of documents given by rule 103(3) and (4).

The same power was originally given by rule 141 [1968] and in *Petrie and McNaught's Application* ([1966] FSR 234), where prior use by the applicants was alleged, the Applicants were ordered to give a list of documents to the Comptroller so that he could decide which should be produced, but discovery was refused as unnecessary in *Temmler-Werke's Patent* ([1966] RPC 187) and in *Ajinomoto's Patent* ([1965] FSR 95). In *Beecham Group's [Amoxycillin] Application* ([1980] RPC 261) it was decided, without establishing any general rule as to the cut-off date for discovery of documents relevant to validity, that the applicants should give discovery (under the 1949 Act in relation to an opposition alleging obviousness) of their internal documents coming into existence before the filing date of the complete specification, the principle of giving some discovery in that case having been conceded.

The increased powers of the Comptroller given under the present Act and rule 103(3) and (4) ought to result in discovery and other evidential procedures before the Comptroller becoming increasingly aligned with court procedure, for which see the discussion on "Discovery" in para. 61.28, especially the cases concerning production of the inventor's research notes and of evidence of commercial success, though the Comptroller will not (in the exercise of his discretion) order discovery of documents under rule 103 unless this is necessary "in order to dispose fairly of the matter or to save costs", see *John Guest's Patent* ([1987] RPC 259). However, in *Halcon's Patent* (SRIS O/118/86, *noted* IPD 9081 and SRIS C/98/97, *noted* IPD 11008) discovery was ordered (in compulsory licence proceedings under s. 48) of a document concerning the costs and profitability of working the invention, but other requests for discovery were stayed until after determination of the pending appeal proceedings ([1989] RPC 1).

Rule 106 was invoked in *Waddington's Application* ([1986] RPC 158) to require an applicant for amendment to identify the prior art which had occasioned the application. The rule has also been applied, in an application to settle the terms of a licence of right under section 46(3), to require production of previous licence agreements, see *Smith Kline & French's Cimetidine Patents* ([1988] RPC 148). Here it was observed that documents produced on an order made under rule 106 became available as evidence in the case even if not relied upon by either party to a contested proceeding.

Most patent forms draw specific attention to rule 106, presumably as the basis on which the Comptroller could require to be satisfied that an agent was properly authorised to act in a particular matter before him, see para. 115.03.

If discovery is ordered, claims to "privilege" can be made which (if successful) result in non-disclosure of the documents held, or conceded, to be privileged. The question of privilege is mainly discussed in paras. 104.06–104.09. A claim for privilege for documents in opposition proceedings before the Comptroller (under s. 14 [1949]) was upheld in *Cooper Mechanical Joints' Application* ([1958] RPC 295).

—Restrictions on disclosure of discovered documents **72.44A**

Where discovery is ordered, or rule 106 is invoked to require documents to be produced, confidentiality orders may be, and often are, imposed. As regards the

Patent Office file, confidentiality orders under rule 94 (reprinted at para. 118.06) can be requested, see para. 118.17. However, where circumstances so require, because documents disclose commercially sensitive information which would be valuable in the hands of the other parties to the proceedings for reasons unconnected therewith, it has become commonplace for the Comptroller to order that a party should have limited access to the documents produced on discovery or under rule 106. This follows the position established by the court in *Warner-Lambert* v. *Glaxo* ([1975] RPC 354 at 361) concerning disclosure of the Defendant's secret, allegedly non-infringing, process, see also *Centri-Spray* v. *Cerosa* ([1979] FSR 175).

Thus, in *Heathway Machine's Compulsory Licence Application* (SRIS O/111/80), discovery of a licence agreement between the patentee and another was produced, but with disclosure limited to the Applicant's legal advisers and a chosen representative after that person had signed and returned an undertaking "not to divulge the information, or any part of it, to any person, firm or company save with the consent of the patentee and not to use the information or permit it to be used for any purpose other than a purpose connected with the present proceedings". For other examples, concerning accountancy evidence, see *Geigy's Patent* ([1964] RPC 391); *Smith Kline & French's Patent* ([1965] RPC 98); and *Ibstock Building Products' Patent* (SRIS O/1/89), where disclosure (in a claim for employee-inventor compensation under s. 40) was limited to a single named accountant.

Another example (in court proceedings) is *Format Communications* v. *ITT* ([1983] FSR 473 (CA)) where a party seeking inspection by one of its employees of a complex computer software code offered certain safeguards to minimise the risk of trade secrets being obtained as a result of the inspection. An order was made accordingly.

Objections to patent agents receiving confidential information have not been accepted, provided that the patent agent, if an employee of one of the parties or of a company associated therewith, has first signed a specific undertaking to receive the information only in his professional capacity (*Unilever* v. *Pearce*, [1985] FSR 475), and see *Schering's Patent* ([1986] RPC 30) where not only was a stringent undertaking required from the employed patent agent, but his employer and the patentee were each required to give undertakings to respect the confidentiality undertaking given by the patent agent. In *Halcon's Patent* (SRIS O/118/86, *noted* IPD 9081 and SRIS O/98/87, *noted* IPD 11008) the document (an assessment of costs and profitability) was to be handed over to the patent agent of a compulsory licence applicant but to be seen only by counsel, solicitors and patent agents within the jurisdiction and with eventual return to the Patent Office.

In *Roussel-Uclaf* v. *ICI* (SRIS C/67/89) a "confidentiality club" of lawyers and an independent expert had been formed under the *Warner-Lambert* principles. The Defendant objected to any employee of the Plaintiff joining this "club" and thereby receiving information of its secret process which it alleged was different to that claimed in the patent. It was held that a party seeking to restrict disclosure had to justify his request, but that a balance had to be maintained between the interests of both parties, the Plaintiff here being hampered by non-disclosure as to experiments that could usefully be done to advance its case. The order made provided that: one member of the Plaintiff's patent department (in France) should receive the information in the strictest confidence, but that person had then to have no further involvement in the parallel litigation in France (where discovery is not available); the Plaintiff had to give an undertaking to pay damages in the United Kingdom for any breach of the confidentialty undertaking by it or its designated employee; and the documents could not be copied, nor could they be removed from the United Kingdom except in the custody of a solicitor.

It would seem probable that disclosure of documents on discovery takes place under the same conditions as apply in relation to discovery under the Rules of the

Supreme Court. Here there is an implied undertaking that the discovered documents will not be used for *any* purpose other than the conduct of the proceedings in which they are discovered, see para. 61.31.

—Evidence of experiments   **72.45**

Evidence of experiments can be given, but this should normally be done in evidence in chief, see *Union Carbide's (Hostettler's) Application* ([1972] RPC 601) and *Scragg's Application* ([1972] RPC 679). The other party could seek to have such experiments repeated in their presence as this accords with practice in proceedings before the court, see RPC Ord. 104, rule 12 (reprinted at para. E104.12). Otherwise, such experiments may be given less than full weight (*British Cast Iron's Patent*, [1976] RPC 33 at 48), or not admitted at all, as in *British Railways' Patent* (SRIS O/41/85). Indeed, in *Raufos' Patent* (SRIS C/102/86, *noted* IPD 12036) the Patents Court observed that experiments carried out in proceedings before the Comptroller should always comply with the Rules of Court. The question of experiments performed for the purposes of litigation is further considered in para. 61.35.

—Onus of proof   **72.46**

In *Dunlop's Application* ([1979] RPC 523) there are useful remarks on the onus of proof. The legal burden of this always rests on he who has to prove his allegations, *e.g.* on an applicant for revocation, but the evidential burden can shift, sometimes quite readily, to the patentee and then, perhaps, re-shift back to the applicant for revocation. On the sufficiency of proof of prior use, see also *O'Shei's Application* ([1958] RPC 72). Where a witness gives affidavit evidence in relation to anticipation or obviousness, and in doing so makes assertions in relation to his experience and that of his employer, it is possible that the witness or the employer could be issued with a subpoena to produce internal documents of a specified class which relate thereto, see *Lucas* v. *Hewitt [Australia]* ([1980] FSR 208).

If an apparent admission of prior use is made in written evidence, the onus lies on the party producing that evidence to establish that the admission was not properly made (*Fernberg's Patent*, [1958] RPC 133).

As regards the provision of evidence of background knowledge of the art in question, the hearing officer can be assumed to have a general, but not a detailed, knowledge of the art in question (*Eickhoff Maschinenfabrik's Patent*, SRIS O/31/87).

Amendments   **72.47**

Any amendments in revocation proceedings are subject to the limitations imposed by sections 72(1)(*d*), 75 and especially 76. There appears to be no obligation on the Comptroller to advertise the amendment, because any amendment is not under section 27 where advertisement is called for, but the Comptroller has a discretionary power under section 75 to do so. If the amendment is not advertised, or if advertised and there is no opponent, the amendment proceedings will normally be consolidated into the revocation proceedings. This is an example of the flexible procedure permitted by rule 75(7). In *Eickhoff Maschinenfabrik's Patent* (SRIS O/31/87), it was held that an applicant for revocation does not need to file opposition to an application to amend the patent in suit made under section 75 because he is already a party to proceedings before the Comptroller.

When any amendment is offered during the course of the proceedings, *i.e.* before any decision has been given on the merits of the case, the proprietor should indicate whether or not the offer to amend is firm and unconditional. If so, it would seem that the Comptroller's decision should deal both with the allowability of the offered amendments and with the objections to validity on the basis of the specifications as notionally amended in accordance with *Nippon Seal's Application* ([1973] FSR 276). If thought appropriate, the amendment application could be taken to a pre liminary hearing. This was done in *Beecham Group's (Amoxycillin) Application* ([1980] RPC 261) where amendments were provisionally allowed subject to the issue of discretion being left for decision at the substantive hearing on the validity issue. It is also possible to offer amendments conditional on an adverse finding being made. *Owens-Corning's Application* ([1973] FSR 451), in which case the sub stantive issues should be considered first on the basis of the unamended claim.

An unconditional offer to amend should be formally pleaded (*Clading-Boel' Application*, [1975] FSR 119) and such amendments may only be resiled from in an application to amend the pleadings. Where an unconditional offer is made, the Comptroller will normally indicate his prima facie view on the allowability of the amendments and then leave their consideration to the substantive hearing (*Dust Suppression's Application*, [1974] FSR 438), but the Comptroller's attitude may lead to some variation of the amendment proposals and thereby shorten the pro ceedings as a whole.

In *Osterman's Patent* ([1985] RPC 579) the counter-statement contained an offer to amend. It was held not necessary that the proprietor should give reasons for pro posing amendments as it was presumed (thus differing from proceedings under s. 27) that these were put forward to meet the alleged grounds of revocation. It was also held that there was no reason to depart from the normal procedure, so that the proprietor should not be required to file evidence until after that filed by the appli cant for revocation.

When a finding of prior use affects the question only of novelty, and is not rel evant to the question of obviousness because no teaching resulted from the prior use, a simple disclaimer of the prior use has been held (under the 1949 Act) to be effective to validate the patent (*Yates Industries' Application*, SRIS O/83/81).

When an amendment offered by the patentee causes the applicant for revocation to modify his case, the pleadings should be amended, or a supplementary statement filed, before the evidence is closed (*Horville Engineering's Application*, [1969] RPC 266).

An amendment will be disallowed if it does not meet the grounds of attack estab lished (*Bristol-Myers' (Johnson's) Application (No. 2)*, [1979] RPC 450). Other wise the saving of a patent by amendment is a matter of discretion.

When a claim has been disallowed, the patentee's attempts to save it by amend ment will be limited by the exercise of discretion according to the facts of each case Thus, in *Philips' (Bosgra's) Application* ([1974] RPC 241) the former Patent Appeal Tribunal indicated that, where broad original claims are maintained from the outset with no part taken in the proceedings after filing a counter-statement and the broad claims are found to be wholly lacking in merit, subsidiary claims should be approached with caution and the onus of establishing invention therein has shifted. Accordingly, when no assistance is given on the determination of ques tions raised on the subsidiary claims, it may well be that there should not be an unfettered opportunity to amend the application. In another case when, after three years, no effective attempt to meet the Hearing Officer's objections had been made, refusal to consider further amendments was held to be justified, *Scholl' Application* ([1974] RPC 383). However, limitation to a specified feature was per mitted in similar circumstances in *Firth Cleveland's Application (No. 2)* ([1974] RPC 377), though the proprietor's conduct was criticised. Nevertheless, the prim ary and overall onus of establishing obviousness always rests on the applicant for revocation and in *ICOS's Application* ([1976] FSR 551) it was indicated that it is only the onus of establishing the truth of particular matters, to be taken into account when deciding the general issue, that might shift from party to party. On this basis the shifting onus in the *Philips'* case (*supra*) arose from the unusual facts of that case where no attempt had been made to defend the amended claims.

In arguing a patentee's case, one should be wary in admitting that, if a main claim is lost, a particular sub-claim cannot be supported. In *Firth Cleveland's Application* ([1973] RPC 202) such an admission led to refusal of an amended claim, but the former Patents Appeal Tribunal allowed the admission to be withdrawn as having been made by mistake.

Hearings   **72.48**

When a case is ready for hearing, notification is given before a date is fixed so as to allow the parties to agree on a mutually convenient date if possible. Once a date is fixed, either with or without agreement, the Comptroller is normally prepared to change it by a few days, but is reluctant to postpone the hearing for any considerable time, whether for the convenience of counsel or otherwise. If any substantial postponement is granted, only very strong grounds will be accepted for any further change.

The provisions for fixing hearings and the practice in relation thereto are dealt with in para. 101.09.

As regards the right of audience at hearings, see para. 102.14. As regards the procedure at hearings before the Comptroller, see para. 101.11. It has long been the tradition that, except in cases of obtaining, the patentee should open the proceedings at a hearing in the Patent Office. Attempts to change this procedure have been unsuccessful, see *Du Pont's (Hull's) Patent* ([1979] FSR 128) and *Jackson and Molloy's Patent* (SRIS O/88/83).

When late-filed evidence is not admitted, and the party putting forward that evidence indicates his intention to appeal that decision, the Comptroller has felt obliged to postpone the substantive hearing, see *Upjohn's and Tadeda's Patents* (SRIS O/21/87).

For the possibility of holding a hearing in Scotland, see para. 98.07.

Advisers   **72.49**

Under rule 109 (reprinted at para. 72.10 *supra*, made under the authority of s. 123(2)(*g*)), the Comptroller may appoint one or more advisers to assist him in any particular case. The provision was new in the present Act and does *not* extend to proceedings under the 1949 Act (r. 124(1)(*d*) [1978], reprinted in para. 127.04). Section 123(2)(*g*) may reflect the increased power of the Comptroller to revoke patents for lack of inventive step under the provisions of section 72, and the desirability of affording the Comptroller expert assistance in the same way as the court may have under the re-enactment of section 96, though the choice of the Comptroller is unfettered and is not limited to scientific advisers as in the case of advisers to the court, see para. 96.25.

While the rule explicitly gives the Comptroller power to settle the question of instructions to be given to the adviser, there is no direction as to the manner in which assistance is to be given, for example whether the adviser will appear at any hearing and, if so, whether the parties will have the right to address the adviser. It is not even clear whether the advice given by the adviser will be disclosed to the parties. In the past, where an assessor has assisted the judge or judges in infringement actions, the assessor has remained tacit, but an assessor has a different legal function to an adviser. It is not clear that the adviser must come from outside the Patent Office, and the rule might legitimise the practice of an examiner sitting with the hearing officer in hearings before the Comptroller, though otherwise no instance of an appointment of an adviser to assist the Comptroller has been noted.

The appointment of a scientific adviser to assist the court is discussed in para. 96.25. For a discussion of the role to be played by such an adviser, see particularly *Beecham Group* v. *Bristol-Myers* [*Amoxycillin*] [New Zealand] [1980] 1 NZLR 185 and 192).

In the debates on the Bill which led to the 1977 Act the impression was given that the Comptroller would often wish to appoint lay advisers in proceedings under section 40 for inventor compensation (H.C. Official report, Standing Committee D, July 5, 1977 (AM), cols. 120–128).

The remuneration of an adviser appointed under rule 109 is to be met out of public funds and be determined by the Secretary of State with the consent of the Minister for the Civil Service (s. 123(5)).

72.50 *Decisions*

The mode of giving decisions is dealt with in para. 101.06 and the publication of decisions in para. 101.12. The Comptroller may give an interim decision, and it is his practice to do so if he thinks that any amendment could save part of the patent. The question of costs is normally deferred to the final decision. An interim decision is subject to appeal as if it were a final decision, and if appeal is lodged the revocation proceedings are suspended pending its resolution. Thus a proprietor faced with an interim decision of patent invalidity must decide whether he wishes to appeal or apply to amend, but if he chooses the latter, he will forfeit his right to the former, see *Nachf's Application* ([1983] RPC 87), discussed in para. 72.51 *infra*.

Because the Comptroller is guardian of the public interest, he may of his own motion take the point that an invention is clearly anticipated by some document or rendered unpatentable by common general knowledge of which he may be aware. However, if such an objection is one of obviousness the Comptroller must give the parties a chance to comment and a full opportunity of filing any necessary evidence. If it appears to a hearing officer, while writing his decision, that a claim is objectionable on grounds not argued before him, he ought to recall the parties for further argument after first drawing their attention to the point and giving them the opportunity of dealing with it first by filing evidence (*BOC International's Application*, [1980] RPC 122).

Very rarely a hearing before the Comptroller will result in an *extempore* decision. In such circumstances the parties can only obtain a copy of the decisions by application to the shorthand writers, see the notice in O.J. May 2, 1973 which also explains that applications for extension of time for lodging appeal will then be entertained while the decision is studied, if this is requested within 14 days of the decision being given.

72.51 *Appeals*

For the time for lodging appeal and the procedure thereon, see para. 97.12. The procedure is governed by RSC Ord. 104, r. 19 reprinted at para. E104.19 discussed in paras. 97.12–97.19. The period for lodging appeal is normally six weeks from the date of the decision, but only 14 days if the decision is on a point of procedure (RSC Ord. 104, r. 9(3)). A first extension of this time may be granted by the Comptroller on application made within the period set for appeal, but thereafter any application for further extension of time must be made to the Patents Court, as also must any application for leave to appeal out of time (Ord. 104, r. 9(8)). The principles upon which an extension of time for appeal is given by the Comptroller have been summarised (O.J. September 23, 1970).

The Patents Court has stated that a general extension of time for lodging appeal against an interim decision of the Comptroller normally cannot be granted, either to a proprietor or applicant for revocation, while the question of submission of amendments which may overcome the finding of invalidity are considered in the Patent Office (*Nachf's Application*, [1983] RPC 87). It was pointed out that if the interim decision is wrong, the amendments submitted to meet it might be wrong and time would be wasted in considering them. Also it is wrong for the Office to consider any amendments to the patent until it is known what the objections to validity are so that, when an appeal on the issues of validity remains possible, consideration of any amendment is a waste of time. Only if the parties are in agreement, or the circumstances are exceptional, should some other procedure be followed.

The difficulty of submitting further evidence on appeal is discussed in para. 97.16.

The advancing of arguments on appeal which were not raised at the hearing below is not to be encouraged and an appellant may not be permitted to raise points which were never argued below by anybody. Nevertheless, when one of two applicants for revocation takes no part in the appeal, the other applicant has been permitted to argue points raised by the other applicant at the hearing below (*Standard Oil's (Fahrig's) Application* [1980] RPC 359).

For the practice of appointment of a scientific adviser to assist the court on appeal, see para. 97.21.

Costs   **72.52**

The question of costs (and the giving of security therefore) in proceedings before the Comptroller is governed by section 107. The principles for such awards of costs and the amounts that are normally allowed and of security required are discussed in paras. 107.03–107.05. In proceedings before the Comptroller the costs awarded are only a contribution to actual costs. However, on appeal, costs (taxed if not agreed) are awarded to the successful party on the normal "standard" basis for proceedings in the High Court, even if that party be the Comptroller, as discussed in para. 97.24.

The question of costs may be affected by rule 76 (reprinted at para. 72.04 *supra*) if prior notice of the intention to apply for revocation is not given to the proprietor and he decides not to contest the application by offering to surrender the patent under section 29. Presumably, this would only apply if the surrender offer is made at an early stage in the proceedings, *i.e.* before a counter-statement is filed. In any case, rule 76 gives the Comptroller a wide discretion.

A party may be awarded costs, even if he does not appear and was not represented, if he expended time and labour on the preparation of his case (*Rhodes (Edgar's) Patent*, [1975] FSR 135).

Legal aid is not available for proceedings before the Comptroller, but see para. 107.02.

SECTION 73

Comptroller's power to revoke patents on his own initiative   **73.01**

73.—(1) If it appears to the comptroller that an invention for which a patent has been granted formed part of the state of the art by virtue only of section 2(3) above, he may on his own initiative by order revoke the patent, but shall not do so without giving the proprietor of the patent an opportunity of making any observations and of amending the specification of the patent so as to exclude any matter which formed part of the state of the art aforesaid without contravening section 76 below.

(2) If it appears to the comptroller that a patent under this Act and a European patent (UK) have been granted for the same invention having the same priority date, and that the applications for the patents were filed by the same applicant or his successor in title, he shall give the proprietor of the patent under this Act an opportunity of making observations and of amending the specification of the patent, and if the proprietor fails to satisfy the comptroller that there are not two patents in respect of the same invention, or to amend the specification so as to prevent there being two patents in respect of the same invention, the comptroller shall revoke the patent.

(3) The comptroller shall not take action under subsection (2) above before—

(a) the end of the period for filing an opposition to the European patent (UK) under the European Patent Convention, or

(b) if later, the date on which opposition proceedings are finally disposed of;

and he shall not then take any action if the decision is not to maintain the European patent or if it is amended so that there are not two patents in respect of the same invention.

(4) The comptroller shall not take action under subsection (2) above if the European patent (UK) has been surrendered under section 29(1) above before the date on which by virtue of section 25(1) above the patent under this Act is to be treated as having been granted or, if proceedings for the surrender of the European patent (UK) have been begun before that date, until those proceedings are finally disposed of; and he shall not then take any action if the decision is to accept the surrender of the European patent.

[(2) *If it appears to the comptroller that a patent under this Act and a European patent (UK) have been granted for the same invention having the same priority date and that the applications for both patents were filed by the same applicant or his successor in title, the comptroller may, on his own initiative but only after the relevant date, consider whether to revoke the patent granted under this Act and may, after giving the proprietor of the patent an opportunity of making any observations and of amending the specification of the patent, revoke the patent.*]

[(3) *In this section "the relevant date" means whichever of the following dates is relevant, that is to say—*

(a) *the date on which the period for filing an opposition to the patent under the European Patent Convention expires without an opposition being filed;*

(b) *the date when any opposition proceedings under that convention are finally disposed of by a decision to maintain the European patent;*

(c) *if later then either of the foregoing dates, the date when the patent under this Act is granted.*]

Note. Subsections (2)–(4) were prospectively substituted for previous subsections (2) and (3) by the 1988 Act (Sched. 5, para. 19). For the commencement of the changes, see the latest Supplement to this Work *re.* this para.

RELEVANT RULE

Procedure on decision to revoke patents under section 73

77. Where it appears to the comptroller in accordance with section 73(1)   **73.02**
or (2) that the patent ought to be revoked, the proprietor of the patent shall be so notified and afforded an opportunity, within a period of three months of such notification, of making observations and of amending the specification of the patent.

Note. See the latest Supplement to this Work *re.* this para. for the amended form of rule 77 to be made consequent upon the bringing into force of the amendments to section 73, for which see para. 73.01 *supra.* The amended rule will probably contain a requirement to supply a copy of the amended specification similar to the requirement of rule 40(7) (reprinted in para. 27.02.

COMMENTARY ON SECTION 73

General   **73.03**

Section 73 gives the Comptroller power to revoke a patent on his own initiative, either: (1) where, as a result of the "whole contents" provision of section 2(3), the invention forms part of the state of the art, thus enabling him to deal with cases where conflict between concurrent applications comes to light after grant of the junior patent (subs. (1)); and (2) in cases of double patenting arising from the same priority where a European patent (UK) has been granted for the same invention (subs. (2)). In the latter situation somewhat similar provisions will apply when simultaneous protection arises from a Community patent, see section 86 implementing CPCa. 80 which provides that "the national patent shall be ineffective to the extent that it covers the same invention as the Community patent".
In either of the revocation situations covered by section 73, the proprietor is afforded (by r. 77, reprinted at para. 73.02 *supra*) an opportunity to submit observations and/or to amend the patent to overcome the objection, and thereby avoid revocation under the section. Practice under the section is, therefore, akin to a reopening of substantive examination, but conducted post-grant.
The action of the Comptroller under section 73 is not regarded as proceedings putting validity in issue (s. 74(8)). Section 73 does not apply to "existing patents" (Sched. 2, para. 1(2)). The proprietor has the right to be heard before any action adverse to him under the section is taken (s. 101), and appeal against the Comptroller's finding is possible under section 97(1) and then, with leave, to the Court of Appeal whether or not a question of law is involved (s. 97(3)(*a*)).

Amendment under section 73   **73.04**

If revocation under section 73 is to be avoided by an amendment of the patent, such must not be one which results in the amended specification describing additional subject-matter or which would extend the extent of protection conferred by the patent (s. 76(3)). The reference in new section 76(3) to amendment under section 27(1), 73 or 75 makes it clear that amendment to meet an objection under section 73 is distinct from amendment under either section 27(1) or 75. Thus, no form or fee is required and there is no requirement for advertisement of the amendment sought, nor provision for lodging opposition against the requested amendment. In the case of an objection under subsection (1), these lacuna could prejudice the position of the proprietor of the cited specification, but any improper amendment would provide a ground of revocation under either section 72(1)(*d*) or (*e*), for which see paras. 72.24–72.26.

73.05 *Revocation of patent for anticipation by prior-dated patent specification (subs. (1))*

Section 2(3), as discussed in paras. 2.19–2.24, provides that the contents of an application of earlier priority date, which is an application under the Act or an application for a European patent (UK) or an international application (UK), and which was unpublished at the priority date of an invention claimed in the application or patent-in-suit, shall be regarded as part of the state of the art against that later application or patent, though only effective to destroy the novelty of the later application and having no effect as regards the requirement for this to have an inventive step (see section 3). The test for according priority is set out in section 5 and discussed in the commentary thereon; and it is to be noted that, in an objection by the Comptroller under section 73(1), such test may need to be applied both to the patent-in-suit and to the cited prior application or patent in order to determine whether the latter is truly to be regarded as part of the state of the art against the former. If this is so, the proprietor may, nevertheless, be able to contend successfully that the invention claimed in the patent-in-suit is not deprived of novelty by the contents of the prior-dated specification. Otherwise, amendment (as discussed in para. 73.04 *supra*) will have to be considered to overcome the objection, failing which the Comptroller will order the revocation of the patent, subject to appeal (for which see para. 73.03 *supra*).

73.06 *Revocation for double patenting in corresponding European patent (UK) (subss. (2)–(4))*

Subsection (2) is to be amended, together with its qualifying subsection (3), and new subsection (4) is to be introduced in a purported attempt to overcome the rigour of the decision in *Turner & Newall's Patent* ([1984] RPC 49) and enable the proprietor to have more time to choose, but *prior to the date of grant of the patent under the Act*, which of his two patents, *i.e.* a patent granted under the Act or a corresponding European patent (UK) should be maintained, the eventual maintenance of both not being possible if they are each "for the same invention". This phrase is also used in section 18(5) which prohibits grants of two patents on two applications of the same priority to the same applicant, for which see para. 18.11. Care therefore needs to be taken if the proprietor wishes to retain his national patent, for example where he wishes to register this in territories that do not register a European patent (UK), for which see para. 77.10. For present purposes it is presumed that the new provisions are in force, but as to their commencement see the latest Supplement to this Work *re.* para. 73.01.

In *Turner & Newall*, the Comptroller held (particularly having regard to CPCa. 80(1)) that he had no discretion, at least in respect of matter contained in both a European (UK) and a patent granted under the Act and, accordingly, subject to the proprietor filing amendments (which were in that case unsuccessful), ordered revocation under the former subsection (2). The absence of any discretion under the subsection is now reinforced in the revised form of subsection (2) which uses "shall" rather than "may".

While it might be thought worthwhile to pursue the United Kingdom national patent in respect of the omnibus claims, which are not allowed by the practice of the EPO, the Comptroller has regarded these as claims to "the same invention" as contained in the claims of the existing European patent (UK) (*Turner & Newall's Patent, supra*), even when, as in that case, there was a drawing in the patent under the Act which had been omitted from the European patent. Also, in *Maag Gear's Patent* ([1985] 532), it was stated that claims do not have to be directed to an invention which has been defined in the two patents in identical terms and that mere differences in scope, such as limitation to an omnibus claim, would not avoid the application of section 73(2).

Avoiding effect of subsection (2)   **73.07**

Although the Comptroller cannot take action under new subsection (2) before the later of the two dates referred to in new subsection (3), the proprietor must take action as to the European patent (UK) *before* the grant of the patent under the Act if he is to be *certain* of avoiding revocation under subsection (2) of the patent granted under the Act. Under new subsection (3) the earliest date when the Comptroller can initiate proceedings under subsection (2) is the later of: (*a*) the last date for lodging opposition to the European patent (UK), *i.e.* nine months after the date of publication of the mention of its grant in the EPB (EPCr. 99(1)); or (*b*), if any such opposition is lodged, the date when such opposition proceedings are finally disposed of by a decision to maintain the European patent. Before the date when notice of the grant of the patent under the Act is published in the O.J., in accordance with section 25(1), it is also now made expressly possible to be able to avoid revocation under subsection (2) by abandoning the European patent (UK), or by amending the European patent by deletion of the United Kingdom designation therefrom (subs. (3)).

Furthermore, revocation under subsection (2) is now to be capable of being avoided (as is not possible with the unamended wording of s. 73) by a surrender of the granted European patent (UK) under section 29, but this action is only to be effective to avoid revocation if application to surrender the European patent (UK) is made *before* the date of grant under section 25(1) (subs. (4)). This is because such surrender does not take place with retro-active effect, see para. 29.06, though subsection (4) will now have the effect (but for the purposes of s. 73(2) only) of back-dating the surrender to the date of application therefor. New subsection (3), in contrast to subsection (4), makes it quite clear that not only successful opposition under EPCa. 100, but also amendment in the course of such opposition, is of retroactive effect. It may, accordingly, in certain circumstances be possible to make use of the "self opposition" procedure to amend (or even revoke) the European patent (UK) (as to which see para. 72.15) so that two patents are not maintained in the United Kingdom in respect of the same invention.

It may also be possible to avoid the effect of subsection (2) by taking action to amend (under section 19) the application under the Act before grant takes place thereon so that two patents for the same invention do not come into effect, but note that any such amendment is precluded once the notice of compliance with the Act and Rules has been issued under section 18(4), see para. 24.11.

If a patent is granted under the Act before the grant of the corresponding European patent (UK) then to avoid the possibility of revocation under subsection (2) with certainty, the United Kingdom designation for the European application must be relinquished before the European patent is granted, irrespective of any opposition subsequently lodged, though revocation under subsection (2) is postponed until the opposition proceedings are concluded. New subsection (3) means that such postponement may be of practical value if the opposition (including presumably "self opposition") succeeds or in response to it the European patent (UK) is amended so that it is in respect of a different invention.

73.08   PRACTICE UNDER SECTION 73

If the Comptroller is minded to revoke the patent under either subsection (1) or (2), the proprietor is required to be notified and be given a period of three months in which to submit observations and/or amend the specification (r. 77). This period is extensible under rule 110(1). It would seem that the right to amend may be lost if unsuccessful appeal is first taken against the decision of the Comptroller to revoke without amendment. Perhaps the amendment should be requested as an initial alternative and the Comptroller asked to stay consideration of it pending determination of the issue of revocation. Amendment under section 73 requires no form or fee and is not, apparently, subject to advertisement or to any opposition procedure, see para. 73.04 *supra*. If the patent is revoked under section 73, this is noted in the O.J., see para. 123.27.

74.01   **SECTION 74**

Proceedings in which validity of patent may be put in issue

74.—(1) Subject to the following provisions of this section, the validity of a patent may be put in issue—

(*a*) by way of defence, in proceedings for infringement of the patent under section 61 above or proceedings under section 69 above for infringement of rights conferred by the publication of an application;

(*b*) in proceedings under section 70 above;

(*c*) in proceedings in which a declaration in relation to the patent is sought under section 71 above;

(*d*) in proceedings before the court or the comptroller under section 72 above for the revocation of the patent;

(*e*) in proceedings under section 58 above.

(2) The validity of a patent may not be put in issue in any other proceedings and, in particular, no proceedings may be instituted (whether under this Act or otherwise) seeking only a declaration as to the validity or invalidity of a patent.

(3) The only grounds on which the validity of a patent may be put in issue (whether in proceedings for revocation under section 72 above or otherwise) are the grounds on which the patent may be revoked under that section.

(4) No determination shall be made in any proceedings mentioned in subsection (1) above on the validity of a patent which any person puts in issue on the ground mentioned in section 72(1)(*b*) above unless—

(*a*) it has been determined in entitlement proceedings commenced by that person or in the proceedings in which the validity of the patent is in issue that the patent should have been granted to him and not some other person; and

(*b*) except where it has been so determined in entitlement proceedings, the proceedings in which the validity of the patent is in issue are commenced before the end of the period of two years beginning with the date of the grant of the patent or it is shown that any person registered as a proprietor of the patent knew at the time of the grant or of the transfer of the patent to him that he was not entitled to the patent.

(5) Where the validity of a patent is put in issue by way of defence or counterclaim the court or the comptroller shall, if it or he thinks just to do so, give the defendant an opportunity to comply with the condition in subsection (4)(*a*) above.

(6) In subsection (4) above "entitlement proceedings", in relation to a patent, means a reference under section 37(1)[(*a*)] above on the ground that the patent was granted to a person not entitled to it or proceedings for a declaration or declarator that it was so granted.

(7) Where proceedings with respect to a patent are pending in the court under any provision of this Act mentioned in subsection (1) above, no proceedings may be instituted without the leave of the court before the comptroller with respect to that patent under section 61(3), 69, 71 or 72 above.

(8) It is hereby declared that for the purposes of this Act the validity of a patent is not put in issue merely because the comptroller is considering its validity in order to decide whether to revoke it under section 73 above.

Note. Subsection (6) was prospectively amended by the 1988 Act (Sched. 5, para. 10). For commencement of the amendment, see the latest Supplement to this Work *re.* this para.

COMMENTARY ON SECTION 74

General   **74.02**

This is an important section and sets out in subsection (1) the proceedings (but subject to the exclusion of proceedings under s.73 (subs. (8)) under which the validity of a patent may be put in issue. By subsection (2) these are the only proceedings in which the validity of a patent can be put in issue, and then only on the grounds upon which a patent can be revoked under section 72(1) (subs. (3)). Subsections (4)–(6) provide further specialist provisions for entitlement contests and relate to section 72(1)(*b*): sections 37 and 72(2) are also relevant in this connection. Subsection (7) prevents the commencement, without leave, of proceedings before the Comptroller for infringement, or for a declaration of non-infringement, or for revocation, if any proceedings with respect to the patent are already pending before the court. There is, therefore, now a concise statement of the circumstances in which validity can be contested.

Section 74 does not apply to "existing patents" (Sched. 2, para. 1(2)), see *Martinez's Patent* ([1983] RPC 307). In this it was held that section 74 is of a declaratory nature which explained the absence of reference thereto in the transitional provisions of Schedules 2 and 4. Section 74 was also held to be inapplicable to an "existing patent" in *Reckitt & Colman* v. *Biorex* ([1985] FSR 94), and also in *Dow Chemical* v. *Ishihara Sangyo* ([1985] FSR 4), but in the latter case the validity of an alleged prior claiming European patent was allowed to be pleaded despite subsection (2). There is no directly corresponding provision in the EPC, but subsection (4) corresponds to CPCa. 27 and 56(1), and is referred to in section 130(7) as having been intended to have the same effect.

74.03   *Proceedings in which validity may be put in issue (subss. (1)–(3) and (8))*

Subsection (1) lists the proceedings in which the validity of a patent may be challenged: *infringement* (ss. 61 and 69); *threats* (s. 70); *declaration of non-infringement* (s. 71); *revocation* (s. 72); and *disputes as to Crown use* (s. 58). Section 73, where the Comptroller revokes on his own initiative, is specifically excluded (subs. (8)). Subsection (2) excludes all other proceedings, and also prohibits proceedings for a mere declaration of validity or invalidity, thereby making statutory previous decisions of the court to this effect.

Subsection (3) repeats section 72(1) in that it limits the grounds of revocation to those specified in section 72.

74.04   *Estoppel against challenge to validity*

There can be circumstances in which a party to proceedings may be estopped from contesting validity therein. Thus, in *Heinemann* v. *Dorman & Smith* ((1955) 72 RPC 60 and 162 (CA)), the Plaintiff agreed to discontinue an action for infringement in return for a contractual undertaking by the defendant not to infringe. The Plaintiff subsequently sued the Defendant for breach of that contract and it was held that the Defendant could not defend that action by counterclaiming for revocation of the patent. A consent judgment may, similarly, lead to an estoppel against further challenge to validity on the normal principles of *res judicata*, see para. 60.09. Likewise, there cannot be a challenge to validity in contempt of court proceedings for breach of an injunction, see *Multiform* v. *Whitmarley* ([1956] RPC 143 and 338 (CA) and [1957] RPC 260 (HL)).

However, a provision in a patent licence agreement that the licensee may not challenge the validity of the patent is invalid under TRa. 85(1), with exception under TRa. 85(3) not being possible (see para. D23). Indeed, the mere presence of such a clause can render the parties liable to fines by the E.C. Commission, see *Windsurfing International* v. *E.C. Commission (Case 193/83)* ([1986] ECR 643; [1986] 3 CMLR 489; [1988] FSR 139 (ECJ)) and para. C19. However, in the special case of a royalty-free licence, a "no challenge" clause has been held valid, see *Bayer* v. *Süllhöffer* (OJEC 27.9.88, L281/17, *noted* [1989] EIPR D–14; (1989) 20 IIC 127 and *The Times*, October 11, 1988) discussed more fully in para. D23. Nevertheless, much the same effect as a "no challenge" clause may be possible by providing for immediate termination of a licence if the licensee initiates or otherwise becomes involved in a challenge to validity of the licensed intellectual property right, see *Du Pont's (Blades') Patent (Licence of Right)* ([1988] RPC 479). Also, there is nothing inconsistent in seeking a compulsory licence under a patent while the applicant continues to challenge its validity (*Halcon's Patent*, [1989] RPC 1).

For further discussion of questions of estoppel in relation to challenge to validity, see para. 72.28.

Allegations of non-entitlement (subss. (4)–(6))   **74.05**

Subsections (4), (5) and (6) relate to revocation under section 72(1)(*b*) for non-entitlement and provide that this ground may not be raised by any person unless *it has been determined*, in entitlement proceedings under sections 8, 12 and 37(1), or in court proceedings for a declaration, that the patent was granted to a person not entitled (subs. (6)); or it is so determined in the proceedings in which validity is in issue. However, except where it has been determined otherwise, the proceedings in which validity is in issue must be commenced within two years of grant of the patent unless the proprietor of the patent knew at the time of grant or on transfer of the patent to him that he was not entitled to the patent. The meaning of "knew" in this context is discussed in paras. 37.13 and 72.17.

Subsection (5) allows a defendant to an allegation of invalidity to be given an opportunity of raising the question of entitlement and provides that consent may be given to an alleviation of the two year time limit in section 72(2)(*b*) and subsection (4)(*b*), but it is not clear whether subsection (5) is broad enough to permit entitlement proceedings to be *commenced* after the end of the two year period if such applies.

In *Dolphin Showers Ltd.* v. *Farmiloe* ([1989] FSR 1) it was held that a defence of non-entitlement could be raised under subsection (1) notwithstanding that there had been no determination under section 72(2); this could be dealt with, under subsection (5), as a preliminary issue or at the same time as the other attacks on validity. It was also held that only a person with a claim that the patent should have been granted to him had the necessary locus to raise the defence; thus a successor in title by virtue of a post-grant assignment has no *locus standi* to raise such a plea.

Concurrency of proceedings before the Comptroller and the court (subs. (7))   **74.06**

Subsection (7) prohibits the institution of proceedings before the Comptroller under sections: 61(3) (*Infringement of a patent*); 69 (*Infringement before grant*); 71 (*Declaration of non-infringement*); and 72 (*Revocation*) while proceedings under any of the provisions specified in subsection (1), *i.e.* those under sections 58, 61, or 69–72, are already pending before the court, unless the court gives leave. This provision applies even if the putative applicant before the Comptroller is not a party to the court proceedings. Presumably, to obtain leave he would first need to apply to the court to intervene in the proceedings already before the court and it seems that he would do this by way of an originating motion. It appears that the court is only likely to exercise discretion in favour of allowing proceedings for revocation (under s. 72), or for a declaration of non-infringement (under s. 71), to take place in the Patent Office rather than before the court if one party is unable to afford the costs of High Court proceedings, as in *Hawker-Siddley* v. *Real Time* ([1983] RPC 395), see *Gen Set* v. *Mosarc* ([1985] FSR 302).

It should be noted that there is no general reverse practice with regard to the practice when court proceedings are commenced during the pendency of proceedings before the Comptroller, but the effect of section 27(2) appears to be that any amendment proceedings under section 27 must be stayed on the commencement of any proceedings before the court. Thus, in *Wilkinson Sword* v. *Warner-Lambert* (SRIS C/122/87), proceedings under section 27 for amendment of the patent were already in being when proceedings for a declaration of non-infringement (under s. 71) and for revocation (under s. 72) were commenced before the court. The Patents Court refused to stay the proceedings before it pending resolution of the amendment proceedings, and indicated that the amendment proceedings should be recommenced before the court under section 75. Subsequently the court allowed the amendments and found the patent valid, but not infringed.

74.07 *Stay of proceedings pending determination of opposition at the EPO*

In *Amersham International* v. *Corning Limited* ([1987] RPC 53; OJEPO 12/1987, 558) a writ for infringement of a European patent (UK) was issued shortly after its grant. The Defendants later lodged opposition in the EPO and asked for the infringement proceedings to be stayed pending determination of the EPO opposition. A stay was refused, it being held that the EPO is not a forum for the issue of infringement and anyway the *forum conveniens* was the English court where infringement and validity could be determined together, and that a stay would only lead to delay if the opposition failed because infringement would then have to be tried in the English court. Similar decisions were subsequently given in *Improver Corp.* v. *Innovations* (SRIS C/16/88, *noted* IPD 11002), where the Patents Court commented that the EPO opposition seemed to it likely to fail; and in *Pall Corp.* v. *Commercial Hydraulics* [1988] FSR 274 and SRIS C/80/89 (CA)). In the *Amersham* case it was also considered irrelevant that a multiplicity of infringement actions in the EEC countries might be avoided if the opposition in the EPO were successful. However, it does not seem to have been fully appreciated in either case that the English proceedings would be futile, irrespective of their result, if the opposition in the EPO were successful and the European patent became revoked thereby so that it is deemed never to have existed (EPCa. 69). In the *Amersham* case the Defendants had also agreed not to seek revocation nationally if the opposition in the EPO were to fail, but in neither the *Amersham* nor the *Pall Corp.* case did the Defendant concede the issue of infringement.

Similar issues have arisen in the national courts of other contracting states to the EPC, as to which see the various cases reported in OJEPO 9/1988, 357–363, in some of which a stay of national proceedings was ordered.

75.01   SECTION 75

Amendment of patent in infringement or revocation proceedings

75.—(1) In any proceedings before the court or the comptroller in which the validity of a patent is put in issue the court or, as the case may be, the comptroller may, subject to section 76 below, allow the proprietor of the patent to amend the specification of the patent in such manner, and subject to such terms as to advertising the proposed amendment and as to costs, expenses or otherwise, as the court or comptroller thinks fit.

(2) A person may give notice to the court or the comptroller of his opposition to an amendment proposed by the proprietor of the patent under this section, and if he does so the court or the comptroller shall notify the proprietor and consider the opposition in deciding whether the amendment or any amendment should be allowed.

(3) An amendment of a specification of a patent under this section shall have effect and be deemed always to have had effect from the grant of the patent.

(4) Where an application for an order under this section is made to the court, the applicant shall notify the comptroller, who shall be entitled to appear and be heard and shall appear if so directed by the court.

RELEVANT RULE

Procedure on advertisement of proposed amendment under section 75

78.—(1) Where in proceedings before the comptroller a proposed **75.02** amendment under section 75 is advertised, notice of opposition to such an amendment shall, within the period of three months from the date of advertisement in the Journal, be filed on Patents Form No. 15/77.

(2) Such notice shall be accompanied by a copy thereof and be supported by a statement in duplicate setting out fully the facts upon which the opponent relies and the relief which he seeks. The comptroller shall send a copy of the notice and statement to the proprietor of the patent and any other party to the proceedings before the comptroller.

(3) The comptroller may give such directions as he may think fit with regard to the subsequent procedure.

Note. It is thought that, upon the next general revision of the Rules, the opportunity will be taken to require the filing of a copy of the amended specification (and any translation thereof) similar to that contained in rule 40(7) (reprinted in para. 27.02) so that such can more readily be republished.

COMMENTARY ON SECTION 75

General   **75.03**

Section 75 is the third of the three sections relating to the amendment of specifications: section 19 relates to amendment before grant and sections 27 and 75 relate to amendment post-grant, the latter applying to proceedings in which the validity of the patent *is* put in issue. However, section 27(2) precludes amendment under that section when proceedings are pending in which validity *may be* put in issue, such proceedings being (by s. 74(1)) under any of sections 58, 61 or 69–72. This suggests a possible lacuna preventing application for amendment under either section if proceedings, such as infringement proceedings, are pending in which validity could be, but is not, put in issue, see further para. 27.09. Amendment can also occur in proceedings initiated by the Comptroller under section 73, see para. 73.04, as well as in opposition proceedings before the EPO, see *infra*. "Amendment" is, however, not to be confused with "correction". Correction of errors in patents and applications is provided for by section 117, see the commentary thereon. Section 75 does not apply to "existing patents" (Sched. 2, para. 1(2) when read with the definition of "patent" in section 130(1)). For such patents sections 29–31 [1949] continue to apply (Sched. 1, para. 1(2)), see the commentaries thereon in Appendix A.

EPCa. 123 provides for amendment of a European patent under conditions laid down in the European Regulations, but at present the only relevant regulations concern amendment of European patent applications or of European patents during opposition proceedings in the EPO under EPCa. 99. Thus amendment of a European patent (UK) is (apart from amendment during such opposition proceedings) governed by the Act. However, CPCa. 51 would provide for limitation of a community patent, as also would CPCaa. 57(2) and 59(3) during revocation proceedings before the EPO.

527

75.04   *Applicability of section 75*

The proceedings which govern the applicability of section 75 need not be revocation or infringement proceedings as the section heading would suggest, but can relate to any of the matters listed in section 74(1), herein called "validity proceedings". These proceedings can also be before either the Comptroller or the court. Otherwise amendment of a granted patent is effected by application to the Comptroller under section 27. This is a different split of jurisdiction than for existing patents under the 1949 Act where section 30 [1949] (*Application to the court*) only applies when the amendment is requested in the course of infringement or revocation proceedings before the court. Section 63(3) further provides for directions as to amendment when validity has been put in issue and the patent has been found only partially valid.

Proceedings can be said to be "pending" at all times from their commencement until expiration of the time for lodging appeal against a final order of the court and disposal of any appeal timely brought thereon (*Lever Bros.' Patent*, (1955) 72 RPC 198 (CA)). Where proceedings are concluded by consent, the proceedings remain pending until the court has approved the proposed consent order (*Critchley* v. *Engelmann*, [1971] RPC 346). Also section 75 would still seem to be applicable if an application to amend is made during the course of "validity proceedings", but these are concluded without disposing of the application to amend (*Congoleum* v. *Armstrong Cork*, [1977] RPC 77) Thus, the stratagem used in *Condor International's Patent* (SRIS O/25/85, *noted* IPD 8107 and discussed in para. A030.02) would not seem applicable under section 75, there now being no apparent way in which the court can transfer amendment proceedings to the Comptroller if the "validity proceedings" before it are to remain even theoretically in being, nor is there provision for transfer of such validity proceedings by the court to the Comptroller. However, the court can order amendment under section 63(3), even if all issues in the proceedings have been determined, but there must first be a finding of partial invalidity.

75.05   *Limitations on amendment*

Amendments under section 75 are subject to the severe restraints of section 76 now to be imposed by new section 76(3). Thus no amendment is to be allowed which (*a*) results in the specification disclosing additional matter or (*b*) which extends the protection conferred by the patent, see paras. 76.08–76.18. If any amendment should be made under section 75 which does contravene new section 76(3), a basis is provided for revocation of the patent under section 72(1)(*d*) or (*e*), see paras. 72.25 and 72.26. An application for revocation on such a ground may be made by anyone, even if not a party to the proceedings under section 75 in which the amendment was made.

75.06   *Discretion*

The power of amendment under section 75 is discretionary by virtue of the words "may allow" in subsection (1). The question of discretion is discussed in paras. 27.05–27.07 and (in relation to grounds of invalidity arising only under the 1949 Act) in para. A031.15; see particularly para. 27.06 as regards refusal of amendment because of unreasonable delay in applying to amend, once the need to do so has been appreciated by the proprietor.

However, delay in seeking amendments in court proceedings can also arise when the proprietor chooses to try and support his claims first, especially on appeal, and, when he fails, then applies to amend. Thus, in *Raleigh* v. *Miller* ((1948) 65 RPC 141 HL)) the grounds on which claims were found invalid had become apparent at an early stage before a lower court, but the patentee had elected to attempt to support its claims through to a final judgment. A subsequent application to amend was refused, see *Raleigh* v. *Miller* ((1950) 67 RPC 226 (HL)), on the basis that the patentee, having failed to enforce his rights, should in the court's discretion not be given a second chance.

Nevertheless, as by section 63(3) the court is specifically given power (and usually exercises it) to direct amendment (under s. 75) of a specification of a patent held by it to be only partially valid, a distinction has been drawn between an amendment designed to validate an invalid claim (as in *Raleigh* v. *Miller, supra*) and an amendment designed to assist in the enforcement of a valid claim. Thus, in *Van der Lely* v. *Bamfords* ([1964] RPC 54 (CA)), the patentee was permitted to make amendments by mere excision of invalid claims (with minimum consequential amendment). A similar line was followed in *Bentley Engineering's Patent* ([1981] RPC 361) where simple excision of claims 1–3 was allowed, but where a recasting amendment was disallowed having regard to the patentees' conduct in asserting the patent in unamended form and their failure to justify their conduct by clear explanation. In *Windsurfing International* v. *Tabur Marine* ([1985] RPC 59 (CA)) leave to amend was refused because the patentee had not sought by his pleadings to support a claim to monopoly on some alternative basis and adduce appropriate evidence for this purpose at the trial. Moreover, the effect of the proposed amendment was to elevate to the status of an essential component the one feature of the allegedly inventive combination previously described in terms which made it entirely clear that it was non-essential, and this was putting forward substantially a different concept. As in *Raleigh* v. *Miller* (*supra*), leave to amend was refused in *Procter & Gamble* v. *Peaudouce (No. 2)* (SRIS C/47/89, *noted* IPD 12064 (CA)) because no attempt had been made during the trial and appeal to put forward an alternative plea involving amendment.

On the issue of discretion it should not be forgotten that in court proceedings there is normally discovery of relevant documents, see paras. 61.28–61.32. Moreover, to obtain the court's discretion to allow an amendment, it will be incumbent on the proprietor to make a full disclosure, see para. 27.05.

In such circumstances it is likely that a proprietor will find himself forced to waive any professional privilege which he might otherwise have claimed against disclosure of certain documents, *e.g.* citations made against corresponding foreign applications, since if he does not do this then it can at least be argued that he has not made a full disclosure of the circumstances underlying the amendment request, see C. P. Tootal ((1984–85) 14 CIPA 362) and *Smith Kline & French's (Bavin's) Patent (No. 2)* (SRIS C/49/89) where opinions from patent agents that the claims were invalid had to be disclosed and were a major factor in discretion to amend being refused.

Imposition of conditions   **75.07**

Subsection (1) gives to the court or the Comptroller power to allow amendments in validity proceedings on such conditions "as to advertising", "costs, expenses or otherwise" as are thought fit. It is not apparent that "otherwise" can extend beyond a requirement to give notice to the public of the proposed or allowed amendments and to provide for financial compensation to opponents or other parties involved in the validity proceedings, and therefore it is curious that the conditions which the court can impose under section 75 appear to be more limited than those which the Comptroller can impose on amendment under section 27, see para. 27.08. Nevertheless, the imposition of "other" conditions for permitting amendment could arise as part of the exercise of general discretion (for which see paras. 27.05–27.07): namely that amendment will not be permitted unless the applicant for amendment agrees to do specified matters now or in the future, but the imposition of conditions should not be predicated on the perceived merits of the invention, see *Autoliv Development's Patent* ([1988] RPC 425) and para. 27.08. For other comments on amendment subject to conditions see paras. 58.05 and 62.05.

75.08 *Opposition*

Subsection (2) provides for opposition, with provision for the proprietor to be notified of the opposition and for this to be considered before decision on the application to amend is made, see paras. 75.11, 75.13 and 75.14 *infra*. Such opposition is only lodged under rule 78 (reprinted at para. 75.02 *supra*) if the application to amend is made in proceedings before the Comptroller and was advertised. The opposition period is then three months (r. 78(1)) which is inextensible (r. 110(2)). When rule 78(1) is inapplicable, because there has been no advertisement (see para. 75.13 *infra*), acceptance of any opposition under subsection (2) would seem to be in the Comptroller's discretion. Opposition in proceedings before the court is governed by RSC, Ord. 104, r. 3, see para. 75.11 *infra*. An opponent does not have to show an interest in the patent and can be an agent for an undisclosed principal, see para. 27.12.

75.09 *Effect of amendment (subs. (3))*

Subsection (3) provides that, where amendment is allowed, it is considered to have had effect from the date of the patent. This point is discussed in para. 27.10. Amendment may also have an effect on the award of damages for infringing acts committed before amendment (s. 62(3)), see para. 62.05.

75.10 *Notice of application made to the court (subs. (4))*

Subsection (4) requires that, where application is made to the court under section 75, notice of the application for an order is to be given to the Comptroller, see para. 75.11 *infra*. The Comptroller is also given the right to be heard if he wishes and the court can order him to appear if the court so desires. However, the Comptroller does not normally take an active part in the court proceedings, leaving the parties thereto to raise all appropriate objections, but the Patent Office will from time to time enquire about progress of the proceedings and the Comptroller normally requires to be notified of the date of the hearing of the amendment application, though he rarely exercises his right to be represented thereat.

PRACTICE UNDER SECTION 75

75.11 *Application to the court*

The procedure for making application to the court under section 75 is governed by RSC, Ord. 104, r. 3 (reprinted at para. E104.03). RSC, Ord. 104, r. 3(1) requires any proprietor applying to amend his patent during the course of pending proceedings first to give notice of his intention to apply for leave to amend his specification with a copy of a proposed advertisement. This must: identify the pending proceedings in which it is intended to seek leave to amend; state the title of the patent (*Practice Direction*, [1965] RPC 481); give particulars of the amendments sought; state an address for service within the United Kingdom; and state that any person intending to oppose the amendment (other than a party to the proceedings) must give written notice of that intention to the applicant within 28 days. That advertisement appears in the O.J. Thereafter, and not less than 35 days thereafter and "as soon as may be" (see *Phillips Petroleum's Patent*, [1966] RPC 243), the applicant must apply by notice to the court for further directions. A copy of the specification certified by the Comptroller, and showing in coloured ink (normally red for the first set of amendments) the amendments sought, should be attached to the notice of motion (*Phillips Petroleum's Patent, supra*) and copies served upon the Comptroller, upon any person who has given notice of intended opposition, and upon all parties to the pending proceedings (Ord. 104, r. 3(2)). Existing parties to the proceedings need not give formal notice of opposition. The directions which must be given are set out in RSC Ord. 104, rule 3(3). An amendment is occasionally allowed by the court in the course of contested proceedings. This then becomes the subject of a special order permitting subsequent opposition to be made (for an example, see O.J. July 13, 1988, p. 2069).

A common form of order is to provide for the parties successively to exchange: (1) statement of reasons for amendment; (2) statement of opposition; (3) evidence in support of the amendments, together with discovery of relevant documents; (4) evidence in support of the opposition, together with any discovery of relevant documents by the opponent; (5) evidence in reply by the applicant; and (6) directions that such evidence be by affidavit with liberty to cross-examine at the hearing, and for that hearing to come before the court either immediately before, or at the same time as, the substantive hearing of the pending proceedings. However, a person who has given affidavit evidence in the amendment proceedings, and who is called for cross-examination on that evidence, will not necessarily be exposed to cross-examination on issues solely related to the other proceedings (*Du Pont* v. *Enka*, [1986] RPC 417). In any event the procedure is flexible and it will be adapted by the court to fit particular circumstances. Thus, in *Farmhand* v. *Spadework* ([1974] FSR 425), the application to amend was only made shortly before the trial of an infringement action: the action was ordered to proceed on the basis of the specification as notionally amended, with the question of amendment being stood over for decision thereafter.

Allowance of amendment by the court   **75.12**

If the court allows amendment, the proprietor must forthwith file at the Patent Office PF 25/77 (no fee) together with an office copy of the court order (RSC, Ord. 104, r. 3(4) and r. 53(*c*), reprinted in para. 32.11, or under r. 150 [1968] in the case of an "existing patent" amended under s. 30 [1949]). The practice is discussed in para. 32.20. If so required by either the court or the Comptroller, the proprietor must provide a new specification conforming to the typographical requirements of rule 20. Now that specifications are published by reproduction of a text supplied by the proprietor, such a request is normally to be expected. However, rule 40(7) (reprinted in para. 27.02) only applies to amendments allowed by the Comptroller.

If the court allows amendment of a European patent (UK) with an authentic text in the French or German language, the requirements of section 77(6)(*b*) should automatically be met following the required filing of PF 25/77, because rule 113(1) will then apply. However, presumably the Comptroller will also require that the amended translation to be filed should comply with rules 79A(1), (3) and (4) and rule 79F (for which see para. 77.16), but the time limit in rule 79B(2) would not apply because the amended specification has not been published by the EPO.

Notice of the order is inserted at least once in the O.J. (RSC Ord. 104, r. 3(4)).

75.13 *Application to the Comptroller*

There are no rules relating to the manner of proposing amendments in proceedings under section 75 before the Comptroller. There is also no automatic advertisement of the amendments proposed, just as section 29(6) [1949] provides for dispensation of advertisement when amendments are offered during the course of proceedings already in being before the Comptroller. However, where there is advertisement of the proposed amendment, rule 78(1) (reprinted in para. 75.02 *supra*) applies and then any opposition must be lodged within an inextensible period of three months (r. 110(2)).

75.14 *Opposition before the Comptroller*

Opposition to amendment under section 75 is governed by rule 78 (reprinted at para. 75.02 *supra*). Any such opposition is lodged on PF 15/77 (reprinted at para. 141.15), this being the same form as is used to oppose an amendment under section 27. The form has to be supported by a statement of case to be filed within 14 days of PF 15/77 (r. 107, reprinted at para. 72.09). However there is no requirement for lodging a counter-statement as such, no doubt in order that the subsequent procedure can be flexible to meet the particular circumstances which prevail in the pending validity proceedings, and whether the opponent is a party thereto or not. Nor, apparently can a non-United Kingdom resident opponent be required to give security for costs, see section 107(4). The procedure to be followed is therefore generally at the discretion of the Comptroller (r. 78(3)). Procedure in all *inter partes* proceedings before the Comptroller is discussed in paras. 72.32–72.52.

Opposition is also permitted even if there has been no advertisement, see subsection (2) and there then appears to be no time limit within which such opposition has to be filed. This is because rule 78(1) only applies where there has been an advertisement.

75.15 *Costs in an opposition*

Where an opponent to an application to amend brought before the court does not present a frivolous case, the practice has been to award him his costs at first instance even if the amendment is allowed (*Mullard* v. *British Belmont*, (1938) 55 RPC 197 at 226 and (1939) 56 RPC 1 at 22). Before the Comptroller, the normal order of a contribution to the costs of the successful party (see para. 107.03) can be expected, but the absence of a requirement to give security noted above could be argued as a basis for departing from the normal practice before the Comptroller.

SECTION 76 [Prospectively substituted]

76.01 **Amendments of applications and patents not to include added matter**

76.—(1) An application for a patent which—
- **(a) is made in respect of matter disclosed in an earlier application, or in the specification of a patent which has been granted, and**
- **(b) discloses additional matter, that is, matter extending beyond that disclosed in the earlier application, as filed, or the application for the patent, as filed,**

may be filed under section 8(3), 12 or 37(4) above, or as mentioned in section 15(4) above, but shall not be allowed to proceed unless it is amended so as to exclude the additional matter.

(2) No amendment of an application for a patent shall be allowed under section 17(3), 18(3) or 19(1) if it results in the application disclosing matter extending beyond that disclosed in the application as filed.

(3) No amendment of the specification of a patent shall be allowed under section 27(1), 73 or 75 if it—

(a) results in the specification disclosing additional matter, or

(b) extends the protection conferred by the patent.

Note. Section 76, as reprinted above, was prospectively substituted for the original form of the section (now reprinted in the next para.) by the 1988 Act (Sched. 5, para. 20). For the commencement of the changes, see the latest Supplement to this Work *re.* this para.

SECTION 76 [Prospectively replaced]   76.02

Before its substitution, as indicated in the proceeding para., section 76 was in the form:

[**76.**—(1) *An application for a patent (the later application) shall not be allowed to be filed under section 8(3), 12, or 37(4) above or as mentioned in section 15(4) above, in respect of any matter disclosed in an earlier application or the specification of a patent which has been granted, if the later application discloses matter which extends beyond that disclosed in the earlier application, as filed, or the application for the patent, as filed.*

(2) *No amendment of an application or the specification of a patent shall be allowed under any of the provisions of this Act to which this subsection applies if it—*

(a) *results in the application or specification disclosing any such matter, or*

(b) *(where a patent has been granted) extends the protection conferred by the patent.*

(3) *Subsection (2) above applies to the following provisions of this Act, namely, sections 17(3), 18(3), 19(1), 27(1), 73 and 75.*]

ARTICLES   76.03

M.G. Harman "Amendment of Specifications—Ss.72 and 76", (1981–82) 11 CIPA 23;

R. Schulte, "Amendment of the European patent after grant and the law on extending the protection conferred", (1989) 20 IIC 323.

COMMENTARY ON SECTION 76

General   76.04

Section 76 specifies the limitations on permissible amendment of applications and patents granted under the Act, including European patents (UK), see section

533

77(1). While the marginal note (shown above as a headnote to the section) refers exclusively to amendments, subsection (1) relates not to amendments as such, but to the content of new applications, *i.e.* "divisional applications" under section 15(4) and "replacement applications" under sections 8(3), 12(6) or 37(4) by a person being granted leave to file such as the result of entitlement proceedings brought under section 8, 12 or 37. If an amendment should be allowed which is contrary to the provisions of subsection (2) or (3), a ground for revocation ensues under section 72(1)(*d*) or (*e*), see paras. 72.25 and 72.26.

Section 76 does not apply to "existing patents" (Sched. 2, para. 1(2) as read with the definition of "patent" in s.130(1)). For such patents the different, and probably less rigid, restrictions of section 31 [1949], rather than those of subsection (2), continue to apply (Sched. 1, para. 1(2)), see the commentary on that section at paras. A031.07–A031.14.

For European divisional applications, corresponding provisions can be found in EPCa. 76(1) and these provisions also apply in relation to a new "replacement" European application under EPCa. 61(1)(*b*) and EPCr. 15 by a person becoming entitled (EPCa. 61(2)). Section 76(2) and (3) now respectively correspond to EPCa. 123(2) and (3). Similar provisions are to be found in PCTaa. 28(2) and 41(2). Section 76 is not one of those sections intended under section 130(7) to have the same meaning as the corresponding provisions of EPC, etc., but see para. 76.19 *infra*.

76.05   *The change in wording of section 76*

The wording of the section, as to be substituted by the 1988 Act (see para. 76.01 *supra*), is more logically presented than in its original wording (see para. 76.02 *supra*) in that subsection (2) will now relate solely to amendment of pending applications, which can arise under sections 17(3), 18(3) and 19(1); whereas subsection (3) will relate to amendment of granted patents, which can arise under sections 27(1), 73 or 75 and for which there is an additional restriction on amendment: subsection (1) continues to relate to the permissible content of divisional and replacement applications (under sections 15(4) or 8(3), 12(6) or 37(4)), but is to be amended to alleviate the previous effect of contravention of the provision, as discussed in para. 76.07 *infra*. For all three subsections, there remains the restriction on any amendment which would have the effect of adding matter to the specification, as discussed in paras. 76.11–76.14 *infra*; and (for amendment of granted patents under subsection (3)) there remains the further restriction that the amendment must not extend the protection conferred by the patent, as discussed in para. 76.17 *infra*.

In the original form of the section, subsection (2)(*a*) dealt with amendment of pending applications and subsection (2)(*b*) with that of granted patents, subsection (3) merely listing the sections to which subsection (2) applied. Thus, in cases decided before the commencement of the revisions, references to subsection (2)(*b*) should be read as references to present subsection (3).

No transitional provision was included in the 1988 Act in relation to section 76 and, therefore, the substituted provisions would appear to apply: in the case of subsection (1), to any divisional or replacement application filed after the date of commencement of the new wording (for which see the *Note* to para. 76.01 *supra*); and, for amendment under subsections (2) or (3), to any decision as to amendment made after that date, even if the application therefor had been filed before then. The following commentary presumes that the amendments to section 76 have been brought into effect.

Divisional and replacement applications, not to contain additional matter (subs. (1))   **76.06**

Subsection (1) applies to all new applications; and specifically, to "replacement" applications made under: (*a*) section 8(3) (*Determination of entitlement to patents resulting in the Comptroller ordering any person to make a new application for a patent based on matter disclosed in an earlier application*); (*b*) section 12(6) (*Determination of questions of entitlement to foreign and convention patents, resulting in a new application being filed*); or (*c*) section 37(4) (*Grant of a patent to a person not entitled to it, resulting in a new application being filed*); as well as (*d*) to divisional applications made under section 15(4). New subsection (1) requires that any such new application must as a first step be amended if, when filed, it discloses "additional matter", that is "matter extending beyond that disclosed in the earlier application, as filed".

Such "earlier application" is the parent application in the case of a divisional application and is the application (or patent) involved in the entitlement proceedings in the case of a replacement application. Also, the reference in subsection (1) to an application "as filed" is to that application in the state it was on the date of filing (s. 130(4)). Such application may be one under the Act (ss. 14 and 15(1)), or an international application which has entered the United Kingdom phase (ss. 89A and 89B), or a European application which has been converted into a United Kingdom application (s. 81). It may also itself be a divisional or replacement application under section 15(4) or under section 8(3), 12(6) or 37(4).

The term "date of filing" is defined in section 130(1): this definition is discussed in para. 15.07.

Effect of breach of subsection (1)   **76.07**

The original wording of subsection (1) stated that, if a new application disclosed "matter which extends beyond that disclosed in the earlier application, as filed" then that application "shall not be allowed to be filed", see para. 76.02 *supra*. This wording meant that, unless the text of the new application was exactly the same as the basic application (except perhaps for excised matter, the excision of which did not itself result in matter being deemed to be added to the basic disclosure), the application was likely to be forfeited, there being no possibility of saving this, see *Hydroacoustics' Application* ([1981] FSR 438).

This came to be appreciated as an unduly harsh provision and, consequently, the new form of subsection (1) will allow correction of the situation by providing that the new application "shall not be allowed to proceed unless it is amended to exclude the additional matter". Therefore if, on a preliminary examination of a new application, it is thought that it does contain "additional matter", presumably this will give rise to an official objection requiring amendment before the application can proceed. Such an objection can then, if desired, be contested in the usual way by: argument; a hearing (for which see para. 101.04); and, if necessary, an appeal to the Patents Court (for which see para. 97.04).

Since any purported divisional application accompanied by the proper documents and prescribed fees must inevitably meet the requirements of section 15(1) for the application to be accorded a filing date, it would appear that the first question to be decided by the Comptroller is what the filing date should be. If the purported divisional application does not contravene subsection (1), section 15(4) overrides section 15(1) and the new application is accorded the date of filing of the parent application. If subsection (1) is contravened, then the actual date of filing must be accorded unless the application is amended, either by excision of the added matter from the specification or by deleting the claim to an earlier filing date made in Section VIII of PF 1/77 (reprinted at para. 141.01, see Note 7 therein). However, if a divisional application is erroneously allowed to proceed with additional matter contained therein over that present in the parent application, and the application proceeds to the grant of a patent, the proprietor may be permitted to excise that additional matter by amendment under section 27 or 75. Certainly there is an implication in section 72(1)(d) that the Comptroller may make a mistake, but such an amendment could be refused in the exercise of discretion if it were thought that the additional matter had been included in bad faith: the discretionary element involved in all questions of permissible amendment is discussed in paras. 27.05–27.07.

What constitutes "additional matter" is discussed in paras. 76.09–76.15.

For the precautions to be taken when preparing a divisional application, see paras. 15.31–15.21 and 15.38–15.32. Similar remarks would seem also to apply to "replacement applications" under sections 8(3), 12(6) and 37(4).

76.08 *Prohibited amendments to applications and granted patents (subss. (2) and (3))*

New subsection (2) prohibits amendment of a pending application in a manner which would result in this "disclosing matter extending beyond that disclosed in the application as filed". This subsection applies to amendments sought under: section 17(3) (*Amendment resulting from formal objections during examination proceedings*); section 18(3) (*Amendment as a result of objections raised during substantive examination proceedings*); and section 19(1) (*Voluntary amendment before grant*) Subsection (3)(a) likewise prohibits amendment of a granted patent in a manner which would result "in the specification disclosing additional matter". This subsection applies to amendments sought under: section 27(1) (*Amendment after grant*); section 73 (*Amendment pursuant to power of Comptroller to revoke of his own initiative*); and section 75 (*Amendment in the course of pending validity proceedings*). Subsection (3)(b) also prohibits amendments under any of these three sections from extending "the protection conferred by the patent". If any amendment contrary to subsection (2) or (3)(a) is allowed, a ground for revocation arises under section 72(1)(d), and an amendment contrary to subsection (3)(b) similarly gives rise to a ground for revocation under section 72(1)(e), see paras. 72.25 and 72.26 respectively. The meaning of "matter extending beyond that disclosed in the application as filed" (subs. (2)) and of "disclosing additional matter" (subs. (3)(a)) is discussed in para. 76.09 *infra*; and the meaning of "extends the protection conferred by the patent" (subs. (3)(b)) is discussed in para. 76.17 *infra*.

Neither subsection (2) nor (3) lists section 117 (*Correction of errors*). What is permissible under section 117 is therefore discussed in the commentary thereon. It would seem that the Act draws a clear distinction between "amendment" which must be permissible under subsection (2) and or (3) as the case may be, and the "correction" of errors, which is entirely governed by section 117.

76.09 *Definition of "additional matter" for section 76*

It will have been noted that subsections (1), (2) and (3) each have slightly different wording in relation to "additional matter". Subsection (1) defines "additional matter" as that "extending beyond that disclosed [in the earlier application]", and subsection (2) is in terms of that definition [in relation to the application as filed]. However, subsection (3) merely refers to "additional matter". Nevertheless, it is believed that nothing turns on this different wording.

Section 76 in its original form likewise used somewhat different wording, for which see para. 76.02 *supra*, but again there would seem to have been little or no difference from that now employed. Therefore, the decisions given under the former wording would seem to be equally applicable under the present form of section

76. These decisions are discussed in paras. 76.11–76.14 and show that the prohibition on the inclusion in a specification of additional matter is one that has been strictly construed, with the consequent failure of many such amendments. This is in contrast to a more lenient attitude which appears to have been shown by the EPO, see paras. 76.20–76.24.

The concept of "additional matter" contained in other sections   **76.10**

The concept of "additional matter" within section 76 has similarities with concepts present in other sections. Thus, there is the question of "matter contained [in an earlier application]" when considering lack of novelty under section 2(3), for which see paras. 2.19–2.24; and the concept of wording "supported by matter disclosed [in a priority document]" required to accord an earlier priority date under section 5(2). Indeed the EPO has stated that EPO Guidelines C-IV, 7.2 and C-V, 2.4 (primarily respectively relevant to the test of novelty and for according priority from an earlier application) are each analogous to the test of added subject matter prohibited under EPC. 123(2), see para. 76.22. Decisions under sections 2(3) or 5(2) may, therefore, assist in questions arising under section 76; and, as is shown in para. 76.11 *infra*, the test of support for claims which is required by section 14(5)(*c*) is also relevant.

Also, in *Liversidge's Application* (SRIS O/99/88), the test of "support" was likened to the concept of "fair basis" under the 1949 Act, reference being made to *Van der Lely* v. *Ruston's Engineering* ([1985] RPC 461 (CA)) and the need there expressed that claims will only be fairly based if they deal with any problem with which the invention was intended to deal. However, the test of "support" required by the present Act may not equate with the test of "fair basis" required for priority (under s.5 [1949]) and for validity (under s.32(1)(*i*) [1949]), see para. 5.04.

Examples of impermissible "additional matter"

—The general principles   **76.11**

Van der Lely's Application ([1987] RPC 61) involved a divisional application specifying "at least one swingable conveyor", when the parent application claimed a baling machine with "three swingable conveyors". In rejecting divisional status, the Comptroller stated that "the fundamental principle in determining additional subject-matter is to decide whether any document presents the informed reader with information relevant to the invention which the other document does not". This statement appears in conformity with EPO Guideline C-V1, 5.4 which suggests that added matter is present if an amendment results in an overall change in the content of the application, whether by way of addition, alteration or excision, which results in the skilled man being presented with information which differs from that previously presented.

Another statement of principle is to be found in *Ward's Applications* ([1986] RPC 50) where the Comptroller stated that "matter must not be disclosed which extends, in the sense of enlarging upon, the original disclosure, *i.e.* which increases the specificity or particularisation of that disclosure"; and, in *B & R Relay's Application* ([1985] RPC 1), the Patents Court stated that the question to be asked is whether the skilled person would find in the original description an indication that it was important to have the feature now sought to be deleted.

In the *B & R Relay* case, the court noted that section 14(5)(*c*) requires claims to be supported by the description and that there was nothing in the original description which could conceivably support a claim omitting those features, so that the proposed divisional application would include additional matter; and, in *Raychem's Applications* ([1986] RPC 547), it was held that an amended claim not supported by the original description must offend against section 76. Thus, decisions under section 14(5)(c) are also relevant, for which see para. 14.25 and *Glatt's Application* ([1983] RPC 122). In *Liversidge's Application* (SRIS O/99/88) "method" claims would have been allowed in an application divided from an application with claims only to a tool if (as was not the case) the method claims had included all the features which the parent specification had indicated the tool should achieve.

76.12 —*Expansion of the previously stated inventive concept*

In *Plantronics' Application* (SRIS O/153/84 and C/96/85) it was held that a drawing had to be construed in conformity with the passage entitled "Summary of the invention"; and, in *RCA Corp.'s Application* (SRIS O/33/87) there was no disclosure in the parent application of the subject-matter of the proposed divisional application, having regard to the previously stated "object of the invention".

In *L.B. (Plastics)' Application* (SRIS O/90/86), a *per se* claim in a divisional application to a component specified in the parent application as part of a combination was held to contravene the prohibition against addition of matter because there was no suggestion in the parent application that the component was, or could be, of independent applicability.

76.13 —*Adding to the implicit disclosure*

In accordance with the principle of not expanding the inventive concept, discussed in the preceding paragraph, it should be realised that it is also possible to add new matter by implication when an excision to the text or disclaimer to the claims is made. Thus, in *Protoned BV's Application* ([1983] FSR 110), amendment to change "mechanical compression spring" to "mechanical spring" was refused, *inter alia* for adding new matter, at least by implication from the mere fact of deleting the word "compression".

Thus, in *Schering AG's Patent [Amendment]* (SRIS O/116/84), it was stated that an applicant or patentee may not later seek to draw from an originally generalised disclosure in such a manner as to create *post hoc* a teaching, or a specific disclosure, or a specific combination, which could not have been plainly derived from the specification at its filing date. Also, in *Air Products' Application* (SRIS O/189/83), the explicit and implicit disclosures of the two specifications were taken into account: the relevant test for whether a generalisation of a previous claim was allowable was whether or not the proposed claim included within its scope workable subject matter not previously described, reference being made to the *Protoned* case. In accordance with these views, an attempt to file a divisional application for the use of "a hydrazone" from a parent specification which referred to hydrazones of a specified general formula failed, the Comptroller being unable to find a positive indication that any hydrazone other than those covered by that formula was contemplated when the original specification was drafted (*Canon KK's Application*, SRIS O/14/85, *noted* IPD 9095). Similar cases are: *RTL Contractor's Application* (SRIS O/152/83); *L.B. (Plastics)' Application* (SRIS O/90/86); *Picker International's Application* (SRIS O/3/84); and *Hepworth Electrical's Application* (SRIS O/40/86, *noted* IPD 9028). D. W. Stanley has discussed and criticised the concept of "implied added subject matter" ((1987–88) 17 CIPA 108).

In *Université René Descartes' Application* (SRIS O/146/88) the Comptroller indicated that, in principle, it would be possible to derive a numerical value, not expressly stated in the specification, by calculation or interpolation from the contents of the specification, but such value had to be unequivocally derivable therefrom and this was not so in this case: to insert the requested value into the claim would also make this objectionable under section 14(5)(c).

—Introducing matter from known sources   **76.14**

The Comptroller does not appear to accept, at least readily, the view (which the EPO does, see para. 76.21) that addition of matter which would be obvious, in the sense of being part of the inherent stock of knowledge of the addressee, the man skilled in the art, does not involve "additional matter". Thus, in *Chinoin's Application* ([1986] RPC 39), the Comptroller observed: "the fact that information sought to be added is obvious, as distinct from being already known, does not in my view justify its admission without objection arising under section 76"; and, in *Mayflower Products' Application* (SRIS O/129/86, *noted* IPD 10002), the Comptroller had recourse to EPO Guidelines C-VI, 5.4 and 5.8 and asked the question whether a proposed divisional application would present the skilled reader with information which the earlier application did not, even if that information were obvious to the skilled reader. For alternative applications of these Guidelines, see paras. 76.22 and 76.23.

In *Armco's Application* (SRIS O/84/85) an attempt was made, which failed on its facts, to find basis for claims of a divisional application in the abstract for its parent. This would seem possible, in theory, because section 76 refers to an "application" as filed and, though an abstract is not part of the "specification" (s. 14(2)(b)), it is part of an "application" (s. 14). However, the EPO has decided that EPCa. 85 precludes consideration of the abstract as providing support for an amendment (*EPO Decision T 407/86*, "Memory circuit/FUJITSU," [1988] 4 EPOR 254). In any event, it is difficult to see how a proper abstract could be regarded as expanding the disclosure of that which it purports to summarise, though an argument based on reasonable generalisation in the abstract might succeed.

The EPO has held that, while a priority document has evidentiary effect, it cannot be taken into account in establishing the content of the application as filed, even if filed at the same time as the European application (*EPO Decision T 260/85*, "*Coaxial connecter/AMP*", OJEPO 4/1989, 105). The same philosophy should apply under the Act in view of section 14(2).

Comparison with cases decided under the 1949 Act   **76.15**

The *Van der Lely* case (discussed in para. 76.11 *supra*) specifically adopted reasoning used in cases under the 1949 Act, in particular the decisions in *Garrod's Application* ([1968] RPC 314); *International Playtex's Application* ([1969] RPC 362; and *Unilever's (Smeath's) Application* ([1978] RPC 617). On appeal in the *Van der Lely* case, the Patents Court noted that the requirements for divisional applications under the Act were now different, and much more restrictive, than under the 1949 Act. The rationale of these cases, where amendments were rejected, would therefore still seem applicable.

Further examples of cases of attempts to add matter decided under section 31 [1949] are *Bristol-Myers' (Johnson and Hardcastle's Application)* ([1974] RPC 389)), where an attempt to limit a chemical process claim to the use of a particular form of starting material was refused as there was no true disclosure in the unamended specification that the use of such form was to be preferred, and *Bristol-Myers' (Johnson's) Application* (No. 2) ([1979] RPC 450) where, after a finding of anticipation of a claim to a chemical compound, restriction of that claim to exclude the compound when made by the particular process previously used was rejected, though amendment to the process particularly described in the specification would have been allowed.

Another case where it was held that the amendment lacked sufficient support in the unamended specification was *Fuji Photo's (Kiritani's) Application* ([1979] RPC 413).

76.16 *The possibility of claim broadening during prosecution*

The fact that the prohibition of "extending the protection conferred by the patent" applies only post-grant (see subs. (3) compared with subs. (2)) suggests that it should be possible to broaden a claim during prosecution of an application. Such was a fairly common practice under the 1949 Act. However, the interpretation that has been put on the prohibition against including "additional matter" by amendment, or in a divisional or replacement application, makes it likely that few broadening amendments will be allowed. Moreover, even if such an amendment should be allowed, the patentee is then liable to have the amendment challenged in any plea for revocation of the patent under section 72(1)(*d*) and/or (*e*).

Thus, in *Honda's Application* (SRIS O/122/86, *noted* IPD 9105) the Comptroller, in response to a contention that section 69(2)(*b*) specifically contemplates claim broadening during examination of the application, held that the amended claims were no longer directed to what was originally contemplated as the inventive concept, and that claim amendment could not be permitted unless there were some indication in the specification as filed that the subject matter of the amended claim "was considered as an inventive concept at the time of filing".

Then, in *Sidco's Application* (SRIS O/173/86) the Comptroller, while accepting that section 76 refers to "matter" and not to "subject-matter", held that an attempt to change the broad description of the invention from one based on "eddy currents" to one which is "electromagnetic" would be a change of substance and therefore not allowable. Thus, the question perhaps has to be asked: if the proposed amendment does not involve additional matter, why is it necessary at all?

In *L.B. (Plastics)' Application* (SRIS O/90/86), a claim to "any novel subject matter disclosed in the specification" was held to have no effect upon the reader and therefore to provide no basis for the divisional application.

76.17 *Extending scope of granted patent (subs. (3)(b))*

New subsection (3)(*b*) prohibits the claims of a granted patent being amended (under the provisions of sections 27(1), 73 or 75) in such a way as to extend the protection conferred by the patent. However, this limitation does not apply to amendment made pre-grant, *i.e.* under the provisions specified in subsection (2), *viz*, under sections 17(3), 18(3) or 19(1), nor apparently to a correction made under section 117 as the Act seems not to regard corrections (of self-evident mistakes in specifications) under section 117 as amendments at all. If an amendment is made which does extend the protection conferred by a patent after grant, this constitutes a ground of revocation under section 72(1)(*e*) as discussed in para. 72.26. It must also be remembered that any amendment is subject to discretion, for which see paras. 25.05–25.07.

While section 76(3)(*b*) has similar wording to part of section 31 [1949], it must also be remembered that, whereas under section 31 [1949] determination of the scope of the protection conferred by the patent depends on a strict interpretation of the claims of the patent, see para. 125.07 (though see para. 125.09 for a possible contrary view), section 125 now makes it necessary to apply the Protocol to EPCa. 69 when determining the total scope of the protection conferred by the patent, see paras. 125.11–125.13. Consequently, excision of descriptive matter from the specification may have the effect of impliedly extending the scope of the patent. Consequently, there may be few amendments prohibited under subsection (3)(*b*) that would not be prohibited under the remainder of section 76 as involving "additional matter", as discussed in paras. 76.11–76.14.

It was suggested ((1980–81) 10 CIPA 316 and 403) that the words "extends the protection conferred by the patent" can only apply to a valid claim, as an invalid claim would confer no protection with the result that allowable amendment would be limited to combining an invalid claim with the whole of one or more sub-claims. If true, this would preclude the curing of invalidity by incorporating into the claims a feature of any specific sub-claim. It would also preclude amendment to a generalisation intermediate between the scope of the invalid claims and that of the valid ones. This seems an unduly rigid view of section 76(3)(*b*), and it may turn out to be a false one. Thus, in *Harding's Patent* ([1988] RPC 515) the Comptroller indicated *obiter* that, in the absence of bad faith, discretion to validate an invalid claim by amendment should be permitted, even if the invalidity arose from an amendment previously made in contravention of section 76, but held that there had been no matter added by the previous amendment. This finding was reversed on appeal but the case was remitted to the Patent Office for consideration of a validating amendment, there being no apparent indication that amendment would be impermissible in the circumstances. Nevertheless, the question remains in some doubt. Certainly, it can be argued that an invalid claim confers "protection" which stands so long as the claims and specification in question remain in a patent which is in force. Thus it is thought that the protection conferred relates to the terms of the specification and claims as these stand immediately before amendment, irrespective of the validity of the unamended claims.

Amendments allowed without contravention of section 76   **76.18**

It must be appreciated that most applications for amendment occur during the prosecution stage and that, if they should succeed, no reasoned decision will be issued. The only formal decisions which are likely to appear on allowability of amendment will, therefore, arise from: successful appeals; contested, *inter partes*, proceedings; or unsuccessful applications for revocation under section 72(1)(*d*) or (*e*). Nevertheless, the paucity of such decisions indicates that amendments which are not merely of a disclaiming nature are unlikely to succeed. However, more cases where amendment has been allowed in the EPO are noted in paras. 76.19–76.24.

Nevertheless, it can be noted that, in *Smith's Patent* (SRIS O/16/86), an objection, in revocation proceedings, that the Comptroller had previously allowed an impermissible amendment during prosecution was rejected on its facts, see further paras. 72.25 and 72.26.

The Comptroller also permitted amendment in *Philips Electronic's Patent* ([1987] RPC 244) to remove reference numerals in the granted claims of a European patent (UK); and to add an omnibus claim of specific wording, neither amendment in the circumstances adding new matter or broadening the claims. Deletion of the French and German translations of the granted claims was also permitted as these served no useful purpose because the authentic text of the specification was in English.

Prohibition of amendments under the EPC

—Effect of EPC on section 76   **76.19**

EPCa. 123(2) and (3) correspond respectively to the prohibitions on amendments based on no "additional matter" and not "extending the protection conferred by the patent". However, section 76 is *not* listed in section 130(7) as one of the provisions of the Act intended to have, as nearly as practicable, the same effects as under the EPC. As a result, the Comptroller has usually refused to take into account EPO decisions (or lack of objection) on amendment or division, even in relation to corresponding applications, see *Air Products' Application* (SRIS O/189/83) and *L.B. (Plastics)' Application* (SRIS O/90/86). However, the Comptroller has not been averse to quoting the EPO Guidelines concerning amendment (EPO Guidelines C-VI, 5.2–5.8), see *Mayflower Products' Application* (SRIS O/129/86), though in that case the Comptroller also stated that, though section 76 and EPCa. 123(2) each proscribe "added subject matter", the meaning of that term is a matter to be decided under national patent law.

This view of the Comptroller appears unduly restrictive. Quite apart from section 130(7), section 91 requires judicial notice to be taken of the EPC and decisions made under it. For cases in which this has been done see para. 91.03. Also, if amendment is improperly allowed under section 76, a ground for revocation arises under section 72(1)(*d*) and/or (*e*) and these provisions are listed in section 130(7). Thus, if the Comptroller disallows an amendment under section 76 which would not, if allowed, lead to revocation under section 72, he is in effect imposing a higher standard of invalidity than is required by EPCa. 138(1) which stipulates the only grounds which the Member States of the EPC have agreed shall be available for the revocation of patents granted under their national laws. Also, in *B & R Relay's Application* ([1985] RPC 1), the Patents Court indicated, in relation to section 76, that an attempt should be made to give the same meaning to any provision of the Act as that given to relevant EPC provisions, whichever jurisdiction is being invoked.

Therefore, the principal cases decided in relation to EPCa. 123(2) (*Prohibition of amendment whereby specification contains "subject-matter which extends beyond the contents of the specification as filed"*) and EPCa. 123(3) (*Prohibition of amendment "in such a way as to extend the protection conferred"*) are discussed in paras. 76.20–76.24 *infra*, particularly with reference to EPO Guidelines C-VI, 5.2–5.8. Amendment in the EPO is more fully discussed in *EPH*.

76.20 *—Acknowledgment of prior art (EPO Guideline C-VI, 5.3)*

EPO Guideline C-VI, 5.3 makes it clear that addition of further reference to the prior art can only serve to define the invention in relation to the prior art and that such added reference cannot be regarded as added "subject-matter", see *EPO Decision T* 11/82, *"Control circuit/LANSING BAGNALL"* (OJEPO 12/1983, 479). It would appear that, in this way, the EPO may even have allowed correction of an alleged insufficiency concerning preparation of starting materials for a claimed chemical process, itself adequately described, see *EPO Decision T* 51/87 (*noted* [1989] 5 IPBB 7). Although section 76 refers to "matter", rather than to "subject matter", this probably introduces no difference of substance. The EPO will also allow correction of an erroneous acknowledgment of prior art (*EPO Decision T* 22/83, *"Surface wave acoustic device/FUJITSU"*. [1988] 4 EPOR 234).

However, since British, as distinct from EPO, practice does not require prior art to be described in the specification, provided the invention is delimited therefrom by its claims, the only reason for making this type of amendment under section 76 would probably be by way of explanation of a latent ambiguity in the claim wording to clarify that it is not intended that the claims cover the acknowledged prior art. For example, prior art amounting to an "accidental anticipation" (such as in *Molins v. Industrial Machinery* ((1937) 54 RPC 94 and (1938) 55 RPC 31) should still be capable of being overcome under section 76, provided that no obviousness argument is applicable over that prior art.

—Permissible addition of well-known matter (EPO Guidelines C-VI, 5.6, 5.7)   **76.21**

EPO Guideline C-VI, 5.6 indicates that, under the EPC, subject-matter can be added by amendment if that matter, in the context of the invention, is so well-known to the person skilled in the art that its introduction can be regarded as an obvious clarification. Thus, in *EPO Decision T* 32/84, *"Redefining an invention . . . /COMMISARIAT . . . "* (OJEPO 1/1986, 9; [1986] 2 EPOR 94), it was held that questions under EPCa. 123(2) do not arise in defining an invention in terms of features which have not been shown explicitly in the specification, provided that the invention can be put into practice without need for additional explicit description. However, the requirement for the amendment to be an "obvious clarification" would appear to be the key here and it will not be sufficient, at least under section 76, merely to show that the additional matter is well-known to the skilled man, see para. 76.14 *supra*.

Thus, where a technical feature has been clearly described in the application, but the effect arising therefrom has not been so mentioned, or not mentioned fully, and yet that effect is readily deducible by the skilled man from the specification, the addition of wording elaborating that effect has been held by the EPO to be mere clarification rather than the addition of new matter, see *EPO Decision T* 37/82, *"Low-tension switch/SIEMENS"* (OJEPO 2/1984, 71). A further case of a permitted clarificatory amendment is *EPO Decision T* 271/84, *"Removal of hydrogen sulphide . . . /AIR PRODUCTS"* (OJEPO 9/1987, 405; [1987] 1 EPOR 23). However, if the true construction of a claim effectively removes an alleged ambiguity, then there appears no need to amend it, see *EPO Decision T* 127/85, *"Blasting composition/IRECO"* (OJEPO 7/1989, 271; [1989] 6 EPOR 358). In a number of EPO decisions it has been permitted to import into the claims features depicted in the drawings but not explicit mentioned in the description, though the imported feature must be one "clearly, unmistakably and fully derivable from the drawings by the person skilled in the art and so be relatable by him to the content of the description as a whole as to be manifestly part of the invention" (*EPO Decision T* 169/83, *"Wall element/VEREINIGTE METALLWERKE"*, OJEPO 7/1985, 193), see also *EPO Decision T* 75/82, *"Transducer head/IBM"* ([1986] 2 EPOR 103). However, such an amendment will be refused if the selected element has truly only been disclosed in combination with some other element which it is not proposed to incorporate in the amended claim (*EPO Decision T* 17/86, *"Refrigeration plant/SATAM BRANDT"*, OJEPO 7/1989, 297; [1989] 6 EPOR 347), see also *EPO Decision T* 174/86, *"Brush assembly/BLACK & DECKER"* ([1989] 5 EPOR 277). Likewise, it is not permissable to replace a specific feature by a functional expression because the latter will cover equivalents of that feature, which the original disclosure did not (*EPO Decision T* 416/86, *"Reflection photometer/BOEHRINGER"*, OJEPO 7/1989, 308; [1989] 6 EPOR 327).

Matter can also be imported from a document to which there is specific reference in the specification, because its contents are deemed always to have been included in the original contents of the specification. An example is *EPO Decision T* 6/84, *"Amendment of claims/MOBIL"* (OJEPO 8/1985, 238), though here a warning was given that the imported feature must not single out a particular feature from a set of features which the referenced document indicated belonged to each other, see also *EPO Decision T* 288/84, *"Activated support/STAMICARBON"* (OJEPO 5/1986, 128; [1986] 4 EPOR 217).

Thus, amendment by introducing a feature from a referenced document must not involve an act of selection which had not been made in the specification as filed. It is therefore not permissible to derive *specific* information from drawings stated to be "diagrammatic" or "perspective" (*EPO Decision T* 17/84, "*Manufacture of fuse-cord/ICI*", [1986] 5 EPOR 274).

While "correction" is to be considered quite separately (under s. 117) from amendment, see para. 117.08, if an error can be perceived and rectified by the skilled person from his common general knowledge, amendment to correct the error would not seem to involve adding new matter to the specification; at least this seems to be so in the light of *EPO Decision T* 171/84, "*Redox catalyst/AIR Products*" (OJEPO 4/1986, 95; [1986] 4 EPOR 210).

76.22 —*Relation of test for additional subject-matter to tests of novelty and priority (EPO Guidelines C-VI, 5.4, 5.5)*

The principle under EPCa. 123(2) is basically similar to that for lack of novelty (*EPO Decision T* 133/85, "*Amendments/XEROX*", [1989] 2 EPOR 116), *i.e.* no new subject matter must be generated by the amendment (*EPO Decision T* 17/86, "*Refrigeration plant/SATAM BRANDT*", OJEPO 7/1989, 297; [1989] 6 EPOR 347), and see EPO Guideline C-VI, 5.4. Thus, according to EPO Guideline C-IV, 7.2, a document destroys the novelty of subject-matter "if that matter is derivable directly and unambiguously from that document, including any features implicit to a person skilled in the art, in what is expressly mentioned in the document", but a warning that care is necessary in applying the lack of novelty test to permissable amendment was given in *EPO Decision T* 133/85 (*supra*). Guideline C-IV, 7.2 cites, as its support for this proposition, *EPO Decision T* 201/83, "*Lead alloy/SHELL*" (OJEPO 10/1984, 481). In this case amendment was allowed to restrict the lower end of a numerical range to a figure illustrated in one of the examples. In contrast, in *EPO Decision T* 54/82, "*Disclosure/MOBIL*" (OJEPO 11/1983, 446), a disclosure of a range of compounds with "10–50 carbon atoms" did not impliedly disclose, and therefore did not provide a basis for amendment to, a range of "18–24 carbon atoms" in the absence of explicit reference to such a range.

Also, the test for added matter is stated in the Guidelines to be the same as that for determining whether a claim is entitled to the date of a priority document, see EPO Guideline C-V 2.4. For example, in *EPO Decision T* 07/80, "*Copying process*" (OJEPO 3/1982, 95), an amended claim was rejected because the characterising clause was held not to find sufficient support in the specification as originally filed.

However, the test under EPCa. 123(2) is not the same as that of support for breadth of claim required by EPCa. 84 (*EPO Decision T* 133/85, *supra*), because it is possible to support something which is broad from a narrower base, but an amendment to provide support under EPCa. 84 must contravene EPCa. 123(2) by adding matter to the disclosure as filed. Thus, use of the word "supported" is inappropriate in relation to EPCa. 123(2) and *EPO Decision T* 52/82, "*Winding apparatus/RIETER*" (OJEPO 10/1983, 416), where a term in the claim preamble was replaced by a more generic term held to be more apt to define a feature present, was expressly disapproved.

Other cases where a lack of support for the amendment in the original specification was found, the amendment not being derivable from the explicit, or implicit, disclosure of that specification include: *EPO Decision T* 188/83, "*Vinyl acetate/FERNHOLZ*" (OJEPO 11/1984, 555); and *EPO Decision T* 32/85, "*Biomass preparation/GIST-BROCADES*" ([1986] 5 EPOR 267).

Nevertheless, amendment to exclude prior art by positive restriction of a numerical range has been permitted even in the absence in the specification of any support for the excluded matter, see *EPO Decision T* 433/86, "*Modified diisocyanates/ICI*" ([1982] 2 EPOR 97), but it was here recognised that such an amendment could alternatively have been made by express disclaimer of the prior art, and therefore the amendment may have been allowed because of a preference for an exclusionary amendment to be expressed in positive, rather than negative, terminology.

The EPO Enlarged Board of Appeal has been asked to consider whether, in opposition proceedings, a claim to a chemical compound (X) can be amended to the form "Use of X as a friction-reducing oil additive" to overcome a reference which describes X as an oil additive for a different purpose, see *EPO Decision T* 59/87, *"Friction reducing additive/MOBIL II"* (OJEPO 9/1988, 347) and para. 2.13.

—Addition of subject matter by excision of text (EPO Guideline C-VI, 5.8)   **76.23**

EPO Guideline C-VI, 5.8 warns that "Alteration or excision of text, as well as the addition of further text, may introduce fresh subject-matter". As has been shown in para. 76.11 *supra*, this is a principle which has resulted in disallowance of an amendment (or the filing of a divisional application) in a number of cases decided under the Act. However, examples of disallowance in EPO amendment decisions appear to be rare, though in *EPO Decision T* 260/85, *"Coaxial connector/ AMP"* (OJEPO 4/1989, 105) it was clearly stated that deletion of a feature from an independent claim will violate EPCa. 123(2) if that feature was originally presented as an essential feature of the invention. Thus, in *EPO Decision T* 66/85, *"Connector/AMP"* (OJEPO 5/1989, 167; [1989] 5 EPOR 283), claim broadening was accepted because the skilled person would have seen that, otherwise, some of the illustrated embodiments would have been outside the scope of the claims.

Indeed, on at least two occasions, the EPO has permitted removal of a feature from claim wording in a pre-grant amendment, thereby resulting in its broadening. Thus, in *EPO Decision T* 190/83, *Otto Bock's Application* (reported only in *EPH*, Chapter 103), it was permitted to omit two features from the original claim on the basis that the totality of the original disclosure constitutes a "reservoir" from which the applicant can draw when amending the specification. This view was approved in *EPO Decision T* 133/85, *"Amendment/XEROX"* ([1989] 2 EPOR 116) where it was pointed out that such reservoir is that of the original application and that it cannot be expanded after the date of filing. Then, in *EPO Decision T* 151/84, *"Thomson-CSF's Application"* ([1988] 1 EPOR 29), a feature was permitted to be deleted from the characterising portion of the main claim because the specification as a whole made it clear that this was an advantageous, but not indispensible, characteristic of the invention. However, a decision seemingly inconsistent with these is *EPO Decision T* 147/85, *"Interchangeable disks/PHILLIPS"* ([1988] 2 EPOR 111) where it was stated that it did not assist the Applicant that the skilled person would immediately appreciate that a particular feature was unnecessary, see also *EPO Decision T* 24/85, *"Lens assembly/DISCOVISION"*, ([1988] 4 EPOR 247).

EPO Decision T 161/86, *"Antibiotic/ELI LILLY"* ([1988] 6 EPOR 366) should also be noted. In this, a structural formula in the claim, found after filing to be incorrect, was allowed to be deleted and the claim converted to claim a product "obtainable" by a stated process and possessing certain specified characteristics, each of which had been mentioned in the original specification. This is similar to the amendment allowed, though under the 1949 Act, in *Egyt's Patent* ([1981] RPC 99), discussed in para. A031.13.

—Amendment extending the protection conferred (EPCa. 123(3))   **76.24**

The paper by R. Schulte (listed in para. 76.03 *supra*) has reviewed the operation of EPCa. 123(3). The EPO has held that this provision only permits a change in claim category after grant in exceptional circumstances because of the Protocol to EPCa. 69 (*EPO Decision T* 378/86, *"Change of category/MOOG"*, OJEPO

10/1988, 386; [1989] 2 EPOR 85). In this decision it was stated that EPCa. 123(3) is contravened when it is obvious that an act can be considered as an infringement of the amended claim, but could not have been so considered in respect of the claims before amendment. However, change of a process claim to an apparatus claim was there permitted because the means of carrying out the process had been described in such detail that the skilled person could readily deduce from the disclosure the apparatus which the amendment sought to claim.

Examples where amendment has been refused under EPCa. 123(3) are *EPO Decision T* 20/84, *"Annular shaft kiln/WARMSTELLE . . . "* ([1986] 3 EPOR 197), where the deletion of several lines from a claim was held to be an impermissible broadening amendment; and *EPO Decision T* 898/85,, *"Vehicle brakes/SAB"* ([1988] 2 EPOR 105), where an amendment to change a feature from being "stabilized in a substantially vertical position" to being "stabilized in a position parallel to the tread of a wheel" was likewise not permitted.

However, it has been permitted to delete a feature from a claim on the basis that its removal clarified and/or resolved an inconsistency in the original claim and did not therefore, in the factual circumstances, result in the scope of the protection being extended (*EPO Decision T* 172/82, *"Particle analyzer/CONTRAVES"*) OJEPO 12/1984, 493). For other claim broadening cases, see para. 76.23 *supra*.

76.25   *Effect of amendment on damages*

It should here be noted that, by section 62(3), the making of any amendment to the specification of the patent after grant (whether under s. 27 or 75) will have the effect of depriving the propietor of damages for infringement of the patent before amendment, unless the court or Comptroller is satisfied that the specification as published was framed in good faith and with reasonable skill and knowledge. However, it is rare for it to be found that such criteria were not met in the drafting of the specification, but see para. 62.05 for the effect of the section and the method and onus of proof required, see also para. 63.03.

PART II

PROVISIONS ABOUT INTERNATIONAL CONVENTIONS

SECTION 77   77.01

Effect of European patent (UK)

77.—(1) Subject to the provisions of this Act, a European patent (UK), shall, as from the publication of the mention of its grant in the European Patent Bulletin, be treated for the purposes of Parts I and III of this Act as if it were a patent under this Act granted in pursuance of an application made under this Act and as if notice of the grant of the patent had, on the date of that publication, been published under section 24 above in the journal; and—

(*a*) the proprietor of a European patent (UK) shall accordingly as respects the United Kingdom have the same rights and remedies, subject to the same conditions, as the proprietor of a patent under this Act;

(*b*) references in Parts I and III of this Act to a patent shall be construed accordingly; and

(*c*) any statement made and any certificate filed for the purposes of the provision of the convention corresponding to section 2(4)(*c*) above shall be respectively treated as a statement made and written evidence filed for the purposes of the said paragraph (*c*).

(2) Subsection (1) above shall not affect the operation in relation to a European patent (UK) of any provisions of the European Patent Convention relating to the amendment or revocation of such a patent in proceedings before the European Patent Office.

(3) Where in the case of a European patent (UK)—

(a) proceedings for infringement, or proceedings under section 58 above, have been commenced before the court or the comptroller and have not been finally disposed of, and

(b) it is established in proceedings before the European Patent Office that the patent is only partially valid,

the provisions of section 63 or, as the case may be of subsections (7) to (9) of section 58 apply as they apply to proceedings in which the validity of the patent is put in issue and in which it is found that the patent is only partially valid.

[(3) *Sections 58(7) to (9) and 63 above shall apply to the case where, after proceedings for the infringement of a European patent have been com-*

547

menced before the court or the comptroller but have not been finally disposed of, it is established in proceedings before the European Patent Office that the patent is only partially valid as those provisions apply to proceedings in which the validity of a patent is put in issue and in which it is found that the patent is only partially valid.]

(4) Where a European patent (UK) is amended in accordance with the European Patent Convention, the amendment shall have effect for the purposes of Parts I and III of this Act as if the specification of the patent has been amended under this Act; but subject to subsection (6)(b) below.

[*(4) Subject to subsection (6) below, where a European patent (UK) is amended or revoked in accordance with the European Patent Convention, the amendment shall be treated for the purposes of Parts I and III of this Act as if it had been made, or as the case may be the patent shall be treated for those purposes as having been revoked, under this Act.*]

(4A) Where a European patent (UK) is revoked in accordance with the European Patent Convention, the patent shall be treated for the purposes of Parts I and III of this Act as having been revoked under this Act.

(5) Where—

(*a*) under the European Patent Convention a European patent (UK) is revoked for failure to observe a time limit and is subsequently restored; and

(*b*) between the revocation and publication of the fact that it has been restored a person begins in good faith to do an act which would, apart from section 55 above, constitute an infringement of the patent or makes in good faith effective and serious preparations to do such an act;

he shall have the rights conferred by section **28A(4) and (5) above, and subsections (6) and (7)** [*28(6) above, and subsection (8) and (9)*] of that section shall apply accordingly.

(6) While this subsection is in force—

(*a*) subsection (1) above shall not apply to a European patent (UK) the specification of which was published in French or German, unless a translation of the specification into English is filed at the Patent Office and the prescribed fee is paid before the end of the prescribed period;

(*b*) subsection (4) above shall not apply to an amendment made in French or German unless a translation **into English of the specification as amended** [*of the amendment into English*] is filed at the Patent Office and the prescribed fee is paid before the end of the prescribed period.

(7) Where **such a translation is not filed** [*a translation of a specification or amendment into English is not filed in accordance with subsection (6)(a) or (b) above*], the patent shall be treated as always having been void.

(8) The comptroller shall publish any translation filed at the Patent Office under subsection (6) above.

(9) Subsection (6) above shall come into force on a day appointed for the purpose by rules and shall cease to have effect on a day so appointed, without prejudice, however, to the power to bring it into force again.

Note. Subsections (3)–(7) were each prospectively amended, and subsection (4A) prospectively added, by the 1988 Act (Sched. 5, paras. 8 and 21). For the commencement of these changes, see the latest Supplement to this Work *re.* this para.

RELEVANT RULES

Translations   **77.02**

4 [1987].—(1) 1st September 1987 is the day appointed under section 77(9) of the Patents Act 1977 for the purpose of the coming into force of subsection (6) of that section.

(2) This rule shall not apply in the case of a European patent (UK) mention of whose grant is published in the European Patent Bulletin before that day.

Note. This is rule 4 of the Patents (Amendment) Rules 1987 (S.I. 1987 No. 288).

Translations of European patents (UK) filed under section 77(6)   **77.03**

79A.—(1) A translation filed under section 77(6) shall be filed in duplicate and shall be accompanied by Patents Form No. 54/77 in duplicate, in the case of a translation filed under section 77(6)(*a*), or by Patents Form No. 55/77 in duplicate, in the case of a translation filed under section 77(6)(*b*).

(2) A translation filed under section 77(6)(*a*) shall comprise a translation of the entirety of the published specification of the patent, irrespective of whether a translation of all or any part of the claims contained in the specification has previously been filed under section 78(7) but subject to paragraph (5) below, and shall include any drawings in the specification, irrespective of whether the drawings contain textual matter.

(3) A translation filed under section 77(6) shall comply with the following requirements as to presentation, subject to paragraph (4) below in the case of any drawings:

(*a*) it shall permit of direct reproduction by photography, electrostatic processes, photo offset and micro-filming, in an unlimited number of copies;

(*b*) it shall be on A4 paper (29.7cm. × 21cm.) which shall be pliable, strong, white, smooth, matt and durable;

(*c*) each sheet of paper shall be free from cracks, creases and folds and used on one side only;

(*d*) each sheet shall be used with its short sides at the top and bottom (upright position);

549

(*e*) the minimum margins shall be:

top	2 cm.
left side	2·5 cm.
right side	2 cm.
bottom	2 cm.;

(*f*) the margins of the sheets shall be completely blank;

(*g*) the translation shall be typed or printed in single-line spacing (unless the comptroller otherwise permits), in a dark, indelible colour and in characters of which the capital letters are not less than 0.21cm. high, save that graphic symbols and characters and chemical and mathematical formulae may, instead of being typed or printed, be written or drawn;

(*h*) the translation shall be reasonably free from deletions and other alterations, overwritings and interlineations and shall, in any event, be legible;

(*i*) each sheet (other than a sheet of drawings) shall be numbered consecutively in arabic numerals.

(4) Where a translation including any drawings is filed, the sheets of drawings shall correspond exactly in content and presentation to the sheets of drawings which were published by the European Patent Office, except that—

(*a*) each sheet shall be numbered consecutively in arabic numerals, as a separate series from that used for the other sheets of the translation, if not so numbered when published by the European Patent Office; and

(*b*) any textual matter contained in the published drawings shall be replaced with a translation into English.

(5) For the purposes of paragraph (2) above, the published specification of the patent shall be taken not to include—

(*a*) anything which does not consist of, or form part of, the description of the invention, the claims or the drawings referred to in the description or the claims, or

(*b*) any claim not having effect in the United Kingdom, or

(*c*) anything published in a language other than the language of the proceedings (within the meaning of Article 14 of the European Patent Convention).

Note. Rule 79A will need some consequent amendment on the bringing into force of the amendments to section 77 (for which see para. 77.01 *supra*). The latest Supplement to this Work *re.* this para. should therefore be consulted.

77.04   *Periods described under section 77(6)*

79B.—(1) The period prescribed under section 77(6)(*a*) for filing a translation of the specification of a European patent (U.K.) and paying the prescribed fee shall be three months from the date of publication of the mention of the grant of the patent in the European Patent Bulletin.

(2) The period prescribed under section 77(6)(*b*) for filing a translation of an amendment to a European patent (U.K.) and paying the prescribed fee shall be three months from the date of publication by the European Patent Office of the specification of the patent as amended.

Note. The *Note* to para. 77.03 applies likewise to rule 79B.

Verification of translation **77.05**

79E. A translation shall be verified to the satisfaction of the comptroller as corresponding to the original text of—

(*a*) the specification, in the case of a translation filed under section 77(6)(*a*), or

(*b*) the amendment, in the case of a translation filed under section 77(6)(*b*), or

(*c*) the claims of the specification of the application, in the case of a translation filed under section 78(7), or

(*d*) the specification of the patent or the claims of the application, as the case may be, in the case of a translation filed under section 80(3);

and if such verification does not accompany the translation when filed it shall be filed within one month of the sending by the Comptroller of a written request for such verification.

Note. The *Note* to para. 77.03 applies likewise to rule 79E.

Inspection of translations **77.06**

79F. A request for inspection of a translation published under section 77(8), 78(7) or 80(3) shall be made on Patent Form No. 23/77.

Notes. Rules 79A, 79B, 79E and 79F reprinted above were added by the Patents (Amendment) Rules 1987 to have effect from September 1, 1987 (S.I. 1987 No. 288, rr. 1(3) and 6). Also relevant are: rule 30 (*Address for service*), reprinted at para. 32.03; rule 79(1) (*European patents: Entries in the register*), reprinted in para. 32.12; and rule 113(4) and (5) (*Translations*), reprinted in para. 123.12. **77.07**

COMMENTARY ON SECTION 77

General **77.08**

Sections 77 to 95 constitute Part II of the Act and relate to international conventions. Section 77 is the first of a group of sections 77–89, which are concerned with patents and applications under EPC and PCT, to give effect to them under British domestic patent law, and to provide for related matters. EPCaa. 63–70 are generally relevant, and section 77 arises from EPCa. 64.

The terms "European Patent Convention", "European Patent", "European Patent (U.K.)", "European Patent Bulletin" and "European Patent Office" are each defined in section 130(1) and (6) (see para. 130.08), though these definitions are largely self-evident.

The purpose of section 77 is to give the proprietor of a European patent (UK) the same rights as he would have had if he had applied for the patent under the Act and to give the court and the Comptroller jurisdiction over a European patent (UK). Section 78 deals likewise with an application for a European patent (UK). These sections are not concerned with a Community patent which is dealt with in sections 86 and 87. Neither section 77 nor section 78 gives the court or the Comptroller any jurisdiction over the prosecution of the application for, and the grant of, the European patent, although jurisdiction over entitlement is provided under section 12, subject to section 82.

77.09   *Effect of European patent (UK) (subs. (1))*

Section 77(1) provides that a European patent (UK) has the same effect as a patent granted under the Act, as from publication of the grant in the EPB, as if such publication had taken place under section 24. The proprietor has the same rights and remedies as a proprietor of a patent under the Act; Parts I and III of the Act apply (*viz.*: ss.1–76 and 96–132) and where there is a prior disclosure at an international exhibition any certificate filed under EPCa. 55(2) is deemed to comply with section 2(4)(*c*). The Patents Rules have effect to govern European patents (UK) from their date of grant, even when these rules have effect by virtue of Part I of the Act (*Deforeit's Patent*, [1986] RPC 142).

It has been pointed out ((1984–85) 14 CIPA 14) that, apparently, the Comptroller is required to publish the specification of a European patent (UK) because the provisions of section 24(3) seem to apply thereto in view of the wording of section 77(1). However, this is not the practice and the Official Journal merely lists the numbers of European patents (UK) that have been granted, together with the corresponding EPO application number and the name of the proprietor ((1983–84 13 CIPA 405). This would seem to raise a problem when a European patent (UK) is amended in proceedings under either of sections 27 or 75.

77.10   *Registration of European patents (UK) in other countries*

It is by no means certain that the effect of a European patent (UK) is the same as one granted under Part I of the Act as regards the obtaining of patents in some of those countries which provide for patent rights to be obtained therein by registration of granted United Kingdom patents, see (1988–89) 18 CIPA 226. The EPO has also published information on the point (OJEPO 8/1986, 292). The position is further summarised in *EPH* as a note to the reprinting of EPCa. 168. Although there may be some doubt as to the exact date of grant of patents granted under Part I of the Act when computing the period permitted for such foreign registrations of the patent (see para. 24.11), no such doubt arises with regard to European patents (UK) because section 77(1) makes it clear that the date of grant of such patents for all purposes is the date of publication of grant in the European Patents Bulletin.

77.11   *Effect of subsections (2)–(5)*

Subsections (2), (4) and (4A) assimilate the effects of any amendments or revocation made under EPCaa. 102, 111, 112 or 123 as if they had been made under Parts I and III of the Act. It is only possible to revoke or amend a European patent by proceedings in the EPO by way of opposition lodged under EPCa. 99, and such can only be done within nine months of the publication in the EPB of the notice of grant of the European patent. If no such opposition is timely filed, then (since January 1984) an entry to this effect has been made in the European register; and an analogous entry is also now made when errors in the specification are allowed by the EPO to be rectified (OJEPO 11/1983, 458). The European register also contains much information on the progress of European patent applications and of the prior art coming to light after the European search report has been established, see OJEPO 2/1986, 61. Access to the European register is discussed in para. 32.34.

Subsection (3) assimilates for the purposes of section 58(7)–(9) (*patent found partially valid in Crown use proceedings*) and section 63 (*relief for infringement of a partially valid patent*) an EPO decision resulting in partial invalidity. The amendment to subsection (3) will serve to clarify the way in which the provisions in the Act for infringement proceedings and section 58 operate in the case of a European patent (UK) which is amended as a result of opposition proceedings before the EPO and also makes it clear that subsection (3) relates only to a European patent (UK).

Subsection (4) (as revised) will equate the amendment of a European patent (UK) as a result of opposition proceedings before the EPO with amendment under the Act, but subject to the filing of the amendment when the European patent is in French or German, see para. 77.16. Although there is no procedure laid down under the EPC for the proprietor of a European patent to apply to the EPO to amend the specification of his patent, the same effect may be achieved within the first nine months after grant by the proprietor filing opposition to his own patent (*EPO Decision Gr* 01/84, *"Opposition by proprietor/MOBIL OIL"*, OJEPO 10/1985, 199; [1986] 1 EPOR 39).

However, an amendment made during EPO opposition proceedings does not take effect until the opposition decision has finally issued. Meanwhile, it would appear that the European patent (UK) may be enforced by the bringing of infringement proceedings and that the court hearing those proceedings must treat the patent as unamended until a final EPO decision is given, if necessary after resolution of any appeal therefrom timely brought. Of course, amendment can be sought in concurrent proceedings before the court under section 75, but there is no obligation that this be done. Nevertheless, when the EPO decision is finally given, it thereafter has binding effect on legal proceedings under the patent, though probably without effect on awards of damages already ordered. The position is likewise if the EPO orders total revocation of the patent. In principle, these are no different positions from those which already exist under United Kingdom law because of the possibility of concurrent proceedings before courts of different jurisdiction, *e.g.* those of England and Scotland, but concurrent infringement and EPO proceedings are more frequent.

Similarly, subsection (4A) will equate the revocation of a European patent (UK) as the result of opposition proceedings before the EPO with revocation under the Act. The previous version of subsection (4) purported to embrace both amendment and revocation.

These revisions of section 77 are to take effect from a commencement date, for which see the *Note* to para. 77.01.

Subsection (5) provides for the application of intervening rights to a European patent (UK) which has been revoked for failure to observe a time limit and has been restored on the same basis as in section 28(6), (8) and (9), now to be replaced by section 28A(4)–(7), that is the right to continue intervening acts or acts that would otherwise infringe or fall under section 55 (*Crown use*) between expiry and an application to restore a lapsed patent, as discussed in paras. 28A.04–28A.06.

Translation of European patents (UK) (subss. (6)–(9))   **77.12**

Subsections (6)–(8) are concerned with translations where the European patent (UK) is in French or German (see EPCa. 65). They apply to European patents

(UK) the mention of the grant of which was published on or after September 1, 1987, see para. 77.02. Subsections (6)–(8) do not apply to European patents (UK) whose mention of grant was published before September 1, 1987 irrespective of any amendment made in opposition proceedings at the EPO and published by the EPO after that date.

Subsection (9) would allow the provisions of subsections (6)–(8) to be removed, and subsequently reimposed, on an appointed day by rules. Rules 79A, 79B, 79E and 79F were made consequent upon bringing subsection (6) into effect from September 1, 1987.

Rules 79A (reprinted at para. 77.03) and 79E (reprinted at para. 77.05) prescribe the requirements for providing translations of European patents (U.K.) having their text in the French or German language. These rules are dealt with in para. 77.16.

Rule 79B (reprinted at para. 77.04) prescribes the period within which subsection (6) must be satisfied: otherwise the European patent (UK) is treated "as always having been void" (subsection (7)). Thus, rule 79B(1) prescribes that the translations now required by subsection (6)(a) are to be filed, and the prescribed fee paid, within three months of the date of mention of the grant of the European patent (UK) in the European Patent Bulletin (the "EPB"), and rule 79B(2) likewise requires a translation of any amendment of such a patent to be filed within three months from the date of publication by the EPO of the amended specification.

The result of subsection (6) is that, until the translation has been filed as required, the European patent (UK) has no effect in the United Kingdom. Thus all formal requisites for the filing of the translation may need to be met before the proprietor is able to take advantage of his patent rights.

It is again stressed that failure to supply a required translation within the prescribed period, unless the period can be extended, renders the patent void, and retroactively so (subs. (7)). However, the period for filing the translation is extensible by one month as of right by filing PF 50/77 under rule 110(3); and for a longer period if discretion can be exercised under rule 110(3C) after application on PF 52/77 under rule 110(3A). The application of rules 110(3A) and (3C) is discussed in para. 123.36.

The translations filed under subsection (6) are published, in accordance with subsection (8), by printing them in the same manner as the B-specifications of patents granted under Part I of the Act and are distributed to the same libraries in the United Kingdom as those B-specifications. For this reason the translation must be filed in conformity with the presentation requirements of rule 79A(3), discussed in para. 77.16. The original translation can be inspected, and copies provided, under rule 79F (reprinted at para. 77.06) by filing PF 23/77 in the usual way, see para. 118.20.

77.13 *Legal effect of translation filed under subsection (6)*

The legal effect of a translation filed under subsection (6) is obscure. The authentic text of a European patent (UK) for the purposes of any proceedings in the United Kingdom remains that of the specification of the European patent in the language of the proceedings before the EPO (s. 80(1), but see the discussion in para. 80.04. Only if the translation filed under section 77(6) is narrower than the protection conferred by the authentic text is the translation to be substituted for that authentic text until this is corrected, and even then not in proceedings for the revocation of the patent (s. 80(2), discussed in para. 80.05). If and when so corrected, the new translation replaces the original translation of the authentic text (s. 80(3), discussed in para. 80.06), but subject to interim loss of rights, see sections

80(3) and (4), discussed in paras. 80.06 and 80.07. Therefore, if the translation is of the same, or wider, scope than the authentic text, it is the authentic text which has effect. Thus, the translation under section 77(6) mainly has effect for information purposes and can only be relied upon in legal proceedings if it is admitted that this is of narrower scope than the authentic text, and even then not in revocation proceedings.

In proceedings before the Comptroller, no further translation needs to be filed under rule 113(4) (reprinted in para. 123.12), see para. 77.16. Thus, the translation filed under section 77(6) is prima facie accepted by the Comptroller, but its existence is evidential and, as with any evidence, is subject to challenge, even though the translation has been verified to the satisfaction of the Comptroller under rule 79E (reprinted at para. 77.05). Otherwise, and especially in proceedings before the court, a translation will need to be provided and supported by evidence, unless it has been made the subject of a formal admission or agreement between the parties, see para. 77.17.

General obligations on proprietor of European patent (UK)   **77.14**

A note on EPO Form 2005 (*Communication under EPCr. 51(6)*) reminds proprietors of the need to supply an address for service for every European patent (UK) (in compliance with rule 30, reprinted at para. 32.03, and discussed in para. 32.16); and also points out the need to file an English translation if the authentic text of the European patent (UK) is not in the English language. It has been suggested that the address for service should be notified as soon as it becomes apparent that an application for a European patent (UK) is going to mature into a patent, *e.g.* upon the issue of the letter under EPCr. 51(6). This can have the advantage that any reminders concerning the filing of a translation, or the payment of a renewal fee, are sent to the United Kingdom agent. Should an English translation be required, but not supplied within the prescribed three months' period, as extended by one month (r. 110(3)), the Patent Office sends a letter to the address for service, notifying that the European patent (UK) is deemed void. This gives an early opportunity to apply for a further extension under rule 110(3A), should the voiding have been unintentional.

There is no need to provide any form of authorisation of agent: provision of an address suffices for this purpose, see para. 115.03. However, if opposition proceedings are commenced against the European patent in the EPO within the permitted nine months' period from the notification of grant in the EPB under EPCa. 99, the representative who is to act before the EPO will need to be authorised in accordance with normal EPO practice, see, *e.g.* O.J. July 19, 1989.

Providing the address for service   **77.15**

When proprietors of European patents (UK) have complied with rule 30 and furnished an address for service, presently within the United Kingdom but with an address elsewhere in the EEC to be permitted (see para. 32.16), this information is added to the register of European patents (UK), for details of which see para. 32.18. No form or fee has been prescribed for entering an address for service in the United Kingdom register for a European patent (UK): a simple letter suffices. However, it is recommended to use PF 51/77 (in duplicate), even though this is not a prescribed use of this form (O.J. December 2, 1987). The publication number of the European patent should be quoted in preference to its application number. Such letter or form can be signed by an agent. If no address for service has been furnished, an address outside the EEC will be treated by the Office as an address for the first communication only. Thereafter, an address within the EEC must be provided, see para. 32.16.

If no address for service has been formally supplied but a communication in respect of the European patent (UK) has been sent to the Patent Office from an address elsewhere within the EEC, the current Patent Office practice is to record as the address for service the address from which the first of such communications was sent to it. Thus, the filing of a required translation under rule 79A from such an address results in that address being recorded as the address for service under rule 30 unless and until some other address is supplied (O.J. December 2, 1987). The legal effect of an address recorded in this way seems doubtful, see para. 32.16.

Although there is no direct sanction against failure to furnish an address for service under rule 30, such failure could be fatal to a restoration application under section 28, see para. 28.09.

77.16 *Translations*

Unless a translation has been filed as required under subsection (6), rule 113(4) requires that any party commencing proceedings before the Comptroller (*e.g.* the proprietor in the case of an application to amend a European patent (UK) under s. 27, or an applicant for revocation under s. 72) must furnish a verified English translation of the European patent if the latter is published in French or German. Only one copy is required if the proceedings are *ex parte*, but two copies are necessary if there is another party to the proceedings (r. 112).

However, for European patents (UK) granted in the French or German language on or after September 1, 1987 it has been necessary to file an English translation thereof within three months of the mention of grant in the European Patent Bulletin, even if a translation of the claims of the application for that patent has previously been filed under section 78(7) (r. 79A(2)). The translation must be filed in duplicate and be accompanied by PF 54/77 (reprinted at para. 141.54), also in duplicate. The translation must be provided in compliance with the formal requirements of rule 79A(3), reprinted in para. 77.03. These requirements are similar to those of rule 20, reprinted at para. 14.05, except that the translation is to be provided in *single-line spacing* unless the Comptroller otherwise permits. Although single-line spacing is preferred $1\frac{1}{2}$ spacing will be accepted at the discretion of the Comptroller, provided that all other requirements of rule 79A(3) are met (O.J. December 2, 1987).

The translation must be of the entire specification, including the drawings (with pages also serially numbered, but in a separate series from that of the description), with any textual matter in the drawings likewise translated (rr. 79A(2) and (4)).

The document to be translated is the text to which the applicant has agreed in response to the communication under EPCr. 51(4) (EPO Form 2004), or that to which proposed amendments have been accepted by the Examining Division in the communication under EPCr. 51(6) (EPO Form 2005), *i.e.* the *"Druckexemplar"* text, rather than the B-specification published by the EPO.

However, there is no need to translate the frontsheet and, if the European patent contains separate claims, *e.g.* for Spain and/or Greece, having no force in the United Kingdom, these need not be translated. Also, if the authentic text of the patent is in the German language, the French translation of its claims need not be separately translated, and likewise as regards the German language translation of the claims when the authentic text is in the French language, because they are not in the language of the proceedings.

On the other hand, the translation filed under subsection (6) must include an English translation of the claims, even though the published specification will already include a translation thereof. The translation published with the European patent will not normally have been verified (EPO Guideline A–VIII, 6) and is of no legal significance (EPO Guideline A–VIII, 5.1).

The translation must be verified (r. 79E, reprinted at para. 77.05) and, if the verification does not accompany the filing of the translation, such must be filed within one month of a request so to do, this period being extensible with discretion under rule 110(1), see para. 123.35. The verification should be in a form acceptable under rule 113(1), see para. 123.42.

Since the date of publication of the grant of the European patent in the European Patent Bulletin has to be included in PF 54/77, it is not possible to file the translation before the decision to grant the European patent has been notified to the applicant (O.J. December 2, 1987). If the date of publication of the grant is omitted from PF 54/77, the form and accompanying translation will be rejected.

The filing of the translation is advertised in the O.J. (O.J. March 1, 1989) and copies of the filed translations are available for inspection in the SRIS.

Use of translation in legal proceedings   **77.17**

The need to provide an English translation of a European patent (UK), or of an application therefor, in any legal proceedings in the United Kingdom involving it, and to support this by evidence, is discussed in para. 77.13. In proceedings before the Comptroller the translation filed under section 77(6) satisfies the requirements of rule 113(4) which would otherwise require a verified translation to be filed, but the accuracy of that translation may be challenged. However, the Comptroller may not have the power at this stage to call for another translation under rule 113(6) (reprinted in para. 123.12) as he will already have, impliedly, accepted the translation as an accurate one.

In court proceedings it would be sensible for the parties to try to agree a translation before the trial, perhaps as the result of a request to admit facts under RSC Ord. 104, r. 10 (see para. E104.10). *Terson* v. *Primeline* (SRIS C/183/88, *noted* IPD 7005) was a case involving a European patent (UK) in the French language. Here the court observed that no translation had been agreed between the parties and indicated that the question of translation was therefore a matter to be proved in evidence.

Amendment   **77.18**

Now that section 77(6) has been brought into force then, when a European patent (UK) with an authentic text in the French or German language is amended in the EPO after grant, which can occur as the result of opposition proceedings before the EPO, a translation of the amended specification must likewise be filed within three months from the date of publication by the EPO of the amended specification (s. 77(6)(*b*)). For this purpose PF 55/77 (reprinted at para. 141.55) is to be used. That translation must comply with the requirements of rule 79A(1), *i.e.* be filed in duplicate, and be verified in compliance with rule 79E. It must also comply with the formal requirements for presentation set out in rules 79A(3) and (4), but it need not comply with the requirements of rules 79A(2) and (5). Thus, only those parts of the specification and drawings affected by the amendment need be translated when supplying a translation under section 77(6)(*b*).

For the procedure for amending a European patent (U.K.) which is not in the English language, see para. 27.15.

Failure to file the required translation of an amended European patent (UK) has the same effect of rendering the patent unenforceable initially, and void eventually, as with the failure to file a translation of the patent as granted, as discussed *supra*. When amendment takes place before the Comptroller under section 27 these requirements will be automatically met, but there will need to be compliance with section 77(6)(*b*) if a European patent (UK) with an authentic text in the French or German language is amended in infringement or revocation proceedings before the court under section 75. However, there appears to be no time limit for this as rule 79B(2) does not apply because the amended specification will not be published by the EPO.

77.19 *Renewal fees*

If four or more years have elapsed following the filing date of an application for a European patent (UK), annual renewal fees are payable to the Patent Office but not in respect of any period before publication of the mention of grant of the European patent (UK) in the European Patent Bulletin (r. 39(2), reprinted in para. 25.02). If the anniversary for payment falls less than two months after the date of publication of the grant, the renewal fee may still be paid within this two months' period. These matters are discussed in para. 25.07 and are the subject of periodic notices in the O.J., *e.g.* in O.J. July 19, 1989.

78.01

SECTION 78

Effect of filing an application for a European patent (UK)

78.—(1) Subject to the provisions of this Act, an application for a European patent (UK) having a date of filing under the European Patent Convention shall be treated for the purposes of the provisions of this Act to which this section applies as an application for a patent under this Act having that date as its date of filing and having the other incidents listed in subsection (3) below, but subject to the modifications mentioned in the following provisions of this section.

(2) This section applies to the following provisions of this Act:—

section 2(3) and so much of section 14(7) as relates to section 2(3);
section 5;
section 6;
so much of section 13(3) as relates to an application for and issue of a certificate under that subsection;
sections 30 to 33;
section 36;
sections 55 to 69;
section 74, so far as relevant to any of the provisions mentioned above;
section 111; and
section 125.

(3) The incidents referred to in subsection (1) above in relation to an application for a European patent (UK) are as follows:—

(*a*) any declaration of priority made in connection with the application under the European Patent Convention shall be treated for the purposes of this Act as a declaration made under section 5(2) above;

(*b*) where a period of time relevant to priority is extended under that convention, the period of twelve months specified in section 5(2) above shall be so treated as altered correspondingly;

(*c*) where the date of filing an application is re-dated under that convention to a later date, that date shall be so treated as the date of filing the application;

(*d*) the application, if published in accordance with that convention, shall, subject to subsection (7) and section 79 below, be so treated as published under section 16 above;

(*e*) any designation of the inventor under that convention or any statement under it indicating the origin of the right to a European patent shall be treated for the purposes of section 13(3) above as a statement filed under section 13(2) above;

(*f*) registration of the application in the register of European patents shall be treated as registration under this Act.

(4) Rules under section 32 above may not impose any requirements as to the registration of applications for European patents (UK) but may provide for the registration of copies of entries relating to such applications in the European register of patents.

(5) Subsections (1) to (3) above shall cease to apply to an application for a European patent (UK), except as mentioned in subsection (5A) below, if

(a) the application is refused or withdrawn or deemed to be withdrawn, or

(b) the designation of the United Kingdom in the application is withdrawn or deemed to be withdrawn,

but shall apply again if the rights of the applicant are re-established under the European Patent Convention, as from their re-establishment.

[(5) Subsections (1) to (3) above shall cease to apply to an application for a European patent (UK) when the application is refused or withdrawn or deemed to be withdrawn, or the designation of the United Kingdom in the application is withdrawn or deemed to be withdrawn, but if the rights of the applicant are re-established under the European Patent Convention, subsections (1) to (3) above shall as from the re-establishment of those rights again apply to the application.]

(5A) The occurrence of any of the events mentioned in subsection (5)(a) or (b) shall not affect the continued operation of section 2(3) above in relation to matter contained in an application for a European patent (UK) which by virtue of that provision has become part of the state of the art as regards other inventions.

(6) Where between those subsections ceasing to apply to any such application and the re-establishment of the rights of the applicant a person begins in good faith to do an act which would, apart from section 55 above, constitute an infringement of the application if those subsections then applied, or makes in good faith effective and serious preparations to do such an act, he shall have the rights conferred by section **28A(4) and (5)**

above, and subsections (6) and (7) of that section shall apply [*28(6) above, and section 28(8) and (9) above shall apply to the exercise of any such right*] accordingly.

(7) While this subsection is in force, an application for a European patent (UK) published by the European Patent Office under the European Patent Convention in French or German shall be treated for the purposes of sections 55 and 69 above as published under section 16 above when a translation into English of the claims of the specification of the application has been filed at and published by the Patent Office and the prescribed fee has been paid, but an applicant—

(*a*) may recover a payment by virtue of section 55(5) above in respect of the use of the invention in question before publication of that translation; or

(*b*) may bring proceedings by virtue of section 69 above in respect of an act mentioned in that section which is done before publication of that translation;

if before that use or the doing of that act he has sent by post or delivered to the government department who made use or authorised the use of the invention, or, as the case may be, to the person alleged to have done the act, a translation into English of those claims.

(8) Subsection (7) above shall come into force on a day appointed for the purpose by rules and shall cease to have effect on a day so appointed, without prejudice, however, to the power to bring it into force again.

Note. Subsections (5) and (6) were prospectively amended, and subsection (5A) prospectively added, by the 1988 Act (Sched. 5, paras. 8 and 22). For the commencement of these changes, see the latest Supplement to this Work *re.* this para.

RELEVANT RULES

Translations

78.02   **5 [1987].**—(1) 1st September 1987 is the day appointed under section 78(7) of the Patents Act 1977 for the purpose of the coming into force of subsection (7) of that section.

(2) This rule shall not apply in the case of an application for a European patent (UK) which is published by the European Patent Office before that day.

Note. This is rule 5 of the Patents (Amendment) Rules 1987 (S.I. 1987 No. 288).

Translations of claims of applications for European patents (UK) filed under section 78(7)

78.03   **79C.**—(1) A translation filed under section 78(7) shall be filed in duplicate and shall be accompanied by Patents Form No. 56/77 in duplicate.

(2) The translation shall comply with the requirements contained in rule 79A(3).

Notes. Rule 79C was added by the Patents (Amendment) Rules 1987 to have effect **78.04**
from September 1, 1987 (S.I. 1987 No. 288, rr. 1(3) and 6). Also relevant are: rule
79 (*European patents: Entries in the register*), reprinted at para. 32.12; rule 79E
(*Verification of translation*), reprinted at para. 77.05); and rule 79F (*Inspection of
translations*), reprinted at para. 77.06.

COMMENTARY ON SECTION 78

General **78.05**

Section 78 concerns an application for a European patent in which that application has designated the United Kingdom as a country in which protection is
sought by that application. Such application is termed by the Act an "application
for a European patent (UK)", see definition thereof and of "designate" in section
130(1).
Section 78 makes an application for a European patent (UK) equivalent to an
application under the Act for certain purposes, particularly in respect of the so-
called provisional protection conferred on publication and possible conflict
between concurrent United Kingdom and European applications. It implements
EPCa. 67.

Effect of application for European patent (U.K.) (subss. (1)–(4)) **78.06**

Subject to the other relevant provisions, subsection (1) provides that an application for a European patent (UK) has the same effect as an application for a
patent under the Act as to its filing date and for the purposes of the sections listed in
subsection (2). Certain incidents in such applications are to be treated in the same
manner as corresponding incidents under the Act: these are listed in subsection (3).
The sections listed in subsection (2) are: section 2(3) (*Contents of copending
application*); section 5 (*Priority date*); section 6 (*Disclosure between earlier and later
applications*); section 13(3) (*Mention of inventor*); section 14(7) (*Abstracts*); sections 30–33 (*Property in patents, register, registration*); section 36 (*Co-ownership*);
sections 55–69 (*Crown use, infringement and right of prior use*); section 74 (*Validity
proceedings*); section 111 (*Unauthorised claim to patent rights*); and section 125
(*Definition of invention*).
The incidents listed in subsection (3) are:

(*a*) Declaration of priority, to be treated as if made under section 5(2);
(*b*) Extended priority period, the 12-month period of section 5(2) is to be altered
correspondingly;
(*c*) Redated application, to be treated as redated accordingly;
(*d*) Publication under EPCa. 91, to be treated as published under section 16
(subject to any intervening rights, and taking PCT into account as provided
by s. 79);
(*e*) Designation of inventor and statement of entitlement, to be treated as a
statement under section 13(2) for the purposes of section 13(3) (*Rectification
of inventorship*); and
(*f*) Registration, to be treated as registration under the Act.

Subsection (4) prohibits imposition of formal requirements for registration of
applications for European patents (UK) by rules made under section 32.
Under rule 79(1) (reprinted in para. 32.13), when a European application (UK)
is published by the EPO, the Comptroller is required to make in the register an
entry corresponding to the entry at that time in the European Register, and under
rule 79(2), where an application to that effect is made on PF 39/77 to make an entry

in the register corresponding to any other entry in the European Register; a certified copy of that entry is required. However, the register of applications for European patents (UK) is constituted by making use of the EPO register and, consequently, PF 39/77 is redundant in practice, see para. 78.09.

78.07 *Effect of refusal, etc. and reinstatement (subss. (5), (5A) and (6))*

New subsection (5) will nullify the enabling provisions of subsections (1)–(3) when the application, or designation of the United Kingdom in it, ceases to exist, and restore them if the rights of the applicant are re-established under EPC, but in that case subject to subsection (6) (*intervening rights as under section 28(6), (8) and (9) or the replacement section 28A(4)–(7)*), for which see paras. 28A.04–28A.06. The operation of new subsection (5) raises problems but, if it is not retrospective, the subsection is only of practical significance to the third-party rights arising under subsection (6) if the European application is restored under EPCa. 122.

The prior art effect of an application for a European patent (UK), arising on its publication, is now to be maintained by virtue of subsection (5A), irrespective of the ultimate fate of the application. Thus, the bizarre effect of the former wording of subsection (5), according to the decision in *L'Oreal's Application* ([1986] RPC 19) should become removed, but see C. Jones ((1987–88) 17 CIPA 130). These matters are discussed further at para. 2.22. The prospective amendments to subsection (5) are consequential upon the introduction of the new subsection (5A). For the commencement of these amendments, see the latest supplement to this Work *re*. para. 78.01.

78.08 *Translations (subss. (7) and (8))*

Subsection (7) is concerned with translations of claims of a published application for a European patent (UK) when these are published in the French or German language (see EPCa. 67(3)). The application is given the effect of publication for the purposes of section 55 (*Crown use*) and 69 (*Infringement of application*) only when a translation of its claims into English has been filed and a fee paid. If the applicant has done this, he may recover compensation for Crown use under section 55(5) or may bring proceedings under section 69 in respect of acts done before publication of the translation, if and as from when he has sent a translation of the claims to the Government department or to the infringer, see paras. 55.12 and 69.03. It should be noted that section 78 requires only the claims of the application to be translated. Filing of the translated claims is governed by rule 79C (reprinted at para. 78.03) and is discussed in para. 78.10.

Subsection (8) would allow the provision of subsection (7) concerning translations to be removed and subsequently restored by rule.

PRACTICE UNDER SECTION 78

78.09 *Register*

No separate register of applications for a European patent (UK) is maintained at the Patent Office. Instead, use is made for this purpose of direct access to the computerised register at the EPO. As a consequence, any application under rule 79(2) (reprinted at para. 32.12) on PF 39/77 (reprinted at para. 141.39) to make an entry in the United Kingdom register corresponding to one already made in the EPO register, *e.g.* for recording an assignment or licence, is returned because the requisite entry will already effectively have been made. Also, it is understood that, if an attempt is made to register an assignment or licence under a published application for a European patent (UK) without prior application to the EPO, PF 39/77 is returned with the request that application be made to record the translation, instrument or event in question in the EPO. It therefore appears that PF 39/77 no longer serves any useful purpose, but the validity of the practice seems doubtful.

On grant of the European patent (UK) a register entry is created at the Patent Office. This consists initially of a computerised print-out of the EPO register for that patent. Thereafter, any update of the United Kingdom register is made by filing PF 20/77 and/or PF 21/77, see paras. 32.24–32.31.

The procedure and documents required for registering in the EPO an assignment of an application for a European patent has been the subject of an official notice from the EPO (OJEPO, 9/1980, 305). EPCr. 72 requires that such assignment is in writing and signed by "the parties to the contract". This condition is not satisfied when counterparts of an assignment were each signed by the separate parties, but not exchanged between them, though both counterparts were supplied to the EPO (*EPO Decision J* 18/84, *"Register of European patents—Entries in"*, OJEPO 6/1987, 215; [1987] 5 EPOR 321). This case also pointed out that it is sufficient if a certified copy of a relevant extract of the instrument of transfer is supplied to the EPO, see EPCr. 20, and in this case this had been done by a jointly signed declaration as part of the application's "Request for grant", even though the signatures on this had been only carbon copies.

The register of European patents can be inspected in the Patent Office in respect of a European patent (UK) or a published application therefor by filing PF 23/77 to obtain a current extract, see para. 118.20. Information can also be obtained by direct contact with the EPO, see para. 32.34.

Translation of claims   **78.10**

If advantage is to be taken of section 78(7), the English translation of the claims of the application for a European patent (UK) must be filed in duplicate under rule 79C (reprinted at para. 78.03) accompanied by PF 56/77 (reprinted at para. 141.56), also in duplicate. The translation must comply with the requirements of rule 79A(3) (reprinted in para. 77.03), but no translation of the specification (apart from its claims) is required by section 78(1): any attempt to file a complete translation may, therefore, be rejected. The filing of the translation is advertised in the O.J. (O.J. March 1, 1989) and copies of translations filed under section 78(7) are made available for inspection in the SRIS.

If application is made under section 78(7) prior to publication of the application for the European patent (UK), the Patent Office requests that the expected date of publication be provided. This is because the Office has no ready means of ascertaining that date because at the time there will be no entry in the EPO register (O.J. September 23, 1987).

SECTION 79   **79.01**

Operation of section 78 in relation to certain European patent applications

79.—(1) Subject to the following provisions of this section, section 78 above, in its operation in relation to an international application for a patent (UK) which is treated by virtue of the European Patent Convention as an application for a European patent (UK), shall have effect as if any reference in that section to anything done in relation to the application under the European Patent Convention included a reference to the corresponding thing done under the Patent Co-operation Treaty.

(2) Any such international application which is published under that treaty shall be treated for the purposes of section 2(3) above as published only when a copy of the application has been supplied to the European Patent Office in English, French or German and the relevant fee has been paid under that convention.

(3) Any such international application which is published under that treaty in a language other than English, French or German shall, subject to section 78(7) above, be treated for the purposes of sections 55 and 69 above as published only when it is re-published in English, French or German by the European Patent Office under that convention.

COMMENTARY ON SECTION 79

79.02 *General*

The purpose of section 79 is to render an application made under the PCT which designates a European patent (UK) equivalent to an application for a European patent filed in the EPO, but subject to certain language requirements and other conditions being met. The general provision contained in subsection (1) provides that, for a Euro-PCT application, any requirement of section 78 arising under the EPC is to be met if a corresponding thing is done under the PCT. The European phase of a "Euro-PCT" application is discussed in detail in *EPH*.

79.03 *Prior art effect of Euro-PCT application (subs. (2))*

Section 2(3) (*conflicting applications*) only applies to Euro-PCT applications when: the relevant fee has been paid to the EPO; *and* either the international application has been published under PCTa. 21 in English, French or German or a translation into one of those languages has been filed at the EPO if the international application was published in another language. Thus, if a Euro-PCT application is withdrawn, or is deemed to be withdrawn, during the international phase, it never forms part of the state of the art for the purposes of section 2(3). The relevant fee for this purpose is not defined, but is presumably the "national fee" mentioned in PCTa. 22(1) and EPCa. 158(2). Subsection (2) is equivalent to EPCa. 158(1). There are good reasons for arguing that the "relevant fee" does not include the designation fee for the United Kingdom or the European search fee, if payable. Such fees may still be paid to the EPO after valid entry into the European phase and failure to pay them results in the UK designation, or the European application, being withdrawn in the European phase (EPCaa. 90(3), 91(4)). The provisions of new section 78(5A) should then apparently apply, for which see para. 78.07.

Note that re-publication by the EPO of any necessary translation into English, French or German is not necessary to establish the prior art effect under section 2(3). Note also that, if the application is not published in the international phase (*e.g.* because the international application was deemed withdrawn and subsequently converted into a European application under PCTa. 25), the prior art effect under section 2(3) will arise by virtue of section 78(2) on publication of the application by the EPO. Also, any amendments made during the international phase are irrelevant to the prior art effect of a Euro-PCT application.

Provisional protection arising from Euro-PCT application (subs. (3))   **79.04**

If the international application for a European patent (UK) is published under PCTa. 21 in English, the application enjoys so-called "provisional protection", *i.e.*, is treated as published for the purposes of section 55 (*Crown use*) or section 69 (*infringement of application*) as of the international publication date. If it is published in French or German, then, to secure provisional protection, it is necessary first to file PF 54/77 and an English translation of the claims at the Patent Office or to supply such translation to the alleged infringer (see s. 78 and para. 78.08). Since an international application, in which a European patent is requested with a designation of the United Kingdom, is regarded *ab initio* as a European patent application (EPCa. 150(3)), it is unnecessary for any fees to be paid to the EPO before such provisional protection can commence. On the other hand, if the international application is published in a language other than English, French or German, provisional protection cannot be secured until a translation has been filed at, and republished by, the EPO: this entails the payment of the above-mentioned fees to the EPO (EPCa. 158(3)). Furthermore, if the international application is republished by the EPO in French or German, compliance with the section 78 procedure is also necessary to secure provisional protection (EPCa. 67(3)). For further comment on these provisions, see C. Jones ((1987–88) 17 CIPA 130).

EPO procedure   **79.05**

After 18 months from the earliest declared priority date, international applications filed in English, French, German, Japanese, Russian or Spanish are published in that language by the International Bureau or, if filed in any other language, are translated by and published by the International Bureau in English (PCTr. 48.3). If the EPO is a designated office, the conditions for commencement of processing by the EPO must be met at the 20 months stage under PCTa. 22, or at the 30 months stage under PCTa. 39. There may, therefore, be a delay of either two or 12 months, sometimes more, following publication of the international application before it has the above-mentioned effects under sections 2(3), 55 and 69. This delay can be reduced, if needed, by meeting the above-mentioned conditions early and requesting early processing of the international application before the EPO under PCTa. 23(2) or 40(2).

International applications for patents (UK) which are not designated as applications for a European patent (UK) do not involve the EPO. Such applications are governed by sections 89, 89A and 89B, see the Commentaries thereon.

SECTION 80   80.01

Authentic text of European patents and patent applications

80.—(1) Subject to subsection (2) below, the text of a European patent or application for such a patent in the language of the proceedings, that is to say, the language in which proceedings relating to the patent or the application are to be conducted before the European Patent Office, shall be the authentic text for the purposes of any domestic proceedings, that is to say, any proceedings relating to the patent or application before the comptroller or the court.

(2) Where the language of the proceedings is French or German, a translation into English of the specification of the patent under section 77 above or of the claims of the application under section 78 above shall be treated as the authentic text for the purpose of any domestic proceedings, other than proceedings for the revocation of the patent, if the patent or application as translated into English confers protection which is narrower than that conferred by it in French or German.

(3) If any such translation results in a European patent or application conferring the narrower protection, the proprietor of or applicant for the patent may file a corrected translation with the Patent Office and, if he pays the prescribed fee within the prescribed period, the Patent Office shall publish it, but—

(a) any payment for any use of the invention which (apart from section 55 above) would have infringed the patent as correctly translated, but not as originally translated, or in the case of an application would have infringed it as aforesaid if the patent had been granted, shall not be recoverable under that section,

(b) the proprietor or applicant shall not be entitled to bring proceedings in respect of an act which infringed the patent as correctly translated, but not as originally translated, or in the case of an application would have infringed it as aforesaid if the patent had been granted,

unless before that use or the doing of the act the corrected translation has been published by the Patent Office or the proprietor or applicant has sent the corrected translation by post or delivered it to the government department who made used* or authorised the use of the invention or, as the case may be, to the person alleged to have done that act.

(4) Where a correction of a translation is published under subsection (3) above and before it is so published a person begins in good faith to do an act which would not constitute an infringement of the patent or application as originally translated but would (apart from section 55 above) constitute an infringement of it under the amended translation, or makes in good faith effective and serious preparations to do such an act, he shall have the rights conferred by **section 28A(4) and (5) above, and subsections (6) and (7) of that section shall apply** [*section 28(6) above, and section 28(8) and (9) above shall apply to the exercise of any such right*] accordingly.

Notes. In subsection (3) the Queens Printer's text states "use" where asterisked. Subsection (4) was prospectively amended by Schedule 5, paragraph 8 [1988]. For commencement of the amendment, see the latest Supplement to this Work *re.* this para.

Corrected translations filed under section 80(3)

79D.—(1) A corrected translation filed under section 80(3) shall be filed **80.02**
in duplicate.

(2) The corrected translation shall comply with the requirements contained in rule 79A(3) and (4).

(3) Publication of the corrected translation shall be requested on Patents
Form No. 57/77, which shall be filed in duplicate.

(4) The period prescribed under section 80(3) for payment of the prescribed fee shall be fourteen days from the day on which the corrected
translation is filed.

Notes. Rule 79D was added by the Patents (Amendment) Rules 1987 to have effect
from September 1, 1987 (S.I. 1987 No. 288, rr. 1(3) and 6). Also relevant are: rule
79E (*Verification of translation*), reprinted at para. 77.05; and rule 79F (*Inspection
of translations*), reprinted at para. 77.06.

ARTICLE **80.02A**

C. Jones, "Language of the proceedings and authentic text", (1987–88) 17 CIPA
130.

COMMENTARY ON SECTION 80

General **80.03**

Section 80 stipulates the authentic text of European patents (UK) and applications therefor and is intended to realise the provisions of EPCa. 70. Where
European patents (UK) and applications therefor are not in the English
language, section 80 also provides for differences between their authentic text
and a purported translation thereof filed under section 77(6), or of the claims of
an application for a European patent (UK) filed under section 78(7), and for
correction of such translations.

Authentic text of European patents and applications therefor (subs. (1)) **80.04**

According to subsection (1), pursuant to EPCa. 70(1), the authentic text for proceedings before the Comptroller or the court is the text in the language of the proceedings before the EPO. This, under EPCa. 14(3), is the official language
(English, French or German) in which the European patent application was filed,
or into which it was translated if it was filed, under EPCa. 14(2) or as an international application, in a non-official language. In the event of filing in an non-
official language, EPCa. 70(2) provides that the text in the language of filing must
be taken into account for the purposes of determining whether the subject-matter
of the application or patent extends beyond the content of the application as filed.
In any event, section 76 (*Amendments of applications and patent not to include
added matter*) does not apply, see section 76(2) and (3).

As pointed out by C. Jones ((1987–88) 17 CIPA 130), the language of subsection
(1) does not clearly take into account the possibility, provided by EPCr. 3, of

567

changing the language of the proceedings before the EPO after a text has been filed in one of the three official languages. As explained in EPO Guideline A–VIII, 1.3, the application nevertheless remains in the initial official language of the proceedings and is published in that language. Accordingly, the definition in subsection (1) of the term "the language of the proceedings" in relation to the language in which the proceedings are to be conducted before the EPO is unfortunate and inconsistent with EPCa. 70(1) where "language of the proceedings" must mean that determined by EPCa. 14(3), *i.e.* the initial official language of the proceedings when the language of the proceedings before the EPO is changed.

The translations of the claims filed pursuant to EPCa. 14(7), and appearing after the specification of the European patent published under EPCa. 98 are for information only and are not part of the authentic text, see para. 77.16. Where the authentic text is in English, the French and German translations of the claims may be deleted by amendment under section 27 (*Philips Electronic's Patent*, [1987] RPC 244).

80.05 *Narrower translation (subs. (2))*

For European patents (UK) on which a translation has been filed under section 77 or applications for European patents (UK) on which a translation of the claims has been filed or supplied to an alleged infringer under section 78, such translation is regarded as the authentic text for all purposes, other than revocation proceedings, but *only* if the protection afforded by the translation is narrower than that afforded by the text in the language of the proceedings (subs. (2): this closely follows EPCa. 70(3)). By "narrower" is meant the possibility of a product, process or article infringing the claims of the text in the language of the proceedings but not infringing the claims in the translation, see para. 80.06 *infra*. Revocation proceedings within the meaning of subsection (2) would include proceedings under section 72 (*Power to revoke patents on application*) or section 73 (*Comptroller's power to revoke patents on his own initiative*), but it is not clear that they would include proceedings in which validity is put in issue (see s.74) unless revocation is sought.

The effect of subsection (2) therefore is that, in legal proceedings in the United Kingdom, the proprietor will normally wish to rely upon the authentic, foreign language, text since he would not wish to admit that a translation provided narrower, not merely the same, protection. There will then be the need, as there is in all revocation proceedings, to produce a translation of the authentic text into English as part of the evidence, see para. 77.17.

80.06 *Correction of translation (subs. (3))*

Subsection (3), which has been included in the Act pursuant to EPCa. 70(4)(*a*), allows translations which afford narrower protection than the authentic text (see the discussion in para. 80.05 *supra*) to be corrected by broadening to bring the translation into conformity with the text in the language of the proceedings. This amounts to a specific derogation to the provisions of section 76(2) and (3) which, it is to be noted, do not apply to section 80.

A request for publication of a corrected translation is made on PF 57/77 under rule 79D. The practice is discussed in para. 80.10. Presumably, the corrected translation will be laid open to public inspection on the date of receipt of the prescribed fee, or 14 days after receipt of the corrected translation if the fee is not paid (r. 93(5) reprinted in para. 118.05). However, unless the corrected translation is published pursuant to the filing of PF 57/77 and payment of the prescribed fee, it is of no effect, see para. 80.07 *infra*.

In contrast to procedure under section 117 (*Correction of errors in patents and applications*), there is no provision for opposition to the filing and publication of a corrected translation filed under subsection (3). Also, it seems that the proprietor may file a corrected translation together with PF 55/77 requesting its publication as of right and the Comptroller has no power of refusal, unless he considers the corrected translation to be inaccurate whereupon he may request a further translation under rule 113(6), reprinted in para. 123.12.

Intervening rights (subs. (4))   **80.07**

Subsection (4) follows the provisions of EPCa. 70(4)(*b*) and enables any third party, who has in good faith commenced to do an act which infringes the European patent (UK) in the language of publication, but not the published translation, or has made serious preparations so to do before a corrected translation has been published under subsection (3) (discussed in para. 80.06 *supra*), to continue doing or commence to do that act. The position is much the same as that, under section 28(6), (8) and (9) (to be replaced in section 28A), of a third party who has commenced to work the invention of a lapsed patent which is subsequently restored under section 28. These rights are to be assignable under section 28A(5), but may not be licensed, see paras. 28A.04–28A.06.

Older European patents (UK) and applications therefor   **80.08**

In the case of European patents (UK) published under EPCa. 98 before September 1, 1987, or applications for European patents (UK) published under EPCa. 93 before that date, the provisions of subsections (2)–(4) discussed *supra* do not apply (Patents (Amendment) Rules 1987 (S.I. 1987 No. 288), rr. 4(2) and 5(2), reproduced in paras. 77.02 and 78.02 respectively). Thus any proceedings before the Comptroller in relation to a European patent published before that date, or the application for which was published before that date in French or German, will be conducted on the basis of the translation required to be filed under rule 113(4), see para. 77.16.

Other corrections to the translation   **80.09**

The provisions of subsections (2)–(4) involving the filing of a corrected translation are *only* concerned with the event of the original translation affording a narrower scope of protection than the authentic text. Consequently, the filing of PF 54/77 with a corrected translation which does not broaden the scope of protection as compared with the uncorrected translation is not appropriate. Instead, such corrections should be requested under section 117 by filing PF 47/77 and paying the prescribed fee. The corrected translation should be verified under rule 113(1) but it is thought that no additional evidence to support the correction should be required. For further details, see the commentary and practice notes under section 117.

PRACTICE UNDER SECTION 80

Filing of corrected translation (r. 79D)   **80.10**

Rules 79D(1) and (2) (reprinted in para. 80.02) require that a corrected translation under section 80 be filed in duplicate and comply with the formal requirements of rules 79A(3) and (4) (reprinted in para. 77.03), and be verified (r. 79E, reprinted in para. 77.05). However, the corrected translation need not comply with rules 79A(2) and (3) (see rule 79D(2)), and therefore need not be of the entirety of the specification and drawings. Therefore, apparently, only those pages of the specification and drawings of the original translation filed under section 77(6), or of the claims under section 78(7) (and rr. 79A and 79C), need be filed under section 80(3) and rule 79D. The requirements of rules 79A(3) and (4) are discussed in para. 77.16.

If it is desired that the corrected translation be published, PF 57/77 (reprinted at para. 141.57) is to be filed in duplicate (r. 79D(3)). Rule 79D does not say that this form *must* be filed with the corrected translation, but a note on PF 57/77 itself says that the form should be accompanied by the corrected translation in duplicate. However, the Comptroller must publish the corrected translation when filed, provided that the prescribed fee is paid within 14 days of filing the corrected translation (r. 79D(4)). This period would appear to be extensible by discretion under rule 110(1), for which see para. 123.35.

80.11   *Use of translation of European patent (UK) in proceedings before the Comptroller*

In the case of proceedings before the Comptroller under a European patent (UK) published before September 1, 1987 in French or German, such proceedings will be conducted on the basis of the translation then required to be provided under rule 113(4) (see para. 77.16), with the possibility of challenge to the accuracy of the translation in which case the Comptroller could perhaps reject any translation which in his current opinion is inaccurate and require another to be furnished (r. 113(6)) despite his previous acceptance of it. If leave is given to amend the European patent (UK), a translation of the amendment into French or German is required to be furnished under rule 113(5). This will then be substituted for the previous translation filed either under rule 113(4) or section 77(6).

80.12   *Use of translation of European patent (UK) in proceedings before the court*

RSC Ord. 104 contains no specific rule relating to court proceedings instituted on the basis of a European patent (UK) where the authentic text is not in English. On general principles, the party relying on the patent should put forward as part of his evidence a translation into English and, if this does not become a document agreed between the parties, there will be a need to introduce it by the testimony of the testator. The accuracy of the translation into English could then be tested by cross-examination, with the opposing party putting forward its own translation in similar fashion. For discussion on the effect of a translation filed under section 77(6) and rule 79A in court proceedings, see para. 77.13.

81.01   **SECTION 81**

Conversion of European patent applications

81.—(1) The comptroller may direct that on compliance with the relevant conditions mentioned in subsection (2) below an application for a European patent (UK) shall be treated as an application for a patent under this Act in the following cases:–

(*a*) where the application is deemed to be withdrawn under the provisions of the European Patent Convention relating to the restriction of the processing of applications;

(*b*) where under the convention the application is deemed to be withdrawn because it has not, within the period required by the convention, been received by the European Patent Office.

(2) The relevant conditions referred to above are that—

(*a*) in the case of an application falling within subsection (1)(*a*) above, the European Patent Office transmits a request of the applicant to the Patent Office that his application should be converted into an application under this Act, together with a copy of the files relating to the application;

(*b*) in the case of an application falling within subsection (1)(*b*) above—

   (i) the applicant requests the comptroller within the relevant prescribed period (where the application was filed with the Patent Office) to give a direction under this section, or

   (ii) the central industrial property office of a country which is party to the convention, other than the United Kingdom, with which the application was filed transmits within the relevant prescribed period a request that the application should be converted into an application under this Act, together with a copy of the application; and

(*c*) in either case the applicant within the relevant prescribed period pays the filing fee and if the application is in a language other than English, files a translation into English of the application and of any amendments previously made in accordance with the convention.

(3) Where an application for a European patent falls to be treated as an application for a patent under this Act by virtue of a direction under this section—

(*a*) the date which is the date of filing the application under the European Patent Convention shall be treated as its date of filing for the purposes of this Act, but if that date is re-dated under the convention to a later date, that later date shall be treated for those purposes as the date of filing the application;

(*b*) if the application satisfies a requirement of the convention corresponding to any of the requirements of this Act or rules designated as formal requirements, it shall be treated as satisfying that formal requirement;

(*c*) any document filed with the European Patent Office under any provision of the convention corresponding to any of the following provisions of this Act, that is to say, sections 2(4)(*c*), 5, 13(2) and 14, or any rule made for the purposes of any of those provisions, shall be treated as filed with the Patent Office under that provision or rule; and

(*d*) the comptroller shall refer the application for only so much of the examination and search required by sections 17 and 18 above as he considers appropriate in view of any examination and search carried out under the convention, and those sections shall apply with any necessary modifications accordingly.

RELEVANT RULES

81.02 *Conversion of European patent applications under section 81(1)(a)*

    80.—[*Revoked*]

Procedure for making request under section 81(2)(b)(i)

81.03   **81.**—(1) A request referred to in section 81(2)(*b*)(i) shall be made on Patents Form No. 41/77 and the period within such a request may be made shall be three months from the date on which the applicant is notified by the European Patent Office that his application for a European patent (UK) has been deemed to be withdrawn.

    (2) In such a case, the applicant shall file Patents Form No. 40/77, and, where necessary, a translation in duplicate into English of the application, within a period of two months from the date on which the comptroller receives the request mentioned in paragraph (1) above.

    (3) The applicant shall also, within the period referred to in paragraph (2) above, for the purposes of section 15(5)(*b*), file Patents Form No. 9/77, and, for the purposes of section 13(2), file Patents Form No. 7/77.

Procedure where section 81(2)(b)(ii) applies

81.04   **82.**—(1) Where section 81(2)(*b*)(ii) applies, the period within which a request may be transmitted to the comptroller shall be the twenty months calculated from the declared priority date or, where there is no declared priority date, the date of filing of the application for the European patent (UK).

    (2) Upon receipt of the request, the comptroller shall notify the applicant thereof and Patents Form No. 40/77 and, where necessary, a translation in duplicate into English of the application shall be filed by the applicant within the period of two months calculated from the date of the notification.

    (3) The applicant shall also, within the period referred to in paragraph (2) above, for the purposes of section 15(5)(*b*), file Patents Form No. 9/77 and, for the purposes of section 13(2), file Patents Form No. 7/77.

Procedure for making request for substantive examination where section 81(2) applies

81.05   **83.**—(1) The period within which a request may be made to the comptroller for substantive examination of any application for a patent to which section 81(2) applies shall be two years from the declared priority date or, where there is no declared priority date, the date of filing of the application for the European patent (UK).

(2) The request shall be made on Patents Form No. 10/77.

(3) Where an application for a European patent (UK) is to be treated as an application for a patent under the Act, the period prescribed for the purposes of sections 18(4) and 20(1) shall be the period which expires four years and six months after the declared priority date or, where there is no declared priority date, the date of filing of the application for the European patent (UK).

Notes. Rule 80, which related to conversion of an application for a European patent **81.06** (UK) which the EPO was unable to process during its start-up period, became redundant and was revoked by the Patents (Amendment) Rules 1987 (S.I. 1987 No. 288, r. 1(4)). The following rules are also relevant:

rule 6(4) (*Declaration of priority for the purposes of section 5*) reprinted in para. 5.02;

rule 15(3) (*Procedure where applicant not the inventor or sole inventor*) reprinted in para. 13.03;

rule 30 (*Address for service*) reprinted at para. 32.03;

rule 31 (*Formal requirements*) reprinted at para. 17.03; and

rule 113 (*Translations*) reprinted at para. 123.12.

COMMENTARY ON SECTION 81

General **81.07**

Section 81 concerns the conversion of European patent applications into applications under the Act, and implements EPCaa. 135, 136 and 137. This subject is more comprehensively discussed in *EPH* in relation to "Abandonment" and "Conversion to National Applications".

When conversion is possible (subs. (1)) **81.08**

Subsection (1) permits conversion only in the circumstances of EPCa. 135(1)(*a*) that is: (*a*) where the EPO could not examine the application; or (*b*) where the European application is deemed to have been withdrawn because the application was not received by the EPO within 14 months after the earliest priority date, when priority has been claimed, or otherwise within 14 months after filing at a national patent office (EPCa. 77(5)).

There has been no restriction of the processing of European patent applications since December 1979 and subsections (1)(*a*), 2(*a*) and (3)(*c*) then became obsolete, enabling rule 80 to be revoked. The provisions of rule 102(1)(*a*) (reprinted in para. 123.09) and rule 113(3) (reprinted in para. 123.12) are similarly exhausted, though only in so far as they would relate to a search report drawn up under the EPC and to section 81(2)(*a*).

In the case where the application was not received by the EPO within the 14-month period, in accordance with EPCa. 136(2), the request for conversion may be filed at the national patent office at which the European patent application was filed, and that office then sends the request and application papers to the patent offices of the other designated countries. This must be effected within 20 months of the earliest priority date (or the filing date where priority is not claimed) if the equivalence of the European patent application to national filings in the designated countries under EPCa. 66 is not to be lost. Alternatively, where the European patent application was filed at the United Kingdom Patent Office, the applicant may (by filing PF 41/77 under r. 81 and subss. (1)(*b*) and (2)(*b*)(i)) request the Comptroller to give a direction under this section. In either case, and assuming that the United Kingdom was designated, to maintain in the United Kingdom the effect of the European patent application, the applicant must pay the filing fee, request preliminary examination and search, and file any necessary translations into English.

Subject to the provisions of sections 22 and 23, the receipt and forwarding of an application for a European patent under EPCa. 75(1)(*b*) is an administrative procedure as between the Patent Office and the EPO. The Act does not prescribe any procedures pursuant to EPCa. 136(2) (see *EPH*), but PF 41/77 includes a request to the Patent Office to transmit copies of the application to the patent offices of the EPC Member States specified by the applicant on the form, in accordance with EPCa. 136(2). These States must have been designated in the European application. It seems that, if the applicant does not wish to pursue the application in the United Kingdom, he should simply not file PF 40/77 and may even delete the first part of PF 41/77.

81.09 *Conditions for conversion (subs. (2))*

The conditions for conversion set out in subsection (2) define the procedure to be employed for conversion to be effected. This procedure is dealt with in para. 81.11.

The German Federal Supreme Court has held that, under the comparable provision of German law, the filing date of the national application and any priority claimed is to be determined solely from the provisions of the EPC ("*Roll and Wippbrett*" ("*Roller and seesaw board*") [*Germany*], OJEPO 2/1982, 66).

81.10 *Date of filing of converted application (subs. (3))*

Subsection (3) provides that for a converted application: (*a*) the date of filing (provided that the application meets the minimum requirements prescribed under EPCa. 80) is treated as the date of filing under the Act; and (*b*) it is deemed to satisfy the formal requirements under the Act and Rules if it satisfies the corresponding EPC requirements. If the minimum requirements to establish a date of filing under EPCa. 80 are not met, presumably a date of filing can be accorded once the application complies with the minimum requirements set out in section 15(1).

PRACTICE UNDER SECTION 81

Procedure for conversion

81.11 *—Initiation of conversion*

In the circumstances of subsection (2)(*b*)(i), where the application was not received by the EPO in time and was first filed at the United Kingdom Patent Office, the applicant must file PF 41/77 (reprinted at para. 141.41) within three months of notification by the EPO that his application is deemed withdrawn. PF 40/77 (reprinted at para. 141.40) and PF 9/77 (*preliminary examination and search*) (reprinted at para. 141.09) must be filed within a further two months, together with any translations if these are required (r. 81).

In the circumstances of subsection (2)(*b*)(ii), where the application was not received by the EPO in time and was first filed at a national patent office outside the United Kingdom which transmits the applicant's request for conversion and a copy of the application to the United Kingdom Patent Office within 20 months of the declared priority date or filing date, the Comptroller notifies the applicant of receipt of the request and the applicant files PF 40/77 and PF 9/77 (*preliminary examination and search*) and any translations within two months of such notification (r. 82). PF 41/77 is not required in this case. It should be noted that this period runs from the date of the "notification" from the foreign patent office and, bearing in mind that communications from that office may be required to be by diplomatic courier, the period of two months is very short. It is understood that rule 82 may be varied to provide for a longer period (for which see the latest Supplement to this Work *re.* para. 81.04), but meanwhile extensions of time are available (at heavy cost) under rule 110(3) and (3A)).

The term "declared priority date" in rules 81 and 82 is defined in rule 2 (reprinted at para. 123.04), definition (*c*) being the one applicable under section 81.

It is to be noted that the applicant has no means of ensuring that the 20-month period prescribed under rule 82(1) and EPCa. 136(2) is observed, since it is up to the national office at which the European application was filed to transmit the copy of the application to the United Kingdom office. The applicant is, therefore, advised to lodge his request for conversion in that national office as soon as possible and not to wait until close to expiry of the three-month term prescribed by EPCa. 135(2) and rule 81(1).

In completing PF 40/77, the surname or family name of the individual applicant should be underlined. In the case of a corporate applicant the country (and, where necessary, the state) of its incorporation should also be stated, but trading styles or former names should not be given, see Note 1 on PF 40/77. An address for service must be given (r. 30, discussed in paras. 32.16 and 32.22).

The period for filing PF 41/77, and the period within which the conversion request is to be transmitted from the patent office at which the European patent application was filed to the United Kingdom Patent Office under rule 82(1), are not extensible because these periods are pursuant to EPCaa. 135(2) and 136(2), see rule 110(2) (reprinted in para. 123.10). It would appear doubtful whether failure to meet either of these periods could form the subject of an application for *restitutio in integrum* under EPCa. 122 but, even if such application were to succeed, the Comptroller apparently has no power under rule 100 or rule 110 to implement it in the United Kingdom, and discretionary extension under rule 110(3A) is also not possible because rule 82(1) is not specified in rule 110(3).

The period for filing PF 40/77 under rule 82(1) or 82(2) and any translation of the application, may be extended by one month as of right by filing PF 50/77 under rule 110(3) and further, at the Comptroller's discretion, by filing PF 52/77 with a supporting statement and evidence under rule 110(3A).

—Other forms required   **81.12**

The two-month period prescribed in rules 81(3) and 82(3) for filing a statement of inventorship on PF 7/77 and paying the search fee on PF 9/77 is extensible by one month under rule 110(3) by filing PF 50/77, and further under rule 110(3A) at the Comptroller's discretion by filing PF 52/77.

The translation to be filed with PF 40/77 is a verified translation of the European application, if it is not in English. If such translation is not filed, rule 113(1) makes it clear that the application will not be further processed unless the Comptroller otherwise directs.

If priority is claimed, a certified copy of the priority application will also be required (r. 6(4)), within 16 months from the declared priority date (r. 6(2)). A verified translation of the certified copy, if not in English, is also required within 21 months of the declared priority date (r. 6(6)). Each of these periods is extensible under rule 110(3) by one month on filing PF 50/77, and further, at the Comptroller's discretion under rule 110(3A), by filing PF 52/77 with a supporting statement and evidence. These periods need to be watched very carefully as conversion could take place as late as 22 months after the declared priority date (the sum of the periods prescribed in rr. 82(1) and (2)).

81.13 *Request for substantive examination on converted application*

Under rule 83 the request for substantive examination must be made on PF 10/77 within two years from the priority date, if any, or otherwise two years from the date of filing the application for the European patent (U.K.). Rather surprisingly, rule 83(1) is not listed under either rule 110(2) or (3). This two-year period would therefore seem to be extensible under rule 110(1) without fee but at the Comptroller's absolute discretion (as discussed in para. 123.35) or under rule 100 when there has been an irregularity of procedure due to error, default or omission in the Patent Office (as discussed in para. 123.21).

Rule 83 also provides that the period prescribed by sections 18(4) (*complying with requirements*) and 20(1) (*failure of application*) is now four-and-a-half years from the declared priority date (r. 83(3)), whereafter the application lapses. This period can be extended by one month on filing PF 50/77 (r. 110(3)) and further, at the Comptroller's discretion, by filing PF 52/77 under rule 110(3A), supported by a statement and evidence. During the last six months of this period, it is prudent to mark correspondence to the examiner prominently with the word "URGENT" as the filing number of the application will not itself alert the examiner to the imminence of expiry of the period, see, *e.g.* O.J. April 20, 1988.

The extensions of time that may, or may not, be obtainable under the various provisions of rule 110 are discussed in paras. 123.30–123.39. The procedure for making such applications is discussed in para. 123.32 (for application under r. 110(3)) and in para. 123.36 (for an application under rule 110(3A)).

81.14 *Result of conversion*

A United Kingdom filing number is allocated to the converted application when PF 40/77 or PF 41/77 has been filed and the usual particulars of filing are then published in the O.J. In due course the Patent Office will make an entry in the register under section 32 and will also publish the application or translation in English. The United Kingdom file is not laid open to inspection until such publication by the Patent Office has taken place (EPCr. 103).

82.01   **SECTION 82**

Jurisdiction to determine questions as to right to a patent

82.—(1) The court shall not have jurisdiction to determine a question to which this section applies except in accordance with the following provisions of this section.

(2) Section 12 above shall not confer jurisdiction on the comptroller to determine a question to which this section applies except in accordance with the following provisions of this section.

(3) This section applies to a question arising before the grant of a European patent whether a person has a right to be granted a European patent, or a share in any such patent, and in this section "employer-employee question" means any such question between an employer and an employee, or their successors in title, arising out of an application for a European patent for an invention made by the employee.

4) The court and the comptroller shall have jurisdiction to determine any question to which this section applies, other than an employer-employee question, if either of the following conditions is satisfied, that is to say—

(*a*) the applicant has his residence or principal place of business in the United Kingdom; or

(*b*) the other party claims that the patent should be granted to him and he has his residence or principal place of business in the United Kingdom and the applicant does not have his residence or principal place of business in any of the relevant contracting states;

and also if in either of those cases there is no written evidence that the parties have agreed to submit to the jurisdiction of the competent authority of a relevant contracting state other than the United Kingdom.

(5) The court and the comptroller shall have jurisdiction to determine an employer-employee question if either of the following conditions is satisfied, that is to say—

(*a*) the employee is mainly employed in the United Kingdom;

(*b*) the employee is not mainly employed anywhere or his place of main employment cannot be determined, but the employer has a place of business in the United Kingdom to which the employee is attached (whether or not he is also attached elsewhere);

and also if in either of those cases there is no written evidence that the parties have agreed to submit to the jurisdiction of the competent authority of a relevant contracting state other than the United Kingdom or, where there is such evidence of such an agreement, if the proper law of the contract of employment does not recognise the validity of the agreement.

(6) Without prejudice to subsections (2) to (5) above, the court and the comptroller shall have jurisdiction to determine any question to which this section applies if there is written evidence that the parties have agreed to submit to the jurisdiction of the court or the comptroller, as the case may be, and, in the case of an employer-employee question, the proper law of the contract of employment recognises the validity of the agreement.

(7) If, after proceedings to determine a question to which this section applies have been brought before the competent authority of a relevant contracting state other than the United Kingdom, proceedings are begun before the court or a reference is made to the comptroller under section 12 above to determine that question, the court or the comptroller, as the case may be, shall stay or sist the proceedings before the court or the comptroller unless or until the competent authority of that other state either—

(a) determines to decline jurisdiction and no appeal lies from the determination or the time for appealing expires, or

(b) makes a determination which the court or the comptroller refuses to recognise under section 83 below.

(8) References in this section to the determination of a question include respectively references to—

(a) the making of a declaration or the grant of a declarator with respect to that question (in the case of the court); and

(b) the making of an order under section 12 above in relation to that question (in the case of the court or the comptroller).

(9) In this section and section 83 below "relevant contracting state" means a country which is a party to the European Patent Convention and has not exercised its right under the convention to exclude the application of the protocol to the convention known as the Protocol on Recognition.

Article

82.02   G. Le Tallac, "The Protocol on jurisdiction and the recognition of decisions in respect of the right to the grant of a European patent (Protocol on recognition)", (1985) 16 IIC 318 and 356.

Commentary on Section 82

82.03   *General*

Section 82 concerns the jurisdiction of the court and of the comptroller to determine questions arising before the grant of a European patent as to the right to such a patent or a share therein. Such questions may involve the grant of a declaration or the making of an order under section 12 (subs. (8)). It may be possible to argue that the term "share in the patent" (in subs. (3)) is broad enough to embrace the question of an application to be named as an inventor in the patent, particularly if questions of possible employee-inventor compensation could then arise. It definitely includes a beneficial (equitable) interest under a trust, as distinct from a legal one, as was decided in *Kakkar* v. *Szelke* ([1989] FSR 225; [1989] 4 EPOR 184 (CA)) where it was held the section should be applied to all questions the substance of which is "Who is the true owner of the invention?".

82.04   *Effect of EPC Protocol on Recognition*

The EPC Protocol on Recognition (which is reproduced and discussed in *EPH*) provides, as between the relevant countries (which subs. (9) defines as those EPC countries bound by the Protocol, which appears to be all present EPC countries), that the judicial authorities of one of the countries shall have exclusive jurisdiction over questions of entitlement to a European patent arising before grant, and that the final decision given in that country shall be recognised in all the others. Section 82 serves to comply with Section I (Jurisdiction) (aa. 1–8) of the Protocol, and is stated in section 130(7) to be so framed as to have, as nearly as practicable, the same effects. It governs the jurisdiction of the Comptroller under section 12(1) of the Act (and of the court under section 12(2)) to decide such questions, but this is only possible if jurisdiction is given thereto under the section (subss. (1) and (2)). This Protocol is discussed in the paper by G. Le Tallac, listed in para. 82.02 *supra*.

—Jurisdiction under section 82 when there is an agreement between the parties   **82.05**

If there is written evidence that the parties in dispute have agreed that the United Kingdom court or the Comptroller shall decide the question, then the court or the Comptroller has jurisdiction (subs. (6)). If the question is an employer-employee question (which is defined in subs. (3)), this is subject to the agreement being valid under the proper law of the contract of employment (under subs. (5)). Conversely, there is no jurisdiction in the United Kingdom to decide a question of entitlement if there is written evidence of a valid agreement between the parties to have it decided in another relevant country.

It has, however, been decided by the ECJ (*Duijnstee* v. *Goderbauer*, [1985] FSR 221; [1985] 1 CMLR 220) that questions of entitlement, to national patents at least, are to be dealt with under national law and within the EEC by that court which has jurisdiction under the Brussels Convention (which in the United Kingdom is made law by the Civil Jurisdiction and Judgments Act 1982 (c. 27)), that is usually by the court within whose jurisdiction the defendant is domiciled. This case also decided that article 16(4) of that Convention (reproduced as Schedule 1, Art. 16(4) of that Act), which deals with exclusive jurisdiction in proceedings concerned with the registration and validity of patents, has no applicability to issues of entitlement to the grant of a patent.

—Jurisdiction under section 82 when there is no prior agreement between the parties   **82.06**

In the absence of any agreement between the parties, the general position is that jurisdiction lies in the United Kingdom for an employer-employee question only if the employee is mainly employed in the United Kingdom (subs. (5)(*a*)), and for other questions only if the applicant for the European patent has his residence or principal place of business in the United Kingdom (subs. (4)(*a*)). Thus, in *Kakkar* v. *Szelke* ([1989] FSR 225; [1989] 4 EPOR 184 (CA)), where the European patent application had been assigned to a Swedish company, it was conceded that subsection (3), presumably when read with subsection (4), precludes an entitlement dispute (being one which did not involve an employer-employee dispute, for which see *infra*) from being determined by the Patents Court, though it was questioned whether the concession was appropriate because the applicability of section 82 had arisen by a post-application assignment, the spectre of oscillatory assignments being envisaged. It was then held, by a majority of the Court of Appeal, that equitable, as well as legal, instruments fall under subsection (3) so that section 82 precluded the English courts from considering the case further, a claim based on a constructive trust being held to be synonymous with a claim to entitlement to a share in the patent.

In an employer-employee question, jurisdiction also lies in the United Kingdom if the employee has no main place of employment or such place cannot be determined, provided that the employer has a place of business in the United Kingdom to which the employee is attached (subs. (5)(*b*)).

In other questions, jurisdiction lies in the United Kingdom if the applicant does not reside or have his main place of business in any of the relevant countries, provided that the party claiming to be entitled to the patent has his residence or main place of business in the United Kingdom (subs. (4)(*b*)). If neither party resides or has a main place of business in a relevant country, jurisdiction lies in the German Federal Republic (EPC Protocol on Recognition, a. 6).

82.07   *Stay of proceedings*

If entitlement proceedings are first brought in another relevant country and afterwards in the United Kingdom, subsection (7) requires a stay (sist in Scotland) of the United Kingdom proceedings unless or until jurisdiction is declined in the other country or a decision is given for which recognition is refused under section 83.

However, subsection (7) does not apply when the United Kingdom proceedings were commenced first, nor when the court or the Comptroller is asked to decide a different question from that in another EPC Member State because subsection (7) is limited to proceedings brought "to determine that question", *i.e.* the question brought before the competent authority of a relevant contracting state.

If proceedings are commenced and it is later held that jurisdiction does not, by virtue of subsection (3), exist to determine any question in issue, then the proceedings are struck out, rather than merely stayed, see *Kakkar* v. *Szelke* ([1989] FSR 225; [1989] 4 EPOR 184 (CA)).

82.08   Practice under Section 82

Rule 84 (reprinted at para. 83.02) requires that, where section 82 applies, any person seeking recognition of a relevant decision, etc., from another EPC country under the terms of section 83 must file a certified copy thereof, see further para. 83.04.

83.01   **SECTION 83**

Effect of patent decisions of competent authorities of other states

83.—(1) A determination of a question to which section 82 above applies by the competent authority of a relevant contracting state other than the United Kingdom shall, if no appeal lies from the determination or the time for appealing has expired, be recognised in the United Kingdom as if it had been made by the court or the comptroller unless the court or he refuses to recognise it under subsection (2) below.

(2) The court or the comptroller may refuse to recognise any such determination that the applicant for a European patent had no right to be granted the patent, or any share in it, if either—

(*a*) the applicant did not contest the proceedings in question because he was not notified of them at all or in the proper manner or was not notified of them in time for him to contest the proceedings; or

(*b*) the determination in the proceedings in question conflicts with the determination of the competent authority of any relevant contracting state in proceedings instituted earlier between the same parties as in the proceedings in question.

RELEVANT RULES

Recognition of determinations in proceedings before comptroller

84. Any person seeking recognition in proceedings before the comptrol-   **83.02**
ler of a determination by a competent authority of a relevant contracting
state other than the United Kingdom of a question to which section 82
applies shall furnish the comptroller with a copy thereof certified as a true
copy by an official of the said authority.

COMMENTARY ON SECTION 83   **83.03**

Section 83 gives effect to Section II (*Recognition*) (aa. 9–11) of the EPC Protocol
on Recognition (reprinted in *EPH*), that Protocol being described in para. 82.04.
A question of entitlement to the grant of a pending application for a European
patent, if determined by the competent authority of another EPC country bound by
the Protocol (which appears to be all present EPC member states), is recognised as
if it had been made in the United Kingdom (subs. (1)), subject to natural justice
(subs. (2)(*a*)), as to which see para. 101.04.
Recognition may also be refused of a decision which is in conflict with the determination of the question in earlier proceedings between the same parties in any relevant country (subs. (2)(*b*)). There is no provision, however, for the court or
Comptroller to consider whether the authority in another relevant country should
have declined jurisdiction but has refused to do so.
Section 83 predates the Civil Jurisdiction and Judgments Act 1982 (c. 27) which
enacted into the law of the United Kingdom the Brussels Convention on the mutual
recognition of civil judgments within the EEC. Section 83 is consistent with the provisions of this Convention and Act, but extends these to the recognition of judgments on entitlement to the grant of European patents given by a competent
authority in an EPC contracting state, whether or not such is a member of the EEC.
If there is any conflict between the provisions of section 83 and those of the Brussels
Convention, then the latter will probably prevail, at least as regards the recognition
of a judgment on patent entitlement arising from a competent authority in an EEC
Member State. In *Duijnstee* v. *Goderbauer* ([1985] FSR 231; [1985] 1 CMLR 220),
the ECJ decided that in such matters a defendant should be sued only in his place of
domicile (in the sense of the place where he is habitually resident), even though
only the courts of States within, or for, which patents are registered have jurisdiction over the validity of such patents, see the Civil Jurisdiction and Judgments Act
1982 (c. 27) (Sched. 1, art. 16(4), reproducing that article of the Brussels Convention).
Note, however, that sections 82 and 83 concern only applications for European
patents.

PRACTICE UNDER SECTION 83   **83.04**

To obtain recognition in the United Kingdom during proceedings under section
82 of a judgment of a competent authority within another EPC contracting state
with regard to entitlement to the grant of a European patent, a certified copy of the
foreign judgment must be obtained and this produced to the court or Comptroller
as the case may be (r. 84 reprinted in para. 83.02 *supra*). The certification must be
by an official of that authority and, if the judgment is not in English, in proceedings
before the Comptroller a certified translation will be required under rule 113

581

(reprinted at para. 123.12 and discussed in para. 123.41). Before the court a translation should be agreed between the parties if possible, but otherwise will need to be the subject of formal evidence.

84.01   **SECTION 84 [Prospectively repealed]**

[Patent agents and other representatives

84.—(1) *No individual shall carry on for gain in the United Kingdom, alone or in partnership with any other person, the business of acting as agent or other representative of other persons for the purpose of applying for or obtaining European patents or for the purpose of conducting proceedings* **in relation to applications for or otherwise** *in connection with such patents before the European Patent Office or the comptroller, or hold himself out or permit himself to be held out as so carrying on such a business, unless he satisfies the condition that his name and that of each of his partners appears on the European list.*

(2) *Subsection (1) above shall not prohibit a barrister, advocate or solicitor of any part of the United Kingdom from conducting or otherwise taking part in any proceedings in connection with European patents before the European Patent Office or the comptroller to the same extent as he is entitled to take part in the corresponding proceedings in connection with patents under this Act before the Patent Office or the comptroller.*

(3) *A body corporate shall not for gain act or describe itself or hold itself out as entitled to act as agent or other representative of other persons for any purpose mentioned in subsection (1) above unless permitted to do so under the European Patent Convention.*

(3A) *in so far as it imposes any prohibition in relation to the business of acting as agent of other persons for the purpose of conducting proceedings before the Comptroller in connection with European patents (UK) to which section 77(1) above for the time being applies—*

(*a*) *subsection (1) above does not apply to any individual who carries on such a business alone if he is registered as a patent agent in the register of patent agents, or to an individual who carries on such a business in partnership if he and each of his partners is so registered; and*

(*b*) *subsection (3) above does not apply to any body corporate which satisfies the condition specified in paragraph (a) or (b) of section 114(2) below (as the case may require).*

(4) *Any person who contravenes subsection (1) or (3) above shall be liable on summary conviction to a fine not exceeding* **level 5 on the standard scale** *[£1,000].*

(5) *Proceedings for an offence under this section may be begun at any time within twelve months from the date of the offence.*

(6) *A person who does any act mentioned in subsection (1) above, but satisfies the condition mentioned in that subsection, shall not be treated as*

contravening section 114 below so long as he does not describe himself as a patent agent without qualification and does not hold himself out or permit himself to be held out as carrying on any business other than one mentioned in that subsection.

(7) *In this section "the European list" means the list of professional representatives maintained by the European Patent Office in pursuance of the European Patent Convention.*]

Note. Section 84 (in which subs. (1) was amended, and subs. (3A) added, by the Administration of Justice Act 1985 (c. 61, s.60); and in which subs. (4) was amended by the Criminal Justice Act 1982 (c. 48, s.46)) has been prospectively repealed (Sched. 8 [1988]). Its provisions are largely, but not completely, to be re-enacted in substituted section 102(4) (reprinted in para. 102.02) and section 274 [1988] (reprinted at para. 102.04), each read in conjunction with section 276 [1988] (reprinted at para. 102.06) and the definitions of section 286 [1988] (reprinted at para. 102.11). These provisions are discussed in paras. 102.13 *et seq.*, particularly in paras. 102.14 and 102.19. However, these 1988 Act changes have not yet taken effect, for which see the latest Supplement to this Work *re.* this para. Meanwhile, therefore, section 84 continues to have effect, but no separate commentary thereon is provided, but see the Second Edition of this work.

SECTION 85 [Prospectively repealed] 85.01

[**European patent attorneys**

85.—(1) *For the avoidance of doubt, it is hereby declared that any person whose name appears on the European list shall not be guilty of an offence under section 21 of the Solicitors Act 1974, section 10 of the Advocates Act 1976 (Act of Tynwald) or Article 22 of the Solicitors (Northern Ireland) Order 1976 by reason only of his describing himself as a European patent attorney.*

(2) *A person whose name appears on the European list shall not be guilty of an offence under any of the enactments mentioned in subsection (3) below by reason only of the preparation by him of any document (other than a deed) for use in proceedings before the comptroller under this Act, in relation to a European patent or application for such a patent.*

(3) *The enactments referred to in subsection (2) above (which prohibit the preparation for reward of certain instruments or writs by persons not legally qualified) are—*

(a) *section 22 of the Solicitors Act 1974;*
(b) *section 39 of the Solicitors (Scotland) Act 1933; and*
(c) *Article 23 of the Solicitors (Northern Ireland) Order 1976; and*
(d) *section 11 of the Advocates Act 1976 (Act of Tynwald).*

(4) *In this section "the European list" means the list of professional representatives maintained by the European Patent Office in pursuance of the European Patent Convention.*]

Note. Section 85 (as amended by S.I. 1978 No. 621) has been prospectively repealed (Sched. 8 [1988]). Its provisions are to be re-enacted in: substituted section 102(2) (reprinted in para. 102.02); section 277 [1988] (reprinted at para. 102.07); and section 278(2) [1988] (reprinted in para. 102.08), each read in conjunction with the definitions of section 286 [1988] (reprinted at para. 102.11). These provisions are discussed in paras. 102.13 *et seq.*, particularly in paras. 102.34–102.38. However, these 1988 Act changes have not yet taken effect, for which see the latest Supplement to this Work *re.* this para. Meanwhile, therefore, section 85 continues to have effect, but no separate commentary thereon is provided, but see the Second Edition of this work.

86.01

SECTION 86

Implementation of Community Patent Convention

86.—(1) All rights, powers, liabilities, obligations and restrictions from time to time created or arising by or under the Community Patent Convention and all remedies and procedures from time to time provided for by or under that convention shall by virtue of this section have legal effect in the United Kingdom and shall be used there, be recognised and available in law and be enforced, allowed and followed accordingly.

(2) The Secretary of State may by regulations make provision—

(*a*) for implementing any obligation imposed by that convention on a domestic institution or enabling any such obligation to be implemented or enabling any rights or powers conferred on any such institution to be exercised; and

(*b*) otherwise for giving effect to subsection (1) above and dealing with matters arising out of its commencement or operation.

(3) Regulations under this section may include any incidental, consequential, transitional or supplementary provision appearing to the Secretary of State to be necessary or expedient, including provision amending any enactment, whenever passed, other than an enactment contained in this Part of this Act, and provision for the application of any provision of the regulations outside the United Kingdom.

(4) Sections 12, 73(2), 77 to 80, 82 and 83 above shall not apply to any application for a European patent which under the Community Patent Convention is treated as an application for a Community patent, or to a Community patent (since any such application or patent falls within the foregoing provisions of this section).

(5) In this section "domestic institution" means the court, the comptroller or the Patent Office, as the case may require.

Note. The section has not been brought into force, see para. 132.08.

86.02

ARTICLES

J. U. Neukom, "Report on the outcome of the Diplomatic Conference held at Luxembourg, December 4–18, 1985", (1985–86) 15 CIPA 173;

C. J. Everitt, "Report of a hearing by the Interim Committee at Brussels, June 26, 1986", (1986–87) 16 CIPA 133;
R. C. Petersen, "Community Patents—Translations", (1986–87) 16 CIPA 217;
A. Krieger, "The Luxembourg Convention on the Community Patent: A challenge and a duty", (1988) 19 IIC 143.

COMMENTARY ON SECTION 86

General   **86.03**

The Community Patent Convention ["the CPC"] is defined in section 130(6), see para. 130.08. This Convention was formulated at a diplomatic conference in Luxembourg in 1975, but it remains to be ratified and political agreement on its acceptability to Member States of the European Community is not forthcoming, though discussions to bring the Convention into effect for some, if not all, the Community's Member States continue. The object of the CPC is to establish a "Community Patent" to be granted as a European patent and to have uniform, and indivisible, effect throughout the Member States of the CPC.

Of the group of sections 86–88 in the Act which related solely to the CPC, section 88 is to be repealed (see para. 88.01). Also, sections 86 and 87 have not been brought into force and may need to be amended before the CPC can be ratified by the United Kingdom. This is because the CPC itself will undoubtedly be amended before agreement is reached to give it any effect.

There is already in existence an "Agreement Relating to Community Patents", resulting from a diplomatic conference held in Brussels in December 1985. This is reported, briefly, in an article by J. U. Neukom, and discussed in an article by A. Krieger, each listed in para. 86.02 *supra*. Further developments are reported in the articles by C. J. Everitt and R. C. Petersen, also listed in para. 86.02 *supra*. These developments included agreement on a new "Protocol on Settlement of Litigation concerning the Infringement and Validity of Community Patents". This is mentioned further in para. 87.04.

The following commentary is based upon the present provisions of section 86 and ignores the above-mentioned later developments. The section will only be brought into force when the CPC is ratified and is about to become operative.

Section 86 will then give effect to the CPC and, by virtue of CPCa. 2(3), also those provisions of the EPC which govern all European patents and are consequently deemed to be provisions of the CPC. However, certain EPC provisions are inapplicable to Community patents. These are EPCaa. 135–7, 142–158, 160(1), 162 and 167 (see also CPCa. 91) and EPCrr. 104–106, the Protocol on Recognition and the Protocol on Centralisation, each reprinted in *EPH*.

Section 86 provides only outline legislation for bringing the CPC into effect. No doubt some detailed regulations will then need to be made under subsection (3) to give specific effect to the CPC and the Regulations made thereunder.

Section 86 is expressed as applicable to "existing patents" (Sched. 2, para. 1(2)).

Basis for giving effect to Community patents under United Kingdom law   **86.04**

Subsections (1)–(3) and (5) are modelled on section 2(1), (2) and (4) of the European Communities Act 1972 (c. 68). They create a legal order for Community patents that is independent of all other United Kingdom legislation (except for Part II of the present Act), including the European Communities Act 1972 (c. 68) except, by virtue of CPCa. 93, in so far as it enacts the Treaty of Rome. Nevertheless, the CPC relies on United Kingdom law on matters for which it does not specifically provide, such as: United Kingdom law on infringement (principally that concerning civil remedies), other than that concerning the effects of the Community patent or application (which are specified in CPCaa. 29–35, see CPCa. 36(1) and (3)): laws of property where United Kingdom law applies (see CPCaa. 39, 41 and 43), except in respect of transfer (CPCa. 40), bankruptcy (CPCa. 42) contractual licensing (CPCa. 43) and licences of right (CPCa. 44); United Kingdom law on compulsory licences, except in so far as it is modified by CPCa. 47 should a reservation under CPCa. 89 not be made by the United Kingdom (see CPCaa. 46–48, 69(4)(*a*), 70(2), 72 and 89); United Kingdom law concerning the right to a Community patent or applicaion, *i.e.* sections 39–43 (employer-employee questions), by virtue of EPCa. 60(1) (see CPCaa. 49(4)(*b*) and 72); United Kingdom procedural law relating to infringement actions, actions concerning compulsory licences and actions concerning the right to a patent, other than rules on burden of proof (CPCa. 75); obligation to treat the patent as valid (CPCa. 76), except in so far as this is reserved (CPCa. 90); stay of proceedings (CPCa. 77); an opinion on extent of protection (CPCa. 78) (see CPCaa. 36(2) and 74); and United Kingdom law concerning contempt of court (see CPCa. 79).

Subsection (4) excepts the operation in relation to community patents and applications therefor of section 12 (*Entitlement questions on foreign and convention patent applications*), section 73(2) (*Revocation for double patenting (simultaneous protection)*), sections 77–80 (*Effects of European patents and applications*), section 82 (*Jurisdiction to determine the right to a European patent application*) and section 83 (*Recognition of decisions on the right to a European patent made outside the United Kingdom*). This is because these matters will instead be dealt with by rules made under this section.

86.05   *Effect of independence of Community patents*

A practical effect of the independence of Community patents in relation to Parts I and III of the Act is that decisions may well be given by Community bodies that conflict as to legal principle with decisions of the United Kingdom courts. This possibility is acute in relation to validity and infringement, particularly on questions of obviousness, sufficient description, what constitutes new matter, and extent of protection. Section 130(7) tends to reduce such conflicts by providing that certain sections of the Act are framed to have as nearly as practicable the same effects in the United Kingdom as the corresponding provisions of the EPC and CPC have in the territories to which they apply. The sections concerned are those on: patentability (ss. 1–6); sufficiency of description other than in relation to the use of new micro-organisms, support for claims, and unity of invention (s. 14(3), (5) and (6)); no application for transfer of a patent or rights to be made more than two years after grant unless the original proprietor knew he was not entitled to the patent (s. 37(5)); no compulsory licence for insufficient working when demand in the United Kingdom is met by working elsewhere in the EEC (s. 54); infringement (ss. 60 and 69); revocation (s. 72(1) and (2)); no determination of entitlement on an application made more than two years after grant unless the original proprietor knew he was not entitled to the patent (s. 74(4)); jurisdiction on entitlement to a European patent (s. 82); recognition of decisions on entitlement to a European patent (s. 83); burden of proof (s. 100); and extent of protection (s. 125).

Section 86 is referred to in section 53(1) to make the compulsory licence provisions of the Act (ss. 48–51) subject to the CPC, and in section 60(4) to make the doctrine of exhaustion of rights under the CPC applicable to infringement under section 60(1)–(3). Neither section 53(1) nor section 60(4) is yet in force, but the doctrine of exhaustion of rights is discussed in paras. 60.17 and C. 15.

SECTION 87   87.01

Decisions on Community Patent Convention

87.—(1) For the purposes of all legal proceedings, including proceedings before the comptroller, any question as to the meaning or effect of the Community Patent Convention, or as to the validity, meaning and effect of any instrument made under or in implementation of that convention by any relevant convention institution shall be treated as a question of law (and if not referred to the relevant convention court, be for determination as such in accordance with the principles laid down by and any relevant decision of that court).

(2) In this section—

"relevant convention institution" means any institution established by or having functions under the Community Patent Convention, not being an institution of the United Kingdom or any other member state, and

"relevant convention court" does not include—

(*a*) the European Patent Office or any of its departments; or

(*b*) a court of the United Kingdom or of any other member state.

Note. The section has not been brought into force, see para. 132.08.

ARTICLES   87.02

C. Wadlow, "The Community Patent Appeal Court", [1986] ELR 295;

K. Bruckhausen, "Institutions and procedures involved in actions involving Community patents", (1987) 18 IIC 682.

COMMENTARY ON SECTION 87

General   87.03

Section 87 has not yet been brought into force and may need to be amended before this is done to take account of changes to be made to the CPC before this is ratified, see para. 86.03.

For example, agreement was reached, in principle, at the Diplomatic Conference in Brussels in December 1985 to revise the original CPC provisions with regard to proceedings before national courts and appeals therefrom, including final arbitration on validity by the EPO Appeal Boards, and instead provide for appeals from "Community Patent Courts", which would decide cases at first instance on a national basis, to be taken to a Common Appeal Court (colloquially known as COPAC) to be set up on a Community basis. In their papers, each listed in para. 87.02 *supra*, K. Bruckhausen compared the 1975 and 1985 CPC texts and C. Wadlow comprehensively described the 1985 proposals. These have also been summarised in *EPH*, see also para. 88.04.

The present provisions of section 87   87.04

The following brief commentary is based upon the present provisions of the section.

As presently worded, section 87 provides that questions on the meaning or effect of the CPC are to be treated as questions of law. Questions as to the validity, meaning or effect of any rules made by the Select Committee of the EPOAC (see CPCa. 20) are to be treated similarly. All such matters are to be decided on principles laid down by the "convention court" if not decided by that court. The term "relevant convention court" is defined differently from the normal definition in section 130(1) so that, for the purpose of operation under the CPC, the term excludes the EPO and its departments and the national courts of all CPC countries. It includes the ECJ at Luxembourg (CPCaa. 63 and 73). It would also include any Central Community Infringement Court set up under the CPC Resolution on Litigation of Community Patents and now the later-proposed Common Appeal Court (COPAC) referred to in para. 87.03 *supra*. Although this is far from clear, it appears to exclude the special departments of the EPO as well as those under EPCa. 15, *i.e.* the Patent Administrative Division, Revocation Divisions and Revocation Boards; it was the Government's intention that not all EPO decisions should be binding and that, *e.g.* practice directions issued by the Comptroller in relation to the CPC should not be subject to section 87, see H.L.Deb., Vol. 380, ser. 42, cols. 1568–1569 (March 15, 1977) and Vol. 383, ser. 62, col. 77 (May 9, 1977).

88.01

SECTION 88 [Prospectively repealed]

Jurisdiction in legal proceedings in connection with Community Patent Convention

[88.—*(1) For the purposes of the application in the United Kingdom of Article 69 of the Community Patent Convention (residence of a party as founding jurisdiction in actions for infringement, etc.) the residence of a party shall be determined in accordance with the following provisions of this section until such date as the Secretary of State may by order appoint for the repeal of those provisions.*

(2) For the purpose of determining whether a person is resident in any part of the United Kingdom the court shall apply the law of that part of the United Kingdom.

(3) A company within the meaning of the Companies Act **1985** *[1948]* **or the Companies Act 1931 (Act of Tynwald)** *shall be treated for the purposes of subsection (2) above as resident in that part of the United Kingdom where its registered office is situated or where it has a principal place of business.*

(4) any other body corporate or any unincorporated body of persons shall be so treated as resident in that part of the United Kingdom where it has a principal place of business.

(5) Where any body has a principal place of business in two or more parts of the United Kingdom it shall be so treated as resident in all those parts.

(6) If the court determines that a person is not resident in the United Kingdom, then, in order to determine whether he is resident in a country which is a party to the Community Patent Convention the court shall, except in a case falling within subsection (7) below, apply the law which would be applied by the courts of that country in order to found jurisdiction under that convention.

(7) The question whether a person is to be taken for the purposes of this section as resident in the United Kingdom or any other country shall be determined in accordance with the law of that country of which he is a citizen if by that law his residence depends on that of another person or on the location of an authority.]

Note. Section 88 was never brought into force (see para. 132.08) and has now been prospectively repealed by the 1988 Act (Sched. 5, para. 23 and Sched. 8). For the effective date of repeal, see the latest Supplement to this Work *re.* this para. The section is printed above with subsection (3) as amended by S.I. 1978 No. 621 and by the Companies Consolidation (Consequential Provisions) Act 1985 (c. 9) (s. 30 and Sched. 2).

BOOKS   88.02

P. Kaye, "Civil Jurisdiction and Enforcement of Foreign Judgments" (Professional Books, 1987);

A. Dashwood, R. Hacon and R. White, "A Guide to the Civil Jurisdiction and Judgments Convention" (Kluwer, 1987);

T. C. Hartley, "Civil Jurisdiction and Judgments" (Sweet and Maxwell, 1984);

L. Collins, "The Civil Jurisdiction and Judgments Act 1982" (Butterworths, 1983).

ARTICLES AND LETTERS   88.03

E. W. E. Micklethwaite, "Convention on Jurisdiction and Enforcement of Judgments", (1978–79) 8 CIPA 489;

M. Burnside, "Civil Jurisdiction and Judgments Act 1982", (1986–87) 16 CIPA 66;

A. W. White, "Civil Jurisdiction and Judgments Act 1982", (1986–87) 16 CIPA 94;

G. W. White, "Civil Jurisdiction and Judgments Act 1982", (1986–87) 16 CIPA 137;

M. Burnside, "Civil Jurisdiction and Judgments Act 1982", (1986–87) 16 CIPA 178;

C. Tritton and G. Tritton, "The Brussels Convention and intellectual property", [1987] 12 EIPR 349;

M. Burnside and A. Burnside, "Patent litigation under the Judgments Convention", *Patent World*, March 1988, 18.

COMMENTARY ON SECTION 88 [Prospectively repealed]

Reasons for repeal of section 88   88.04

Section 88 related to jurisdiction in legal proceedings in connection with the CPC and prospectively made provisions for the determination of the residence of a party for the purposes of CPCa. 69 which was intended to determine which court or courts would have jurisdiction in specified circumstances, particularly based on the habitual residence of the defendant. However, the section became superseded by the provisions of the Civil Jurisdiction and Judgments Act 1982 (c. 27) ["the CJJA"] which came into force on January 1, 1987. This Act has brought into effect in the United Kingdom the 1968 Brussels "Convention on Jurisdiction and

Enforcement of Judgments in Civil and Commercial Matters". The texts of this "Enforcement Convention," and its subsequent amendments are set out in Schedules 1–3 of the CJJA.

The whole content and effect of the CJJA is the subject of the books listed in para. 88.02 *supra*, and is discussed particularly in relation to patent litigation in *EPH*, and referred to in the various articles and letters likewise listed in para. 88.03 *supra*. Its effect on the jurisdiction of United Kingdom courts *inter se* is discussed in para. 96.24 and illustrated in para. 98.05 in relation to patent litigation in Scotland.

Moreover, the intended effect of section 88 was to a large extent superseded by the "Protocol on the Settlement of Litigation concerning the Infringement and Validity of Community Patents" ["the CPC Litigation Protocol"] agreed in December 1985 to be annexed with other documents to a revised "Agreement relating to Community Patents", see the papers by C. Wadlow and K. Bruckhausen listed in para. 87.02. Central among these proposals is to leave the initial stage of litigation under Community patents (including determination of the extent of protection, infringement and validity) to a national court, but with final appeal thereupon proceeding, not to a national court, but necessarily to a Common Appeal Court ("COPAC") which is to be a new institution of the European Community.

89.01   **SECTION 89 [Prospectively substituted]**

Effect of international application for patent

89—(1) An international application for a patent (UK) for which a date of filing has been accorded under the Patent Co-operation Treaty shall, subject to—

   section 89A (international and national phases of application), and
   section 89B (adaptation of provisions in relation to international application),

be treated for the purposes of Parts I and III of this Act as an application for a patent under this Act.

(2) If the application, or the designation of the United Kingdom in it, is withdrawn or (except as mentioned in subsection (3)), deemed to be withdrawn under the Treaty, it shall be treated as withdrawn under this Act.

(3) An application shall not be treated as withdrawn under this Act if it, or the designation of the United Kingdom in it, is deemed to be withdrawn under the Treaty—

   (a) because of an error or omission in an institution having functions under the Treaty, or

   (b) because, owing to circumstances outside the applicant's control, a copy of the application was not received by the International Bureau before the end of the time limited for that purpose under the Treaty,

or in such other circumstances as may be prescribed.

(4) For the purposes of the above provisions an application shall not be treated as an international application for a patent (UK) by reason only of its containing an indication that the applicant wishes to obtain a European patent (UK), but an application shall be so treated if it also separately designates the United Kingdom.

(5) If an international application for a patent which designates the United Kingdom is refused a filing date under the Treaty and the comptroller determines that the refusal was caused by an error or omission in an institution having functions under the Treaty, he may direct that the application shall be treated as an application under this Act, having such date of filing as he may direct.

Note. Section 89 was prospectively substituted, and new sections 89A and 89B prospectively added, by the 1988 Act (Sched. 5, para. 25), but for commencement of these changes see the latest Supplement to this Work *re.* this para.

SECTION 89 [Prospectively repealed]   89.02

Before its prospective substitution, as indicated in para. 89.01 *supra*, section 89 was in the form:—

[89.—*(1) Subject to the provisions of this Act, an international application for a patent (UK) for which a date of filing has been accorded (whether by the Patent Office or by any other body) under the Patent Co-operation Treaty (in this section referred to as the Treaty) shall, until this subsection ceases to apply to the application, be treated for the purposes of Parts I and III of this Act as an application for a patent under this Act having that date as its date of filing and—*

    (a) the application, if published in accordance with the Treaty and if it satisfies relevant conditions, shall be so treated as published under section 16 above, subject, however, to subsection (7) below;

    (b) where the date of filing an application is re-dated under the Treaty to a later date, that date shall be so treated as the date of filing the application;

    (c) any declaration of priority made under the Treaty shall be so treated as a declaration made under section 5(2) above;

    (d) where a period of time relevant to priority is extended under the Treaty, the period of twelve months specified in section 5(2) above shall be treated as altered correspondingly;

    (e) any statement of the name of the inventor under the Treaty shall be so treated as a statement filed under section 13(2) above: and

    (f) an amendment of the application made in accordance with the Treaty shall, if it satisfies the relevant conditions, be so treated as made under this Act.

(2) Accordingly, until subsection (1) above ceases to apply to an application filed or published in accordance with the Treaty, the applicant shall, subject to subsection (7) below, have the same rights and remedies in relation to the application as an applicant for a patent under this Act has in relation to a filed or, as the case may be, a published application for such a patent.

(3) *Notwithstanding anything in subsection (1) above, the provisions of the Treaty and not those of this Act relating to publication, search, examination and amendment shall apply to any such application until all the relevant conditions are satisfied and, if those conditions are not satisfied before the end of the prescribed period, the application shall be taken to be withdrawn.*

(3A) **If the relevant conditions are satisfied with respect to an application which is amended in accordance with the Treaty and the relevant conditions are not satisfied with respect to any amendment, that amendment shall be disregarded.**

(4) *The relevant conditions—*

(a) *in the case of an application, are that a copy of the application and, if it is not in English, a translation into English has been filed at the Patent Office and the filing fee has been paid to the Patent Office by the applicant; and*

(b) *in the case of an amendment, are that a copy of the amendment and, if it is not in English, a translation into English have been filed at the Patent Office.*

(4A) **In subsection (4)(a) "a copy of the application" includes a copy of the application published in accordance with the Treaty in a language other than that in which it was filed.**

(5) *The comptroller shall on payment of the prescribed fee publish any translation filed at the Patent Office under subsection (4) above.*

(6) *Before the relevant conditions are satisfied, subsection (1) above shall not operate so as to secure that an international application for a patent (UK) is to be treated for the purposes of section 8 above as an application for a patent under this Act and shall not affect the application of section 12 above to an invention for which an international application of [sic] a patent is made or proposed to be made, but when the relevant conditions are satisfied the international application shall be so treated and accordingly section 12 above shall not apply to it.*

(7) *For the purposes of sections 55 and 69 above an international application for a patent (UK) published in accordance with the Treaty—*

(a) *shall, if published in English, be treated as published under section 16 above on its publication in accordance with the Treaty;*

(b) *shall, if published in any other language and if the relevant conditions are satisfied, be treated as published under section 16 above on the publication of a translation of the application under subsection (5) above;*

but, if the application is published in a language other than English, the applicant may recover a payment by virtue of section 55 above in respect of the use of the invention in question before publication of that translation, or may bring proceedings by virtue of section 69 above in respect of an act mentioned in that section which is done before publication of that translation, if before that use or the doing of that act he has sent by post or delivered to the

592

government department who made use or authorised the use of the invention, or, as the case may be, to the person alleged to have done the act, a translation into English of the specification of the application.

(8) Subsection (1) above shall cease to apply to an international application for a patent (UK) if—

(a) the application is withdrawn or deemed to be withdrawn; or
(b) the designation of the United Kingdom in the application is withdrawn or deemed to be withdrawn;

except where the application or the designation of the United Kingdom in the application is deemed to be withdrawn under the Treaty because of an error or omission in the Patent Office or any other institution having functions under the Treaty or of an application not being received by the International Bureau, owing to circumstances outside the applicant's control, before the end of the time limited for that purpose by the Treaty.

(9) Where the relevant conditions are satisfied before the end of the prescribed period, the comptroller shall refer the application for so much of the examination and search as is required by sections 17 and 18 above as he considers appropriate in view of any examination and search carried out under the Treaty, and those sections shall apply with any necessary modifications accordingly.

(10) **The foregoing provisions of this section do not apply to an application which falls to be treated as an international application for a patent (UK) by reason only of its containing an indication that the applicant wishes to obtain a European patent (UK); but without prejudice to the application of those provisions to an application which also separately designates the United Kingdom.**

[(10) The foregoing provisions of this section shall not apply to an international application for a patent (UK) which is treated by virtue of the European Patent Convention as an application for a European patent (UK) or which contains an indication that the applicant wishes to obtain a European patent (UK).]

(11) If an international application for a patent which purports to designate the United Kingdom is refused a filing date under the Treaty and the comptroller determines that the refusal was caused by an error or omission in the Patent Office or any other institution having functions under the Treaty, he may direct that the application shall be treated as an application under this Act.]

Note. Subsections (3A) and (4A) were added, and subsection (10) replaced, by the 1988 Act (Sched. 5, para. 24). These amendments came into force on the Royal Assent of that Act (s. 305(1) [1988]) and are deemed always to have had effect (Sched. 5, para. 24(5) [1988]). Section 89, as so amended, was then prospectively replaced (according to Sched. 5. para. 25 [1988]) by a substituted section 89 and new sections 89A and 89B (reprinted respectively in paras. 89.01 *supra*, 89A.01 and 89B.01). However, for the commencement of these changes see the latest Supplement to this Work *re*. para. 89.01.

Relevant Rules

International applications for patent: section 89

89.03   85.—(4) Where, in relation to an international application for a patent (UK), the applicant desires that section 89(1) ahall not cease to apply to the application by virtue of the operation of section 89(8) because the application or the designation of the United Kingdom in the application has been deemed to be withdrawn under the said Treaty on account of an error or omission in the Patent Office or any other institution having functions under the said Treaty or of an application not being received by the International Bureau owing to circumstances outside his control, before the end of the time limited for that purpose by the said Treaty, application shall be made to the comptroller on Patents Form No. 44/77, accompanied by a statement of the facts upon which the applicant relies.

(4A) Where, because of an error made by the receiving office, an international application for a patent (UK) has been accorded a date of filing which is not correct, or where the declaration made under Article 8(1) of the Patent Co-operation Treaty has been cancelled or corrected by the receiving office or by the International Bureau because of an error made by the office or the Bureau, the Comptroller may amend any document received by the Patent Office from the receiving office or the International Bureau or alter any period of time which is specified in the Act or these rules as if the error were an error on the part of the Patent Office.

(5) Where an international application for a patent (UK) purports to designate the United Kingdom and the applicant alleges that it has been refused a filing date under the said Treaty on account of an error or omission in the Patent Office or any other institution having functions under the said Treaty, he may apply to the comptroller for it to be treated as an application under the Act by filing Patents Form No. 44/77, accompanied by a statement of the facts upon which he relies.

(6) In this rule, "receiving office" has the same meaning as in the Patent Co-operation Treaty.

Note. Only sub-rules 85(4)–(6) have been reprinted above because sub-rules 85(1)–(3) are more pertinent to prospective new section 89A and are therefore reprinted at para. 89A.02. In both instances the rule is reprinted as amended by S.I. 1985 No. 1166. However, the whole of rule 85 will need to be revised when the prospective changes to section 89, and the new sections 89A and 89B, are brought into effect. When this has occurred (for which see the *Note* para. to para. 89.01), the latest Supplement to this Work should be consulted under this para. 89.03 (in relation to practice under the new section 89) and under para. 89A.02 (in relation to practice under the new section 89A) to ascertain the replacement wording for the former rule 85. At that time the whole of the commentaries on sections 89 and 89A will need to be read in the light of the new rule wording, particularly as to time limits and documents required to be filed.

RELEVANT RULES FOR INTERNATIONAL APPLICATIONS

Filing of applications

117.—(1) Where the Patent Office is the competent receiving office **89.04** under the Patent Co-operation Treaty, an international application shall be filed at it in English in triplicate.

(2) If less than three copies of the international application are so filed, upon preparation by the Patent Office of the number of copies of it required to bring the total to three, the applicant shall on demand pay to the Patent Office the appropriate charge.

Designation and search fees

118.—(1) Payment of the transmittal fee and the basic fee referred to in **89.05** rule 15.1(*i*) of the Regulations under the Patent Co-operation Treaty shall be made to the Patent Office not later than one month after the date on which the application to which they relate is filed at the Patent Office.

(1A) Payment of designation fees referred to in rule 15.1(ii) of the said Regulations shall be made to the Patent Office in the amount provided for in rule 15.2(b) thereof not later than—

(*a*) one year after the date of which the application to which they relate is filed at the Patent Office in a case in which there is no date to be treated, by virtue of section 89B(1)(*b*), as the declared priority date, or

(*b*) one month after that date or, if later, one year after the date to be treated, by virtue of section 89B(1)(*b*), as the declared priority date in any other case.

(2) Payment of the search fee referred to in rule 16.1 of the said Regulations shall be made to the Patent Office in the amount fixed by the Administrative Council of the European Patent Organisation and published in the Journal.

Certified copies

119. A request under rule 20.9 of those Regulations for a certified copy **89.06** of an international application as filed with the Patent Office as receiving office and of any corrections thereto shall made on Patents Form No. 24/77 and shall be accompanied by the appropriate fee.

Fees for international preliminary examination

120. A demand for international preliminary examination made under **89.07** Article 31 of the said Treaty to the Patent Office as International Preliminary Examining Authority shall be accompanied by payment of the handling fee referred to in rule 57 of those Regulations and the international preliminary examination fee and, upon request by the Patent Office, payment shall also be made to it of an amount which is the equivalent in sterling of the search fee referred to in rule 118(2) above.

Additional fees for further inventions

89.08   121. Where under rule 68.2 of those Regulations the Patent Office as International Preliminary Examining Authority reports to the applicant that the requirement of unity of invention is not complied with, and the applicant decides to pay an additional fee in respect of each invention other than the main invention, the additional fee payable to the Patent Office in respect of each invention shall not exceed the international preliminary examination fee.

Fees to be paid in sterling

89.09   122. The fees referred to in rules 118 to 121 shall be paid in sterling.

89.10   OTHER RELEVANT RULE

The following rule is also relevant:
rule 2(*d*) (*Interpretation*) reprinted in para. 123.04.

89.11   SECTION 89—BOOK

J. Lahore, "The Patent Co-operation Treaty—A New Era" (Centre for Commercial Law Studies, Queen Mary College, London 1986).

89.12   SECTION 89—ARTICLE

B. Bartels, "PCT: The advantages for the applicant in the United Kingdom", (1983–84) 13 CIPA 3.

COMMENTARY ON SECTION 89 [Prospectively substituted]

89.13 *General*

Sections 89, 89A and 89B concern the application of the Act to international applications filed under the provisions of the PCT. These three sections were each prospectively introduced by the 1988 Act and will together replace entirely the former, to be repealed, section 89 which is briefly discussed at paras. 89.38–89.42, *infra*, see *Note* to para. 89.02. The general remarks *infra* apply to all three new sections, as if these changes were already in force. However, for the date of their commencement, see the latest Supplement to this Work *re*. para. 89.01. Rule 85 was made in respect of the wording of section 89 now to be repealed. This rule will need to be largely recast and considerably changed to apply its contents to the substituted section 89 and new section 89A, but it is not thought that any particular rule will be required for the operation of new section 89B.

Accordingly, as the text of the replacement wording for rule 85 was not available at the time of going to press, the text of the then existent rule 85 has been reprinted (at para. 89.03 in respect of r. 85(4)–(6), and at para. 89A.02 in respect of r. 85(1)–(3)) and the commentaries on sections 89 and 89A have perforce had to be written with respect to this form of rule 85. When available, the replacement wording for this rule will be set out in the Supplement to this Work *re.* paras. 89.03 and 89A.02 respectively, and attention will be drawn to significant changes in the effect of the new wording by supplements to the commentaries on sections 89–89B. Thus, apart from pars. 89.38–89.42 (which deal with the existing wording of s. 89), the commentary herein on these three sections assumes that the changes have been brought into effect with the reservation that the text of the rules in respect thereof will not be correct to reflect the changes when these are made.

The terms "international application for a patent (UK)" (herein more simply called an "international application (UK)"); "international application for a patent" (herein abbreviated to "international application"); "International Bureau"; "designate"; and "Patent Co-operation Treaty" are each defined in section 130(1), see para. 130.08, as regards the PCT. The term "receiving office" is defined in rule 85(6) (reprinted in para. 89.03) as having the same meaning as in the PCT. The PCT definition is at PCTr. 19 made under PCTa. 10 (see para. 89.16, *infra*).

"Declared priority date" in relation to an international application (UK) is defined at rule 2(*d*) (reprinted in para. 123.04). "Priority date" is defined differently in the PCT (see PCTa. 2(xi)). Thus, in the language of the PCT, "priority date" includes the international filing date except when repugnant to the context. The term "priority date" is used herein, in relation to the international phase in the same sense.

The objects of subsections 89(1)–(3) and (5), and sections 89A and 89B(1)–(3) and (5) are: (i) to provide for the recognition of international applications (UK) as being applications under the Act; (ii) to enable the transfer of the international application from the international phase to the United Kingdom or national phase; and (iii) to provide for the recognition of the processing of the application in the international phase. Although the PCT does not anywhere use the expressions "international phase" and "national phase", they have been adopted widely for the purposes of quickly identifying the two distinct stages of the international application. The terms "international phase" and "national phase" are used in sections 89A and 89B and in rule 85. They are defined for this purpose in section 89A(2) and (3), for which see para. 89A.04 *et seq.* However, the term "UK phase" is used herein in preference to "national phase" where the latter might give rise to ambiguity. It is also convenient to speak of "valid entry into the United Kingdom phase" to denote the transfer of the international application (UK) from the international phase to the United Kingdom phase.

A detailed discussion on the filing of an international application under the PCT and its prosecution in the international phase are outside the scope of this book. The *PCT Applicant's Guide*, published by WIPO, is extremely helpful. Vol. 1 of this covers the international phase and Vol. 2 contains basic information on the national phases before the designated offices. The *EPH* (2nd edition) at chapter 15 also contains a discussion of the international phase. However, paras. 89.16–89.21 *infra*, contain a brief synopsis of the principal stages in the international phase, mainly for the purpose of clarifying the terminology used in the PCT. Also, paras. 89.22–89.32 *infra* discuss aspects of practice before the Patent Office, in its role as an international authority, and comment on rules 117–122 which relate to those matters which, under the PCT, are to be prescribed by the receiving office and the international preliminary examining authority.

While the United Kingdom Patent Office will commonly be the PCT receiving office for an applicant for an international application normally resident in the United Kingdom, the international searching authority for such applications is the EPO and not the United Kingdom Patent Office. However, the United Kingdom Patent Office is an international examining authority, though not when the EPO is the receiving office, see para. 89.22 *infra*.

89.14 *Synopsis of substituted section 89*

The provisions of the substituted form of section 89 are first summarised for convenience. Subsection (1) enables an international application (UK) to be regarded as generally equivalent to an application filed under the Act. Subsection (2) is to ensure that a withdrawal in the international phase is fully equivalent to a withdrawal under the Act. Subsection (3) provides for a review of an allegedly wrongful decision made by an international authority whereby the international application or a designation of the United Kingdom was deemed withdrawn in the international phase. The purpose of subsection (4) is to prevent subsections (1) to (3) (but not subsection (5)) being operative in the case of a designation of the United Kingdom in the international application coupled with a request that such designation be treated as a request for a European patent (UK) (often, and herein, called a "Euro/PCT application").

Subsection (5) is to enable an international application purporting to designate the United Kingdom to be saved when the application has wrongfully been refused an international filing date. As noted at para. 89.37 *infra*, an international application allowed to proceed in the United Kingdom by virtue of subsection (5) is not subject to the provisions of subsections (1)–(4) or to sections 89A and 89B.

89.15 *Advantages of the PCT*

Advantages of the PCT include the relatively low *initial* cost and the delay in the commencement of the national processing and the expense thereof. If the international search report or commercial considerations arising after filing make further prosecution not worthwhile, the application can be abandoned without incurring any of the costs and expenses involved with national filings abroad. For other expositions of the advantages put forward in favour of filing international applications under the PCT, see the book by J. Lahore and the article by B. Bartels, listed respectively in paras. 89.11 and 89.12, *supra*. The usefulness of the PCT is also described in the *PCT Applicant's Guide*, at Vol. I, paras. 14 to 38.

Despite the advantages of the PCT, its facilities are not fully exploited, understandably because of the complexity of the PCT and of the legislations of various contracting countries, whereby the risks involved in filing an international application are often considered unacceptably high. Indeed, there have been many cases where the effect of an international application has been lost in the United Kingdom through failure to take an essential procedural step. For example, the national fee may not have been paid in time (as in *E's Applications*, [1983] EPC 231). In other cases, the translation of the international application has been filed belatedly because: the wrong document had been filed (*Masuda's Application*, [1987] RPC 37); or because the patent agent wrongly thought that the period for filing the translation of the international application was the same as that prescribed for filing a verified translation of the priority document (*Mitsubishi Jidosha's Application*, [1988] RPC 449). Another common mistake has been a failure to file PF 10/77 because there was no United Kingdom publication under section 16 to trigger a period for paying this fee (*Daviero and Katz and Fogel's Applications*, SRIS C/102/85). A further mistake which has occurred was a failure to file a verified translation of the priority document through the misapprehension that such a translation had been filed at the International Bureau (*Application des Gaz's Application*, [1987] RPC 279). Another cause of a loss of priority in the United Kingdom has been a failure to file a priority document in the international phase (*Matsushita's Application*, [1983] RPC 105 and *Brossmann's Application*, [1983] RPC 109).

In most of these cases, the Comptroller or Court sympathised with the application but had no power under rule 100, 101 or 110 (as these then stood) to rectify the situation. However, it is thought that the introduction of rule 110(3A) and (3C) in 1987 (discussed in para. 123.33) should result in a dramatic fall in the number of lost PCT applications, so far as the United Kingdom is concerned. This is because all prescribed periods relevant to valid entry into the United Kingdom phase are now extensible at the Comptroller's discretion, either under rule 110(3A) and (3C) or (less usually, but without fee when applicable) under rule 110(1), for which see para. 123.35. Accordingly, cases on missed time limits, based on the rules before the 1987 amendments thereto came into force, no longer provide useful precedents, so far as practice under sections 89, 89A and 89B is concerned.

The international phase

—*International filing*   **89.16**

An international application may only be filed at the competent receiving office (PCTa. 10). The competent receiving office is determined by the nationality or country of residence of the applicant or of any one of the applicants, if there are more than one (PCTr. 19.1.(*a*), 19.2). Thus, for a sole applicant normally resident in the United Kingdom, the PCT receiving office will be the United Kingdom Patent Office.

The necessary bibliographical and other data must be included in the PCT Request Form (PCT/RO/101). The countries for which patents are required must be designated on filing. (The PCT, like the EPC, uses the word "state", rather than "country"). If a regional patent, such as a European patent, is desired for any of the designated countries, this must also be indicated at the time of filing.

—*International search*   **89.17**

After the filing of the international application, it is referred to the appropriate international searching authority (PCTa. 16), resulting in the establishment of the international search report (PCTa. 18). Thereafter, it is possible to file amended claims (but no amendments to the description) and a statement explaining the amendments (PCTa. 19(1)).

—*International publication*   **89.18**

The international application, including the international search report, is published by the International Bureau 18 months after the priority date (PCTa. 21). It is published in pamphlet form (PCTr. 48.1(*a*)). Normally, any amendments made to the claims are published with the application, but occasionally the preparations for publication are completed before expiry of the applicable time limit under PCTr. 46.1 for filing amended claims. In the latter event, the amended claims are published later (PCTr. 48.2(*h*)). When the international application is filed in English, French, German, Japanese, Russian or Spanish, it is published in the language of filing (PCTr. 48.3(*a*)). When it is filed in any other language it is published in English translation (PCTr. 48.3(*b*)).

The frontsheet of the published PCT pamphlet contains all the usual bibliographical data, including a list of the designated countries (PCTr. 48.2(*b*)). When the application is published before the time limit for filing amended claims has expired, this is stated. The data included on the frontsheet is also published separately on the same day in the *PCT Gazette* (PCTr. 86.1(*i*) of which there are both English and French editions.

89.19   *—Communication under PCTa. 20*

The international application is communicated to the designated offices as soon as possible after the international publication (PCTa. 20, PCTr. 47.1(*a*), (*b*)). The applicant is notified (on Form PCT/IB/308) that such communication has taken place (*PCT Application's Guide* at Vol. II—General Part, para. 33). All designated countries are obliged to accept receipt of such notification by the applicant as conclusive proof that the communication under PCTa. 20 has taken place (PCTr. 47.1(*c*)). This communication consists of a copy of the international application as published (in pamphlet form mentioned at para. 89.18, *supra*); or of a copy of the international application as filed, if the application is published in a language different from that in which it was filed; or both, depending upon the requirements of the designated offices (PCTr. 47.3).

A copy of the priority document (if filed in the international phase) is also furnished to the designated offices (normally with the communication under PCTa. 20) unless the designated office does not require one (PCTr. 17.2(*a*)).

89.20   *—Commencement of national phase*

The PCT national phase normally begins 20 months from the priority date (PCTa. 22). However, in relation to any designated country which has been elected within 19 months from the priority date for the purposes of international preliminary examination under Chapter II of the PCT (see para. 89.21, *infra*), the national phase normally commences 30 months from the priority date (PCTa. 39(1)).

There is no time limit to the period for filing a demand for international preliminary examination (discussed in para. 89.21 *infra*) or for electing offices, but any election after expiry of 19 months from the priority date is *not* effective to postpone entry into the national phase from 20 months after the priority date to 30 months after the priority date.

89.21   *—International preliminary examination*

International preliminary examination, if demanded under Chapter II of the PCT, is conducted by the appropriate international preliminary examining authority (PCTa. 32) and results in the issuance of an international preliminary examination report (PCTa. 35) which is communicated by the International Bureau to the elected offices (PCTa. 36). Amendments may be made to the description and claims during international preliminary examination and such amendments are annexed to the international preliminary examination report (PCTa. 34(2)(*b*), PCTr. 70.16). The international preliminary examination report is not binding on the elected office (PCTa. 33(1)). The report is not published and remains confidential in the international phase (PCTa. 38). However, after the national phase has commenced, this obligation of confidentiality does not extend to the elected offices.

Patent Office as an international authority

—*General*   89.22

The Act does not contain any provisions prescribing the conduct of proceedings before the Patent Office in its capacities either as a receiving office or as an international preliminary examining authority: the Patent Office is *not* an international searching authority. The filing and prosecution of international applications are governed entirely by the PCT, the Regulations and Administrative Instructions thereunder and, for Chapter II of the PCT, by the Guidelines for examination under the Treaty (for each of which see *EPH*, 2nd ed., Chapter 82). Rules 117–122 are made under the authority of section 123 for the purpose of regulating the *business of the United Kingdom Patent Office* in relation to international applications. These rules do not give the Patent Office any jurisdiction under the Act in relation to international applications. Jurisdiction is *delegated* to the United Kingdom Patent Office by the PCT itself and its Regulations (PCTaa. 10 and 32; PCTrr. 19.1(*a*) and 59) and by an agreement between the Patent Office and the International Bureau (see PCTa. 55(5) and the definition of "national office" at PCTa. 2 (xii)).

Rules 117–122 (reprinted at paras. 89.04–89.09 *supra*) prescribe the requirements which pertain to the filing of an international application and to the filing of a demand for international preliminary examination, each as required by the PCT and its Regulations to be respectively determined by the receiving office and the international preliminary examining authority.

The United Kingdom Patent Office is the competent receiving office for nationals or residents of the United Kingdom, the Isle of Man and Hong Kong (*PCT Applicant's Guide*, at Vol. I, Annex A). If there are several applicants, it is sufficient for one to be a resident of one of these countries. United Kingdom residents and nationals have the option of choosing the EPO as receiving office (*PCT Applicant's Guide*, at Vol. I, Annex B1 (GB)) but the secrecy provisions of sections 22 and 23 then apply (PCTa. 27.8) and the earliest international filing date available is that upon which the application actually reaches the EPO.

The EPO is the only competent international searching authority for international applications filed at the United Kingdom Patent Office as receiving office.

The United Kingdom Patent Office is the only competent international preliminary examining authority when that office is the receiving office. The United Kingdom Patent Office is also a competent international preliminary examining authority for applications filed at some other receiving offices, but not for international applications filed at the EPO (see *PCT Applicant's Guide*, at Vol. I, Annex C); and see para. 89.31 below as regards right of representation.

—*Number of copies (r. 117)*   89.23

Pursuant to PCTr. 11.1(*b*), rule 117(1) prescribe that international applications filed at the United Kingdom Patent Office as receiving office shall be filed in triplicate. This applies to the request (form PCT/RO/101) as well as to the description, claims and abstract, and drawings (if any). Rule 117(2) enables the Patent Office to demand a fee for making the necessary copies if the applicant does not comply with rule 117(1).

—*Transmittal, international and search fees (r. 118)*   89.24

Pursuant to PCTr. 14, rule 118(1) prescribes that a transmittal fee (which is for the benefit of the United Kingdom Patent Office) is required, but this may be paid up to one month after the date on which the international application is filed at the Patent Office. This is an administrative convenience, as well as a convenience to the applicant, because the Patent Office is obliged to allow up to one month after filing for payment of the PCT basic, designation and search fees, and the designation fees may be paid up to one year after the priority date if this expires later (PCTrr. 15.4(*a*), (*b*), 16.1(*b*)). Thus, the reference to the basic fee in rule 118(1) and the whole of rule 118(1A) and rule 118(2) are superfluous.

The amount of the transmittal fee is prescribed in the current Patents (Fees) Rules (see paras. 144.01 and 144.02). The amounts of the international fee (made up of the basic and designation fees), and of the search fee, are determined respectively by the Assembly of the PCT Union (PCTa. 58, PCTr. 96), and by the EPO (PCTr. 16.1(a)), for which see para. 89.28 *infra*.

89.25   —*Supply of certified copies (r. 119)*

The purpose of rule 119 is simply to prescribe that PF 24/77, accompanied by the prescribed fee, shall be filed when requesting the Patent Office, in its capacity of a receiving office, to supply to the applicant a certified copy of an international application (and of any correction thereto), *e.g.* for filing to support a claim to priority arising from that international application.

89.26   —*Handling and preliminary examination fees (r. 120)*

Under PCTr. 57.1, the handling fee is due at the time of filing the demand for international preliminary examination but, if this fee does not accompany the demand, it may be paid up to one month after the date of receipt of an invitation to pay it (PCTr. 57.4). Under PCTr. 58.1(*b*), the United Kingdom Patent Office, as international preliminary examining authority, shall prescribe the *due date* for payment of the preliminary examination fee (which is for the benefit of the examining authority); but, if this fee is not paid by the due date, it may still be paid within one month after the date of an invitation to pay it (PCTr. 58.2). Rule 120 is, therefore, in error in referring to the handling fee and in requiring that the examination fee *shall accompany* the demand. In practice, the Patent Office regards the date of filing the demand as being the date on which the examination fee is due: it also follows the other provisions of PCTrr. 57 and 58.

Rule 120 also prescribes that the Patent Office, as international preliminary examining authority, may request a fee amounting to the sterling equivalent of the international search fee. Presumably, this latter fee would be requested if no international search report has been drawn up (PCTa. 17(2)(*a*)), or if the international search report does not cover all of the claims being subjected to preliminary examination (PCTa. 17(2)(*b*), (3)(*a*)). This might particularly apply where the claims are directed to more than one invention, in which case rule 121 may also apply (for which see para. 89.27 *infra*).

The amount of the handling fee is determined by the Assembly of the PCT Union (PCTa. 58, PCTr. 96), for which see para. 89.28, *infra*. The amount of the international preliminary examination fee is prescribed in the current Patents (Fees) Rules (see paras. 144.01 and 144.02.

89.27   —*Additional fees for further inventions (r. 121)*

When the Patent Office, as international preliminary examining authority, considers that the claims are directed to more than one invention, it may, under rule 121, request an additional examination fee for each invention after the first. It may also, under rule 120 (for which see para. 89.26 *supra*), request an additional fee for a further search against each further invention, if the international search report did not cover that invention. Failure to pay such fees will result in the relevant claims being excluded from the international preliminary examination report (PCTa. 34(3)(*c*)). Additional fees may be paid under protest accompanied by a reasoned argument (PCTr. 68.3(*c*)). The protest must be considered by a three-member board or special instance or higher authority. The rules contain no provisions for the composition of such three-member board or special instance of the Patent Office but presumably "competent higher authority" within the meaning of PCTr. 68.3(*c*) could include a judge hearing a request for a judicial review under RSC Ord. 53 (reprinted in part at para. E053.1).

—Fees to be paid in sterling (r. 122)   **89.28**

Pursuant to PCTrr. 15.3, 16.1(*b*), 57.3(*c*), all fees payable to the Patent Office as receiving office, or as international preliminary examining authority, shall be paid in sterling. The amounts, in sterling, of the basic fee, the designation fee, the international search fee and the handling fee are determined by agreement with the International Bureau and the EPO (as international searching authority) and are published from time to time in the *PCT Gazette* and in the O.J. They are also listed in the *PCT Applicant's Guide*, at the appropriate Annexes to Vol. I. However, these may change at very short notice and, unless a constant check on the *PCT Gazette* has been kept, it may be prudent to check the sums required with the International Unit at the Patent Office (tel. 071–829 6906).

—Delay or loss in mail (PCTr. 82.1)   **89.29**

Rule 97 (*postal delays*), reprinted at para. 119.02 does not apply to international applications in the international phase. However, by virtue of PCTr. 82(1), items addressed to the United Kingdom Patent Office as "Receiving Office" or as "International Preliminary Examining Authority", and sent *by registered post*, using airmail from abroad where available, at least five days before the end of a prescribed period, will be deemed to have been filed in time.

—Interruption in the mail service (PCTr. 82.2)   **89.30**

Similarly, rule 111 (*Interruption in postal services*), reprinted at para. 123.11, does not apply to international applications in the international phase. Instead, PCTr. 82.2 prescribes that, in the event of an interruption of postal services in the locality of the applicant or his agent, a delay in receipt by an international authority of any letter or document or payment by post from such applicant or agent may be excused *provided* that the applicant or agent, as the case may be, proves that such interruption commenced within any of the 10 days preceding the due date for that letter or document or payment and that he posted it within the next five days following resumption of mail services. Presumably, registered mail should be used, although this is not expressly stated.

—Right of representation (PCTa. 49)   **89.31**

The PCT does not impose any positive obligations upon national offices as receiving offices with regard to a right of representation, but it is implied in PCTa. 49 that anyone entitled to represent applicants before a national office in the filing and prosecution of national patent applications is also entitled to represent applicants in the international phase of international applications filed, searched or examined at that office (see also *PCT Applicants' Guide*, at Vol. 1, paras. 72 and 225). Thus, to ascertain who is entitled to represent applicants before the United Kingdom Patent Office in its role as receiving office or international preliminary examining authority, it will now be necessary to refer to substituted section 102, new section 102A and section 274 [1988] (reprinted respectively at paras. 102.02–102.04). These provisions will permit representation by any person, other than one subject to specific prohibition under section 281 [1988] (for which see paras. 115.04–115.06). It is submitted that it would be wrong to interpret these provisions as limiting freedom to practise before the United Kingdom Patent Office to applications filed under the Act and impose any stricter requirement for international applications when the PCT itself does not do so. Specifically, it should make no difference whether or not the United Kingdom Patent Office is a designated office, or whether or not the EPO is a designated office, so that in the latter case representation by a European patent attorney should not be required. Certainly no such distinction is made in the *PCT Applicant's Guide*, at Vol. 1, Annex C, GB.

A representative entitled to represent applicants before the United Kingdom Patent Office also has the right, by virtue of PCTa. 49, to represent applicants before the EPO as international searching authority, and before the International Bureau in connection with international applications filed at the United Kingdom Patent Office as receiving office. This is also irrespective of the offices designated and, so far as the EPO as international searching authority is concerned, is not dependent on the representative being on the "European list", for which see para. 102.43.

Anyone having a right of representation before the United Kingdom Patent Office in respect of patent applications filed under the Act has the right to represent applicants before the United Kingdom Patent Office in its capacity as international preliminary examining authority whether or not that Office was the receiving office (PCTa. 49 and *PCT Applicant's Guide*, at Vol. 1, para. 225).

However, in all these cases, it is possible to interpret PCTa. 49 as limiting the right of representation on international applications to persons, if any, who may already have been appointed for the purpose so that a further specific appointment, or amendment of an existing appointment, may be necessary for the national phase.

89.32 *—No appeal*

Adverse decisions (negative determinations) of the Patent Office acting as an international authority are not appealable (although the practice of the Office is to afford a hearing before making a negative determination). This is because the PCT deliberately does not provide for such an appeal. Any application for redress against a negative determination must be made to the designated offices by way of a request for review under PCTa. 25. For the United Kingdom Patent Office acting as designated office for the purpose of such a review, see para. 89.37 *infra*. Decisions after such a review are appealable in the usual way, since invoking the provisions of subsection (3) or (5) brings the international application within the provisions of the Act, *but only so far as the designation of the United Kingdom is concerned*. A separate review, and the consequent expense, before each designated office is necessary. The decision in *Vapocure Technologies' Application* (SRIS O/178/87 and C/30/88 and C/74/89, *noted The Times*, August 25, 1989 (CA)) is an example of such a review before the Office (though apparently PF 44/77 was not filed, see para. 89B.13).

The *PCT Applicant's Guide*, at Vol. I, para. 163 warns that, if an appeal is entertained by a higher national authority from a decision by an office acting in its capacity as an international authority, then there is no obligation on designated offices to accept the outcome of such an appeal. In *Hemosol's Application* (SRIS O/51/87, *noted* IPD 10111), the Comptroller expressed the view that there is no right to appeal to the Patents Court from a decision of the Comptroller acting as a receiving office, but that the possibility exists of a request to the High Court for judicial review of a negative determination under RSC Ord. 53 (for which see para. E053.1). However, the applicant would be very ill-advised to contemplate such a step. Quite apart from the warning in the *PCT Applicant's Guide, supra*, time limits in the international phase are very tight and prescribed periods for seeking reviews under PCTa. 25 will run from the date of the negative determination by the Comptroller and not from any later date, whatever the High Court might decide on judicial review. Also other time limits will continue to run, particularly the 20 month period and the 19 and 30 month periods mentioned at PCTaa. 22 and 39, respectively.

Effect of an international application (UK) (subs. (1)) **89.33**

The effect of subsection (1) is that an international application (UK) is equivalent to a United Kingdom application immediately on filing at a competent receiving office *and* being accorded an international filing date. This is subject to the savings of sections 898A and 89B, particularly section 89A(1) (*Procedure in the international phase*), for which see paras. 89A.05, and 89B(3) (*Provisional protection arising on publication*), for which see para. 89B.11. Section 89B(1) specifically concerns the filing date, declaration of priority and statement of inventorship, for which see respectively paras. 89B.05, 89B.06 and 89B.08.

If a purported international application designating the United Kingdom is not accorded an international filing date, whereby it is *not* treated as an international application (PCTr. 20.7(i)), then it does not come within the provisions of subsection (1), and cannot be treated as an application under the Act by virtue of these provisions. However, it does fall for review under the provisions of subsection (5), for which see para. 89.37 *infra*.

Withdrawal in the international phase (subs. (2)) **89.34**

Subsection (2) expressly provides that an international application (UK), which is withdrawn or considered withdrawn under the PCT, *i.e.* in the international phase, shall be regarded as withdrawn under the Act. The same applies to the withdrawal, or considered withdrawal, of a designation of the United Kingdom. Having regard to section 14(9) (*Withdrawal*), (for which see para. 14.39), which is in Part I of the Act, and subsection (1) (for which see para. 89.33 *supra*), the reference to withdrawal in subsection (1) appears superfluous. However, subsection (2) is necessary in so far as it covers withdrawal of the United Kingdom designation and deemed withdrawal in the international phase under circumstances to which there is no equivalent in the Act. Nevertheless, subsection (2) does not apply in the case of wrongful deemed withdrawal (for which see subsection (3) and para. 89.35 *infra*).

Patent Office review of deemed withdrawal (subs. (3)) **89.35**

As mentioned at para. 89.32 *supra*, the PCT does not provide for any appeal in the international phase, but PCTa. 25 enables the applicant to have any "negative determination" by an international authority reviewed by each of the designated offices.

Subsection (3)(*a*) provides for a review of a decision by the receiving office (which could be the United Kingdom Patent Office), that the international application has been deemed withdrawn or that the designation of the United Kingdom has been deemed withdrawn when the applicant alleges that such decision results from an error or omission made by that receiving office.

Subsection (3)(*b*) provides for a review of a finding by the International Bureau that the international application has been deemed withdrawn because the record copy of the international application did not reach the International Bureau within the time limit prescribed at PCTr. 22.3, but only when the applicant alleges that such decision results from an error or omission made by the International Bureau, or that an error or omission made by the applicant and resulting in such decision arose through a time limit being missed by the applicant when, in comparable circumstances, a failure to meet such time limit would be excused under the Act.

Although subsection (3)(*a*) and (*b*) appears to be worded more broadly than as stated above, particularly in relation to the references to "an institution having functions under the Treaty", and "circumstances outside the applicant's control", it is believed that the above remarks describe the practical effect of these two clauses of subsection (3), having regard to the provision of PCTa. 25.

The last part of subsection (3) will be the basis for a new sub-rule whereby the applicant can apply to proceed with the United Kingdom phase if the application has been deemed withdrawn when an application filed under the Act would not have been deemed withdrawn in comparable circumstances. Thus, subsection (3) will enable the provisions of the Act and the Rules, particularly rules 100, 101 and 110 (reprinted respectively at paras. 123.07, 123.08 and 123.10), to be applied to the circumstances in the international phase leading to the deemed withdrawal. Rule 85(4A) (reprinted in para. 89.03 *supra*) confirms the Comptroller's entitlement to make any necessary corrections to the documents filed in the international phase, but such corrections would not be effective for any designated country other than the United Kingdom.

The correction of errors and omissions (including failures to meet time limits) made by the applicant, or by an international authority, in the international phase is discussed more fully at para. 89B.14. Such errors and omissions do not necessarily lead to the international application or the designation of the United Kingdom being considered withdrawn.

The request for review of the decision of deemed withdrawal is made by filing PF 44/77, together with a supporting statement, and paying the national fee which, in this case, is the fee prescribed for PF 44/77. The time limit for filing this form is two months from the date of the letter from the relevant international authority indicating that the international application or designation is deemed withdrawn (PCTr. 51.3). Rule 85(4) refers to this time limit but rule 85(5) presently omits to do so. The applicant must also file a translation of the international application, if not in English, within the same two month time limit (PCTr. 51.3). Rules 85(4) and (5) both omit to say this, but see section 89A(2) and (3). The PCT does not require the applicant to file a copy of the international application at the Patent Office (see PCTa. 25(2)(*a*)), but it does require the applicant to request the International Bureau to transmit a copy of the international application to the Patent Office, again within the same two month period (PCTa. 25(1)(*b*) and PCTr. 51.1), such request being in English or French (PCT Applicant's Guide, at Vol. II, General Part, para. 54(i)). Since this last task must be done by the applicant or his representative in the international phase, *e.g.* in Japan or Australia, and the other steps must be done by the agent in the United Kingdom, good and speedy liasion is essential if a successful application for review is to be made.

It is not clear whether a failure to file PF 44/77, pay the national fee and file the translation, if required, or a failure to request the International Bureau to transmit a copy of the international application within the two month period, will prejudice the international application so far as the United Kingdom is concerned. Rule 100 or 110(1) may give the Comptroller power to grant an appropriate extension in either case.

An application to which subsection (1) continues to apply, by virtue of the subsection (3), becomes subject to the provisions of sections 89A and 89B, except that those of subsection 89A(3) will already have been met. The application will effectively be in the same position as one for which early national processing has been expressly requested under PCTa. 23(3), and the comments at paras. 89A.15, 89A.16 and 89B.15–89B.21 become applicable.

The other circumstance embraced in PCTa. 25, *i.e.* a refusal to accord an international filing date, is covered by subsection (5) (for which see para. 89.37 *infra*).

International application designating the EPO (subs. (4))   **89.36**

In the case of an international application in which a European patent is requested in respect of the designation of the United Kingdom, subsection (4) ensures that subsections (1)–(3) and sections 89A and 89B do not operate in respect of such designation. The application is then governed by the provisions of section 79, see the commentary thereon.

It is interesting that subsection (4) does not apply to subsection (5). The way therefore appears to be open to apply for a review under subsection (5) (see para. 89.37 *infra*) even in the case of an international application in which the United Kingdom is designated but only in conjunction with a request for a European Patent. However, there appears to be a major impediment to the implementation of this possibility. PCTa. 25(1)(*a*) requires that the International Bureau shall, at the applicant's request, supply a copy of the international application to designated offices. The latter is defined at PCTa. 2 (xii) and (xiii) and excludes the United Kingdom Patent Office when a European patent is requested in conjunction with the designation of the United Kingdom. Thus, there appears to be no way for the Office to receive an official copy of the international application in these circumstances. If a request is made to the EPO for a review of a refusal to accord a filing date and leads to a favourable result, section 79 then applies to the application (for which see the commentary thereon) and the Comptroller has no jurisdiction under subsection (5).

For a review under PCTa. 25 by the EPO as a designated office, see *EPH*.

Patent Office review of refusal to accord international filing date (subs. 5)   **89.37**

Whereas subsection (3) covers a wrongful deemed withdrawal of an international application (UK) in the international phase, subsection (5) provides for a review of a decision by the receiving office (which could be the United Kingdom Patent Office) to refuse to accord an international filing date so that, in the absence of a successful review, the international application would fail to come into existence.

The procedure for review is the same as that under subsection (3) and likewise, involves the filing of PF 44/77, together with a supporting statement, payment of the national fee, the filing of a translation, if required, and requesting the International Bureau to transmit a copy of the application to the Office, all as described at para. 89.35 *supra*.

However, an application which has been refused an international filing date and allowed to proceed as a United Kingdom application under subsection (5) is *never* to be regarded as an international application for the purposes of subsections (1)–(4) and sections 89A and 89B, since subsection (1) requires the international application to be accorded a filing date for that subsection to apply. Therefore, an application refused an international filing date becomes treated *ab initio* as an application under section 14 *et seq.* and all time limits will be those prescribed under Part I of the Act and described in the commentaries on the relevant sections.

Note that an international application accorded an international filing date, and later deemed withdrawn under PCTa. 14(4) because the receiving office later found that the international application did not meet the minimum requirement of PCTa. 11(1), will be entitled to review under subsection (3) and not under subsection (5).

COMMENTARY ON SECTION 89 [Prospectively repealed]

89.38 *General*

Upon the Royal Assent of the 1988 Act on November 15, 1988, the (now to be repealed) section 89 (reprinted in para. 89.02 *supra*) was amended retrospectively back to June 1, 1978 (by virtue of ss. 295 [1988] and 305(1) [1988]) by para. 24 of Schedule 5 [1988]. These amendments comprised the introduction of subsections (3A) and (4A) and the re-writing of subsection (10) and are discussed at paras. 89.39–89.41 *infra*. The retrospective effect of these three amendments regularised the position in respect of many patents (UK) which had already been granted.

The prospectively substituted sections 89, 89A and 89B avoid shortcomings in the repealed section 89, as briefly described in para. 89.42 *infra*. When brought into effect the prescribed rules can be written more simply.

The correlation between the subsections of the repealed section 89 and those of the substituted sections, 89, 89A and 89B is as follows:

Repealed section 89	Substituted sections 89–89B
89(1)	89(1)
(*a*)	89B(2)
(*b*)–(*e*)	89B(1)
(*f*)	89A(5)
89(2)	89B(3)
89(3)	89A(1), (2), (4)
89(3A)	89A(5)
89(4)(*a*)	89A(3)
(*b*)	90A(5)
89(4A)	89A(3)
89(5)	89A(6)
89(6)	89B(4)
89(7)	89B(3)
89(8)	89(2), (3)
89(9)	89B(5)
89(10)	89(4)
89(11)	89(5)

89.39 *Repealed subsection (3A)*

The effect of repealed section 89(4)(*b*) in conjunction with repealed section 89(1)(*f*) (each reprinted in para. 89.02 *supra*) has been that, in the event of a copy of an amendment made in the international phase (or a translation of such amendment, if required) not being filed at the United Kingdom Patent Office within the prescribed 20 or 30 month period, such amendment would not be deemed to have been made under the Act. The effect of now to be repealed subsection (3A) was then to make it clear that such amendment should be disregarded. It might be inferred from now to be repealed subsection (4)(*b*), in conjunction with now to be repealed subsection (3), that the effect of such amendment or translation not being filed at the Office was that the application was to be taken as withdrawn. The presence of subsection (3A) implies that this was not so.

Repealed subsection (4A)   **89.40**

The effect of this now to be repealed subsection has been that, in the case of an international application published in English translation (see para. 89.18 *supra*), a failure to file a *verified* translation (r. 113(1)) did not result in the application being taken to be withdrawn.

Repealed subsection (10)   **89.41**

The retrospective amendment to the original subsection (10), now to be repealed, ensured that, where the United Kingdom had been designated twice in an international application, *i.e.* for a patent (UK) and for a European patent (UK), the repealed subsections (1)–(9) applied to the one designation but not to the other. Without this amendment, the original section 89(10) did not recognise that the two designations could exist simultaneously.

Shortcomings of the repealed section 89   **89.42**

The principal shortcoming in the now to be repealed section 89 lay in an inconsistency between the old subsection (4) and PCTa. 22. The latter only requires a copy of the international application to be filed when the communication under PCTa. 20 has not taken place. It has been the practice in the past for the word "filed" as used in old subsection (4) at (*a*) and (*b*) to be interpreted so as to include receipt by the Patent Office of the communication under PCTa. 20. Another shortcoming was that the repealed section 89 did not enable the full implementation of PCTa. 26 (*Opportunity to correct before designated Offices*) and PCTa. 48 (*Delay in meeting certain time limits*). The substituted sections 89, 89A and 89B will also remove other less significant shortcomings and deficiencies of the now to be repealed section 89 which are too numerous to mention.

Also, the present form of rule 85 (reprinted in paras. 89.03 and 89A.02) under the now to be repealed section 89 is complicated and difficult to apply. In particular, it has not enabled rule 110 (*Extensions of time*) to be applied satisfactorily to time limits in the international phase, as required by PCTr. 82*bis*.

PRACTICE UNDER SECTION 89

International phase   **89.43**

Readers wishing to file an international application are strongly recommended to refer to Vol. I of the *PCT Applicant's Guide* for guidance on all essential procedures relating to the filing of an international application and its prosecution in the international phase. Blank forms, such as the international request form (PCT/RO/101) and the demand for international preliminary examination form (PCT/IPEA/401) are available from the Patent Office. These forms are accompanied by respective annexes which comprise fee calculation sheets. The forms are also accompanied by respective notes. If meticulous attention is paid to these notes, the applicant should be able to avoid any serious mistakes in preparing and filing an international application. The International Unit at the Patent Office (tel. 01–829 6906) is also very helpful and should be consulted in any event to check on the current amounts of the fees payable, for which see also para. 89.28 *supra*.

All documents other than the fee calculation sheet should be filed in triplicate (r. 117(1)). The Office also requires the usual fee sheet in addition to the fee calculation sheet. Contrary to practice under the Act, when the applicant is represented by an agent, a signed appointment of agent (power of attorney) must be filed (PCTr. 90). Such power of attorney is recognised by all the competent international authorities, see para. 89.31 *supra*, as regards right of representation, but no special form is prescribed for appointment of an agent under the PCT. Suitable forms of specific and general powers of attorney can be found in the *PCT Applicant's Guide*, Vol. 1 at Annexes G1 and G2.

If priority is claimed from an earlier application filed at the Patent Office, a request for the Office to make a certified copy to be transmitted to the International Bureau should be made by checking "Box No. VI" on form PCT/RO/101, filing PF 24/77 with the prescribed fee and filing Sales Form 3 to cover the copying cost.

Any amendments to the claims under PCTa. 19(1), *i.e.* after receipt of the international search report, and any explanatory statement, should be filed in single copy but must be filed directly at the International Bureau.

A demand for international preliminary examination should be filed at the Patent Office as examining authority (PCTa. 31(6)(*a*)). It can be filed in single copy. Amendments to the description and claims during international preliminary examination can also be filed in single copy.

It is recommended that the transmittal fee, the basic fee, the designation fee and the search fee payable in respect of an international application should all be paid when the application is filed and that, if a demand for international preliminary examination is filed, the handling fee and the examination fee are paid when filing that demand, in order that none of these should be overlooked.

The above deals with points which are to a certain extent peculiar to the United Kingdom Patent Office when the latter is acting as an international authority. A fuller description of practice under the PCT is beyond the scope of this book.

89.44 *Request for review (subss. (3) and (5))*

This para. has been written on the basis of the practice at the time of going to press, but it is thought that the practice may be substantially changed by the rule revisions to be made when the substituted section 89 is brought into effect, as to which see the latest Supplement to this Work re. para. 89.01.

A request to the Comptroller for a review under subsection (3) or (5) following a negative determination by an international authority (which may be the Patent Office) is presently made by filing PF 44/77 together with a supporting statement of the facts on which the applicant relies. The statement should give details of the alleged error or omission of the international authority by which the international application or the designation of the United Kingdom was deemed withdrawn or by which no international filing date was accorded, or alternatively of the circumstances by which the international application was not timely received by the International Bureau, or alternatively of the other circumstances by which the international application (UK) should be given more favourable treatment, as appropriate.

A copy of the international application is supplied to the Office by the International Bureau on a request from the applicant to the International Bureau pursuant to PCTa. 25(1) or (2) and PCTr. 51. Such request can at the same time ask

610

the International Bureau to transmit copies to other designated offices. This request must be accompanied by a copy of the negative determination from the receiving office (PCTr. 51.2).

It is not clear whether, in fact, such a request need be sent to the International Bureau when the Patent Office is the receiving office and therefore already has a copy of the international application.

The period for requesting the International Bureau to transmit a copy of the international application is two months from the date of the letter notifying the applicant of the negative determination (PCTr. 51.1). The periods for filing PF 44/77, filing the supporting statement, paying the national fee; and filing a verified translation (if required) of the international application at the Office each expire at the same time (PCTr. 51.3; r. 85(4)). Both these periods may be extensible either under rule 100, or at the Comptroller's discretion under rule 110(1). The national fee in this case is the fee paid on PF 44/77. For an explanation of the translation, see para. 89A.19.

For particulars of other forms and documents which may be required after a request under subsection (3), e.g. PF 7/77, PF 9/77, PF 10/77, priority document(s) and translation(s) thereof, see paras. 89A.24–89A.31. After a successful request under subsection (5), the application is to be treated as one under the Act, the documentary requirements for which are listed in para. 14.32. Under subsection (5) the date of filing for such an application is to be as the Comptroller may direct, and this date will determine the time limits within which these requirements are to be met, subject to such extensions as may be possible under rule 110.

SECTION 89A 89A.01

International and national phases of application

89A.—(1) The provisions of the Patent Co-operation Treaty relating to publication, search, examination and amendment, and not those of this Act, apply to an international application for a patent (UK) during the international phase of the application.

(2) The international phase of the application means the period from the filing of the application in accordance with the Treaty until the national phase of the application begins.

(3) The national phase of the application begins—

(a) when the prescribed period expires, provided any necessary translation of the application into English has been filed at the Patent Office and the prescribed fee has been paid by the applicant; or

(b) on the applicant expressly requesting the comptroller to proceed earlier with the national phase of the application, filing at the Patent Office—

(i) a copy of the application, if none has yet been sent to the Patent Office in accordance with the Treaty, and

(ii) any necessary translation of the application into English,

and paying the prescribed fee.

For this purpose a "copy of the application" includes a copy published in accordance with the Treaty in a language other than that in which it was originally filed.

(4) If the prescribed period expires without the conditions mentioned in subsection (3)(a) being satisfied, the application shall be taken to be withdrawn.

(5) Where during the international phase the application is amended in accordance with the Treaty, the amendment shall be treated as made under this Act if—

> (a) when the prescribed period expires, any necessary translation of the amendment into English has been filed at the Patent Office, or
>
> (b) where the applicant expressly requests the comptroller to proceed earlier with the national phase of the application, there is then filed at the Patent Office—
>
>> (i) a copy of the amendment, if none has yet been sent to the Patent Office in accordance with the Treaty, and
>>
>> (ii) any necessary translation of the amendment into English;

otherwise the amendment shall be disregarded.

(6) The comptroller shall on payment of the prescribed fee publish any translation filed at the Patent Office under subsection (3) or (5) above.

Note. Section 89A was prospectively added by the 1988 Act (Sched. 5, para. 25). For its commencement see the latest Supplement to this Work *re.* this para.

RELEVANT RULE

89A.02 **85.**—(1) Subject to the provisions of paragraph (1A) below, an international application for a patent (UK) shall be treated as an application for a patent under the Act if the relevant conditions of section 89(4) are satisfied before the end of—

> (a) the period of twenty months calculated from the date which, by virtue of section 89(1)(c), is to be treated as the declared priority date or, where there is no declared priority date, the date of filing of the internation application for a patent (UK), or
>
> (b) in a case where the United Kingdom has been elected in accordance with Chapter II of the Patent Co-operation Treaty before the expiry of nineteen months calculated from the declared priority date, the period of thirty months calculated from the declared priority date or, where there is no declared priority date and the United Kingdom has been so elected before the expiry of nineteen months calculated from the date of filing of the internation application for a patent (UK), the period of thirty months calculated from the date of filing of that international application,

and in either case the national fee (being the fee referred to in section 89(4)(a)) is paid to the Patent Office within the relevant period:

Provided that where the relevant conditions of section 89(4) are not satisfied before the end of the relevant period because, for any reason outside the control of the applicant or any person acting on his behalf, the Patent Office has not received the communication provided for in Article

20 of the Patent Co-operation Treaty, the relevant period shall be extended until actual receipt by the Patent Office of the said communication or until the expiry of a further period of two months commencing on the date on which the Comptroller sends to the applicant notice that the Patent Office has not received the said communication, whichever is the sooner.

(1A) Where, in accordance with rule 17 above, the information specified in paragraph (1)(*a*) (iii) of that rule is added to an international application for a patent (UK), rule 113(1) below shall not apply in respect of that information; and where the translation of that information the filing of which is required to satisfy the relevant condition of section 89(4) has not been filed at the Patent Office before the end of the relevant period referred to in paragraph (1) above—

(*a*) the comptroller shall give notice to the applicant at the address furnished by the applicant in accordance with rule 30 above requiring the applicant to file the translation within the period of two months commencing on the day on which the letter containing the notice is sent, and

(*b*) the relevant period shall be treated in respect of the translation as not expiring until the end of the relevant period specified in the notice given under subparagraph (*a*) above.

(2) The Patent Office shall publish any translation supplied in accordance with section 89(4) following the filing of Patents Form No. 43/77.

(2A) In the case of an international application for a patent (UK)—

(*a*) rule 5(1) above shall not apply if the applicant, on filing the application, states in writing to the receiving office that the invention has been displayed at an international exhibition;

(*b*) rule 5(2) above may be complied with at any time before the end of the period of two months commencing with the expiry of the relevant period referred to in paragraph (1) above; and

(*c*) verification of translation as required by rule 113(1) below may be given to the comptroller at any time before the end of the said period of two months when the translation is of a document or part of a document required by the Act or these rules to be filed at the Patent Office before the end of the relevant period referred to in paragraph (1) above.

(3) In the case of an international application for a patent (UK) in respect of which the conditions specified in section 89(4) are satisfied, the period prescribed—

(*a*) for the purposes of sections 13(2), 15(5)(*b*) and 17(1) shall be the period which expires two months after the end of the relevant period referred to in paragraph (1) above;

(*b*) for the purposes of section 18(1) shall, except in a case in which the relevant period is extended in accordance with the proviso to paragraph (1) above, be—

613

(i) where subparagraph (*a*) of paragraph (1) applies, the period which expires two years after the declared priority date or, if there is no declared priority date, the date of filing of the international application for a patent (UK), and

(ii) where subparagraph (*b*) of paragraph (1) applies, the period of thirty-three months calculated from the declared priority date or, if there is no declared priority date, the date of filing of the international application for a patent (UK),

and, in a case in which the relevant period is so extended, be the period mentioned in subparagraph (i) or (ii) above, as the case may be, or the period which expires three months after the end of the relevant period as so extended, whichever may expire the later; and

(*c*) for the purposes of section 18(1) and 20(1) shall be the period which expires four years and six months after the declared priority date or, where there is no declared priority date, the date of filing of the international application for a patent (UK).

Note. Only sub-rules 85(1)–(3) have been reprinted above because sub-rules 85(4)–(6) are more pertinent to the substituted section 89 and are therefore reprinted at para. 89.03. In each case the rule is reprinted as amended by S.I. 1985 No. 1166. However, for the revision of the whole of rule 85 which will be required when the prospective changes to section 89, and the new sections 89A and 89B, are brought into effect, and the basis on which the following commentary on section 89A has been prepared, see the *Note* to para. 89.03. This explains that the latest Supplement to this Work should be consulted under this para. 89A.02 to ascertain the replacement wording for the former rule 85 made in relation to practice under this new section 89A when this was brought into effect. At that time the whole commentary on this section will need to be read in the light of the new rule wording.

89A.03   OTHER RELEVANT RULES

The following rules are also relevant:

rule 6(5), 6(6)	(*Declaration of priority for the purposes of section 5*) reprinted in para. 5.02;
rule 15(4)	(*Procedure where the applicant is not the inventor or sole inventor*) reprinted in para. 13.03;
rule 30	(*Address for service*) reprinted at para. 32.03;
rule 31(1)	(*Formal requirements*) reprinted in para. 17.03;
rule 100	(*Correction of irregularities*) reprinted at para. 123.07;
rule 102(1)(*b*), (2)	(*Remission of fees*) reprinted in para. 123.09;
rule 110	(*Alteration of time limits*) reprinted at para. 123.10; and
rule 113	(*Translations*) reprinted at para. 123.12.

COMMENTARY ON SECTION 89A

General   **89A.04**

This is the second of the three sections which will concern international applications (UK), and the general remarks at para. 89.13 are relevant to this section
and to section 89B. Subsection (1) will ensure that the provisions of the PCT relating to the progress of the application in the international phase override the corresponding provisions under the Act, notwithstanding section 89(1) (for which see
para. 89.33). Subsection (2) will define the international phase and subsection (3)
will define the national phase and outline the procedures to secure valid entry into
the United Kingdom phase. Subsection (4) will ensure that an international application does not enter the United Kingdom phase if the procedures prescribed in
and under subsection (3) are not completed. Subsection (5) will concern the effect
of amendments made in the international phase. Subsection (6) will concern publication of a translation of the application and of any amendment made in the international phase and will be relevant to so-called provisional protection arising on
publication, for which see para. 89B.11.

Effect of proceedings in the international phase (subs. (1))   **89A.05**

Whilst in principle an international application (UK) is to be treated *ab initio* as
an application under the Act (s. 89(1), see para. 89.33), subsection (1) will prescribe that the PCT provisions for publication, search, examination and amendment take precedence in the international phase. The PCT provisions are mainly
contained in PCTaa. 15–19, 21, 31–35, 38 and 41. International search, international publication and international preliminary examination are briefly described at paras. 89.17, 89.18 and 89.21 respectively. Amendment is discussed in
each of these paragraphs. The provisions in the Act relating to publication, search,
examination and amendment appear principally in sections 16–19, for which see the
commentaries on those sections.
The effect of publication in the international phase is to be specified in section
89B(2) (for which see para. 89B.09). The effects of search and examination in the
international phase are taken into account in section 89B(5) (for which see
paras. 89B.16 and 89B.17). The effect of amendment in the international phase is
to be subject to subsections 89A(5) and (6) (for which see para. 89A.14 *infra*). It
has been held, in relation to the corresponding provisions of the now repealed section 89(3) (for which see para. 89.02), that "the provisions of the PCT relating to
publication, search, examination and amendment" are to be construed narrowly so
as to exclude the provisions of the PCT relating to all other matters, such as corrections of errors and irregularities in procedure (*Prangley's Application*, [1988] RPC
187 (CA)), for which see 89B.13.

Supply of copy of international application to the Patent Office   **89A.06**

A copy of the international application is supplied by the International Bureau to
the Patent Office, as the so-called "communication under PCTa. 20" (see
para. 89.19), between 18 and 19 months after the priority date and it is not normally necessary for the applicant to file a copy. An exception is discussed in
para. 89A.12 *infra*. This communication comprises a copy of the PCT pamphlet
(see para. 89.18) when the application is both filed and published in the same
language. It comprises both a copy of the application as filed and a copy of the published PCT pamphlet when the application is published in English translation
(subs. (3)).

89A.07   *The applicant in the United Kingdom phase*

The applicant in the international phase becomes the applicant for the commencement of the United Kingdom phase. This is because an international application (UK) is treated as an application under Part I of the Act (s. 89(1)). It is not possible simply to add or substitute some other person as applicant for the purpose of commencing proceedings in the United Kingdom. If there are several applicants, they are treated as joint applicants in the international phase. If the international application designates different applicants for different designated countries (PCTr. 18.4(a)), only applicant(s) who were designated for the United Kingdom are treated as applicant(s) at the commencement of the United Kingdom phase. If the international application, or at least the United Kingdom part thereof, is assigned, or the applicant changes his name, and application to record the assignment or name change reaches the International Bureau while the application is still in the international phase, the recordal is effective for the international application (UK) (PCT rule 92*bis*). The United Kingdom patent office is entitled to call for evidence of such assignment or name change, but only after the application has entered the United Kingdom phase (PCTr. 51*bis* (*a*)(ii) and *PCT Applicant's Guide*, at Vol. 1, para. 264).

Valid entry into the United Kingdom phase (subss. (2) and (3)(a))

89A.08   *—General*

The transfer of the international application (UK) from the international phase into the national or United Kingdom phase at the end of the prescribed 20 or 30 month period is achieved by paying the national fee and by filing an English translation of the international application if it was neither filed nor published in English. It is not normally necessary expressly to request national processing nor is it necessary to file a special form (PCTr. 49.4). The payment of the national fee, the filing of the translation and the prescribed 20 or 30 month period are discussed respectively in paras. 89A.09, 89A.10 and 89A.11 *infra*.

Subsection (3)(*a*) will ensure that valid entry into the United Kingdom phase can be secured at the end of the prescribed 20 or 30 month period without the applicant filing a copy of the international application (or any amendments thereto) even if the communication under PCTa. 20 has been delayed, as envisaged at PCTr. 49.1(*a-bis*). It will also ensure, pursuant to PCTaa. 23(1) and 40(1), that the United Kingdom phase does not commence until expiry of the prescribed 20 or 30 month period, even if the national fee is paid (para. 89A.09 *infra*) and the translation, if required (para. 89A.10 *infra*) is filed sooner, save that earlier entry into the United Kingdom phase can be obtained at the *express* request of the applicant (subs. (3)(*b*), for which see para. 89A.12 *infra*.

89A.09   *—Payment of the national fee*

It is left to the designated offices to prescribe what is meant by the "national fee" within the meaning of PCTa. 22. For the United Kingdom as a designated office, it is the fee to be paid under subsection (3) and now prescribed at rule 85(1), reprinted in para. 89A.02 *supra*. The national fee is equivalent to the filing fee, which is the fee payable on PF 1/77, as indicated in para. 144.02. The filing of PF 9/77, and payment of the United Kingdom search fee, are not necessary for the purpose of securing valid entry into the United Kingdom phase. The filing of PF 9/77 and PF 10/77 are discussed at paras. 89A.24 and 89A.25 *infra*. No form is prescribed for paying the national fee but it is recommended to use PF NP.1 (reprinted at para. 143.01).

—Filing of translation of the international application   **89A.10**

When the international application (UK) was filed in a language other than English, it becomes necessary to file an English translation at the Patent Office to secure valid entry into the United Kingdom phase, unless the international application has already been published in English translation (subs.(3)). Such translation must be verified (r. 113(1)), but the verification can be filed later (r. 85(2A)(*c*)) as discussed in the practice notes at para. 89A.21 *infra*. If the international application is published in English translation (see para. 89.18), such translation becomes a part of the international application to be communicated under PCTa. 20 and no separate translation need be filed at the Patent Office by the applicant and no verification is necessary. For the content of the translation, see para. 89A.19 *infra*. If a translation of the wrong document is filed, then a translation of the correct document cannot be substituted by way of correction of a clerical error under section 117 (*Masuda's Application*, [1987] RPC 37).

The securing of valid entry into the United Kingdom phase is not dependent on the filing of a translation of any amendment made in the international phase because amendments in the international application are covered separately at subsection (5). The furnishing of a translation of amendments is discussed at 89A.14 *infra*.

—Time limits   **89A.11**

The time limit, to be prescribed under subsection (3) for paying the national fee (para. 89A.09 *supra*) and for filing a translation, if required (para. 89A.10 *supra*), is 20 months from the declared priority date (or from the international filing date if no priority is claimed), unless a demand for international preliminary examination has been filed and the United Kingdom has been elected within 19 months from the declared priority (or filing) date (r. 85(1)(*a*)). If a demand has been so filed and the United Kingdom has been so elected, then the time for paying the national fee and filing the translation, if required, is deferred until 30 months after the declared priority (or filing) date (r. 85(1)(*b*)). For the supply of a copy of the priority document and, if necessary, its translation, see para. 89A.15 *supra*. The time limits for filing PF 9/77, PF 10/77 and other documents, if needed, are discussed at paras. 89A.24–89A.31 *infra*. An extension of one month under rule 110(3) can be obtained to the 20 or 30 month period for paying the national fee and for filing the translation, if required, and a further discretionary extension may be obtained under rule 110(3A), as discussed at para. 89A.35 *infra*. Rule 110 is reprinted at para. 123.10.

An omission to elect the United Kingdom within 19 months of the priority date may be excused under rule 100 (*Prangley's Application*, [1988] RPC 187 (CA), see also para. 89B.13).

In the case of documents mailed to the Patent Office for commencement of the national phase, it is thought that the operation of rule 97 (reprinted at para. 119.02) will be effective in conjunction with the provisions of PCTr. 82. Thus the Office may consider that any document sent to it from abroad will be deemed to be received by it by the due date if sent registered airmail at least five days before the due date.

Early entry in the United Kingdom phase (subs. (3)(b))   **89A.12**

Notwithstanding the 20 or 30 month prescribed period for valid entry into the United Kingdom phase, the applicant has the right expressly to request commencement of national processing before the Patent Office as soon as he wishes after international filing (PCTaa. 23(2) and 40(2)). When requesting early processing, the applicant must pay the national fee and file the translation, if required, as described at paras. 89A.09 and 89A.10 *supra*. Also, the applicant himself must file a copy of the international application at the United Kingdom Patent Office if the communication under PCTa. 20 has not yet taken place (subs. 3(*b*)(ii)), and see *PCT Applicant's Guide*, at Vol. II, General Part, paras. 9 and 34), even if the international application were initially filed therewith as receiving office.

Reasons why the applicant might want to request early national processing include: a desire for early grant to enable infringement proceedings to commence; a desire to have early publication in English to secure provisional protection (see para. 89B.11); and a wish to have an adverse decision by an international authority reconsidered, especially before publication. This last point is discussed further at para. 89B.14.

89A.13   *Failure to pay the national fee and file a translation (subs. (4))*

Failure to pay the national fee (as discussed at para. 89A.09 *supra*), or to file a translation if required (as discussed at para. 89A.10 *supra*), within the prescription period (as described at para. 89A.11 *supra*), results in the international application being deemed to be withdrawn (subs. (4)). Also, if the international application has been published under PCTa. 21, such publication is not regarded as published under the Act (s. 89B(2), see para. 89B.09) and has no prior art effect under section 2(3) as against other United Kingdom patents and applications (see para. 89B.10).

89A.14   *Amendments in the international phase (subss. (5) and (6))*

Amendments made to the claims under PCTa. 19(1) and any explanatory statement are normally included in the communication under PCTa. 20 (see para. 89.19) and the applicant does not need to file such amendments at the Patent Office. In the event that the applicant requests early national processing under PCTa. 23(2) (see para. 89A.12 *supra*), *and* the amendment or explanatory statement has not yet been communicated to the Patent Office under PCTa. 20, then the applicant must supply a copy of such amendment to the Patent Office when requesting early processing.

If the amended claims are not in English, a translation must be filed within the prescribed 20 or 30 month period, though the point is not specifically covered in present rule 85.

If the above conditions are not complied with, the amendments to the claims and explanatory statement, if any, are disregarded but the validity of the entry into the United Kingdom phase is not jeopardised.

Note that, if amended claims published with the international application are so disregarded, the provisional protection afforded by sections 55 and 69 (see para. 89B.11) is then based on the scope of the unamended claims. This should be considered before making any decision as to whether to refrain deliberately from filing a translation of amended claims.

Amendments made to the description and claims during international preliminary examination under PCT Chapter II are annexed to the international preliminary examination report and are communicated to the United Kingdom Patent Office with such annex (see para. 89.21). However, if the applicant requests early national processing under PCTa. 40(2) (see para. 89A.12 *supra*), such amendments must be filed when requesting early processing. If the international preliminary examination report is not in English, it is translated into English by the International Bureau (PCTa. 36(2)(*b*) and PCTr. 72.1) and the English translation is included in the above-mentioned communication. However, the applicant is responsible for filing an English translation of the amendments at the Patent Office before the expiry of the prescribed 30 month period. If a translation is not timely filed, or in the event of a request for early national processing, a copy of the amendments is not filed, the amendments are disregarded (subs. (5)), but the validity of the application itself is not jeopardised.

Translations of claims amended under PCTa. 19(1) and translations of amendments annexed to the international preliminary examination report must be verified (r. 113(1)), but verification can be filed after expiry of the prescribed 20 or 30 month period (r. 85(2A)(c), see para. 89A.21 *infra*).

Any amendments which are made in the international phase, but which are disregarded so far as the United Kingdom phase is concerned, can still be requested under section 19(1) in the United Kingdom phase (see para. 89A.32 *infra*).

Copy and translation of priority document   89A.15

A copy of the priority document is normally forwarded to the Patent Office by the International Bureau (see para. 89.19): the Patent Office cannot then require the applicant to file a certified copy of the priority document (PCTr. 17.2). When the priority document is not in English, a verified translation must be filed but this can be filed *after* commencement of the United Kingdom phase, as described in more detail in para. 89A.27 *infra*. The Patent Office is entitled to ask for a verified translation of the priority document to be accompanied by an uncertified copy of that document, but does not do so (PCTr. 17.2(a) and *PCT Applicant's Guide*, at Vol. II, General Part, para. 44). However, this practice may change under the revised wording for rule 85: the latest Supplement to this Work *re*. this para. should therefore particularly be consulted on the supply of copy priority documents and translations thereof.

It should also be noted that the Patent Office is not required to, and does not, issue any reminder of the need to comply with the time limit imposed by rule 6(6) for filing any necessary translation of the priority document, see *Application des Gaz's Application* ([1987] RPC 279).

Priority is discussed more fully at para. 89B.06.

Further formalities after entry into the United Kingdom phase   89A.16

In addition to paying the national fee and filing the translation, if required, as described at paras. 89A.09 and 89A.10 *supra*, the applicant must also file PF 9/77 and PF 10/77 and pay the prescribed search and examination fees. PF 9/77 can be filed up to two months after expiry of the relevant 20 or 30 month period (r. 85(3)(a)), but it is advisable to file it when paying the national fee in order that the formalities officer can commence his preliminary examination under section 17(2) and (3) and so enable any noted deficiencies to be corrected within the one month extension available under rule 110(3) or the discretionary extension available under rule 110(3A). However, the Office is not obliged to commence its preliminary examination within the first month (*Masuda's Application*, [1987] RPC 37). The period for filing PF 10/77 is somewhat longer (see r. 85(3)(b)), but it is safest to file PF 10/77 along with PF 9/77 lest it be forgotten.

If the inventor is not named in the international application then PF 7/77 must be filed (r. 85(3)(a)).

If the performance of the invention claimed in an international application involves the use of a micro-organism not available to the public at the international filing date, then the information concerning deposit of the micro-organism (for which see para. 125A.11) must have been filed with the international application or within such further time as permitted by PCTr. 13*bis*.4. This information forms part of the international application and, if not filed or published in English, must be translated. Pursuant to PCTr. 49.5(*h*), the period prescribed for filing such a translation is two months from the date of an invitation to furnish a translation (r. 85(1A)). Failure to furnish such a translation will apparently result in the application being deemed withdrawn, a harsher penalty than that imposed by section 125A.

If the invention was displayed at an international exhibition within six months preceeding the international filing date, then the applicant has two months after the expiry of the prescribed 20 or 30 month period in which to file the necessary certificate (r. 85(2A)(*b*)).

If a translation of the international application or of any amendment is not verified, then verification can be submitted up to two months after expiry of the prescribed 20 or 30 month period (r. 85(2A)(*c*)).

The above time limits and possible extensions thereto under rule 110 are detailed in the practice notes at paras. 89A.17–89A.36 *infra*.

Practice under Section 89A

89A.17   *Valid entry into the United Kingdom phase*

Paras. 89A.18 and 89A.19 *infra* set out briefly the steps to be taken to ensure valid entry into the United Kingdom phase and the subsequent paragraphs describe the other steps required for continued prosecution in the United Kingdom phase. Possible extensions under rule 110 are the subject of para. 89A.35. It is no longer necessary to check whether the Patent Office has received a copy of the international application.

89A.18   *National fee and prescribed 20 or 30 month period*

The national fee, being the fee prescribed at rule 85(1) pursuant to section 85A(3), is due to be paid within the prescribed 20 or 30 month period. This period is extensible under rule 110(3) and 110(3A), see para. 89A.35 *infra*. It is recommended to use PF NP. 1 (reproduced at para. 143.01) when paying this fee, though such form is not compulsory (PCTr. 49.4). PF NP. 1 contains reminders of the procedural steps to be taken on and after entry into the United Kingdom phase. It also contains spaces for insertion of an address for service (r. 30, discussed at para. 32.16) and the nationality of the applicant. When the applicant is an Australian or United States body corporate, the Patent Office requires to know the state of incorporation before preparations for the *ex-officio* re-publication (see para. 89B.15) can be completed.

The prescribed 20 or 30 month period mentioned above, and elsewhere, is: the period of 20 months from the priority date if the United Kingdom has not been elected (r. 85(1)(*a*)); or the period of 30 months from the priority date if the United Kingdom has been elected for the purpose of international preliminary examination (r. 85(1)(*b*)). Priority date here has the meaning ascribed to it by the PCT (PCTa. 2(xi)), *i.e.* either the declared priority date (for which see r. 2(*d*) reprinted in para. 123.04) or the international filing date when no priority is claimed.

89A.19   *Translation of the international application*

When the international application is neither filed nor published in English, it is necessary to file an English translation (in duplicate) within the prescribed 20 or 30 month period mentioned at para. 89A.18 *supra*. This period is extensible under rule 110(3) and 110(3A), see para. 89A.35 *infra*, but it should be noted that it is *less* than that allowed for filing a translation of a priority document (for which see para. 89A.27 *infra*). This fact was overlooked in *Mitsubishi Jidosha's Application* ([1988] RPC 449), but this application was eventually saved by an application of rule 100.

The translation must include the description and the claims. If the drawings contain textual matter not in English, the translation must include a copy of the drawings in which the textual matter is translated into English. Informal drawings will suffice (PCTr. 49.5(*e*). Notwithstanding PCTr. 49.5(*a*), the translation need not normally include the abstract or the request (PCT Applicant's Guide, at Vol. II, General Part, paras. 20 and 21 and National Chapter, GB, Summary).

The bibliographic data can always be identified in the frontsheet by virtue of use of the INID code (for which a summary is published periodically in the O.J., see para. 123.45), and the abstract is always published in English (PCTr. 48.3(*c*)). However, if the communication under PCTa. 20 has not taken place, *e.g.* in the event of early entry into the United Kingdom phase (for which see para. 89A.23 *infra*), or after a review under section 89(3) (for which see para. 89.44), the translation should include a translation of the request (PCT/RO/101) and a translation of the abstract. An English language version of the blank form of the request may be completed to provide a translation of the request (PCTr. 49.5(*b*)). As to later filing of the verification of the translation, see para. 89A.21 *infra*.

Translation of amendments and explanatory statement   **89A.20**

When the application has been amended in the international phase, and the amendments were not filed in English, an English translation (in duplicate) of the amendments should be filed within the prescribed 20 or 30 month period mentioned at para. 89A.18 *supra*. This period is extensible under rule 110(3) and 110(3A), see para. 89A.35 *infra*. If this time limit is not met, the amendments will be disregarded (subs. 89A(5)). Such amendments are those made to the claims under PCTa. 19(1) (see para. 89.17), or those made to the description and claims during international preliminary examination under PCT Chapter II (see para. 89.21).

If amendments to the claims under PCTa. 19(1) were accompanied by an explanatory statement, not in English, an English translation of such statement should also be filed within the prescribed 20 or 30 month period, since the explanatory statement is part of the application (PCTr. 49.3). However, failure to furnish a translation merely results in the explanatory statement being disregarded (PCTr. 49.5(*c*)). See para. 89A.21 *infra*, with reference to possible later filing of verification of the translation.

Verification of translation of application   **89A.21**

It will be usual for a translation of the international application and of any amendment thereto, filed as described in paras. 89A.19 and 89A.20 *supra*, to be verified, for which see para. 123.42. However, verification can be filed up to two months after expiry of the prescribed 20 or 30 month period mentioned in para. 89A.18 *supra*. For the calculation of this two month period, see para. 89A.36 *infra*. This two month period is only extensible at the Comptroller's discretion under rule 110(1), for which see para. 89A.35 *infra*.

Publication of translation (subs. (6))   **89A.22**

When the international application was neither filed nor published in English, provisional protection under sections 55 and 69 (see para. 89B.11) during the

United Kingdom phase can be secured by filing PF 43/77 (reprinted at para. 141.43). The translation is laid open to public inspection immediately both it and PF 43/77 have been filed (O.J. February 20, 1980). There is no time limit for filing this form but it is recommended to file it along with the translation of the international application. The laying open of the translation to public inspection under section 118(1) and rule 94(1) does not give the applicant any legal rights.

89A.23 *Early national processing (subs. (3)(b))*

To secure early national processing before the Patent Office, it is necessary to carry out the steps described at paras. 89A.18 and 89A.19 *supra*, and *expressly* request the Comptroller to proceed with the national phase. Also, if the communication under PCTa. 20 has not taken place, it is necessary to file a copy of the international application with such express request; and see para. 89A.19 *supra*, for the content of a translation of the application, if required. To enable the Comptroller to proceed it is also necessary to file PF 9/77 and PF 10/77.

89A.24 *Request for preliminary examination and search (PF 9/77)*

PF 9/77 must be filed within two months after expiry of the prescribed 20 or 30 month period mentioned in para. 89A.18 *supra*. This period is extensible under rule 110(3) and 110(3A), see para. 89A.35 *infra*. For determining the date of commencement of this two month period, see para. 89A.36 *infra*. However, it is recommended to file PF 9/77 when paying the national fee, especially when expressly requesting early national processing (para. 89A.23 *supra*). The search fee must be paid in full on PF 9/77, even if the applicant is entitled to later remission (see para. 89A.33, *infra*).

89A.25 *Request for substantive examination (PF 10/77)*

PF 10/77 must be filed within two years of the priority date (r. 85(3)(*a*)), unless the United Kingdom Patent Office has been elected for international preliminary examination, in which case the period is 33 months from the priority date (r. 85(3)(*b*)). This two year or 33 month period is extensible under rule 110(3) and 110(3A), see para. 89A.35 *infra*. "Priority date" here has the same meaning as in para. 89A.18 *supra*. It is best to file PF 10/77 along with PF 9/77 when paying the national fee. There is no event subsequent to commencement of the United Kingdom phase to trigger a reminder. The examination fee must initially be paid in full on PF 10/77, even if the applicant is entitled to a later remission (see para. 89A.33 *infra*). The above applies even in the rare event of publication taking place under section 16 (see para. 89B.15), since rule 85(3) still applies and measures the period from the priority date.

89A.26 *Priority document*

It is not normally necessary to file a priority document, since this should have been filed in the international phase within 16 months of the priority date. For the procedure when the priority document is not filed in time in the international phase, see para. 89B.07. In the event of an express request for early commencement of United Kingdom processing (see para. 89A.23 *supra*) before 16 months have elapsed from the priority date and the priority document having not yet been filed in the international phase, or in the event of a review under section 89(3) (see para. 89.44), a certified copy of the earlier application must be filed within 16 months of the priority date to support a claim to priority (r. 6(2)).

Translation of priority document   **89A.27**

When the priority document is not in English, a verified translation of the prior-ity document must be filed within two months after the expiry of the prescribed 20 or 30 month period mentioned in para. 89A.18 *supra* (r. 85(2A)(*c*)). Each of these periods is extensible under rule 110(3) and 110(3A), see para. 89.35 *infra*. The determination of the date from which this two months period commences is des-cribed at para. 89A.36 *supra*. The Office is not obliged to, and does not, remind the applicant that a translation of the priority document is outstanding when such trans-lation is required and has not been filed (see para. 89A.15, *supra*).

Statement of inventorship (PF 7/77)   **89A.28**

If indications concerning the inventor were omitted from the request form (PCT/RO/101) pursuant to PCTa. 4(i)(v) and PCTr. 4.6, a statement of inventorship (including the details of the right to the grant of a patent) on PF 7/77 must be filed, but (pursuant to PCTr. 51*bis*.1(*a*)(iv) and 51*bis*.2(*a*)) this may be filed up to two months after expiry of the prescribed 20 or 30 month period (r. 85(3)(*a*)), a period which is extensible under rule 110(3) and 110(3A), see para. 89A.35 *infra*. For the mode of determining the date from which this two month period commences, see para. 89A.36 *infra*.

Indications concerning micro-organisms   **89A.29**

The provisions relating to inventions whose performance requires the use of micro-organisms not available to the public at the (international) filing date are dis-cussed at para. 125A.11. If the information concerning the deposit of the micro-organism required by rule 17(1)(*a*)(iii) (*i.e.* the name of the culture collection, the date of the deposit and the accession number) is only added to the international application after filing and if this information is not in English, a verified translation is required to be filed. Pursuant to PCTr. 49.5(*h*), such translation may be filed up to two months after a notice has been sent by the Comptroller, calling for such translation (r. 85(1A)). This period is extensible at the Comptroller's discretion under rule 110(1).

International exhibition certificate   **89A.30**

If it is desired that disclosure of the invention at an international exhibition (for which see para. 2.27) in the six months preceding the international filing date shall be excluded from the state of the art, due notice must have been included in the supplemental box of the request form (PCT/RO/101) as filed with the application or must have been included in the description (*cf.* r. 5(1) for which see para. 2.32). Also, pursuant to PCTr. 51*bis*.1(a)(vi) and 51*bis*.2(*a*), a certificate from the auth-ority organising the exhibition must be filed in the United Kingdom phase within two months after the expiry of the prescribed 20 or 30 month period (r. 85(2A)(a)), a period which is extensible at the Comptroller's discretion under rule 110(1), see para. 89A.35 *infra*. For the determination of the date of commencement of this two month period, see para. 89A.36 *infra*.

Formal drawings   **89A.31**

It is not normally necessary to file drawings when entering the United Kingdom phase, since these are included in the communication under PCTa. 20. However, when the drawings contain textual matter which must be translated (see para. 89A.19 *supra*), it becomes necessary to file drawings complying with the formal requirements of rule 18 (reprinted at para. 14.03). Drawings filed with the translation may be informal (PCTr. 49.5(*d*)). When such drawings filed with the translation do not comply with the formal requirements, the formalities officer must specify a reasonable period for the applicant to file formal drawings (PCTr. 49.5(*e*)(i)). Similarly, when the international application enters the United Kingdom phase early, *i.e.* before the international publication, the formalities officer may call for formal drawings for the purposes of publication under section 16 (see para. 89B.15).

89A.32 *Prosecution and amendment*

A United Kingdom application number is allotted to the international application upon payment of the national fee and a receipt is issued. A United Kingdom publication number is allotted when preparations for re-publication are about to be completed (see para. 89B.15). In due course, filing particulars are published in the O.J.

It is the usual practice for the examiner to conduct his search under section 17 and substantive examination under section 18 simultaneously in respect of an international application (UK) and the search report (if drawn up separately) accompanies the substantive examination report.

If any citation in the international search report is not in English, the Comptroller can call for a verified translation (for which see para. 123.42) of all or part of the citation to be filed within two months of the direction to furnish such translation (r. 113(3), reprinted in para. 123.12). This period may be extended at the Comptroller's discretion under rule 110(1), for which see para. 89A.35 *infra*. In practice in the case of a foreign patent specification, the Office may accept an English language equivalent.

The conduct of the prosecution in the United Kingdom phase is the same as for an application filed under the Act, for which see paras. 17.17 *et seq.* and 18.14, *et seq.* Amendments can be made under section 19, for which see the commentary thereon. However, prosecution is more compact because there is less time available (see para. 89A.34 *infra*), even though the international filing date and the declared priority date are taken into account when deciding what precedence the application should be given in relation to other applications within the responsibility of the relevant examining group.

89A.33 *Refunds and remission of fees*

As in the case of an application filed under the Act, it is the practice for the Patent Office to refund the search and examination fees in full if the application is withdrawn unconditionally before the United Kingdom search report or first examination report is issued, respectively (see paras. 17.11 and 18.06). Additionally, the Office remits part of the search fee when benefit is obtained from the international search report (r. 102(1)(*b*), reprinted in para. 123.09), and remits an amount equal to the fee paid for international preliminary examination when the Office has drawn up an international preliminary examination report (r. 102(2)). It is not necessary to apply for such remissions. No remission of the United Kingdom examination fee is made when an authority other than the Office has drawn up an international preliminary examination report. Refunds are discussed further at para. 123.25.

Placing application in order   **89A.34**

The period prescribed at rule 85(3)(*c*) under sections 18 and 20 for bringing an international application (UK) into compliance with the Act and Rules is four-and-a-half years from the priority date. This leaves only two years to complete the examination in the case of an application proceeding via Chapter II of the PCT. It is thus necessary to prosecute such applications diligently and correspondence with the Patent Office during the last six months of this period should be marked "URGENT" (see *e.g.* O.J. April 20, 1988). The four-and-a-half year period is extensible under rule 110(3) and 110(3A), see para. 89A.35 *infra*.

Extensions of time   **89A.35**

Virtually all of the periods mentioned in paras. 89A.17 to 89A.34 *supra*, are extensible under rule 110, reprinted at para. 123.10. Specific mention is made where extension is available under rule 110(3) and also where discretionary extension under rule 110(1), or 110(3A) and 110(3C), is possible. Also, where a period is specified in an official report, it may be extended in exceptional circumstances. For obtaining; (i) a discretionary extension under rule 110(1), see para. 123.35; (ii) an automatic extension of one month under rule 110(3), by filing PF 50/77 (reprinted at para. 141.50) with its heavy fee, see para. 123.32; and (iii) a discretionary extension under rule 110(3A) by filing PF 52/77 (reprinted at para. 141.52), together with evidence as to why the relevant date was missed, and later (under r. 110(3C)) PF 53/77 (reprinted at para. 141.53), each with their heavy fee, see para. 123.33.

Only a single PF 50/77, or a single PF 52/77, is required to extend the prescribed 20 or 30 month period mentioned in paras. 89A.18, 89A.19 and 89A.20 *supra* for: paying the national fee; filing the translation, if required, both of the application and of amendments thereto; and filing the verified translation, if required, of the priority document. Similarly, a single PF 50/77, or a single PF 52/77, is sufficient for all of the steps for which a period of two months after expiry of the prescribed 20 or 30 month period is prescribed.

For the effect of a one month extension of the precribed 20 or 30 month period under rule 110(3); and on the calculation of the two month period for filing: (i) PF 9/77 (para. 89A.24); (ii) PF 7/77, if required (para. 89A.28); (iii) a certificate of exhibition, if required (para. 89A.30); (iv) verification of a translation, if required (para. 89A.21); and (v) the verified translation of the priority document (para. 89A.27), see para. 89A.36 *infra*.

Aggregate time limits   **89A.36**

Rule 85(3)(*a*) prescribes that the two month period for filing PF 9/77 runs from the *expiry* of the 20 or 30 month period prescribed at rule 85(1). Such periods are often referred to as "aggregate time limits". To determine the expiry of the prescribed 20 or 30 months period, it is necessary to take into account that the 20 or 30 month period may fall to end on an excluded day, or on the 31st day of a month having only 30 or fewer days, or may be extended under rule 110(3) or 110(3A). For excluded days under section 120(2) and rule 99, see para. 120.05 and for the practice as to calculation of a calender month see RSC Ord. 3, rule 1 (reprinted at para. E003.1), discussed at para. 123.37. The effect of aggregate time limits upon practice under section 89A is best understood by reference to examples.

The following examples all relate to an international application with a priority date (within the meaning of the PCT) as shown and all assume that early national processing was not requested and that the United Kingdom was not elected. The 20 month period prescribed at rule 85(1)(*a*) is thus applicable.

Example 1

 (i) Priority date—Friday, February 12, 1988;
 (ii) Start of United Kingdom phase—Thursday, October 12, 1989;
 (iii) (*a*) PF 9/77 due—Tuesday, December 12, 1989, or
   (*b*) PF 9/77, together with PF 50/77, due—Friday, January 12, 1990.

Example 2

 (i) Priority date—Monday, November 23, 1987;
 (ii) Start of United Kingdom phase—Monday July 24, 1989 (because July 23, 1989 is a Sunday);
 (iii) (*a*) PF 9/77 due—Monday, September 25, 1989 (because September 24, 1989 is a Sunday), or
   (*b*) PF 9/77, together with PF 51/77, due—Tuesday, October 24, 1989.

Example 3

 (i) Priority date—Thursday, March 31, 1988;
 (ii) Start of United Kingdom phase—Thursday, November 30, 1989 (because November has no 31st day);
 (iii) (*a*) PF 9/77 due—Tuesday, January 30, 1990, or
   (*b*) PF 9/77, together with PF 50/77, due Wednesday, February 28, 1990 (because February has no 29th or 30th day).

Example 4

 (i) Priority date—Monday, February 8, 1988;
 (ii) Start of United Kingdom phase when PF 50/77 filed—Wednesday, November 8, 1989;
 (iii) (*a*) PF 9/77 due—Monday, January 8, 1990, or
   (*b*) PF 9/77, together with PF 50/77, due—Thursday, February 8, 1990.

Example 5

 (i) Priority date—Friday, November 27, 1987;
 (ii) Start of United Kingdom phase when PF 50/77 filed—Tuesday, August 29, 1989 (because August 27, 1989 is a Sunday, and Monday, August 28, 1989 is a public holiday in England and Wales);
 (iii) (*a*) PF 9/77 due—Monday, October 30, 1989 (because October 29, 1989 is a Sunday), or
   (*b*) PF 9/77, together with PF 50/77, due—Wednesay, November 29, 1989.

Example 6

 (i) Priority date—Tuesday, May 31, 1988;
 (ii) Start of United Kingdom phase when PF 50/77 filed—Wednesday, February 28, 1990 (because February 1990 has no later day);
 (iii) (*a*) PF 9/77 due—Monday April 30, 1990 (because April 28 and 29, 1990 are a Saturday and a Sunday), or

(b) PF 9/77, together with PF 50/77, due—Monday, May 28, 1990.

These examples show that, in the case of aggregate time limits, the two periods in question should *not* be simply added together.

Although the above examples relate to the filing of PF 9/77 (see para. 89A.24), they are equally valid for the filing of a verified translation of the priority document and PF 7/77 (see paras. 89A.27 and 89A.28 *supra*). They also apply to the filing of a verification of the translation of the application itself (see para. 89A.21) and of a certificate of an international exhibition (see para. 89A.30), except that the two month period for filing these documents is extensible under rule 110(1), rather than requiring the filing of PF 50/77.

All the above examples assume that the filing of PF 50/77 automatically gives an extension of one month. It is not considered whether an extension of less than one month might be obtained. The Patent Office may take the view that, in the case of an extension of the prescribed 20 or 30 month period, the requested extension expires on the date of receipt of PF 50/77, together with the national fee and the translation (if required), thereby advancing the other due dates. Early confirmation of the extension accorded on the filing of PF 50/77 is therefore recommended.

SECTION 89B   89B.01

Adaptation of provisions in relation to international applications

89B.—(1) Where an international application for a patent (UK) is accorded a filing date under the Patent Co-operation Treaty—

(a) **that date, or if the application is re-dated under the Treaty to a later date that later date, shall be treated as the date of filing the application under this Act,**

(b) **any declaration of priority made under the Treaty shall be treated as made under section 5(2) above, and where in accordance with the Treaty any extra days are allowed, the period of 12 months specified in section 5(2) shall be treated as altered accordingly, and**

(c) **any statement of the name of the inventor under the Treaty shall be treated as a statement filed under section 13(2) above.**

(2) If the application, not having been published under this Act, is published in accordance with the Treaty it shall be treated, for purposes other than those mentioned in subsection (3), as published under section 16 above when the conditions mentioned in section 89A(3)(a) are complied with.

(3) For the purposes of section 55 (use of invention for service of the Crown) and section 69 (infringement of rights conferred by publication) the application, not having been published under this Act, shall be treated as published under section 16 above—

(a) **if it is published in accordance with the Treaty in English, on its being so published; and**

(b) **if it is so published in a language other than English—**

(i) **on the publication of a translation of the application in accordance with section 89A(6) above, or**

627

(ii) on the service by the applicant of a translation into English of the specification of the application on the government department concerned or, as the case may be, on the person committing the infringing act.

The reference in paragraph (*b*)(ii) to the service of a translation on a government department or other person is to its being sent by post or delivered to that department or person.

(4) During the international phase of the application, section 8 above does not apply (determination of questions of entitlement in relation to application under this Act) and section 12 above (determination of entitlement in relation to foreign and convention patents) applies notwithstanding the application; but after the end of the international phase, section 8 applies and section 12 does not.

(5) When the national phase begins the comptroller shall refer the application for so much of the examination and search under section 17 and 18 above as he considers appropriate in view of any examination or search carried out under the Treaty.

Note. Section 89B was prospectively added by the 1988 Act (Sched. 5, para. 25). For the commencement of this new section, see the latest Supplement to this Work *re.* this para.: see also the *Note* to para. 89.03.

89B.02   RELEVANT RULES

The following rules are relevant:

rule 6(5)   (*Declaration of priority for the purposes of section 5*) reprinted in para. 5.02;

rule 15(4)   (*Procedure where the applicant is not the inventor or sole inventor*) reprinted in para. 13.03;

rule 85   (*International applications for patents*) reprinted at paras. 89.03 and 89A.02;

rule 100   (*Correction of irregularities*) reprinted at para. 123.07;

rule 101   (*Dispensation by Conptroller*) reprinted at para. 123.08;

rule 102(1)(*b*), (2) (*Remission of fees*) reprinted in para. 123.09; and

rule 110   (*Alteration of time limits*) reprinted at para. 123.10.

89B.03   SECTION 89B—ARTICLE

G. Gall, "Excusal of Failure to Comply with Time Limits under the New Rule 82*bis* PCT and Application of Means of Redress under the EPC", (1986) 17 IIC 618.

COMMENTARY ON SECTION 89B

89B.04   *General*

This is the last of the three sections which are now to deal with international applications (UK). The general remarks at para. 89.13 also apply to the present section, particularly as regards its commencement. Subsection (1) will equate: (*a*) the international filing date with a United Kingdom filing date; (*b*) a declaration of priority under the PCT with a declaration of priority under the Act; and (*c*) indications concerning the inventor under the PCT with a declaration of inventorship under the Act. Subsection (2) will provide that publication under the PCT is not equated with publication under the Act unless and until the application enters the United Kingdom phase. Nevertheless, subsection (3) will ensure that the provisional protection arising on publication may commence as early as the international publication date. Subsection (4) will deal with the Comptroller's power to consider entitlement to international applications. Subsection (5) will concern the search and examination in the United Kingdom phase.

Additionally, correction (in the United Kingdom phase) of errors made in the international phase is discussed at para. 89B.13 *infra*, and the application of more favourable provisions in the United Kingdom phase forms the subject of para. 89B.14 *infra*.

Filing date (subs. (1)(a))   **89B.05**

The object of subsection (1)(*a*) is to ensure that the filing date for the purposes of the Act is the international filing date (PCTa. 11(3)). According to PCTa. 11(1), (2)(*b*), an international filing date is accorded when the minimum requirements set forth in PCTa. 11(1) are met. However, PCTr. 20.2 provides for re-dating of the international application and, in the event of such re-dating, the newly accorded date is regarded as the filing date for the purposes of the Act. If the minimum requirements are not met within 30 days of an invitation to comply with such minimum requirements, the application is not accorded an international filing date and is not regarded as an international application (PCTr. 20.7).

Declaration of priority (subs. (1)(b))   **89B.06**

A declaration of priority under PCTa. 8(1) is, by virtue of subsection (1)(*b*), to be treated as a declaration of priority made under the Act. This is subject to the provision of rule 6(1) (reprinted in para. 5.02) that the declaration of priority be made at the time of filing of the application. This is because PCTa. 8(2) refers to the provisions of Article 4 of the Paris Convention (as revised in the Stockholm Act). Here Article 4D(1) leaves it to member countries to decide when the declaration of priority should be made.

Subsection (1)(*b*) takes into account that the priority term of 12 months may be extended under the PCT. Such extension may, for example, be granted pursuant to PCTr. 82.2 (*Interruption in the mail service*). Similarly, rule 6(5) (reprinted in para. 5.02) equates the filing of a priority document in accordance with the regulations under the PCT with the filing of a priority document under the rules. PCTr. 17.1(*a*) requires that the priority document be filed either at the receiving office, or at the International Bureau, within 16 months of the priority date; or no later than the date of requesting early national processing (see para. 89A.12), if this occurs sooner.

Whereas the priority date within the meaning of the PCT is established at the time of filing, the declared priority date within the meaning of the Act (for which see r. 2(*d*) reprinted in para. 123.04) is only established for an international application (UK) on the condition that a certified copy of the basic application has been filed with the appropriate international authority within 16 months after the priority date claimed (r. 6(5) and PCTr. 17.1).

The filing of a verified translation of the priority document, when required (r. 6(6)), is discussed at para. 89A.27.

89B.07   *Effect of late filing or non-filing of priority document in international phase*

For expected changes to this text consult the latest supplement *re.* this para.

The priority claim is *not* deemed to be withdrawn in the international phase if the certified copy is filed late or not at all (PCTr. 17.1(*c*)); and other time limits prescribed in the PCT, and in particular the date for calculating the 20 or 30 months time limits prescribed in PCTaa. 22 and 39 for meeting the relevant conditions for valid entry into the national phase, are not changed. Some designated offices, *e.g.* the EPO and that of the United States, will still recognise the priority claim if the priority document is filed there in the regional or national phase. It is worth noting that no information is published with the international application as to whether a priority document was filed after expiry of the prescribed 16 month period (PCTr. 17.1) or at all; and all information about the filing and content of priority documents is kept strictly confidential by the International Bureau. The latter does, however, notify the designated offices of the date of receipt of a priority document if this date is after expiry of the 16 month period.

However, so far as the United Kingdom Patent Office (as a designated or elected office) is concerned, the date used for calculating the relevant 20 or 30 months period prescribed in rule 85(1) *is* changed if priority is denied so far as the United Kingdom is concerned on account of the certified copy not having been timely filed in the international phase. Loss of priority, with corresponding displacement of the date for calculating the 20 or 30 month period, occurs in both the international and the United Kingdom phase if a notice of withdrawal of the claim to priority reaches the International Bureau or the receiving office within 20 months of the would-be priority date (PCTr. 32*bis*).

It would seem that, if the priority document is filed with the relevant international authority, but later than expiry of the prescribed 16 month period, the applicant has (by virtue of PCTa. 48(2)(*a*) and PCTr. 82*bis*) the possibility of requesting one month's extension under rule 110(3) and/or a discretionary extension under rule 110(3A) by filing PF 50/77 and/or PF 52/77 when entering the United Kingdom phase, for which see para. 89A.35. Such form or forms must accompany the national fee and the translation, if required, or otherwise their belated filing would also have to be excused. The Office cannot require the filing of any forms prior to entry into the United Kingdom phase (PCTa. 23(1)).

It is moot as to whether the applicant can file the priority document together with PF 52/77 at the Patent Office when paying the national fee and filing the translation, if required, or thereafter. Such a possibility was not available at the time of the decisions in *Matsushita's Application*, ([1983] RPC 105) and *Brossman's Application* ([1983] RPC 109). In both cases it was held that the then rule 6(5) did not enable the option under PCTr. 17.1(*c*), that designated offices may still recognise the priority claim when the priority document has not been timely filed, to be recognised for the designation of the United Kingdom. In the latter decision it is implied that a one month extension could have been obtained under a previous version of rule 110(3) but that there was no power under a previous version of rule 100 to extend further the period for filing the priority document.

The *PCT Applicant's Guide*, at Vol. I, Annex B1, GB, states that the priority claim is disregarded in the United Kingdom if the priority document is not filed within the prescribed 16 month period. The *PCT Applicant's Guide* at Vol. II, National Chapter, GB, para. GB.18, describes time limits which relate to entry into the United Kingdom phase and which are extensible under rule 110(3) or 110(3A) but makes no reference to the priority document itself. However, the preceding para. GB.17 refers to paras. 57 to 61 of the General Part to *PCT Applicant's Guide*, Vol. II. There, at para. 57, it is expressly stated that "All national provisions relating to the excusing of delays must be applied to international appli-

cations in the same way and under the same conditions as they are to national applications". The authority for this lies in PCTa. 48(2)(*a*) and PCTr. 82*bis*.

The designation of the inventor for the United Kingdom (subs. (1)(c))   **89B.08**

If the inventor is the applicant, or one of several applicants for an international
application (UK), then the international request form (PCT/RO/101) may say so
(PCTa. 4(1)(v) and PCTr. 4.6), and no action is then required in the United Kingdom phase to name the inventor. If the inventor is not an applicant, but he is
named on the international request form (PCT/RO/101), again no action is needed
in the United Kingdom phase. If the inventor is not named in the international
phase, then PF 7/77 must be filed at the Patent Office on or shortly after entry into
the United Kingdom phase (see para. 89A.28).

Effect of international publication (subs. (2))   **89B.09**

When international publication under PCTa. 21 takes place in the international
phase, as it normally does, then this replaces publication under section 16
(s. 89A(1)). However, if the application enters the United Kingdom phase before
international publication, as may happen when requesting early commencement of
national processing (see para. 89A.12), then the Office must publish the application under section 16. Subsection (2) ensures that, even when international publication takes place after valid entry into the United Kingdom phase, such
international publication is equivalent to publication under section 16, notwithstanding section 89A(1), but subject to subsection (3), unless actual publication
under section 16 takes place before international publication. These matters are
relevant to the prior art effect (for which see para. 89B.10 *infra*) and to the provisional protection arising on publication, for which see para. 89B.11 *infra*).

Prior art effect under section 2(3)   **89B.10**

The prior art effect of an international application (UK), for the purposes of section 2(3), is to come into effect immediately on entry into the United Kingdom
phase, assuming that international publication has taken place, and cannot subsequently be lost, even if the application is withdrawn in the United Kingdom
phase. This is consequential to subsection (2). Conversely, an international application (UK) which is withdrawn or deemed withdrawn in the international phase
(s. 89(2)), or otherwise does not enter the United Kingdom phase (s. 89A(4)), is
never to form part of the state of the art for the purposes of section 2(3). The prior
art effect under section 2(3) is discussed more fully in paras. 2.19–2.24.

For international applications which entered the United Kingdom phase before
the new sections 89, 89A and 89B are brought into force by applying Sched. 5,
para. 25 [1988]), the question as to whether the prior art effect under section 2(3) is
lost if the application was withdrawn or deemed withdrawn after entry into the
United Kingdom phase depends on whether a withdrawal or deemed withdrawal in
the United Kingdom phase was under section 14(9) or under the original section
89(8) (reprinted in para. 89.02). Since at this stage the application would have been
proceeding under Parts I and III of the Act, an argument could be developed that
the original section 89(8) could not be operative after entry into the United Kingdom phase. In any case, this original provision does not cover refusal of the application. It would be strange if a different result would obtain, depending on whether
the application was withdrawn or refused.

89B.11 *Provisional protection arising on publication (subs. (3))*

The provisions of subsection (3) are to be an exception to the generality of subsection (2) according to which an international application (UK) is not to be deemed to be published for the purposes of the Act (as discussed at para. 89B.09 *supra*) until valid entry into the United Kingdom phase has taken place. If the international application is published in the international phase in English, the provisional protection (*i.e.* the right to recover payment under s. 55 (*Crown use*), and the right to recover damages under s. 69 (*Infringement after publication*)) is to be retrospective back to the international publication date (subs. (3)(*a*)). If the international application is published in the international phase in any other language, the provisional protection is to be obtained by meeting the relevant conditions and by requesting publication of a translation by filing this with PF 43/77 (reprinted at para. 141.43) (subs. (3)(*b*) and r. 85(2)). Routine re-publication by the Patent Office (see para. 89B.15) is of no consequence since it is not under section 16 (*PCT Applicant's Guide*, at Vol. II, National Chapter, GB, para. GB.07). Nevertheless, earlier protection can still be obtained by sending a translation to the relevant government department or to the infringer, as the case may be. In view of the references to publication in sections 55(4), 69(1) and 89A(3)(*b*), it is not possible to recover payment or damages in respect of any Crown use or infringement before the international publication date. If the international application (UK) enters the United Kingdom phase, and the application is published under section 16 (see para. 89B.15 *infra*), before international publication has taken place, the provisional protection arising on publication by virtue of sections 55 and 69 commences when publication under section 16 takes place.

89B.12 *Disputes as to entitlement (subs. (4))*

Subsection (4) ensures that a dispute as to the right to be granted a patent or patents pursuant to an international application is governed in the international phase by section 12 and not by section 8. However, once the application has entered the United Kingdom phase (assuming it does), the dispute is then conducted under section 8. Nevertheless, section 12 will continue to apply in respect of a European phase (even if a United Kingdom designation is included in the Euro-PCT application) and in respect of the continued processing of the international application in other countries.

It has been held that the repealed subsection 89(6) (reprinted in para. 89.02) concerns only the question of whether an entitlement dispute should be brought under section 8 or under section 12; thus the wording of the repealed subsection 89(6) could not be used to affect the meaning of the repealed subsection 89(1) (*Masuda's Application*, [1987] RPC 37). Subsection (4) replaces the repealed subsection 89(6).

89B.13 *Correction of errors arising in international phase*

Corrections of obvious clerical errors can be authorised by the international authorities (PCTr. 91), as described in the *PCT Applicant's Guide*, at Vol. I, paras. 276–278. The correction of clerical errors does not fall within the expression "publication, search, examination and amendment" as used in subsection 89A(1), so that the United Kingdom Patent Office may consider that it has a right to review any corrections authorised in the international phase, just as it has been held that rule 100 can be applied to correct a demand for international preliminary examination even though this would have retrospective effect (*Prangley's Application*,

[1988] RPC 187 (CA)). As the conditions for correction of a clerical error under the PCT are more stringent than those under section 117 and rule 91(2), the Office is unlikely to refuse to recognise a correction authorised by an international authority unless the international authority itself was wrong to authorise the correction. However, in the absence of replacement wording for rule 85 to be made consequent on bring into effect new sections 89–89B, the statements *infra* are rather speculative and the latest Supplement to this Work should particularly be consulted in relation to this para. 89B.13.

With at least one important exception, it is open to the applicant to apply under section 117 during the United Kingdom phase for correction of a clerical error made in the international phase, even when an international authority has refused to authorise correction. The Patent Office is obliged to afford the applicant the more favourable conditions available under section 117 and rule 91(2), particularly in relation to documents other than the specification (PCTa. 26). This is discussed further at para. 89B.14, *infra*. Rule 85(4A) (reprinted in para. 89.03) empowers the Comptroller to enter corrections on documents filed in the international phase.

If authorisation to correct a clerical error is refused by an international authority, the fact of refusal may, at the applicant's request, be published with the international application (PCTr. 91.1(*f*)). In the absence of any publication of the fact that correction was applied for, it may be essential or advisable to commence early national processing (see para. 89A.12) in order to have the request for correction considered as soon as possible by the Patent Office as the Office must consider the effect on third parties of a correction material to the information revealed by the pamphlet published by the International Bureau (for which see para. 89.18). Important matters in this connection are a correction to a claim to priority (discussed at para. 89B.06, *supra*), and a correction by adding the designation of the United Kingdom to the international request, as next discussed. If the fact of refusal to authorise a correction appears in the international publication of the application, the need to request early national processing may be less pressing.

The addition of the designation of the United Kingdom to an international application is a correction that can be authorised by an international authority (see *Vapocure Technologies' Application*, SRIS O/178/87 and C/30/88 and C/74/89, noted *The Times*, August 25, 1989 (CA)). However, any authorisation for correction of a clerical error must (except in the case of a correction authorised by an international preliminary examining authority) reach the International Bureau before preparations for publication of the international application have been completed if it is to be effective (PCTr. 91.1(*g*)(ii) and 91.1(*g-bis*)), see the *Vapocure* case (*supra*) and also *Hemosol's Application* (SRIS O/15/87, noted IPD 10111). In the *Vapocure* case (*supra*), the authorisation of correction reached the International Bureau too late so that the United Kingdom was not included among the designated countries listed in the published pamphlet. The relevant conditions were complied with at the Patent Office within the prescribed 20 month period. The Comptroller held that there was no United Kingdom application in existence upon which he could exercise any discretion in favour of the applicant and that he had no power to add the United Kingdom to the countries designated in the international application. The first of these reasons is no longer applicable in view of the insertion of section 123(3A) (for which see para. 123.36); and, as regards the second reason, it may be inferred that, had the authorisation for the correction reached the International Bureau in time, all would have been well, particularly in view of the decision in *Prangley's Application* (*supra*).

It may be assumed that, had the new subsection 123(3A) been in force at the time of the *Vapocure* case (*supra*), the Comptroller would have had power to exercise discretion but he would still likely have refused the correction in the public interest as the published pamphlet did not mention the United Kingdom. There would have been a parallel with *EPO Decision J* 03/81 (OJEPO 3/1982, 100), where the adding of a country designation by way of a correction of a clerical error would have been allowed but for the need to protect the interests of the public in being able to rely upon the information given in officially published documents.

89B.14 *More favourable law and excusing delay (PCTaa. 26, 27 and 48)*

PCTa. 26 requires that the Patent Office shall not reject an international application (UK) for non-compliance with the PCT or its Regulations without first giving the applicant time to correct the application to the extent that is permissible under the Act and Rules in comparable circumstances. This provision cannot be used to overcome an objection on the ground of non-compliance with an express provision of the Act or Rules pursuant to the PCT but it does allow the provisions of Parts I and III of the Act and the Rules thereunder to be applied to things done or not done in the international phase. In connection with PCTa. 27(4), (5) and (6), the provisions of the Act relating to such things as novelty, inventive step, industrial application, exclusion from patentability and unity of invention are essentially the same as those of the PCT. Accordingly, the opportunities to use PCTa. 26 are not great and are confined mainly to errors made by the international authorities, clerical errors and time limits. However, it may be that the new wording to replace present rule 85 when sections 89–89B are brought into effect will deal with some of the deficiencies noted *infra*. The latest Supplement to this Work should therefore be particularly consulted in relation to this para. 89B.14.

Certain errors made by international authorities are covered by rule 85(4A) (reprinted in para. 89.03). Under this, the international filing date and the particulars of the claim to priority can be corrected and, in view of the power of the Comptroller under this rule to alter *any* prescribed period, he can extend any specified period for filing documents and paying fees, when such period becomes exceeded following the correction. It is, however, unlikely that he can extend the priority period under the Paris Convention, as this is determined by PCTa. 8(2)(*a*) by virtue of subsection (1)(*b*) (see also para. 89B.06 *supra*).

Clerical errors made in the international phase can be corrected under section 117 after the application has entered the United Kingdom phase because the international application is deemed to be a United Kingdom application for the purposes of Part III of the Act (s.89(1)).

Time limits must be considered in conjunction with PCTa. 48(2)(*a*) and PCTr. 82*bis* whereby the Comptroller must extend any time limit prescribed by the PCT or its Regulations or specified by any office (including the Patent Office) acting as an international authority, if an extension would be available under the Act or the Rules or by virtue of practice thereunder. Periods coming into consideration here include the period prescribed for filing the priority document and the periods specified for correcting deficiencies revealed during the examination by the Receiving Office. The latter deficiencies would include failure to file a specification and/or drawings complying with the physical requirements of PCTr. 11 within the period specified by the receiving office or as extended by that office under PCTa. 14 and PCTr. 26. Since a failure to correct such deficiencies will result in the international application being withdrawn (PCTa. 14(1)(*b*)), PCTaa. 26 and 48 can in such circumstances only be pleaded before the Patent Office in conjunction with a simultaneous request for a review under PCTa. 25 and subsection 89(3) involving the filing of PF 44/77, for which see para. 89.35.

Since the failure to file the priority document within the prescribed time limit in the international phase does not result in the international application being deemed withdrawn, the filing of a PF 50/77 or PF 52/77 at the Patent Office to seek an appropriate extension does not (on the present wording of r. 85) entail a simultaneous request on PF 44/77. This is discussed at para. 89B.07 *supra*, where there is a quotation from the *PCT Applicant's Guide*.

In such a case as does not entail a request for review by filing PF 44/77 (reprinted at para. 141.44), it may be desirable to request early national processing before the Patent Office under PCTa. 23(2) or 40(2) (for which see para. 89A.12) in order to give an opportunity for appropriate advertisements, *e.g.* under rule 91(3), to be inserted in the O.J. before or as soon as possible after international publication.

Rule 85(4A) implements PCTr. 82*ter*, although it might be thought that rules 100 and 101 and section 117 already give the Comptroller the necessary powers. It is not clear why there is no express provision to implement PCTr. 82*bis*, especially having regard to the difficulty of applying the provisions of rule 110 to the international phase, but perhaps the point will be dealt with in the replacement wording for rule 85.

It is to be observed that any decision of the Comptroller after valid entry into the United Kingdom phase, and involving the applicability of PCTaa. 26 and 48 and PCTrr. 82*bis* and 82*ter*, is appealable to the Patents Court and to higher authorities.

The article by G. Gall (listed in para. 89B.03 *supra*), discusses the inter-relationship between PCTaa. 25 and 48 and PCTrr. 82*bis* and 82*ter*.

Publication and re-publication   **89B.15**

Normally, international publication (para. 89.18) takes place before entry into the United Kingdom phase and, in this event, there is *no* publication under the provisions of section 16 (see para. 89B.09, *supra*). Nevertheless, it is the policy of the Patent Office then to re-publish the application as soon as convenient after entry into the United Kingdom phase. When the international application is published in English, such re-publication takes the form of a single sheet containing a reference to the international publication, all the usual bibliographical data (see para. 16.07) and the abstract, together with one or more accompanying figures of the drawings, if any. When a translation of the international application has to be filed to secure valid entry into the United Kingdom phase, the re-publication includes such translation in its entirety.

The re-publication just described is of *no* legal significance. In particular, re-publication including a translation *cannot* establish provisional protection under the provisions of sections 55 and 69, for which see para. 89B.11 *supra*.

Entry into the United Kingdom phase may take place before international publication takes place, *e.g.* on conversion into a United Kingdom application after review under section 89(3) (for which see para. 89.35), or after an express request for early national processing under section 89A(3)(*b*) (for which see para. 89A.12). Because section 89A(1) then ceases to apply, the Comptroller must publish the application in full under section 16 by virtue of section 89(1). Unless the international application (UK) or the designation of the United Kingdom was wrong-fully deemed withdrawn and the application proceeded in the United Kingdom by virtue of section 89(3), publication under PCTa. 21 will also take place in due course.

Such international publication, or publication under section 16, whichever occurs first, establishes the prior art effect (for which see para. 89B.10 *supra*) and (subject to any language requirement) the provisional protection arising on publication (for which see para. 89B.11 *supra*).

Search in the United Kingdom phase (subs. (5))   **89B.16**

This subsection gives the Comptroller discretion to restrict the search made under section 17, having regard to the extent of the international search. It will always be necessary to search United Kingdom, European and international applications published after the international search commenced, in case any such recently published applications have a priority or filing date earlier than the international filing date, which may make them citable under section 2(1) or 2(3).

The Comptroller may remit all or a part of the United Kingdom search fee, depending upon the benefit obtained from the international search report (r. 102(1)(*b*), and see para. 89A.33). It would seem that, in the occasional event of the international search report being established after the application has entered the United Kingdom phase (*e.g.* when there has been an express request for early national processing as described at para. 89A.23), whereby the United Kingdom provisions as to search under section 17 apply rather than those under the PCT, the Comptroller may still take note of the resulting international search report and remit part of the United Kingdom search fee.

89B.17 *Examination in the United Kingdom phase (subs. (5))*

The search in the United Kingdom phase is covered by para. 89B.16 *supra*. Pursuant to the filing of PF 10/77, the Examiner conducts the substantive examination under section 18(2), or just so much examination as is deemed necessary having regard to any international preliminary examination report established under Chapter II of the PCT (subs. (5)). Evidently, notice can be taken of such report even if it is not established before or does not reach the Patent Office before the commencement of the United Kingdom phase. See para. 89A.33 for remission of the examination fee under rule 102(2).

Nevertheless, amendments made during international preliminary examination must be disregarded unless they reach the Patent Office by commencement of the United Kingdom phase, either by virtue of the timely communication of the international examination report or by being filed by the applicant (see para. 89A.14). However, such amendments may still be filed under section 18 as described at para. 89B.18 *infra*.

If any document cited in the international search report is not in English, the Comptroller is, apparently, not entitled to ask for an English translation of all or a part of such documents ((see the wording of r. 113(3), reprinted in para. 123.12), but he is likely to do so if no corresponding English text is available to him.

The examination under section 18 must include a check to ensure that any amendments made in the international phase as well as any amendments made in the United Kingdom phase do not contravene new section 76(2) (see para. 89B.18 *infra*).

89B.18 *Amendment in the United Kingdom phase*

As soon as the application enters the United Kingdom phase, amendment becomes subject to section 19 and rule 36 thereunder (for which see paras. 19.03 and 19.05). Thus, voluntary amendments can be lodged at any time up to issuance of the first examination report or when responding thereto. These amendments can comprise or include amendments filed in the international phase but disregarded because they did not reach the Patent Office in time, or because a translation did not reach the Patent Office in time (see para. 89A.14). The Patent Office is obliged to give the applicant at least one opportunity to amend (PCTa. 28(1)). All amendments, whether made in the international or United Kingdom phase must not contravene new section 76(2) (*Amendment of applications not to include new subject matter*), see also PCTa. 28(2)).

Division **89B.19**

The PCT contains no provisions as to the filing of divisional applications, but an international application (UK) can be divided in the United Kingdom phase in the same way as any application filed under the Act (see paras. 15.13–15.21 and 15.28–15.32). Note that the time available for placing such a divisional application in order (see para. 89B.21 *infra*) may be very short, especially if the patent application was subjected to international preliminary examination under PCT Chapter II.

Withdrawal in the United Kingdom phase **89B.20**

Withdrawal in the United Kingdom phase is effected under section 14(9) (discussed at paras. 14.31 and 14.39). Withdrawal or deemed withdrawal in the international phase is governed by section 89(2) (for which see para. 89.34) and by section 89A(4) (for which see para. 89A.13).

Compliance with the Act and Rules **89B.21**

An international application (UK) must be placed in order under sections 18 and 20 within the four-and-a-half years prescribed by rule 85(3)(*c*). Because of the "delay" obtained by use of the PCT, the time available for examination by the Patent Office is reduced as compared with an application initially filed under the Act.

PRACTICE UNDER SECTION 89B

Prosecution in the United Kingdom phase **89B.22**

Search, examination and amendment in the United Kingdom phase are covered by paras. 89A.32 *et seq.* which are closely interrelated with the formalities upon, and after, entry into the United Kingdom phase.

SECTION 90 **90.01**

Orders in Council as to convention countries

90.—(1) Her Majesty may with a view to the fulfilment of a treaty or international convention, arrangement or engagement, by Order in Council declare that any country specified in the Order is a convention country for the purposes of section 5 above.

(2) Her Majesty may by Order in Council direct that any of the Channel Islands, any colony [*or any British protectorate or protected state*] shall be taken to be a convention country for those purposes.

(3) For the purposes of subsection (1) above every colony, protectorate, and territory subject to the authority or under the suzerainty of another country, and every territory administered by another country under the trusteeship system of the United Nations shall be taken to be a country in the case of which a declaration may be made under that subsection.

Note. Subsection (2) was amended by the Statute Laws (Repeals) Act 1986 (c. 12).

COMMENTARY ON SECTION 90

90.02 *General*

Section 90 corresponds to section 68 [1949] and provides for countries, by Order in Council, to be declared "convention countries" for the purposes of the claiming of priority under section 5. Similar Orders made under previous patent statutes are continued as if made under the Act (Sched. 4, para. 9(1)). Such countries are mainly, although not completely, the member countries of the Paris Convention (1883, as revised). Thus, Bangladesh, India and Pakistan are three countries made convention countries under the Act but which are not members of the Paris Union. Other countries in this category are some of those which provide patent protection within their territory only by way of registration of United Kingdom patents. These and other countries may effectively be designated more for the purpose of registering trade marks with priority rather than for patents. Normally, a territory is designated a convention country in respect of patents, trade marks and designs.

The United Kingdom is itself not a convention country for the purposes of the Act, see *Agfa-Gevaert's Application* ([1982] RPC 441).

There are also minor differences between the list of countries to which exempting powers with regard to infringement exist under section 60(4)–(7) and to which section 90 does not apply, see further para. 60.22.

90.03 *Countries designated as "convention countries"*

The list of convention countries currently designated as such by effective Orders in Council is:

Algeria	Finland	Kenya
Argentina	France	Korea
Australia	Gabon	(Republic of [South])
Austria	German Democratic	Lebanon
Bahamas	Republic	Libya
Bangladesh*	(East Germany)	Liechtenstein
Barbados	German Federal	Luxembourg
Belgium	Republic	Madagascar
Belize	(West Germany)	Malaysia
Benin	Ghana	Malawi
Brazil	Greece	Mali
Bulgaria	Guinea	Malta
Burkino Faso	Guinea-Bissau	Mauritania
Burundi	Haiti	Mauritius
Cameroon	Hong Kong*	Mexico
Canada	Hungary	Monaco
Central African	Iceland	Mongolia
Republic	India*	Morocco
Chad	Indonesia	Netherlands
China	Iran	New Zealand
Congo	Iraq	Niger
Cuba	Ireland	Nigeria
Cyprus	Israel	Norway
Czechoslovakia	Italy	Pakistan*
Denmark	Ivory Coast	Philippines
Dominican Republic	Japan	Poland
Egypt	Jordan	Portugal

Roumania	Sweden	U.S.A.
Ruanda	Switzerland	U.S.S.R.
San Marino	Syria	Uruguay
Senegal	Tanzania*	Vatican (Holy See)
Singapore*	Togo	Viet Nam
South Africa	Trinidad and	Yugoslavia
Spain	Tobago	Zaire
Sri Lanka	Tunisia	Zambia
Sudan	Turkey	Zimbabwe
Surinam	Uganda	

The countries marked with an asterisk are *not* members of the Paris Convention. In addition, Ecuador is recognised as a convention country for trade marks and designs only. It should be noted that, though the Democratic People's Republic of [North] Korea is a member of the Paris Convention, this country is not recognised by H.M. Government. Also, there is some doubt as to the status, as convention countries, of Myanmar (Burma), Honduras and Pakistan.

Effect of incorrect designation of convention country on Patent Office **90.04**

The Patent Office is not in a position to question whether the wording of an Order in Council is *ultra vires*. Therefore, if it is felt that, because of political changes in the status of a country, such ought not to have been treated as a "convention country" under section 90 so that priority under section 5 was improperly accorded by the Comptroller, relief from the court should be sought by way of judicial review under RSC Ord. 53, r. 1 (reprinted at E53.1), see *Dirks' Applications* ([1960] RPC 1).

SECTION 91

Evidence of conventions and instruments under conventions

91.—(1) Judicial notice shall be taken of the following, that is to say— **91.01**
(*a*) the European Patent Convention, the Community Patent Convention and the Patent Co-operation Treaty (each of which is hereafter in this section referred to as the relevant convention);
(*b*) any bulletin, journal or gazette published under the relevant convention and the register of European or Community patents kept under it; and
(*c*) any decision of, or expression of opinion by, the relevant convention court on any question arising under or in connection with the relevant convention.
(2) Any document mentioned in subsection (1)(*b*) above shall be admissible as evidence of any instrument or other act thereby communicated of any convention institution.
(3) Evidence of any instrument issued under the relevant convention by any such institution, including any judgment or order of the relevant convention court, or of any document in the custody of any such institution or

639

reproducing in legible form any information in such custody otherwise than in legible form, or any entry in or extract from such a document, may be given in any legal proceedings by production of a copy certified as a true copy by an official of that institution; and any document purporting to be such a copy shall be received in evidence without proof of the official position or handwriting of the person signing the certificate.

(4) Evidence of any such instrument may also be given in any legal proceedings—

(*a*) by production of a copy purporting to be printed by the Queen's Printer;

(*b*) where the instrument is in the custody of a government department, by production of a copy certified on behalf of the department to be a true copy by an officer of the department generally or specially authorised to do so;

and any document purporting to be such a copy as is mentioned in paragraph (*b*) above of an instrument in the custody of a department shall be received in evidence without proof of the official position or handwriting of the person signing the certificate, or of his authority to do so, or of the document being in the custody of the department.

(5) In any legal proceedings in Scotland evidence of any matter given in a manner authorised by this section shall be sufficient evidence of it.

(6) In this section—

"convention institution" means an institution established by or having functions under the relevant convention;

"relevant convention court" does not include a court of the United Kingdom or of any other country which is a party to the relevant convention; and

"legal proceedings", in relation to the United Kingdom, includes proceedings before the comptroller.

COMMENTARY ON SECTION 91

91.02   *General*

   Section 91 is the first of a group of sections (ss. 91–95) the effect of which is to give statutory force to certain provisions relating to the EPC, CPC and PCT and to provide for various consequential matters and publications.
   Subsection (1) provides that judicial notice is to be taken of: the EPC, CPC and PCT ("the relevant convention") (para. (*a*)), for further details of which see para. 130.08; any bulletin or publication under the EPC, CPC or PCT and including the European register (para. (*b*)); and any decision or opinion by a relevant court (para. (*c*)). By subsection (2), any document under subsection (1)(*b*) is to be admissible as evidence; and, by subsection (3), certified copies of instruments issued by a "convention institution" (as defined in subs. (6)) are to be accepted in evidence. By subsection (4) copies of such instruments printed by the Queen's Printer are to be accepted in evidence, as are certified copies of documents in the custody of a government department, without proof of the signature of the officer

certifying the copy. Subsection (5) provides for evidence in proceedings in Scotland.

Subsection (6) defines (though only for the purposes of section 91): "convention institution" as an institution established under the relevant convention; "relevant convention court" to exclude any national court in the EEC, and therefore (for the purposes of section 91) to be a supra-national tribunal established by a "convention institution"; and "legal proceedings" to include proceedings before the Comptroller.

Application of section 91 in practice   **91.03**

In *Rotocrop* v. *Genbourne* ([1982] FSR 241) the Patents Court noted that under section 91(1) judicial notice had to be taken of *inter alia* the EPC. Accordingly, the principles of the Protocol to EPCa. 69 were taken into account in considering the question of infringement of a patent granted under the 1949 Act, on which see para. 125.12. Section 91(1) was also relied upon in *John Wyeth's and Schering's Applications* ([1985] RPC 545) where the Patents Court decided to follow a decision of the EPO Enlarged Board of Appeal in preference to a well-established precedent under British law in order to achieve a harmonious interpretation of the EPC, see para. 2.29.

However, as K. Bruckhausen (of the Patent Senate of the German Supreme Court) has stated, "The EPO must accept the national courts' judgment as to the validity and interpretation of the patents it grants and their assessment of the ambit of protection" (*EPI Information* 2–1988, 148 at 164); and, in *Genentech's Patent* ([1989] RPC 147 (CA)), it was observed that section 91(1)(*c*) is directed to evidentiary matters, so that a judgment under the relevant convention does not have to be proved as foreign law, but the provision does not give other courts any greater status than they would otherwise have possessed. Also, the EPO Guidelines do *not* have binding authority (*EPO Decision T 42/84*, "*Alumina spinel/EXXON*", [1988] 6 EPOR 387).

SECTION 92   92.01

Obtaining evidence for proceedings under the European Patent Convention

92.—(1) Sections 1 to 3 of the Evidence (Proceedings in Other Jurisdictions) Act 1975 [c. 34] (provisions enabling United Kingdom courts to assist in obtaining evidence for foreign courts) shall apply for the purpose of proceedings before a relevant convention court under the European Patent Convention as they apply for the purpose of civil proceedings in a court exercising jurisdiction in a country outside the United Kingdom.

(2) In the application of those sections by virtue of this section any reference to the High Court, the Court of Session or the High Court of Justice in Northern Ireland shall include a reference to the comptroller.

(3) Rules under this Act may include provision—

(*a*) as to the manner in which an application under section 1 of the said Act of 1975 is to be made to the comptroller for the purpose of proceedings before a relevant convention court under the European Patent Convention; and (*b*) subject to the provisions of that Act as to the circumstances in which an order can be made under section 2 of that Act on any such application.

(4) Rules of court and rules under this Act may provide for an officer of the European Patent Office to attend the hearing of an application under section 1 of that Act before the court or the comptroller, as the case may be, and examine the witnesses or request the court or comptroller to put specified questions to the witnesses.

(5) Section 1(4) of the Perjury Act 1911 [1 & 2 Geo. 5, c. 6] and **article 3(4) of the Perjury (Northern Ireland) Order 1979** [S.I. 1979 No. 1714], [*section 1(4) of the Perjury Act (Northern Ireland) 1946*] (statements made for the purposes, among others, of judicial proceedings in a tribunal of a foreign state) shall apply in relation to proceedings before a relevant convention court under the European Patent Convention as they apply to a judicial proceedings in a tribunal of a foreign state.

Note. Amendment of subsection (5) was effected by S.I. 1979 No. 1714.

RELEVANT RULE

Obtaining evidence for proceedings under European Patent Convention

92.02   86.—(1) An application to the comptroller under section 1 of the Evidence (Proceedings in Other Jurisdictions) Act 1975 [c. 34], as applied by section 92 of the Act for an order for evidence to be obtained in the United Kingdom shall be made *ex parte* on Patents Form No. 45/77 and shall be accompanied by an affidavit made by a person duly authorised in that behalf by the relevant convention court, evidencing that the request is made in pursuance of a request issued by or on behalf of that court and that the evidence to which the application relates is to be obtained for the purposes of civil proceedings before it.

(2) After such an application as is mentioned in paragraph (1) above has been made, an *ex parte* application for a further order or directions in relation to the same matter may be made to the comptroller in writing.

(3) The comptroller may allow an officer of the European Patent Office to attend the hearing of such an application as is mentioned in paragraph (1) above and examine the witnesses or request the comptroller to put specified questions to them.

92.03   COMMENTARY ON SECTION 92

Section 92 is the second of the group of sections (ss. 91–92) which give statutory force to certain provisions relating to the EPC, CPC and PCT.

Sections 1–3 of the Evidence (Proceedings in Other Jurisdictions) Act 1975

(c. 34) provide for dealing with "letters of request" ("letters rogatory") by which foreign courts ask a United Kingdom court to assist it in the taking of evidence in matters proceeding before the foreign court. Section 92(1) extends the operation of the 1975 statute to proceedings in a relevant convention court under the EPC. In court proceedings, this operation is governed by RSC Order 70, rule 2 (reprinted at para. E070.2). By subsection (2) the provisions of these sections of the 1975 Act apply also to proceedings before the Comptroller. The relevant procedure is set out in rule 86 (reprinted in para. 92.02 *supra*) which was made under the authority of subsection (3).

The term "relevant convention court" is defined in section 130(1) and is discussed in para. 103.02.

Subsection (4) is an independent provision which provides for rules to permit the attendance at a hearing before the court or the Comptroller of an officer of the EPO. Rule 86(3) has been made accordingly. On such attendance the EPO office may examine witnesses or require the Comptroller to put specified questions to a witness. RSC, Ord. 70, r. 2(3) (reprinted in para. E070.2) provides the court with a similar power.

Subsection (5) is a further provision independent of the remainder of the section. It extends the application of the perjury statutes to any evidence given before a relevant convention court under the EPC, thereby permitting proceedings for perjury to be brought in the United Kingdom in respect of evidence given under the EPC abroad, for example in proceedings before the EPO.

PRACTICE UNDER SECTION 92   **92.04**

An application to the Comptroller under section 92(2) and rule 86 is made on PF 45/77 (reprinted at para. 141.45) by the relevant convention court or its representative and must be accompanied by an affidavit. This must have been made by a person duly authorised for the purpose by the relevant convention court which seeks assistance in obtaining evidence for proceedings before it under the EPC, CPC or PCT as the case may be. This affidavit should set out the nature of the request made and aver that the evidence requested is required for the purposes of civil proceedings before that court. The request may, for example, be for the attendance of named witnesses, who may be required to produce specified documents and things and who may be required to submit to cross-examination. RSC Ord. 70, rule 2(1) and (2) makes similar provisions for corresponding procedure before the High Court.

The application, whether before the court or the Comptroller, is to be made by or on behalf of the convention court *ex parte*, and will normally lead to the giving of further directions for the procedure to be followed and the scope of the enquiry permitted. Before the Comptroller such requirement may be made in writing (r. 86(2)). The convention court should take care to formulate its request in sufficiently broad terms, as the tribunal may not permit evidence to be given before it which goes beyond the scope of the request, as established by the accompanying affidavit.

Llewelyn and Small have discussed ([1985] EIPR 81) the probable absence of privilege against self-incrimination during evidence given in response to a request from a foreign court by letters rogatory, and the effect on such evidence of section 72 of the Supreme Court Act 1981 (c. 54), for which see para. 104.06.

The normal practice on the taking of evidence will be for a transcript of the proceedings before the tribunal to be signed as a correct record of the proceedings and for this then to be transmitted to the court which made the request for assistance.

93.01   SECTION 93

Enforcement of orders for costs

93. If the European Patent Office orders the payment of costs in any proceedings before it—

(a) in England and Wales the costs shall, if a county court so orders, be recoverable by execution issued from the county court or otherwise as if they were payable under an order of that court;

(b) in Scotland the order may be enforced in like manner as a recorded decree arbitral,

(c) in Northern Ireland the order may be enforced as if it were a money judgment;

(d) in the Isle of Man the order may be enforced in like manner as an execution issued out of the court.

Note. Amendment of this section was effected by S.I. 1978 No. 621.

93.02   COMMENTARY ON SECTION 93

Section 93 is the third of the group of sections (ss. 91–95) which give statutory effect to certain provisions and operation of the EPC, CPC and PCT. It provides for the enforcement of payment of costs awarded by the EPO; payment can be enforced by a county court order or the equivalent in Scotland, Northern Ireland or the Isle of Man in like manner as for costs awarded by the Comptroller, for which see para. 107.06.

                                    SECTION 94

Communication of information to the European Patent Office, etc.

94. It shall not be unlawful by virtue of any enactment to communicate the following information in pursuance of the European Patent Convention to the European Patent Office or the competent authority of any country which is party to the Convention, that is to say—

(a) information in the files of the court which, in accordance with rules of court, the court authorises to be so communicated;

(b) information in the files of the Patent Office which, in accordance with rules under this Act, the comptroller authorises to be so communicated.

                              RELEVANT RULE

Communication of information to European Patent Office

94.02   **87.** The comptroller may authorise the communication to the European Patent Office or the competent authority of any country which is party to the European Patent Convention of such information in the files of the

Patent Office as may be disclosed in accordance with section 118 and rule 93 below.

COMMENTARY ON SECTION 94

General   **94.03**

Section 94 is the fourth of the group of sections (ss. 91–95) which makes statutory provision for miscellaneous matters arising under the EPC, CPC and PCT. It provides that it is not to be unlawful to convey, in pursuance of the EPC, to the EPO or to the competent authority of any country party to the EPC, information in the files of a court which the court orders to be communicated, or information in the files of the Patent Office which the Comptroller authorises to be communicated.

Disclosure by the Comptroller   **94.04**

Rule 87 (reprinted at para. 94.02 *supra*) authorises the Comptroller to act under section 94, though there is no specific authority for this rule. The rule provides that the Comptroller may authorise the communication to any competent authority of any country party to the EPC of information as may be disclosed under section 118 or rule 93 (reprinted at para. 118.05).

Disclosure by the Patents Court   **94.05**

The operation of section 94 in relation to proceedings before the court is provided (in respect of the Patents Court) by RSC Ord. 104, r. 20 (reprinted at para. E104.20). Presumably, similar rules will apply to the other courts which are defined in section 130(1) as a "court" within the meaning of the Act. While, for the Patents Court, RSC Ord. 104, rule 20(1) seems to permit the court to disclose any information which it thinks fit, rule 20(2) appears to envisage that there must be a prior request for disclosure because rule 20(2) requires the court to afford any party affected "by the request" the opportunity of making representations on whether the information should be disclosed. It should also be noted that section 94 is limited to information "in the files of the court". However, (except on an appeal from the Comptroller) the file of the Patents Court will contain only the pleadings and affidavits in the case, but not the exhibits thereto nor any transcript of any evidence given orally to the court, this being the normal way in which an English court receives evidence.

SECTION 95

Financial provisions

95.—(1) There shall be paid out of moneys provided by Parliament any   **95.01**
sums required by any Minister of the Crown or government department to meet any financial obligation of the United Kingdom under the European Patent Convention, the Community Patent Convention or the Patent Co-operation Treaty.

(2) Any sums received by any Minister of the Crown or government department in pursuance of either of those conventions or that treaty shall be paid into the Consolidated Fund.

95.02   Commentary on Section 95

Section 95 is the last of the group of sections (ss. 91–95) which give statutory provision for miscellaneous matters concerning the operation of the EPC, CPC and PCT. Subsection (1) enables H.M. Government and Parliament to provide funds for the meeting of monetary obligations imposed upon the United Kingdom by these Conventions and Treaty. Subsection (2) provides for any income from these sources to be paid into the Consolidated Fund. Thus, any surplus funds at the end of the financial year do not remain available for use by the Patent Office in ensuing years.

It seems that it is subsection (1) which enables the Patent Office to act under PCTr. 19.1 as a receiving office and under EPCa. 75(1)(*b*) as an authority with which European patent applications may be filed.

Section 95 is supplementary to unrepealed sections 62 and 63 of the Patents and Designs Act 1907 (7 Edw. 7, c. 29) (Paras. B02–B03) which authorise the provision of funds for the running of the Patent Office and for the appointment of the Comptroller, its officers and examiners.

PART III

MISCELLANEOUS AND GENERAL

SECTION 96 [Repealed]   96.01

The Patents Court

[**96.**—*(1) There shall be constituted, as part of the Chancery Division of the High Court, a Patents Court to take such proceedings relating to patents and other matters as may be prescribed by rules of court.*

(2) The judges of the Patents Court shall be such of the puisne judges of the High Court as the Lord Chancellor may from time to time nominate.

(3) The foregoing provisions of this section shall not be taken as prejudicing the provisions of the Supreme Court of Judicature (Consolidation) Act 1925 which enable the whole jurisdiction of the High Court to be exercised by any judge of that court.

(4) Rules of court shall make provision for the appointment of scientific advisers to assist the Patents Court in proceedings under this Act and for regulating the functions of such advisers.

(5) The remuneration of any such adviser shall be determined by the Lord Chancellor with the consent of the Minister for the Civil Service and shall be defrayed out of moneys provided by Parliament.]

Note. Section 96 was repealed by the Supreme Court Act 1981 (c. 54, Sched. 7) ["the SCA"]. At the same time the section was in substance re-enacted and supplemented by provisions in sections 6, 54, 62 and 70 of that Act, which provisions are reprinted in paras. 96.02–96.05 *infra*.

In addition to these provisions, sections 287–292 of the 1988 Act prospectively provide a framework for Patents County Courts as an alternative jurisdiction to the Patents Court of the High Court for patent and design proceedings (including proceedings ancillary thereto) in England and Wales of generally lesser character. These sections are reprinted at paras. 96.06–96.11 *infra*, but remain to be brought into effect at some later date.

SUPREME COURT ACT 1981 (c. 54)

The Patents, Admiralty and Commercial Courts

6.—(1) There shall be—   96.02

(*a*) as part of the Chancery Division, a Patents Court; and

(*b*) as parts of the Queen's Bench Division, an Admiralty Court and a Commercial Court.

(2) The Judges of the Patents Court, of the Admiralty Court and of the

Commercial Court shall be such of the puisne judges of the High Court as the Lord Chancellor may from time to time nominate to be judges of the Patents Court, Admiralty Judges and Commercial Judges respectively.

Court of Appeal: Court of civil division

96.03   **54.**—(9) Subsections (3) and (4) of section 70 (scientific advisers to assist the Patents Court in proceedings under the Patents Act 1949 and the Patents Act 1977) shall apply in relation to the civil division of the Court of Appeal and proceedings on appeal from any decision of the Patents Court in proceedings under those Acts as they apply in relation to the Patents Court and proceedings under those Acts.

Business of Patents, Admiralty and Commercial Courts

96.04   **62.**—(1) The Patents Court shall take such proceedings relating to patents as are within the jurisdiction conferred on it by the Patents Act 1977, and such other proceedings relating to patents or other matters as may be prescribed.

Assessors and scientific advisers

96.05   **70.**—(3) Rules of court shall make provision for the appointment of scientific advisers to assist the Patents Court in proceedings under the Patents Act 1949 and the Patents Act 1977 and for regulating the functions of such advisers.

   (4) The remuneration of any such adviser shall be determined by the Lord Chancellor with the concurrence of the Minister for the Civil Service and shall be defrayed out of money provided by Parliament.

COPYRIGHT, DESIGNS AND PATENTS ACT 1988 (c. 48)

["THE 1988 ACT"]

PART VI—PATENTS

PATENTS COUNTY COURTS

Patents county courts: special jurisdiction

96.06   **287 [1988].**—(1) The Lord Chancellor may by order made by statutory instrument designate any county court as a patents county court and confer on it jurisdiction (its "special jurisdiction") to hear and determine such descriptions of proceedings—

(*a*) relating to patents or designs, or

(*b*) ancillary to, or arising out of the same subject matter as, proceedings relating to patents or designs,

as may be specified in the order.

(2) The special jurisdiction of a patents county court is exercisable throughout England and Wales, but rules of court may provide for a matter pending in one such court to be heard and determined in another or partly in that and partly in another.

(3) A patents county court may entertain proceedings within its special jurisdiction notwithstanding that no pecuniary remedy is sought.

(4) An order under this section providing for the discontinuance of any of the special jurisdiction of a patents county court may make provision as to proceedings pending in the court when the order comes into operation.

(5) Nothing in this section shall be construed as affecting the ordinary jurisdiction of a county court.

Financial limits in relation to proceedings within special jurisdiction of patents county court

288 [1988].—(1) Her Majesty may by Order in Council provide for limits   **96.07**
of amount or value in relation to any description of proceedings within the special jurisdiction of a patents county court.

(2) If a limit is imposed on the amount of a claim of any description and the plaintiff has a cause of action for more than that amount, he may abandon the excess; in which case a patents county court shall have jurisdiction to hear and determine the action, but the plaintiff may not recover more than that amount.

(3) Where the court has jurisdiction to hear and determine an action by virtue of subsection (2), the judgment of the court in the action is in full discharge of all demands in respect of the cause of action, and entry of the judgment shall be made accordingly.

(4) If the parties agree, by a memorandum signed by them or by their respective solicitors or other agents, that a patents county court shall have jurisdiction in any proceedings, that court shall have jurisdiction to hear and determine the proceedings notwithstanding any limit imposed under this section.

(5) No recommendation shall be made to Her Majesty to make an Order under this section unless a draft of the Order has been laid before and approved by a resolution of each House of Parliament.

Transfer of proceedings between High Court and patents county court

289 [1988].—(1) No order shall be made under section 41 of the County   **96.08**
Courts Act 1984 [c. 28] (power of High Court to order proceedings to be transferred from the county court) in respect of proceedings within the special jurisdiction of a patents county court.

(2) In considering in relation to proceedings within the special jurisdiction of a patents county court whether an order should be made under section 40 or 42 of the County Courts Act 1984 [c. 28] (transfer of proceedings from or to the High Court), the court shall have regard to the financial position of the parties and may order the transfer of the proceedings to a patents county court or, as the case may be, refrain from ordering their transfer to the High Court notwithstanding that the proceedings are likely to raise an important question of fact or law.

Limitation of costs where pecuniary claim could have been brought in patents county court

96.09   **290 [1988].**—(1) Where an action is commenced in the High Court which could have been commenced in a patents county court and in which a claim for a pecuniary remedy is made, then, subject to the provisions of this section, if the plaintiff recovers less than the prescribed amount, he is not entitled to recover any more costs than those to which he would have been entitled if the action had been brought in the county court.

(2) For this purpose a plaintiff shall be treated as recovering the full amount recoverable in respect of his claim without regard to any deduction made in respect of matters not falling to be taken into account in determining whether the action could have been commenced in a patents county court.

(3) This section does not affect any question as to costs if it appears to the High Court that there was reasonable ground for supposing the amount recoverable in respect of the plaintiff's claim to be in excess of the prescribed amount.

(4) The High Court, if satisfied that there was sufficient reason for bringing the action in the High Court may make an order allowing the costs or any part of the costs on the High Court scale or on such one of the county court scales as it may direct.

(5) This section does not apply to proceedings brought by the Crown.

(6) In this section "the prescribed amount" means such amount as may be prescribed by Her Majesty for the purposes of this section by Order in Council.

(7) No recommendation shall be made to Her Majesty to make an Order under this section unless a draft of the Order has been laid before and approved by a resolution of each House of Parliament.

Proceedings in patents county court

96.10   **291 [1988].**—(1) Where a county court is designated a patents county court, the Lord Chancellor shall nominate a person entitled to sit as a judge of that court as the patents judge.

(2) County court rules shall make provision for securing that, so far as is practicable and appropriate—

    (*a*) proceedings within the special jurisdiction of a patents county court are dealt with by the patents judge, and

    (*b*) the judge, rather than a registrar or other officer of the court, deals with interlocutory matters in the proceedings.

(3) County Court rules shall make provision empowering a patents county court in proceedings within its special jurisdiction, on or without the application of any party—

    (*a*) to appoint scientific advisers or assessors to assist the court, or

    (*b*) to order the Patent Office to inquire into and report on any question of fact or opinion.

(4) Where the court exercises either of those powers on the application of a party, the remuneration or fees payable to the Patent Office shall be at such rate as may be determined in accordance with county court rules and shall be costs of the proceedings unless otherwise ordered by the judge.

(5) Where the court exercises either of those powers of its own motion, the remuneration or fees payable to the Patent Office shall be at such rate as may be determined by the Lord Chancellor with the approval of the Treasury and shall be paid out of money provided by Parliament.

Rights and duties of registered patent agents in relation to proceedings in patents county court

292 [1988].—(1) A registered patent agent may do, in or in connection   **96.11** with proceedings in a patents county court which are within the special jurisdiction of that court, anything which a solicitor of the Supreme Court might do, other than prepare a deed.

(2) The Lord Chancellor may by regulations provide that the right conferred by subsection (1) shall be subject to such conditions and restrictions as appear to the Lord Chancellor to be necessary or expedient; and different provision may be made for different descriptions of proceedings.

(3) A patents county court has the same power to enforce an undertaking given by a registered patent agent acting in pursuance of this section as it has, by virtue of section 142 of the County Courts Act 1984 [c. 28], in relation to a solicitor.

(4) Nothing in section 143 of the County Courts Act 1984 [c. 28] (prohibition on persons other than solicitors receiving remuneration) applies to a registered patent agent acting in pursuance of this section.

(5) The provisions of county court rules prescribing scales of costs to be paid to solicitors apply in relation to registered patent agents acting in pursuance of this section.

(6) Regulations under this section shall be made by statutory instrument which shall be subject to annulment in pursuance of a resolution of either House of Parliament.

96.12   Books

T. C. Hartley, "Civil Jurisdiction and Judgments", Sweet and Maxwell, 1984;
L. Collins, "The Civil Jurisdiction and Judgments Act 1982", Butterworths 1983;
P. Kaye, "Civil Jurisdiction and Enforcement of Foreign Judgments", Professional Books, 1987.

96.13   Article

Sir Patrick Graham, "The Patents Court in the United Kingdom", (1980) 11 IIC 585;
P. R. B. Lawrence, "The new Patents County Court", (1988–89) 18 CIPA 78;
D. Gladwell, "Patent litigation", [1989] EIPR 128.

Commentary on Section 96 [Repealed]

96.14 *General*

Although section 96 has been repealed, its provisions have been re-enacted and extended by the provisions of the Supreme Court Act 1981 (c. 54) ["the SCA"], reprinted in paras. 96.02–96.05 *supra*. It is therefore convenient to discuss these replacement provisions in the present commentary, as well as the further prospective county court jurisdiction in England and Wales provided for by sections 287–292 of the 1988 Act, reprinted at paras. 96.06–96.11 *supra*.

Section 96 provided for the establishment in 1978 of a "Patents Court", as part of the High Court of Justice in England and Wales, to deal with all matters relating to patents (including "existing patents" (Sched. 2, para. 1(2))) brought before the High Court, including appeals from the Comptroller. The former Patents Appeal Tribunal (PAT) was therefore abolished, for the history of which see the article by Sir Patrick Graham listed in para. 96.13 *supra*. It may be doubted whether the abolition was entirely desirable, since the change has meant that (apart from a few matters still decided under the 1949 Act) the unsuccessful appellant is likely to have to pay costs on the court scale as opposed to a mere contribution as previously, see para. 97.24. Such prospect naturally favours the financially strong over the financially weak, so far as contentious proceedings in the Patent Office are concerned, and makes it more difficult for the private inventor or small company to challenge a decision of the Comptroller given *ex parte*.

Section 130(1) (as amended) defines "court" as having different meanings for the different parts of the United Kingdom (see para. 130.01). For England and Wales "court" presently means the High Court, the jurisdiction of which has been assigned to the Patents Court (SCA, s. 62, reprinted in para. 96.04 *supra*) as part of the Chancery Division (SCA, s. 6, reprinted in para. 96.02 *supra*). However, the 1988 Act has made provision for an alternative jurisdiction in "patents county courts" to be created within the format of the county court system, as now established under the County Courts Act 1984 (c. 28), see sections 287–292 [1988] referred to *supra*, but these provisions (although formally in force from August 1, 1989 by S.I. 1989 No. 816) remain to be brought into effect at some later date. The origin of these provisions is explained by P. R. B. Lawrence and D. Gladwell in their papers each listed in para. 96.13 *supra*. They are briefly discussed therein and in paras. 96.17–96.23 *infra*, see also D. Gladwell and S. Wilcox (1988–89) 18 CIPA 422.

The jurisdiction of the court for patent proceedings in Scotland is dealt with by section 98; and sections 131 and 132(2) relate respectively to Northern Ireland and the Isle of Man, but do not deal with jurisdiction as such: this arises under the general law pertaining therein.

The appropriate rules of court in relation to patent matters brought before the High Court in England and Wales (including the Patents Court) are contained in RSC Ord. 104, reprinted in paras. E104.1–E104.22. For appeals from the Comptroller, see section 97 and paras. 97.04 and 97.12–97.23.

Jurisdiction of the Patents Court   **96.15**

RSC Ord. 104, rule 2 (reprinted in para. E104.2) not only requires that all proceedings in the High Court under the Patents Acts 1949 to 1961 and 1977 should be taken by the Patents Court, but also that this exclusive jurisdiction shall apply "to all proceedings for the determination of a question or the making of a declaration relating to a patent under the inherent jurisdiction of the High Court": this presumably includes any dispute concerning ownership of a patent. Disputes concerning assignments and licensing of patents are normally heard in the Patents Court in any event, an example being *BICC* v. *Burndy* ([1985] RPC 273). By rule 2 the Patents Court is also required to take all proceedings in the High Court under the Registered Designs Acts 1949 to 1961, and also under the Defence Contracts Act 1958 (reprinted at paras. B10–B17): presumably this jurisdiction will be extended to matters concerning the new design right created under Part III of the 1988 Act. It is also possible to request an order of the High Court that any particular matter should be referred to, and determined in, the Chancery Division by one of the judges assigned to the Patents Court. Such an order could be useful, for example in cases involving complex technology and has been used for proceedings relating to trade marks, copyrights and trade secrets. Note, however, that the exclusivity of the Patents Court's jurisdiction will come to be sharply affected by the new Patents County Court, for which see paras. 86.17–96.23 *infra*.

Nominated judges for Patents Court   **96.16**

Section 84 [1949] provided for patent matters in the High Court to be dealt with "by such judges of the High Court as the Lord Chancellor may select for the purpose". Lloyd-Jacob J. was the first incumbent of this position and it was not until 1969 that a second "Patents Judge" (Graham J.) was appointed. The practice of nominating two such judges then continued, with Whitford J. being appointed in 1970 on the death of Lloyd-Jacob J., and Falconer J. on the retirement of Graham J. in 1981, by which time the two "Patents Judges" had become the nominated Judges of the Patents Court under section 96, now replaced by section 6(2) of the SCA. Following the retirement of Whitford J. in 1988, Aldous J. became the second nominated judge of the Patents Court, for "Wellcome" see [1988] FSR 525, Falconer J. then becoming the senior patents judge. However, on his retirement in 1989 Aldous J. became the primary assigned judge for the Patents Court, with Hoffmann, Morritt and Mummery JJ. being nominated judges to take the place of Aldous J. as necessary. Other judges are nominated from time to time for particular cases, and leading counsel (*i.e.* Queen's Counsel) are occasionally appointed as deputy judges of the Patents Court on an *ad hoc* basis, for example where there is a conflict of interest for a newly-appointed judge or a need to reduce a back-log of cases awaiting trial.

Patents county courts

—Nature and jurisdiction (s. 287 [1988])   **96.17**

Sections 287–292 of the 1988 Act make provision for a jurisdiction to be created which is alternative to the High Court for proceedings in England and Wales relating to patents and designs, and matters ancillary to, or arising out of the same subject matter as, such proceedings. Such is to be part of the present system of county courts, now organised under the County Courts Act 1984 (c. 28), with one or more of such courts being designated as a "patents county court" and given a "special jurisdiction" to "hear and determine such descriptions of proceedings relating to patents and designs as may be specified" in an Order made by the Lord Chancellor (s. 287(1) [1988]). Thus, while jurisdiction to bring proceedings under section 60 (*Infringement*) and section 72 (*Revocation*) is clearly envisaged, it is uncertain whether patents county courts will be given jurisdiction in proceedings under section 37 (*Entitlement*); section 40 (*Employee-inventor compensation*); section 58 (*Crown use compensation*); section 70 (*Threats*); section 71 (*Declaration of non-infringement*); or even section 75 (*Amendment*). The definition of court for the purposes of the Registered Designs Act 1949 (12, 13 & 14 Geo. 6, c. 88, s. 27) has also been extended to cover the new Patents County Courts (Sched. 3, para. 16 [1988]).

Many of the provisions of sections 287–292 [1988] are merely enabling ones and, obviously, before they can be rendered effective in practice will require appropriate full County Court Rules to be made. But it can be expected that, wherever possible, the provisions of the County Courts Act 1984 (c. 28) and the County Court Rules made thereunder will be given effect: these are set out in *"The County Court Practice"* (the "Green Book") and often follow the Rules of the Supreme Court, for which see Appendix E hereto. It is likely that a separate chapter of the County Court Rules, analogous to RSC Order 104, will be promulgated.

The powers of a patents county court can also be expected to be generally similar to those given to a county court under the above-mentioned County Courts Act. However, any doubts as to the ability of such a court to grant an injunction are removed by section 287(3) [1988], even if no damages or an account of profits is claimed. A patents county court should therefore have power to grant interlocutory injunctions, as well as *Anton Piller* Orders and *Mareva* injunctions. Appeals from decision of a patents county court to the Court of Appeal should be possible in the normal way under section 77 of the County Courts Act, but there is power (under s. 77(2)) for the Lord Chancellor, by Order, to limit appeals on specified matters unless leave therefore is granted either by the county or the Court of Appeal.

It will be clear from the foregoing that the eventual introduction of the Patents County Court will constitute a major change in the patent law of the United Kingdom as regards the fora available for the determination of disputes concerning patents, and perhaps also related intellectual property rights. However, only time will tell whether the innovation proves successful in its aim of providing a cheaper, and quicker, forum for the resolution of patent disputes. Much will depend on the judge(s) appointed, the form and application of the rules governing its procedure, and the manner in which the parties are represented, but the opportunity is there to be grasped. The enabling powers so far provided for the envisaged Patents County Courts are discussed further in paras. 96.18–96.23 *infra*.

96.18 —*Financial limits to jurisdiction (s. 288 [1988])*

Section 288 [1988] envisages an Order in Council, which can only be made after recommendation to the Crown by positive resolution of each House of Parliament (subs. (5)), fixing a maximum limit on damages claimable in the patents county court jurisdiction, but a plaintiff can abandon any damages in excess of this limit in order that the patents county court may retain jurisdiction over his claim (subs. (2)), such abandonment being final (subs. (3)). Alternatively, jurisdiction can be conferred on a Patents County Court by agreement of the parties and there will be no financial limit, unless agreed otherwise (subs. (4)).

—Transfer of proceedings between Patents Court and a patents county court (s. 289 **96.19**
[1988])

Section 289(1) [1988] prevents the High Court from ordering of its own motion transfer of proceedings from a Patents County Court to itself under section 41 of the County Courts Act 1984 (c. 28). Sections 40 and 42 of that Act provide for transfer of cases from or to a county court, but in making any order under these provisions in relation to its special jurisdiction the court is required to have regard to the financial position of the parties, even when the proceedings are likely to raise an important question of fact or law (subs. (2)).

—Limitation on costs (s. 290 [1988])   **96.20**

While section 288 [1988] envisages an upper limit on damages which may be awarded by a Patents County Court (unless the excess is waived or the parties otherwise agree, see para. 96.18 *supra*), section 290 [1988] sets an effective minimum ("the prescribed amount") on damages recovery from patent proceedings commenced in the High Court because, if this amount is not recovered, the High Court can limit the costs to be paid to the successful plaintiff by reference to the scales of costs applicable to proceedings before a county court under the County Court Rules (subs. (1)). However, this limit is not to apply if the High Court is satisfied that there was sufficient reason for bringing the action in the High Court (subs. (4)). The High Court is then given a wide discretion as to awards of costs, including power to award costs according to any county court scale. The "prescribed amount" is to be fixed by Order in Council made following positive resolution of each House of Parliament.

—Judges in the Patents County Courts (s. 291 [1988])   **96.21**

Section 291 [1988] provides for the Lord Chancellor to nominate a person entitled to sit as a county court judge as "the patents judge" for a particular Patents County Court (subs. (1)), so that it would appear that all patent cases in that court should be heard by the same person, so far as is practicable and that the patents judge (rather than a registrar or other court officer) should deal with interlocutory matters in such proceedings (subs. (2)).

—Procedure in the Patents County Courts   **96.22**

As indicated above, special rules for dealing with patents and designs litigation within the "special jurisdiction" of a Patents County Court will need to be made under the County Courts Act 1984 (c. 28). However, section 291(3) [1988], corresponding to section 70 of the SCA (reprinted at para. 96.05 *supra*), will enable similar rules to be made for the appointment of scientific advisers or assessors to assist a Patents County Court, see RSC Ord. 104, r. 15, reprinted at para. E104.15). The powers and duties of such persons are discussed in para. 96.25 *infra*.

Section 291(3) [1988] also provides power (as do the new sections 99A and 99B similarly for the High Court and Court of Session respectively) for a Patents County Court, even on its own initiative, to ask the Patent Office to "inquire into and report on any question of fact or opinion" which arises in proceedings before it, see paras. 99A.02–99A.04. The costs of such an inquiry or report, which are to be payable to the Patent Office, are to be costs of the proceedings unless otherwise ordered by the judge (s. 291(4) [1988]), or unless such was ordered by the court of its own initiative, in which case the costs will be borne out of central funds (s. 291(5) [1988]).

96.23 —*Representation in the Patents County Courts*

Whereas only counsel (besides non-corporate litigants in person) normally have a right of audience in the High Court, and for such are required to be instructed by a solicitor (except in relation to proceedings before the Patents Court by way of appeal from the Comptroller, for which see para. 97.14), in proceedings before a county court solicitors also have a right of audience. Section 280 [1988] provides for registered patent agents to do anything in proceedings before a Patents County Court which a Solicitor of the Supreme Court may do (subs. (1)), other than prepare a deed, but subject to such conditions and restrictions as the Lord Chancellor may deem necessary or expedient (subs. (2)), as set out in regulations to be made by statutory instrument subject to negative resolution by either House of Parliament (subs. (6)).

It is significant that the wording of the side-note to section 292 [1988] refers to the "rights and duties" of registered patent agents. Clearly, registered patent agents who practise before a patents county court will become subject to similar disciplinary rules and procedures, and to the need to have professional indemnity insurance, as apply to solicitors in their role as Officers of the Supreme Court. Subsection (3) makes specific reference to the enforcement of undertakings given by a registered patent agent in such proceedings as such would be enforced against a solicitor under section 142 of the County Courts Act (c. 28).

The term "registered patent agent" is defined in section 275(1) [1988], see section 286 [1988] (reprinted respectively in paras. 102.04 and 102.11), and is discussed in para. 102.31.

96.24 *Jurisdiction of various United Kingdom courts*

It is necessary to distinguish between: (i) the provisions contained in the Act for courts other than the Patents Court to have local jurisdiction in the parts of the United Kingdom in which they operate; and (ii) the impact of the Civil Jurisdiction and Judgments Act 1982 (c. 27) [the "CJJA"].

As to (i), reference may be made to the provisions of section 98 (*Proceedings in Scotland*), and sections 131 and 132(2) concerning application of the Act to Northern Ireland and the Isle of Man respectively. For England and Wales an alternative forum to the Patents Court is also to be provided when sections 287–292 [1988] are brought into practical effect to provide a "special jurisdiction" to "patents county courts", see paras. 96.17–96.25 *supra*.

As to (ii), the CJJA (which came into effect on January 1, 1987) enacted the 1968 Brussels Convention on Jurisdiction and Enforcement of Judgments between EEC Member States, as amended by the Accession Convention of 1971. The CJJA, however, did not alter the jurisdiction for the courts of Scotland, Northern Ireland and the Isle of Man to consider and, if appropriate, revoke a United Kingdom patent. This is because proceedings concerned with the registration or validity of patents, trade marks, service marks, designs or other similar rights required to be deposited or registered are excluded (by Sched. 5, para. 2 of the CJJA, amended by the 1986 Act, Sched. 2, para. 1(2)(*f*)) from the provisions of Sched. 4 of the CJJA (which governs questions of jurisdiction within the component parts of the United Kingdom): for Scotland see also Sched. 8, paras. 2(14) and 4(2) of the CJJA).

The CJJA (by Sched. 1, art. 16(4)) also prevents actions concerning registration or validity of United Kingdom patents (including a European patent (UK)) being determined by a court outside the United Kingdom and the Isle of Man. Also, the provisions of arts. 21–23 of the Brussels Convention concerning a stay of parallel, or connected, proceedings, while enacted into United Kingdom law as regards the Contracting States to that Convention (by the CJJA, Sched. 1, arts. 21–23), have no effect with regard to parallel, or connected, actions within component parts of the United Kingdom since these articles of the Convention are excluded from Sched. 4 of the CJJA. The question whether a court in one United Kingdom jurisdiction will stay its proceedings while a court in another of such jurisdictions has before it the same, or a connected, case will therefore continue to be decided according to the test of *forum conveniens*, for which see *The Spiliada* ([1987] AC 460; [1986] 3 All ER 843 (HL)) and *MacShannon* v. *Rockware Glass* ([1978] AC 795; [1978] 1 All ER 625 (HL)), though this test has no application when the Brussels Convention applies.

It must also be realised that it is now possible for courts and tribunals in other Contracting States to the Brussels Convention to adjudicate in proceedings relating to the infringement of a United Kingdom patent. If they do so their judgments must be recognised and enforced by United Kingdom courts under the CJJA.

The CJJA is also discussed in paras. 61.07 and 88.04 and attention is drawn to the articles listed in para. 88.03 which particularly discuss the application of the CJJA to patent litigation. For comprehensive coverage of the CJJA generally, see the books listed in para. 96.12, especially that by P. Kaye.

Appointment of scientific advisers **96.25**

Section 70(3) and (4) of the SCA (reprinted in para. 96.05 *supra*) re-enacts the repealed section 96(4) and (5) and extends those provisions to proceedings under the 1949 Act. By section 54(9) of the SCA (reprinted in para. 96.03 *supra*), the same provisions are made to apply to the appointment of scientific advisers to assist the Court of Appeal. The rule relating to the appointment of scientific advisers is RSC, Ord. 104, r. 15 (reprinted at para. E104.15). By this the Patents Court is given power, by its own motion if it so wishes, or otherwise on the application of any party, to appoint such an independent adviser either (*a*) to sit with the judge at the trial, or (*b*) to enquire and report on any question of fact or opinion not involving a question of law or construction.

By RSC Ord. 104, r. 14(3)(*b*) (reprinted in para. E104.14), at the hearing of the summons for directions, the court is required to consider, if necessary of its own motion, whether a scientific adviser should be appointed pursuant to Ord. 104, r. 15, and in *International Electronics* v. *Weigh Data* (SRIS C/58/80, but see [1980] FSR 423 for other aspects) the Patents Court regretted that this had not been done in that case. Insofar as parties normally attempt to agree, so far as possible, on a draft of the Order they would like the court to make, they should also seek to agree whether or not they consider it would be desirable to appoint a scientific adviser, and, if so, whom this should be. Clearly, the question should be raised on the summons for directions by any party who thinks an adviser would materially assist the court.

A scientific adviser has been appointed on a number of occasions to sit with the Patents Court, see: *Western Electric* v. *Racal-Milgo* ([1981] RPC 253); *Compagnie Française de Télévision* v. *Thorn* ([1981] FSR 306 and SRIS C/181/83); and *Codex* v. *Racal-Milgo* (SRIS C/135/81 *noted* IPD 4150 and C/77/83, *noted* IPD 6025). In *Valensi* v. *British Radio* ([1973] RPC 337) the Court of Appeal appointed a scientific adviser for the first time since the corresponding rule was introduced under section 84(2) [1949]. For the hearing of the appeal in *Codex* v. *Racal-Milgo* (noted *supra*) the Court of Appeal appointed two scientific advisers, of whom one was new to the case and the other had sat with Whitford J. at first instance. Likewise, there were two scientific advisers in *Compagnie Française de Television* v. *Thorn (supra)* at the appeal stage (SRIS C/98/85); and in *Genentech's Patent* ([1989] RPC 147 (CA)), the scientific adviser prepared that part of one of the judgments which set out the scientific background to the case.

The principles to be followed in appointing a scientific adviser to assist a court on appeal from the Patent Office were extensively considered in *Beecham Group* v. *Bristol-Myers (Amoxycillin) (New Zealand)* ([1980] 1 NZLR 185), as also was the restricted role which the adviser should play, though this was subsequently expanded by agreement (*Beecham Group* v. *Bristol-Myers (Amoxycillin) No. 2) (New Zealand)* ([1980] 1 NZLR 192). In that case the same adviser also similarly assisted during the hearing of the appeal to the New Zealand Court of Appeal ([1982] FSR 181).

In the Australian case of *Minnesota Mining* v. *Beiersdorf* ([1980] FSR 449) a court expert was appointed under a provision similar to that of RSC, Ord. 104, r. 15. The functions of a court expert are different from those of a scientific adviser in that he is asked to present a report to the court on scientific questions or issues, but (as the Australian decision points out and Ord. 104, r. 15(1)(*b*) requires) a court expert should not be asked questions which can only be decided by the court itself.

Attention is also drawn to sections 99A and 99B of the Act (inserted by the 1988 Act) which (when brought into effect) will provide for rules of court to be made for the Patents Court, and the Court of Session in Scotland, to order the Patent Office to inquire into and report on any question of fact or opinion. Section 291(3) [1988] (reprinted at para. 96.10 *supra*) contains similar provisions in respect of Patents County Courts.

96.26 *Decisions of the Patents Court, etc.*

For the availability of decisions of the court on patent matters and the publication of law reports, see para. 123.48.

Though there is no specific rule on the matter, the court has an inherent jurisdiction to correct an error in the reasons (*i.e.* in its decision) given as the basis for its judgment (strictly only the resulting court order), see *Hazeltine Corp.* v. *International Computers* ([1980] FSR 521).

97.01

SECTION 97

Appeals from the comptroller

97.—(1) Except as provided by subsection (4) below, an appeal shall lie to the Patents Court from any decision of the comptroller under this Act or rules except any of the following decisions, that is to say—

(*a*) a decision falling within section 14(7) above;

(*b*) a decision under section 16(2) above to omit matter from a specification;

(*c*) a decision to give directions under subsection (1) or (2) of section 22 above;

(*d*) a decision under rules which is excepted by rules from the right of appeal conferred by this section.

(2) For the purpose of hearing appeals under this section the Patents

Court may consist of one or more judges of that court in accordance with directions given by or on behalf of the Lord Chancellor [*; and the Patents Court shall not be treated as a divisional court for the purposes of section 31(1)(f) of the Supreme Court of Judicature (Consolidation) Act 1925 (appeals from divisional courts)*].

(3) An appeal shall not lie to the Court of Appeal from a decision of the Patents Court on appeal from a decision of the comptroller under this Act or rules—

(*a*) except where the comptroller's decision was given under sections 8, 12, 18, 20, 27, 37, 40, 61, 72, 73 or 75 above; or

(*b*) except where the ground of appeal is that the decision of the Patents Court is wrong in law;

but an appeal shall only lie to the Court of Appeal under this section if leave to appeal is given by the Patents Court or the Court of Appeal.

(4) An appeal shall lie to the Court of Session from any decision of the comptroller in proceedings which under rules are held in Scotland, except any decision mentioned in paragraphs (*a*) to (*d*) of subsection (1) above.

(5) An appeal shall not lie to the Inner House of the Court of Session from a decision of an Outer House judge on appeal from a decision of the comptroller under this Act or rules—

(*a*) except where the comptroller's decision was given under section 8, 12, 18, 20, 27, 37, 40, 61, 72, 73 or 75 above; or

(*b*) except where the ground of appeal is that the decision of the Outer House judge is wrong in law.

Note. Subsection (2) was amended by the Supreme Court Act 1981 (c. 54) (Sched. 7).

RELEVANT RULES   **97.02**

Note. The rules of court governing appeals from the Comptroller to the Patents Court are contained in RSC Ord. 104, r. 19 (reprinted at para. E104.19). A specimen Notice of Appeal is reprinted at para. E104.19B. Further appeals to the Court of Appeal are governed by RSC Ord. 59, the main applicable rules thereof being rules 17 and 18 (reprinted at paras. E059.17 and E059.18).

COMMENTARY ON SECTION 97

General   **97.03**

Section 97 relates to appeals from the Comptroller to the Patents Court (subss. (1) and (2)) and to further appeals to the Court of Appeal (subs. (3)). Subsections (4) and (5) provide for corresponding appeals from proceedings before the Comptroller held in Scotland. Section 97 is generally applicable also to appeals from decisions of the Comptroller given under the still effective provisions of the 1949 Act, see particularly Schedule 4, para. 15.

97.04   *Right of appeal from Comptroller (subs. (1))*

Subsection (1)(*a*)–(*d*) specifies certain decisions (in matters mainly of an administrative nature) from which no appeal lies. These are: section 14(7) (*Amendment of abstract by Comptroller*); section 16(2) (*Omission of offensive matter from specification before publication*); section 22(1) and (2) (*Prohibition of publication of information prejudicial to defence or public safety*); and any other decisions made unappealable by rule, these at present being rule 102 (reprinted at para. 123.09) and rule 108 (reprinted at para. 98.02). However, the process of judicial review of such decisions may still be possible leading to the remedies of certiorari, mandamus or prohibition in appropriate circumstances.

In *Omron Tateisi's Application* ([1981] RPC 125) the Patents Court held that there is a general right of appeal to it on all decisions of the Comptroller (save those excepted by subs. (1)(*a*)–(*d*)) and, *obiter*, that a litigant is under no obligation to exercise a right of appeal to the Patents Court from such a decision before having recourse to the Queen's Bench Division for judicial review under RSC Ord. 53, r. 1 (reprinted at para. E053.1). Such an application will, in fact, be heard by a judge of the Patents Court sitting as an additional judge of the Queen's Bench Division, as in the *Omron* case. While judicial review is normally commenced by making *ex parte* an application for leave therefor, in *R. v. Comptroller ex p. Bayer* (SRIS C/67/85) the court indicated that notice of intention to seek such leave ought to be given to the Comptroller so that he could be represented if he thought his appearance would assist the court, see also *NETWORK 90 Trade Mark* ([1984] RPC 549).

97.05   *Composition of Patents Court (subs. (2))*

Subsection (2) relates to the composition and status of the Patents Court when hearing appeals from the Comptroller. Normally the Patents Court consists of a single judge, but (for the purpose of hearing appeals) it may consist of two of the nominated judges (including by the provisions of the Supreme Court Act, 1981 deputy judges appointed *ad hoc*) sitting *in banc* if the senior judge or, in his absence, another nominated judge so directs (*Practice Direction*, [1978] FSR 449). An example of this practice was *John Wyeth's and Schering's Applications* ([1985] RPC 545).

97.06   *Further appeals from the Patents Court (subs. (3))*

Subsection (3) concerns further appeals from the Patents Court in relation to appeals from the Comptroller. The provision is expressed in terms that no further appeal shall lie *except* (*a*) where the Comptroller's original decision relates to: sections 8, 12 or 37 (*Entitlement*); sections 18 or 20 (*Refusal of application*); sections 72 or 73 (*Revocation of patent*); sections 27 or 75 (*Amendment*); section 40 (*Inventor compensation*); or section 61 (*Infringement*), when appeal may be taken both on questions of fact and law, and (*b*) in any other case on the ground that the decision of the Patents Court is wrong in law. However, in all cases such further appeal lie only if specific leave to appeal is given either by the Patents Court or (on application thereto) by the Court of Appeal. Subsection (3) also applies to appeals in proceedings under section 33 [1949] (*Revocation*) and sections 55–56 [1949] (*Co-ownership* and *Employee-inventor disputes*) (Sched. 4, para. 11(6)). It may be noted that subsection (3) does *not* provide for further appeal on questions of fact arising in proceedings under sections 46, 48 or 51 (*Licences of Right* and *Compulsory licences*), nor under section 71 (*Declaration of non-infringment*), but at least in section 46 proceedings this absence does not seem to have had significant inhibitory effect, see *Allen & Hanburys' (Salbutamol) Patent* ([1987] RPC 327). Also, for possible assistance on the construction of subsection (3) when apparently no appeal is possible (*e.g.* questions of fact, under the specified sections), see *Beecham Group's Irish Application* ([1983] FSR 355).

A final appeal to the House of Lords is also possible, though only by leave of the Court of Appeal or, if the Court of Appeal refuses leave, by the House of Lords itself. An example of such an appeal is *Du Pont's (Witsiepe's) Application* ([1982] FSR 303).

The possibility also exists of direct "leapfrog" appeal from the Patents Court to the House of Lords under the Administration of Justice Act 1969 (c. 58, ss. 12 and 13), provided that the parties agree and the court certifies that certain conditions are met. An applicable Practice Direction was issued ([1971] RPC 71), now embodied in *Direction No. 21 for Civil Appeals to the House of Lords*. The procedure was first used in *American Cyanamid's (Dann's) Patent* ([1971] RPC 425) when some doubt was expressed at the desirability of avoiding consideration of the matter by the Court of Appeal. The applicable conditions have more recently been discussed, see *York Trade Mark* ([1981] FSR 33).

Principles affecting exercise of appellate jurisdiction

—General   **97.07**

The principles affecting the exercise of appellate jurisdiction are among the most subtle, and important, for the patents practitioner to grasp. They can only be dealt with here in outline. The discussion below is centred upon appeals to the Patents Court from the Comptroller. Much of this is applicable also to subsequent appeals from the Patents Court to the Court of Appeal, but the equivalence is not total; such differences as there are spring largely from the fact that generally (although not always) the judges of the Court of Appeal lack the scientific and technical background of the Comptroller and judges of the Patents Court.

The *locus classicus* on the role of the Patents Court in hearing appeals from the Comptroller is now provided by the decision in *Allen & Hanburys' (Salbutamol) Patent* ([1987] RPC 327). This emphasised that the appeal is a re-hearing, section 99 indicating that the Patents Court is not limited merely to the exercise of a supervisory jurisdiction. Thus, the Patents Court can decide *de novo* all questions which arise, irrespective of whether these are of law, fact or the exercise of discretion. Due weight will, of course, be given to the Comptroller's decision below, and the reasons therefor. The Patents Court, though it re-hears the case (which might notionally suggest that it should ignore the decision below in order that it may come to the matter with an untrammelled mind), does not work in a vacuum: indeed, an appellant will normally devote a considerable part of his argument to criticising that decision.

—Weight given to Comptroller's decision   **97.08**

The degree of weight attached to the Comptroller's decision may vary sharply according to the nature of the dispute. The three-fold classification as between law, fact and discretion can be refined further, as shown in the following explanatory Table:—

661

TABLE

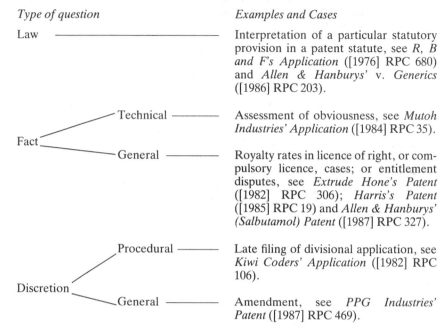

Type of question		Examples and Cases
Law ———————————		Interpretation of a particular statutory provision in a patent statute, see *R, B and F's Application* ([1976] RPC 680) and *Allen & Hanburys'* v. *Generics* ([1986] RPC 203).

Fact
- Technical ——— Assessment of obviousness, see *Mutoh Industries' Application* ([1984] RPC 35).
- General ——— Royalty rates in licence of right, or compulsory licence, cases; or entitlement disputes, see *Extrude Hone's Patent* ([1982] RPC 306); *Harris's Patent* ([1985] RPC 19) and *Allen & Hanburys' (Salbutamol) Patent* ([1987] RPC 327).

Discretion
- Procedural ——— Late filing of divisional application, see *Kiwi Coders' Application* ([1982] RPC 106).
- General ——— Amendment, see *PPG Industries' Patent* ([1987] RPC 469).

Broadly speaking, the least weight will be accorded to any decision depending at root on law, since this is a field in which the disparity between the qualifications of the Comptroller and Patents Court is at its greatest. On questions of fact, the weight on technical issues may be marginally higher than on non-technical ones since undoubtedly the Comptroller is likely to have superior technical expertise to the Patents Court; the Comptroller has a pool of individually more qualified specialist Hearing Officers on whom to call. But on certain non-technical issues also, for example licence royalty rates, the Comptroller has a vast experience and he will not lightly be upset—unless, of course, some error in his underlying legal approach can be demonstrated, as in *Shiley's Patent* ([1988] RPC 97) and *Smith Kline & French's Patent [Generics' Application]* (SRIS C/12/89, *noted* IPD 12036). On discretion, the Patents Court is reluctant to upset in cases involving what might be termed the procedural mechanics of handling patent applications or patent disputes, see *Kiwi Coders' Application* (*supra*) and also *Owens-Corning's Patent* ([1972] RPC 684), which concerned additional citations at a late stage in revocation proceedings.

Great weight is also accorded where there has been cross-examination before the Comptroller on disputed issues of technical fact, and the Comptroller has relied upon the demeanour and manner of the witnesses in resolving such conflict. This consideration may be of increasing importance in the future, with the wider use of cross-examination before the Comptroller.

97.09   —*By the Court of Appeal*

In the Court of Appeal, it is difficult to upset concurrent findings of technical fact in both tribunals below, see *Johns-Manville's Patent* ([1967] RPC 479); *Du Pont's (Werner's) Patent* ([1976] FSR 47) and *Tetra Molectric's Application* ([1977] RPC

290). But a more adventurous attitude may be taken when the findings below are in conflict, as in *Technic's Application* ([1973] RPC 383) and *Du Pont's (Dahlstrom and Bunting's) Patent* ([1976] RPC 177). In *Hauni-Werke's Patent of Addition* ([1982] RPC 327), the Court of Appeal confirmed that an experienced judge of the Patents Court was entitled to say that a particular technical fact was within his own knowledge, hence equating him in this respect to the Comptroller. However, the Court of Appeal (in *Genentech's Patent*, [1989] RPC 147), following the House of Lords in *Benmax* v. *Austin* ((1955) 72 RPC 39), have held themselves entitled to evaluate the evidence heard by the Patents Court afresh and form their own opinion.

Similar (if not greater) difficulty may be experienced in upsetting concurrent exercises of discretion below; the decision in *General Tire* v. *Firestone* ([1976] RPC 197 at 229 (HL)) may be invoked here by a respondent.

But the position is open when the issue is one of law, and it may even be possible to launch an attack upon a technical finding under a legal umbrella, as in *Technic's Application* (*supra*) where the Court of Appeal was prepared to hold that the finding of the Appeal Tribunal as to fortuitous prior performance of a process was unsupported by any evidence at all and hence was erroneous in law.

—Effect of prior decisions   **97.10**

Generally, the position is not entirely clear. To begin with, it is reasonably well-established that the Comptroller's own decisions have persuasive, but not compelling, impact upon subsequent cases in the Patent Office involving comparable facts. The strength of the persuasion may depend upon the length of time for which the preceding decision has been extant and followed; also upon the status, as a matter of historical perspective, of the personification of the Comptroller involved. Some Hearing Officers, like some judges, are regarded as more equal than others. *R, B and F's Application* ([1976] RPC 28) is of general interest on the topic.

The Patents Court (just like the Patents Appeal Tribunal before it) is fully entitled to overrule an existing precedent of the Comptroller, being the higher forum. But it is not yet certain as to whether the Patents Court regards itself as bound by its own precedents. In the High Court generally, judges are not so bound, though naturally close attention is paid thereto. In *Hoffmann-La Roche's Patent* ([1971] RPC 311), concerning a licence to import as part of a compulsory licence, the Tribunal explicitly found that it was bound by an earlier decision of the Tribunal on the same point. It is suggested that future perpetuation within the Patents Court of such rigidity would be regrettable, as well as being incompatible with the Patents Court's rank as part of the Chancery Division of the High Court.

Nor is the precedential power of previous decisions of the Patents Appeal Tribunal upon the Patents Court yet settled. It can be argued that, being a mere Tribunal as opposed to the High Court and hence coming lower in the overall heirarchy of the legal system, decisions of the Tribunal (even though made by a Patents Judge) were on an inherently lower plane than those of the Patents Court.

As between the Patents Court, the Court of Appeal and the House of Lords, the normal rules of precedent apply. The Patents Court is bound by decisions of the Court of Appeal and House of Lords. The Court of Appeal is normally bound by its own decisions (though there are certain categories of exceptional cases) and in any event by those of the House of Lords. The House of Lords does have power to depart from its own previous decisions, but rarely does so. Decisions of foreign courts, especially those of the Privy Council, have persuasive effect, but are not binding. However, in *John Wyeth's and Schering's Applications* ([1985] RPC 545) the Patents Court preferred to follow a decision of the EPO Enlarged Board of

Appeal for the sake of harmony under the EPC, and in so doing departed from a long-standing authority of the High Court, see para. 4.05.

97.11 *Proceedings in Scotland (subss. (4) and (5))*

Rule 108 (reprinted at para. 98.02) provides for the Comptroller to hear certain proceedings in Scotland, see para. 98.07. When this has occurred, appeal from the Comptroller lies (subject to the same limitations as in subsection (1)) not to the Patents Court but to the Outer House of the Court of Sessions in Scotland (subs. (4)) with further appeal possible (in analogous circumstances to those under subs. (3)) to the Inner House of the Court of Session (subs. (5)), see further para. 98.08. For court procedure in Scottish cases, see para. 98.09.

Practice under Section 97

Appeals from the Comptroller to the Patents Court

97.12 *—Lodging and serving notice of appeal*

The procedure on appeal to the Patents Court from the Comptroller is governed by RSC Ord. 104 r. 19 (reprinted at para. E104.19). The time for lodging appeal is usually six weeks from the date the decision is given, but only 14 days when the Comptroller states that his decision is one of procedure, which decision is itself unappealable (Ord. 104, r. 19(2) and (3)), see also para. 72.51), where the possible extension of time for lodging appeal under Order 104, r. 19(8) is discussed and the procedure of applying for this explained.

Much of the practice under the 1949 Act for appeals from the Comptroller to the former Patents Appeal Tribunal remains valid, though with change of terminology. This previous practice was reviewed by B. C. Reid ((1974–75) 4 CIPA 131.

In order to appeal to the Patents Court, it is necessary to bring the proceedings formally into the High Court. For the purposes of the Supreme Court Rules generally, the document by which this is done is termed an originating motion (Ord. 14, r. 9)), but in the specific context of appeals to the Patents Court the originating motion is described as a "notice of appeal". The suggested form of this notice has been set out in a *Practice Direction* ([1979] RPC 56) and this form is reprinted in Appendix E at para. E104.19B.

RSC Order 104, r. 19(2) requires that the notice of appeal be lodged with the "proper officer". This term refers, at present, to the Chancery Chambers in Room 157 at the Royal Courts of Justice, Strand, London WC2A 2LL. Notice of appeal, and Respondent's notices, should be taken or sent to this Room; receipt by the due date in the central post room at the courts is not sufficient. If the Registrar of Patent Appeals and his deputy are not there available, the copies may be lodged in the Chief Master's Secretariat (Room 169). Two copies of the notice of appeal are required, one being stamped as regards the appeal fee. Cheques should be made payable to "H.M. Paymaster-General". Room 163 remains the Room to which enquiries should be made for listing of appeal hearings, see para. 98.14. During court vacations, particularly during August, the court offices close early. Care must, therefore, be taken at such times when lodging notice of appeal on the last day of the time within which an appeal should be lodged, since otherwise it may be necessary to seek leave to lodge the appeal out of time. For days when the court office is entirely closed (for which see RSC Ord. 64, r. 7, reprinted at para. E064.7) actions due thereon may be taken on the next day that the office is open for business (RSC Ord. 3, r. 4, reprinted at para. E003.4). At the time of writing the fee payable is £15.00 (S.I. 1980 No. 821), but this should be checked as increases may occur without notice. Where the decision appealed from is in respect of proceedings relating to two or more patents or applications therefore, a single notice of appeal may be lodged; however, the precribed fee must be paid in respect of each patent or application involved.

Notice of appeal may be given in respect of the whole or any specific part of the appealed decision and normally, the grounds of appeal and the relief sought will be limited according to the terms of the notice of appeal (Order 104, r. 19(4) and (5)).

By Ord. 104, r. 19(6) an appellant must within five days of lodging notice of appeal serve a copy on the Comptroller and any other party to the proceedings. Although service may be effected by post, care should be taken to ensure the notice arrives within the specified period of five days.

—Respondent's notice and cross-appeal   **97.13**

A respondent's notice (fee £10.00 at the time of writing. S.I. 1980 No. 821, Sched., para. 11(*d*)) should be filed wherever the non-appealing party desires to contend that the decision should be varied either in any event or in the event of the appeal being allowed in whole or in part; such a notice should specify the grounds of the contention and the relief sought (Ord. 104, r. 19(9)). A respondent's notice should likewise be filed where it is intended to contend that the Comptroller's decision should be affirmed on alternative grounds (Ord. 104, r. 19(10)). Any such notice must be served on the Comptroller, on the appellant, and on any other party within 14 days of receipt by the respondent of the notice of appeal (Ord. 104, r. 19(1)) and lodged in duplicate at the Chancery Chambers within five days after such service (Ord. 104, r. 19(12)). If a party wishes to vary a decision in a different direction to the other party, a separate appeal should be filed and the hearing will deal with the two appeals as separate matters.

Once an appeal has been lodged, the Comptroller's file is transferred to the Chancery Chambers as the "proper officer" under Order 104, r. 19(7). Thereafter the Comptroller can take no action on the file, *e.g.* he cannot then consider an application to amend the patent.

—Hearings and representation thereat   **97.14**

Representation at the appeal is now governed by section 102A and Order 104, r. 19(16): a patent agent has a right of audience before the Patents Court when (but only when) it is hearing an appeal from the Comptroller, see para. 102.17. Normally the Comptroller appears by counsel (instructed by the Treasury Solicitor) to support his decision when this has been given in an *ex parte* proceeding.

Chancery practice also requires that a certificate signed by counsel (or other person permitted to appear) for each of the parties should be lodged with the Clerk to the Lists for the Chancery Division in Room 163 at the Royal Court of Justice giving an estimate for the length of the hearing. For the form of certificate formerly used before the Patents Appeal Tribunal, and still appropriate with suitable changes for the Patents Court, see [1970] RPC 102. The Clerk to the Lists in Room 163 should also be consulted with regard to the fixing of a date for the hearing of the appeal. Notice must also be given to him if the appeal is withdrawn and such notice should also be served on the Comptroller. The respondent will then be asked if he consents to the formal dismissal of the appeal and thereafter he is unlikely to be awarded costs if his consent is unconditional, see former *Practice Direction* ([1973] RPC 75).

97.15   —*Decisions and resulting orders*

The formal order of the court is drawn up automatically, supplied to the parties, and entered in the court records. A copy of the Order should then be served upon the Comptroller under rule 53 (reprinted at para. 32.11), see para. 32.20. The Order then appears in the public file at the Patent Office. The decision itself does not, however, appear on the patent file. Indeed, it should be noted that copies of the decision (as distinct from the formal Order) are not supplied to the parties automatically unless the decision is reserved and handed down in writing. Copies of the oral judgment must be ordered from the official shorthand writers, see *Practice Direction* ([1973] RPC 74), still applicable in principle, but see para. 123.48 for the availability of transcripts of court decisions in the SRIS.

97.16   —*Admission of new evidence on appeal*

The appeal is by way of rehearing, see para. 97.07 *supra*, but further evidence can only be admitted on appeal with the leave of the court (Ord. 104, r. 19(14)). Such leave is only likely to be obtained for good cause, though it may be that the strict criteria, generally applied for admission of new evidence in the Court of Appeal on appeal from the High Court, can be ameliorated in the circumstances of the case in question. These criteria are that it should be shown: that the evidence could not have been obtained with reasonable diligence for use at the original hearing; that, if given, the evidence would probably have had an important influence on the result of the case, though it need not be decisive; and that the evidence is such as presumably to be believed, *i.e.* it must be apparently credible, although it need not be incontrovertible (*Ladd* v. *Marshall*, [1954] 1 WLR 1489; [1954] 3 All ER 745).

Hence, it may be somewhat easier to adduce fresh evidence (or evidence in the first place) in appeals based on *ex parte* prosecution matters where the rules, though not excluding the presentation of evidence to the Comptroller, do not make formal provision for an evidence stage, than in *inter partes* proceedings where there has been such evidence. The *Ladd* v. *Marshall* rules were formulated against the background (as is normal in a High Court case) of the full complement of oral evidence (evidence-in-chief, cross-examination and re-examination). There may also be prayed in aid the public interest factor present in proceedings before the Comptroller, see *Oxon Italia's Trade Mark Application* ([1981] FSR 408). Also, the courts can be expected to "allow fresh evidence when to refuse it would affront common sense, or a sense of justice (*Mulholland* v. *Mitchell*, [1971] AC 666 (HL)).

Fresh evidence was refused admission in relation to an obviousness rejection in *Wistar Institute's Application* ([1983] RPC 255), and in relation to restoration in *Winventive's Patent* (SRIS O/55/83, *noted* IPD 6034), but was allowed on a late hearing of an obviousness rejection in *PCUK Produits' Application* ([1984] RPC 482). A request to cross-examine a witness on the hearing of the appeal is generally to be considered as an application to admit new evidence (*Sainsbury's Application*, [1981] FSR 406). In *Wellcome Foundation's Application* (SRIS O/72/83, *noted* IPD 6066) an applicant was allowed to submit a primer of background facts by way of explanation, rather than as evidence. As for cases under the 1949 Act, see *Mediline's Patent* ([1973] RPC 91); *Du Pont's Patent* ([1968] RPC 193); and *Kiashek's Patent* ((1954) 71 RPC 339), which generally are in keeping with the 1977 Act cases discussed above.

97.17   —*Intervention by third party*

It may be possible for a person, who was not a party to the original proceedings, to intervene in any appeal by action under RSC, Ord. 15, r. 6(2), but only when the question in issue is one which actually affects the proposed intervenor, a mere point of law not being sufficient for this purpose (*Spelling Goldberg* v. *BPC Publishing*, [1981] RPC 283).

—Other relevant rules of court   **97.18**

Attention is drawn to some of the rules of court which, though they appeared in the former Patents Appeal Tribunal Rules, are now not included within Order 104, r. 19 and yet can have considerable relevance to appeals from the Comptroller. Such rules relate to:

Hearings in camera: There is a general principle that a hearing can be held in camera where a public hearing would defeat the ends of justice: the court has complete discretion in the matter and an application should be made to the court in any appropriate case. For further information, see *The Supreme Court Practice*, para. 33/4/3. The *in camera* arrangement may persist throughout the hearing or during only part thereof (as where confidential financial information in a licensing situation is being discussed).

Cross-examination: Order 38, r. 2(3) empowers the court to order cross-examination of a witness who has made an affidavit: an application must be made to the court and if such an order is made and the witness does not attend, his affidavit may not be used without leave of the court. However, the use of the power may be restricted by the rules against the admission of new evidence on appeal, see para. 97.16 *supra*.

Scientific advisers: Order 104, r. 15 (reprinted at para. E104.15) is apt to cover the appointment of a scientific adviser on an appeal to the Patents Court, for which see para. 96.25.

New section 99A also provides power for the Patents Court (even on appeal from the Comptroller) to order the Patent Office to inquire into and report on any question of fact or opinion, see para. 99A.02.

—Non-applicable rules of court   **97.19**

Certain of the rules are expressly stated in Order 104, r. 19(18) not to apply to appeals from the Comptroller. These are, therefore, not reprinted herein but are noted as:—

Order 42, r. 7, relating to the formalities for having orders in the Chancery Division drawn up: an order will be drawn up in the Chancery Chambers (under Ord. 42, rule 7(1)), but this is done automatically;

Order 55, which is concerned with other appeals to the High Court (from, *e.g.* a tribunal), except in relation to certain powers of the Court set out in Order 55, rule 7(2), (3) and (5)–(7); and

Order 57, relating to proceedings before a Divisional Court.

Appeals from the Patents Court to the Court of Appeal

—General   **97.20**

The practice is governed generally by RSC Ord. 59, all relevant parts of which are reprinted in Appendix E at paras. E059.1–E059.18. Leave to appeal under subsection (3) must first be sought from the Patents Court and, if refused, it can then be sought by *ex parte* application to the Court of Appeal, initially in writing (see RSC Ord. 59, r. 14(2)–(2B)). Leave should first be requested at the conclusion of the judgment of the Patents Court. There is no commitment to proceed with an appeal, and it is much more convenient to request leave when all the parties are already in Court. Such an application may subsequently be made *ex parte*, but the hearing may be adjourned to be heard *inter partes*, and where this happens an unsuccessful applicant can expect to be required to pay the other side's costs (*International Paint's Application*, [1982] RPC 247).

Where leave to appeal is granted by the Patents Court, the notice of appeal must be served within four weeks following the date on which the judgment of the Patents Court was signed, entered or otherwise perfected (*i.e.* when the relevant order is entered in the court records, *not* from the date when the judgment was given by the court). Where leave to appeal is refused by the Patents Court, application for leave to appeal is made by summons to the Court of Appeal under RSC Ord. 59, r. 14(1) and within seven days of the refusal of leave by the Patents Court (Ord. 59, r. 14(2) and (3)), see para. E059.14. Where leave is then granted, the notice of appeal may be lodged within seven days of the leave being granted (Ord. 59, r. 4(3), reprinted in para. E059.4).

Where the order appealed from is one relating to the revocation of a patent, RSC Ord. 59, rule 17 (reprinted at para. E059.17) governs service of the notice of appeal and any respondent's notice on the Comptroller and the Comptroller's right to appear. Otherwise RSC Ord. 59, rule 18 (reprinted at para. E059.18) governs the procedure.

The Court of Appeal may appoint a scientific adviser in the same manner as the Patents Court, see para. 96.25.

A patent agent has no right of audience before the Court of Appeal and counsel must be instructed by a solicitor for the purposes of this further appeal or when leave to appeal is sought (often at short notice) from the Court of Appeal. A solicitor, likewise, has to be in charge of the day-to-day handling of the appeal while awaiting hearing, including such matters as the setting down of the appeal for hearing, lodgment of bundles of documents for the court, and the like. Para. E059.9A reprints the relevant parts of a Practice Statement made in 1986 relating to the preparation of bundles, etc. Such topics are beyond the scope of this work and, accordingly, no complete account of Court of Appeal practice is presented herein. Nevertheless, some comments on matters of particular interest to patent agents are given below.

97.21 —*Scientific advisers*

The question of scientific advisers is discussed in para. 96.25. It may be particularly acute in the Court of Appeal, especially in the instance of a case of substantial scientific complexity, on account of the selected members of that Court lacking any technical comprehension of the art involved, as they have been known at times openly to admit.

97.22 —*Evidence*

The *Ladd* v. *Marshall* rules, discussed in para. 97.16 *supra*, concerning the admissibility of fresh evidence on appeal, will normally be applied. For a case under the 1949 Act, see *Zakarias' Patent* ([1956] RPC 254). However, the presentation of an agreed statement of background facts, or a scientific primer, for the instruction of the Court of Appeal, as in *Johns-Manville's Patent* ([1967] RPC 479), has to be distinguished from fresh evidence.

97.23 —*Skeleton arguments*

Since about 1983 each party to an appeal before the Court of Appeal has been required to submit in advance of the hearing a "skeleton argument". This constitutes a distinctive, and useful, feature of current Court of Appeal procedure. It is discussed in the *Practice Notes* dated April 12, 1983 ([1983] 1 WLR 1055; [1983] 2 All ER 34) October 17, 1985 ([1985] 1 WLR 1156); and now see particularly the more comprehensive *Practice Direction (Court of Appeal: Presentation of Arguments)* of March 24, 1989 ([1989] 1 WLR 281; [1989] 1 All ER 89) which in an introduction explains the basis for the Practice Direction. The 1989 Direction also relates to the scope of oral argument now permitted before the Court of Appeal.

The main purpose of the skeleton argument is to provide the court with an *aide memoire* as to the main points of the party's submissions. It is provided to the court in advance, in order that the court may have a clearer idea of the issues likely to be argued before it. The skeleton argument is not intended to be a detailed dissertation, but instead (as the name of the document implies) just an outline of the party's case. Too lengthy a document may well prove to be counter-productive. Points of law should be accompanied by cross-references to the relevant authorities; and points of fact by cross-reference to relevant passages in the written or oral (transcript) evidence below. A chronology of relevant dates has also to be provided as a separate document. However, there is no overall set form for the presentation of skeleton arguments.

The skeleton argument is normally prepared by counsel, since he has the responsibility of providing the actual oral argument at the hearing, but there may well be room for the patent agent and solicitor to provide substantial assistance in its preparation and in checking its factual accuracy and that of the cross-references to the evidence. The skeleton arguments are simultaneously exchanged between the parties, and lodged with the Court of Appeal, four weeks or 10 days before the hearing according to the estimated length of the hearing (*Practice Direction of 1989, supra*). This procedure was introduced in order that there should be substantial pre-reading of the papers by the court before the hearing which should therefore be shorter than under the previous procedure.

Costs on appeal   **97.24**

Neither the Patents Court nor the Court of Appeal has power (other than in proceedings under section 40 for employee-inventor compensation, for which see para. 106.02) to award a fixed sum by way of costs unless the parties consent. The normal rule for most proceedings in the High Court is that the successful party is entitled to his costs on the "standard basis" (*i.e.* all reasonable costs reasonably incurred, but with doubts resolved in favour of the paying party, see para. E062.12). This basis is more favourable to the successful party, and correspondingly less favourable to the unsuccessful one, than was the "party and party" basis (*i.e.* all costs necessarily incurred) which prevailed prior to April 28, 1986. For the matters that are taken into account in assessing taxed costs, see paras. E062A2.1–E062A2.3. In the absence of agreement, the successful party's bill should be lodged with the Taxing Office of the High Court for taxation by a Taxing Master. It would be prudent for a patent agent to have this bill drawn up by an experienced costs clerk.

When the 1977 Act first came into force, the Patents Court continued the practice of the former Patents Appeal Tribunal and awarded a lump sum as a contribution to costs, and the Comptroller likewise continued his practice of not seeking costs whatever the result. However, it came to be appreciated that this was no longer appropriate with appeals being heard by the High Court. Consequently, in appeals from the Comptroller, whether in *ex parte* or *inter partes* proceedings, the successful party is now awarded costs to be taxed according to the normal practice in the High Court. The Court of Appeal likewise awards costs against the unsuccessful party, see *Associated British Combustion's Application* ([1978] RPC 581). It follows that the Comptroller now gives, and receives, costs when he appears on an appeal, see *Associated British Combustion's Application* (*supra*); *Omron Tateisi's Application* ([1981] RPC 125); and *ICI's (Richardson's) Application* ([1981] FSR 609). If an appeal from the Comptroller on an *ex parte* matter is lodged and then not proceeded with, the Treasury Solicitor now makes a claim for costs incurred up to withdrawal of the appeal.

Nevertheless, any award of costs remains within the ultimate discretion of the court, and the Patents Court stated in the *Omron* case (*supra*) that "There may well be instances when the Court will make variations from the normal rules, for example where the court has itself invited the Comptroller to come and assist". Thus, where an *ex parte* appeal has been taken to clarify a point of law, the Comptroller *may* be prepared to settle costs by the award of a realistic sum in lieu of taxation ((1981–82) 11 CIPA 351). In *Smith (T.J.) and Nephew's Patent (No. 2)* (SRIS C/21/88), an appellant in a compulsory licence case achieved only a minor fraction of his requested reduction from the royalty rate awarded by the Comptroller: no award of costs was made. Other special costs questions arose in *Bradley's Patent* (SRIS C/41/86) and *PPG Industries' Patent* (SRIS C/116/85).

On taxation of the costs of an appeal to the Court of Appeal there will normally be no allowance for a patent agent's assistance or attendance. However, where a patent agent has assisted the Court, for example by the provision of a background technical explanation, the Court of Appeal can be requested to signify that such assistance has been given so that the taxing master may give the question special consideration, see *Toppan Printing's Application*, SRIS C/116/83).

97.25   *Legal aid*

Legal aid is not available in proceedings before the Comptroller, see para. 107.02, but is in principle available on appeal therefrom.

In *Tiefenbrun's Application* ([1979] FSR 97) the unsuccessful appellant was legally aided with a nil contribution. The Court of Appeal ordered the costs of the respondent to be paid out of the Legal Aid Fund subject to time being given for the Law Society to make representations if it so wished. However, the Court also indicated that it had no power to order that the costs of attendance of the appellant's instructing patent agent should be covered by the legal aid certificate.

98.01   **SECTION 98**

Proceedings in Scotland

98.—(1) In Scotland proceedings relating primarily to patents (other than proceedings before the comptroller) shall be competent in the Court of Session only, and any jurisdiction of the sheriff court relating to patents is hereby abolished except in relation to questions which are incidental to the issue in proceedings which are otherwise competent there.

(2) The remuneration of any assessor appointed to assist the court in proceedings under this Act in the Court of Session shall be determined by the Lord President of the Court of Session with the consent of the Minister for the Civil Service and shall be defrayed out of moneys provided by Parliament.

Proceedings in Scotland

108.—(1) Where there is more than one party to proceedings under sec-   **98.02**
tion 8, 12, 37, 40(1) or (2), 41(8), 61(3), 71 or 72, any party thereto may
request the comptroller to direct that any hearing in such proceedings shall
be held in Scotland and—
- (*a*) the comptroller shall so direct in the following cases—
    - (i) where one party resides in Scotland and all the parties to the
      proceedings agree to a hearing being held there; or
    - (ii) where all the parties to the proceedings reside in Scotland and
      one of them requests a hearing there, unless it is shown to the
      comptroller' satisfaction that it would be unduly burdensome to
      any other party to hold the hearing there; and
- (*b*) the comptroller may direct that a hearing be held in Scotland (even
  where none of the parties resides in Scotland) where one party to
  the proceedings requests it and the balance of convenience is in
  favour of holding the hearing there.

(2) A request under paragraph (1) above shall be made in duplicate and
shall—
- (*a*) be in writing;
- (*b*) be accompanied by a statement of facts in duplicate setting out the
  grounds upon which the request is made; and
- (*c*) be filed at any time before the comptroller issues notification to the
  parties that a hearing has been appointed, or, with the leave of the
  comptroller, within fourteen days thereafter.

(3) The comptroller, upon a request being made under paragraph (1)
above, shall send a copy of the request and the statement to any party to
the proceedings who has not indicated that he consents to the request.

(4) Any party or parties to the proceedings having objection to a request
made under paragraph (1) above may, within three months of notification
of the request, file at the Patent Office a counter-statement in duplicate setting out the grounds upon which objection is taken, and the comptroller
shall send a copy of the counter-statement to any person who is not party to
it.

(5) The comptroller may give such directions as he may think fit with
regard to the subsequent procedure.

(6) Where the comptroller, after consideration of a request made under
paragraph (1)(*a*)(ii) or (*b*) above, is satisfied that any hearing thereon
should be held in Scotland, he shall grant the request and issue such directions as shall seem to him appropriate.

(7) No appeal shall lie from any decision of the comptroller under this
rule.

Commentary on Section 98

98.03 *General*

Section 98 provides for jurisdiction in Scotland in relation to proceedings under the 1977 or 1949 Act brought before the court in that country, including proceedings relating to "existing patents" (Sched. 2, para. 1(2)). By section 130(1) "court" in relation to Scotland means "the Court of Session" and initially means the Outer House of that Court. The former jurisdiction believed to have resided in the sheriff court was specifically abolished by subsection (1) and the provisions of sections 287–292 [1988], for establishing Patents County Courts, do so only for England and Wales (s. 304 [1988]).

Section 31 makes specific provision for the transfer of patent rights under Scots law, see the commentary on that section. The "territorial scope of infringement" is discussed in para. 60.28; the statutory limitation period for actions under Scots law is discussed in para. 60.28; and special provision for privilege in patent proceedings in Scotland is provided by section 105. Parallel provisions to section 98 exist in relation to proceedings in Northern Ireland, see section 131 and the commentary thereon; and to proceedings in the Isle of Man, see section 132(2) and para. 132.05.

Subsection (2) corresponds to section 70(2) of the Supreme Court Act 1981 (c. 54) discussed in para. 96.25.

98.04 *Terminology*

Cases decided under Scots law use legal terminology with which patent agents may be unaccustomed. The corresponding terms were previously set out in section 103(6) [1949] as follows, with Scottish terms in parentheses: "injunction" ("interdict"); "chose in action" ("right of action or an incorporeal moveable"); "account of profits" ("accounting and payment of profits"); "arbitrator" ("arbiter"); "plaintiff" ("pursuer"); and "defendant" ("defender"). Other Scots law terms include: "assignation" (for assignment); "delict" (for a tort); "declarator"(for a declaration); and "expenses" (for costs).

98.05 *Jurisdiction of the Court in Scotland*

Since January 1, 1987, the Civil Jurisdiction and Judgments Act 1982 (c. 27) [the "CJJA"] has regulated, *inter alia*, jurisdiction between the component parts of the United Kingdom, as discussed in para. 96.24 and see also the books listed in para. 96.12. Schedule 4 of the CJJA regulates the cases where persons must, or may, be sued in the courts of a particular component part of the United Kingdom. The primary rule is that persons "domiciled" in one particular component part *shall* be sued in the courts of that part (Sched. 4, art. 2), but a court of a component part also has jurisdiction in cases of tort, delict or quasi-delict where the harmful event occurred in that part or, in the case of a threatened wrong, where this is likely to occur in that component part (Sched. 4, art. 5).

"Domiciled" for this purpose is defined in the CJJA (ss. 41–46). In the case of an individual, a person is domiciled in a particular part of the United Kingdom "if and only if (*a*) he is resident in that part; *and* (*b*) the nature and circumstances of his residence indicates that he has a substantial connection with that part" (s. 41(3)), though (*b*) is not required if its provisions are not satisfied in relation to *any* particular part of the United Kingdom (s. 41(5)). In the case of a company incorporated under any of the United Kingdom Companies Acts, the company must have its "seat" in that particular part of the United Kingdom and this is so if it has its registered office in that part (ss. 42(1) and 43(5)). For any other company or corporation, it is sufficient if such has its "seat" in the United Kingdom; and (a) its registered office is in the particular part of the United Kingdom in question; or (b) its central management and control is exercised in that part; or (c) it has a place of business in that part (s. 42(4)). For further discussion of "domicile" for the purposes of the CJJA (which differs from the normal concept of domicile under English law), see the books listed in para. 96.12.

These general rules are applied to proceedings in Scotland by Schedule 8 of the CJJA (paras. 1 and 2(3) thereof). Also, proceedings may be taken for an interdict [injunction in English terminology] before a Scottish court where a wrong is likely to be committed in Scotland (Sched. 8, para. 2(10)); and the Court of Session expressly maintains jurisdiction to adjudicate in proceedings principally concerned with the registration or validity of United Kingdom patents (Sched. 8, paras. 2(14) and 4(2)).

Here it should be noted that an interdict (injunction) granted by a Scottish court has no effect in another component part of the United Kingdom, and *vice versa*. Separate proceedings have hitherto had to be commenced for a parallel interdict or injunction, but it is possible that, under the new law of the CJJA, a court in one part of the United Kingdom will now feel able to impose an injunction effective throughout the United Kingdom, at least in respect of a person resident within the jurisdiction of that court.

Omitted from Schedule 4 of the CJJA are provisions corresponding to articles 21–23 of the Brussels Convention (CJJA, Sched. 1, arts. 21–23) which would, otherwise, require or suggest a stay of proceedings in a court when parallel, or connected, proceedings are commenced in different parts of the United Kingdom. Thus, whether any particular litigation should be brought, or continued, in Scotland or England, where similar causes of action occur in both jurisdictions may (although the CJJA permits such actions to be commenced without leave) continue to be decided on considerations based on the doctrine of *forum conveniens*, for which the leading cases are *MacShannon* v. *Rockware Glass* ([1978] AC 795 (HL)) and *The Spiliada* ([1987] AC 460; [1986] 3 All ER 843 (HL)).

—Types of patent proceedings justiciable in Scotland   **98.06**

Where infringement, or threatened infringement, occurs in Scotland, proceedings under section 61 can be brought before the Court of Session. Such proceedings can also be brought against a person domiciled in Scotland, even in respect of infringements occurring, or threatened, in some other part of the United Kingdom. It is also possible to bring action in Scotland against a person domiciled in Scotland for infringement of a foreign patent, see para. 61.06.

Proceedings can also be brought before the Court of Session in Scotland under: section 58 (*Compensation for Crown use*); section 69 (*Infringement of rights conferred by publication of a patent application*); section 70 (*Remedy for groundless threats of infringement proceedings*); or section 71 (*Declaration of non-infringement*). Moreover, where a patent proprietor is domiciled in Scotland, revocation proceedings under section 72 (or register rectification proceedings under s. 34) can be brought in the Court of Session, but it is not clear that a Scottish court is required to accept jurisdiction over such proceedings when there is no nexus of any of the parties with Scotland, despite that Court being rendered competent for this purpose (CJJA, Sched. 8, paras. 2(14) and 4(2)). The Court of Session can also be expected to hear claims for employee-inventor compensation under section 40, though again probably only when the employee or employer is domiciled in Scotland.

If the Comptroller orders employee-inventor compensation under section 40, this can be enforced in Scotland as a recorded decree arbitrarl (s. 41(10)).

An example of an infringement action decided in Scotland in recent years is that of *Plasticisers* v. *Stewart* ([1975] RPC 491). Other cases are: *Christian Salvesen* v. *Odfejeld Drilling [Scotland]* ([1985] RPC 569), discussed in para. 68.02 in relation to the entitlement of an exclusive licencsse to institute infringement proceedings; and *Brupat* v. *Smith* ([1985] FSR 156), discussed in para. 65.02 in relation to the grant of a certificate of contested validity. Other reported cases since 1949 are: *Speedcranes* v. *Thomson* ([1978] RPC 221), a case of threats discussed in paras. 70.04 and 74.09; and *Anemostat* v. *Michaelis* ([1957] RPC 167), an alleged employee-inventor case decided under the common law, now more relevant as an illustration of the use of Scots legal terminology.

The rules of court applicable to patent proceedings before the Court of Session are discussed in para. 98.09.

98.07 *Proceedings before the Comptroller in Scotland*

Under rule 108 (reprinted at para. 98.02, *supra*), made under the authority of section 123(2)(*f*) referred to in para. 123.28, the Comptroller has power to hold in Scotland a hearing in proceedings under certain specified sections of the Act. These are (as listed in r. 108) proceedings under sections: 8, 12 or 37 (*Entitlement proceedings*); 40(1), 40(2) or 41(8) (*Employee-inventor compensation*); 61(3) (*Infringement proceedings before the Comptroller*); 71 (*Declaration of non-infringement by Comptroller*); and 72 (*Revocation by Comptroller*). Rule 108 also applies to proceedings under the 1968 Rules (r. 124(1)(*d*) [1978], reprinted at para. 127.04) and, therefore, can apply to a hearing for the determination of a co-ownership or employee-inventor dispute in relation to an "existing patent" under respectively section 55 or 56 [1949].

The holding in Scotland of a hearing in such proceedings requires a direction of the Comptroller made after request and requires at least one of the parties to reside in Scotland. Where only one party resides in Scotland, all the parties must agree to a hearing there (r. 108(1)(*a*)(i)), and where all the parties reside in Scotland the hearing is to be held there if any party so requests, unless it is shown to the Comptroller's satisfaction that it would be unduly burdensome to *any* other party to hold the hearing there (r. 108(1)(*a*)(ii)). However, even when no party resides in Scotland, the Comptroller has power to order a hearing there if one party so requests and "the balance of convenience is in favour of having that hearing there".

Nevertheless, no case is known in which the Comptroller has yet held a full hearing in Scotland, either under the Act or under the 1949 Act which gave (for the first time) a similar power, but in *Tiefenbrun's Application* ([1979] FSR 97) the Comptroller sat in Scotland to hear a witness who was unable to travel on medical grounds.

There is no appeal from a decision of the Comptroller under rule 108 (r. 108(7)).

The practice for requesting a hearing before the Comptroller in Scotland is described in para. 98.10, *infra*.

98.08 *Appeals in Scottish proceedings*

Any appeal from a decision of the Comptroller after a hearing in Scotland has to be taken to the Court of Session (s. 97(4)), the Patents Court now having no jurisdiction (s. 97(1)). A further appeal from the Outer House of the Court of Session to the Inner House thereof is only possible in certain circumstances (s. 97(5). These are analogous to those in which a further appeal from a decision of the Comptroller may be taken from the Patents Court to the (English) Court of Appeal, see section 97(3).

As regards proceedings initiated in the Court of Session, an appeal therefrom may be taken, as of right, to the Inner House of that Court and then, with leave, to the House of Lords (in Scotland), but leave is not required when the appeal relates to a final judgment disposing of the whole case.

For an example of parallel actions against different defendants on the same patent which proceeded contemporaneously before the courts of England and Scotland leading (after opposite conclusions in the respective appeal courts) to eventual appeals to the House of Lords, which were heard together, see *British Thomson-Houston* v. *Charlesworth, Peebles* and *Same* v. *British Insulated Cables* ((1925) 42 RPC 180).

PRACTICE UNDER SECTION 98

Proceedings before the Court **98.09**

The rules of court applicable to proceedings in Scotland under the Act are those set out in the Act of Sederunt. The rules mainly applicable are those first made after the coming into force of the Act by the Act of Sederunt (Rules of Court Amendment No. 8) (Patents Rules) 1978 (S.I. 1978 No. 955 (s. 84)), (reprinted at [1979] RPC 188). These rules originally generally followed those of RSC Ord. 104 (reprinted at paras. E104.1–E104.22) with appropriate changes in terminology, but they have not, as yet, been revised to follow the changes to RSC Ord. 104 made in 1986 for proceedings in the Patents Court. Section 99B, introduced by the 1988 Act, makes provision (analogously as does s. 99A for the Patents Court and s. 291(3)(*b*) [1988] for Patents County Courts) for the Court of Session to be able to order the Patent Office to inquire into and report on any question of fact or opinion, see the commentaries on sections 99A and 99B.

The Rules of Sederunt provide (in like manner to RSC Ord. 104, r. 2, reprinted at para. E104.2) for a Lord Ordinary of the Court of Session (to be known as "the Patent Judge") to be assigned to determine all proceedings in Scotland under the 1949 and 1977 Acts, as well as under the Registered Designs Acts 1949–61 and the Defence Contracts Act 1958. The present incumbent of that position is Lord Dervaird.

Hearings by the Comptroller in Scotland **98.10**

By rule 108(2) (reprinted in para. 98.02 *supra*) a request for the Comptroller to hold a hearing in Scotland is to be made to the Comptroller in duplicate; in writing; and be accompanied by a statement of facts (also in duplicate) setting out the grounds upon which the request is made. No special forms are prescribed for such a request or statement and there is no fee. The request must be made before the Comptroller issues notice to the parties that a hearing has been appointed, or (if the Comptroller gives leave) within 14 days after the date when the hearing is appointed.

Upon receipt of such a request, the Comptroller sends a copy of the request and statement to each other party to the proceedings who has not indicated his consent to the request (r. 108(3)). If any party objects to the holding of the hearing in Scotland, he must within three months file (in duplicate) a counter-statement setting out the grounds of his objection. This counter-statement is then sent by the Comptroller to any person not party to it (r. 108(4)). Thereafter, the Comptroller may give such directions as he thinks appropriate (r. 108(5)). When the Comptroller is satisfied that a hearing should be held in Scotland, he is required to grant the request and issue appropriate directions (r. 108(6)). No appeal lies against this decision (r. 108(7)). Clearly, if a request for a hearing before the Comptroller in Scotland is not made with the consent of all parties, the determination of that request is likely to be a time-consuming (and expensive) process.

SECTION 99

99.01 General powers of the Court

99. The court may, for the purpose of determining any question in the exercise of its original or appellate jurisdiction under this Act or any treaty or international convention to which the United Kingdom is a party, make any order or exercise any other power which the comptroller could have made or exercised for the purpose of determining that question.

99.02 COMMENTARY ON SECTION 99

Section 99 is a general provision ensuring that the court may exercise original jurisdiction in relation to any matter where such could have been done by the Comptroller. It applies also to "existing patents" (Sched. 2, para. 1(2)). An example of exercise of this power is *Omron Tateisi's Application* ([1981] RPC 125) where the court held that, under section 99, it had itself the power to grant a certificate of postal delay which the Comptroller could have granted under rule 111 (reprinted at para. 123.11 and discussed at para. 123.39). Similarly, in *Allen & Hanburys' (Salbutamol) Patent* ([1987] RPC 327 (CA)), it was held that, where the Comptroller has exercised his discretion, the Patents Court (and the Court of Appeal on further appeal) is entitled to exercise a fresh discretion of its own, see further at para. 97.07. Presumably such power could be exercised by any of the courts designated by section 130(1) as a "court" for the purposes of the Act.

99A.01 SECTION 99A

Power of Patents Court to order report

99A.—(1) Rules of court shall make provision empowering the Patents Court in any proceedings before it under this Act, on or without the application of any party, to order the Patent Office to inquire into and report on any question of fact or opinion.

(2) Where the court makes such an order on the application of a party, the fee payable to the Patent Office shall be at such rate as may be determined in accordance with rules of court and shall be costs of the proceedings unless otherwise ordered by the court.

(3) Where the court makes such an order of its own motion, the fee payable to the Patent Office shall be at such rate as may be determined by the Lord Chancellor with the approval of the Treasury and shall be paid out of money provided by Parliament.

Note. Section 99A was prospectively inserted by the 1988 Act (Sched. 5, para. 26). For commencement of the section, see the latest Supplement to this work *re* this para.

COMMENTARY ON SECTION 99A

General   **99A.02**

Section 99A (to be inserted into the Act by the 1988 Act) is an enabling provision to provide for rules of court to empower the Patents Court to call for a inquiry or report from the Patent Office on any fact or opinion in a matter before it. Section 99B provides a similar enabling power for proceedings in the Scottish Court of Session, and section 291(3)–(5) [1988] (reprinted in para. 96.10 and discussed in para. 96.22) is analogous for proceedings in a Patents County Court. No such rules have yet been made.

Request for inquiry and report   **99A.03**

Under each of the provisions listed in para. 99A.02 *supra*, the court will be able to request the Patent Office to inquire into, and report on, any question of fact or opinion arising in proceedings before it, and may do so on the request of any party to the proceedings or on the initiative of the court itself. It is envisaged that fees will be payable to the Patent Office for any such inquiry and report, and that these will, in due course, become costs allowable on taxation to the successful party, except when the referral to the Patent Office is made on the initiative of the court when the fees are to be paid out of central funds.

Purpose of inquiry and report   **99A.04**

It remains to be seen whether, and to what extent, the provisions of sections 99A, 99B and 291(3) [1988] will be given effect. The purpose would seem to be to model patent litigation in future more on the investigative basis used in Continental systems of law and in the EPO, and therefore to move away from the traditional British adversarial style of litigation. Such change could have a profound effect on the determination of questions of obviousness where, at least hitherto, determination by the courts has been firmly based upon the evidence given at trial by persons skilled in the relevant art at the relevant date, often with especial emphasis on the sequence of contemporaneous events at the date of the patent which may rank as indicia of obviousness or non-obviousness, see paras. 3.07–3.14. It is not immediately clear as to how the concept of a report from the Patent Office could be properly married together with the concept of wholly oral evidence stages, given that the former stage would, logistically, necessarily have to come in advance of the latter.

However, if there is a move to evidence-in-chief being presented in writing (as seems at least likely in the Patents County Court), then it may be that a factual report from the Patent Office on that evidence (and/or on the case generally) could serve to focus the issues which the court has to decide, in a manner similar to the role of the Advocate-General in proceedings before the European Court of Justice in Luxembourg. Here the Advocate-General prepares for the Court a written opinion in which he analyses the issues before the Court and suggests the decision that should be given. Then, at the oral hearing, the parties tend to concentrate their arguments by supporting, or criticising, the views of the Advocate-General and, though the eventual decision does not always adopt the view of the Advocate-General, it does so in a majority of cases. Another model is provided by the kind of provisional report often issued in opposition proceedings before the EPO, for which see *EPH*.

99A.05 *Opinion from the European Patent Office*

Under EPCa. 25 a national court trying an infringement action on a European patent can request the EPO to give a technical opinion concerning that patent. The procedure is governed by EPO Guidelines E-XII. Note that such an opinion can only be given on "technical" matters. The opinion is given by the Examining Division of the EPO and is not regarded as a decision and so is not subject to any appeal in the EPO. The Guidelines indicate that the EPO will accept submissions from the parties prior to rendering its opinion which, however, must be objective; moreover, care must be taken not to impinge on the decision-making powers of the court which has requested the opinion.

At the time of writing, there does not appear to have been any request, from any national court, for an EPO technical opinion under EPCa. 25.

99B.01

SECTION 99B

Power of Court of Session to order report

99B.—(1) In any proceedings before the Court of Session under this Act the court may, either of its own volition or on the application of any party, order the Patent Office to inquire into and report on any question of fact or opinion.

(2) Where the court makes an order under subsection (1) above of its own volition the fee payable to the Patent Office shall be at such rate as may be determined by the Lord President of the Court of Session with the consent of the Treasury and shall be defrayed out of monies provided by Parliament.

(3) Where the court makes an order under subsection (1) above on the application of a party, the fee payable to the Patent Office shall be at such rate as may be provided for in rules of court and shall be treated as expenses in the cause.

Note. Section 99B was prospectively inserted by the 1988 Act (Sched. 5, para. 26). For its commencement, see the latest Supplement to this Work *re.* this para.

99B.02   COMMENTARY ON SECTION 99B

Section 99B is exactly analogous to section 99A in that it will provide power for the Court of Session in Scotland to request the Patent Office to make an inquiry or report on any fact or opinion in proceedings before the Court under the Act. A similar power also exists for the patents county courts in England and Wales (s. 291(3) [1988], reprinted in para. 96.10 and discussed in para. 96.22). The scope of the provision is discussed in para. 99A.03, and its possible use and effect in para. 99A.04.

Note also the power of the Court of Session to request a technical opinion from the EPO in proceedings involving a European patent, as discussed in para. 99A.05.

Litigation in Scotland is generally discussed in the commentary on section 98. At the time of writing no Rule of Sederunt (rule of court for Scottish proceedings in the Court of Session) has been made which would bring section 99B into effect.

SECTION 100

Burden of proof in certain cases

100.—(1) If the invention for which a patent is granted is a process for obtaining a new product, the same product produced by a person other than the proprietor of the patent or a licensee of his shall, unless the contrary is proved, be taken in any proceedings to have been obtained by that process.

(2) In considering whether a party has discharged the burden imposed upon him by this section the court shall not require him to disclose any manufacturing or commercial secrets if it appears to the court that it would be unreasonable to do so.

100.01

COMMENTARY ON SECTION 100

General

100.02

Section 100 was a new provision in the present Act. It concerns the onus of proof in cases of infringement where the patent is for a process for obtaining a *new* product. If the same product is produced, there is an assumption that that product is made by the patented process, unless the contrary is proved. Thus, in such a case, the onus of proof of infringement is shifted from the plaintiff and it falls upon the defendant to prove non-infringement. There is a provision for protection of the defendant's confidential information (subs. (2)), see para. 100.04 *infra*. The section, by section 130(7), is intended to have, as nearly as practicable, the same effects in the United Kingdom as CPCa. 75.

The section has obvious application to chemical cases but, because chemical process patents that result in new products that are chemically definable usually have claims to the product *per se*, the section may have little practical application to such cases. The section therefore mainly applies to a patent that includes no claim to the product *per se*. Otherwise, by section 60(1)(*c*), disposal of the product of a claimed process is infringement of the patent.

Doubts as to the ambit of subsection (1)

100.03

The section is not clear in several respects. "Products" is not defined and there is no guide as to whether it is intended to be given a meaning, appropriate to chemical cases, of a new composition of matter, or whether it is intended to have a broader meaning of anything that is produced; there is no obvious limitation of the section to chemical cases. "New" is not defined in the context of the section; section 1 defines an invention as new if it does not form part of the state of the art and this definition could be appropriate to "a new product", but in that event a product could be considered new if it is not exactly the same as anything comprised in the state of the art, that is it could be a known product modified or improved in some respect, such as a magnetic material having properties superior to any previously known. It is not clear what is meant by a process for "obtaining" the new product.

This could mean that the process must be directed to synthesising or fabricating the product, but it would seem to be an arbitrary definition of this expression to exclude a process of, say, making a melt of materials and heat treating the melt on cooling in such way as to produce the improved magnetic materials referred to. Whether the section would apply to a patent directed to the method of heat treatment is even more difficult to discern.

There is also doubt in chemical cases as to the meaning of "the same product". Such difficulty has arisen in those countries where there has been a similar provision. It is beyond the scope of this commentary to examine the law in such countries, but the "*Alkylenediamine II*" decision of the German Federal Supreme Court ((1977) 8 IIC 350) gives an indication of the kinds of problems that may arise. In that case the *d*-isomer used in the defendant's drug was held to be a material of the same composition as the racemic mixture produced by the patented method. The extent to which "the same product" will permit application of the section to a non-identical product, as in this German case, must be a matter for speculation. "The same product" is likely to give rise to difficulty in other cases.

100.04   *Protection of confidential information (subs. (2))*

Subsection (2) provides that a defendant under this section may not be forced to disclose manufacturing or commercial secrets if the court thinks this would be unreasonable in all the circumstances. In this context "disclose" presumably means disclose to the plaintiff. Nevertheless, if the defendant is to discharge the burden of proof imposed upon him by subsection (1), some disclosure must presumably be made. Thus, subsection (2) indicates that such disclosure could be in confidence, for example to legal advisers only, or perhaps also to the plaintiff under conditions preventing further disclosure, as in *Warner-Lambert* v. *Glaxo* ([1975] RPC 354); *Centri-Spray* v. *Cera* ([1979] FSR 175); *Roussel-Uclaf* v. *ICI* (SRIS C/67/89); and other cases as noted in para. 72.44A. Without such a safeguard, there would be the possibility of a plaintiff starting an action mainly to obtain details of a defendant's secret process. The rather different wording of CPCa. 75(2) is interesting.

100.05   *Operation of the section in practice*

Although, as yet, there appears to be no instance of section 100 being pleaded in any specific case, *Farmos* v. *Wellcome Foundation* (SRIS C/55/84 (CA)) may be noted for a case where the Defendant-patentee was able to prove, without the benefit of the section, infringement of a process claim by importation of a resulting product. This was done by showing the presence of impurities in the imported product, it being held that these indicated (in the absence of a satisfactory explanation from the other party) that the claimed process had been used abroad to make that product.

SECTION 101

Exercise of comptroller's discretionary powers

101.01   **101.** Without prejudice to any rule of law, the comptroller shall give any party to a proceeding before him an opportunity of being heard before exercising adversely to that party any discretion vested in the comptroller by this Act or rules.

Comptroller's discretionary powers

88.—(1) The comptroller shall, before exercising any discretionary **101.02**
power vested in him by the Act or these Rules adversely to any party to a
proceeding before him, give that party at least fourteen days' notice of the
time when he may be heard.

(2) If in *inter partes* proceedings a party desires to be heard he shall
notify the comptroller on Patents Form No. 46/77 and the comptroller may
refuse to hear any party who has not filed the said form prior to the date of
hearing.

(3) If in *inter partes* proceedings a party intends to refer at the hearing to
any document not already mentioned in the proceedings, he shall give to
the other party and to the comptroller at least fourteen days' notice of his
intention, together with details of every document to which he intends to
refer.

(4) After hearing the party or parties desiring to be heard or, if neither
so desires, then without a hearing, the comptroller shall decide the application and notify his decision to the parties, giving reasons for his decision
if so required by either party.

Hearings in public

89. Where a hearing before the comptroller of any dispute between two **101.03**
or more parties relating to any matter in connection with a patent or an
application for a patent takes place after the publication of the application
under section 16, the hearing of the dispute shall be in public, unless the
comptroller, after consultation with those parties to the dispute who
appear in person or are represented at the hearing, otherwise directs.

COMMENTARY ON SECTION 101

General **101.04**

Section 101 (which applies also to "existing patents", Schedule 2, para. 1(2))
provides that the Comptroller, before exercising his discretion in any matter under
either the 1949 or 1977 Acts adversely to any party to the proceedings, must afford
that party an opportunity of being heard. The section is similar to provisions in the
former patents statutes. It statutorily expresses the general rule of natural justice in
British administrative law that no one may be penalised by a decision of a tribunal
unless he has been given a fair opportunity to know and answer the case against
him. A corollary of this rule is that the person must also be given proper and prior
notice of the case he has to meet before the tribunal, *e.g.* an examiner must have set
out adequately his objection to allowing an application to proceed to grant. A
further consequence of section 101 is that an application may not be rejected (*e.g.*
under s. 18(3)) without the applicant (or his agent) having been given the chance to
be heard (*S's Application*, [1977] RPC 367).

The EPO appears to be following a similar principle. Thus, in *EPO Decision J04/82*, *"Priority Declaration/Yoshida"* (OJEPO 10/1982, 385), it was stated that there was a substantial procedural violation when a decision was issued without having fixed a time limit for submissions or without having waiting for a reasonable time for these. Also, an appeal was allowed where the decision was based on a ground on which the appellant had had no opportunity to present his comments (*EPO Decision J 07/82*, *"Cause of non-compliance/Cataldo"*, OJEPO 10/1982, 391).

101.05 *Procedure for hearings*

The procedure under section 101 is governed by rule 88 (reprinted at para. 101.02 *supra*), unless the hearing is under the 1949 Act when rule 45 [1968] (reprinted at para. A033.09) applies. Before exercising his discretion adversely to a party, the Comptroller must give a party 14 days' notice of the time when he may be heard (r. 88(1)). This applies to all hearings, including matters under the 1949 Act (r. 124(1)(*d*) [1978], reprinted at para. 127.04). Unfortunately, there appears to be no power whereby an applicant could waive this requirement. In addition, in *inter partes* proceedings only, each party wishing to be heard should be filed before the hearing PF 46/77 (reprinted at para. 144.46), or PF No. 13 (reprinted at para. A122) if the hearing is under the 1949 Act, failing which that party may not be, but in practice is, heard (r. 88(2); r. 45(2) [1968]).

Also the Comptroller, and any other party, must be given fourteen days' notice of any document not already mentioned in the proceedings, together with "details of every document" to which it is intended to refer at a hearing (r. 88(3)), though under the 1949 Act, rule 45(3) [1968] requires only at least 10 days' notice of each "publication" to which it is intended to refer. It is also customary to give notice of any legal precedents to which reference may be made in argument. For further information on procedure at hearings, see para. 72.48; and for the right of audience at hearings, see substituted section 102 (reprinted at para. 102.02) and paras. 102.14 and 102.16.

101.06 *Communication of decisions*

The Comptroller decides the matter in issue, with a hearing if any party requests it, or otherwise without a hearing, and informs the parties of his decision, giving his reasons if required by either party to do so. The practice with regard to written decisions in *ex parte* hearings under the 1949 Act was stated to be as follows:

"If a decision adverse to the applicant is made orally at a hearing, then notwithstanding the applicant's acceptance of that decision, he may request a written decision in order that he may consider the possibility of appealing. Equally, a decision adverse to the applicant issued subsequent to the hearing is always in the form of a written decision. If, however, a finding is made in the applicant's favour, a written decision is not issued. Even if judgment is reserved, an ordinary official letter stating that the objection is withdrawn is all that is required so that action by the Examiner may be resumed or concluded."

A consequence of this practice is that written precedents favourable to applicants are only available from successful appeals, and not from Patent Office decisions. Nevertheless it would seem that a party could require the Comptroller to give a reasoned decision on any case by virtue of the provisions of the Tribunals and Inquiries Act 1971 (c. 62, s. 12(1) and Sched. 1).

Public access to hearings and decisions   **101.07**

The access of the public to hearings in proceedings before the Comptroller is largely governed by rule 89 (reprinted at para. 101.03 *supra*). The origin of this rule is rule 156 [1968] which was then new. Rule 156 [1968] (reprinted at para. A117), is still applicable to proceedings under the 1949 Act. By these rules, where a hearing is in respect of a matter concerning a patent or application which takes place after publication of the application, the hearing will normally be in public, unless after consultation with the parties concerned at the hearing the Comptroller decides otherwise. However, note that a decision whether a hearing should be *in camera* can only be given after the representations in respect thereof have themselves been made in public. Cases in which the public has been excluded for at least part of the hearing are believed to be those in which sensitive financial information has been disclosed during an application for a compulsory licence or for settlement of the terms of a "licence of right"; and where details of secret manufacturing processes have been given as incidental to an allegation of prior user. An order for *in camera* proceedings may also arise in entitlement or inventorship disputes under any of sections 8, 12, 13, 37 and 82, or in applications for employee-inventor compensation under section 40, each where commercially sensitive information may be disclosed during oral evidence or need to be discussed during the proceedings.

While a written decision will necessarily be made available to the public, if only by inspection of the file in the Patent Office, there are precedents for confidential information to be contained in an appendix to the decision which is made available to the parties and their advisers only, see *Geigy's Patent* ([1964] RPC 391).

Appealability of decisions of the Comptroller   **101.08**

Any decision of the Comptroller given under section 101 is appealable (*Omron Tateisi's Application*, [1981] RPC 125). However, clear errors in a decision have been corrected by the Comptroller by following RSC Order 20, rule 11 (reprinted at para. E020.11) without the need for appeal (*Eli Lilly's Patent (No. 4)*, SRIS O/180/88).

PRACTICE UNDER SECTION 101

Fixing of hearing date   **101.09**

The Patent Office will normally try to be helpful in fixing a hearing date which is convenient to all the parties and their chosen representatives. A preliminary notice is normally sent out indicating that the case is now ready for hearing. An agent should then promptly inform the hearings clerk as to the manner of intended representation. Then, if counsel is to appear, that clerk will normally liaise directly with counsel's clerk in an attempt to find a date mutually convenient for all concerned. However, without agreement of the parties, hearing dates will not be unduly delayed because of the unavailability of chosen counsel.

Notice of hearings   **101.10**

Notification of hearings whether *ex parte* or *inter partes*, is given on the board inside the front door of the former Patent Office at 25 Southampton Buildings. The hearing will take place in the Court Room at that address, unless otherwise stated. However, *ex parte* hearings are often held in the Patent Office itself, at State House, High Holborn. For these, the room notified as that in which the hearing will take place is in fact a waiting room, where the examiner will be encountered, the hearing itself often taking place in the room of the hearing officer chosen to take it.

101.11 *Procedure at hearings*

An examiner will normally be in attendance; a tape recording will be made; and a shorthand writer will be present in most contested cases. The longstanding practice of the court in requiring the applicant/proprietor to open the hearing (except in cases of "obtaining") is followed in accordance with the *Comptroller's Ruling 1910* (F) ((1910) 27 RPC Appendix vii, following p. 184), but the continuing reason for this has been unsuccessfully questioned (*Du Pont's (Hull's) Application*, [1979] FSR 128 and *Jackson and Molloy's Patent*, SRIS O/88/83), see further para. 72.48.

For representation at hearings, see substituted section 102 (reprinted at para. 102.02) and paras. 102.14 and 102.16.

101.12 *Publication of decisions*

When a written decision is given on behalf of the Comptroller on an application which has previously been published, a copy of the decision is normally passed to the Science Reference and Information Service. The SRIS collection of Patent Office decisions extends back to 1965. The SRIS will prepare photocopies of such decisions on request. This is in contrast to decisions of the court where copies can only be obtained on request to the shorthand writers involved. For further discussion on the public availability of decisions, see para. 123.48.

102.01   **SECTION 102 [Prospectively replaced]**

Right of audience in patent proceedings

[**102.**—(1) *Any party to any proceedings before the comptroller under this Act or any treaty or international convention to which the United Kingdom is a party may appear before the comptroller in person or be represented by counsel or a solicitor (of any part of the United Kingdom) or a patent agent or, subject to rules under section 115 below, by any other person whom he desires to represent him.*

(2) Subsection (1) above, in its application to proceedings **in relation to applications for, or otherwise in connection with, European patents** *[under any such treaty or convention]* **shall have effect subject to section 84(1) or (3) above.**

(3) **Without prejudice to the right of counsel to appear before the High Court, a member of the Bar of England and Wales who is not in actual practice, a solicitor of the Supreme Court and a patent agent shall each have the right to appear and be heard on behalf of any party to an appeal under this Act from the comptroller to the Patents Court.**]

Note. Section 102 (subsection (2) of which was amended by the Administration of Justice Act 1985 (c. 61, s. 60)) has been prospectively replaced by a new substituted section 102 and by a new section 102A (reprinted respectively at paras. 102.02 and 102.03 *infra.*) (Sched. 5, para. 27 [1988]). These provisions are prospectively supplemented by sections 274–279, 285 and 286 [1988] contained in Part V of the 1988 Act in the section thereof entitled "Patent agents", and are reprinted at paras. 102.04–102.11 *infra*. These latter sections (when brought into force) will also replace sections 84, 85, 114 and 115, each prospectively repealed, and for convenience all these new provisions are now dealt with in the commentary which follows. Also concerned with "patent agents" are: section 104 (*Privilege*), now prospectively repealed and replaced by s. 280 [1988] and dealt with in paras. 104.02 *et seq.*; and section 115 (*Refusal to deal with certain agents*), now prospectively repealed and replaced by s. 281 [1988] and dealt with in paras. 115.04 *et seq.* All of these new provisions, however, remain to be brought into effect at a date yet to be specified, for which the latest Supplement to this Work should be consulted *re.* this para. Until then the original provisions continue to have effect. No commentary thereon has been provided, but see the Second Edition of this work.

SECTION 102 [Prospectively substituted]   102.02

Right of audience, &c. in proceedings before comptroller

102.—(1) A party to proceedings before the comptroller under this Act, or under any treaty or international convention to which the United Kingdom is a party, may appear before the comptroller in person or be represented by any person whom he desires to represent him.

(2) No offence is committed under the enactments relating to the preparation of documents by persons not legally qualified by reason only of the preparation by any person of a document, other than a deed, for use in such proceedings.

(3) Subsection (1) has effect subject to rules made under section 281 of the Copyright, Designs and Patents Act 1988 (power of comptroller to refuse to recognise certain agents).

(4) In its application to proceedings in relation to applications for, or otherwise in connection with, European patents, this section has effect subject to any restrictions imposed by or under the European Patent Convention.

SECTION 102A   102.03

Right of audience &c. in proceedings on appeal from the comptroller

102A.—(1) A solicitor of the Supreme Court may appear and be heard on behalf of any party to an appeal under this Act from the comptroller to the Patents Court.

(2) A registered patent agent or a member of the Bar not in actual practice may do, in or in connection with proceedings on an appeal under this Act from the comptroller to the Patents Court, anything which a solicitor of the Supreme Court might do, other than prepare a deed.

(3) The Lord Chancellor may by regulations—

(*a*) provide that the right conferred by subsection (2) shall be subject to such conditions and restrictions as appear to the Lord Chancellor to be necessary or expedient, and

(*b*) apply to persons exercising that right such statutory provisions, rules of court and other rules of law and practice applying to solicitors as may be specified in the regulations;

and different provision may be made for different descriptions of proceedings.

(4) Regulations under this section shall be made by statutory instrument which shall be subject to annulment in pursuance of a resolution of either House of Parliament.

(5) This section is without prejudice to the right of counsel to appear before the High Court.

102.04   SECTION 274 [1988]

Persons permitted to carry on business of a patent agent

274.—(1) Any individual, partnership or body corporate may, subject to the following provisions of this Part, carry on the business of acting as agent for others for the purpose of—

(*a*) applying for or obtaining patents, in the United Kingdom or elsewhere, or

(*b*) conducting proceedings before the comptroller relating to applications for, or otherwise in connection with, patents.

(2) This does not affect any restriction under the European Patent Convention as to who may act on behalf of another for any purpose relating to European patents.

102.05   SECTION 275 [1988]

The register of patent agents

275.—(1) The Secretary of State may make rules requiring the keeping of a register of persons who act as agent for others for the purposes of applying for or obtaining patents; and in this Part a "registered patent agent" means a person whose name is entered in the register kept under this section.

(2) The rules may contain such provision as the Secretary of State thinks fit regulating the registration of persons, and may in particular—

(*a*) require the payment of such fees as may be prescribed, and

(*b*) authorise in prescribed cases the erasure from the register of the name of any person registered in it, or the suspension of a person's registration.

(3) The rules may delegate the keeping of the register to another person, and may confer on that person—

(a) power to make regulations—

(i) with respect to the payment of fees, in the cases and subject to the limits prescribed by rules, and

(ii) with respect to any other matter which could be regulated by rules, and

(b) such other functions, including disciplinary functions, as may be prescribed by rules.

(4) Rules under this section shall be made by statutory instrument which shall be subject to annulment in pursuance of a resolution of either House of Parliament.

SECTION 276 [1988]

102.06

Persons entitled to describe themselves as patent agents

276.—(1) An individual who is not a registered patent agent shall not—

(a) carry on a business (otherwise than in partnership) under any name or other description which contains the words "patent agent" or "patent attorney"; or

(b) in the course of a business otherwise describe himself, or permit himself to be described, as a "patent agent" or "patent attorney".

(2) A partnership shall not—

(a) carry on a business under any name or other description which contains the words "patent agent" or "patent attorney"; or

(b) in the course of a business otherwise describe itself, or permit itself to be described as, a firm of "patent agents" or "patent attorneys",

unless all the partners are registered patent agents or the partnership satisfies such conditions as may be prescribed for the purposes of this section.

(3) A body corporate shall not—

(a) carry on a business (otherwise than in partnership) under any name or other description which contains the words "patent agent" or "patent attorney"; or

(b) in the course of a business otherwise describe itself, or permit itself to be described as, a "patent agent" or "patent attorney",

unless all the directors of the body corporate are registered patent agents or the body satisfies such conditions as may be prescribed for the purposes of this section.

(4) Subsection (3) does not apply to a company which began to carry on business as a patent agent before 17th November 1917 if the name of a director or the manager of the company who is a registered patent agent is

mentioned as being so registered in all professional advertisements, circulars or letters issued by or with the company's consent on which its name appears.

(5) Where this section would be contravened by the use of the words "patent agent" or "patent attorney" in reference to an individual, partnership or body corporate, it is equally contravened by the use of other expressions in reference to that person, or his business or place of business, which are likely to be understood as indicating that he is entitled to be described as a "patent agent" or "patent attorney".

(6) A person who contravenes this section commits an offence and is liable on summary conviction to a fine not exceeding level 5 on the standard scale; and proceedings for such an offence may be begun at any time within a year from the date of the offence.

(7) This section has effect subject to—

(*a*) section 277 (persons entitled to describe themselves as European patent attorneys, &c.), and

(*b*) section 278(1) (use of term "patent attorney" in reference to solicitors).

102.07

SECTION 277 [1988]

Persons entitled to describe themselves as European patent attorneys &c.

277.—(1) The term "European patent attorney" or "European patent agent" may be used in the following cases without any contravention of section 276.

(2) An individual who is on the European list may—

(*a*) carry on business under a name or other description which contains the words "European patent attorney" or "European patent agent", or

(*b*) otherwise describe himself, or permit himself to be described, as a "European patent attorney" or "European patent agent".

(3) A partnership of which not less than the prescribed number or proportion of partners is on the European list may—

(*a*) carry on a business under a name or other description which contains the words "European patent attorneys" or "European patent agents", or

(*b*) otherwise describe itself, or permit itself to be described, as a firm which carries on the business of a "European patent attorney" or "European patent agent".

(4) A body corporate of which not less than the prescribed number or proportion of directors is on the European list may—

(*a*) carry on a business under a name or other description which contains the words "European patent attorney" or "European patent agent", or

(b) otherwise describe itself, or permit itself to be described as, a company which carries on the business of a "European patent attorney" or "European patent agent".

(5) Where the term "European patent attorney" or "European patent agent" may, in accordance with this section, be used in reference to an individual, partnership or body corporate, it is equally permissible to use other expressions in reference to that person, or to his business or place of business, which are likely to be understood as indicating that he is entitled to be described as a "European patent attorney" or "European patent agent".

SECTION 278 [1988]   102.08

Use of the term "patent attorney": supplementary provisions

278.—(1) The term "patent attorney" may be used in reference to a solicitor, and a firm of solicitors may be described as a firm of "patent attorneys", without any contravention of section 276.

(2) No offence is committed under the enactments restricting the use of certain expressions in reference to persons not qualified to act as solicitors—

(a) by the use of the term "patent attorney" in reference to a registered patent agent, or

(b) by the use of the term "European patent attorney" in reference to a person on the European list.

(3) The enactments referred to in subsection (2) are section 21 of the Solicitors Act 1974 [c. 37], section 31 of the Solicitors (Scotland) Act 1980 [c. 46] and Article 22 of the Solicitors (Northern Ireland) Order 1976 [S.I. 1976 No. 582 (N.I. 12)].

SECTION 279 [1988]   102.09

Power to prescribe conditions, &c. for mixed partnerships and bodies corporate

279.—(1) The Secretary of State may make rules—

(a) prescribing the conditions to be satisfied for the purposes of section 276 (persons entitled to describe themselves as patent agents) in relation to a partnership where not all the partners are qualified persons or a body corporate where not all the directors are qualified persons, and

(b) imposing requirements to be complied with by such partnerships and bodies corporate.

689

(2) The rules may, in particular—

(a) prescribe conditions as to the number or proportion of partners or directors who must be qualified persons;

(b) impose requirements as to—

(i) the identification of qualified and unqualified persons in professional advertisements, circulars or letters issued by or with the consent of the partnership or body corporate and which relate to it or to its business; and

(ii) the manner in which a partnership or body corporate is to organise its affairs so as to secure that qualified persons exercise a sufficient degree of control over the activities of unqualified persons.

(3) Contravention of a requirement imposed by the rules is an offence for which a person is liable on summary conviction to a fine not exceeding level 5 on the standard scale.

(4) The Secretary of State may make rules prescribing for the purposes of section 277 the number or proportion of partners of a partnership or directors of a body corporate who must be qualified persons in order for the partnership or body to take advantage of that section.

(5) In this section "qualified person"—

(a) in subsections (1) and (2), means a person who is a registered patent agent, and

(b) in subsection (4), means a person who is on the European list.

(6) Rules under this section shall be made by statutory instrument which shall be subject to annulment in pursuance of a resolution of either House of Parliament.

102.10   **SECTION 285 [1988]**

Offences committed by partnerships and bodies corporate

285.—(1) Proceedings for an offence under this Part alleged to have been committed by a partnership shall be brought in the name of the partnership and not in that of the partners; but without prejudice to any liability of theirs under subsection (4) below.

(2) The following provisions apply for the purposes of such proceedings as in relation to a body corporate—

(a) any rules of court relating to the service of documents;

(b) in England, Wales or Northern Ireland, Schedule 3 to the Magistrates' Courts Act 1980 [c. 43] or Schedule 4 to the Magistrates' Courts (Northern Ireland) Order 1981 [S.I. 1981 No. 1675 (N.I. 26)] (procedure on charge of offence).

(3) A fine imposed on a partnership on its conviction in such proceedings shall be paid out of the partnership assets.

(4) Where a partnership is guilty of an offence under this Part, every partner, other than a partner who is proved to have been ignorant of or to have attempted to prevent the commission of the offence, is also guilty of the offence and liable to be proceeded against and punished accordingly.

(5) Where an offence under this Part committed by a body corporate is proved to have been committed with the consent or connivance of a director, manager, secretary or other similar officer of the body, or a person purporting to act in any such capacity, he as well as the body corporate is guilty of the offence and liable to be proceeded against and punished accordingly.

SECTION 286 [1988]

102.11

Interpretation

286. In this Part—
"the comptroller" means the Comptroller-General of Patents, Designs and Trade Marks;
"director", in relation to a body corporate whose affairs are managed by its members, means any member of the body corporate;
"the European list" means the list of professional representatives maintained by the European Patent Office in pursuance of the European Patent Convention;
"registered patent agent" has the meaning given by section 275(1);
"registered trade mark agent" has the meaning given by section 282(1).

ARTICLES CONCERNING PATENT AGENTS

102.12

"Centenary of the Chartered Institute of Patent Agents", (1981–82) 11 CIPA 470 (Commemorative Issue);
Sir David Napley, "Professional ethics and the public interest", (1982–83) 12 CIPA 178;
B. I. Cawthra, "The disciplinary bodies for professional representatives before the European Patent Office", (1983–84) 13 CIPA 46;
D. L. Cannon, "Interdisciplinary partnerships between patent agents and solicitors", (1984–85) 14 CIPA 66;
F. W. B. Kittel, "Register of patent agents: A historical review", (1986–87) 16 CIPA 195;
W. E. Caro, "Professional idemnity insurance", (1986–87) 16 CIPA 150;
K. Weatherald, "The OFT and DTI versus the British patent profession", *Patent World*, July 1987, p. 50;
Report on seminar, "Professional indemnity insurance", (1986–87) 16 CIPA 399;
R. P. Lloyd, "Patent agent's lien", (1988–89) 18 CIPA 30;
P. R. B. Lawrence, "Representation in intellectual property cases", (1988–89) 18 CIPA 88.

Commentary on Sections 102 [Prospectively repealed] and Sections 102, 102A and 274–279, 285 and 286 [1988]

102.13 *The basis of the new provisions*

The recommendations contained in Chapter 6 of the "Review of Restrictions on the Patent Agents' Profession" published by the Office of Fair Trading on September 25, 1986, *noted* [1986] EPOR 348 (and commented on in the article by K. Weatherald in *Patent World* listed in para. 102.12 *supra*) led to the prospective repeal of sections 84, 85, 102, 104, 114, 115, 123(2)(*k*) and the definition of "patent agent" in section 130(1) and their replacement by new sections 102 and 102A and by provisions in Part V of the 1988 Act, *viz.* sections 274–281, 285 and 286 [1988]. These new sections (apart from ss. 280 and 281 [1988]) are reprinted at paras. 102.02–102.11 *supra* and discussed in the commentary *infra*. Section 280 [1988] is reprinted at para. 104.02 and discussed in para. 104.04, and section 281 [1988] is reprinted at para. 115.02 and discussed in paras. 115.04 *et seq.* Paragraphs 7 and 8 of Schedule 5 have also been replaced by further amendment of the other statutes to which they referred, see para. 137.01.

As a result, the so-called "monopoly" on representation before the Comptroller (which was to some extent illusory, see para. 102.15 *infra*) is to be removed in order "to minimise the anti-competitive effects of the Register", that is the Register of Patent Agents. However, that Register is retained, see section 275 [1988].

Commentary on substituted section 102

102.14 *—General*

The new form of section 102 (reprinted at para. 102.02) stipulates a general freedom for a party to proceedings before the Comptroller now to appear before him in person instead to be represented by any person whom he desires should so act for him (subs. (1)); and without committing an offence with regard to the preparation of documents (other than a deed) for use therein (subs. (2)), for which see para. 102.25 *infra*. Subsection (1) is complementary to section 274 [1988] (reprinted at para. 102.04) and is therefore primarily discussed in relation thereto at paras. 102.18–102.25 *infra*. The section applies to proceedings involving "existing patents" (Sched. 2, para. 1(2)).

The section is subject to the provisions of the EPC in relation to European patents (subs. (4)) and there is again a parallel provision in section 274(2) [1988]. These preserve the position under EPCa. 134 according to which proceedings before the EPO must be conducted either in person or by a person on the "European List" (*i.e.* a "European patent attorney", for which see para. 102.34 *infra*), or by a duly qualified legal practitioner (*i.e.* in England and Wales a solicitor or counsel). However, proceedings before the Comptroller concerning a European patent (UK) fall outside the scope of EPCa. 134.

Section 102 is also subject to possible non-recognition by the Comptroller of certain agents, see section 281 [1988] (reprinted at para. 115.02 and discussed in paras. 115.04 *et seq.*).

Representation in appeals from the Comptroller to the Patents Court is now to be governed by new section 102A (reprinted at para. 102.03 and discussed at para. 102.17 *infra*).

102.15 *—Original scope of section 102*

Under the original form of section 102 (reprinted at para. 102.01 *supra*), any person *could* represent a party in proceedings before the Comptroller, but subject to rules made under section 115 (now repealed, see para. 115.01). The rule that was so made (r. 90 [1982]), besides providing for the Comptroller to refuse to deal with persons guilty of criminal activity or professional misconduct (as with the present rule, for which see para. 115.03), also entitled the Comptroller to refuse to deal with any person, other than a solicitor (of any part of the United Kingdom), counsel, or a registered patent agent who in the Comptroller's opinion was "engaged wholly or mainly in acting as agent in applying for patents in the United Kingdom or elsewhere in the name of or for the benefit of a person by whom he [was] employed". Moreover (by prospectively repealed s. 114), only a registered patent agent has been able to practise, describe himself, or hold himself out as a "patent agent", as that term has been defined in section 130(1) (for which see para. 130.01), a definition which required operations to be carried on "for gain".

Thus, in practice, patent proceedings before the Comptroller have been largely handled by registered patent agents, with occasional matters handled by solicitors or counsel, or by an applicant appearing in person, or by a corporate applicant appearing by an "agent" appointed to be the company for the purposes of the proceedings.

While, in recent years at least, there does not appear to have been any non-recognition by the Comptroller of persons acting as agent contrary to the former rule 90 [1982], nevertheless the provision has acted as a deterrent. As explained in para. 102.13 *supra*, that position is now to change by a shift of emphasis towards representation by "anyone", but it remains to be seen to what extent this will result in a shift in practice, other than perhaps to open the way to representation in proceedings before the Comptroller by foreign patent professionals, particularly those situated elsewhere in the EEC.

As originally enacted, the wording of section 102 was deficient as regards the right of representation before the Comptroller in matters relating to European patents. This was corrected in 1985, as indicated in para. 102.01 *supra*.

—Hearings before the Comptroller   **102.16**

Although the Act refers to proceedings "before the Comptroller", all hearings to determine matters arising from such proceedings are entrusted to a "hearing officer", who acts in the name of the Comptroller under authority conferred by virtue of section 63 of the Patents & Designs Act 1907 (7 Edw. 7, c. 29), for which see paras. B05 and B06 in Appendix B. Such hearing officer will normally be a Principal Examiner but, for cases of particular principle may be an Assistant Comptroller. Accordingly, references herein to decisions of the "Comptroller" are normally to decisions of a hearing officer given under a delegated power.

While *ex parte* hearings are normally held in the Patent Office at State House, 66–71 High Holborn, London WC1, *inter partes* hearings continue to be held in the Court Room at the former location of the Office at 25 Southampton Buildings, London WC1.

Representation on appeal from the Comptroller to Patents Court (s. 102A)   **102.17**

New section 102A will express more clearly the intended meaning of former section 102(3) (reprinted in para. 102.01 *supra*), namely that (besides practising counsel) registered patent agents, solicitors (of the Supreme Court), and non-practising barristers should each have both a right of representation of a party to an appeal from the Comptroller to the Patents Court and of audience before that Court on the hearing of any such appeal. However (under the to be repealed s. 102), that intention was put in doubt by a decision of a Taxing Master to disallow the costs of a patent agent who had instructed counsel to appear at the hearing of an appeal to the Patents

Court from a decision of the Comptroller. Although that decision was reversed on appeal (*Reiss Engineering* v. *Harris*, [1987] RPC 171), the revised wording of section 102A (over the previous s. 102(3)) is intended to put the position (as stated above) beyond doubt.

It should be noted that section 102A (in contrast to the general power of representation in proceedings before the Comptroller now conferred by s. 102) will *not* permit a party to an appeal to the Patents Court from a decision of the Comptroller to be represented other than by counsel, a solicitor of the Supreme Court, a registered patent agent or a non-practising barrister. It is perhaps strange that Scottish solicitors have not been given a right of representation or appearance in appeals to the Patents Court. However, if appeal from the Comptroller were to the Court of Session, for which see para. 97.11 (following proceedings in Scotland under r. 108), representation and audience would, presumably, be covered by the rules of that Court, for which see para. 98.09.

Note however, that the right of appearance of the persons specified in section 102A(1) and (2) does not extend to their appearance on the hearing of any subsequent appeal to the Court of Appeal: nor are registered patent agents permitted to brief counsel directly on such an appeal to the Court of Appeal, although this was recommended by the Royal Commission of Legal Services (Cmnd. 7648), see (1979–80) 9 CIPA 155. The right of appearance of the persons specified in section 102A(1) and (2) also does not extend to appearance before the Patents Court in proceedings which are *not* appeals from the Comptroller.

Also, the right of appearance on such an appeal of persons other than practising counsel (whose position continues to be regulated by the practice of the High Court, see subs. (5)) is now potentially circumscribed (as it was not previously) by rules which the Lord Chancellor may make under the power therefor conferred by subsections (3) and (4). No such Rules have yet been made, but the latest Cumulative Supplement to this work should be consulted on this point since it is expected that advocates before the High Court should be subject to the disciplinary jurisdiction of the court (as is the case with solicitors who are *ipso facto* "officers of the court").

When a patent agent appears before the Patents Court, he should wear a gown of approved design. The Chartered Institute has a small stock of such gowns which may be hired by patent agents for this purpose ((1977–78) 7 CIPA 398).

Persons entitled to carry on business of a patent agent (s. 274 [1988])

102.18   —*General*

Section 274 [1988] is complementary to substituted section 102 (reprinted at para. 102.02 *supra*). That section will provide a general freedom of representation and appearance in proceedings before the Comptroller, including absolution in respect of any offence of preparation of documents (other than a deed) by legally unqualified persons, see section 102(2), each discussed in para. 102.14 *supra*. Section 274 [1988] will provide a like freedom for anyone to carry on practice as if he were a "patent agent" as that term was formerly defined in section 130(1), for which see para. 102.15 *supra*. Thus, section 274 [1988] will confirm the freedom of those not on the Register of Patent Agents to carry on the business of a "patent agent", but extended to cover business relating to European patents and patent applications (except in proceedings before the EPO). However, that freedom is to be considerably circumscribed in practice, see para. 102.23 *infra*. The prepared new rules and freedom for representation in intellectual property cases are discussed by P. R. B. Lawrence in his paper listed in para. 102.12 *supra*.

—Agency under the EPC   **102.19**

But for the presence of subsection (2) (which parallels new section 102(4)), section 274 [1988] would have been in conflict with EPCa. 134. This restricts representation before the EPO to those on the List of Professional Representatives maintained by the EPO ("the European list", as defined in s. 286 [1988] reprinted in para. 102.11 *supra*), or a duly qualified legal practitioner, see para. 102.14 *supra*. Accordingly, while a person not covered by EPCa. 134 may be refused recognition by the EPO, he or she is apparently free under the present statutes to carry on in the United Kingdom the business of acting as agent for others for the purpose of applying for European patents. However, if the applicant does not act personally, an authorisation for a duly qualified representative to act must be filed under EPCr. 101(4).

It is not clear whether any person not on the European list is free to file in the United Kingdom an international application for a European patent. It would seem that such a person is free because PCTa. 49 provides that any "person, having the right to practice before the national office with which the international application was filed, shall be entitled to practise in respect of that application before: the International Bureau (WIPO); the competent International Searching Authority [EPO]; and the competent International Preliminary Examination Authority [also EPO]". It would seem wholly illogical for someone so entitled not to be free to file the application itself, and this view must be strengthened by the provision in EPCa. 150(2) that, in the case of conflict, the provisions of the PCT prevail over those of EPC.

—Location of agent   **102.20**

Section 281(5) [1988] (reprinted in para. 115.02) will (when brought into effect) require the Comptroller not to recognise as agent a person appointed to represent another in "business under the Patents Act 1949, the Registered Designs Act 1949 (12, 13 & 14 Geo. 6, c. 88) or the Patents Act 1977" unless such person resides, or has a place of business, in the United Kingdom, the Isle of Man or a Member State of the EEC. This is a broadening of the present position, as prospectively repealed section 115(2) requires such location to be "in the United Kingdom". Rule 30 (reprinted at para. 32.03) requires an address for service to be specified in all cases, but this can be expected to be amended likewise, see para. 32.16, so that the location of such address could also then be in another EEC Member State, as an alternative to the United Kingdom (or Isle of Man). This point is discussed further at para. 115.06.

—Authorisation of agent   **102.21**

Rule 90 (reprinted at para. 115.03) was amended in 1982 to make it unnecessary to file at the Patent Office a formal authorisation of agent when an application is filed or proceedings commenced. This brought proceedings before the Comptroller into line with the position as regards authorisation of a solicitor to bring proceedings before the court. However, when the Patent Office is acting as receiving office under the PCT, an authorisation must be filed under PCTr. 90.3, see para. 89.43.

Nevertheless, attention is drawn (as it is by a note on most of the Patents Forms) to rule 106 (reprinted at para. 72.08). This enables the Comptroller to direct that there should be furnished to him, within a period which he specifies, such documents and/or evidence as he may require. Accordingly, under the power of rule 106, the Comptroller can at any time require that he be satisfied that an agent was duly authorised by his principal to file the application or instigate the proceeding in question. Presumably, if the form naming the agent is directly signed by the principal that will suffice, as also would the provision of a pre-dated authorisation or a statutory declaration (or other acceptable evidence) from the principal that the agent had been duly authorised: for example by oral instructions or by implication from the nature of the relationship between the agent and principal, or as a result of the requests made by the principal to the agent. There seems no reason why the authorisation should not arise by sub-delegation and it may even be possible for the principal to adopt the actions of his agent retro-actively. However, a prudent agent may wish to protect himself against a subsequent repudiation of authority from the principal, for example in dispute over payment of costs, and he may therefore deem it a wise precaution to seek a signed authorisation from the principal and retain this on his file. The signing of an authorisation is also a useful way of an agent ensuring that he has correctly stated the name and address of the principal.

In *General Motors (Longhouse's) Application* ([1981] RPC 41) it was held that a signature of an employee on behalf of an authorised agent had been made with at least implied authority unless it could be shown that the employee had acted "on a frolic of his own".

If an authorisation is provided, care should be taken that its terms are broad enough to cover the acts performed, or to be performed, by the agent. For example, a general authorisation for the filing of applications, for obtaining grant and for subsequent proceedings in respect of the patent so obtained may not have broad enough wording (unless modified) to authorise the agent to act in proceedings against third parties, such as in applications for revocation under section 72.

102.21A   *—Exercise of agency*

If it is desired to have the principal execute an authorisation, a suitable form, which can be adapted as either a specific or general authorisation, has been published in the O.J. March 30, 1978. This is reproduced *infra*, but modification of this is necessary if it is intended to provide an authorisation to act in proceedings relating to third party patents.

Many of the Patent Forms now provide space for entry of an ADP number for the specified agent. This is an automatic data processing number which is being assigned to agents in order to aid computerisation of Patent Office procedures. If the agent's ADP number is known this should be used, but care is necessary to insert this correctly.

It is important to note that in proceedings before the EPO, documents (if not signed personally by the applicant) must be signed personally by a duly authorised representative. However, personal signature is not, in practice, required by the United Kingdom Patent Office. It is sufficient that the person appending a requisite signature has authority, express or implied, to sign on behalf of the authorised agent. It is on this basis that a partnership or firm may be authorised to act collectively.

PATENTS ACT 1977

Authorisation of Agent

I/We (a) ....

have appointed (b) ....

to act for me/us in proceedings concerning

696

(d) {
  (1) my/our application for a patent or a patent identified as follows
     (c) ....
     ....
  (2) all applications for patents and patents in my/our name.

and request that notices, requisition and communications relating thereto be sent to
such agent at the above address
I/We hereby revoke all previous authorisations given by me/us in this connection.

Dated this ....day of ....19 ......

(e) ....

Notes:
  (a) State name and address of applicant (s).
  (b) State name and address of agent.
  (c) State here the title of the invention if not yet filed or the application
      or patent number if available.
  (d) Delete (1) or (2) whichever is inapplicable.
  (e) To be signed by the person(s) appointing the agent.

—Change of agency   **102.22**

Rule 90(2) requires that, where an agent is appointed for the first time or there is
a change of agent during pending proceedings, the newly appointed agent must file
a declaration of agency on PF 51/77 (for which no fee is required) "on or before"
such person acts as agent for the first time. Since rule 90(2) is not mentioned in
either rule 110(2) or (3), an extension of time for filing PF 51/77 is, in principle,
obtainable by discretion exercised under rule 110(1). PF 51/77 is to be filed in duplicate so that the Comptroller can send one copy to the agent formerly acting to
inform him of the new agency, thereby giving him the chance to object if appropriate.

It has been suggested that the procedure of being able to nominate oneself as a
new agent during the course of proceedings is open to abuse (A. J. Hewlett,
((1981–82) 11 CIPA 417), see also N. J. Flower ((1982–83) 12 CIPA 119). However, any such abuse by a patent agent would constitute gross professional misconduct leading to possible penalty under the Register of Patent Agents Rules (for
which see Appendix F) and possible refusal of recognition under rule 90(3)(*c*).
Such actions as envisaged would also be likely to be criminal as being part of a con-
spiracy to defraud and possibly theft, or obtaining a pecuniary advantage by deception, or even forgery. Moreover, the persons concerned would be liable to civil law
actions for damages for deceit and breach of warranty of authority.

If the new agent is to act only in a limited manner and the previous agency is not
to be revoked, or at least not totally, this should be made clear on PF 51/77, if
necessary with deletion or amendment of the instruction to send *all* correspondence
to the address of the new agent. When PF 51/77 relates to a published patent application or to a granted patent, it is *not* treated as a change of the address for service
recorded in the register. For this, the filing of PF 20/77 is required, see *e.g.* O.J.
July 19, 1989 and para. 32.23.

—Obstacles to practice by unqualified person   **102.23**

While, as stated *supra*, the practice of patent agency is no longer to be restricted to
registered patent agents (and solicitors), others (here termed "unqualified persons")
are to suffer disadvantages compared to registered patent agents (and solicitors).

Thus: only registered patent agents (*i.e.* those on the Register of Patent Agents, for which see paras. 102.26–102.36 *infra*) are to be able to use the term "patent agent", and similar expressions including "patent attorney" (s. 276 [1988], discussed in paras.102.31–102.33 *infra*), though solicitors may use the term "patent attorney" (s. 278 [1988], see para. 102.39 *infra*) and the term "European patent attorney" is restricted to those on the European list (s. 277 [1988], discussed in paras. 102.34–102.38 *infra*); "patent agents" have a right to conduct and appear in appeals to the Patents Court from decisions of the Comptroller (s. 102A, discussed in para. 102.17 *supra*); and "patent agents" enjoy the legal privilege of solicitors in respect of communications relating to inventions, etc. (s. 280 [1988], discussed in paras. 104.06–104.09), though an unqualified person may come to enjoy a like privilege under Scots law, see para. 105.03. There may also be a problem over the availability of professional indemnity insurance (for which see the paper by W. E. Caro and the Seminar Report listed in para. 102.12 *supra*) to unqualified persons, though this has, apparently, not yet been fully explored.

Also, agreements relating to services provided by "patent agents" and "European patent attorneys" as such are exempt from being made the subject of an order under sections 107 and 108 of the Fair Trading Act 1973 (c. 41) (see s. 109(3) and Sched. 4, paras. 10 and 10A thereof) or of an order under sections 11 and 12 of the Restrictive Trade Practices Act 1976 (c. 34) (see section 13(3) and Sched. 1, paras. 10 and 10A thereof), the respective amended texts of the provisions noted from these Schedules being set out in para. 137.01 in relation to Schedule 5, paragraphs 7 and 8 [1977].

While a registered patent agent need not be a member of the Chartered Institute of Patent Agents, the vast majority of registered patent agents are members of this professional body. As such, they are bound by the rules of professional conduct imposed by the Chartered Institute upon its patent agent members. These rules embody the general ethical principles expected of any truly professional body, for which see the paper by Sir David Napley listed in para. 102.12 *supra*. They are now expressed in simplified form as a set of principles, rather than detailed rules. These principles have been reprinted in *Patent World* (May 1989, p. 10). However, those members of the Chartered Institute who are also European patent attorneys (as most of them are) are also bound (at least in respect of their activities before the EPO) by the Code of Professional Conduct of the Institute of Professional Representatives before the EPO (EPI), for which see para. 102.43 *infra*, of which membership for European patent attorneys is compulsory. The restrictions therein are more restrictive, for example as regards freedom to offer services by way of advertisements, particularly in view of the Chartered Institute's new rules of professional conduct see *supra* made with a view to a greater latitude as regards professional advertising, see (1987–88) 17 CIPA 203.

102.24   —*General liability*

Any person providing a service for the benefit of another is liable to that other person (either in contract or in tort) for any negligence in the performance of these duties, or actions in respect thereof, because a general duty of care is assumed to exist in such circumstances (*Hedley Byrne* v. *Heller*, [1964] AC 465 (HL)). Also, under section 13 of the Supply of Services and Goods Act 1982 (c. 20) there is an implied term in a contract for the supply of a service, where the supplier is acting in the course of a business, that the supplier will carry out the service with reasonable care and skill. However, there has been exempted from this particular provision "the services of an advocate in court or before any tribunal, inquiry directly affecting the conduct of the hearing" (Supply of Services (Exclusion of Implied Terms)

Order, S.I. 1982 No. 1771): this would appear to cover anyone appearing before the Comptroller under section 102(1) (reprinted in para. 102.02 *supra*).

Under section 2(2) of the Unfair Contracts Terms Act 1977 (c. 50) [the "UCTA"], liability for negligence cannot be excluded by a contract term or a notice except (other than for death or personal injury) as such term or notice satisfies a requirement for reasonableness (as defined in s. 11 of UCTA). However, the UCTA does not extend to "any contract so far as it relates to the creation or transfer of a right or interest in any patent, trade mark, service mark, copyright or design right, (including a "topography right"), registered design, technical or commercial information or other intellectual property, or relates to the termination of any such right or interest" (UCTA, Sched. 1, para. 1(*c*), as amended) by Sched. 1, para. 1(2)(*f*) [1986] and Sched. 7, para. 24 [1988] including S.I. 1989 No. 1100). Thus, agents acting for others in matters relating to patents *could* exclude, or limit, liability for their negligence in respect of much of the work carried out by them. However, most "patent agents" are unlikely at least totally to exclude such liability, regarding it as inimical to their professional character and relying instead on professional indemnity insurance, a subject which is discussed in various articles as listed *inter alia* in para. 102.12 *supra*. Unqualified persons, to whom such insurance is unlikely to be available (see para. 102.23 *supra*) are more likely to adopt such a practice.

Andrew Master Hones v. *Cruikshank and Fairweather* ([1980] RPC 16) was a case of negligence against a firm of patent agents. A breach of contract between client and patent agent was held to have occurred when the agent did not exercise the degree of knowledge and care to be expected from a notional duly qualified person practising in the profession. The agent in question was negligent in that he had taken a superficial and incorrect view of the prior art and had failed to apply these to all the claims. He had also failed to ascertain from his client the features which distinguished the invention from the prior art and which resulted in its practical success. Moreover, on the evidence, the patent could have been effective against competitors irrespective of its validity. Consequently, the agent should not have assumed, without further inquiry, that the applicant, by his silence, had taken the agent's advice to abandon the application. An inquiry into damages was ordered on the basis that there was good reason to think that valid claims could have been obtained which would not readily have been circumvented by competitors. On appeal ([1981] RPC 389) it was conceded that there had been some degree of negligence and a breach of contract, but it was held that the degree of negligence was much less than the judgment at first instance indicated. Thus, none of the claims of the specification in the form which existed when the application lapsed were valid and the claims could easily be avoided. The Court of Appeal did not accept the view at first instance that there were advantages in the use of adjustable spacers and pointed out that, anyway, this point should not have been taken into account as it had not been pleaded. In these circumstances the Court of Appeal thought that damages, though not purely nominal, were unlikely to be large.

Another case of negligence on the part of a patent agent is *Lee* v. *Walker* ((1872) LR 7 CP 121) where negligence was held to arise when the patent agent had failed, through ignorance, to act in accordance with a recent legal decision.

—Offences relating to document preparation **102.25**

Under section 22 of the Solicitors Act 1974 (c. 47), and similar provisions in Scotland (Solicitors (Scotland) Act 1980 (c. 46, s. 32)); in Northern Ireland (Solicitors (Northern Ireland) Order 1976, S.I. 1976 No. 582, art. 23); and in the Isle of Man (Advocates Act 1976 (Act of Tynwald), s. 11), it is an offence for a person not qualified under any of these provisions (which are no longer to be specified as such) to draw or prepare for personal benefit (that is for, or in expectation of, any fee, gain or reward) any instrument relating to the transfer or charge of real or personal estate or to any legal proceeding.

However, there are certain exceptions, particularly for the preparation of an agreement not under seal. These exceptions are to be extended by section 102(2) (reprinted at para. 102.02 *supra*) to "any document (other than a deed)" for use in proceedings covered by section 102(1), that is proceedings before the Comptroller under the Patents Act 1977 (which extends to proceedings under the 1949 Act by virtue of Sched. 2, para. 1(2)), or under any treaty or international convention to which the United Kingdom is a party (*e.g.* the EPC and PCT), but the corresponding exemption for documents prepared for the purposes of legal proceedings by way of appeal to the Patents Court from a decision of the Comptroller is to be limited to "registered patent agents" and non-practising barristers, see section 102A(2) (reprinted in para. 102.03 *supra*).

Thus, it is an offence ior any person (including a "patent agent"), not legally qualified under any of the above-mentioned enactments, to prepare for personal benefit an agreement under seal (or any other deed) for assignment, charge or grant of patent rights, though assignment by deed only now seems to be required in relation to "existing patents", see para. 30.07. Although, there is a general exception to all these provisions for "European lawyers" by the European Communities (Services of Lawyers) Order 1978 (S.I. 1978 No. 1910), it is not certain that this covers activities by a "European patent attorney".

The register of patent agents (s. 275 [1988])

102.26   *—General*

Section 275 [1988] is an enabling section providing for rules to be made concerning the maintenance of the Register of Patent Agents, including admission to, and removal from, the Register. Thus, this Register (first established by section 1 of the Patents, Designs and Trade Marks Act 1888 (51 & 52 Vict. c. 50)), the history of which was reviewed by F. W. B. Kittel in his article listed in para. 102.12 *supra*, continues to provide the public with information of those who are specifically qualified by examination (for which see para. 102.30 *infra*) to act for others as agents in relation to matters concerning patents (and indeed most other forms of intellectual property as well).

Section 275 [1988] will replace section 123(2)(*k*) in providing for rules governing the Register of Patent Agents and will define the term "registered patent agent" as a person entered in this Register. This definition will replace the definition of "patent agent" originally contained in section 130(1) which is in terms of functions performed and activity carried out, though by section 114 the title "patent agent" has been for use only by a person entered in this register. Now that anyone is to be permitted to perform such functions and carry out such activity, the definition of "patent agent" becomes available to be fully equated with the term "registered patent agent". This is because it will remain the position that only a registered patent agent is entitled to use the term "patent agent", see section 276 [1988], discussed in paras. 102.31–102.33 *infra*.

There is now no nationality requirement for entry in the Register of Patent Agents, but the Comptroller is to be required to refuse to recognise a patent agent who neither resides nor has a place of business in the United Kingdom, the Isle of Man or a Member State of the EEC (s. 281(5) [1988], discussed in paras. 102.20 and 115.06).

—*The Register of Patent Agents Rules (subss. (2)–(4))*   **102.27**

Subsection (2) repeats part of the substance of original section 123(2)(*k*), to give power for Rules ("the Register of Patent Agents Rules" or "RPA Rules") to be made by the Secretary of State for the keeping and regulation of the Register, including power to erase or suspend entries therein, but adds formal power to prescribe fees which are required to be paid. These RPA Rules will replace the Register of Patent Agents Rules 1978 (S.I. 1978 No. 1093, as amended) and will then be reprinted in relation to Appendix F and commented upon in the supplementary commentary under the present para. 102.27. These Rules are to be subject to annulment by positive resolution of either House of Parliament (subs. (4)).

Subsection (3) will give powers of delegation (including power to make rules) in respect of payment of fees and of disciplinary and other matters and functions as may be prescribed in the primary RPA Rules, subject to fee limits as prescribed in these primary rules. A similar power of delegation has existed in previous forms of the RPA Rules and has, since 1889, been delegated to the Chartered Institute of Patent Agents, though the power to delegate disciplinary functions is new.

Under the previous delegations, the Chartered Institute has been entrusted with the responsibility for the preparation and maintenance, and sale to the public of copies, of the Register of Patent Agents and in return has been permitted to retain the registration fees levied under the RPA Rules. Copies of the register may, therefore, be obtained from the Registrar, The Chartered Institute of Patent Agents, Staple Inn Buildings, London WC1V 7PZ.

The Chartered Institute has also had delegated responsibility for the regulations governing the examinations qualifying for entry in the Register (subject to the approval of the Comptroller), and for the conduct of those examinations, for which see para. 102.30 *infra.*

—*The privileges of a registered patent agent*   **102.28**

The entry of an individual's name in the Register of Patent Agents is to entitle him or her to use the title "patent agent" or "patent attorney" as a description in the course of business, which use would otherwise be an offence under section 276(1) [1988], see para. 102.31 *infra.* Also, a registered patent agent may be a partner in a partnership, or a director in a body corporate, which describe themselves as a firm or company of patent agents or patent attorneys, provided that the provisions of section 276(2) or (3) [1988] are met, for which also see para. 102.31 *infra.* The terms "patent agent" and "patent attorney" are not to be used otherwise, except that a solicitor and his firm may use the term "patent attorney" or "patent attorneys" (s. 278(1) [1988]), see para. 102.39 *infra.*

Other privileges of registered patent agents (to be possessed in common with counsel and solicitors), but denied to persons not falling within any of these categories, are those referred to in para. 102.23 *supra, viz.* rights as regards representation and appearance in, and document preparation for, appeals from a decision of the Comptroller to the Patents Court (s. 102A, discussed in para. 102.17 *supra*); rights as regards legal privilege (s. 280 [1988], discussed in paras. 104.06–104.09) perhaps also enjoyed in Scotland by unqualified persons, see para. 105.03; and certain freedoms (as noted in para. 102.23 *supra*) under the Fair Trading Act 1973 (c. 41, Sched. 4, paras. 10 and 10A) and the Restrictive Trade Practices Act 1976 (c. 34, Sched. 1, paras. 10 and 10A). The extent of the lien which a patent agent may have over the papers of his client who has failed to make proper payment to him is explained by R. P. Lloyd in his article listed in para. 102.12 *supra*, see also (1988–89) 18 CIPA 133 and 135.

It also appears that, whilst an individual's name remains in the Register of Patent

Agents, the Comptroller will not be able to refuse to recognise that individual as an agent in respect of business under the Patents and Registered Designs Acts, see section 281 [1988] (reprinted at para. 115.02 and dealt with in paras. 115.04 *et seq.*).

102.29   *—The Chartered Institute and "Chartered Patent Agents"*

The Chartered Institute of Patent Agents is a professional body incorporated under a Royal Charter granted in 1891. The history of the Chartered Institute was described in a special Centenary Issue of CIPA as referenced in para. 102.12 *supra*. The term "Chartered Patent Agent" is a title approved by the Privy Council for use by those Fellows of the Chartered Institute who are also registered patent agents (Charter of Incorporation of the Institute, 1891, clause 29). The Privy Council has approved and recommended use of the abbreviation "C.P.A." to designate such a person. The abbreviation "F.C.I.P.A." is not approved by the Privy Council, see (1973–74) 3 CIPA 170 and 265. However, note that Fellows of the Chartered Institute who have retired from practice and are no longer "registered patent agents" will apparently, strictly speaking, be committing an offence if they continue to describe themselves as a "Chartered Patent Agent", though only if this is done "in the course of a business", see section 276(1)(*b*).

Chartered Patent Agents are bound by the Rules of Professional Conduct adopted from time to time by the Chartered Institute, see para. 102.23 *supra*. These rules have been recognised by the Patents Court, who drew no distinction between those Chartered Patent Agents in private practice and those employed in industry, the Government or public service. Thus, in *Schering's Patent* ([1986] RPC 30, it was held that because all such Agents are bound by the same rules of professional conduct, there was no good reason why an employed patent agent, as regards the receipt of evidence in confidence in proceedings under section 46, should be put in a different position from that of an independent patent agent, though conditions were imposed on his employer to ensure his independence, see also *Unilever* v. *Pearce* ([1985] FSR 475 and para. 72.44A).

102.30   *—Examinations for entry into the Register of Patent Agents*

The Register of Patent Agents Rules 1978 (S.I. 1978 No. 1093), by rules 8 and 9, provided for examination requirements to be met as the basis for qualification for entry in the Register of Patent Agents, with responsibility for the entire management and control of these examinations being delegated to the Chartered Institute of Patent Agents (r. 8(1)). These pre-entry requirements have consisted of preliminary, intermediate and final examinations, together with a required period of service (of up to three years according to prior educational and professional qualifications) as a pupil or technical assistant to a registered patent agent practising in the United Kingdom.

The preliminary examinations have been examinations organised by other bodies, success in which has been recognised as evidence of a satisfactory background (in English, a foreign language, mathematics and science or technology) for entry (after satisfaction of the applicable service requirement) into the intermediate and final examinations organised by the Chartered Institute.

It is not expected that the principles underlying this qualification route will be varied by the new form of the Register of Patent Agents Rules (for which see under Appendix F), these principles being that the Chartered Institute should have a prominent management role in the pre-entry examinations and that entry into the register should indicate a competent knowledge of intellectual property law and practice both for the United Kingdom and for overseas countries generally. However, at the time of writing, the position is fluid and the latest Supplement to this Work should therefore particularly be consulted *re*. this para.

Examination Regulations are issued by the Chartered Institute dealing in detail with each of the four pre-entry requirements as indicated above. Copies of the current form of these Regulations can be obtained from The Registrar, The Chartered Institute of Patent Agents, Staple Inn Buildings, London WC1V 7PZ. At the time of writing, the form of these Regulations was that issued (with the approval of the Comptroller) on March 2, 1988. However, the form of these examinations is presently under review (see (1987–88) 17 CIPA 152) with a modular form of examination covering patents, trade marks, designs and general law being proposed to replace the present system of an intermediate examination consisting of four papers covering United Kingdom patent law and procedure, overseas patent law and procedure, trade marks and industrial designs, and patent agents' practice; and a final examination consisting of five papers, two covering preparation of specifications for United Kingdom and overseas patents, two covering infringement and validity of United Kingdom patents, and one covering patent agents' practice. Changes will also need to take into account the new statutory provisions set out in paras. 102.02–102.11 *supra* relating to the Register and representation and practice in patent matters, as well as changes which may arise from the introduction of a Register of Trade Mark Agents and protection of the designation of "registered trade mark agent" contained in sections 282–284 [1988]. Accordingly, the Examination Regulations are not being reprinted herein, but when the position becomes clearer it is intended to include these in the next Supplement to this Work in relation to Appendix G.

For qualification as a "European patent attorney", see para. 102.44 *infra*.

The titles of "patent agent" and "patent attorney" (s. 276 [1988])

—General   **102.31**

Section 276 [1988] (reprinted at para. 102.06 *supra*) will replace section 114 then to be repealed, but with one notable omission consequent upon the Government's acceptance of part of recommendation 6.6c of the Report of the Office of Fair Trading of September 1986 (for which see para. 102.13 *supra*), *viz.* criminal sanctions against the practice of patent agency by unqualified persons. This omission follows naturally from the provisions of substituted section 102 and section 274 [1988], discussed respectively in paras. 102.14–102.16 and 102.18–102.25 *supra*. However, the second arm of that recommendation, to remove all protection from the title "patent agent" was not accepted. Indeed, the Government eventually went further than the protection for this provided by the former section 114 by providing protection also for the term "patent attorney", and for other expressions indicating activity in the area of patent agency, and by officially sanctioning the use (by registered patent agents and solicitors) of the term "patent attorney", see section 278(2) [1988] and para. 102.39 *infra*.

Subsection (1) will prohibit an individual from practising under, or using in the course of a business, the title "patent agent" or "patent attorney", unless registered in the Register of Patent Agents, for which see section 275 [1988] and paras. 102.26–102.30 *supra*. The prohibition is clear and would presumably apply to foreign patent agents and patent attorneys not on the register, though those persons on the European list (for which see para. 102.43 *infra*) may use the title of "European patent attorney" or "European patent agents" (s. 277 [1988]), see para. 102.34 *infra*.

Subsections (2) and (3) will extend the prohibition of subsection (1) respectively to partnerships and bodies corporate, unless all the partners or directors thereof are registered, or satisfy as yet unspecified conditions. The ability to specify exempting conditions by secondary legislation lays the ground for so-called mixed practices, for which see para. 102.40 *infra*. The previous exemption (in s. 114(2)(*a*)) in favour of companies which started business "as a patent agent" before November 17, 1917 is to be retained by subsection (4), but at least one director or the manager must be a registered patent agent and the name of at least one of these must be mentioned in all professional advertisements, circulars or letters issued by the company on which its name appears.

Subsection (5) will extend the prohibitions of section 276 [1988] to expressions "which are likely to be understood as indicating that [the person in question] is entitled to be described as a 'patent agent' or 'patent attorney' ". In this way it is hoped that the gap revealed by litigation under former statutes has been closed. It was especially inserted to deal with the problem of unregistered persons using expressions in reference to themselves which, whilst not including the forbidden words, imply that they are registered, or otherwise qualified, as "patent agents" or "patent attorneys", for which see para. 102.33 *infra*.

102.32   —*Penalty for offence under the section (subs. (6))*

Section 276(6) will prescribe that an offence under the section is triable only summarily and proceedings must be commenced within a year from the date of the offence. However, this latter provision is not clear in respect of an offence of a continuing, rather than isolated, nature. The maximum penalty is prescribed as a fine "not exceeding level 5 on the standard scale". The term "standard scale" is defined by section 37(2) of the Criminal Justice Act 1982 (c. 48). The amount of the fine corresponding to stated levels on the standard scale may be increased by order made under section 143 of the Magistrates' Courts Act 1980 (c. 43), and "level 5" presently stands at £2,000 by virtue of the Criminal Penalties Etc. (Increase) Order 1984 (S.I. 1984 No. 447, Sched. 4).

102.33   —*Improper use of titles of "patent agents" and "patent attorney" and analogous expressions*

Not only can a registered patent agent use (to the exclusion of all others) the title of "patent agent", but the propriety of use of the term "patent attorney" (also reserved under s. 276(1) [1988]) to a registered patent agent in the course of business is now not to be in doubt (as it was before the 1988 Act) because section 278(2)(*a*) [1988] makes specific provision for use of this term alone by a registered patent agent, just as use of the title "European patent attorney" by a person on the European list will continue to be sanctioned (by s. 278(2)(*b*) [1988]), as it originally was under now to be repealed section 85(1). However (by s. 278(1)), the title "patent attorney" may also be used by any solicitor, even if not also a registered patent agent.

While the term "registered trade mark agent" is likewise to be reserved for use by persons entered in the Register of Trade Marks to be created under the 1988 Act, there is to be no reservation of, or authorisation for, the term "registered trade mark attorney", see sections 282 and 283 [1988].

Because, section 274 [1988] (without subsection (5) thereof), together with sections 276(1)–(3) [1988], would have merely changed the law back to the unsatisfactory position which obtained between 1888 and 1919, concern was felt as to titles which might be used by persons acting for others in patent matters, but who are not registered patent agents or solicitors. Past decisions on appeal during the former period suggested that the use of names very similar to "patent agents" would not be held to be prohibited, as it did not then prove possible for the Chartered Institute to stop the use of titles which were very close to, but not precisely the same as, the term "patent agents". Thus, for example, prosecutions by the Chartered Institute failed in the following instances: *Graham* v. *Fanta* ((1892) 9 RPC 164), "Agent for the Applicant"; *Graham* v. *Eli, Hughes and Barlow* ((1898) 15 RPC 259), "Patent Office", "Inventors' Medium Limited", "patent expert" and "If you want a patent agent, I am the man for you"; *Graham* v. *Tanner* ((1912) 29 RPC 683), "Agent for preparing patent specifications"; and *Hans* v. *Graham* ([1914] 3 KB 400), "Patent Agency". After 1919, when the statute was amended into a form substantially similar to that of now to be repealed section 114, further prosecutions failed to prove that the defendant was acting "as a patent agent", see: *Thompson* v. *Bettinger (No. 2)* (1929) 46 RPC 189), "negotiation of all foreign Patents"; *Thompson* v. *Joseph Benton* (1932) 49 RPC 33, acting as agent for a foreign patent attorney; and *Thompson* v. *Arthur Edward Brown* ((1933) 50 RPC 389), assisting applicant by attending interview with Patent Office examiner.

While it is not thought that these decisions would necessarily be repeated in modern times, a criminal statute is construed strictly and therefore it is appropriate for the protection of the title of "patent agent" to be safeguarded against the use of other expressions implying registration when this is not the case. Also, with the increasing interest in other forms of intellectual and industrial property, the public is beginning to recognise the term "intellectual property" as covering patents, trade marks, service marks, designs (both registered and unregistered) and copyrights. Nevertheless, it remains to be seen whether the term "intellectual property agent" will be held as being understood as indicating that its user is a registered patent agent. Of even more concern, would be a decision which permitted the use of foreign language terms corresponding to the prohibited wording, such as "Patentanwalt", "Conseil en brevets", "Patentombud" or "Octrooigemachtigde".

It may be noted that, while the term "registered trade mark agent" is (by s. 283 [1988]) likewise to be reserved to persons entered in the register of trade mark agents being created by section 282 [1988], there is no provision corresponding to section 276(5) [1988] making it an offence to use similar expressions indicating that the person is a registered trade mark agent when such is not the case. Thus, it remains to be seen whether the former cases in relation to "patent agents" will still be applied in modern times in relation to trade mark agents.

The title of "European patent attorney" (s. 277 [1988])

—General   **102.34**

A person is only qualified to use the title "European patent attorney" (or "European patent agent") if he or she is on the "European list, as defined in section 286 [1988] and discussed in paras. 102.43–102.45 *infra*. But for section 277 [1988], use of either of these titles by persons on the "European list", but who are not registered patent agents, would be a contravention of section 276 [1988]; and, but for section 278(2) and (3) [1988], there could then have been a contravention of other statutes, see para. 102.39 *infra*. The recommended title is "European patent attorney", see para. 102.37 *infra*.

Section 277(2)–(4) [1988] sets out in positive terms the use that may be made of these titles by a person on the European list, rather than negatively forbidding certain actions to those not on the European list as with the former section 84. The unintended effect of this seems to be that a registered patent agent, who is not on the European list, commits no offence under the 1988 Act by using the title "European patent attorney", but the terms of section 278(2)(*b*) [1988] seem to be such than an offence as to use of the word "attorney" may then be committed under the enactments specified in section 278(3) [1988], as to which see para. 102.39 *infra*, unless exemption could be claimed under section 278(2)(*a*) [1988].

102.35   —*Use by partnerships and bodies corporate (subss. (3) and (4))*

Section 277(3) [1988] refers specifically to partnerships, and subsection (4) to bodies corporate, in both cases requiring a prescribed number or proportion of partners, or directors, to be on the European list, if the partnership, or body corporate, is to be permitted to use the title "European patent attorney(s) [or agent(s)]". These, again, are provisions laying ground for mixed practices by rules to be prescribed under section 279 [1988], as discussed in para. 102.40 *infra*.

However, though authorisation of partnerships or associations of professional representatives before the EPO is provided for in undeleted EPCr.101(9), this provision has not been put into effect (OJEPO 4/1978). Authorisation of individuals is preferred by the EPO, though EPCr.101(8) permits authorisations of more than one person, who may act jointly or singly. An association (whether a partnership or a body corporate) of representatives is allowed to practise before the EPO as such, but such must consist solely of named persons on the European list in private practice (OJEPO 3/1979, 92). Any change in the composition of that association requires notification to, and approval by, the EPO. Section 285(5) [1988] is relevant to the liability of officers thereof for offences committed by a body corporate, for which see para. 102.41 *infra*.

102.36   —*Penalties arising from section 277 [1988]*

As section 277 [1988] is permissive and introduces no offence, there are no penalties under the section as there were under repealed section 84. However, an individual, partnership or body corporate using the title "European patent attorney(s)" (or "European patent agent(s)"), and not satisfying any of section 277(2)–(4), would contravene section 276 [1988] and therefore be liable for penalty under section 276(6) [1988], for which see para. 102.33 *supra*.

102.37   —*Approval of titles under the EPC*

The use of the title "European patent attorney" was eventually approved by EPOAC (OJEPO 11–12/1979, 452) and by the EPI Council ((1979–1980) 9 CIPA 453, 455), though only after considerable controversy. see (1979–80) 9 CIPA 100. However, as these notices indicate, use by a person on the European list of a national title, together with the designation "European" (*e.g.* "European patent agent"), has been disapproved of by both EPOAC and the EPI Council.

102.38   —*Privileges of a "European patent attorney"*

Legal professional privilege, now accorded (by s. 280 [1988]) to communications with "patent agents" (and discussed in para. 104.07) is likewise accorded to persons "on the European list", and to partnerships and bodies corporate thereof (s. 280(3) [1988]). However, it is not certain that a person on the European list, who is not also a registered patent agent, benefits from the exceptions to the prohibition on document preparation by legally unqualified persons provided by section 102(2), see para. 102.25.

102.39   *Use of term "attorney" (s. 278 [1988])*

Section 21 of the Solicitors Act 1974 (c. 37), as well as section 31 of the Solicitors (Scotland) Act 1980 (c. 46) and Article 22 of the Solicitors (Northern Ireland)

Order 1977 (S.I. 1976 No. 582 (N.I. 12)), make it an offence for legally-unqualified persons to use a title suggesting that such qualification is possessed. It was uncertain whether the term "attorney" was embraced by these provisions, at least as regards use in England and Wales, because of its apparent disuse as an expression of legal qualification, see J. C. H. Ellis ((1987–88) 17 CIPA 289). However, Section 278(2) [1988] will put the matter beyond doubt so far as the terms "patent attorney" and "European patent attorney" are concerned by expressly legalising such use under these three statutes (as listed in subss. (3)).

Also (by s. 278(1) [1988]), a solicitor is to be permitted to use the term "patent attorney" without contravention of section 276 [1988], for which see paras. 102.31–102.33 *supra*.

Provision for mixed professional practices (s. 279 [1988]) **102.40**

Section 279 [1988] contains enabling provisions so that effect can be given to the recommendation in the Report of the Office of Fair Trading (September 1986), for which see para. 102.13 *supra*, that the provisions in sections 84 and 114 preventing patent agents from practising in mixed partnerships be deleted. The OFT Report also recommended corresponding changes in other statutes, for example those in the Solicitors Act 1974 (c. 37) presently being some of the bars to solicitors engaging in mixed practices. The paper by D. L. Cannon listed in para. 102.12 *supra* discussed the restraints upon mixed partnerships of patent agents and solicitors that existed in 1984 both under statute and under the professional rules of conduct and practice involving, respectively, the two professions.

Unfortunately, the 1988 Act will make no change in other enactments as regards mixed practices. It may be, therefore, that section 279 [1988] will not be given effect to by appropriate secondary legislation until further consideration has been given to the subject. No doubt strong pressure will be brought to bear upon professional organisations to alter their conduct and practice rules if the Government is to follow through its present objective of encouraging inter-professional mixed practices but, before Rules under section 279 [1988] are made, careful consideration will also need to be given as regards the responsibilities and privileges of registered patent agents, as discussed in paras. 102.23 and 102.28 *supra*. Nevertheless, the OFT Report clearly envisaged mixed practices between patent and trade mark agents and perhaps also with "exploitation brokers", but it should be appreciated that mixed practices with other professions subject to similar statutory protection as patent agents raises rather different problems to those involving other so-called professions which are under no sort of specific statutory control.

The eventual effect of section 279 [1988] will only become clear when rules are made under it. In particular, these rules can be expected to prescribe the number or proportion of partners or directors who must be registered patent agents or European patent attorneys in a firm or company entitled to describe themselves as "patent agents" (subs. (2)(*a*) and (5)).

Patent agents are excused from the limitation on partnerships to a maximum of 20 persons as contained in section 715 of the Companies Act 1985 (c. 6), by virtue of the Partnerships (Unrestricted Size) No. 1 Regulations 1968 (S.I. 1968 No. 1222).

Offences concerning patent agents committed by partnerships and bodies corporates **102.41**
   (s. 285 [1988])

Section 285 [1988] (reprinted in para. 102.10 *supra*) concerns the handling of offences committed under Part V of the 1988 Act (*i.e.* under sections 276 [1988] and

283 [1988] by partnerships and bodies corporate. Section 113 covers offences by corporations under the 1977 Act, but does not refer to partnerships.

Subsection (1) will simplify proceedings for such offences by partnerships by requiring these to be brought in the name of the partnership, rather than against each individual partner named as such, though (by subs. (4)) each individual partner is likewise to be guilty of the offence unless it is proved that he was ignorant of the offence or tried to prevent its commission.

Subsection (2) will enable partnerships to be treated on the same basis as bodies corporate as regards rules of court, as to service of documents upon them and as to procedure by the application thereto of Schedule 3 to the Magistrates' Courts Act 1980 (c. 43) in England and Wales, and in Northern Ireland of Schedule 4 to the Magistrates' Court (Northern Ireland) Order 1981 (S.I. 1981 No. 1675 (N.I. 26)): Scottish partnerships are, anyway, to be treated as bodies corporate. Subsection (3), likewise, will make the partnership as such responsible for the payment of any fine imposed upon it, in lieu of or in addition to any fines imposed on the individual partners under subsection (4).

Subsection (5) will concern bodies corporate and repeats (for the purposes of ss. 276 [1988] and 283 [1988]) the substance of section 113, for discussion of which see para. 113.02. However, proof of guilt of any individual charged under section 285 [1988] will require the connivance or consent of that person, rather than the mere "neglect" required for offence by an individual under section 113. This appears to be the equivalent of the defence of ignorance afforded to individual partners by subsection (4).

102.42   *Definitions for Part V of the 1988 Act (s. 286 [1988])*

Section 286 [1988] provides certain definitions for use with sections 274–285 [1988]. Of these: the definition of "the comptroller" repeats that in section 130(1), for which see para. 130.04; the definition of "director" in relation to a body corporate is made sufficiently broad as to cover any member of that body who plays a role in the management of that body; and the definitions of "registered patent agent" and "registered trade mark agent" are merely references respectively to sections 275(1) and 282(1) [1988] which themselves state these meanings. The remaining definition is that of the "European list", for which see paras. 102.43–102.45 *infra*.

102.43   *Definition of the "European list"*

Section 286 [1988] defines the "European list" as the list of professional representatives maintained by the EPO in pursuance of the EPC. The provisions for such a list are to be found in ERPCaa. 133 and 134, with EPCrr. 91(1)(*h*), 101 and 102 also making reference to "representatives" (*i.e.* agents who act for others in proceedings before the EPO).

The European list was established in January 1978 (OJEPO 2/1978), together with: (i) a "Regulation on the Establishment of an Institute of Professional Representatives before the EPO" (which has officially adopted the acronym "EPI", for which see para. 102.45 *infra*, and a "Code of Professional Conduct", the latest version of which was published OJEPO 9/1986, 331); and (ii) a "Regulation on Discipline for Professional Representatives", published OJEPO 7/1980, 183. The texts of these Regulations, and the Code of Professional Conduct, are reprinted in *EPH* (see 2nd. ed., Chapters 96 and 98).

The EPO will not permit an unqualified person to present an argument at an oral hearing before it, even though the authorised representative has so requested and is himself present (*EPO Decision T* 80/84, "*Representation/MITA*," OJEPO 9/1985, 269).

Qualification for entry to the European list **102.44**

The transitional period under EPCa. 163, during which admission to the European list was open to representatives by virtue of national qualifications or practice, ended on October 5, 1981 (except for nationals of newly-joining EPC Member States). From that date entry to the European list has been solely by the European qualifying examination under EPCa. 134, for which a "Regulation on the European Qualifying Examination for Professional Representatives before the EPO" was adopted, the latest version of which was published OJEPO 7/1983, 282 and is reprinted in *EPH* (see 2nd. ed., Chapter 97). For this examination, four years service in "full-time" training "under supervision" is a prerequisite. This will present considerable difficulty to any person practising under the provisions of sections 274 [1988] and 102 who has not already satisfied this service requirement, particularly in view of *EPO Decision D* 04/86 (OJEPO 1–2/1988, 26).

The European Patents Institute or "EPI" **102.45**

The EPI, or "Institute of Professional Representatives before the EPO" (see para. 102.43 *supra*) has a General Secretariat in an office within the EPO and has the postal address: Postfach 28 01 12, D–8000 München 2, German Federal Republic, see *EPH*. Membership of the EPI is compulsory for those on the European list. Such persons are subject to certain disciplinary rules, including the requirement to pay annual subscriptions and notify changes of address in due time, and adherence to the Code of Professional Conduct referred to in para. 102.43 *supra*. The paper by B. I. Cawthra, listed in para. 102.12 *supra*, describes the bodies which enforce these disciplinary rules and the fines which have been imposed, for example for late or non-payment of subscriptions.

SECTION 103

Extension of privilege for communications with solicitors relating to patent proceedings

103.—(1) It is hereby declared that the rule of law which confers privilege from disclosure in legal proceedings in respect of communications made with a solicitor or a person acting on his behalf, or in relation to information obtained or supplied for submission to a solicitor or a person acting on his behalf, for the purpose of any pending or contemplated proceedings before a court in the United Kingdom extends to such communications so made for the purpose of any pending or contemplated— **103.01**

(*a*) proceedings before the comptroller under this Act or any of the relevant conventions, or

(*b*) proceedings before the relevant convention court under any of those conventions.

(2) In this section—

"legal proceedings" includes proceedings before the comptroller; the references to legal proceedings and pending or contemplated proceedings include references to applications for a patent or a European patent and to international applications for a patent; and "the relevant conventions" means the European Patent Convention, the Community Patent Convention and the Patent Co-operation Treaty.

(3) This section shall not extend to Scotland.

103.02 COMMENTARY ON SECTION 103

Section 103 concerns only the privilege of solicitors in a matter before the Patent Office. Their privilege in court proceedings is a matter of general law discussed in paras. 104.06–104.09. The privilege of patent agents is the subject of section 280 [1988] (reprinted at para. 104.02), which privilege is extended for Scotland by sections 280(4) [1988] and 105 (as amended), see para. 105.03. Section 103 applies to "existing patents" and therefore also to proceedings under the 1949 Act (Sched. 2, para. 1(2)).

Section 103 provides that solicitors are to have, in respect of proceedings before the Patent Office, or a relevant convention court, the same privilege from disclosure of documents as they have in connection with any pending or contemplated proceedings before a court in the United Kingdom, for which see para. 104.07. Apart from the reference to "convention courts", the provisions of section 103 were previously to be found in section 15 of the Civil Evidence Act 1968 (c. 64), repealed by Schedule 6 of the present Act.

Subsection (2) defines "legal proceedings", to which subsection (1) refers, as including *any* proceedings before the Comptroller, including applications for a European patent and international applications for patents. Section 103 is therefore relevant where an application for employee compensation is made to the Comptroller under section 40 with the applicant being represented by a solicitor.

"Relevant conventions" are defined in subsection (2) as meaning the EPC, CPC and PCT, these being themselves defined in section 130(1) (for which see para. 130.08). Section 130(1) also defines the term "relevant convention court". For discussion of privilege in relation to proceedings under these conventions see para. 104.05.

By subsection (3), section 103 does not extend to Scotland, but similar privilege under Scots law is provided by section 105, see para. 105.03.

SECTION 104 [Prospectively repealed]

Privilege for communications with patent agents relating to patent proceedings

104.01 [*104.*—(1) *This section applies to any communication made for the purpose of any pending or contemplated patent proceedings, being either—*

    (a) *a communication between the patent agent of a party to those proceedings and that party or any other person; or*

    (b) *a communication between a party to those proceedings and a person other than his patent agent made for the purpose of obtaining, or in response to a request for, information which that party is seeking for the purpose of submitting it to his patent agent.*

(2) *For the purposes of subsection (1) above a communication made by or to a person acting—*

(i) on behalf of a patent agent; or

(ii) on behalf of a party to any pending or contemplated proceedings,

shall be treated as made by or to that patent agent or party, as the case may be.

(3) In any legal proceedings other than criminal proceedings a communication to which this section applies shall be privileged from disclosure in like manner as if any proceedings before the comptroller or the relevant convention court for the purpose of which the communication was made were proceedings before the court (within the meaning of this Act) and the patent agent in question had been the solicitor of the party concerned.

(4) In this section—

"legal proceedings" includes proceedings before the comptroller;

"patent agent" means an individual registered as a patent agent in the register of patent agents, a company lawfully practising as a patent agent in the United Kingdom or a person who satisfies the condition mentioned in section 84(1) or (3) above;

"patent proceedings" means proceedings under this Act or any of the relevant convention before the court, the comptroller or the relevant convention court, whether contested or uncontested and including an application for a patent;

"party", in relation to any contemplated proceedings, means a prospective party to the proceedings; and

"the relevant conventions" means the European Patent Convention, the Community Patent Convention and the Patent Co-operation Treaty.

(5) This section shall not extend to Scotland.]

Note. Section 104 was prospectively repealed by the 1988 Act (Sched. 8) to be replaced by section 280 [1988] reprinted at para. 104.02 *infra*. However, these changes remain to be brought into effect at a date to be specified, as to which the latest Supplement to this Work should be consulted *re.* this para. Meanwhile the original provisions continue to have effect, but no commentary thereon is provided, though much of the commentary on the new provisions applies also to the original provisions, and see the Second Edition to this work.

SECTION 280 [1988]

Privilege for communications with patent agents

280.—(1) This section applies to communications as to any matter relating to the protection of any invention, design, technical information, trade mark or service mark, or as to any matter involving passing off.　　**104.02**

(2) Any such communication—

(a) between a person and his patent agent, or

(b) for the purpose of obtaining, or in response to a request for, information which a person is seeking for the purpose of instructing his patent agent, is privileged from disclosure in legal proceedings in England, Wales or Northern Ireland in the same way as a communication between a person and his solicitor or, as the case may be, a communication for the purpose of obtaining, or in response to a request for, information which a person seeks for the purpose of instructing his solicitor.

(3) In subsection (2) "patent agent" means—

(*a*) a registered patent agent or a person who is on the European list,

(*b*) a partnership entitled to describe itself as a firm of patent agents or as a firm carrying on the business of a European patent attorney, or

(*c*) a body corporate entitled to describe itself as a patent agent or as a company carrying on the business of a European patent attorney.

(4) It is hereby declared that in Scotland the rules of law which confer privilege from disclosure in legal proceedings in respect of communications extend to such communications as are mentioned in this section.

Commentary on Sections 104 [Prospectively repealed] and 280 [1988]

104.03 *General*

Section 280 [1988] (reprinted at para. 104.02 *supra*), which will replace section 104, which itself had its origin in the Civil Evidence Act 1968 (c. 64, s. 15), extends to "patent agents" (as defined in subs. (3) discussed in para. 104.04 *infra*) the same rights of privilege in relation to disclosure of communications in legal proceedings in England, Wales and Northern Ireland (subs. (2)), and in Scotland (subs. 4)), as apply to a solicitor. The legal professional privilege which applies to solicitors is discussed in paras. 104.07–104.09 *infra*, and note that this now extends (by s. 103) to proceedings before the Comptroller or a "relevant convention court", as discussed in para. 103.02.

However, the extension of privilege to be provided by section 280 [1988] is only for activities in relation to "the protection of any invention, design, technical information, trade or service mark, or as to any matter involving passing off" (subs. (1)), herein called "the relevant fields", as discussed in para. 104.05 *infra*. Outside these fields, communications by or to a patent agent will not enjoy legal professional privilege, as was decided (under the original s. 104) in *Wilden Pump* v. *Fusfield* [*Privilege*] ([1985] FSR 159 (CA)).

104.04 *Persons entitled to privilege under section 280 [1988]*

Privilege under section 280 [1988] is to be accorded only in relation to communications by or to "patent agents", as that term is defined in subsection (3). By this definition "patent agents" are: either registered patent agents, *i.e.* those on the register of patent agents under section 275 [1988] (reprinted at para. 102.05 and discussed in paras. 102.26–102.30); or those on the "European list" of persons entitled to practice before the EPO (as defined in s. 286 [1988], reprinted at para. 102.11 and discussed in paras. 102.42–102.45), *i.e.* "European patent attorneys" (a term defined by s. 277 [1988], reprinted at para. 102.07 and discussed in paras. 102.34–102.38) (subs. (3)(*a*)). However, privilege is also to be accorded to "partnerships" and "bodies corporate", as defined in section 276(2) and (3) [1988] in relation to "patent agents", and as defined in section 277(3) and (4) [1988] in relation to "European patent attorneys" (subs. (3)(*b*) and (*c*)).

While, in contrast to section 103(1), the reference to "patent agent" does not explicitly include "a person acting on his behalf" (such as a technical assistant or a secretary), these words are presumably to be imported into the section. Otherwise, the protection accorded by the section would be severely limited, and in particular would make the section of no effect in relation to bodies corporate since these have no natural *persona* and must, therefore, act through their officers and servants.

The "relevant field"   **104.05**

By section 280 [1988] the extension of privilege to "patent agents" will be limited to "any matter relating to the protection of any invention, design, technical information, trade mark or service mark, or as to any matter involving passing off" (herein "the relevant field"). This is an extension over the scope of the repealed section 104 which accorded such privilege only "for the purpose of pending or contemplated patent proceedings", which did however include proceedings "whether contested or uncontested and including an application for a patent" (s. 104(4)). Clearly, the scope of the relevant field is now to be much broader than merely "patent proceedings", but also it would not seem so broad as to extend to any matter relating to "intellectual property" as that term has been defined, for example in the Supreme Court Act 1981 (c. 54, s. 72(5)), as set out in para. 61.32.

For present purposes, it is sufficient to note that the privilege will not extend to matters of copyright, unrelated to designs; and that there is an apparent limitation of the privilege to communications relating to "protection" of an intellectual property right. The presence of this word certainly provides scope for argument that in proceedings other than those of the types obviously intended to be covered, such as patent procurement, contests on validity and infringement proceedings, communications with a patent agent may perhaps not fall within the scope of section 280 [1988], but see the Governmental assurances described by J. Needle ((1988–89) 18 CIPA 130). However, this section contains no geographical limitation and, therefore, it would appear that privilege may now be accorded, under English law, to documents prepared in connection with foreign patent applications, this not being so (except for proceedings under the EPC or PCT) under the former section 104, see *Sonic Tapes' Patent* ([1987] RPC 251).

The nature of privilege

—General and the grounds of privilege   **104.06**

The question of privilege is closely allied to that of discovery of documents during the course of litigation. Thus, as part of the pre-trial litigation process in court proceedings a party is required to prepare a list (and, if requested, verify such list by affidavit) of those documents which he has, or has had in the past, in his possession, custody, control or power which are relevant to any issue in the proceedings (RSC Ord. 24, r. 1, reprinted at para. E024.1). Other parties to those proceedings may then require production and inspection of the listed documents (RSC Ord. 24, r. 9, reprinted at para. E024.9), *except* to the extent that the particular documents are covered by one of the grounds of "privilege."

The mere fact that a document contains confidential information is not a basis for a claim to privilege and thus, of itself, no excuse against production of that document (*Crompton (Alfred)* v. *Customs & Excise Commissioners (No. 2)*, [1974] AC 405; [1973] 2 All ER 1169 (HL)). However, the court may limit inspection of such documents to legal or independent advisers in cases where trade secret material is disclosed in the documents, see para. 72.44A, but it is up to the party disclosing a

713

document to indicate to, and satisfy, the court that the general right of the public to know all the evidence upon which a case is decided (subject to the limitation on use of discovered documents discussed in para. 61.31) should be varied by an order of some more limited disclosure (*Hoechst* v. *Phillips Petroleum*, SRIS C/07/89, *noted* IPD 12030). However, it is permissible to mask out those portions of documents which contain confidential matter which is irrelevant for the purposes of the discovery, but inferences may then be drawn from the extent of that masking, see the judgment of Buckley LJ in *Beecham Group's (Amoxycillin) Application* ([1980] RPC 261 (CA)).

Privilege against discovery of documents can be claimed on any of three broad grounds; "legal professional privilege" (discussed in paras. 104.07–104.09 *infra*), "self-incrimination" and "public policy". Little needs to be said about the last two: except to note that privilege against self-incrimination (*i.e.* against disclosing documents which may tend to show the commission of a criminal offence by the discovering party) has been virtually abolished for proceedings relating to "intellectual property", *e.g.* for England and Wales by section 72 of the Supreme Court Act 1981 (c. 54), see para. 61.32; and that a claim to public policy privilege usually only arises when a government department (whether or not a party to the proceedings in question) thinks disclosure of a document would be inimical to the public interest, which is most likely in proceedings for Crown use compensation under section 58 or in proceedings relating to inventions having a national defence purpose.

Legal professional privilege itself involves two distinct classes of documents depending on whether or not litigation was pending or contemplated at the time the document came into existence.

104.07   —*Legal professional privilege arising from request for, or giving of, legal advice*

First, irrespective of whether or not proceedings are pending or contemplated, documents which have passed between a party and its legal adviser (which term includes a patent agent if the document relates to the relevant fields) for the purpose of seeking, or the passing of, advice on the party's legal position are privileged against production even if the documents pass through an intermediate hand, unless it appears to the court that the party may have engaged in fraudulent or dishonest conduct, see *Gamlen* v. *Rochem* ([1983] RPC 1). The term "legal advice" is here to be construed broadly (*Balabel* v. *Air India*, [1988] 2 WLR 1036; [1988] 2 All ER 246 (CA)), but clearly not all communications with a legal adviser are capable of exclusion under this head.

104.08   —*Legal professional privilege arising from actual or contemplated proceedings*

Secondly, legal professional privilege also attaches to documents which are communications between a solicitor (or, for proceedings in the relevant fields, a "patent agent") and a non-professional agent or third party, whether communicated directly or through an agent, *provided* that these documents have come into existence for the purpose of obtaining or giving advice in relation to pending or contemplated proceedings, or for obtaining or collecting evidence to be used in such proceedings, or for obtaining information which may lead to the obtaining of such evidence. However, such purpose must be the dominant purpose for which the document was created, see *Waugh* v. *British Railways Board* ([1980] AC 521; [1979] 2 All ER 1169 (HL)). The proceedings must also actually be in contemplation. This apparently requires that a decision has already been taken that proceedings should be instituted or defended (*Crompton (Alfred)* v. *Customs & Excise Commissioners (No. 2)*, [1974] AC 405; [1973] 2 All ER 1169 (HL)). The Patents Court has held that such contemplation must be genuine (*Bishop* v. *Advest*, SRIS

C/20/83); and there must be more than a mere fear of litigation (*Rockwell* v. *Serck*, [1987] RPC 89), where it was observed that a contemplated patent application would bring proceedings within the terms of the former section 104.

It should be noted that, under this head of privilege, communications between a solicitor and a patent agent will be privileged whether or not these relate to the relevant field, see *Cooper Mechanical Joints' Application* ([1958] RPC 459) and *Hydroplan* v. *Naan Metal Works [Israel]* ([1985] FSR 255).

Communications between the parties, conducted on a "without prejudice" basis, are privileged and may be disclosed to the court only in reserved circumstances, for example as to an eventual award of costs as in *Cutts* v. *Head* ([1984] Ch. 290; [1984] 1 All ER 597 (CA)) or, after settlement, in relation to a dispute as to the terms of that settlement (*Rush & Tompkins* v. *GLC*, [1988] 3 All ER 737 (HL)).

—Limitations on privilege   104.09

Privilege can only stem from a party to the proceedings, see *Reeves* v. *Reed (Lewis)* ([1971] RPC 355) where a licensee could not claim privilege in proceedings in which the licensor, but not the licensee, was a party. However, once a document has become privileged in one set of proceedings, it remains privileged in future proceedings, unless the party from whom the privilege stems chooses to waive the claim to that privilege.

In *Sonic Tapes' Patent* ([1987] RPC 251) the personal recipient of letters from a patent agent was an employee of the applicant. After leaving that employment the recipient sought to make use of copies of the letters in an inventorship dispute under section 13. It was held that he had received those letters both in a personal capacity and as a representative of his employer and, on this basis, the employer could claim privilege for their contents as against third parties, but not as against that person. Letters received solely by the employer could not be used in the dispute upon privilege being claimed. However, no similar privilege was accorded in respect of communications relating to a United States' patent application, even though filed initially under the PCT, but on this point the decision may become over-ruled by the new wording of section 280 [1988], see para. 104.05 *supra*.

The protection to be afforded by section 280 [1988] is broad within the relevant field, but where the patent agent is acting for a foreign client the effect may be reduced by the client being called upon to comply with an order for discovery in his native country and against which the United Kingdom legislation is ineffective so far as his client is concerned. Here it may be noted that in the United States the scope of legal professional privilege is probably considerably less than in the United Kingdom. However, in *Detection Systems* v. *Pittway [USA]* ((1984) 220 USPQ 716), it was suggested that United States courts should not insist on disclosure of documents prepared by a foreign patent agent which are privileged according to his own law. Here it may be important that section 280 [1988] now appears to provide privilege in respect of foreign patent applications, which was not formerly the case, as noted *supra*.

It should also be noted that, under European law arising from the Treaty of Rome, privilege is not accorded to lawyers unless they are independent, that is not bound to their client by a relationship of employment (*Australian Mining & Smelting* v. *E.C. Commission (Case No. 155/79)*, [1982] 2 CMLR 264; [1982] FSR 474 (ECJ)). Whether the term "lawyer" here includes a patent agent or European patent attorney is uncertain ((1981–82) 11 CIPA 416). English law does not discriminate between independent and employed lawyers in this way, though an employed lawyer may only claim privilege for communications which have arisen in his capacity as lawyer and not as employee. In any event, all legal advice given on matters which may come to the attention of the E.C. Commission should be clearly headed "Professional Legal Advice: Private and Confidential", and should not be given by employed legal advisers.

SECTION 105

Extension of privilege in Scotland for communications relating to patent proceedings

105.01   **105.**—(1) It is hereby declared that in Scotland the rules of law which confer privilege from disclosure in legal proceedings in respect of communications, reports or other documents (by whomsoever made) made for the purpose of any pending or contemplated proceedings in a court in the United Kingdom extend to communications, reports or other documents made for the purpose of patent proceedings [*within the meaning of section 104 above*].

(2) In this section—

"patent proceedings" means proceedings under this Act or any of the relevant conventions, before the court, the comptroller or the relevant convention court, whether contested or uncontested and including an appliation for a patent; and

"the relevant conventions" means the European Patent Convention, the Community Patent Convention and the Patent Cooperation Treaty.

Note. Section 105 was prospectively amended by the 1988 Act (Sched. 7, para. 21 and Sched. 8), but the amendment remains to be brought into effect. The *Note* to para. 104.01 therefore applies also to section 105.

Commentary on Section 105

105.02   *General*

Section 105 provides for privilege in patent proceedings under Scots law, apparently whether or not these proceedings are held or contemplated in Scotland. The section is to be amended in consequence of the intended replacement of section 104 by section 280 [1988], but section 280(4) [1988] (reprinted in para. 104.02) seems largely to overlap section 105. In particular, it should be noted that section 280 [1988] is of broader scope than section 105 in that section 280 [1988] is not limited to "patent proceedings", or to proceedings before the Comptroller or a "relevant convention court", though such proceedings are covered thereby because of the extension of privilege of a solicitor to such proceedings by virtue of section 103. The commentaries at paras. 103.02 and 104.03–104.09 are, therefore, also relevant with adaptation to the principles of Scots law.

Section 105 extends to proceedings in relation to "existing patents" (Sched. 2, para. 1(2)). It has also been held to have effect even to communications which came into existence before June 1, 1978 when the section became effective (*Santa Fe* v. *Napier Shipping* [*Scotland*], [1985] SLT 430; [1986] RPC 72).

Extent of privilege under sections 105 and 280(4) [1988]　　　　　**105.03**

Section 105 refers to "the rules of law which confer privilege from disclosure in legal proceedings in respect of communications, reports or other documents". Section 280(4) [1988] (reprinted in para. 104.02) declares that, in Scotland, these rules of law in respect of communications (though not, it is noted, in respect of "reports or other documents") are those set out in that section. Section 280(4) [1988], therefore, has the effect of extending privilege under Scots law to the circumstances mentioned in section 103 (*Extension of privilege for communications with solicitors relating to patent proceedings*), discussed in para. 103.02; and also to communications wih respect to the "relevant field", as discussed in para. 104.05.

However, because subsection (1) refers to "communications, reports and other documents (*by whomsoever made*)", the effect of section 105 *may* be to extend, under Scots law, the privilege provided by sections 103 and 280 [1988] to a wider class of persons than is stated therein, though of course only in relation to proceedings in Scotland. Thus, it is possible that persons, other than solicitors, registered patent agents and European patent attorneys (and firms and bodies corporate practising thereas), may be able to claim a privilege under section 105 not available in proceedings elsewhere in the United Kingdom, though this would be only in respect of "patent proceedings" as defined in subsection (2). Note that this subsection does *not* require these proceedings to take place in Scotland.

Scottish cases on privilege in connection with intellectual property matters　　**105.04**

As with privilege under English law, the mere fact that a document has been provided in confidence to a party to proceedings is not sufficient reason for according it privilege, see para. 104.06. This has been specifically confirmed under section 105 in *Sante Fe* v. *Napier Shipping [Scotland]* ([1985] SLT 430; [1986] RPC 72). Here it was held that, where one party to patent proceedings had entered into contracts with third parties which contained clauses binding that party to hold certain information in strict confidence and not to disclose it to others without the consent of the third party, nonetheless that promise of confidentiality must yield to the public interest that, in the administration of justice, the truth should be established. Therefore, the other party to the litigation was entitled to see those contracts, despite the provisions making the technical contents confidential. However, for cases where disclosure of confidential information has been ordered to be disclosed on a restricted basis, *e.g.* to legal advisers only, see para. 72.44A.

SECTION 106　　　　　**106.01**

Costs and expenses in proceedings before the Court under section 40

106.—(1) In proceedings before the court under section 40 above (whether on an application or on appeal to the court), the court, in determining whether to award costs or expenses to any party and what costs or expenses to award, shall have regard to all the relevant circumstances, including the financial position of the parties.

(2) If in any such proceedings the Patents Court directs that any costs of one party shall be paid by another party, the court may settle the amount of the costs by fixing a lump sum or may direct that the costs shall be taxed

on a scale specified by the court, being a scale of costs prescribed by the Rules of the Supreme Court or by the County Court Rules.

106.02   COMMENTARY ON SECTION 106

Section 106 *only* applies to employee-inventor compensation proceedings under section 40, and then only in proceedings brought before the court, whether *ab initio* or on appeal from the Comptroller. The "court" (which is defined in s. 130(1), as amended, see para. 130.01 as discussed in para. 96.14) is here given broad discretion as regards awarding costs (or expenses) "to any party". It can therefore be concluded that in such proceedings costs (on even the "standard basis") are not automatically to be awarded in a normal case to the successful party as is now the position with other proceedings brought before the Patents Court, for which see paras. 61.18 and 97.24. A wide discretion is instead given to the court to make such order for costs as it may deem appropriate (including the award of a lump sum). However, no rule for a special scale of costs as envisaged by subsection (2) has yet been made, see RSC, Ord. 104, rule 18 (reprinted at para. E104.181) which concerns the procedure for an application to the court under section 40.

The origin of section 106 lies in the pleas made during the debates on the Patents Bill that an employee should not find himself saddled with a heavy burden of costs by the actions of the employer using his superior economic strength. The terms of section 106 do not, however, necessarily rule out an order for costs on the normal taxed basis, but it is clear from the parliamentary debates (H.L.Deb. Vol. 386, ser. 102, cols. 1078–1080, July 27, 1977) that it was expected that such an order would rarely be made. It was here noted that the provision is similar to that pertaining before the Lands Tribunal.

If Legal Aid has been granted to the employee, this will clearly be a factor for the court to consider. Whether Legal Aid will be available for section 40 proceedings is as yet unclear. In principle it is available (unlike in proceedings before the Comptroller) as it is before the Lands Tribunal (Legal Aid Act 1988 (c. 34), s. 14 and Sched. 2, Part 1). Nevertheless, legal aid has been refused in proceedings aimed to secure a personal benefit from ownership of a patent (*Halpern and Ward's Patent*, [1974] FSR 242). The availability of legal aid may influence the choice of forum for section 40 proceedings, see para. 40.08.

Costs in proceedings before the Comptroller are dealt with in paras. 107.03 and 107.04.

107.01   SECTION 107

Costs and expenses in proceedings before the comptroller

107.—(1) The comptroller may, in proceedings before him under this Act, by order award to any party such costs or, in Scotland, such expenses as he may consider reasonable and direct how and by what parties they are to be paid.

(2) In England and Wales any costs awarded under this section shall, if a county court so orders, be recoverable by execution issued from the county court or otherwise as if they were payable under an order of that court.

(3) In Scotland any order under this section for the payment of expenses may be enforced in like manner as a recorded decree arbitral.

(4) If any of the following persons, that is to say—

(a) any person by whom a reference is made to the comptroller under section 8, 12 or 37 above;

(b) any person by whom an application is made to the comptroller for the revocation of a patent;

(c) any person by whom notice of opposition is given to the comptroller under section 27(5), 29(2), 47(6) or 52(1) above, or section 117(2) below;

neither resides nor carries on business in the United Kingdom, the comptroller may require him to give security for the costs or expenses of the proceedings and in default of such security being given may treat the reference, application or notice as abandoned.

(5) In Northern Ireland any order under this section for payment of costs may be enforced as if it were a money judgment.

(6) **In the Isle of Man any order under this section for the payment of costs may be enforced in like manner to an execution issued out of the court.**

Note. Amendment of the section was effected by S.I. 1978 No. 621.

COMMENTARY ON SECTION 107

General   **107.02**

Section 107 provides for the award of costs by the Comptroller in proceedings before him and for a mechanism whereby payment of the award may be enforced. It also provides that the Comptroller can require security for such costs to be given in certain circumstances. Section 107 applies also to "existing patents" and therefore to proceedings under the 1949 Act (Sched. 2, para. 1(2)).

It should be noted that costs on appeal from the Comptroller are taxed according to normal High Court practice, see para. 97.24. Also, Legal Aid is not available in proceedings before the Comptroller (Legal Aid Act 1988, c. 34, s. 14 and Sched. 2, Part I), but may be available on appeals therefrom, see para. 97.25.

Awards of costs

—Basis of awards   **107.03**

The terms of subsection (1) give the Comptroller a broad discretion in awarding costs, but the taxation procedure of the court is not required to be followed. Instead, the long-standing practice of the Comptroller is to make a lump sum award which is intended to be only a contribution to the costs of the successful party, rather than compensation therefor, as it is felt that persons should not be inhibited by the prospect of having to pay heavy costs, if unsuccessful after commencing or defending proceedings in the Patent Office.

The Comptroller has declined to depart from this practice in compulsory licence proceedings under section 48 (*Extrude Hone's Patent*, [1984] FSR 105), and in entitlement proceedings under sections 8 and 37 (*Harris's Patent*, [1985] RPC 19), but whether a party has funds to pay costs is *not* a material consideration for the Comptroller in deciding upon an award of costs (*Pelling and Campbell's Application (No. 2)*, SRIS O/174/88).

While subsection (1) does not preclude an award of costs for or against a party in *ex parte* proceedings, this would be most unusual because here the Comptroller is not merely fulfilling a judicial role: a member of his staff will have made a prima facie ruling which the applicant/proprietor wishes to challenge at a formal hearing before a hearing officer appointed for the purpose.

On the determination of an *inter partes* case (otherwise than by a decision after a hearing) any party claiming costs may make application for an award. Detailed bills should not be sent, but particulars of any special expenses claimed may be supplied, *e.g.* for attendance of witnesses for cross-examination, discovery or experiments (O.J. October 26, 1988).

In *Nippon Shinyaku's Application* (SRIS O/1/83) a claim for extra costs was apparently successful based on the opponent's failure to respond to evidence or inform the applicant until shortly before the hearing that he would not be present thereat without making it clear whether the opposition was withdrawn. As a general rule costs will follow the event, but in deciding upon an award the hearing officer will consider the extent to which costs to be awarded one party following success on one or more grounds raised should be offset by costs to be awarded against the other party on any grounds on which that other party was successful. For example, where a patentee amends his patent during revocation proceedings he will not receive a full award of costs, and indeed usually will not receive any award even if thereafter he was totally successful. Where a party unilaterally withdraws from legal proceedings, he can as a normal rule expect to have costs awarded against him, see *Godin's Application* (SRIS O/122/86) where an applicant failed to request preliminary examination after entitlement proceedings had been commenced on his application; and *Science Research's Patent* (SRIS O/7/89) where an application for a licence of right was withdrawn after the Patentee had been involved in some work on it.

Costs will not be awarded against any party until he has had an opportunity of submitting to the Comptroller any relevant considerations and, if he wishes has been heard on the matter (s. 101). In cases determined by decision after a hearing, a finding of costs will be included in the decisions. Any submission of costs should therefore be brought forward for consideration at the hearing. In cases determined by agreement between the parties before hearing, the settlement should deal with the costs of the proceedings. The amount of an award of costs is at the discretion of the Comptroller and, since normally no reasoned decision thereon is given, any appeal on the quantum of the award will normally fail (*Ford's (Runyon's) Application*, [1968] RPC 400).

107.04 *—Extent of awards*

It has been customary for the Comptroller to award costs according to a fixed scale. The most recent scale was published O.J. October 26, 1988. This was expressed to act as a guide for all *inter partes* patent proceedings before the Comptroller and for similar proceedings under the Registered Designs Act 1949 and the Trade Marks Act 1938 (as amended). The notice reiterates the long-established practice that "costs in proceedings before the Patent Office are not intended to compensate parties for the expense to which they may have been put". The following sums are given and are stated to be a guide and not maxima:

1.	Notice of Opposition or application for Revocation and accompanying Statement	£75 plus statutory fee
2.	Perusing Counterstatement	£25

or

1.	Perusing Notice of Opposition or Application for Revocation and accompanying Statement	£25
2.	Counterstatement	£75
3.	Preparing and filing evidence	£150–£300
4.	Perusing evidence	one-half of Item 3
5.	Preparation for and attendance at Hearing	£250–£700
6.	Where the Applicant or Opponent appears in person and where attendance of witnesses is required by the opposite party, allowance will be made for general expenses and travelling, but the allowance for general expenses will not normally exceed £20 per day.	

Security for costs (subs. (4)) 107.05

Subsection (4) provides for security for costs to be required in certain specified proceedings, namely from applicants under sections 8, 12 or 37 (*Entitlement to apply or right to grant*); applications for revocation to the Comptroller under 72; and by opponents under sections 27(5) (*Amendment*), 29(2) (*Surrender*), 47(6) (*Cancellation of "licence of right" entry*), 52(1) (*Compulsory licence*), and 117(2) (*Correction of error*). Note that there is no provision for requiring such security in proceedings under section 40 (*Employee-Inventor Compensation*). Also, in infringement proceedings which are brought before the Comptroller by agreement of the parties under section 61(3), that agreement should deal with security for costs if appropriate.

Security is only required when the applicant/opponent/proprietor neither resides nor carries on business in the United Kingdom (including the Isle of Man by virtue of section 132(2)). Though the Comptroller has a discretion whether to require security in the specified circumstances, it is his usual practice to do so when the proceedings are initiated. This is done by requiring security for a fixed sum, which is at present £700 (O.J. October 26, 1988). It is customary for this sum to be guaranteed by the authorised agent, though he may decline to do so unless he has satisfied himself that he would be reimbursed if necessary. Alternatively, money could be deposited in an interest-bearing bank account in the joint names of the authorised agents of both parties to the proceedings, or a guarantee could be given by a bank in the United Kingdom.

Enforcement of award of costs (subss. (2), (3), (5) and (6)) 107.06

Subsections (2), (3), (5) and (6) provide a new mechanism for the enforcement of an award of costs made by the Comptroller against a person resident respectively in England or Wales, Scotland, Northern Ireland, or the Isle of Man. The mechanism corresponds to that applicable for debt payment enforcement for relatively small sums in the various areas of the United Kingdom, and this should be capable of being operated at little cost to the person in whose favour the award was made. For the similar provision on costs awarded by the EPO, see section 93 and para. 93.02.

SECTION 108 108.01

Licences granted by order of comptroller

108. Any order for the grant of a licence under section 11, 38, 48 or 49 above shall, without prejudice to any other method of enforcement, have effect as if it were a deed, executed by the proprietor of the patent and all other necessary parties, granting a licence in accordance with the order.

108.02
Commentary on Section 108

This section removes any doubt as to validity, for want of proper execution, of a licence granted or modified by order of the Comptroller under the provisions of sections 11 or 38 (*Order for substitution of an existing licence following an order for change of applicant or proprietor*), or sections 48 or 49 (*Grant of compulsory licence or substitution of an existing licence by a new compulsory licence*). Section 108 applies also to "existing patents" (Sched. 2, para. 1(2)). The licence would seem to take effect from the making of the Order, so that the Order could take effect though an appeal is filed against it.

Curiously, section 108 does not appear to apply to cases where the Comptroller has settled or ordered the terms of a "licence of right" under section 46(3)(*a*) or (*b*), or if a modification of an existing licence is ordered under the substituted section 51(3).

SECTION 109

Falsification of register, etc.

109.01   **109.** If a person makes or causes to be made a false entry in the register kept under this Act, or a writing falsely purporting to be a copy or reproduction of an entry in any such register, or produces or tenders or causes to be produced or tendered in evidence any such writing, knowing the entry or writing to be false, he shall be liable—

(*a*) on summary conviction, to a fine not exceeding **the prescribed sum** [*£1,000*];

(*b*) on conviction on indictment, to imprisonment for a term not exceeding two years or a fine, or both.

Note. Section 109 was amended by section 32(2) of the Magistrates' Courts Act 1980 (c. 43).

Commentary on Section 109

109.02 *General*

The offences under section 109 concern false entries in the register of patents and false copies thereof. Such an offence has existed since 1883 but no case appears to have been brought in respect of it.

The offence is one triable "either way", *i.e.* by summary conviction or on indictment. The "prescribed sum" for the maximum fine on summary conviction is specified as the "statutory maximum" fine (Criminal Justice Act 1982 (c. 48, s. 74). This can be increased by order under section 143 of the Magistrates' Courts Act 1980 (c. 43) and was raised to £2,000 by Sched. 1, para. 4 of the Criminal Penalties Etc. (Increase) Order 1984 (S.I. 1984 No. 447). Although there is no limit specified for the fine on conviction on indictment, it must not be excessive (Bill of Rights 1688,

s. 1) and must be within the offender's capacity to pay (*R. v. Churchill (No. 2)*, [1967] 1 QB 190 (CCA)).

Where a company commits the offence, its officers may be liable under section 113, see para. 113.02.

Knowing the entry or writing to be false   **109.03**

The offences under section 109 require the offender to have knowledge that the register entry or copy is false. A statement which is literally true may be false if an omission creates clearly and intentionally a belief which is wrong (*R. v. Bishirgian*, [1936] 1 All ER 586 (CCA)). Whether the person responsible for the falsehood gains by it is not relevant (*Barrass* v. *Reeve*, [1980] 3 All ER 705).

Proof of a person's knowledge can be based on evidence that he "deliberately shut his eyes to the obvious or refrained from inquiry because he suspected the truth but did not wish to have his suspicions confirmed" (*Westminster City Council* v. *Croyalgrange*, [1986] 2 All ER 353; [1986] 1 WLR 674 (HL) *per* Lord Bridge). The knowledge of an employee or agent may be imputed to his employer or principal where control of the work was delegated to him (*Vane* v. *Yiannopoullos*, [1965] AC 486; [1964] 3 All ER 820 (HL), but, in the absence of control or delegation, criminal acts by an employee are not imputed to his employer (*Tesco* v. *Natrass*, [1972] AC 153; [1971] 2 All ER 127 (HL)).

SECTION 110

Unauthorised claim of patent rights

110.—(1) If a person falsely represents that anything disposed of by him   **110.01** for value is a patented product he shall, subject to the following provisions of this section, be liable on summary conviction to a fine not exceeding **level 3 on the standard scale** [*£200*].

(2) For the purposes of subsection (1) above a person who for value disposes of an article having stamped, engraved or impressed on it or otherwise applied to it the word "patent" or "patented" or anything expressing or implying that the article is a patented product, shall be taken to represent that the article is a patented product.

(3) Subsection (1) above does not apply where the representation is made in respect of a product after the patent for that product or, as the case may be, the process in question has expired or been revoked and before the end of a period which is reasonably sufficient to enable the accused to take steps to ensure that the representation is not made (or does not continue to be made).

(4) In proceedings for an offence under this section it shall be a defence for the accused to prove that he used due diligence to prevent the commission of the offence.

Note. Section 110 was amended by section 46 of the Criminal Justice Act 1982 (c. 48).

COMMENTARY ON SECTION 110

110.02 *General*

The offence under section 110 is a false representation that a product disposed of for value is "patented". It applies also to "existing patents" (Sched. 2, para. 1(2)) and to European patents (UK) (s. 77(1)). For a false representation that a patent has been applied for, see section 111.

110.03 *Penalties*

Offences under section 110 are triable only summarily. The amount of the maximum fine is now stated with reference to a stated level on the "standard scale". This is defined by section 37(2) of the Criminal Justice Act 1982 (c. 48). The sums applicable to the five specified levels may be increased by order made under section 143 of the Magistrates' Courts Act 1980 (c. 43). "Level 3" presently stands at £400 (Criminal Penalties Etc. (Increase) Order 1984 (S.I. 1984 No. 447), Sched. 4).

Where a company commits an offence under section 110, its officers may be liable under section 113, see para. 113.02.

110.04 *Other effects of false marking*

For the effect of marking on infringement proceedings and why it is desirable, see para. 62.03.

Besides giving rise to possible criminal penalties, false marking may also disentitle the marker to discretionary relief from the court, *e.g.* an injunction against trade mark infringement or passing off (*Cheavin* v. *Walker*, (1877) 5 Ch.D. 850 (CA) and *Cochrane* v. *MacNish*, (1896) 13 RPC 100 (PC)). False marking is not, however, an offence under the Trade Descriptions Act 1968 (c. 29) in view of the definition of "trade description" in section 2(1) of that Act.

No company, firm or individual may trade under a name which incorporates the word "patent" or "patentee" without the consent of the Secretary of State for Trade and Industry (Companies and Business Names Regulations 1981 (S.I. 1981 No. 1685), r. 3, now effective under sections 2(1) and 3(1) of the Business Names Act 1985 (c. 6)).

110.05 *Patented product*

An offence under section 110 is only committed by reference to a "patented product". This term is defined in section 130(1) and discussed in para. 60.11. It includes a product to which a patented process has been applied, as well as the products of section 60(1)(*a*) and (*c*). The fact that sales of the article could be restrained as a contributory infringement under section 60(2) (see paras. 60.14–60.16) does not make the article a "patented product".

The patent in question must be subsisting at the time. A fine for unauthorised marking was imposed in *Cassidy* v. *Eisenmann* ([1980] FSR 381) where a toy imported from Italy was marked "Brevettato Italia, Espania, Great Britain, France, Deutschland" and only a pending application existed in the United Kingdom. The decision was in line with earlier cases where there had once been a patent which had expired, or where there was at the time only a pending application (*R.* v. *Wallis*, (1886) 3 RPC 1; *R.* v. *Crampton*, (1886) 3 RPC 367).

Falsely represents (subss.(2) and (3)) **110.06**

Subsection (2) defines the representation required for an offence to be committed. There is however ancient authority that use of the word "patent" is not objectionable where the patent expired long ago and the word has become part of the description of the article (*Sykes* v. *Sykes*, (1824) 3 B & C 641; 107 E.R. 834).

It is irrelevant that the vendor of an article believes it to be a patented product if this is not so (*Esco* v. *Rolo*, (1923) 40 RPC 471). The patent does not have to be represented as his.

Subsection (3) now provides a reasonable period of grace after expiry or revocation of a patent for marking to cease.

The effect of section 110 on trade in second-hand goods is obscure.

Defence of due diligence (subs. (4)) **110.07**

The burden of proof for the defendant under subsection (4) is a preponderance of probability. A company may have a defence by proving that the false marking was carried out without its consent (*Tesco* v. *Natrass*, [1972] AC 153; [1971] 2 All ER 127 (HL)).

SECTION 111

Unauthorised claim that patent has been applied for

111.—(1) If a person represents that a patent has been applied for in **111.01** respect of any article disposed of for value by him and—

(*a*) no such application has been made, or

(*b*) any such application has been refused or withdrawn,

he shall, subject to the following provisions of this section, be liable on summary conviction to a fine not exceeding **level 3 on the standard scale** [*£200*].

(2) Subsection (1)(*b*) above does not apply where the representation is made (or continues to be made) before the expiry of a period which commences with the refusal or withdrawal and which is reasonably sufficient to enable the accused to take steps to ensure that the representation is not made (or does not continue to be made).

(3) For the purposes of subsection (1) above a person who for value disposes of an article having stamped, engraved or impressed on it or otherwise applied to it the words "patent applied for" or "patent pending", or anything expressing or implying that a patent has been applied for in respect of the article, shall be taken to represent that a patent has been applied for in respect of it.

(4) In any proceedings for an offence under this section it shall be a defence for the accused to prove that he used due diligence to prevent the commission of such an offence.

Note. Section 111 was amended by section 46 of the Criminal Justice Act 1982 (c. 48).

Commentary on Section 111

111.02 *General*

The offence under section 111 is a false representation that, in respect of an article disposed of for value, a patent has been applied for which will cover that article. It therefore complements section 110 which concerns false representation that a product is "patented". Section 111 applies also to applications for a European patent (UK) (s. 78(2)) and to international applications for a patent (UK) (s. 89(1)). However, an earlier application in another country from which priority may be claimed under the Paris Convention is not an "application" for the purpose of section 111, and an offence may therefore be committed by a prospective applicant during the priority interval.

111.03 *Effect and limitations of section 111*

An offence under the section is committed if there is no application subsisting when an article, marked for example "patent applied for", is disposed of for value. Disposal by gift, *e.g.* distribution of free samples, is outside the ambit of the section.

The subsisting application need not have been published under section 16 or under the EPC or PCT.

The Act does not define what is meant by a patent applied for "in respect of" an article. The definition of section 69(2)(*b*) is evidently not intended (*cf.* "patented product" in s. 110, see para. 110.05).

For the effect of marking and why it is desirable, see the discussion on section 62 at para. 62.03, which provision is extended to published applications by section 69(1), discussed at para. 69.04. For the purpose of section 111 (unlike under s. 69(3) discussed at para. 69.05), the likelihood of grant of the application is immaterial.

Where a company commits an offence under section 111 its officers may be liable under section 113, see para. 113.02.

111.04 *Defences and penalties*

Subsection (3) gives a period of grace to cease marking after refusal or withdrawal of the application.

The defence under subsection (4) is analogous to that discussed under section 110(4), see para. 110.07.

An offence under section 111 is triable only summarily. The maximum fine is now defined with reference to "level 3 on the standard scale". This term is explained at para. 110.03.

SECTION 112

Misuse of title "Patent Office"

112.01 112. If any person uses on his place of business, or on any document issued by him, or otherwise, the words "Patent Office" or any other words suggesting that his place of business is, or is officially connected with, the

Patent Office, he shall be liable on summary conviction to a fine not exceeding **level 4 on the standard scale** [*£500*].

Note. Section 112 was amended by section 46 of the Criminal Justice Act 1982 (c. 48).

The offence under section 112 is misuse of the words "Patent Office" to suggest some connection with "The Patent Office" and is thus analogous to a case of passing off in relation to these words. "Patent Office" is defined in unrepealed section 62 of the Patents and Designs Act 1907, see para. B04.

The offence is triable only summarily. The maximum fine is now defined by reference to "level 4 on the standard scale". This term is explained at para. 110.03. "Level 4" was increased to £1,000 in 1984 in the manner described in that paragraph.

Where a company commits an offence under section 112, its officers may be liable under section 113, see para. 113.02.

For control of unauthorised display of the Royal Arms, see section 92 [1949] (reprinted at para. A092.1) and section 61 of the Trade Marks Act 1938 (1 & 2 Geo. 6, c. 22), both discussed at para. A092.2.

Care should be taken not to contravene section 112 in the wording of advertisements for staff, *e.g.* inserted in the O.J., referring to recruitment for the "patent office" of a particular company or firm.

SECTION 113

Offences by corporations

113.—(1) Where an offence under this Act which has been committed by   **113.01** a body corporate is proved to have been committed with the consent or connivance of, or to be attributable to any neglect on the part of, a director, manager, secretary or other similar officer of the body corporate, or any person who was purporting to act in any such capacity, he, as well as the body corporate, shall be guilty of that offence and shall be liable to be proceeded against and punished accordingly.

(2) Where the affairs of a body corporate are managed by its members, subsection (1) above shall apply in relation to the acts and defaults of a member in connection with his functions of management as if he were a director of the body corporate.

Section 113 makes an officer, or any person managing the affairs of a body corporate, liable for any offence which that company commits under the Act, but only on proof that the offence was committed with the consent or connivance of that person or was attributable to his neglect. Such offences may arise under section 22(9) (discussed at para. 22.08), section 23(3) (discussed at para. 23.07) and sections 109–112 (discussed in the commentaries on those sections). A similar provision exists in section 273(5) [1988] in relation to offences under provisions of the 1988 Act which will replace sections 84, 85, 114 and 115 of the present Act when their prospective repeals are given effect, for which see *Note* in para. 102.01. Section 113 does not apply to offences under section 92 [1949] (discussed in para. A092.2), but otherwise does apply to "existing patents" (Sched. 2, para. 1(2)). Section 113 places the onus of proof on the prosecutor, in contrast to section 93 [1949] which it replaced and which provided a possible defence to be proved by the accused.

A company may be convicted for the criminal acts (including those requiring *mens rea*) of a director or manager, but only when that person can be identified with the controlling mind and will of the company and was in actual control of its operations (*Tesco* v. *Natrass*, [1972] AC 153; [1971] 2 All ER 127 (HL)).

In a case under a statute similarly requiring the consent, connivance or neglect of an officer of the company, it was held that "neglect" did not mean a failure to see that the law was observed and, where a director had no reason to distrust another officer of the company, she could properly leave matters to him and could not be said to have neglected her duty because she had failed to inquire specifically as to whether a certain statutory requirement had been complied with (*Huckerby* v. *Elliott*, [1970] 1 All ER 189).

114.01   SECTION 114 [Prospectively repealed]

Restrictions on practice as patent agent

[**114.**—(1) *An individual shall not, either alone or in partnership with any other person, practise, describe himself or hold himself out as a patent agent, or permit himself to be so described or held out, unless he is registered as a patent agent in the register of patent agents or (as the case may be) unless he and all his partners are so registered.*

(2) *A body corporate shall not practise, describe itself or hold itself out or permit itself to be described or held out as mentioned in subsection (1) above unless*—

    (a) *in the case of a company within the meaning of the Companies Act* **1985** *[c. 6] [1948]* **or the Companies Act 1931 (Act of Tynwald)** *which began to carry on business as a patent agent before 17th November 1917, a director or the manager of the company is registered as a patent agent in the register of patent agents and the name of that director or manager is mentioned as being so registered in all professional advertisements, circulars or letters issued by or with the consent of the company in which the name of the company appears;*

    (b) *in any other case, every director or, where the body's affairs are managed by its members, every member of the body and in any event, it if has a manager who is not a director or member, the manager, is so registered.*

(2A) **Notwithstanding the definition of "patent agent" in section 130(1) below, subsections (1) and (2) above do not impose any prohibition in relation to the business of acting as agent for other persons for the purpose of** *conducting proceedings before the comptroller in connection with European patents (UK) to which section 77(1) above for the time being applies.*

(3) *Any person who contravenes the provisions of this section shall be liable on summary conviction to a fine not exceeding level 5 on the standard scale [£1,000].*

(4) *Proceedings for an offence under this section may be begun at any time within twelve months from the date of offence.*

(5) *This section shall not be construed as prohibiting solicitors from taking such part in proceedings relating to patents and applications for patents as has heretobefore been taken by solicitors and, in particular, shall not derogate from the provisions of section 102 above as it applies to solicitors.*

(6) *A patent agent shall not be guilty of an offence under section 22 of the Solicitors Act 1974 [c. 47], section 11 of the Advocates Act 1976 (Act of Tynwald) or section 32 [39] of the Solicitors (Scotland) Act 1980 [c. 46] [1933] [23 & 24 Geo. 5, c. 21] (which prohibit the preparation for reward of certain instruments or writs by persons not legally qualified) by reason only of the preparation by him for use in proceedings under this Act before the comptroller or on appeal under this Act to the Patents Court from the comptroller of any document other than a deed.*

(7) *For Article 23(2)(d) of the Solicitors (Northern Ireland) Order 1976 [S.I. 1976 No. 582] there shall be substituted the following paragraph—*

> *"(d) a patent agent within the meaning of the Patents Act 1977 preparing, for use in proceedings under that Act or the Patents Act 1949 before the comptroller (as defined in the former Act) or on appeal under either of those Acts to the Patents Court from the comptroller, any document other than a deed;"*

Note. Section 114 was prospectively repealed by Schedule 8 [1988] to be replaced by sections 274 [1988] (reprinted at para. 102.04 and discussed in paras. 102.18–102.25) and 276 [1988] (reprinted at para. 102.06 and discussed in paras. 102.31–102.33). However, the repeal has not yet taken effect, for which the latest Supplement to this Work should be consulted *re.* this para. Meanwhile, section 114 (as amended) continues to have effect, but no separate commentary thereon is provided, though see the Second Edition of this work.

The indicated amendments to the section were made: by the Companies Consolidation (Consequential Provisions) Act 1985 (c. 9, s. 30 and Sched. 2), as to subsection (2)(*a*); by the Administration of Justice Act 1985 (c. 61, s. 60), as to insertion of subsection (2A); by the Criminal Justice Act 1982 (c. 48, s. 46), as to subsection (3); and by the Solicitors (Scotland) Act 1980 (c. 46), as to subsection (6).

SECTION 115 [Prospectively repealed]   115.01

Power of comptroller to refuse to deal with certain agents

[**115.**—(1) *Rules may authorise the comptroller to refuse to recognise as agent in respect of any business under this Act—*

(*a*) *any individual whose name has been erased from, and not restored to, the register of patent agents, or who is for the time being suspended from acting as a patent agent;*

(*b*) *any person who has been convicted of an offence under section 114 above or section 88 of the 1949 Act (which is replaced by section 114);*

(*c*) *any person who is found by the Secretary of State to have been convicted of any offence or to have been guilty of any such misconduct as, in the case of an individual registered in the register of patent agents, would render him liable to have his name erased from it;*

(*d*) *any person, not being registered as a patent agent, who in the opinion of the comptroller is engaged wholly or mainly in acting as agent in applying for patents in the United Kingdom or elsewhere in the name or for the benefit of a person by whom he is employed;*

(*e*) *any company or firm, if any person whom the comptroller could refuse to recognise as agent in respect of any business under this Act is acting as a director or manager of the company or is a partner in the firm.*

(2) *The comptroller shall refuse to recognise as agent in respect of any business under this Act any person who neither resides nor has a place of business in the United Kingdom.*

(3) *Rules may authorise the comptroller to refuse to recognise as agent or other representative for the purpose of applying for European patents any person who does not satisfy the condition mentioned in section 84(1) above and does not fall within the exemption in subsection (2) of that section.]*

Note. Section 115 was prospectively repealed by Schedule 8 [1988] to be replaced by section 281 [1988] (reprinted at para. 115.02 and discussed in paras. 115.04 *et seq., infra*). However, the repeal and replacement has not yet taken effect, for which the latest Supplement hereto should be consulted *re.* this para. Meanwhile, section 115 (as amended) continues to have effect, but no separate commentary thereon is provided, though much of the commentary on the new provisions also applies to the original provisions, and see the Second Edition of this work.

115.02   **SECTION 281 [1988]**

Power of comptroller to refuse to deal with certain agents

281.—(1) This section applies to business under the Patents Act 1949, the Registered Designs Act 1949 or the Patents Act 1977.

(2) The Secretary of State may make rules authorising the comptroller to refuse to recognise as agent in respect of any business to which this section applies—

(*a*) a person who has been convicted of an offence under section 88 of the Patents Act 1949, section 114 of the Patents Act 1977 or section 276 of this Act;

(*b*) an individual whose name has been erased from and not restored to, or who is suspended from, the register of patent agents on the ground of misconduct;

(*c*) a person who is found by the Secretary of State to have been guilty of such conduct as would, in the case of an individual registered in the register of patent agents, render him liable to have his name erased from the register on the ground of misconduct;

(*d*) a partnership or body corporate of which one of the partnes or directors is a person whom the comptroller could refuse to recognise under paragraph (*a*), (*b*) or (*c*) above.

(3) The rules may contain such incidental and supplementary provisions as appear to the Secretary of State to be appropriate and may, in particular, prescribe circumstances in which a person is or is not to be taken to have been guilty of misconduct.

(4) Rules made under this section shall be made by statutory instrument which shall be subject to annulment in pursuance of a resolution of either House of Parliament.

(5) The comptroller shall refuse to recognise as agent in respect of any business to which this section applies a person who neither resides nor has a place of business in the United Kingdom, the Isle of Man or another member State of the European Economic Community.

Relevant Rule

Agents

90.—(1) Unless the comptroller otherwise directs in any particular **115.03** case—

(*a*) all attendances upon him may be made by or through an agent; and

(*b*) every notice, application or other document filed under the Act may be signed by an agent.

(2) Where after a person has become a party to proceedings before the comptroller he appoints an agent for the first time or appoints one agent in substitution for another, the newly appointed agent shall file Patents Form No. 51/77 in duplicate on or before the first occasion when he acts as agent.

(3) The comptroller may refuse to recognise as such an agent in respect of any business under the Act—

(*a*) any individual whose name has been erased from, and not restored to, the register of patent agents, or who is for the time being suspended from acting as a patent agent;

(*b*) any person who has been convicted of an offence under section 88 of the 1949 Act or section 114;

(*c*) any person who is found by the Secretary of State to have been convicted of any offence or to have been guilty of any such misconduct as, in the case of an individual registered in the register or patent agents, would render him liable to have his name erased from it;

(*d*) any person, not being registered as a patent agent, who in the opinion of the comptroller is engaged wholly or mainly in acting as agent in applying for patents in the United Kingdom or elsewhere in the name or for the benefit of a person by whom he is employed;

(*e*) any company or firm, if any person whom the comptroller could refuse to recognise as agent in respect of any business under the Act is acting as a director or manager of the company or is a partner in the firm.

(4) The comptroller may refuse to recognise as agent or other representative for the purpose of applying for European patents any person who does not satisfy the condition mentioned in section 84(1) and does not fall within the exemption in subsection (2) of that section.

Note. This rule will require considerable amendment when the repeal of section 115, and section 281 [1988], each becomes effective, for which see the *Note* to para. 115.01.

COMMENTARY ON SECTION 281 [1988]

115.04   *General*

Section 281 [1988] will replace section 115, when this is repealed, and has its origin in section 89 [1949]. However, various changes are to be made to suit the new provisions as regards persons acting as agents for others in matters relating to patents, for which see sections 274 [1988] (reprinted at para. 102.04 and discussed in paras. 102.18–102.25) and substituted section 102 (reprinted in para. 102.02 and discussed in paras. 102.14–102.16). Rule 90 (reprinted at para. 115.02 *supra*), which was originally made under section 115, is now discussed at paras. 102.21–102.22.

Because section 32 of the Registered Designs Act 1949 (12, 13 & 14 Geo. 6, c. 88) was repealed by Schedule 8 [1988], section 281(1) [1988] will extend the application of the section to business under that Act, as well as covering business under the Patents Acts 1949 and 1977.

115.05   *Rules for refusal of recognition of agent (subss. (2)–(4))*

Subsections (2)–(4) will authorise the making of rules in terms quite similar to those in the repealed section 115 and rule 90 [1982] made thereunder. Subsection (2)(*a*) will require a prior conviction for an offence under the patent statutes and corresponds to section 115(1)(*b*) with addition of reference to section 276 [1988] which will replace repealed section 114 [1977]. Subsection (2)(*b*) arises from erasure or suspension of the individual from the Register of Patent Agents and corresponds to section 115(1)(*a*), but with the important proviso that that removal or suspension must have been on the ground of misconduct. This flows naturally from the provisions of section 274(1) [1988] that it will not be necessary to be on the Register in order to act as agent for another in matters relating to patents, but appears too narrow, see *infra*. Subsection (2)(*c*) corresponds to section 115(1)(*c*), but is likewise limited to equivalence to erasure from the Register on the ground of misconduct and omits reference to conviction "of any offence", again probably unduly narrowing the provision, see *infra*. However, subsection (3) refers specifically to the "circumstances" in which a person may be taken to have been guilty or not of misconduct, and its wording suggests that the rules may come to use different language from that of the statutory provision, rather than use identical language as did rule 90 [1982]. Subsection (2)(*d*) corresponds to section 115(1)(*e*) in extending the circumstances for non-recognition of individuals to the firms or companies through which they practise. Section 115(1)(*d*) has no counterpart in the new section because unregistered persons may be employed full-time as agents under section 274 [1988]. Subsection (3) will give the Secretary of State a new power to make other rules incidental and supplementary to those specifically set out in subsection (2), whilst subsection (4) will provide for annulment of the rules by negative resolution of either House of Parliament.

It should, however, be realised that the Comptroller does not appear in the past to have taken any action either under section 115 or its predecessor section 89 [1949]. Nor, apparently, were any cases brought in respect of alleged offences under section 114 or its predecessor section 88 [1949]. Also, in particular, it is to be noted that, apparently, a person remaining on the Register, and not suspended therefrom, must be recognised by the Comptroller in the absence of a conviction under section 276 [1988] (or its predecessors), see subsection (2)(*a*); and that the misconduct now referred to in subsection (2)(*c*), and perhaps also in subsection (3), is linked to conduct such as would render a person liable to actual or possible erasure from the register of patent agents. Thus, though an unregistered person describing himself as a "patent agent" would commit a criminal offence under section 276 [1988], it is not clear that that person would be considered as having committed such "misconduct" as would entitle the Comptroller to refuse to recognise that person as an "agent," unless and until a conviction has been obtained for an offence under section 276 [1988], thereby enabling non-recognition under subsection (2)(*a*).

Residence or place of business of agent   **115.06**

Subsection (5) will mandatorily require the Comptroller to refuse recognition, in respect of "business" under the patent and registered design statutes, to an agent who neither resides nor has a place of business in the United Kingdom, the Isle of Man or another EEC Member State. In comparison with prospectively repealed section 115(3), this will add the possibility that an agent may have a residence or place of business outside the United Kingdom but elsewhere within the EEC (the Isle of Man being included by virtue of section 132(2)). However, a recognisable agent may not be located solely in the Channel Islands as such are not part of the "United Kingdom" nor of an EEC Member State. Also, the provision will only apply to "business" activity and, hitherto at least, the Comptroller is understood to have taken the prima facie view that the payment of renewal fees is not a "business".

Subsection (5) would seem to be tied in practice to rule 30 (reprinted at para. 32.03) which requires an agent to give an address for service, but this can be expected to be amended to permit that address to be within the same territory as specified in subsection (5), see para. 32.16. However, such extension will raise problems as regards rules made, in particular, in respect of subsections (2)(*c*) and (3) when the alleged misconduct, which would bring these provisions into play, is alleged to have occurred outside the jurisdiction of the Comptroller or the United Kingdom courts.

116.01   SECTION 116

Immunity of department as regards official acts

116. Neither the Secretary of State nor any officer of his—

(*a*) shall be taken to warrant the validity of any patent granted under this Act or any treaty or international convention to which the United Kingdom is a party; or

(*b*) shall incur any liability by reason of or in connection with any examination or investigation required or authorised by this Act or any such treaty or convention, or any report or other proceedings consequent on any such examination or investigation.

116.02   COMMENTARY ON SECTION 116

Although the 1977 Act makes no statement generally on any presumption of validity of a patent granted under the Act, section 116 protects the Secretary of State and his officers from any implication that the grant of a patent carries with it any warranty of validity. It also excludes all liability arising from any examination or investigation (which would include the search carried out during the preliminary examination of an application) under the Act or any treaty or convention. The section would not, however, appear to absolve the Comptroller from acts of negligence arising in other connections, for example recording that a patent has lapsed when the required renewal fee had been duly paid. Section 116 applies to "existing patents" (Sched. 2, para. 1(2)).

Under the Interpretation Act 1978 (c. 30, Sched. 1), "Secretary of State" means any one of Her Majesty's Principal Secretaries of State, see paras. 22.03 and 130.04.

117.01   SECTION 117

Correction of errors in patents and applications

117.—(1) The comptroller may, subject to any provision of rules, correct any error of translation or transcription, clerical error or mistake in any specification of a patent or application for a patent or any document filed in connection with a patent or such an application.

(2) Where the comptroller is requested to correct such an error or mistake, any person may in accordance with rules give the comptroller notice of opposition to the request and the comptroller shall determine the matter.

                                    RELEVANT RULE

Correction of errors in patents and applications

117.02   **91.**—(1) A request for the correction of an error of translation or transcription, a clerical error or mistake in any specification of a patent or application for a patent or any document filed in connection with a patent or such an application shall be made on Patents Form No. 47/77.

(2) Where such a request relates to a specification, no correction shall be made therein unless the correction is obvious in the sense that it is immediately evident that nothing else would have been intended than what is offered as the correction.

(3) Where the comptroller requires notice of the proposed correction to be advertised, the advertisement shall be made by publication of the request and the nature of the proposed correction in the Journal and in such other manner (if any) as the comptroller may direct.

(4) Any person may, at any time within three months after the date of the advertisement, give notice to the comptroller of opposition to the request on Patents Form No. 48/77.

(5) Such notice shall be accompanied by a copy thereof and be supported by a statement in duplicate setting out fully the facts on which the opponent relies and the relief which he seeks. The comptroller shall send a copy of the notice and the statement to the person making the request who, if he desires to proceed with the request, shall within three months of the receipt of the copies file a counter-statement in duplicate setting out fully the grounds on which he contests the opposition and the comptroller shall send a copy of the counter-statement to the opponent.

(6) The comptroller may give such directions as he may think fit with regard to the subsequent procedure.

ARTICLE

117.03

R. P. Lloyd, "Correction of Clerical Errors and Obvious Mistakes", (1980–81) 10 CIPA 226.

COMMENTARY ON SECTION 117

General

117.04

Section 117 gives the Comptroller power to correct errors in various documents filed in connection with a patent or application therefor. Application is made on PF 47/77 (reprinted at para. 141.47) under rule 91 (reprinted at para. 117.02 *supra*).

Section 117 does not apply to "existing patents" (Sched. 2, para. 1(2) read in conjunction with the definition of "patent" in section 130(1)). For such patents sections 31 [1949] and 76 [1949] continue to apply respectively to the amendment and correction of "existing patents" (Sched. 1, para. 1(2)). Errors in the register in respect of "existing patents" can, however, be corrected either under section 76 [1949] or under section 32, see para. 32.32. Translations of European patents (UK) can also be corrected in two ways, either under section 80(3), which provides specifically for this, or under the present section, but proceeding under section 80(3) is likely to be preferred, see paras. 80.06 and 80.09.

Subsection (1) is similar to section 76(1) [1949], but with some differences. Thus, subsection (1) specifies correction of documents generally (other than of the register, which is dealt with in para. 32.32 and rule 47, reprinted at para. 32.07) in respect of any error of translation or transcription or any clerical error or mistake, whereas section 76(1) [1949] is limited to correction of clerical errors in patents, applications therefor (including any document filed in pursuance thereof) and of any error in the register of patents. Correction of mistakes in "existing patents" is also permitted under section 31 [1949].

The paper by R. P. Lloyd, listed in para. 117.03 *supra*, discussed generally the correction of clerical errors under section 117 and the extent to which cases decided under section 76 [1949] may still be applicable. He noted that, while rule 91(2) appears to be in conformity with EPCr. 88 (for correction of documents filed under the EPC), PCTr. 91.1(*b*) has different wording. In any event section 130(7) does *not* list section 117 as one of those intended to conform with the provisions of the EPC, CPC and PCT.

Subsection (2) provides for opposition to any request for correction and requires the Comptroller to determine any opposition, whereas under section 76 [1949] opposition is only possible if the Comptroller decides to advertise the correction request, and then only by a "person interested". Though the procedure on application to correct, and on opposition, each resembles that under section 76 [1949], there is a substantial change of presentation of the provisions, which are largely transferred to the rules. Subsection (2) essentially concerns practice and is discussed thereunder *infra*.

117.05   *Who may apply for correction*

There is, apparently, no restriction on who may apply for correction under section 117. Thus, it would seem that any person able to give evidence on the occurrence of the error may apply for its correction. For example, PF 47/77 can apparently be filed in the name of an agent, rather than that of an applicant or proprietor.

117.06   *Nature of permissible correction (r. 91(2))*

Rule 91(2) (reprinted in para. 117.02 *supra*) is important in that, where a specification is to be corrected, the rule explicitly limits the correction thereof to one which is obvious in the sense that it is "immediately evident" that nothing else but the correction offered would have been intended. There is no similar restriction in section 76 [1949], which merely requires the mistake to be corrected to be a "clerical error".

In at least three decisions (*Antiphon's Application*, [1984] RPC 1; *Dukhovskoi's Applications*, [1985] RPC 8; and *VEB Kombinat Walzlager's Application*, [1987] RPC 405) the Comptroller has held that rule 91(2) requires, not only that it is immediately evident from the specification that something has gone wrong, but also that it is immediately evident from the specification what has gone wrong. This is similar to the test for correction of an obvious mistake under section 31 [1949] as propounded in *Holtite* v. *Jost* ([1979] RPC 81 (HL)), namely that it should be obvious: (a) that there has been some mistake; (b) what the mistake is; and (c) what is the correction needed, see para. A031.13. However, if that criterion is strictly construed, then correction is scarcely needed because the skilled reader would mentally read the document as if already corrected. It seems significant that, in each of these three decisions under section 117, the Patents Court specifically refused to endorse the expressed view of the Comptroller as to the requirements for rule 91(2) to be satisfied and decided each of them on some other ground.

In the *Antiphon* and *VEB* cases, the Patents Court held that to allow correction to deal with missing drawings would, in the circumstances, circumvent the statutory requirement under section 15(3), but both these decisions will become overruled on this point when new subsection 15(3A) is brought into effect, for which see the *Note* to para. 15.01. This new provision will specifically permit correction under section

117 to take place despite any failure to meet the requirements of section 15(2) or (3) as to missing drawings, on which see para. 15.09.

Nevertheless, there have been instances where correction has been refused because to allow correction would have the effect of circumventing some statutory provision. Thus: in *Payne's Application* ([1985] RPC 193) correction would have circumvented section 15(5)(*b*) (*Filing request for preliminary examination and search*); in *Masuda's Application* ([1987] RPC 37) correction of a translation of an international application was refused because statutory withdrawal was deemed already to have occurred; in *BOC's Application* (SRIS O/113/86, *noted* IPD 9072) correction of PF 10/77 was refused because the application was already deemed withdrawn under section 18(1); and in *Moskovsky Nauchno-Isseldovatelsky's Application* (SRIS O/5/88) a notice of withdrawal filed in error could not be corrected because such is irrevocable under section 14(9). However, it may be that, if the circumstances of some (though not all) of these cases were now repeated, it might be possible to save the application by seeking, instead of correction, an extension of time for filing a new document under rule 110(3A), for which see para. 123.33. The availability of extensions of time under this rule should, in any event, reduce the need to try to apply section 117 to circumstances where the aim in correcting a document is to overcome a deemed failure of an application because of some action not timely taken.

EPO decisions on correction   **117.07**

EPCr. 88 is similar in terms to rule 91(2), except that its limitations do not apply to "linguistic errors or errors of transcription". However, section 117 is not listed in section 130(7) as being a provision intended to be in harmony with the EPC. Thus, EPO decisions under EPCr. 88 are only illustrative of a parallel way of thought in another jurisdiction on a similar, though not necessarily analogous, law.

On this basis it is noted that the EPO has held that there is no insufficiency of description when an error in the sole illustrative example of the specification could be seen and rectified by the skilled reader using his common general knowledge (*EPO Decision T* 171/84, *"Redox catalyst/AIR PRODUCTS"*, OJEPO 4/1986, 95; [1986] 4 EPOR 210), but the EPO indicated that this was an exceptional case. Such an error would, therefore, appear to be of the type that is correctable under rule 91(2), but the EPO has held that such correction must be an unequivocal one from the specification as filed, see *EPO Decision T* 32/85, *"Biomass preparation/GIST-BROCADES"* ([1986] 5 EPOR 267) where correction was refused.

The EPO has also held that a priority document is of assistance in determining an applicant's intention and, on this basis, allowed replacement of an incorrect drawing initially filed (*EPO Decision J* 04/85, *"Correction of drawings/ETAT FRANÇAIS"*, OJEPO 7/1986, 205; [1986] 6 EPOR 331).

However, EPCr. 88 does not give the EPO power to correct a mistake unless this is in a document, or is a linguistic error or an error of transcription (*EPO Decision T* 152/85, *noted* [1986] EIPR D–180). *EPO Decision T* 3/88, *"Melting point/HOECHST"* ([1988] 6 EPOR 377) is a case where a typing error in which two numerals were transposed was permitted to be corrected as an error of transcription, but it is not clear that such a correction would have been within the more restricted terms of rule 91(2).

In *EPO Decision T* 13/83. *"Erroneous technical calculation"* (OJEPO 9/1984, 428) it was held that EPCr. 88 requires the nature of the correction to a specification to be obvious and, therefore, if more than one possibility of correction can be envisaged, the correction chosen must be the one which the application as a whole clearly implies. However, the British test of rule 91(2) would seem to require that the correction be made to the only, not merely to the most obvious, possibility.

Before the EPO can accede to a request for correction under EPCr. 88, it must be satisfied that a mistake has been made, what the mistake was and what the correction should be (*EPO Decision J* 08/80, OJEPO 9/1980, 293, also reported as *Appeal Practice Decision No. 4*, [1981] RPC 60). However, this is not the same test as requiring the correction to be self-evident, as it must also be if a specification is to be corrected. Also, this decision stresses the need to present evidence of the relevant facts fully and frankly, and states that, where the alleged mistake is not self-evident and where it is not immediately evident that nothing else would have been intended than what is offered as the correction, the burden of proving the facts must be a heavy one. This decision also warns that, if the evidence put forward is incomplete, obscure or ambiguous, the request for correction should be rejected.

The limitation in EPCr. 88 (like that in rule 91(2)) for an allowable correction to be a self-evident one only applies to a correction to a description, drawing or claim; and the EPO has shown a fairly benevolent attitude to corrections of other documents where it has been satisfied that the document as filed did not accord with the applicant's intention, and where the correction could be made in time for the public not to be prejudiced by it, on which point see para. 117.11 *infra*. For example, the EPO has permitted correction of omissions in the designation of States on the application form (*EPO Decision J 08/80, supra*; and *EPO Decision J 04/80*, OJEPO 10/1980, 351, reported also as *Appeal Practice Decision No. 5*, [1981] RPC 65). Further, in *EPO Decision J 07/80* (OJEPO 5/1981, 137), correction was allowed of the identity of the applicant in a case where the wrong and correct applicants were both companies within the same group, but full evidence was required to substantiate the correction.

Moreover, *EPO Decision J 19/80* (OJEPO 3/1981, 65, reported also as *Appeal Practice Decision No. 6* [1981] RPC 277), allowed correction under EPCr. 88 where half a sheet of drawings was missing from the application as filed, but where the nature of the correction was unambiguous from the priority document which contained the full drawing and where the relevant portion of the text was in identical terms to the specification as filed at the EPO: thus it was clear that nothing else would have been intended than what was offered as the correction. However, this case is probably to be considered as special to its own facts having regard to refusal of correction under EPCr. 88 in a later case where a sheet of drawings with a complete figure was omitted: post-dating for late filing of the drawings was then the remedy (*EPO Decision J 01/82*, OJEPO 8/1972, 293).

The EPO has also allowed correction of a priority declaration (*EPO Decision J 04/82*, "*Priority Declaration/Yoshida*," OJEPO 10/1982, 385), but see para. 117.11 *infra* for further comment on this decision.

The EPO has left open whether an error of law can be recognised as a mistake, see *EPO Decision J 03/81* (OJEPO 3/1982, 100), but in *EPO Decision D 06/82* (OJEPO 8/1983, 337) it was indicated that a mistake in law does not, as a general rule, constitute a ground for re-establishment of rights under EPCa. 122.

117.08   *"Correction" as contrasted with "Amendment"*

Section 117 refers to "correction" and not to "amendment". Moreover, section 117 is not mentioned in section 76(2) or (3) as one of the sections to which the limitations contained in section 76 apply. The question nevertheless arises whether objections could be raised under section 72(1)(*d*) or (*e*) that the correction was in contravention of these provisions, for example because it offended against rule 91(2). It is thought that this should be unlikely because correction is not amendment and correction can only be made to a specification in obvious and evident circumstances, in which case the content of the specification and the effective scope of protection as determined by section 125 will probably not have been altered. Furthermore, since an application to correct under section 117 is normally advertised and can be opposed, it is not seen that the point should necessarily be one that can be raised at a later date, in the absence of fraud, see also paras. 72.25 and 72.26.

Documents which can be corrected **117.09**

Section 117 is general in its application to all documents filed in connection with a patent or an application, but the Comptroller has now held, in at least three cases (*Klein Schanzlin's Application*, [1985] RPC 241; *Allibert's Application*, SRIS O/22/83; and *Tokan Kogyo's Application*, [1985] RPC 244), that section 117 relates to mistakes in documents and not to procedural errors or omissions, such as mistakes in the *filing* of documents. However, correction of an incorrect number on PF 10/77 was allowed in *Minnesota Mining's Application* (SRIS O/86/86) after rule 100 had been invoked to correct the notice of deemed withdrawal which had been entered in the register, thereby allowing the rationale of *Payne's Application* ([1985] RPC 193, *noted* in para. 117.06 *supra*) to be overcome. For discussion of rule 100, see para. 123.20. Thus, the provisions of the section are unlikely to be invoked to reinstate an application that has, in error, been allowed to lapse, though an example of such a case would seem to have been advertised in the O.J. April 23, 1981 under rule 91(3) where the advertisement stated "If no notice of opposition is received, the reinstatement will be allowed".

Correction to documents other than specifications **117.10**

Rule 91(2) relates only to corrections in specifications. Accordingly, corrections to documents other than specifications are not required to be obvious in the sense that it is immediately evident that nothing else would have been intended than what is offered as the correction. EPCr 88 is to like effect and, on this basis, the EPO Boards of Appeal have allowed correction of non-evident mistakes in documents other than specifications, see para. 117.07 *supra*.

Discretion **117.11**

The allowability of a correction is essentially a matter of the exercise of discretion. This involves drawing a balance between the interests of the applicant (or proprietor) and that of the public who may have acted in reliance on the uncorrected document. It was on this basis that the EPO refused to consider whether an application could be corrected after its publication when the correction could have had a profound effect on the public, see *EPO Decision J 03/81* (OJEPO 3/1982, 100), and see also *EPO Decision J 04/82*, "*Priority declaration/Yoshida*" (OJEPO 10/1982, 385) discussed in para. 117.07 *supra*. Here it was important that the correction request had been made sufficiently early for it to be included in the publication of the application, though only decided upon thereafter.

On a similar basis, correction will probably be refused where there has been an inexcusable delay in applying to make it, even in the absence of public interest (*Western Electric* v. *Racal-Milgo*, [1981] RPC 253), see also the discussion on "discretion" in relation to amendment in paras. 27.05–27.07.

117,12 *Proof of mistake or error*

Since section 117 concerns only correction of errors, the fact that an error has occurred will need to be proved. Here the requirements of the EPO (noted in para. 117.07 *supra*) for submission of strict proof of the mistake and the appropriate correction therefor should be borne in mind. A similar standard of proof may well be required under section 117, particularly as correction involves the exercise of discretion, and such in turn requires that the applicant for correction must have acted, and be seen to have acted, with the utmost good faith, *i.e. uberrimae fidei*.

In English law there is the maxim that all are presumed to know the law. It would therefore seem doubtful that "error" in section 117(1) can extend to an error of law. This point has been left open by the EPO, see para. 117.07 *supra*.

It may be noted that in *Western Electric* v. *Racal-Milgo* ([1981] RPC 253) amendment was not allowed to correct (under the 1949 Act) what was agreed to be an obvious mistake on the ground that this has remained undetected for many years and so was not a mistake apparent on the face of the document. Presumably the same decision would have been reached under the 1977 Act in view of the terms of rule 91(2).

PRACTICE UNDER SECTION 117

117.13 *Request for correction*

The procedure is governed by rule 91 (reprinted at para. 117.02 *supra*). By rule 91(1) a request for correction has to be made on PF 47/77 (reprinted at para. 141.47). Advertisement of the request is not obligatory (see s. 117(1) and r. 91(3)), but can be regarded as usual in all but the most trivial case. Advertisement is in the O.J. and in such other manner (if any) as the Comptroller may direct (r. 91(3)) and sets out the nature of the correction sought. In any event the filing of an application, as well as its eventual outcome, are each now advertised in the O.J., see O.J. November 9, 1988, a complete back-list of such applications being published in the issues of the O.J. from November 23, 1988 to February 8, 1989.

117.14 *Opposition to correction*

The period for opposition is three months after advertisement (r. 91(4)); this time is inextensible (r. 110(2), reprinted in para. 123.10). It is not clear within what time opposition can be lodged should the Comptroller decide to dispense with advertisement. Any person may oppose, *e.g.* a nominee for an undisclosed principal, and he need not show an interest, see para. 27.11, but a non-United Kingdom resident opponent will be required to give security for costs (s. 107(4)).

Opposition to the request is filed on PF 48/77 (reprinted at para. 141.48) supported by a statement. Both are filed in duplicate, but the statement can be filed within 14 days after PF 48/77 (r. 107, reprinted at para. 72.09). The copy of the PF 48/77 and statement are sent by the Comptroller to the person making the request who, if he desires to proceed, must file within three months a counter-statement in duplicate, of which the Comptroller will send a copy to the opponent (r. 91(5)). Both statement and counter-statement must set out fully the facts relied upon. The subsequent procedure is at the discretion of the Comptroller (r. 91(6)), but is likely to be similar to that in other *inter partes* proceedings before the Comptroller. This is discussed generally in paras. 72.32–72.52.

Under the corresponding section 76 [1949], there is no appeal from the Comptroller's decision, but under section 117 there is provision for appeal under the general terms of section 96(1).

SECTION 118

Information about patent applications and patents, and inspection of documents

118.—(1) After publication of an application for a patent in accordance   **118.01**
with section 16 above the comptroller shall on a request being made to him
in the prescribed manner and on payment of the prescribed fee (if any) give
the person making the request such information, and permit him to inspect
such documents, relating to the application or to any patent granted in pursuance of the application as may be specified in the request, subject, however, to any prescribed restrictions.

(2) Subject to the following provisions of this section, until an application for a patent is so published documents or information constituting or
relating to the application shall not, without the consent of the applicant,
be published or communicated to any person by the comptroller.

(3) Subsection (2) above shall not prevent the comptroller from—

(*a*) sending the European Patent Office information which it is his duty
to send that office in accordance with any provision of the European
Patent Convention; or

(*b*) publishing or communicating to others any prescribed bibliographic
information about an unpublished application for a patent;

nor shall that subsection prevent the Secretary of State from inspecting or
authorising the inspection of an application for a patent or any connected
documents under **section 22(6)** [*section 22(6)(a)*] above.

(4) Where a person is notified that an application for a patent has been
made, but not published in accordance with section 16 above, and that the
applicant will, if the patent is granted, bring proceedings against that person in the event of his doing an act specified in the notification after the
application is so published, that person may make a request under subsection (1) above, notwithstanding that the application has not been published, and that subsection shall apply accordingly.

(5) Where an application for a patent is filed, but not published, and a
new application is filed in respect of any part of the subject-matter of the
earlier application (either in accordance with rules or in pursuance of an
order under section 8 above) and is published, any person may make a
request under subsection (1) above relating to the earlier application and
on payment of the prescribed fee the comptroller shall give him such information and permit him to inspect such documents as could have been given
or inspected if the earlier application had been published.

Note. Subsection (3) was prospectively amended by the 1988 Act (Sched. 5, para. 28). For the commencement of the amendment, see the latest Supplement to this work *re.* this para.

RELEVANT RULES

Request as to payment of renewal fee

118.02   **48.** A request for information about the date of payment of any renewal fee shall be made on Patents Form No. 23/77 and shall be accompanied by the appropriate fee.

Inspection of register

118.03   **49.**—(1) The register or entries or reproductions of entries in it shall be made available for inspection by the public on payment of the prescribed fee between the hours of 10 a.m. and 4 p.m. on weekdays, other than Saturdays and days which are specified as excluded days for the purposes of section 120.

(2) A request to be allowed to inspect the register shall be made on Patents Form No. 23/77 and shall be accompanied by the appropriate fee.

Request for information under section 118

118.04   **92.**—(1) A request under section 118 for information relating to any patent or application for a patent may be made—

    (*a*) as to when a request for substantive examination has been filed or the prescribed period for doing so has expired without the request having been filed;

    (*b*) as to when the specification of a patent or application for a patent has been published;

    (*c*) as to when a published application for a patent has been withdrawn, taken to be withdrawn, treated as having been withdrawn or refused by the comptroller;

    (*d*) as to when a renewal fee has not been paid within the period prescribed for the purposes of section 25(3);

    (*e*) as to when a renewal fee has been paid within the period of six months referred to in section 25(4);

    (*f*) as to when a patent has ceased to have effect and/or an application for restoration of a patent has been filed;

    (*g*) as to when an entry has been made in the register or application has been made for the making of such entry;

    (*h*) as to when any application or request is made or action taken involving an entry in the register or advertisement in the Journal, if the nature of the application, request or action is specified in the request;

(*i*) as to when any document may be inspected in accordance with the provisions of rule 93 or 94 below.

(2) As regards information relating to any existing patent or existing application for a patent, a request may also be made—

(*a*) as to when a complete specification following a provisional specification has been filed or when the period of fifteen months from the date of the application has expired and a complete specification has not been filed;

(*b*) as to when a complete specification is or will be published, or when an application for a patent has become void;

(*c*) as to when a patent has been sealed or when the time for requesting sealing has expired.

(3) Any such request shall be made on Patents Form No. 49/77 and a separate form shall be used in respect of each item of information required.

Inspection of documents under section 118

93.—(1) Subject to paragraph (6) below and to the restrictions pre- **118.05**
scribed in paragraph (5) below, after the date of the publication of an application for a patent in accordance with section 16, the comptroller shall, upon request made on Patents Form No. 23/77 and payment of the appropriate fee, permit all documents filed at or kept in the Patent Office in relation to the application or to any patent granted in pursuance of it to be inspected at the Patent Office.

(2) Subject to the same restrictions and to rule 96 below, where the circumstances specified in section 118(4) or (5) exist, the comptroller shall, upon request made on Patents Form No. 23/77 and payment of the appropriate fee, permit inspection of such documents before the publication in accordance with section 16.

(3) . . .

(4) Where a declaration has been made in accordance with section 5(2) or 127(4), inspection of any application referred to therein and of any translation thereof shall be permitted upon request under paragraph (1) or (2) above without payment of any fee.

(5) The restrictions referred to in paragraph (1) above are—

(*a*) that no document shall be open to inspection until fourteen days after it has been filed at the Patent Office;

(*b*) that documents prepared in the Patent Office solely for use therein shall not be open to inspection;

(*c*) that any document sent to the Patent Office, at its request or otherwise, for inspection and subsequent return to the sender, shall not be open to inspection;

(*d*) that no document filed at the Patent Office in connection with an application under section 40(1) or (2) or section 41(8) shall be open to inspection unless the comptroller otherwise directs;

743

(*e*) that no request made under rule 48, 49(2), 52(2), 92 or this rule shall be open to inspection; and

(*f*) that documents in respect of which the comptroller issues directions under rule 94 below that they are to be treated as confidential shall not be open to inspection, save as permitted in accordance with that rule.

(6) Nothing in this rule shall be construed as imposing upon the comptroller the duty of making available for public inspection any documents filed with or sent to or by the Patent Office before 1 June 1978.

Note. Rule 93(3) was omitted, and rule 93(5)(*e*) amended, by S.I. 1988 No. 2089.

Confidential documents

118.06   **94.**—(1) Where a document other than a Patents Form is filed at, or sent to, the Patent Office, and the person filing or sending it or any party to the proceedings to which the document relates so requests, giving his reasons, within fourteen days of the filing or sending of the document, the comptroller may direct that it be treated as confidential, and the document shall not be open to public inspection while the matter is being determined by the comptroller.

(2) Where such a direction has been given and not withdrawn, nothing in this rule shall be taken to authorise or require any person to be allowed to inspect the document to which the direction relates except by leave of the comptroller.

(3) The comptroller shall not withdraw any directon given under this rule nor shall he give leave for any person to inspect any document to which a direction which has not been withdrawn relates without prior consultation with the person at whose request the direction was given, unless the comptroller is satisfied that such prior consultation is not reasonably practicable.

(4) Where such a direction is given or withdrawn a record of the fact shall be filed with the document to which it relates.

(5) Where the period referred to in paragraph (1) above is extended under rule 110, the relevant document shall not be, or, if the period is extended after it has expired, shall cease to be, open to public inspection until the expiry of the extended period, and if a request for a direction is made the document shall not be open to public inspection while the matter is being determined by the comptroller.

Bibliographic data for purposes of section 118(3)(b)

118.07   **95.**—The following bibliographic data is prescribed for the purposes of section 118(3)(*b*)—

(*a*) the number of the application;

(*b*) the date of filing of the application and, where a declaration has been made under section 5(2) or 127(4), the filing date, country and file number when available of each application referred to in that declaration;

(c) the name of the applicant or applicants;

(d) the title of the invention;

(e) if the application has been withdrawn, taken to be withdrawn or refused or is treated as having been refused, that fact.

Note. Rule 95 is reprinted as amended by S.I. 1985 No. 1166, rule 6.

Request for information where section 118(4) applies

96.—(1) Where the circumstances specified in section 118(4) exist, a **118.08** request under section 118(1) shall be accompanied by a statutory declaration verifying their existence and such documentary evidence (if any) supporting the request as the comptroller may require.

(2) The comptroller shall send a copy of the request, the declaration and the evidence (if any) to the applicant for the patent and shall not comply with the request until the expiry of fourteen days thereafter.

RELEVANT 1968 RULES

Note. Rules 32 and 158 [1968] below are each reprinted as amended by rule 124(1)(*c*) [1978] (reprinted at para. 127.04) and Schedule 4 of these 1978 Rules (S.I. 1978 No. 216).

32 [1968]. An application for disclosure of the result of a search made **118.09** under sections 7 and 8 [of the 1949 Act] shall be made on Patents Form No. 8.

158 [1968]. Notwithstanding the provisions of rule 93 of the Patents **118.10** Rules 1978 the Comptroller may at any time after three months from the date of publication of the complete specification or other document refuse further inspection of any application, specification or other document in respect of which the Secretary of State has certified that further inspection thereof could in his opinion be prejudicial to the safety of the public; provided that no such certificate shall be valid for a period in excess of twelve months unless renewed by the Secretary of State.

COMMENTARY ON SECTION 118

General **118.11**

Section 118 concerns the information relating to applications and patents which the Comptroller is required to give on request. There are no directly corresponding provisions in EPC or CPC, and the section is not one of those referred to in section 130(7). Subsections (1)–(3) apply to "existing patents" (Sched. 2, para. 1(2)), as also do rules 92–95 (r. 124(1)(*d*) [1978] reprinted at para. 127.04).

745

Whatever may have been the position previously, no infringement of copyright now takes place when copies of documents are made available at the request of a third party from the file of a patent or published application by an appropriate person (*e.g.* by the Comptroller), see sections 47, 48 and 50(1) [1988]. The saving provision of section 47 [1988] has been extended to copies provided by the Comptroller of documents open to public inspection in the EPO under the EPC, or at WIPO under the PCT (Copyright (Material Open to Public Inspection) (International Organisations) Order 1989 (S.I. 1989 No. 1098)).

It should be noted that public access to papers filed at the Patent Office is in marked contrast to the rules and practice of the court. Here only the writ (or other originating pleading) and judgments and orders in the proceedings are available, other than to parties to the proceedings or with the leave of the court (RSC Ord. 63, rr. 4 and 5, reprinted at paras. E063.4 and E063.5).

118.12 *Access to register and to documents filed at Patent Office (subs. (1))*

Subsection (1) gives the right to obtain information and inspect documents of, or relating to, a patent or an application after its publication under section 16. The information which can be requested by a specific inquiry is set out in rule 92(1)(*a*)–(*i*) (reprinted at para. 118.04), the request being made on PF 49/77 (reprinted at para. 141.49), see further para. 118.19. As regards "existing patents," the information which can be requested is set out in rule 92(2). By rule 92(3) a request for information (whether under rr. 92(1) or 92(2)), is made on PF 49/77 (reprinted at para. 141.49), but a separate form is required in respect of each request. Such a request is often called a *caveat*.

The time when, and the manner in which, the register can be inspected is set out in rule 49 (reprinted at para. 118.03). This requires the use of PF 23/77 (reprinted at para. 141.23), see further para. 118.20. However, the register for all patents (but not "existing patents") and published applications in force on and from November 8, 1989, is now computerised with data print-outs available and the previous book registers no longer updated, see O.J. November 8, 1989.

Rule 93 (reprinted at para. 118.05) provides that all documents filed or kept at the Patent Office in relation to a published application, or to a patent granted thereon, can be inspected, but (by rule 93(6)) such inspection does not extend to documents sent to, or by, the Patent Office before June 1, 1978. Rule 52(3) (reprinted in para. 32.10) contains a similar limitation as regards requesting copy documents from the Comptroller.

Rule 92(1)(*h*) provides that information can be requested as to when any application or request is made, or action taken, involving an entry in the register or advertisement in the Journal. Thus, information can be requested on most of the matters affecting an application, see further para. 118.19 below.

In *Wisconsin Alumni Research Foundation's Patent* (SRIS C/45/88, *noted* IPD 11024), the Patents Court upheld the Comptroller's decision that evidence filed during subsequently abandoned proceedings for revocation (under s. 33 [1949]) should not be removed from the file and returned to the parties as had been requested.

118.13 *—Documents available concerning "existing patents"*

As indicated above, the availability of documents from the files of "existing patents" is likewise governed by rule 93(1), but the result of rule 93(6) is that only certain documents filed before June 1, 1978 are available for inspection from these files, these being determined by rule 146 [1968], not reprinted herein. Official forms, with a few exceptions, are available for inspection from the Patent Office files; and so is the specification as amended at, but not before, acceptance. The reports of the examiner and correspondence from the applicant prior to publication of an existing patent are not available. However, the results of the examiner's search carried out on an existing patent under sections 7 and 8 [1949] are obtainable by filing PF No. 8 (reprinted at para. A120) under rule 32 [1968] (reprinted at para. 118.09).

Prior to November 1, 1968 (when rule 146 [1968] was made) the availability of documents for public inspection from Patent Office files was considerably more restricted. The then new rule explicitly preserved the position of documents filed before that date, see *Rouseel-Uclaf's Patent* ([1969] FSR 131).

Restrictions on access to documents filed at Patent Office   **118.14**

Subsection (2) provides that documents of an application can be inspected only after the application has been published under section 16, but this is subject to the exceptions of subsections (3)–(5). These subsections do not appear wide enough to avoid a problem arising under subsection (2) when entitlement proceedings are commenced (under section 8 or 12) in relation to an unpublished application: these difficulties may make it difficult for these proceedings to continue until publication has taken place and yet a party to such proceedings may be seeking to avoid publication of details of an invention to which he is alleging title.

Subsection (3) empowers the Comptroller to provide certain information concerning an application in specified circumstances, and also confirms the right of the Secretary of State to inspect, or authorise the inspection of, an unpublished application for the purposes of section 22(5)(c). Thus, subsection (3)(a) states that subsection (2) shall not operate to prevent the Comptroller from fulfilling his duties in accordance with the EPC.

Subsection (3)(b) permits the publication or communication of prescribed bibliographic data about an unpublished application. This data consists of the items specified in rule 95 (reprinted at para. 118.07), being: (a) the number; (b) priority date, country and country file number, where priority has been claimed; (c) name of applicant(s); and (d) title, of the application; and (e) its (deemed) withdrawal or refusal. The first four of these items are published in the O.J. about five weeks after filing, and this data is supplied on cards which form a card index in the SRIS. The SRIS also creates a numerical register of the state of progress of the application and an entry is made in this when information is published in the O.J. that an application has been withdrawn. However, such an entry does not appear until a date when reinstatement of the application would be unlikely.

The data given in the SRIS card index can, however, be incorrect because of changes to the data which may be allowed after the application has been filed and the original card created, but the O.J. does contain "errata" data from time to time.

If a secrecy order is imposed on an application under section 22, the above bibliographic data is not published, but when the order is lifted a card is placed in the SRIS card index, though no entry appears in the O.J.

Subsection (3) also permits the Secretary of State to inspect application papers in his annual review of the continuance of a secrecy order pursuant to section 22(5)(c). For this purpose he may now submit these papers to the United Kingdom Atomic Energy Authority under section 22(6)(a) for evaluation where the invention relates to the production or use of atomic energy, or research into matters connected therewith. Indeed, when the amendment to subsection (3) is given effect (for which see the *Note* to para. 119.01 *supra*), no doubt will remain as to the power of the Secretary of State to inspect any application (and the documents relating thereto) from the date when publication under section 16 could have taken place but for the secrecy order, and even before that date if the applicant consents.

118.15   *Inspection of unpublished documents (subss. (4) and (5))*

Subsection (4) provides that, where a person has been warned that proceedings will be instituted for infringement of a patent to be granted upon an application not published at the date of the warning, the person warned may inspect the unpublished documents. Whether this right of inspection extends to a threat of infringement proceedings on a patent to be granted on an application the subject of a secrecy order under section 22(2) is not explicit, but logic would suggest that an order under section 22 extinguishes the right under section 118(2).

Subsection (5) relates to a further circumstance in which the documents of an unpublished application can be examined. In the case of a divisional application, or of an application filed as a result of an order made under the entitlement provisions of section 8, if that application but not the earlier application has been published, the earlier application can be inspected as though it had been published.

A request for inspection in the circumstances of subsections (4) or (5) is made on PF 23/77 together, in the case of an application under subsection (4), with evidence as required by rule 96(1) (reprinted in para. 118.08). Compliance with the request is delayed until the applicant has been notified of the request (r. 96(2)), see para. 118.20 *infra*. It is not apparent whether the applicant of the relevant application may, on receipt of such documents, contest the request for inspection, for example by disputing the statements of the person making the request; under subsection (5) the Comptroller is not given any discretion, and compliance with the request is mandatory and not permissive. In this case also there would appear to be conflict with a secrecy order under section 22, as mentioned *supra*.

It is not clear what record, if any, will be made of the actual inspection of any documents in accordance with the provisions of subsection (4) or (5), as distinct from authority to inspect having been given, and there may be doubt as to the effect of a nominal publication of this kind in consideration of patent novelty in countries abroad and, in view of rule 96, the effective date of such publication.

118.16   *Documents not available (r. 93(5))*

Subsection (3)(*b*) limits publication of details of applications not yet published under section 16 to the bibliographic data listed in rule 95 (reprinted at para. 118.07).

Not all the documents generated in the application can be inspected, and rule 93(1) states that the inspection is subject to restrictions. These are set out in rule 93(5) (reprinted in para. 118.05), as supplemented by rule 52(3) (reprinted in para. 32.10), *viz*: providing (*a*) a delay of 14 days after their filing before documents can be examined; and excluding documents which are: (*b*) internal Patent Office papers, (*c*) documents filed for inspection only and subsequent return, (*d*) documents filed in connection with applications under sections 40 and 41 (*compensation of inventors*), though it is understood that decisions on such applications will be made available, (*e*) requests for information, and (*f*) documents which are accepted to be treated as confidential.

It is understood that the Comptroller has occasionally refused to lay open to public inspection, under rule 93, a document lodged at the Patent Office, though required to do so by the terms of the Act and Rules, on the ground that, by doing so, he could be exposed to an action for defamation for publishing a disparaging or otherwise libellous statement. Such practice would appear to be both *ultra vires* and unnecessary as any such publication would surely be the subject of qualified privilege in view of the statutory duties of the Comptroller, see further at para. 21.06.

Rule 158 [1968] (reprinted in para. 118.10) provides a general power for any document published or made available to the public by the Comptroller in connection with an "existing patent" to be removed from further public inspection if the document has been open to inspection for three months and the Secretary of State certifies that further inspection would, in his opinion, be prejudicial to the safety of the public. Such certificate has a maximum life of 12 months, unless rescinded. This rule was introduced in 1975 (S.I. 1975 No. 1021), when it was discovered that specifications describing the preparation of a banned hallucinogenic drug and a chemical warfare agent had been published. It remains effective (despite formal repeal), but only in relation to "existing patents", see rule 124 [1978] (reprinted at para. 127.04).

Confidentiality   **118.17**

Rule 94 (reprinted at para. 118.06) provides for documents lodged at the Patent Office to be treated as confidential and therefore not available for public inspection. By rule 94(1), where a document (other than a patents form) is filed or sent to another party and the person filing or sending it so requests, giving his reasons, within 14 days of the filing or sending of the documents, the Comptroller *may* then direct that the document be treated as confidential and not be laid open to public inspection while the matter is being determined. It is not clear that the other party receiving the document would be under an obligation of confidentiality during the 14 days or until the Comptroller issues his direction. Coupled with the fact that under rule 93(5) documents can normally be inspected 14 days after filing, it is clearly prudent to make a request for confidentiality when a document is filed, and to indicate to any party to whom the document is sent that the document is to be treated as "confidential", at least until the Comptroller has given a ruling, which could then be appealed. It appears that the question of confidentiality relates to the content of the document, and not to the proceedings to which the document relates.

Evidence and information in *inter partes* proceedings are made confidential only when good reason is established and the risk of commercial harm to the parties overrides the Comptroller's responsibility to keep proceedings before him as open to public view as possible (*Schering's Patent*, [1986] RPC 30). In *Diamond Shamrock's Patent*, ([1987] RPC 91), the Patents Court allowed information to remain confidential where its disclosure would be against the wish of a third party or would have no relevance to any interest of the public in the case, but not simply because one of the parties regarded it as "commercially sensitive". Under the analogous provisions of EPCa. 128(4) and EPCr. 93(*d*) the EPO has excluded medical documents and other information about personal circumstances from inspection (OJEPO 10/1985, 316).

When a confidentiality order is imposed under rule 94, it has become quite common also to limit disclosure to specified categories of persons independent of the other parties to the proceedings, for which see para. 72.44A.

Rule 94(2)–(5) further concerns confidentiality. Paragraph (2) provides that only with leave of the Comptroller can a document be inspected which has been declared confidential, and by paragraph (3) such leave, or a decision to remove the direction, is to be made only after consultation with the person at whose request the direction was made, if consultation is reasonably practicable. By paragraph (4) a record of the direction, or its withdrawal, is to be filed with the document.

The period of 14 days allowed under rule 94(1) can be extended under rule 110(1), and paragraph (5) provides that, where there is such an extension, the confidentiality is to remain until the end of the extended period; if the extension is granted after the expiry of the 14 days allowed, there is no right to inspect during the extended period, or until the matter is determined by the Comptroller. Any person affected by a request for confidentiality, or removal of a confidentiality direction under paragraph (3), is entitled to be heard before a decision adverse to him is made under rule 94, see section 101 and para. 101.04.

Practice under Section 118

118.18 *Information given on a request*

Information under rule 92(1) is obtained by filing PF 49/77 (r. 92(3)) and information can also be obtained likewise in respect of European patents (UK) and patents granted on international applications (O.J. March 30, 1978), but not in respect of applications for European patents.

An answer to a request under rule 92(1)(*b*) as to when a specification of a United Kingdom application has been published will include the case where that specification has been made available as a priority document in the file of a subsequent application upon publication of the later application. A forward reference to such later application will also be made against the earlier application in the informal records maintained by the SRIS, provided such information is supplied on the filing of the later application ((1978–79) 8 CIPA 43).

118.19 *Caveats*

It is important to note that a *caveat* request under rule 92(1) or (2), made on PF 49/77 (reprinted at para. 14.49, is exhausted as soon as one answer has resulted even if an event giving rise to a second answer subsequently occurs. Thus careful wording of *caveats* is required to minimise the number necessary to cover eventualities. The following 10 suggested wordings for PF 49/77 for patents and applications under the 1977 Act were agreed in 1980 between the Chartered Institute and the Patent Office ((1979–80) 9 CIPA 243), though it is not certain that the Patent Office continues to adhere to them:-

1. As to when the application has been or will be published under secton 16, or the application is or has been withdrawn, treated as having been withdrawn or refused by the Comptroller.
2. As to when the application is or has been specified in a declaration made under section 5(2).
3. As to when notification of grant of the patent has been or will be published under section 24 or the application is or has been withdrawn, taken to be withdrawn, treated as having been withdrawn or refused by the Comptroller.
4. As to when any patent application is made in respect of subject-matter divided from it.
5. As to when the request for substantive examination is or has been filed or the prescribed period for doing so has expired without the request having been filed.
6. As to when a renewal fee has not been paid within the period prescribed for the purposes of section 25(3).
7. As to when a renewal fee has not been paid within the period of six months referred to in section 25(4).
8. As to when an application for restoration of the patent has been filed.
9. As to when an application is or has been made to register or to give notice of a transaction, instrument or event affecting the rights in the patent application or patent.

10. As to when any application or request is made or action taken involving any entry in the register or advertisement in the Journal under or arising out of any one of sections 27, 29, and 72 to 75 of the Patents Act 1977.

PF 49/77 is also used for *caveats* in respect of existing patents (or indeed of any existing application still subsisting) (r. 92(2)(3)). Analogous wording should then be used as indicated above for *caveats* under rule 92(1).

A *caveat* can also be filed for information whether a request for one or more certified copies of the application has been requested, even if the application has been withdrawn. Such request may assist in ascertaining whether corresponding foreign applications, for example a European or international application, were filed, though the Office will probably not indicate for what countries the copies have been requested, but that information may perhaps be available on the file of the application which can be inspected if published, for which see para. 32.33 and (1980–81) 10 CIPA 411.

As the register becomes computerised, it is understood that it will also become possible to file PF 49/77 to request information on whether or not, or when, a translation of a European patent (UK) has been filed.

It is important to note that the information given in response to a *caveat* request on PF 49/77 is only correct as at the date on which it is given, and that, in particular, leave may subsequently be given under rule 110(3C) to extend the period for taking any action which has not been timely taken, for which see para. 123.33, so that an application indicated to be treated as withdrawn might subsequently be revived under this rule. Presumably, it is also possible to file a *caveat* to be informed if PF 52/77 were to be filed under rule 110(3A) as a request to extend retrospectively under rule 110(3C) a time limitation period that has apparently expired.

Inspection of register and file **118.20**

PF 23/77 and 49/77 can each be filed by an agent without disclosing the identity of his principal. Since June 14, 1982, these forms do not subsequently become open to inspection (r. 93(5)(e)). Where action is required on PF 23/77 under both (*a*) (*inspection of the register and/or documents*) and (*b*) (*supply of copies of register entries or filed documents*), a single form may be filed, but a separate fee for each item is required, even if the same patent is involved, see General Note on PF 23/77. Section (*c*) on PF 23/77 requests information whether a particular renewal fee has been paid and the date of payment pursuant to rule 48 (reprinted at para. 118.02). Since June 14, 1982 this information has no longer been recorded in the register itself, see para. 32.17. However, the information under (*c*) will be supplied free of charge if a request is made under either (*a*) or (*b*) on PF 23/77 in respect of the same patent, see Note 3 on PF 23/77, but the date on which the renewal fee was due must be specified as the Patent Office records are maintained on a day-by-day diary system, see para. 32.33.

As a matter of administrative convenience, PF 12/77 and PF 13/77 (filed when a renewal fee is paid or paid late) are not placed on the patent file, nor are copies of the statutory reminder letters of non-payment of renewal fees issued under rules 39(4) and 42. However, it is understood that these forms can be made available for inspection if a specific request is made therefor.

Where a request is made for inspection of documents in the special circumstances of subsection (4), PF 23/77 must be accompanied by a statutory declaration of the facts and any supporting documentary evidence which the Comptroller may require (r. 96(1)). The Comptroller then sends a copy of the documents to the applicant in question and compliance with the request is delayed for 14 days (r. 96(2)).

Rule 93(4) provides that priority documents may be inspected free of charge, but PF 23/77, with its fee, is needed if a copy is required. The copying charge may be paid from a deposit account by supplying a form "Sales 3". For obtaining certified copies of priority documents PF 24/77 is required, see para. 32.37; and for copies of provisional specifications of "existing patents", see para. 32.38.

Personal inspection of the register is made upon application to the Public Search Room at the Patent Office (Ground Floor), between 10 a.m. and 4 p.m. on normal weekdays, see rule 49 (reprinted at para. 118.03), accompanied by a receipted PF 23/77. Files are not normally available on demand and may take a day or two to be produced. It is recommended to make a telephone request to the Public Search Room (071–829 6844) to locate a file and then to ascertain, again by telephone, that it is available before making a visit for inspection. A request (on a fresh PF 23/77) for copies of documents in the file can then be left in the Search Room, together with a form "Sales 3" for payment from a deposit account. The documents can then be copied "while you wait" or posted when ready: otherwise they can be collected and payment made on collection. Information in response to PF No. 8 can, however, be obtained almost immediately for all patents granted under the 1949 Act.

The register for all patents (including European patents (UK)) is available on demand at the Public Search Room (Patents). Hitherto, the register has been maintained by entries in bound volumes, but details of live patents and applications, and of European patents (UK), but not of "existing patents", are now entered into a computerised data base to which access is available via visual display units in the Public Search Room (Patents) accompanied, if desired, by a simultaneous print-out of the data shown thereon, but PF 23/77 is still required (O.J. November 8, 1989).

Although rule 93(1) provides for inspection of the file of a published application, in practice this is difficult if the file is with the examiner or the Printing Branch. Problems may also be experienced in relation to the files of divisional applications where publication under section 16 has been deferred to enable examination to proceed and consequently the divisional file may not be publicly available, although the parent file is available. Access to the divisional file may, however, be granted on written request.

118.21 *Requesting confidentiality*

Any request for confidentiality under rule 94(1) should be made as early as possible, and certainly no later than 14 days after the receipt by the Patent Office of the document in question (O.J. May 28, 1987). A request by the person filing the document should be by letter accompanying it, and parties to whom copies of the document are sent directly should be sent a copy of that letter or otherwise informed of the request. Sometimes, it will be such recipient who will wish to seek an order under rule 94 and any such request should be made promptly, and in any event within 14 days of the date of filing, preferably in a letter marked "URGENT", and preferably supported by a telephone request and notification to the party which filed the document in question.

If a request is made belatedly, or in an obscure manner, the document in question is likely to have been laid open to inspection and made available for copying in accordance with rule 93. Once this has happened, it is not clear whether a confidentiality order under rule 94 can then be made.

It is quite common in making requests for confidentiality, not only to seek to keep documents off the public file under rule 94, but also to seek restricted availability to other parties to the proceedings in which the document has been lodged, for example by seeking restrictions on access to persons (including the parties themselves) other than their legal advisers, including patent agents. Obviously, such an order will only be made where there are strong reasons for so doing, for example when information in the document would disclose valuable commercial information to a competitor.

Where a patent agent has been an employee of a party who is to be restricted as to access, he has been required to give undertakings to receive the documents solely in a personal professional capacity, not to copy them and to return them at the end of the proceedings; and his employer has been required to give an undertaking not to seek disclosure from him, see *Unilever* v. *Pearce* ([1985] FSR 475) and *Schering's Patent* ([1986] RPC 30). Presumably similar undertakings would be required if an employee solicitor were involved in the proceedings.

Requests of this nature are discussed in para. 72.44A. They are most likely to arise in licence proceedings under section 46 or 48, but can also arise in entitlement proceedings, and perhaps in revocation proceedings when evidence of commercial success is lodged to indicate unobviousness of the invention.

Where possible, a request for confidentiality should be sought for only part of a document and a copy of that document, with the confidential parts thereof obliterated, should be supplied so that this "masked" copy document can be placed on the public file. Alternatively, the confidential information can sometimes be conveniently presented in an exhibit for which confidentiality can then be requested as a separate document.

SECTION 119 $\qquad$ 119.01

Service by post

119. Any notice required or authorised to be given by this Act or rules, and any application or other document so authorised or required to be made or filed, may be given, made or filed by post.

RELEVANT RULE

97. Any notice, application or other document sent to the Patent Office **119.02** by posting it in the United Kingdom shall be deemed to have been given, made or filed at the time when the letter containing it would be delivered in the ordinary course of post.

COMMENTARY ON SECTION 119

General $\qquad$ 119.03

Section 119 provides for the sending of notices and documents by postal delivery, and rule 97 reprinted at para. 119.02 *supra*) states that a document posted to the Patent Office is deemed to arrive in the ordinary course of post. These provisions are applicable to "existing patents" and to proceedings under the 1949 Act (Sched. 2, para. 1(2) and r. 124(1)(d) [1978] (reprinted in para. 127.04).

Rule 111 (reprinted at para. 123.11) provides for periods of interruption of the postal services or the normal operation of the Patent Office, permitting the Comptroller to extend periods allowed for any acts to the day which follows the end of the interruption of services, see paras. 123.38 and 123.39. For the computation of time limits, see para. 123.37.

Service in the ordinary course of the post (r. 97) $\qquad$ 119.04

Section 7 of the Interpretation Act 1978 (c. 30) requires that section 119 is only applicable when a letter containing the document(s) in question has been properly addressed and posted with pre-paid postage. Thus in *Fujisawa's Application* ([1978] FSR 187), it was held that, where delivery of documents to the Patents Office was made by an employee of a patent agent, this did not constitute "service by post".

Revision of rule 97 is presently under consideration: therefore see the latest supplement to this Work *re.* this para. At present, rule 97 stipulates that documents sent to the Patent Office by post will be deemed delivered "in the ordinary course of the post". For proceedings before the High Court, this phrase is now interpreted according to *Practice Direction (Service of Documents: First and Second Class Mail)* ([1985] 1 WLR 489; [1985] 1 All ER 889) under which, unless the contrary is proved, there is deemed service on the second working day after posting in the case of First Class Mail, and on the fourth working day after posting in the case of Second Class Mail, with "working days" being Monday to Friday, excluding any Bank Holiday. However, it is understood that the Comptroller actually ante-dates first class mail automatically to the first working day after posting provided that the postmark is legible, but that there is no corresponding ante-dating of second class mail (which includes that sent under official paid labels and foreign mail). Most Saturdays are working days of the Patent Office, though only for certain purposes, see rules 98 and 99 (reprinted at paras. 120.02 and 120.03).

Thus, it is desirable always to use first class mail and to obtain a certificate of posting (or to use recorded delivery or registered post), because in the case of a dispute the onus of proving the fact and date of posting lies on the sender (*Westinghouse's Application*, SRIS O/13/85). While, in view of the *Practice Direction* (*supra*), it may be possible to contend that there should be a deemed date of receipt four days after posting if the date of actual receipt is later than this (or two days after posting if the use of first class mail can be proved, and the Comptroller changes his previous practice indicated above), the Comptroller is not obliged to follow a Practice Direction of the High Court, though he usually does so if the Patents Rules do not provide to the contrary.

"Expresspost" is recognised as a service by post (O.J. August 2, 1978), and presumably "Datapost" would also be recognised, but it is thought that a telex communication cannot be said to be "posted".

119.05   *Postal delays under the EPC and PCT*

It should be noted that rule 97 has no applicability to the international phase for an international application filed at the Patent Office as PCT receiving office, see para. 89.29, but it *could* be applicable as regards such application entering the United Kingdom national phase, see para. 89A.11.

Rule 97 has, however, no applicability at all under the EPC and so cannot be prayed in aid against late receipt of documents by the EPO (*EPO Decision T 18/86*, *"Filing date/ZOUEKI"*, [1988] 5 EPOR 338), and this applies even if papers for the EPO are lodged with the United Kingdom Patent Office (*EPO Decision J 4/87*, *"Delays in post/ELTON,"* [1988] 5 EPOR 346).

119.06   PRACTICE UNDER SECTION 119

If a filing date is altered as the result of a successful application under rule 97, nevertheless the O.J. and the SRIS card index will have recorded the original date of filing. Consequently, in an important case, the date of filing recorded in these ways should be checked against the file of the application once this has been published.

SECTION 120   **120.01**

Hours of business and excluded days

120.—(1) Rules may specify the hour at which the Patent Office shall be taken to be closed on any day for purposes of the transaction by the public of business under this Act or of any class of such business, and may specify days as excluded days for any such purposes.

(2) Any business done under this Act on any day after the hour so specified in relation to business of that class, or on a day which is an excluded day in relation to business of that class, shall be taken to have been done on the next following day not being an excluded day; and where the time for doing anything under this Act expires on an excluded day that time shall be extended to the next following day not being an excluded day.

RELEVANT RULES

Hours of business

98.—The Patent Office shall be deemed to be closed at the following   **120.02** hours for the transaction of business of the classes specified—
- (*a*) on weekdays other than Saturdays, at midnight for the filing of applications, forms and other documents, and at 4 p.m. for all other business;
- (*b*) on Saturdays, at 1 p.m. for the filing of new applications for patents in respect of which no declaration for the purposes of section 5(2) or 127(4) is made.

Excluded days

99.—(1) The following shall be excluded days for all purposes under the   **120.03** Act:
- (a) all Sundays;
- (b) Good Friday and Christmas Day;
- (c) any day specified as or proclaimed to be a bank holiday in England in or under section 1 of the Banking and Financial Dealings Act 1971 [c. 80];
- (d) any Saturday immediately preceded by one of the above.

(2) Saturdays not falling within paragraph (1) above shall be excluded days for all purposes except the filing of applications in respect of which no declaration for the purposes of section 5(2) is made.

COMMENTARY ON SECTION 120

General   **120.04**

Section 120 provides for the making of rules concerning the working times of the Patent Office, and concerning days which are to be *dies non*. Section 120 and rules

98–99 apply to "existing patents" and therefore also to proceedings under the 1949 Act (Sched. 2, para. 1(2) and r. 124(1)(*d*) [1978], (reprinted in para. 127.04). Rules 98 and 99 (reprinted respectively at paras. 120.02 and 120.03 *supra*) are the rules made under section 120 and detail the hours (r. 98), and days (r. 99), during which documents may, and may not, be lodged at the Patent Office.

Subsection (2) provides that any business done, or due to be done, on an excluded day is considered to have been done, or due to be done, on the next day not being an excluded day. Similar rules obtain under the EPC and PCT, see EPCr. 80(1) and (3) and PCTr. 80.5.

Rule 111 (reprinted at para. 123.11 and discussed in paras. 123.38 and 123.39) provides a separate power to deal with interruption of postal services and (since August 1, 1989) when other disruption of Patent Office business occur, for example as a result of strike action or weather problems.

120.05 *The statutory "excluded days"*

Since rule 99(1) was revised in 1987, the only "excluded days" for the purposes of section 120 are those set down in this rule. These excluded days are now defined as being: all Sundays; Good Friday and Christmas Day; the days specified as a "bank holiday" in England and Wales in or under section 1 of the Banking and Financial Dealings Act 1971 (c. 80), and any Saturday immediately preceded by one of those days. Section 1(1) of this 1971 Act specifies the regular "bank holidays" as: "Easter Monday; The Last Monday in May; The last Monday in August; 26th December, if it be not a Sunday; and 27th December in a year in which 25th or 26th December is a Sunday", unless a proclamation be issued to the contrary. In addition, there is a power to declare further "bank holidays" by proclamation and, since 1974, it has been customary to declare "New Year's Day"; and, since 1978, "The first Monday in May", to be additional bank holidays.

Since it is not usual to declare any Friday (other than Good Friday) to be a bank holiday, the effect of rule 99(1)(*d*) is that the only Saturdays on which the Patent Office is closed for *all* classes of business are the Saturday following Good Friday and December 27, if that be a Saturday. Thus, over the Christmas and Easter holiday periods, there may be a period of some days when it is not possible to secure a priority date by an initial filing at the Patent Office. Perhaps in these circumstances, an initial filing in some other country could be made to secure priority over a projected disclosure of the invention, with permission then being sought retroactively under section 23(1) for the foreign filing made in the circumstances.

120.06   PRACTICE UNDER SECTION 120

The procedure for filing documents at the Patent Office between the hours of 4 p.m. and midnight on Mondays to Friday is as follows:
(1) All documents must be in sealed packages.
(2) Between 4.00 p.m. and 9.00 p.m. packages must be handed to the person on duty at the front reception desk.
(3) Between 9.00 p.m. and midnight the front doors are locked; the bell should be rung for attention and the package handed to the person answering.
(4) All packages handed in under the above procedures will be stamped with the date and time of receipt.
On Saturdays packages are accepted up to 1.00 p.m. at the front reception desk, but that date is only accorded in the case of originating applications for which no priority is claimed, see rule 98(*b*). In all cases, payment must be enclosed for any fees which are due, see O.J. December 31, 1980.

SECTION 121   121.01

Comptroller's annual report

121. Before 1st June in every year the comptroller shall cause to be laid before both Houses of Parliament a report with respect to the execution of this Act and the discharge of his functions under the European Patent Convention, the Community Patent Convention and the Patent Co-operation Treaty, and every such report shall include an account of all fees, salaries and allowances, and other money received and paid by him under this Act, those conventions and that treaty during the previous year.

Book   121.02

N. Davenport, "The United Kingdom patent system: A brief history" (Kenneth Mason, 1979).

Commentary on Section 121   121.03

Section 121 requires the Comptroller to make an annual report to be placed before Parliament. The section is in similar terms to provisions which have appeared in the patent statutes since the office of Comptroller was established in 1883, except that under the 1977 Act, the Report must include reference to the discharge of the functions of the Comptroller under the EPC, CPC and PCT, and the accounts of fees, etc., must also refer to these treaties. The Annual Report also covers matters arising under: the 1949 Act (Sched. 2, para. 1(2)); the Trade Marks Act 1938 (1 & 2 Geo. 6, c. 22), see section 45 thereof; and under the Registered Designs Act 1949 (12, 13 & 14 Geo. 6, c. 88), see section 42 thereof (amended for the purpose by Sched. 5, para. 3 [1988]).

These Annual Reports, copies of which may be inspected at the central desk in the SRIS, provide a wealth of statistical data concerning the operations of the Patent Office and, therefore, of the relative levels of activity from time to time occurring in relation to various provisions of the patent statutes, and of the geographical origin of applications filed thereunder. Much of this statistical data has been summarised, and commented upon, by N. Davenport in his book containing a brief summary of the historical development of the United Kingdom patent system, as listed in para. 121.02 *supra*.

SECTION 122   122.01

Crown's right to sell forfeited articles

122. Nothing in this Act affects the right of the Crown or any person deriving title directly or indirectly from the Crown to dispose of or use articles forfeited under the laws relating to customs or excise.

Commentary on Section 122   122.02

Section 122 provides that nothing in the Act affects the right of the Crown to dispose of articles seized by the Customs and Excise; and forfeited under the laws relating to customs and excise. It extends to "existing patents" (Sched. 2, para. 1(2)). Without this provision, such disposal would be an act of infringement of the patent having regard to the limited powers of the Crown as regards sale of patented products under section 55, see para. 55.05, nor would such disposal be absolved by section 129 which defines the liability of the Crown for acts of patent infringement for which see para. 129.02.

123.01   **SECTION 123**

Rules

123.—(1) The Secretary of State may make such rules as he thinks expedient for regulating the business of the Patent Office in relation to patents and applications for patents (including European patents, applications for European patents and international applications for patents) and for regulating all matters placed by this Act under the direction or control of the comptroller; and in this Act, except so far as the context otherwise requires, "prescribed" means prescribed by rules and "rules" means rules made under this section.

(2) Without prejudice to the generality of subsection (1) above, rules may make provision—

    (a) prescribing the form and contents of applications for patents and other documents which may be filed at the Patent Office and requiring copies to be furnished of any such documents;

    (b) regulating the procedure to be followed in connection with any proceeding or other matter before the comptroller or the Patent Office and authorising the rectification of irregularities of procedure;

    (c) requiring fees to be paid in connection with any such proceeding or matter or in connection with the provision of any service by the Patent Office and providing for the remission of fees in the prescribed circumstances;

    (d) regulating the mode of giving evidence in any such proceeding and empowering the comptroller to compel the attendance of witnesses and the discovery of and production of documents;

    (e) requiring the comptroller to advertise any proposed amendments of patents and any other prescribed matters, including any prescribed steps in any such proceeding;

    (f) requiring the comptroller to hold proceedings in Scotland in such circumstances as may be specified in the rules where there is more than one party to proceedings under section 8, 12, 37 40(1) or (2), 41(8), 61(3), 71 or 72 above;

    (g) providing for the appointment of advisers to assist the comptroller in any proceedings before him;

    (h) prescribing time limits for doing anything required to be done in connection with any such proceeding by this Act or the rules and

providing for the alteration of any period of time specified in this
Act or the rules;

(*i*) giving effect to the right of an inventor of an invention to be mentioned in an application for a patent for the invention;

(*j*) without prejudice to any other provision of this Act, requiring and
regulating the translation of documents in connection with an application for a patent or a European patent or an international application for a patent and the filing and authentication of any such
translations;

[(*k*) *requiring the keeping of a register of patent agents and regulating the
registration of patent agents and authorising in prescribed cases the
erasure from the register of patent agents of the name of any person
registered therein or the suspension of the right of any such person to
act as a patent agent;*]

(*l*) providing for the publication and sale of documents in the Patent
Office and of information about such documents.

(3) Rules may make different provision for different cases.

(3A) It is hereby declared that rules—

(a) authorising the rectification of irregularities of procedure, or

(b) providing for the alteration of any period of time,

**may authorise the comptroller to extend or further extend any period not-
withstanding that the period has already expired.**

(4) Rules precribing fees shall not be made except with the consent of
the Treasury.

(5) The remuneration of any adviser appointed under rules to assist the
comptroller in any proceeding shall be determined by the Secretary of
State with the consent of the Minister for the Civil Service and shall be
defrayed out of moneys provided by Parliament.

(6) Rules shall provide for the publication by the comptroller of a journal (in this Act referred to as "the journal") containing particulars of applications for and grants of patents, and of other proceedings under this Act.

(7) Rules shall require or authorise the comptroller to make arrangements for the publication of reports of cases relating to patents, trade
marks, **service marks,** [*and*] registered designs **or design rights** decided by
him and of cases relating to patents (whether under this Act or otherwise)
trade marks, **service marks**, registered designs [*and*] copyright **and design
right** decided by any court or body (whether in the United Kingdom or
elsewhere).

Note. Subsection (2)(*k*) was prospectively repealed (Sched. 8 [1988]), but for its
coming into effect see the latest Supplement to this Work *re.* this para. Subsection
(3A) was added (Sched. 5, para. 29 [1988]), with effect from the Royal Assent
thereto, November 15, 1988 (s. 305(1) [1988]). The references in subsection (7) to
"service marks" were effectively made by the 1986 Act (s. 2(3) and Sched. 2,
para. 1(2)(*e*)), and the other amendments to subsection (7) were made by the 1988
Act (Sched. 7, para. 22).

123.02   RELEVANT RULES

The original Rules under the 1977 Act were the Patents Rules 1978 (S.I. 1978 No. 216). These were variously amended and (apart from r. 124 [1978], reprinted at para. 124.04) replaced by the Patents Rules 1982 (S.I. 1982 No. 717), this being a consolidation of the 1978 Rules as they then stood. The 1982 Rules have, likewise, since then been amended in numerous respects by various Patents (Amendment) Rules, but the numbering of the 1978 Rules has been retained both in the 1982 Rules and throughout the amendments made thereto.

The individual rules of the 1982 Rules are listed in para. 139.01, together with reference to the paragraphs of this work at which each is reprinted herein. Para. 139.02 provides details of the Amendment Rules by which the various amendments to the 1982 Rules have been made and the particular rules affected thereby. When it is significant, the nature of the previous form of a rule and the date at which its change became effective is given in a *Note* to that rule following its reprinting in this work. Some additional rules of relevance are listed in para. 142.01. In relation to "existing patents" some of the Patents Rules 1968 (S.I. 1968 No. 1389), as amended, remain effective despite the repeal of these Rules: details are given in para. A109.

The fees payable under the Rules are dealt with in paras. 140.01, 144.01 and 144.02, and the Forms for use under the 1982 Rules (as amended) are reprinted in paras. 141.01–141.58.

The following rules are relevant to section 123 itself, and are reprinted below as amended by subsequent Patents (Amendment) Rules:

Citation and commencement

123.03   **1.** These Rules may be cited as the Patents Rules 1982 and shall come into operation—
     (*a*) except for rules 3(1) and 124(2), on 14th June 1982, and
     (*b*) as respects rules 3(1) and 124(2), on 12th July 1982.

Interpretation

123.04   **2.** In these Rules, unless the context otherwise requires—

"the Act" means the Patents Act 1977 and, save where otherwise indicated, any reference to a section is a reference to that section of the Act;

"the 1949 Act" means the Patents Act 1949 [c. 87];

"declared priority date" means—
     (*a*) the date of filing of the earliest relevant application specified in a declaration made for the purposes of section 5 where the priority date claimed in the declaration has not been lost or abandoned and where the declaration has not been withdrawn before preparations for the publication of the application in suit have been completed by the Patent Office in accordance with section 16;
     (*b*) the date of filing of any such application for a patent as is referred to in section 127(4) which is specified in a declaration made for the purposes of that section;

(*c*) where an application for a European patent (UK) is, by virtue of section 8(1), to be treated as an application for a patent under the Act, the date of filing of the earliest previous application mentioned in the declaration of priority filed by the applicant in respect of the application for a European patent (UK) under Article 88(1) of the European Patent Convention where the priority date claimed in the declaration has not been lost or abandoned and where the declaration has not been withdrawn before the comptroller directs that the application for a European patent (UK) shall be so treated; or

(*d*) where an international application for a patent (UK) is to be treated as an application for a patent under the Act, the date of filing of the earliest application filed in or for a State which is a party to the Convention of the Protection of Industrial Property signed at Paris on 20th March 1883 the priority for which is claimed in a declaration filed for the purposes of Article 8 of the Patent Co-operation Treaty, provided that such priority claim has not been lost or abandoned under the provisions of that Treaty;

"existing patent" means a patent mentioned in section 127(2)(*a*) and (*c*) and "existing application" means an application mentioned in section 127(2)(*b*);

"Journal" means the Official Journal (Patents) published in accordance with rule 115.

Fees

3.—[*Repealed.*]   **123.05**

Note. Rule 3 was replaced by rule 3 of the Patents (Fees) Rules 1986 (S.I. 1986 No. 583). This reads:

> "**3.**—The fees to be paid in respect of any matter arising under the Patents Act 1949 or the Patents Act 1977 shall be those specified in the Schedule to these Rules; and in any case where a form specified in the Schedule as the corresponding form in relation to any matter is required by the Patents Rules 1968 or the Patents Rules 1982 to be used, that form shall be accompanied by the fee specified in respect of that matter".

The Schedule to the Patents (Fees) Rules 1986 has itself since been repealed and replaced, see para. 144.01.

Forms

4. The forms mentioned in these Rules, except for those mentioned in   **123.06** rule 124(3), are those set out in Schedule 2 to these Rules. Replicas of the forms complying with these Rules shall be used wherever required by these Rules. The forms shall not be modified without the consent of the comptroller.

Note. The forms of Schedule 2 are reprinted at paras. 141.01–141.5.

Correction of irregularities

123.07 **100.**—(1) Subject to paragraph (2) below, any document filed in any proceedings before the comptroller may, if he thinks fit, be amended, and any irregularity in procedure in or before the Patent Office may be rectified, on such terms as he may direct.

(2) Where the irregularity in procedure consists of a failure to comply with any limitation as to times or periods specified in the Act or the 1949 Act or prescribed in these Rules or the Patents Rules 1968, as they continue to apply, the comptroller may direct that the time or period in question shall be altered where the irregularity is attributable wholly or in part to an error, default or omission on the part of the Patent Office, but not otherwise.

(3) Paragraph (2) above is without prejudice to the comptroller's power to extend any times or periods under rule 110 below.

Note. Rule 100 was replaced, to provide the wording reprinted above, by the Patents (Amendment) Rules 1987 (S.I. 1987 No. 288, rr. 1(2) and 11) with effect from March 24, 1987. Before that date, rule 100 was in the form:

[**100.** *Any document filed in any proceedings before the comptroller may, if he thinks fit, be amended, and any irregularity in procedure in or before the Patent Office may be rectified, on such terms as he may direct:*

Provided that, without prejudice to the comptroller's power to extend any times or periods under rule 110 below and except where such irregularity is attributable wholly or in part to an error, default or omission on the part of the Patent Office the comptroller shall not direct that any time or period specified in the Act or the 1949 Act or prescribed in these Rules or the Patent Rules 1968, as they continue to apply, shall be altered.]

Note. The proviso to this former wording of rule 100 took effect from January 5, 1981 (Patents (Amendment No. 4) Rules 1980, S.I. 1980 No. 1783).

Dispensation by comptroller

123.08 **101.** Where, under these Rules, any person is required to do any act or thing, or any document or evidence is required to be produced or filed, and it is shown to the satisfaction of the comptroller that from any reasonable cause that person is unable to do that act or thing, or that that document or evidence cannot be produced or filed, the comptroller may, upon the production of such evidence and subject to such terms as he thinks fit, dispense with the doing of any such act or thing, or the production or filing of such document or evidence.

Remission of fees

123.09 **102.**—(1) The comptroller may remit the whole or part of a search fee in the following cases—

(*a*) . . .

(*b*) where an international application for a patent (UK) which has already been the subject of a search by the International Searching Authority in accordance with the Patent Co-operation Treaty falls to be treated as an application for a patent under the Act;

(*c*) where a new application is filed in accordance with section 15(4) for a patent for an invention in relation to which the applicant has previously paid the search fee in connection with the earlier application referred to in that subsection.

(2) In a case governed by Chapter II of the Patent Co-operation Treaty, the comptroller may remit the whole or part of the fee for the substantive examination of the international application where its preliminary examination has been carried out by the Patent Office acting as the International Preliminary Examining Authority under Article 32 of the said Treaty.

(3) In cases falling within paragraph (1)(*c*) above the request for remission of the whole or part of the fee shall be made in writing.

(4) No appeal shall lie from any decision of the comptroller under this rule.

Note. Rule 102 is printed as amended by rule 7 of the Patents (Amendment No. 2) Rules 1985 (S.I. 1985 No. 1166).

Alteration of time limits

110.—(1) The times or periods prescribed by these Rules for doing any **123.10** act or taking any proceedings thereunder, other than time or periods prescribed in the rules specified in paragraph (2) below and subject to paragraphs (3) and (3A) below, may be extended by the comptroller if he thinks fit, upon such notice to the parties and upon such terms, as he may direct, and such extension may be granted although the time or period for doing such act or taking such proceeding has already expired.

(2) The rules referred to in paragraph (1) above are rules 6(1), 17(3), 26 (so far as it relates to rule 6(1)), 39(1) and (2), 40(2), 43(2), 60(2), 65(1), 66(1), 71(1), 78(1), 81(1), 82(1) and 91(4).

(3) A time or period prescribed in rules 6(2) and (6), 15(1), 17(2), 23, 25(2), 25(3) (except so far as it relates to the filing of claims for the purposes of the application and the filing of the abstract), 26 (except so far as it relates to rule 6(1)), 33(2), (3) and (4), 34, 79B, 81(2) and (3), 82(2) and (3), 83(3) and 85(1) and (3) above shall, if not previously extended, be extended for one month upon filing Patents Form No. 50/77; and where in any proceedings more than one such time or period expires on the same day (but not otherwise), those times or periods may be extended upon the filing of a single such form.

(3A) Without prejudice to paragraph (3) above a time or period prescribed in the rules referred to in that paragraph may, upon request made

763

on Patents Form No. 52/77, be extended or further extended by the comptroller if he thinks fit, upon such terms as the comptroller may direct, and whether or not the time or period, including any extension obtained under paragraph (3), has expired:

Provided that no extension may be granted under this paragraph in relation to any time or period expiring before 24th March 1987.

(3B) A single request may be made under paragraph (3A) above for the extension of more than one time or period in the same proceedings if the extensions are to be to a common date (but not otherwise).

(3C) If on consideration of a request under paragraph (3A) above the comptroller decides that the extension requested (or, in a case falling within paragraph (3B) above, any or all of the extensions requested) may be granted he shall notify the applicant accordingly and invite him to file Patents Forms No. 53/77, upon receipt of which the comptroller shall effect the extension or extensions in accordance with the decision.

(4) Where the period within which any party to a dispute may file evidence under these Rules is to begin after the expiry of any period in which any other party may file evidence under these Rules and that other party notifies the comptroller that he does not wish to file any or any further evidence, the comptroller may direct that the period within which the first-mentioned party may file evidence shall begin on such date as may be specified in the direction and shall notify all the parties to the dispute of that date.

Notes. 1. Rule 110 is printed as amended by the Patents (Amendment) Rules 1987 (S.I. 1987 No. 288 rr. 1(2) and 12), with effect from March 24, 1987. This amendment introduced paragraphs (3A)–(3C) so that the reference to paragraph (3A) in paragraph (1) was then new. Before that date, from January 5, 1981, paragraphs (2) and (3) were in the forms first reprinted below (Patents (Amendment No. 4) Rules 1980, S.I. 1980 No. 1783), the following forms of these paragraphs reprinted below being those which were present in the original 1978 Rules.

[(2) *The rules referred to in paragraph (1) above are rules 6(1), 17(3), 23, 25(3) (except so far as it relates to the filing of claims for the purposes of the application and also the abstract), 25(4), 26 (in so far as it relates to rule 6), 39(1) and (2), 40(2), 43(2), 60(2), 65(1), 66(1), 71(1), 78(1), 80, 81, 82, 91(4) and 123(1).*]

[(2) *The rules referred to in sub-rule (1) above are rules 6(3) and (6), 15(1), 17(2) and (3), 23, 25, 26, 33(2) and (3), 34, 39(1) and (2), 40(2), 43(2), 60(2), 65(1), 66(1), 71(1), 78(1), 80, 81, 82, 83(1), 85(1)(a) and (b) and (3)(b) and (c), 90, 91(4), 113(3) and 123(1).*]

[(3) *The periods prescribed in rules 6(2) and (6), 15(1), 17(2), 25(2), 26 (in so far as it relates to rule 15), 33(2), (3) and (4), 34, 83(3), 85(1)(a) and (b) and (3)(b) and (c) above may be extended for not more than one month upon filing Patents Form No. 50/77.*]

[(3) *The period prescribed in rule 6(2) above may be extended for not more than one month upon filing Patents Form No. 50/77.*]

2. The latest Supplement to this Work should be consulted *re* this para. for possible amendments to this rule consequent upon the bringing into effect of revised section 28 and new section 89A, for which see the *Notes* to paras. 28.01 and 89A.01 respectively.

Calculation of times or periods

111.—(1) Where, on any day, there is—   **122.11**

  (a) a general interruption or subsequent disclocation in the postal services of the United Kingdom, or

  (b) an event or circumstances causing an interruption in the normal operation of the Patent Office,

the comptroller may certify the day as being one on which there is an "interruption" and, where any period of time specified in the Act or these Rules for the giving, making or filing of any notice, application or other document expires on a day so certified the period shall be extended to the first day next following (not being an excluded day) which is not so certified.

(2) Any certificate of the comptroller given pursuant to this rule shall be posted in the Patent Office.

(3) Where, in or in connection with an application for a patent ("the application in suit"), it is desired to make a declaration specifying for the purposes of section 5(2) an earlier relevant application and the period of twelve months immediately following the date of filing the earlier relevant application ends on a day which is an excluded day for the purposes of section 120, such period shall, if the declaration is made on the first following day on which the Patent Office is open for the transaction of such business, be altered so as to include both the day of filing of the earlier relevant application and the day on which the declaration is made in or in connection with the application in suit.

(4) Where it is desired to make such a declaration and the said period of twelve months immediately following the date of filing the earlier relevant application ends on a day certified under paragraph (1) above as being one on which there is an interruption, the period shall, if the declaration is made on the first day following the end of the interruption, be altered so as to include both the day of filing of the earlier relevant application and the day on which the declaration is made in or in connection with the application in suit.

(5) Where an application for a patent is filed upon the day immediately following a day which is certified under paragraph (1) above as being one on which there is an interruption or which is an excluded day for the purposes of section 120, the period of six months specified in section 2(4) shall be computed from the day following the next preceding day which is neither so certified nor so excluded.

(6) If any particular case the comptroller is satisfied that the failure to give, make or file any notice, application or other document within—

  (a) any period of time specified in the Act or these Rules for such giving, making or filing,

  (b) the period of six months following a disclosure of matter constituting an invention falling within paragraph (a), (b) or (c) of section 2(4), or

(c) the period of twelve months referred to in paragraph (3) above,
was wholly or mainly attributable to a failure or undue delay in the postal
services in the United Kingdom, the comptroller may, if he thinks fit—

>   (i) extend the period of time for the giving, making or filing so that
>   it ends on the day of the receipt by the addressee of the notice,
>   application or other document (or, if the day of such receipt is
>   an excluded day, on the first following day which is not an
>   excluded day),
>
>   (ii) determine that the period of six months referred to in sub-
>   paragraph (b) above shall be altered so that it begins on the day
>   of the disclosure and ends on the day of receipt by the Patent
>   Office of the application for the patent (or, if the day of such
>   receipt is an excluded day, on the first following day which is
>   not an excluded day), or
>
>   (iii) determine that the period of twelve months referred to in para-
>   graph (3) above shall be altered so as to include both the day of
>   filing of the earlier relevant application is received by the
>   Patent Office (or, if the day of such receipt is an excluded day,
>   the first following day which is not an excluded day).

as the case may be, in each case upon such notice to other parties and upon
such terms as he may direct.

Note. Rule 111 was replaced by the form printed above by the Patents (Amendment) Rules 1989 (S.I. 1989 No. 116, r. 3) with effect from August 1, 1989.

Translations

123.12   **113.**—(1) Subject to the provisions of rules 6, 80, 81, 82 and 85 and paragraph (3) below, where any document or part of a document which is in a
language other than English is filed at the Patent Office or sent to the
comptroller in pursuance of the Act or these Rules, it shall be accompanied
by a translation into English of the document or that part, verified to the
satisfaction of the Comptroller as corresponding to the original text.
Where the document is or forms part of an application for a patent, the
Patent Office shall not, in the absence of such a translation, take any
further action in relation to that document, unless the comptroller otherwise directs.

(2) Where more than one copy of that document is required to be so filed
or sent, a corresponding number of copies of the translation shall accompany it.

(3) In a case where a search report drawn up under Article 92 of the
European Patent Convention or Article 18 of the Patent Co-operation
Treaty is filed at the Patent Office in relation to the provisions of section
81(2)(*a*) or 89 and that report refers to any document in a language other
than English, a translation into English of that document or any part
thereof verified to the satisfaction of the comptroller as corresponding to

the original text thereof shall, if the comptroller so directs, be filed within two months of the date on which such direction is given.

(4) Where proceedings are instituted before the comptroller in relation to a European patent (UK) the specification of which was published in French or German, the party who institutes those proceedings shall furnish to the Patent Office a translation into English of the specification of the patent verified to the satisfaction of the comptroller as corresponding to the original text thereof unless such a translation has already been filed under section 77(6).

(5) If, in the course of such proceedings, leave is given for the amendment of the specification of the European patent (UK), the party given leave to amend shall furnish to the Patent Office a translation of the amendment into the language in which the specification of the patent was published, verified to the satisfaction of the comptroller as corresponding to the original text thereof.

(6) The comptroller may refuse to accept any translation which is in his opinion inaccurate and thereupon another translation of the document in question verified as aforesaid shall be furnished, together with the appropriate number of copies thereof.

Notes. 1. Rule 113 is reprinted as amended by: the Patents (Amendment No. 4) Rules 1980 (S.I. 1980 No. 1783); the Patents (Amendment No. 2) Rules 1985 (S.I. 1985 No. 1166, r. 8); and the Patents (Amendment) Rules 1987 (S.I. 1987 No. 288, rr. 1(3) and 7).

2. This rule, and rules 6, 80–82 and 85 to which it is subject, may come to be altered by new rules made when the remainder of Schedule 5 [1988] is brought into effect. The latest Supplement to this Work should therefore be consulted *re.* this para.

Publication and sale of documents

114. The comptroller may arrange for the publication and sale of copies **123.13** of specifications and other documents in the Patent Office and of indexes to and abridgements or abstracts of such documents.

The Journal

115.—(1) The comptroller shall publish a journal containing particulars **123.14** of applications for patents and other proceedings under the Act and any other information that he may deem to be generally useful or important.

(2) The journal shall be entitled "The Official Journal (Patents)".

(3) Unless the comptroller otherwise directs, the Journal shall be published weekly.

Reports of cases

116. The comptroller shall from time to time publish reports of cases **123.15** relating to patents, trade marks and registered designs decided by him and of cases relating to patents (whether under the Act or otherwise), trade marks, registered designs and copyright decided by any court or body (whether in the United Kingdom or elsewhere), being cases which he considers to be generally useful or important.

123.16   Patent Office (Address) Rules 1985

(S.I. 1985 No. 1099)

2.—(1) The address of the Patent Office shall be State House, 66–71 High Holborn, London WC1R 4TP.

(2) [*Not reprinted, relevant only to trade marks*]

Note. This rule was effective from September 23, 1985.

Commentary on Section 123

123.17   *General*

Section 123 empowers the Secretary of State to make rules for the purpose of implementing the various provisions of the Act and is applicable to "existing patents" (Sched. 2, para. 1(2)). For an explanation of the present state of these rules, see para. 123.02. For a listing of the Patents Rules 1982, indicating where each is reprinted in this work, see para. 139.01, and likewise para. 142.01 for additional relevant rules which are reprinted herein. Separate Patents (Fees) Rules now exist, see para. 144.01.

Subsection (1) refers to the making of rules for regulating the business of the Patent Office in connection with patent matters, and includes reference to European patent matters; the subsection also defines "prescribed" and "rules", for the purpose of section 130(1).

Subsection (2) lists at length various matters on which rules can be made, without prejudice to the generality of subsection (1), and these rules can make different provision for different cases (subs. (3)). These matters are discussed herein in relation to the particular rules made under these provisions. In general, such rules are printed herein following the main section to which they relate, with a location listing in para. 139.01. Thus, in this commentary under section 123, there are only discussed below rules 100–102, 110, 111 and 113–116 (reprinted respectively in paras. 123.07–123.15 *supra*). Rules 100, 101 and 114–116 apply also to proceedings under the 1949 Act (r. 124(1)(*d*) [1978], reprinted at para. 127.04).

New subsection (3A) declares the Comptroller to have an important power to deal with an application or patent, even if it had, apparently, ceased to exist, and is discussed in para. 123.36 *infra*. Subsections (4)–(7) relate respectively to: fees, for which see para. 123.24 *infra*); remuneration of advisers, for which see para. 123.29 *infra*); and the publication of the O.J. and the RPC law reports, for which see respectively paras. 123.47 and 123.48 *infra*. Under the Tribunals and Inquiries Act 1971 (c. 62, ss. 1, 10 and Sched. 1) the Secretary of State may not make "procedural rules" for the Comptroller without prior consultation with the Council on Tribunals established under that Act.

123.18   *Definitions for Patents Rules (r. 2)*

Rule 2 (reprinted at para. 123.04, *supra*) defines various terms used in the Patents Rules 1982. These include:

Defined Term	Definition
"The Act"	Patents Act 1977 (c. 37);
"section"	section of the Patents Act 1977, unless otherwise indicated;
"1949 Act"	Patents Act 1949 (12, 13 & 14 Geo. 6, c. 62), see Appendix A;
"declared priority date"	see para. 5.07;
"existing patent"	Subsisting patent granted under the Patents Act 1949, see para. 127.07;
"existing application"	Application filed under the 1949 Act as yet ungranted [*Note*. Few such applications still exist, see para. 127.07];
"Journal"	The Official Journal (Patents') [abbreviated herein as "O.J."], see para. 123.47.

Note. By section 11 of the Interpretation Act 1978 (c. 30) the definitions contained in the Patents Act 1977 itself apply also for the purposes of the Rules made under its provisions. Thus, the term "United Kingdom" in the Patents Rules includes the Isle of Man by virtue of section 132(2).

Form and content of documents (subs. (2)(a))   123.19

Subsection (2)(*a*) specifies the form and content of applications and documents, and the supply of copies. This could be taken as the authority for many of the rules, especially rules 16 and 18–20 (reprinted at paras. 14.02–14.05) and rule 21 (reprinted at para. 72.02), and for the Patent Forms (r. 4 and Sched. 2 to the Rules), which are herein termed "PF" and are reprinted in paras. 141.01–141.57, with additional forms in paras. 142.01–143.02, and forms for use in connection with "existing patents" in paras. A119–A138. Subsection (2)(*a*) is also authority for the many instances where documents are required to be filed in duplicate.

The Comptroller permits home-made forms to be used provided that these present him with the required information, *e.g.* agents can reproduce the forms without the explanatory notes. However, since many of the forms have been designed for easy reading by Patent Office staff, the general layout of a home-made form has to be closely similar to the official form if such is to be found acceptable.

Procedure before the Comptroller (subs. (2)(b) and r. 100)

General   123.20

Subsection (2)(*b*) specifies the regulation of procedure before the Comptroller and the Patent Office and the rectification of irregularities of procedure. This, together with section 117(1), is the direct authority for rule 100 which gives the Comptroller discretion to amend any document filed in proceedings before him (whether under the 1977 or 1949 Act) and to rectify any irregularity of procedure in or before the Office.

Since 1981 the use of rule 100 to obtain an extension of time has been strictly limited to cases where the irregularity is attributable wholly or in part to an error, default or omission on the part of the Patent Office (see now r. 100(2)), but this is without prejudice to the grant of extensions of time under rule 110. However, until 1987, the provisions of rule 100 were strict and thus recourse was often had (usually without success) to the provisions of rule 100 (the wording of which was merely clarified in 1987) to try and save an application or patent for which a time limit had expired due to some error or oversight but, with the introduction in 1987 of sub-rules 110(3A)–(3C), extensions of time are now much more readily obtainable, though only under the rules specified under rule 110(3). Thus, there is now much less need to try and invoke rule 100(2) to obtain an extension of time, though this can be of importance in the case of periods prescribed by the rules listed in rule 110(2) as being inextensible. The grant of extensions of time is, therefore, now discussed in contiguous paras. 123.30–123.39 *infra*, with the seminal decisions relating to "error, default or omission on the part of the Patent Office" (as required under rule 100(2)) being discussed in para. 123.34.

As an alternative to the use of rule 100, it should be noted that section 117(1) provides that the Comptroller may, subject to any rules, correct an error of translation, or a clerical error or a mistake in any document filed in connection with a patent or application, see the commentary on section 117. While rule 100 does not specifically limit amendment to that sought by an applicant, comparison with the wording of section 19 suggests that it is not the intention to give the Comptroller power under this rule to amend of his own volition and a proprietor/applicant has a right to be heard, see para. 101.04.

123.21   *—Irregularity in procedure*

An "irregularity in procedure" is required for operation of rule 100, but the rule cannot itself be used to over-ride any limitation imposed by virtue of any statute or other rule, as was uncompromisingly laid down in *E's Applications* ([1983] RPC 231 (HL)). The "irregularity" may, perhaps, be something which occurs in an agent's office (or elsewhere as a result), see *Fater's Application* ([1979] FSR 647) which, though overruled by *E's Applications* (*supra*), may still be relevant on this point. However, there is no irregularity of procedure when there has merely been a change of mind of the applicant (or his agent) (*P's Application*, [1983] RPC 269).

Examples of procedural irregularities which have led (or which would have led but for the proviso of present rule 100(2)) to the grant of relief under rule 100 are: wrongly according priority in a published application when the necessary certified priority document had not been filed (*Brossmann's Application*, [1983] RPC 109); failure by the Patent Office to send out promptly a statutory reminder of failure to pay a renewal fee or of lapsing of the patent (*Daido Kogyo's Patent*, [1984] RPC 97); receipt of renewal fees for some years though the patent should have been recorded as lapsed because of a failure to pay such a fee in some earlier year (*Phillips Petroleum's Patent*, SRIS O/20/84, *noted* IPD 7069); failure to request substantive examination (*Elf Union's Application*, SRIS O/96/81, *noted* IPD 5011, but decided prior to *E's Applications*, *supra*); non-receipt by the agent of a complimentary copy of the patent specification contrary to expected and advertised practice (*Mills' Application*, [1985] RPC 339 (CA)); Patent Office receipt issued causing agent to believe, according to custom and practice, that all necessary papers had been duly filed (*Mitsubishi Jidosha's Application*, [1988] RPC 449); application wrongly recorded as being withdrawn (*Alsthon-Atlantique's Application*, SRIS O/49/84; and *Akebono Brake's Application*, SRIS O/2/85, where the agent had understood the application to have been placed in order; and *Minnesota Mining's Application*, SRIS O/86/86, where PF 10/77 had been mis-filed because it bore an incorrect number); letter of further objections never received by the agent (*Coal Industry's Application*, [1986] RPC 57 and *Opatowski's Application*, SRIS O/74/88)); non-receipt of response to substantive examination objections (*Bosch's Application*, SRIS O/175/86); likewise loss of a letter in the Patent Office (*Kangeroos USA's Application*, SRIS O/136/85); and omission of "UK" from the list of designated States for an international application though "United Kingdom (EPO)" had been listed (*Prangley's Application*, [1988] RPC 187 (CA)). Apparently, rule 100 has also been successfully invoked when the necessary fee had been paid by a cheque received in an unsigned state ((1984–85) 14 CIPA 363).

However, there is no irregularity in procedure, at least within the Patent Office, where the Comptroller fails to draw attention to a mistake by the applicant or his agent where the Comptroller is not under a legal duty so to do (*M's Application*, [1985] RPC 249 (CA)), as in: *Masuda's Application* ([1987] RPC 37), where a wrong translation of an international application was filed; and in *Borg-Warner's Patent* ([1986] RPC 137), where a renewal fee refund was authorised without attention being drawn to the lapsing of the patent. However, the position is different where the Comptroller has a moral duty to act in a certain way because he has previously indicated he will do so, see *Mills' Application (supra)*; or by virtue of custom and expected practice, see *Mitsubishi Jidosha's Application (supra)*. A further example may be where the Patent Office gives erroneous advice, as has been accepted by the EPO, see *EPO Decision J 06/79* ([1980] RPC 515; OJEPO 7/1980, 225). Nevertheless, in these cases there *may* have been an "irregularity of procedure", albeit in an agent's office, but the case came for decision under what is now rule 100(2) under which it is necessary to show specifically that the irregularity occurred "in the Patent Office".

As to allegations of loss of papers in the Patent Office after alleged due filing, it should be noted that the Office keeps copies of receipts issued on Form "P Ack. 6" in bound books, and that they are able to retrieve the fee sheets which should have accompanied the filing of fee-bearing forms (*Sanyo's Application*, SRIS O/31/88).

—Relief under rule 100 is discretionary and may be conditional   **123.22**

It must, however, be remembered that application of rule 100 is a matter of discretion. Thus, in *Lebelson's Application* ([1984] RPC 136), the Patents Court observed that in such circumstances it is important to see what had been done by the applicant and his agent to secure compliance with the requirements of the Act and Rules. Also, in *Application des Gaz's Application* ([1987] RPC 279), it was pointed out that applicants for the exercise of discretion are under an obligation to make a full disclosure of all relevant matters and it has to be seen whether the activities and actions of the applicants (and their agents, both in this country and abroad) have been such as to justify the exercise of discretion in their favour. In particular the blameworthiness of the agent(s) cannot be separated from that of the applicants themselves, but see now *Textron's Patent* ([1989] RPC 441 (HL)) discussed in para. 28.09.

Since relief under rule 100 involves an exercise of discretion, it may be granted only subject to conditions, see *Roussel-Uclaf's (Clemence & Le Martret's) Patent* ([1987] RPC 109) where the Comptroller held that rule 100 provides him with authority to rectify any irregularity in procedure (other than as regards time limits, unless r. 100(2) is satisfied) on such terms as he may direct. Thus, where information as to the status of an application or patent has been given to the public which then falls to be corrected under rule 100, the Comptroller appears, almost invariably, to make his order subject to conditions to protect third parties similar to those now imposed under new section 28A when a patent is restored, for which see paras. 28A.04–28A.06.

Examples where such conditions have been imposed are: *Elf Union's Application* (SRIS O/96/81, *noted* IPD 5011); *Coal Industry's Application (No. 2)* (SRIS O/10/86) and *Kangeroos USA's Application* (SRIS O/136/85). In the *Kangeroos* case there had been no fault at all by the Applicant, the Patent Office having lost a letter, but nevertheless restoration of the application was made subject to the third party conditions.

Where the Comptroller purports to have exercised his discretion to extend a time period, and it can be shown that he had in fact no power to do so under the Act or Rules, it can be argued that the subsequent grant of a patent was made *ultra vires* and that, consequently, the patent is a nullity, see para. 34.02.

123.23 —*Dispensation by Comptroller (r. 101)*

Rule 101 is also made under subsection (2)(*b*) and applies to proceedings under the 1977 or 1949 Act. It permits the Comptroller to dispense with the performance of any act or production of any document where it is not reasonably possible to do so; evidence is required and conditions can be imposed.

Rule 101 is worded in the present tense and, therefore, its applicability to matters past is precluded (*Allibert's Application*, SRIS O/22/83). Also, the rule only applies if an action cannot be taken and not when a choice is made not to do so (*Lebelson's Application*, [1984] RPC 136), and its use is only appropriate when there is some tangible restraint, and not a mere mental inhibition, having a permanent effect in preventing fulfilment of a statutory requirement and this requirement has to be dispensed with altogether (*Thermo Technic's Application*, [1985] RPC 109). This case also held that rule 101 cannot be used to circumvent rule 110, see also *Brossmann's Application* ([1983] RPC 109). It seems, therefore, that rule 101 can only have effect when no other rule is directly in point to control the factual situation which prevails.

The exercise of the Comptroller's discretion in connection with any amendment or dispensation under rule 101 is subject to section 101 and rule 88 giving the party concerned the right to be heard, and appeal lies to the Patents Court under section 97, see paras. 101.04 and 97.04 respectively.

Fees and remission of fees (subss. (2)(c) and (4))

123.24 —*Fees*

Subsection (2)(*c*) now authorises the current form of the Patents (Fees) Rules, see para. 123.05. The current fees are discussed in para. 144.01. They are required to be made with Treasury consent (subs. (4)).

It may be noted that no rule pertaining to fees is mentioned in rule 110(2) and, therefore, if a form (such as PF 50/77) is timely filed, other than under a specific provision in the Act or in a rule specified in either of rules 110(2) or (3), and the fee is omitted from that form, the time for paying that fee might be extensible by discretion exercised under rule 110(1).

The Department of Trade and Industry (Fees) Order 1988 (S.I. 1988 No. 93), made under section 102 of the Finance (No. 2) Act 1987 (c. 51), has given power to the Secretary of State to fix Patent Office fees at levels which not only cover the direct cost of providing the service in question, but also to cover deficits incurred or to be incurred, as well as to secure a return on an amount of capital, and in respect of depreciation of assets.

123.25 —*Remission of fees (r. 102)*

Subsection (2)(*c*) also authorises rule 102 which now only provides for the remission of the search fee where this has already been paid by the applicant under the PCT (r. 102(1)(*b*)), or in the case of a divisional application which has already been paid on an earlier application under section 15(4) (r. 102(1)(*c*)). Similarly, the substantive examination fee may be remitted wholly or in part in the case of a PCT application where a preliminary examination for patentability has been carried out by the United Kingdom Patent Office under Chapter II of the PCT, for which see para. 89A.33. A request for fee remission need only be in writing in the case of a divisional application (*i.e.* one filed under section 15(4)) (r. 102(3)), but in other cases the refund should be automatic. No appeal on fee remission is permitted (r. 102(4)).

In practice, the fee remitted under rule 102(1)(*b*) is a sum equal to the fee paid for an International Preliminary Examination under rule 120 (reprinted at para. 89.07). On a divisional application filed under section 15(4) the search fee is remitted in full upon written application, but no remission of the examination fee is allowed. However, it should be noted that there is no provision for remission of the search fee on a later application when a corresponding search has been made on an earlier United Kingdom application from which the later application claims priority, rule 102(1)(c) being limited to the case of divisional applications filed under section 15(4). Also, when an examination report on an international application (UK) is drawn up by some International Preliminary Examination Authority other than the United Kingdom Patent Office, the circumstances fall outside both rules 102(1)(c) and 102(2) and, therefore, no part of the United Kingdom examination fee (paid on PF 10/77) can then be refunded, see O.J. October 17, 1979 and para. 89A.33. The EPO has also ruled that remission of fees is not a matter of equity and can only take place where a rule so provides (*EPO Decision J* 20/87, "*Refund of search fee/UPJOHN*", OJEPO 3/1989, 67; [1989] 5 EPOR 298).

Though there is power to do so, it is the present practice not to refund any part of the fee for substantive examination when an international preliminary examination report has already been established on an international application before this enters its national phase before the Office, see para. 89A.03.

Evidence (subs. (2)(d))   **123.26**

Subsection (2)(d) regulates the mode of giving evidence, the attendance of witnesses and the power of discovery, etc., in proceedings before the Comptroller. It is the direct authority for rules 103–107 and 112 (reprinted at paras. 72.06–72.11). These rules are also applicable to proceedings under the 1949 Act in relation to "existing patents". Rules 103–107 and 112 are discussed in paras. 72.40–72.46.

Advertisements (subs. (2)(e))   **123.27**

Subsection (2)(e) requires the Comptroller to make certain advertisements. Under the following rules the Comptroller is required to advertise in the O.J. certain proceedings, *viz.* those under: section 27 and rule 40 (*Amendment*), for which see para. 27.02; section 28 and rule 41 (*Restoration*), for which see para. 28.02; section 29 and rule 43 (*Surrender of patent*), for which see para. 29.02; section 46 and rule 62 (*Making "licence of right" entry*), for which see para. 46.02; section 47 and rule 66 (*Cancellation of "licence of right" entry*), for which see para. 47.04; and section 48 and rule 70 (*Compulsory licence application*), for which see para. 48.03. The Comptroller is also required by sections 16 and 24 to advertise in the O.J. publication of an application and grant of a patent, and details of applications withdrawn are published in the O.J. under the authority of section 118(3)(b) and rule 95(e) (reprinted in para. 118.07), as discussed in para. 118.14.

Under rule 50 (reprinted at para. 32.08) the Comptroller has a general discretionary power to advertise things done under the Act or rules in relation to the register. Under this power the Comptroller advertises in the O.J. those patents for which notice of transactions, instruments or events have been entered in the register under section 32, see para. 32.19. Also, it has long been the practice to publish in the O.J. details of revocation proceedings under sections 72 or 73.

Since the end of 1986 the O.J. has also published details of applications filed under section 46(3) (*Settlement of licences of right*) and, subsequently, the outcome of such applications (O.J. December 10, 1986, which also published a first retrospective list back to August 1, 1983 with further such lists appearing in subsequent issues). Since November 1988 there has been a further expansion of information published in the O.J. by the inclusion therein of details of proceedings under sections: 8, 10, 12(1) and (4) (*Entitlement to application*); 13 (*Inventorship*); 27(5) (*Opposition to amend-*

ment); 29(2) (*Opposition to surrender*); 37(1) (*Entitlement to patent*); 40 (*Employee-inventor compensation*); and 117 (*Correction*) (O.J. November 9, 1988, with retrospective lists of such proceedings published in this and subsequent issues). Details of declarations which could, after January 15, 1989, be filed under Schedule 1, para. 4A (for which see paras. 47.10–47.14) have also been published.

However, apparently, no notice is to be published of proceedings under: section 61(3) (*Infringement proceedings before the Comptroller*); section 71 (*Declaration of non-infringement*); or section 82 (*Entitlement disputes under European patent*).

123.28   *Proceedings in Scotland (subs. (2)(f))*

Subsection (2)(*f*) is the authority for rule 108 (reprinted at para. 98.02 and discussed in paras. 98.07 and 98.10) in relation to proceedings in Scotland under the Act.

Under the Act hearings in proceedings before the Comptroller can be conducted in Scotland, where the conditions of rule 108 are met, in matters under sections 8, 12 and 37 (*Entitlement*), sections 40 and 41 (*Rewards to inventors*), section 61 (*Action for infringement*), and sections 71 and 72 (*Revocation*), but not apparently in proceedings under any other section. Rule 108 also applies to proceedings under the 1949 Act in relation to "existing patents" (r. 124(1)(*d*) [1978] reprinted at para. 127.04.

123.29   *Advisers (subss. (2)(g) and (5))*

Subsection (2)(*g*) is the authority for the appointment by the Comptroller under rule 109 (reprinted at para. 72.10) of an adviser or advisers to assist him. The provision is discussed in para. 72.49. It does *not* extend to proceedings under the 1949 Act (r. 124(1)(*d*) [1978] reprinted in para. 127.04). The remuneration of such an adviser is determined by the Secretary of State with the consent of the Minister for the Civil Service, and is defrayed from monies provided by Parliament (subs. (5)).

Time limits (subs. (2)(h) and rr. 110 and 111)

123.30   *—General*

Subsection (2)(*h*) is the authority for rules 110 and 111 (reprinted respectively at paras. 123.10 and 123.11 *supra*). Rule 110 (discussed in paras. 123.31–123.35 *infra*) provides for extensions of time, while rule 111 (discussed in paras. 123.38 and 123.39 *infra*) deals with the calculation of time limits, particularly where there has been a disruption in postal services. These rules are *not* applicable to "existing patents" (r. 124(1)(*d*) [1978], reprinted in para. 127.04), but rule 154 [1968] (reprinted at para. A116, and still applicable by r. 124(1)(*a*) [1978]) provides for these patents a general discretionary power to grant extensions of time.

Extensions of time are now obtainable in the following ways: (1) by general discretion exercised under rule 110(1), which however is only applicable in the case of time periods arising under rules (*other than* those listed in rule 110(2) and (3)); (2) by automatic extension of up to one month of the periods specified in the rules listed under rule 110(3); (3) by further discretionary extension in the cases covered by rule 110(3) under rule 110(3A)–110(3C); and (4) in cases of "error, default or omission by the Patent Office" under rule 100(2). These are discussed in the following paragraphs, but note that extensions under heads (2) and (3) above require the payment of heavy fees, while extensions under heads (1) and (4) are obtainable without fee.

—The inextensible time periods under rule 110 (r. 110(2)) **123.31**

Rule 110(2) stipulates the rules whereunder the prescribed time periods are inextensible under rule 110, though for these there remain a faint possibility of extension of these periods under rule 100(2), for which see para. 123.34 *infra*. Since January 1981, these rules are: rule 6(1) (*priority declaration*); rule 17(3) (*new deposit of micro-organism*); rule 26 (in relation to r. 6(1) only, *i.e. priority declaration in new divisional or replacement priority application*); rules 39(1) and (2) (*renewal fees*); rule 40(2) (*opposing amendment*); rule 43(2) (*opposing surrender*); rule 60(2) (*employee's application for compensation*); rule 65(1) (*cancellation of licence of right by third party*); rule 66(1) (*opposition to cancellation*); rule 71(1) (*opposition to compulsory licence*); rule 78(1) (*opposition to amendment*); rules 81(1) and 82(1) (*conversion of European application*); and rule 91(4) (*opposition to correction*).

—Automatic limited extension of certain time periods (r. 110(3)) **123.32**

Under rule 110(3) an extension of one month is obtainable for certain other time limits, *viz.* those specified in: rule 6(2) (*priority document*); rule 6(6) (*translation of priority document*); rule 15(1) (*statement of inventorship*); rule 17(2) (*information concerning deposit of micro-organism*); rule 23 (*late filing of drawings*); rule 25(2) (*request for search and fee*); rules 25(3) and 26(1) (*filing of divisional application, or new application after entitlement proceedings and meeting requirements therefor*, but *excluding* the periods for the filing of claims and an abstract and the claiming of priority under r. 6(1)); rules 33(2), (3) and (4) (*request for examination*); rule 34 (*acceptance period*); rule 79B (*filing translation of granted European Patent (UK)*); rules 81(2) and (3) and 82(2) and (3) (*meeting requirements on conversion of application for European patent (UK)*); rule 83(3) (*acceptance period for converted European application*); rule 85(1) (*entering UK phase of international application*); and rule 85(3) (*examination request and acceptance period for international application*).

The one month extension under rule 110(3) is obtainable as of right by filing PF 50/77 (reprinted at para. 141.50), but is subject to payment of a large fee for each extension sought (see Note 2 on PF 50/77). A single form may be used for expiry of a number of different time periods provided that these co-expire, but only one extension of each period is permitted under rule 110(3). However, PF 50/77 must be filed before the end of the extended period (*Konishiroku's Application*, SRIS O/16/83). While PF 50/77 can be filed during the one month extension period, if it is not then filed the application is deemed to have been withdrawn at the end of the normal extended period (*P's Application*, [1983] RPC 269), though now with the possibility of further extension under rule 110(3A)–(3C), see para. 123.33 *infra*. Note that, because extension under rule 110(3) is obtainable as of right, there is no question of the imposition of any third party rights (for which see para. 123.23 *supra*) as a condition for permitting extension as there is with extensions granted by the exercise of discretion, as in all other cases, as discussed *infra*.

An interesting situation arises where PF 50/77 is timely filed together with the form required by a rule specified in rule 110(3), but the fee only paid on this latter form. The filing of PF 50/77 would appear itself to provide the extension, and extra time for paying the missing fee on the PF 50/77 could then be allowed by discretion under rule 110(1) on the basis that rule 3 of the Patents (Fees) Rules 1986 (reprinted at para. 123.05 *supra*), under which fees are now prescribed and which requires that a form be accompanied by the specified fee, is not listed in either of sub-rules 110(2) or (3). A similar position may arise when any form, other than one filed under rule specified in either of sub-rules 110(2) or (3), is filed but the fee omitted thereon.

123.33 *—Further discretionary extension of the time periods covered by rule 110(3) (r. 110(3A)–(3C))*

Until rule 110(3A)–110(3C) was introduced in 1987, the limitations of rule 110(3) in restricting extension to only one month caused great hardship and led to many efforts to invoke rule 100 to save an application from being deemed withdrawn, or a patent from being deemed to have lapsed, and particularly in the presentation of ingenious arguments to contend that what is now rule 100(2) could be invoked, for which see para. 123.34 *infra*. However, rule 110(3A)–110(3C) greatly alleviates the hardship situations, with the consequence that little need should now exist to seek an extension under rule 100(2), but see para. 123.34 *infra*.

Rule 110(3A) grants the Comptroller full discretion to extend the time periods under the rules listed in rule 110(3) (for which see para. 123.33 *supra*), though subject to such terms as he may choose to direct, and whether or not that time period has already expired. The legality of a provision permitting extension even though the application or patent has apparently ceased to exist has now been removed by new subsection (3A) (for which see para. 123.36 *infra*).

Application for an extension under rule 110(3A)) is made on PF 52/77 (reprinted at para. 141.52). This carries a heavy fee and is required to be accompanied by a statement setting out *fully* the reasons for requesting the extension. There is no need to file PF 50/77 as well, unless there is a desire to reduce the period of third party rights which can be expected to accompany an extension granted under rule 110(3C) unless the application is as yet unpublished. If both PF 50/77 and PF 52/77 are filed, an offer of a refund of the fee on the former can be expected.

In practice, the statement accompanying PF 52/77 is required to be supported by evidence (in the form of a statutory declaration or affidavit) attesting to the reason(s) why the particular time limit in question was not met. It is thought that this evidence should squarely (and of course honestly) address two issues: *viz.* that the time limit was not met because of inadvertence; and that there was no undue delay in seeking the requested extension after the failure to meet that time limit had come to light. In particular, the Comptroller will be looking for any evidence that the extension is being sought because of a change of mind of the applicant or his agent, as in *P's Application* ([1983] RPC 269): extension would then be likely to be refused, as presumably it would if undue delay in seeking it had occurred.

However, it is understood that, since the rule was introduced, almost all applications made thereunder have succeeded. Certainly, no cases of refusal of extension under rule 100(3A) have been reported. This indicates that the Comptroller is not exercising his discretion under the rule (for which see para. 123.22 *supra*) in a restrictive manner. Nevertheless, it seems doubtful whether a missed priority date could be retrieved under rule 110(3A), not only because such action would probably be contrary to the Paris International Convention, but also because at the relevant time there would have been no application in existence under the Act to which rule 110(3A) could be applied.

After rule 110(3A) was introduced, the Patent Office started to send out warning letters when time periods are about to expire, or have just expired. These include a request that any desired restorative action be taken promptly, *e.g.* within the one month period allowed for extension under rule 110(3), or within a week or so thereafter, If, thereafter, restorative action is not promptly requested, it will obviously be more difficult to obtain a discretionary extension under rule 110(3A).

Rule 110(3B) permits a single request to be made under rule 110(3A) for multiple extensions on the same application/patent, provided that time periods in issue co-expire.

If the Comptroller allows extension after an application under rule 110(3A), then the extension is only obtained upon the filing of PF 53/77 (reprinted at para. 141.53) with which a further heavy fee is required. However, the availability of extensions at a price is more advantageous to an agent who has suffered from human error, than the alternative of facing the prospect of heavy damages in an action for professional negligence, as was the position prior to the introduction of rule 110(3C) in 1987.

Needless to say, PF 53/77 should be filed promptly, and of course within any time period set in the communication advising that the requested extension(s) is/are allowable, but any such period would appear to be extensible under the general discretionary provision of rule 110(1) (discussed in para. 123.35 *infra*) because rule 110(3C) is not itself listed in rule 110(3).

It is customary for the Comptroller to make the grant of restorative relief under rule 110(3C) conditional in all cases, other than those involving unpublished applications, on the imposition of conditions giving rise to third party rights similar to those imposed, now to be under section 28A, upon patent restoration being allowed under section 28, for which see paras. 28A.04–28.06. Similar conditions are imposed when rule 100 is invoked, for which see para. 123.22 *supra*.

—Extension because of error, default or omission in the Patent Office (r. 100(2))   **123.34**

As previously noted in para. 123.20 *supra*, there is also the possibility of obtaining a discretionary extension (and without fee) under rule 100(2), though only when it is proved that the need for the extension was due to an "irregularity of procedure" (for which see para. 123.21), and when that irregularity has occurred due to an "error, default or omission in the Patent Office", and when the time period in question has already elapsed. Between 1978 and 1987 many decisions were given indicating that an applicant has a heavy onus to discharge if he is to be successful on this ground. However, these cases are not reviewed herein because it is felt that there will now be little, or no, need to seek to rely on rule 100(2) to obtain restorative relief because such can now much more easily be obtained under rule 100(3A), as discussed in para. 123.33 *supra*.

Nevertheless the possibility remains and could perhaps be sought, in parallel with a precautionary application under rule 110(3A), when there is clear evidence of some failure by the Patent Office, with a view to obtaining restorative relief without the payment of the heavy fees required by the filing of PF 52/77 and 53/77: presumably, if successful, such application under rule 100(2) would then lead to refund of the fee paid on PF 52/77 in the recommended parallel application. Examples of failures which in the past have occurred in the Patent Office are indicated in para. 123.21 *supra*.

Rule 100(2) may also need to be invoked in a situation where rule 110(3A) does not apply because the missed time limit is not one under a rule listed in rule 110(3), and where extension under the general discretionary provision of rule 110(1) (for which see para. 123.35 *infra*) is not available because that rule cannot be used to vary a time limit which is stipulated in the Act, rather than the Rules, see *ITT's Application* ([1984] RPC 23).

—Discretionary extension without fee (r. 110(1))   **123.35**

Extension of prescribed periods (other than those of r. 110(2) and (3)) is permitted under rule 110(1), but only at the absolute discretion of the Comptroller. This may be exercised at any time. A reported example is *Brockhouse's Patent* ([1985]

RPC 332) where extension was granted under rule 14(3) on the basis that this rule is not mentioned in either rule 110(2) or (3). However, rule 110(1) cannot be used to extend the one-month extension permitted by rule 110(3) (*Nippon Gaishi's Application*, [1983] RPC 388). Also, rule 110(1) provides no discretion to vary a time limit which is stipulated by the Act, rather than by the Rules (*ITT's Application*, [1984] RPC 23), so that in such an instance recourse may have to be had to rule 100(2) discussed in para. 123.34 *supra*. This is because rule 110(3A) is also then not applicable, this being limited to the time periods set under the rules listed in rule 110(3), see para. 123.34 *supra*.

Under the 1949 Act and the corresponding rule 154 [1968], the time for paying the fee for a convention application, which had been inadvertently omitted from the papers and was filed after expiry of the Convention year, was extended in an exceptional case (*A's Application*, [1974] RPC 663). Section 15(1)(*d*) [1977] may not wholly exclude this possibility, particularly because the Fees Rules are not mentioned elsewhere in rule 110, see para. 123.24 *supra*.

A further instance where rule 110(1) is applied is where a sole applicant has died. Discretionary extensions of periods not covered by rule 110(2) or (3) are then allowed until after probate has been granted or letters of administration issued.

A request for time extension under rule 110(1) should be made as soon as the need therefor is seen and while time still remains for taking the necessary action. The request should be supported by full reasons why discretion should be exercised in the applicant's favour and it should not be presumed that the extension will be granted. The request is made by letter and no fee is required. It may be noted that a request for an extension of time for the term set for response to an official letter issued during substantive examination under section 18(3) does not fall within rule 110(1) as this is not a time limit set by the Act or Rules. It is thought that the same principles apply to the exercise of discretion under rule 110(1) as have been applied under section 18(3), for which see para. 18.15.

123.36   *—Extension after lapsing (subs. (3A))*

Subsection (3A) was inserted by the 1988 Act and became effective on the Royal Assent thereto on November 15, 1988 (s. 305(1) [1988]), but no transitional provision was made. The subsection formally permits the Comptroller (subject to the Patent Rules) to extend any period of time specified in the Act or Rules notwithstanding that such period may already have expired, and hence the application or patent has apparently become void. The subsection is expressed in declaratory form, but this still leaves open the question whether a period which expired before the commencement of the subsection could validly be extended under the provision, or whether any extension granted before that commencement in respect of an already expired period was one granted *ultra vires*, thereby rendering void any patent granted thereafter, as noted in para. 34.02.

Previously it had been held that the Comptroller had no authority over an application or patent once it had gone void (*T's Application*, [1982] FSR 172 (CA)), but nevertheless an extension in respect of an application that was apparently already deemed to be withdrawn was subsequently permitted in *Daido Kogyo's Patent* ([1984] RPC 97). These cases may, therefore, still be relevant in respect of events which occurred prior to commencement of subsection (3A).

123.37   *—Calculation of time limits*

The Patents Rules do not contain any rule indicating how time limits are to be computed, other than in the specific circumstances set out in rule 111 (discussed in paras. 123.38 and 123.39 *infra*). Therefore, in cases of doubt the Rules of the Supreme Court are likely to be followed.

These are set out in RSC Ord. 3, rules 1, 2 and 4 (reprinted in Appendix E at paras. E003.1, E003.2 and E003.4 respectively). Under these rules: a "month" means a calendar month, unless the context otherwise requires (r. 1); the period for an act which is required to be done "within a specified period *after or from* a specified date" begins immediately after that date (r. 2(2)), so that the specified date itself does not count; but a period for an act which is required to be done within a specified period *before* a specified date ends immediately before that date (r. 2(3)), so that the specified date then does count; and, for an act which is required to be done a specified number of *clear* days *before or after* a specified date, at least that number of days must intervene between that date and the day when the act is done (r. 2(4)). In all these cases, but only when the period in question is seven days or less, an act due on a Saturday, Sunday, bank holiday (as defined in Banking and Financial Dealings Act 1971 (c. 80, s. 1), Christmas Day or Good Friday, may be done on the next non-excluded day (r. 2(5)): compare rule 99(1) (reprinted in para. 120.03 and discussed in para. 120.05). However, where documents have to be filed at an office of the Supreme Court on a day when the office is closed (which includes all Sundays), these may be filed on the day when the office is next open (RSC Ord. 3, r. 4). For filing notices of appeal from decisions of the Comptroller, note that during a court vacation the court office may close early, see para. 97.12. For the calculation of time limits under the EPC and PCT, see respectively EPCr. 83 and PTCr. 80, each discussed in *EPH*.

When a time limit is to be calculated from a "declared priority date", this date is to be determined according to the definition thereof in rule 2 (reprinted in para. 123.04 *supra*). In this rule: sub-paragraph (*a*) normally applies; sub-paragraph (*b*) is now spent; sub-paragraph (*c*) relates to applications for a European patent (UK) converted under section 81; and sub-paragraph (*d*) relates to international applications (UK) converted under section 89, but it has been held that rule 2(*d*) only applies where priority is lost under the provisions of the PCT, *e.g.* under PCTr. 4.10(*e*).

Rule 110(4) allows the Comptroller to set a time limit for filing evidence by one party to proceedings where the other party notifies the Comptroller that its evidence is complete or no evidence will be filed.

—Automatic extensions of time (r. 111)   **123.38**

Rule 111 (in the form effective from August 1, 1989, see *Note* to para. 123.11 *supra*) provides automatic extensions of time where there is a certified general or subsequent dislocation in the postal services of the United Kingdom, or (since August 1, 1989) an interruption in the normal operation of the Patent Office (r. 111(1), (2), (4) and (5), discussed in para. 123.39 *infra*); and (by r. 111(3) and (4)) where the year for claiming priority under section 5(2) (either under the Paris International Convention or from an earlier application filed under the Act) expires on a *dies non* under section 120, for which see rule 99 (reprinted at para. 120.03 and discussed in para. 120.05), or on a day of certified disruption under rule 111(1). In each case the time period in question is automatically extended to the *first* day after the end of the postal dislocation or the excluded days, as the case may be, though rule 111(3) uses the word "altered" rather than "extended", presumably in deference to Article 4C(3) of the Paris Convention which uses "extended" only in relation to days when a patent office is not open.

Rule 111(6) was new in 1989 and provides for discretionary extension or alteration of any of the periods designated in rule 111(1) and (3) when the Comptroller is satisfied in any particular case that a failure to give, make or file any notice, application or other document within the normal specified period "was wholly or mainly attributable to a failure or undue delay in the postal services in the United Kingdom", but "upon such notice to other parties and upon such terms as he may direct". This discretionary extension is also discussed in para. 123.39 *infra*, but note that rule 111(6) refers to postal services "in" (and not "of") the United Kingdom, as in r. 111(1).

Rule 111 does not apply to "existing patents" (r. 124(1) [1968], reprinted in para. 127.04) and, though r. 154 [1968] (reprinted at para. A116) continues to apply thereto (r. 124(1)(*a*) [1978]), the exclusion from that rule of certain time limits could cause problems, because rule 110 also does not apply to existing patents (r. 124(1)(*d*) [1978]).

123.39   *—Extensions arising from postal dislocation or interruption in Patent Office operations (r. 111(1), (2) and (4)–(6))*

Rule 111(1) is a rule which experience has shown to be increasingly necessary. It now allows the Comptroller to make provisions where postal services are interrupted by what is certified by him as being a general interruption or subsequent dislocation, but the rule applies to interruptions in the postal service of, and not necessarily in, the United Kingdom. However, rule 111 has been held to apply only to postal delays occurring *within* the United Kingdom (*Koehring's Application*, SRIS O/91/86). Here it was stated that the rule protects an applicant from the effects of delays incurred in the United Kingdom on documents posted outside of the United Kingdom "just as rule 97 protects United Kingdom residents from the effects of delays incurred within the United Kingdom in relation to documents posted therein". This seems to suggest that there is no need to apply rule 111 if it is possible to apply rule 97. This rule (reprinted at para. 119.02) provides that documents sent by post are deemed to have been received at the time when the document would have been received in the ordinary course of post, see para. 119.04.

Rule 111(1) now also provides for an extension of time periods likewise to be certified when "an event or circumstance" causes an interruption "in the normal operations of the Patent Office". While clearly intended to provide for the possibility of industrial action within the Patent Office, the provision can also be applied when the event or circumstances are external to the Patent Office, for example dislocation of transport services due to weather conditions.

Rule 111(4) combines rule 110(1) and (3) further to extend the priority period under section 5(2) to the next available day after taking into account the days excluded under section 120 or rule 111(1), and rule 111(5) likewise extends the six months' grace period under section 2(4).

While an interruption or subsequent dislocation of postal services of the United Kingdom must be certified by the Comptroller before rule 111(1), (4) or (5) can have effect, it appears that such a certificate can be issued retroactively and, if the Comptroller refuses so to do, by the court on appeal to it under section 97(1), see *Omron Tateisi's Application* ([1981] RPC 125). The certificate must be posted in the Patent Office (r. 111(2)), and presumably it will also be published, in due course, in the O.J.

Rule 111(1) cannot be used to give additional time to an individual whose problem is of a purely personal kind. It is concerned only with exceptional circumstances where there has been a *general* interruption or subsequent dislocaton in the postal service over and above the provisions for excluded days (r. 99) which might bring about such an interruption, see *Armaturjonsson's Application* ([1985] RPC 213). Here mail was delayed over the Christmas holiday period, but this did not amount to a "dislocation" in the postal service. The Post Office was then misinformed as to the day when the agent's office would re-open after the holiday period with the consequence that delivery was further delayed, but the Comptroller and the court each held that this did not amount to a "subsequent" dislocation in the post enabling the convention priority date to be saved. However, the harshness of this situation is now alleviated by rule 111(6) which (since August 1989) has provided scope for individual extensions of time by exercise of the Comptroller's discretion, when the Comptroller is satisfied that failure timely to lodge a document in the Patent Office is attributable (at least to a major extent) to a failure or undue delay in the postal service *within the United Kingdom*.

The onus of proof will be on the applicant and proof of timely posting can be expected to be required. If an extension is granted under rule 111(6) (as distinct from a general extension arising under the other sub-rules of r. 111), the Comptroller can require notification of the extension to other parties (presumably including insertion of a notice in the O.J.). He can also make the extension subject to terms, for example by granting third parties certain rights, such as those that arise under section 28A when a patent is restored, for which see paras. 28A.04–28A.06. Previously, it had been held that rule 111 (in its former form) could not be invoked in respect of an isolated instance of failure to deliver a letter, see *Tiszai Vegyi's Application* (SRIS O/109/87) where again the end of the Christmas period was involved, but presumably this (and the *Armaturjonsson* case (*supra*) would now be differently decided under new rule 111(6).

General interruptions in the postal service were certified to have occurred: from June 28 to August 18, 1979 (O.J. August 15, 1979); from July 11 to August 17, 1984 (O.J. September 19, 1984); from November 15 to December 5, 1985 (O.J. January 22, 1986); from January 12 to 17, 1987 (O.J. February 11, 1987); from June 25 to July 17, 1987 (O.J. July 21, 1987); from July 21 to August 5, 1987 (O.J. August 12, 1987); from October 16 to 22, 1987 (O.J. November 4, 1987); and from August 31 to October 17, 1988 (O.J. November 2, 1988).

The EPO has held that the provisions of EPCr. 85(2), which are analogous to those of rule 111(1), may be invoked whenever a general interruption in the postal service has been certified and that it is not necessary for the applicant to show that his non-observance of the set time limit was due to that disruption (*EPO Decision T 192/84*, "*Interruption in delivery of mail/DAIKIN KOGYO*," OJEPO 2/1985, 39). A similar conclusion would seem to be possible under rule 111(1).

Naming of inventor (subs. (2)(i))   **123.40**

Subsection (2)(*i*) provides for rules to be made to give an inventor the right to be named in an application. Such right is inherent in the procedure of section 13 and rules 14 and 15 and is discussed in para. 13.04. The right to be named was previously given by section 16 [1949] and this section (discussed in paras. A016.3 and A016.4) remains alive for the removal of a named inventor from an "existing patent". The difficulties arising from the meaning of "invention" are discussed in para. 1.06. The concomitant difficulty with "inventor" is discussed in para. 7.07.

Translations (subs. (2)(j) and r. 113)   **123.41**

Subsection (2)(*j*) is the authority for rule 113 (reprinted at para. 123.12, in which see the *Note* as to likely effective amendment). Continuing rule 44(2) [1968] (reprinted in para. A033.07) provides for translation of foreign language documents supplied to the Comptroller in proceedings under the 1949 Act.

Any document which is sent to the Patent Office which is not in English must be "accompanied" by an English translation, which must be "verified" (r. 113(1)); and be supplied in the same number of copies as the document translated (r. 113(2)). Verification and the form of the translation are discussed in para. 123.42 *infra*.

The word "accompanied" in rule 113(1) can be regarded as defining an infinitely short period of time which may perhaps be extended under rule 110(1) (*Rohde and Schwarz's Application*, [1980] RPC 155). While discretion with respect to rule 113(1) was not exercised in that case, the decision of the hearing officer does contain the more general statement that "the Comptroller must allow a period of time to put the description into conformity with rule 20(1) [as it now is]".

Rule 113(1) now stipulates that, if the foreign language document is, or forms part of, an application for a patent, the Patent Office shall not, in the absence of the translation required by rule 113(1), take any further action in relation to that document, unless the Comptroller otherwise directs.

Rule 113(1) does not apply to the provision of translations of priority documents for which separate periods are set by rule 6(6) (reprinted in para. 5.02), *viz.*: 21 months from priority date (or 31 months therefrom in the case of an international application (UK) for which an international preliminary examination has been requested), and by rules 80–82 (reprinted in paras. 81.02–81.04), *viz.*: two months from the date of notification of, or request for, conversion of a European or international application (UK), see paras. 5.21 (and 89A.27) and 81.12 respectively. Nor does it apply to the supply of the required verification of the translation of an international application under rule 85(2A)(*c*), for which see para. 89A.15. However, when a new application is filed under sections 8(3), 12(6), 15(4) or 37(4), the translated priority document, if this is required at all, must be filed with the new application or within an extension period already allowed, see rule 26(2) and (3) reprinted in para. 15.05 and discussed in para. 15.21.

Rule 113(3) does not now require automatic submission of translations of foreign language documents cited in a European or international search report and filed at the Patent Office, but allows the Comptroller to call for translations of such documents, or parts thereof, as he thinks appropriate, setting a two month term for compliance. This term is extensible under rule 110(1).

Since September 1, 1987, when section 77(6) came into effect, it has been necessary to file translations of European patents (UK) under rule 79A (reprinted at para. 77.03) within three months from the date of publication of the mention of the grant thereof in the European Patent Bulletin (r. 79B, reprinted at para. 77.04), see paras. 77.12 and 77.16. Such translation must be verified (r. 79E, reprinted at para. 77.05). Unless such a translation has been supplied, rule 113(4) requires that a person instituting proceedings before the Comptroller in relation to such a patent must furnish a verified translation thereof. Note that (for European Patents (UK) granted before September 1, 1987), if such proceedings are commenced by a person other than the patentee, for example by an applicant for revocation of the patent, that person has the duty of supplying the translation under rule 113(4) and not the patentee. If such European patent (UK) is to be amended in the course of those proceedings (which proceedings could be one solely for amendment under section 27), a verified translation of the amendment must then be furnished (r. 113(5)).

Rule 113(6) gives the Comptroller power to reject a translation which is in his opinion inaccurate and to demand an improved translation.

For amendment of a European patent (UK) not in the English language, see para. 27.15. For the correction of translations initially filed under section 77(6) and rule 79A, see section 80(3) and rule 79D (reprinted at para. 80.02) as discussed in paras. 80.06, 80.09 and 80.10. For the legal effect in proceedings before the court of a translation filed under section 77(6) or rule 113(4), see para. 77.13.

—Verification of translations and form thereof   **123.42**

A notice in the O.J. (March 18, 1981) drew attention to rule 113(1) and pointed out that all documents sent to the United Kingdom Patent Office in a language other than English should be accompanied by a *verified* translation into English. The notice states: "The requirement for translations to bear a verification is of general application even though it may not be expressly provided in all the references to translations contained in the Act and Rules".
A suitable form of verification is given in the *PCT Applicants' Guide* (*Annex GB-IV*). It reads:
> "re Patent Application. . . . I, [name and address of translator], hereby declare that I am the translator of the documents attached and certify that the following is a true translation to the best of my knowledge and belief.
> Signature of translator . . . . . . Dated this . . . day of. . . . "

The form of verification previously acceptable under rule 15(2) [1968], when signed and dated by the translator, read:
> I, [name and address of translator], hereby certify that to the best of my knowledge and belief the following is a true translation made by me (or *compared by me*) and for which I accept responsibility of the documents attached (or *listed*) (O.J. April 11, 1973; (1973–74) 3 CIPA 6).

This form would appear still to be applicable under the 1977 Act because rule 113(1) is in less strict terms than rule 15(2) [1968].
The Patent Office has stated (see (1975–76) 5 CIPA 380) that, in the case of convention documents from France where introductory pages contain mainly formal data, the only information which need be translated is the title(s) and any special remarks supplementing the usual standard information. In such cases the translator should add below his certification:
> Translator's note—The only matter requiring translation on the standard introductory pages is the title:
> "Improved . . . . "

A similar practice may also be used in the case of a convention document from Belgium drawn in standard form and in the French language (see (1976–77) 6 CIPA 189).

Register of patent agents (subs. (2)(k) [repealed]   **123.43**

Subsection (2)(*k*) provided for rules concerning the maintenance of the Register of Patent Agents. The subsection was prospectively repealed by the 1988 Act (Sched. 8) to be replaced by section 275 [1988], reprinted at para. 102.05. The Register of Patent Agents, and rules made in relation thereto are discussed in paras. 102.26–102.30. For the Register of Patent Agents Rules, now made under section 275 [1988], see Appendix F.

Publications by Patent Office (subs. (2)(l))   **123.44**

Subsection (2)(*l*) is the authority for rule 114 (reprinted at para. 123.13). It applies also to matters continuing to arise under the 1949 Act (r. 124(1)(*d*) [1978] reprinted in para. 124.04). The historical evolution of this rule was discussed by R. M. C. Arnot ((1978–79) 8 CIPA 287) where he deplored the removal of the reference to the provision of indexes, previously present in the statute itself (s. 94(1)(*d*) [1949]), into a rule from which it could readily be deleted.
Patent Office publications are available from the Sales Branch, The Patent Office, Orpington, Kent BR5 3RD. Holders of deposit accounts may now make

purchases by telephone orders to the Sales Branch, Orpington (0689) 32111, extn. 309 (O.J. January 22, 1986).

The Science Reference and Information Service has published a comprehensive pamphlet, "Industrial property publications in SRIS" (ISSN 0306–4301, January 1985) describing the official publications held by SRIS for patents, designs, trade marks and plant breeders rights for the United Kingdom and the patent publications arising from the EPC and PCT, together with the various unofficial indexes maintained by the SRIS from information taken from these patent publications.

123.45   *—Specifications and abstracts*

Specifications are published in two series, the specification as filed published under section 16 which is given a 2 million series number with the suffix "A" (the "A-specification"), and the specification of the granted patent under the same number with the suffix "B" (the "B-specification"). Although both forms of specification were initially printed in letterpress, neither form is now typeset but is reproduced directly from the typed specification provided by the applicant: hence the rigid requirement of rule 20 discussed in para. 14.35.

The front page of both publications carries bibliographic data identified by the international INID code numbers. These are explained in a booklet obtainable from the Patent Office Classification Section and the SRIS, and have been published in OJEPO 10/88, 395 and explained in O.J. April 27, 1988 at p. 983. For specifications filed under the present Act, the suffix -A is used to designate a patent application which has been searched but not examined; the suffix -B designates a granted patent; and -C designates a patent specification which has been amended after grant. For patents granted under the 1949 Act, the suffix -A designates a specification which has been searched, examined and accepted (but is only used in Patent Office subject matter file lists) and the suffix -B has been used to designate a specification which has been amended after grant, but only on reprinted specifications issued from March 1976, see O.J. April 26, 1989.

The front page of the "A-specification" also carries the abstract with an associated drawing and these pages are available separately as "Abstracts". The weekly batches of "A-specifications" are arranged according to the divisions of the classification scheme before the seven figure number is allotted.

123.46   *—Indexes*

Details of applications are printed on individual cards which are filed alphabetically by name of applicant in annual sequence and made available in the SRIS. This information is usually available before the corresponding entry in the O.J.

For the "A-Specifications" the index available in the SRIS is in the form of a computer print-out which is up-dated weekly.

An annual name index to printed "A-specifications" for past years is published by the Patent Office and is available in the SRIS. However, this does not include the "B-specifications" for which there is no present index. Also, the 1979 name index is defective in not giving any index entry in respect of second and subsequent joint inventors ((1980–81) 10 CIPA 520). The same defect occurred in the weekly indexes for 1981, but the 1981 defect was corrected when the consolidated index was published. The indexing rules used by the Patent Office for the compilation of these name indexes, together with particulars of the abbreviations used for various corporate entities and the anglicised versions used for Slavic organisations, are periodically explained (*e.g.* in O.J. July 26, 1989). For further details of publications of the Patent Office, see para. 123.47 *infra*.

A card index of pre-grant assignments is available in the SRIS. This, like other indexes referred to above, is made up of material provided by the Patent Office and merely recorded or filed in order by the SRIS. The SRIS also compiles various registers of the progress of United Kingdom, European and PCT applications based on the information published in the relevant journals (*i.e.* the O.J., EPB and International Gazette), but these registers, while most useful as a readily available tool, have no official status.

The Journal (subs. (6)) **123.47**

Subsection (6) defines "the Journal" for the purpose of section 130(1) and is the authority for rule 115 (reprinted at para. 123.14). These provisions apply also to matters continuing to arise under the 1949 Act (r. 124(1)(*d*) [1978], reprinted at para. 127.04). The journal is published as "The Official Journal (Patents)" or "O.J.(P)" (herein termed the "O.J."). The previous requirement that the Comptroller also publish in the O.J. rules made under the Registered Designs Act 1949 (12, 13 and 14 Geo. 6, c. 88), contained in section 37(1) thereof (as amended by Schedule 5, para. 3 [1977]) was removed in the amendment of that section by Schedule 3, para. 27 [1988].

The Journal normally appears each Wednesday and contains details of proceedings under both the 1949 and 1977 Acts. Apart from an alphabetical index of new applications and information on publication under section 16, which is given fully and with indexes, much of the other information is in the form of lists of patent or application numbers in respect of which some event has occurred. The extent of information provided in the O.J., as regards various proceedings before the Comptroller, was expanded during 1988 beyond that which the Comptroller is *required* to publish, see para. 123.27; and, from May 11, 1988 (though not previously), the O.J. has contained bibliographic details of granted patents, *i.e.* of the "B-specifications", in numerical order together with details of inventors, priorities claimed, etc., but the title is restricted to 158 characters, see also para. 24.10. The O.J. also contains numerical lists of European patents (UK) that have been granted, and of translations of European patents (UK) and applications therefor filed respectively under sections 77(6) and 78(7). The Journal further: provides details of the classification of patent specifications; advertises the commercial services available from the Patent Office; and provides details of the libraries in the United Kingdom which maintain collections of United Kingdom patent specifications.

Patent law reports (subs. (7)) **123.48**

Subsection (7) is the authority for rule 116 (reprinted at para. 123.15) and provides for the official publication of reports of patent and other cases (the "RPC"), including those arising under the 1949 Act (r. 124(1)(*d*) [1978], reprinted at para. 127.04). Subsection (7) was amended by Schedule 7, para. 22 [1988] and now provides for reports of cases on patents (whether or not granted under the Act) and of cases on copyrights, trade marks, service marks, registered designs and design rights in the United Kingdom and elsewhere. The Comptroller can require publication of such cases as he considers "generally useful or important", but in practice the selection of cases from the court is made by the editor who is appointed from among the practising members of the patent bar.

The RPC commenced publication in 1883 with Vol. 1 and its volumes were numbered annually up to Vol. 72 (1955). Thereafter, the volumes have been designated solely by their year of publication. The RPC appears irregularly in about 25 issues per year together with an annual Digest which, until 1985, contained classified abridgements of the cases reported in the volume for that year. This Digest continues to include various lists of cases and statutes cited in those cases. A consolidated Digest of Volumes 1–71 (1883–1955) was issued in three volumes, which has now been independently reprinted. Copies of each individual issue of the RPC are kept in print and are available for purchase from the Patent Office Sales Branch. The RPC is rare among United Kingdom law reports as being sanctioned by statute and published thereunder, unlike most other law reports whch are organised privately.

The Fleet Street Law Reports ("FSR") is a privately produced series of law reports which has been published since 1963. It presently has the same editor as the RPC, but aims to produce its reports more quickly, though with a less authoritative headnote, and to publish in addition cases of lesser or more transient importance than those generally reported in RPC as well as including cases arising under EEC law.

Decisions of the European Commission and of the European Court of Justice ("ECJ") in Luxembourg are reported in Common Market Law Reports ("CMLR"), but the authentic reports of cases decided by the ECJ are contained in the European Court Reports ("ECR").

Decisions of the EPO and its Appeal Boards are published in the OJEPO and in a private series of law reports, European Patent Office Reports ("EPOR"). These decisions are not now reported in the RPC or FSR.

Copies of transcripts of decisions of the High Court, Court of Appeal and House of Lords in proceedings relating to intellectual property should be sent automatically to the Science Reference and Information Service ("SRIS"), see (1983–84) 13 CIPA 411 and (1985–86) 15 CIPA 155. Here they are numbered, and the names of the parties indexed, in a "C/–/–" series. Copies of decisions in the Patent Office are also supplied to the SRIS and filed in a separate "O/–/–" series and indexed accordingly. The transcripts are eventually bound into yearly volumes. Photocopies of Patent Office decisions contained in this collection can be obtained from the SRIS, but for six years after judgment transcripts of court decisions can only be obtained by application to the firm of shorthand writers responsible for providing the transcript. To obtain these, the date of the judgment and the name of the judge should be identified, as well as the names of the parties. It should, however, be noted that the cost of obtaining such copies is quite high as the shorthand writers base their charges on transcription, rather than copying, cost. All the court transcripts on intellectual property cases are also placed on the "LEXIS" data base of law reports where they will be found in its "UKIP" library. This can be accessed at a computer terminal by subscribers to this service.

124.01   **SECTION 124**

Rules, regulations and orders; supplementary

124.—(1) Any power conferred on the Secretary of State by this Act to make rules, regulations or orders shall be exercisable by statutory instrument.

(2) Any Order in Council and any statutory instrument containing an order, rules or regulations under this Act, other than an order or rule required to be laid before Parliament in draft or an order under section 132(5) below, shall be subject to annulment in pursuance of a resolution of either House of Parliament.

(3) Any Order in Council or order under any provision of this Act may be varied or revoked by a subsequent order.

Commentary on Section 124

General **124.02**

Under the Interpretation Act 1978 (c. 30, Sched. 1), "Secretary of State" means any one of Her Majesty's Principal Secretaries of State. In relation to the operation of the patent statutes, the powers of the "Secretary of State" are normally exercised by the Secretary of State for Trade and Industry.

Rule-making powers **124.03**

General rule-making powers are conferred by section 123 and are discussed in the commentary thereon. Powers to make specific rules are also contained in: section 25(5) (*notice of overdue renewal*); section 32(3) (*entries in the register*); sections 92(3) and (4) (*evidence for use under the EPC*); section 120(1) (*hours of business*); prospectively in section 125A (*availability of samples of micro-organisms*); and section 130(2) (*statement of international exhibition*). The rules made, or to be made, under these powers are discussed in the commentaries on these sections. There is an accepted convention that proposed changes in the Patents Rules are discussed, at least in principle, with the Chartered Institute and the Government's Standing Advisory Committee on Patents prior to their promulgation.

Variation of Act by executive order **124.04**

Powers to vary provisions of the Act by executive order are given by: section 1(5) (*non-inventions*); section 25(2) (*date of commencement of patent*), but subject to affirmative resolution of each House of Parliament; section 48(2) (*period before compulsory licence application*); section 77(9) (*translation of European patent*); section 78(8) (*translation of claims of European application*); and Schedule 1, para. 4A (*licences of right in respect of certain patents*). The only exercise of these powers to date has been the implementation of sections 77(9) and 78(8), see paras. 77.12 and 78.08 respectively. Section 86(2) and (3) (not yet in force) provides for the making of "regulations" for implementing the CPC. There are also provisions for Orders in Council in: section 54 (*foreign working of inventions*); section 59(3) and (4) (*declaration of period of emergency,* after affirmative resolution by each House of Parliament); and section 90 (*designation of convention countries*). For designations made under section 90, see para. 90.03. The Act itself can also be modified by Order in Council for its application to the Isle of Man (s. 132(2)) and has been so modified (as noted appropriately throughout this work) by S.I. 1978 No. 621 and S.I. 1989 Nos. 493 and 1292.

Annulment of amendments made by secondary legislation (subs. (2)) **124.05**

Subsection (2) provides that, unless otherwise stated, any Order in Council or statutory instrument made under the Act (or the 1949 Act by virtue of Sched. 2, para. 1(2)) is subject to negative resolution (*i.e.* a prayer for annulment) by either House of Parliament, but in the absence of any such resolution the Order or instrument comes into force automatically on the date specified therein. A prayer for annulment of an Order in Council or a statutory instrument can, however, only relate to the Order or instrument as a whole, so that Parliament cannot debate any specific variation thereof.

125.01   **SECTION 125**

Extent of invention

125.—(1) For the purposes of this Act an invention for a patent for which an application has been made or for which a patent has been granted shall, unless the context otherwise requires, be taken to be that specified in a claim of the specification of the application or patent, as the case may be, as interpreted by the description and any drawings contained in that specification, and the extent of the protection conferred by a patent or application for a patent shall be determined accordingly.

(2) It is hereby declared for the avoidance of doubt that where more than one invention is specified in any such claim, each invention may have a different priority date under section 5 above.

(3) The Protocol on the Interpretation of Article 69 of the European Patent Convention (which Article contains a provision corresponding to subsection (1) above) shall, as for the time being in force, apply for the purposes of subsection (1) above as it applies for the purposes of that Article.

RELEVANT PROVISION OF THE EUROPEAN PATENT CONVENTION

125.02   Article 69

Extent of protection

(1) The extent of the protection conferred by a European patent or a European patent application shall be determined by the terms of the claims. Nevertheless, the description and drawings shall be used to interpret the claims.

125.03   Protocol on the Interpretation of Article 69 of the Convention

Article 69 should not be interpreted in the sense that the extent of the protection conferred by a European patent is to be understood as that defined by the strict, literal meaning of the wording used in the claims, the description and drawings being employed only for the purpose of resolving an ambiguity found in the claims. Neither should it be interpreted in the sense that the claims serve only as a guideline and that the actual protection conferred may extend to what, from a consideration of the description and drawings by a person skilled in the art, the patentee has contemplated. On the contrary, it is to be interpreted as defining a position between these extremes which combines a fair protection for the patentee with a reasonable degree of certainty for third parties.

BOOK

125.04

"Patent claim drafting and interpretaton" (Ed. J. A. Kemp, Oyez Longman, 1983): Chapter 2A, "Claim drafting and significance: An Anglo-German industrial view" by J. L. Beton and K. J. Heimbach.

ARTICLES

125.05

B. C. Reid, "The Catnic decision: The construction of patent claims", [1981] EIPR 56;

T. A. Blanco White, "The Catnic case: The test of infringement of a patent", [1981] EIPR 90;

W. R. Cornish and M. Vitoria, "Catnic in the House of Lords: A new approach to infringement"; [1981] JBL 136;

M. Pendleton, "Catnic: Signpost to where?" [1982] EIPR 79;

A. M. Walton, "Purposive construction", [1984] EIPR 93;

B. C. Reid, "CATNIC: Further case notes", (1984–85) 14 CIPA 254;

P. Prescott, "*Improver Corp.* v. *Remington Consumer Products Ltd.*", [1989] EIPR 259.

COMMENTARY ON SECTION 125

General

125.06

Section 125 defines the extent, or scope, of protection provided under the Act by a patent or application therefor. Application of the section is therefore fundamental to: considerations of infringement (sections 60 and 69); validity in the light of prior art (sections 2 and 3); the according of priority (section 5); and permissible amendment (section 76). Unless a uniform interpretation is given to the extent of protection provided by a patent claim in these various circumstances, then serious difficulties arise. For instance, a claim could be found infringed on the basis of an act to be found described in the prior art. Clearly, this should not be so, absent some special statutory exception, and it is suggested that the following maxim be borne in mind: "What would infringe, if later, anticipates, if sooner". A similar theme has been developed by B. C. Reid in his article "The right to work" ([1983] EIPR 6).

However, the EPO has held that determination of the extent of protection is not a matter for the EPO (*EPO Decision T 175/84, "Combination claim/KABEL-METAL"*, OJEPO 3/1989, 71), though objections to clarity of claims can be raised in EPO opposition proceedings, though only as far as they can influence the decision in issues under EPCa. 100 (*EPO Decision T 127/85, "Blasting composition/IRECO"*, OJEPO 7/1989, 271; [1989] 6 EPOR 358). Nevertheless, such may create a file wrapper estoppel, see para. 125.18 *infra*.

The "extent of protection" is not defined in section 125 in terms of the claims of the patent, as was more or less the position under the former law, but is in terms of "an invention for a patent". Unless the context otherwise requires, this is to be taken to be that specified in the claims of the specification "as interpreted by the description and any drawings contained in that specification" (subs. (1)). However,

789

this provision is modified, to an extent which will only become clearer as jurisprudence develops, so as (by subs. (3)) specifically to conform to the Protocol to the interpretation of EPCa. 69 annexed to the EPC. EPCa. 69 and the Protocol are reprinted respectively, in paras. 125.02 and 125.03 *supra*.

By subsection (2) each invention covered by the patent may have a different priority date under section 5, even if these different inventions are contained within the same claim of the specification.

125.07   *The scope of protection under former patent statutes*

Under former patent statutes, the scope of protection provided by a patent was left to be determined by the Common Law based on the wording of the Letters Patent grant with its royal command that others "do not directly or indirectly make use of or put into practice the said invention, nor in anywise imitate the same". While this was generally construed to limit the extent of protection to the subject-matter defined by a literal interpretation of the claims of the patent (*EMI* v. *Lissen*, (1939) 56 RPC 23 (HL)), so that "What is not claimed, is disclaimed" (*Nobel* v. *Anderson*, (1895) 12 RPC 164 (HL)), there have been occurrences (albeit rare) when a claim has been held infringed when this would not have been so on a literal interpretation of the claim, invoking doctrines sometimes called "taking the pith and marrow of the invention" or using a chemical or mechanical "equivalent" of, or even disregarding, some (inessential) integer of the claim, see *Raleigh* v. *Miller* ((1948) 65 RPC 141 (HL)) and *Rotocrop* v. *Genbourne* ([1982] FSR 241), but these decisions can be seen as exceptions to the usual adherence to a strict rule of literal claim construction, see *Van der Lely* v. *Bamfords* ([1963] RPC 61 (HL) and *Rodi & Wienenberger* v. *Showell* ([1969] RPC 367 (HL)).

However, since the passing of the Act, the former ways of construing patent claims have been codified into what is probably a single, and apparently less restrictive, test of "purposive" construction, see para. 125.10.

125.08   *Meaning of "invention"*

Except where the context otherwise requires, section 125 defines what is meant by an "invention"; and, by section 130(1), "patented invention" means an invention for which a patent is granted. The applicability of section 125 to the definition of "invention" is discussed in para. 1.06. It appears that when an "invention" has not yet been defined by claims it can have any meaning which suits the context in which the word is used, and such meaning can be specific or general, tangible or conceptual, in circumstances where the "invention claimed" is not the meaning intended. For example, this is so when claims have not yet been drawn up (ss. 7(3)), 15(1), 22, 23, 39, 42(2) and 43(1), (2) and (3)), and also where references to the invention appear to be to its specific and tangible aspects (ss. 14(1)(*b*) and (3), 15(1)(*c*) and 72(1)(*c*)) as indicated in the disclosure in the specification, rather than general or conceptual ones indicated by the claims. Thus, in *Viziball's Application* ([1988] RPC 213) (in entitlement proceedings), "invention" was held to encompass anything devised by the inventor and to include both patentable and non-patentable discoveries. The term "invention" is, therefore, *not* synonymous with a "patentable invention": see further para. 1.06.

In contrast to these exceptions, subsection (1) states that (the context not requiring a different meaning) an invention for which an application has been made or a patent granted shall be taken to be that specified in a claim as interpreted by the description and any drawings. This appears to refer to the extent of the invention as a logical definition in the general sense and to be related to that of "the invention as claimed in any claim of the complete specification" found in the 1949 Act and is somewhat similar to the "alleged invention" of that Act. Examples of sections of the Act where this is plainly the meaning intended are: section 1 *Patentability*); section 2 (*Novelty*); section 3 (*Inventive step*); section 4 (*Industrial application*); sections 5 and 6 (*Priority*); sections 7–13 and 36–38 (*Inventorship and entitlement, though only when dealing with an invention which has been defined by one or more claims*); sections 14(5)(*d*) and (6), 17(6) and 26 (*Unity of invention*); section 18(5) (*Double patenting*); section 21 (*Observations by a third party*); sections 40–41 (*Compensation in respect of patented inventions*); sections 60, 69 and 100 (*Infringement*); sections 72 and 73 (*Revocation*); and section 130 (*Definitions of patented invention and patented product*).

It would appear that a claim which extends beyond what has been invented cannot be regarded as defining an "invention" at all within the meaning of section 1(2) as being a mere discovery unpatentable under section 1(2)(*a*), see *Genentech's Patent* ([1989] RPC 147 (CA)), discussed in paras. 1.08, 3.07 and 14.21.

A special rule of construction arises from the decision in *Adhesive Dry Mounting* v. *Trapp* ((1910) 27 RPC 341). This held that a claim for an article "suitable for use" in a specified method is a claim to an article *per se* whatever might be the purpose for which it is used. This decision has more recently been applied in *Furr* v. *Truline* ([1985] FSR 553). Nevertheless, special circumstances now appear to alter this rule of novelty (which presumably applies also to the question of infringement) when the specified method is one specifically precluded from patent protection under section 4(2), see *John Wyeth's and Schering's Applications* ([1985] RPC 545) discussed in para. 2.29. In both these applications claims directed to methods of making a medicament suitable for use in (novel) therapeutic treatments of the human body were held to possess novelty even though the medicaments as such were not novel.

A further special rule arises from section 100, the provisions of which have the effect of reversing the onus of proof for infringement of a claim to a process for making a *new* product, see paras. 100.02–100.05.

Application of section 125 to "existing patents"   **125.09**

It can be seen from Schedule 2, para. 1(2) that most of the sections listed above do not apply to "existing patents". However, section 36 (*Co-ownership*) and section 130 (*Definitions*) do apply thereto. More importantly, by Schedule 4, para. 3(2), sections 60–71 apply to "infringement" of "existing patents" and, while this should also make subsections (1) and (3) applicable thereto, this is not necessarily so because "patent", as used in the body of the Act, means only a patent granted under the Act (section 130(1)), unless Schedule 2 applies (Sched. 2, para. 2(2)(*d*)). For further discussion of Schedule 4, para. 3(2) and its varying applicability to "existing patents", see para. 136.05. However, while the applicability of section 125 to infringement of existing patents is obscure, the point may be of little significance because the way in which the extent of protection of an existing patent has been determined since 1978 would seem to be little different from that which appears to be the position under section 125.

In contrast, however, there seems no basis for the application of subsection (2) to "existing patents". It seems, therefore, that *Thornhill's Application* ([1962] RPC 199) will continue to apply thereto so that each claim of an existing patent can have but a single priority date, see para. A005.4.

Infringement test of "purposive construction"   **125.10**

The most authoritative decision in recent years on the extent of protection conferred under the former law is that involving the "purposive construction" test propounded by Lord Diplock in *Catnic v. Hill and Smith* ([1982] RPC 183 (HL)). Although this test was propounded under the former Common Law regime, it has been equated with that under the present Act, see *Improver Corp. v. Remington* ([1989] RPC 69 (CA)) holding that the effect of the Protocol to EPCa. 69 (discussed in para. 125.12 *infra*) is the same as the test of purposive construction set out in the *Catnic* case.

In the *Catnic* case, Lord Diplock declared that a patent specification should be given a "purposive", rather than a "purely literal", construction. He then stated that textual infringement and infringement of the "pith and marrow" of an invention are but a single matter to be decided in each case on the basis whether persons of relevant practical knowledge and experience would understand that strict compliance with a particular descriptive word or phrase was intended by the patentee to be an essential requirement of the invention so that *any* variant would fall outside the monopoly claimed, even though it could have no material effect upon the way the invention worked. Such question could only be answered in the negative when it would be apparent to a reader skilled in the art that such a descriptive word or phrase could not have been intended to exclude minor variants which would have no material effect upon the working of the invention. On the facts of the *Catnic* case no plausible reason had been advanced why the word "vertical" should be given a meaning so as to exclude a member not positioned at precisely 90 degrees to the horizontal yet close enough to make no material difference to its function. Accordingly infringement was found, the decision of the Court of Appeal reversed, and the decision at first instance restored, though the reasoning at first instance, which had denied textual infringement, but found infringement on the basis of the "pith and marrow" doctrine, was not approved. The case, its effect on earlier decisions, and the test of "purposive construction" are dealt with in the articles by B. C. Reid, T. A. Blanco White, W. R. Cornish and M. Vitoria, M. Pendleton and A. M. Walton, each listed in para. 125.05 *supra*.

Following the *Catnic* decision, the Court of Appeal (in *Codex v. Racal-Milgo*, [1983] RPC 369) stated:

"First, therefore, we must construe the specification and the claims in the present case purposively, through the eyes and minds of those skilled in the art and not by applying to them an over-meticulous verbal analysis . . . with the learning of a person skilled in the art, rather than with the meticulous verbal analysis of the lawyer alone."

In this case the Court of Appeal observed that the speech of Lord Diplock in *Catnic v. Hill and Smith* ([1982] RPC 183) is so authoritative that in future it would usually be unnecessary to take a court through the previous cases referred to in that speech. The previous finding of infringement was confirmed largely on the basis that the defendant's device produced the same result with the Court of Appeal giving a broad purposive construction to the means specified in the claim for attaining that result. Contemporaneously, a different Court of Appeal also applied the *Catnic* decision and allowed an appeal to make a finding of infringement by purposively construing a claim so that its features were considered functionally and therefore broadly (*Soc. Nouvelle des Bennes Saphem v. Edbro*, [1983] RPC 345), a decision applied in *Harrison v. Project & Design (No. 2)* ([1987] RPC 151 (CA)).

In *SKM v. Wagner-Spraytech (No. 2)* (SRIS C/22/84) the Court of Appeal restated the relevant principles for construction of a specification [of an existing patent] as:

1. The court must construe the specification and claims purposively and through the eyes and minds of those skilled in the art at the material time and not by applying an over-meticulous verbal analysis (*Codex v. Racal-Milgo, supra*; *Catnic v. Hill and Smith, supra*);
2. The function of claims is to define clearly and with precision the monopoly

claimed so that others may know the exact boundaries in which they will be trespassers (*EMI* v. *Lissen*, (1939) 56 RPC 23);

3. If claims have a plain meaning in themselves then advantage cannot be taken of the language used in the body of the specification to make their meaning something different (*EMI* v. *Lissen, supra*); and

4. If any part of the claim is ambiguous, then what is said in the body of the specification can be referred to to resolve the ambiguity (*British Hartford-Fairmount* v. *Jackson*, (1966) 49 RPC 495 at 556).

In the *SKM* case the Court of Appeal then allowed an appeal against a previous finding of infringement which had arisen from the term "nozzle" being given a broad meaning at first instance, which the Court of Appeal did not feel was justified. It is thought that this judgment gives an indication of some of the limitations which should be put on a wholly "purposive" construction of the claims: other such limitations are indicated in para. 125.13 *infra*.

The extent of protection under subsections (1) and (3)

—*General*   **125.11**

Subsection (1), taken with subsection (3), defines the "extent of protection" conferred by a patent or patent application and this definition was indicated in *Genentech's Patent* ([1989] RPC 147 (CA)) to supplant the former rule of construction laid down in *EMI* v. *Lissen* ((1939) 56 RPC 231 (HL)), see para. 125.07 *supra*.

The expression "extent of protection" is similar to that used in new section 76 by which an amendment after grant is not allowable if it "extends the protection conferred by the patent" (s. 76(3)). Section 125 makes no reference to validity and, accordingly, the definition of invention evidently includes an alleged invention, as noted in para. 125.08 *supra*. Consequently, the "extent of protection conferred" can be defined by an invalid claim. This is relevant to the operation of new section 76(3), see para. 76.16.

A difficulty arises in that neither section 125(1) nor EPCa. 69 takes into account contributory, or indirect, infringement under section 60(2). CPCa. 30 contains language similar to section 60(2), but CPCa. 29 refers to "the subject matter of a patent". It is therefore possible to conclude that the scope of the monopoly enjoyed by the proprietor is larger than the extent of protection conferred. On this point, see *Monsanto's Patent* (SRIS O/45/88) where a compulsory licence was refused for lack of jurisdiction in respect of acts which, unless authorised, would have constituted indirect infringement under section 60(2) by the licensee applicant.

The contents of the abstract may not be used to determine the scope of protection because this is not part of the description of the patent, see section 14(2)(*b*) and (1984–85) 14 CIPA 93).

—*Conformity of interpretation with EPC and CPC*   **125.12**

Section 125 is qualified by section 130(7) so that it has been framed to have, as nearly as practicable, the same effects in the United Kingdom as the corresponding provisions of the EPC, CPC and PCT. Judicial notice is also to be taken of the EPC, CPC, PCT and decisions and opinions of convention courts (s. 91). Hence, there is an obligation to construe section 125 in a manner which will harmonise as far as possible with such decisions and opinions. In view of the wording of subsection (1) difficulties are to be expected, since it is usual in many Continental jurisdictions to include obvious equivalents within the extent of protection whereas subsection (1) indicates that the extent of protection is defined by the claims, but with some flexibility in the interpretation of terms used in view of the description and any drawings. Thus, it has been stated (*Rotocrop* v. *Genbourne*, [1982] FSR 241) that (by virtue of s. 91) a patent specification should not be construed as strictly as a conveyancing document, as sometimes was the case under the former law. The wording of subsection (1) indeed may in some cases lead to a narrower scope of protection than was afforded by the wording of Letters Patent under the 1949 Act (for which see para. A021.3) with its command, quoted in para. 125.06 *supra*, which was construed by the courts to bring some equivalent constructions (as well as the products of patented processes) within the extent of protection.

These difficulties may be resolved by not attempting to construe subsection (1) in detail at all, but applying it in a broad manner by relying directly on the Protocol to EPCa. 69 which, by subsection (3), applies for the interpretation of subsection (1). Briefly, this Protocol requires EPCa. 69 (and hence s. 125 also) to be interpreted neither as defining the extent of protection according to a strict, literal meaning of the claim wording (as was generally the former British philosophy), nor using the claim merely as a guideline (or signpost) to what the patentee intended (as was more the philosophy under German law), but "defining a position between these extremes which combines a fair protection for the patentee with a reasonable degree of certainty for third parties". A way in which this could be done to arrive at a European standard of interpretation that is acceptable to German views is indicated in the article by J. L. Beton and K. J. Heimbach referred to in para. 125.04 *supra*. Briefly this suggests that, where it would be obvious to the skilled person at the priority date that the claims are defective, the tribunal should apply a doctrine of equivalents which would extend to find infringement in cases involving unmeritorious disguised evasions and manifestly evident or plain equivalents (as would seem to have been so in *Van der Lely* v. *Bamfords* ([1963] RPC 61 (HL) and *Rotocrop* v. *Genbourne* (*supra*). Indeed, such a concept now seems to have been adopted by the German Supreme Court, see *"Formstein" ("Moulded Curbstone")*, *[Germany]* (OJEPO 12/1987, 551).

125.13   —*Limitation of literal wording*

While it is generally thought that the "fair position" required by the Protocol to EPCa. 69 (see paras. 125.02 and 125.03 *supra*) will often result in claims being interpreted more broadly than their literal construction, there may be occasions where the court would limit to the literal wording of the claim in the interests of fairness and certainty. An example of this under the former law may be the restricted meaning given to "fluid" in *Barking Brassware* v. *Allied Ironfounders* ([1962] RPC 210) in order to find the claim valid, with a broad meaning then being given to "concentric" to find the claim infringed; and the restricted meaning given to the word "workbench" in *Hickman* v. *Andrews* ([1983] RPC 147) in order to limit the claim and avoid a finding of lack of novelty.

Here it may also be noted that in *Du Pont's (Witsiepe's) Application* ([1982] FSR 303 (HL)) two law lords specifically left open the point that, where a patent is in respect of a selection invention, the use of the selected member for the purpose described for the prior art class may perhaps be regarded as outside the extent of the protection conferred by the patent for an invention of selection based on previously unspecified advantages. On this point, see the comments by J. G. Drysdale and J. Woolard ((1981–82) 11 CIPA 262 and 328 respectively).

125.14   *Extension of claim wording to penumbra of equivalents*

Whether, for the purpose of examining patent claims and determining validity after grant, the extent of the "invention" includes, in addition to that which is claimed as a matter of language, a penumbra of equivalents such as might (in the absence of considerations of the validity of such a penumbra and estoppel) be included for infringement purposes, remains to be seen. This depends very much on the decisions and opinions of convention courts. The EPO Guidelines at C-IV, 7.2, however, indicate that this is not intended by the EPO. Plainly it could lead to practical difficulties during examination and could prejudice the operation of sections 2(3) and 3 by including obviousness considerations in novelty determination for "whole contents" purposes. This problem is further discussed in paras. 2.19, 3.26 and 5.14 in relation respectively to the requirements of novelty, inventive step and support for priority of invention, each of which falls to be decided on the basis of the extent of protection afforded by the claims.

Meaning of technical terms   **125.15**

Under the former law, the courts never felt difficulty in construing technical and functional terms in the pragmatic manner which they felt would have been that of the skilled addressee of the specification. It is not thought that section 125 requires any different application in this regard. The classic case is *BTH* v. *Corona* ((1922) 39 RPC 49 (HL)) where a "filament of large diameter" can now be seen to have been given a purposive construction, *i.e.* the meaning which it enjoyed in the mind of the skilled addressee of the specification. Some further examples are mentioned in para. 125.13 *supra*.

In *American Cyanamid* v. *Ethicon* ([1979] RPC 215) there was considerable discussion in the judgment of the way in which a modern court should treat expert evidence on the meaning of technical terms. It was held that the word "polymer" was not necessarily a precise term excluding copolymers and that, on the facts of the case and the construction to be placed on the specification, a claim which referred to "a polyhydroxyacetic ester" was infringed by use of a copolymer of "PHAE" with about 10 per cent. of a co-monomer. Likewise, in *Minnesota Mining* v. *Beiersdorf* [*Australia*] ([1980] FSR 449), the court construed the word "inextensible" not in absolute terms, but as a practical matter in the light of its context. Further examples of the modern mode of construction of the scope of protection under the former law are given by: *Monsanto* v. *Maxwell Hart* ([1981] RPC 201) where the phrase "secured essentially upright" was construed as a relative expression to be understood and given an appropriate meaning in the context in which it had been used so that the quoted phrase could not therefore be limited so as to import some particular angle specified precisely; and by *Poseidon* v. *Cerosa (No. 2)* (decided in 1975 but only reported [1982] FSR 209) where a functional phrase was given a purposive construction so that it covered the patentee's own commercial article and infringement was then found on the similar construction of the two commercial articles.

In *Dow Chemical* v. *Spence Bryson (No. 2)* ([1984] RPC 359) the Court of Appeal can be seen to have construed "rapid" in a purposive manner. They also gave "pourable" a pragmatic meaning, but defined the term "elevated temperature" as meaning "a temperature above room temperature". On these constructions the claims were found invalid and not infringed. In *Halcon* v. *BP Chemicals* (*unrep.*, SRL C/100/87, *noted* IPD 10072) the words "under substantially anhydrous conditions" were held to have a restrictive effect on a chemical process claim, a contention that the words merely excluded an inutility being rejected. The claims were then held not to be infringed because the defendants' feedstock was a wet feedstock.

Mention should also be made of *Beecham* v. *Bristol-Myers* ([1978] RPC 153 (HL)) where it was held to be infringement of a claim to ampicillin (a chemical intended for use as an oral antibiotic drug) to sell a different compound, hetacillin, which decomposed to ampicillin in the stomach of the patient. This was on the basis that "as a matter of reality hetacillin is to be regarded as a reproduction of ampicillin which was but temporarily masked in hetacillin".

Monsanto v. Stauffer ([1984] FSR 574) appears to be a similar case, in that the alleged infringing chemical compound was not described as such in the specification and arguably fell outside the literal wording of the claim. Nevertheless, an interlocutory injunction was granted on the basis that the plaintiff clearly had an arguable case of infringement. The court in New Zealand took a similar line (*Monsanto v. Stauffer [New Zealand]*, [1984] FSR 559).

125.16 *Applicability of former test to the present law*

It can now be seen that the test of "purposive construction" (discussed in para. 125.10 *supra*) continues to apply to patents granted under the present Act, and to European patents (UK). Thus, in interlocutory proceedings in *Improver Corp. v. Remington* ([1989] RPC 69 (CA)), on which see the Case Comment by P. Prescott listed in para. 125.05 *supra*, and previously in *Unilever v. Schöller Lebensmittel* ([1988] FSR 596), the effect of the Protocol to EPCa. 69 was stated to be the same as the test of purposive construction in *Catnic v. Hill and Smith* ([1982] RPC 183 (HL)). In the *Unilever* case the question of infringement was then posed in the form: "Would the specification make it obvious to a person skilled in the relevant art that the description of the invention could not have been intended to exclude the alleged infringement?"

On the substantive decision in the *Improver* case (SRIS C/61/89, *noted* IPD 12076), it was noted that, in the *Catnic* case, it had been indicated that there would be no infringement of a claim by a variant falling outside its literal wording if: (1) the variant had a material effect upon the way the invention works; (2) it would not have been obvious at the date of publication of the patent that the variant had no material effect; and (3) if the skilled reader would understand from the language of the claim that the patentee intended that strict compliance with its primary meaning was an essential requirement of the invention. The alleged infringement was then held to avoid the first two of these exclusions, but not the third, so that non-infringementthe configuration according to the preferred embodiment of the invention so that the variant should be regarded as impliedly excluded from the claim in the absence of explicit broadening wording. A contrary decision in Germany was explained as apparently not having considered this third factor of the *Catnic* analysis. The position was likewise in *Jacques Dory v. Richard Wolf* (SRIS C/37/89, *noted* IPD 12077) where it was held that had the claim been broadened on one point to cover the alleged infringement, it would have been invalid for obviousness; and on another point the broadening feature would not have been seen by the addressee as an equivalent.

Nevertheless, it remains somewhat of an open question whether the *Catnic* test will be held to cover the unmeritorious disguised evasions which appear to have occurred under the former law, see para. 125.12 *supra*; and also whether, despite being ill-adapted for the purpose, it will deal with equivalents. It is, however, opined that subsections (1) and (3), when interpreted in the light of the Protocol to EPCa. 69, will be interpreted to extend the protection of the patent so as to cover evasions of the type that was held to be infringement under the former law in *Beecham v. Bristol-Myers* ([1978] RPC 153), see para. 125.15 *supra*. Nevertheless, it is thought there will remain difficulty in persuading a court to depart from unambiguous, but unnecessarily restrictive, claim wording to find infringement, even when an obvious equivalent thereto is involved, as was the situation in relation to claim 11 in *Van der Lely v. Bamfords* ([1963] RPC 61 (HL); and in relation to claim 1 in *Rotocrop v. Genbourne* ([1982] FSR 241).

The "squeeze argument" **125.17**

As indicated in para. 125.06 *supra*, the determination of the extent of protection conferred by a patent must be applied consistently both to infringement and validity of its claims: otherwise considerable problems arise with the possibility of a claim being given an "elastic" interpretation, *i.e.* a broad construction for a finding of infringement and a narrower construction for a finding of validity. This possibility is a serious problem in these European countries (such as, *e.g.* Germany, the Netherlands, and Sweden) where the forum for consideration of validity is different from that for consideration of infringement. Thus, in an ideal world, the extent of protection should be determined without looking at the alleged infringement, that is "as if the defendant had never been born" (*Nobel* v. *Anderson*, (1894) 11 RPC 519 (CA)).

The "elastic" interpretation of a claim can also be applied in reverse by a defendant who contends that a claim will be invalid if construed broadly, and not infringed if construed more narrowly. This is often called the "squeeze argument" and a good example of its use is in *Fairfax* v. *Filhol* ([1986] RPC 499 (CA)) because here the argument failed, the court finding a construction of claim which left it neither anticipated nor obvious and yet infringed by a modification of the illustrated embodiment, a decision criticised by D. R. Cowan ((1986–87) 16 CIPA 179). Thus, while the squeeze argument is a powerful way for a defendant to plead his case, it can sometimes contain an inherent fallacy which is avoided when validity and infringement are separately considered. Perhaps one test is to consider whether the alleged infringement could itself have been patented over the prior art, as the German Supreme Court has apparently now held should be done, see *"Formstein"* (*"Moulded Kerbstone"*) (OJEPO 12/18987, 561).

Another example of the "squeeze" argument is *Compagnie Française de Télévision* v. *Thorn* (SRIS C/181/83, *noted* IPD 7018 and C/98/85 (CA)) where the decision was in favour of the narrower, not infringed, construction (albeit of an existing patent). In rejecting one of the broader constructions, it was stated that "it is well settled that a patent specification will be construed so as to avoid an absurd or foolish result or one which the patentee would not have contemplated".

File wrapper estoppel **125.18**

The concept of "file wrapper estoppel" appears to have been introduced into British patent law (*Furr* v. *Truline*, [1985] FSR 553). Here an interlocutory injunction was refused on the basis that the applicant in prosecuting his application had made an admission against interest which had become available to the public in the Patent Office file. Accordingly, the claims could not be construed to include single-flange members when they had been limited to exclude such members from their ambit in order to meet the objections raised by the examiner. Also, as a matter of language, a member specified as having a double flange could not be construed so as to cover a "member consisting of two single-flange plates".

Reference numerals in claims **125.19**

The Act does not contain any equivalent to EPCr. 29(7) which indicates that reference signs present in claims in parentheses, and relating to features of the drawings, are not to be construed as limiting the claims, although that effect may, but not necessarily does, arise by virtue of section 130(7) applying EPC principles to section 125, see the satirical article by J. C. H. Ellis ((1982–83) 12 CIPA 2).

The effect of reference numerals in claims was analysed in *Philips Electronic's*

Patent ([1987] RPC 244). On the basis that such numerals did not limit the scope of protection, having regard to section 125(1) and the Protocol to EPCa. 69, amendment was permitted to remove the numerals from the claims of a European patent (UK). In *EPO Decision T* 237/84, *"Reference signs/PHILIPS"* (OJEPO 7/1987, 309; [1987] 5 EPOR 302) the EPO would not allow deletion of reference numerals from the claims but did allow the insertion into the specification of a statement that these numerals were not to be regarded as limiting the scope of the claims, though the view was expressed that the applicant's fears in this regard were probably groundless, at least for the United Kingdom, having regard to the decision in *Philips Electronic's Patent (supra)*.

125.20 *Technical opinion by EPO on extent of protection*

EPCa. 25 provides that, on request from a national court trying an infringement or revocation action, the EPO can give a technical opinion concerning a European patent the subject of such action. The procedure is governed by EPO Guidelines E-XII and is discussed further at para. 99A.05.

125.21 *Priority dates of inventions (subs. (2))*

Subsection (2) appears to contain difficulties not yet manifested in a reported decision. The provision was intended to overrule *Thornhill's Application* ([1962] RPC 199) and to harmonise with EPCa. 88(2) following section 5 which accords priority to an "invention", whereas formerly priority was attributed to a claim (s. 5 [1949]) so that (as was held in the *Thornhill* case) a claim in an "existing patent" can only have a single priority date. On a literal construction, subsection (2) provides for "claim splitting" such as has been allowed in numerous amendment decisions under the 1949 Act, but on an automatic and notional basis. Thus, if more than one invention is "specified" as an alternative in a claim, each so specified invention can take its own priority date in the same manner as if the claim had been "split" by amendment. No difficulty arises if the separately specified inventions can be seen as specific linguistic alternatives in the claim (as in American *Markush*-type claims), but difficulty can be expected if the claim is truly generic, for instance it specifies a range or a continuum of species rather than alternative subgenera. However, the "alternatives" construction was adopted in *Hallen* v. *Brabantia (No. 2)* (SRIS C/40/89), see para. 63.02.

Cases where the EPO has applied multiple priorities to a single claim are: *EPO Decision T* 85/87, *"Arthropodicidal compositions/CSIRO"* ([1989] 1 EPOR 24; and *EPO Decision T* 310/87, *"Alpha-interferons/BIOGEN"* (unreported).

125A.01   SECTION 125A

Disclosure of invention by specification: availability of samples of micro-organisms

125A.—(1) Provision may be made by rules prescribing the circumstances in which the specification of an application for a patent, or of a patent, for an invention which requires for its performance the use of a micro-organism is to be treated as disclosing the invention in a manner which is clear enough and complete enough for the invention to be performed by a person skilled in the art.

(2) The rules may in particular require the applicant or patentee—

(*a*) to take such steps as may be prescribed for the purposes of making available to the public samples of the micro-organism, and

(*b*) not to impose or maintain restrictions on the uses to which such samples may be put, except as may be prescribed.

(3) The rules may provide that, in such cases as may be prescribed, samples need to be made available to such persons or descriptions of persons as may be prescribed; and the rules may identify a description of persons by reference to whether the comptroller has given his certificate as to any matter.

(4) An application for revocation of the patent under section 72(1)(*c*) above may be made if any of the requirements of the rules cease to be complied with.

Note. Section 125A was prospectively inserted into the Act by the 1988 Act (Sched. 5, para. 30). For the commencement of the section, see the latest Supplement to this Work *re.* this para.

RELEVANT RULE

Micro-organisms

17.—(1) Without prejudice to the provisions of section 14(3), to the **125A.02** extent that the specification of an application for a patent or of a patent discloses an invention which requires for its performance the use of a micro-organism which is not available to the public at its date of filing, the specification shall be treated for the purposes of the Act as disclosing the invention in a manner which is clear enough and complete enough for the invention to be performed by a person skilled in the art if either of the following conditions is satisfied, that is to say—

(*a*) (i) a culture of the micro-organism has been deposited in a culture collection not later than the date of filing the application;

  (ii) the application as filed gives such relevant information as is available to the applicant on the characteristics of the micro-organism; and

  (iii) the name of the culture collection, the date when the culture was deposited and the accession number of the deposit are given in the specification of the application; or

(*b*) in the case of a European patent (UK) or an application for a European patent (UK) which is treated, by virtue of section 77 or 81, as a patent under the Act, or, as the case may be, an application for a patent under the Act, that the corresponding provisions of the Implementing Regulations to the European Patent Convention have been complied with,

and where paragraph (3) below applies, that the applicant or proprietor makes a new deposit in accordance with that paragraph.

799

(2) Where the information specified in paragraph (1)(*a*)(iii) above is not contained in an application for a patent as filed, it shall be added to the application within the period of two months after the date of filing the application. The giving of this information shall be considered as constituting the unreserved and irrevocable consent of the applicant to the culture deposited being made available to any person who, on or after the date of publication of the application in accordance with section 16, makes a valid request therefor to the culture collection with which the micro-organism is deposited. A request shall be valid if it is accompanied by the comptroller's certificate authorising the release of the sample to that person. An application for such a certificate shall be submitted to the comptroller on Patents Form No. 8/77, together with—

(*a*) an undertaking not to make the culture available to any other person until the application for the patent is refused or withdrawn or deemed to be withdrawn or, if a patent is granted, until it ceases to have effect without the possibility of renewal or restoration in accordance with sections 25 and 28; and

(*b*) an undertaking to use the culture for experimental purposes only until the application is refused or withdrawn or deemed to be withdrawn until the date of publication in the Journal of a notice that the patent has been granted:

Provided that the undertaking specified in sub-paragraph (*b*) of this paragraph shall not be required from any government department or person authorised in writing by a government department to make the request, where the request is being made in order to enable any act specified in section 55 to be done in relation to the culture for the services of the Crown.

(3) Where a culture collection notifies the applicant or proprietor that it cannot, for any reason, satisfy a valid request, made in accordance with paragraph (2) above, for a sample of a culture which has been deposited with it, and in particular because the furnishing of the sample would require that it be sent outside the country in which the culture collection is situated and the sending or the receipt of the sample is prevented by export or import restrictions, the applicant or proprietor may, unless the culture has been transferred to another culture collection which is able to satisfy a request for a sample of that culture, make a new deposit of a culture of that micro-organism and if, within three months of receipt of such notification—

(i) he makes the new deposit;

(ii) he furnishes to the culture collection with which the new deposit is made a declaration claiming that the culture so deposited is of the same micro-organism as was the culture originally deposited; and

(iii) he amends the specification as to indicate the accession number of the new deposit and, where applicable, the name of the culture collection with which the new deposit has been made, the new deposit shall be treated as always having been available for the purposes of this rule.

(4) The new deposit referred to in paragraph (3) above shall be made with the same culture collection as was the original deposit, except in the particular case described in that paragraph, when the new deposit shall be made with a culture collection which is able to satisfy the request.

(5) The comptroller shall send a copy of Patents Form No. 8/77 to the applicant for, or proprietor of, the patent.

Note. Rule 17 has been reprinted to indicate the form of that rule which prevailed under the original provisions of section 14(4) and (8), to be repealed (by Sched. 8 [1988]) when new section 125A is brought into effect. However, at that time, rule 17 will need very extensive amendment, but the revised wording was not available at the time of going to press. Therefore, the latest Supplement to this Work should be particularly consulted as to when section 125A was brought into effect and for the replacement wording for rule 17 (as printed *supra*) which then ensued. Meanwhile, the present commentary has, perforce, been written in terms of the existing rule 17, as a guide to the possible operation of the new section, but to be read with considerable circumspection.

It is thought that the replacement wording for rule 17 will more closely accord with EPCrr. 28 and 28A and, where applicable, with the Budapest Treaty. However, some differences will probably remain. Thus, it is understood that there will continue to be no list of approved culture collections and that amendment of the specification will continue to be required when a new deposit is made (as under present r. 17(3)(iii)), whereas the EPO has such a list and only requires "notification" that a new deposit has been made (EPCr. 28(1)). Also the time periods may be revised, and provisions made for revival of undertakings given on PF 8/77 when an application/patent has lapsed (when the undertaking also lapses) and is subsequently restored at some quite later date under rule 110(3C) or section 28.

BOOKS   125A.03

S. A. Bent, R. L. Schwab, D. G. Cronin and D. D. Jeffrey, "Intellectual property rights in biotechnology worldwide" (Stockton Press, New York, 1987);

P. W. Grubb, "Patents in chemistry and biotechnology" (Clarendon Press, Oxford, 1986)

ARTICLES   125A.04

R. S. Crespi, "Biotechnology and patents", [1981] EIPR 134;

R. Teschemacher, "Patentability of micro-organisms *per se*", (1982) 13 IIC 27;

D. L. T. Cadman, "The protection of micro-organisms under European patent law", (1985) 16 IIC 311 and 352;

I. Purvis, "Patents and genetic engineering: Does a new problem need a new solution?" [1987] EIPR 347;

R. Teschemacher, "The practice of the European Patent Office regarding the grant of patents for biotechnological inventions", (1988) 19 IIC 18;

J. Mellor, "Patents and genetic engineering: Is it a new problem?", [1988] EIPR 159;

P. G. Cole, "Genentech loses battle in British patent war", *Patent World*, January 1989, p. 31;

J. P. Thurston, "The commercial and legal impact of the Court of Appeal decision in *Genentech* v. *Wellcome*", [1989] EIPR 66.

COMMENTARY ON SECTION 125A

125A.05   *General*

Section 125A was prospectively inserted by the 1988 Act and relates to inventions which require for their performance the use of micro-organisms. As indicated by the *Note* to para. 125A.01 *supra*, the latest Supplement to this Work will need to be consulted as to the commencement of the new section. The new section will replace the former subsections 14(4) and (8) (reprinted in para. 14.01 but now to be repealed by Schedule 8 to the 1988 Act) and in respect of which the form of rule 17 reprinted at para. 125A.02 *supra* was made. The terms of the new section will require considerable amendment of this rule. A *Note* to that para. therefore warns of the circumspection to be applied to the wording of rule 17 as so reprinted and discussed in the commentary *infra*. Nevertheless this commentary has been prepared on the basis that the new section has been brought into effect. The provisions of section 125A (and of the former section 14(4) and (8)) can be regarded as superseding (for patents granted under the present Act) case law on inventions involving micro-organisms decided under the 1949 Act.

Subsection (1) will authorise, as did former section 14(4), the necessary rules for ensuring that the specification in such a case complies with section 14(3) as to the adequate disclosure of the way in which the invention is to be performed. Subsection (2) will authorise, as did former section 14(8), rules concerning the availability to the general public of samples of the micro-organisms; and subsection (3) (which had no counterpart in the original provisions) will authorise rules concerning the availability of the samples to nominated experts.

The relevant rules under the section will be contained in a new form of rule 17, but the original form of rule 17 should have effect to determine the validity of patents on applications filed before the commencement of the new section. Failure to comply with the terms of rule 17 is a ground for revocation under section 72(1)(*c*), see section 125A(4), but it is not clear what will be the position of a patent filed under the original terms of rule 17 when the requirements of the new form thereof were not met at the date of filing. No transition provision was made in the 1988 Act to deal with this point, but attention is drawn to para. 127.09 (*Accrued rights*).

Rule 17 in both forms is, and will be, confined to the case when the micro-organism is not available to the public at the time of filing the application. Thus, not all applications for inventions which require the use of a micro-organism require the making available of the micro-organism to the public. Accordingly, there is no need to deposit a sample of the micro-organism if the specification is already sufficient to indicate how the claimed substance can be made (*Genentech's Patent*, [1987] RPC 553 and [1989] RPC 147 (CA)).

The effect of comparable, though not exactly analogous, provisions of the EPC and PCT to the new section is discussed in para. 125A.14 *infra*.

125A.06   *Types of claim*

Under the 1949 Act the form of claim customarily used for inventions of a microbiological nature was of the process type, *e.g.* "The process of producing X which comprises cultivating a strain of micro-organism Y designated as A.T.C.C. No. Z under submerged aerobic conditions in an aqueous nutrient medium containing P, Q and R", see *American Cyanamid* v. *Berk* ([1976] RPC 231) and *American Cyanamid's (Dann's) Patent* ([1971] RPC 425). However, the difficulty of proving infringement of a claim in process form makes this type of claim unattractive, particularly when (as was shown in *American Cyanamid* v. *Berk*, *supra*)) the claim was not fairly based on the disclosure unless limited to the precise strain(s) which had been deposited.

The field of genetic engineering has developed very rapidly in recent years and with this increased interest in the value of inventions of a microbiological nature much effort has been expended to find more useful forms of claim wording, particularly with claims of the "product" type. However, as the cases have continued to show, there remains difficulty in obtaining a claim which is both broad enough to deter competitors and yet not so broad as to render the claim invalid, see para. 125A.08 *infra*.

Indeed, since 1978, a wide variety of types of claims for products obtained by microbiological methods, particularly by genetic engineering techniques, (*i.e.* recombinant DNA technology) have been granted both in the United Kingdom and under the EPC. These include claims directed to micro-organisms *per se*, whether or not naturally occurring though not of course previously disclosed as such; cell lines *per se* (including hybridoma cells); natural products which have undergone alteration through the intervention of man such as bacterial mutants and attenuated viruses and protozoa; natural products which have been isolated from micro-organisms such as enzymes and other proteins; the products of recombinant DNA technology such as DNA and polypeptides produced therefrom; and materials useful in recombinant DNA technology such as vectors, promoters and transformable micro-organisms, see the books and articles listed in paras. 125A.03 and 124A.04 listed *supra*.

Particular forms of claim for microbiological products   **125A.07**

The United Kingdom Patent Office will ordinarily accept claims in the form "Micro-organism of species X, deposited in culture collection ABC as No. 12345, or a mutant or variant thereof having the property Y." This claim does not limit the mutants and variants to those of the same species. The practice was established in *Queen Elizabeth College's Application* (No. 2,093,017 (*unreported*). The EPO has not yet established a consistent practice, although several European patents have been granted which claim mutants in a similar way; at least one patent which claims variants derived from the parent deposited strain; and at least two patents which have broader claims not dependent on the deposit.

In the recombinant DNA field, difficulties have arisen over the extent of claims to alleles of genes and antigenically functional sub-units of expression product proteins, but the United Kingdom Patent Office and the EPO have taken a generally sympathetic line towards broad claims at the examination stage, see *EPO Decision T 292/85, "Polypeptide expression/GENENTECH I"* (OJEPO 7/1989, 275; [1989] 1 EPOR 1) and *EPO Decision T 301/87, "Alpha-interferons/BIOGEN"* (*unreported*).

For proteins isolated from natural sources the EPO has accepted "obtainable by" claims if a more precise definition cannot be formulated, see *EPO Decision T 93/83, "Ethylene polymers/MONTEDISON"* ([1987] 3 EPOR 144) and *EPO Decision T 161/86, "Antibiotic/ELI LILLY"* ([1987] 6 EPOR 366).

It appears that claims to hybridoma cell lines made by the conventional mouse myeloma/mouse spleen cell fusion method will usually have to be limited to a particular cell line that has been deposited if the antigen is *per se* known; but, where the antigen is novel, the hybridoma will normally also be claimable in broad terms because such is dependent for its novelty on the previously unknown antigen. In such a case it is believed that a deposit is unnecessary, because the conventional method is employed and invention does not lie in any specific hybridoma.

The book by S. A. Bent *et al.*, listed in para. 125A.03 *supra*, contains (at pages 228–251) exemplary case histories of prosecution of biotechnological patent applications in the United States and comments on the scope of claim obtained.

125A.08   *Prior art issues applicable to biotechnology*

The issue of whether a known protein (more precisely, an artificial analogue of a known protein), prepared by a recombinant DNA process of a kind known *per se*, can be validly claimed seems to have been resolved by the invalidation of broad product claims in *Genentech's Patent* ([1989] RPC 147 (CA)). Previously, many such patents had been granted under the Act. Also, the EPO has granted some patents with broad product claims of this type despite the fact that the end product is useful for an expected purpose and is an obvious *desideratum*. The process of prering it, although broadly known, requires high experimental skill and a great deal of time, particularly if the structure of the protein must first be elucidated. Unless there is some particular difficulty which has to be overcome by some non-routine step, claims to the protein or to complementary DNA encoding it are vulnerable to the "obvious to try" test and it was for these (as well as other) reasons that a patent to "Human tissue plasminogen activator as produced by recombinant DNA technology" was invalidated in the *Genentech* case (*supra*), as discussed in para. 3.07. Even before this decision several commentators had cast doubt on the validity of such claims, see, *e.g.* page 160 of the book by P. W. Grubb listed in para. 125A.03 *supra* where the author suggested that it may no longer be possible to obtain a valid patent for a recombinant product whose structure was even partially known. Even if the structure of the protein is unknown, there are still obviousness problems: the determination of a partial structure (the N-terminal amino acid sequence) of a protein is often only a routine operation and there are standard ways of overcoming obstacles to such sequencing. In the *Genentech* case (*supra*) all but the most specific claims were revoked on various grounds arising from their undue breadth, though failure to comply with section 14(5) was held not to be an objection available post-grant, see paras. 1.08, 3.07 and 14.21 and the papers by P. G. Cole and J. P. Thurston listed in para. 125A.04 *supra*. However, in *Genentech*, the courts indicated that some limited claim to the particular recombinant DNA process described could have been upheld, but the specific claims in that case had no commercial value.

The fundamental problem, at the centre of the *Genentech* case, is that recombinant DNA technology is expensive in terms of the high degree of skill and amount of labour involved and, consequently, the investment required is seen as something which perhaps ought to be rewarded and encouraged by the grant of effective patent protection. Yet the benefit to the public is merely information, namely the DNA and amino acid sequences which would enable a competitor to prepare the product much more quickly than the original researchers could. The value of the information was recognised by the court in the *Genentech* case (*supra*), but both the Patents Court and the Court of Appeal felt able to hold out hope of only a limited claim to the process. In his article listed in para. 125A.04 *supra*, I. Purvis commented on the *Genentech* case and suggested that it exposed the limitations of patent law and proposed a separate form of protection for naturally occurring living material produced by artificial methods. J. Mellor in a response paper, likewise listed *supra*, gives further interesting background information on the *Genentech* case.

Nevertheless, there will be cases in which it can reasonably be argued that the conventional recombinant DNA technology was not obvious to try, *e.g.* if it were not known how to detect the gene of interest, or if the gene were so similar to others that subtle means of discrimination would be required.

In the hybridoma field (*ex parte Old et al. [USA]*, (1985) 229 USPQ 196) an obviousness objection was reversed on the ground of lack of predictability of the nature of the monoclonal antibodies from a particular deposited hybridoma cell line. However, in this case the United States Board of Patent Appeals specifically pointed out that "obvious to try" is not an available objection under United States law. It appears that EPO examiners now question such claims, asking for evidence of unexpectedness in the properties of the antibodies, see also para. 125A.10 *infra*.

Insufficiency issues in relation to biotechnology   **125A.09**

Issues relating to deposition of micro-organisms are dealt with in para. 125A.11 *infra*, while more general issues relating to the application of sections 14(3) and 14(5) to biotechnological patenting are dealt with in connection with section 14(5) at para. 14.21 and at para. 125A.11 *infra*. It must be stressed that failure to meet the prescribed conditions constitutes a ground of revocation under section 72(1)(c), see subsection (4) (and para. 125A.05 *supra* for patents filed under the previous form of rule 17). However, there is doubt as to the precise requirements of the prescribed conditions and, in *Sankyo* v. *Merck* (SRIS C/128/88) pleadings were allowed to remain of: (1) insufficiency due to failure to disclose culture conditions and products of metabolism in addition to growth and morphological characteristics of a micro-organism; and (2) that the sufficiency conditions are automatically met for a micro-organism if this has been properly deposited.

Trade secrecy in relation to biotechnology   **125A.10**

The alternative to patenting, of keeping a new invention secret, is often attractive. Trade secrecy has been used for hybridoma cell lines (since the antibodies which they secrete do not assist a third party to copy the cell line by any simple means) and for cloned genes (because of the problems associated with patent protection. The book by S. A. Bent *et al.* (listed in para. 125A.03 *supra*) contains two chapters on the subject, Chapter 7 (pages 346–383) dealing with general issues of non-patent forms of protection, including questions of ownership of biological material, and Chapter 11 (pages 555–586) summarising the applicable law in major countries. The authors warn however:

"The problem is that there is little or no law dealing with the rights and liabilities of ownership of micro-organisms, their progeny and their products. It is therefore extremely important to define the rights of the parties dealing with genetically valuable biological materials via contractual agreements that envision the many different circumstances involving such materials, and for each party to such agreements to take all practical precautions in safeguarding the materials against theft, 'escape' or other loss".

Deposit of micro-organism   **125A.11**

Rule 17(1) (as reprinted in its original form in para. 125A.02 *supra*) required, in the case of an invention which involves for its performance the use of a micro-organism not available to the public at the time of filing of the application, that a sample of the micro-organism shall have been deposited in a culture collection not later than the date of filing. Rule 17 does not require that the sample shall have been deposited by the applicant but, clearly, if a micro-organism not available to the public has been deposited by someone other than the applicant, there must exist some contractual relationship between the depositor and the applicant.

The application as filed must give such relevant information as is available to the applicant on the characteristics of the micro-organism. The specification must also identify the culture collection and give the date of deposit and the accession number, but this information can be added to the specification within two months after filing (r. 17(2)), a period which is extensible as of right by a further one month by filing PF 50/77 under rule 110(3), and further extensible at the Comptroller's discretion by filing PF 52/77 under rule 110(3A).

The inclusion in the application of this information is regarded as the unreserved and irrevocable consent of the applicant to the culture deposited being made available to any person who makes a request in the prescribed manner, but that person must undertake neither to use a sample so obtained for commercial purposes without licence nor make a sample available to a third party prior to the application being refused or withdrawn prior to the patent lapsing or expiring (r. 17(2)).

In *Chinoin's Application* ([1986] RPC 39) a new micro-organism had been isolated from a soil sample. From this a new strain had been derived by breeding and a sample of this strain had been deposited in a culture collection. Other strains had been mutated or modified from the isolated micro-organism, but not deposited. The applicant attempted to claim all such strains as a new species, *Micromonospora rosea*. A claim to the deposited strain was allowed, together with a claim to strains of *Micromonospora rosea* derived therefrom, but a broader claim to all strains of this species was disallowed. The invention of the broader claim was thus held insufficiently disclosed in the specification under section 14(3) and rule 17(1), whereas that of the narrower claims was held sufficiently disclosed. However, it was held that rule 17 does not require the deposit of every strain of a new species to support a claim directed to that species, nor does it require the deposit of the best strain known to the applicant for the intended purpose of the invention. The case is discussed in more detail at pages 246–249 of the book by S. A. Bent *et al.* listed in para. 125A.03 *supra*.

125A.12 *Obtaining a sample of a deposited micro-organism*

A request for a sample of the culture to be made available is made by filing PF 8/77 (reprinted at para. 141.08). Although rule 17(2) implied that an undertaking by a person wanting the sample should accompany the PF 8/77, the form itself has not included the undertaking. This undertaking is: first, not to make a sample available to any third party prior to withdrawal or refusal of the application or earlier than one year after lapse of the patent for failure to pay a renewal fee or prior to expiry of the patent; and, secondly, to use the sample for experimental purposes only, prior to refusal or withdrawal of the application or prior to publication of the grant of the patent under section 24(1). After such grant of the patent, the use of the sample without licence is prevented by the patent itself, but only in so far as a valid claim protects such use. The second part of the undertaking is not required when the sample is wanted in connection with proposed Crown use (s. 55) (r. 17(2) proviso). On receipt of a valid request on PF 8/77, and having sent a copy thereof to the applicant/proprietor (r. 17(5)) and presumably allowed time or objection by him, though there is no provision for opposition to the request, the Comptroller issues a certificate which the requestor needs when applying to the culture collection for the release of a sample to him.

An application on PF 8/77 for a certificate can be filed prior to publication under section 16, in particular if the person filing the form has become entitled to inspect the file under section 118(4) or (5) because he has been threatened with infringement proceedings or because the invention has been obtained from him. This is clear from paragraph (iii) of the declaration at (*a*) on PF 8/77 and from Note 2 thereon. Since rule 17(2) has referred exclusively to the date of publication under section 16, and since section 118 makes no reference to cultures, it is not certain that the Comptroller would issue a certificate of entitlement to a sample prior to such publication.

The United Kingdom has ratified the Budapest treaty on the International Recognition of the Deposit of Micro-organisms for the Purposes of Patent Procedure

(Cmnd. 8136). The Budapest Treaty with up-to-date Regulations under the Treaty is reprinted in Chapter 82 of *EPH* and discussed in the article by R. S. Crespi listed in para. 125A.04 *supra*.

The United Kingdom Patent Office is apparently prepared to recognise any culture collection (depositary institution) in the world for the purposes of subsection (4) and rule 17(1) (PCT Gazette No. 13/1982, pp. 1378 and 1379, particularly note 5). However, it is up to the applicant to satisfy himself that the chosen culture collection is able and willing to comply with the relevant provisions of rule 17 (O.J. April 19, 1979), since the failure of the culture collection to release a sample on being presented with a request for a sample together with the Comptroller's certificate issued pursuant to the filing of PF 8/77 is to be taken as equivalent to failure of the application to meet the requirements of subsection (3) and to this extent to give rise to a ground for revocation under section 72(1)(*c*). As to the choice of culture collections, see para. 125A.18 *infra*.

If both the applicant and the culture collection are agreeable to the release of a sample, there is no need for PF 8/77 to be filed, (see Budapest Treaty, r. 11(2)). In such a case, it would be up to the applicant and the person wanting the sample to negotiate what undertakings should be given in relation to use of that sample.

Nothing has been prescribed as to what remedy might be available to the applicant or proprietor for a breach of any undertaking given on PF 8/77 and no case has yet appeared to deal with the effect of such undertaking, though it is thought that such would be construed as a contractual (or quasi-contractual) undertaking given by the requester. However, there are obvious difficulties in seeking relief against persons not resident within the United Kingdom.

Renewal of deposited micro-organism   **125A.13**

Rule 17(3) has contained provisions to protect the applicant or proprietor in the event that the deposit ceases to be viable or the culture collection for any other reason ceases to be able to supply a sample on receipt of a valid request. To take advantage of these provisions, which comply in principle with article 4 of the Budapest Treaty, the applicant or proprietor must, within three months of receiving notification from the culture collection that it can no longer supply samples, transfer the culture, if still viable, to another collection, or, if no longer viable, make a new deposit in the same collection, furnish a declaration that the micro-organism of the new deposit is the same as that of the old deposit and amend the patent specification to indicate the accession number and name of the culture collection at which the new deposit is made. This three-month period is inextensible (r. 110(2)). Although the wording of rule 17(3) is not entirely clear, it is to be assumed that this three-month term is applicable in the case of the transfer of the culture from one collection to another. If the applicant/proprietor fails to comply with any obligation to make a new deposit under these provisions, the specification will be taken as not complying with section 14(3) *ab initio* in respect of the relevant invention.

Comparison with EPC and PCT provisions   **125A.14**

EPCr. 28 and PCTr. 13*bis* contain provisions corresponding generally to those of rule 17(1), (2) and (5), and EPCr. 28 corresponds to rule 17(3) and (4). The original form of rule 17 contained no provisions corresponding to EPCr. 28(4) and (5). However, the original form of rule 17 provides the same option that an applicant for a European patent has of ensuring that a sample of a deposited micro-organism, during the period following publication of the European patent application up to grant of a patent or withdrawal of the application, may only be made available to a nominated expert.

This option (sometimes called the "expert solution") is virtually equivalent to maintaining inaccessibility of the deposit during that period, since the expert is independent and must not make the culture available to the requester or any other third party. The provisions of the EPC, rather than those of the 1977 Act, apply to a European patent (UK) for an invention which involves the use of a micro-organism not available to the public at the date of filing (r. 17(1)(b)). On the other hand, the United Kingdom provisions apply in the case of an international application for a patent (UK); but the differences between the United Kingdom and EPC rules are now likely to be greatly reduced, if not eliminated, by the replacement form of rule 17 made under this new section 125A, in particular, by allowing an applicant under the Act to opt for pre-grant availability of a sample only to a nominated expert. However, whereas under the Act a time limit exists for putting the application in order for grant (s. 20, r. 34, see para. 18.10), no such time limit is provided under the EPC. Therefore, an applicant wishing to keep his deposit inaccessible for as long as possible might continue to find the EPC or Euro-PCT route more advantageous than the national or PCT(UK) route under the Act, even though revised rule 17 will now allow the "expert solution", see para. 125A.21 *infra*.

125A.15   *Micro-organisms already available to the public*

If the invention involves the use of a micro-organism which is available to the public at the date of filing of the application, a deposit for patent purposes is not necessarily required, and therefore there is no relevant rule. For compliance with section 14(3) the specification as originally filed must still give such relevant information as is available to the applicant at the date of filing, including mention of how a culture of that micro-organism can be obtained. It appears to be the responsibility of the applicant, and subsequently the proprietor of the patent, to ensure that the culture remains available to the public at least until the lapse or expiry of the patent: otherwise the specification would not continue to enable a person skilled in the art to perform the invention. Applicants should, therefore, beware of relying upon the continuing availability or viability of a micro-organism deposited by others, sold or available by gift, but should themselves make a deposit. Generally, a deposit under the Budapest Treaty is greatly to be preferred for this purpose: under this, the deposit is kept for at least 30 years or five years after the most recent request for a sample, whichever is the longer (Treaty, r. 9.1). Unless the duplicate deposit is made before the patent application is filed, there is the risk of an interruption of availability which would probably be regarded as fatal, at least if occurring after section 16 publication, see para. 125A.17 *infra*.

PRACTICE UNDER SECTION 125A

Procedure for deposit of micro-organisms

125A.16   —*General*

The term micro-organism should be assumed to include any material of a micro-biological nature that is not consistently reproducible. Thus, plant and animal cells, phages and plasmids are regarded by the Patent Office, and by the EPO, as equivalent to micro-organisms.

—Time limits for deposit of micro-organism in culture collection   **125A.17**

If an invention, for which a United Kingdom patent application is about to be filed, requires the use of a micro-organism not available to the public, rule 17 will usually require a sample culture of the micro-organism to have been deposited in a culture collection before the United Kingdom application is filed, see para. 125A.11 *supra*. Where a corresponding application has already been filed in another country, the situation should be checked carefully for full compliance with rule 17. Any deficiency might require urgent action to be taken to deposit before the deadline for filing the application. The deposition process is likely to take at least a week, longer for animal cells, in order to have the viability checked (essential for a Budapest Treaty deposit) before the application is filed. It is *not* adequate to rely on a mere mention in the specification of the culture collection, deposit number and filing date. Unless the specification states that the deposit was made for the purposes of a United Kingdom patent application or under the Budapest Treaty, it is not necessarily a valid deposit. Thus, where an applicant had made a deposit in the American Type Culture collection and had paid the lower fee for a deposit valid only for United States patent purposes, a higher fee being required for an EPO or Budapest Treaty deposit, and the specification gave no indication of this limitation of the deposit, it was held that such a deposit did not fulfil the EPC requirements, see *EPO Decision T* 239/87, *"Micro-organisms/NABISCO"* ([1988] 5 EPOR 311) where a short-time failure to meet the EPO requirements was excused, though as an exceptional case. The EPO then warned applicants (OJEPO 8/1986. 269) that an application should indicate clearly at the time of filing the legal status of a deposited micro-organism. A "US-only" deposit should therefore be converted before filing other applications.

—Factors influencing choice of culture collection   **125A.18**

Consideration should also be given, where appropriate, to the relative merits of national and EPC applications, if it is desired to keep the deposit inaccessible for as long as possible, see para. 125A.14 *supra*. The same choice applies in the case of an international application designating the United Kingdom or the EPO. Careful thought should be given to the earliest date in any foreign country when the deposit can be accessed by application to the foreign patent office. A summary of foreign laws is given at pages 471–554 of the book by S. A. Bent *et al.* listed in para. 125A.03 *supra*.

The responsibility for arranging for deposit will devolve directly on the United Kingdom patent agent when he is entrusted with the first filing of a patent application on the invention. The later filing of corresponding applications in other countries is also an important consideration. Wherever possible, it is advisable to choose a culture collection which is an International Depositary Authority (IDA) under the Budapest Treaty on the International Recognition of the Deposit of Micro-organisms for the purposes of Patent Procedure. This will ensure that the collection meets the requirements of the EPO (EPCrr. 28 and 28A) United Kingdom (r. 17), United States, Japan, Australia, Denmark, Finland, Norway, and many other foreign countries which have ratified the Treaty. The choice of IDA will depend largely on: (1) whether the IDA is authorised to accept micro-organisms of the kind in question; (2) whether it can store, re-culture and check for viability the particular micro-organism; and (3) the convenience of making the deposit. Use of an IDA situated in the United Kingdom will obviously be more convenient for a United Kingdom resident depositor, especially if the organism has any tendency to detioriate in transit.

There are at present six United Kingdom-domiciled IDAs and each is authorised under the Budapest Treaty to accept certain defined micro-organisms only. The location, telephone number and the broad outline of what they can accept are as follows: (1) the National Collection of Industrial and Marine Bacteria Ltd. in Aberdeen (tel. 0224 877071) which accepts non-pathogenic bacteria, bacteriophages and plasmids, including recombinant plasmids, naked and cloned in a bacterial host; (2) the European Collection of Animal Cell Cultures at Porton Down, Wiltshire (tel. 0980 610391) which accepts cell lines including hybridomas, and certain viruses; (3) the Commonwealth Mycological Institute at Kew (tel. 081–940 4086) which accepts most non-pathogenic fungi, other than yeasts; (4) the National Collection of Yeast Cultures in Norwich (tel. 0603 56122) which accepts non-pathogenic yeasts; (5) the National Collection of Type Cultures at Colindale, London NW9 (tel. 081–200 4400) which accepts pathogenic bacteria; and (6) the Culture Collection of Algae and Protozoa, principally at Ambleside Cumbria (tel. 09662 2468) which accepts algae and non-pathogenic protozoa. There are no United Kingdom IDAs for plant cells (including seeds). In difficult cases, for example pathogenic protozoa and viruses, it is always worth checking thoroughly with United Kingdom IDAs before trying abroad. Before using a foreign IDA it is essential to check that no problems will arise in importing the organism into the foreign country. Official clearances are particularly likely to be needed where a virus is involved and obtaining such could be very time-consuming.

Where the collection used is not an IDA, it is advisable to check that it complies with the requirements of the relevant foreign laws and practice, at least in so far as they affect priority, especially with regard to permanence of deposit and ensuring that the deposit will be released to the public at the time required by national law, see particularly the United States "Manual of Patent Examining Practice", the Notice of the EPO dated July 18, 1986 (OJEPO 8/1986, 269) and the Notice of the President of the German Patent Office dated November 10, 1987 (Blatt für PMZ [Germany], December 1987, *89*, 365). The same warning applies to micro-organisms which are publicly available or have been deposited by a third party, see para. 125A.15 *supra*.

Lists of culture collections including non-IDAs, which are believed by the United Kingdom Office to be willing to meet the obligations prescribed in rule 17 are published in the O.J. at the end of each quarter. Lists of IDAs are published by WIPO in January in *"Industrial Property"* and similar lists including other depositary institutions appear in a January issue of the PCT Gazette and periodically in the OJEPO. The OJEPO lists those few culture collections abroad which are not IDAs but are recognised by the EPO.

125A.19 *—Inadequate deposit*

In West Germany, a non-Budapest Treaty deposit of a micro-organism in a collection potentially controlled by the applicant itself was held to be an insufficient deposit (*"Methylomonas" [Germany]*, OJEPO 8/1986, 285; [1986] 6 EPOR 325). While such an "incestuous" deposit is not explicitly prohibited by the Treaty or under the United Kingdom or EPC rules, there is a danger that, if no transfer of control of the micro-organism takes place, no "deposition" will be construed to have occurred.

When deposit is made, the date of the deposit will be that on which the sample is received by the culture collection. However, if the sample turns out to be of the wrong micro-organism, heavily contaminated or non-viable, the date is likely to be refused. Therefore it is extremely important to allow enough time for possible re-deposit before filing. An IDA must issue the depositor with a receipt (Budapest

Treaty, r. 7.1) and viability statement (Budapest Treaty, r. 10.2) which should be carefully checked to ensure that the micro-organism is correctly identified.

—Fees for deposit   125A.20

Most culture collections, including all the IDAs in the Western world, require payment of fees. These vary greatly. It should be ascertained whether the fees must be paid at the time of deposit in order for the deposit to be validly made.

Obtaining sample of deposited micro-organism   125A.21

To obtain a culture of a micro-organism to which a United Kingdom patent specification (including an international application designating the United Kingdom Patent Office) refers and which was not available to the public at the time of filing of the application, PF 8/77 (reprinted at para. 141.08) must first be completed in accordance with the Notes on the form and filed at the Patent Office in order to obtain a certificate authorising the release of the culture. The Patent Office sends a copy of the PF 8/77 to the applicant or proprietor (r. 17(5)). The certificate must be presented to the Culture Collection in which the deposit was made, together with the request for a sample of a specified culture.

When the culture collection is an international depositary authority, form PF 8/77 must be accompanied by form BP/12 (Note 5 to PF 8/77). Form BP/12 (reprinted at para. 143.02) must be filed in duplicate, is one prescribed under rule 11.3(*a*) of the Budapest Treaty. It is a combined certificate (to be signed by the Patent Office) and request for release of a culture. Blank forms BP/12 are available from the United Kingdom Patent Office.

SECTION 126   126.01

Stamp duty

126.—(1) An instrument relating to a Community patent or to an application for a European patent shall not be chargeable with stamp duty by reason only of all or any of the provisions of the Community Patent Convention mentioned in subsection (2) below.

(2) The said provisions are—

(*a*) Article 2.2 (Community patent and application for European patent in which the contracting states are designated to have effect throughout the territories to which the Convention applies);

(*b*) Article 39.1(*c*) (Community patent treated as national patent of contracting state in which applicant's representative has place of business);

(*c*) Article 39.1(*c*) as applied by Article 45 to an application for a European patent in which the contracting states are designated.

COMMENTARY ON SECTION 126   126.02

Section 126, though in force, will have no effect until the CPC is implemented. It will then apply to relieve from liability to United Kingdom stamp duty a disposition of rights in a Community patent or an application for a European patent which is to have effect as a Community patent.

Section 126 is not applicable to European patents (UK), nor to applications therefor which are not destined to become Community patents. The payment of stamp duty on dispositions of rights in other patents and applications is discussed in para. 30.12.

127.01   **SECTION 127**

Existing patents and applications

127.—(1) No application for a patent may be made under the 1949 Act on or after the appointed day.

(2) Schedule 1 to this Act shall have effect for securing that certain provisions of the 1949 Act shall continue to apply on and after the appointed day to—

(*a*) a patent granted for that day;

(*b*) an application for a patent which is filed before that day, and which is accompanied by a complete specification or in respect of which a complete specification is filed before that day;

(*c*) a patent granted in pursuance of such an application.

(3) Schedule 2 to this Act shall have effect for securing that (subject to the provisions of that Schedule) certain provisions of this Act shall apply on and after the appointed day to any patent and application to which subsection (2) above relates, but, except as provided by the following provisions of this Act, this Act shall not apply to any such patent or application.

(4) An application for a patent which is made before the appointed day, but which does not comply with subsection (2)(*b*) above, shall be taken to have been abandoned immediately before that day, but, notwithstanding anything in section 5(3) above, the application may nevertheless serve to establish a priority date in relation to a later application for a patent under this Act if the date of filing the abandoned application falls within the period of 15 months immediately preceding the filing of the later application.

(5) Schedule 3 to this Act shall have effect for repealing certain provisions of the 1949 Act.

(6) The transitional provisions and savings in Schedule 4 to this Act shall have effect.

(7) In Schedules 1 to 4 to this Act "existing patent" means a patent mentioned in subsection (2)(*a*) and (*c*) above, "existing application" means an application mentioned in subsection 2(*b*) above, and expressions used in the 1949 Act and those Schedules have the same meanings in those Schedules as in that Act.

RELEVANT RULES

Patent Rules 1982 (S.I. 1982 No. 717)

Revocation of existing rules and transitional provision

124.—(1) The Patents Rules 1978 [S.I. 1978 No. 216], except for rule   **127.02**
124 and Schedule 4, and Patents (Amendment No. 3) Rules 1980 [S.I. 1980
No. 1146] and the Patents (Amendment No. 4) Rules 1980 [S.I. 1980
No. 1783] except for Rule 2 (*bb*) and (*cc*) are hereby revoked.
    (2) The Patents (Amendment) Rules 1981 [S.I. 1981 No. 72] are hereby
revoked.
    (3) The reference to Schedule 2 to the Patents Rules 1968 [S.I. 1968
No. 1389] in paragraph (*a*) of the proviso to rule 124 of the Patents Rules
1978 shall be construed as a reference to that Schedule with the substitution for forms 7, 9, 14 to 21, 23, 27, 28, 32 to 39, 43 to 46, 53 to 55, 63 to 65
and 69 of the correspondingly numbered forms in Schedule 4 hereto.
    (4) In rule 124 of the Patents Rules 1978—
    (*a*) for the words "these rules" in each place where they occur there
         shall be substituted the words "the Patents Rules 1982"; and
    (*b*) for the words "In rule 39(1)" in paragraph (4) there shall be substi-
         tuted the words "In rule 39(1) of the Patents Rules 1982".

Schedule 2   **127.03**

Note. Schedule 2 to the 1982 Rules sets out the Patent Forms to be used. These
are reprinted at paras. A119–A138.

Patents Rules 1978 (S.I. 1978 No. 216)

Revocation of existing Rules

124. [1978]—(1) The Patents Rules 1968, [S.I. 1968 No. 1389], the   **127.04**
Patents (Amendment) Rules 1970, [S.I. 1970 No. 955], the Patents
(Amendment No. 2) Rules 1971 [S.I. 1971 No. 1917], the Patents
(Amendment) Rules 1973 [S.I. 1973 No. 66], the Patents (Amendment
No. 2) Rules 1975 [S.I. 1975 No. 891], the Patents (Amendment No. 3)
Rules 1975 [S.I. 1975 No. 1021] and the Patents (Amendment No. 4)
Rules 1975 [S.I. 1975 No. 1262] are hereby revoked:
    Provided that in relation to existing patents and existing applications—
    (*a*) subject to sub-rule (2) below, rules 1, 5, 9(2) and (4), 10 to 31, 33 to
         37, 40 to 63, 69 to 77, 84 to 97, 103, 105 to 107(1), 113, 114, 116 to
         118, 128 to 132, 136, 150, 153, 154, 156 and 157 of, and Schedule 4
         and, to the extent necessary for the purposes of this rule, Schedule 2
         to, the Patents Rules 1968, as amended, shall continue to apply;
    (*b*) rule 83 of those Rules shall continue to apply only for the purposes
         of rule 89 of those Rules;

(*c*) rules 2, 9(1) and (3), 32, 104, 107(2), 112, 115 and 158 of those Rules shall apply as if they were in the form set out in Schedule 4 hereto; and

(*d*) subject to sub-rules (3) and (4) below, rules 30, 39(1) and (3) to (6), 41 to 50, 52, 62 to 74, 76, 88(1), 90, 92 to 95, 97 to 101, 103 to 108 and 114 to 116 of the Patents Rules 1982 shall apply.

(2) In the rules specified in proviso (*a*) to sub-rule (1) above, as they continue to apply by virtue of that sub-rule, a reference to any of the Patents Rules 1968, as amended, or to any Schedule thereto, which is not specified in the said proviso or in proviso (*c*) to that sub-rule shall be taken to be a reference to the corresponding provisions of the Patents Rules 1982 (any provision of the Patents Rule 1982 being treated as a corresponding provision of those Rules if it was made for purposes which are the same as or similar to that provision of those Rules).

(3) In the rules specified in proviso (*d*) to sub-rule (1) above, as they apply by virtue of that sub-rule—

(*a*) a reference to the Act shall include a reference to the 1949 Act;

(*b*) a reference to a specified provision of the Act other than one of the provisions referred to in paragraph 1(2) of Schedule 2 to the Act shall be construed as a reference to the corresponding provision of the 1949 Act (any provision of that Act being treated as corresponding to a provision of the Act if it was enacted for purposes which are the same as or similar to that provision of the Act);

(*c*) a reference to any of the Patents Rules 1982 which is not specified in the said proviso (*d*) shall be taken to be a reference to the corresponding provisions of the Patents Rules 1968, as amended, (any provision of those Rules being treated as corresponding to a provision of the Patents Rules 1982 if it was made for purposes which are the same as or similar to that provision of the Patents Rules 1982);

(*d*) references to a patent under the Act and to an application for such a patent shall include respectively a reference to an existing patent and application;

(*e*) references to the grant of a patent under the Act shall include a reference to the sealing and grant of an existing patent; and

(*f*) references to a published application for a patent under the Act, and to publication of such an application, shall include respectively references to a complete specification which has been published under the 1949 Act and to publication of such a specification (and a reference to an application for a patent under the Act which has not been published shall be construed accordingly).

(4) In rule 39(1) of the Patents Rules 1982, as it applies by virtue of sub-rule (1) above, the reference to the date of filing an application for a patent as determined in accordance with section 15 shall be treated as being a reference to the date of a patent.

Notes

1. Rule 124 [1978] is printed as amended by S.I. 1980 No. 1783, 1983 No. 180 and 1986 No. 583 as well as by rule 124(3) [1982].
2. The commentary hereunder contains reference to unrepealed Schedule 4 of the 1978 Rules and those of the 1968 Rules (S.I. 1968 No. 1389) which continue to have effect, but neither this Schedule 4 nor these Rules are reprinted *in extenso* in the present work, but those of these 1968 Rules considered to be still effective are reprinted following the section of the 1949 Act to which each such rule mainly relates, with a list of such rules, and the section under which each is reprinted, being listed in Appendix A at para. A109, followed at paras. A119–A138 by those forms to the 1968 Rules which remain applicable.

ARTICLES   **127.05**

W. R. Farwell, "Patent Rules: Continuing application of 1968 Rules and 1978 Rules", (1981–82) 11 CIPA 531;
A. W. White, "Transitional provisions of the United Kingdom Patents Act 1977", [1983] EIPR 5.

COMMENTARY ON SECTION 127

General   **127.06**

Section 127 provides transitional provisions defining the applicability of the Act to patents and applications therefor granted or filed under the 1949 Act, referred to in the Act as "existing" patents and applications (subs. (7)). The detailed provisions are in Schedules 1 to 4 and in this edition these are specifically considered either under the sections of the Act to which the transitional provision particularly pertains or in separate commentaries at paras. 133.02–136.09. The present commentary is therefore restricted to comments of a general nature. The points of greatest importance which arose under the section are discussed in the paper by A. W. White listed in para. 127.05 *supra*.
Section 132 deals with repeals and amendments of previous statutes, as detailed in Schedules 5 and 6, and these are dealt with in the commentaries on these schedules at paras. 137.02 and 138.02. Unrepealed provisions of other patent or patent-related statutes are dealt with at para. 138.04 and reprinted as necessary in Appendix B.

Application of Act to existing patents and applications   **127.07**

The term "existing patent" as used in the Act (and also in the Patents Rules, see para. 123.18) means a patent granted under the Patents Act 1949 (12, 13 & 14 Geo. 6, c. 62), either as granted before the "appointed day" (subs. (2)(*a*)) or when later granted on an application then existing (subs. (2)(*c*)). The term "existing application" refers to such an application provided that a complete specification had by the appointed day been filed (subs. (2)(*b*)). However, the term "existing application" is virtually spent because only a few applications pending on June 1, 1978 are now subsisting and ungranted, these being those still subject to secrecy orders.

The continuing effect of the 1949 Act to "existing patents", and "existing applications" is discussed in Appendix A commencing at p. 919.

From the "appointed day" (which was June 1, 1978 for all but a few of the Act's provisions, see para. 132.07) no further applications could be filed under the 1949 Act (subs. (1)). However, Schedule 1 provided (subject to Sched. 4) for the continued application of certain provisions of the 1949 Act, (*i.e.* those listed in Sched. 1, para. 1(2)) to "existing patents" and applications then pending, provided that a complete specification thereon had by then been filed (subs. (2)). Schedule 1 also amended certain provisions of the 1949 Act for the purpose of its continuing applicability and section 32(3) [1949] ceased to have any effect (Sched. 1, para. 1(3) and Sched. 3).

Subsection (3) applies (by Sched. 2) certain provisions of the Act (as specified in Sched. 2, para. 1(2)) to existing patents and applications, but is subject to the provisions of Schedule 4, as described *infra* with reference to subsection (6). Although the term "patent" is used in the 1977 Act as normally meaning only a patent granted under that Act (s. 130(1)), the term also includes an existing patent when Schedule 2 applies (Sched. 2, para. 2(*d*)).

Where on June 1, 1978 an application existed, but on which only a provisional specification had been filed, that application became abandoned but it could, nevertheless, have served to establish a priority right under section 5(2) (subs. (4)). Section 128 provided a specialist transitional provision for resolving questions of conflicting priorities between applications filed respectively under the two Acts.

Subsection (5) introduced Schedule 3 providing that certain sections of the 1949 Act would cease to have any effect on existing patents and applications. These and other sections of the 1949 Act were repealed by Schedule 6 introduced by section 132(7). For further comments, see paras. 132.09, 135.02 and 138.02.

Subsection (6) introduced Schedule 4 which modifies the provisions of Schedules 1 and 2 in certain specified circumstances. The most important of these make sections 55–59 and sections 60–71 applicable respectively to acts of "Crown user" or of "infringement" done on or after June 1, 1978 (Sched. 4, paras. 2(2) and 3(2)). However, not all of sections 60–71 relate to acts of "infringement" as such. This leads to considerable uncertainty as to the extent to which some of sections 62–71 apply, if at all, in relation to existing patents, see para. 136.05.

127.08   *Precedent cases*

Decisions in which the interpretation of a transitional provision has been considered are mentioned in paras. 133.04, 133.05 and 136.05. However, general comment on the transitional provisions is to be found in *Therm-a-Stor* v. *Weatherseal* ([1981] FSR 579(CA)) where these provisions were described as a masterpiece of anfractuosity and a paradigm of convoluted draftsmanship. This decision also commented on the general object of the Schedules. It noted that the transitional provisions had to deal with three quite separate problems:

(1) The 1977 Act defines a "patent" by reference to a patent granted thereunder, but it was necessary to ensure that relevant provisions also applied to "old" patents;

(2) it was necessary to deal with applications made under the 1949 Act which proceeded to grant after the appointed day; and

(3) it was necessary to provide for rights which had accrued in relation to old patents or applications pending on the appointed day which would fall to be dealt with under the old law.

The decision noted that this was done in part by preserving the continued operation of specified sections of the 1949 Act, even though some of those provisions are specifically repealed, and in part by the application of parts of the new Act to old patents and pending applications.

Accrued rights **127.09**

Where the wording of the transitional provisions is not clear, certain provisions of section 16(1) of the Interpretation Act 1978 (c. 30) may be applicable. These read:—

"**16.**—(1) . . . where an Act repeals an enactment, the repeal does not, unless the contrary intention appears,—

(c) affect any right, privilege, obligation or liability acquired, accrued or incurred under that enactment;

(d) . . .

(e) affect any investigation, legal proceeding or remedy in respect of any such right, privilege, obligation, liability, penalty, forfeiture or punishment,

and any such investigation, legal proceeding or remedy may be instituted, continued or enforced, and any such penalty, forfeiture or punishment may be imposed, as if the repealing Act had not been passed".

These provisions were applied in *Convex's Patent* ([1980] RPC 437). The precedent cases on what constitutes an "accrued right" were also reviewed in *Bristol-Myers* v. *Nassau Agencies [Bahamas]* ([1981] FSR 126) where it was held, by the Bahamian Court of Appeal, that the grant of a patent gave rise to an accrued right or privilege which was not abstract and which enured to the benefit of the patentee when the law changed. It was said here that it was unthinkable that any patent granted under the old Bahamian patent law should become open to attack under a new statute for prior non-Bahamian use or publication in the absence of the clearest indication in the body of the Act or in transitional provisions.

Continuing effect of 1968 Rules and Forms thereunder **127.10**

Apart possibly from a few existing applications which remain subject to secrecy discretions, all "existing applications" have either matured into granted patents or have been rejected or withdrawn. Many of the transitional provisions of Schedules 1–4 can therefore be regarded as spent. In this edition detailed commentary on such provisions has, therefore, been omitted or curtailed.

Where the 1949 Act continues to have applicability (Sched. 1, para. 1(2)) the 1968 Rules (S.I. 1968 No. 1389) continue to be applicable by virtue of unrepealed rule 124 [1978]. These include the 1968 Rules specified in provisos (a) to (e) to rule 124(1) [1978], with proviso (c) thereto amending some of these rules into the form set out in Schedule 4 to the 1978 Rules. Otherwise, the 1982 Rules are to apply (r. 124(2) [1978], as amended see note to para. 127.04). Most of those of the 1968 rules which were continued relate to prosecution of applications and these can now be regarded as virtually spent. The particular 1968 Rules which appear to have any significant continuing effect are listed in Appendix A at para. A109. These rules are reprinted and commented on as indicated in that listing.

The patent forms referred to in those continuing 1968 Rules (herein denoted as "PF No. . . . ") are also reprinted in Appendix A at paras. A119–A138 to the extent that such forms continue to have any significant effect. Many of these forms were amended by rule 124 [1982] (see para. 127.02), and subsequently as noted in para. A109. They are reprinted as so amended.

128.01

SECTION 128

Priorities between patents and applications under 1949 Act and this Act

128.—(1) The following provisions of this section shall have effect for the purpose of resolving questions of priority arising between patents and applications for patents under the 1949 Act and patents and applications for patents under this Act.

(2) A complete specification under the 1949 Act shall be treated for the purposes of sections 2(3) and 5(2) above—

(*a*) if published under that Act, as a published application for a patent under this Act;

(*b*) if it has a date of filing under that Act, as an application for a patent under this Act which has a date of filing under this Act;

and in the said section 2(3), as it applies by virtue of this subsection in relation to any such specification, the words "both as filed and" shall be omitted.

(3) In section 8(1), (2) and (4) of the 1949 Act (search for anticipation by prior claim) the references to any claim of a complete specification, other than the applicant's, published and filed as mentioned in section 8(1) shall include references to any claim contained in an application made and published under this Act or in the specification of a patent granted under this Act, being a claim in respect of an invention having a priority date earlier than the date of filing the complete specification under the 1949 Act.

(4) In section 32(1)(*a*) of the 1949 Act (which specifies, as one of the grounds of revoking a patent, that the invention was claimed in a valid claim of earlier priority date contained in the complete specification of another patent), the reference to such claim shall include a reference to a claim contained in the specification of a patent granted under this Act (a new claim) which satisfies the following conditions:—

(*a*) the new claim must be in respect of an invention having an earlier priority date than that of the relevant claim of the complete specification of the patent sought to be revoked; and

(*b*) the patent containing the new claim must be wholly valid or be valid in those respects which have a bearing on that relevant claim.

(5) For the purposes of this section and the provisions of the 1949 Act mentioned in this section the date of filing an application for a patent under that Act and the priority date of a claim of a complete specification under that Act shall be determined in accordance with the provisions of that Act, and the priority date of an invention which is the subject of a patent or

application for a patent under this Act shall be determined in accordance with the provisions of this Act.

Commentary on Section 128

General   128.02

Section 128 is in the nature of a specialised transitional provision for resolving the question of priority between patents or applications filed respectively under the 1949 and 1977 Acts and having conflicting dates, that is for resolving questions of the prior claiming type. The provision is no longer active, except to the extent that such conflicts remain to be resolved in the course of disputes concerning the validity of patents with priority dates lying respectively on either side of June 1, 1978.

Existing patents and applications as part of the state of the art under section 2(3)   128.03

Subsection (2) provides that complete specifications filed under the 1949 Act are to be considered under the 1977 Act as constituting part of the state of the art (to the extent permitted by section 2(3) [1977]), and as if published and filed under the terms of the Act. Correspondingly, subsections (3) and (4) provide that, in determining questions of prior claiming under sections 8 or 32(1)(*a*) [1949], applications filed and patents granted under the 1977 Act are also to be considered, provided that the claims thereof have an earlier priority date (in proceedings under section 32(1)(*a*) [1949]) are at least valid in those respects which have a bearing on the relevant claim.

Subsection (5) provides, however, that the priority date of a claim in an existing patent or application is to be determined according to the provisions of the 1949 Act, *viz.* section 5 [1949] thereof, whereas the priority date of applications filed and patents granted under the present Act is to be determined according to the provisions of the Act, *viz.* section 5 [1977]. These provisions are each discussed and compared in para. 5.04 and discussed in the commentaries on the two sections, that for section 5 [1949] being in Appendix A. In *Hydroacoustics' Application* ([1981] FSR 538) it was held that subsection (2) did not modify the definition of "relevant application" in section 5(2) [1977].

SECTION 129   129.01

Application of Act to Crown

129.—This Act does not affect Her Majesty in her private capacity but, subject to that, it binds the Crown.

Commentary on Section 129   129.02

Prior to 1947, the Crown was immune from actions in tort on the legal principle that the Crown could do no wrong. The Crown Proceedings Act 1947 (c. 44) [the

"CPA"] altered that principle, and (by s.3) provided that the Crown could be sued for acts of infringement of specified forms of intellectual property. However, rights of Crown use of patents were maintained so that the right of action under the CPA could only be used for acts outside the scope of the permitted Crown user rights. Moreover, because patents then resulted from a Royal Grant made by Letters Patent, the patent would in any event have no effect against the Crown acting in a private capacity as one cannot infringe one's own grant. Section 129 has effect to maintain the former position as regards patents now granted under statute, rather than as a Royal Grant. Consequently, the section has no need to apply to "existing patents" and does not do so (Sched. 2, para. 1(2) and Sched. 4, para. 3(2)).

The change in the legal status of a patent grant also led (by Sched. 5, para. 1 of the present Act) to revision of section 3 of the CPA to provide that acts of permitted Crown user (for which see s. 55) do not rank as acts of "infringement". The 1988 Act (by Sched. 7, para. 4) has further amended section 3 of the CPA to refer to various new forms of intellectual property and, consequently, this section now reads:—

3.—(1) Civil proceedings lie against the Crown for an infringement committed by a servant or agent of the Crown, with the authority of the Crown, of—
   (a) a patent,
   (b) a registered trade mark or registered service mark,
   (c) the right in a registered design,
   (d) design right, or
   (e) copyright;
but save as provided by this subsection no proceedings lie against the Crown by virtue of this Act in respect of an infringement of any of those rights.

(2) Nothing in this section, or any other provision of this Act, shall be construed as affecting—
   (a) the rights of a government department under section 55 of the Patents Act 1977, Schedule 1 to the Registered Designs Act 1949 or section 240 of the Copyright, Designs and Patents Act 1988 (Crown use of patents and designs), or
   (b) the rights of the Secretary of State under section 22 of the Patents Act 1977 or section 5 of the Registered Designs Act 1949 (security of information prejudicial to defence or public safety.

The reference in section 3(1) of this Act to "design right" also extends to a topography right (Design Right (Semiconductor Topographies) Regulations (S.I. 1989 No. 1100).

Thus, the overall effect with regard to patents is that, while section 129 (and the wording of the Letters Patent Grant of an "existing patent") prevents a patent being applied against acts of the Crown in a private capacity, the Crown can be sued (by virtue of s. 3 of the CPA) for acts of infringement which were *not* for the "services of the Crown" under the terms of section 55, for which see paras. 55.04–55.09. Nevertheless, in any event, no injunction can be obtained against the Crown (CPA, s. 21). The right of action conferred by section 129 is, therefore, a narrow one, most likely to be used against acts of "sale" by the Crown carried out in a public, or Governmental, capacity because these generally lie outside the terms of section 55. However, even then, an exception exists as regards sale of articles forfeited under the laws relating to the customs and excise, see section 122.

Just as the Crown, when representing the State, is liable for patent infringements, so also is a foreign state as no immunity is conferred thereon by the State Immunity Act 1978 (c. 33), see section 7 thereof.

SECTION 130

Interpretation

130.—(1) In this Act, except so far as the context otherwise requires— **130.01**
"application for a European patent (UK)" and "international application for a patent (UK)" each mean an application of the relevant
description which, on its date of filing, designates the United Kingdom;
"appointed day", in any provision of this Act, means the day
appointed under section 132 below for the coming into operation of
that provision;
"Community Patent Convention" means the Convention for the
European Patent for the Common Market and "Community
patent" means a patent granted under that convention;
"comptroller" means the Comptroller-General of Patents, Designs
and Trade Marks;
"Convention on International Exhibitions" means the Convention
relating to International Exhibitions signed in Paris on 22nd
November 1928, as amended or supplemented by any protocol to
that convention which is for the time being in force;
"court" means
   (a) as respects England and Wales, the High Court **or any patents**
   county court having jurisdiction by an order under section 287
   of the Copyright, Designs and Patents Act 1988 [c. 48];
   (b) as respects Scotland, the Court of Session;
   (c) as respects Northern Ireland, the High Court in Northern Ireland:
   (d) **as regards the Isle of Man, Her Majesty's High Court of Justice**
   in the Isle of Man;
"date of filing" means—
   (a) in relation to an application for a patent made under this Act,
   the date which is the date of filing that application by virtue of
   section 15 above; and
   (b) in relation to any other application, the date which, under the
   law of the country where the application was made or in
   accordance with the terms of a treaty or convention to which
   that country is a party, is to be treated as the date of filing that
   application or is equivalent to the date of filing an application
   in that country (whatever the outcome of the application);
"designate" in relation to an application or a patent, means designate
the country or countries (in pursuance of the European Patent Convention or the Patent Co-operation Treaty) in which protection is
sought for the invention which is the subject of the application or
patent;

"employee" means a person who works or (where the employment has ceased) worked under a contract of employment or in employment under or for the purposes of a government department **or a person who serves (or served) in the naval, military or air forces of the Crown**;

"employer", in relation to an employee, means the person by whom the employee is or was employed;

"European Patent Convention" means the Convention on the Grant of European Patents, "European patent" means a patent granted under that convention, "European patent (UK)" means a European patent designating the United Kingdom, "European Patent Bulletin" means the bulletin of that name published under that convention, and "European Patent Office" means the office of that name established by that convention;

"exclusive licence" means a licence from the proprietor of or applicant for a patent conferring on the licensee, or on him and persons authorised by him, to the exclusion of all other persons (including the proprietor or applicant), any right in respect of the invention to which the patent or application relates, and "exclusive licensee" and "non-exclusive licence" shall be construed accordingly;

"filing fee" means the fee prescribed for the purposes of section 14 above;

"formal requirements" means those requirements designated as such by rules made for the purposes of section 17 above;

"international application for a patent" means an application made under the Patent Co-operation Treaty;

"International Bureau" means the secretariat of the World Intellectual Property Organisation established by a convention signed at Stockholm on 14th July 1967;

"international exhibition" means an official or officially recognised international exhibition falling within the terms of the Convention on International Exhibitions or falling within the terms of any subsequent treaty or convention replacing that convention;

"inventor" has the meaning assigned to it by section 7 above;

"journal" has the meaning assigned to it by section 123(6) above;

"mortgage", when used as a noun, includes a charge for securing money or money's worth and, when used as a verb, shall be construed accordingly;

"1949 Act" means the Patents Act 1949; [12, 13 & 14 Geo. 6, c. 87]

"patent" means a patent under this Act;

[*"patent agent" means a person carrying on for gain in the United Kingdom the business of acting as agent for other persons for the purpose of applying for or obtaining patents (other than European patents) in the United Kingdom or elsewhere or for the purpose of conducting proceedings before the comptroller—*

(a) in relation to applications for, or otherwise in connection with, such patents, or

(b) in connection with European patents (UK) to which section 77(1) above for the time being applies;]

"Patent Co-operation Treaty" means the treaty of that name assigned at Washington on 19th June 1970;

"patented invention" means an invention for which a patent is granted and "patented process" shall be construed accordingly;

"patented product" means a product which is a patented invention or, in relation to a patented process, a product obtained directly by means of the process or to which the process has been applied;

"prescribed" and "rules" have the meanings assigned to them by section 123 above;

"priority date" means the date determined as such under section 5 above;

"published" means made available to the public (whether in the United Kingdom or elsewhere) and a document shall be taken to be published under any provision of this Act if it can be inspected as of right at any place in the United Kingdom by members of the public, whether on payment of a fee or not; and "republished" shall be construed accordingly;

"register" and cognate expressions have the meanings assigned to them by section 32 above;

"relevant convention court", in relation to any proceedings under the European Patent Convention, the Community Patent Convention or the Patent Co-operation Treaty, means that court or other body which under that convention or treaty has jurisdiction over those proceedings, including (where it has such jurisdiction) any department of the European Patent Office;

"right", in relation to any patent or application, includes an interest in the patent or application and, without prejudice to the foregoing, any reference to a right in a patent includes a reference to a share in the patent;

"search fee" means the fee prescribed for the purposes of section 17(1) above;

"services of the Crown" and "use for the services of the Crown" have the meanings assigned to them by section 56(2) above, including, as respects any period of emergency within the meaning of section 59 above, the meanings assigned to them by the said section 59.

(2) Rules may provide for stating in the journal that an exhibition falls within the definition of international exhibition in subsection (1) above and any such statement shall be conclusive evidence that the exhibition falls within that definition.

(3) For the purposes of this Act matter shall be taken to have been disclosed in any relevant application within the meaning of section 5 above or

in the specification of a patent if it was either claimed or disclosed (otherwise than by way of disclaimer or acknowledgement of prior art) in that application or specification.

(4) References in this Act to an application for a patent, as filed, are references to such an application in the state it was on the date of filing.

(5) References in this Act to an application for a patent being published are references to its being published under section 16 above.

(6) References in this Act to any of the following conventions, that is to say—

    (*a*) The European Patent Convention;

    (*b*) The Community Patent Convention;

    (*c*) The Patent Co-operation Treaty;

are references to that convention or any other international convention or agreement replacing it, as amended or supplemented by any convention or international agreement (including in either case any protocol or annex), or in accordance with the terms of any such convention or agreement, and include references to any instrument made under any such convention or agreement.

(7) Whereas by a resolution made on the signature of the Community Patent Convention the governments of the member states of the European Economic Community resolved to adjust their laws relating to patents so as (among other things) to bring those laws into conformity with the corresponding provisions of the European Patent Convention, the Community Patent Convention and the Patent Co-operation Treaty, it is hereby declared that the following provisions of this Act, that is to say, sections 1(1) to (4), 2 to 6, 14(3), (5) and (6), 37(5), 54, 60, 69, 72(1) and (2), 74(4), 82, 83, [*88(6) and (7)*], 100 and 125, are so framed as to have, as nearly as practicable, the same effects in the United Kingdom as the corresponding provisions of the European Patent Convention, the Community Patent Convention and the Patent Co-operation Treaty have in the territories to which those conventions apply.

(8) The Arbitration Act 1950 shall not apply to any proceedings before the comptroller under this Act.

(9) Except so far as the context otherwise requires, any references in this Act to any enactment shall be construed as a reference to that enactment as amended or extended by or under any other enactment, including this Act.

Notes.

1. The definition of "court" was amended: as to (*a*) by the 1988 Act (Sched. 7, para. 23); and as to (*d*) by S.I. 1978 No. 621.

2. The definition of "employee" was amended by the Armed Forces Act 1981 (c. 55) (s. 22).

3. The definition of "patent agent" (printed as amended by the Administration of Justice Act 1985 (c. 61), s. 60) was prospectively repealed by the 1988 Act (Sched. 8). The defined terms is now to be "registered patent agent", see the 1988 Act (s. 275 [1988], reprinted at para. 102.05); and the terms "patent agent", "patent attorney", or the like, may not be used by anyone who is not a registered

patent agent as so defined (s. 276 [1988], reprinted at para. 102.06), see further at paras. 102.18–102.33. The definition of "search fee" was prospectively amended by Schedule 5, paragraph 5 [1988], and subsection (7) was prospectively amended by Schedule 8 [1988], but for commencement of these amendments, and the repeal of the definition of "patent agent", see the latest Supplement to this Work *re.* this para.

COMMENTARY ON SECTION 130

General 130.02

Subsection (1) defines many of the various terms used in the Act and the whole of section 130 has an important bearing on the interpretation of many sections of the Act. The definitions are, however, qualified by the proviso in the preamble to section (1) "except so far as the context otherwise requires". The corresponding section of the 1949 Act is section 101 [1949], discussed at paras. A101.03—A101.10, but section 130 [1977] applies to "existing patents" as appropriate (Sched. 2, para. 1(2)).

Specific definitions (subs. (1)) 130.03

Most of the specific definitions for use in various parts of the Act are listed in subsection (1). So far as possible these definitions are dealt with herein in the commentaries of the particular section to which they relate. The definitions of subsection (1) are listed below with an indication of the section under which the principal commentary thereon will be found herein together with a note of the other sections where the term in question will be found (other than in Scheds. 5 and 6), unless the use of the term is too great for individual mention:

Term	Main Commentary (para.)	Term mentioned in sections
"application for a European patent (UK)"	78.05	12, 22, 78, 80, 81, 89, 123, 126
"appointed day"	132.07	127, 132, Schedules 1, 2, 4
"Community Patent Convention"	86.03	53, 60, 86–88, 91, 95, 103, 104, 121
"Community patent"	86.03	86, 126
"comptroller"	130.04	121
"Convention on International Exhibitions"	2.27	2
"court"	96.14 98.05 131.03 132.05	34, 37, 40, 41, 52, 58, 61, 63, 65, 71, 75, 82, 88, 96, 98, 99, 106, 107, 131, 132, Schedule 4
"date of filing"	15.07	15, 17, 78, 81, 89, 128

Term	Main Commentary (para.)	Term mentioned in sections
"designate"	78.06 89.16	78, 89
"employee"	39.07	39, 43, 82
"employer"	41.05	39, 43, 82
"European Patent Convention"	130.08	22, 73, 77–79, 81, 89, 91, 92, 94, 95, 103, 104, 118, 121, 125
"European patent"	77.08	73, 77, 80, 83–86, 123
"European patent (UK)"	77.08	77–79, 89
"European Patent Bulletin"	77.08	77
"European Patent Office"	77.08	22, 77–81, 84, 85, 92–94, 118
"exclusive licence"	67.03	57, 57A, 58, 67, Schedule 4
"filing fee"	14.09	14, 81, 89, 123
"formal requirements"	17.07	17, 81
"international application for a patent"	89.13	22, 79, 89, 123
"international application for a patent (UK)"	89.13	12, 79, 89
"International Bureau"	89.13	89
"international exhibition"	2.27	2
"inventor"	7.07	7, 13, 78, 89, 123
"journal"	123.07	16, 24, 25, 50, 91, 123, Schedule 2
"mortgage"	30.10	30, 33, 36
"1949 Act"	130.05	various
"patent"	130.06	various
"Patent Co-operation Treaty"	130.08	79, 89, 91, 95, 103, 104, 121
"patented invention"	125.08	28, 43–45, 48, 55, 57, 57A, 125
"patented process"	60.13	44, 48, 49, 55, 57A, 60, 100, Schedule 2
"patented product"	60.11	28, 36, 44, 45, 48, 49, 51, 55, 57A, 60, 110, Schedule 2

Term	Main Commentary (para.)	Term mentioned in sections
"prescribed"	123.17	various
"priority date"	5.05	2, 5, 127, 128, Schedule 2
"published"	2.05	*See also Note, infra.*
"register"	32.15	32, 46, 48, 51, 52, 58, 78, 109, 123
"relevant convention court"	103.02	12, 87
"right"	30.06	30, 31, 33, 40, 41, 42, 46, 51, 70, 123
"rules"	123.02	119, 123, Schedule 2
"search fee"	17.09	17
"services of the Crown"	56.03	55–59, Schedule 4
"use for the services of the Crown"	56.03	55–59

Notes. The term "published" in respect of a patent application under the Act has a special meaning, see subsection (5) and para. 130.07.

Definition of "comptroller"   **130.04**

The office of Comptroller-General of Patents, Designs and Trade Marks referred to in this definition is authorised by section 62 of the Patents and Designs Act 1907 (7 Edw. 7, c. 29) which remains in force, see paras. B03, B04. By section 62(3) [1907] (as amended), any officer in the Patent Office may be authorised by the Secretary of State to act instead of the Comptroller. It is under this provision that the powers of the Comptroller are delegated to others in the Patent Office, particularly to take hearings and issue decisions in the name of the Comptroller. The manner of this delegation was tabulated in the O.J. June 28, 1978. Hearings involving the exercise of the Comptroller's judicial functions are normally taken, not by the Comptroller himself, but by a "hearing officer" appointed to act for the Comptroller. Thus, while throughout this Work the convention has been adopted of referring to "decisions of the Comptroller", it should be realised that these decisions will normally have been given by a Superintending Examiner, or occasionally by an Assistant Comptroller, acting for the Comptroller under such delegated powers. For the appointment of other officers in the Patent Office, see section 63 [1907], reprinted at para. B05.

By the Interpretation Act 1978 (c. 30, Sched. 1) the term "Secretary of State" in any statute means "one of Her Majesty's Principal Secretaries of State". The powers of the Secretary of State under the Act are administered (unless otherwise stated) by the Secretary of State for Trade and Industry, the Patent Office coming within the Department of Trade and Industry ("the DTI").

Definition of "1949 Act"   **130.05**

The term "1949 Act" means the Patents Act 1949 (12, 13 & 14 Geo. 6, c. 87). It may be noted that the previous patent statute was the Patents and Designs Act 1907

(7 Edw. 6, c. 29) which had been amended by various Acts in: 1908 (8 Edw. 7, c. 4); 1914 (4 & 5 Geo. 5, c. 18); 1919 (9 & 10 Geo. 5, c. 80); 1928 (18 & 19 Geo. 5, c. 3); 1932 (22 & 23 Geo. 5, c. 32); 1938 (1 & 2 Geo. 6, c. 29); 1939 (2 & 3 Geo. 6, c. 32 and c. 107) 1942 (5 & 6 Geo. 6, c. 6); 1946 (9 & 10 Geo. 6, c. 26 and c. 44); and 1947 (11 & 12 Geo. 6, c. 10). This Act was then further amended by the Patents and Designs Act 1949 (12, 13 & 14 Geo. 6, c. 62), but before this was brought into force the Patents Act 1949 (12, 13 & 14 Geo. 6, c. 87) and the Registered Designs Act 1949 (12, 13 & 14 Geo. 6, c. 88) were each passed in order to split the two subjects and consolidate the various provisions. These two Acts were then brought into force and the Patents and Designs Act 1949 was itself almost entirely repealed by the Patents Act 1949. The surviving provisions of the 1949 Act are the subject of Appendix A to this work commencing at p. 919.

130.06 *Definition of "patent"*

The term "patent" as used throughout the sections of the Act normally means only a patent granted under the 1977 Act, see *Wellcome's Two Patent Applications* ([1983] RPC 200). However, a European patent (UK) is to be treated as a patent granted under the Act, though only for the purposes of Parts I and III of the Act, *i.e.* excluding the provisions of sections 77–95. An existing patent granted under the 1949 Act also falls within the definition of "patent", but only when the provisions of those sections listed in Schedule 2, para. 1(2) are under consideration (Schedule 2, para. 2(*d*)), see para. 134.05.

A Community patent granted under the CPC will not be subject to the present Act at all, but will be governed for all purposes by the terms of the CPC and any regulations made under section 86(2) to give this effect under United Kingdom law, see para. 86.04.

The Act contains no definition of "patentee", as did s.101 [1949], and indeed does not use this term. The owner of a patent granted under the Act is termed a "proprietor", though this is not a term defined in the Act. It would, therefore, appear to be the better practice to use the term "patentee" only in relation to an "existing patent", (*i.e.* one applied for under the 1949 Act), and otherwise to use the term "proprietor" to refer to a beneficial owner and, in respect of a title entered in the patent register, to refer to a "registered" proprietor or other types of rights ownership.

130.07 *Miscellaneous further definitions (subss. (2)–(5))*

Subsection (2) provides for rules defining an international exhibition. This is for the purpose of section 2(4)(*c*), and only very large international exhibitions can qualify (O.J., February 23, 1977). No such rule was made until the 1982 Rules when rule 5(3) was made. For further discussion, see para. 2.27.

Subsection (3) corresponds to section 69(2) [1949]. It is of relevance to section 5 and is discussed in the commentary on section 5(2) at para. 5.06. Subsection (3) defines the extent of the disclosure in an application for the purpose of providing priority based thereon and excludes matter present in the application "by way of disclaimer or acknowledgment of prior art". There is no decision whether the "disclaimer" can be implied, *e.g.* by inference such as absence of claim, but certainly express words of disclaimer are to be discounted when determining priority as also are acknowledgments of prior art, presumably whether or not these are accurately stated. The presence of claims in an application has been held to limit the scope of its disclosure so that a divisional application with a broader claim was not permitted (*Van der Lely's Application*, [1987] RPC 61).

Subsection (4) provides that an application "as filed" is an application in the state it was on the date of filing. This is presumably of importance in determining whether an impermissible amendment has been made, for which see paras. 76.04 *et seq.*

Subsection (5) defines "publication of an application" as that which occurs pursuant to section 16, for which see para. 16.05.

Definitions of EPC, CPC and PCT (subs. (6))   **130.08**

Subsection (6) defines the terms "European Patent Convention" ("EPC"), "Community Patent Convention" ("CPC") and "Patent Co-operation Treaty" ("PCT") for the purpose of references thereto in the Act. The definitions, in each case, extend to future agreements replacing, amending or supplementing any of these conventions, including any annexes, or protocols annexed or to be annexed thereto, and also any instrument made under any such convention or agreement. The full titles of these conventions and their official publications in English are:

EPC: "Convention on the Grant of European Patents", signed in Munich October 5, 1973, published November 1974 as Cmnd. 5657;

CPC: "Convention of the European Patent of the Common Market (Community Patent Convention)", signed in Luxembourg December 15, 1975, published August 1976 as Cmnd. 6553; and

PCT: "Patent Co-operation Treaty", signed in Washington June 19, 1970, published December 1970 as Cmnd. 4530.

The English language texts of each of these Conventions, together with their protocols and regulations (as amended), are set out fully in *EPH*. It must be borne in mind that the CPC has not yet been ratified and so is not yet in force, and that amendatory documents have been agreed, see para. 86.03.

The long title of the Act (reprinted at p. 1) indicates that an object of the Act is to give effect to certain conventions, that is to the EPC, CPC and PCT. As a result the title of the Act gives rise to the applicability of the rule of statutory construction laid down by the House of Lords in *The Escherheim (sub nom The Jade)* ([1976] 1 All ER 920) that, where there is any difference between the language of the statutory provision and that of the corresponding provision of the convention which the statutory provision is to enact, the statutory language should be construed in the same sense as that of the convention if the words of the statute are reasonably capable of bearing that meaning. However, this decision has no applicability if the wording of the statute (or rule made thereunder) is "plain", even if this wording leads to breach of an international obligation under a Convention or Treaty. Thus, in *E's Applications* ([1983] RPC 231 (HL)), it was held that the wording of section 89(3) and rule 110 (each as they then stood) was too "plain" for a reference to the wording of the PCT to be made. Nevertheless, the *Escherheim* (or *Jade*) rule has found use, see para. 130.09, *infra*.

Meaning and effect of subsection (7)   **130.09**

Subsection (7) is an important provision since it specifies those sections of the Act which, being deemed to have equivalents in the EPC, CPC or PCT, are to be taken as having been intended to be framed so as to have, as nearly as practicable, the same effect in the United Kingdom as the corresponding provision of the relevant convention. This adds some specificity to the general object of the Act noted above. At the time of its enactment, the provision of subsection (7) was unique in United Kingdom statute law, but other examples will arise as the strict interpretation of United Kingdom statutes has to be adapted to the interpretation of Continental civil law which is often expressed in terms of principles rather than means. Another more recent example of this new legislative technique is the Civil Jurisdiction and Judgments Act 1982 (c. 27), outlined in para. 96.24.

The effect of subsection (7) would seem to be that, in interpreting those sections of the Act listed therein, due weight should be given not only to the wording of the corresponding provisions in the EPC, CPC and PCT, but also to their *travaux preparatoires*, for example the official minutes of the conferences which led to the adoption of the final wording of these conventions. Subsection (7), in effect, directs the Comptroller and the courts to treat the wording of these conventions, their *travaux preparatoires* and foreign decisions construing these as persuasive authorities. Indeed in *Fothergill* v. *Monarch Airlines* ([1980] 2 All ER 696; [1981] AC 251) the House of Lords, reversing previous authorities, held that such preparatory works could be taken into account in interpreting any statute which purported to enact into United Kingdom law the terms of an international convention ratified by the United Kingdom. Another decision of similar effect is *The Jade* ([1976] 1 All ER 920 (noted *supra*), see also the note by I. C. Baillie ((1979–80) 9 CIPA 526) and *Wavin* v. *Hepworth [Ireland]* ([1982] FSR 32).

Section 91 requires judicial notice to be taken of the three Conventions as well as any decision of, or expression of opinion by, a "relevant convention court" of an organisation set up under the Convention, such as the EPO and its Boards of Appeal. The decisions thereof in interpreting the provisions of the EPC are required to be taken into account in construing those provisions of the Act listed in section 130(7), but such decisions would appear to be of persuasive, rather than of decisive, authority under English law.

Likewise, the International Convention of Paris is only a guide to, but not a rule of, interpretation of the Act. The EPO takes a similar view as regards any conflict between this Convention and the EPC, the latter being regarded by the EPO as a self-contained code, see *EPO Decision J* 15/80, (OJEPO 7/1981, 213).

130.10   *Provisions of Act required to conform with EPC, CPC and PCT (subs. (7))*

The provisions of the Act to which subsection (7) is now to apply are the following:

   (*a*) those defining patentability (*i.e.* ss. 1(1)–(4), 2–6 and 14(3), (5) and (6));
   (*b*) those limiting the period within which allegations of improper ownership of the patent may be raised (ss. 37(5) and 74(4));
   (*c*) those treating use abroad as local use when considering abuse of monopoly (s. 54);
   (*d*) those concerning infringement of patents and applications (ss. 60 and 69);
   (*e*) those relating to the grounds of revocation (s. 72(1)(2));
   (*f*) those determining the right to a European patent application (U.K.) and the recognition of foreign judgments thereon (ss. 82 and 83); and
   (*g*) those concerning the scope of protection of the patent and the burden of proof in relation to patented processes (ss. 100 and 125).

The most important of these provisions is the application of subsection (7) to section 125 which defines the scope of protection of a patent for the purposes of the Act. This is because section 125(3) applies to the Act the Protocol to EPCa. 69, just as the Protocol modifies the meaning of ECPa. 69. This makes it clear that the scope of patents granted under the Act (and of European patents (UK) by virtue of section 77(1)) is not to be limited to the strict wording of their claims. The point is more fully dealt with in paras. 125.11 *et seq.*, as also is the question whether (by virtue of the reference to section 130 in Schedule 2, para. 1(2)) the Protocol to EPCa. 69 can be taken into account in determining the scope of an existing patent for the purpose of infringement under section 60 and Schedule 4, para. 3(2), see para. 125.16.

Application of subsection (7) in decided cases   **130.11**

The first application of section 130(7) was in *Smith, Kline & French* v. *Harbottle* ([1980] RPC 363), where section 60(1)(*a*) was construed in conformity with CPCa. 29, see para. 60.12; and, in *Monsanto* v. *Stauffer (No. 2)* ([1985] RPC 515 (C.A.)), CPCa. 31 was used as an interpretive aid to section 60(5)(*b*), see para. 60.20. In *Rotocrop* v. *Genbourne* ([1982] FSR 241) the Protocol to EPCa. 69 was considered as an aid to claim interpretation, and this on an existing patent, see para. 125.12.

A controversy has arisen whether sections of the Act should be construed in accordance with the EPC, or EPO decisions applied *mutatis mutandis*, even where section 130(7) does not specify the section in question. A particular problem arises here concerning the allowability of amendments under section 76, which is not listed in section 130(7), while section 72 (covering the question of recovation for unlawful amendment) is so listed. This dichotomy was rationalised by the Comptroller, in *Mayflower Products' Application* (SRIS O/129/86), *noted* IPD 10002) on the basis that, while original section 76(1) and EPCa. 123(2) each proscribe "added matter", the meaning of that phrase is to be decided under national law.

However, by contrast, in *Daido Kogyo's Patent* ([1984] RPC 97), the Patents Court and Court of Appeal each indicated, *obiter*, that section 28 should be construed in conformity with the EPC because of the Long Title to the Act, notwithstanding absence of reference to this section in section 130(7). Moreover, in *B & R Relay's Application* ([1985] RPC 1); the Patents Court stated that in this jurisdiction "it is of the greatest importance to take note of the decisions of the EPO" and that "an attempt should be made to give the same meaning to relevant provisions, whichever the jurisdiction which is being invoked". Accordingly, the better view would seem to be that, whether or not a provision of the Act is referred to in section 130(7), interpretations given by the EPO to analogously worded provisions of the EPC or its rules should be taken into consideration in construing provisions intended to have a similar effect. This was done in *John Wyeth's and Schering's Applications* ([1985] RPC 545) see para. 4.06.

Arbitration (subs. (8))   **130.12**

Subsection (8) states that the Arbitration Act 1950 (c. 27) does not apply to proceedings before the Comptroller who is defined as a "tribunal" for the purposes of the Tribnals and Inquiries Act 1971 (c. 62, Sched. 1). Proceedings before the Comptroller are therefore to be considered as taking place in a tribunal which should follow fully the legal principles of natural justice and the legal principles and practices used in the High Court, unless the Act should imply otherwise. Appeals from the Comptroller are entirely governed by the Act (s. 97) and the Rules of the Supreme Court, see paras. 97.12–97.19.

Amendment of, and reference to, other statutes (subs. (9))   **130.13**

Subsection (9) provides that, where the Act refers to another enactment, the relevant provision is to be construed as a reference to any amendment or extension of that enactment by any subsequent enactment. The other enactments referred to in the present Act (as amended), other than those deleted by amendment or cited in the amendment and repeal provisions of Schedules 5 and 6, are as follows:

Year	Enactment cited	Section of Act where cited
1911	Perjury Act (1 & 2 Geo. 5, c. 6), s. 1(4)	92(5)
1937	Arbitration Act (Northern Ireland) (1 Edw. 8 & 1 Geo. 6, c. 8 (NI))	52(4), 131(*e*)
1946	Atomic Energy Act (9 & 10 Geo. 6, c. 80), s. 12	Sched. 4, para. 5(3)
1949	Patents Act (12, 13 & 14 Geo. 6, c. 87)	130(1) and elsewhere
1950	Arbitration Act (14 Geo. 6, c. 27), s. 21	52(4), 130(8)
1957	Patents Act (5 & 6 Eliz. 2, c. 13)	Sched. 4, para. 18(2)
1964	Continental Shelf Act (c. 29)	132(4)
1965	Science and Technology Act (c. 4)	41(3)
1968	Medicines Act (c. 67), s. 130	Sched. 1, para. 4A
1973	Fair Trading Act (c. 41)	51, 53(2)
1974	Consumer Credit Act (c. 39)	45(4)
"	Trade Union and Labour Relations Act (c. 52)	40(6)
1975	Evidence (Proceedings in other Jurisdictions) Act (c. 34), ss. 1–3	92(1)
1977	National Health Services Act (c. 49)	56(4)
1978	National Health Services (Scotland) (c. 29)	56(4)
"	Interpretation Act (c. 30), ss. 12, 14, 16	41(7), Sched. 4, para. 7(2)
1979	Perjury (Northern Ireland) Order (S.I. 1979 No. 1714)	92(5)
1980	Competition Act (c. 21)	51
1982	Civil Aviation Act (c. 16), Sched. 15, para. 19	60(7)
"	Oil and Gas (Enterprise) Act (c. 23), ss. 22, 23	132
1985	Companies Act (c. 6)	131(*d*)
1988	Income and Corporation Taxes Act (c. 1), s. 839	43(8)
"	Copyright, Designs and Patents Act (c. 48), ss. 293, 294	Sched. 1, paras. 4A, 4B

Tables of statutes and statutory instruments referred to in the present work are included at the front of the work. A table of amendments to the Act is set out at the end of the preliminary pages of this Work.

SECTION 131   131.01

Northern Ireland

131. In the application of this Act to Northern Ireland—

(*a*) "enactment" includes an enactment of the Parliament of Northern Ireland and a Measure of the Northern Ireland Assembly;

(*b*) any reference to a government department includes a reference to a Department of the Government of Northern Ireland;

(*c*) any reference to the Crown includes a reference to the Crown in right of Her Majesty's Government in Northern Ireland;

(*d*) any reference to the Companies Act 1985 [c. 6] [*1948*] includes a reference to the corresponding enactments in force in Northern Ireland; and

(*e*) the Arbitration Act (Northern Ireland) 1937 shall apply in relation to an arbitration in pursuance of this Act as if this Act related to a matter in respect of which the Parliament of Northern Ireland had power to make laws.

Note. The amendment to section 131(*d*) was made by the Companies Consolidation (Consequential Provisions) Act 1985 (c. 9, s. 30 and Sched. 2).

COMMENTARY ON SECTION 131

General   131.02

Northern Ireland has its own judicial system distinct from those of the rest of the United Kingdom. The Act extends to Northern Ireland and section 131 provides for references in the Act to certain terms to apply correspondingly when the Act is applied to Northern Ireland. However, the Northern Ireland legal system generally differs from that of England and Wales only procedurally, rather than substantively as does the law of Scotland, and even then in only relatively minor respects. Consequently, few special provisions are required for patent proceedings in Northern Ireland and there are no special provisions corresponding to those of section 31 (*Transfer of patent rights under Scots law*) or section 105 (*Privilege in patent proceedings in Scotland*). However, sections 287–292 [1988] (*Patents County Courts jurisdiction*) apply only to England and Wales (s. 304 [1988]).

The enactment referred to in section 131(*d*) is now the Companies (Northern Ireland) Order 1986 (S.I. 1986 No. 1032 (NI 6)).

Jurisdiction of the Court in Northern Ireland   131.03

By section 130(1) "court" means, in relation to Northern Ireland, the High Court in Northern Ireland. That Court has jurisdiction in all matters under the Act which can be brought before "the court". Thus, provided that there is sufficient nexus with Northern Ireland of the parties or the acts involved, that Court has, *e.g.* jurisdiction in relation to infringement (s. 61), revocation (s. 72) and employee-inventor compensation (s. 40).

This question of jurisdiction is discussed in general terms in para. 96.24 where the effect of the Civil Jurisdiction and Judgments Act 1982 (c. 27) ["the CJJA"], effective from January 1, 1987, is indicated. Schedule 4 of the CJJA regulates the intra-jurisdiction of the courts of the various component parts of the United Kingdom (*i.e.* England and Wales, Scotland and Northern Ireland, with provision for extension to other territories, such as the Isle of Man), and its provisions are discussed in relation to patent proceedings in Scotland in para. 98.05. These comments apply, *mutatis mutandis*, to patent proceedings before the Court in Northern Ireland, except that no parallel provisions to those for Scotland contained in Schedule 8 of the CJJA were needed. The power of the High Court in Northern Ireland to determine revocation proceedings under section 72 appears to have been maintained by the absence from Schedule 4 of the CJJA of a provision corresponding to article 16(4) of the Brussels Convention which would otherwise have restricted such proceedings to the court for that part of the United Kingdom where the register of patents is kept, (*i.e.* in England and Wales) (see CJJA, s. 16(2)(*a*); Sched. 1, art. 16(4) and Sched. 4, art. 16).

Under the CJJA it may no longer be possible for a defendant domiciled in Northern Ireland, and sued for an act of patent infringement commited in that territory, voluntarily to submit to the jurisdiction of the court in England, as happened in *Dow Chemical* v. *Spence Bryson* ([1982] FSR 397).

An award of employee-inventor compensation by the Comptroller may be enforced in Northern Ireland as if it were a money judgment (s. 41(11).

131.04   *Hearings before the Comptroller in Northern Ireland*

Unlike the position in Scotland (for which see s. 123(2)(*f*) and r. 108 made thereunder, as discussed in para. 98.07) there is apparently no power for the Comptroller to conduct proceedings before him in Northern Ireland. This seems an unfortunate omission, at least in respect of claims for employee-inventor compensation under section 40.

132.01   SECTION 132

Short title, extent, commencement, consequential amendments and repeals

132.—(1) This Act may be cited as the Patents Act 1977.

(2) This Act shall extend to the Isle of Man, subject to any modifications contained in an Order made by Her Majesty in Council, and accordingly, subject to any such order, references in this Act to the United Kingdom shall be construed as including references to the Isle of Man.

(3) For the purposes of this Act the territorial waters of the United Kingdom shall be treated as part of the United Kingdom.

(4) This Act applies to acts done in an area designated by order under section 1(7) of the Continental Shelf Act 1964 [c. 29], **or specified under section 22(5) of the Oil and Gas (Enterprise) Act 1981 [c. 23] in connection with any activity falling within section 23(2) of that Act,** [*in connection with the exploration of the sea bed or of subsoil or exploitation of their natural resources*] as it applies to acts done in the United Kingdom.

(5) This Act (except sections 77(6), (7) and (9), 78(7) and (8), this subsection and the repeal of section 41 of the 1949 Act) shall come into operation on such day as may be appointed by the Secretary of State by order,

and different days may be appointed under this subsection for different purposes.

(6) The consequential amendments in Schedule 5 shall have effect.

(7) Subject to the provisions of Schedule 4 of this Act, the enactments specified in Schedule 6 to this Act (which include certain enactments which were spent before the passing of this Act) are hereby repealed to the extent specified in column 3 of that Schedule.

Note. The amendments to subsection (4) were effected by the Oil and Gas (Enterprise) Act 1982 (c. 23, Sched. 3, para. 39).

COMMENTARY ON SECTION 132

General   **132.02**

Section 132 provides the official title to the Act (subs. (1)) and extends operation of the Act to the Isle of Man (subs. (2)), to territorial waters (subs. (3)) and to other designated areas (subs. (4)), including operation in respect to "existing patents" (Sched. 2, para. 1(2)). It also provided for the commencement of the provisions of the Act on varying dates (subs. (5)) and for certain consequential amendments to, and repeals of, other statutes by Schedules 5 and 6 (subss. (6) and (7)).

Title (subs. (1))   **132.03**

Subsection (1) provides that the official title of that Act is "The Patents Act 1977": the Act is Chapter 37 in the 1977 volume of Public General Acts and it can be cited more fully as "The Patents Act 1977 (c. 37)". The "long title" of the statute is that given as the preamble to the Act, see p. 1.

Extension of the Act outside the United Kingdom   **132.04**

The "United Kingdom" consists of the countries of England, Wales, Scotland and Northern Ireland and, in the absence of any statement to the contrary, the Act applies automatically thereto. Subsections (2)–(4) provide for extension of the Act outside the United Kingdom as such, but it should be noted that the Act has no direct applicability to other territories for which the United Kingdom has some responsibility, for example its remaining colonies, protected territories or the Channel Islands.

However, patent protection in such areas is, for many of these territories, obtainable by registration therein of a granted United Kingdom patent within a specified period from grant, that registration then having effect (with or without the payment of renewal fees) so long as the United Kingdom patent remains in force. Further reference to such registration will be found in the commentary on section 77 at para. 77.10. It may be noted that United Kingdom patents, but not necessarily European patents (UK), have automatic effect in Botswana and Swaziland; and more recently the same position has been effected in the British Indian Ocean Territory ((1983–84) 13 CIPA 459).

—Isle of Man (subs. (2))   **132.05**

By subsection (2) the Act is extended to the Isle of Man with provision for modification of the Act, by Order in Council, to adapt its provisions to Manx legislation and terminology. Such an Order is The Patents Act 1977 (Isle of Man) Order 1978 (S.I. 1978 No. 621) which amended, or affected, the operation of sections 41, 52, 58, 85, 88, 93, 107, 114 and 130 to the extent stated in the reprinting of these sections in this work. The PCT was not, however, extended to the Isle of Man until October 29, 1983 (OJEPO 11/1983, 465); and the amendments to section 32, and the repeal of section 35, effected by the 1986 Act (ss. 1 and 3(1)) and operative from January 1, 1989 (see para. 32.01), were not effective in the Isle of Man until April 1, 1989 (S.I. 1989 No. 493).

Also, while sections 293 [1988] and 294 [1988] (*Amendment of licence of right provisions for certain existing patents*), and Schedule 5, paras. 24 and 29 thereof (*Amendment of s. 89 for international applications*) and *Power to extend time limits*), applied to the Isle of Man automatically (s. 305(1) [1988]), the other provisions of the 1988 Act are only extended to the Isle of Man, with possible amendment thereof, when a further Order in Council is made..

By section 130(1) (as so amended) "court", in relation to the Isle of Man, means "Her Majesty's High Court of Justice in the Isle of Man", and that Court is therefore given the same powers under the Act as the other United Kingdom courts designated in section 130(1). Thus, for example, jurisdiction is extended to the Isle of Man for infringement (s. 61), revocation (s. 72) and employee-inventor compensation (s. 40), though there must be sufficient nexus with the Isle of Man of the parties of the acts involved for the Isle of Man Court to assume this jurisdiction given to it. The question of jurisdiction between the various United Kingdom courts is discussed in general terms at para. 96.24. Here reference is made to the Civil Jurisdiction and Judgments Act 1982 (c. 27), an Act under which there is power to extend its provisions by Order in Council to the Isle of Man. Final appeal from the court in the Isle of Man would be to the Judicial Committee of the Privy Council. It should be remembered that, for some purposes at least, the Isle of Man is not part of the EEC. This could, for example, affect the application of the doctrine of "exhaustion of rights" in relation to products first, or subsequently, placed on the market in the Isle of Man.

An order for employee-inventor compensation made by the Comptroller can be enforced in the Isle of Man in like manner as an execution issued out of the court (s. 41(12)).

132.06   —*Territorial waters and continental shelf (subss. (3) and (4))*

Subsection (3) states explicitly that the Act applies to the territorial waters of the United Kingdom, while subsection (4) was new in terms, giving a United Kingdom patent effect on the United Kingdom continental shelf as defined by Orders made under section 1(7) of the Continental Shelf Act 1964 (c. 29), thereby removing a doubt whether this 1964 Act had had its intended effect of extending section 21 [1949] to acts carried out in areas of the continental shelf as defined by the 1964 Act. The "United Kingdom continental shelf" is the area around the United Kingdom designated as such by the Geneva Convention on the High Seas (1958); a "designated area" is one designated by Order in Council under section 1(7) of the 1964 Act. Various such Orders, known as the Continental Shelf (Jurisdiction) Orders, have designated specified areas of the United Kingdom Continental Shelf as areas to which English, Scottish and Northern Ireland civil law is to apply. Such Orders may govern which court has jurisdiction under the Civil Jurisdiction and Judgments Act 1982 (c. 27) over acts of patent infringement committed in one of these designated areas.

The amendment made to subsection (4) has been stated to have the effect (broadly speaking) of extending the application of the Act to specified areas which are in a foreign sector of the continental shelf and which comprise part of a geological structure which extends into the foreign sector from an area designated under section 1(7) of the Continental Shelf Act 1964; and also as redefining the off-shore activities to which the Act applies in a way which corresponds to other off-shore legislation (O.J. August 11, 1982).

Thus, subsections (3) and (4) extend possibly infringing acts to those done in connection with the exploration of specified areas of the sea bed or subsoil or of exploitation of their natural resources. Also, in connection with areas specified under the said 1982 Act, the infringing acts also include activities carried out from, by means of, or on, or for purposes connected with, installations for carrying out such exploitation, the storage or recovery of gas, the conveyance by a pipe and the provision of accommodation for workers on an off-shore installation (Oil and Gas (Enterprise) Act 1982 (c. 23, s. 23(2) and (3)).

Commencement (subs. (5))   **132.07**

The Act received the Royal Assent on July 29, 1977, but this brought into operation only subsection (5) and the provisions specified therein so that the only effect of the Royal Assent was the repeal of section 41 [1949] with immediate effect, other than as regards existing licences.

On December 31, 1977 sections 84, 85, 114 and 130 were brought into operation by The Patents Act (Commencement No. 1) Order 1977 (S.I. 1977 No. 2090) which also repealed section 88 [1949]; and on June 1, 1978 all the remaining provisions of the Act (except for ss. 53(1), 60(4) and 86–88) were brought into operation by The Patents Act (Commencement No. 2) Order 1978 (S.I. 1978 No. 586).

By section 130(1) the term "appointed day" in any provision of the Act means "the day appointed under section 132 for the coming into operation of that provision." Accordingly, June 1, 1978 is "the appointed day" for all provisions of the Act with the exceptions noted above.

While section 77(6) and (7) (requiring the proprietor of a European patent (UK) to file at the Patent Office a translation of the specification into Engish if this is not already its language, and for the patent to become void if this is not done within the time specified), and section 78(7) (enabling applicants for such patents to file such a translation in order to take advantage of s. 69) were "in operation" from June 1, 1978, these provisions had no effect before September 1, 1987 when rules were made under sections 77(9) and 78(8) (Patents (Amendment) Rules 1987, S.I. 1987 No. 288, r. 1(3) and (6)). Provision exists in sections 77(9) and 78(8) for such rules to be revoked and, if desired, reimposed at a subsequent date, without the need for further primary legislation, see further the commentaries on these sections.

Provisions of the Act not yet in operation   **132.08**

The provisions of sections 53(1), 60(4), 86 and 87 are not yet in operation and will not be made effective, if at all, until the CPC comes into effect. There is no specific provision in the Rules with regard to a requirement to file translations of patents granted under the CPC (see s. 86), but doubtless such rules could, if thought desirable, be made within the scope of section 86(3) if and when section 86 is brought into operation.

Amendments to, and repeals of, other statutes (subss. (6) and (7))   **132.09**

Subsection (6) introduced Schedule 5 which made amendments to certain statutes in order that references therein to earlier patent enactments were replaced with references to the corresponding provisions of the present Act. Further comment thereon is at para. 137.02.

Subsection (7) introduced Schedule 6 which repealed the enactments listed to the extent specified therein. Schedule 6 repealed, *inter alia*, those provisions of the 1949 Act rendered ineffective by Schedule 3, but the provisions of Schedules 3 and 6 are each made subject to the provisions of Schedule 4 so that, in some respects, the repealed provisions had some continuing effect. Schedule 6 is reprinted at para. 138.01 and is followed by a commentary on its specific provisions.

Section 47(1) of the Patents & Designs Act 1907 provided for the Patent Museum. This has now been transferred to, and made part of, the Science Museum (National Heritage Act 1983 (c. 47, ss. 12, 13 and Sched. 1, para. 15).

132.10   *Unrepealed former patent statutes*

Besides the provisions of the 1949 Act which remain in force and which are dealt with in Appendix A commencing at p. 919, certain provisiosn of other patent or patent-related statutes remain in force. These provisions are reprinted, or summarised, in Appendix B at pp. 1062–1071 and are here listed as follows:—

Statute of Monopolies 1623 (21 Jac. 1, c. 3): section 6 has relevance to the definition of invention in section 101 [1949], see the commentary thereon at para. B02.

Patents and Designs Act 1907 (7 Edw. 7, c. 29): sections 62(1)–(3) and section 63 provide for the existence of the Patent Office, and of the Comptroller-General and the staff of the Office as discussed in the commentary in section 130 [1977] at para. 130.04, and at paras. B04 and B06; and section 64 which provides for recognition of the seal of the Patent Office, this having relevance to the granting of Letters Patent under the 1949 Act, as discussed in the commentary on section 21 [1949] in para. A021.4. Sections 88, 91 and 91A of the 1907 Act also remain in force, but each has been amended so that these now relate only to trade marks.

Patents, Designs, Copyright and Trade Marks (Emergency) Act 1939 (2 & 3 Geo. 6, c. 107): the provisions of this are inactive until a "state of emergency" should be declared. This Act is not reprinted herein, but its existence is mentioned in para. B09, and see the commentary on section 59.

Defence Contracts Act 1958 (6 & 7 Eliz 2, c. 38), sections 2–4, 6, 7(2) and (3) and 8(1) and (4) (reprinted in paras. B10–B17, and discussed in para. B18) relate to Crown user of intellectual property for which see the commentaries on sections 55–58.

SCHEDULES

133.01   Section 127   **SCHEDULE 1**

APPLICATION OF 1949 ACT TO EXISTING PATENTS AND APPLICATIONS

1.—(1) The provisions of the 1949 Act referred to in subparagraph (2) below shall continue to apply on and after the appointed day in relation to existing patents and applications (but not in relation to patents and applications for patents under this Act).

(2) The provisions are sections 1 to 10, 11(1) and (2), 12, 13, 15 to 17, 19 to 21, 22(1) to (3), 23 to 26, 28 to 33, 46 to 53, 55, 56, 59 to 67, 69, 76, 80, 87(2), 92(1), 96, 101, 102(1) and 103 to 107.

(3) Sub-paragraph (1) above shall have effect subject to the following provisions of this Schedule, paragraph 2(*b*) of Schedule 3 below and the provisions of Schedule 4 below.

2.—(1) In section 6 of the 1949 Act, at the end of the proviso to subsection (3) (post-dating of application) there shall be inserted "and—

(c) no application shall on, or after the appointed day, be post-dated under this subsection to a date which is that of the appointed day or which falls after it",

and there shall be inserted at the end of subsection (4) "; but no application shall on or after the appointed day be post-dated under this subsection to a date which is that of the appointed day or which falls after it".

(2) At the end of subsection (5) of that section (ante-dating) there shall be inserted "; but a fresh application or specification may not be filed on or after the appointed day in accordance with this subsection and those rules unless the comptroller agrees that he will direct that the application or specification shall be ante-dated to a date which falls before the appointed day".

3.—(1) This paragraph and paragraph 4 below shall have effect with respect to the duration of existing patents after the appointed day, and in those paragraphs—

(a) "old existing patent" means an existing patent the date of which fell eleven years or more before the appointed day and also any patent of addition where the patent for the main invention is, or was at any time, an old existing patent by virtue of the foregoing provision;

(b) "new existing patent" means any existing patent not falling within paragraph (a) above; and

(c) any reference to the date of a patent shall, in relation to a patent of addition, be construed as a reference to the date of the patent for the main invention.

(2) Sections 23 to 25 of the 1949 Act (extension of patents on grounds of inadequate remuneration and war loss) shall not apply to a new existing patent.

(3) The period for which the term of an old existing patent may be extended under section 23 or 24 of that Act shall not exceed in the aggregate four years, except where an application for an order under the relevant section has been made before the appointed day and has not been disposed of before that day.

4.—(1) The term of every new existing patent under section 22(3) of the 1949 Act shall be twenty instead of sixteen years from the date of the patent, but—

(a) the foregoing provision shall have effect subject to section 25(3) to (5) above; and

(b) on and after the end of the sixteenth year from that date a patent shall not be renewed under section 25(3) to (5) above except by or with the consent of the proprietor of the patent.

(2) Where the term of a new existing patent is extended by this paragraph,—

(a) any licence in force under the patent from immediately before the appointed day until the end of the sixteenth year from the date of the patent shall, together with any contract relating to the licence, continue in force so long as the patent remains in force (unless determined otherwise than in accordance with this sub-paragraph) but, if it is an exclusive licence, it shall after the end of that year be treated as a non-exclusive licence;

(b) notwithstanding the terms of the licence, the licensee shall not be required to make any payment to the proprietor for working the invention in question after the end of that year;

(c) every such patent shall after the end of that year be treated as endorsed under section 35 of the 1949 Act (licences of right).

(3) Where the term of a new existing patent is extended by this paragraph and any government department or any person authorised by a government department—

(a) has before the appointed day, used the invention in question for the services of the Crown; and

(b) continues to so use it until the end of the sixteenth year from the date of the patent,

any such use of the invention by any government department or person so authorised, after the end of that year, may be made free of any payment to the proprietor of the patent.

(4) Without prejudice to any rule of law about the frustration of contracts, where any person suffers loss or is subjeced to liability by reason of the extension of the term of a patent by this paragraph, the court may on the application of that person determine how and by whom the loss or liability is to be borne and make such order as it thinks fit to give effect to the determination.

(5) No order shall be made on an application under sub-paragraph (4) above which has the effect of imposing a liability on any person other than the applicant unless notification of the application is given to that person.

4A.—(1) If the proprietor of a patent for an invention which is a product files a declaration with the Patent Office in accordance with this paragraph, the licences to which persons are entitled by virtue of paragraph 4(2)(c) above shall not extend to a use of the product which is excepted by or under this paragraph.

(2) Pharmaceutical use is excepted, that is—

(a) use as a medicinal product within the meaning of the Medicines Act 1968 [c. 67], and

(b) the doing of any other act mentioned in section 60(1)(a) above with a view to such use.

(3) The Secretary of State may by order except such other uses as he thinks fit; and an order may—

(a) specify as an excepted use any act mentioned in section 60(1)(a) above, and

(b) make different provision with respect to acts done in different circumstances or for different purposes.

(4) For the purposes of this paragraph the question what uses are expected, so far as that depends on—

(a) orders under section 130 of the Medicines Act 1968 [c. 67] (meaning of "medicinal product"), or

(b) orders under sub-paragraph (3) above,

shall be determined in relation to a patent at the beginning of the sixteenth year of the patent.

(5) A declaration under this paragraph shall be in the prescribed form and shall be filed in the prescribed manner within the prescribed time limits.

(6) A declaration may not be filed—

(a) in respect of a patent which has at the commencement of section 293 of the Copyright, Designs and Patents Act 1988 [c. 48] passed the end of its fifteenth year; or

(b) if at the date of filing there is—

(i) an existing licence for any description of excepted use of the product, or

(ii) an outstanding application under section 46(3)(a) or (b) above for the settlement by the comptroller of the terms of a licence for any description of excepted use of the product,

and, in either case, the licence took or is to take effect at or after the end of the sixteenth year of the patent.

(7) Where a declaration has been filed under this paragraph in respect of a patent—

(a) section 46(3)(c) above (restriction of remedies for infringement where licences available as of right) does not apply to an infringement of the patent in so far as it consists of the excepted use of the product after the filing of the declaration; and

(b) section 46(3)(d) above (abatement of renewal fee if licences available as of right) does not apply the patent.

4B.—(1) An application under section 46(3)(a) or (b) above for the settlement by the comptroller of the terms on which a person is entitled to a licence by virtue of paragraph 4(2)(c) above is ineffective if made before the beginning of the sixteenth year of the patent.

(2) This paragraph applies to applications made after the commencement of section 294 of the Copyright, Designs and Patents Act 1988 [c. 48] and to any application made before the commencement of that section in respect of a patent which has not at the commencement of that section passed the end of its fifteenth year.

5. In section 26(3) of the 1949 Act (no patent of addition unless date of filing of complete specification was the same as or later than the date of filing of complete specification in respect of main invention) after "main

invention" there shall be inserted "and was earlier than the date of the appointed day".

6. Notwithstanding anything in section 32(1)(*j*) of the 1949 Act (ground for revocation that patent was obtained on a false suggestion or representation), it shall not be a ground of revoking a patent under that subsection that the patent was obtained on a false suggestion or representation that a claim of the complete specification of the patent had a priority date earlier than the date of filing the application for the patent, but if it is shown—

(*a*) on a petition under that section or an application under section 33 of that Act; or

(*b*) by way of defence or on a counterclaim on an action infringement;
that such a suggestion or representation was falsely made, the priority date of the claim shall be taken to be the date of filing the application for that patent.

7.—(1) In section 33 of the 1949 Act (revocation of patent by comptroller), in subsection (1) for the words preceding the proviso there shall be substituted—

"(1) Subject to the provisions of this Act, a patent may, on the application of any person interested, be revoked by the comptroller on any of the grounds set out in section 32(1) of this Act."

(2) At the end of the said section 33 there shall be added the following subsection:—

"(5) A decision of the comptroller or on appeal from the comptroller shall not estop any party to civil proceedings in which infringement of a patent is in issue from alleging that any claim of the specification is invalid on any of the grounds set out in section 32(1) of this Act, whether or not any of the issues involved were decided in that decision".

8. In section 101(1) of the 1949 Act (interpretation) there shall be inserted in the appropriate place—

"appointed day" means the day appointed under section 132 of the Patents Act 1977 for the coming into operation of Schedule 1 to that Act;".

Note. Paragraphs 4A and 4B were respectively inserted by sections 293 [1988] and 294 [1988]. By virtue of section 305(2) [1988] these provisions became effective from January 15, 1989. An Order has been made under paragraph 4A (S.I. 1989 No. 1202, reprinted at para. 133.01A *infra*) which became effective on August 14, 1989.

STATUTORY ORDERS UNDER SCHEDULE 1, PARAGRAPH 4A

133.01A   **The Patents (Licences of Right) (Exception of Pesticidal Uses) Order 1989**
(S.I. 1989 No. 1202)

The Secretary of State, in exercise of the powers conferred upon him by section 127(2) of, and paragraph 4A(3) of Schedule 1, to the Patents Act 1977, hereby makes the following Order:

1. This Order may be cited as the Patents (Licences of Right) (Exception of Pesticidal Use) Order 1989 and shall come into force on 14th August 1989.

2.—(1) The following uses of a product are excepted under paragraph 4A of Schedule 1 to the Patents Act 1977—

(a) use of a product as a pesticide, and

(b) the doing of any other act mentioned in section 60(1)(a) of the Patents Act 1977 with a view to such use.

(2) In paragraph (1)(a) above "pesticide" means—

any substance, preparation or organism prepared or used for any of the following purposes:

(a) destroying any pest;

(b) protecting plants or wood or other plant products from harmful organisms;

(c) regulating the growth of plants;

(d) giving protection against harmful creatures;

(e) rendering such creatures harmless;

(f) controlling organisms with harmful or unwanted effects on water systems, buildings or other structures, or on manufactured products;

(g) protecting animals against ectoparasites;

other than:

(aa) organisms other than bacteria, protozoa, fungi, viruses and mycoplasmas, used for destroying or controlling pests;

(bb) substances whose use or sale within the United Kingdom is controlled under any of the following enactments—

Medicines Act 1968 [c. 67];

Agriculture Act 1970, Part IV [c. 40);

Food Act 1984 [c. 30];

Food and Drugs (Scotland) Act 1956 [c. 30];

The Cosmetics Products (Safety) Regulations 1984 [S.I. 1984 No. 1260];

when those substances are used or sold for the purpose over which control under that enactment is exercised;

(cc) substances prepared or used for the purpose of disinfecting, bleaching or sterilising any substance (including water), other than soils, compost or other growing medium;

(dd) substances used in laboratories for the purpose of the micropropagation of plants or substances used in the production of novel food;

(ee) substances designed and used for—

(i) the stimulation of the growth of plants, excluding materials which act as plant growth hormones, or which mimic the action of such materials;

843

(ii) the modification of micro-biological processes in soil, excluding soil sterilants;

(iii) assistance in the anaerobic fermentation of silage;

(*ff*) substances, preparations or organisms, prepared or used for destroying any pest.—

(i) used in adhesive pastes, decorative paper or textiles;

(ii) used as part of a manufacturing process, other than for the purpose of preserving timber or timber products or in the production of food;

(iii) used in preparations intended for topical application to human beings for the purpose of repelling insects;

(iv) used in metal working fluids;

(v) used in paint;

(vi) used in water supply systems or in swimming pools.

(3) Notwithstanding sub-paragraph (*ff*)(ii) and (v) above the expression "pesticide" when used in paragraph (1)(*a*) above includes paints used to prevent the fouling of the hulls of vessels or structures below the waterline, or applied to nets, floats or other apparatus used in the cultivation of fish.

(4) In this Order—

"agricultural" is to be construed in accordance with section 109(3) of the Agriculture Act 1947 [10 & 11 Geo. 6, c. 48];

"creature" means any living organism other than a human being or a plant;

"Crops" includes any form of vegetable produce;

"food" has the meaning assigned to it by section 131 of the Food Act 1984, except that it includes water which is—

(*a*) bottled; or

(*b*) an ingredient of food;

"metal working fluid" means any fluid used to facilitate the cutting, drilling, forming or machining of metal;

"micropropagation" means the growth of plantlets from tissue culture or small parts of a plant in culture solution and under conditions which are sterile apart from the presence of that plant;

"mycoplasma" means a genus of organisms which have a unit membrane without a rigid cell wall and are highly pleomorphic, having no independent form or spore stage in the life cycle;

"novel food" means any food or food ingredient produced from raw material which hitherto has not been used for human consumption or has been so used only in small amounts, or produced by new or extensively modified processes not previously used in the production of food;

"paint" includes surface coatings;

"pest" means—

(*a*) any organism harmful to plants or to wood or other plant products;

(*b*) any undesired plant; and

(*c*) any harmful creature;

"plants" means any form of vegetable matter, while it is growing and after it has been harvested, gathered, felled or picked, and in particular, but without prejudice to the generality of this definition, includes—

(*a*) agricultural crops;

(*b*) tress and bushes grown for purposes other than those of agriculture;

(*c*) wild plants; and

(*d*) fungi;

"soil sterilant" means a substance used to control harmful organisms in soil or compost;

"vessel" has the meaning assigned to it by section 742 of the Merchant Shipping Act 1894 [57 & 58 Vict., c. 60].

ARTICLE 133.02

A. W. White, "Transitional Provisions of the United Kingdom Patents Act 1977", [1983] EIPR 5.

COMMENTARY ON SCHEDULE 1

General (paras. 1 and 8) 133.03

Schedule 1 is introduced by section 127(2) and concerns the application of the 1949 Act to existing patents and applications. As indicated in para. 127.07, the general purpose of Schedule 1 is given by paragraph 1, sub-para. (1) stating that the provisions of the 1949 Act listed in sub-paragraph (2) are to continue to have effect after the appointed day (June 1, 1978 as defined by para. 8), but (by sub-para. (3)) subject to the following provisions of Schedule 1 and those of Schedule 3, para. (2)(*b*) (repeal of s. 32(3) [1949]) and of Schedule 4 (*Transitional provisions*), see the commentary thereon. Many of these 1949 Act provisions are now spent, but those relating to patents of addition (s. 26), amendment (ss. 29 to 31 and 76), validity (ss. 32, 33), co-owners (s. 55), and inventions made by employees (s. 56) continue to have a significant effect, are dealt with in the commentaries thereon in Appendix A.

Prohibition on post-dating (paras. 2 and 5) 133.04

Paragraph 2 amended section 6 [1949] to prevent post-dating of an application after the appointed day in order to ensure that all existing patents would have a priority date prior to June 1, 1978. The provision is spent, but sub-paragraph (2) was considered in *Hydroacoustics' Application* ([1981] FSR 538). Likewise, paragraph 5 amended section 26(3) [1949] so that no patent of addition would be dated on or after June 1, 1978.

Terms of "old" and "new" "existing patents" (paras. 3–4B) 133.05

Paragraphs 3 and 4 are most important provisions. They define the meaning of "old existing patents" and "new existing patents" (para. 3(11)) in terms that the former were patents with complete specifications dated on or before June 1, 1967, and the latter were patents with complete specifications dated after June 1, 1967 and before June 1, 1978. "Old existing patents" could continue to be extended under sections 23 to 25 [1949], though not for a total period exceeding four years (para. 3(2)(3)), but without prejudice to extentions already applied for or granted before June 1, 1978 (para. 3(3) and Sched. 4, para. 18). All "old existing patents" have now expired.

Although the term of a "new existing patent" is automatically extended to 20 years, this is subject to renewal under section 25(3)–(5) [1977] and with limitations on: the method of renewal; the effect of the patent as a result of its automatic endorsement "licences of right"; and licences already in force on June 1, 1978 (para. 4). The provisions relating to "new existing patents" are discussed in greater detail in paras. 25.10 and 25.11, and see the article by A. W. White listed in para. 133.02 *supra*. The operation of the "licence of right" provisions is discussed in the Commentary on section 46 at paragraphs 46.07–46.27.

Paragraphs 4A and 4B were respectively inserted by sections 293 [1988] and 294 [1988]. They came into force on January 15, 1988 (by virtue of s. 305(2) [1988]). These provisions provided, in effect, means for the partial revocation of the "licence of right" provisions on certain types of existing patents, (*viz.* those for "products": though only for the "pharmaceutical uses" of a "medical product" (as defined in para. 4A); and (from August 14, 1989) also for the "pesticidal uses" (as defined in S.I. 1989 No. 1202, reprinted in para. 133.01A *supra*) of products), but without effect upon licences of right, the terms of which had been settled by those dates or for which applications for settlement had by then been filed; and stipulated that no application made under section 46(3)(*a*) or (*b*) for settlement of terms of licence of right can, at least since January 15, 1989 effectively be made before the end of the 15th year of the life of the existing patent. These provisions are dealt with in paragraphs 47.10–47.14 for paragraph 4A, and para. 46.12 for paragraph 4B. These new provisions have given rise to new rule 67A (reprinted at para. 47.06) and to new PF 58/77 (reprinted at para. 141.58), as discussed in para. 47.19.

133.06 *Revocation of "existing patents" (paras. 6 and 7)*

Paragraph 6 amended section 32(1)(*j*) [1949] on the effect of an existing patent being found to have been obtained on a false suggestion. Its effect was in issue in *Masi* v. *Coloroll* ([1986] RPC 483) as discussed in para. A32.30 *infra*.

Paragraph 7 is also a most important provision because it amended section 33 [1949] to provide that an application to revoke an existing patent can now be made to the Comptroller at any time during the life of an existing patent and on any of the grounds specified in section 32 [1949] (as amended by Sched. 1, para. 6 and Scheds. 3 and 6). A new section 33(5) [1949] was also added in similar terms to section 72(5) [1977] in order to prevent a decision of the Comptroller under section 33 [1949] creating an estoppel in subsequent court proceedings. These provisions are discussed in paras. A033.12 and 72.28 respectively, see also the article by A. W. White listed in para. 13302 *supra*.

134.01 **Section 127** **SCHEDULE 2**

APPLICATION OF THIS ACT TO EXISTING PATENTS AND APPLICATIONS

1.—(1) Without prejudice to those provisions of Schedule 4 below which apply (in certain circumstances) provisions of this Act in relation to existing patents and applications, the provisions of this Act referred to in sub-paragraph (2) below shall apply in relation to existing patents and applications on and after the appointed day subject to the following provisions of this Schedule and the provisions of Schedule 4 below.

(2) The provisions are sections 22, 23, 25(3) to (5), 28 to 36, 44 to 54, 86, [96], 98, 99, 101 to 105, 107 to 111, 113 to 116, 118(1) to (3), 119 to 124, 130 and 132(2), (3) and (4).

2. In those provisions as they apply by virtue of this Schedule—

(*a*) a reference to this Act includes a reference to the 1949 Act;

(*b*) a reference to a specified provision of this Act other than one of those provisions shall be construed as a reference to the corresponding provision of the 1949 Act (any provision of that Act being treated as corresponding to a provision of this Act if it was enacted for purposes which are the same as or similar to that provision of this Act);

(*c*) a reference to rules includes a reference to rules under the 1949 Act;

(*d*) references to a patent under this Act, and to an application for such a patent include respectively a reference to an existing patent and application;

(*e*) references to the grant of a patent under this Act includes a reference to the sealing and grant of an existing patent;

(*f*) a reference to a patented product and to a patented invention include respectively a reference to a product and invention patented under an existing patent;

(*g*) references to a published application for a patent under this Act, and to publication of such an application, include respectively references to a complete specification which has been published under the 1949 Act and to publication of such a specification (and a reference to an application for a patent under this Act which has not been published shall be construed accordingly);

(*h*) a reference to the publication in the journal of a notice of the grant of a patent includes a reference to the date of an existing patent;

(*i*) a reference to the priority date of an invention includes a reference to the priority date of the relevant claim of the complete specification.

Note. The amendment to paragraph 1(2) was effected by the Supreme Court Act, 1981 (c. 54, Sched. 7).

COMMENTARY ON SCHEDULE 2

General   **134.02**

Schedule 2 is introduced by section 127(3) and concerns the application of the present Act to "existing patents and applications", but subject to the specific provisions of Schedule 4. As indicated in the commentary on section 127, the general purpose of the Schedule is given by paragraph 1 which (by sub-para. (1)) applied after the appointed day (June 1, 1978) to existing patents and applications those provisions of the present Act which are listed in sub-paragraph (2), but subject to the transitional provisions of Schedule 4, see below and the commentary thereon.

134.03 *Applicability of Act to "existing patents"*

The most important of the 1977 Act provisions applicable to "existing" patents are those of sections: 22 (*secrecy orders*), see also Schedule 4, para. 5; 25(3)–(5) (*patent renewal*); 28 (*restoration*); 29 (*surrender*); 30–36 (*patents as an object of property*); 44–54 (*licences, licences of right and compulsory licences*); 96–108 (*legal proceedings*), other than sections 97, 100 and 106 which are inapplicable to existing patents; 109–113 (*offences*), other than section 112 not applicable to patents as such; 114–115 (*agents*), now to be replaced by sections 274–281, 285 and 286 [1988]; 116 (*immunity*); 118(1)–(3) (*information concerning patents*); 119–124 (*administrative provisions*); 130 (*definitions*) and 132(2)–(4) (*territorial scope*). The individual commentaries on these sections refer to their applicability to "existing" patents as appropriate, and also mention any special considerations which arise under these sections in relation to such patents.

Although sections 55–71 (*Crown user and infringement*) are not listed in paragraph 1(2), these sections mostly apply to acts done in relation to existing patents after June 1, 1978 by virtue of Schedule 4, paras. 2 and 3, see the commentary at para. 136.05.

134.04 *Non-applicability of the Act to "existing patents"*

However, sections: 1–5 and 14(3) (*patentability*); 19, 27, 75 and 117 (*amendment and correction*); and 39–43 (*employee compensation*) do not apply to existing patents in any circumstance. The first two of these matters are therefore dealt with more fully in Appendix A hereto in relation respectively to sections 32 [1949] (*invalidity*); 29–31 [1949] (*amendment*); and 76 [1949] (*correction*), there being no counterpart to sections 39–43 in the 1949 Act.

134.05 *Extension of definitions to "existing patents" (para. 2)*

Paragraph 2 of Schedule 2 extends, in relation to existing patents and applications, various definitions so as to include for the purposes of Schedule 2 references to the provisions of the 1949 Act, rules made thereunder and definitions employed therein. The most important of these provisions is in paragraph 2(*d*) which, in relation to the provisions of the Act listed in paragraph 1(2), extends the definition of a "patent" as used therein to include an "existing patent". Otherwise the term "patent" when used in the 1977 Act means only a patent granted under the Act, see the definition in section 130(1) and para. 130.06. The existence of the provisions of paragraph 2 may also exist in resolving any ambiguity with regard to the application of the Act to existing patents. However, these extended definitions do not appear to apply to the terms when used in Schedule 4.

135.01 Section 127   **SCHEDULE 3**

REPEALS OF PROVISIONS OF 1949 ACT

1. Subject to the provisions of Schedule 4 below, the provisions of the 1949 Act referred to in paragraph 2 below (which have no counterpart in the new law of patents established by this Act in relation to future patents and applications) shall cease to have effect.

2. The provisions are:—

(a) section 14 (opposition to grant of patent);

(b) section 32(3) (revocation for refusal to comply with Crown request to use invention);

(c) section 41 (inventions relating to food or medicine, etc.);

(d) section 42 (comptroller's power to revoke patent after expiry of two years from grant of compulsory licence);

(e) section 71 (extension of time for certain convention applications);

(f) section 72 (protection of inventions communicated under international agreements).

COMMENTARY ON SCHEDULE 3

General 135.02

Schedule 3 is introduced by section 127(5) which refers to repealing certain provisions of the 1949 Act. However, Schedule 3, by paragraph 1, merely rendered these provisions ineffective as from the appointed day (June 1, 1978), it being specified that these provisions have no counterpart in the present Act. The actual repeal of these provisions on the same day occurred under Schedule 6, see the commentary thereon and also para. 132.09, but both Schedules 3 and 6 are subject to Schedule 4 (para. 1) and section 132(7).

Continuing effect of repealed provisions (para. 2) 135.03

The provisions of the 1949 Act in issue hence are those listed in paragraph 2. The provisions of section 14 [1949] (*opposition before grant*) had some continuing effect (Sched. 4, paras. 4, 11–13, 15 and 17(a)), as also did those of section 41 [1949] (*compulsory licences for food or medicine*) (Sched. 4, para. 8). There were no continuing provisions in respect of sections: 32(3) [1949] (*revocation for refusal to supply Crown*); 42 [1949] (*power to revoke after compulsory licence grant*); 71 [1949] (*extension of time for certain covention applications*); and 72 [1949] (*inventions protected under certain international agreements*), presumably because no need for such was seen.

| Section 127 | **SCHEDULE 4** | 136.01 |

TRANSITIONAL PROVISIONS

General

1. In so far as any instrument made or other thing done under any provision of the 1949 Act which is repealed by virtue of this Act could have been made or done under a corresponding provision of this Act, it shall not be invalidated by the repeals made by virtue of this Act but shall have effect as if made or done under that corresponding provision.

Use of patented invention for services of the Crown

2.—(1) Any question whether—

(*a*) an act done before the appointed day by a government department or a person authorised in writing by a government department amounts to the use of an invention for the services of the Crown; or

(*b*) any payment falls to be made in respect of any such use (whether to a person entitled to apply for a patent for the invention, to the patentee or to an exclusive licensee);

shall be determined under section 46 to 49 of that Act and those sections shall apply accordingly.

(2) Sections 55 to 59 above shall apply to an act so done on or after the appointed day in relation to an invention—

(*a*) for which an existing patent has been granted or an existing application for a patent has been made; or

(*b*) which was communicated before that day to a government department or any person authorised in writing by a government department by the proprietor of the patent or any person from whom he derives title;

and shall so apply subject to sub-paragraph (3) below, the modifications contained in paragraph 2 of Schedule 2 above and the further modification that sections 55(5)(*b*) and 58(10) above shall not apply in relation to an existing application.

(3) Where an act is commenced before the appointed day and continues to be done on or after that day, then, if it would not amount to the use of an invention for the services of the Crown under the 1949 Act, its continuance on or after that day shall not amount to such use under this Act.

Infringement

3.—(1) Any question whether an act done before the appointed day infringes an existing patent or the privileges or rights arising under a complete specification which has been published shall be determined in accordance with the law relating to infringement in force immediately before that day and, in addition to those provisions of the 1949 Act which continue to apply by virtue of Schedule 1 above, section 70 of that Act shall apply accordingly.

(2) Sections 60 to 71 above shall apply to an act done on or after the appointed day which infringes an existing patent or the privileges or rights arising under a complete specification which has been published (whether before, on or after the appointed day) as they apply to infringements of a patent, and shall so apply subject to sub-paragraph (3) below, the modifications contained in paragraph 2 of Schedule 2 above and the further modification that section 69(2) and (3) above shall apply in relation to an existing application.

(3) Where an act is commenced before the appointed day and continues to be done on or after that day, then, if it would not, under the law in force immediately before that day, amount to an infringement of an existing patent or the privileges or rights arising under a complete specification, its continuance on or after that day shall not amount to the infringement of that patent or those privileges or rights.

Notice of opposition

4.—(1) Where notice of opposition to the grant of a patent has been given under section 14 of the 1949 Act before the appointed day, the following provisions shall apply:

(*a*) if issue has been joined on the notice before the appointed day, the opposition, any appeal from the comptroller's decision on it and any further appeal shall be prosecuted under the old law, but as if references in the 1949 Act and rules made under it to the Appeal Tribunal were references to the Patents Court;

(*b*) in any other case the notice shall be taken to have abated immediately before the appointed day.

(2) Sub-paragraph 1(*a*) above shall have effect subject to paragraph 12(2) below.

Secrecy

5.—(1) Where directions given under section 18 of the 1949 Act in respect of an existing application (directions restricting publication of information about inventions) are in force immediately before the appointed day, they shall continue in force on and after that day and that section shall continue to apply accordingly.

(2) Where sub-paragraph (1) above does not apply in the case of an existing application section 18 of the 1949 Act shall not apply to the application but section 22 of this Act shall.

(3) Where the comptroller has before the appointed day served a notice under section 12 of the Atomic Energy Act 1946 [9 & 10 Geo. 6, c. 80] (restrictions on publication of information about atomic energy, etc.) in respect of an existing application that section shall continue to apply to the application on and after that day; but where no such notice has been so served that section shall not apply to the application on and after that day.

Revocation

6.—(1) Where before the appointed day an application has been made under section 33 of the 1949 Act for the revocation of a patent (the original application), the following provisions shall apply:

(*a*) if issue has been joined on the application before the appointed day, the application, any appeal from the comptroller's decision on it and any further appeal shall be prosecuted under the old law, but as if references in the 1949 Act rules made under it to the Appeal Tribunal were references to the Patents Court;

(b) if issue has not been so joined, the original application shall be taken to be an application under section 33 of the 1949 Act for the revocation of the patent on whichever of the grounds referred to in section 32(1) of that Act corresponds (in the comptroller's opinion) to the ground on which the original application was made, or, if there is no ground which so corresponds, shall be taken to have abated immmediately before the appointed day.

(2) Sub-paragraph (1)(a) above shall have effect subject to paragraph 11(3) below.

7.—(1) This paragraph applies where an application has been made before the appointed day under section 42 of the 1949 Act for the revocation of a patent.

(2) Where the comptroller has made no order before that day for the revocation of the patent under that section, the application shall be taken to have abated immediately before that day.

(3) Where the comptroller has made such an order before that day, then, without prejudice to section **16**[*38*] of the Interpretation Act **1978** [c.30] [*1889*] section 42 shall continue to apply to the patent concerned on and after that day as if this Act had not been enacted.

Licences of right and compulsory licenses

8.—(1) Sections 35 to 41 and 43 to 45 of the 1949 Act shall continue to apply on and after the relevant day—

(a) to any endorsement or order made or licence granted under sections 35 to 41 which is in force immediately before that day; and

(b) to any application made before that day under sections 35 to 41.

(2) Any appeal from a decision or order of the comptroller instituted under sections 35 to 41 or 43 to 45 on or after the relevant day (and any further appeal) shall be prosecuted under the old law, but as if references in the 1949 Act and rules made under it to the Appeal Tribunal were references to the Patents Court.

(3) In this paragraph "the relevant day" means, in relation to section 41, the date of the passing of this Act and, in relation to sections 35 to 40 and 43 to 45 the appointed day.

Convention countries

9.—(1) Without prejudice to paragraph 1 above, an Order in Council declaring any country to be a convention country for all purposes of the 1949 Act or for the purposes of section 1(2) of that Act and in force immediately before the appointed day shall be treated as an Order in Council under section 90 above declaring that country to be a convention country for the purpose of section 5 above.

(2) Where an Order in Council declaring any country to be a convention country for all purposes of the 1949 Act or for the purposes of section 70 of that Act is in force immediately before the appointed day, a vessel registered in that country (whether before, on or after that day) shall be treated for the purposes of section 60 above, as it applies by virtue of paragraph 3(2) above to an existing patent or existing application, as a relevant ship and an aircraft so registered and a land vehicle owned by a person ordinarily resident in that country shall be so treated respectively as a relevant aircraft and a relevant vehicle.

Appeal from court on certain petitions for revocation

10. Where the court has given judgment on a petition under section 32(1)(*j*) of the 1949 Act before the appointed day, any appeal from the judgment (whether instituted before, on or after that day) shall be continued or instituted and be disposed of under the old law.

Appeals from comptroller under continuing provisions of 1949 Act

11.—(1) In this paragraph "the continuing 1949 Act provisions" means the provisions of the 1949 Act which continue to apply on and after the appointed day as mentioned in paragraph 1 of Schedule 1 above.

(2) This paragraph applies where—

(*a*) the comptroller gives a decision or direction (whether before or on or after the appointed day) under any of the continuing 1949 Act provisions, and

(*b*) an appeal lies under those provisions from the decision or direction;

but this paragraph applies subject to the foregoing provisions of this Schedule.

(3) Where such an appeal has been instituted before the Appeal Tribunal before the appointed day, and the hearing of the appeal has begun but has not been completed before the day, the appeal (and any further appeal) shall be continued and disposed of under the old law.

(4) Where such an appeal has been so instituted, but the hearing of it has not begun before the appointed day, it shall be transferred by virtue of his sub-paragraph to the Patents Court on that day and the appeal (and any further appeal) shall be prosecuted under the old law, but as if references in the 1949 Act and rules made under it to the Appeal Tribunal were references to the Patents Court.

(5) Any such appeal instituted on or after the appointed day shall lie to the Patents Court or, where the proceedings appealed against were held in

Scotland, the Court of Session; and accordingly, the reference to the Appeal Tribunal in section 31(2) of the 1949 Act shall be taken to include a reference to the Patents Court or (as the case may be) the Court of Session.

(6) Section 97(3) of this Act shall apply to any decision of the Patents Court on an appeal instituted on or after the appointed day from a decision or direction of the comptroller under any of the continuing 1949 Act provisions as it applies to a decision of that Court referred to in that subsection, except that for references to the sections mentioned in paragraph (*a*) of that subsection there shall be substituted references to sections 33, 55 and 56 of the 1949 Act.

Appeals from comptroller under repealed provisions of 1949 Act

12.—(1) This paragraph applies where an appeal to the Appeal Tribunal has been instituted before the appointed day under any provision of the 1949 Act repealed by this Act.

(2) Where the hearing of such an appeal has begun but has not been completed before that day, the appeal (and any further appeal) shall be continued and disposed of under the old law.

(3) Where the hearing of such an appeal has not begun before that day, it shall be transferred by virtue of this sub-paragraph to the Patents Court on that day and the appeal (and any further appeal) shall be prosecuted under the old law, but as if references in the 1949 Act and rules made under it to the Appeal Tribunal were references to the Patents Court.

Appeals from Appeal Tribunal to Court of Appeal

13. Section 87(1) of the 1949 Act shall continue to apply on and after the appointed day to any decision of the Appeal Tribunal given before that day, and any appeal by virtue of this paragraph (and any further appeal) shall be prosecuted under the old law.

Rules

14. The power to make rules under section 123 of this Act shall include power to make rules for any purpose mentioned in section 94 of the 1949 Act.

Supplementary

15. Section 97(2) of this Act applies to—
(*a*) any appeal to the Patents Court by virtue of paragraph 4(1)(*a*), 6(1)(*a*), 8(2) or 11(5) above, and
(*b*) any appeal which is transferred to that Court by virtue of paragraph 11(4) or 12(3) above,

as it applies to an appeal under that section; and section 97 of this Act shall apply for the purposes of any such appeal instead of section 85 of the 1949 Act.

16. In this Schedule "the old law" means the 1949 Act, any rules made under it and any relevant rule of law as it was or they were immediately before the appointed day.

17. For the purposes of this Schedule—

(*a*) issue is joined on a notice of opposition to the grant of a patent under section 14 of the 1949 Act when the applicant for the patent files a counter-statement fully setting out the grounds on which the opposition is contested;

(*b*) issue is joined on an application for the revocation of a patent under section 33 of that Act when the patentee files a counter-statement fully setting out the grounds on which the application is contested.

18.—(1) Nothing in the repeals made by this Act in sections 23 and 24 of the 1949 Act shall have effect as respects any such application as is mentioned in paragraph 3(3) of Schedule 1 above.

(2) Nothing in the repeal by this act of the Patents Act 1957 shall have effect as respects existing applications.

(3) Section 69 of the 1949 Act (which is not repealed by this Act) and section 70 of that Act (which continues to have effect for certain purposes by virtue of paragraph 3 above) shall apply as if section 68 of that Act has not been repealed by this Act and as if paragraph 9 above had not been enacted.

Note. The amendment to paragraph 7(2) was effected by the Interpretation Act 1978 (c. 30, s. 25(2)).

COMMENTARY ON SCHEDULE 4

General   **136.02**

Schedule 4 is introduced by section 127(6) and contains transitional provisions which modify the provisions of Schedules 1–3 and 6, each of which is subject to the provisions of Schedule 4 (see Sched. 1, para. 1(3), Sched. 2. para. 1(1). Sched. 3, para. 1(1) and s. 132(7)). The term "old law" as used in Schedule 4 means the 1949 Act, the rules made thereunder and any rules of law as applicable on the appointed day (para. 16), the repeal of the Patents Act 1957 (5 & 6 Eliz. 2, c. 74) having no effect (para. 18(2) and Sched. 6).

Instruments made and things done before the appointed day (para. 1)   **136.03**

Paragraph 1 refers to "any instrument made or other thing done under any provision of the 1949 Act repealed by virtue of this Act" and provides that such is to have continuing effect in so far as it could have been made or done under the present Act as if had been so made or done under a corresponding provision of the present Act. In this way, assignments and licences executed before June 1, 1978 continue to have effect. While it could be argued that the provision renders ineffective instruments made or things done before June 1, 1978 which can be longer be made or done under the 1977 Act, *e.g.* execution of assignments by the assignor only (s. 30(6) [1977]) or an assignment for a part of the United Kingdom only (s. 21(1) [1949]) not apparently continued for patents granted under the present Act, see section 30 [1977]—such will generally continue to be effective because the benefit of the transaction will probably be an "accrued right," see para. 127.09.

The Comptroller has stated that Schedule 4, paragraph 1 affords no power to vary the provisions of the Act so as to accommodate the possibility of an application acquiring an earlier priority date as a remedy in a successful revocation action for a patent granted without entitlement thereto (*Georgia Pacific's Application*, [1984] RPC 467).

136.04 *Spent provisions*

Many of the provisions of Schedule 4 have ceased to have any practical effect because they relate to proceedings which were, or might have been, in being on the appointed day (generally June 1, 1978) and these proceedings should now have been concluded or no longer be actionable under the Limitation Act 1980 (c. 58). These provisions are: acts of Crown use and of infringement (paras. 2(1) and 3(1)), other than possibly continuing acts as discussed in para. 136.05 *infra*; oppositions and revocation proceedings lodged before the Comptroller before the appointed day, and appeals therefrom (paras. 4, 6, 7, 10–13, 15, 17 and 18(1) and (2)). It may, however, be noted that paragraphs 6(1)(*a*) and 11(6) were in issue in *Standard Brands' Patent* ([1980] RPC 187) where the Court of Appeal held that interpretation of paragraph 6(1)(*a*) probably denied any effect to paragraph 11(6). The term "issue has been joined," as used in paragraph 17, was interpreted in *Standard Oil's (Fahrig's) Application* ([1980] RPC 359).

Provisions with continuing effect

136.05 —*Crown use and infringement (paras. 2 and 3)*

As for acts of Crown use and infringement occurring after June 1, 1978 in relation to "existing patents", sections 55–59 and 60–71 respectively apply (paras. 2(2) and 3(2)), despite the absence of reference to these provisions in Schedule 2, paragraph 1(2). However, if such acts are ones which were carried out before June 1, 1978 and "continue" thereafter, then these would continue to be considered under the 1949 Act (paras. 2(3) and 3(3)). The nature of a continuing act was discussed in *Rotocrop* v. *Genbourne* ([1982] FSR 241).

The stated applicability (by para. 3(2)) of sections 62–71 to acts of infringement occurring on or after June 1, 1978 causes some difficulty as some of these sections do not pertain to "infringement" as such. While these sections have generally been held to apply to "existing patents", see *Therm-a-stor* v. *Weatherseal* ([1981] FSR 579), *Martinez's Patent* ([1983] RPC 307) and *Reckitt & Colman* v. *Biorex* ([1985] FSR 94), an exception is that section 65 (*certificate of validity*) has been held not to apply to revocation actions before the Comptroller under section 33 [1949] (*Canon K. K.'s Patent*, [1982] RPC 549). The applicability of section 64 (*right to continue prior secret use*) remains unsettled, see para. 64.07 and an article by A. W. White ([1983] EIPR 5).

In *Masi* v. *Coloroll* ([1986] RPC 483) it was put forward, but not there decided, that, in a case where validity of an existing patent obtained on a false suggestion was saved (subject to loss of priority date) by Schedule 1, paragraph 6, Schedule 4, paragraph 3(3) would provide an alternative argument that the patent would be unenforceable after the appointed date because the act in question would not have been an infringement before that date due to the then invalidity of the patent.

—Secrecy provisions (para. 5)   **136.06**

Paragraph 5 provides for the continuing effect of secrecy directions made under section 18 [1949] or under section 12(1) of the Atomic Energy Act 1946 (9 & 10 Geo. 6, c. 80) (now repealed by Sched. 6), but otherwise section 22 [1977] is to apply to existing applications (para. 5(2)). This leads to the result that (by virtue of section 18(1) [1949]) the provisions of the 1949 Act continue to apply to the grant of patents on "existing applications" upon which secrecy orders have been imposed. However, if such applications are withdrawn, there is now to be no requirement for the Comptroller to advertise acceptance of the application or to publish the complete specification, see the amendment to be made to section 13(2) [1949] by Schedule 5, paragraph 1 [1988]) noted in para. A013.1. It is understood that, in the absence of this amendment, a number of files have had to be kept open and secrecy directions thereon reviewed annually because there has been no mechanism for abandoning an accepted application, other than by failing to pay the sealing fee after publication, but publication could not take place because of the need to continue the secrecy directions. The amendment to section 13(2) [1949] will allow these applications to be abandoned.

—Licences of right and compulsory licences (para. 8)   **136.07**

Paragraph 8 provides for the continuing effect of "licence of right" endorsements and compulsory licences already granted, or for which applications had already been made, under sections 35–41 [1949] and 43–45 [1949] by the relevant day, which was July 20, 1977 in the case of section 41 [1949] and June 1, 1978 otherwise, see para. 132.07. However, paragraph 8 does not extend to "licence of right" endorsements which, after June 1, 1978, are deemed to occur when existing patents are maintained in force after their sixteenth year (Sched. 1, para. 4(2)(*c*)) or to licences the terms of which are settled after such deemed endorsement has occurred. For such patents the terms of section 46 apply (*Allen & Hanburys* v. *Generics*, [1986] RPC 203 (HL)). The extent to which section 36 [1949] could continue to have effect for the cancellation of a licence of right endorsement made before June 1, 1978 is discussed in a note at para. A036.6.

—Designation of Convention Countries (para. 9)   **136.08**

Paragraph 9 continued the effect of Orders in Council made under the 1949 Act, and earlier patent statutes, designating certain countries as "Convention Countries" for the purposes of the Acts, but without effect on the continuing effect of sections 69 and 70 [1949] which also are not affected by the repeal of section 68 [1949] (para. 18(3)), see para. 90.02.

Power to make rules (para. 14)   **136.09**

Paragraph 14 adds to section 123 the power to make rules for any purpose mentioned in section 94 [1949]. It is under this power that any amendment is made to the Patents Rules 1968 (as amended) (for which see para. A109) and the forms used in connection therewith (for which see para. A119—A138).

137.01 **Section 132** **SCHEDULE 5**

Consequential Amendments

Crown Proceedings Act 1947 (10 & 11 Geo. 6, c. 44)

1. . . .

Note. The amendment to section 3 of the Crown Proceedings Act 1947 (c. 44) made by this para. 1 has been superseded by a new section 3 thereof. This is reproduced in para. 129.02.

Registered Designs Act 1949 (12, 13 & 14 Geo. 6, c. 88)

2. . . .

Note. The amendment to section 32 of the Registered Designs Act 1949 (c. 88) made by this para. 2 has been superseded by repeal of that section (Sched. 8 [1988]).

3. In sections 42 [*and 44(1)*] of the Registered Designs Act 1949, for "the Patents Act 1949" there shall be substituted [*, in each case,*] "the Patents Act 1977".

Note. The further amendments indicated were made by Schedule 8 [1988].

Defence Contracts Act 1958 (6 & 7 Eliz. 2, c. 38)

4. In subsection (4) of section 4 of the Defence Contracts Act 1958, for the words from "Patents Act 1949" to the end there shall be substituted "Patents Act 1977".

Administration of Justice Act 1970 (c. 31)

5.—(1) In subsections (2) and (3) of section 10 of the Administration of Justice Act 1970 for "either" there shall be substituted, in each case, "the".

(2) In subsection (4) of the said section 10, for "(as so amended)" there shall be substituted "(as amended by section 24 of the Administration of Justice Act 1969) [c. 58]".

(3) For subsection (5) of the said section 10, there shall be substituted:—

"(5) In subsection (8) of the said section 38 [of the Registered Designs Act 1949 (c. 88)] (which confers power on the Tribunal to make rules about procedure etc.), there shall be inserted at the end of the subsection the words "including right of audience".

Atomic Energy Authority (Weapons Group) Act 1973 (c. 4)

6. In section 5(2) of the Atomic Energy Authority (Weapons Group) Act 1973—

(*a*) after the first "Patents Act 1949" there shall be inserted, "the Patents Act 1977"; and

(*b*) after the second "Patents Act 1949" there shall be inserted "section 55(4) of the Patents Act 1977."

Fair Trading Act (c. 41)

7. . . .

Note. This provision amended paragraph 10 of, and added new paragraph 10A to, Schedule 4 of the Fair Trading Act 1973 (c. 41), but these paragraphs have been further amended by the Administration of Justice Act 1985 (c. 6, s. 60), and prospectively by Schedule 7, paragraph 15, and Schedule 8 [1988], so that paragraph 7 to Schedule 5 will be repealed when Schedule 7, para. 15 [1988] and Schedule 8 [1988] are brought into effect (for which see the latest Supplement to this Work *re.* the present para.). These paragraphs in the Fair Trading Act 1973 will then read:-

"**10.** The services of registered patent agents (within the meaning of Part V of the Copyright, Designs and Patents Act 1988 [c. 48]) in their capacity as such."; and

"**10A.** The services of persons carrying on for gain in the United Kingdom the business of acting as agents or other representatives of other persons for the purpose of applying for or obtaining European patents or for the purpose of conducting proceedings in relation to applications for or otherwise in connection with such patents before the European Patent Office or the comptroller and whose names appear on the European list (within the meaning of Part V of the Copyright, Designs and Patents Act 1988 [c. 48]) in their capacity as such persons".

Note. The above-mentioned services are discussed at paras. 102.18–102.25 for "patent agents", and at paras. 102.34–102.38 for "European patent attorneys".

Restrictive Trade Practices Act 1976 (c. 34)

8 . . .

Note. This provision amended paragraph 10 of, and added new paragraph 10A to, Schedule 1 of the Restrictive Trade Practices Act 1976 (c. 34), but these paragraphs have been further amended by the Administration of Justice 1985 (c. 61, s.60), and prospectively by Schedule 7, para. 18(2) [1988] and Schedule 8 [1988], so that, when these provisions are brought into effect (for which see the latest Supplement to this Work *re.* the present para.), paragraph 8 to Schedule 5 will be repealed and the amended substituted paragraphs in the Restrictive Trade Practices Act 1976 will then have identical wording to the revised paragraphs 10 and 10A of Schedule 4 of the Fair Trading Act 1973 (c. 41), reprinted *re.* paragraph 7 of Schedule 5 *supra*. Thus, the *Note* thereto applies also hereto, *mutatis mutandis*.

COMMENTARY ON SCHEDULE 5   **137.02**

Schedule 5 is introduced by section 132(6) and made some consequential amendments in certain other statutes so that these would apply, or be applied, to the modern patent statute. Notes in para. 137.01 *supra* indicate where these amendments have been further amended or otherwise superseded.

As regards such of these amendments as they continue to have effect, it is noted that:

Paragraph 1, amending section 3 of the Crown Proceedings Act 1947 (c. 44), is discussed in para. 129.02;

Paragraph 3, amending section 42 of the Registered Designs Act 1949 (c. 88), is discussed in para. 121.03;

Paragraph 4, amending section 4(4) of the Defence Contracts Act 1958 (c. 38), is noted in para. B.11;

Paragraph 5 (together with the partial repeal set out in Schedule 6) had the effect of confining section 10 of the Administration of Justice Act 1970 (c. 31) to making provision for the Registered Designs Tribunal to hear appeals from the Comptroller under the Registered Designs Act 1949 (c. 88), appeals under the Patents Act 1977 (and now also the Patents Act 1949) now being heard by the Patents Court by virtue of section 97, see para. 97.03;

Paragraph 6, amending section 5(2) of the *Atomic Energy Authority (Weapons Group) Act 1973* (c. 4), may have some relevance to Crown uses and is mentioned in para. 55.11; and

Paragraphs 7 and 8 made amendments to the Fair Trading Act 1973 (c. 41) and the Restrictive Trade Practices Act 1976 (c. 34) which, in a further revised form (as noted *supra*), continue to have effect in relation to the powers of registered patent agents and European patent attorneys: these are discussed in paras. 102.18–102.25 and 102.34–102.38 respectively.

138.01   Section 132   **SCHEDULE 6**

ENACTMENTS REPEALED

Chapter	Short Title	Extent of Repeal
7 Edw. 7. c. 29.	The Patents and Designs Act 1907.	Section 47(2).
9 & 10 Geo. 6. c. 80.	The Atomic Energy Act 1946.	In section 12, subsections (1) to (7).
12, 13, & 14 Geo. 6. c. 87.	The Patents Act 1949.	Section 11(3). Section 14. Section 16(6). Section 18. Section 22(4) and (5). In section 23(1), the words from "(not exceeding" to "ten years)". In section 24, in subsection (1), the words "(not exceeding ten years)" and, in subsection (7), the words from "but" to the end. Section 27. In section 32, subsection (3). In section 33(3), the proviso. Sections 34 to 45. Sections 54, 57 and 58. Section 68.

Chapter	Short Title	Extent of Repeal
		Sections 70 to 75.
		Sections 77 to 79.
		Sections 81 to 86.
		Section 87(1) and (3).
		Sections 88 to 91.
		Sections 93 to 95.
		Sections 97 to 100.
		Section 102(2).
		Schedule 1.
		Schedule 3, except paragraphs 1 and 26.
5 & 6 Eliz. 2. c. 13.	The Patents Act 1957.	The whole Act, except in relation to existing applications.
9 & 10 Eliz. 2. c. 25.	The Patents and Designs (Renewals, Extensions and Fees) Act 1961.	In section 1(1), the words from "subsection (5)" to "and in". Section 2.
10 & 11 Eliz. 2. c. 30.	The Northern Ireland Act 1962.	In Schedule 1, the entry relating to section 84 of the Patents Act 1949.
1967 c. 80.	The Criminal Justice Act 1967.	In Schedule 3, in Parts I and IV, the entries relating to the Patents Act 1949.
1968 c. 64.	The Civil Evidence Act 1968.	Section 15.
1969 c. 58.	The Administration of Justice Act 1969.	In section 24, in subsection (1), the words "85 of the Patents Act 1949 and section" and "each of", in subsections (2), (3) and (4) the words "of each of those sections" and in subsection (4) the words from "as subsection (11)" to "and" and the words "in the case of the said section 28".
1970 c. 31.	The Administration of Justice Act 1970.	In section 10, in subsection (1), the words "Patents Appeal Tribunal or the" and in subsection (4), the words from "the Patents Appeal" to "and".
1971 c. 23.	The Courts Act 1971.	Section 46.
1971 c. 36 (N.I.).	The Civil Evidence Act (Northern Ireland) 1971.	Section 11.
1973 c. 41.	The Fair Trading Act 1973.	Section 26. In Schedule 3, in paragraph 16(2), the words from "of section 40" to "Commission" where first occurring. In Schedule 12, the entry relating to the Patents Act 1949.
1974 c. 47.	The Solicitors Act 1974.	In Schedule 3, paragraph 3.

138.02   COMMENTARY ON SCHEDULE 6

General

Schedule 6 is introduced by section 132(7) and is subject to the provisions of Schedule 4. It repealed, to the extent specified in column 3 of the Schedule, the enactments specified in columns 1 and 2 thereto. The provisions so repealed were either: (a) spent or would be so once the transitional provisions of Schedule 4 ceased to have effect; or (b) arose because it was desired to delete altogether a particular provision from the statute book. It should be noted that a repealed provision, despite its repeal, can be given continuing effect if other statutory provisions so provide or where there is a question of an "accrued right" as discussed in para. 127.09. However, the repeal of a provision which itself repealed a previous enactment does not revive that enactment, and a repeal does not (unless the contrary intention appears) revive anything not then in force or affect the previous operation of any enactment (Interpretation Act 1978 (c. 30, ss. 15 and 16).

138.03   *Appendices A and B to this work*

Appendix A, commencing at p. 919, deals with the unrepealed provisions of the 1949 Act with commentaries on those sections which appear to have some practical continuing effect, and where the commentary thereon could not conveniently be incorporated in the commentary on a corresponding provision of the present Act. Appendix B commencing at p. 1062 makes reference to, and reprints as appropriate, other patent and patent-related statutes which also continue to remain in operation.

138.04   *Unrepealed provisions of Patents Act 1949*

The unrepealed provisions of the 1949 Act are: sections 1–13 (except s. 11(3)); 15–17 (except s. 16(6)); 19–26 (except ss. 22(4) and (5) and with amendment of ss. 23 and 24); 28–33 (except s. 32(3) and the proviso to s. 33(3)); 46–53; 55; 59–67; 69; 76; 80; 87(2); 92; 96; 101–107 (except s. 102(2)); Schedule 2 (as previously amended); and Schedule 3 (paras. 1 and 26 only). Commentaries and notes on these provisions are provided in Appendix A.

139.01   THE PATENTS RULES 1982

S.I. 1982 No. 717
(as amended)

ARRANGEMENT OF RULES

(*For amendment and revocations, see para. of reprint*)

Miscellaneous

International applications

SCHEDULES:

139.02 *Notes on Patents Rules 1982.*

1. Because of the copious amendments made to the Patents Rules 1982, it is expected that these will shortly be reissued in a new consolidation. The entry in the Supplement under this paragraph No. 139.02 should therefore be checked in case the consolidation may have changed the numbers of these rules.

2. At the time of going to press, the Patents Rules 1982 had been amended (other than by amendments which have since been superseded) by:

   (*a*) the Patents (Amendment) Rules 1985 (S.I. 1985 No. 785), amending Schedule 2 (all forms amended from September 23, 1985);

   (*b*) the Patents (Amendment No. 2) Rules 1985 (S.I. 1985 No. 1166), revoking rule 123 and amending rules 5, 6, 15, 85, 95, 102, 113, 117, 118,

122 and Schedule 2 (amending PF 1/77 and withdrawing PF 42/77), each from September 1, 1985;

(c) the Patents (Fees) Rules 1986 (S.I. 1986 No. 583), revoking rule 3 and Schedule 1 to provide for separate Patents (Fees) Rules (for which see para. 144.01); and amending rules 85, 118, 120, 121 and Schedule 2 (PF 23/77 amended), each from May 26, 1986;

(d) the Patents (Amendment) Rules 1987 (S.I. 1987 No. 288), revoking rules 28 and 80 and amending rules 20, 25, 26, 99, 100, 110 and Schedule 2 (PF 40/77 and 50/77 amended and new PF 52/77 and PF 53/77 added), with effect from March 24, 1987; and adding rules 79A–79F, amending rule 113 and Schedule 2 (PF 23/77 amended and PF 54/77–PF 57/77 added), with effect from September 1, 1987;

(e) the Patents (Amendment) Rules 1988 (S.I. 1988 No. 2089) amending rules 52 and 93 and PF 23/77 and 24/77, with effect from January 1, 1989; and adding new rule 63A and PF 58/77, with effect from January 15, 1989; and

(f) the Patents (Amendment) Rules 1989 (S.I. 1989 No. 1116 amending rules 69 and 111, with effect from August 1,1989.

For further changes, see the latest Supplement to this Work under this para. 139.02.

2. Details of those of the 1968 Rules (as amended) which still have effect are given in para. A109.

3. Details of rules additional to the 1982 and 1968 Rules, and of fees and other forms, will be found at paras. 142.01–144.02 respectively.

FEES 140.01

SCHEDULE 1 TO THE PATENTS RULES 1982 [Revoked]

This Schedule listed the various fees payable under the Rules and was revoked and replaced by the Patents (Fees) Rules 1986 (S.I. 1986 No. 583). A note on the current Fees Schedule will be found in paragraph 144.01.

FORMS

SCHEDULE 2 TO PATENTS RULES 1982 140.02

Note. The address of the Patent Office was removed from each of the Forms by S.I. 1985 No. 785. The Patent Office address is now stipulated by the Patent Office (Address) Rules 1985 (S.I. 1985 No. 1099, reprinted at para. 123.02), but this address is no longer part of the wording of the Forms. Any amendments noted below to the forms of Schedule 2 are in addition to the deletion of the former Patent Office address.

FORMS OF SCHEDULE 2

141.01   **PATENTS ACT 1977**

PATENTS FORM No. 1/77 (Revised 1982)
(Rules 16, 19)

The Comptroller
The Patent Office

REQUEST FOR GRANT OF A PATENT

THE GRANT OF A PATENT IS REQUESTED BY THE UNDERSIGNED ON THE BASIS OF THE PRESENT APPLICATION

I   Applicant's or Agent's Reference (*Please insert if available*)

II   Title of Invention

III   Applicant or Applicants (*see note 2*)

Name (First or only applicant) ....
Country .... State.................... ADP Code No. ....
Address ....
Name (of second applicant, if more than one)...
.... Country.............. State...........
Address ....

IV   Inventor (*see note 3*)   (a) The applicant(s) is/are the sole/joint inventor(s) or
                                   (b) A statement on Patents Form No. 7/777 is/will be furnished

	ADP CODE NO.
V Name of Agent (if any) (*see note 4*)	

VI   Address for Service (*see note 5*)

VII   Declaration of Priority (*see note 6*)

Country	Filing data	File number

....
....

VIII   The Application claims an earlier date under Section 8(3), 12(6), 15(4), or 37(4) (*see note 7*)

Earlier application or patent number........................... and filing date..............

IX   Check List (*To be filled in by applicant or agent*)

A   The application contains the following number of sheet(s)

B   The application as filed is accompanied by:-

1   Request .... Sheet(s)   1   Priority document ....
2   Description .... Sheet(s)   2   Translation of priority document ......

868

3	Claim(s) .... Sheet(s)	3	Request for Search ....
4	Drawing(s) .... Sheet(s)	4	Statement of Inventorship and Right to Grant....................................
5	Abstract .... Sheet(s)		

X   It is suggested that Figure No. .... of the drawings (if any) should accompany the abstract when published.

XI   Signature (*see note 8*)

NOTES:
1. This form, when completed, should be brought or sent to the Patent Office together with the prescribed fee and two copies of the description of the invention, and of any drawings.
2. Enter the name and address of each applicant. Names of individuals should be indicated in full and the surname or family name should be underlined. The names of all partners in a firm must be given in full. Bodies corporate should be designated by their corporate name and the country of incorporation and, where appropriate, the state of incorporation within that country should be entered where provided. Full corporate details, eg "a corporation organised and existing under the laws of the State of Delaware, United States of America," trading styles, eg "trading as xyz company", nationality, and former names, eg "formerly [known as] ABC Ltd." are *not* required and should *not* be given. Also enter applicant(s) ADP Code No. (if known).
3. Where the applicant or applicants is/are the sole inventor or the joint inventors, the declaration (a) to that effect at IV should be completed, and the alternative statement (b) deleted. If, however, this is not the case the declaration (a) should be struck out and a statement will then be required to be filed upon Patent Form No. 7/77.
4. If the applicant has appointed an agent to act on his behalf, the agent's name and the address of his place of business should be indicated in the spaces available at V and VI. Also insert agent's ADP Code No. (if known) in the box provided.
5. An address for service in the United Kingdom to which all documents may be sent must be stated at VI. It is recommended that a telephone number be provided if an agent is not appointed.
6. The declaration of priority at VII should state the date of the previous filing and the country in which it was made and indicate the file number, if available.
7. When an application is made by virtue of section 8(3), 12(6), 15(4), or 37(4) the appropriate section should be identified at VIII and the number of the earlier application or any patent granted thereon identified.
8. Attention is directed to rules 90 and 106 of the Patent Rules 1982.
9. Attention of applicants is drawn to the desirability of avoiding publication of inventions relating to any article, material or device intended or adapted for use in war (Official Secrets Acts, 1911 and 1920). In addition after an application for a patent has been filed at the Patent Office the comptroller will consider whether publication or communication of the invention should be prohibited or restricted under section 22 of the Act and will inform the applicant if such prohibition is necessary.
10. Applicants resident in the United Kingdom are also reminded that, under the provisions of section 23 applications may not be filed abroad without written permission or unless an application has been filed not less than six weeks previously in the United Kingdom for a patent for the same invention and no direction prohibiting publication or communication has been given or any such direction has been revoked.

Notes 1. Note 10 was amended by S.I. 1985 No. 1166, r. 14.

2. It is understood that PF 1/77 is being redesigned. The latest Supplement to this Work *re*. this para. 141.01 should therefore be consulted.

141.02 **PATENTS ACT 1977**

PATENTS FORM No. 2/77 (Revised 1982)
(Rules 7, 8, 54, 55)

The Comptroller
The Patent Office

REFERENCE UNDER SECTION 8(1), 12(1) OR 37(1)

NOTES:
1. The person making the reference should complete the form by entering his name and address and indicating the section (8, 12 or 37) and the sub-section ((1) (a) or (b)) under which the reference is brought in the spaces provided.
2. Attention is directed to rules 90 and 106 of the Patents Rules 1982.

I/We ....
refer to the comptroller under subsection ....
of section .... of the Patents Act 1977, the question set out in the accompanying statement.

Signature ....
(*see note 2*)

Name of Agent (if any) and   ....
address for service in the   ....
United Kingdom to which all   ....
communications should be sent   ....

141.03 **PATENTS ACT 1977**

PATENTS FORM No. 3/77 (Revised 1982)
(Rules 11, 56)

The Comptroller
The Patent Office

APPLICATION UNDER SECTION 8(5) OR 37(3) FOR AUTHORISATION BY COMPTROLLER

NOTES:
1. This form should be completed by the person(s) making the application who should identify the names and addresses of the parties to the proceedings and the relevant patent application or patent number.
2. The applicant should also indicate whether the directions were given upon a reference under section 8(1)(a), 8(1)(b), 37(1)(a) or 37(1)(b).
3. Attention is directed to rules 90 and 106 of the Patents Rules 1982.

I/We ....
declare that ....
has failed to carry out within 14 days the directions of the comptroller given upon a reference made under section .... in respect of Patent Application/Patent No. .... as set out in the accompanying statement:
And I/we accordingly request that the comptroller authorise me/us to carry out the said directions on behalf of the person to whom the directions were given.

Signature ....
(*see note 3*)

Name of Agent (if any) ....

Address for service in the ....
United Kingdom to which all ....
communications should be sent ....
....

PATENTS ACT 1977

141.04

PATENTS FORM No. 4/77 (Revised 1982)
(Rule 15)

The Comptroller
The Patent Office

REQUEST FOR DIRECTIONS UNDER SECTION 10 OR 12(4)

NOTES:
1. The form should be completed by the person making the application entering his own name and address and those of the joint applicant(s) where appropriate, and quoting the relevant application number in the space provided.
2. Where application is made under section 12(4) the relevant country, international convention or treaty should be identified together with the number of the application for a patent.
3. Attention is directed to rules 90 and 106 of the Patents Rules 1982.

I ....
....
....

being a joint applicant with ....
....

in Patent Application No. ....
declare that a dispute has arisen between us and request that an order of the comptroller be made giving directions for enabling the application to proceed.

Signature ....
(*see note 3*)

Name of Agent (if any) and ....
address for service in the ....
United Kingdom to which all ....
communications should be sent ....

PATENTS ACT 1977

141.05

PATENTS FORM No. 5/77 (Revised 1982)
(Rules 13, 59)

The Comptroller
The Patent Office

REFERENCE UNDER SECTION 11(5) OR 38(5) TO DETERMINE THE QUESTIONS OF A LICENCE

NOTES:
1. This form is to be completed by the person making the reference, entering his name and address, the number of the relevant patent application or patent and the name and address of the person to whom the licence is to be granted in the spaces provided.
2. The two inappropriate categories in the second paragraph should be deleted.

3.   Attention is directed to rules 90 and 106 of the Patents Rules 1982.

I/We ....
....
....
refer to the comptroller the question whether:-
(a) a licence should be granted on Patent Application/Patent No. ....
.... to ....
....
.... and/or
(b) the period or terms of the proposed licence (of which a copy is attached) are reasonable
     and I also request that the comptroller should determine the question and, if he considers
     it appropriate, order the grant of such a licence.

I am/We are the
(a) applicant(s) for the patent
(b) proprietor(s) of the patent
(c) person(s) claiming entitlement to the grant of a licence.

Signature ....
(see note 3)

Name of Agent (if any) and   ....
address for service in the   ....
United Kingdom to which all   ....
communications should be sent   ....

141.06   PATENTS ACT 1977

PATENTS FORM No. 6/77 (Revised 1982)
(Rule 14)

The Comptroller
The Patent Office

APPLICATION TO COMPTROLLER UNDER SECTION 13(1) AND/OR 13(3)

NOTES:
1.   The person making the application should indicate on the form the published appli-
      cation or patent in respect of which the application is being made, state his name and
      address and then complete parts (a) and/or (b) as appropriate.
2.   Where a certificate is sought under section 13(3), the name of the person who, in the
      opinion of the applicant, ought not to have been mentioned as sole or joint inventor
      should be entered in the space provided in part (b).
3.   If the application is being brought under one only of subsections (1) and (3) of section
      13, either part (a) or part (b) should be cancelled as appropriate.
4.   Attention is directed to rules 90 and 106 of the Patents Rules 1982.

In the matter of Patent Application/Patent No. ....
I/We ....
....
declare that:-
(a) I am/we are the inventor(s) of the invention which is the subject of the said application for
     a patent or patent and accordingly have a right to be mentioned as such in accordance
     with the terms of section 13(1); and/or
(b) ....
     ....
     ought not to have been mentioned in pursuance of section 13(1) as the sole or joint inven-
     tor of the invention which is the subject of the said application; and I/We apply for a
     certificate to that effect.

Signature ....
(*see note 4*)

Name of Agent (if any) and ....
address for service in the ....
United Kingdom to which all ....
communications should be sent ....

PATENTS ACT 1977   **141.07**

PATENTS FORM No. 7/77 (Revised 1982)
(Rules 15, 82)

The Comptroller
The Patent Office

STATEMENT OF INVENTORSHIP AND OF RIGHT TO THE GRANT OF A PATENT

I	Application No.

II	Title

III   I/We ....
the applicant(s) in respect of the above mentioned application for a patent declare as follows:-
   (i) I/We believe the person(s) whose name(s) and address(es) are stated on the reverse
        side of this form (and supplementary sheet if necessary) is/are the inventor(s) of the
        invention in respect of which the above mentioned application is made;
   (ii) The derivation of my/our right to be granted a patent upon the said application is as
        follows:-
        ....
   (iii) I/We consent to the publication of the details contained herein to each of the inventors
        named on the reverse side of this form.

IV	Signature
	(*see note 3*)
	....

NOTES:
1.   The name(s) and address(es) of the inventor(s) are to be entered in the spaces provided
      alongside.
2.   Where more than 3 inventors are to be named, the names of the 4th and any further
      inventors should be given on the reverse side of an additional blank copy of Patents
      Form No. 7/77 and attached to this form.
3.   Attention is directed to rules 90 and 106 of the Patents Rules 1982.
4.   The surnames or family names of individuals should be underlined.

Note. 1. It is understood that this form is being revised. The latest Supplement to
         this Work *re*. this para. 141.07 should therefore be consulted.

141.08 PATENTS ACT 1977

PATENTS FORM No. 8/77 (Revised 1982)
(Rule 17)

The Comptroller
The Patent Office

REQUEST FOR COMPTROLLER'S CERTIFICATE AUTHORISING THE RELEASE OF A SAMPLE FROM A CULTURE COLLECTION

I/We ....
  (a) declare as follows:
      (i) that the micro-organism deposited at ....
          under the accession No. ....
          is referred to in the specification of Patent Application/Patent No. ....
      (ii) that the invention disclosed in the said specification requires for its performance the use of the micro-organism identified above; and
     (iii) that, although the said application has not yet been published, I am/we are, for the reasons established by the accompanying evidence and the virtue of section 118(4) or (5), entitled to receive information and inspect documents relating to the said application; and
  (b) undertake, if a sample of the said micro-organism is released to me/us,
      (i) not to make the culture available to any other person until the application for the patent is refused or withdrawn or deemed to be withdrawn or, if a patent is granted, until it ceases to have effect without the possibility of renewal or restoration in accordance with sections 25 and 28; and
      (ii) to use the culture for experimental purposes only until the application is refused or withdrawn or deemed to be withdrawn or until the date of publication in the Journal or a notice that the patent has been granted; and
  (c) accordingly request that the comptroller's certificate authorising the release of a sample of the said micro-organism may be forwarded to me/us.

Signature ....
(*see note 4*)

Name of Agent (if any) and   ....
address in the United Kingdom ....
to which Comptroller's certifi-   ....
cate is to be sent   ....

NOTES:
1.   This form should be completed by the person making the request entering his name and address and information identifying the relevant culture collection, accession number and patent application or patent number in the spaces provided.
2.   Unless the above reference is to a patent application which has not been published under section 16(1) and the person making the request seeks by virtue of section 118(4) or (5) to secure release of a sample prior to the publication of the said application, part (iii) of the declaration at (a) should be deleted.
     Where section 118(4) is invoked, evidence substantiating the facts relied on must also be furnished.
     Where section 118(5) is relied on the reference to the accompanying evidence should be deleted.
3.   The undertaking at (b)(ii) may be deleted either:
      (a) where the reference to the micro-organism in question appears in the specification of a granted patent; or
      (b) where the person making the request is a government department or person authorised in writing by a government department to make the request and the request is made in order to enable any act specified in section 55 to be done in relation to the culture in question for the services of the Crown.

4. Attention is directed to rules 90 and 106 of the Patents Rules 1982.
5. If the micro-organism of which a sample is required is deposited with an International Depository Authority under the Budapest Treaty, form BP/12, for certification by the Comptroller, should be filed with this form.

Notes 1. Form BP12 is reprinted at para. 144.02.
2. This form will need revision when section 125A is brought into effect and rule 17 revised, for which see *Notes* to paras. 125A.01 and 125A.02. The latest Supplement to this Work *re.* this para. 141.08 should therefore be consulted.

PATENTS ACT 1977   **141.09**

PATENTS FORM No. 9/77 (Revised 1982)
(Rules 29, 32, 80, 81, 82)

The Comptroller
The Patent Office

REQUEST FOR PRELIMINARY EXAMINATION AND SEARCH OR REQUEST FOR FURTHER SEARCH

NOTES:
1. Paragraph I or paragraph II should be completed by the applicant for a patent according to whether request is made for a preliminary examination and search under section 17(1) or for a further search under section 17(6).
2. Paragraph II should be completed so as to identify the invention in relation to which the further search is being requested. Reference should be made to the claims in which that invention is specified. If this is not done the further search will be made in relation to the second invention specified in the search report previously made under section 17(5).
3. The application number to be quoted should be that assigned to the application when first filed.
4. Attention is directed to rules 90 and 106 of the Patents Rules 1982.

I   I/We ....
request the Comptroller to refer my/our Patent Application No. ....
to an examiner for a preliminary examination and search in accordance with section 17(1) of the Patents Act 1977.

II   I/We ....
      ....
      ....
request that in addition to the search carried out by the examiner in relation to the first invention specified in the claims of my/our Patent Application No. .... a search shall also be carried out in relation to the following other invention specified therein, viz.

Signature ....
(*see note 4*)

Notes 1. It is understood that this form may be revised. The latest Supplement to this Work *re.* this para. 141.09 should therefore be consulted.

141.10 **PATENTS ACT 1977**

PATENTS FORM No. 10/77 (Revised 1982)
(Rules 33, 83)

The Comptroller
The Patent Office

REQUEST FOR SUBSTANTIVE EXAMINATION

NOTES:
1. The application number to be quoted should be that assigned to the application when first filed.
2. Attention is directed to rules 90 and 106 of the Patents Rules 1982.

I/We ....
request the comptroller to refer my/our Patent Application No. ....
to an examiner for substantive examination in accordance with section 18(1) of the Patents Act 1977.

Signature ....
(*see note 2*)

Notes 1. It is understood that this form may be revised. The latest Supplement to this Work *re*. this para. 141.10 should therefore be consulted.

141.11 **PATENTS ACT 1977**

PATENTS FORM No. 11/77 (Revised 1982)
(Rules 35, 36)

The Comptroller
The Patent Office

REQUEST TO AMEND APPLICATION BEFORE GRANT

NOTES:
1. The application number to be quoted should be that assigned to the application when first filed.
2. Attention is directed to rules 90 and 106 of the Patents Rules 1982.

I/We ....
seek leave to amend my/our Patent Application No. ....
as shown in red ink in the annexed copy of the original application.

My/Our reasons for making this amendment are as follows ....
....

Signature ....
(*see note 2*)

Notes 1. It is understood that this form may be revised. The latest Supplement to this Work *re*. this para. 141.11 should therefore be consulted.

PATENTS ACT 1977   141.12

PATENTS FORM No. 12/77 (Revised 1982)
(Rules 39, 41, 64, 67, Schedule 4)

The Comptroller
The Patent Office

PAYMENT OF RENEWAL FEE

I/We ....
transmit the renewal fee due on .... which is prescribed for the
continuance in force for its ....th year of Patent No. ....
standing in the name(s) of ....
and request that the Certificate of Payment below may be sent to me/us at the address specified.

NOTE: Where the proprietor of the patent requires the notice specified in rule 39(4) to be
sent in accordance with rule 39(5) to him at an address in the United Kingdom other
than the address for service specified in the register, he shall give the address in the
space following and add his signature thereto.

....

Signature ....

- -

CERTIFICATE OF PAYMENT OF RENEWAL FEE

This is to certify that the prescribed fee has been duly paid and Patent No. ....
renewed until ....when the next renewal fee will be due.

Patent Office
date stamp.

Please do not detach this certificate. If it is completed, the Patent Office will date and return it
to the address given in the above box.

Note It is understood that this form will probably be amended at the next revision
of the Rules, and perhaps then combined with PF 13/77. The latest Supplement to
this Work *re.* this para. 141.12 should therefore be consulted.

PATENTS ACT 1977   141.13

PATENTS FORM No. 13/77 (Revised 1982)
(Rule 39)

The Comptroller
The Patent Office

PAYMENT OF ADDITIONAL FEE UNDER SECTION 25(4)

I/We ....
hereby transmit the additional fee payable in respect of an extension of ....
month(s) for the payment of the renewal fee due in respect of Patent No. ....

NOTES:
1.   The person tendering the fee should insert his name and address in the space provided.
2.   The number of months in respect of which the additional fee is payable should be
      stated.
3.   Patents Form No. 12/77 in respect of the corresponding unpaid renewal fee should
      accompany this form.

Note The Note to para. 141.12 *supra* is also applicable to this form.

141.14 **PATENTS ACT 1977**

PATENTS FORM No. 14/77 (Revised 1982)
(Rule 40)

The Comptroller
The Patent Office

APPLICATION TO AMEND SPECIFICATION AFTER GRANT

NOTE: Attention is directed to rules 90 and 106 of the Patents Rules 1982.

I/We ....
seek leave to amend the specification of Patent No. ....
as shown in red ink in the annexed copy of the printed specification thereof.

I declare that no proceedings are pending before the Court or the comptroller in which the validity of the patent may be in issue.

My/Our reasons for making this amendment are as follows ....
....

Signature ....
(*see note*)

Name of Agent (if any) and   ....
address for service in the   ....
United Kingdom to which all   ....
communications should be sent   ....

Note It is understood that this form may be revised. The latest Supplement to this Work *re*. this para. 141.14 should therefore be consulted.

141.15 **PATENTS ACT 1977**

PATENTS FORM No. 15/77 (Revised 1982)
(Rules 40, 78)

The Comptroller
The Patent Office

NOTICE OF OPPOSITION TO AMENDMENT OF SPECIFICATION AFTER GRANT

NOTES:
1.   The person giving the notice should complete the form by entering his name and address in the space provided.
2.   Attention is directed to rules 90 and 106 of the Patents Rules 1982.

I/We ....
give notice of opposition to the proposed amendment of the specification of Patent No. ....
....

Signature ....
(*see note 2*)

Name of Agent (if any) and   ....
address for service in the   ....
United Kingdom to which all   ....
communications should be sent   ....

PATENTS ACT 1977   **141.16**

PATENTS FORM No. 16/77 (Revised 1982)
(Rule 4)

The Comptroller
The Patent Office

APPLICATION FOR THE RESTORATION OF A PATENT

NOTE: Attention is directed to rules 90 and 106 of the Patents Rules 1982.

I/We ....
apply for an order for the restoration of Patent No. ....

My/Our reasons for applying for this restoration are as follows:

Signature ....
(*see note*)

Name of Agent (if any) and   ....
address for service in the   ....
United Kingdom to which all   ....
communications should be sent   ....

Note It is understood that this form may be revised. The latest Supplement to this
Work *re*. this para. 141.16 should therefore be consulted.

PATENTS ACT 1977   **141.17**

PATENTS FORM No. 17/77
(Rule 41)

The Comptroller
The Patent Office

ADDITIONAL FEE ON THE APPLICATION FOR RESTORATION OF A PATENT

I/We ....
hereby transmit the prescribed additional fee in connection with the restoration of Patent
No. .... together with Patents Form No. 12/77, duly completed.

Signature ....

PATENTS ACT 1977   **141.18**

PATENTS FORM No. 18/77 (Revised 1982)
(Rule 43)

The Comptroller
The Patent Office

OFFER TO SURRENDER A PATENT

NOTES:
1.   If an action before the court is pending, the declaration below should be deleted and
      full particulars of such action furnished in writing to the comptroller.

2.   Attention is directed to rules 90 and 106 of the Patents Rules 1982.

I/We ....
offer to surrender Patent No. ....

I/We declare that no action is pending before the Court for infringement or for revocation of the patent.

My/Our reasons for making this offer are as follows:
....

Signature ....
(*see note 2*)

Name of Agent (if any) and   ....
address for service in the   ....
United Kingdom to which all   ....
communications should be sent   ....

141.19   **PATENTS ACT 1977**

PATENTS FORM No. 19/77 (Revised 1982)
(Rule 43)

The Comptroller
The Patent Office

NOTICE OF OPPOSITION TO OFFER TO SURRENDER A PATENT

NOTES:
1.   The person giving the notice should complete the form by entering his name and address in the space provided.
2.   Attention is directed to rules 90 and 106 of the Patents Rules 1982.

I/We ....
give notice of opposition to the offer to surrender Patent No. ....

Signature ....
(*see note 2*)

Name of Agent (if any) and   ....
address for service in the   ....
United Kingdom to which all   ....
communications should be sent   ....

141.20   **PATENTS ACT 1977**

PATENTS FORM No. 20/77 (Revised 1982)
(Rule 45)

The Comptroller
The Patent Office

REQUEST FOR ALTERATION OF NAME, ADDRESS OR ADDRESS FOR SERVICE IN THE REGISTER OF PATENTS

NOTES:
1.   The person(s) making the request should complete the form indicating whether the request relates to an application for a patent or to a granted patent by appropriate deletion and by insertion of the number of the application or patent as the case may be.

2. Any of categories (a)–(c) which are inapplicable should be deleted and the desired alteration specified.
3. Where the request is for alteration in a name evidence of the alteration must be furnished.
4. Attention is directed to rules 90 and 106 of the Patents Rules 1982.

In the matter of Patent Application/Patent No. ....

I/We ....

request that the (a) name
                  (b) address
                  (c) address for service

now on the register of patents be altered to:

....

Signature ....
(*see note 4*)

Name of Agent (if any)   ....
Address for service in the   ....
United Kingdom to which all ....
communications should be sent   ....

Note. It is understood that this form may be revised. The latest Supplement to this Work *re*. this para. 141.20 should therefore be consulted.

PATENTS ACT 1977   **141.21**

PATENTS FORM No. 21/77 (Revised 1982)
(Rule 46)

The Comptroller
The Patent Office

APPLICATION TO REGISTER OR TO GIVE NOTICE OF A TRANSACTION, INSTRUMENT OR EVENT AFFECTING THE RIGHTS IN A PATENT OR APPLICATION FOR A PATENT

NOTES:
1. The name and address of the person making the application should be entered in the space provided.
2. Details of the transaction, instrument or event to be registered, i.e. whether it is an assignment, a licence or a mortgage etc, should be stated where appropriate together with its date and the parties to the same.
3. Attention is directed to rules 90 and 106 of the Patents Rules 1982.

I/We ....
give notice to the comptroller of or apply for an entry to be made in the register of patents of a transaction, instrument or event (details of which are given below) affecting the rights in or under Patent Application/Patent No. ....

The details are as follows:- ....
....

I/We submit the accompanying certified copy, official document or extract establishing the transaction, instrument or event.

Signature ....
(*see note 3*)

881

Name of Agent (if any) ....
Address for service in the ....
United Kingdom to which all ....
communications should be sent ....

Note. It is understood that this form may be revised. The latest Supplement to this Work *re*. this para. 141.21 should therefore be consulted.

141.22   PATENTS ACT 1977

PATENTS FORM No. 22/77 (Revised 1982)
(Rule 47)

The Comptroller
The Patent Office

REQUEST FOR THE CORRECTION OF AN ERROR IN THE REGISTER OR IN ANY CONNECTED DOCUMENT

NOTES:
1.   The person making the request should clearly identify in the space provided, the document containing the error to be corrected and should also supply a copy thereof with the desired corrections shown in red ink, unless it is not convenient to do so, in which case the correction sought may be stated in the space provided.
2.   Attention is directed to rules 90 and 106 of the Patents Rules 1982.

I/We ....
request:-
    (a) That the entry made in the register in relation to Patent Application/Patent No. ....
        and/or
    (b) that the undermentioned document filed in connection with such registration be corrected
        (i) as shown in red ink on the annexed copy of ....or
        (ii) as follows ....

Signature ....
(*see note 2*)

Name of Agent (if any) and ....
address for service in the ....
United Kingdom to which all ....
communications should be sent ....

PATENTS FORM No. 23/77 (Revised 1982)   **141.23**

For official use

Your reference

The Patent Office

Request for Miscellaneous Information

Patents
Act 1977

Form 23/77

1. Inspection of register or documents

1. If you want to inspect the register and/or the original
documents filed at or kept in the Patent Office in relation
to any patent or patent application, please give full details.

2. Supply of copies or extracts.

2. If you want copies of, or extracts from, the register or
documents relating to any patent or patent application, please
give full details.

Revised 1988

dti
the department for Enterprise

Please Turn Over ▶

883

3 If a request is made under 1 or 2, the information under 3 will be provided at no extra charge if requested in respect of the same patent.

3. Information about renewal.

3. Please give the number of any patent for which you want to know whether, and when, a renewal fee has been paid.

4. Details of the person making the request(s)

4. Please give your name and address.

Name

Address

Postcode

Please Sign Here ▶ Signed _____ Date _____

                                                                    day   month   year

Note. PF 23/77 was revised by S.I. 1988 No. 2089, r. 2(4).

PATENTS FORM No. 24/77 (Revised 1982)   **141.24**

For official use

Your reference

Notes

Please type, or write in dark ink using BLOCK LETTERS. The fees for a rubber stamp impression and for a separate, sealed certificate are different. For details of prescribed fees please contact the Patent Office.

Please use a separate form for each application or patent.

Rules 6, 52 and 119 of the Patents Rules 1982 are the main rules governing the completion and filing of this form.

3 Include any special requirements such as the need for patent register extracts or details of renewal payments made.
If you do not have enough space please continue on the back of this form.

Please Sign Here ▶

The Patent Office

Request for Certificate of the Comptroller

Patents Act 1977

Form 24/77

1. Please give the patent application or patent number.

2. Please give the full name and address of the person making the request.
Name

Address

Postcode.

3. Please give details of the contents of the certificate(s)

4. Please give the number and type of certificates required.

Rubber stamp impressions ☐

Signed and sealed certificates ☐

Signed _____ Date _____
                                  day   month   year

Revised 1988

dti
the department for Enterprise

Note. PF 24/77 was revised by S.I. 1988 No. 2089, r. 2(4).

141.25 **PATENTS ACT 1977**

PATENTS FORM No. 25/77 (Revised 1982)
(Rule 53)

The Comptroller
The Patent Office

APPLICATION FOR ENTRY OF ORDER OF COURT IN THE REGISTER

NOTE: Attention is directed to rules 90 and 106 of the Patents Rules 1982.

I/We ....
transmit an office copy of an Order of the Court with reference to ....
....

Signature ....
(*see note*)

141.26 **PATENTS ACT 1977**

PATENTS FORM No. 26/77 (Revised 1982)
(Rule 60)

The Comptroller
The Patent Office

APPLICATION FOR COMPENSATION BY EMPLOYEE

NOTES:
1.   The name and address of the person making the application should be entered in the
     space provided.
2.   Attention is directed to rules 90 and 106 of the Patents Rules 1982.

I/We ....
apply to the comptroller for an award of compensation under section 40 in respect of
Patent No. ....

Signature ....
(*see note 2*)

Name of Agent (if any) and   ....
address for service in the   ....
United Kingdom to which all   ....
communications should be sent   ....

141.27 **PATENTS ACT 1977**

PATENTS FORM No. 27/77 (Revised 1982)
(Rule 61)

The Comptroller
The Patent Office

APPLICATIONS UNDER SECTION 41(8) IN CONNECTION WITH AN ORDER MADE UNDER SECTION 40(1) OR 40(2)

NOTES:
1.   The form should be completed by the person making the application who should enter
     the names of the employer and employee in the previous proceedings under section
     40(1) or 40(2) and his own name, in the spaces provided.

2.   Attention is directed to rules 90 and 106 of the Patents Rules 1982.

In the matter of Patent No. ....
and of the order made under section 40(1) or 40(2) and dated ....
between the employer, viz: ....
and the employee, viz:
I/We, the said ....
hereby apply to the comptroller as set out fully in the accompanying statement.

Signature ....
(*see note 2*)

Name of Agent (if any) and   ....
address for service in the   ....
United Kingdom to which all   ....
communications should be sent   ....

PATENTS ACT 1977   **141.28**

PATENTS FORM No. 28/77 (Revised 1982)
(Rule 62)

The Comptroller
The Patent Office

**APPLICATION BY PROPRIETOR FOR ENTRY TO BE MADE IN THE REGISTER TO
THE EFFECT THAT LICENCES UNDER THE PATENT ARE TO BE AVAILABLE
AS OF RIGHT**

NOTE: Attention is directed to rules 90 and 106 of the Patents Rules 1982.

I/We ....
request that an entry may be made in the register in the respect of Patent No. ....
entitled ....
to the effect that licences under the patent are to be available as of right.
I am/We are not precluded by contract from granting licences under the patent.

Signature (*see note*) ....
Name of Agent (if any) ....

CONFIRMATION OF MAKING AN ENTRY

This is to confirm that an entry has been made in the Register to the effect that licences under
Patent No. .... are to be available as of right.

Patent Office
date stamp

Please do not detach this confirmation slip. If it is completed, the Patent Office will date and
return it to the address, which must be within the United Kingdom, given in the above box.

141.29 PATENTS ACT 1977

PATENTS FORM No. 29/77 (Revised 1982)
(Rule 63)

The Comptroller
The Patent Office

APPLICATION FOR SETTLEMENT OF THE TERMS OF A LICENCE OF RIGHT

NOTES:
1. The applicant or applicants should complete the form entering his/their name(s) and address(es) in the space provided.
2. *Delete as appropriate.
3. Attention is directed to rules 90 and 106 of the Patents Rules 1982.

I/We ....
apply to the comptroller for settlement of the terms of a licence to be exchanged or granted under Patent No. .... being a patent in respect of which an entry has been made in the register of patents to the effect that licences thereunder are to be available as of right.

I am/We are
(a)* the proprietor(s) of the patent
(b)* the person(s) requiring the licence
(c)* the holder(s) of a licence under the patent before the said entry was made.

Signature ....
(*see note 3*)

Name of Agent (if any) and   ....
address for service in the   ....
United Kingdom to which all   ....
communications should be sent   ....

141.30 PATENTS ACT 1977

PATENTS FORM No. 30/77 (Revised 1982)
(Rule 64)

The Comptroller
The Patent Office

APPLICATION BY PROPRIETOR UNDER SECTION 47(1) FOR CANCELLATION OF ENTRY IN THE REGISTER

NOTES:
1. Either (a) or (b) below should be deleted as appropriate.
2. Attention is directed to rules 90 and 106 of the Patents Rules 1982.

I/We ....
apply for cancellation of the entry in the register to the effect that licences under Patent No. .... are to be available as of right.
I/We enclose Patents Form No. 12/77 accompanied by the balance of all renewal fees which would have been payable if the entry had not been made.

I/We declare (*see note 1*)
(a) that there is no existing licence under the patent;
(b) that all licensees consent to this application.

Signature ....

(*see note 2*)

Name of Agent (if any) ....

- -

CONFIRMATION OF CANCELLATION OF ENTRY

This is to confirm the cancellation of an entry in the Register to the effect that licences under Patent No. .... were to be available as of right.

<table>
<tr><td>

</td><td>Patent Office
date stamp</td></tr>
</table>

Please do not detach this confirmation slip. If it is completed, the Patent Office will date and return it to the address, which must be within the United Kingdom, given in the above box.

PATENTS ACT 1977   **141.31**

PATENTS FORM No. 31/77 (Revised 1982)
(Rule 65)

The Comptroller
The Patent Office

APPLICATION UNDER SECTION 47(3) BY PERSON INTERESTED FOR CANCELLATION OF ENTRY IN THE REGISTER

NOTES:
1. The name and address of the person making the application should be entered in the space provided.
2. Attention is directed to rules 90 and 106 of the Patents Rules 1982.

I/We ....
claim that the proprietor of Patent No. .... made an entry in the register to the effect that licences under it are to be available as of right but is, and was at the time of the entry, precluded by a contract in which I am/we are interested from so doing, and I/we apply for the cancellation of the entry.

Signature ....

(*see note 2*)

Name of Agent (if any) and   ....
address for service in the   ....
United Kingdom to which all   ....
communications should be sent   ....

141.32 PATENTS ACT 1977

PATENTS FORM No. 32/77 (Revised 1982)
(Rule 66)

The Comptroller
The Patent Office

NOTICE OF OPPOSITION TO AN APPLICATION UNDER SECTION 47(1) OR 47(3) FOR CANCELLATION OF ENTRY IN THE REGISTER

NOTES:
1. The name and address of the opponent should be entered in the space provided.
2. Attention is directed to rules 90 and 106 of the Patents Rules 1982.

I/We ....
give notice of opposition to the application for the cancellation of the entry in the register of patents to the effect that licences under Patent No. .... are to be available as of right.

Signature ....
(*see note 2*)

Name of Agent (if any) and   ....
address for service in the   ....
United Kingdom to which all   ....
communications should be sent   ....

141.33 PATENTS ACT 1977

PATENTS FORM No. 33/77 (Revised 1982)
(Rule 68)

The Comptroller
The Patent Office

APPLICATION UNDER SECTION 48(1) FOR A COMPULSORY LICENCE OR ENTRY IN THE REGISTER

NOTES:
1. The applicant should complete the form entering his name and address in the space provided and deleting whichever of items (a), (b) and (c) are inapplicable.
2. Attention is directed to rules 90 and 106 of the Patents Rules 1982.

I/We ....
apply to the comptroller in respect of Patent No. ....
   (a) for a licence under the patent;
   (b) for an entry to be made in the register to the effect that licences under the patent are to be available as of right;
   (c) for the grant of a licence under the patent to ....
      on the grounds set out in the accompanying statement.

Signature ....
(*see note 2*)

Name of Agent (if any) and   ....
address for service in the   ....
United Kingdom to which all   ....
communications should be sent   ....

PATENTS ACT 1977

141.34

PATENTS FORM No. 34/77 (Revised 1982)
(Rule 69)

The Comptroller
The Patent Office

APPLICATION BY CROWN IN CASE OF MONOPOLY OR MERGER

NOTE: Attention is directed to rules 90 and 106 of the Patents Rules 1982.

I/We ....
apply to the comptroller in respect of Patent No. .... for his order for the
relief set out in the accompanying statement or for such other relief as he may direct.

Signature ....
(*see note*)

Name of Agent (if any) and ....
address for service in the ....
United Kingdom to which all ....
communications should be sent ....

PATENTS ACT 1977

141.35

PATENTS FORM No. 35/77 (Revised 1982)
(Rule 71)

The Comptroller
The Patent Office

NOTICE OF OPPOSITION TO APPLICATION MADE UNDER SECTION 48 OR 51

NOTES:
1. This form is to be completed in duplicate by the proprietor of the patent or other
   person(s) wishing to oppose the application made under section 48 or 51, and should
   show in addition to the name and address of the opponent and the patent number the
   name(s) of the applicant under section 48 or 51.
2. *Delete as appropriate.
3. Where the application has been made under section 48 by a government department for
   the grant of a licence to another person, the name and address of that other person
   should be inserted at (c).
4. Attention is directed to rules 90 and 106 of the Patents Rules 1982.

I/We ....
give notice of opposition to the application made in respect of Patent No. ....
by ....
for:
  (a) *a licence under the patent
  (b) *an entry to be made in the register to the effect that licences under the patent are to be
     available as of right.

(c) *the grant of a licence under the patent to..

....

(d) the order of the comptroller under sub-section (4) or (5) of section 51.

Signature ....
(*see note 4*)

Name of Agent (if any) and   ....
address for service in the   ....
United Kingdom to which all   ....
communications should be sent   ....

141.36   PATENTS ACT 1977

PATENTS FORM No. 36/77 (Revised 1982)
(Rule 72)

The Comptroller
The Patent Office

REFERENCE TO THE COMPTROLLER OF A DISPUTE AS TO INFRINGEMENT

NOTES:
1. The parties to the reference should enter their names and addresses in the appropriate spaces and the status of the first party should be indicated.
2. The parties should submit a joint statement, setting out fully the matters on which they are in agreement and those upon which they are in dispute.
3. Attention is directed to rules 90 and 106 of the Patents Rules 1982.

We, ...
the proprietor of Patent No. ....
or the exclusive licensee under Patent No. ....
and ....
the person(s) alleged by the proprietor or exclusive licensee to have infringed the patent, refer to the comptroller the question whether such infringement has in fact taken place. We submit herewith a joint statement giving full particulars of the matters which are in dispute and those on which we are in agreement.

Signature of proprietor or   ....
exclusive licensee   ....
(*see note 3*)   ....

Name of Agent (if any) and   ....
Address for service in the   ....
United Kingdom to which all   ....
communications should be sent   ....
Signature of other party to the   ....
reference   ....
(*see note 3*)   ....

Name of Agent (if any) and   ....
address for service in the   ....
United Kingdom to which all   ....
communications should be sent   ....

PATENTS ACT 1977   **141.37**

PATENTS FORM No. 37/77 (Revised 1982)
(Rule 74)

The Comptroller
The Patent Office

APPLICATION FOR DECLARATION OF NON-INFRINGEMENT

NOTES:
1.   The name and address of the applicant should be entered in the space provided.
2.   Attention is directed to rules 90 and 106 of the Patents Rules 1982.

I/We ....
seek the declaration of the comptroller that the act or proposed act described fully in the
accompany statement does not, or would not, constitute an infringement of Patent
No. .... whose present registered proprietor(s)
is/are ....

I/We confirm that I/we have written to the said proprietor(s) for a written acknowledgement
to the effect of the declaration claimed and have furnished him/them with particulars in
writing of the said act or proposed act; and further confirm that he has/they have refused or
failed to give any such acknowledgement.

Signature ....
(*see note 2*)

Name of Agent (if any) and   ....
address for service in the   ....
United Kingdom to which all   ....
communications should be sent   ....

PATENTS ACT 1977   **141.38**

PATENTS FORM No. 38/77 (Revised 1982)
(Rule 75)

The Comptroller
The Patent Office

APPLICATION FOR THE REVOCATION OF A PATENT

NOTES:
1.   The notice and accompanying statement are to be furnished in duplicate. The
      statement should not only set out clearly which of the grounds (a) to (e) of section 72(1)
      is being relied on, but it should also set out fully the facts upon which the applicant
      relies in support of his case and the relief sought.
2.   Attention is directed to rules 90 and 106 of the Patents Rules 1982.

I/We ....
apply for the revocation of Patent No. ....
standing in the name of ....

Signature ....
(*see note 2*)

Name of Agent (if any) and   ....
address for service in the   ....
United Kingdom to which all   ....
communications should be sent   ....

141.39 PATENTS ACT 1977

PATENTS FORM No. 39/77 (Revised 1982)
(Rule 79)

The Comptroller
The Patent Office

APPLICATIONS TO REGISTER COPY OF ENTRY MADE IN THE EUROPEAN REGISTER OF PATENTS

NOTES:
1. The name and address of the applicant should be entered in the space provided.
2. Attention is directed to rules 90 and 106 of the Patents Rules 1982.

I/We ....

apply for a copy of an entry made in the Register of European Patents in relation to European Patent Application No. ....
to be entered in the register of patents.
A copy of the relevant entry, duly certified, accompanies this application.

Signature ....
(see note 2)

Name of Agent (if any) and ....
address for service in the ....
United Kingdom to which all ....
communications should be sent ....

141.40 PATENTS ACT 1977

PATENTS FORM No. 40/77 (Revised 1982)
(Rules 81, 82)

The Comptroller
The Patent Office

PAYMENT OF FILING FEE UPON CONVERSION OF EUROPEAN PATENT APPLICATION TO AN APPLICATION UNDER THE ACT

NOTES:
1. Enter the name and address of each applicant. Names of individuals should be entered in full and the surname or family name should be underlined. The names of all partners in a firm must be given in full. Bodies corporate should be designated by their corporate name and the country of incorporation and, where appropriate, the State of incorporation with that country should be entered. Full corporate details, eg "a corporation organised and existing under the laws of the State of Delaware, United States of America," trading styles, eg "trading as XYZ company", nationality, and former names, eg "formerly [known as] ABC Ltd." are *not* required and should *not* be given.
2. Attention is directed to rules 90 and 106 of the Patents Rules 1982.
3. Enter agent's ADP Code No. (if known) in the space provided.

I/We ....
(see note 1)
the applicant(s) in respect of European Patent Application No. ....
in respect of which a request for conversion to an application under the Patents Act 1977 has been made, transmit herewith the filing fee.

Signature ....
(*see note 2*)

Name of Agent (if any)   .... ADP Code No. ....
(*see note 3*)

Address for service in the   ....
United Kingdom to which all   ....
communications should be sent   ....

Note. This form is printed as amended by S.I. 1987 No. 288, r. 1(4).

PATENTS ACT 1977   **141.41**

PATENTS FORM No. 41/77 (Revised 1982)
(Rule 81)

The Comptroller
The Patent Office

REQUEST FOR CONVERSION OF EUROPEAN PATENT APPLICATION

NOTES:
1.   Enter the name and address of each applicant; continue on a separate sheet if
      necessary.
2.   Attention is directed to rules 90 and 106 of the Patents Rules 1982.

I/We ....
(*see note 1*)
the applicant(s) in respect of European Patent Application No. ....
filed at the Patent Office on .... request that a direction be given
converting the application into an application for a patent under the Patents Act 1977.

I/We also request that a copy of my/our European Patent Application, together with a copy of
this request, be sent in accordance with Article 136, paragraph 2, of the European Patent
Convention to the central industrial property office of the following Contracting States
designated in my/our said application:
....

In support of this request, I/we submit the notification issued to me/us by the European Patent
Office to the effect that my/our said application has been deemed to be withdrawn pursuant to
Article 77, paragraph 5, of the European Patent Convention.

Signature ....
(*see note 2*)

Name of Agent (if any) and   ....
address for service in the   ....
United Kingdom to which all   ....
communications should be sent   ....

PATENTS ACT 1977   **141.42**

PATENTS FORM No. 42/77

**REQUEST FOR NATIONAL PROCESSING OF AN INTERNATIONAL APPLICATION
FOR A PATENT (UK)**

Note. This form was withdrawn by S.I. 1985 No. 1166. However, an informal form
(Form NP. 1) (reprinted at para. 143.01) was then introduced for the same purpose. Its use is recommended, but not obligatory, see para. 89A.18.

141.43 PATENTS ACT 1977

PATENTS FORM No. 43/77 (Revised 1982)
(Rule 85)

The Comptroller
The Patent Office

PAYMENT OF PRESCRIBED FEE AND REQUEST FOR PUBLICATION OF TRANSLATION

NOTES:
1. The application relevant to the translation to be published should be identified on the form by entering the number assigned to it by the Patent Office for use in connection with pre-grant proceedings.
2. Attention is directed to rules 90 and 106 of the Patents Rules 1982.

I/We ....
herewith transmit the prescribed fee required under section 89(5) and request that the translation of the application/amendment filed at the Patent Office under section 89(6) in respect of application number .... should be published.
(*see note 1*)

Signature ....
(*see note 2*)

Note. This form will need revision when new section 89A is brought into effect, for which see para. 89A.01. Rule 85 will then need revision, for which see para. 89A.02. The references to section 89(5) and 89(6) will then also need to be changed to section 89A(6) and 89A(5) respectively. Other changes in the form are also likely to be made. The latest Supplement to this Work *re.* this para. 141.43 should therefore be consulted.

141.44 PATENTS ACT 1977

PATENTS FORM No. 44/77 (Revised 1982)
(Rule 85)

The Comptroller
The Patent Office

APPLICATION TO THE COMPTROLLER FOR AN INTERNATIONAL APPLICATION TO BE TREATED AS AN APPLICATION UNDER THE ACT

NOTES:
1. The number of the international application should be entered in the relevant items (a), (b) or (c) and the remaining two items deleted.
2. Attention is directed to rules 90 and 106 of the Patents Rules 1982.

I/We ....
claim that the fact that (*see note 1*)
   (a) international application No. .... has been deemed to be withdrawn;
   (b) the designation of the United Kingdom in international application No. ....
       has been deemed to be withdrawn;
   (c) a filing date has been refused to the international application having an international
       application No. ....
was due to an error or omission in the Patent Office or other institution having functions

under the Patent Co-operation Treaty or circumstances beyond my/our control as set out more fully in the accompanying statement.

I/We also request that the comptroller should treat the said application as an application under the Patents Act 1977 by virtue of section 89(3) or 89(5) as appropriate.

Signature ....
(*see note 2*)

Name of Agent (if any) and ....
address for service in the ....
United Kingdom to which all ....
communications should be sent ....

Note. This form will need some amendment when section 89A is brought into effect, for which see para. 89A.01. Rule 85 will then need revision, for which see para. 89A.02. The references to section 89(3) or 89(5) will also need to be changed to references to section 89A(1), (2), (4) and (6). Other changes to the form are also likely. The latest Supplement to this Work *re.* this para. 141.44 should therefore be consulted.

PATENTS ACT 1977

141.45

PATENTS FORM No. 45/77 (Revised 1982)
(Rule 86)

The Comptroller
The Patent Office

APPLICATION FOR ORDER FOR EVIDENCE TO BE OBTAINED IN THE UNITED KINGDOM

NOTES:
1. The applicant should enter his name and address in the space provided.
2. Attention is directed to rules 90 and 106 of the Patents Rules 1982.

I/We ....
apply to the comptroller for an order under section (1) of the Evidence (Proceedings in other Jurisdictions) Act 1975, as applied by section 92 of the Patents Act 1977, for evidence to be obtained in the United Kingdom for the purpose of proceedings before a relevant convention court under the European Patent Convention in respect of the matter particulars of which are given in the accompanying affidavit.

The evidence desired is ....
....

Signature (*see note 2*) ....

Address to which the evidence ....
should be sent ....

141.46 PATENTS ACT 1977

PATENTS FORM No. 46/77 (Revised 1982)
(Rule 88)

The Comptroller
The Patent Office

NOTICE THAT HEARING BEFORE THE COMPTROLLER WILL BE ATTENDED

NOTES: Attention is directed to rules 90 and 106 of the Patents Rules 1982.

I/We ....
give notice that the hearing fixed for the ....
in reference to ....
will be attended by myself/ourselves or by some person on my/our behalf.

Signature ....
(*see note*)

141.47 PATENTS ACT 1977

PATENTS FORM No. 47/77 (Revised 1982)
(Rule 91)

The Comptroller
The Patent Office

REQUEST FOR THE CORRECTION OF AN ERROR OF TRANSLATION OR TRANSCRIPTION CLERICAL ERROR OR MISTAKE

NOTES:
1. The person making the request should clearly identify in the space provided the document containing the error or mistake to be corrected and should also supply a copy thereof with the desired corrections shown in red ink, unless it is not convenient to do so, in which case the correction sought may be stated in the space provided.
2. *Delete as appropriate.
3. Attention is directed to rules 90 and 106 of the Patents Rules 1982.

I/We ....
request that the error ....
relating to Patent Application/Patent No.............may be corrected:–
    (a) *as shown in red ink in the annexed copy of the said ....
        or
    (b) *as follows ....
....

Signature ....
(*see note 2*)

Name of Agent (if any) and   ....
address for service in the   ....
United Kingdom to which all ....
communications should be sent ....

Note. It is understood that this form may be revised. The latest Supplement to this Work *re.* this para. 141.47 should therefore be consulted.

PATENTS ACT 1977   **141.48**

PATENTS FORM No. 48/77 (Revised 1982)
(Rule 91)

The Comptroller
The Patent Office

NOTICE OF OPPOSITION TO THE CORRECTION OF AN ERROR, CLERICAL ERROR OR MISTAKE

NOTES:
1.   The name and address of the opponent should be entered in the space provided, and details of the request being opposed furnished where indicated.
2.   Attention is directed to rules 90 and 106 of the Patents Rules 1982.

I/We ....
give notice of opposition to the request, dated .... made by ....
.... for
the correction of an error or mistake made in connection with Patent Application/Patent
No. ....

Signature ....
(*see note 2*)

Name of Agent (if any) and   ....
address for service in the   ....
United Kingdom to which all   ....
communications should be sent   ....

PATENTS ACT 1977   **141.49**

PATENTS FORM No. 49/77
(Rule 92)

The Comptroller
The Patent Office

REQUEST FOR INFORMATION RELATING TO A PATENT OR AN APPLICATION FOR A PATENT

I/We hereby request the comptroller to furnish me/us with the following information relating
to Patent Application/Patent No. ....
viz; as to when ....

Signature ....

Name of Agent to which   ....
information is to be sent   ....

Note. It is understood that this form may be revised. The latest Supplement *re.* this
para. 141.49 should therefore be consulted.

For official use only

141.50 THE PATENT OFFICE

PATENTS ACT 1977   **PATENTS FORM NO. 50/77**

REQUEST FOR EXTENSION OF TIME OR PERIOD UNDER RULE 110(3)

Please write or type in BLOCK LETTERS using dark ink. For details of current fees please contact the Patent Office

1. Application Number

Enter the full name(s) of the person(s) making the request

2. Name

Mark the appropriate box(es) with an 'x'. This form may not be used to extend more than one time or period unless the times or periods expire on the same day

3. Rule(s) prescribing the time(s) or period(s) to be extended

☐ 6(2)   ☐ 25(2)   ☐ 33(4)   ☐ 82(2)
☐ 6(6)   ☐ 25(3)   ☐ 34   ☐ 82(3)
☐ 15(1)   ☐ 26   ☐ 79B   ☐ 83(3)
☐ 17(2)   ☐ 33(2)   ☐ 81(2)   ☐ 85(1)
☐ 23   ☐ 33(3)   ☐ 81(3)   ☐ 85(3)

Please sign here ▶

4. Signature:

Attention is drawn to rules 90 and 106 of the Patents Rules 1982

Date: _____

Day Month Year

Notes 1. The original form PF 50/77 was withdrawn and replaced by the version printed above by S.I. 1987 No. 288, r. 2.
2. It is understood that this form is to be further revised. The latest Supplement to this Work *re.* this para. 141.50 should therefore be consulted.

141.51 **PATENTS ACT 1977**

PATENTS FORM No. 51/77
(PLEASE FILE IN DUPLICATE)
(Rule 90)

The Comptroller
The Patent Office

FORM OF DECLARATION OF AUTHORISATION WHERE AN AGENT IS APPOINTED DURING THE PROGRESS OF AN APPLICATION OR WHERE ONE AGENT IS SUBSTITUTED FOR ANOTHER

NOTES:
1.   Enter name and address in the United Kingdom of agent and agent's ADP Code No. (if known).

2.   Enter in full, name and address of applicant, proprietor or other person who has authorised agent. The full names of all partners in a firm must be entered.
3.   State the application or other proceeding in relation to which the authorisation was made, quoting the application number or patent number as appropriate.

I/We (*see note 1*) ....

.... ADP Code No. ....

declare that I/we have been authorised by (*see note 2*) ....

....

....

to act as agent in the matter of (*see note 3*) ....

and request that all communications relating thereto be sent to me/us at my/our address given above.

Signature ....

Note. It is understood that this form may be revised. The latest Supplement to this Work *re*. this para. 141.51 should therefore be consulted.

	For official use only
THE PATENT OFFICE	**141.52**
PATENTS ACT 1977 PATENTS FORM NO. 52/77	
REQUEST FOR EXTENSION OF TIME OR PERIOD UNDER RULE 110(3A)	

Please write or type in BLOCK LETTERS using dark ink. For details of current fees please contact the Patent Office	1. Application Number	
Enter the full name(s) of the person(s) making the request	2. Name	

Mark the appropriate box(es) with an 'x'. This form may not be used to extend more than one time or period unless the times or periods are to be extended to a common date

3. Rule(s) prescribing the time(s) or period(s) to be extended

☐ 6(2)   ☐ 25(2)   ☐ 33(4)   ☐ 82(2)
☐ 6(6)   ☐ 25(3)   ☐ 34   ☐ 82(3)
☐ 15(1)   ☐ 26   ☐ 79B   ☐ 83(3)
☐ 17(2)   ☐ 33(2)   ☐ 81(2)   ☐ 85(1)
☐ 23   ☐ 33(3)   ☐ 81(3)   ☐ 85(3)

Enter the date on which the extension would expire if allowed

4. Extension required:

Day Month Year

Please sign here ▶ | 5. Signature:

Date: _____
Day Month Year

Attention is drawn to rules 90
and 106 of the Patents Rules
1982

**This form must be
accompanied by a statement
setting out fully the reasons for
requesting the extension**

Reminder

Have you attached

Statement of reasons for requesting
an extension of time or period ☐

Notes 1. This form was introduced by S.I. 1987 No. 288, r. 2.
2. It is understood that this form may be revised. The latest Supplement to
this Work *re*. this para. 141.52 should therefore be consulted.

For official use only

141.53 THE PATENT OFFICE

PATENTS ACT 1977   **PATENTS FORM NO. 53/77**

**ADDITIONAL FEE FOR EXTENSION OF TIME
OR PERIOD UNDER RULE 110(3C)**

Please write or type in BLOCK
LETTERS using dark ink. For
details of current fees please
contact the Patent Office

1. Application Number

Enter the full name(s) of the
applicant(s)

2. Name

Please sign here ▶ | 3. Signature:

Date: _____
Day Month Year

Attention is drawn to rules 90
and 106 of the Patents Rules
1982

Notes 1. This form was introduced by S.I. 1987 No. 288, r. 2.
2. It is understood that this form may be revised. The latest Supplement to
this Work *re*. this para. 141.53 should therefore be consulted.

For official use only

THE PATENT OFFICE

141.54

PATENTS ACT 1977   **PATENTS FORM NO. 54/77**

**FILING OF TRANSLATION OF EUROPEAN
PATENT (UK) UNDER SECTION 77(6)(a)**

Please write or type in BLOCK LETTERS using dark ink. For details of current fees please contact the Patent Office	1. European Patent Number
Enter the name and address of the proprietor(s) of the European Patent (UK). If you do not have enough space please continue on a separate sheet	2. Name Address
Enter the date on which the mention of the grant of the European Patent (UK) was published in the European Patent Bulletin, or, if it has not yet been published, the date on which it will be published	3. European Patent Bulletin Date: Day Month Year
	4. Name of Agent (if any) Agent's Patent Office ADP number (if known)
A UK Address for Service MUST be provided to which all communications from the Patent Office will be sent	5. Address for Service Postcode
Please sign here ▶	6. Signature:
Attention is drawn to rules 90 and 106 of the Patents Rules 1982	Date: _____ Day Month Year
This form must be filed in duplicate and must be accompanied by a translation into English in duplicate of: **1) the whole description**	Reminder Have you attached One duplicate copy of this form ☐
2) those claims appropriate to the UK (in the language of the proceedings)	Two copies of the Translation ☐

3) all drawings, whether or not these contain any textual matter

Any continuation sheets (if appropriate) [ ]

but *excluding* the front page which contains bibliographic information. The translation must be verified to the satisfaction of the comptroller as corresponding to the original text

Notes 1. This form was introduced by S.I. 1987 No. 288, r. 2.
2. It is understood that this form may be revised. The latest Supplement to this Work *re*. this para. 141.54 should therefore be consulted.

For official use only

141.55   THE PATENT OFFICE

PATENTS ACT 1977   **PATENTS FORM NO. 55/77**

FILING OF TRANSLATION OF AMENDMENT OF EUROPEAN PATENT (UK) UNDER SECTION 77(6)(b)

Please write or type in BLOCK LETTERS using dark ink. For details of current fees please contact the Patent Office

1. European Patent Number [ ]

Enter the name and address of the proprietor(s) of the European Patent (UK). If you do not have enough space please continue on a separate sheet

2. Name

   Address

Enter the date on which the amended European Patent (UK) was published by the European Patent Office, or, if it has not yet been published, the date on which it will be published

3. Amended European Patent Publication Date:

   _____
   Day Month Year

4. Name of Agent (if any)

   Agent's Patent Office ADP number (if known) [ ]

A UK Address for Service MUST be provided to which all communications from the Patent Office will be sent

5. Address for Service

   Postcode

Please sign here ▶

6. Signature:

Date: _____
Day Month Year

Attention is drawn to rules 90 and 106 of the Patents Rules 1982

This form must be filed in duplicate and must be accompanied by a translation into English in duplicate of either the amendment or preferably the whole of the amended European Patent (UK). The translation must be verified to the satisfaction of the comptroller as corresponding to the original text

Reminder

Have you attached

One duplicate copy of this form ☐

Two copies of the Translation ☐

Any continuation sheets (if appropriate) ☐

Notes 1. This form was introduced by S.I. 1987 No. 288, r. 2.
2. It is understood that this form may be revised. The latest Supplement to this Work *re*. this para. 141.55 should therefore be consulted.

For official use only

THE PATENT OFFICE

141.56

PATENTS ACT 1977   **PATENTS FORM NO. 56/77**

REQUEST FOR PUBLICATION OF TRANSLATION OF CLAIMS OF APPLICATION FOR EUROPEAN PATENT (UK) FILED UNDER SECTION 78(7)

Please write or type in BLOCK LETTERS using dark ink. For details of current fees please contact the Patent Office

1. European Publication Number

Enter the name and address of the applicant(s) of the European Patent (UK). If you do not have enough space please continue on a separate sheet

2. Name

Address

3. Name of Agent (if any)

Agent's Patent Office ADP number (if known)

A UK Address for Service MUST be provided to which all communications from the Patent Office will be sent	4. Address for Service
	Postcode

Please sign here ▶	5. Signature:
Attention is drawn to rules 90 and 106 of the Patents Rules 1982	Date: _____ Day Month Year

This form must be filed in duplicate and must be accompanied by a translation into English in duplicate of the claims of the Application for a European Patent (UK). The translation must be verified to the satisfaction of the comptroller as corresponding to the original text	Reminder Have you attached One duplicate copy of this form ☐ Two copies of the Translation ☐ Any continuation sheets (if appropriate) ☐

Notes 1. This form was introduced by S.I. 1987 No. 288, r. 2.

2. It is understood that this form may be revised. The latest Supplement to this Work *re.* this para. 141.56 should therefore be consulted.

For official use only

141.57 THE PATENT OFFICE

PATENTS ACT 1977   **PATENTS FORM NO. 57/77**

REQUEST FOR PUBLICATION OF CORRECTED TRANSLATION OF EUROPEAN PATENT (UK) OR APPLICATION FOR EUROPEAN PATENT (UK) FILED UNDER SECTION 80(3)

Please write or type in BLOCK LETTERS using dark ink. For details of current fees please contact the Patent Office	1. European Patent or Publication Number
Enter the name and address of the proprietor(s) of, or the applicant(s) for, the European Patent (UK). If you do not have enough space please continue on a separate sheet	2. Name Address

3. Name of Agent (if any)

Agent's Patent Office
ADP number (if known)

A UK Address for Service
MUST be provided to which
all communications from the
Patent Office will be sent

4. Address for Service

Postcode

Please sign here ▶

5. Signature:

Date: _____
Day Month Year

Attention is drawn to rules 90
and 106 of the Patents Rules
1982

**This form must be filed in
duplicate and must be
accompanied by a corrected
version, in duplicate, of the
whole of the incorrect
translation. The translation
must be verified to the
satisfaction of the comptroller
as corresponding to the
original text**

Reminder

Have you attached

One duplicate copy of this form

Two copies of the Translation

Any continuation sheets (if appropriate)

Notes 1. This form was introduced by S.I. 1987 No. 288, r. 2.
2. It is understood that this form may be revised. The latest Supplement to
this Work *re.* this para. 141.57 should therefore be consulted.

141.58 PATENTS FORM No. 58/77

Declaration that
Licences of Right   Patents
Shall not Extend to   Act 1977
Excepted Uses   **Form 58/77**

For official use

Notes

Please type, or write in dark ink using
BLOCK LETTERS. No fee is required
with this form. However, there will be
no reduction of renewal fees for the
final years of the patent's life.

Rule 67A of the Patents Rules 1982
is the main rule governing the
completion and filing of this form.

If an agent has been newly
authorised, form 51/77 should be filed.

Please complete the confirmation slip
below. The Patent Office will stamp
and return it to the address in the
United Kingdom given in the box
below.

Please Sign Here

1a. Please give the patent number.

1b. Please give full name(s) of proprietor(s).

2. Please give the full name and address in the United
Kingdom to which all correspondence will be sent.
Name

Address

Postcode

ADP Number(if known)

I/We declare that licences of right under paragraph 4(2)(c) of
Schedule 1 to the Patents Act 1977 shall not extend to a use
which is excepted by or under paragraph 4A. I/We also declare
that there is no existing licence for any description of
excepted use, which took or is to take effect at or after the
end of the sixteenth year of the patent.

Signed   Date

day   month   year

Confirmation of Making an Entry

Patent number

This is to confirm that an entry has been made in the register under
rule 67A(2) (Licences of right not to extend to an excepted use).

The Patent Office

Your Reference

Patent Office
date stamp

dti
the department for Enterprise

Note. This form was introduced by S.I. 1988 No. 2089, r. 3.

ADDITIONAL RULES   142.01

The following rules are relevant (in addition to the Patents Rules (as amended), as listed in para. 139.01, and the Rules of the Supreme Court, set out in Appendix E), *viz*:

Statutory Instrument	*Rule*	*Reprinted in para.*
Patents Rules 1978 (S.I. 1978 No. 216)	124	127.04
Patent Office (Address) Rules 1985 (S.I. 1985 No. 1099)	2	123.16
Patents (Fees) Rules 1986 (S.I. 1986 No. 583)	3	123.05
Patents (Amendment) Rules 1987 (S.I. 1987 No. 288)	4	77.02
	5	78.02

ADDITIONAL FORMS

The following forms are also available for use in connection with proceedings in the Patent Office.

FORM NP 1 (for optional use under Rule 85)   143.01

National Fee for National Processing of an International Application for a Patent (UK)

Patents Act 1977

Notes	Applicants Details
Please type or write in dark ink using BLOCK LETTERS	1a Name of Applicant
For details of current fees please contact the Patent Office	
Give the full name of each Applicant. The names of all partners in a firm must be given in full. Bodies Corporate should be designated by their Corporate Name. If you do not have enough room. please continue on a separate sheet of paper.	1b Address
	Postcode/Zipcode
	Country/State of incorporation
If applicant is a body corporate give country of incorporation ▶	Country
	1c Please give ADP No. (if known)

2 Please give international
   Application Number

3a Name of Agent (if any)

3b Please give ADP No.
   (if known)

A UK Address for Service
must be given, to which all
correspondence from the
Patent Office will be sent

Address for Service
4 Please give Address for Service in the UK

_____

A check list is provided for your
use overleaf

_____

_____ Postcode _____

Please sign here.
Attention is drawn to Rules ▶
90 and 106 of the Patent
Rules 1982

Signed _____ Date _____19___
                                          Day Month Year

Name (BLOCK LETTERS) _____

This Form cannot be accepted without the Prescribed Fee.

CHECK LIST (items filed with this form
should be ticked in the appropriate box

NOTE: The rules referred to are those of the
       Patent Rules 1982 as amended by
       the Patent (Amendment No 2)
       Rules 1985.

WARNINGS* If any of these items are not
       filed within their appropriate
       prescribed periods the appli-
       cation will be taken to be
       withdrawn.
       Care should be taken that the
       translation of the right docu-
       ment and not some other
       document is filed.

Rule 85(1)   The following items must be
             filed within the prescribed
             period before an inter-
             national application can
             satisfy the relevant con-
             ditions for national process-
             ing:

       * Copy of the international
          application. (Note: the
          copy should have been
          sent to the UK Patent
          Office by the Inter-
          national Bureau).

       □* Translation of the inter-

national application if
not in English.

□* Filing Fee.

  * A copy of any amend-
     ment of the international
     application made in
     accordance with the
     Patent Co-operation
     Treaty.
     (Note: this copy should
     have been sent to the
     UK Patent Office by the
     International Bureau).
□* Translation of any such
    amendment if not in
    English.

Rule 85(1A) □* Where applicable trans-
                lation of information, if
                not in English, filed
                with the International
                Bureau, and relating to
                the deposit of a micro-
                organism.

The following items must
also be filed within their
appropriate prescribed
periods:

Rule 85(3)(a) □* Request for preliminary
                  examination and search
                  (Patent Form No 9/77),
                  and prescribed fee.

910

Rules 15(4) and 85(3)(a)	□*	Where required information specifying the inventor and derivation of right to apply (Patents Form No 7/77).	Rule 85(2A)(b) □	Where applicable a certificate relating to the display of the invention of an international exhibition.
Rules 85(3)(b)	□*	Request for substantive examination (Patents Form 10/77) and prescribed fee.	Rule 85(2) □	Request for publication of translation (Patents Form 43/77).
Rule 6(6)	□	Translation of any priority application if not in English.	Rule 85(2A)(c) □	Translations should be verified as required by the Rules.

Notes 1. This form was introduced to replace PF 42/77. It is mentioned in the Fees Schedule, see Para. 144.02.
2. This form will need amendment when rule 85 is revised, for which see para. 89A.02. The latest Supplement to this Work *re.* this para. 143.01 should therefore be consulted.

FORM BP/12 (for use with PF 8/77 under r. 17)   143.02

| I.   IDENTIFICATION OF THE MICROORGANISM |
| Accession number of the deposit: |
| II.   PATENT APPLICATION OR PATENT REFERRING TO THE MICROORGANISM |
| □[2]   Patent application No.   filed on
       Filed by (name, address): |
| □[2]   International Application (PCT) No. Filed   filed on
       by (name, address): |
| □[2]   Patent[3] No.   granted on
       Granted to (name, address): |

[1] The request must be sent to the competent industrial property office which, in conformity with its own applicable procedure, will either transmit it directly to the international depositary authority or send it back to the certified party for transmission to the international depositary authority.
[2] Mark with a cross the applicable box.
[3] References to a "patent" shall be construed as references to patents for inventions, inventors' certificates, utility certificates, utility models, patents or certificates of addition, inventors' certificates of addition, and utility certificates of addtion.

| III.   REQUEST FOR INFORMATION |
| The undersigned |
| □[2]   requests |
| □[2]   does not request |
| an indication of the conditions which the international depositary authority employs for the cultivation and storage of the microorganism. |

IV. CERTIFIED PARTY

Name: Signature[4]:

Address:

                                            Date:

---

[2] Mark with a cross the applicable box.
[4] Where the signature is required on behalf of a legal entity, the typewritten name(s) of the natural person(s) signing on behalf of the legal entity should accompany the signature(s).

CERTIFICATION

It is hereby certified that:

(1) ☐[2]   the patent application specified under II above, referring to the deposit of the microorganism identified under I above, has been filed with this Office for the grant of a patent and its subject matter involves the said microorganism or the use thereof

    ☐[2]   the international application specified under II above, referring to the deposit of the microorganism identified under I above, designates for the grant of a patent the State party to the Patent Cooperation Treaty (PCT) for which this Office is the "designated Office" within the meaning of the said Treaty, and the subject of that international application involves the said microorganism or the use thereof

    ☐[2]   the patent specified under II above, referring to the deposit of the microorganism identified under I above, has been granted by this Office and its subject matter involves the said microorganism or its use thereof

(2) ☐[2]   publication for the purposes of patent procedure has been effected
           ☐[5] by this Office
           ☐[5] by the International Bureau of the World Intellectual Property Organization as an international publication under the Patent Cooperation Treaty (PCT)

    or

    ☐[2]   the certified party has a right to a sample before publication in accordance with[6]:

(3) ☐[2]   the certified party has a right to a sample of the microorganism identified under I above under the law governing patent procedure before this Office and this Office is satisfied that the conditions, if any, prescribed by the said law have actually been fulfilled

    or

    ☐[2]   the certified party has affixed his signature on a form before this Office and, as a consequence of the signature of the said form, the conditions for furnishing a sample of the microorganism identified under I above to the certified party are deemed to be fulfilled in accordance with the law governing patent procedure before this Office

---

Industrial Property Office Street City [Country]	Signature: Date:

[2] Mark with a cross the applicable box.
[5] If only one box applies, mark with a cross that box; if both boxes apply, mark with a cross one of the two boxes (choose one).
[6] Cite the applicable provision of the law, including any court decision.

Notes 1. This is a form approved for use internationally under the Budapest Treaty for International Recognition of Deposit of Microorganisms.
2. This form is for use under rule 17. For the revision of this rule, see para. 125A.02.

FEES

Illustrative fee schedule   **144.01**

The Patents (Fees) Rules 1986 (S.I. 1986 No. 583) introduced a new schedule of fees payable, replacing Schedule 1 to the Patents Rules 1982 (S.I. 1982 No. 717) which was revoked thereby. When the fees are altered, as seems to be the annual position about May of each year, the Schedule to the Fees Rules is amended or revoked and replaced by new Patents (Fees) Rules. Because of this frequent change it would be inappropriate for this Work to attempt to keep track of the current fees. A pamphlet setting out the fees currently payable can be obtained from the Patent Office. At the time of printing the current fees payable under the Patents Rules 1982 will be found in Part A of the Schedule to the Patents (Fees) Rules 1989 (S.I. 1989 No. 899) and, as an indication of the level of fees which obtained immediately after July 3, 1989, and the relation of the various fees one to another, this Schedule is reproduced in para. 144.02 below. Part B of this Schedule deals with fees payable under the Patents Rules 1968, for matters still governed by the Patents Act 1949, and this Part (likewise as applicable immediately after July 3, 1989) is reproduced, likewise, in para. A139.

144.02

PATENTS (FEES) RULES 1989
(S.I. 1989 No. 899)

SCHEDULE

FEES PAYABLE

PART A

(In this Part of this Schedule, any reference to a section is a reference to that section of the Patents Act 1977 and any reference to a rule is a reference to that rule of the Patents Rules 1982.)

Number of corresponding Patents Form	Item	Amount
		£
1/77	On request for the grant of a patent (the filing fee)	15
2/77	On reference under section 8(1), 12(1) or 37(1)	30
3/77	On application under section 8(5) or 37(3) for authorisation by comptroller	30
4/77	On request for directions under section 10 or 12(4)	30
5/77	On reference under section 11(5) or 38(5) to determine the question of a licence	30
6/77	On application to comptroller under section 13(1) and/or 13(3)	22
7/77	Statement of inventorship and of right to the grant of a patent	—
8/77	On request for comptroller's certificate authorising the release of a sample for a culture collection	10
9/77	On request for preliminary examination and search or request for further search	95
10/77	On request for substantive examination	110
11/77	On request to amend application before grant	25
12/77	*On payment of renewal fee—	
	Before the expiration of the 4th year from the date of filing of the application for the patent or, in the case of an existing patent, the date of the patent and in respect of the 5th year	86
	Before the expiration of the 5th year from the date of filing of the application for the patent or, in the case of an existing patent, the date of the patent and in respect of the 6th year	92
	Before the expiration of the 6th year from the date of filing of the application for the patent or, in the case of an existing patent, the date of the patent and in respect of the 7th year	100
	Before the expiration of the 7th year from the date of filing of the application for the patent or, in the case of an existing patent, the date of the patent and in respect of the 8th year	110

914

Number of corresponding Patents Form	Item	Amount
	Before the expiration of the 8th year from the date of filing of the application for the patent or, in the case of an existing patent, the date of the patent and in respect of the 9th year	120
	Before the expiration of the 9th year from the date of filing of the application for the patent or, in the case of an existing patent, the date of the patent and in respect of the 10th year	132
	Before the expiration of the 10th year from the date of filing of the application for the patent or, in the case of an existing patent, the date of the patent and in respect of the 11th year	146
	Before the expiration of the 11th year from the date of filing of the application for the patent or, in the case of an existing patent, the date of the patent and in respect of the 12th year	160
	Before the expiration of the 12th year from the date of filing of the application for the patent or, in the case of an existing patent, the date of the patent and in respect of the 13th year	180
	Before the expiration of the 13th year from the date of filing of the application for the patent or, in the case of an existing patent, the date of the patent and in respect of the 14th year	200
	Before the expiration of the 14th year from the date of filing of the application for the patent or, in the case of an existing patent, the date of the patent and in respect of the 15th year	220
	Before the expiration of the 15th year from the date of filing of the application for the patent or, in the case of an existing patent, the date of the patent and in respect of the 16th year	242
	Before the expiration of the 16th year from the date of filing of the application for the patent or, in the case of an existing patent, the date of the patent and in respect of the 17th year	264
	Before the expiration of the 17th year from the date of filing of the application for the patent or, in the case of an existing patent, the date of the patent and in respect of the 18th year	286
	Before the expiration of the 18th year from the date of filing of the application for the patent or, in the case of an existing patent, the date of the patent and in respect of the 19th year	318
	Before the expiration of the 19th year from the date of filing of the application for the patent or, in the case of an existing patent, the date of the patent and in respect of the 20th year	350
13/77	On extension of the period for payment of a renewal fee under section 25(4)—	

915

Number of corresponding Patents Form	Item	Amount
	Not exceeding one month	18
	Each succeeding month	18
	(but not exceeding six months)	
14/77	On application to amend specification after grant	52
15/77	On notice of opposition to amendment of specification after grant	22
16/77	On application for the restoration of a patent	105
17/77	Additional fee on the application for restoration of a patent	105
18/77	An offer to surrender a patent	—
19/77	On notice of opposition to offer to surrender a patent .	22
20/77	On request for alteration of name, address or address for service in the register, for each patent or application	3
21/77	On application to register or to give notice of a transaction, instrument or event affecting the rights in a patent or application for a patent	22
	On each application covering more than one patent or application for a patent, the devolution of title being the same as in the first patent or application for a patent. For each additional request	3
22/77	On request for the correction of an error in the register or in any connected document	16
23/77	On request for the furnishing of or access to miscellaneous information .... Each	2
24/77	On request for certificate of the comptroller— (a) by impressed stamp .... (b) sealed and attached to documents	3 11
25/77	On application for entry of order of court in the register	—
26/77	On application for compensation by employee	30
27/77	On application under section 41(8) in connection with an order made under section 40(1) or 40(2)	30
28/77	On application by proprietor for entry to be made in the register to the effect that licences under the patent are to be available as of right	12
29/77	On application for settlement of terms of licence of right	52
30/77	On application by proprietor under section 47(1) for cancellation of entry in the register	22
31/77	On application under section 47(3) by person interested for cancellation of entry in the register	22
32/77	On notice of opposition to an application under section 47(1) or 47(3) for cancellation of entry in the register	22

Number of corresponding Patents Form	Item	Amount
33/77	On application under section 48(1) for a compulsory licence or entry in the register	52
34/77	On application by Crown in case of monopoly or merger	52
35/77	On notice of opposition to application made under section 48 or 51	22
36/77	On reference to the comptroller of a dispute as to infringement	52
37/77	On application for declaration of non-infringement	52
38/77	On application for the revocation of a patent	22
39/77	On application to register copy of entry made in European Register of Patents	9
40/77	On payment of filing fee upon conversion of European patent application to an application under the Act ...	15
41/77	On request for conversion of European patent application	15
43/77	On payment of prescribed fee and request for publication of translation	9
44/77	On application to the comptroller for an international application to be treated as an application under the Act	15
45/77	On application for order for evidence to be obtained in the United Kingdom	30
46/77	On notice that hearing before the comptroller will be attended	—
47/77	On request for the correction of an error of translation or transcription, clerical error or mistake	32
48/77	On notice of opposition to the correction of an error, clerical error or mistake	22
49/77	On request for information relating to a patent or an application for a patent	8
50/77	On request for extension of time or period under rule 110(3) .... Each	105
51/77	On declaration of authorisation where agent appointed during progress of application or in substitution for another	—
52/77	On request for extension of time or period under rule 110(3A)	105
53/77	Additional fee for extension of time or period under rule 110(3C)	105
54/77	On filing of translation of European Patent (UK) under section 77(6)(a)	26
55/77	On filing of translation of amendment of European Patent (UK) under section 77(6)(b)	26

917

Number of corresponding Patents Form	Item	Amount
56/77	On request for publication of translation of claims of application for European Patent (UK) filed under section 78(7)	26
57/77	On request for publication of a corrected translation filed under section 80(3)	26
58/77	On declaration that licence of right shall not extend to excepted uses	—
—	National fee (rule 85(1))	15
	As Receiving Office or International Preliminary Examining Authority under the Patent Co-operation Treaty—	
—	Transmittal Fee (rule 118(1))	15
—	Preliminary Examination Fee (rule 120)	50
—	Additional fee (rule 121) .... Maximum	50

APPENDIX A

THE 1949 ACT

Scope of Appendix A   A000.1

This Appendix A deals with the unrepealed provisions of the Patents Act 1949 (12, 13 & 14 Geo. 6, c. 87), as amended by subsequent enactments, including the 1977 Act, and known as the Patents Acts 1949 to 1961, see Patents and Designs (Renewals, Extensions and Fees) Act 1961 (9 & 10 Eliz. 2, c. 25, s. 3(2)), at least so far as these appear to have some present effect. In relation to this amended statute those provisions which are considered to be effectively spent are usually merely noted, but some sections, though spent, are reprinted in order to provide an explanation of terminology which still has effect. Cross-references to replacement provisions in the 1977 Act are given where appropriate and, throughout Appendix A, there is indicated the extent to which the 1949 Act continues to apply to "existing patents", that is to those patents having a complete specification dated before June 1, 1978. The 1949 Act also remains alive to deal with any applications filed before that date and not yet granted. This can arise from applications which remains subject to secrecy directions (under s. 18 [1949]), but the amendment now to be made to section 13 [1949] (noted in para. A013, *infra*) should make the number of these *de minimis*, and therefore they are not dealt with in this Work. The historical background to the 1949 Act is set out in para. 130.05.

The Patents Rules 1968   A000.2

In relation to proceedings for which the 1949 Act continues to have effect, the Patents Rules 1968 (S.I. 1968 No. 1389) remain effective, despite their repeal. Those of such rules which are not effectively spent are reprinted under the section under which they have their greatest effect, in some cases under a section of the 1977 Act. These 1968 Rules are summarised in paragraph A109 and those of the forms to the 1968 Rules which may still need to be used are reprinted at paras. A119–A138.

Other patent statutes still effective   A000.3

Appendix B contains details of other former patent statutes which still have some effect in relation to patent matters.

PATENTS ACTS 1949 TO 1961
(12, 13 & 14 Geo. 6, c. 87)

ARRANGEMENT OF SECTIONS   A000.4

Application, investigation, opposition, etc.

SECTION

  1. Persons entitled to make application.

SCHEDULES:

First Schedule—Maximum Fees. [*Repealed*]
Second Schedule—Enactments Repealed. [*Repealed*]
Third Schedule—Transitional Provisions. [*Partially Repealed*]

AN ACT TO CONSOLIDATE CERTAIN ENACTMENTS RELATING TO PATENTS.

A000.5

[16th December 1949.]

Be it enacted by the King's most Excellent Majesty, by and with the advice and consent of the Lords Spiritual and Temporal, and Commons, in this present Parliament assembled, and by the authority of the same, as follows:

SECTION 1 [1949]

A001.1

Persons entitled to make application

1.—(1) An application for a patent for an invention may be made by any of the following persons, that is to say:
  (*a*) by any person claiming to be the true and first inventor of the invention;
  (*b*) by any person being the assignee of the person claiming to be the true and first inventor in respect of the right to make such an application;
and may be made by that person either alone or jointly with any other person.

(2) Without prejudice to the foregoing provisions of this section, an application for a patent for an invention in respect of which protection has been applied for in a convention country may be made by the person by whom the application for protection was made or by the assignee of that person;

Provided that no application shall be made by virtue of this subsection after the expiration of twelve months from the date of application for protection in a convention country or, where more than one such application for protection has been made, from the date of the first application.

(3) An application for a patent may be made under subsection (1) or subsection (2) of this section by the personal representative of any deceased person who, immediately before his death, was entitled to make such an application.

(4) An application for a patent made by virtue of subsection (2) of this section is in this Act referred to as a convention application.

A001.2

J. C. H. Ellis, "Convention applications", Trans. Chart. Inst., LXXXVII, C75 and B81 (1968–69);

R. L. Andrews, "Wrongly claimed convention priority", CIPA, May 1973, p. 344.

COMMENTARY ON SECTION 1 [1949]

A001.3 *General*

Subsection (1) is of historical significance because it provided for the first time in United Kingdom patent law that an application not claiming convention priority could be filed, initially, solely in the name of an assignee: before 1950 the inventor had to be at least a joint applicant. By subsection (3) the right to apply was also given to the personal representatives of a deceased inventor or assignee. Subsections (2) and (4) enabled "convention applications" to be filed by an applicant (or his assignee) for an application for protection in a convention country (as defined by s. 68), provided that the application under the 1949 Act was filed within 12 months of the *first* application for protection in a convention country. Subsections (1) and (3), therefore, have continuing significance in relation to objections to validity of existing patents arising from non-entitlement to apply; and subsections (2) and (4) as regards improper claiming of convention priority.

Allegations of improper claiming of convention priority could previously be raised pre-grant under the specific provision of section 14(1)(*h*) and also post-grant by an objection under section 32(1)(*j*) that the patent had been obtained on a false suggestion. A successful objection under the latter head used to lead to revocation without any opportunity of amendment. This was considered a harsh result and section 32(1)(*j*) was amended by Schedule 1, para. 6 [1977] so that the penalty now for mis-claiming of convention priority in an existing patent is merely loss of that priority, see para. A032.31.

As can be seen from the commentary on section 5 [1977], particularly from para. 5.04, under the 1977 Act the matter of convention priority is treated rather differently, no distinction now being drawn between a "convention application" and any other application from which priority may be claimed. Moreover, the test for according priority is no longer stated as one of "fair basis."

A001.4 *Nature and disclosure of priority application*

For determining whether convention priority has properly been accorded, section 1 must be read in conjunction with section 69. Section 69(1) provided for convention priority to be claimed, not merely from a normal patent application but also from applications for other forms of protection, such as German Gebrauchsmusters and other utility models. Also, in considering the disclosure of the earlier foreign application as the basis for according priority, account is to be taken of both the claims and disclosure of that application, otherwise than disclosure by way of disclaimer or acknowledgment of prior art (s. 69(2)).

A001.5 *The "fair basis" test for according convention priority*

The test of whether convention priority can properly be accorded has now been decided to be whether the claims of the convention application are "fairly based" on the foreign application in a convention country filed within the preceding 12 months, see *Polaroid's (Land's) Patent* ([1981] RPC 111 (CA) and [1981] FSR 578 (HL)), *Canon K.K.'s Application* ([1980] RPC 133) and *International Paint's Application* ([1982] RPC 247) and the discussion in para. A005.9 of the test of "fair basis" for determination of priority under section 5 [1949]. This test is similar to that required by section 4(4) and section 32(1)(*i*) for "fair basis" of claims over the disclosure of the corresponding specification and, in these contexts, the test is discussed respectively in paras. A004.05 and A032.29.

Status of the foreign priority application   **A001.6**

In *Stauffer's Application* ([1977] RPC 33 (CA)) it was held that the test for fair basis was only applicable after it had been decided whether the application could be regarded as being a "convention application" within the terms of section 1(2). Here an attempt to claim priority from a feature, disclosed in the priority application as one well-known, failed on the basis that that application was not an application for protection of the invention subsequently claimed in the alleged "convention application". In *Polaroid's (Land's) Patent* ([1981] RPC 111 (CA) and [1981] FSR 578 (HL)) it was clarified, in accordance with Article 4H of the Paris Convention, that a convention application could properly be founded on a disclosure in the foreign application that have been included only incidentally, provided that such disclosure could be seen as included with a view to provisional protection against adverse effects of disclosure or use after filing which might then prejudice the applicant's chance of obtaining a patent: for example, such might be an obvious development over the main disclosure and hence become unpatentable in a later application.

However, it is immaterial whether the priority application is patentable under the law of its own country, provided that it can be regarded as one made with regularity under its own law (*Ishihara Sangyo* v. *Dow Chemical*, [1987] FSR 137 (CA)). In this case a pleading that the priority application was not an initiatory step towards obtaining a patent for the invention subsequently claimed in the United Kingdom was permitted to remain to be decided as a matter of the foreign law, but that pleading was not permitted to be supported by evidence that the compound(s) in question had neither then been made or tested.

Both in the *Ishihara* case, and in *Compagnie Française de Télévision* v. *Thorn* (SRIS C/181/83, *noted* IPD 7018), it seems to have been accepted that the foreign application ought to be construed in the manner in which it would be construed under its own law, but on appeal in the latter case (SRIS C/95/85 (CA)) English principles appear to have been applied.

Effect of abandoned foreign application   **A001.7**

It was held in *Van de Poele's Patent* ((1890) 7 RPC 69) that, if an earlier abandoned application had no effect whatever, priority could be claimed from a later substitute application. Because of this and other decisions (*Whitin's Application* ((1937) 54 RPC 278) and *Poly-Resin's Application* ([1961] RPC 228)), it was unnecessary for the United Kingdom to amend the 1949 Act when the Paris Convention was amended at Lisbon in 1958 to introduce a new Article, *viz.*

4C(4) A subsequent application for the same subject as a previous application filed in the same country of the Union shall be considered as a first application within the meaning of paragraph (2), the filing date of which shall be the starting point of the period of priority, provided that, at the time of filing the subsequent application, the previous application has been withdrawn, abandoned or refused, without being open to public inspection and without leaving any rights outstanding, and has not served as a basis for claiming a right of priority. The previous application may not thereafter serve as a basis for claiming a right of priority".

A common assignee of two different applicants who made separate applications for the same invention in a convention country could apply within 12 months of the later of the two foreign applications (*Minnesota Mining's Application*, (1952) 69 RPC 163). But an applicant abroad who made two different applications (not abandoned) for the same invention, or his assignee, had to apply for a patent within 12 months of the earlier of the two applications (*Gumbel's Patent*, 1958 RPC 1).

A001.8   *United States continuation-in-part applications as priority documents*

A United States continuation-in-part application normally derives some right from the earlier application so, as a generality, a convention application based on a continuation-in-part application filed more than 12 months after the original application could only validly claim matter disclosed for the first time in the continuation-in-part application. However, in *Monsanto's Applications* ([1964] RPC 6) evidence showed that the disclosure in an original United States application was insufficient to support allowable claims and, therefore, a continuation-in-part application based thereon was not entitled to the benefit of the filing date of the original application. It was held that the continuation-in-part was therefore a proper basis for a convention application under section 1(2).

It can now be seen that this decision is probably in accord with the "fair basis" test expounded in the more recent cases. The same may also be true with *Union Carbide's (Bailey and (O'Connor's) Application* ([1972] RPC 854) and *Minnesota Mining's (Vogel's) Application* ([1973] RPC 578), both of which involved United States continuation-in-part applications for specific subject matter falling within the more general disclosure of the original United States application. The question thus seems to be whether the later application can be regarded as a valid selection of novel subject matter over the disclosure of the basic application. However, it can be questioned whether these decisions are in accord with the subsequent decision in *Polaroid's (Land's) Patent*, discussed in para. A001.6 *supra*.

A002.1   **SECTION 2 [1949]**

Application

2.—(1) Every application for a patent shall be made in the prescribed form and shall be filed at the Patent Office in the prescribed manner.

(2) If the application (not being a convention application) is made by virtue of an assignment of the right to apply for a patent for the invention, there shall be furnished with the application or within such period as may be prescribed after the filing of the application a declaration, signed by the person claiming to be the true and first inventor or his personal representative, stating that he assents to the making of the application.

(3) Every application (other than a convention application) shall state that the applicant is in possession of the invention and shall name the person claiming to be the true and first inventor; and where the person so claiming is not the applicant or one of the applicants, the application shall

contain a declaration that the applicant believes him to be the true and first inventor.

(4) Every convention application shall specify the date on which and the convention country in which the application for protection, or the first such application, was made, and shall state that no application for protection in respect of the invention had been made in a convention country before that date by the applicant or any person from whom he derives title.

(5) Where applications for protection have been made in one or more convention countries in respect of two or more inventions which are cognate or of which one is a modification of another, a single convention application may, subject to the provisions of section four of this Act, be made in respect of those inventions at any time within twelve months from the date of the earliest of the said applications for protection:

Provided that the fee payable on the making of any such application shall be the same as if separate applications had been made in respect of each of the said inventions; and the requirements of the last foregoing subsection shall in the case of any such application apply separately to the applications for protection in respect of each of the said inventions.

COMMENTARY ON SECTION 2 [1949] A002.2

Section 2 [1949] has present interest only for indicating the procedure and terminology for filing applications under the 1949 Act.

It should be noted that under subsection (2) the inventor's consent to the making of the application had to be supplied and, by subsection (3), the applicant (other than one for a convention application) had to name the inventor and the application had to contain a statement by the applicant that he believed such person(s) to be the true and first inventor(s). If that declaration can be shown to have been untrue, then objection leading to revocation under section 32(1)(b), (c) or (j) [1949] would be possible.

The prescribed application form (required by subs. (1)) normally contained a declaration that the applicant knew of no lawful ground of objection to the grant of a patent to him, although such declaration could be (but rarely was) avoided by use of Application Forms 1A and 1B under The Strasbourg Convention on Patent Formalities of December 11, 1953. A side note on the normal application form stated that "Use of the invention in the United Kingdom before the date of the application for a patent is a lawful ground of objection". Therefore, when it can be shown that the applicant made such a declaration, knowing at the time that it was false because there had been prior publication or prior use of the claimed invention within the United Kingdom, the patent is revocable under section 32(1)(j) for having been obtained on a false suggestion and amendment to cure such an objection is not normally permitted, see *Armco's Application* ([1969] FSR 33). In *Parry-Husband's Application* (1965] RPC 382) full evidence was called for as to the state of knowledge of the applicant as to the prior use within his own organisation, but amendment was allowed (*unreported*) on a showing that the persons who knew of the prior use did not know of the application and vice versa.

Subsection (4) relates to convention applications and is the basis for the claiming of convention priority, for which see the commentary on section 1 [1949] at para. A001.2 where possible objections based on improper claiming of such priority are discussed.

Subsection (5) permitted the claiming of multiple convention priorities and section 4(6) permitted the claiming of partial priority from a provisional specification or convention application. However, under the 1949 Act, it was not possible to claim multiple priority from both a United Kingdom provisional specification and a foreign application because the United Kingdom was (and is) not a convention country within the meaning of the United Kingdom patent statutes.

A003.1   **SECTION 3 [1949]**

Complete and provisional specifications

3.—(1) Every application for a patent (other than a convention application) shall be accompanied by either a complete specification or a provisional specification; and every convention application shall be accompanied by a complete specification.

(2) Where an application for a patent is accompanied by a provisional specification, a complete specification shall be filed within twelve months from the date of filing of the application and if the complete specification is not so filed the application shall be deemed to be abandoned:

Provided that the complete specification may be filed at any time after twelve months but within fifteen months from the date aforesaid if a request to that effect is made to the comptroller and the prescribed fee paid on or before the date on which the specification is filed.

(3) Where two or more applications accompanied by provisional specifications have been filed in respect of inventions which are cognate or of which one if a modification of another, a single complete specification may, subject to the provisions of this and the next following section, be filed in pursuance of those applications, or, if more than one complete specification has been filed, may with the leave of the comptroller be proceeded within respect of those applications.

(4) Where an application for a patent (not being a convention application) is accompanied by a specification purporting to be a complete specification, the comptroller may, if the applicant so requests at any time before the acceptance of the specification, direct that it shall be treated for the purpose of this Act as a provisional, and proceed with the application accordingly.

(5) Where a complete specification has been filed in pursuance of an application for a patent accompanied by a provisional specification or by a specification treated by virtue of a direction under the last foregoing subsection as a provisional specification, the comptroller may, if the application so requests at any time before the acceptance of the complete specification, cancel the provisional specification and post-date the application to the date of filing of the complete specification.

Section 3 is effectively spent, but it explains the terminology of "provisional" and "complete" specifications found with existing patents.

Under subsection (1) every application under the 1949 Act had to have a "complete" specification, but (except in the case of a convention application) this could be preceded by one or more "provisional" specifications filed within the previous 15 months (subss. (2) and (3)). Under subsection (4) it was also possible to convert a complete specification into a provisional specification and then file a new complete specification (within 15 months thereof), and under subsection (5) it was possible to cancel a provisional specification and post-date the application to the date when a complete specification had been filed thereon and this could itself then be treated as a provisional specification under subsection (4) and a new complete specification then filed, all provided that the maximum time limit of 15 months between the earliest effective provisional specification and the eventual complete specification was not exceeded.

These provisions had no application to convention applications which had to be filed (with a complete specification in the first instance) within an inextensible period of 12 months from the first application for protection in a convention country, see the commentary on section 1 [1949] at para. A001.1.

SECTION 4 [1949]   A004.01

Contents of specification

4.—(1) Every specification, whether complete or provisional, shall describe the invention, and shall begin with a title indicating the subject to which the invention relates.

(2) Subject to any rules made by the Board of Trade under this Act, drawings may, and shall if the comptroller so requires, be supplied for the purposes of any specification, whether complete or provisional; and any drawings so supplied shall, unless the comptroller otherwise directs, be deemed to form part of the specification, and references in this Act to a specification shall be construed accordingly.

(3) Every complete specification—

(a) shall particularly describe the invention and the method by which it is to be performed;

(b) shall disclose the best method of performing the invention which is known to the applicant and for which he is entitled to claim protection; and

(c) shall end with a claim or claims defining the scope of the invention claimed.

(4) The claim or claims of a complete specification must relate to a single invention, must be clear and succinct, and must be fairly based on the matter disclosed in the specification.

(5) Rules made by the Board of Trade under this Act may require that in such cases as may be prescribed by the rules, a declaration as to the inventorship of the invention, in such form as may be so prescribed, shall be fur-

nished with the complete specification or within such period as may be so prescribed after the filing of that specification.

(6) Subject to the foregoing provisions of this section a complete specification filed after a provisional specification, or filed with a convention application, may include claims in respect of developments of or additions to the invention which was described in the provisional specification or, as the case may be, the invention in respect of which the application for protection was made in a convention country, being developments or additions in respect of which the applicant would be entitled under the provisions of section one of this Act to make separate application for a patent.

(7) Where a complete specification claims a new substance, the claim shall be construed as not extending to that substance when found in nature.

A004.02   ARTICLE

A. W. White, "The patentability of naturally occurring products", [1980] EIPR 37.

COMMENTARY ON SECTION 4 [1949]

A004.03

General

Section 4 prescribes the basic requirements for the sufficiency of provisional and complete specifications under the 1949 Act. It therefore has effect for construing the scope of protection conferred by the patent, as discussed in paras. A004.06 and A004.07 *infra*; and has continuing applicability to questions of the priority date to be accorded to a claim under section 5 [1949], as discussed in the commentary thereon; as well as for the consideration of questions of validity under section 32(1)(*b*), (*c*), (*h*), (*i*) and (*j*) [1949], as discussed in the paragraphs cited in para. A004.05 *infra*.

Also, subsection (7) provides a special rule for claim interpretation in relation to inventions of a product which is also "found in nature".

A004.04   *Functions of provisional specification, drawings and complete specification (subss. (1)–(4)*

By subsection (1) a provisional specification was simply required to describe the invention. The real function of such a specification was to establish a priority date for one or more of the claims in the complete specification or for any application abroad. It is, however, matter actually described therein which is rendered harmless by section 52, for which see para. A052.2. Thus, an intervening publication of an undescribed way of carrying out an invention might not be rendered harmless by section 52 even though it was covered by a broad statement of invention.

By subsection (2) drawings form part of a specification if supplied therewith and drawings supplied with a provisional specification could be used also for a subsequent complete specification.

However, a complete specification must not only describe the invention (as required by subs. (i)), it must also comply with the requirements of subsections (3) and (4). The requirements of subsection (3) are that a complete specification of an existing patent must: (a) particularly describe the invention and the method by which the invention is to be performed; (b) describe the best method of performing the invention which is known to the applicant and for which he is entitled to claim protection; and (c) have a claim or claims defining the scope of the invention claimed. By subsection (4) such claims must: (1) relate to a single invention, (2) be clear and and succinct, and (3) be fairly based on the matter disclosed in the specification.

Effect of non-compliance with subsections (3) and (4)   **A004.05**

The requirement of subsection (3)(a) is one of sufficiency of description and a failure to meet this leads to invalidity under section 32(1)(h), as discussed in paras. A032.17–A.032.22.

The requirement of subsection (3)(b) as to disclosure of the best method known of performing the invention can lead to invalidity under 32(1)(h) [1949], as discussed in paras. A032.23–A032.26. However, an applicant who learned of an improved method of carrying out his invention was under no obligation to describe it if he was not entitled to claim protection for it, but if he was so entitled he ought to have included it and failure to have done so will be a ground of revocation under section 32(1)(h).

The requirements of subsections (3)(c) and (4) relate to the grounds of invalidity under section 32(1)(i), namely "ambiguity of claim", as discussed in paras. A032.27 and A032.28, and "lack of fair basis", as discussed in para. A032.29. The latter requirement has been equated, see *Stauffer's Application* [1977] RPC 33 (CA)), with the criterion for a claim to have a priority date earlier than the date of the complete specification which also requires that such is "fairly based" on a specification of earlier date (whether a provisional specification or that of a foreign specification) from which priority is claimed, for which see para. A005.3. However, the two tests are not necessarily the same. In all cases the claims are to be construed in accordance with the general rules summarised in para. A004.06 *infra*.

No objection can be taken to an existing patent on the ground that it was granted for more than one invention (s. 21(4)), but this presumption may have an effect on the interpretation of multiple independent claims, see para. A021.6.

General rules of construction for patent claims   **A004.06**

In the oft-cited case of *EMI* v. *Lissen* ((1938) 56 RPC 23 (HL)) it was stated (at p. 41) that there is "no canon or principle which would justify one in departing from the unambiguous and grammatical meaning of a claim and narrowing or extending its scope by reading into it words which are not in it", see also *Norton and Gregory* v. *Jacobs* ((1937) 54 RPC 58 and 271 (CA)). However, the specification must be read as a whole so that the meaning of its claims can be influenced by the wording of the description, see *Henriksen* v. *Tallon* ([1965] RPC 434 (HL)) and *Ransburg* v. *Aerostyle* ([1968] RPC 287 (HL)). Also, technical terms are to be construed as they would be by men skilled in the art (*British Thomson-Houston* v. *Corona*, (1929) 39 RPC 49 (HL) and *Cleveland Graphite* v. *Glacier Metal*, (1950) 67 RPC 149 (HL)), and as discussed in para. 125.15. In particular, the claims should not be construed as strictly as a conveyancing document (*Rotocrop* v. *Genbourne*, [1982] FSR 241).

The claims of a patent granted under the 1949 Act are now to be given a "purposive" construction (*Catnic* v. *Hill and Smith*, [1982] RPC 183 (HL)), as discussed in para. 125.10, but they should be construed *in vacuo*, *i.e.* without reference to either the alleged infringement, "as if . . . before the defendant was born" (*Nobel* v.

Anderson, (1894) 11 RPC 519 at 524 (CA)), or to prior art not acknowledged in the specification (*Molins* v. *Industrial Machinery*, (1938) 55 RPC 31 (CA)).

Attention is also drawn to the "squeeze argument" discussed in para. 125.17, *i.e.* the contention that if the claim is given a broad interpretation it is invalid, and if a narrow construction is preferred the claim is not infringed.

The application of these points of general construction to the particular grounds of invalidity is discussed in the paragraphs referred to in para. A004.05 *supra*.

A004.07 *Functional claims*

In a sense all claims are functional in nature, but this term is usually reserved for claims the scope of which is limited by a statement of expressed function which the claim is required to perform, or result which the claimed product or method has to achieve, *e.g.* as in *No-Fume* v. *Pitchford* ((1935) 52 RPC 231 (CA)). However, such a claim will be invalid if it is a "free beer" claim, *i.e.* one which claims all solutions to a known problem as in *British United Shoe Machinery* v. *Simon Collier* ((1909) 26 RPC 21).

A claim may also be limited by a reference to it being of a particular type, *e.g.* as in *Raleigh* v. *Miller* ((1948 65 RPC 141 (HL)) where a claim to "A dynamo for a cycle . . . " was construed as being one for an article of such dimensions and weight as would make it suitable to be fitted to a bicycle, but *not* limited to a dynamo which was necessarily suitable for the stated object of the invention, *viz.* for producing a steady light.

Other, more recent, examples where descriptive words have been used in a claim and held there to have a clarificatory or limiting effect are: *Beloit's Application* ([1974] RPC 467), where the addition to a claim of the words "dimensioned and arranged substantially as and for the purposes herein set forth" to a paper-making roll was allowed, it being held that the relevant public (the makers and users of the roll) would have no difficulty in deciding whether any given roll was an infringement; *Hayashibara's Patent* ([1977] FSR 582), where the inclusion in the claim of the words "so that the products obtained have an increased sweetness without an increase in the calorific value of the food materials" were held not to be mere surplusage but to have a limiting effect on the claim; and *ICI's (Whyte's) Patent* ([1978] RPC 11), where full limiting effect was given to a functional statement that the claimed grey film should be "suitable for use as a photographic film base," though without decision whether an identical film, not stated to be suitable for the stated purpose, would be considered as an anticipation, or indeed as an infringement.

A004.08 *Declaration of inventorship (subs. (5))*

Subsection (5) required a declaration of inventorship to be filed on PF No. 4, see also section 2(3) [1949] discussed in para. A002.2. The contents of this declaration can have effect for objection under section 32(1)(*b*) and (*c*) (*Patent granted to person not entitled to apply or in contravention of right*), discussed in para. A032.08; or under section 32(1)(*j*) (*Patent obtained on false suggestion or representation*), discussed in paras. A032.30–A032.33.

A004.09 *Development of invention of priority specification (subs. (6))*

Subsection (6) allowed a complete specification to include matter not contained in a basic provisional specification or prior foreign application so long as the claims were for a single invention. This provision introduced a doctrine of "legitimate development" of an invention and finally abolished the former ground of invalidity due to "disconformity between a provisional and its complete specification, or between a foreign application and the complete specification from which priority was claimed. Such a ground had existed, to a diminishing degree, under the former statutes. Section 4(6), and the provision for cognating the contents of two (or more) foreign applications (under s. 2(5)), or of two (or more) provisional applications (under s. 3(3)), gives rise to the requirement to determine the "priority date" to be accorded to a claim. This is done under the provisions of section 5, discussed in the commentary thereon, see particularly para. A005.3 where cases involving legitimate development are noted. Just as section 4(4) requires a valid claim to be "fairly based" on its complete specification, with failure on this point leading to possible revocation under section 32(1)(i), so also the test for according priority under section 5 is, likewise, stated to be one of "fair basis," as is also discussed in para. A005.3. However, the two tests are not necessarily the same, though such was indicated in *Stauffer's Application* ([1977] RPC 33 (CA)).

Special rule of construction for claims relating to naturally-occurring products   **A004.10**
(subs. (7))

Subsection (7) is a special requirement relating to claims to products of the type which also exist in a natural environment. This was a new provision in the 1949 Act and there is no corresponding provision in the 1977 Act, though a similar result could result by claim construction under section 125(1)[1977].

Subsection (7) provides that, where a new substance is claimed, the claim "shall be construed as not extending to that substance when found in nature". This appears to be a statutory limitation on the total scope of a claim by a specific exclusion from the scope thereof. Presumably, such exclusion relates to the consideration of both validity and infringement of the claim, but the effect of the provision has not been clarified by a court in the United Kingdom. However, in South Africa, it has been held that a claim to a substance which also exists in a natural environment is valid, but does not extend to the substance when taken from the place where it is found (*American Cyanamid* v. *Continental Ethicals,* South Africa Patent Journal, January 17, 1962, p. 17) Also, in Ireland it has been held that, where a product is an unaltered substance occurring as such in nature, it was precluded from patent protection by virtue of a provision corresponding to subsection (7) (*Rank Hovis McDougall* v. *Controller [Ireland]*, [1978] FSR 588). However, the question whether a substance is one "found in nature" is quite different to the question whether that substance is a living organism. Thus, a non-natural micro-organism would appear to be patentable under the 1949 Act irrespective of the precise meaning of subsection (7), see *NRDC's Irish Application [Ireland]* ([1986] FSR 620), distinguishing the *Rank Hovis* case in that country.

The effect of subsection (7) is discussed further in the article by A. W. White listed in para. A004.02 *supra*.

SECTION 5 [1949]   A005.1

Priority date of claims of complete specification

5.—(1) Every claim of a complete specification shall have effect from the date prescribed by this section in relation to that claim (in this Act referred to as the priority date); and a patent shall not be invalidated by reason only of the publication or use of the invention so far as claimed in any claim of the complete specification, on or after the priority date of that calim, or by the grant of another patent upon a specification claiming the same invention in a claim of the same or later priority date.

(2) Where the complete specification is filed in pursuance of a single application accompanied by a provisional specification or by a specification which is treated by virtue of a direction under subsection (4) of section three of this Act as a provisional specification, and the claim is fairly based on the matter disclosed in that specification, the priority date of that claim shall be the date of filing of the application.

(3) Where the complete specification is filed or proceeded with in pursuance of two or more applications accompanied by such specifications as are mentioned in the last foregoing subsection, and the claim is fairly based on the matter disclosed in one of those specifications, the priority date of that claim shall be the date of filing of the application accompanied by that specification.

(4) Where the complete specification is filed in pursuance of a convention application and the claim is fairly based on the matter disclosed in the application for protection in a convention country or, where the convention application is founded upon more than one such application for protection, in one of those applications, the priority date of that claim shall be the date of the relevant application for protection.

(5) Where, under the foregoing provisions of this section, any claim of a complete specification would, but for this provision, have two or more priority dates, the priority date of that claim shall be the earlier or earliest of those dates.

(6) In any case to which subsections (2) to (5) of this section do not apply, the priority date of a claim shall be the date of filing of the complete specification.

COMMENTARY ON SECTION 5 [1949]

A005.2 *General*

Section 5 provides the test for determining the date to be accorded to each claim of a complete specification, *i.e.* its "priority date" (subs. (1)). The section must be read in conjunction with section 52, which preserves claims not entitled to a priority date from attack based on intervening publication or use of matter disclosed in a priority document. Unless an earlier priority date can be accorded under any of subsections (2)–(5), the priority date of a claim is the date of its complete specification (subs. (6)).

Whether a claim is entitled to a priority date earlier than the date of the complete specification depends on whether such claim is "fairly based" on the disclosure of an earlier priority document, be this a "provisional specification" as defined in s. 3), or a foreign application the priority date of which has been claimed in a "convention application" (as defined in s. 1). For a general discussion on the claiming of convention priority, see the commentary on section 1 [1949] and see para. A069.2 on the nature and content of a prior foreign application which is to be considered in relation to according convention priority under section 5(4). In a contested case on priority the onus is on a patentee to establish that he is entitled to priority earlier than the date of his complete specification (*Stauffer's Application*, [1977] RPC 33 (CA)).

Section 128 [1977] provides a special transitional provision for resolving conflicts of priority between claims having possible priority dates which straddle the "appointed day", *i.e.* June 1, 1978.

The test of "fair basis" for according a priority date   **A005.3**

To accord a priority date to a claim which is earlier than that of its complete specification, the claim must be "fairly based" on the disclosure of a prior filed application (including the claims of a priority foreign application, see s. 69(2)). That prior application must have been filed within the 12 months prior to the complete specification in the case of a "convention application", see paras. A001.6–A001.8, or within 15 months of that date where the complete specification had been preceded by a provisional specification, see para. A003.2.

It must also be noted that a claim will be invalid under section 32(1)(*i*) [1949] unless it is "fairly based" on the disclosure of the complete specification, as discussed in para. A032.29. The "fairly based" tests under sections 5 and 32(1)(*i*) have been stated to be the same (*Stauffer's Application*, [1977] RPC 33 (CA)), but the matter perhaps deserves further consideration. However, under the 1977 Act, the tests for priority (under s. 5 [1977]) and of permissible breadth of claim (under s. 14(5)(*c*) [1977]) are expressed in terms of the claims "being supported by the description". That may be a different test from that of "fair basis" under the 1949 Act, as discussed in para. 5.04.

The guide rules for the operation of section 5 [1949] were initially laid down in *Mond Nickel's Application* ([1956] RPC 189) as: "(1) Is the invention claimed broadly described in the provisional? (2) Is there anything in the provisional which is inconsistent with the invention as claimed? (3) Does the claim include as a characteristic of the invention a feature not mentioned in the provisional?" These guide rules were, however, given a broad interpretation. For example, otherwise, the factual decision in *Mond Nickel* is contrary to the rules laid down therein. This perhaps follows because of the doctrine of "legitimate development" which had been provided for by section 4(6), see para. A004.O9.

However, in *ICI's Patent* ([1960] RPC 223), these rules were more strictly applied to find a claim to the use of cathodes (whether solid or of molten metal) not fairly based on a provisional specification which had described the invention in terms of a molten metal cathode only, though it had described the use of a solid anode. In a similar case, a generic claim was held to have been fairly based on three examples in the priority documents (*Hercules' Application*, [1968] RPC 203).

Later, the emphasis was placed on the word "fairly" and the court construed this, and similar provisions wherein the words "fairly based" are also used in the 1949 Act, as requiring that there should be a fair balance between the patentee and the public, see: *Letraset* v. *Rexel* ([1974] RPC 175 at p. 196); *CIBA's Patent* ([1971] FSR 616), decided on the basis of whether an earlier application and the claim in question in essence relate to the same invention; *UCB's Application* ([1973] FSR 433), which regarded fair basis as a matter of substance and not of form; and *Muto Industrial's Application* ([1978] RPC 70), which stated that the Patents Appeal Tribunal would not be astute to deprive an applicant of his claimed priority by the harsh application of linguistic or legal canons but would interpret the priority document in the same way as it would be by the skilled unimaginative addressee (*i.e.* priority was to be decided on the basis of the obviousness, or implicit disclosure, of the feature or generalisation in question). In *Union Carbide's Application* ([1968] RPC 371) one of the two foreign priority applications featured a copolymer having an alkyl acrylate content of 2 to 65 per cent., and the other a copolymer having a vinyl alkanoate content of 2 to 50 per cent. The claim in the complete specification, which embraced both copolymers, reduced the alkyl acrylate range of the one copolymer to 2 to 50 per cent. In dismissing a contention that this change had resulted in loss of the priority date it was stated: "The applicants, in thus jetisoning for the sake of uniformity the upper values in this original range, are merely disclaiming part of the monopoly to which their disclosures would entitle them. There is no question here of any selection being made, or of an inducement provided by subsequently acquired knowledge".

In *Olin Mathieson* v. *Biorex* ([1970] RPC 157 at 193) the term "fair basis" was equated (under s. 32(1)(*i*)) with the words "sound prediction" and it is thought that this view is also applicable for according priority under section 5. This is consistent with *Mond Nickel* and with the subsequent judgment in *Stauffer's Application* ([1977] RPC 33 (CA)) where it was stated:

> "If a new feature were a development along the same line of thought which constitutes or underlies the invention described in the earlier document, it might be that that development could properly be regarded as fairly based on the matter disclosed in the earlier document, and that the new process described in the later document which incorporates that development could as a whole be regarded as fairly based upon the matter disclosed in the earlier document. If, on the other hand, the additional feature involves a new inventive step or brings something new into the combination which represents a departure from the idea of the invention described in the earlier document, it could not, I think, be properly described as fairly based upon the earlier document."

It is further stated in *Stauffer* that the answer to the question: "Did what was disclosed in the priority document afford a fair basis for the claims in the application?" depends upon the contents and language of the relevant documents. What was required to be fair was not the applicant's claim to priority, but the basis which one document afforded for a claim in the other. This follows from *American Cyanamid's (Dann's) Patent* ([1971] RPC 425 at 437 (HL)). However, a mention of the subject matter subsequently claimed is not to be equated with "basis" for the claim if this is seen to be a further or different invention from that claimed in the priority document (*Coopers Animal Health* v. *Western Stock [Australia]* ((1988) 11 IPR 20).

Other cases in which it has been considered that fair basis could be provided having regard to legitimate development of the invention initially disclosed are: *Ronson* v. *Lewis* ([1963] RPC 103); *Farbenfabriken Bayer's (Zirngibl's) Application* ([1973] RPC 698); and *Canon K.K.'s Application* ([1980] RPC 133). Also, in *Wellcome Foundation's Application* (SRIS O/72/83, *noted* IPD 6066), a wrongly-assigned chemical formula in the provisional specification was ignored on the basis that the product, whatever structure it actually had, had been adequately described by the method of preparation there given; and the addition of non-inventive variants did not deprive it of priority. However, in *Rousell-Uclaf's (Nomine's) Patent* ([1974] RPC 405), priority was refused for a claim to a group of chemical compounds when only one such compound had been fairly disclosed in the priority document.

Also, a mere disclosure, even if speculative, is enough for fair basis under section 5 [1949]. In *Ishihara Sango* v. *Dow Chemical* ([1987] FSR 137 (CA)), it was held that a chemical compound is disclosed if sufficiently indicated. Such compound does not need to have been made and tested. This case also held that there is an effective disclosure even if such is shown to be erroneous. Thus, if a later document is identical with the earlier, section 5(4) is satisfied even if the date displayed in the documents is wrong. This seems to follow from section 4, which merely requires a provisional specification to describe an invention but not to particularly describe it or give a method for performing it, while provisional protection has to be equally accorded to the contents of an application for protection in a convention country, for which see the commentary on section 1 [1949]. "Protection" was explained in *Polaroid's (Land's) Patent* ([1981] RPC 111 (CA) and [1981] FSR 578 (HL)) as embracing both the monopoly which will be secured if and when a patent is granted and the "provisional protection" against adverse effects of disclosure or use after filing which would otherwise prejudice the applicant's chance of securing patent protection therefor.

Multiple priorities   A005.4

A claim of an existing patent cannot have more than one date, so that if a claim specifically mentions alternatives. only some of which are to be found in the priority document, that claim cannot bear the date of that document (*Thornill's Application*, [1962] RPC 199). This is in contrast to the position under section 5 [1977] where it is the priority date of an "invention", rather than that of a "claim", which is in issue. The *Thornhill* decision led to several cases in which amendments were allowed which had the effect of claim splitting in order to accord each claim a single, and the earliest possible, priority date, see *Farbenfabriken Bayer's Patent* ([1966] RPC 278). Also, *Union Carbide's Application* ([1968] RPC 44 and 371) was founded on two United States applications of the same date, and the main claim embraced the subject-matter of both. It was held that in subsection (4) the word "application" must be confined to the singular despite the provisions in the Interpretation Act that the singular includes the plural, and that the claim was not entitled to the priority date. The applicants were allowed to split the claim into two by way of correction. *SCM's Application* ([1979] RPC 341) is a similar case. Here the specification cognated subject matter from two foreign applications filed on the same day and priority was lost as no claim was fairly based on the subject matter of *one* of those applications.

SECTION 6 [1949]   A006.1

Examination of application

6.—(1) When the complete specification has been filed in respect of an application for a patent, the application and specification or specifications shall be referred by the comptroller to an examiner.

(2) If the examiner reports that the application or any specification filed in pursuance thereof does not comply with the requirements of this Act or any rules made by the Board of Trade thereunder, or that there is lawful ground of objection to the grant of a patent in pursuance of the application, the comptroller may either—

(*a*) refuse to proceed with the application; or

(*b*) require the application or any such specification as aforesaid to be amended before he proceeds with the application.

(3) At any time after an application has been filed under this Act and before acceptance of the complete specification, the comptroller may, at the request of the applicant and upon payment of the prescribed fee, direct

that the application shall be post-dated to such date as may be specified in the request:

Provided that:

(*a*) no application shall be post-dated under this subsection to a date later than six months from the date on which it was actually made or would, but for this subsection, be deemed to have been made, and

(*b*) a convention application shall not be post-dated under this subsection to a date later than the last date on which, under the foregoing provisions of this Act, the application could have been made, **and**

(*c*) **no application shall, on or after the appointed day, be post-dated under this subsection to a date which is that of the appointed day or which falls after it.**

(4) Where an application or specification filed under this Act is amended before acceptance of the complete specification, the comptroller may direct that the application or specification shall be post-dated to the date on which it is amended or, if it has been returned to the applicant, to the date on which it is refiled; **but no application shall on or after the appointed day be post-dated under this subsection to a date which is that of the appointed day or which falls after it.**

(5) Rules made by the Board of Trade under this Act may make provision for securing that where, at any time after an application or specification has been filed under this Act and before acceptance of the complete specification, a fresh application or specification is filed in respect of any part of the subject matter of the first-mentioned application or specification, the comptroller may direct that the fresh application or specification shall be ante-dated to a date not earlier than the date of filing of the first-mentioned application or specification; **but a fresh application or specification may not be filed on or after the appointed day in accordance with this subsection and those rules unless the comptroller agrees that he will direct that the application or specification shall be ante-dated to a date which falls before the appointed day.**

(6) An appeal shall lie from any decision of the comptroller under subsection (2) or subsection (4) of this section.

Note. Amendments were effected by Patents Act 1977, Sched. 1, para. 2.

A006.2   COMMENTARY ON SECTION 6 [1949]

Section 6 is effectively spent. It provided the basis for the official examination of applications under the 1949 Act. Subsections (3) and (4) provided for post-dating of an application in certain circumstances and subsection (5) was the basis for filing divisional applications under that Act. The amendments made to subsections (3)–(5) by the 1977 Act ensured that all "existing applications" should have a date earlier than the appointed day, *i.e.* before June 1, 1978. When on that day an application was pending, but on which only a provisional specification had been filed, that application then lapsed, but it could still serve as a priority document in respect of an application filed thereafter under the 1977 Act, see section 127(4) [1977].

However, the priority date of a claim in such an application is then to be determined under section 5 [1977], see section 128(5) [1977].

SECTION 7 [1949]

Search for anticipation by previous publication

7.—(1) Subject to the provisions of the last foregoing section, the examiner to whom an application for a patent is referred under this Act shall make investigation for the purpose of ascertaining whether the invention, so far as claimed in any claim of the complete specification, has been published before the date of filing of the applicant's complete specification in any specification filed in pursuance of an application for a patent made in the United Kingdom and dated within 50 years next before that date.

(2) The examiner shall, in addition, make such investigation as the comptroller may direct for the purpose of ascertaining whether the invention, so far as claimed in any claim of the complete specification, has been published in the United Kingdom before the date of filing of the applicant's complete specification in any other document (not being a document of any class described in subsection(1) of section 50 of this Act).

(3) If it appears to the comptroller that the invention, so far as claimed in any claim of the complete specification, has been published as aforesaid, he may refuse to accept the specification unless the applicant either—

(a) shows to the satisfaction of the comptroller that the priority date of the claim of his complete specification is not later than the date on which the relevant document was published; or

(b) amends his complete specification to the satisfaction of the comptroller.

(4) An appeal shall lie from any decision of the comptroller under this section.

COMMENTARY ON SECTION 7 [1949]

Section 7 provided the basis for the search carried out on applications filed under the 1949 Act and for objections arising therefrom. The search was mandatory for United Kingdom patent specifications dated within 50 years prior to the date of the complete specification (subs. (1)), but other documents could be cited if published in the United Kingdom and not excluded by section 50(1) (subs. (2)). However, under subsection (3), objection was limited to objections of lack of novelty. This matter is considered in the commentaries under section 32(1)(e) [1949] at paras. A032.10–A032.12 and under section 2 [1977] at paras. 2.06–2.11. While objections of "prior claiming" in conflicting applications of earlier priority date could be raised under section 8 [1949], it is important to appreciate that, under the 1949 Act, the examiner was powerless at the application stage before acceptance to raise any objection based on alleged lack of inventive step ("obviousness") and that, in practice, the search was normally limited to prior United Kingdom patent specifications. Moreover, there was a well-established practice that the applicant should be

939

given the benefit of any doubt as regards any objection raised by the examiner: thus, refusal of an application under section 7 [1949] occurred only in rare cases.

SECTION 8 [1949]

Search for anticipation by prior claim

8.—(1) In addition to the investigation required by the last foregoing section, the examiner shall make investigation for the purpose of ascertaining whether the invention, so far as claimed in any claim of the complete specification, is claimed in any claim of any other complete specification published on or after the date of filing the applicant's complete specification, being a specification filed—

(a) in pursuance of an application for a patent made in the United Kingdom and dated before that date; or

(b) in pursuance of a convention application founded upon an application for protection made in a convention country before that date.

(2) If it appears to the comptroller that the said invention is claimed in a claim of any such other specification as aforesaid, he may, subject to the provisions of this section, direct that a reference to that other specification shall be inserted by way of notice to the public in the applicant's complete specification unless within such time as may be prescribed either—

(a) the applicant shows to the satisfaction of the comptroller that the priority date of his claim is not later than the priority date of the claim of the said other specification; or

(b) the complete specification is amended to the satisfaction of the comptroller.

(3) If in consequence of the investigation under section 7 of this Act or otherwise it appears to the comptroller—

(a) that the invention, so far as claimed in any claim of the applicant's complete specification, has been claimed in any such specification as is mentioned in subsection (1) of that section; and

(b) that the other specification was published on or after the priority date of the applicant's claim,

then unless it has been shown to the satisfaction of the comptroller under that section that the priority date of the applicant's claim is not later than the priority date of the claim of that other specification, the provisions of subsection (2) of this section shall apply in relation to a specification published on or after the date of filing of the applicant's complete specification.

(4) The powers of the comptroller under this section to direct the insertion of a reference to another specification may be exercised either before or after a patent has been granted for the invention claimed in that other specification, but any direction given before the grant of such a patent shall be of no effect unless and until such a patent is granted.

(5) An appeal shall lie from any direction of the comptroller under this section.

COMMENTARY ON SECTION 8 [1949] A008.2

,FCP-02-01

Section 8 provided for objections of "prior claiming" to be raised as the result of an official search for possible conflicting applications with claims of earlier priority date to those of the application in suit. However, section 8 [1949] did not provide for refusal of an application from objections arising thereunder: only a specific reference in statutory form could be inserted. This was in the following terms:

> "Reference has been directed, in pursuance of Section 8 of the Patents Act 1949, to specification No. —." (r. 31 [1968]).

The history of the provision is set out in *GEC's Patent* ([1959] RPC 103 and 109) which also held that such a reference became part of the specification. It would, therefore, seem that a statutory reference ordered to be made under section 8 [1949] might be removed by a correcting or explanatory amendment under section 31 [1949] if the basis for its insertion no longer exists, for example because the cited patent has been revoked. This is because prior claiming only exists if the earlier claim is a valid one (s. 32(1)(*a*)[1949]). However, in contrast with a statutory reference inserted under section 9 [1949] (see para. A009.2), no specific provision was made for deletion of a statutory reference inserted under section 8.

It seems doubtful if a reference under section 8 [1949] would now be ordered to be inserted. The point could only arise in an application for revocation before the Comptroller under section 33 [1949]. But, if "prior claiming" were found to exist, the present jurisdiction under section 32(1)(*a*) [1949] (for which see paras. A032.03–A032.07) would presumably require its definitive resolution by amendment or revocation.

It is important to appreciate that the objection of "prior claiming" under the 1949 Act require a comparison of the claims of the respective patents: their disclosure is irrelevant except in so far as this aids the construction of the scope of the claims. This is a quite different position from that arising under the 1977 Act where the "whole contents" of the earlier specification are deemed to have been published at the date thereof, but permitting that notional publication to be effective only as regards the consideration of the novelty of the latter invention and with the notional publication being ineffective as regards the consideration of the presence of "inventive step," see section 2(3) [1977] and the commentary thereon in paras. 2.19–2.24.

SECTION 9 [1949] A009.1

Reference in case of potential infringement

9.—(1) If, in consequence of the investigations required by the foregoing provisions of this Act or of proceedings under section 14 or section 33 of this Act, it appears to the comptroller that an invention in respect of which application for a patent has been made cannot be performed without substantial risk of infringement of a claim of any other patent, he may direct that a reference to that other patent shall be inserted in the applicant's complete specification by way of notice to the public unless within such time as may be prescribed either—

    (*a*) the applicant shows to the satisfaction of the comptroller that there are reasonable grounds for contesting the validity of the said claim of the other patent; or

    (*b*) the complete specification is amended to the satisfaction of the comptroller.

(2) Where, after a reference to another patent has been inserted in a complete specification in pursuance of a direction under the foregoing subsection,—

    (*a*) that other patent is revoked or otherwise ceases to be in force; or

    (*b*) the specification of that other patent is amended by the deletion of the relevant claim; or

    (*c*) it is found, in proceedings before the court or the comptroller, that the relevant claim of that other patent is invalid or is not infringed by any working of the applicant's invention.

the comptroller may, on the application of the applicant, delete the reference to that other patent.

(3) An appeal shall lie from any decision or direction of the comptroller under this section.

RELEVANT 1968 RULES

A009.2   **34. [1968]** When, pursuant to such procedure, the Comptroller directs that reference to a patent shall be inserted in the applicant's complete specification, the reference shall be inserted after the claims and shall be in the following form: "Reference has been directed in pursuance of section 9, subsection (1) of the Patents Act 1949, to Patent No. . . . .".

A009.3   **35. [1968]** An application under section 9(2) for the deletion of a reference inserted pursuant to a direction under section 9(1) shall be made on Patents Form No. 9, and shall state fully the facts relied upon in support of the application.

A009.4   **36. [1968]** In the application of Rules 28 to 31, 33 and 34 to proceedings subsequent to the grant of a patent, references to the patentee shall be substituted for references to the applicant.

A009.5   COMMENTARY ON SECTION 9 [1949]

Section 9 remains applicable to existing patents, but it has no counterpart under the 1977 Act. Section 9 provided for the insertion of a reference in statutory form when it was considered by the examiner or Comptroller that the alleged invention of the specification could not be performed without substantial risk of infringement of a claim of some other patent that was apparently valid and subsisting. That reference was in the form prescribed by rule 34 [1968] reprinted in para. A009.2 *supra*. As the powers of the Comptroller under subsection (1) are exercisable after grant (s. 11(1) [1949]) such reference could still arise as a result of an application for revocation made to the Comptroller under the provisions of amended section 33 [1949].

Subsection (2) still has effect because it provides for the removal of such reference if the basis for its insertion can be shown no longer to exist because of the revocation, lapsing or amendment of the cited patent or because of a finding that such is not infringed by the performance of the invention described in the patent in suit.

The manner of performance of the invention is to be ascertained from the body of the complete specification of the patent in suit and not from its claims (*Ministry of Supply's Application*, (1953) 70 RPC 219), see also *Pittsburgh's Application*, ([1969] RPC 628).

PRACTICE UNDER SECTION 9 [1949]	A009.6

Application to remove a statutory reference inserted under subsection (1) is made on PF No. 9 (reprinted at para. A121) and full supporting facts must be supplied. The Comptroller may require these to be supported by written evidence. There is no provision for advertisement of an application under subsection (2), nor for any opposition thereto. Appeal against refusal to delete the reference is possible under subsection (3). Such appeal would now be to the Patents Court under section 97 [1977], see Schedule 4, para. 11 [1977].

SECTION 10 [1949]	A010

Refusal of application in certain cases

[Spent]

Note. Section 10 is spent because it applied only to pre-grant objections. It provided for refusal of applications in three specified circumstances, but these had no direct counterparts in the provisions of revocation under section 32(1) [1949]. Nevertheless: objection under subsection (1)(*a*) (*Alleged invention frivolous or obviously contrary to well-established natural laws*) could no doubt be raised under section 32(1)(*g*) (*Inutility*) or under 32(1)(*h*) (*Insufficiency*); objection under subsection (1)(*b*) (*Use of invention contrary to law or morality*) would give rise to objection under section 32(1)(*k*) (*Intended use or exercise contrary to law*), though not apparently if the objection were only on the ground of morality; and objection under subsection (1)(*c*) (*Claims being mere mixture of known ingredients capable of being used as food or medicine*) would probably give rise to objection under section 32(1)(*d*) (*No invention within the meaning of the Act*) or section 32(1)(*f*) (*Invention obvious and not involving any inventive step*), for all of which see the respective commentaries on these provisions of section 32 [1949].

SECTION 11 [1949]	A011.1

Supplementary provisions as to searches, etc.

11.—(1) The powers of the comptroller under section 8 or section 9 of this Act may be exercised either before or after the complete specification has been accepted or a patent granted to the applicant, and references in those sections to the applicant shall accordingly be construed as including references to the patentee.

(2) [*Spent*]

(3) [*Repealed*]

A011.2   Commentary on Section 11 [1949]

The provisions of section 11 [1949] are effectively spent, though in theory they would enable objections to be raised under sections 8 or 9 [1949] against existing patents.

Subsection (3) [*repealed*] provided for immunity of the Board of Trade in relation to the grant of a patent. It has been replaced by section 116 [1977] effective with regard to existing patents by Schedule 2, para. 1(2) [1977].

A012.   **SECTION 12 [1949]**

Time for putting application in order for acceptance

[*Spent*]

Note. Section 12 related solely to the time within which an application filed under the 1949 Act had to be put in order for acceptance. Originally this time was specified as 12 months, but the Patents Act 1957 changed this to a period not shorter than this and not longer than four years as may be prescribed. The prescribed period varied, but for applications filed before January 1, 1962 it was three-and-a-half years; thereafter and before January 1, 1964 it was three years; and thereafter it was two-and-a-half years.

A013.1   **SECTION 13 [1949]**

Acceptance and publication of complete specification

13.—(1)[*Spent*]

(2) On the acceptance of a complete specification the comptroller shall give notice to the applicant and **unless the application is withdrawn** shall advertise in the Journal the fact that the specification has been accepted and the date on which the application and the specification or specifications filed in pursuance thereof will be open to public inspection.

(3) Any reference in this Act to the date of the publication of a complete specification shall be construed as a reference to the date advertised as aforesaid.

(4) After the date of the publication of a complete specification and until the sealing of a patent in respect thereof, the applicant shall have the like privileges and rights as if a patent for the invention had been sealed on the date of the publication of the complete specification:

Provided that an applicant shall not be entitled to institute any proceedings for infringement until the patent has been sealed.

Note. Subsection (2) was prospectively amended by the 1988 Act (Sched. 5, para. 1). For its commencement, see the latest Supplement to this Work.

COMMENTARY ON SECTION 13 [1949] A013.2

Subsection (1) required the Comptroller to accept an application when the requirements of the Act were met within the period specified in section 12(1) [1949] or as soon as may be thereafter, but with power for the applicant to request a short postponement. The provision is spent.

Subsection (2), in its original form, required the Comptroller upon acceptance to advertise the complete specification in the O.J. and lay it open to public inspection. When secrecy directions (under s. 18 [1949] remained in force, the application proceeded to acceptance but publication had to be postponed until the secrecy directions were lifted, perhaps after the end of the permitted life of the patent, but there was no mechanism to avoid eventual publication of the specification. The amendment now to be made will rectify that position and enable an accepted application to be withdrawn, with publication then being avoided. An unknown number of still secret applications remained in existence when the amendment was made in 1988, and many of these will probably be withdrawn when the amendment becomes effective.

Subsection (3) may have effect if publication of the printed specification happened to be delayed. It provided for deemed publication on the date advertised in the O.J.

Subsection (4) prevented infringement proceedings being instituted until a patent had been sealed (under s. 19 [1949]). Where an opposition delayed sealing for more than six years, the Limitation Act 1980 (c. 58, s.2) created an inability to claim full monetary relief for acts of infringement committed before the patent was sealed (*Sevcon* v. *Lucas*, [1986] RPC 609 (HL)).

SECTION 14 [1949] [*Repealed*] A014

Opposition to grant of patent

Note. Section 14 provided for pre-grant opposition to the grant of a patent by any person having an "interest" on the grounds specified in subsection (1). These grounds were much less extensive than those provided for possible revocation by the court under section 32 [1949]. In particular, objection on the ground of obviousness was limited to the case where any claim of the complete specification "clearly does not involve any inventive step", and objections on the grounds of inutility, false promise and lack of fair basis for the claims could not be raised under section 14. Moreover, an opposition would only succeed in a clear case as an applicant was given the benefit of any doubt. In *General Electric's (Cox's) Patent* [1977] RPC 421) the Court of Appeal stated that "section 14 is designed to clear the register of patents which are manifestly untenable. It is not intended to provide a method of disposing of truly contentious cases". These factors need to be borne in mind in reading reported cases decided under either section 14 [1949] or section 33 [1949].

While objections under section 14 could only be raised pre-grant, section 33 [1949] provided for an application to be made to the Comptroller for revocation of a patent within one year of its date of grant, but only on the grounds of opposition listed in section 14 [1949]: an application for revocation under section 33 [1949] was, therefore, commonly-known as a "belated opposition". The 1977 Act repealed section 14. It also amended section 33 [1949] to enable applications for revocation of existing patents to be brought before the Comptroller at any time during the life of the patent and on any of the grounds of revocation prescribed for court proceedings under section 32 [1949], see the commentary on section 33 [1949] at paras. A033.12–A033.20.

A015.1   **SECTION 15 [1949]**

Refusal of patent without opposition

[*Spent*]

A015.2   Commentary on Section 15 [1949]

Section 15 contained provisions for prior publications to be brought to the attention of the Comptroller by third parties and for the Comptroller to raise objection thereon which could lead to refusal of the application despite its previous acceptance. The replacement section 21 [1977] is in similar vein, but its provisions are more extensive than the limited ones previously provided by section 15 [1949].

A016.1   **SECTION 16 [1949]**

Mention of inventor as such in patent

16.—(1) If the comptroller is satisfied, upon a request or claim made in accordance with the provisions of this section—
  (*a*) that the person in respect of or by whom the request or claim is made is the inventor of an invention in respect of which application for a patent has been made, or of a substantial part of that invention; and
  (*b*) that the application for the patent is a direct consequence of his being the inventor.
the comptroller shall, subject to the provisions of this section, cause him to be mentioned as inventor in any patent granted in pursuance of the application, in the complete specification, and in the register of patents:
  Provided that the mention of any person as inventor under this section shall not confer or derogate from any rights under the patent.
  (2) For the purposes of this section the actual deviser of an invention or a part of an invention shall be deemed to be the inventor, notwithstanding that any other person is for any of the other purposes of this Act treated as the true and first inventor; and no person shall be deemed to be the inventor of an invention or a part of an invention by reason only that it was imported by him into the United Kingdom.
  (3) [*Spent*]

(4) [*Spent*]
(5) [*Spent*]
(6) [*Repealed*]
(7) [*Spent*]
(8) Where any person has been mentioned as inventor in pursuance of this section, any other person who alleges that he ought not to have been so mentioned may at any time apply to the comptroller for a certificate to that effect, and the comptroller may, after hearing, if required, any person whom he may consider to be interested, issue such a certificate, and if he does so, he shall rectify the specification and the register accordingly.

(9) An appeal shall lie from any decision of the comptroller under this section.

RELEVANT 1968 RULE   A016.2

54. [1968]—(1) An application under section 16(8) for a certificate shall be made on Patents Form No. 17 and shall be accompanied by statement setting out fully the facts relied upon.

(2) A copy of the application and of the statement shall be sent by the Comptroller to each patentee (not being the applicant), to the person mentioned as the actual deviser, and to any other person whom the Comptroller may consider to be interested and the applicant shall supply a sufficient number of copies for that purpose.

(3) The Comptroller may give such directions (if any) as he may think fit with regard to the subsequent procedure.

COMMENTARY ON SECTION 16 [1949]   A016.3

Section 16 remains only partly applicable to existing patents. Subsections (1)–(5) and (7) are spent and subsection (6) was repealed by the 1977 Act.

Subsection (1) provided for application to be made for the patent to mention the inventor who, for this purpose, was to be regarded as the actual deviser of the invention (or part thereof) (subs. (2)), notwithstanding the previous naming of some other person as inventor under the now abolished doctrine of regarding the first importer of an invention into the United Kingdom as an inventor in law. The mention of such an inventor was in the form:

> "The inventor of this invention in the sense of being the actual deviser thereof within the meaning of Section 16 of the Patents Act 1949 is—of—", or "The inventor of a substantial part of this invention in the sense of being the actual deviser thereof within the meaning of Section 16 of the Patents Act 1949 is— of—".

as the case required (r. 55 [1968]).

However, subsection (8) remains effective for possible application to delete a mention of inventor made under section 16 by anyone (not necessarily the named deviser) who desires that that mention be deleted. Appeal from a decision of the Comptroller lies under subsection (9), but now to the Patents Court under section 97 [1977] (Sched. 4, para. 11 [1977]).

A016.4   Practice under Section 16 [1949]

An application under subsection (8) would be made under rule 54 [1968] (reprinted at para. A016.2 *supra*) by filing PF No. 17 (reprinted at para. A123) accompanied by a statement of the facts relied upon, this to be supplied in a sufficient number of copies for one copy to be sent to each patentee and to the deviser mentioned if he is not the applicant under subsection (8). The Comptroller notifies any other person he considers may be interested (r. 54(2) [1968]), and, thereafter, the procedure is flexible (r. 54(3) [1968]).

A017.1   **SECTION 17 [1949]**

Substitution of applicants, etc.

[*Spent*]

A017.2   Commentary on Section 17 [1949]

Section 17 provided for substitution of applicants prior to grant to take account of assignment of rights under a pending application. Section 17 also provided for disputes between joint applicants to be resolved by the Comptroller. After grant such disputes may be resolved under section 55 [1949] which remains effective, see para. A055.4.

A018   **SECTION 18 [1949]** [*Repealed*]

Provisions for secrecy of certain inventions

Relevant 1968 Rule

69. [1968] Where directions given by the Comptroller under section 18(1) of the Act or under section 12 of the Atomic Energy Act 1946, prohibiting the publication of information with respect to an invention forming the subject of an application for a patent have been revoked and a patent is granted on the application, no renewal fees shall be payable in respect of any year which commenced in the period during which directions were in force.

Notes. 1. Section 18 provided for directions to be given restricting publication of inventions relevant for defence purposes. Similar provisions existed in relation to inventions concerning the use of atomic energy under the Atomic Energy Act 1946 (c. 80, s. 12(4), also now repealed). All these provisions have now been replaced by section 22 [1977]. Restrictions on the filing of patent applications abroad by persons normally resident in the United Kingdom, previously provided by section 18(5) [1949], are now to be found in section 23 [1977].

2. Secrecy orders already in being on June 1, 1978 remain effective: otherwise section 22 [1977] applies to existing patents (Sched. 4, para. 5 [1977]). The effect of continuing secrecy orders on applications filed under the 1949 Act is that such

applications may remain ungranted for many years. This is the reason why this Appendix often refers to provisions as being "effectively spent": many of them remain alive solely for the purpose of unpublished applications still subject to directions under section 18 [1949]. If and when such directions are lifted, the patent is granted in accordance with the 1949 Act unless withdrawn, see para. A013.2. Renewal fees then become payable under section 25(3)–(5) [1977] (Sched. 2, para. 1(2) [1977]), other than for the period during which a direction was in force (r. 69 [1968] reprinted *supra*).

SECTION 19 [1949]

A019

Grant and sealing of patent

[Spent]

Note. Section 19 provided for grant of the patent as "Letters Patent" under the seal of the Patent Office provided the prescribed request was made within the specified time of four months from publication of the application (or some other time in certain circumstances, for example after the termination of such proceedings as opposition under s. 14 [1949] or appeals against refusal) and the prescribed "sealing fee" was paid, also within this time. The date of sealing has no significance except that a patentee could only commence infringement proceedings once the patent had been sealed, and for starting the period under unamended section 33 [1949] under which "belated opposition" proceedings could be commenced. Also, a compulsory licence under section 37 [1949] could not be granted until three years had elapsed from the date of sealing. For the importance of the grant in the form of "Letters Patent", see para. A021.4 *infra*.

The date of sealing of an existing patent can be ascertained by inspection of the register, for which see para. 32.33. The date of sealing was also advertised in the O.J., but the date recorded in the informal registers kept in the SRIS is *not* the actual date of sealing but the date of the O.J. in which this was advertised.

SECTION 20 [1949]

A020.1

Amendment of patent granted to deceased applicant

20. Where, at any time after a patent has been sealed in pursuance of an application under this Act, the comptroller is satisfied that the person to whom the patent was granted had died, or (in the case of a body corporate) had ceased to exist, before the patent was sealed, he may amend the patent by substituting for the name of that person the name of the person to whom the patent ought to have been granted; and the patent shall have effect, and shall be deemed always to have had effect, accordingly.

RELEVANT 1968 RULE

63. [1968] An application under section 20 for the amendment of a patent shall be made on Patents Form No. 23 and shall be accompanied by evidence verifying the statements therein and by the Letters Patent.

A020.2

A020.3
Commentary on Section 20 [1949]

Section 20 gives the Comptroller power to correct a grant of an existing patent where the original grant was made to a deceased person or to a corporation which had ceased to exist at the date of sealing, and thus prevent the grant being incurably invalid. However, section 20 has no applicability where the grant was made to joint patentees, not all of whom had at the date of sealing died or ceased to exist. Section 20 also has no applicability where a patentee dies or ceases to exist after grant has taken place. Such matters are now resolved under section 36 [1977] (*Co-ownership of patents, etc.*) or under section 32 [1977] and rule 46 [1982] (*Registration of transactions, instruments and events*).

A020.4
Practice under Section 20 [1949]

Application is made under rule 63 [1968] (reprinted at para. A020.3 *supra*) using PF No. 23 (reprinted at para. A124). The Comptroller requires to be satisfied by documentary evidence, such as probate or a certificate from the Registrar of Companies. Such evidence, together with the incorrect Letters Patent, must accompany this form. The Comptroller may also require an explanation as to why he was not informed of the circumstances, and, although there are no reported cases under the section, it should be noted that the use of the word "may" suggests that the Comptroller's power under section 20 is discretionary.

A021.1

SECTION 21 [1949]

Extent effect and form of patent

21.—(1) A patent sealed with the seal of the Patent Office shall have the same effect as if it were sealed with the Great Seal of the United Kingdom, and shall have effect throughout the United Kingdom and the Isle of Man:

Provided that a patent may be assigned for any place in or part of the United Kingdom or Isle of Man as effectually as if it were granted so as to extend to that place or part only.

(2) Subject to the provisions of this Act and of subsection (3) of section 3 of the Crown Proceedings Act 1947, a patent shall have the same effect against the Crown as it has against a subject.

(3) A patent shall in such form as may be authorised by rules made by the Board of Trade under this Act.

(4) A patent shall be granted for one invention only; but it shall not be competent for any person in an action or other proceedings to take any objection to a patent on the ground that it has been granted for more than one invention.

Relevant 1968 Rule

A021.2   **62. [1968]** A patent shall be in the Form A or Form B (whichever is applicable) set out in the Fourth Schedule to these Rules, or such modification of either of these forms as the Comptroller directs.

Note. Rule 30 [1982] (*Address for service*), reprinted at para. 32.03 is also applicable.

SCHEDULE 4 [1968 RULES] A021.3

FORM OF PATENT

Form A

ELIZABETH the Second by the Grace of God of the United Kingdom of Great Britain and Northern Ireland and of Her other Realms and Territories, Queen, Head of the Commonwealth, Defender of the Faith: To all of whom these presents shall come greeting:

WHEREAS a request for the grant of a patent has been made by for the sole use and advantage of an invention for

AND WHEREAS We, being willing to encourage all inventions which may be for the public good, are graciously pleased to condescend to the request:

KNOW YE THEREFORE, that We, of our especial grace, certain knowledge, and mere motion do by these presents, for Us, our heirs and successors, give and grant unto the person(s) above named and any successor(s), executor(s), administrator(s) and assign(s) (each and any of whom are hereinafter referred to as the patentee) our especial licence, full power, sole privilege, and authority, that the patentee or any agent or licensee of the patentee and no others, may subject to the conditions and provisions prescribed by any statute or order for the time being in force at all times hereafter during the term of years herein mentioned, make, use, exercise and vend the said invention within our United Kingdom of Great Britain and Northern Ireland, and the Isle of Man, and that the patentee shall have and enjoy the whole profit and advantage from time to time accuring by reason of the said invention during the term of sixteen years from the date hereunder written of these presents: AND to the end that the patentee may have and enjoy the sole use and exercise and the full benefit of the said invention, We do by these presents for Us, our heirs and successors, strictly command all our subjects whatsoever within our United Kingdom of Great Britain and Northern Ireland, and the Isle of Man, that they do not at any time during the continuance of the said term either directly or indirectly make use of or put in practice the said invention, nor in anywise imitate the same, without the written consent, licence or agreement of the patentee, on pain of incurring such penalties as may be justly inflicted on such offenders for their contempt of this our Royal command, and of being answerable to the patentee according to the law for damages thereby occasioned:

PROVIDED ALWAYS that these letters patent shall be revocable on any of the grounds from time to time by law prescribed as grounds for revoking letters patent granted by Us, and the same may be revoked and made void accordingly:

PROVIDED ALSO that nothing herein contained shall prevent the granting of licences in such manner and for such considerations as they may by law be granted: AND lastly, We do by these presents for Us, our heirs and successors, grant unto the patentee that these our letters patent shall be construed in the most beneficial sense for the advantage of the patentee.

IN WITNESS whereof We have caused these our letters to be made patent as of the [day of one thousand nine hundred and [ ] and to be sealed.

Comptroller-General of Patents,
Designs and Trade Marks.

Seal of
Patent Office.

FORM OF PATENT OF ADDITION

Form B

ELIZABETH the Second by the Grace of God of the United Kingdom of Great Britain and Northern Ireland and of Her other Realms and Territories, Queen, Head of the Commonwealth, Defender of the Faith: To all to whom these presents shall come greeting:

WHEREAS a request for the grant of a patent has been made by
for the sole use and advantage of an invention for
and it has been further requested that the patent may be granted as a patent of addition to Patent No.   dated the   day of   19   (hereinafter referred to as the main patent):

AND WHEREAS We, being willing to encourage all inventions which may be for the public good, are graciously pleased to condescend to the request:

KNOW YE, THEREFORE, that We, of our especial grace, certain knowledge, and mere motion do by these presents for Us, our heirs and successors, give and grant unto the person(s) above named and any successor(s), executor(s), administrator(s) and assign(s) (each and any of whom are hereinafter referred to as the patentee) our especial licence, full power, sole privilege, and authority, that the patentee or any agent, or licensee of the patentee and no others, may subject to the conditions and provisions prescribed by any statute or order for the time being in force at all times hereafter during the terms of years herein mentioned, make, use, exercise and vend the said invention within our United Kingdom of Great Britain and Northern Ireland, and the Isle of Man, and that the patentee shall have and enjoy the whole profit and advantage from time to time accruing by reason of the said invention during a term beginning on the date hereunder written of these presents and ending at the expiration of sixteen years from the [   ] day of [   ] one thousand nine hundred and [   ] the date of said main patent:

AND to the end that the patentee may have and enjoy the sole use and exercise and full benefit of the said invention. We do by these presents for Us, our heirs and successors strictly command all our subjects whatsoever within our United Kingdom of Great Britain and Northern Ireland, and the Isle of Man, that they do not at any time during the continuance of the said term either directly or indirectly make use of or put in practice the said invention, nor in anywise imitate the same, without the written consent, licence or agreement of the patentee, on pain of incurring such penalties as may be justly inflicted on such offenders for their contempt of this our Royal command, and of being answerable to the patentee according to law for damages thereby occasioned:

PROVIDED ALWAYS that these letters patent shall be revocable on any of the grounds from time to time by law prescribed as grounds for revoking letters patent granted by Us, and the same may be revoked and made void accordingly:

PROVIDED ALSO that nothing herein contained shall prevent the granting of licences in such manner and for such considerations as they may by law be granted:

AND lastly, We do by these presents for Us, our heirs and successors, grant unto the patentee that these letters patent shall be construed in the most beneficial sense for the advantage of the patentee.

IN WITNESS whereof We have caused these letters to be made patent as of the [   ] day of [   ] one thousand nine hundred and [   ] and to be sealed.

Comptroller-General of Patents,
Designs, and Trade Marks.

Seal of
Patent Office.

COMMENTARY ON SECTION 21 [1949]

Effect, extent and assignment of existing patents (subss. (1)–(3)) **A021.4**

Section 21 continues to have effect as the basis for existing patents granted under the royal prerogative (see s. 102(1) 1949]) and the seal of the Patent Office.

By subsection (1) an existing patent is sealed under the seal of the Patent Office. It is, therefore, a "deed" and, as such, can only be assigned by a deed so that an assignment of an existing patent should be executed under seal, at least by the assignor. Execution under seal is, however, not necessary for patents granted under the 1977 Act because such are created under statute (s. 24(2) [1977] and r. 38 [1982] (reprinted at para. 24.02) with prescribed formalities for their assignment, requiring only optional execution under seal (s. 30(6) [1977], see para. 30.07.

Use of the seal of the Patent Office has the same effect as if the patent had been sealed under the Great Seal of the United Kingdom, as was so prior to 1883. This means that existing patents are (as patents granted under the 1977 Act are not) "Letters Patent". Such term is therefore inappropriate except in relation to "existing patents". Perhaps for this reason, the 1977 Act uses the term "proprietor", rather than "patentee", to refer to the owner of a patent granted under the 1977 Act.

An existing patent has legal effect throughout the United Kingdom and the Isle of Man. It also extends to territorial waters, the continental shelf etc. because section 132(2)–(4) [1977] applies to existing patents, see Schedule 2, paras. 1(2) and 2(*d*) [1977] and the commentary on section 132 [1977] at para. 132.06. However, like patents granted under the 1977 Act, an existing patent does not extend to the Channel Islands or to any British colony other than if the patent has been registered therein under some local ordinance, see para. 132.04.

An existing patent must have an address for service (r. 30 [1982] (reprinted at para. 32.03) made applicable by rule 124(1)(*d*) [1978] reprinted at para. 127.04, see paras. 32.16 and 32.22.

Subsection (1) permits assignment of an existing patent for part only of the territory to which it extends. In *Reitzman* v. *Grahame-Chapman* ((1950) 67 RPC 179) a patent had been assigned for a limited territory and the assignees were not before the court. Doubt was expressed whether a patent could be revoked for only part of the United Kingdom, but the point was not there decided.

Subsection (2) corresponds to section 129 [1977]. so that, as regards use of inventions by the Crown, the position is as with patents granted under the 1977 Act, for which see the commentary on section 55 [1977]. Section 3 of the Crown Proceedings Act 1947 (c. 44), as amended, is reprinted at para.129.02 and commented thereon therein.

Subsection (3), and rule 62 [1968], reprinted *supra*, provides for the form of the Letters Patent grant reprinted at para. A021.3, *supra*, in the form as altered by the 1968 Rules. By these Rules the former reference to a declaration by the applicant that no lawful ground of objection exists was then omitted, as was the statement that the complete specification had particularly described the invention: the reference to a prayer for the grant of a patent was also replaced by one to a request. The patentee is now defined as including any successors, executors, administrators and assigns of the person named in the patent. The requirements of the Act and the effect of the patent, however, apparently remained unchanged by these changes.

Infringement of existing patents **A021.5**

What constitutes infringement of an existing patent was not defined in the 1949 Act. This was decided under the Common Law on the basis of the wording of the

Letters Patent grant and particularly that the patentee "may have and enjoy the whole profit and advantage from time to time accruing by reason of the said invention . . . and the sole use and exercise and the full benefit of the said invention", and of the Royal command therein that persons "do not at any time . . . either directly or indirectly make use of or put in practice the said invention". In general, the tests of infringement seem little different to those employed under the 1977 Act, for which see the commentaries under sections 60 and 125 [1977]. Importation was held to be an infringing act in *Pfizer* v. *Minister of Health* ([1965] RPC 261 (HL)).

A021.6 *Patent granted for single invention only*

Subsection (4) prevents any objection that an existing patent was granted for more than one invention. It corresponds to section 26 [1977]. The provision may have the effect of causing an independent claim to be interpreted as if it were dependent on some earlier independent claim on the basis that, by the statute, a patent must relate to a single invention and must therefore be interpreted accordingly, see *Vaisey* v. *Toddlers Footwear* ([1957] RPC 90).

A022.1 **SECTION 22 [1949]**

Date and term of patent

22.—(1) Every patent shall be dated with the date of filing of the complete specification:

Provided that no proceeding shall be taken in respect of an infringement committed before the date of the publication of the complete specification.

(2) The date of every patent shall be entered in the registrar of patents.

(3) Except as otherwise expressly provided by this Act, the term of every patent shall be 16 years from the date of the patent.

(4) [*Repealed*]

(5) [*Repealed*]

A022.2 COMMENTARY ON SECTION 22 [1949]

Section 22 deals with the dating of an existing patent. Formerly, it also dealt with the renewal fee system, but this is now dealt with by section 25(3)–(5) [1977] which applies to existing patents (Sched. 2, paras. 1(2) and 2(*d*) [1977]). Renewal fees on existing patents are payable on anniversary dates reckoned from "the date of the patent" (r. 124(4) [1978], reprinted at para. 127.04).

As regards the term of an existing patent, subsection (3) is effectively amended by Schedule 1, paras. 3 and 4 [1977]. For all practical purposes the term of a subsisting existing patent is now 20 years from the date of filing its complete specification, but with severe restrictions on the effect on the patent, particularly its deemed endorsement "Licences of right" under section 35 [1949] by Schedule 1, para. 4 [1977]. This matter is discussed at length in the commentaries on sections 25 [1977] at para. 25.11 and on section 46 [1977] at paras. 46.07 *et seq*. However, the effect of this deemed endorsement can now be overcome so far as the invention relates to a product for a pharmaceutical or pesticidal use, see paras. 47.10–47.14. Also, the term of a patent of addition is limited to that of its parent patent, see section 26 [1949] and the commentary thereon.

The date of an existing patent is the date of filing its complete specification as defined in section 101 [1949]. This is not always so and prior to 1950 the date of a patent was its application date or earliest claimed Convention priority date. This can have an effect on the operation of the 50 year rule on prior publication, for which see section 50 [1949] and the commentary thereon. The term of a patent was originally 14 years from its date. This was extended to 16 years by the Patents and Designs Act 1919, section 6 (9 & 10 Geo. 5, c. 80) but, after the Patents, etc. (International Conventions) Act 1938 (1 & 2 Geo. 6, c. 26, s. 2), this 16 year period was computed from the date of the complete specification of the patent.

For the effect of the proviso to subsection (1), see para. A013.2. For renewal of an existing patent, see para. 25.10.

SECTION 23 [1949]   A023

Extension on ground of inadequate remuneration

[*Spent*, but see para. A025].

SECTION 24 [1949]   A024

Extension on ground of war loss

[*Spent*, but see para. A025]

SECTION 25 [1949]   A025

Extension on ground of war loss of licensee

[*Spent*, but see *Note, infra*]

Note. Sections 23–25 provided for the extension of the term of patents in certain circumstances. However, by Schedule 1, para. 3 [1977], these sections were limited, in effect, to "old existing patents" as defined therein and, for these, any extension of term granted after June 1, 1978 was limited to a maximum of four years, unless application for extension was pending on that date, but all patents extended under these provisions have now expired. Nevertheless, the case law developed under section 23 [1949] remains applicable in some Commonwealth countries where analogous provisions continue to exist. For this case law, see *PLUK* and its Supplements and the First Edition of this Work and its Supplements.

SECTION 26 [1949]   A026.0[1]

Patents of addition

26.—(1) Subject to the provisions of this section, where application is made for a patent in respect of any improvement in or modification of an invention (in this Act referred to as "the main invention") and the applicant also applies or has applied for a patent for that invention or is the patentee in respect thereof, the comptroller may, if the applicant so requests, grant the patent for the improvement or modification as a patent of addition.

(2) Subject to the provisions of this section, where an invention, being an improvement in or modification of another invention, is the subject of an independent patent and the patentee in respect of that patent is also the patentee in respect of the patent for the main invention, the comptroller may, if the patentee so requests, by order revoke the patent for the improvement or modification and grant to the patentee a patent of addition in respect thereof, bearing the same date as the date of the patent so revoked.

(3) A patent shall not be granted as a patent of addition unless the date of filing of the complete specification was the same as or later than the date of filing of the complete specification in respect of the main invention **and was earlier than the date of the appointed day**.

(4) . . .

(5) A patent of addition shall be granted for a term equal to that of the patent for the main invention, or so much thereof as is unexpired, and shall remain in force during that term or until the previous cesser of the patent for the main invention and no longer:

Provided that—

(a) . . . ; and

(b) if the patent for the main invention is revoked under this Act, the court or comptroller, as the case may be, may order that the patent of addition shall become an independent patent for the remainder of the term of the patent for the main invention, and thereupon the patent shall continue in force as an independent patent accordingly.

(6) No renewal fees shall be payable in respect of a patent of addition; but, if any such patent becomes an independent patent by virtue of an order under the last foregoing subsection, the same fees shall thereafter be payable, upon the same dates, as if the patent had been originally granted as an independent patent.

(7) The grant of a patent of addition shall not be refused, and a patent granted as a patent shall not be revoked or invalidated, on the ground only that the invention claimed in the complete specification does not involve any inventive step having regard to any publication or use of—

(a) the main invention described in the complete specification relating thereto; or

(b) any improvement in or modification of the main invention described in the complete specification of a patent of addition to the patent for the main invention or of an application for such a patent of addition; and the validity of a patent of addition shall not be questioned on the ground that the invention ought to have been the subject of an independent patent.

(8) An appeal shall lie from any decision of the comptroller under this section.

Notes. Subsections (4) and (5)(*a*) are spent and are therefore not reprinted. Subsection (1) has no new applicability. Subsection (3) was amended by Sched. 1, para. 5 [1977].

RELEVANT 1968 RULE

9. [1968] . . .   **A026.02**

(4) An application for the grant of a patent of addition in lieu of an independent patent shall be made on Patents Form No. 1 Add.

Note. The remainder of rule 9 [1968] is spent.

COMMENTARY ON SECTION 26 [1949]

General   **A026.03**

Section 26 provides for patents of addition. The section remains effective not only because of subsisting patents of addition (a term not known under the 1977 Act) granted under subsection (1), but also because of the possibility of converting an existing patent into a patent of addition under subsection (2) in order to obtain the considerable benefit in relation to validity provided by subsection (7), discussed in para. A026.08 *infra*. While subsections (4) and (5)(*a*) are spent, there remains the possibility of conversion of a patent of addition into an independent patent if the parent patent should be revoked, but with a term limited to that of its parent patent (subs. (5)(*b*)). Once a patent of addition has been granted, no renewal fees are payable thereon (subs. (6)). The form of the Letters Patent document for a patent of addition is that of Form B of the Fourth Schedule to the 1968 Rules (as reprinted at para. A021.3).

Subject matter requirements for patents of addition   **A026.04**

The test of suitability for a patent of addition (whether granted originally under subs. (1), or newly granted in substitution for a previously granted independent patent under subs. (2), is whether the invention is an improvement in or modification of the invention of the parent patent, and in *Elliott Brothers' Application* ([1967] RPC 1) the Patents Appeal Tribunal said:

> "The meaning of the words 'modification' and 'improvement' is clear enough. A modification is an alteration which does not involve a radical transformation and an improvement is a variation whether by addition, omission or alteration, to secure a better performance, whilst retaining some characteristic part".

In that case it was also held that account must be taken of the novelty of the manner of manufacture and, on the facts, the second application transformed the essential novelty of the first and was thus not suitable for a patent of addition.

The claims of a patent of addition must be for novel matter not disclosed in the specification of the main invention, since otherwise the patent of addition would not be for "an improvement in or modification of" the invention disclosed in the

957

specification of the main invention (*P & S's Application* (1952) 69 RPC 249 and *Georgia Kaolin's Application*, [1956] RPC 121). In the *Georgia Kaolin* case it was held that the phrase "main invention" means the invention "disclosed and described" in the complete specification and not the invention claimed, with the consequence that a patent of addition could not be granted for matter already disclosed in the parent patent but not claimed. Similarly, in *Welwyn's Application* ([1957] RPC 143), it was held impermissible to claim the main invention (a method of making a condenser) from a different aspect, *i.e.* as the condenser itself; or to claim subject-matter *contained*, but not *claimed*, in the earlier specification.

It is not necessary that a patent of addition should be more limited in scope than the parent patent (*Hughes* v. *Ingersoll*, [1977] FSR 406).

Two or more patents of addition to a single patent may be granted, and a patent of addition to an earlier patent of addition may be granted (*McFeely's Application*, (1912) 29 RPC 386), but such would not then have the advantage of subsection (7) with regard to the original main invention.

A026.05   *Conversion of independent patent of addition (subs. (2))*

Subsection (2) allows an independent patent granted under the 1949 Act to be converted into a patent of addition at any time, provided that the patentee is the same. It follows that a patentee can take an assignment of a patent granted to another person for an invention which is in fact an improvement in or modification of his own patented invention and can convert it to a patent of addition. The advantages of subsection (7) can thereby be obtained in order to avoid an obviousness attack over the disclosure of the main invention.

Where there is more than one patentee of the parent patent, it is not necessary for all the patentees to apply for the patent of addition, but the applicants for the patent of addition may not include anyone who is not a patentee of the parent patent.

The decision of the Comptroller whether to grant a patent of addition is one for him alone. Thus, once a patent of addition has been granted, it would not appear that the propriety of its grant as such can then be challenged. Accordingly, if an applicant for revocation of a patent which the patentee desires to convert into a patent of addition is permitted to address remarks on the propriety of permitting this, he does so only as *amicus curiae* and no appeal on the point by the applicant for revocation is permitted (*Hauni-Werke's Patent of Addition*, [1980] FSR 121). An applicant for revocation of the patent ought to be able to make submissions, at least in writing, against the propriety of allowing conversion of the patent under attack into a patent of addition, but the Comptroller is under no obligation to invite such submissions (*Polysius' Application*, SRIS, SRL O/106/80, *noted* IPD 3121), or perhaps even to inform the applicant for revocation of the patentee's application under subsection (2) to have the patent converted into a patent of addition. In *Aktiebolaget Celloplast's Application* ([1978] RPC 239) the Patents Appeal Tribunal held, contrasting the wording of sections 26 and 29 [1949] that, if the Comptroller was satisfied that the provisions of the statute were met, he had no discretion under subsection (2) whether or not to convert a patent of addition into an independent patent, so that in effect the word "may" in subsection (2) should be read as the word "must".

A026.06   *Date of patent of addition (subs. (3))*

By subsection (3) a patent of addition may be granted even though the application was made before the application for the parent patent, provided that the complete specification of the patent of addition is not filed earlier than that of the parent patent. This is possible because of the provision in section 22(1) [1949] that the date of a patent is the date of filing of the complete specification.

The amendment to subsection (3) ensures that no patent granted on an application filed under the 1977 Act can become converted to a patent of addition to an existing patent.

Conversion of patent of addition to independent patent (subs. (5)(b))   **A026.07**

If a parent is revoked, it may be ordered that a patent of addition thereto shall become converted into an independent patent. Renewal fees are then payable thereon (subs. (6)). In *Ronson* v. *Lewis* ([1963] RPC 103 at 139) a request under subsection (5)(*b*) upon revocation by the court of the parent patent was ordered to be dealt with in separate proceedings.

Variation in validity requirements of patent of addition (subs. (7))   **A026.08**

According to subsection (7), no publication or use of the main invention (or of the invention of any intermediate patent of addition) as described in the complete specification of the parent patent (or for the intermediate patent of addition) can be used to deprive the patent of addition of invention step. It seems, therefore, that the patent of addition might be deprived of inventive step by reason of prior publication or use of matter described in the provisional, but not in the complete specification of the parent patent or earlier patent of addition. This subsection applies only to matter in the complete specification of the main invention, or of another patent of addition thereto, as accepted and not as originally filed (*P & S's Application*, (1952) 69 RPC 249). In *Letraset* v. *Rexel* ([1974] RPC 175) additional matter in the French equivalent of the parent patent was held not covered by the exception.

The word "only " in subsection (7) is used also in section 50(4) [1949] and was considered in *Bloxham* v. *Kee-Less* ((1922) 39 RPC 195), in which a specification more than 50 years old was taken into account in conjunction with other specifications, but in *Page* v. *Brent Toy Products* ((1950) 67 RPC 4) leave to rely on a specification more than 50 years old was refused. It therefore appears that, in an attack on the inventive step of a patent of addition, the complete specification of the parent patent must be wholly disregarded. However, the distinction between consideration of novelty and obviousness is not clear-cut where an implied disclosure is in question. Similar points arise under section 2(3) [1977] and section 32(1)(*i*) [1949], see paras. 2.19 and A032.35 respectively.

In *Monsanto's (Salyer's) Application* ([1969] RPC 75), it was held that the exception provided for in subsection (7)(*b*) covers publication whether by the patentee or by third parties.

Miscellaneous   **A026.09**

The Comptroller will accept a separate assignment of a patent of addition, but the assignee would be wise to file a caveat for the payment of each renewal fee on the parent patent so as to assure himself that his patent is kept in force, for which see para. 118.19.

A parent patent and a patent of addition may be licensed separately.

PRACTICE UNDER SECTION 26 [1949]   **A026.10**

A request for conversion of granted existing patent into a patent of addition to another existing patent (for which the date and ownership requirements mentioned above are met) is made on PF No. 1 Add (reprinted at para. A119) under Rule 9(4) [1968] (reprinted at para. A026.02 *supra*). This form has not been revised, but rule 90 [1982] (reprinted at para. 115.03) obviates the previous requirement for personal signature by the patentee. There is no provision for opposition, but subsection (8) and Schedule 4, para. 11 [1977]. Renewal fees continue to be payable until a patent of addition has actually been granted.

A027   **SECTION 27 [1949]** *[Repealed]*

Restoration of lapsed patents

Note. Section 28 [1977] now applies for the restoration of existing patents, but with much more stringent requirements than under section 27 [1949] so that the previous case law is not inapplicable.

A028   **SECTION 28 [1949]**

Restoration of lapsed applications for patents

[Spent]

A029.01   **SECTION 29 [1949]**

Amendment of specification with leave of comptroller

29.—(1) Subject to the provisions of section 31 of this Act, the comptroller may, upon an application made under this section by a patentee, or by an applicant for a patent at any time after the acceptance of the complete specification, allow the complete specification to be amended subject to such conditions, if any, as the comptroller thinks fit:

Provided that the comptroller shall not allow a specification to be amended under this section upon an application made while any action before the court for infringement of the patent or any proceeding before the court for the revocation of the patent is pending.

(2) Every application for leave to amend a specification under this section shall state the nature of the proposed amendment and shall give full particulars of the reasons for which the application is made.

(3) Any application for leave to amend a specification under this section, and the nature of the proposed amendment, shall be advertised in the prescribed manner:

Provided that where the application is made before the publication of the complete specification, the comptroller may, if he thinks fit, dispense with advertisement under this subsection or direct that advertisement shall be postponed until the complete specification is published.

(4) Within the prescribed period after the advertisement of an application under this section, any person may give notice to the comptroller of opposition thereto; and where such a notice is given within the period aforesaid, the comptroller shall notify the person by whom the application under this section is made and shall give to that person and to the opponent an opportunity to be heard before he decides the case.

(5) An appeal shall lie from any decision of the comptroller under this section.

(6) This section shall not apply in relation to any amendment of a specification effected in proceedings in opposition to the grant of a patent or on a reference to the comptroller of a dispute as to the infringement or validity of a claim, or effected in pursuance of any provision of this Act authorising the comptroller to direct a reference to another specification or patent to be inserted, or to refuse to grant a patent, or to revoke a patent, unless the specification is amended to his satisfaction.

RELEVANT 1968 RULES

90. [1968]—An application to the Comptroller for leave to amend an accepted complete specification under Section 29 shall be made on Patents Form No. 35, and, subject to the proviso to Section 29(3), shall be advertised by publication of the application and the nature of the proposed amendment in the Journal, and in such other manner, if any, as the Comptroller may in each case direct.   **A029.02**

91. [1968]—(1) Any person wishing to oppose the application shall, within one month from the date of the advertisement in the Journal, or such further period not exceeding three months from the said date as the Comptroller may in special cases allow, give notice to the Comptroller on Patents Form No. 36.   **A029.03**

(2) Such notice shall be accompanied by a copy thereof and shall be supported by a statement (in duplicate) setting out fully the nature of the opponent's interest, the facts and of the statement shall be sent by the Comptroller to the applicant.

92. [1968]—Upon such notice of opposition being given and a copy thereof sent to the applicant the provisions of Rules 40 to 45 shall apply.   **A029.04**

93. [1968]—Unless the Comptroller otherwise directs, an application or proposal for amendment of an accepted complete specification shall be accompanied by a copy of the printed specification and drawings clearly showing in red ink the amendment sought.   **A029.05**

94. [1968]—Where leave to amend a specification is given the applicant shall, if the Comptroller so requires, and within a time to be fixed by him,   **A029.06**

file a new specification and drawings as amended, which shall be prepared in accordance with Rules 5 and 18 to 23.

A029.07 *Note to Relevant Rules.* The following rules are also relevant to amendment under section 29 [1949]: rules 40–45 [1968], reprinted at paras. A033.04–A033.09 respectively (for opposition proceedings); rules 153, 154 and 156 [1968], reprinted at paras. A115–A117 respectively (for time limits, extensions of time and hearings in public); and rules 88, 100 and 101 [1982], reprinted at paras. 101.02, 123.07 and 123.08 respectively (for the exercise of the Comptroller's discretion and correction of irregularities).

COMMENTARY ON SECTION 29 [1949]

A029.08 *General*

Section 29 is concerned with the procedure on amendment in the Patent Office of existing patents. It also applies to applications filed under the 1949 Act and still pending as a result of a "secrecy order". Amendment of an "existing patent" in proceedings before the court is carried out under section 30 [1949]. The conditions which an allowable amendment of an existing patent must satisfy are contained in section 31 [1949]. The corresponding sections of the 1977 Act are sections 27, 75 and 76 [1977] respectively.

Under the proviso to subsection (1), the Comptroller cannot act under section 29 if any action for infringement or revocation is pending before the court, in which event section 30 [1949] applies and the amendment is dealt with by the court instead of the Comptroller. The meaning of "pending" is considered in para. 75.04. If the application is presented to the Comptroller prior to any infringement or revocation action, but one is started subsequently, this will not prevent the Comptroller proceeding in his discretion with the section 29 application (*Western Electric's Patent*, (1933) 50 RPC 59). A revocation action is not commenced until the patentee is given notice of it (*Foseco's Patent*, [1976] FSR 244).

A029.09 *Opposition*

An application to amend under section 29 is advertised by the Comptroller (see para. A029.14 *infra*), and opposition may be lodged within one month (extensible to three months) of the advertisement (r. 91 [1968], reprinted at para. A029.03 *supra*). An opposition may be lodged by "any person", see *Braun AG's Application* ([1981] RPC 355) and para. 27.12. Under subsection (5) appeal now lies to the Patents Court (Sched. 4, paras. 11(5) and 15 [1977] and s. 97 [1977]).

A029.10 *Discretion*

The Comptroller's power to allow amendment is, by virtue of the word "may" in subsection (1), a discretionary one which he can refuse to exercise if he considers that the circumstances so demand. This may be so where there has been undue delay in applying for the amendment once its desirability is known, or where the original claim was "covetous" or deliberately "ambiguous." "Discretion" is considered more fully in paras. 27.05–27.07.

A029.11 *Conditions*

Under subsection (1) the Comptroller has the power to impose conditions in allowing an amendment. Though this power is not usually exercised, the court in

Dorr's Application ((1942) 59 RPC 113) under the 1907 Act prohibited the applicant from bringing any action in respect of machines the manufacture of which was begun prior to the application for leave to amend, the makers of the machines having been advised that they did not infringe the unamended claim, which was prima facie restricted to a drum, and the amendment being allowed on the ground that in the light of the detailed description the word "drum" was used to include various equivalents.

However, in neither *General Tire's (Frost's) Patent* ([1972] RPC 259 and [1974] RPC 207) nor *Wilkinson Sword* v. *Gillette* ([1975] RPC 101) were any conditions imposed. The facts in the *General Tire* case were somewhat similar to those in the *Dorr* case, but the Court of Appeal pointed out that there was no evidence that anyone had infringed the amended claim only because of reliance on his belief that the unamended claim was more limited and, despite allegations of widespread infringement, there had only been one opponent to the amended application. In the *Wilkinson* case, the court noted that normally section 59(3) [1949] (see now s. 62(3) [1977]) would provide adequate protection to infringers.

For further discussion on amendments permitted subject to imposed conditions, see para. 27.08.

Objections to validity of amended claims   A029.12

The extent to which an opponent to amendment proceedings may be permitted to argue that the amendments, if made, would nevertheless leave the claims invalid is discussed in para. 27.13.

Amendments during revocation proceedings before the Comptroller (subs. (6))   A029.13

Subsection (6) lays down in particular that section 29 does not apply to amendments introduced in proceedings already in being before the Comptroller, for example in an application for revocation under section 33 [1949]. This means that amendments can be made in such proceedings without previous advertisement, so that non-parties to the proceedings are not informed or given the opportunity to oppose them, though periodic inspection of the file can be carried out under section 118 [1977] to monitor the submission and processing of any application for amendment put forward in existing, *inter partes*, proceedings. It is not clear that a caveat (for which see para. 118.19) could be used for this purpose as the filing of an amendment application is not one of the actions listed in rule 92 [1982], see para. 118.04 or one notified by the Patent Office as acceptable, see para. 118.19. However, no doubt such persons could seek to intervene in the proceedings, but it is by no means certain that such intervention would be entertained.

PRACTICE UNDER SECTION 29 [1949]

Filing of application with Comptroller for amendment of existing patent   A029.14

The procedure for requesting amendment of an existing patent from the Comptroller under section 29 [1949] is governed by rules 90–93 and 95 [1968] (reprinted at paras. A029.02–A029.06 *supra*) and by the general rules for oppositions, see para. A029.07. Because the practice under section 29 [1949] is essentially the same as that under section 27 [1977], only points of difference are noted here and paras. 27.14–27.19 should be consulted otherwise.

The application to amend under section 29 [1949] is made on PF No. 35 (reprinted at para. A125). This must give full particulars of the reasons for which the application is made (subs. (2)). Particulars must include a statement as to whether each amendment is by way of disclaimer, correction or explanation (*Warnant's Application* ([1956] RPC 205). The application is then examined and any objections are raised prior to advertisement in the O.J. under rule 90 [1968] (reprinted at para. A029.02 *supra*). If necessary, the advertisement will indicate that advertisement is taking place prior to determination of the allowability of the advertised amendments.

A029.15 *Opposition to amendment application made to Comptroller*

The period for opposition after advertisement in the O.J. is only one month, but this can be extended up to a total of three months following application to the Comptroller as a special case (r. 91(1) [1968]). Opposition is lodged on PF No. 36 (reprinted at para. A126). The statement need not accompany PF No. 36, but can be filed within 14 days thereof (r. 153 [1968]) (reprinted at para. A115). The counter-statement is not filed in duplicate (as under r. 40(4) [1982]), but one copy is sent directly to the opponent. Otherwise, the procedure is similar to that generally used in *inter partes* proceedings before the Comptroller, for which see paras. 72.32–72.52.

A030.1 **SECTION 30 [1949]**

Amendment of specification with leave of court

30.—(1) In any action for infringement of a patent or any proceeding before the court for the revocation of a patent, the court may, subject to the provisions of the next following section, by order allow the patentee to amend his complete specification in such manner, and subject to such terms as to costs, advertisements or otherwise, as the court may think fit; and if in any such proceedings for revocation the court decides that the patent is invalid, the court may allow the specification to be amended under this section instead of revoking the patent.

(2) Where an application for an order under this section is made to the court, the applicant shall give notice of the application to the comptroller, and the comptroller shall be entitled to appear and be heard, and shall appear if so directed by the court.

A030.2 Commentary on Section 30 [1949]

Subsection (1) provides that, in any action before the court for infringement or revocation, the court may at its discretion permit the amendment of the complete specification of an existing patent. Similar considerations apply to this section as to section 29 [1949], and likewise the limitations of section 31 [1949] apply. The court is entitled to impose such conditions as it may think fit and to require advertisement of the proposed amendments.

The sections of the 1977 Act corresponding to sections 29–31 [1949] are respectively sections 27, 75 and 76 [1977], while the procedure under section 30 [1949] is little different from that of section 75 [1977], so that the commentary thereon provides also the requisite commentary on section 30 [1949], but the jurisdictional split between the pairs of sections is different. The proviso to section 29(1) [1949] precludes the Comptroller from proceeding with an amendment of an "existing patent" thereunder if any action is pending before the court for infringement or revocation thereof, whereas section 75 [1977] provides for amendment of a patent by the court or Comptroller when "validity proceedings" are pending before it: otherwise only the Comptroller is competent (under s. 27 [1977]) to amend a patent, see section 27(2) [1977] and para. 27.09. The meaning of "pending proceedings" is discussed in para. 75.04.

In *Condor International's Patent* (O/25/85 SRIS *noted* IPD 8107) an order for revocation made by the court was ordered by the court to be stood over and not to be effective if an application to amend was timely filed before the Comptroller (under s. 29 [1949]) and allowed. In this way the need for the court to consider the amendment was avoided despite the formal continuance of court proceedings.

As with all amendment proceedings, amendment may be allowed subject to conditions and involves an exercise of discretion. The imposition of conditions is discussed in para. A029.11 with "discretion" generally dealt with in paras. 27.05–27.07. However, para. 75.06 deals with the question whether amendments will be allowed if the patentee chooses to support his claims before the court and then fails, and also when the court finds a patent only partially valid. In this latter case section 63(3) [1977] is relevant, see para. 63.04.

When an application to amend is made to the court under section 30 the applicant is required to inform the Comptroller, who is entitled to appear and may be directed by the court to do so (subs. (2)). However, the Comptroller usually does not exercise his right to appear when the amendment application is made during the course of contested *inter partes* proceedings, but requires to be kept informed of the date of the hearing.

PRACTICE UNDER SECTION 30 [1949] A030.3

The procedure for seeking leave of the court during infringement or revocation proceedings for amendment of a patent-in-suit is governed by RSC Ord. 104, r. 3 (reprinted at para. E104.3) and is the same as that under section 75 [1977], see para. 75.11. However, any order of the court allowing amendment must be notified to the Patent Office on PF No. 69 (no fee) (reprinted at para. A138) under rule 150 [1968] (reprinted at para. 32.12).

SECTION 31 [1949] A031.01

Supplementary provisions as to amendment of specification

31.—(1) After the acceptance of a complete specification no amendment thereof shall be effected except by way of disclaimer, correction or explanation, and no amendment thereof shall be allowed, except for the purpose of correcting an obvious mistake, the effect of which would be that the specification as amended would claim or describe matter not in substance disclosed in the specification before the amendment, or that any claim of the specification as amended would not fall wholly within the scope of a claim of the specification before the amendment.

(2) Where, after the date of the publication of a complete specification, any amendment of the specification is allowed or approved by the comp-

965

troller, the court or the Appeal Tribunal under this Act, the right of the patentee or applicant to make the amendment shall not be called in question except on the ground of fraud; and the amendment shall in all courts and for all purposes be deemed to form part of the specification:

Provided that in construing the specification as amended reference may be made to the specification as originally published.

(3) Where, after the date of the publication of a complete specification, any amendment of the specification is allowed or approved as aforesaid, the fact that the specification has been amended shall be advertised in the Journal.

A031.02   ARTICLES

R. P. Lloyd, "Correction of Clerical Errors and Obvious Mistakes", (1980–81) 10 CIPA 266;
G. Aggus, "The Equities of Amendment", (1980–81) 10 CIPA 399.

COMMENTARY ON SECTION 31 [1949]

A031.03   *General*

Section 31 applies to "existing patents", and also to applications filed under the 1949 Act and still pending as a result of a "secrecy order". It governs amendments applied for under section 29 [1949] and also amendments proposed in the course of revocation proceedings under section 33 [1949]. It further governs amendments made under section 30 [1949] during court proceedings.

There is no provision under section 31 for the amendment of a provisional specification, though such a specification may be amended by excision or the title may be corrected (*Brackett & McLay's Application*, (1930) 47 RPC 335); clerical errors therein can also be corrected under section 76 [1949].

A031.04   *Nature of permissible amendments (subs. (1))*

Under subsection (1) the only permitted amendments are those by way of disclaimer, correction or explanation. These are key words in interpreting the section, but they are not used in the 1977 Act. In addition, there are prohibitions against adding "matter not in substance disclosed" and against broadening the scope of the claims; these last two prohibitions do not apply to correction of an "obvious mistake". These two prohibitions find echoes in section 76 [1977], but no broadening is permitted except, possibly, by the making of a correction under section 117 [1977]. Under the 1949 Act there is also a separate power of correction under section 76 [1949], but thereunder only "clerical" errors can be corrected, see para. A076.09.

A031.05   *Challenge to, and construction of, amended specification (subs. (2))*

Under subsection (2) an amendment once allowed by the Comptroller or court cannot be challenged except on the ground of fraud. The meaning of "fraud" in this context is not clear and there appears to be no case on the point.

The proviso to subsection (2) permits the amended specification to be construed by reference to its form as originally published, but not in the light of the reasons for seeking amendment (*Dow Chemical* v. *Spence Bryson (No. 2)*, [1982] FSR 598 and [1984] RPC 359 (CA)). Here the insertion of the word "fluid" into the claim was held to limit the phrase "fluid foam" to one that is pourable, *i.e.* not normally solid. However, in *Corning Glassworks' and Corning Ltd.'s Patent* ([1984] RPC 459 (CA)), it was indicated, *obiter*, that subsection (2) would not prevent evidence being given that statements made in the original specification constituted admissions against the interest of the patentee even if these statements had been subsequently deleted by an allowable amendment.

Advertisement and publication of amended specification (subs. (3))　　　　**A031.06**

Subsection (3) requires that, where any complete specification of an existing patent is allowed to be amended (whether under ss. 29 or 30 [1949]), this fact is to be advertised in the O.J. The specification is itself then usually reprinted, or at least an amendment slip is issued when subsequently copies of the specification are supplied by the Patent Office or are sent to those libraries supplied with specifications on a regular basis. Since March 1976 the suffix "B" has been added to the number of an existing patent that has been reprinted after amendment, see O.J. April 26, 1989.

Prohibition on adding new matter or extending scope of claim　　　　**A031.07**

Dominating section 31 is the over-riding provision that no amendment is permissible (other than to correct an obvious mistake) which would claim or describe matter not in substance disclosed, or render any claim not wholly within the scope of a claim existing in the specification before amendment. This means that no amendment, apart from the above exception, can widen the scope of a specification. While section 31 does not specifically require an amended claim to be fairly based on the original specification, it seems that the reference to "matter not in substance disclosed" may have this effect. Because of the obvious similarities of these provisions with those of section 76 [1977], the questions arising therefrom have been discussed in paras. 76.09–76.15. Cases in which the provisions have been a cause of rejection of proposed amendments are also to be found in the cases discussed *infra* under the separate headings of "disclaimer", "correction" and "explanation".

Disclaimer

—Meaning of "disclaimer"　　　　**A031.08**

If an amendment has the effect of curtailing the monopoly, it will normally be regarded as a disclaimer (*AMP* v. *Hellerman*, [1962] RPC 55). The word "disclaimer" can also cover the idea of repudiating a connection with, or of renouncing in more general terms without reference to, any legal claim: provided that the claims are not widened, new matter is not introduced, and there is no material false suggestion thereby (*American Cyanamid* v. *Ethicon*, [1979] RPC 215). With the same provisos, language could also be removed which might mislead the reader or suggest to him unfruitful manufacture or experimentation. Conversion of an optional requirement into an essential one is a disclaimer (*Schwank's Patent*, [1958] RPC 53). However, adding words which are only explanatory of what is already present does not constitute a disclaimer and therefore does not meet the object of overcoming an anticipation (*Bentley Engineering's Patent*, [1981] RPC 361); but, when an amendment is seen to do no more than add an extra feature to the combination of an unamended claim, it must then be a disclaimer and, accordingly, the amended claim must then fall wholly within the claim before amendment (*Wilkinson Sword* v. *Gillette*, [1975] RPC 101).

In *Bentley Engineering's Patent* (*supra*) a proposed amendment was not allowed as a disclaimer on a finding of fact that the additional words were only explanatory of what was already present, so that they did not meet the object of overcoming an anticipation.

In *Farbwerke Hoechst's Application* (decided in 1963, but only published [1972] RPC 703) leave was given to replace a claim for a fungicidal preparation by one for a method of treating seeds or living plants with such a preparation on the ground that the protection given by the unamended claim would have extended to this use of the preparation and, therefore, the amended claim would not render any act an infringement which would not have been an infringement of the unamended claim. Likewise, in *Beecham Group's (Amoxycillin) Application* ([1980] RPC 261), a claim to a compound X was allowed to be replaced by a claim to "A pharmaceutical composition adapted for oral administration to human beings containing an active ingredient compound Y". However, such change from a claim of the "product" type to one of the "use" type will not be possible if the use is not one patentable under section 101 [1949], for example because it is for medical treatment of the human body, see para. A010.08.

Limitation of a claim to an article to incorporate its intended purpose was allowed in *Beloit's Application* ([1974] RPC 467), but the amendment must do no more than merely mention the purpose in a non-limiting way because there is generally no novelty in mere purpose (*Adhesive Dry Mounting* v. *Trapp*, (1910) 27 RPC 341).

A031.09   —*Overcoming of invalidity by disclaimer*

Where there has been a finding that a claim to a chemical compound *per se* is anticipated by a prior use, it is not possible to secure by amendment a claim to that compound with exclusion of the circumstance when that compound has been made by that particular process used in the prior use, though it is possible that the claim can be limited to the compound when made by a particular and advantageous process that has been disclosed (*Bristol-Myers' (Johnson's) Application (No. 2)* ([1979] RPC 450).

It is sometimes possible to cut out inoperative matter (*Du Pont's Patent* [1968] RPC 193) if this has been mentioned only as a mere possibility, but it is not possible to cure insufficiency of a description of a chemical process by limiting the claim to the use of a particular form of starting material when there was no true disclosure in the unamended specification that use of such form was to be preferred (*Bristol-Myers' (Johnson and Hardcastle's) Application*, [1974] RPC 389).

A "definite affirmation of utility" was not permitted to be removed as a disclaimer (*Antiference* v. *Telerection*, ([1957] RPC 31). Likewise, deletion of a statement of alleged advantage was refused in the exercise of discretion (*Wulfing's Patent*, SRIS C/91/81), as also a statement of promise which had been shown to be false (*Suwa Seikosha's Patent*, SRIS O/86/82, *noted* IPD 5065), and deletion of an apparent definition of the invention claimed (*Bristol-Myers' (Johnson's) Application (No. 2)*, *supra*).

In *Union Carbide's (Bailey and O'Connor's) Application* ([1972] RPC 854) the applicants were embarrassed in claiming convention priority by a description of process steps which were claimed in a sub-claim, and they sought to delete both the description and the sub-claim. It was held that, though the sub-claim could be deleted by way of disclaimer, the deletion of the description was not a disclaimer, and if its presence was an embarrassment that was a good reason for not exercising discretion in the applicant's favour.

This decision was effectively followed in *Corning Glassworks' and Corning Ltd.'s Patent* ([1984] RPC 459 (CA)) where the specification specifically described five alternative methods of making a particular product and it was sought to limit the claims to two only of these alternatives. Although the restriction of the claims was allowed as a disclaimer, the patentee was not permitted to excise the description of these alternative methods, now not claimed, on the ground that the proposed excision was not itself disclaimer and because a potential applicant for revocation was entitled to rely upon the presence of the passage sought to be deleted. It was argued that the amendment was allowable as consequential upon a disclaimer and also to avoid inconsistency between the text and the claims, but it was held that the proposed deletion went "substantially beyond what is necessary or desirable for the purpose of avoiding any such inconsistency" and was therefore not merely consequential.

Thus, whether a particular amendment will be permitted to overcome invalidity is essentially a question of discretion which is discussed generally in the commentary on section 27 [1977] at paras. 27.05–27.07.

Limitation to an intermediate generalisation by disclaiming amendment   **A031.10**

In *Rose Bros.' Application* ([1960] RPC 247) an attempt to include in claim 1 generalised forms of integers not generalised in the specification failed. In contrast, in *Baker Perkins' Application* ([1958] RPC 267) an amendment to introduce integers into claim 1 was allowed because each such integer was disclosed. Thus, the question is essentially one of whether the proposed amendment would, by implication, add new matter to the specification: the commentary on section 76(2) [1977] is therefore relevant, see paras. 76.11–76.15.

However, limitation of a broad claim to an intermediate generalisation, not described in so many words in the specification, has occasionally been allowed, *e.g.* in *Ethyl Corp.'s Patent* ([1972] RPC 169 (CA)), where a numerical range not found in the specification as such was inserted into a claim; in *Matbro* v. *Michigan* ([1973] RPC 823); and in *Screen Printing's Application* ([1974] RPC 628), where it was observed that, if a broad claim is found to be anticipated, an applicant ought not to be forced into a position of having to make so restrictive an amendment that he would lose the benefit of the protection to which he ought to be entitled. However, the allowability of all amendments of this type seems to depend on the *inherent* disclosure of the unamended specification, and in *Bristol-Myers* v. *Manon* ([1973] RPC 836 at 860) amendment of a sub-claim was refused either as not being a true disclaimer or as being one which should be refused in the exercise of the court's discretion. Restriction to an intermediate generalisation was also refused in *Lucas* v. *Gaedor* ([1978] RPC 297 at 351) on the ground that it would then be a claim to matter which was not in substance disclosed in the original specification.

Disclaimer in relation to sub-claims   **A031.11**

The deletion of an independent claim can be regarded as a disclaimer, but the deletion of an appendant claim was not allowed in *Standard Telephones' Patent* ((1955) 72 RPC 19). In *Plastics' Patent* ([1970] RPC 22) deletion of a sub-claim, which was directed to a feature known in itself, was allowed although the process of the deleted claim remained covered by claim 1, but the deletion of two further sub-claims was refused on the ground that their presence assisted in construing claim 1.

In *Chilowsky's Application* ([1957] RPC 43) the deletion of an alternative from a dependent claim was allowed only when the alternative was also deleted from the description, but in *Gallay's Application* ([1959] RPC 141) an omnibus claim was directed to two constructions, one shown in the provisional and the other not, the latter having been published before the date of the complete specification, and amendment of the claim to restrict it to the first construction and so to change its priority date was allowed as a disclaimer, even though the second construction remained covered by claim 1. These cases suggest that special considerations apply to a claim amendment intended to change a priority date.

When a main claim is amended by way of limitation, there is no objection to the introduction of fresh appendant claims relating to features added to the main claim, the position being different when an attempt is made to add new subsidiary claims in the absence of any limitation of the main claim (*ICI's (Whyte's) Patent*, [1978] RPC 11).

Correction

A031.12 *—Meaning of "correction"*

The term "correction" implies a mistake of the nature of an unobserved error: it does not embrace an error of judgment (*Distillers' Application*, (1953) 70 RPC 221) or an error of drafting (*Standard Telephones' Patent*, (1955) 72 RPC 19), though in the former case it was observed, *obiter*, that the addition of a claim that did not extend the scope of the monopoly might be allowable, presumably if the draftsman could prove that he intended to include it. On the other hand, in *Sinkler's Application* ([1967] RPC 155), in which the scope of claim 1 was limited in opposition proceedings, simultaneous amendment of claim 7 to make it appendant to any preceding claim instead of to claim 6 was refused on the ground that limitation of part of a claim cannot justify its extension in other respects. It is somewhat difficult to reconcile the *Distillers* and *Sinkler* cases, except on the assumption that the desired object in the *Sinkler* case might have been attained by the addition of a new claim that was a combination of claim 7 with the amended claim 1. The question of error of judgment was also considered in *General Tire's (Frosts's) Patent* ([1972] RPC 259 and [1974] RPC 207), and the *Distiller's* decision (*supra*) was doubted, *obiter*, in *Polymer Corp.'s Patent* ([1972]).

In *Alliance Flooring* v. *Winsorflor* ([1961] RPC 95) the deletion of a passage inconsistent with the claims was permitted as a correction. There is, however, at least one unreported case where the existence of such a passage was regarded as restricting the claims and its deletion was refused as a broadening amendment.

Whatever the meaning of "correction", it is not necessarily intended to refer to clerical errors, for the correction of these is provided for separately under section 76 [1949], see paras. A076.08 *et seq.* (and also para. 117.06 for correction under s. 117 [1977]). However, since a clerical error to be corrected under section 76 [1949] must have been made in the course of the preparation of the actual documents to be corrected (see para. A076.09), it seems that a clerical error made at an earlier stage of an existing patent, can only be corrected, if at all, under sections 29–31 [1949].

Unless the existence of a mistake is obvious on the face of the specification, the Comptroller, as a matter of practice, requires evidence that there is a mistake to be corrected. Such evidence is desirably given by the draftsman of the specification and by the patent agent who prosecuted the application if he was not the original draftsman.

A wrong title can be corrected under section 31 [1949].

—Correction of obvious mistake **A031.13**

Only when an amendment is to correct an obvious mistake can the scope of claims be broadened, other than by correction of a clerical error under section 76. The authoritative view on amendment by correction of an obvious mistake is that of the House of Lords in *Holtite* v. *Jost* ([1979] RPC 81): *viz.* "What must be obvious is not simply that there has been some mistake, but also what the mistake is and what is the correction needed". However, the existence of alternative correcting amendments did not prevent the mistake from being obvious. If extraneous evidence is required, other than to equip the court with knowledge of the skilled addressee, it was stated the mistake cannot be obvious. In this case it was obvious that the only specific embodiment described was intended to fall within the claims and amendment was allowed, as it had been in a somewhat similar case on the facts in *Farmhand* v. *Spadework* ([1975] RPC 617). These, and other cases on "obvious mistake", are discussed in the paper by R. P. Lloyd listed in para. A031.02 *supra*.

Correction of a self-evident error was allowed in *Codex* v. *Racal-Milgo* (SRIS C/135/81, *noted* IPD 4100) and a broadening correction of an obvious mistake was allowed in *Plows* v. *Cambridge Instruments* (SRIS C/100/84). However, amendment was refused in *Western Electric* v. *Racal-Milgo* ([1981] RPC 253) as the mistake in that case was not obvious on the face of the document. Moreover, since this error was one that had not occurred to the inventors or to the draftsman, the text reflected their intentions and correction was only possible if there had been a failure in this regard.

Amendment was also refused in *PPG Industries' Patent* ([1987] RPC 469 (CA)) because, though it was obvious that mistakes were present in the specification, it was not obvious to an informed reader what the mistake was and how it should be corrected. It was there indicated that correction of an obvious mistake was appropriate when an inadequately skilled reader might be misled, though the mistake and its method of correction were obvious to the skilled reader.

Egyt's Patent ([1981] RPC 99) was a chemical case where the product was claimed in terms of a structural formula which was later found to be incorrect. The Patents Court allowed an amendment to delete from the claim the incorrect structural formula while adding thereto certain other characterising data which the specification described the compound in question to possess. It was held that an obvious mistake existed in the unamended specification since practice of the clearly described process of the examples did not give a product having the stated formula, though it did have the other stated characteristics. It was held that it was obvious that what was intended to be claimed was a product having these characteristics and evidence that to any competent chemist the existence of the mistake would have been obvious on reading the specification was sufficient to distinguish the case from that of *Zambon's Patent* ([1971] RPC 95), while adhering to the principles of *Holtite* v. *Jost* (*supra*).

In *General Tire's (Frost's) Patent* ([1972] RPC 259) the Comptroller held that there was an obvious mistake since the main claim was not consonant with the inventive concept, but the PAT, observing that a difference in scope between the description and the claim would not necessarily enable the instructed reader to appreciate that a mistake had been made, held that the correction required was certainly not obvious so that the amendment would not be allowed. The Court of Appeal ([1974] RPC 207) did not deal with the question of obvious mistake, but allowed the amendment as one of explanation. *NRDC's Application* ([1957] RPC 344), where the facts were similar to those of *Egyt's Patent (supra)* and of *Zambon's Patent (supra)*, is also best seen as an amendment allowed by way of "explanation" rather than as correction of an obvious mistake.

In considering the question of the correction of an obvious mistake it is, apparently, permissable to look at the convention document, *Minnesota Mining's (Vogel's) Application* [1973] RPC 578, at 580).

It was observed in *Kyowa's Application* ([1968] RPC RPC 101 and [1969] RPC 259) that an amendment by way of correction to remove insufficiency must describe matter not in substance disclosed in the specification before amendment and hence is unallowable; accordingly the possibility of amendment by way of correction appears to arise only in respect of an obvious mistake. But the presence of an apparent insufficiency is not to be equated with the presence of an obvious mistake, as the reader of the specification may simply suppose that the specification is insufficient (*Wilson's Patent*, [1968] RPC 197).

A031.14 *Amendment by "Explanation"*

An amendment by explanation is permissable only if it does not involve the addition of subject matter. Thus, in *Merck's Application* ((1952) 69 RPC 285) amendment to add a phrase to a claim was allowed as this only expressed with clarity the true construction of the unamended specification. It would seem, therefore, that the elaboration of a test procedure would be permissable as explanation, as also would the insertion of a reference to prior art. Also, in *Kyowa's Application* ([1968] RPC 101 and [1969] RPC 259) the PAT said (*obiter*) that, if a manufacturer's reference number for a micro-organism were "shown in a catalogue of a recognised culture number for a micro-organism were "shown in a catalogue of a recognised culture collection available to the public at the priority date to be identifiable under a culture collection number", then it could be permissable to add the culture collection number to the specification, which had only contained the manufacturer's number, as an explanatory amendment.

In *Lucas* v. *Gaedor* ([1978] it was permitted to add wording to the claim which, in effect, explained more fully the nature of the article claimed, this being a construction which the Court had anyway already placed on the unamended claim, see also *Jamesign's Application* ([1983] RPC 68) where a change of technical expression was held to express only what would have been understood by a person skilled in the art.

A statement of advantages was cancelled by way of explanation in *Plastics' Patent* ([1970] RPC 22).

The amendment disallowed in *Corning Glassworks' and Corning Ltd.'s Patent* ([1984] RPC 459 (CA)) as not being a disclaimer (see para. A031.09 *supra*) was deletion of wording can amount to "explanation" of the wording which remains where the deletion serves to cure an ambiguity. Thus, in *Polymer's Corp.'s Patent* ([1972] RPC 34), the deletion of sentences inconsistent with claim 1, and introduced into examples at the request of the examiner, was allowed by way of explanation. It was remarked that the sentences introduced uncertainty and that their deletion turned an ambiguous specification into a clear specification.

In *General Tire's (Frost's) Patent* ([1972] RPC 259 and [1974] RPC 207) the claim was limited to a dihyroxy-terminated compound, but the specification suggested that compounds with more than two hydroxy terminal groups could be used and actually recommended use of some compounds which the evidence showed to have four to five such groups on average. The patentees applied to amend "dihydroxy-terminated" to "having at least two terminal hydroxy groups," contending that the amendment was allowable either by way of explanation or as correction of an obvious mistake. On opposition the Hearing Officer allowed the amendment on either basis, the PAT refused them on either basis, and the Court of Appeal allowed them by way of explanation, construing the phrase as a threshold and not a ceiling.

Discretion **A031.15**

It is well established that amendment is not available as of right, but requires the exercise of discretion by the Comptroller of court, see para. 27.05. As already noted in para. A031.09 *supra*, even if an amendment is otherwise allowable, it may still be refused by refusal to exercise discretion. The exercise of discretion is discussed in the papers by R. P. Lloyd and G. Aggus listed in para. A031.02 *supra* and, because the discretionary nature of amendment remains under the 1977 Act, discretionary considerations in relation to permitted amendment are discussed in the commentary on section 27 [1977] at paras. 27.05–27.07. A difference in practice between mere excision of invalid claims and more extensive amendment to validate a claim found to be invalid is also noted in para. 75.06. However, there are noted here cases in which would not arise as such under the 1977 Act.

In *American Cyanamid's (Wilkinson and Shepherd's) Patent* ([1977] RPC 349) the patentees were permitted in section 30 proceedings to restrict their broad claims covering a vast group of chemical compounds to claims relating to a single compound which had become the drug of choice for treating tuberculosis. This was in order to avoid arguments of inutility and lack of fair basis. The amendment was opposed by the petitioner for revocation on the grounds of lack of candour in framing originally a claim alleged to be covetous, and also of unreasonable delay in applying for amendment. The court stated that, in the absence of proof to the contrary, it was bound to assume that the statements made in the specifications were originally framed as a fair generalisation from the necessarily limited experimental data then available to the patentees. Indeed, evidence showed that the claims as originally framed did not include any compounds which were known to have no activity whatsoever, although for some of them activity was very low indeed. Thus the question of delay did not properly arise. The court also declines to consider solely on affidavit evidence the question whether the amended claim would be invalid.

In *ICI's (Whyte's) Patent* ([1978] RPC 11) it was held that discretion should not be exercised against amendment merely because the patentee wished to improve its position as regards raising a possible prior claiming objection against a claim of later date. Moreover, amendments should not be refused on the grounds that the original claims were covetously broad unless it were proved that the patentee had knowingly and deliberately obtained claims of unjustified width, though the Office could, and should, demand evidence from patentees where there is good ground for suspecting covetousness in contrast to mere breadth of claim.

In *SCM's Application* ([1979] RPC 341), amendment by way of claim splitting to preserve a priority date was refused pending submission of evidence showing that a drafting mistake had truly been made. It would not be a drafting mistake, but rather an error of professional judgment, if the United Kingdom agent had given to draft the original claims in the unified form. It was stated that amendment is an indulgence which requires the fullest disclosure of the underlying facts.

ICI's (Small's) Patent ([1979] FSR 78) was a case where the patent had previously been unsuccessfully asserted as a prior claim in the *Daikin* case ([1974] RPC 589) in which the validity of the ICI claim in suit was doubted by the Court of Appeal. Amendment to overcome this criticism was then permitted even though (a) the claim had been asserted in the previous proceedings, (b) a previous more ambitious attempt at amendment had failed, and (c) the amendment only partially corrected the original intention of the draftsman. In allowing an amendment to the omnibus claim by partial disclaimer, the comment was made that the amended claim, like the unamended claim, was not of the kind susceptible to a notional splitting into discrete alternatives.

In *PPG's Industries Patent* (SRIS, O/119/85 and C/11/85, *noted* [1985] EIPR

973

D–212) discretion would have been refused by the Comptroller where the proposed amendment would have left the claim open to an objection of disunity of invention and, by the Patents Court because the specification should not set puzzles for its readers and because the proposed amendment was a broadening one to cure an alleged obvious mistake but the broadened scope would not have been subjected to search by the examiner. In dismissing a further appeal the Court of Appeal declined to comment on these views ([1987] RPC 469).

A031.16 *Withdrawal of requested amendment*

The Comptroller also has discretion to refuse to allow withdrawal of an application to amend (*Upjohn's (Beal's) Patent*, [1973] RPC 77), but if withdrawal is permitted, perhaps on the basis that the underlying circumstances are anyway recorded on the file of the patent, any subsequent attempt to seek that amendment is likely to be rejected in the exercise of discretion, see *GEC's Patent* ([1959] RPC 103 and 109).

A031.17   PRACTICE UNDER SECTION 31 [1949]

Where amendment is made by way of specific disclaimer of the claims of an earlier patent, for example to overcome an objection of "prior claiming", the disclaimer should be inserted at the end of the specification and the preamble to the claims amended to read: "Subject to the foregoing disclaimer, what is claimed is:".

A032.01   **SECTION 32 [1969]**

Revocation of patent by court

32.—(1) Subject to the provisions of this Act, a patent may, on the petition of any person interested, be revoked by the court on any of the following grounds that is to say,—

(*a*) that the invention, so far as claimed in any claim of the complete specification, was claimed in a valid claim of earlier priority date contained in the complete specification of another patent granted in the United Kingdom;

(*b*) that the patent was granted on the application of a person not entitled under the provisions of this Act to apply therefor;

(*c*) that the patent was obtained in contravention of the rights of the petitioner or any person under or though whom he claims;

(*d*) that the subject of any claim of the complete specification is not an invention within the meaning of this Act;

(*e*) that the invention, so far as claimed in any claim of the complete specification, is not new having regard to what was known or used, before the priority date of the claim, in the United Kingdom;

(*f*) that the invention, so far as claimed in any claim of the complete specification, is obvious and does not involve any inventive step having regard to what was known or used, before the priority date of the claim, in the United Kingdom;

974

(g) that the invention, so far as claimed in any claim of the complete specification, is not useful;

(h) that the complete specification does not sufficiently and fairly describe the invention and the method of which it is to be performed, or does not disclose the best method of performing it which was known to the applicant for the patent and for which he was entitled to claim protection;

(i) that the scope of any claim of the complete specification is not sufficiently and clearly defined or that any claim of the complete specification is not fairly based on the matter disclosed in the specification;

(j) that the patent was obtained on a false suggestion or representation;

(k) that the primary or intended use of exercise of the invention is contrary to law;

(l) that the invention, so far as claimed in any claim of the complete specification, was secretly used in the United Kingdom, otherwise than as mentioned in subsection (2) of this section, before the priority date of that claim.

(2) For the purposes of paragraph (l) of subsection (1) of this section, no account shall be taken of any use of the invention—

(a) for the purpose of reasonable trial or experiment only; or

(b) by a Government department or any person authorised by a Government department, in consequence of the applicant for the patent or any person from whom he derives title having communicated or disclosed the invention directly or indirectly to a Government department or person authorised as aforesaid; or

(c) by any other person, in consequence of the applicant for the patent or any person from whom he derives title having communicated or disclosed the invention, and without the consent or acquiescence of the applicant or of any person from whom he derives title;

and for the purposes of paragraph (e) or paragraph (f) of the said subsection (1) no account shall be taken of any secret use.

(3) [*Repealed*]

(4) Every ground on which a patent may be revoked shall be available as a ground of defence in any proceeding for the infringement of the patent.

Note. Subsection (1)(j) is effectively amended by Schedule 1, para. 6 [1977] reprinted in para. 133.01. Subsection (3) was repealed by Schedules 3 and 6 [1977].

COMMENTARY ON SECTION 32 [1949]

General   A032.02

Section 32 contains the provisions for the revocation of an existing patent. Since June 1, 1978 these provisions have applied both to revocation by the court and also in proceedings before the Comptroller under section 33 [1949] (as amended). However, before the 1977 Act, the Comptroller's powers to refuse an application on opposition under section 14 [1949] (or on "belated opposition" under section 33 [1949]) were much more restricted, see para. A014.

An existing patent may, on the petition of any person interested, be revoked by the court under section 32 on any of the 12 grounds specified under subsection (1) (with the limitations of subsection (2) in the case of objection under subsection (1)(e), (f) and (l)). Each of these grounds is also available as a ground of defence in an action for infringement of the patent (subs. (4)). Subsection (3) has been repealed as being otiose now that Crown use of a patent is no longer regarded as infringement thereof, see para. 55.03. The list of grounds for revocation in subsection (1) is exhaustive (*American Cyanamid's (Dann's) Patent*, [1971] RPC 425 (HL)).

Revocation actions under the section are normally by way of counterclaim in infringement proceedings, formerly under section 61 [1949] and now under section 74(1)(a) [1977]. The existence of such proceedings automatically provides the applicant for revocation with the necessary interest. Under other circumstances, application to the court for revocation is permitted, but most such actions will be brought as applications to the Comptroller under section 33 [1949]. Accordingly, for further discussion on the *locus standi* necessary under the present section, see para. A033.13.

Prior claiming (subs. (1)(a))

A032.03 —*General*

"Prior claiming" concerns the effect of a prior unpublished application on the validity of a claim of later date. The ambit of the ground of objection is one of considerable difficulty and, in *ICI's (Whyte's) Patent* ([1978] RPC 11 at 23), the Patents Appeal Tribunal, sitting *in banc* referred to:

> "unfortunate decisions which have been given upon the question of prior claim, of which *Kromschröder's Patent* ([1960] RPC 75 (CA)) is the prime example. The effect of these decisions has led to illogical and unreal results so far as concerns the legal position of earlier and later patents which are in prior claiming relationship."

It should also be noted that, with the exception of the *Kromschröder* decision, all the decisions discussed below have arisen under the opposition provisions of sections 14 and 33 [1949] under which a finding of invalidity was made only in a clear case.

Under the 1977 Act, the situation is dealt with quite differently by the provisions of section 2(3) [1977], see paras. 2.19–2.24.

From the *Kromschröder* case (*supra*) it would appear that revocation will only occur if there is found substantial identity of invention between distinct claims of the two patents having different priority dates. The *Kromschröder* case concerned two patents both in the name of *Kromschröder*. Claim 1 of the earlier patent was for a combination of parts which included one part claimed *per se* in the later patent. It was held by the Court of Appeal that there was no prior claiming on the ground that claims to A + B and to A are not identical with each other.

In earlier cases (but re-affirmed since in *Xerox Corp.'s (Chatterji's) Application*, [1979] RPC 375) prior claiming had been found on the basis of interpretation of a claim in the light of disclosure implicit in its specification. Thus, in *Babcock & Wil-*

cox's Application ((1952) 69 RPC 224) the recitation in a later apparatus claim of a feature of common general knowledge, which a competent designer would naturally have introduced, did not avoid substantial identity of claim. Again, when the two inventions claimed were processes and the difference between them lay in the inclusion in the later claim of a condition of operation of the process, the importance of which was common general knowledge at the date of publication of the earlier patent and which the reader of the earlier specification would have determined by routine experiments, the later claim was refused (*Commercial Solvents' Application*, (1954) 71 RPC 143). In this case the Patents Appeal Tribunal observed that the matter to be determined is "whether the difference between the two claims as a matter of language imports any real differentiation as a matter of inventive step".

—The "remonopolisation" test A032.04

From the *Xerox* case (*supra*) it seems that the present test of prior claiming involves the question whether the later claim, in fact, remonopolises the same invention as the earlier claim, and that this will occur when the later claim embraces the subject matter of the earlier claim in a manner in which the earlier invention can be identified in the later claim. This was the situation in *Merck's (Macek's) Patent* ([1967] RPC 157) where prior claiming was found and the *Kromschröder* case was explained and distinguished as involving a situation in which the prior patent claimed only a number of integers in combination and made no claim to one of such integers separately whilst the later patent claimed one of these integers independently of its association with the others. *Merck's (Macek's) Patent* was quoted and followed in *Wilkinson Sword's Application* ([1970] RPC 42) in which the applicant's main claim was wider than and included the subject matter of an earlier claim and, as a result, the later claim was held to be prior claimed.

A similar situation of apparent remonopolisation can now be seen also to explain the earlier decisions of: *Organon's Application* ([1962] RPC 119), where a later broad claim to a chemical product was held to be prior-claimed by a claim to the product made by a particular process; *Union Carbide's (Cuthbertson's) Application*, [1971] RPC 81), in which a claim to a mould with a particular surface was held to be in part prior-claimed by a claim to a method of making an alloy in such a mould, the inventive step being the same in both cases; and *Merck's (Arth's) Application* ([1973] RPC 220) where a claim to a chemical intermediate was held to overlap, and therefore to be prior-claimed by, an earlier claim for a limited use of that intermediate.

—Claims considered as bundle of discrete alternatives A032.05

The decisions discussed in paras. A032.04 *supra* need to be treated with some caution because the Court of Appeal decision in *Daikin Kogyo's (Shingu's) Application* ([1974] RPC 559) seems to have returned to the *Kromschröder* test of near identity of claims (discussed in para. A032.03 *supra*), though the decisions discussed in para. A032.04 can perhaps be rationalised on the basis of whether a claim should be regarded as a claim to a unitary group or class (which has to be considered as a whole) or as a list or collection of discrete alternative entities, prior claiming being more readily found in the latter type of case where the claim can be notionally split into those entities, as was done in *Merck (Macek's) Patent* [1967] RPC 157).

The major difficulty arises when the earlier claim is a broad one and the later claim more narrow. If the later claim could have been validly obtained as a selection if that earlier claim had been prior published, it must be allowed (*Ethyl Corp.'s*

Patent, [1970] RPC 227), but failure to pass this test is not necessarily fatal (*Westinghouse's (Frost's) Application*, [1973] RPC 139). The test is then not whether the later claim could have been framed from the disclosure of the earlier specification, but whether it was in fact so framed, see *Montecatini Edison's Patent* ([1975] FSR 446).

What is clear is that a mere infringement situation is not sufficient. Thus, in the *Daikin* case (*supra*), it was stated:

"Where an earlier claim is wider in scope than a later claim and there is no separate claim in the earlier specification restricted to the subject matter of the later claim, the claimant of the earlier claim cannot assert that he has made a prior claim to the subject matter of the later claim."

However, it should be noted that, in the *Daikin* case, only some of the experiments covered in a single omnibus claim would have infringed the later claim. All the experiments were stated to illustrate "our invention" and also, in view of its precise wording, the omnibus claim was held not to be notionally divisible as had been done in *Merck's (Macek's) Patent* ([1967] RPC 157): thus in the *Daikin* case there was no prior claiming. Also, in *Lucas* v. *Gaedor* ([1978] RPC 297), infringement was found in respect of an article which was described in a patent of earlier date, but it was held that the claims of the two patents were so wholly different that the objection of prior claiming could not be upheld. Similarly, in *British Cast Iron's Patent* ([1976] RPC 33), there was no prior claiming because no claim of the prior specification contained as a distinct feature a limitation corresponding to the distinguishing feature of the later claim.

In *Badische Anilin's (Distler's) Application* ([1977] FSR 137) a broad claim to a class of chemical compounds was held not to be a prior claim to a later claim to one specific member of the class. The broad claim was held not to be notionally divisible, particularly because of the breadth of the class involved. The Patents Appeal Tribunal was obviously much influenced by the fact that the earlier specification contained no specific mention of the single compound which was the subject of the later claim. This case also contains some remarks pertinent to the question of the later claim fulfilling the requirements of a selection patent.

In *Allen & Hanburys' (Hayes') Application* ([1977] RPC 113) it was said that there was no single test of prior claiming, but that each case had to be decided on its merits. Thus, whether a general chemical formula ought to be regarded as a convenient way of specifying a number of discrete alternatives, which would occur to the reader on seeing the formula must, in each case, be a matter of degree. In this case, in contrast to the *Badische* case (*supra*), it was held to be proper to rewrite a claim to a general chemical formula so that it included specifically within its scope such particular compounds, the specific formula of which "would as a matter of course occur to the reader as being within and disclosed by the general formula". However, other formulae within the general formula should not be regarded as having been specifically disclosed so that, following *Westinghouse's (Frosts's) Application* (*supra*), in respect of these there was no prior claim, at least so far as opposition proceedings were concerned.

It is suggested that prior claiming will only be found to exist where the features of the later claim are to be found within a single claim of the earlier patent and preferably, as a discrete alternative within the scope of that claim. Otherwise, the *Kromschröder* case will continue to be followed as was done in the *Daikin* case, see also *Esso Research's Application* ([1971] FSR 118) which involved a somewhat similar fact situation in relation to an omnibus claim. Also, in *Standard Telephones' Patent* (SRIS C/19/85, *noted* [1985] EIPR D-48), it was stressed that it is not sufficient for prior claiming that the concepts of the two claims should be the same:

equivalent wording must be used and this was not so here where the term "element" was construed in a manner such that the claim was fairly based on its priority document.

—Prior claim must be valid   **A032.06**

It should be remembered that subsection (1)(*a*) requires that the prior claim be valid. However, the onus on proving invalidity will be on him who seeks to defend his claim against an objection of prior claiming otherwise likely to be upheld, see *EMI* v. *Radio and Allied Industries* ([1960] RPC 115). Likewise, a revoked patent cannot be the basis of a prior claim (*Techniservice's Application*, [1968] FSR 389). The question of a lapsed prior grant is less clear, but note the use of the words "was claimed" in subsection (1)(*a*). In *Dow Chemical* v. *Ishihara Sangyo* ([1985] FSR 4) the validity of an alleged prior claim was allowed to be put in issue despite the provisions of section 74(2) [1977].

—Avoiding prior claim by disclaimer   **A032.07**

Because the objection of prior claiming, if upheld, is one of identity of invention, there is no necessity for the subject matter of the later claim to involve an inventive step over the invention of the earlier claim. Therefore, where the earlier claim is narrower than the later claim, it will normally be possible to overcome the prior claiming objection by a direct disclaimer of the subject matter of the earlier claim (*Comptroller's Ruling, 1922(C)*, (1922) 39 RPC Appendix v, following p. 340). However, care should be taken in making this type of amendment not to introduce an ambiguity into the amended claim by virtue of an ambiguity present in the earlier claim which is being disclaimed from the scope of the later claim.

Applicant not entitled to apply (subs. (1)(b)), and patent obtained in contravention   **A032.08**
    of the rights of the petitioner (subs. (1)(c))

These two grounds of objection overlap and can be considered together. Most of the cases relevant to subsection (1)(*b*) and (*c*) are those which arose under the opposition ground that the applicant for the patent had "obtained" the invention or any part thereof from the opponent, but see *Loben* v. *Bader Machinery* ([1965] RPC 548) for an unsuccessful attack under subsection (1)(*b*). The word "contravention" in subsection (1)(*c*) replaced the word "fraud" used in the 1907 Act thus indicating that fraud is not a necessary ingredient of the objection. This is supported by *Usher* v. *Nordhoff* [*New Zealand*] ([1972] RPC 636) which states that "obtaining" need not be intentional. Under the 1977 Act the corresponding ground of revocation is that of section 72(1)(*b*), for which see para. 72.17.

Subsection (1)(*b*) matches section 1 [1949] which defines the persons who may apply for a patent. It is therefore effective when an existing patent has been granted on a non-convention application made without the true inventor, or his assignee or the personal representative of a deceased person who was entitled to apply, being an applicant therefor. However, in *Beumer (Bernhard) Maschinenfabrik's Patent* (SRIS O/120/83), the Comptroller refused to allow a pleading under section 32(1)(*b*) based on an allegation that the applicant had failed to comply with the provisions of section 1(2) [1949] required for convention applications, see para. A032.31 *infra*.

Following the ideas expressed in the article "The right to work" by B. C. Reid ([1982] EIPR 6), it is perhaps worthy of consideration whether objection under subsection (1)(*c*) could provide a useful alternative to a plea of prior grant under subsection (1)(*a*) and thereby avoid the restrictive effect of some of the decisions discussed in paras. A032.03–A032.07 *supra*.

There is authority that "obtaining" arises where the applicant found out about the nature of the invention claimed from someone else and filed the application without the consent of that person (*International Carbon's Application*, [1975] RPC 365). That case apparently involved a factual situation in which the invention was made at a time when the inventor was employed by the opponents, but the application had been filed by a subsequent employer of the inventor: "obtaining" was held to exist where the inventor's service agreement with the first employer prevented him from giving consent to the filing by the second employer. Also, if an applicant for revocation can show communication of the invention to the public, the onus of proof is shifted to the patentee to show that he had made the invention prior to the communication (*Perrett's Application*, (1932) 49 RPC 406 and *Jackson and Molloy's Patent*, SRIS O/88/83).

In proceedings before the Patent Office, no account has been taken of obtaining abroad (*Dicker's Application*, (1934) 51 RPC 392 and *Du Pont's Application* [1965] RPC 582). However, an invention was held to have been obtained when information about it was received by post from a company abroad in response to a written request from the United Kingdom and an ordinary application was made without the knowledge or consent of the foreign company (*H's Application*, [1956] RPC 197). The question of "obtaining" abroad is complicated by two factors: the concept under the 1949 Act that the first importer of an invention into the United Kingdom is to be regarded in law as the inventor; and whether the action of the "obtainer" would amount to unlawful conduct, such as theft, according to the law of the place in which the alleged act of obtaining took place. Subject to consideration of these factors, however, there would seem no inherent objection to raising an objection of foreign obtaining under subsections (1)(*b*) or (*c*).

A032.09 *Claim not for invention as defined by the 1949 Act (subs. (1)(d))*

For the purposes of the 1949 Act the term "invention" is defined in section 101 [1949] mainly by reference to section 6 of the Statute of Monopolies (reprinted at para. B01) and discussed in paras. A101.05–A101.09. The objection is one that has rarely been successfully taken in proceedings under section 32 [1949] because it has been the Patent Office practice to consider the question closely during the examination before the Comptroller. Nevertheless, the objection was carefully considered, and the main precedent cases reviewed, in *American Cyanamid* v. *Berk* ([1976] RPC 231), though then rejected.

In *Reitzman* v. *Grahame-Chapman* ((1950) 67 RPC 178 and (1951) 68 RPC 25), it was held that a process of separating articles cemented together by rust was a mere discovery that an old process would produce its result under more difficult conditions and was not a patentable manner of manufacture.

It would seem possible under this head to argue that a patent should be revoked on the ground that it is, or has become, contrary to section 6 of the Statute of Monopolies as "mischievous to the State . . . or generally inconvenient", see *Rolls Royce's Application* ([1963] RPC 251).

A032.10 *Lack of novelty (subs. (1)(e))*

Subsection (1)(*e*) covers the objection of lack of novelty by either prior publication or use and would seem to include oral publication by its reference to knowledge". However, knowledge must have been gained, and any prior use practised, by a member of the public acting as such, on which point see *Catnic* v. *Evans* ([1983] FSR 410), *Bristol-Myers' Application* ([1969] RPC 146) and para. A101.10.

The objection is closely similar in principle to that arising from failure to comply with section 2(1) and (2) [1977], for which see paras. 2.06–2.11. However, the major difference is that, under the 1949 Act, knowledge and use outside the United Kingdom are specifically excluded from consideration. Other differences from the novelty requirements of section 2 [1977] are the saving provisions of sections 50–52 [1949] discussed in the commentaries thereon. As with the position under the 1977 Act, prior secret use is not destructive of novelty as such (subs. (2)) but, unlike the position under the 1977 Act, prior secret use may be a separate ground of invalidity in certain circumstances, see subsection (1)(*l*) and para. A032.35 *infra*.

—Prior use   **A032.11**

The importance of deciding whether a prior use falls under subsection (1)(*e*) (*public prior use*) or under subsection (1)(*l*) (*secret prior use*) is that an objection of obviousness under sections (1)(*f*) can lie in the former, but not the latter, case, as discussed in para. A032.13 *infra*. Since the opposite of "public" is "private" (and not "secret"), considerable difficulties can arise in determining whether a given non-public prior use, which is not a direct anticipation, (*i.e.* novelty-destroying), can be relied upon to render a claim obvious.

The extent to which use in a factory is secret is clearly one of fact. In *Reitzman* v. *Grahame-Chapman* ((1950) 67 RPC 178) it was held that prior use inside a factory to which the public had no access was a secret use not invalidating the patent. In the *Reitzman* case it was also held that a demonstration of the invention to government officials was not a prior use invalidating the patent, but this decision might well be regarded as flowing from section 51(1). In contrast, in *Fomento* v. *Mentmore* ((1955) 72 RPC 287 and [1956] RPC 87), the gift of a pen to an airforce officer was held to be prior use because the pen was given to him in his capacity as a member of the public.

The unconditional sale of a substance on the open market is prior use, even if the substance is unidentifiable. If no steps intended to conceal what is being done are taken, the use is not a secret use: "secret use" means a use intentionally concealed by the user, see *Bristol-Myers' (Johnson's) Application* ([1973] RPC 157 (CA), particularly the judgment of Lord Denning; and [1975] RPC 127 (HL), particularly the judgment of Lord Diplock giving the principal judgment for the narrow 3–2 decision on this point). In that case the Patents Appeal Tribunal had held that an accidental, unappreciated production of a substance did not qualify as a use at all, but all subsequent courts hearing the case disagreed, see [1973] RPC 147 and the Court of Appeal and House of Lords judgments (*supra*). An offer for sale made after a demonstration becomes a public use immediately the offer is accepted, even if the goods are only delivered after a patent application has been filed. (*Wheatley's Application*, [1985] RPC 91 (CA)). Here it was held: that "used" should be given the meaning it has in ordinary usage; that, by agreeing to sell, the applicant had used his invention to achieve his commercial object; and that to hold otherwise would enable an inventor to reap the benefit of his monopoly for a period longer than the Act prescribes. For a further instance of anticipation by an isolated instance of prior use, see *Windsurfing International* v. *Tabur Marine* (SRIS C/136/82; and [1985] RPC 59 (CA)).

Prior importation of a product made abroad by a subsequently patented process anticipates a claim to that process even if examination of the product would not reveal the method by which it had been made (*Gore (W.H.)* v. *Kimal*, [1988] RPC 137). The question whether it is a requirement that prior use under the 1949 Act should pass the means of knowledge for it to be anticipatory is further discussed in para. 2.17.

A032.12 *—Single instance of prior publication or use*

A single instance of publication suffices to deny novelty to a subsequent claim (*Bristol-Myers' Application*, [1969] RPC 146), as does a single instance of prior use (*Fomento* v. *Mentmore*, (1955) 72 RPC 287 and (1956) 73 RPC 87 (CA)). However, surprise has been expressed by the Court of Appeal that this should be so (*Laguerre's Patent*, [1971] RPC 384 (CA)). To this should perhaps be added the remark of the same court in *Woven Plastics* v. *British Ropes* ([1970] FSR 47 (CA)) that it was unrealistic that Japanese utility model specifications could be said to be "known" in the United Kingdom when merely received in the Science Reference Library a few days before the priority date of the patent claim in issue, although counsel declined to argue the case from such a standpoint.

A032.13 *Obviousness and lack of inventive step (subs. (1)(f))*

This ground of revocation is sometimes referred to in the older cases as involving a lack of subject matter. It would appear to be the same objection to validity as now arises under section 3 [1977] and the commentary thereon therefore constitutes the main commentary on subsection (1)(f).

There is, however, the important difference that prior knowledge, publication or use outside the United Kingdom are specifically excluded from consideration of inventive step under the present subsection (1)(f). Nevertheless, use abroad can be used to corroborate an argument of obviousness over common general knowledge to show that others have done the same thing independently, see *Lucas* v. *Gaedor* ([1978] RPC 297), but obviousness is primarily to be judged against the knowledge of a person skilled in the relevant art at the priority date of the claim and then resident in the United Kingdom (*Rockwell International* v. *Cape Insulation*, SRIS C/17/80).

Subsection (2) makes it clear that no secret use can be taken into account for the purposes of the present provision, and sections 50–52 [1949] likewise prevent certain other prior art from destroying inventive step, despite the fact that sections 50 and 51 use the word "anticipated" which usually, but not apparently here, refers to a lack of novelty only, see para. A050.2.

In *Technograph* v. *Mills and Rockley* ([1972] RPC 346 (HL)) there was disunity as to whether "having regard to what was known or used" has the same meaning in subsection (1)(e) (*lack of novelty*) as in subsection (1)(f) (*obviousness*), but in *Windsurfing International* v. *Tabur Marine* ([1905] RPC 59 (CA)), it was stated:

> "We can see no context for giving the words 'having regard to what was used' any different meaning for the purposes of sub-paragraph (f) [than for the purposes of sub-paragraph (e)]."

This judgment has been criticised by S. Gratwick ((1986) 102 LQR 403 in a sequel to his 1972 paper written after the *Technograph* case ((1972) 88 LQR 341–356.

The distinction between heads (e) and (f) was also drawn in an indirect way in *Minnesota Mining* v. *Bondina* ([1973] RPC 491) where it was pointed out that under head (e) a publication must be construed as at its date of publication, whereas under head (f) it will be considered at the priority date of the patent, but in relation to the prior art as a whole in the light of all the surrounding circumstances as a kind of jury question. The "circumstances of publication" presumably include not only the relative obscurity of the prior art in question, but also the persons who would be likely to become aware of it, as well as its degree of antiquity. On these points, see para. 3.17.

Inutility (subs. (1)(g))

—*General* **A032.14**

The objection that the invention as claimed is not useful does not appear as such in the 1977 Act, but may fall to be considered thereunder as a lack of sufficient description, for which see paras. 14.15–14.18, particularly para. 14.18. However, under the 1949 Act, the objection is a separate one and, therefore, needs to be distinctly pleaded and argued, it normally being unwise to rely solely on an objection of insuffiency under subsection (1)(*h*) (discussed at paras. A032.17–A032.22 *infra*). In pleading an objection under subsection (1)(*g*) no particulars need be given, though before trial the patentee will normally have acquired knowledge of the nature of the objection as a result of being given notice of pre-trial experiments. It should also be noted that intutility as such was not a ground of opposition under repealed section 14 [1949], though it may now be raised in revocation proceedings before the Comptroller under the revised form of section 33 [1949]. Thus, it is only since 1978 that the Patent Office has had any jurisdiction to consider intutility pleaded as such and, as yet, the Comptroller has not apparently given any decision on the point.

—*Types of inutility, and overlap with other grounds* **A032.15**

Occurrences of inutility can be divided roughly into two types. In the first type, the invention as claimed cannot be performed, or something falling within the claim does not function. In such cases, the objection tends to overlap the grounds of insufficiency (subs. (1)(*h*)), as it can be said that the specification does not describe how to perform the invention. In the second type, the claim covers an embodiment which, though it may work and may even be of practical use, does not provide a benefit claimed for the invention, see for example *Horville* v. *Clares* ([1976] RPC 411), where the alleged infringement fell within the scope of the claims but did not have the advantage stated for the invention in the description. This type of inutility may result from over-enthusiastic "objects" clauses in the patent specification. In cases of this type, the objection tends to overlap the ground of false suggestion (subs. (1)(*j*)), as it can be said that the patent includes a representation (that a certain advantage flows from the invention) which is not true (see para. A032.32 *infra*), and possibly also lack of fair basis, for which see para. A032.29 *infra*.

The overlap of inutility with insufficiency was discussed in *Valensi* v. *British Radio* ([1973] RPC 337 at 378). Inutility requires proof that the claimed invention will not work as described, or with any modification which the addressee can properly be expected to make; whereas, if a proposed modification is one which he cannot be expected to make, the specification is insufficient. The *Valensi* case contains detailed observations (at pp. 375–377) on the expertise which the notional addressee of a specification can be expected to have, on which point see para. 14.17.

Although the objection of inutility also often overlaps with that of "false suggestion" under subsection (1)(*j*), it is usually necessary to distinguish between these two heads because inutility may be curable by restrictive amendment, whereas a finding of false suggestion may amount to a finding that the Crown has been deceived in its grant, in which case discretion to permit amendments is unlikely to be exercised.

—*Scope of the objection of inutility* **A032.16**

Objection under subsection (1)(*g*) is only likely to succeed if it is shown that an embodiment falling fairly within the claim will not perform or function as stated in the specification. It is not possible to construe a claim so as to exclude obviously inoperative embodiments (*Norton and Gregory* v. *Jacobs* (1937) 54 RPC 58 and 271 and *Minerals Separation* v. *Noranda*, (1952) 69 RPC 81 at 95). In *Sonotone* v. *Multitone* ((1955) 72 RPC 131 at 146) (CA)), the specification contained a promise which was not fulfilled, but which would not have misled anyone expert in the art. Nevertheless, the claims to which the promise related were held to be invalid. Subsequently, in *Henriksen* v. *Tallon* ([1965] RPC 434 (HL)), it was held that a construction of the claim which led to an absurd result must be rejected and that, consequently, the attack of inutility failed. Thus, the question of inutility is closely linked to the question of construction of claim and a court can avoid the objection by giving the claim a limited scope, if its wording should so permit. Perhaps, therefore, a claim defined by being limited by a requirement that its subject matter must function in a stated manner can never be invalid on the ground of inutility, although such a functional claim may fail under heads (*h*) (*insufficiency*) or (*i*) (*ambiguity or indefiniteness of claiming*), for which see respectively paras. A032.17–A032.22 and A032.28 *infra*. Thus, in *American Cyanamid* v. *Berk* ([1976] RPC 231), the invention claimed was defined by reference to an experimental test. The test was not sufficiently clearly defined and the patent was found invalid for insufficiency, ambiguity, inutility and false suggestion.

While inutility was found in *Reymes-Cole* v. *Elite Hosiery* ([1965] RPC 102), where it was shown that the method claimed could not be carried out, and also in *Horville* v. *Clares* ([1976] RPC 411), it was indicated in *American Cyanamid* v. *Ethicon* ([1979] RPC 215) that inutility does not exist where a satisfactory material is obtained after the use of certain purification steps which the instructed reader desirous of achieving success would be expected to perform.

It is, therefore, important to demonstrate an alleged inutility by evidence, see *Rosedale* v. *Carlton* ([1959] RPC 189 and [1960] RPC 59 (CA)) and *Olin Mathieson* v. *Biorex* ([1970] RPC 157). If there is a conflict of evidence on inutility, the court will favour the evidence of an expert rather than that of the theorist who challenges the expert conclusion (*Chevron Research's Patent*, [1975] FSR 1). Nevertheless, the fact of inutility can be admitted and the argument presented that the inoperative embodiment is outside the construction of the claim. This argument has been tried, but unsuccessfully, both in *Raleigh* v. *Miller* ((1948) 65 RPC 141 (HL)) and in *Dow Chemical* v. *Spence Bryson (No. 2)* ([1982] FSR 598 and [1984] RPC 359 (CA)). In the latter case an argument that the claim should be construed functionally was rejected as being contrary to *Norton and Gregory* v. *Jacobs* (*supra*).

Insufficiency of description (subs. (1)(h))

A032.17   —*General*

This objection to validity also includes a failure to comply with the requirements of section 4(3)(*b*) [1949] with regard to the specification describing the best method of performing the invention, but this particular objection is discussed separately in paras. A032.23–A032.26 *infra*. Otherwise, the objection under subsection (1)(*h*) has obvious similarities with the requirements of section 14(3) [1977] so that the commentary thereon at paras. 14.15–14.18 is also relevant. Nevertheless, the ambit of the objection under the two Acts may be somewhat different as discussed in para. 14.18.

The issue of insufficiency under subsection (1)(*h*) raises two distinct issues, *viz*: (1) that the complete specification does not sufficiently and fairly describe *the invention*; and (2) that the complete specification does not sufficiently and fairly describe the *method by which the invention is to be performed* (*Edison and Swan* v. *Holland*, (1889) 6 RPC 243).

Some of the difficulties that can arise in the pleading and defence of allegations of insufficiency are illustrated by two interlocutory decisions given on *Polaroid Corp.'s Patent* ([1977] FSR 233 and 243). Also, in *Halcon* v. *Shell* ([1977] FSR 458), requests for further and better particulars of a plea of insufficiency were rejected as relating more to the construction of the specification and also because it is for the defendants to make out their allegations of invalidity without assistance from the patentees.

—Insufficient or unfair description of the "invention"   A032.18

Revocation will be ordered under the first limb of subsection (1)(*h*) if the claims of the patent are broad to the point of speculation, or if the reader is not told adequately what the invention is (*Amchem's Patent*, [1978] RPC 271). However, the specification is not insufficient if there is an adequate description of a method of operation, even though objections may be levelled at the language used (*Reitzman* v. *Grahame-Chapman*, (1950) 67 RPC 178 at 188).

The question of an unfair description was considered in *Fuji Photo's (Kiritani's) Application* ([1978] RPC 413) where the distinction drawn in *Edison* v. *Holland* (*supra*) was again drawn. In the *Fuji Photo* case the opposed claim concerned the use of defined compounds as solvents for making colour-former solutions for use in pressure-sensitive recording materials. Some of these defined compounds were solid at working temperatures and it was therefore unclear whether or not the use of such compounds was included within the scope of the claim. The Patents Appeal Tribunal endorsed the Comptroller's decision that the presence in the specification of a statement that certain compounds, now admitted by the applicant's witness to be solid at working temperatures, had certain properties, including viscosity, which were required for the stated purpose, was entirely misleading so that in this respect the description of the invention was unfair.

An unusual definition in a specification does not render a description of the invention insufficient or unfair, provided that the definition is not lacking in clarity (*Warnant's Application* [1956] RPC 205). Nor is the description insufficient because it fails to set out details of re-design which are necessary in the adoption of the invention (*Patchett's Applications* [1959] RPC 57). Also in *Holliday's Application* ([1978] RPC 27) an allegation of insufficiency was rejected on the ground that the term "synergistic effect" was one which had a meaning well understood in the art. In *Eastman Kodak's Application* ([1970] RPC 548) the claim referred to the "limiting melting point" of a polymer and the specification indicated that this should be determined in the manner described in a foreign publication. An allegation of insufficiency resulting from the non-availability of that publication in the United Kingdom was rejected because the witness appeared to be familiar with the analytical technique and there was no evidence that copies could not be obtained on request.

In *Du Pont* v. *Enka* ([1988] FSR 69) a claim lacked fair basis by being open-ended, and the description was held to be insufficient in relation to that part of the scope of the claim which extended beyond the specific description, see also *Eastman Kodak's Application* (*supra*) for another example of an open-ended claim found invalid for lack of fair basis.

An unjustified statement derogatory of a prior art patent may cause insufficiency (*Raufos' Patent*, SRIS O/12/85 and C/102/86, *noted* IPD 10036, applying *Ehrig and Keilhauer's Application*, (1933) 50 RPC 176).

In *Wilson's Patent* ([1968] RPC 197), however, an opposition based on insufficiency succeeded when the applicant was forced to admit that a compound required by the claim as starting material was unknown at the relevant date and incapable of being made according to the instructions contained in the specifications. An attempt at correction failed as it was not obvious that there was a mistake: the reader may simply suppose that the specification was insufficient, see para. A031.13. However, the decision, on this ground, may perhaps be doubted in view of the later decision in *American Cyanamid's (Dann's) Patent* ([1971] RPC 425 (HL)) where it was held that the grounds of revocation set out in section 32 are exhaustive and do not include the objection that a necessary starting material was not available to the public. Nevertheless, the starting material must be adequately described, which in *Wilson's Patent (supra)* it was not, see also *Bristol-Myers' (Johnson and Hardcastle's) Application* ([1974] RPC 389).

In *American Cyanamid v. Berk* ([1976] RPC 231) insufficiency was also found because the claimed invention depended upon an experimental test which was not clearly defined.

A032.19   —*Insufficient description of the method of performing the invention*

The question under the second limb of subsection (1)(*h*) is whether the description which has been given is sufficient to enable a person, who (at a relevant date) was reasonably skilled in the particular field, to make an embodiment of the invention which would make it fall within the objects of the invention (*Dual Manufacturing's Patent* [1977] RPC 189), see also *Procter & Gamble's Application* ([1982] RPC 473). There is no objection to carrying out experiments within the competence of the addressee, but evidence of what the man skilled in the art might be able to do will be of vital importance in establishing an insufficiency. Also "normal use", if referred to as such, must be such as to ensure that the user should take care to carry out the method which he was instructed to use, that is on the basis that the notional skilled workman reading the specification was trying to get the result which the draftsman told him was required (*Blendax-Werke's Application* [1980] RPC 491), see also *American Cyanamid v. Ethicon* ([1979] RPC 215).

The *Dual Manufacturing* and *Procter & Gamble* cases also stated that such points as: whether the scope of the monopoly claimed is unclear; or whether inconsistencies exist between claims and disclosure; or whether there is no, or an erroneous, explanation of the function of a particular mechanism, where such an explanation was not necessary for the purpose of instructing the reader to build an embodiment of the invention as described, were all irrelevant to the plea of insufficiency as such. Accordingly, care should be taken to plead such objections under the appropriate provisions of section 32(1), particularly in proceedings before the Comptroller under the revised section 33 [1949], see *Wülfing's Patent* (SRIS O/91/81, *noted* IPD 4107), where an objection of inutility failed, but it was indicated that a plea of insufficiency might have succeeded if it had been raised.

A032.20   —*Date for determination of sufficiency*

In *American Cyanamid's (Dann's) Patent* ([1971] RPC 425 (HL)) Lord Diplock indicated, in his dissenting judgment, that the date when a specification should be sufficient is the date when it is published, and the Court of Appeal has held that sufficiency should be determined in the light of the common general knowledge of the public at the date of publication of the specification because until then the public is not at all concerned with the question (*Standard Brands' Patent (No. 2)*, [1981] RPC 499 (CA)). For further discussion of this point, see para. 14.15. Nevertheless, in determining the question of priority date it has been held that the priority document should be construed without having any regard to knowledge arising later than its date of filing (*Mutoh Industrial's Application*, [1978] RPC 70), but in such a case the priority document is being construed as a document of record as of its filing date, rather than as a document supporting the claims of a patent monopoly.

—Overcoming insufficiency may give rise to other objections　　　　　**A032.21**

In the *Standard Brands'* case (*supra*) the specification described the invention only in the broadest terms without any particularity. It was argued that by the date of publication it would have been obvious to the man skilled in the art how to perform the invention without further description to obtain the results promised. The argument was unsuccessful, the court observing that an inventor was not entitled to set the reader of his specification a puzzle and call it a complete specification. The patent was revoked. Although no decision on obviousness was given, the court pointed out that, in view of the argument on insuffiency, the patentee would have had serious difficulty in establishing that the invention claimed was not obvious at the date of filing. A similar case involving a potential overlap between the objections of insufficiency and obviousness, so that if one fails the other is the more likely to succeed, was *Amchem's Patent* ([1978] RPC 271).

—Inventions relating to micro-organisms　　　　　**A032.22**

The special provisions for specifications relating to the use of micro-organisms applicable under the 1977 Act, for which now see section 125A and the commentary thereon at para. 125A.05 *et seq.*, are not applicable as such to existing patents, though there is little doubt that the provisions of the 1949 Act will be met if the more stringent requirement of the 1977 Act and Rules made thereunder have been met. Thus, where a micro-organism required for a claimed fermentation process had been deposited in a culture collection, it was held that the micro-organism was sufficiently described in the specification and the specification was held to be sufficient (*Dann's Application*, [1966] RPC 532) even though a sample was not available to the public at the date of publication of the specification, a feature which would now invalidate a patent granted under the 1977 Act. The sufficiency of this specification was subsequently upheld by the House of Lords in *American Cyanamid's (Dann's) Patent* ([1971] RPC 425), see para. A032.19 *supra*. However, in another fermentation process the applicants identified the micro-organism solely by reference to their own code, which was not available to the public; the application was, consequently, rejected (*Kyowa's Application* [1966] FSR 108). In an appeal thereon ([1968] RPC 101) it was held that if the reference numbers of the applicant's code had been bracketed with those in a culture collection catalogue available to the public at the priority date, the insufficiency could have been cured. The application was refused for lack of adequate evidence to this effect.

Best method not disclosed

—General　　　　　**A032.23**

The requirement of section 4(3)(*b*) [1949] is that the complete specification shall disclose the best method of performing the invention which is known to the applicant and for which he is entitled to claim protection. This is not a requirement for patents granted under the 1977 Act, but failure of an existing patent to meet it is a ground of revocation under section 32(1)(*h*) [1949].

There is little authority on the ambit of this objection because there are few cases, but in *Norton and Gregory* v. *Jacobs* ((1937) 54 RPC 58 and 271) the facts emerged during the trial and the patent was revoked. Nowadays, the greater scope of the pre-trial discovery of documents is more likely to reveal information leading to the plea.

In *American Cyanamid* v. *Berk* ([1976] RPC 231) a description of certain strains of micro-organisms taken from the inventor's notes prior to filing the application showed that two strains not deposited gave better results than four strains that were deposited and the patent was revoked, *inter alia*, for failure to disclose the best method.

In the case where a product or article is claimed by reference to its shape, "the best method of performing the invention" means the most advantageous form of the product or article (*Illinois Tool Works* v. *Autobars*, [1974] RPC 337 at 369). Where the claim is to a process, the specification need not state how or where the starting material therefor may be obtained (*American Cyanamid's (Dann's) Patent*, [1971] RPC 425).

The question of "best method" is one not merely to be decided on the language of the specification, and evidence can be put forward to show that the disclosure, in whatever terms it was made, was in fact a disclosure of the best method, though difficulty will no doubt arise where the language of the specification is entirely general with little or no specific disclosure of any particular way of carrying out the invention (*Garlock's Application*, [1979] FSR 604), see also *Udylite's Application* ([1968] RPC 225).

Note also that the applicant must be entitled to claim protection for the method. In *Du Pont* v. *Enka* ([1988] FSR 69) this was interpreted as requiring that the applicant must be entitled to claim protection for the "best method" by virtue of the same right as his right to the invention, so that it can properly be described in the same specification. See also *Monsanto* v. *Maxwell Hart* ([1981] RPC 201), where the non-disclosed feature was the contribution of a different inventor and had not been assigned to the applicant on the United Kingdom filing date, though the applicant was entitled to call for an assignment.

A032.24   *—Date of knowledge of "best method"*

The question whether failure to disclose is to be determined as of the priority date of the claim or at the date of filing the complete specification has not been authoritatively decided. In *American Cyanamid* v. *Ethicon* ([1979] RPC 515) an allegation of non-disclosure of the best method of performing the invention was rejected on a holding that there is no obligation on an applicant to incorporate in the complete specification improvements made after the filing of the priority application. However, in *Monsanto* v. *Maxwell Hart* ([1981] RPC 201) the relevant date of knowledge of the best method was taken as the period shortly before the filing of the complete specification. In South Africa, it has been held that the relevant date is the date of filing the application (*Enka* v. *Du Pont* [*South Africa*], noted [1987] EIPR D-106).

A032.25   *—Nature of knowledge of "best method"*

In *Monsanto* v. *Maxwell Hart* ([1981] RPC 201) it was held that "known" in section 32(1)(*h*) required a degree of certainty such that the patentee has defrauded the public by his non-disclosure, and that the section was directed against dishonest conduct. However, in *Du Pont* v. *Enka* ([1988] FSR 69), it was held that the objection is not restricted to cases of dishonest conduct and defrauding the public, but applies to any case of non-disclosure, "whatever the reason for the omission". In *Enka* v. *Du Pont* [*South Africa*] (*noted* [1987] EIPR D-106) it was also held that bad faith is irrelevant.

In *Du Pont* v. *Enka* (*supra*) it was held that in the case of a body corporate, the relevant knowledge is that of the person who gave instructions for the application, and controlled it on the company's behalf. properly instructed so as to be in possession of the relevant information. In *Enka* v. *Du Pont* [*South Africa*] (*supra*) it was held to be necessary for the patentee to know that the non-disclosed method was better: this was then established by a contemporaneous note written by the inventor.

—Nature of the non-disclosed method   **A032.26**

The alleged non-disclosed method must be a method of performing the invention, and it must be better than any method described in the specification, see *Enka* v. *Du Pont* [*South Africa*] (*noted* [1987] EIPR D-106).

"Ambiguity" and lack of fair basis (subs. (1)(i))

—General   **A032.2**

Subsection (1)(*i*) provides for revocation of an existing patent if the scope of a claim is not sufficiently and clearly defined, or if any claim is not fairly based on the matter disclosed in the specification: the latter ground of objection is considered in para. A032.29 *infra*. There is a similar requirement for clarity under section 14(5)(*b*) [1977], see para. 14.24.

—When ambiguity arises   **A032.28**

The ground of ambiguity arises particularly when there are two literal constructions of a claim and a court is unable to distinguish between them. The plea is often made, but in modern times has rarely succeeded: the court seems to prefer to find for a particular construction of a claim and then consider its validity on the basis of the other objections available. Thus, in *Van der Lely* v. *Ruston's Engineering* ([1985] RPC 461 (CA)), it was held that the claims were either so vague as to be ambiguous, or otherwise had such breadth as to lack fair basis. In *Dow Chemical* v. *Spence Bryson (No. 2)* ([1984] RPC 359 (CA)) the claims were construed in a manner which avoided the pleaded objection of ambiguity. However, this was not possible in *Minerals Separation* v. *Noranda* ((1952) 69 RPC 81) where the claim used the phrase "akaline xanthate" which could have either of two distinct meanings: the claim was held to be invalid. In *Henriksen* v. *Tallon* ([1965] RPC 434 (HL)) it was held that the mere fact that a part of a claim was capable of more than one construction was not sufficient to invalidate it for ambiguity. In *Poseidon* v. *Cerosa (No. 2)* ([1982] FSR 209 (CA)) it was stated that it would be strange to construe a claim in a manner such that neither the patentees' own commercial embodiment of a genuine invention, nor the alleged infringement, are within the true construction of the claim, and accordingly relative terms contained in a claim should not be given a meaning which no person skilled in the art would have attributed to them. This was a case where a purposive construction was given to a claim containing a relative term, namely that a diving suit should be a "close fit". It was held that this phrase did not require the suit to be skin-tight or have only the minimum of air space between the suit and the skin of the diver. In similar vein, in *American Cyanamid* v. *Ethicon* ([1979] RPC 215), the court first construed the meaning of technical terms, not in a literal fashion, but as they would be understood in normal parlance by the skilled addressee, which was here held to be a multi-disciplinary term of workers rather than any single person, the court accepting expert evidence on these matters. Having done this, the court resolved objections of ambiguity and lack of fair basis in favour of the patentee.

Note also that the objection is strictly one of lack of clarity. It is not necessary for the claim to have alternative meanings: the objection of ambiguity will succeed if it is not possible to construe the claim at all. Thus, in *Proctor & Gamble* v. *Peaudouce* ([1989] FSR 180 (CA)), a claim was found invalid because of failure of the required functional test at the limit of the claim rendering it indeterminate whether or not the claim was then infringed but, as this limit was greatly exceeded in the alleged infringement, the claim would have been·held infringed had it been valid.

A032.29   —*Lack of fair basis*

The words "fair basis" occur also in section 5 [1949] in relation to the determination of priority date and there has been an increasing tendency to apply the same tests in relation thereto, see para. A005.3. There is also a relation to the requirement of section 14(5)(*c*) [1977], see para. 14.25, but under the 1977 Act, the objection can only be raised during the substantive examination, the objection not being a ground for revocation permitted by section 72(1) [1977], see para. 72.20.

In *Letraset* v. *Rexel* ([1974] RPC 175 at 196) it was stated that the requirement of "fair basis" indicates that a fair balance should be drawn between the interests of the patentee and of the public. Lack of fair basis was also an important issue in *Olin* v. *Biorex* ([1970] RPC 157), in which it was held that a chemical claim is fairly based if it does not go beyond the limits of a sound prediction and there is no proof that the prediction was unsound. A question of lack of fair basis is one to be decided after the claim has been construed and its ambit determined: discovery of documents relating to the differing wording of claims in corresponding foreign applications or patents therefore serves no useful purpose (*Schering Agrochemicals* v. *ABM Chemicals*, [1987] RPC 185).

In *Van der Lely* v. *Ruston's Engineering* ([1985] RPC 461 (CA)) it was stated that, for a claim to be fairly based on the disclosure in the specification, the invention claimed must, in fairness to the public, be only that which the inventor had described as his invention and which dealt with any problem with which the invention was intended to deal. The specification should be construed in a purposive way and then the question asked whether the material in the specification provides a fair ground or base as between the patentee and the public for the claims made. On these criteria the patent was held invalid. The practicability of considering fair basis before obviousness, on which ground the *Van der Lely* patent was also found invalid, has been criticised by A. C. Serjeant ((1986–87) 16 CIPA 34) with further comment by G. Aggus and A. J. A. Bubb (1986–87) 16 CIPA 109 and 219).

In *Kahn (David)* v. *Conway Stewart* ([1974] RPC 279) it was also stated that a patentee is not entitled to claim a monopoly more extensive than is necessary to protect what he has himself said is his invention, and that only if invention lies in identification of a problem can he claim all solutions thereto. In *British United Shoe Machinery* v. *Collier (Simon)* ((1909) 26 RPC 21 and 834 and (1910) 27 RPC 567) the patent was held invalid because it claimed all solutions to a known problem. In Australia it has been held that a claim is not fairly based if it covers products that do not possess the stated advantages (*AMP* v. *Utilux* [*Australia*] ([1973] RPC 175), and in *Horville* v. *Clares* ([1976] RPC 411 (CA)) claims were held invalid as not being fairly based because they covered devices (actually the infringing device) which did not achieve the stated object of the invention.

American Cyanamid v. *Berk* ([1976] RPC 231) was a case in which a microbiological process was claimed in broad terms on a meagre disclosure. It was alleged that the claims were obvious. The experts agreed that the object of the invention was obvious as also was the way in which the research should be carried out. However, an enormous burden of research could be involved and there was no certainty that the object could ever be achieved. On that basis, on the facts of the case, the allegation of obviousness failed, but the claim was, however, held to lack fair basis because it was not limited to the particular way that had been discovered of achieving the obviously desirable objective. The court stated:

> "While it is vital to give inventors the fullest possible protection in respect of the contribution which they have made, it must be to my mind wrong to give them a monopoly which will cover something to which they have really made no genuine contribution at all."

However, in *Soc. Industrielle Lasaffre's Patent* (SRIS C/97/85 and C/106/86, *noted* IPD 10037 (CA)), an attack of lack of fair basis failed, when it was held that nothing more was needed than mere experimentation to find micro-organism strains which would produce the claimed product additional to those specific strains which had been identified.

The case of *Mullard* v. *Philco* ((1936) 53 RPC 323 (HL)) often seems to cause great difficulty because in it a claim to the pentode thermionic valve was held invalid because its utility extended beyond the particular electrical circuit in which it was intended to be used with no wider use disclosed. However, the case was carefully analysed in *Letraset* v. *Dymo* ([1976] RPC 65) and explained on the basis that in *Mullard* the pentode valve *per se* was obvious whereas its application in a particular circuit was not. In any case, the *Mullard* decision was given at a time when claims to chemical products *per se* were excluded by the terms of the then statute and it has generally been recognised that this decision has no direct applicability to the validity of such claims, even if only a single use therefor may be disclosed.

In *Letraset* v. *Dymo* (*supra*) it was argued that the claim lacked fair basis because the claimed article could be used according to both the new and the prior art techniques, but this was held to be immaterial because the article was itself both novel and unobvious.

A claim can be revoked for lack of fair basis if it is open-ended in the sense that it has no limit to its scope at one end and is therefore indeterminate and speculative, see *Eastman Kodak's Application* ([1970] RPC 548) and *Du Pont* v. *Enka* ([1988] FSR 69). In the latter case, this also caused a finding of insufficiency, see para. A032.19 *supra*.

False suggestion (subs. (1)(j))

—General   **A032.30**

This ground can be pleaded in respect of incorrect or misleading statements in the specification, as well as in respect of false statements or declarations in any of the formal documents filed at the Patent Office, for example as regards a false claim to priority as considered in para. A032.31 *infra*. If the objection is upheld, the consequence is that the Crown was deceived in its grant so that it would be inappropriate to exercise discretion to permit a validating amendment. Conversely, if the court is minded to permit amendment, it is unlikely to uphold an objection under this provision. There is no corresponding provision in the 1977 Act. Under that Act reliance will need to be placed on the other grounds for revocation available under section 72(1) [1977], that of insufficiency under section 14(3) [1977] being the most likely to succeed where, under the 1949 Act, the objection would have been one of "false suggestion".

A032.31   —*False claims to convention priority*

The effect of the provision of subsection (1)(*j*) in relation to revocation has, however, been reduced by Schedule 1, para. 6 [1977] (reprinted at para. 133.01). Under this provision, where there is a finding that the false suggestion or representation relates to a false claim to entitlement to a priority date earlier than the filing of the complete specification, the patent is not to be revoked, but instead the priority date of the claim is to be taken to be the date of filing the application for the patent. Thus, no longer will a false claim to convention priority lead to revocation as it did, *e.g.* in *Gumbel's Patent* ([1958] RPC 1) and *Kopat's Patent* ([1965] RPC 404). However, revocation may still be possible if an application were prosecuted in full knowledge that the priority claim was not valid, see *Beumer (Bernhard) Maschinenfabrik's Patent* (SRIS C/120/83) where a pleading to this effect was allowed to remain. Also, in *Masi* v. *Coloroll* ([1986] RPC 483), pleadings were allowed to remain that an existing patent could be revoked for a false claim to priority, or at least that acts which fell within its claims would not be infringements by virtue of the effect of Schedule 4, paragraph 3(3) [1977]. The question of false claiming of convention priority date is considered in paras. A001.4–A001.8.

A032.32   —*Materiality of the false suggestion*

It has been held that assertions in the specification which are immaterial to the grant of a patent do not lead to its invalidity even if the assertions are false, see *American Cyanamid* v. *Ethicon* ([1979] RPC 215) and *Intalite* v. *Cellular Ceilings (No. 2)* ([1987] RPC 537). However, in *American Cyanamid* v. *Berk* ([1976] RPC 231), the patent was invalidated, *inter alia*, on this ground.

An objection under subsection (1)(*j*) often overlaps with that of inutility under subsection (1)(*g*) discussed in para. A032.14–A032.16 *supra*. This was the position in *Dow Chemical* v. *Spence Bryson (No. 2)* ([1982] FSR 598 and [1984] RPC 359 (CA)), where the objection was upheld on both grounds after it was admitted that the method described would not produce a thick foam, there being nothing in the specification to indicate this practical limitation on the process claimed.

The ground of objection under subsection (1)(*j*) was not previously available in proceedings before the Comptroller, but since 1978 the Comptroller has had authority to revoke on this ground under the revised form of section 33 [1949]. Under this power, in *Suwa Seikosha's Patent* (SRIS O/86/82, *noted* IPD 5065) a patent was invalidated on a finding that it contained a false promise in that its stated object was that the battery of an electronic watch should last for at least one year, it being irrelevant that the skilled reader would see that this was not so. Amendment was refused, the Hearing Officer stating:

> "In the absence of mitigating circumstances, it is not in the public interest that a patentee should hold out a promise in his specification and then merely be allowed to remove it when it is shown to be untenable, even though the presence of the promise may have been the result of careless drafting at some stage."

A032.33   —*False declaration on application form*

Besides the case of a false claim to priority discussed in para. A032.31 *supra*, an instance of a false declaration on an application form arose in *Armco's Application* ([1969] FSR 33). American patentees who applied for amendment were found to have been aware, when applying for the patent, of a prior-published United States specification which anticipated the main claim, but to have supposed that the law in the United Kingdom was the same as that in the United States under which the prior specification was ineffective. The amendment was refused because the patent had been obtained on a false representation, namely the statement in the printed wording on the application form declaring that the applicant knew of no lawful ground of objection to the grant of a patent to him. oIgnorance of the law is no excuse, as all are presumed to know the law.

The declaration on the application form that the applicant is in possession of the invention is made in respect of the invention described in the specification lodged with the application and cannot be rendered false by subsequent amendment (*Martin* v. *Scribal* [*Australia*], [1956] RPC 215 at 224).

Use contrary to law (subs. (1)(k))   **A032.34**

An existing patent can, in theory, be revoked if its primary or intended exercise would be contrary to law. However, there appears to be no case of revocation under the provision. It is insufficient that the invention *could* be used in a manner contrary to law (*Walton* v. *Ahrens*, (1939) 56 RPC 195); its primary or intended use must be illegal. A similar objection arises under the 1977 Act by the provisions of section 1(3) and (4) [1977], but it is now provided that patentability is not affected merely because use of the invention is prohibited by any law in force in the United Kingdom or any part of it.

Secret prior use (subs. (1)(l))   **A032.35**

Subsection (1)(*l*) covers prior secret use in the United Kingdom by the patentee or by a third party. It will be noted that this ground of invalidity is not limited to use on a commercial scale. However, by subsection (2), secret use is ineffective if it was: (*a*) for the purpose of reasonable trial or experiment only; (*b*) by a Government department in consequence of a disclosure by the patentee; or (*c*) by anyone else in breach of confidence. Also, by subsection (2) secret prior use only invalidates as such: no account thereof is to be taken in objections under grounds (*e*) (*prior knowledge or public use*) or (*f*) (*obviousness thereover*).

There is no corresponding ground of invalidity under the 1977 Act. Instead, the secret prior user obtains a personal right to continue with the acts carried out before the priority date of the invention and likewise where there had been serious and effective preparations to do such an act, see section 64 [1977]. Thus, under each Act, the secret prior user may continue with his previous (non-experimental) activities, though he may not be able to make any changes in the previously utilised product or process because, under the 1949 Act, of his inability to argue invalidity due to obviousness and the restriction in section 64 [1977] to "continuation" of the prior acts. Note that section 64[1977] also, apparently applies to existing patents, see para. 64.07.

Whether the test of secrecy is objective or subjective was strictly not decided in *Bristol-Myer's (Johnson's) Application* ([1973] RPC 157; [1975] RPC 127), but a majority of the House of Lords held that the deliberate sale of a product constituted a non-secret use of that product irrespective of the lack of knowledge concerning its constitution, see the discussion of this case in para. A032.11 *supra*.

It would appear from *Wheatley's Application* ([1985] RPC 91) that, once an applicant has dealt with the invention in a commercial manner, in this case by making an offer for sale, his use is not secret. Indeed, it was indicated that, even though a use may have preserved the inventor's power to prevent his purchaser discovering, if he can, the manner in which the invention works, such use was not necessarily a secret use.

In *Harrison* v. *Project & Design* ([1978] FSR 81) the patented stair lift had been used for a short time in the private house of the designer. This use was held not to be *de minimis*, but was excused as secret and by way of reasonable trial or experiment only. The test for such trial or experiment was held to be an objective one.

In *Lucas* v. *Gaedor* ([1978] RPC 297) allegations of prior user were rejected on the ground that the use was secret and experimental, there having been a policy of concealment by the prior user.

In *Andrew Master Hones* v. *Cruikshank & Fairweather* ([1980] RPC 16) it was indicated, *obiter*, that secrecy would seem to exist when precautions were taken to prevent persons who might be interested from seeing the apparatus in question, and here others were in fact not able to find out how the machine worked. It was also considered that the alleged prior use could be regarded as for the purpose of reasonable trial or experiment, but this was doubted on appeal ([1981] RPC 389).

On the meaning of the words "reasonable trial or experiment" in subsection (2), see *Cave-Brown-Cave's Application* ([1958] RPC 429) where, under section 51(3) [1949], six-months' constant use was held to be more than was reasonably necessary for reasonable trial, and *International Paint's Application* ([1982] RPC 247), decided under section 52 [1949].

With regard to subsection (2)(*b*) and (*c*), it should be noted that secret use by a government department, otherwise than as a result of disclosure by the patentee, is available as an attack under subsection (1)(*l*), as also is secret use by anyone which is not a breach of confidence.

For completeness it is noted that, when the Post Office and British Telecom respectively ceased to be Government departments, special transitional provisions were enacted to preserve the position under section 32(2)(*b*) in respect of inventions previously communicated thereto, see Post Office Act 1969 (c. 48, Sched. 10) and British Telecommunications Act 1981 (c. 38, Sched. 5).

A032.36   PRACTICE UNDER SECTION 32 [1949]

The procedure for presenting a petition for revocation of an existing patent to the Patents Court is governed by RSC Ord. 104, rules 4 and 6–14 (reprinted at paras. E104.04–E104.14). This is the same as with an application to the court under section 72 [1977]. However, since an application for revocation made to the court is usually made as a counterclaim in an action for infringement, this procedure is discussed in relation to Practice under section 61 [1977] at paras. 61.21–61.38.

When the court makes an order for the revocation of an existing patent, rule 150 [1968] (reprinted at para. 32.13) applies, requiring the order to be notified to the Comptroller on PF No. 69 (no fee) reprinted at para. A138, as is discussed in paras. 32.20 and 32.29.

SECTION 33

Revocation of patent by comptroller

A033.1   33.—(1) [*At any time within twelve months after the sealing of a patent,
               any person interested who did not oppose the grant of the patent may apply
               to the comptroller for an order revoking the patent on any one or more of the
               grounds upon which the grant of the patent could have been opposed:*] **Sub-
               ject to the provisions of this Act, a patent may, on application of any person
               interested, be revoked by the comptroller on any of the grounds set out in
               section 32(1) of this Act;**

Provided that when an action for infringement, or proceedings for revocation, of a patent are pending in any court, an application to the comptroller under this section shall not be made except with the leave of the court.

(2) Where an application is made under this section, the comptroller shall notify the patentee and shall give to the applicant and the patentee an opportunity to be heard before deciding the case.

(3) If on an application under this section the comptroller is satisfied that any of the grounds aforesaid are established, he may by order direct that the patent shall be revoked either unconditionally or unless within such time as may be specified in the order the complete specification is amended to his satisfaction:

[*Provided that the comptroller shall not make an order for the unconditional revocation of a patent under this section unless the circumstances are such as would have justified him in refusing to grant the patent in proceedings under section fourteen of this Act.*]

(4) An appeal shall lie from any decision of the comptroller under this section.

(5) **A decision of the comptroller or on appeal from the comptroller shall not estop any party to civil proceedings in which infringement of a patent is in issue from alleging that any claim of the specification is invalid on any of the grounds set out in section 32(1) of this Act, whether or not any of the issues involved were decided in that decision.**

Note. The amendments to subsections (1) and (5) were effected by Schedule 1, para. 7 [1977] and that to subsection (3), by Schedule 6 [1977].

RELEVANT 1968 RULES

96. [1968]—(1) An application for the revocation of patent shall:—   A033.2
  (*a*) be made on Patents Form No. 39,
  (*b*) state the ground or grounds for the application, and
  (*c*) be accompanied by a copy thereof and shall be supported by a statement (in duplicate) setting out fully the nature of the applicant's interests, the facts upon which he relies, and the relief which he seeks.

(2) A copy of the application and of the statement shall be sent by the Comptroller to the patentee.

97. [1968] Upon such application being made and a copy thereof sent to   A033.3
the patentee the provisions of Rules 40 to 46 shall apply with such consequential adaptations as the case requires and in particular with the substitution of references to the patentee for references to the applicant and of references to the applicant for references to the opponent.

40. [1968] If the applicant desires to proceed with his application, he   A033.4
shall, within three months of the receipt of such copies, file a counterstate-

ment setting out fully the grounds upon which the opposition is contested and deliver to the opponent a copy thereof.

A033.5   **41. [1968]** The opponent may within three months from the receipt of the copy of the counterstatement file evidence in support of his case and shall deliver to the applicant a copy of the evidence.

A033.6   **42. [1968]** Within three months from the receipt of the copy of the opponent's evidence or, if the opponent does not file any evidence, within three months from the expiration of the time within which the opponent's evidence might have been filed, the applicant may file evidence in support of his case and shall deliver to the opponent a copy of the evidence and within three months from the receipt of the copy of the applicant's evidence the opponent may file evidence confined to matters strictly in reply and shall deliver to the applicant a copy of the evidence.

A033.7   **43. [1968]** No further evidence shall be filed by either party except by leave or direction of the Comptroller.

A033.8   **44. [1968]**—(1) Copies of all documents, other than printed United Kingdom specifications, referred to in the notice of opposition, or in any statement or evidence filed in connection with the opposition, authenticated to the satisfaction of the Comptroller, shall be furnished (in duplicate) for the Comptroller's use unless he otherwise directs. Such copies shall accompany the notice, statement or evidence in which they are referred to.

(2) Where a specification or other document in a foreign language is referred to, a translation thereof, certified by the translator as being true to the best of his knowledge and belief, shall also be furnished, together with a further copy of the translation. The Comptroller may refuse to accept any translation which is in his opinion inaccurate and thereupon another translation of the specification or other document certified as aforesaid shall be furnished, together with a further copy of such other translation.

A033.9   **45. [1968]**—(1) On completion of the evidence (if any), or at such other time as he may see fit, the Comptroller shall appoint a time for the hearing of the case, and shall give the parties at least fourteen days' notice of the appointment.

(2) If either party desires to be heard he shall notify the Comptroller on Patents Form No. 13 and the Comptroller may refuse to hear either party who has not filed the said form prior to the date of hearing.

(3) If either party intends to refer at the hearing to any publication not already mentioned in the proceedings, he shall give to the other party and to the Comptroller at least ten days' notice of his intention, together with details of each publication to which he intends to refer.

(4) After hearing the party or parties desiring to be heard or, if neither party desires to be heard, then without a hearing, the Comptroller shall decide the case and notify his decision to the parties giving reasons for his decision if so required by any party.

46. [1968] If in consequence of the proceedings the Comptroller directs that a reference to another patent shall be inserted in the applicant's specification under section 9(1), the reference shall be as prescribed by Rule 34. **A033.10**

47. [1968] If the applicant notifies the Comptroller that he does not desire to proceed with the application, the Comptroller, in deciding whether costs should be awarded to the opponent, shall consider whether proceedings might have been avoided if the opponent had given reasonable notice to the applicant before the opposition was filed. **A033.11**

COMMENTARY ON SECTION 33 [1949]

General **A033.12**

Section 33 in its original form provided a limited possibility of bringing invalidity proceedings before the Comptroller within one year after grant of the patent. Such proceedings were restricted to persons who had not opposed the application under section 14 [1949] before grant and were confined to the same limited range of grounds as applicable thereunder. Consequently, such proceedings under section 33 (before its amendment) were known as "belated oppositions" and much of the law and practice relevant to section 33 arose from pre-grant oppositions under section 14 [1949].

The effect of the amendment made to subsection (1) is that applications for the revocation of existing patents may now be made to the Comptroller at any time during the life of the patent and on any of the grounds applicable in actions for revocation of existing patents brought before the court, that is those set out in section 32 [1949]. The position is, therefore, now the same for "existing patents" as for patents granted under the 1977 Act; applications for the revocation of such patents may be made either to the court or to the Comptroller under a common section 72 [1977].

The grounds upon which application can now be made under section 33 [1949] (as amended), being the same as those under section 32 [1949], are, therefore, not discussed here, but see the commentory on section 32 [1949]. For an indication of the previous limitations on the grounds available under the unamended section 33, see para. A014.

Locus standi **A033.13**

Unlike the position under section 72 [1977], application under section 33 can only be brought by a person "interested". The meaning of the phrase "interested person" in this context was considered by the Court of Appeal in *Globe Industries' Patent* ([1977] RPC 563) where the decisions in *Kessler's Application* ([1971] RPC 360) and *Mediline's Patent* ([1973] RPC 91) were generally approved. The *Globe* case held that the applicant for revocation must show "(a) that his objection is not frivolous, vexatious or blackmailing in character; and in addition (b) that he has a real, definite and substantial commercial interest which may be prejudiced", though it is not necessary that actual prejudice be shown. In the case in question the interest was more potential than actual, the opponents being at risk if the patent were used as the basis for obtaining by registration a patent in Hong Kong for which they had shown a real commercial interest. It was held that the necessary interest need not be in the United Kingdom provided it arose from the existence of the United Kingdom patent. Two prior decisions which suggested to the contrary were criticised.

A person who does not believe that he is an infringer, but recognises that he may be wrong, also would appear to have sufficient *locus standi* to apply under the section by analogy with *Glaverbel's Application* ([1987] RPC 73 (CA)) which concerned the interest of an opponent to the cancellation of a "licences of right" endorsement.

An interest in a patent for similar subject-matter will always suffice to provide *locus standi*. In its absence an allegation of manufacturing or trading in the United Kingdom is sufficient. In general, a trade or research association is entitled to apply for revocation. In *Baigent's Application* ((1954) 71 RPC 441) an association whose finances were dependent to a substantial extent on admission charges made to the public when running entertainment which used the invention was considered to have an interest in the nature of a trading interest which provided a *locus standi* for opposition by the secretary of the association.

The *locus* must exist when the application for revocation is filed, and it appears from *Bamford's Application* ([1959] RPC 66) and *American Cyanamid's (Yarrow's) Application* ([1967] FSR 79) that *locus*, once established, cannot be destroyed by subsequent events. In the *American Cyanamid* case the opponents failed to establish *locus*. Before the publication of the patent application they had been engaged in importation which would have given them *locus*, but they failed to prove any importation after the publication of the application and they had gone into voluntary liquidation, thus showing that they could have no intention to resume the importation.

The financial interest of a holding company whose subsidiary is a person interested suffices to enable the holding company to apply (*Badische Anilin's Application*, [1963] RPC 19). A manufacturer of raw materials related to the products of an invention has a sufficient interest for the section and so does a holding company having a controlling interest in such a manufacture (*Continental Oil's Application*, [1963] RPC 32).

An assignor has no *locus standi*. In *Wantoch and Wray's Patent* ([1968] RPC 394) it was held on appeal that, as the assignment conveyed the full benefit of any patent which might be granted, assignor-opponents could not derogate from their assignment by prosecuting an opposition to restrict the scope of what they had assigned.

A033.14 *Conflict with proceedings before the court*

The proviso to subsection (1) prevents an application for revocation being made to the Comptroller when any proceedings for infringement or revocation of the patent are already pending before the court, unless the court gives leave. The corresponding provision under the 1977 Act is section 74(7) [1977] and is in somewhat broader terms, see para. 74.06. However, there is no specific provision which enables the Comptroller to decline to deal with applications under section 33 [1949] even if he is of the opinion that the matter ought to be dealt with by the court, though there is such a provision, under section 72(7)(*b*) [1977], for patents granted under the 1977 Act.

The proviso to subsection (1) only applies at the time the application under section 33 is made. In *Foseco's Patent* ([1976] FSR 244) two notices under section 33 were filed on the same day as a writ for infringement was issued against one of the proposed belated opponents, though the writ was only served later. It was held that for the purpose of section 33(1) an action was not "pending" unless a writ had been both issued and served. Accordingly, the notice of belated oppositions were to be accepted by the Patent Office.

For the position when court proceedings are commenced while section 33 proceedings are pending, see para. A033.18 *infra*.

Lack of estoppel   **A033.15**

Under the unamended section 33, no issue estoppel arose when an application for revocation was dismissed. This was because the grounds for revocation were limited in scope and the benefit of any doubt was given to the patentee in order that he could, if he wished, subsequently have his day in court by bringing an infringement action, see *Bristol-Myers* v. *Beecham* [*Israel*] ([1978] FSR 553). New subsection (5) maintains the previous position so that an applicant for revocation who fails under section 33 need not find his position jeopardised in a subsequent challenge to validity before the court under section 32 [1949]. A similar provision applies to applications for revocation under section 72 [1977] which are brought before the Comptroller rather than the court, see section 72(5) [1977] and paras. 72.28 and 72.31.

Certificate of contested validity   **A033.16**

No certificate of contested validity can be granted after an unsuccessful application to revoke under section 33 [1949], see *Canon K.K.'s Application* ([1982] RPC 549) holding that Schedule 4, para. 3(2) [1977], and therefore also section 65 [1977], has no applicability to proceedings under section 33 [1949] which do not relate to "infringement" as Schedule 4, para. 3 [1977] requires.

PRACTICE UNDER SECTION 33 [1949]

General procedure   **A033.17**

An application for revocation under section 33 [1949] is initiated under rule 96 [1968] by the filing (in duplicate) of PF No. 39 (reprinted at para. A127) and supported by a statement of case (also in duplicate) setting out fully the nature of the applicant's interests, the facts relied upon and the relief sought. This statement can be filed within the following 14 days (r. 153 [1968]) further extensible under rule 154 [1968], reprinted respectively at paras. A115 and A116. Rule 96 [1968] corresponds to rule 75(1) and (2) [1982] (reprinted in para. 72.03) for an application for revocation made to the Comptroller under section 72 [1977]. PF No. 39 may be signed by an agent who need not supply any authorisation unless so requested by the Comptroller, see rule 90 [1982] reprinted at para. 115.02 discussed at para. 115.03. Thereafter rules 40–46 [1968] (reprinted at paras. A033.4–A033.10 *supra*) are to apply with substitution of references to the "applicant" and "opponent" by respective references to the "patentee" and "applicant [for revocation]" as appropriate (r. 97 [1968], reprinted at para. A033.3 *supra*).

This procedure closely follows that applicable to an application for revocation made to the Comptroller under section 72 [1977]. Therefore, the present Practice notes concentrate on the differences from that procedure and the commentary on Practice under section 72 at paras. 72.32–72.52 is otherwise to be applied hereunder.

The still applicable 1968 rules provide first for the filing of a counterstatement if the patentee wishes to contest the application. This must set out fully the grounds upon which the application is contested and a copy is sent directly to the applicant for revocation (r. 40 [1968], corresponding to r. 75(3) [1982], except that thereunder the second copy is filed at the Patent Office for onward transmission). There is provision for: successive filing of evidence in support of the application for revocation; evidence in support of the patent by the patentee and replying to the evidence of the applicant for revocation; and evidence in reply thereto by the applicant for revocation (r. 41 [1968], corresponding to r. 75(3)–(5) [1982]). The periods for filing the counterstatement and each round of evidence are specified as three months in each case, but these periods are extensible under rule 154 [1968] (reprinted at para. A116) at the Comptroller's discretion. No further evidence may be filed without leave of the Comptroller (r. 42 [1968] corresponding to r. 75(6) [1982]).

A copy of the counterstatement and all evidence is required to be supplied directly to the other party by the party filing the same. With this is also to be supplied a copy of any document (other than printed United Kingdom patent specifications) referred to in the notice of opposition or in any statement and evidence filed, together with a certified translation of any such document not in English (r. 44 [1968]). This is less rigid than the corresponding r. 112 [1982], see para. 72.37. The form of the evidence filed and its manner of attestation is governed by rules 103–106 [1982], reprinted at paras. 72.05–72.08 made applicable by rule 124(1)(*d*) [1978] (reprinted at para. 127.04). These provisions are discussed in more detail in paras. 72.36–72.46.

On completion of the evidence: a hearing is to be appointed with at least 14 days notice; PF No. 13 (reprinted at para. A122) is then to be filed by any party desiring to be heard. At least 10 days notice must be given of any intention to rely on any publication not already mentioned in the proceedings and details thereof given. The Comptroller then decides the case and notifies his decision to the parties, giving reasons therefor if so required by any party (r. 45 [1968], corresponding to r. 88 [1982]). The hearing will normally be in public, though there is provision for *in camera* hearings (r. 156 [1968], reprinted at para. A117, corresponding to r. 89 [1982]). Rules 88 and 89 [1982] are reprinted respectively at paras. 101.02 and 101.03 and are discussed in the commentary on section 101 [1977] because this section is applicable to hearings in proceedings arising under the 1949 Act (Sched. 2, para. 1(2) [1977]).

There is power for the Comptroller to order as part of his decision the insertion of a statutory reference under section 9(1) [1949] (r. 46 [1968]), for which see para. A009.5. There is no corresponding provision under the 1977 Act or the Rules applicable thereto.

Costs may be awarded to the successful party under section 107 [1977], see para. 107.02, but may be refused where the patentee does not contest the action and reasonable notice of the revocation application was not given assuming that rule 47 [1968] (reprinted at para. A033.11 *supra*, and still applicable by r. 124(1)(*a*) [1978] reprinted at para. 127.04) would apply despite the absence of reference thereto in rule 97 [1968], see para. A033.3.

For a more detailed discussion on many of these points, see paras. 72.32–72.46 and 72.50–72.52.

A033.18 *Concurrency of proceedings*

While section 33 proceedings cannot be commenced if court proceedings for infringement or revocation are already pending, see the proviso to subsection (1) and para. A033.14 *supra*, the position can be different if the proceedings before the court are commenced subsequently. The matter is then at the discretion of both the court and the Comptroller. Thus, concurrent proceedings against the same patent under sections 32 and 33 by different parties and involving different issues may be allowed to proceed together but, if one party initiates proceedings against a patent under both sections, he may be restrained from proceeding under section 32 until the section 33 proceedings are terminated (*Lever Bros., Patent*, (1952) 69 RPC 117). However, if during proceedings under section 33 the patent is attacked by another party, either by way of petition or counterclaim in an infringement action, the Comptroller will, in general, stay the section 33 proceedings until the section 32 proceedings have been concluded. Thus, in *Regal International's Patents* (SRIS O/125/84), infringement proceedings were commenced after some of the evidence stages in existing proceedings under section 33 had been completed. Nevertheless, the Comptroller ordered a stay of these proceedings, noting that proceedings before the court would be likely in any event.

Leave to start section 33 proceedings after an infringement action had been instituted was granted in *Concept Engineering's Application* ([1968] RPC 487) and also in *Telesco Brophey's Patent* ([1972] RPC 805). In the latter case a suggestion that the application for revocation should be stayed, while the infringement action proceeded, was not accepted; the court observed that the Patent Office proceedings might go much faster than those in the High Court.

When two proceedings before the Comptroller are pending together (for example under s. 29 for amendment and under s. 33 for revocation), the Comptroller has power to decide which of the two proceedings should be heard first (*Gibbons' Patent*, [1957] RPC 155).

Withdrawal of application for revocation   A033.19

The Rules contain no provision for the withdrawal of an application for revocation. Accordingly, the former Patents Appeal Tribunal ruled, *in banc*, that an applicant for revocation can only indicate his intention to take no further part in the proceedings, thereby leaving the Comptroller, if he thinks it appropriate in the public interest, to continue to consider the pleaded grounds of attack (*General Motors' (Turney and Barr's) Application*, [1976] RPC 659 at 665). A patentee can no longer evade a finding of invalidity by surrendering his patent since section 29 [1977], applicable to "existing patents", would leave some rights intact, see paras. 29.03 and 29.06.

Amendments   A033.20

If the patentee wishes to amend the specification he must indicate clearly (whether in the counterstatement or otherwise) all the amendments he desires. Before the hearing, a copy of the printed specification showing the amendments in red is required by the Comptroller, and a copy should be sent to the applicant for revocation. It is necessary to specify the ground under section 31 [1949] (*disclaimer, correction or explanation*) upon whch the amendment is sought (*Warnant's Application*, [1956] RPC 205). A formal application to amend under section 29 [1949] is not required (*GEC's Patent*, [1959] RPC 109). However, amendments will not be allowed in the section 33 proceedings unless they arise strictly out of the proceedings (*Roussel-Uclaf's (Nomine's) Patent*, [1974] RPC 405 at 427) and unless they are vital to the result of the proceedings (*Owen-Illinois' (Baker and Bode's) Application*, [1976] FSR 437).

A patentee should state whether his offer to amend is made conditionally or unconditionally and, if the latter, a patentee can only be allowed to resile from the proposals by an application to amend the pleadings, on which and other points on amendment in revocation proceedings, see para. 72.47.

SECTION 34 [1949] [*Repealed*]

Surrender of patent

Note. Section 34 has been replaced by section 29 [1977] applicable to existing patents.

SECTION 35 [1949] [*Repealed*]

Endorsement of patent "licences of right"

[**35.**—(1) . . .

(2) *Where a patent is endorsed under this section—*

(a) *Any person shall, at any time thereafter, be entitled as of right to a licence under the patent upon such terms as may, in default of agreement, be settled by the comptroller on the application of the patentee or the person requiring the licence;*

(b) *the comptroller may, on the application of the holder of any licence granted under the patent before the endorsement, order the licence to be exchanged for a licence to be granted by virtue of the endorsement upon terms to be settled as aforesaid;*

(c) *if in proceedings for infringement of the patent (otherwise than by the importation of goods) the defendant undertakes to take a licence upon terms to be settled by the comptroller as aforesaid, no injunction shall be granted against him, and the amount (if any) recoverable against him by way of damages shall not exceed double the amount which would have been payable by him as licensee if such a licence had been granted before the earliest infringement;*

(d) *the renewal fees payable in respect of the patent after the date of the endorsement shall be one half of the renewal fees which would be payable if the patent were not so endorsed.*

(3) *The licensee under any licence granted by virtue of the endorsement of a patent under this section shall (unless, in the case of a licence the terms of which are settled by agreement, the licence otherwise expressly provides) be entitled to call upon the patentee to take proceedings to prevent any infringement of the patent; and if the patentee refuses or neglects to do so within two months after being so called upon, the licensee may institute proceedings for the infringement in his own name as if he were patentee making the patentee a defendant:*

Provided that a patentee so added as defendant shall not be liable for any costs unless he enters an appearance and takes part in the proceedings.

(4) . . .

(5) . . .

(6) . . .

(7) *An appeal shall lie from any decision of the comptroller under this section.*]

RELEVANT 1968 RULE A035.2

103. [1968]—(1) An application under Section 35(2)(*a*) or section 35(1)(*b*) for settlement of the terms of a licence under a patent endorsed "Licences of Right" shall be made on Patents Form No. 43, and shall be accompanied by a copy thereof and a statement (in duplicate) setting out fully the facts upon which the applicant relies, and the terms of the licence which he is prepared to accept or grant.

(2) A copy of the application and statement shall be sent by the Comptroller to the patentee or the person requiring a licence, as the case may be, who, if he does not agree to the terms set out in the statement, shall, within six weeks of the receipt of such copies, file a counterstatement setting out fully the grounds of his objection and send a copy thereof to the applicant.

(3) The Comptroller shall give such directions as he may think fit with regard to the filing of evidence and the hearing of the parties.

COMMENTARY ON SECTION 35 [1949] [Repealed] A035.3

Section 35 has been replaced by section 46 [1977], which is applicable to existing patents, though only as regards those endorsed "licences of right" on or after "the appointed day" (June 1, 1978). The 1977 Act likewise applies to existing patents after the end of their 16th year when they become deemed to be so endorsed by virtue of Schedule 1, para. 4(2)(*c*) [1977], as decided in *Allen & Hanburys* v. *Generics* ([1986] RPC 203 (HL)).

However, subsections (2), (3) and (7) are to be applied, despite their repeal, to any existing patent endorsed before June 1, 1978 (Sched. 4, para. 8 [1977]). For this reason these subsections are reprinted above and PF No. 43 (reprinted at para. A128) would apply. Nevertheless, no separate commentary is provided on these provisions because the commentary on section 46 [1977] can be taken to apply likewise, with the possible exception that, under rule 103 [1968], only six weeks is allowed for filing a counterstatement, though subject to possible extension under rule 154 [1968] (reprinted at para. A116), whereas under the replacement rule 63 [1982] (reprinted at para. 46.03) the prescribed period for this purpose is three months.

Also, for such patents, section 36 [1949] likewise continues to apply to any attempt to cancel the endorsement (*Glaverbel's Patent*, [1987] RPC 73). In that case such cancellation was permitted even though by that date the patent had automatically received a deemed endorsement under Schedule 1, para. 4(2)(*c*) [1977], see *Glaverbel's Patent (No. 2)* (SRIS O/82/88).

Any appeal from a decision of the Comptroller under repealed section 35 would lie to the Patents Court (Sched. 7 [1977] and Sched. 4, para. 8 [1977]) with further repeal to the Court of Appeal possible, with leave, on a point of law or excess of jurisdiction (Sched. 4, para. 13 [1977] and repealed section 87(1)(*aa*) [1949].

A036.1   **SECTION 36 [1949]** [*Repealed*]

Cancellation of endorsement under section 35

[**36.**—*(1) At any time after a patent has been endorsed under the last fore-going section, the patentee may apply to the comptroller for cancellation of the endorsement; and where such an application is made and the balance paid of all renewal fees which would have been payable if the patent had not been endorsed, the comptroller may, if satisfied that there is no existing licence under the patent or that all licensees under the patent consent to the application, cancel the endorsement accordingly.*

(2) Within the prescribed period after a patent has been endorsed as afore-said, any person who claims that the patentee is, and was at the time of the endorsement, precluded by a contract in which the claimant is interested from granting licences under the patent may apply to the comptroller for cancellation of the endorsement.

(3) Where the comptroller is satisfied, on application made under the last foregoing subsection, that the patentee is and was precluded as aforesaid, he shall cancel the endorsement; and thereupon the patentee shall be liable to pay, within such period as may be prescribed, a sum equal to the balance of all renewal fees which would have been payable if the patent had not been endorsed, and if that sum is not paid within that period the patent shall cease to have effect at the expiration of that period.

(4) Where the endorsement of a patent is cancelled under this section, the rights and liabilities of the patentee shall thereafter be the same as if the endorsement had not been made.

(5) The comptroller shall advertise in the prescribed manner any application made to him under this section; and within the prescribed period after such advertisement—

    (a) in the case of an application under subsection (1) of this section, any person interested; and

    (b) in the case of an application under subsection (2) of this section, the patentee,

may give notice to the comptroller of opposition to the cancellation.

(6) Where any such notice of opposition is given, the comptroller shall notify the applicant, and shall give to the applicant and the opponent an opportunity to be heard before deciding the case.

(7) An application made under this section for the cancellation of the endorsement of a patent of addition shall be treated as an application for the cancellation of the endorsement of the patent for the main invention also, and an application made under this section for the cancellation of the endorsement of a patent in respect of which a patent of addition is in force shall be treated as an application for the cancellation of the endorsement of the patent of addition also.

(8) An appeal shall lie from any decision of the comptroller under this section.]

Note. This section has been replaced by section 47 [1977] and that section applies to the cancellation of "licences of right" endorsements of, or in respect of, existing patents made or deemed to be made on or after June 1, 1978, see para. A035.3. Section 36, however, continues to apply in the limited circumstances described in that para. For this purpose section 36 is reprinted above and rules 104–107 [1968] are reprinted in paras. A036.2–A036.5, *infra*. Nevertheless, no separate commentary is provided as that of paras. 47.15–47.18 would apply *mutatis mutandis*. However, for such a purpose, PF Nos. 44–46 (reprinted at paras. A129–A131) remain applicable, and rule 104 [1968] requires the filing of evidence rather than a declaration by the proprietor contained on PF 30/77. Such a case was *Fabran's Patent* (SRIS O/103/88). For extensions of time and appeals, see para. A035.3 which applies likewise to any proceedings under repealed section 36 [1949].

RELEVANT 1968 RULES

104 [1968]. An application under section 36(1) for the cancellation of an   **A036.2**
endorsement shall be made on Patents Form No. 44, and shall be accompanied by evidence verifying the statement in the application, and by Patents Form No. 12/77 accompanied by fees to the amount of the balance of all renewal fees which would have been payable if the patent had not been endorsed.

105 [1968]. An application under section 36(2) for the cancellation of an   **A036.3**
endorsement shall be made on Patents Form No. 45 within two months after the patent has been endorsed and shall be accompanied by a copy and a statement (in duplicate) setting out fully the nature of the applicant's interest, and the facts upon which he relies.

106 [1968].—(1) Every application under section 36(1) or 36(2) shall be   **A036.4**
advertised in the Journal, and the period within which notice of opposition to the cancellation of an endorsement may be given under section 36(5) shall be one month after the advertisement.

2. Such notice shall be given on Patents Form No. 46 and shall be accompanied by a copy thereof, and shall be supported by a statement (in duplicate) setting out fully the facts upon which the opponent relies and, in the case of opposition to an application under section 36(1), the nature of his interest.

107 [1968].—(1) A copy of the notice and of the statement shall be sent   **A036.5**
by the Comptroller to the applicant for cancellation of the endorsement and thereafter Rules 40 to 45 shall apply.

(2) Where the Comptroller cancels the endorsement pursuant to section 36(3), the patentee shall, within one month from the cancellation of the endorsement, file Patents Form No. 12/77 accompanied by fees to the amount of the balance of all renewal fees which would have been payable if the patent had not been endorsed.

A036.6 *Note.* Rules 104 and 107(2) [1968] are printed as amended by rule 124(1)(*c*) [1978].

A037   SECTION 37 [1949] [*Repealed*]

Compulsory endorsement

For *Note*, see para. A045.

A038   SECTION 38 [1949] [*Repealed*]

Provisions as to licences under section 37

For *Note*, see para. A045.

A039   SECTION 39 [1949] [*Repealed*]

Exercise of powers on applications under section 37

For *Note* see para. A045.

A040   SECTION 40 [1949] [*Repealed*]

Endorsement, etc. on application of Crown

For *Note*, see para. A045.

A041   SECTION 41 [1949] [*Repealed*]

Inventions relating to food or medicine, etc.

For *Note*, see para. A045.

A042   SECTION 42 [1949] [*Repealed*]

Revocation of patent

For *Note*, see para. A045.

A043   SECTION 43 [1949] [*Repealed*]

Procedure on application under sections 37 to 42

For *Note*, see para. A045.

A044   SECTION 44 [1949] [*Repealed*]

Appeal and references to arbitrator

For *Note*, see para. A045.

SECTION 45 [1949] [*Repealed*]   A045

Supplementary provisions

Note. Sections 37–45 [1949] provided for the grant of compulsory licences or compulsory endorsement of patents "licences of right". The provisions of sections 37–40 and 43–45 have been replaced by those of sections 48–54 [1977] while the provisions of section 41 (*Compulsory licences on patents relating to food or medicine*) and section 42 (*Revocation where endorsement proved ineffective*) were not re-enacted. Any compulsory licences granted or applied for by June 1, 1978 remain effective (Sched. 4, para. 8 [1977]), though no further application for licences under section 41 [1949] was possible after the Royal Assent to the 1977 Act on July 29, 1977, see para. 132.07.

SECTION 46 [1949]   A046

Use of patented inventions for services of the Crown

[*Spent*, see para. A049]

SECTION 47 [1949]   A047

Rights of third parties in respect of Crown use

[*Spent*, see para. A049]

Note. Section 47, despite being effectively spent, was amended by the 1988 Act (Sched. 7, para. 5) to add "design right" after "copyright" in subsection (1), a term which includes a "topography right" (Design Right (Semiconductor Topographies) Regulations 1989, S.I. 1989 No. 1100).

SECTION 48 [1949]   A048

Reference of disputes as to Crown use

[*Spent*, see para. A049]

SECTION 49 [1949]   A049

Special provisions as to Crown use during emergency

[*Spent*]

Note. Sections 46–49 have been replaced by sections 55–59 [1977].

SECTION 50 [1949]

Previous publication

50.—(1) An invention claimed in a complete specification shall not be deemed to have been anticipated by reason only that the invention was published in the United Kingdom—

    (*a*) in a specification filed in pursuance of an application for a patent made in the United Kingdom and dated more than fifty years before the date of filing of the first-mentioned specification;

    (*b*) in a specification describing the invention for the purposes of an application for protection in any country outside the United Kingdom made more than fifty years before that date; or

    (*c*) in any abridgement of or extract from any such specification published under the authority of the comptroller or of the government of any country outside the United Kingdom.

(2) Subject as hereinafter provided, an invention claimed in a complete specification shall not be deemed to have been anticipated by reason only that the invention was published before the priority date of the relevant claim of the specification, if the patentee or applicant for the patent proves—

    (*a*) that the matter published was obtained from him or (where he is not himself the true and first inventor) from any person from whom he derives title, and was published without his consent or the consent of any such person; and

    (*b*) where the patentee or applicant for the patent or any person from whom he derives title learned of the publication before the date of the application for the patent or (in the case of a convention application) before the date of the application for protection in a convention country, that the application or the application in a convention country, as the case may be, was made as soon as reasonably practicable thereafter.

Provided that this subsection shall not apply if the invention was before the priority date of the claim commercially worked in the United Kingdom, otherwise than for the purpose of reasonable trial, either by the patentee or applicant for the patent or any person from whom he derives title or by any other person with the consent of the patentee or applicant for the patent or any person from whom he derives title.

(3) Where a complete specification is filed in pursuance of an application for a patent made by a person being the true and first inventor or deriving title from him, an invention claimed in that specification shall not be deemed to have been anticipated by reason only of any other application for a patent in respect of the same invention, made in contravention of the rights of that person, or by reason only that after the date of filing of that other application the invention was used or published, without the consent

of that person, by the applicant in respect of that other application, or by any other person in consequence of any disclosure of the invention by that applicant.

(4) Notwithstanding anything in this Act, the comptroller shall not refuse to accept a complete specification or to grant a patent, and a patent shall not be revoked or invalidated, by reason only of any circumstances which, by virtue of this section, do not constitute an anticipation of the invention claimed in the specification.

COMMENTARY ON SECTION 50 [1949]

General   **A050.2**

This section, together with section 51 [1949], defines (in subss. (1)–(3)) the circumstances in which a prior publication, prior application or prior use, each in the United Kingdom, may (by subs. (4)) be saved from constituting an "anticipation" of the claims of an existing patent. Subsection (1)(*a*) has no counterpart in the 1977 Act, but some of the circumstances provided for in subsections (2) and (3) are dealt with by the provisions of subsections (4)(*a*) and (*b*) and (5) of section 2 [1977], see paras. 2.25 and 2.26.

If only because the word "anticipated" is used in subsection (3) in relation to the "other application", thus apparently bringing "prior claiming" within the group of circumstances which are excused thereunder, and because the provisions of the section would have little value if "anticipated" and "anticipation" in each of the provisions of section 50 referred only to the consideration of novelty, it appears that the word "anticipation" in subsection (4) (used also in s. 51(4) [1949]) is to be interpreted broadly, so that the debarred anticipating publication or use cannot alone destroy either novelty or inventive step, on which point see para. A026.08.

In any situation where relief from "anticipation" is sought, each of the saving provisions of sections 50 and 51, together with those of section 32(2) [1949], should be considered because it may be possible to overcome a particular anticipating event under one provision even though the requirements of other provisions are not met, see *Ethyl Corp.'s Patent* ([1963] RPC 155 and [1966] RPC 205).

The 50 year publication rule (subs. (1))   **A050.3**

Subsection (1) provides that patent specifications and official abridgements or extracts thereof published more than 50 years earlier do not constitute an anticipation, but the subsection provides no saving provision with regard to other forms of publication, or with regard to prior use, nor against republication in a later patent specification, for example by way of acknowledgment of prior art, provided such republication is itself sufficient as discussed *infra*.

Subsection (1)(*a*) prescribes that, in relation to prior British patents, the 50 year period runs from the *date* of the earlier patent to the date of filing the complete specification of the claims in issue. Here, it should be noted that, prior to 1950, a British patent was dated with the date of filing of the first of any provisional specifications or with the earliest convention date claimed, whereas from 1950 the patent was dated with the date of its complete specification. In subsection (1)(*b*) the 50 year period runs from the date when the foreign application was made. Under subsection (1)(*c*) the date of the abridgement or extract is irrelevant provided it is of a specification which qualifies under either of heads (*a*) or (*b*) of subsection 1.

In *AMP* v. *Hellerman* ([1966] RPC 159 at 183) a mere reference by number in a specification within the 50 year limit to an earlier specification outside the 50 year limit was held not to constitute "republication" of the earlier specification. This was followed in *Beecham's Patent* ([1966] FSR 238) where the later specification contained a brief description of the earlier specification, but did not depend on and direct the reader to the earlier specification for the further necessary information.

The term "published" is defined in section 101 [1949] and this is discussed in para. A101.10 and also in para. 2.05.

The operation of the 50 year rule has been determined by the ECJ not to constitute a disguised restriction on trade within the EEC contrary to TRaa. 30 and 36 (*Thetford* v. *Fiamma (Case 35/87)*, [1988] 3 CMLR 549; [1989] FSR 57 (ECJ)), for case comment on which see R. Eccles ([1989] EIPR 26).

A050.4   *Unauthorised publication or use derived from the inventor (subs. (2))*

Subsection (2) protects a patentee against the unauthorised publication of matter "obtained" from him or his predecessor. The meaning of "obtained" is discussed in para. A032.08. However, for the purposes of this subsection, the obtaining may have occurred in the United Kingdom or abroad (*Ethyl Corp.'s Patent*, [1966] RPC 205). The unauthorised publication is not limited to patent specifications.

Tiefebrun's Application ([1979] FSR 97) contains observations that, to take advantage of the relevant provisions of section 50, the published matter must have been obtained from the patentee, applicant or predecessor in title and that such persons must not have consented to the prior publication. The onus of proof in such cases was considered and it was noted that the failure to impose an obligation of confidence did not necessarily mean that there had been consent to publication. In *Ralph Parsons' Application* ([1978] FSR 226) a paper by the inventor had been read at a scientific meeting in Canada, and copies of this paper had been made widely available to those attending the meeting with the result that details had subsequently appeared in four scientific journals. It was held that, though the subject matter of the prior publication had been obtained (*i.e.* had been "got") from the inventor, the circumstances were such that he had effectively given his consent to world-wide publication. Accordingly, protection under the subsection could not be afforded.

It should be noted that subsection (2) is governed by the words "by reason only", on which see *Bloxham* v. *Kee Less* ((1922) 39 RPC 195).

There is no mention in subsection (2) of unauthorised use which does not itself amount to publication, a point discussed in *Chemithon's Patent* ([1966] RPC 365). Unauthorised *secret* use consequent on disclosure by the patentee is excused under section 32(2)(*c*) [1949] as discussed in para. A032.35. However, unauthorised *public* use can only be excused under subsection (3) as discussed in para. A050.5 *infra*. Public use or publication by the patentee (or by anyone from whom he has derived title) is not excused at all (except for reasonable trial under section 51(3) [1949], discussed in para. A051.5), but secret commercial use by the patentee, etc., can be used against the patent under section 32(1)(*l*) [1949] and can also be invoked under the proviso to subsection (2). This proviso applies the saving provisions of subsection (2) only if there has been no commercial working of the invention in the United Kingdom by or with the consent of the inventor or his successors in title to his patent rights, unless this was for the purposes of reasonable trial and experiment.

To take advantage of subsection (2), the application for the patent in issue must have been filed (or based on a filing of an application itself filed) "as soon as practicable" after knowledge of the unauthorised publication may have come to the attention of the applicant or person from whom he derived the right to apply (subs. (2)(*b*)).

Unauthorised prior application (subs. (3))   **A050.5**

Subsection (3) deals with cases where there is another application for a patent made in contravention of the rights of the proper applicant. In this case unauthorised use resulting from the other application, as well as authorised publication or use, is debarred from being an application provided that that publication or use occurred after the filing of the wrongful application. The circumstances under which subsection (3) can be invoked are probably those on which a patent which has been granted on the wrongful application can be revoked under section 32(1)(*b*) or (*c*) [1949]. In such a case the rightful patentee may also be able to rectify the position by acquiring the date of the unauthorised application under section 53 [1949]. Provisions similar to those of subsection (3) were in issue in *Dickinson's Application* ((1927) 44 RPC 79).

SECTION 51 [1949]   A051.1

Previous communication, display or working

51.—(1) An invention claimed in a complete specification shall not be deemed to have been anticipated by reason only of the communication of the invention to a Government department or to any person authorised by a Government department to investigate the invention or its merits, or of anything done, in consequence of such a communication, for the purpose of the investigation.

(2) An invention claimed in a complete specification shall not be deemed to have been anticipated by reason only of—

(*a*) the display of the invention with the consent of the true and first inventor at an exhibition certified by the Board of Trade for the purposes of this section, or the use thereof with his consent for the purposes of such an exhibition in the place where it is held;

(*b*) the publication of any description of the invention in consequence of the display or use of the invention at any such exhibition as aforesaid;

(*c*) the use of the invention, after it has been displayed or used at any such exhibition as aforesaid and during the period of the exhibition, by any person without the consent of the true and first inventor; or

(*d*) the description of the invention in a paper read by the true and first inventor before a learned society or published with his consent in the transactions of such a society.

if the application for the patent is made by the true and first inventor or a person deriving title from him not later than six months after the opening of the exhibition or the reading or publication of the paper as the case may be.

(3) An invention claimed in a complete specification shall not be deemed

to have been anticipated by reason only that, at any time within one year before the priority date of the relevant claim of the specification, the invention was publicly worked in the United Kingdom.

(*a*) by the patentee or applicant for the patent or any person from whom he derives title; or

(*b*) by any other person with the consent of the patentee or applicant for the patent or any person from whom he derives title,

if the working was effected for the purpose of reasonable trial only and if it was reasonably necessary, having regard to the nature of the invention, that the working for that purpose should be effected in public.

(4) Notwithstanding anything in this Act, the comptroller shall not refuse to accept a complete specification or to grant a patent, and a patent shall not be revoked or invalidated, by reason only of any circumstances which, by virtue of this section, do not constitute an anticipation of the invention claimed in the specification.

Note. Section 5(4) of the Food Act 1984 (c. 30) is in the following terms:

"(4) Section 51 of the Patents Act 1949 (which secures inventions against anticipation in certain cases) applies in relation—

(*a*) to the disclosure of any invention made in pursuance of an order under this section, and

(*b*) to anything done in consequence of any such disclosure,

as it applies in relation to such communications of inventions as are therein mentioned, and to anything done in consequence of such communications".

Section 5(4) of the Food and Drugs (Scotland) Act 1956 (c. 30) has equivalent wording in respect of invention disclosures made in Scotland.

COMMENTARY ON SECTION 51 [1949]

A051.2 *General*

This section defined the circumstances in which certain previous communications, display, publications or use do not constitute anticipation of the claims of an existing patent. It therefore extends the saving provisions of section 50 [1949] discussed in paras. A050.2–A050.5. Subsection (4) repeats the wording of section 50(4) [1949] and, for the reasons given in the commentary on section 50 [1949], the effect of the saving provisions of the section is that the circumstances covered by its subsections (1)–(3) (and also by the note on extending legislation, *supra*) do not themselves affect the validity of an existing patent. There are no corresponding provisions in the 1977 Act, except as regards display at an international exhibition under section 2(4)(*c*) [1977], on which see para. 2.28.

A051.3 *Communications to Government department (subs. (1))*

Subsection (1) refers to communications to a Government department. It should be noted that it covers any invention and is not limited to inventions for defence purposes. It is not clear whether the provision applies to communications to statutory bodies who are responsible to a Minister of the Crown but are not Government departments as such but, when the Post Office and British Telecom each became public corporations, saving provisions were provided to preserve the effect of prior communications to these former Government departments, though not to communications made after privatisation, see the Post Office Act 1969 (c. 48, Sched. 10) and the British Telecommunications Act 1981 (c. 38, Sched. 5).

Note that any such prior communication (unless expressly made in confidence) will give rise to the possibility of Crown use of any invention disclosed in the communication without compensation therefor, see section 55(3) as discussed in para. 55.10. While there are no corresponding provisions under the 1977 Act, it can be argued that a communication to a government department does not make the details of that communication available to the public and therefore that those details do not become part of the state of the art under section 2 [1977].

Under section 5 of the Food Act 1984 (c. 30) (and similarly under section 5 of the Food and Drugs (Scotland) Act 1956 (c. 30)) an Order can be made requiring persons to furnish to the Secretary of State particulars (as may be specified in the Order) of the composition and use of any substance of any specified class sold in the course of a business which includes the production, importation or use of such substances in the preparation of food for human consumption or used for that purpose in the course of that business. However, the furnishing of such particulars brings into play (by s. 5(4) of these Acts, see Note to para. A051.1 *supra*) the saving provisions of section 51 in relation thereto. Nevertheless, it might be thought that furnishing of such particulars would anyway be regarded as a communication to a government department and therefore be already covered by subsection (1). The section 5(4) provisions are spent as regards any new Orders made under these provisions. The position under section 55(3) [1977] in respect of any such forced disclosure now made is, however, not clear, though if the Order is one made in respect of a product on sale, any subsequently filed patent would anyway presumably be invalid for prior use.

Prior publication and use at exhibitions and by learned societies (subs. (2)) **A051.4**

Subsection (2) refers to (*a*) display, (*b*) publication and (*c*) use, each at a certified exhibition, and (*d*) to papers read before, or published or reported in the transactions of, a learned society. The exhibitions are those certified by the Department of Trade, but retrospective certification is no longer given, see O.J. August 23, 1967. There is no definition of what constitutes a learned society or of its "transactions". However, in *Ethyl Corp.'s Patent* ([1963] RPC 155) it was observed that "transactions" means the published record of the proceedings of a learned society and so includes an abstract published as an advance notice of a paper to be read before it. Presumably, disclosure in a discussion following such a reading is similarly protected, but there would seem to be no protection for a paper read by someone other than the true and first inventor.

In *Ralph Parsons' Application* ([1978] FSR 226) questions arose concerning a paper read to a scientific society in Canada which had given rise to four reports in scientific journals. It was held that whatever the exact meaning to be given to the words "learned society", protection under subsection (2)(*d*) could not be given because the reading of the paper had not occurred in the United Kingdom; nor was it published in the transactions of such a society, there being no evidence that the paper had been edited by anyone appointed by the society in question; nor that the publication had in any way been approved by or issued under the aegis of the society.

In *Steel's Application* ([1958] RPC 411) it was held that publication in an exhibition catalogue issued prior to the opening of the exhibition was not something published "in consequence" (*i.e.* "after") the exhibition.

It should be noted that in order to invoke the section in the case of an exhibition the inventor must have given his consent to the invention being displayed. No reference is made to the consent of anyone but the inventor. It therefore appears that a display with the consent of an assignee of the inventor and without the actual inventor's consent would constitute an anticipation.

It is also most important to note that subsection (2) contains the general provision that the saving it may provide can only operate if application for the invention in issue was filed within six months of the otherwise anticipating event. The "date of application" means the date of the United Kingdom application and not the date of some foreign application from which priority is claimed (*Ethyl Corp's Patent, supra*).

In some foreign countries it has been possible to have an application, filed later, accorded the prior date of an excepted disclosure such as display at an exhibition. However, it is not possible to claim such a date as a priority date for a United Kingdom application (*Soudre Electrique's Application*, (1939) 56 RPC 218), though the actual date of filing the foreign application can be claimed.

The corresponding provision of section 2(4)(*c*) [1977] is of much more restricted scope than section 51(2) [1949]. This is discussed in paras. 2.27 and 2.32.

A051.5   *Prior necessary working in public (subs. (3))*

Subsection (3) provides a saving for prior public working of an invention provided that: this has taken place within one year before the priority date of the claim; it was carried out by or with the consent of the patentee or his predecessors in title; the working was for the purpose of reasonable trial only; *and* the nature of the invention made it reasonably necessary for the working to be effected in public. This saving provision goes further than section 32(2)(*a*) [1949] which refers to trials and experiments carried out in secret.

In *Cave-Brown-Cave's Application* ([1958] RPC 429) it was held that it was reasonable to send to a school for the purpose of trial a gymnast unit designed to be assembled by children, but that a six months' period was in excess of that required for reasonable trial. Thus the words "any time" are qualified.

The words "for the purpose of reasonable trial only" were considered in *Perard Engineering's (Hubbard's) Application* ([1976] RPC 363). It was held that the prior use was with the consent of the applicant and that it was immaterial in the circumstances of the case that commercial benefit had resulted therefrom, the prior use looked at objectively being in the nature of a trial from both the viewpoint of the applicant and that of the user. In *International Paint's Application* ([1982] RPC 247) it was pointed out that use did not cease to be use for purpose of reasonable trial only by mere reason of the fact that the use was for the reasonable trial of more than one party; and that even commercial use may be within the protection of subsection (3) because it may be reasonable to finance the trials of (a) the inventor, and (b) a potential customer, by the potential customer buying some material to test for the inventor. What matters is that such purchase should be for the purpose of the testing of both parties.

A052.1   **SECTION 52 [1949]**

Use and publication after provisional specification or foreign application

52.—(1) Where a complete specification is filed or proceeded with in pursuance of an application which was accompanied by a provisional specification or by a specification treated by virtue of a direction under subsection (4) of section three of this Act as a provisional specification, then, notwithstanding anything in this Act, the Comptroller shall not refuse to grant the patent, and the patent shall not be revoked or invalidated by reason only that any matter described in the provisional specification or in the specification treated as aforesaid as a provisional specification was used or published at any time after the date of filing of that specification.

(2) Where a complete specification is filed in pursuance of a convention application, then, notwithstanding anything in this Act, the comptroller shall not refuse to grant the patent, and the patent shall not be revoked or invalidated by reason only that any matter disclosed in any application for protection in a convention country upon which the convention application is founded was used or published at any time after the date of that application for protection.

COMMENTARY ON SECTION 52 [1949]

General   **A052.2**

This section deals with the use and publication after a provisional specification or foreign application has been filed. It has a counterpart in section 6 [1977].

The section provides that publication or use between the filing of a provisional specification (subs. (1)), or a foreign application from which priority is claimed under the Paris International Convention (subs. (2)), and the filing of a complete specification does not, in either case, invalidate the claims of the complete specification if the matter concerned is disclosed in the provisional specification or foreign application. For an example of the application of the section, see *Letraset* v. *Rexel* ([1976] RPC 51).

Effect of the section   **A052.3**

The section should be read in conjunction with section 5 [1949]. The word "claim" does not appear in the section, though clearly the section is concerned with happenings before the priority date of a claim. The section has no applicability to complete specifications in which all the claims are entitled to the priority date of a single earlier document. Were it not for this section a claim entitled only to the priority date of a complete specification filed after a priority document (provisional or convention specification) might be held to lack novelty or inventive step in view of the publication or use, before the priority date, of matter described in the priority document. In *Ronson* v. *Lewis* ([1963] RPC 103) there was an intervening independent publication of a device which was identical with the invention disclosed in the provisional specification. It was argued that, even if the priority date of the claim was that of the complete specification, this publication was excused under section 52. In fact the priority date was held to be that of the provisional, so the point was not decided, but there was no dissent from the argument in court.

It seems that the scope of the claim is immaterial, that is to say, a claim wider than anything disclosed in the priority document is just as much freed from attack as a claim for matter precisely disclosed in the priority document. On the word "only", see para. A026.08.

In *International Paint's Application* ([1982] RPC 247) it was held that the word "described" in section 52 has the same meaning as "fairly based" in section 5(2).

1015

Moreover, if an earlier priority date in respect of a decription of a class is held established, then any member of that class may be used as from the date of the priority document with protection under section 52. However, if such priority date is lost, then section 52 only provides protection in respect of embodiments specifically disclosed in the priority document. The issue under subsection (1) is whether a specific embodiment within the claim has been described, whether specifically or in general terms, in the priority document. There is no difference in meaning between the words "described" and "disclosed" in relation to a document which is being considered as a whole.

Protection is granted under section 52 against any use after the date of the priority document whether such use was experimental or not: thus reliance on section 51(3) is not necessary. However, it may be that such prior user may now have a personal right (under section 64 [1977]) to continue that use, see para. 64.07.

A053.1   SECTION 53 [1949]

Priority date in case of obtaining

53. Where an application is made for a patent for an invention which has been claimed in a complete specification filed in pursuance of any other such application, then if—

(*a*) the comptroller has refused to grant a patent in pursuance of that other application on the ground specified in paragraph (*a*) of subsection (1) of section fourteen of this Act;

(*b*) a patent granted in pursuance of that other application has been revoked by the court or the comptroller on the ground specified in paragraph (*a*) of subsection (1) of section fourteen or paragraph (*c*) of subsection (1) of section thirty-two of this Act; or

(*c*) the complete specification filed in pursuance of the said other application has, in proceedings under section fourteen or section thirty-three of this Act, been amended by the exclusion of the claim relating to the said invention in consequence of a finding by the comptroller that the invention was obtained by the applicant or patentee from any other person.

the comptroller may direct that the first-mentioned application and any specification filed in pursuance thereof shall be deemed, for the purposes of the provisions of this Act relating to the priority date of claims of complete specifications, to have been filed on the date on which the corresponding document was or was deemed to have been filed in the proceedings upon the said other application.

A053.2   COMMENTARY ON SECTION 53 [1949]

This section relates to the priority date of an application in the case of obtaining, and provides that where a patent has been refused or revoked, or a claim deleted, on the ground of "obtaining" then a specification filed by the later applicant may be accorded the priority date of the offending application.

There appears to be no time limit within which the benefit of section 53 can be obtained, either as regards applying for revocation on the ground of "obtaining" (for which see para. A032.00) or for making the new application after a finding thereof. However, the power of the Comptroller under section 53 is permissive and would doubtless be refused if it was thought generally contrary to the public interest to permit a new patent to be obtained, for example when the public may legitimately have thought the protection originally given by the revoked patent would no longer exist.

A similar effect can be obtained under the 1977 Act by a new application filed under sections 8(3), 12(6) or 37(4) [1977] as appropriate, but here the entitlement proceedings must, normally, though not necessarily, have been brought within a two-year period from grant, see para. 37.13.

It was held in *Page's Application* ([1970] RPC 1), which was belatedly reported, that under the equivalent section in the 1907 Act (and so under the present section) it was not enough for an applicant to withdraw in order to enable a specification filed by an opponent to be afforded the priority date of the offending application; there must be positive refusal of grant. On this analogy, mere surrender of the "obtained patent" under section 29 [1977] would also not suffice since such surrender is not an act of revocation, see para. 29.06.

In *X Ltd.'s Application* ([1982] FSR 143) it was held that an application filed under section 53 cannot contain claims broader in scope than those against which the objection of "obtaining" has succeeded.

SECTION 54 [1949] [*Repealed*]   A054

Co-ownership of patents

Note. Section 54 has been replaced by section 36 [1977].

SECTION 55 [1949]

Power of comptroller to give directions to co-owners

55.—(1) Where two or more persons are registered as grantee or pro-   A055.1
prietor of a patent, the comptroller may, upon application made to him in the prescribed manner by any of those persons, give such directions in accordance with the application as to the sale or lease of the patent or any interest therein, the grant of licences under the patent, or the exercise of any right under the last foregoing section in relation thereto, as he thinks fit.

(2) If any person registered as grantee or proprietor of the patent fails to execute any instrument or to do any other thing required for the carrying out of any direction given under this section within fourteen days after being so requested in writing so to do by any of the other persons so registered the comptroller may, upon application made to him in the prescribed manner by any such other person, give directions empowering any person to execute that instrument or to do that thing in the name of and on behalf of the person in default.

(3) Before giving directions in pursuance of an application under this section, the comptroller shall give an opportunity to be heard—
- (*a*) in the case of an application under subsection (1) of this section, to the other person or persons registered as grantee or proprietor of the patent;
- (*b*) in the case of an application under subsection (2) of this section, to the person in default.

(4) An appeal shall lie from any decision or direction of the comptroller under this section.

(5) No directions shall be given under this section so as to affect the mutual rights or obligations of trustees or of the personal representatives of a deceased person, or their rights or obligations as such.

RELEVANT 1968 RULES

A055.2 **116. [1968]**—(1) An application for directions under Section 55(1) by a co-grantee or co-proprietor of a patent shall be made on Patents Form No. 53 and shall be accompanied by a statement setting out fully the facts upon which the applicant relies and the directions which he seeks.

(2) A copy of the application and of the statement shall be sent by the Comptroller to each other person registered as grantee or proprietor of the patent and the applicant shall supply a sufficient number of copies for that purpose.

(3) Thereafter the Comptroller may give such directions as he may think fit with regard to the subsequent procedure.

A055.3 **117. [1968]**—(1) An application for directions under Section 55(2) by a co-grantee or co-proprietor of a patent shall be made on Patents Form No. 54, and shall be accompanied by a copy thereof, and a statement (in duplicate) setting out fully the facts upon which the applicant relies and the directions which he seeks.

(2) A copy of the application and of the statement shall be sent by the Comptroller to the person in default.

(3) Thereafter the Comptroller may give such directions as he may think fit with regard to the subsequent procedure.

A055.4 COMMENTARY ON SECTION 55 [1949]

Under the 1977 Act, section 37(1) [1977] gives the Comptroller power to settle disputes as to co-ownership of patents, but this provision is inapplicable to existing patents, see para. 37.08. Accordingly, section 55 remains operative for the settlement of disputes between co-owners of "existing patents".

Subsection (1) (which was complementary to repealed section 54 [1949] and now is complementary to section 36 [1977] which replaced it) enables the Comptroller to settle disputes between co-patentees of "existing patents", other than between trustees and personal representatives (subs. (5)), as to which see para. 37.09. The disputes to which the section applies are settled by giving directions procuring the execution of documents if any party fails to do so (subs. (2), corresponding to section 37(3) [1977], but there are no specific provisions (corresponding to those of s. 38 [1977]) for dealing with licences already granted under the patent, and section 38 [1977] does not, on its terms, apply to proceedings under section 55 [1949]).

The matters in respect of which directions may be given under subsection (1) appear to be unlimited, and so does the nature of the directions that may be given thereunder. Thus, it would appear that a co-patentee could be deprived of the right to work the invention, though this seems to be excluded under the 1977 Act, see section 38(3) [1977] the terms of which are not reflected in the 1949 Act. Accordingly, it would appear that directions may be given, not only where the parties have not made any agreement regulating their rights, but also where they have made such an agreement (and, *e.g.* a position of stalemate has arisen), see for example the decision in *Florey's Patent* ([1962] RPC 186) where an order was made that one of the co-patentees should join in the sale of the patent based on a joint invention by himself and several others, as discussed in para. 37.12.

Section 55 concerns only proceedings before the Comptroller. It in no way fetters the powers of the court under its general jurisdiction. Presumably, subsection (5) does not prevent the court from making a declaration in relation to a trust, see *Kakkar* v. *Szelke* ([1989] FSR 225; [1989] 4 EPOR 184 (CA)).

Appeal from the Comptroller under the section lies to the Patents Court or (where the appealed proceedings were held in Scotland, under r. 108 [1982], for which see para. 98.07) to the Court of Session (Sched. 4, para. 11 [1977]); and then respectively, with leave, to the Court of Appeal or the Inner House (s. 97(3)–(5) [1977]), see para. 97.06.

PRACTICE UNDER SECTION 55 [1949] A055.5

The procedure for settling disputes under subsection (1) is governed by rule 116 [1968] (reprinted in para. A055.2 *supra*) requiring the filing of PF No. 53 (reprinted at para. A132). The procedure, when there is failure to carry out directions given under the section, is governed by rule 117 [1968] (reprinted in para. A055.3 *supra*) and application is made by filing PF No. 54 (reprinted at para. A133). In each case the procedure after filing the initiating form and required supporting statement is flexible, but will probably follow that under the analogous rules 55 and 56 [1982] as discussed in paras. 37.14–37.15.

SECTION 56 [1949] A056.01

Disputes as to inventions made by employees

56.—(1) Where a dispute arises between an employer and a person who is or was at the material time his employee as to the rights of the parties in respect of an invention made by the employee either alone or jointly with other employees or in respect of any patent granted or to be granted in respect thereof, the Comptroller may, upon application made to him in the prescribed manner by either of the parties, and after giving to each of them an opportunity to be heard, determine the matter in dispute, and may make such orders for giving effect to his decision as he considers expedient:

Provided that if it appears to the Comptroller upon any application under this section that the matter in dispute involves questions which would more properly be determined by the court, he may decline to deal therewith.

(2) In proceedings before the court between an employer and a person who is or was at the material time his employee, or upon an application made to the Comptroller under subsection (1) of this section, the court or Comptroller may, unless satisfied that one or other of the parties is entitled, to the exclusion of the other, to the benefit of an invention made by the employee, by order provide for the apportionment between them of the benefit of the invention, and of any patent granted or to be granted in respect thereof, in such manner as the court or Comptroller considers just.

(3) A decision of the Comptroller uner this section shall have the same effect as between the parties and persons claiming under them as a decision of the court.

(4) An appeal shall lie from any decision of the comptroller under this section.

Relevant 1968 Rule

A056.02   118. [1968]—(1) An application under Section 56(1) to determine a dispute as to rights in an invention shall be made on Patents Form No. 55 and shall be accompanied by a copy thereof, together with a statement (in duplicate) setting out fully the facts of the dispute and the relief which is sought.

(2) A copy of the application and of the statement shall be sent by the Comptroller to the other party to the dispute, who, within three months after receipt thereof, shall file a counterstatement (in duplicate) setting out fully the grounds on which he disputes the right of the applicant to the relief sought.

(3) The Comptroller shall send a copy of this counterstatement to the applicant and thereafter, subject to such directions as the Comptroller may think fit to give, the provisions of Rule 41 to 45 shall apply with the substitution of references to the applicant for references to the opponent and references to the other party for references to the applicant.

Commentary on Section 56 [1949]

A056.03   *General*

Employee-inventions made before June 1, 1978 (when s. 39 [1977] took replacement effect) remain governed by the Common Law and the terms of the contract of employment. The provisions of section 56 [1949], which were new in the 1949 Act, empower the Comptroller to settle entitlement disputes as between an employee and his employer, with the proviso that the Comptroller can refer the matter to the Court if he thinks fit (proviso to subs. (1)). The only novelty which was introduced by the section was to provide a forum, alternative to the court, before which disputes in cases of invention ownership between an employer and his employee can be determined.

Definitions   **A056.04**

In section 56 [1949] "invention" and "patent" have to be interpreted more narrowly than in sections 39–43 [1977]: these terms are defined in section 101(1)
[1949], see paras. A101.01 and A101.05. The meanings of "employee" and
"employer" are discussed in paras. 39.07 and 39.08 in relation to section 39 [1977],
and it is doubtful if there is any difference between the meaning of these words in
relation to the operation of section 56 [1949] from the meanings of these terms
under sections 39–43 [1977].

Entitlement to ownership

—General   **A056.05**

Two quite different situations must be distinguished in which the ownership of an
invention made by an employee has to be determined: first, where there is an
express contractual provision in the employee's contract of employment; and,
secondly, where there is nothing stipulated at all.

—Under express contractual provision   **A056.06**

In the cases of express contractual provisions the practice of tribunals has been
simply to refer to the contract and construe the relevant clause to determine ownership. From the earliest days of "master and servant" disputes, the general doctrine
of freedom of contract, the sanctity of contract and the fiction of equality of bargaining powers have prevailed, and contract terms were given effect subject only to
the doctrine of restraint of trade.
   It should be remembered that the express contractual terms relevant to an
entitlement dispute need not necessarily be found in a single document headed
"Contract of Employment". The meaning of a given clause may be modified by any
one or more of the following, namely: pre-engagement or post-engagement correspondence; employer's handbook or notices; terms incorporated by collective
agreements between the employer and a Trade Union of which the employee is a
member; and custom and practice.
   Under the Common Law, the so-called "pre-assignment" clauses, which give an
employer sweeping rights in all the inventions of his employees, were broadly considered to be fair and were enforced by the courts for as long as they restricted the
claims of the employer to the duration of the contract of employment. Until about
the late 1960s, courts were not influenced by any notion of fairness or reasonableness, and the doctrine of unreasonable restraint of trade tended to strike down only
those clauses in contracts of employment which interfered with the employee's
freedom to accept other employment after the contract came to an end. However,
contracts requiring employees to hand over all the inventions of any sort that they
might make in the future have been held to be unreasonable (*Electric Transmission*
v. *Dannenberg*, (1949) 66 RPC 183 (CA)) because the net effect was to prevent
employees from accepting any skilled employment elsewhere.
   But, from the beginning of the 1970 decade, a series of cases arose, initially concerning young pop singer composers making unequal employment contracts with
music publishing houses in which they had been required to assign copyright in
future compositions. In these cases, the concept of restraint of trade was trans-
mogrified into that of fairness to the employee, the leading case being *Schroeder
Music* v. *Macaulay*, ([1974] 1 WLR 1308; [1974] 3 All ER 616 (HL)). This case was
cited in *Electrolux* v. *Hudson* ([1977] FSR 312) and, though there distinguished on

its facts, Lord Diplock's dicta at page 63 were adopted: what has to be considered in deciding enforceability of a contract term is (see *Hudson* at p. 323): whether the restrictions imposed were reasonably necessary for the protection of the legitimate interests of the employer; and also whether the restrictions were commensurate with the benefit secured by the employee. In the *Hudson* case an employee's contract of service purported to require him to disclose to his employer any invention relating to the employer's business, which invention would remain the sole property of the employer. This clause was held too wide to be enforceable because it related to *any* product of the employer including any associated company in the United Kingdom or elsewhere. It was suggested that such a clause was probably too wide even if applied to a research worker employed to invent, because such a worker would likely work only in a restricted field. The inventor in question was a storekeeper who, it was held, was not a person paid to invent and, moreover, the invention had been made in the inventor's own time without using the materials of his employer. For all these reasons, it was held that the employer had no claim upon the patent application made by the employee. The employer's argument based on the implied term of good faith and fidelity also failed: the implied duty was held not to extend to preventing the employee from engaging in honest competition with the employer in respect of inventions made outside his course of employment, even if the employer is commercially harmed thereby. There is, however, an *obiter dictum* in this case to the effect that it might have been desirable for Mr. Hudson to have disclosed his invention to the employer.

A056.07 *—Where there is no express contractual provision*

Where there has been no express contractual stipulation, the line of enquiry has been rather different. First, the question has had to be determined whether the invention was made "in the course of [the employee's] employment", a phrase discussed in para. 39.15.

Secondly, if this circumstance prevails, the employer has then had to rely on the implied term of the employee-inventor's contract leading to him holding his invention on a trust in favour of the employer. Such a term has been implied by the courts as arising, *either* by virtue of the employee's position or status, *or* by virtue of the employee's actual contractual duties. These will now be discussed, but the similarities with section 39(1)(*b*) and section 39(1)(*a*) [1977] will be obvious. Subject, therefore, to the caveat in para. 39.15, paras. 39.09–39.13 are also relevant to the questions to be decided under section 56 [1949] when there is no express contractual provision.

A056.08 *Trust implied by virtue of the employee's position or status*

The leading cases where it has been decided that an employee has held patent rights on a constructive trust for the benefit of his employer are *Worthington Pumping* v. *Moore* ((1903) 20 RPC 41) and *British Syphon* v. *Homewood* ([1956] RPC 225). In each of these cases the employee-inventor was not in the "paid to invent" category of employees, but the Court implied a duty owed by the employee to the employer. The enquiry then developed into considering, to quote from *Selz's Application* ((1954) 71 RPC 158), whether "in the circumstances of the case it is inconsistent with the good faith which ought properly to be inferred or implied as an obligation arising from the contract of service" that the employee should hold the patent otherwise than as trustee for his employers, see further para. 39.13A.

It may be noted that a director of a company is in a fiduciary relationship to his company and will not normally be entitled to make use for his own profit of knowledge acquired by him while acting as a director *Regal (Hastings) v. Gulliver* ([1967] 2 AC 134; [1942] 1 All ER 378 (HL)).

Trust implied by virtue of the employee's contractual duties   **A056.09**

A constructive trust can also arise by virtue of an employee's contractual duties. The early cases of this category concentrated on determining whether the invention concerned was made in the course of employment and whether it was something that it was the employee's job to invent. Factors such as whether the invention was made in the employer's time or at the weekend, with or without the employer's materials, or whether the employer has been using the invention with the inventor's consent in his business were merely factors that were weighed alongside other factors without any one of them being determinative on its on. In *Adamson v. Kenworthy* ((1931) 49 RPC 57) a draughtsman was held to have the duty "to prepare the best design for the purpose that he can, and if he has any ingenuity or any inventive ability, to exercise that ingenuity and that inventive ability in order to give effect to the instructions that he has received". Thus the employer could claim ownership of any invention resulting from broad instructions even if it was not foreseen that the employee would make inventions in the carrying out of duties.

The much-criticised apogee of the line of cases holding that every employee has an implied term to serve his employer to the best and most inventive manner was in *Patchett v. Sterling* ((1955) 72 RPC 50 (HL)). Here Viscount Simmonds said that "It is an implied term . . . in the contract of service of any workman that what he produces by the strength of his arm or the skill of his hand or the exercise of his inventive faculty shall become the property of his employer". Despite criticisms of this decision, it is of the highest authority. Nevertheless, it is submitted that the case would nowadays either no longer be followed or at least that its severity would be mitigated by the application of the principle of restraint of trade, as developed to the stage it has now reached, as indicated in para. A056.06 (*supra*).

Apportionment   **A056.10**

Subsection (2) gives either the court or the Comptroller power to apportion the benefit of an invention between an employer and an employee in such manner as the tribunal thinks "just". For the meaning of "just" see para. 40.05. However, no apportionment is possible if the tribunal is satisfied that one of the parties is entitled to the whole of the benefit of the invention. In *Patchett v. Sterling* ((1955) 72 RPC 50 (HL)) the word "entitled" was held to mean "legally entitled". The effect of this decision has resulted in the applicability of the subsection being restricted to cases where some agreement to share the benefit of the invention already existed between the parties. However, apportionment may still be possible where the invention is such that the employer only has a part, not the whole, of it.

Practice under Section 56 [1949]

Procedure   **A056.11**

The procedure under section 56 [1949] is set out in rule 118 [1968] (reprinted in para. A056.02 *supra*). The application is filed on PF No. 55 (reprinted at para. A134). After the filing of the required statement and counterstatement, as is customary in contested proceedings before the Comptroller (for which see rules 41–45 [1968] (reprinted at paras. A033.05–A033.09) and paras. 72.32–72.52), the resulting procedure is flexible but will be likely to follow that adopted in entitlement proceedings under the 1977 Act, for which see paras. 37.14 and 37.15.

An appeal from a decision of the Comptroller under the section lies to the Patents Court (Sched. 4, para. 11(5) [1977]) and thence, with leave, to the Court of Appeal under section 97(3)(*a*) [1977] (Sched. 4, para. 11(6) [1977]). There is also power to hold a hearing in Scotland as rule 108 [1982] applies (r. 124(1)(*d*) [1978]): this is discussed in para. 98.07 with similar appeal provisions, for which see para. 97.06.

A057   **SECTION 57 [1949]** [*Repealed*]

Avoidance of certain restrictive conditions

Note. Section 57 has been replaced by section 44 [1977].

A058   **SECTION 58 [1949]** [*Repealed*]

Determination of certain contracts

Note. Section 58 has been replaced by section 45 [1977].

A059   **SECTION 59 [1949]**

Restrictions of recovery of damages for infringement

[*Spent*]

Note. Section 59 has been replaced by section 62 [1977].

A060   **SECTION 60 [1949]**

Order for account in action for infringement

[*Spent*]

Note. Section 60 has been replaced by section 61(1)(*d*) and (2) [1977].

A061   **SECTION 61 [1949]**

Counterclaim for revocation in action for infringement

[*Spent*]

Note. Section 74(1)(*a*) [1977] now permits validity to be raised as a defence, *inter alia*, to a plea of infringement.

A062   **SECTION 62 [1949]**

Relief for infringement of partially valid specification

[*Spent*]

Note. Section 62 has been replaced by section 63 [1977].

SECTION 63 [1949]   A063

Procedure for infringement by exclusive licensee

[*Spent*]

Note. Section 63 has been replaced by section 67 [1977].

SECTION 64 [1949]   A064.1

Certificate of contested validity of specification

64.—(1) If in any proceedings before the court the validity of any claim of a specification is contested, and that claim is found by the court to be valid, the court may certify that the validity of that claim was contested in those proceedings.

(2) Where any such certificate has been granted, then if in any subsequent proceedings before the court for infringement of the patent or for revocation of the patent, a final order or judgment is made or given in favour of the party relying on the validity of the patent, that party shall, unless the court otherwise directs, be entitled to his costs as between solicitor and client so far as concerns the claim in respect of which the certificate was granted:

Provided that this subsection shall apply to the costs of any appeal in any such proceedings as aforesaid.

COMMENTARY ON SECTION 64 [1949]   A064.2

Section 64 continues to apply to existing patents rather than the, generally corresponding, replacement section 65 [1977] (*Canon K.K.'s Patent*, [1982] RPC 549). The effect of section 64 [1949] is discussed at para. 65.05, but it is here noted that the section provides for the grant of a certificate of validity of a claim contested in any proceedings before the court, whether infringement actions, petitions for revocation or others. The patentee's entitlement to costs in subsequent proceedings is subject to the discretion of the court and applies only to infringement and revocation proceedings, and only in the court of first instance. "Solicitor and client" costs are no longer awarded, see para. 65.04. Presumably, costs on a certificate of validity awarded on an existing patent would now be assessed on the present "indemnity" basis, see para. 65.05.

SECTION 65 [1949]   A065

Remedy for groundless threats of infringement proceedings

[*Spent*]

Note. Section 65 has been replaced by section 70 [1977].

A066

SECTION 66 [1949]

Power of court to make declaration as to non-infringement

[*Spent*]

Note. Section 66 has been replaced by section 71 [1977].

A067

SECTION 67 [1949]

Reference to Comptroller of disputes as to infringement

[*Spent*]

Note. Section 67 has been replaced by section 61(3) [1977].

A068

SECTION 68 [1949] [*Repealed*]

Orders in Council as to convention countries

Note. Section 68 has been replaced by section 90 [1977]. Orders in Council made prior to June 1, 1978 designating countries to be convention countries for the purposes of the Patents Act continue to be effective under the 1977 Act (Sched. 4, para. 9(1) [1977]), see para. 90.02.

A069.1

SECTION 69 [1949]

Supplementary provisions as to convention applications

69.—(1) Where a person has applied for protection for an invention by an application which—
   (*a*) in accordance with the terms of a treaty subsisting between any two or more convention countries, is equivalent to an application duly made in any one of those convention countries, or
   (*b*) in accordance with the law of any convention country, is equivalent to an application duly made in that convention country,
he shall be deemed for the purpose of this Act to have applied in that convention country.

(2) For the purpose of this Act, matter shall be deemed to have been disclosed in an application for protection in a convention country if it was claimed or disclosed (otherwise than by way of disclaimer or acknowledgment of prior art) in that application or in documents submitted by the applicant for protection in support of and at the same time as that application; but no account shall be taken of any disclosure effected by any such

document unless a copy of the document is filed at the Patent Office with the convention application or within such period as may be prescribed after the filing of that application.

Section 69 remains of importance for according convention priority to existing patents and for the definition of "convention application" applicable thereto. Its meaning and effect is more fully discussed in the commentaries on sections 1 and 5 [1949].

Subsection (1) provides that certain applications for protection in convention countries which fell short of regular applications for a patent may, nevertheless, have been equivalent to applications "duly made" in the country concerned and, as such, could validly have served as a basis for a claim to convention priority in existing patents. On this basis, a convention application under the 1949 Act could validly be based on, for example, a German Gebrauchsmuster or Japanese utility model application. Also, an application based on an inventor's certificate in a communist country belonging to the International Convention was also accepted as the basis for convention priority, although it is not clear whether this was under the present section or under section 1 [1949]. However, priority was not validly claimable from the date of display at an exhibition even when this became the accorded filing date under the foreign country in question (*Soudre Electrique's Application*, ((1939) 56 RPC 218).

Subsection (2) provided for the filing of convention documents and states that matter claimed or disclosed in the convention document is deemed to be "matter disclosed" in that document. Such matter is that on which (under s. 5(4) [1949]) a claim must be fairly based in order to have the convention priority date. Thus it is possible to rely on matter disclosed in the body of the foreign specification even if it is not covered by the claims, provided such matter is not by way of disclaimer or acknowledgment of prior art.

Subsection (2) can only be taken into account once it can be decided that the application can be considered as a convention application within the terms of section 1(2), see the discussion on *Stauffer's Application* ([1977] RPC 33) in para. A001.06.

The Orders in Council designating convention countries for the purposes of section 69 are those which were applicable under section 68 [1949] at the relevant time. For this purpose section 68 [1949] continues to have effect despite its repeal (Sched. 4, para. 18(3) [1977]). It is possible, though unlikely, that the court could declare a particular Order in Council invalid as being *ultra vires*, see *Dirk's Applications* ([1960] RPC 1).

SECTION 70 [1949] [*Repealed*]   A070

Special provisions as to vessels, aircraft and land vehicles

Note. Section 70 has been replaced by section 60(5)(*d*)–(*f*) and 60(7) [1977]. Orders in Council previously made under section 70 continue to have effect under the 1977 Act (Sched. 4, para. 9(2) [1977]).

A071   **SECTION 71 [1949]**

Extension of time for certain convention applications

For *Note*, see para. A072.

A072   **SECTION 72 [1949]** [*Repealed*]

Protection of inventions communicated under international agreements

Note. The provisions of sections 71–72 [1949] have not been replaced as such in the 1977 Act, but there is a general rule-making power in section 123(2)(*h*) [1977] which could be used to extend the 12 months' period for claiming convention priority should international circumstances so justify.

A073   **SECTION 73 [1949]** [*Repealed*]

Register of Patents

For *Note*, see para. A075.

A074   **SECTION 74 [1949]** [*Repealed*]

Registration of assignments, etc.

For *Note*, see para. A075.

A075   **SECTION 75 [1949]** [*Repealed*]

Rectification of register

Note. Sections 73–75 [1949] were replaced by sections 32–35 [1977].

A076.01   **SECTION 76 [1949]**

Power to correct clerical errors, etc.

76.—(1) The comptroller may, in accordance with the provisions of this section, correct any clerical error in any patent, any application for a patent or any document filed in pursuance of such an application, or any error in the register of patents.

(2) A correction may be made in pursuance of this section either upon a request in writing made by any person interested and accompanied by the prescribed fee, or without such a request.

(3) Where the comptroller proposes to make any such correction as aforesaid otherwise than in pursuance of a request made under this section, he shall give notice of the proposal to the patentee or the applicant for the patent, as the case may be, and to any other person who appears to him to be concerned, and shall give them an opportunity to be heard before making the correction.

(4) Where a request is made under this section for the correction of any error in a patent or application for a patent or any document filed in pursuance of such an application, and it appears to the comptroller that the correction would materially alter the meaning or scope of the document to which the request relates, and ought not to be made without notice to persons affected thereby, he shall require notice of the nature of the proposed correction to be advertised in the prescribed manner.

(5) Within the prescribed time after such advertisement as aforesaid any person interested may give notice to the Comptroller of opposition to the request, and where such notice of opposition is given the Comptroller shall give notice thereof to the person by whom the request was made, and shall give to him and to the opponent an opportunity to be heard before he decides the case.

RELEVANT 1968 RULES

129. [1968] A request for the correction of a clerical error in an application for a patent or in any document filed in pursuance of such an application or in any patent or in the register, shall be made on Patent Form No. 64. **A076.02**

130. [1968] Where the Comptroller requires notice of the nature of the proposed correction to be advertised, the advertisement shall be made by publication of the request and the nature of the proposed correction in the Journal, and in such other manner (if any) as the Comptroller may direct. **A076.03**

131. [1968]—(1) Any person may, at any time within one month from the date of the advertisement in the Journal, give notice to the Comptroller of opposition to the proposed correction on Patents Form No. 65. **A076.04**

(2) Such notice shall be accompanied by a copy thereof and shall be supported by a statement (in duplicate) setting out fully the nature of the opponent's interest, the facts on which he relies, and the relief which he seeks.

(3) A copy of the notice and of the statement shall be sent by the Comptroller to the person making the request, and thereafter the provisions of Rules 40 to 45 shall apply.

132. [1968] Where in accordance with Section 76(3), a hearing is appointed, at least 14 days' notice of the appointment shall be given to the patentee or the applicant for a patent and to any other person to whom notice of the proposed correction has been given by the Comptroller. **A076.05**

A076.06   *Note to relevant rules*

The following rules are also relevant to correction under section 76 [1949]: rules 40–45 [1968] reprinted at paras. A033.04–A033.09 respectively (for opposition proceedings); rules 153, 154 and 156 [1968], reprinted at paras. A115–A117 respectively (for time limits, extensions of time and hearings in public); and rules 88, 100 and 101 [1982], reprinted at paras. 101.02, 123.07 and 123.08 respectively (for the exercise of the Comptroller's discretion and correction of irregularities).

A076.07   ARTICLE

R. P. Lloyd, "Correction of Clerical Errors and Obvious Mistakes", (1980–81) 10 CIPA 266.

COMMENTARY ON SECTION 76 [1949]

A076.08   *General*

Section 76 provides for the correction of clerical errors in documents filed at the Patent Office under the 1949 Act. It therefore applies to the correction of existing patents as well as to applications filed under the 1949 Act which are still pending owing to a "secrecy order".

Subsection (1) gives the Comptroller a general power to correct clerical errors, including also errors in documents other than specifications, and also errors in the register. It differs from the provisions of section 117 [1977] for correction of documents under the 1977 Act. In particular, section 76 permits only the correction of errors which are "clerical", but it would not appear that the need for correction must be immediately evident (as is required by r. 91(2) [1982] under s. 117 [1977], see para. 117.06). However, it must be noted that section 31 [1949] also permits errors to be corrected, see para. A031.12; and, where such errors are "obvious mistakes", the scope of the claims can then be broadened under that section, see para. A031.13.

A076.09   *Limitations of subsection (1)*

It has been held that a "clerical error" is a mistake made in a mechanical process such as writing or copying, as distinct from the intellectual process of drafting (*Maere's Application*, [1962] RPC 182). It appears to follow that a mistake made by a draftsman in writing one word in a manuscript specification when he had another in mind cannot be corrected under section 76, and any power to correct it must be found under section 31 [1949]. In *Maere's* case, the original error was made in copying matter to produce a specification for filing in Belgium, this specification being that from which the English specification was translated. It was held that this was not an error capable of correction under section 76, and that the error must be in the document to be corrected and not an error made before preparation of the document began.

It was again stressed in *Mobil Oil's (Civic's) Application* ([1974] RPC 507) that section 76 only permits the correction of clerical errors made in the course of preparation of a document filed in pursuance of an application, and that a foreign priority document was not prepared as part of the "course of the preparation" of the United Kingdom complete specification. It was also stressed that the discretion to allow amendment under section 76 should be exercised with extreme caution, particularly where the wording of the specification is completely reasonable in its unamended form.

The power to correct a clerical error under section 76 is not limited by section 31 [1949] (*Heberlein's Application*, [1971] FSR 373). However, the power to permit correction is still discretionary and, in *Heberlein's Application*, correction was refused because the applicants had become aware of the mistake in the course of opposition proceedings, but had made no attempt to correct it until a decision had been given in those proceedings. The question of discretion is discussed more fully in paras. 27.05–27.07 and in para. A031.15. In his paper listed in para. A076.07 *supra*, R. P. Lloyd discusses the differences between section 76 [1949] and section 117 [1977], as well as referring to the exercise of discretion in permitting amendment or correction.

Section 76 does not provide for any appeal from a decision of the Comptroller under the section, but appeal may nevertheless be possible on the rationale of *Omron Tateisi's Application* ([1981] RPC 125) or, failing this, an application for judicial review under RSC Ord. 53, rule 1 (reprinted at para. E053.1) is probably possible.

Application, advertisement and opposition   **A076.10**

Correction under section 76 [1949] may be initiated by a request made by any person interested, who need not apparently be the patentee, or by the Comptroller on his own initiative (subs. (2)), but the Comptroller must give notice of his intention to the patentee and to any other persons who appear to him to be concerned, (*e.g.* because they are already involved in proceedings under the patent), and to give all such persons notified the right to be heard (subs. (3)), after 14 days' notice of the appointed hearing (r. 132 [1968], reprinted at para. A076.05 *supra*). However, the proposed correction is only advertised by the Comptroller if it appears to him materially to alter the meaning the scope of the document to which the request relates and ought not to be made without notice to persons affected thereby (subs. (4)). In such circumstances, the proposed correction is advertised in the O.J. (r. 130 [1968], reprinted at para. A076.03 *supra*): opposition may then be lodged, but apparently only when advertisement has been required. Opposition should be filed within one month of the advertisement (r. 131(1) [1968], reprinted at para. A076.04 *supra*), but this period is apparently extensible under rule 154 [1968], reprinted at para. A116. In contrast to the position on amendments under sections 29–31 [1949], opposition may only be lodged by "a person interested", so that an opponent will be required to show a *locus standi*, presumably as required for proceedings under section 33 [1949], for which see para. A033.13.

Correction of errors in the register   **A076.11**

Section 76 [1949] covers the correction of errors in the register as well as in any other document filed in pursuance of an application, or in any patent, under the 1949 Act. However, by virtue of Schedule 2 to the 1977 Act and rule 124 [1982] (reprinted at para. 127.02), section 32 [1977] and rule 47 [1982] also apply to register entries relating to "existing patents". Thus, such register entries can be corrected either under rule 47 [1982] (using PF 22/77) or under rule 129 [1968] using PF No. 64. However, it would seem that correction under section 76 [1949] may be the less preferred route: first, because of the likelihood that the Comptroller will require the request on PF No. 64 to be advertised for opposition; and, secondly, because the fee on this form is somewhat higher than that on PF 22/77. Correction of the register under section 32 [1977] is discussed in para. 32.32.

There is also power to correct a Letters Patent document which has, in error, issued to a deceased person, see para. A020.3.

A076.12   PRACTICE UNDER SECTION 76 [1949]

An application for correction is made under rule 129 [1968] (reprinted in para. A076.02 *supra*) on PF No. 64 (reprinted at para. A135). If the application is advertised, opposition may be lodged (within one month with possible extension as noted above) on PF No. 65 (reprinted at para. A136) supported by a statement in duplicate setting out fully the nature of the opponent's interest, the facts on which he relies and the relief which he seeks (r. 131(2) [1968], reprinted in para. A076.04 *supra*). Thereafter, the procedure follows rules 40–45 [1968] (reprinted at paras. A033.04–A033.09) which are the rules that generally govern the procedure in contested proceedings before the Comptroller under the 1949 Act. These rules are discussed in paras. A033.17–A033.20, with the procedure applicable to all proceedings before the Comptroller being discussed in paras. 72.32–72.52.

A077   **SECTION 77 [1949]** [*Repealed*]

Evidence of entries, documents, etc.

Note. Section 77 was replaced by section 35 [1977].

A078   **SECTION 78 [1949]** [*Repealed*]

Requests for information as to patent or patent application

For *Note*, see para. A079.

A079   **SECTION 79 [1949]** [*Repealed*]

Restriction of publication of specifications, etc.

Note. Sections 78–79 have been replaced and extended by section 118 [1977]. Rule 32 [1968], which provided for the availability of the examiner's search report under sections 7 and 8 [1949], remains applicable to existing patents and is reprinted in its revised form at para. 118.09. The request under rule 32 [1968] for the search results is made on PF No. 8 (reprinted at para. A120). Attention is also drawn to rule 158 [1968] (as revised), reprinted at para. 118.10. This enables the Comptroller to withdraw from public availability any application, specification, drawing or other document three months after its date of publication if the Secretary of State has certified that further inspection would, in his opinion, be prejudicial to the safety of the public. However, any such certificate has a maximum life of 12 months, unless renewed. The rule is discussed further in para. 118.16.

A080.1   **SECTION 80 [1949]**

Loss or destruction of patent

80. Where the comptroller is satisfied that a patent has been lost or destroyed or cannot be produced, he may at any time cause a duplicate thereof to be sealed.

136. [1968] An application under section 80 for a duplicate of a patent   **A080.2**
shall be made on Patents Form No. 68 and shall be accompanied by evidence setting out fully and verifying the circumstances in which the patent
was lost or destroyed, or cannot be produced.

COMMENTARY ON SECTION 80 [1949]   **A080.3**

This section remains effective should a duplicate of a lost Letters Patent document
of an existing patent be required. However, this document is not required for court
proceedings as the entries in the register control the legal title to a patent (ss. 32(9)
and 68 [1977]), each applicable to existing patents. Formerly, duplicate Letters
Patent were most likely to be needed if it was desired to effect a "Licence of right"
endorsement: the patent document then had to be produced for the endorsement to
be recorded thereon. However, endorsement is now entered instead in the register
(s. 46 [1977]). Thus, section 80 is probably otiose.

The section provides only for loss or destruction and it is not clear if the section
could be relied upon to obtain a duplicate if the patent document has been deliberately destroyed. Presumably any duplicate document issued under the section will
be in the form prescribed in Schedule 4 to the 1968 Rules reprinted at para. A021.3

PRACTICE UNDER SECTION 80 [1949]   **A080.4**

Rule 138 [1968] (reprinted *supra*) governs the procedure requiring the filing of PF
No. 68 (reprinted at para. A137). The accompanying evidence should be prepared
in accordance with rules 103–107 [1982], reprinted at paras. 72.05–72.09, and discussed in paras. 72.40–72.46. PF No. 68 no longer requires personal signature as
rule 90(1) [1982] (reprinted at para. 115.02 and discussed in para. 115.03) applies.

SECTION 81 [1949] [*Repealed*]   **A081**

Exercise of discretionary powers of comptroller

Note. Section 81 has been replaced by section 101 [1977].

SECTION 82 [1949] [*Repealed*]   **A082**

Costs and security for costs

Note. Section 82 has been replaced by section 107 [1977].

SECTION 83 [1949] [*Repealed*]   **A083**

Evidence before comptroller

Note. Section 83 has been replaced by section 123(2)(*d*) [1977] and rules 103–107
[1982] (reprinted at paras. 72.05–72.09) made thereunder, see paras. 72.40–72.46.

A084   **SECTION 84 [1949]** [*Repealed*]

The Court

Note. Section 84 has been replaced by section 96 [1977], itself now repealed, see para. 96.14.

A085   **SECTION 85 [1949]** [*Repealed*]

The Appeal Tribunal

For *Note*, see para. A086.

A086   **SECTION 86 [1949]** [*Repealed*]

Appeals for the decision of the comptroller in Scottish cases

Note. Sections 85 and 86 have been replaced by section 97 [1977].

A087   **SECTION 87 [1949]** [*Repealed in part*]

Appeals to Court of Appeal and Court of Session

Note. Subsections (1) and (3) have been repealed and subsection (2) is spent. The repealed subsections were replaced by section 97 [1977], but section 87(1)(*aa*) could still have effect under sections 35 and 36 [1949], see para. A035.

A088   **SECTION 88 [1949]** [*Repealed*]

Restrictions on practice as patent agent

For *Note*, see para. A089.

A089   **SECTION 89 [1949]** [*Repealed*]

Power of comptroller to refuse to deal with certain agents

Note. Sections 88 and 89 were replaced by sections 114 and 115 [1977]. These sections, together with sections 84 and 85 [1977] concerning the practice of professional representatives in relation to European patents (UK) and applications therefor have themselves each been repealed and replaced, see Note to para. 114.01 and para. 115.04.

SECTION 90 [1949] [*Repealed*]   A090

Falsification of register, etc.

For *Note*, see para. A091.

SECTION 91 [1949] [*Repealed*]   A091

Unauthorised claim of patent rights

Note. Sections 90 and 91 have been replaced by sections 109, 110 and 112 [1977] with section 111 [1977] making further provision of a similar nature.

SECTION 92 [1949]   A092.1

Unauthorised assumption of Royal Arms

92.—(1) The grant of a patent under this Act shall not be deemed to authorise the patentee to use the Royal Arms or to place the Royal Arms on any patented article.

(2) If any person, without the authority of His Majesty, uses in connection with any business, trade, calling or profession the Royal Arms (or Arms so nearly resembling them as to be calculated to deceive) in such manner as to be calculated to lead to the belief that he is duly authorised to use the Royal Arms then, without prejudice to any proceedings which may be taken against him under section 61 of the Trade Marks Act 1938, he shall be liable on summary conviction to a fine not exceeding **level 2 on the standard scale** [*twenty-five pounds*]:

Provided that this section shall not affect the right, if any, of the proprietor of a trade mark containing such Arms to continue to use that trade mark.

Note. Amendment was effected by the Criminal Justice Act 1982 (c. 48, s. 38).

COMMENTARY ON SECTION 92 [1949]

Subsection (1) is applied to existing patents by Schedule 1, para. 1(2) [1977]. A   **A092.2**
patent granted under the 1977 Act is not a grant from the Crown and there is, therefore, no corresponding provision in that Act for such patents. The Crown, however, retains a prerogative to grant licences to use the Royal Arms.

Subsection (2) makes unauthorised use of the Royal Arms a criminal offence. It is included in a patent statute by historical accident and supplements section 61 of the Trade Marks Act 1938 (1 & 2 Geo. 6, c. 22) which provides for an injunction to be granted in respect of such unauthorised use. Under this section 61 it has been held that the "belief" must be on the part of persons who saw the display of the Royal Arms (*Royal Warrant Holders* v. *Edward Deane and Beal*, (1911) 28 RPC 721). A defence that the accused, under the forerunner of section 92 [1949], was a contractor to Government departments failed in *Wood's Case* (*noted, The Times*, May 14, 1903 at p. 15).

The term "standard scale" is defined and explained in para. 110.03. "Level 2" of that scale presently stands at £100 (Criminal Penalties Etc. (Increase) Order 1984 (S.I. 1984 No. 447), Sched. 4).

A093   **SECTION 93 [1949]** [*Repealed*]

Offences by companies

Note. Section 93 has been replaced by section 113 [1977].

A094   **SECTION 94 [1949]** [*Repealed*]

General power of Board of Trade to make rules, etc.

Note. The general rule-making powers of sections 94 and 95 have been replaced by provisions now to be found mainly in section 123 [1977], but section 118 [1977] is also relevant and certain other powers to make rules are also to be found elsewhere in the 1977 Act. There is also the power under section 123 [1977] to make rules under the 1949 Act, see Schedule 2, paras. 1(2) and 2(*c*) [1977].

A095   **SECTION 95 [1949]** [*Repealed*]

Provisions as to rules and Orders

Note. Section 95 has been replaced by section 124 [1977].

A096.1   **SECTION 96 [1949]** [*Repealed in part*]

Proceedings of Board of Trade

96.—(1) [*Repealed*].

(2) All documents purporting to be orders made by the Board of Trade and to be sealed with the seal of the Board, or to be signed by a secretary, under-secretary or assistant secretary of the Board, or by any person authorised in that behalf by the President of the Board, shall be received in evidence, and shall be deemed to be such orders without further proof, unless the contrary is shown.

(3) A certificate, signed by the President of the Board of Trade, that any order made or act done is the order or act of the Board, shall be conclusive evidence of the fact so certified.

A096.2   Commentary on Section 96 [1949]

Section 96(1) was repealed by the Industrial Expansion Act 1968 (c. 32). Subsections (2) and (3) remain alive to provide formal validity for previous orders. The powers of the Board of Trade are now exercisable by the President of the Board of Trade (Industrial Expansion) Act 1968, c. 32, s. 14), whose powers are exercised by the Secretary of State (S.I. 1970 No. 1537).

SECTION 97 [1949] [*Repealed*] {A097}

Service of notices, etc., by post

Note. Section 97 has been replaced by section 119 [1977].

SECTION 98 [1949] [*Repealed*] {A098}

Hours of business and excluded days

Note. Section 98 has been replaced by section 120 [1977].

SECTION 99 [1949] [*Repealed*] {A099}

Fees

Note. Section 99 has been replaced by section 123(2)(*c*) and (4) [1977].

SECTION 100 [1949] [*Repealed*] {A100}

Annual Report of comptroller

Note. Section 100 has been replaced by section 121 [1977].

SECTION 101 [1949] {A101.01}

Interpretation

101.—(1) In this Act, except where the context otherwise requires, the following expressions have the meanings hereby respectively assigned to them, that is to say—

> **"Appeal Tribunal" means the Appeal Tribunal constituted and acting in accordance with section 85 of this Act as amended by the Administration of Justice Act 1969;**
>
> "applicant" includes a person in whose favour a direction has been given under section seventeen of this Act, and the personal representative of a deceased applicant;
>
> **"appointed day" means the day appointed under section 132 of the**

Patents Act 1977 for the coming into operation of Schedule 1 to that Act";

"article" includes any substance or material, and any plant, machinery or apparatus, whether affixed to land or not;

"assignee" includes the personal representative of a deceased assignee, and references to the assignee of any person include references to the assignee of the personal representative or assignee of that person;

"Comptroller" means the Comptroller-General of Patents, Designs and Trade Marks;

"convention application" has the meaning assigned to it by subsection (4) of section one of this Act;

"court" means the High Court;

"date of filing," in relation to any document filed under this Act, means the date on which the document is filed or, where it is deemed by virtue of any provision of this Act or rules made thereunder to have been filed on any different date, means the date on which it is deemed to be filed;

"exclusive licence" means a licence from a patentee which confers on the licensee, or on the licensee and persons authorised by him, to the exclusion of all other persons (including the patentee), any right in respect of the patented invention, and "exclusive licensee" shall be construed accordingly;

"invention" means any manner of new manufacture the subject of letters patent and grant of privilege within section six of the Statute of Monopolies and any new method or process of testing applicable to the improvement or control of manufacture, and includes an alleged invention;

"Journal" has the meaning assigned to it by subsection (2) of section ninety-four of this Act;

"patent" means Letters Patent for an invention;

"patent agent" means a person carrying on for gain in the United Kingdom the business of acting as agent for other persons for the purpose of applying for or obtaining patents in the United Kingdom or elsewhere;

"patent of addition" means a patent granted in accordance with section twenty-six of this Act;

"patentee" means the person or persons for the time being entered on the register of patents as grantee or proprietor of the patent;

"precribed" means prescribed by rules made by the Board of Trade under this Act;

"priority date" has the meaning assigned to it by section five of this Act;

"published", except in relation to a complete specification, means made available to the public; and without prejudice to the generality of the foregoing provision a document shall be deemed for the purposes of this Act to be published if it can be inspected as of right at any place in the United Kingdom by members of the public, whether upon payment of a fee or otherwise;

"the Statute of Monopolies" means the Act of the twenty-first year of the reign of King James the First, chapter three intitled "An Act concerning monopolies and dispensations with penal laws and the forfeiture thereof."

(2) For the purposes of subsection (3) of section one, so far as it relates to a convention application, and for the purposes of section seventy-two of this Act, the expression "personal representative", in relation to a deceased person, includes the legal representative of the deceased appointed in any country outside the United Kingdom.

Note. The definition of "Appeal Tribunal" was inserted by the Administration of Justice Act 1969 (c. 58), Sched. 1 and that of "appointed day" by the 1977 Act, Schedule 1, para. 8.

ARTICLES   **A101.02**

I. Shachter, "Manner of manufacture", Trans. Chart. Inst. LXXV (1956–57), C81;

M. W. Hill, "Date-stamping in the NRLSI", (1972–73) 2 CIPA 408;

A. W. White, "Patentability of medical treatment: Wellcome Foundation's (Hitching's) Application", [1980] EIPR 364;

Y. Cripps, "The refusal of patents for methods of medical treatment: A preference for parliamentary guidance", [1983] EIPR 173.

COMMENTARY ON SECTION 101 [1949]

General   **A101.03**

This section defines certain words and phrases used in the 1949 Act. Many of these definitions are self-explanatory; others are commented on below. The definition of "invention" is fundamental to the whole operation of the 1949 Act and has great historical significance. The definitions in the section apply only for the 1949 Act. Otherwise, the definitions of section 130 [1977] are to be applied if the context so requires, see paras. 130.02–130.07. Consequently, some of the definitions in section 101 are no longer applicable, this depending on whether the provision in which the defined term is used itself remains applicable.

Definition of "article"   **A101.04**

This definition is broad enough to cover any tangible material. There is no exclusion of chemical products *per se* as had existed from 1919 to 1950 under the Patents & Designs Act 1907 (7 Edw. 7, c. 29, s. 38A, as added by the Patents and Designs Act 1919, 9 & 10 Geo. 5, c. 80, s. 11) which for this period restricted protection for chemical products to methods for their production.

Definition of "invention"

A101.05 —*General*

"Invention" for the purposes of the 1949 Act is mainly defined in terms of section 6 of the "Statute of Monopolies" (reprinted at para. B01). However, to the requirement therein that an invention be "a manner of new manufacture", section 100 adds that an invention may be "any new method or process of testing applicable to the improvement or control of manufacture". An "alleged invention" is also included within the statutory definition.

For patents granted under the 1977 Act, a different code of law operates, mainly as set out in section 1 [1977], see para. 1.05. Thus, the present importance of the definition of "invention" in section 101 is limited to the question of possible revocation of an "existing patent" under section 32(1)(*d*) [1949] (*No invention within the meaning of the Act*). There are few court decisions at this level, for which see para. A032.09. Of course, where a claim has been rejected at the application stage as failing to meet the statutory criterion, that decision may suggest that similar subject matter would now be held unpatentable by the court. However, this area of law is one where judicial attitudes have become noticeably more liberal over the years, so that old decisions would not necessarily be followed in more modern times. Also, acceptance of a claim is no more than an approximate guide to an ultimate finding as to its validity, should this come to be judged under section 31(1)(*d*) [1949] because, where there was any doubt as to patentability, the practice was to allow the claim so that this could, if necessary, subsequently be tested before the court, see *R. v. Patents Appeal Tribunal ex p. Swift* ([1962] RPC 37). Nevertheless, the decided cases are the only guide because the interpretation of the phrase "manner of new manufacture" is entirely one of judicial view to be reached in the light of these cases.

In addition to the requirement that patents are only valid if granted in respect of a "manner of new manufacture", section 6 of the Statute of Monopolies stipulates that patents must not be "contrary to the law, nor mischievous to the state, by raising prices of commodities at home, or hurt of trade, or generally inconvenient". This provision led to refusal of grant in *Rolls-Royce's Application* ([1963] RPC 251. Also, where the Act specifically refers to the "invention as claimed", this is to be interpreted as limited to what has been claimed as distinct from what has been described (*Georgia Kaolin's Application*, [1956] RPC 121).

A101.06 —*Meaning of "manner of manufacture"*

In *R. v. Wheeler* ([1819] 2 B & Ald 345; 106 E.R. 392) it was stated that:

Something of a corporeal and substantial nature, something that can be made by man from the matters subjected to his art and skill, or at least some mode of employing practically his art and skill, is requisite to satisfy the word manufacture."

However, decisions in the early part of the present century placed a more restrictive interpretation on the meaning of "manufacture" and, in *GEC's Application* ((1943) 60 RPC 1), Morton J. enunciated the concept that a patentable method or process should result in the production of a "vendible product" or improve or restore or prevent the deterioration of a "vendible product", though he said such tests might not be exhaustive. This "vendible product" test then came to be applied for several years and its application led to the drawing of many artificial distinctions. The cases in this period are reviewed in the article by I. Shachter listed in para. A101.02 *supra*.

In 1960 the full court of the High Court of Australia gave a landmark decision in *NRDC's Application* ([1961] RPC 135) in which a method of eradicating weeds from crop areas was deemed patentable. The strong court stated that the statutory test did not depend on what the words "manner of manufacutre" meant in 1624, but whether the subject matter is "a proper subject of Letters Patent according to the principles which have been developed for the application of Section six of the Statute of Monopolies". This led to a judgment in New Zealand where a method of tenderising meat by injecting a living animal with an enzyme prior to slaughter was held to be patentable, but the corresponding United Kingdom application was rejected (*Swift's Application*, [1961] RPC 129). However, in doing so, the Patents Appeal Tribunal appended the aforesaid Australian and New Zealand decisions to its own decision. This provided basis for the Divisional Court subsequently to quash the PAT decision and find the *Swift* invention patentable on the basis that the difference of judicial opinion under the same statutory test showed that the invention was not clearly unpatentable and should therefore be allowed to proceed to grant, the application stage not being intended as a final determination of validity (*R. v. PAT ex p. Swift*, [1962] RPC 37).

From this date the practice of granting doubtful claims under the definition naturally became more lenient and, for practical purposes, the areas of definite statutory unpatentability now seem to lie in methods of presenting mere information, computer programs and medical treatment, each as such. These, together with the separate aspect of the patentability of methods of testing, are discussed more fully in paras. A101.07–A101.09 *infra*.

—*Presentation of information* **A101.07**

In *Rhodes' Application* ([1973] RPC 243) the PAT sitting *in banc* stated that "a patent cannot be sustained on the basis of novelty in information, for example, artistic or literary content, alone", but it indicated that a novel method of presenting information, or a novel article by which information can be presented, ought to be regarded as an invention within section 101. On this basis a claim to a speedometer showing both speed and the square of speed (the "impact speed") was allowed. This decision is illustrative of the principles applied in the determination of the exclusions from patentability in this area, as has been considered in para. 1.13 with reference to many of the cases decided under the 1949 Act. Other instances of applications rejected as being for mere methods of presenting information as such, additional to those there listed, are: *Rolls-Royce's Application* ([1963] RPC 251); *Hiller's Application* ([1969] RPC 267); and *Dixon's Application* ([1978] RPC 687). A further instance of a case where a claim had a significance beyond the mere presentation of information, and was therefore held patentable, was *Pitmans' Application* ([1969] RPC 646).

As regards the patentability of inventions based upon the use of novel computer programs, the decisions given under the 1977 Act (for which see paras. 1.10 and 1.11) appear largely to be compatible with the developments which had been occurring prior to the new law coming into effect. Therefore, it is thought that modern decisions in this area would also now be held applicable to "existing patents". The development of the law of patentability under section 101 in relation to inventions involving computer programs can be traced through: *Slee and Harris' Application* ([1966] RPC 194); *Badger's Application* ([1970] RPC 36); *Gevers' Application* ([1970] RPC 91); *Burroughs' (Perkins') Application* ([1974] RPC 147); and *IBM's [Revocation] Application* ([1980] FSR 564).

A101.08 —*Medical treatment*

Before the *Swift* decision (referred to para. A101.06 *supra*), claims to agricultural and horticultural processes were refused, though claims to microbiological processes were allowed. The patentability of the latter has since been upheld by the court in a validity, rather than allowability, context (*American Cyanamid* v. *Berk*, [1976] RPC 231). However, while claims to treatment of the animal body have been allowed (as in the *Swift* case), the courts have consistently denied patentability to a method of *medical* treatment of the human body, see *Eli Lilly's Application* ([1975] RPC 438) and *Upjohn's (Robert's) Application* ([1977] RPC 94 (CA)), in each of which claims directed to the medical treatment of humans with a drug already known for some other purpose were refused as not meeting the test of "manner of new manufacture". Subsequently, in New Zealand, a judgment was given allowing this type of claim on the basis that the law should move with the times (see the article by A. W. White listed in para. A101.02 *supra*, which traced the historical development of the previous decisions), but this decision was reversed on appeal on the basis that the grant of patents for inventions of this type, though apparently meritorious, raised issues which were more properly to be debated by the Legislature than decided by the courts (*Wellcome's (Hitching's) Application* [*New Zealand*], [1980] RPC 305 and [1983] FSR 593), see the article by Y. Cripps listed in para. A101.02 *supra*.

Nevertheless, the exclusion was limited to "medical" treatment and claims were allowed where the treatment was not for medical (*i.e.* therapeutic) purposes, *e.g.* for: a method of defence against bodily human attack (*Palmer's Application*, [1970] RPC 597); a method of contraception (*Schering's Application*, [1971] RPC 337), but not for inducing abortion (*Upjohn's (Kirton's) Application*, [1976] RPC 324) or for cleaning teeth (*Blendax-Werke's Application*, [1980] RPC 491); or for removing dental plaque (*Oral Health's (Halstead's) Application*, [1977] RPC 612). However, where the effect of the treatment is clearly only cosmetic, the claimed method could more clearly be seen to be of economic endeavour and to have commercial significance and therefore be patentable, see *Joos* v. *Commissioner of Patents* [*Australia*] ([1973] RPC 59) where it was observed that "cosmetic processes and methods are not of a like kind with medical, prophylactic or therapeutic processes or methods". Nevertheless, in *Lee Pharmaceutical's Application* ([1978] RPC 51), claims were refused to methods of repairing physical defects in teeth as being therapeutic, rather than cosmetic, treatments.

Attempts to obtain patents protecting inventions of new methods of medical treatment have also been made by drafting claims to specified types of package, but such attempts have generally failed because of lack of novelty or technical effect in the claimed package as such, see *Ciba-Geigy's (Dürrs) Applications* ([1977] RPC 83 (CA)) and para. 2.30. However, this type of claim has been held patentable in a few instances where the package has assumed some special form in its own right, see *Organon's Application* ([1970] RPC 574) and *Blendax-Werke's Application* (*supra*).

In considering the validity of claims under the 1949 Act, care must be taken not to be influenced by decisions given on the definition of "invention" under the 1977 Act. The specific exclusion from the test of "patentable invention" under that Act of methods of treatment of the human or animal body by surgery, therapy or diagnosis practised on such a body (s. 4(2) [1977]) is clearly more restrictive if only because of the exclusion of claims to animal treatment which had been allowed without question since the *Swift* decision (*supra*), see *Wellcome Foundation's Australian Application* ([1981] FSR 72) where such claims had been allowed prior to the appeal therein on the rejected "package" claims: for which see para. 2.30. Thus, in *Ciba-Geigy's Application* (SRIS O/30/85, *noted* IPD 8083), the Comptroller refused under the 1977 Act to follow the decision in *Stafford-Miller's Applications* ([1984] FSR 268), wherein claims to methods of using certain compositions for the treatment of ectoparasites, such as head-lice, on humans had been allowed under section 101, holding the criteria under the two statutes to be different. The non-patentability under the 1977 Act of medical and veterinary treatment as such is discussed in paras. 4.05–4.08, but (as indicated in paras. 2.28–2.30) inventions in this field may now be patented under the 1977 Act by casting the claims in a form not envisaged at the time when applications under the 1949 Act were still being prosecuted.

—Method of testing   **A101.09**

Mere testing as such is not patentable. The testing must involve a new method, and a process claim in which the novelty is the use of a new apparatus for obtaining readings to facilitate an old test does not meet the test of the extended definition of being a new "method or process of testing applicable to the improvement or control of manufacture" (*BP's Application*, [1958] RPC 253).

A method of testing is not necessarily unpatentable if it is not a method applied to the improvement or control of manufacture (*Bio-Digital Sciences' Application*, [1973] RPC 668); it may possibly qualify as a "manner of new manufacture" *per se*, as in that case where an analogy was seen with the claim allowed in *Gevers' Application* ([1970] RPC 91) for operations controlled by a computer program.

Definition of "published"   **A101.10**

The term "published" (except for the official publication of a complete specification) means generally "made available to the public [in the United Kingdom]". A sub-test is then provided that a document is to be deemed to be published if it can be inspected as of right at any place in the United Kingdom by members of the public, whether upon payment of a fee or otherwise. The wider definition is, however, the controlling one.

Both the wider and narrower definitions are, prima facie, in conflict with the decision in *Plimpton* v. *Malcolmson* ((1876) 3 Ch.D. 531), in which a book in the British Museum, not indexed, was held not to be published; but it may be questioned whether the present statutory definitions would be so literally interpreted as to overrule the *Plimpton* decision. For example, if a prohibitive fee were asked for the inspection of a document the court might hold that it was not published. However, a single document or instance of prior use suffices, see *Woven Plastics* v. *British Ropes* ([1970] FSR 47) in which a single Japanese utility model specification had been received in the then Patent Office Library only three days before the priority date; *Fomento* v. *Mentmore* ([1956] RPC 87) where a single pen had been given to a public official; and *Bristol-Myers' Application* ([1969] RPC 146) where a South African patent specification was specially imported into the United Kingdom after an abstract of it had been seen. Also, in *Van der Lely* v. *Bamfords* ([1960] RPC 169), the contents of a foreign magazine were held to be communicated to the public on proof that there were five regular subscribers in the United Kingdom, see also *Pickard* v. *Prescott* ((1892) 9 RPC 195 (HL)). However, mere knowledge of an invention by another, without non-confidential disclosure, does not amount to publication (*Dolland's Case*, (1776) 1 WPC 43) and, more recently, *Catnic* v. *Evans* ([1983] FSR 410).

Thus, the most important element in the definition is "made available to the public". Mere communication to one person, whether or not confidential, is unlikely to constitute publication, but multiplication of copies, or the nature or position of the person or persons communicated to, can negate this (*Weir's Application*, (1926) 43 RPC 39) as also shown by the cases cited *supra*.

A document sent to members of a trade association and dealing with their work would presumably always be "published". A document which was marked "confidential" and "not to be disclosed to non-members" and which was sent to members of a trade association, government departments and other scientific workers for them to use the information in it, has been held to be published (*Dalrymple's Application*, [1957] RPC 449). A fairly obvious corollary is that a document in the library of a learned society, and accessible only to members thereof, is published.

The circumstances in which a document is sent are material, and if the sender and receiver are, in effect, collaborators there is no publication even if the document is not said to be confidential (*Gallay's Application*, [1959] RPC 141).

Thus, following *Humpherson* v. *Syer* ([1887] 4 RPC 407 (CA)), an invention is published if any member of the public who is free in law and equity to make use of the information contained in a document comes into possession of it in the United Kingdom, *i.e.* he receives the document in his capacity as a member of the public (*Bristol-Myers' Application, supra*).

Proof of publication will normally require reference to some library or other documentary record of receipt of the document in question in the United Kingdom by a member of the public *qua* member of the public. Often a letter from a responsible librarian referring to the system of recording receipt and, if necessary, producing a copy of the relevant record will be sufficient for the other party in a contested case to admit the facts. If no admission is made, then the librarian should be called as a witness. It may be necessary to make use of the provisions of the Civil Evidence Act 1968 (c. 64, s. 4) for proof by way of documentary hearsay evidence. The SRIS (formerly the Science Reference Library, SRL, and before that the National Reference Library of Science and Invention, NRLSI, and the Patent Office Library) has had a consistent practice of date-stamping documents when received and placed in the library collection. This date-stamping practice is the subject of the article by M. W. Hill listed in para. A101.02 *supra*. Such a stamp is normally accepted as sufficient evidence, but the Library retains further accession records which can be consulted, for example, when a book has been removed from stock. It is not necessary that a document remains published: it is sufficient that it can be proved that it was once published.

A102.1

SECTION 102 [1949] [*Repealed in part*]

Saving for Royal prerogative, etc.

102.—(1) Nothing in this Act shall take away, abridge or prejudicially affect the prerogative of the Crown in relation to the granting of letters patents or to the withholding of a grant thereof.

(2) [*Repealed*].

Note. Section 102(2) has been replaced by section 122 [1977].

A102.1

COMMENTARY ON SECTION 102 [1949]

Section 102(1) provided the basis for the grant of patents under the 1949 Act as an exercise of the royal prerogative giving rise to grant by a Letters Patent document under the seal of the Patent Office. The prerogative was occasionally exercised to refuse grant, presumably on the basis of the presumed interest of the public. Under the 1977 Act the grant of a patent is a statutory obligation, if the conditions for grant are found to have been met. The grant is then recorded in the register, the certificate of grant being secondary, rather than a primary, record of grant as was the Letters Patent document for patents granted under all previous British patent statutes. One result of this change is that the term "patentee" is, strictly speaking, no longer appropriate except in relation to "existing patents", but the term is of such long-standing that it continues to be used. Nevertheless, the correct modern term for a patent owner under the 1977 Act is "proprietor", a term also used there in relation to the owner of a pending application.

SECTION 103 [1949]   A103

Application in Scotland

[*Spent*]

Note. Section 103 has been replaced by section 98 [1977].

SECTION 104 [1949]   A104

Application in Northern Ireland

[*Spent*]

Note. Section 104 has been replaced by section 131 [1977].

SECTION 105 [1949]   A105

Isle of Man

[*Spent*]

Note. Section 105 has been replaced by section 132(2) [1977].

SECTION 106 [1949]   A106

Repeals, transitional provisions and amendment

[*Spent*]

Note. Section 106 introduced the Schedules to the 1949 Act, see para. A108.

SECTION 107 [1949]   A107

Short title and commencement

107.—(1) This Act may be cited as the Patents Act 1949.
(2) This Act shall come into operation on the first day of January, nine-

teen hundred and fifty, immediately after the coming into operation of the Patents and Designs Act 1949.

Note. The 1907–46 Acts were actually amended, not by the present Act, but by the Patents and Designs Act 1949 (12, 13 & 14 Geo. 6, c. 62), a parliamentary device which avoided putting various parts of the 1907–46 Acts into the amending Bill. Most of the unrepealed parts of the 1907–46 Acts and the amended parts were then consolidated and passed without parliamentary debate to become the present Act, which came into force immediately after, and at once repealed, the amending Act. The unrepealed provisions of the 1907–46 Acts are reprinted at paras. B03–B07.

A108   **SCHEDULES TO PATENTS ACT 1949** [*Repealed in part*]

SCHEDULE 1 [1949]: MAXIMUM FEES [*Repealed*]

SCHEDULE 2 [1949]: ENACTMENTS REPEALED [*Repealed*]

SCHEDULE 3 [1949]: [*Repealed in part*]

Transitional provisions

1. Subject to the provisions of this Schedule, any Order in Council, rule, order, requirement, certificate, notice, decision, direction, authorisation, consent, application, request or thing made, issued given or done under any enactment repealed by this Act shall, if in force at the commencement of this Act, and so far as it could have been made, issued, given or done under this Act, continue in force and have effect as if made, issued, given or done under the corresponding enactment of this Act.

[*Paras. 2–25 repealed*]

26. Any document referring to any enactment repealed by this Act shall be construed as referring to the corresponding enactment of this Act.

[*Para. 27 repealed*]

Note. These Schedules are largely repealed. The remaining provisions are formal and duplicate general provisions relating to statutory repeals now to be found in the Interpretation Act 1978 (c. 30). For discussion on unrepealed patent statutes, see para. 132.10 and the reprints thereof in Appendix B.

THE PATENTS RULES 1968

S.I. 1968 No. 1389 [As amended]

A109   *General*

Although the Patents Rules 1968 were entirely repealed by rule 124 [1978] (reprinted at para. 127.04), some of them, by this rule, may continue to have application in respect of existing patents. This includes the forms contained in Schedule 2 of the 1968 Rules (designated herein as "PF No. .."). Nevertheless, many of the 1968 Rules (and forms thereto) can be considered as spent. Accordingly, there is now tabulated those of the 1968 Rules which are considered as, at least potentially, still effective, indicating whereat such rules and their associated forms are reprinted herein. Where possible, this reprinting is presented immediately following the statute section under which the rule now has effect, but rules of an entirely general nature are printed *infra*. The still effective forms are then reprinted as the following paras. A119–A138. Several of the rules were amended by rule 124 [1978] and are reprinted as amended. The forms are reprinted as amended: by rule 124 [1982] (reprinted at para. 127.02); by the Patents (Amendment) Rules 1985 (S.I. 1985 No. 785, r. 4(1)), deleting the Patent Office address; and by the Patents (Amendment No. 2) Rules 1985 (S.I. 1985 No. 1166, r. 15), adding a note to PF No. 1 Add.

Subject and Rules	Reprinted para.	Associated Forms	Forms reprinted at para.
Citation, Commencement and Interpretation			
Rule 1	A110	—	—
Rule 2	A111	—	—
Fees and Forms			
Rule 3	A112	—	—
Rule 4	A113	—	—
Documents			
Rule 5	A114	—	—
Applications for the grant of patents			
Rule 9(4)	A026.00	PF No. 1 Add	A119
Procedure under Sections 7, 8 and 9			
Rule 31	A008.2	—	—
Rule 32	118.09	PF No. 8	A120
Rule 34	A009.2	—	—
Rule 35	A009.3	PF No. 9	A121
Rule 36	A009.4	—	—
Opposition to grant of patent (Section 14)			
Rule 40	A033.04	—	—
Rule 41	A033.05	—	—
Rule 42	A033.06	—	—
Rule 43	A033.07	—	—
Rule 44	A033.08	—	—
Rule 45	A033.09	PF No. 13	A122
Rule 46	A033.10	—	—
Rule 47	A033.11	—	—
Mention of inventor as such (Section 16)			
Rule 54	A016.2	PF No. 17	A123
Secrecy orders (Section 18)			
Rule 69	A018	—	—

Citation, Commencement and Interpretation

1. These Rules may be cited as the Patents Rules 1968 and shall come into operation on November 1, 1968. **A110**

2.—(1) In these Rules unless the context otherwise requires— **A111**
"the Act" means the Patents Act 1949, as amended by the Patents Act 1957 and the Patents and Designs (Renewals, Extensions and Fees) Act 1961 and the Patents Act 1977 and, save where otherwise indicated any reference to a section is a reference to that section of the Act;
"Journal" means the Official Journal (Patents) published in accordance with rule 115 of the Patent Rules 1978;
"Office" means the Patent Office;
"register" means the register of patents kept under the provisions of section 32 of the Patents Act 1977;
"United Kingdom" includes the Isle of Man.
(2) The Interpretation Act 1978 shall apply to the interpretation of these Rules as it applies to the interpretation of an Act of Parliament, and as if these Rules and the Rules hereby revoked were Acts of Parliament.

Note. Rule 2(2) was amended by the Interpretation Act 1978 (c. 30 s. 25(2)).

Fees and Forms

3. The fees to be paid in respect of any matters arising under the Act shall be those specified in Schedule I to these Rules and in any case where a form specified in that Schedule as the corresponding form in relation to any matter is required to be used that form shall be accompanied by the fee specified in respect of that matter. **A112**

Note. Schedule 1 has been successively replaced and now constitutes Part B of the Schedule to the current Patents (Fees) Rules, see para. 144.01. Part B of the Schedule to the Patents (Fees) Rules 1989 (S.I. 1989 No. 899) is reprinted at para. A139 solely as a comparative indication of the level of fees that then prevailed.

4. The forms mentioned in these Rules are those set out in Schedule 2 to these Rules and such forms shall be used in all cases in which they are applicable and may be modified as directed by the Comptroller. **A113**

Note. The relevant forms are reprinted at paras. A119–A138.

Documents

A114   **5.**—(1) All documents and copies of documents, except drawings, filed at the Office shall, unless the Comptroller otherwise directs, be written, typewritten, lithographed or printed in English language—

(*a*) upon strong white paper of a size 330 mm. by 200 to 210 mm. (13 inches by 8 inches to $8\frac{1}{4}$ inches) or of A4 size (297 mm. by 210 mm.: $11\frac{3}{4}$ inches by $8\frac{1}{4}$ inches);

(*b*) in legible characters with a dark indelible ink;

(*c*) with the lines widely spaced;

(*d*) except in the case of statutory declarations and affidavits, on one side only;

(*e*) leaving a margin of at least 25 mm (1 inch) on the left-hand part thereof; and

(*f*) in the case of each of the forms set out in Schedule 2 hereto, leaving a space of about 80 mm. (3 inches) blank at the top of the form.

(2) Duplicate documents required under these Rules may be carbon copies of the original documents provided that they are on paper of good quality and the typing is black and distinct.

Note. Rule 5 would appear to be an alternative to rule 20 [1982] (reprinted at para. 14.05) in relation to documents concerning existing patents. Nevertheless, the use of foolscap paper (apparently permitted by r. 5 [1968], but not by r. 20 [1982]) is not advised.

General

A115   **153.**—(1) Where by virtue of any of the Rules mentioned in sub-rule (2) of this Rule any notice of opposition or application for revocation of a patent is required to be supported by a statement or evidence, such statement or evidence shall be filed on, or within fourteen days after, the date on which the notice is given or the application is made.

(2) The Rules referred to in sub-rule (1) are Rules 39(1), 72(2), 80(2), 86(2), 91(2), 96(1), 100(1), 106(2), 114(3) and 131(2).

A116   **154.** The times prescribed by these Rules for doing any act, or taking any proceedings thereunder, other than the times prescribed by Rules 37, 59, 72(1), 80, 86, 100 and 106, may be extended by the Comptroller if he thinks fit, upon such notice to the parties and upon such terms, as he may direct, and such extension may be granted although the time has expired for doing such act or taking such proceedings.

A117   **156.** Where the hearing before the Comptroller of any dispute between two or more parties relating to any matter in connection with a patent or an application for a patent takes place after the date of the publication of the complete specification, the hearing of the dispute shall be in public unless the Comptroller, after consultation with those parties to the dispute who appear in person or are represented at the hearing otherwise directs.

FIRST SCHEDULE: List of Fees Payable [*Repealed*]   A118

Note. For further details of fees, see para. A139.

SECOND SCHEDULE: *General Forms*

PATENTS ACT 1949   A119
PATENTS FORM No. 1 ADD.

To the Comptroller
The Patent Office

APPLICATION FOR THE GRANT OF A PATENT OF
ADDITION IN LIEU OF AN INDEPENDENT PATENT

(*a*) I/We ....
....
hereby request that patent No. .... of which I am/we are the patentee ..... be revoked and that in lieu thereof a patent of addition to patent No. .... of which I am/we are also the patentee be granted to me/us, such patent of addition to bear the same date as the patent so revoked.

(*b*) ....

(*a*) State full name, address and nationality of patentee or patentees.
(*b*) To be signed by patentee. Attention is directed to Rules 90 and 106 of the Patents Rules 1982.

PATENTS ACT 1949   A120
PATENTS FORM No. 8

To the Comptroller
The Patent Office

APPLICATION UNDER SECTION 79(2) FOR THE RESULT
OF A SEARCH MADE UNDER SECTIONS 7 AND 8

I/We hereby request that I/we may be informed of the result of the search made under Sections 7 and 8 in connection with Application for Patent No. ....

(*a*) ....

(This part to be filled in at the Patent Office.)

Result of the search made under Sections 7 and 8 of the Patents Act, 1949, in connection with Application for Patent No. ....

Specifications or other publications cited as the result of the search made under Section 7	Specifications cited as the result of the search made under Section 8

(*a*) Insert name and full address to which information is to be sent.

A121   **PATENTS ACT 1949**
PATENTS FORM No. 9

The Comptroller
The Patent Office

APPLICATION UNDER SECTION 9(2) FOR DELETION OF REFERENCE

I/We (*a*) ....
apply for deletion of the reference to patent No. .... which has been inserted in the complete specification of my/our (*b*) (application for a) patent No. .... in pursuance of a direction under section 9(1).

The facts relied upon in support of this application are (*c*) ....
Communications should be sent to ....
at (*d*) ....
(*e*) ....

(*a*) State (in full) name and address of applicant(s).
(*b*) Delete the words in brackets if a patent has been granted.
(*c*) The facts must be stated fully.
(*d*) The address must be within the United Kingdom.
(*e*) To be signed by applicant(s) or his or their agent. Attention is directed to Rules 90 and 106 of the Patents Rules 1982.

A122   **PATENTS ACT 1949**
PATENTS FORM No. 13

To the Comptroller
The Patent Office

NOTICE THAT HEARING BEFORE THE COMPTROLLER WILL BE ATTENDED

(*a*) I/We ....
hereby give notice that the Hearing fixed for the (*b*) .... in reference to (*c*) ....
....

1052

.... will be attended by myself/ourselves or by some person on my/our behalf.

(d) ....

(a) State name and address.
(b) Insert date of Hearing.
(c) Give particulars (*i.e.* number of application or patent, names of parties and nature of proceedings).
(d) Signature.

PATENTS ACT 1949
PATENTS FORM No. 17

A123

The Comptroller
The Patent Office

APPLICATION UNDER SECTION 16(8)
(*To be accompanied by copies as required by Rule 54*)

(a) I/We ....
declare that (b) ....
ought not to have been mentioned under section 16 as the inventor in the sense of being the actual deviser of (a substantial part of) the invention covered by Application No. .... dated the .... 19 ....
and entitled (c) ....
and I/we apply for a certificate to that effect.

A statement setting out the circumstances upon which I/we rely to justify this Application is attached together with copies thereof as required by Rule 54.

Communications should be sent to ....
at (d) ....
(e) ....

(a) State (in full) name, address and nationality of the person or persons making this application.
(b) Enter the name of the person mentioned as the actual deviser.
(c) Enter title of invention.
(d) The address must be within the United Kingdom.
(e) To be signed by all the persons making the application. Attention is directed to Rules 90 and 106 of the Patents Rules 1982.

PATENTS ACT 1949
PATENTS FORM No. 23

A124

The Comptroller
The Patent Office

APPLICATION UNDER SECTION 20 FOR AMENDMENT OF LETTERS PATENT
(*To be accompanied by evidence verifying the statements made in this application*)

I/We (a) ....
request that Letters Patent No. .... granted to ....
may be amended by substituting the name of (b) ....
for the name of the grantee.

My/Our address for service in the United Kingdom is ....

(c) ....

(a) State name and address.

(b) State name, address and nationality of person to whom patent should have been granted.

(c) Signature. Attention is directed to Rules 90 and 106 of the Patents Rules 1982.

A125 **PATENTS ACT 1949**
PATENTS FORM No. 35

The Comptroller
The Patent Office

APPLICATION UNDER SECTION 29 FOR AMENDMENT OF
A COMPLETE SPECIFICATION AFTER ACCEPTANCE

(a) I/We ....

seek leave to amend the complete specification No. ....

as shown in red ink in the copy of the printed specification hereunto annexed.

(b) I/We declare that no action for infringement or proceeding before the Court for revocation of the Patent is pending.

My/Our reasons for making this amendment are in details as follows:—

(c) ....

Communications should be sent to ....

at (d) ....

(e) ....

(a) State full name and address of applicant or patentee.

(b) These words are to be struck out when a Patent has not been sealed.

(c) State full particulars of the reasons for seeking amendment. If this space is not sufficient the particulars may be continued on a separate sheet.

(d) The address must be within the United Kingdom.

(e) To be signed by applicant or patentee. Attention is directed to Rules 90 and 106 of the Patents Rules 1982.

A126 **PATENTS ACT 1949**
PATENTS FORM No. 36

The Comptroller
The Patent Office

NOTICE OF OPPOSITION TO AMENDMENT OF SPECIFICATION UNDER SECTION 29
(*To be accompanied by a copy, and a statement of case in duplicate*)

(a) I/We ....

give notice of opposition to the proposed amendment of specification No. ....

for the following reason:

....

Communications should be sent to ....

at (b) ....

(c) ....

(*a*) State full name and address.
(*b*) The address must be within the United Kingdom.
(*c*) To be signed by the opponent. Attention is directed to Rules 90 and 106 of the Patents Rules 1982.

PATENTS ACT 1949
PATENTS FORM No. 39

A127

The Comptroller
The Patent Office

APPLICATION UNDER SECTION 33 FOR THE REVOCATION OF A PATENT
(To be accompanied by a copy, and a statement of case in duplicate)

(*a*) I/We ....
apply for an Order for the revocation of Patent No. .... on the following grounds:
(*b*) ....

(*c*) I/We declare that no action for infringement or proceedings in any Court for the revocation of the patent is pending.

Communications should be sent to ....
.... at (*d*) ....
(*e*) ....

(*a*) State full name and address.
(*b*) State upon which of the grounds the application is based and identify all specifications and other publications relied upon.
(*c*) If such action or proceeding is pending in any Court the application cannot be made without the leave of the Court.
(*d*) The address must be within the United Kingdom.
(*e*) To be signed by applicant.
   Attention is directed to Rules 90 and 106 of the Patents Rules 1982.

PATENTS ACT 1949
PATENTS FORM No. 43

A128

The Comptroller
The Patent Office

APPLICATION UNDER SECTION 35(2) FOR SETTLEMENT OF
TERMS OF LICENCE UNDER PATENT ENDORSED "LICENCES OF RIGHT"
(To be accompanied by a copy, and a statement of case in duplicate)

I/We (*a*) ....
apply for settlement of the terms of a licence to be granted under Patent No. ....

I am/We are the
   (*b*) patentee(s)
   (*c*) person(s) requiring a licence
   (*d*) holder(s) of a licence under the Patent granted before endorsement.

I/We (*e*) request that an Order may be made entitling me/us to exchange my/our existing licence for a licence to be granted upon the terms as settled.

Communications should be sent to ....
.... at (*f*) ....
(*g*) ....

(*a*) State name and address.
(*b*)(*c*)(*d*) Delete the two categories not applicable.
(*e*) Delete if the applicant is not the holder of a licence.
(*f*) The address must be within the United Kingdom.
(*g*) Signature of applicant. Attention is directed to Rules 90 and 106 of the Patents Rules 1982.

A129   **PATENTS ACT 1949**
PATENTS FORM No. 44

The Comptroller
The Patent Office

APPLICATION UNDER SECTION 36(1) BY PATENTEE FOR CANCELLATION OF ENDORSEMENT OF A PATENT "LICENCES OF RIGHT"
(*To be accompanied by evidence in support of the application*)

I/We (*a*) ....
request that the endorsement of Patent No. ....
"Licences of Right" may be cancelled, and I/we enclose Patent Form No. 12/77 accompanied by the balance of all renewal fees which would have been payable if the patent had not been endorsed.

I/We declare (*b*) that there is no existing licence under the Patent, or (*c*) all the licensees consent to this application.

Communications should be sent to ....
.... at (*d*) ....
                                                                                (*e*) ....

(*a*) State name and address.
(*b*)(*c*) Delete whichever is not applicable.
(*d*) The address must be within the United Kingdom.
(*g*) To be signed by the patentee. Attention is directed to Rules 90 and 106 of the Patents Rules 1982.

A130   **PATENTS ACT 1949**
PATENTS FORM No. 45

The Comptroller
The Patent Office

APPLICATION UNDER SECTION 36(2) BY ANY PERSON INTERESTED FOR CANCELLATION OF ENDORSEMENT OF PATENT "LICENCES OF RIGHT"
(*To be accompanied by a copy, and a statement of case in duplicate*)

I/We (*a*) ....
claim that the endorsement of Patent No. ....
"Licences of Right" is and was at the time of the endorsement contrary to a contract in which I am/we are interested and I/we request that such endorsement may be cancelled.

Communications should be sent to ....
.... at (*b*) ....
                                                                                (*c*) ....

(*a*) State name and address.
(*b*) The address must be within the United Kingdom.
(*c*) To be signed by the applicant(s). Attention is directed to Rules 90 and 106 of the Patents Rules 1982.

PATENTS ACT 1949   **A131**
PATENTS FORM No. 46

The Comptroller
The Patent Office

NOTICE OF OPPOSITION BY PATENTEE OR BY ANY PERSON INTERESTED TO CANCELLATION OF ENDORSEMENT OF A PATENT "LICENCES OF RIGHT"
(To be accompanied by a copy, and a statement of case in duplicate)

I/We (*a*) ....
give notice of opposition to the application for the cancellation of the endorsement "Licences of Right" in respect of Patent No. ....

Communications should be sent to ....
.... at (*b*) ....
(*c*) ....

(*a*) State name and address.
(*b*) The address must be within the United Kingdom.
(*c*) To be signed by the opponent. Attention is directed to Rules 90 and 106 of the Patents Rules 1982.

PATENTS ACT 1949   **A132**
PATENTS FORM No. 53

The Comptroller
The Patent Office

APPLICATION FOR DIRECTIONS UNDER SECTION 55(1)
(To be accompanied by a statement of case and by copies of the application and statement as required by Rule 116)

I/We (*a*) ....
apply for the following directions in respect of Patent No. ....
(*b*) ....

Communications should be sent to ....
.... at (*c*) ....
(*d*) ....

(*a*) State name and address.
(*b*) State the directions sought.
(*c*) The address must be within the United Kingdom.
(*d*) To be signed by the patentee seeking directions. Attention is directed to Rules 90 and 106 of the Patents Rules 1982.

A133 PATENTS ACT 1949
PATENTS FORM No. 54

The Comptroller
The Patent Office

APPLICATION FOR DIRECTIONS UNDER SECTION 55(2)
(To be accompanied by a copy, and by a statement of case in duplicate)

I/We (a) ....
apply for directions in respect of the failure of (b) ....
to comply with the directions of the Comptroller given under section 55(1) on the
.... in the following matter:
(c) ....

Communications should be sent to ....
at (d) ....

(e) ....

(a) State name and address of patentee or joint patentees.
(b) State name of person in default.
(c) State the directions sought.
(d) The address must be within the United Kingdom.
(e) To be signed by the patentee. Attention is directed to Rules 90 and 106 of the Patents
Rules 1982.

A134 PATENTS ACT 1949
PATENTS FORM No. 55

The Comptroller
The Patent Office

APPLICATION UNDER SECTION 56 TO DETERMINE A DISPUTE BETWEEN EMPLOYER AND EMPLOYEE AS TO RIGHTS IN AN INVENTION
*(To be accompanied by a copy and a statement in duplicate
setting out the facts of the dispute and the relief sought)*

I/We (a) ....
declare that in respect of the rights in the invention for which an application for a patent was
made by ....
and numbered .... (b) and upon which a patent has been granted, a dispute has risen
between me/us and (c) ....
and I/we apply to the Comptroller to determine the dispute.

The facts of the dispute, and the relief which I/we seek are set out fully in the accompanying
statement.

Communications should be sent to ....
at (d) ....

(e) ....

(a) State name and address.
(b) Delete if a patent has not been granted.
(c) State name and address of other party to dispute.
(d) The address must be within the United Kingdom.
(e) Signature. Attention is directed to Rules 90 and 106 of the Patents Rules 1982.

PATENTS ACT 1949
PATENTS FORM No. 64

The Comptroller
The Patent Office

REQUEST FOR CORRECTION OF CLERICAL ERROR (SECTION 76)

I/We (a) ....
request that the clerical error(s) in the (b) ....
relating to application/patent No. .... indicated in red ink
in the annexed copy of the said (b) ....
or shown as follows:–

....

may be corrected.

Communications should be sent to ....
.... at (c) ....
(d) ....

(a) State full name and address.
(b) State whether in application, specification, entry in register, patent, or the particular relevant document.
(c) The address must be within the United Kingdom.
(c) To be signed by applicant or his authorised agent. Attention is directed to Rules 90 and 106 of the Patents Rules 1982.

PATENTS ACT 1949
PATENTS FORM No. 65

The Comptroller
The Patent Office

NOTICE OF OPPOSITION TO THE CORRECTION OF A CLERICAL ERROR
(To be accompanied by a copy, and a statement of case in duplicate)

I/We (a) ....
give notice of opposition to the correction of an alleged clerical error in ....
....
which said correction has been applied for by ....
....

The grounds upon which the said correction is opposed are as follows:–
....

Communications should be sent to ....
at (b) ....
(c) ....

(a) State (in full) name and address.
(b) The address must be within the United Kingdom.
(c) To be signed by opponents.
    Attention is directed to Rules 90 and 106 of the Patents Rules 1982.

A137 **PATENTS ACT 1949**
PATENTS FORM No. 68

To the Comptroller
The Patent Office

APPLICATION FOR A DUPLICATE OF LETTERS PATENT

I/We have to inform you that the Letters Patent dated (*a*) .... No. ....
...... granted to ....
for an invention the title of which is (*b*) ....
....
has been lost or destroyed, or cannot be produced in the following circumstances:— (*c*) ....
....
....

I/We accordingly apply for the issue of a duplicate of such Letters Patent. (*d*)
(*e*) ....

(*a*) State date, number and full name and address of grantee or grantees.
(*b*) Insert title of invention.
(*c*) State, in full, the circumstances of the case, *which must be verified by evidence.*
(*d*) State interest possessed by applicant or applicants in the Patent.
(*e*) Signature of patentee or patentees and full address to which the duplicate is to be sent.

A138 **PATENTS ACT 1949**
PATENTS FORM No. 69

The Comptroller
The Patent Office

NO FEE

APPLICATION FOR ENTRY OF ORDER OF COURT IN THE REGISTER

(*a*) I/We ....
....
hereby transmit and office copy of an Order of the Court with reference to (*b*) ....
....
(*c*) ....

(*a*) State (in full) name and address of applicant or applicants.
(*b*) State the purport of the Order.
(*c*) Signature. Attention is directed to Rules 90 and 106 of the Patents Rules 1982.

A139   FEES

The fees currently payable on the forms reprinted at paras. A119–A138 *supra* will
be found in Part B of the Schedule to the Patents (Fees) Rules as in force at any
particular time. As a comparative guide to the levels of these fees, the relevant
parts of Part B of the Schedule to the Patents (Fees) Rules 1989 (S.I. 1989 No. 899)
are reprinted below. For other fees, see para. 144.01.

PATENTS (FEES) RULES 1989

(S.I. 1988 No. 899)

SCHEDULE

FEES PAYABLE

PART B

Number of corresponding Patents Form	Item	Amount
1 Add	Application for grant of patent of addition in lieu of independent patent	£ 29
8	On application for result of search made under sections 7 and 8	2
9	On application under section 9(2) for deletion of reference	—
13	On notice that hearing before the comptroller will be attended	—
17	On application for a certificate under section 16(8)	21
23	On application under section 20 for amendment of a patent	52
35	On application to amend specification after acceptance	48
36	On notice of opposition to amendment	22
39	On application for revocation of a patent under section 33	22
43	On application for settlement of terms of licence under patent endorsed "Licences of Right"	52
44	On application by patentee for cancellation of endorsement of patent "Licences of Right"	52
45	On application for cancellation of endorsement "Licences of Right"	52
46	On notice of opposition to cancellation of endorsement of patent "Licences of Right"	52
53	On application under section 55(1) for directions of comptroller	52
54	On application under section 55(2) for directions of comptroller	52
55	On application under section 56(1) to determine dispute	52
64	On request to comptroller to correct a clerical error	32
65	On notice of opposition to the correction of a clerical error	22
68	For duplicate of patent	22
69	On application for entry of order of court in the register	—

OTHER FORMER PATENT STATUTES STILL EFFECTIVE

THE STATUTE OF MONOPOLIES 1623

(21 Jac. 1, c. 3)

B01   **VI.** Provided also, and be it declared and enacted, That any Declaration before-mentioned shall not extend to any Letters Patents and Grants of Privilege for the Term of fourteen Years and under, hereafter to be made, of the sole Working or Making of any manner of new Manufactures within this Realm, to the true and first Inventor and Inventors of such manufactures which others at the Time of Making such Letters Patents and Grants shall not use, so as also they be not contrary to the Law, nor mischievous to the State, by raising Prices of Commodities at home, or Hurt of Trade, or generally inconvenient: the said fourteen Years to be accounted from the Date of the first Letters Patents, or Grant of such Privilege hereafter to be made, but that the same shall be of such Force as they should be, if this Act had never been made, and of none other.

B02   COMMENTARY ON SECTION 6 OF STATUTE OF MONOPOLIES, 1623

Section 6 of the Statute of Monopolies of 1623, unrepealed, has been the foundation stone of the British patent system. This statute generally prohibited the future grant of monopoly privileges by the Crown, but by section 6 an exception was created in respect of "Letters Patent" for the introduction into the Realm of "any manner of new manufacture". This phrase governed the definition of patentable subject matter up to and including the Patents Act 1949, see section 101 [1949] (discussed in paras. A101.05–A101.09). As "existing patents" (*i.e.* those granted under the 1949 Act and still extant) progressively lapse, the provisions of this ancient statute will assume historical importance only.

PATENTS AND DESIGNS ACT 1907

(7 Edw. 7, c. 29)

Patent Office

B03   **62.**—(1) The Treasury may continue to provide for the purposes of this Act, [*and*] the Trade Marks Act **1938** [*1905*] **and the Trade Marks (Amendment) Act 1984** an office with all requisite buildings and conveniences, which shall be called, and is in this Act referred to as, the Patent Office.

(2) The Patent Office shall be under the immediate control of the comptroller, who shall act under the superintendence and direction of **the Secretary of State** [*Board of Trade.*]

(3) Any act or thing directed to be done by or to the comptroller may be done by or to any officer authorised by the **Secretary of State** [*Board of Trade.*]

Note. The amendments indicated were effected by: the Trade Marks Act 1938 (1 & 2 Geo. 6, c. 22); by S.I. 1970 No. 1537 and S.I. 1974 No. 692; and by the Trade Marks (Amendment) Act 1984 (c. 39).

COMMENTARY ON SECTION 62 [1907]   **B04**

This unrepealed section 62 of the 1907 Act provides the statutory basis for the existence of the Patent Office and the requirement that the Treasury provide "all requisite buildings and conveniences". It also provides for the post of "Comptroller" to act at the behest of the Secretary of State, who may himself act in place of the Comptroller. By the Interpretation Act 1978 (c. 30, Sched. 1) the term "Secretary of State" in any statute covers "any of Her Majesty's Principal Secretaries of State". The powers of the Secretary of State under the patent statutes (except for some matters relating to national security or defence applications) are carried out by the Secretary of State for Trade and Industry (Transfer of Functions (Trade and Industry) Order 1983, S.I. 1983 No. 1127), the Patent Office being part of the Department of Trade and Industry ("DTI"). Also associated with the Patent Office is the Industrial Property and Copyright Department of the DTI. This has responsibility for formulating governmental policy in relation to matters of intellectual property law and practice. From the beginning of 1988 correspondence from the various sections of the Patent Office has been on a uniform "DTI" letterhead.

Officers and clerks

63.—(1) There shall continue to be a comptroller-general of patents,   **B05** designs and trade marks, and the **Secretary of State** [*Board of Trade*] may, subject to the approval of the Treasury, appoint the comptroller, and so many examiners and other officers and clerks, with such designation and duties as the **Secretary of State** [*Board of Trade*] thinks fit, and may remove any of those officers and clerks.

Note. The amendments indicated were effected by S.I. 1970 No. 1537 and S.I. 1974 No. 692.

COMMENTARY ON SECTION 63 [1907]   **B06**

The unrepealed section 63 of the 1907 Act provides for the appointment of the Comptroller, "examiners, other officers and clerks", all by the Secretary of State, that is by the Secretary of State for Trade and Industry, see para. B04 *supra*. While the Comptroller and examiners in the Patent Office may be appointed in this manner, their duties are nevertheless often defined in the statutes. It would appear that these persons may not be given instructions to ignore or act in non-compliance with their statutory duties, at least it has so been decided in the Republic of Ireland under a similar statutory provision (*Rajan* v. *Ministry for Industry and Commerce [Ireland]*, [1988] FSR 9).

Seal of the Patent Office

B07 **64.** Impressions of the seal of the Patent Office shall be judicially noticed and admitted in evidence.

B08 COMMENTARY ON SECTION 64 [1907]

Under the 1949 Act, as under the 1907 Act, patents were granted as "Letters Patent" under seal. From 1883 the seal of the Patent Office replaced the use of the Great Seal of the Realm on such documents.

B09 PATENTS, DESIGNS, COPYRIGHT AND TRADE MARKS
(EMERGENCY) ACT 1939

(2 & 3 Geo. 6, c. 107)

This Act, referred to in para. 59.04, remains in force but, as its provisions all relate to intellectual property rights granted to, or licensed to or by, an "enemy" or "enemy subject" (as defined in the Trading with the Enemy Act 1939, 2 & 3 Geo. 6, c. 89, see s. 9), the Act only has effect during a declared "state of war", and so has no present effect. The Act affects patents, registered designs, copyrights and design rights (including "topography rights" (Design right (Semiconductor Topographies) Regulations 1989, S.I. 1989 No. 1100), see Sched. 7, para. 3 [1988], as well as trade marks (including now also service marks, (s. 2(2) and Sched. 2, para. 7 [1986]). The address of a proprietor entered in the appropriate register of patents, designs and trade marks as being in an "enemy" country is prima facie evidence of enemy status under the Act (s. 7).

The Act makes provision for the continued validity of grants, assignments and licences of intellectual property rights arising from "enemy subjects", notwithstanding the terms of the Trading with the Enemy Act 1939, and the Comptroller is given power to revoke or vary such an existing licence upon application to him (s. 1). The Comptroller is also empowered to grant licences (which can be exclusive) under intellectual property rights of "enemy subjects", and any such licensee is given power to bring infringement proceedings thereunder (s. 2).

Despite a "state of war", the grant of intellectual property rights to "enemy" persons can continue (s. 4); and the status of an enemy country as a "convention country" is not affected thereby (s. 5). Section 6, which was amended by the Patents and Designs Act 1946 (9 & 10 Geo. 6, c. 44, s. 6(2)), provides a general power to the Comptroller to extend time limits having regard to circumstances arising out of a person being on active service or otherwise due to a state of war.

Although the Act has not been updated to replace references therein to the Patents & Designs Act 1907 by references to either the 1949 or 1977 Act, section 10(3) appears to be an automatic updating provision. There is power to make Rules and levy fees (s. 9), but no such Rules presently exist.

DEFENCE CONTRACTS ACT 1958

(6 & 7 Eliz. 2, c. 38)

Amendments of statutory provisions for use of patented inventions and registered designs for services of the Crown

1.—(2) Where any models, documents or information relating to an **B10** invention are used in connection with any such use of the invention as is described in subsection (1) of section forty-seven of the Patents Act 1949, subsection (3) of section forty-six of that Act (which regulates in certain cases the terms on which inventions may be used for the services of the Crown under that section) shall, whether or not it applies to the use of the invention, apply to the use of the models, documents or information as if for the reference therein to the patentee there were substituted a reference to the person entitled to the benefit of any provision of an agreement which is rendered inoperative by the said section forty-seven in relation to that use; and in section forty-eight of that Act (which provides for the determination of disputes) the references to terms for the use of an invention shall be construed accordingly.

(3) Nothing in section forty-seven of the Patents Act 1949 shall be construed as authorising the disclosure to a Government department or any other person of any model, document or information to the use of which that section applies in contravention of any such licence, assignment or agreement as is therein mentioned.

(4) The foregoing provisions of this section shall apply in relation to registered designs as they apply in relation to patented inventions, and accordingly—

(a) references to section forty-six of the Patents Act 1949, to subsections (3) and (6) of that section, to section forty-seven of that Act and to subsection (1) of that section shall include references to paragraph 1 of the First Schedule to the Registered Designs Act 1949 [12, 13 & 14 Geo. 6, c. 88], to sub-paragraphs (3) and (6) of that paragraph, to paragraph 2 of that Schedule and to sub-paragraph (1) of that paragraph, as the case may be; and

(b) in relation to registered designs, subsection (1) of this section shall have effect as if for the words "the next following section" there were substituted the words "the next following paragraph" and for the words "make, use and exercise" there were substituted the word "use".

Note. Subsection (1) was spent and has been repealed. The remainder of this section is also spent, save as regards its application (by subs. (4)) to registered designs.

Provision for use of other technical information by Crown contractors for production and supply of defence materials

B11 **2.**—(1) For the purposes of any contract or order for the production of defence materials, any person authorised in that behalf by a competent authority may make use of any technical information to which this section applies of which he is in possession and supply articles produced by means of the use of any such information, discharged—

(*a*) from any restriction imposed by any agreement to which he is party (whether made before or after the commencement of this Act); and

(*b*) from any obligation to make payments to any other person in pursuance of any such agreement in respect of the use or supply.

(2) Any authorisation given for the purposes of subsection (1) of this section shall be given in writing, and shall—

(*a*) describe the defence materials in connection with which the authorisation is given; and

(*b*) identify the restrictions or obligations from which the person to whom the authorisation is given is thereby discharged;

and so much of any agreement (whether made before or after the commencement of this Act) as restricts the disclosure of terms of that or any other agreement shall be of no effect in relation to the disclosure to a competent authority of information required by the authority for the purpose of compliance with paragraph (*b*) of this subsection.

(3) An authorisation given for the purposes of subsection (1) of this section may apply to things done before as well as after the date on which it is given.

(4) Where any person is discharged by virtue of an authorisation under this section from the obligation to make payments in respect of the use of any technical information or the supply of any articles, so much of any agreement (whether made before or after the commencement of this Act) as provides for the making by any other person of payments in respect of the use of the information or the supply of articles of that description shall be of no effect in relation to any use or supply in respect of which the first-mentioned person is so discharged.

(5) Nothing in this section shall affect any restriction or obligation imposed by an agreement to which any Government department are party.

(6) Nothing in this section or in any authorisation given thereunder shall be construed as authorising the disclosure to a competent authority or any other person of any technical information to which this section applies in contravention of any agreement.

(7) The technical information to which this section applies is any specification or design for articles, and any process or technique used in the production of articles (not being in any case a patented invention or registered design), and any drawing, model, plan, document or other information relating to the application or operation of any such specification, design,

process or technique; and references in this Act to the use of technical information include references—

    (*a*) to the production of articles to any such specification or design, or by means of any such process or technique, as aforesaid; and

    (*b*) to the reproduction of any such drawing, model, plan or document as aforesaid.

Procedure in connection with authorisation under section 2

    3.—(1) Subject to subsection (3) of this section, a competent authority **B12** shall, before giving to any person an authorisation under section two of this Act in respect of any restriction or obligation, serve on that person a notice in writing requesting him to treat with the party entitled to enforce that restriction or obligation for such waiver or modification as will enable the technical information to be used or the articles supplied upon terms approved by the competent authority; and the authorisation shall not be given unless either—

    (*a*) at the expiration of such period, not being less than three months beginning with the date of the service of the notice, as may be specified therein, no agreement for such waiver or modification as aforesaid has been concluded to the satisfaction of the competent authority; or

    (*b*) before the expiration of the said period, the person on whom the notice was served has given notice in writing to the competent authority that no such agreement is likely to be concluded within that period.

    (2) Where an authorisation is given under the said section two in respect of any restriction or obligation, the competent authority shall, subject to subsection (3) of this section, give notice to that effect to the person who, apart from the authorisation, would be entitled to enforce that restriction or obligation, and to such other persons (if any) as appear to the authority, after making such enquiries as are reasonably practicable in the circumstances, to be persons whose interests are affected by the authorisation.

    (3) An authorisation under the said section two may be given by a competent authority without compliance with subsection (1) of this section in any case where it appears to the authority, and is certified in the authorisation, that the disclosure of the production or supply of the defence materials concerned would be prejudicial to the safety of the State; and in any such case—

    (*a*) the competent authority shall not be required to give notice of the authorisation in pursuance of subsection (2) of this section unless and until they are satisfied that the disclosure would no longer be prejudicial as aforesaid; and

    (*b*) unless and until the competent authority, being satisfied as aforesaid, otherwise direct, the person to whom the authorisation is given shall be discharged thereby from any obligation to which he would otherwise be subject by virtue of any agreement to give information to any other person in respect of the use of the information or the supply of articles to which the authorisation relates.

Payments for use and determination of disputes

B13   **4.**—(1) A competent authority by whom an authorisation is given under section two of this Act shall pay to the person entitled to the benefit of any restriction or obligation in respect of which the authorisation is given, or of any such provision of an agreement as is mentioned in subsection (4) of that section (whether or not he would himself be entitled, apart from the authorisation, to enforce the restriction, obligation or provision by legal proceedings) such sum (if any) as may be agreed upon between him and the competent authority with the approval of the Treasury or as may, in default of such agreement, be determined by the court under this section to be just having regard—

(*a*) to the extent of the use made in pursuance of the authorisation;

(*b*) to the value of any services performed by that person in connection with the conception, development, improvement or adaptation of any specification, design, process or technique used in pursuance of the authorisation;

(*c*) to any benefit or compensation which that person or any person from whom he derives title may have received, or may be entitled to receive, directly or indirectly from any Government department in respect of any technical information so used; and

(*d*) to any other relevant circumstances.

(2) Any dispute between a competent authority and any other person as to the exercise of powers conferred by section two of this Act, as to the making of a payment under this section, or as to the amount of any such payment, shall be determined by the court upon a reference made by either party to the dispute in such manner as may be prescribed by rules of court.

(3) Without prejudice to any rule of law enabling a court to sit in camera, the court may make such orders for the exclusion of the public from proceedings under this section, and for prohibiting the publication of any technical information to which section two of this Act applies so far as disclosed or recorded in such proceedings, as appear to the court to be necessary or expedient in the public interest or in the interests of any parties to the proceedings.

(4) In this section "the court" has the same meaning as in the **Patents Act 1977** [*Patents Act 1949; and subsection (1) of section eighty-four of that Act (which provides for the allocation to a selected judge of certain proceedings under that Act) shall apply to references to the court under this section as it applies to references under that Act*].

Notes. The amendment to subsection (4) was effected by Patents Act 1977

(Sched. 5, para. 4). In its application to proceedings in Northern Ireland section 4 shall have effect with the omission from subsection (2) of the words "in such manner as may be prescribed by rules of court" (Northern Ireland Act 1962 (c. 30, Sched. 1).

Expenses

5.—There shall be defrayed out of moneys provided by Parliament any increase attributable to section one of this Act in the sums required for making payments on behalf of a Government department under . . . paragraph 1 of the First Schedule to the Registered Designs Act 1949 [12, 13 & 14 Geo. 6, c. 88], and any sums required by a competent authority for making payments under section four of this Act.   **B14**

Note. The omitted words relate to a spent provision.

Interpretation, etc.

6.—(1) In this Act the following expressions have the meaning hereby respectively assigned to them, that is to say: **B15**

"agreement" includes a licence, assignment or assignation;

"article" includes any substance or material, and any plant, machinery or apparatus, whether affixed to land or not;

"competent authority" means a Secretary of State, the Admiralty, the Minister of Supply or the Minister of Defence;

"defence materials" means—

(*a*) articles required for the armed forces of the Crown or for any such supply to the governments of countries outside the United Kingdom, or to the United Nations, as is authorised by the enactments amended by section one of this Act, being articles designed or adapted for the use of armed forces or components of articles so designed or adapted;

(*b*) articles required for purposes of civil defence within the meaning of the Civil Defence Act, 1948 [12, 13 & 14 Geo. 6, c. 5], being articles designed or adapted for use for those purposes or components of articles so designed or adapted;

(*c*) articles required by the Admiralty or the Minister of Supply for the production of any such articles as aforesaid;

"production" includes repair, maintenance, testing and development.

(2) This Act shall apply in relation to restrictions subsisting by reason of the existence of copyright in any work as it applies in relation to restrictions imposed by an agreement.

Repeal and transitional provisions

7.— . . .   **B16**

Note. Section 7 is spent.

Citation, construction, commencement and extent

B17   **8.**—(1) This Act may be cited as the Defence Contracts Act, 1958.

(2) Section one of this Act . . . and so far as it amends the Registered Designs Act 1949 [12, 13 & 14 Geo. 6, c. 88], shall be construed as one with that Act as the Registered Designs Acts 1949 to 1958.

(3) This Act shall come into operation at the expiration of one month beginning with the date on which it is passed.

(4) This Act shall extend to the Isle of Man; and it is hereby declared that this Act extends to Northern Ireland.

Note. The words omitted from subsection (2) relate to a spent provision.

B18   COMMENTARY ON THE DEFENCE CONTRACTS ACT 1958

This Act, to which reference is made in para. 55.02, provides (in s. 2) powers for a Secretary of State (herein called a "competent authority") to authorise persons (conveniently called "suppliers") to make use of technical information for the purpose of any contract or order for the production of "defence materials" without restriction under any agreement which the supplier may have with another (a "licensor"), or restriction arising under copyrights, and free from any obligation thereunder to make payment to such licensor or copyright owner (s. 2(1)). This Act, accordingly, should be read alongside the Crown user provisions now to be found in section 55 [1977], and in the 1988 Act for registered designs and design rights, see para. 55.02.

"Technical information" is defined in section 2(7) to include any specification or design and any drawing, model, plan, document or information, and the power given in respect thereof includes power to "reproduce" the same. Also the "restrictions" which can be overriden by the Act specifically include any arising from the existence of copyrights (s. 6(2)). The references to copyright have also been extended to include "design rights" (Sched. 7, para. 3 [1988]), including "topography rights" (Design Right (Semiconductor Topographies) Regulations 1989, S.I. 1989 No. 1100).

The authorisation must be in writing, define the "defence materials" in question, and identify the restrictions and obligations to be discharged by the authorisation (s. 2(2)). The authority may be given retroactively (s. 2(3)), but the authorisation does not override any obligation which the supplier has to respect confidentiality in the technical information received from his licensor (s. 2(6)). Before any authorisation should be given under section 2, the Secretary of State is required to serve a notice upon the supplier requiring him to treat with his licensor for the purpose of obtaining his agreement to the supply of the defence materials, and to wait for three months (unless the supplier indicates sooner that agreement is unlikely) (s. 3(1) and (2)). However, this requirement can be waived if the Secretary of State certifies that disclosure of the production or supply of the defence materials concerned would (presumably in his opinion) be prejudicial to the safety of the State (s. 3(3)).

Section 4 provides for compensation to be paid to the licensor with regard to the use by the supplier of the technical information, the subject of the authorisation. Such compensation is to be settled by the court in default of agreement. "Court" here has the same meaning as in section 130(1) [1977], for which see para. 96.14. Proceedings in England and Wales can be expected to be heard by the Patents Court under RSC Ord. 104, rr. 2 and 21 (reprinted in paras. E104.2 and E104.21 respectively).

Section 1 of the 1958 Act amended section 46 [1949], but the amended provision can be regarded as effectively spent as Crown use of an "existing patent" is now dealt with under sections 55 and 57 [1977], see para. 55.02. However, the section still has applicability to the Crown use of registered designs.

APPENDIX C

THE TREATY OF ROME

C01 *Introduction*

On January 1, 1973, the United Kingdom joined the European Economic Community. The European Communities Act 1972 (c. 68) provides in section 2(1) that:
"All such rights, powers, obligations and restrictions from time to time created or arising by or under the Treaties, and all such remedies and procedures from time to time provided by for or under the Treaties, as in accordance with the Treaties are without further enactment to be given legal effect or used in the United Kingdom shall be recognised and available in law, and be enforced, allowed and followed accordingly: and the expression 'enforceable Community right' and similar expressions shall be read as referring to one to which this subsection applies".

Section 1(2) of this 1972 Act provides that therein " 'The Communities' means the European Economic Community [the "EEC"], the European Coal and Steel Community and the European Atomic Energy Community" and contains a definition of "the Treaties". These include the Treaty known as the Treaty of Rome ["TR"].

The Treaty was signed in 1957 by the original six Member States of the European Economic Community, *viz*. Belgium, France, German Federal Republic, Italy, Luxembourg and The Netherlands. In 1972, Denmark, Ireland and the United Kingdom acceded to the Treaties. Greece likewise joined the Communities in 1981 and Spain and Portugal in 1986. Thus, "EEC Member State" now means any of these 12 countries.

The provisions of the Treaty of Rome (Cmnd. 5179) are generally outside the scope of this work, but those of its Articles ["TRa."] which have an effect on patent law and practice are reprinted in paras. C02–C08 *infra*. Para. C09 then lists some of the more specialist works which discuss European competition law. The commentary which then follows in this Appendix C provides some basic explanation of the effect of these reprinted Rome Treaty Articles in relation to the exercise, as distinct from the existence, of patent rights. Some further information is given in *EPH*.

The exercise of patent rights by way of licensing is increasingly being controlled by the terms of the Block Exemption Regulations issued by the European Commission with the approval of the Council of Ministers of the European Community. Such of these Regulations as affect the licensing of patents (with or without know-how) are discussed in the following Appendix D, which reprints the main provisions of these Regulations.

In addition, the commentary on section 44 discusses some further limitations on the exercise of patent rights which arise additionally from that section and under other aspects of national United Kingdom competition law.

RELEVANT ARTICLES OF THE TREATY OF ROME

C02 *Article 30*

Quantitative restrictions on imports and all measures having equivalent effect shall, without prejudice to the following provisions, be prohibited between Member States.

1072

Article 34(1)   **C03**

1. Quantitative restrictions on exports, and all measures having equivalent effect, shall be prohibited between Member States.

Article 36   **C04**

The provisions of Articles 30 and 34 shall not preclude prohibitions or restrictions on imports, exports or goods in transit justified on grounds of public morality, public policy or public security; the protection of health and life of humans, animals or plants; the protection of national treasures possessing artistic, historic or archaeological value; or the protection of industrial and commercial property. Such prohibitions or restrictions shall not, however, constitute a means of arbitrary discrimination or a disguised restriction on trade between Member States.

Article 85   **C05**

1. The following shall be prohibited as incompatible with the common market: all agreements between undertakings, decisions, by associations of undertakings and concerted practices which may affect trade between Member States and which have as their object or effect the prevention, restriction or distortion of competition within the common market, and in particular those which:
   (*a*) directly or indirectly fix purchase or selling prices or any other trading conditions;
   (*b*) limit or control production, markets, technical development, or investment;
   (*c*) share markets or sources of supply;
   (*d*) apply dissimilar conditions to equivalent transactions with other trading parties, thereby placing them at a competitive disadvantage;
   (*e*) make the conclusion of contracts subject to acceptance by the other parties of supplementary obligations which, by their nature or according to commercial usage, have no connection with the subject of such contracts.
2. Any agreement or decisions prohibited pursuant to this Article shall be automatically void.
(3) The provisions of paragraph 1 may, however, be declared inapplicable in the case of:
   — any agreement or category of agreements between undertakings;
   — any decision or category of decisions by associations of undertakings;
   — any concerted practice or category of concerted practices:
which contributes to improving the production or distribution of goods or to promoting technical or economic progress, while allowing consumers a fair share of the resulting benefit, and which does not:

(*a*) impose on the undertakings concerned restrictions which are not indispensable to the attainment of these objectives;

(*b*) afford such undertakings the possibility of eliminating competition in respect of a substantial part of the products in question.

C06 *Article 86*

Any abuse by one or more undertakings of a dominant position within the common market or in a substantial part of it shall be prohibited as incompatible with the common market in so far as it may affect trade between Member States. Such abuse may, in particular, consist in:

(*a*) directly or indirectly imposing unfair purchase or selling prices or other unfair trading conditions;

(*b*) limiting production, markets or technical development to the prejudice of consumers;

(*c*) applying dissimilar conditions to equivalent transactions with other trading parties, thereby placing them at a competitive disadvantage;

(*d*) making the conclusion of contracts subject to acceptance by the other parties of supplementary obligation which, by their nature or according to commercial usage, have no connection with the subject of such contracts.

C07 *Article 177*

The Court of Justice shall have jurisdiction to give preliminary rulings concerning:

(*a*) the interpretation of this Treaty;

(*b*) the validity and interpretation of acts of the institutions of the Community;

(*c*) the interpretation of the statutes of bodies established by an act of the Council, where those statutes so provide.

Where such a question is raised before any court or tribunal of a Member State, that court or tribunal may, if it considers that a decision on the question is necessary to enable it to give judgment, request the Court of Justice to give a ruling thereon.

Where any such question is raised in a case pending before a court or tribunal of a Member State, against whose decisions there is no judicial remedy under national law, that court or tribunal shall being the matter before the Court of Justice.

C08 *Article 222*

This Treaty shall in no way prejudice the rules in Member States governing the system of property ownership.

R. Merkin and K. Williams, "Competition law: Antitrust policy in the UK and the EEC", (Sweet & Maxwell, 1984);
R. Whish, "Competition law", (Butterworths, 1985);
E.C. Commission, "Competition law in the EEC and in the ECSC" (Official Publication, 1986);
N. Green, "Commercial agreements and competition law: Practice and procedure in the United Kingdom and EEC" (Grahan and Trotman, 1986);
C. W. Bellamy and G. D. Child, "Common Market law of competition" (3rd ed.) (Sweet & Maxwell, 1987);
I. Van Bael and J-F Bellis, "Competition law of the EEC" (CCH Editions, 1987);
D. Wyatt and A. Dashwood, "The substantive law of the EEC" (2nd ed.) (Sweet & Maxwell), 1987);
D. G. Goyder, "EEC Competition Law" (Clarendon Press, 1988);
P. Oliver, "Free movement of goods in the EEC under Articles 30–36 of the Rome Treaty" (2nd. ed., ELC, 1988).

V. Korah, "The group exemption for know-how licences", [1988] EIPR 134;
J. Ferry, "Patent agreements: No-challenge clauses", [1989] EIPR 138.

COMMENTARY ON THE TREATY OF ROME

Interpretation of the Treaty by the European Court of Justice **C10**

The great majority of cases relevant to intellectual property reach the European Court of Justice ["the ECJ"] in Luxembourg because of requests for preliminary rulings concerning the interpretation of the Treaty under TRa. 177 (reprinted in para. C07 *supra*). Under this Article, any court of a Member State *may* request the ECJ to give a ruling if it considers that this is "necessary" before the court can itself give judgment on the case before it, and a court of final jurisdiction *must* make such request if a question of interpretation of any of the Community Treaties arises. It is by this procedure that litigants can, if successful in such an application, effectively transfer a case from a national court to the ECJ. For example, one party to a British lawsuit may argue that the British court should seek a preliminary ruling and the other party may contend that the law is clear and that therefore no reference should be made. British judges have considered these conflicting contentions in several cases.

The first such cases in which TRa. 177 was considered by the English Court of Appeal were *Löwenbrau München* v. *Grunhalle Lager* ([1974] RPC 49; [1974] CMLR 1) and *Bulmer* v. *Bollinger* ([1975] RPC 321; [1974] CMLR 91). In the latter case the view was expressed that the point of Community law in issue must be decisive of the proceedings, but is is doubtful if that is correct. The reference can take place before full trial. This was done in the patent cases of *Hagen* v. *Moretti* ([1980] FSR 517; [1980] 3 CMLR 253 (CA)) and *Thetford* v. *Fiamma* ([1987] FSR 244; [1987] 3 CMLR 266 (CA)), see also the trade mark case of *EMI* v. *CBS* ([1976] RPC 1; [1975] 1 CMLR 285) and the copyright case of *British Leyland* v. *Wyatt Interpart* ([1979] FSR 39; [1979] 1 CMLR 395 and [1980] FSR 18), but a reference was refused in *British Leyland* v. *Armstrong* ([1982] FSR 481; [1982] 3 CMLR 603). For cases from other jurisdictions, see *Salonia* v. *Poidomani (ECJ Case 126/80)*

([1981] ECR 1563; [1982] 1 CMLR 64 (ECJ)) and *Foglia* v. *Novello (Case 104/79)* ([1980] ECR 745; [1981] 1 CMLR 45 (ECJ)). For a recent English decision where the Court of Appeal made a reference even without full hearing, see *R*. v. *Pharmaceutical Society ex p. Association of Pharmaceutical Importers* ([1987] 3 CMLR 951).

C11 *Anti-trust provisions of the Treaty*

Articles 85 and 86 are the basis of the Community's competition, or anti-trust, policy. Article 85 is concerned with co-operative market behaviour which may have an effect upon trade between Member States, as may be expressed in the form of agreements between undertakings or decisions of associations of undertakings; or of concerted practices; and Article 86 is concerned with instances of an abuse of a dominant position within the European Community. No exemption is provided for under TRa. 86, but an agreement which is objectionable under TRa. 85(1) can be exempted by the European Commission under TRa. 85(3).

However, also important are Regulations made by the European Commission. Particularly relevant to European competition law is Regulation No. 17/1962, under which agreements had originally to be notified if exemption under TRa. 85(3) was to be sought, and the various Block Exemption Regulations relating to Article 85(3) (discussed in Appendix D). These Block Exemption Regulations provide for automatic exemption of agreements which contain only clauses generally considered not to have an anti-competitive effect (the "white" clauses), provided that no clause is present which is *per se* objectionable whatever the circumstances (the "black clauses").

Neither TRa. 85 nor TRa 86 is applicable unless the behaviour in question is one which affects trade between Member States, but the European Commission and the ECJ have each readily been prepared to find that this factor is present if other conditions for the applicability of these Articles exist, see *Vaessen* v. *Morris* ([1979] 1 CMLR 511; [1979] FSR 259) and *Remia* v. *Nutricia* ([1987]) 1 CMLR 1; [1987] FSR 190).

Cases generally dealing with what is meant by agreements between undertakings, decisions of association of undertakings and concerted practices are not cited here, but to offend against TRa. 85 the object or effect of such agreements, etc. must be to prevent, restrict or distort competition. The Rome Treaty assumes that an undertaking acting unilaterally cannot threaten competition unless it occupies a dominant position within the meaning of TRa. 86, and companies in common ownership, such as parent and subsidiary, are not regarded as separate entities in this regard (*Centrafarm* v. *Sterling Drug (Case 16/74)*, [1974] ECR 1147; [1974] 2 CMLR 480), but see *Konica's Agreements* (OJEC 23.3.88, L 78/34) for an exception when subsidiaries did not receive parental instructions for day-to-day running of their businesses.

While only the E.C. Commission is able to grant an exemption under TRa. 85(3) to an agreement which contravenes TRa. 85(1), a national court may rule that TRa. 85(1) is not applicable to a particular situation brought before that court. In practice, there is a growing development by the ECJ of a rule of reason approach to the analysis of cases under TRa. 85, see the philosophy which underlies the Block Exemption Regulations (for which see Appendix D) and particularly the *"Maize Seed"* case (*Nungesser* v. *E.C. Commission (ECJ Case 258/78)* [1982] ECR 2015; [1983] 1 CMLR 278; [1983] FSR 309 (ECJ)) and *Pronuptia* v. *Schillglais, (Case 184/84)* [1986] ECR 374; [1986] 1 CMLR 414, *noted* [1987] FSR 317 (ECJ)), each discussed in para. D32.

Exemption under TRa. 85(3) of prohibited licence clauses   **C12**

The general question of the permissibility of various clauses in an agreement where the agreement may be within the scope of TRa. 85(1), but if so is eligible for exemption under TRa. 85(3), is best studied by referring to the decided cases, and to the Block Exemption Regulations discussed in Appendix D. The Commission's Notice on Agreements of Minor Importance is also relevant, for the latest version of which see OJEC 1986, C 231/2. This Notice exempts automatically from the effects of TRa. 85(1) agreements where the goods or services the subject of the agreement do not represent more than 5 per cent. of the total market for such goods or services in the area of the EEC affected by the agreement, *and* the aggregate annual turnover of the participating undertakings does not exceed 200 million ECU. However, it is unwise to rely on this exception, because it could easily cease to apply if either the licensor or licensee became part of a larger corporate grouping. Also, the Notice has been narrowly construed in a number of cases, see *Henkel* v. *Colgate* (OJEC 1972, L 14/14) where the Commission said that TRa. 85(1) could apply to joint research ventures between two large enterprises. For a recent expression of the official view, see Recital (2) of the Block Exemption Regulation on Research and Development Agreements No. 418/85 (OJEC 22.2.85, L 53/5).

Free movement of goods within the EEC   **C13**

Articles 30 and 34 of the Treaty state that quantitative restrictions on imports and exports between Member States are not permitted, but this is subject to an express derogation stated in TRa. 36. This provides that prohibitions or restrictions on imports, exports, etc. can be justified on the ground of protection of industrial and commercial property, *but provided that* such does not "constitute a means of arbitrary discrimination or a disguised restriction on trade between Member States". Thus, TRa. 36 (which is particularly discussed in the book by P. Oliver listed in para. C09 *supra*) presents a compromise between the rights of an intellectual property holder and the rights of, and the desire for, free movement of goods within the Common Market. The latter has to prevail unless it is the specific subject matter of the right that is in question. Accordingly, section 46(3) of the Act has had to be amended, following the judgment of the ECJ in *Allen & Hanburys* v. *Generics (Case 434/85)* ([1988] 1 CMLR 701; [1988] FSR 312 (ECJ)), so that in the case of a patent bearing a "licence of right" entry those who infringe by importation from another EEC Member State are treated in the same way as a domestic manufacturer infringer, see paras. C15 *infra* and 46.21.

The "existence" and "exercise" of intellectual property rights   **C14**

The ECJ first considered intellectual property rights in *Parke, Davis* v. *Probal (Case 24/67)* ([1968] ECR 55; [1968] CMLR 47). Here the Court observed that the national character of the protection of industrial property was capable of creating obstacles both to the free movement of patented products and to competition within the Common Market, but it was held that the holder of a patent or trade mark right protected under the law of Member State X could properly oppose the importation of an article manufactured by a third party in Member State Y in which he could not obtain a patent. In Germany, the same principle has been held to apply where a patent in State Y could have been, but was not, obtained (*Pfizer* v. *Denkavit, "Carbadox" [Germany]*, (1983) 14 IIC 107). In other words, the holder of intellectual property rights in two Member States can choose in which State to sue an infringer of those rights, but note that in these cases the Defendant had in no way obtained his product from the patentee.

The *Parke, Davis* case was decided in 1968 and there are later cases in which the ECJ has considered more deeply the problem presented by TRa. 222, which states that the Treaty shall in no way prejudice the rules in Member States governing the system of property ownership, in conjunction with TRa. 36 where the derogation from the general provisions of the Treaty is much more circumscribed as indicated above. However, again, the ECJ has construed TRa. 222 quite narrowly, drawing a distinction between the "existence" and "exercise" of the property right.

This was first done in *Deutsche Gramophon* v. *Metro (Case 78/78)* ([1971] ECR 487; [1971] CMLR 631). This case concerned gramophone records manufactured by the Plaintiff in Germany and sold to its subsidiary in France. In turn, *Metro* obtained the records in France and attempted to resell them in Germany. The Court said that the exercise of the industrial property right (copyright) did not fall within TRa. 85, but the compatibility thereof with the Treaty had to be considered with respect to TRa. 86 and with the principle of the free movement of goods so that the re-importation could not be prevented, the "existence" of the right not being called into question.

C15 *The "exhaustion of rights" doctrine*

The concept of the "exhaustion of rights" doctrine has been reviewed by C. T. Harding ((1987–88) 17 CIPA 306). As this doctrine has been developed by the ECJ, the first sale of a product by a holder of an industrial property right (or of a product put on the market with his explicit consent) "exhausts" the industrial property right, see *Centrafarm* v. *Sterling Drug (Case 16/74)* ([1974] ECR 1147; [1974] 2 CMLR 480; [1975] FSR 55 (ECJ)) and *Merck* v. *Stephar (Case 187/80)* ([1981] ECR 2063; [1981] 3 CMLR 463; [1982] FSR 57 (ECJ)). In the latter case the patentee could not at the time have obtained a patent in the country (Italy), where the patented drug was first put on the market, but the Dutch patent could not be enforced against an importer of the *Merck* product from Italy because that product had there been marketed with the express consent of the Patentee and it was immaterial that no patent there existed because the Patentee had had the choice whether to market in that country or not.

However, a distinction was drawn in *Pharmon* v. *Hoechst (Case 19/84)* ([1985] ECR 2281; [1985] 3 CMLR 775; [1986] FSR 108 (ECJ)) where the first sale arose under a United Kingdom compulsory licence and the product was held not to have been put on the market with the patentee's consent so that infringement action could be brought under a parallel patent. As discussed in para. D31, it is a moot point whether this case would apply to a product marketed under a "licence of right" where the royalty has been determined by the Comptroller under section 46(3), particularly where the "licence of right" is involuntary because of the deemed endorsement of an "existing" patent, for which see para. 133.05.

In *Allen & Hanburys* v. *Generics (Case 434/85)* ([1988] 1 CMLR 701; [1988] FSR 312 (ECJ)), discussed in para. 46.21, it was held that a prohibition in a national patent law against importation of a patented product from another EEC Member State was discriminatory and not justified under TRa. 36 when domestic manufacturers would be able to market the product. As a consequence of this decision, section 46(3)(*c*) was amended by the 1988 Act, see para. 46.01. A similar point may well arise over the wording of at least subsection (3)(*b*)(ii) of section 48, see para. 48.08, but that section was left unamended by the 1988 Act.

The "exhaustion of rights" doctrine does not apply to the situation where a disparity in the duration of intellectual property rights permits a product to be lawfully sold in one EEC country where the right has expired without any consent from the rights-holder and then is imported into another EEC country where a protective right still exists. In such a situation the rightsholder can enforce his right in the country of importation because the product has never been marketed with his *explicit* consent, see the copyright case of *EMI Electroler* v. *Patricia (Case 341/87)* ([1989] 2 CMLR 413, *noted* [1989] FSR 444 (ECJ)) and Case Comment thereon by R. Strivens ([1989] EIPR 297). By analogy, a similar position could obtain where a protective right never existed, either as a matter of law or as a matter of choice of the rights-holder, in the country where the first sale took place without consent.

The "exhaustion of rights" doctrine also does not apply where a protected product is first marketed by the rights-holder or his licensee outside the EEC and then imported without the consent of the rights-holder into the EEC (*EMI* v. *CBS (Case No. 51/75)* ([1976] ECR 811; [1976] 2 CMLR 235; [1976] FSR 457 (ECJ)). This is also so where the licensee under a patent outside the EEC lawfully firsts imports the patented product into an EEC Member State where no parallel patent exists and that product is then imported into another Member State where a parallel patent does exist (*Smith Kline & French* v. *Global Pharmaceutics*, SRIS C/107/83, *noted* IPD 6125 and [1986] RPC 394; and *"Patented Bandaging Material [Germany]*, [1988] 2 CMLR 359; [1988] FSR 505).

The *Merck* v. *Stephar, Allen & Hanburys'* and *EMI Electrola* judgments can be contrasted with *Warner Bros.* v. *Christainsen (Case 158/86)* (*The Times*, June 1, 1988 (ECJ)) where the Court upheld a prohibition against the importation of video cassettes from the United Kingdom, where they had been made under licence from the Plaintiff, to Denmark for rental purposes. This was because Danish law (but not then United Kingdom law) permitted an author to oppose the hiring out of recordings of his works. The distinction from the *Merck* case would seem to be that, in *Warner Bros.*, rights of a third party (the author) were involved or that copyright (or at least a rental right thereunder) is to be treated differently from a patent right.

Although Spain and Portugal joined the EEC on January 1, 1986, the doctrine of exhaustion of rights does not apply in relation to these countries under patents for chemical, pharmaceutical or plant-health products until the end of the third year after these products have become patentable in Spain and Portugal, as the case may be (Acts of Accession to EEC of Spain and Portugal, Arts. 47 and 209 respectively).

Because connected companies are deemed not to be separate entities under EEC law, an inter-group transfer of goods does not lead to any exhaustion of intellectual property rights (*Musik-Vertrieb* v. *GEMA [Germany]*, [1982] 1 CMLR 630, *noted* [1982] FSR 355).

Principle of "common origin"   **C15A**

The ECJ has relied on a principle of common origin rather than the principle of "exhaustion" in considering the free movement of goods from one Member State to another where those goods bear the same trade mark. This is true when goods have not previously been marketed in that other State and the trade marks belong to different owners involuntarily. Reliance on the doctrine of common origin is very different from reliance on the doctrine of "exhaustion of rights" and, as yet, has only been used with respect to trade marks, as distinct from patents.

In *Van Zeulen Freres* v. *Hag (Case 192/73)* ([1974] ECR 731; [1979] 2 CMLR 127) the Defendant shipped from Germany to Belgium decaffeinated coffee bearing the trade mark "HAG". Prior to the Second World War, the "HAG" trade mark registrations in Germany and in Belgium belonged to the same proprietor, but during that war the registrations in Belgium and Luxembourg were sequestered as enemy property and eventually came into the hands of the Plaintiff. The ECJ held that, though the marks were now in the hands of totally separate and unrelated companies, the product from Germany could be marketed in Belgium because the trade mark used by the Defendant had a common origin with that of the Plaintiff.

An assignment of parallel patents in different Member States, so that these cease to be commonly owned, may therefore not avoid the exhaustion of rights doctrine discussed in para. C15 *supra*, but there is no authority on the point.

C16   *Special arrangements concerning particular countries*

The Community has Treaties of Association with certain former colonies of Member States and with a number of former members of the European Free Trade Association (EFTA). These include Treaties with Austria, Finland, Norway, Sweden and Switzerland. Questions of the free flow of goods within the Common Market may, therefore, be subject to exemptions in the case of imports from such countries, see *Polydor* v. *Harlequin (Case 270/80)* ([1982] ECR 329; [1982] 1 CMLR 677; [1982] FSR 358 (ECJ)). Here the Court refused to interpret articles of one of those free trade agreements as corresponding substantially to TRaa. 30 and 36, though similar wording was used therein, see also *Bosshard* v. *Sunlight [Switzerland]* ([1980] 3 CMLR 664).

Before Spain and Portugal joined the Community, Treaties of Association also existed between them and the EEC. Of course, these are no longer in effect, but in respect of chemical, pharmaceutical or plant-health products, the doctrine of "exhaustion of rights" wil not apply to such products until the end of the third year after these products have become patentable in Spain or Portugal as the case may be (Acts of Accession to EEC of Spain and Portugal, Articles 47 and 209 respectively).

C17   *Abuse of a dominant position (TRa. 86)*

Article 86 (reprinted in para. C06 *supra*) deals with "abuse of a dominant position". This phrase is not defined as such in the Treaty, but its sub-paragraphs provide some illustrative examples. TRa. 86 has been discussed in a number of cases, most of which do not concern rights of intellectual property. Leading early cases were: *Continental Can* v. *E.C. Commission (Case 6/72)* ([1973] ECR 215; [1973] CMLR 199 (ECJ)); and *United Brands* v. *E.C. Commission (Case 27/76)* ([1978] ECR 207; [1978] 1 CMLR 429 (ECJ)).

TRa. 86(*d*) states that an abuse may exist by making the conclusion of a contract subject to acceptance by the other party of supplementary obligations, which have no connection with the subject of such a contract. This provision reads fairly directly onto a situation where, for example, a purchaser is forced to buy unpatented goods from a patentee when taking a licence: such would be an instance of an illegal tying-in clause. Section 44 provides for sanctions under United Kingdom law in respect of certain types of tying-in provisions in a patent licence contract, for which see paras. 44.05–44.08 but, over and above the provisions of that section, care has to be taken to avoid infringement of TRa. 86, in circumstances where it can be argued that a patent licensor has a "dominant position", which could be the case merely from the existence of his patent.

In *Hugin* v. *E.C. Commission (Case 22/78)* ([1979] ECR 1869; [1979] 3 CMLR 345 (ECJ)), the Court found that *Hugin* did not have a dominant position within the EEC with respect to the sale of cash registers, as their share of the market for this product was only about 12 per cent. However, the spare parts for their registers were mostly not interchangeable with spare parts for other registers, and there therefore existed a dominant position with respect to the reconditioning and repair of *Hugin* registers.

In *Eurofix and Bauco* v. *Hilti A.G.* (OJEC 11.3.88, L 65/19; *abridged* [1988] FSR 473) the Defendant was heavily fined by the Commission for abuse of a dominant position because, *inter alia*, it had attempted to control the supply of unpatented nails for use with its patented fastening guns. Arguments that *Hilti* was only restricting supplies on safety grounds, and/or because the complainants was selling inferior nails, were rejected. A fine was also levied for operating selective and discriminatory practices directed against the business of both competitors and competitors' customers, including "frustrating and delaying legitimately-available licences of right" in proceedings for the settlement of terms thereof under section 46(3). Besides the fine, *Hilti* agreed not to assert its copyrights in respect of present and future operations under "licences of right" obtained on the patents in question. The case is under appeal to the ECJ.

The Commission has also stated that any unfair commercial practice on the part of a dominant enterprise intended to eliminate, discipline or deter small companies is potentially an abuse of monopoly and contrary to TRa. 86 (*Engineering and Chemical Supplies* v. *AKZO*, [1986] 3 CMLR 273), for case comment on which see [1987] EIPR 86.

Mere exercise of rights   **C18**

It is, however, not an abuse of a dominant position merely to exercise an intellectual property right, even though a similar right does not exist in the Member State of first sale, provided that the "exhaustion of rights" doctrine, as expounded in para. C15 *supra*, is not breached. Thus, by *Parke, Davis* v. *Probel (Case 24/67)* ([1968] ECR 55; [1968] CMLR 47 discussed in para. C14 *supra*, a patentee is not obliged to enforce his right in the country where the infringer's first sale occurs. Also, if a rights holder possesses more than one type of right, he may enforce those remaining when others have expired. For example, in *Industrie Diensten* v. *Beele (Case No. 6/81)* ([1982] ECR 707; [1982] 3 CMLR 102; [1983] FSR 119 (ECJ)), action was permitted to be taken under a law against unfair competition to prevent slavish copying of the device of an expired patent.

A lack of compatibility of a national intellectual property law with the principles applicable in other EEC countries is also not be taken into account in the absence of a harmonisation requirement. Thus, in *Keurkoop* v. *Nancy Kean (Case 114/81)* ([1982] ECR 2853; [1982] 2 CMLR 47; [1983] FSR 387 (ECJ)) a Benelux registered design was enforced against an importation from Taiwan, even though the design registered had itself been imported from Taiwan, apparently without the knowledge of the actual designer, this being permitted under the Benelux Designs law. Other cases of a similar kind are *Thetford* v. *Fiamma (Case 35/87)* ([1988] 3 CMLR 549; [1989] FSR 57 (ECJ)) where an "existing patent" was held enforceable even if it would be anticipated but for the "50-year rule" exempting certain prior art from consideration (under s.50(1) [1949]); and *Volvo* v. *Veng (Case 238/87)* ([1989] 4 CMLR 122 (ECJ)) holding that a refusal of a rights owner (of a registered design) to grant licences for the supply of spare parts is not in itself an abuse of a dominant position within the meaning of TRa. 86.

Imposition of fines by European Commission   **C19**

Under Regulation No. 17/62 the European Commission has power to levy fines for breaches of TRaa. 85 and 86. Such fines were first imposed in *Toltec and Dorcet Trade Marks* ([1983] 1 CMLR 412; [1983] FSR 327), but here the fines were rescinded on appeal (*BAT* v. *E.C. Commission (Case 35/83)*, [1985] ECR 363; [1985] 2 CMLR 470); [1985] FSR 533).

However, in *Windsurfing International* v. *E.C. Commission (Case 193/83)* ([1986] ECR 643; [1986] 3 CMLR 489; [1988] FSR 139 (ECJ)), the facts of which are discussed in para. D32, a fine was imposed, *inter alia*, because of the existence of "no challenge" clauses both as to patent and trade mark rights. The ECJ stated that "it is in the public interest to eliminate any obstacle to economic activity which may arise where a patent was granted in error". Other reasons for imposing a fine in this case were:

(a) the existence of effective export restrictions to other parts of the EEC;

(b) the requirement to pay royalties on sales of unpatented components alone, and limitation of a licensee's power to supply components separately;

(c) the limitation of licensed manufacture to a country where a patent existed, with the effect that royalties were paid even on products manufactured and sold in parts of the EEC where no patent protection existed;

(d) the presence of provisions for terminating the licence if the licensee changed his manufacturing location;

(e) the requirement for a licensee's designs to be approved, other than for objective reasons of quality control or safety factors based on the specific subject of the patent; and

(f) provisions requiring marketing to be accompanied by a notice of the licence even when no patent or other right requiring a licence existed in the country of sale and no know-how had been supplied by the licensor. For comment on this case, see G. I. F. Leigh ([1986] EIPR 27); P. A. Stone ([1986] EIPR 242); and J. S. Venit ((1987) 18 IIC 1).

In *Eurofix-Bauco* v. *Hilti* (OJEC 11.3.88, L 65/19) the Commission fined *Hilti* heavily for abusing a dominant position, as noted more fully in para. C17 *supra*, but this case is under appeal.

APPENDIX D

LICENSING OF INTELLECTUAL PROPERTY UNDER EEC LAW

Relationship of Appendix D to Appendix C   **D01**

In Appendix C there has been discussed the relevant provisions of the Treaty of Rome which have an effect on patent law and practice, and also the decisions of the ECJ which have interpreted its articles. However, as explained in para. C12, there was there little discussion of contractual licensing as this is now primarily governed by various Block Exemption Regulations (outlined in para. D03 *infra*) and it has been thought that these are best considered separately.

While these Regulations are now considered in the present Appendix, their treatment has deliberately been kept brief because the subject is peripheral to the main contents of this book, though TRa. 85 (reprinted in para. C05) can be seen as a (very considerable) extention of those prohibitions on certain patent licence agreement provisions defined in section 44 [1977]. Thus, in order to present a balanced account of British patent law and practice, there is now outlined those principles of EEC law which govern the types of provisions which may, validly, appear in a patent licence contract which is to have effect within the EEC, and to point out those which will be ineffective, save to render the parties liable to fines from the E.C. Commission. A fuller discussion of the subject will be found in *EPH* and the books listed in para. C09.

The present Appendix D pays particular attention to the licensing of patents, with or without associated know-how; and to the licensing of know-how, with or without associated patents. The general principles of such types of licensing have been mentioned in paras. C11 and C12. In the present Appendix there are also brief references to the licensing of other forms of intellectual property, though this occurs primarily because the same principles apply as with the licensing of patents.

The basic nature of the Block Exemption Regulations   **D02**

The basic legal position, as discussed in para. C11, is that any provision of a licence agreement which falls within TRa. 85(1) is void unless the agreement is notified to the E.C. Commission and exemption then granted under TRa. 85(3). Thus, an un-notified agreement which falls within TRa. 85(1), and therefore is one which should have been notified to the E.C. Commission for possible exemption under TRa. 85(3), is void; and the Commission may impose fines on the parties for putting it into effect, for which see para. C19. Exemption under TRa. 85(3) cannot be ante-dated before the date of notification, see *Brasserie de Haecht* v. *Wilkin (No. 2) (Case 48/72)* ([1973] ECR 77; [1973] CMLR 287 (ECJ)).

To expedite approval of those agreements which would probably be deemed either to fall outside TRa. 85(1), or would otherwise merit exemption under TRa. 85(3), the Commission has issued a number of Block Exemption Regulations for different types of licences, see para. D03 *infra*. These lead to automatic exemption of agreements covered by a particular Regulation as regards certain types of provisions (the "white clauses"), provided that certain other types of clauses (the "black clauses") are not present. If the parties are in doubt, concerning the applicability of a Regulation to a particular agreement, exemption may be requested in the normal manner. The Regulations usually provide an opposition system under which a notified agreement is deemed to have received approval if no opposition thereto has been indicated by the Commission within a defined time; and, provided it is a suitable agreement, for exemption under that opposition procedure.

D03 *The various Block Exemption Regulations*

Regulation No. 556/89 (OJEC 4.3.89, L 61/1; [1989] 4 CMLR 774) is the latest of the various Block Exemption Regulations and is of particular importance. It is summarised in the article by V. Korah listed in para. C09A and primarily concerned with the licensing of know-how with or without associated patents, and is herein called "the Know-How Exemption Regulation". Regulation 2349/84 (published OJEC 16.8.84 L 219/15; [1984] EIPR Supplement; [1985] FSR 191) is primarily concerned with the licensing of patents with or without associated know-how, and is herein called "the Patent Exemption Regulation".

The Articles of the Know-How Exemption Regulation are reprinted herein at paras. D07–D18 *infra*, but the similarly worded Articles of the earlier Patent Exemption Regulation have not been included for reasons of space and because this Regulation now appears to have relevance only when the Know-How Regulation does not apply. The relationship between these two Regulations is discussed further in para. D28 *infra*.

Also, for reasons of space, the Recitals of the Know-How Regulations are not reprinted, despite the importance of recitals in interpreting the meaning of Community Regulations. Therefore, in many situations the reader should consult the complete text of the appropriate Regulation (either in a publication as noted herein, or in a textbook of EEC law, the main ones of which are listed in para. C09) in order to amplify the brief commentary that is here provided.

The other Block Exemption Regulations (which are mentioned *infra* as necessary) are as follows:

Regulation No. 1983/83, relating to exclusive distribution agreements (OJEC 30.6.83, L 173/1);

Regulation No. 1984/83, relating to categories of exclusive purchasing agreements (OJEC 30.6.83, L 173/5);

Regulation No. 417/85, relating to specialisation agreements (OJEC 22.2.85, L 53/1);

Regulation No. 418/85, relating to joint research and development agreements (OJEC 22.2.85, L 53/5); and

Regulation No. 4087/88, relating to franchising agreements (OJEC 28.12.88, L 359/46; [1989] 4 CMLR 387; [1989] FSR 499; [1989] EIPR 212).

Also, if the agreement is truly one of "minor importance", it may be exempted as such, for which see para. C12.

D04 *Exclusive distribution agreements*

Regulation No. 1983/83 (listed in para. D03 *supra*) relates to exclusive distribution agreements. It may be pertinent to patent licences because the Patent and Know-How Exemption Regulations only apply when there is manufacture by the licensee as is clearly spelled out in their Recitals. A licence agreement, where the licensee only sells and has no intention to manufacture, may thus only qualify for exemption, if at all, under Regulation No. 1983/83.

However, it may be necessary to decide whether a licensee's activities constitute a simple sale or whether there is "manufacture" within the terms of the claims of a licensed patent. Thus, in *Davide Campari-Milano's Agreement* ([1978] 2 CMLR

397), the licensor supplied raw materials to its licensees including a secret mixture of herbs and colouring matters. The licensees had to comply with the licensor's instructions for the manufacture of the products. It was held that this constituted a manufacturing licence, as distinct from a situation where a licensor might simply supply a concentrate which the licensee diluted with water. Thus, it may be possible to contend to the E.C. Commission that what may appear to be a simple sales licence is in fact a manufacturing licence falling within the scope of either the Patent or Know-How Exemption Regulation, depending upon the precise language of the patent claims being licensed.

Franchising agreements   **D05**

Although the definition of franchising is such that it can sometimes be difficult to distinguish a franchising agreement from an exclusive distribution agreement, it is unlikely that there will be doubt as to whether the Patent and/or the Know-How Exemption Regulations are applicable. It is specifically stated in Recital 4 of the Franchising Regulation No. 4087/88 that an agreement which relates to a relationship between producers is outside the scope of that Regulation, and this clearly indicates that such should be considered as manufacturing licences based on patents and/or know-how. This Regulation is the subject of comment by V. Korah ([1989] EIPR 207).

The Know-How Exemption Regulation (Regulation No. 556/89)   **D06**

—General   **D06**

Regulation No. 556/89 is concerned with the licensing of know-how, with or without patents that are not "necessary" to the licensee, while the Patent Exemption Regulation (No. 2349/84) is concerned with the licensing of "necessary" patents with or without know-how. The borderline on relationships between the two Regulations is discussed in para. D28 *infra*, but it may be noted that the Patent Exemption Regulation is due to expire (unless extended) at the end of 1994, whereas the Know-How Exemption Regulation is scheduled to last until the end of 1999.

These two Regulations have a similar structure and, as it is believed that the Know-How Regulation may be of much greater importance in practice, this will be discussed in greater detail than the Patent Exemption Regulation. However, the remarks on the structure of the Know-How Exemption Regulation, which follow (in paras. D19–D25) the reprinting of its Articles in paras. D07–D18 *infra*, are generally applicable also to the Patent Exemption Regulation, the differences being pointed out in paras. D26–D28 *infra* where the Patent Exemption Regulation is explained.

—Articles of the Know-How Regulation

——Article 1 (Scope of the Regulation)   **D07**

(1) Pursuant to Article 85(3) of the Treaty and subject to the provisions of this Regulation, it is hereby declared that Article 85(1) of the Treaty shall not apply to pure know-how licensing agreements and to mixed know-how and patent licensing agreements not exempted by Regulation (EEC) No. 2349/84, including those agreements containing ancillary provisions relating to trade marks or other intellectual property rights, to which only two undertakings are party and which include one or more of the following obligations:

1. an obligation on the licensor not to license other undertakings to exploit the licensed technology in the licensed territory;
2. an obligation on the licensor not to exploit the licensed technology in the licensed territory himself;
3. an obligation on the licensee not to exploit the licensed technology in territories within the common market which are reserved for the licensor;
4. an obligation on the licensee not to manufacture or use the licensed product, or use the licensed process, in territories within the common market which are licensed to other licensees;
5. an obligation on the licensee not to pursue an active policy of putting the licensed product on the market in the territories within the common market which are licensed to other licensees, and in particular not to engage in advertising specifically aimed at those territories or to establish any branch or maintain any distribution depot there;
6. an obligation on the licensee not to put the licensed product on the market in the territories licensed to other licensees within the common market;
7. an obligation on the licensee to use only the licensor's trademark or the get-up determined by the licensor to distinguish the licensed product during the term of the agreement, provided that the licensee is not prevented from identifying himself as the manufacturer of the licensed products;
8. an obligation on the licensee to limit his production of the licensed product to the quantities he requires in manufacturing his own products and to sell the licensed product only as an integral part of or a replacement part for his own products or otherwise in connection with the sale of his own products, provided that such quantities are freely determined by the licensee.

(2) The exemption provided for the obligations referred to in paragraph 1(1), (2) and (3) shall extend for a period not exceeding for each licensed territory within the EEC 10 years from the date of signature of the first licence agreement entered into by the licensor for that territory in respect of the same technology.

The exemption provided for the obligations referred to in paragraph 1(4) and (5) shall extend for a period not exceeding 10 years from the date of signature of the first licence agreement entered into by the licensor within the EEC in respect of the same technology.

The exemption provided for the obligation referred to in paragraph 1(6) shall extend for a period not exceeding five years from the date of the signature of the first licence agreement entered into by the licensor within the EEC in respect of the same technology.

(3) The exemption provided for in paragraph 1 shall apply only where the parties have identified in any appropriate form the initial know-how and any subsequent improvements to it, which become available to the parties and are communicated to the other party pursuant to the terms of the agreement and for the purpose thereof, and only for as long as the know-how remains secret and substantial.

(4) Insofar as the obligations referred to in paragraph 1(1) to (5) concern territories including Member States in which the same technology is protected by necessary patents, the exemption provided for in paragraph 1 shall extend for those Member States as long as the licensed product or process is protected in those Member States by such patents, where the duration of such protection exceeds the periods specified in paragraph 2.

(5) The exemption of restrictions on putting the licensed product on the market resulting from the obligations referred to in paragraph 1(2), (3), (5) and (6) shall apply only if the licensee manufactures or proposes to manufacture the licensed product himself or has it manufactured by a connected undertaking or by a subcontractor.

(6) The exemption provided for in paragraph 1 shall also apply where in a par-

ticular agreement the parties undertake obligations of the types referred to in that paragraph but with a more limited scope than is permitted by the paragraph.

(7) For the purposes of the present Regulation the following terms shall have the following meanings:

1. 'know-how' means a body of technical information that is secret, substantial and identified in any appropriate form;
2. the term 'secret' means that the know-how package as a body or in the precise configuration and assembly of its components is not generally known or easily accessible, so that part of its value consists in the lead-time the licensee gains when it is communicated to him; it is not limited to the narrow sense that each individual component of the know-how should be totally unknown or unobtainable outside the licensor's business;
3. the term 'substantial' means that the know-how includes information which is of importance for the whole or a significant part of (i) a manufacturing process or (ii) a product or service, or (iii) for the development thereof and excludes information which is trivial. Such know-how must thus be useful, i.e. can reasonably be expected at the date of conclusion of the agreement to be capable of improving the competitive position of the licensee, for example by helping him to enter a new market or giving him an advantage in competition with other manufacturers or providers of services who do not have access to the licensed secret know-how or other comparable secret know-how;
4. the term 'identified' means that the know-how is described or recorded in such a manner as to make it possible to verify that it fulfils the criteria of secrecy and substantiality and to ensure that the licensee is not unduly restricted in his exploitation of his own technology. To be identified the know-how can either be set out in the licence agreement or in a separate document or recorded in any other appropriate form at the latest when the know-how is transferred or shortly thereafter, provided that the separate document or other record can be made available if the need arises;
5. 'pure know-how licensing agreements' are agreements whereby one undertaking, the licensor, agrees to communicate the know-how, with or without an obligation to disclose any subsequent improvements, to another undertaking, the licensee, for exploitation in the licensed territory;
6. 'mixed know-how and patent licensing agreements' are agreements not exempted by Commission Regulation (EEC) No. 2349/84 under which a technology containing both non-patented elements and elements that are patented in one or more Member States is licensed;
7. the terms 'licensed know-how' or 'licensed technology' mean the initial and any subsequent know-how communicated directly or indirectly by the licensor to a licensee by means of pure or mixed know-how and patent licensing agreements; however, in the case of mixed know-how and patent licensing agreements the term 'licensed technology' also includes any patents for which a licence is granted besides the communication of the know-how;
8. the term 'the same technology' means the technology as licensed to the first licensee and enhanced by any improvements made thereto subsequently, irrespective of whether and to what extent such improvements are exploited by the parties or the other licensees and irrespective of whether the technology is protected by necessary patents in any Member States;
9. 'the licensed products' are goods or services the production or provision of which requires the use of the licensed technology;
10. the term 'exploitation' refers to any use of the licensed technology in particular in the production, active or passive sales in a territory even if not coupled with manufacture in that territory, or leasing of the licensed products;

11. 'the licensed territory' is the territory covering all or at least part of the common market where the licensee is entitled to exploit the licensed technology;
12. 'territory reserved for the licensor' means territories in which the licensor has not granted any licences and which he has expressly reserved for himself;
13. 'connected undertakings' means:
   (a) undertakings in which a party to the agreement, directly or indirectly;
      — owns more than half the capital or business assets, or
      — has the power to exercise more than half the voting rights, or
      — has the power to appoint more than half the members of the supervisory board, board of directors or bodies legally representing the undertaking, or
      — has the right to manage the affairs of the undertaking;
   (b) undertakings which directly or indirectly have in or over a party to the agreement the rights or powers listed in (a);
   (c) undertakings in which an undertaking referred to in (b) directly or indirectly has the rights or powers listed in (a);
   (d) undertakings in which the parties to the agreement or undertakings connected with them jointly have the rights or powers listed in (a): such jointly controlled undertakings are considered to be connected with each of the parties to the agreement.

D08   ——*Article 2 (The "White List" of exempted clauses)*
(1)   Article 1 shall apply notwithstanding the presence in particular of any of the following obligations, which are generally not restrictive of competition:

1. an obligation on the licensee not to divulge the know-how communicated by the licensor; the licensee may be held to this obligation after the agreement has expired;
2. an obligation on the licensee not to grant sub-licences or assign the licence;
3. an obligation on the licensee not to exploit the licensed know-how after termination of the agreement in so far and as long as the know-how is still secret;
4. an obligation on the licensee to communicate to the licensor any experience gained in exploiting the licensed technology and to grant him a non-exclusive licence in respect of improvements to or new applications of that technology, provided that:
   (a) the licensee is not prevented during or after the term of the agreement from freely using his own improvements, insofar as these are severable from the licensor's know-how, or licensing them to third parties where licensing to third parties does not disclose the know-how communicated by the licensor that is still secret; this is without prejudice to an obligation on the licensee to seek the licensor's prior approval to such licensing provided that approval may not be withheld unless there are objectively justifiable reasons to believe that licensing improvements to third parties will disclose the licensor's know-how; and
   (b) the licensor has accepted an obligation, whether exclusive or not, to communicate his own improvements to the licensee and his right to use the licensee's improvements which are not severable from the licensed know-how does not extend beyond the date on which the licensee's right to exploit the licensor's know-how comes to an end, except for termination of the agreement for breach by the licensee; this is without prejudice to an obligation on the licensee to give the licensor the option to continue to use the improvements after that date, if at the same time he relinquishes the post-term use ban or agrees, after having had an oppor-

tunity to examine the licensee's improvements, to pay appropriate royalties for their use;

5. an obligation on the licensee to observe minimum quality specifications for the licensed product or to procure goods or services from the licensor or from an undertaking designated by the licensor, insofar as such quality specifications, products or services are necessary for:
   (a) a technically satisfactory exploitation of the licensed technology, or
   (b) for ensuring that the production of the licensee conforms to the quality standards that are respected by the licensor and other licensees,
   and to allow the licensor to carry out related checks;

6. obligations:
   (a) to inform the licensor of misappropriation of the know-how or of infringements of the licensed patents, or
   (b) to take or to assist the licensor in taking legal action against such misappropriation or infringements,
   provided that these obligations are without prejudice to the licensee's right to challenge the validity of the licensed patents or to contest the secrecy of the licensed know-how except where he himself has in some way contributed to its disclosure;

7. an obligation on the licensee, in the event of the know-how becoming publicly known other than by action of the licensor, to continue paying until the end of the agreement the royalties in the amounts, for the periods and according to the methods freely determined by the parties, without prejudice to the payment of any additional damages in the event of the know-how becoming publicly known by the action of the licensee in breach of the agreement;

8. an obligation on the licensee to restrict his exploitation of the licensed technology to one or more technical fields of application covered by the licensed technology or to one or more product markets;

9. an obligation on the licensee to pay a minimum royalty or to produce a minimum quantity of the licensed product or to carry out a minimum number of operations exploiting the licensed technology;

10. an obligation on the licensor to grant the licensee any more favourable terms that the licensor may grant to another undertaking after the agreement is entered into;

11. an obligation on the licensee to mark the licensed product with the licensor's name;

12. an obligation on the licensee not to use the licensor's know-how to construct facilities for third parties; this is without prejudice to the right of the licensee to increase the capacity of its facilities or to set up additional facilities for its own use on normal commercial terms, including the payment of additional royalties.

(2) In the event that, because of particular circumstances, the obligations referred to in paragraph 1 fall within the scope of Article 85(1), they shall also be exempted even if they are not accompanied by any of the obligations exempted by Article 1.

(3) The exemption provided for in paragraph 2 shall also apply where in the agreement the parties undertake obligations of the types referred to in paragraph 1 but with a more limited scope than is permitted by that paragraph.

——*Article 3 (The "Black List" of impermissible clauses)* **D09**

Articles 1 and 2(2) shall not apply where:
   1. the licensee is prevented from continuing to use the licensed know-how after

the termination of the agreement where the know-how has meanwhile become publicly known, other than by the action of the licensee in breach of the agreement;

2. the licensee is obliged either:

    (a) to assign in whole or in part to the licensor rights to improvements to or new applications of the licensed technology;

    (b) to grant the licensor an exclusive licence for improvements to or new applications of the licensed technology which would prevent the licensee during the currency of the agreement and/or thereafter from using his own improvements insofar as these are severable from the licensor's know-how, or from licensing them to third parties, where such licensing would not disclose the licensor's know-how that is still secret; or

    (c) in the case of an agreement which also includes a post-term use ban, to grant back to the licensor, even on a non-exclusive and reciprocal basis, licences for improvements which are not severable from the licensor's know-how, if the licensor's right to use the improvements is of a longer duration than the licensee's right to use the licensor's know-how, except for termination of the agreement for breach by the licensee;

3. the licensee is obliged at the time the agreement is entered into to accept quality specifications or further licences or to procure goods or services which he does not want, unless such licences, quality specifications, goods or services are necessary for a technically satisfactory exploitation of the licensed technology or for ensuring that the production of the licensee conforms to the quality standards that are respected by the licensor and other licensees;

4. the licensee is prohibited from contesting the secrecy of the licensed know-how or from challenging the validity of licensed patents within the common market belonging to the licensor or undertakings connected with him, without prejudice to the right of the licensor to terminate the licensing agreement in the event of such a challenge;

5. the licensee is charged royalties on goods or services which are not entirely or partially produced by means of the licensed technology or for the use of know-how which has become publicly known by the action of the licensor or an undertaking connected with him;

6. one party is restricted within the same technological field of use or within the same product market as to the customers he may serve, in particular by being prohibited from supplying certain classes of user, employing certain forms of distribution or, with the aim of sharing customers, using certain types of packaging for the products, save as provided in Article 1(1)(7) and Article 4(2);

7. the quantity of the licensed products one party may manufacture or sell or the number of operations exploiting the licensed technology he may carry out are subject to limitations, save as provided in Article 1(1)(8) and Article 4(2);

8. one party is restricted in the determination of prices, components of prices or discounts for the licensed products;

9. one party is restricted from competing with the other party, with undertakings connected with the other party or with other undertakings within the common market in respect of research and development, production or use of competing products and their distribution, without prejudice to an obligation on the licensee to use his best endeavours to exploit the licensed technology and without prejudice to the right of the licensor to terminate the exlusivity granted to the licensee and cease communicating improvements in the event of the licensee's engaging in any such competing activities and to

1090

require the licensee to prove that the licensed know-how is not used for the production of goods and services other than those licensed;

10. the initial duration of the licensing agreement is automatically prolonged by the inclusion in it of any new improvements communicated by the licensor, unless the licensee has the right to refuse such improvements or each party has the right to terminate the agreement at the expiry of the initial term of the agreement and at least every three years thereafter;

11. the licensor is required, albeit in separate agreements, for a period exceeding that permitted under Article 1(2) not to license other undertakings to exploit the same technology in the licensed territory, or a party is required for periods exceeding those permitted under Articles 1(2) or 1(4) not to exploit the same technology in the territory of the other party or of other licensees;

12. one or both of the parties are required:
   (a) to refuse without any objectively justified reason to meet demand from users or resellers in their respective territories who would market products in other territories within the common market;
   (b) to make it difficult for users or resellers to obtain the products from other resellers within the common market, and in particular to exercise intellectual property rights or take measures so as to prevent users or resellers from obtaining outside, or from putting on the market in the licensed territory products which have been lawfully put on the market within the common market by the licensor or with his consent;
   or do so as a result of a concerted practice between them.

—*Article 4 (Approval in absence of opposition)*   **D10**

(1) The exemption provided for in Articles 1 and 2 shall also apply to agreements containing obligations restrictive of competition which are not covered by those Articles and do not fall within the scope of Article 3, on condition that the agreements in question are notified to the Commission in accordance with the provisions of Commission Regulation No. 27, [OJEC 10.5.62, 35/1118] and that the Commission does not oppose such exemption within a period of six months.

(2) Paragraph 1 shall in particular apply to an obligation on the licensee to supply only a limited quantity of the licensed product to a particular customer, where the know-how licence is granted at the request of such a customer in order to provide him with a second source of supply within a licensed territory.

This provision shall also apply where the customer is the licensee and the licence, in order to provide a second source of supply, provides for the customer to make licensed products or have them made by a sub-contractor.

(3) The period of six months shall run from the date on which the notification is received by the Commission. Where, however, the notification is made by registered post, the period shall run from the date shown on the postmark of the place of posting.

4. Paragraphs 1 and 2 shall apply only if:
   (a) express reference is made to this Article in the notification or in a communication accompanying it; and
   (b) the information furnished with the notification is complete and in accordance with the facts.

(5) The benefit of paragraphs 1 and 2 may be claimed for agreements notified before the entry into force of this Regulation by submitting a communication to the Commission referring expressly to this Article and to the notification. Paragraphs 3 and 4(b) shall apply mutatis mutandis.

(6) The Commission may oppose the exemption. It shall oppose exemption if it

receives a request to do so from a Member State within three months of the transmission to the Member State of the notification referred to in paragraph 1 or of the communication referred to in paragraph 5. This request must be justified on the basis of consideration relating to the competition rules of the Treaty.

(7) The Commission may withdraw the opposition to the exemption at any time. However, where the opposition was raised at the request of a Member State and this request is maintained, it may be withdrawn only after consultation of the Advisory Committee on Restrictive Practices and Dominant Positions.

(8) If the opposition is withdrawn because the undertakings concerned have shown that the conditions of Article 85(3) are fulfilled, the exemption shall apply from the date of notification.

(9) If the opposition is withdrawn because the undertakings concerned have amended the agreement so that the conditions of Article 85(3) are fulfilled, the exemption shall apply from the date on which the amendments take effect.

(10) If the Commission opposes exemption and the opposition is not withdrawn, the effects of the notification shall be governed by the provisions of Regulation No. 17.

D11   ——*Article 5 (Inapplicable agreements)*

(1) This Regulation shall not apply to:
1. agreements between members of a patent or know-how pool which relate to the pooled technologies;
2. know-how licensing agreements between competing undertakings which hold interests in a joint venture, or between one of them and the joint venture, if the licensing agreements relate to the activities of the joint venture;
3. agreements under which one party grants the other a know-how licence and the other party, albeit in separate agreements or through connected undertakings, grants the first party a patent, trademark or know-how licence or exclusive sales rights, where the parties are competitors in relation to the products covered by those agreements;
4. agreements including the licensing of intellectual property rights other than patents (in particular trademarks, copyright and design rights) or the licensing or software except where these rights or the software are of assistance in achieving the object of the licensed technology and there are no obligations restrictive of competition other than those also attached to the licensed know-how and exempted under the present Regulation.

(2) However, this Regulation shall apply to reciprocal licences of the types referred to in paragraph 1(3) where the parties are not subject to any territorial restriction within the common market on the manufacture, use or putting on the market of the products covered by the agreements or on the use of the licensed technologies.

D12   ——*Article 6 (Extension of Regulation beyond pure know-how agreements)*

This Regulation shall also apply to:

1. pure know-how agreements or mixed agreements where the licensor is not the developer of the know-how or the patentee but is authorised by the developer or the patentee to grant a licence or a sub-licence;

2. assignments of know-how or of know-how and patents where the risk associated with exploitation remains with the assignor, in particular where the sum payable in consideration of the assignment is dependent upon the turnover attained by the assignee in respect of products made using the know-how or the patents, the

quantity of such products manufactured or the number of operations carried out employing the know-how or the patents;

3. pure know-how agreements or mixed agreements in which rights or obligations of the licensor or the licensee are assumed by undertakings connected with them.

——Article 7 (Right to withdraw exemption)   **D13**

The Commission may withdraw the benefit of this Regulation, pursuant to Article 7 of Regulation No. 19/65/EEC, where it finds in a particular case that an agreement exempted by this Regulation nevertheless has certain effects which are incompatible with the conditions laid down in Article 85(3) of the Treaty, and in particular where:

1. such effects arise from an arbitration award;

2. the effect of the agreement is to prevent the licensed products from being exposed to effective competition in the licensed territory from identical products or products considered by users as equivalent in view of their characteristics, price and intended use;

3. the licensor does not have the right to terminate the exclusivity granted to the licensee at the latest five years from the date the agreement was entered into and at least annually thereafter if, without legitimate reason, the licensee fails to exploit the licensed technology or to do so adequately;

4. without prejudice to Article 1(1)(6), the licensee refuses, without objectively valid reason, to meet unsolicited demand from users or resellers in the territory of other licensees;

5. one or both of the parties:

(a) without objectively justified reason, refuse to meet demand from users or resellers in their respective territories who would market the products in other territories within the common market; or

(b) make it difficult for users or resellers to obtain the products from other resellers within the common market, and in particular where they exercise intellectual property rights or take measures so as to prevent resellers or users from obtaining outside, or from putting on the market in the licensed territory products which have been lawfully put on the market within the common market by the licensor or with his consent;

6. the operation of the post-term use ban referred to in Article 2(1)(3) prevents the licensee from working an expired patent which can be worked by all other manufacturers;

7. the period for which the licensee is obliged to continue paying royalties after the know-how has become publicly known by the action of third parties, as referred to in Article 2(1)(7), substantially exceeds the lead time acquired because of the head-start in production and marketing and this obligation is detrimental to competition in the market;

8. the parties were already competitors before the grant of the licence and obligations on the licensee to produce a minimum quantity or to use his best endeavours as referred to in Article 2(1)(9) and Article 3(9) have the effect of preventing the licensee from using competing technologies.

——Article 8 (Transitional arrangements)   **D14**

(1) As regards agreements existing on 13 March 1962 and notified before 1 February 1963 and agreements, whether notified or not, to which Article 4(2)(2)(b) of Regulation No. 17 applies, the declaration of inapplicability of Article 85(1) of the Treaty contained in this Regulation shall have retroactive effect from the time at which the conditions for application of this Regulation were fulfilled.

(2) As regards all other agreements notified before this Regulation entered into force, the declaration of inapplicability of Article 85(1) of the Treaty contained in this Regulation shall have retroactive effect from the time at which the conditions for application of this Regulation were fulfilled, or from the date of notification, whichever is the later.

D15 ——*Article 9 (Amendment of ancient agreements)*

If agreements existing on 13 March 1962 and notified before 1 February 1963 or agreements to which Article 4(2)(2)(b) of Regulation No. 17 applies and notified before 1 January 1967 are amended before 1 July 1989 so as to fulfil the conditions for application of this Regulation, and if the amendment is communicated to the Commission before 1 October 1989 the prohibition in Article 85(1) of the Treaty shall not apply in respect of the period prior to the amendment. The communication shall take effect from the time of its receipt by the Commission. Where the communication is sent by registered post, it shall take effect from the date shown on the postmark of the place of posting.

D16 ——*Article 10 (Pre-accession agreements)*

(1) As regards agreements to which Article 85 of the Treaty applies as a result of the accession of the United Kingdom, Ireland and Denmark, Articles 8 and 9 shall apply except that the relevant dates shall be 1 January 1973 instead of 13 March 1962 and 1 July 1973 instead of 1 February 1963 and 1 January 1967.

(2) As regards agreements to which Article 85 of the Treaty applies as a result of the accession of Greece, Articles 8 and 9 shall apply except that the relevant dates shall be 1 January 1981 instead of 13 March 1962 and 1 July 1981 instead of 1 February 1963 and 1 January 1967.

(3) As regards agreements to which Article 85 of the Treaty applies as a result of the accession of Spain and Portugal, Articles 8 and 9 shall apply except that the relevant dates shall be 1 January 1986 instead of 13 March 1962 and 1 July 1986 instead of 1 February 1963 and 1 January 1967.

D17 ——*Article 11 (Confidentiality of information supplied to Commission)*

(1) Information acquired pursuant to Article 4 shall be used only for the purposes of the Regulation.

(2) The Commission and the authorities of the Member States, their officials and other servants shall not disclose information acquired by them pursuant to this Regulation of the kind covered by the obligation of professional secrecy.

(3) The provisions of paragraphs 1 and 2 shall not prevent publication of general information or surveys which do not contain information relating to particular undertakings or associations of undertakings.

D18 ——*Article 12 (Duration of Regulation)*

This Regulation shall enter into force on 1 April 1989.

It shall apply until 31 December 1999.

This Regulation shall be binding in its entirety and directly applicable in all Member States.

D19 —*Summary of the Articles of the Know-How Exemption Regulation*

Article 1 of the Know-How Exemption Regulation sets out certain provisions which, when at least one thereof appears in a know-how agreement (or a mixed know-how/patent agreement where the patents are not "necessary"), brings the agreement within the scope of the Know-How Exemption Regulation, these provisions being deemed to be exempted under TRa. 85(3) whether or not they fall within the prohibition of TRa. 85(1), but exemption under the Regulation is predicated on the other conditions thereof being met. Thus, paragraphs 1, 2, 4 and 5 of Article 1(1) set out permissible territorial restrictions on manufacture and sales that a licensor may, validly, impose on his licensees. Article 2 spells out some further clauses which are generally considered not to be restrictive of competition and so may also be regarded as unobjectionable on whatever basis. Thus, Article 1 defines the scope of the Regulation, and Article 2 sets out the so-called "white clauses".

Article 3 sets out the so-called "black clauses". These are provisions which do fall within TRa. 85(1), and which will not automatically be exempted under TRa. 85(3). The presence of any of these clauses in an unnotified agreement is likely to render the parties liable to fines from the Commission.

Article 1(3) sets out conditions for identification of the know-how, and Article 1(7) contains definitions of 12 terms used in the Regulation. Some of these definitions are very important and are discussed in paras. D20–D23 *infra*.

Article 4 of the Regulation sets out a quick clearance, or opposition, procedure for obtaining individual exemption and this is a feature of several of the other Block Exemption Regulations. General remarks on the usefulness of this procedure are set out in para. D24 *infra*. Articles 5, 6 and 7 contain further qualifications on the scope of the Regulation and are explained herein in para. D25 *infra*, after a detailed analysis (in paras. D20–D23 *infra*) of the critical first three Articles. Only brief references are necessary to the remaining Articles 8–12.

—Permissible provisions for exclusivity and territorial restrictions (Art. 1)   **D20**

One important case decided by the ECJ on permissible territorial restrictions in licence agreements is *Nungesser* v. *E.C. Commission (Case 258/78)* ([1982] ECR 2015; [1983] 1 CMLR 278; [1983] FSR 309), discussed in para. D32 *infra*. There has been much argument on the exact scope of this decision, but this may now be academic in that, if a licence agreement satisfies paragraphs 1, 2, 4 and 5 of Article 1(1) of the Know-How Exemption Regulation, it benefits from an automatic exemption under TRa. 85(3), provided that no "black clauses" according to Article 3 are present. From an analysis of these paragraphs of Article 1, it seems that the following are permissible:

(1) the grant of an exclusive licence for all or part of the Common Market: provided that, if the licensed territory is only part of the Common Market, exclusivity cannot be for more than ten years from the date of signature of the first licence agreement for the territory concerned, though agreements between connected companies should not trigger off this ten year period because the Regulation applies to licences between independent entities;

(2) the exclusive licence of (1) can exclude the licensor himself from all or part of the Common Market for the same period of 10 years;

(3) a licensee may be required not to exploit (manufacture or sell) in a territory reserved to the licensor for the same period of 10 years;

(4) a licensee may be required not to manufacture or use or engage in active sales (*i.e.* sales sought by him) in a territory reserved to other licensees for a period of 10 years from the date of signature of the first licence agreement within the EEC in respect of the same technology;

(5) a licensee may be required not to engage in passive sales (*i.e.* sales resulting from approaches to, rather than by, the selling party) in territories reserved to other licensees for a period not exceeding five years from the date of signature of the first licence agreement within the EEC; and

(6) where the product is protected in some territories by "necessary" patents, the restrictions may extend for the life of those patents.

The possibility of passive sales outside the periods set out in Article 1(1)(6) and Article 1(2) can be deduced from the "black" clauses of Article 3(11) and 3(12).

The above restrictions are only possible when the licensee directly or indirectly engages in manufacture of the licensed product (Art. 1(5)).

The significance of five or ten years as cut-off points on permissible conditions that may be included in licence agreements is arbitrary. They were selected to balance the interests of the holder of the intellectual property right against the benefits to consumers that will follow because of the free flow of goods. These periods are anyway extended for Member States so long as "necessary" patents continue to exist therein (Art. 1(4)).

However, despite the Exemption Regulations, the Commission has stated that objection arises under TRa. 86 if an exclusive licence is granted to an undertaking which is already the world-wide leader in the field (*Tetra Pak's Agreement*, OJEC 4.10.88, L 272/27). Here the exemption (under Regulation No. 2349/84) would have been withdrawn had it not been voluntarily relinquished.

D21 —*Licensed know-how must be secret, substantial and identified (Art. 1(7))*

To benefit from the Regulation, the know-how is required (by Art. 1(7)(1)) to be "non-patented technical information which is secret, substantial and identified in any appropriate form", and there are definitions of "secret" and "substantial" (in Art. 1(7)(2) and (3)). In practice, these definitions should not cause any difficulties in their application. However, the requirement that the know-how should be identified may cause difficulties. How practical it will be for different industries to apply the identification requirement will only become clear with time. There is no similar requirement in the Patent Exemption Regulation No. 2349/84, and no Commission decision which explains the necessity of identification.

While a know-how agreement exempted under the Regulation must be of relatively limited life, if at the end of that time the know-how is still secret and substantial, a new licence can be entered into for continued use of the know-how by the former licensee if the original agreement contained a post-termination prohibition provision.

D22 —*The "white clauses" (Art. 2)*

Many of the clauses set out in Article 2, as well as those of Article 3 (the "black clauses"), find a precise counterpart in the Patent Exemption Regulation (No. 2349/84), as explained in para. D26 *infra*. The Commission's view that the clauses of Article 2 are generally not restrictive of competition has been set out in a number of decisions which mostly ante-date the adoption of Regulation No. 2349/84. These decisions are, therefore, in some ways only now of historic interest because the language of the Block Exemption Regulations has become the definitive Commission law. Nevertheless, there is room for argument as to the precise meaning of some of these white clauses.

Article 2(1) sets out 12 permissible clauses which can be summarised as follows:

The licensee can be obliged not to disclose the secret know-how even after termination of the agreement (para. (1));

Sub-licences may not be granted and the licence may not be assigned (para. (2));

Use of the know-how after the termination of the agreement may be prohibited, but subject to certain important qualifications (para. (3)), see also [1989] FSR 851;

The licensor and licensee can enter into mutual undertakings to communicate

improvements to each other (para. (4)), but the actual wording of this complicated provision should be carefully studied;

The licensee can be required to observe minimum quality specifications and to
procure goods or services from the licensor, provided that these restrictions are
necessary for certain detailed technical reasons (para. (5)); and

The licensee can be required to inform the licensor of any theft of the know-
how or infringement of the patents, but cannot be stopped from challenging the
validity of the licensed patents para. (6)).

Paragraphs (7), (9) and (10) set out permissible restrictions on royalty payments,
while paragraph (8) permits a field of use restriction on the licensee, and paragraphs (11) and (12) set out obligations which are clearly apparent from their wording.

—The "black clauses" (Art. 3) **D23**

To some extent the "black clauses" of Article 3 are the reverse or mirror image
of the "white clauses" of Article 2. Again these are set out in 12 paragraphs. However, these clauses are of prime importance because the presence of any of them in
an agreement will, unless their presence can exceptionally be justified, not only be
regarded void and therefore ineffective, but also render the parties liable to fines
from the Commission, for which see para. C19. Thus, any patent and/or know-how
licence agreement should be carefully vetted against these 12 provisions. The first
four of these can be summarised as follows:

Once the licensed know-how has become truly public knowledge, other than
by the action of the licensee or as otherwise set out in paragraph (1), the licensee
cannot be stopped from using that know-how after termination of the agreement
in contrast to the situation in Article 2(1)(1), see para. D22 *supra*;

A licensee cannot be required to assign rights in improvements to the licensor,
or grant a certain form of exclusive licence to the licensor, and the grant of non-
exclusive licences to use improvements on a reciprocal basis is circumscribed
(para. (2));

Illegal tie-in clauses are prohibited (para. (3)); and

"No challenge" clauses to the secrecy of the know-how, or to the validity of
patents, are not permitted (para. (4)). Such clauses are particularly condemned,
see para. C19, though it may be possible to justify them when they represent a
genuine and reasonable compromise to litigation without effective competitive
disadvantage, for example as in *Bayer and Süllhöfer's Agreement* (OJEC 27.9.88,
L 281/17 *noted* [1989] EIPR D–14; (1989) 20 IIC 127, *The Times*, October 11,
1988) and where the licence was royalty-free and for a technically outdated procedure not used by the licensee and did not prevent the licensee from using its
own technology, see the article by J. Ferry listed in para. C09A.

Otherwise, the wording of para. (5) should be carefully studied as it may mean
that a royalty based on an end product, which is only partially produced by the
licensed technology, is not permitted under the Regulation, on which point see the
discussion on the *Windsurfing* case in para. D32 *infra*. Division of customers, or
other forms of market-sharing, are not permitted (para. (6)), but cross-reference
should be made to Article 1(1)(7), for which see para. D21 *supra*. Also, in general,
there cannot be any quantity restriction on the licensee's output (para. (7)), or any
control on his pricing structure (para. (8)); and covenants requiring the parties not
to compete with each other in certain ways are also not permitted (para. (9)), but
the wording of this provision merits careful study. Finally, the permissible exclusive
licensing practices set out in Article 1(1)(2) and (6), and the permissible prohibitions on passive sales, are respectively qualified by paragraphs (11) and (12).

While neither (a) a requirement to pay royalties after the licensed patent has expired, nor (b) a clause prohibiting manufacture and distribution the licensed products after its termination, is *per se* objectionable under TRa. 85, such may be so if (a) the licensee cannot terminate the licence on reasonable notice and (b) the prohibition has an effect on trade between Member States (*Ottung* v. *Klee (Case 320/87), unreported judgment of May 12, 1989* (ECJ)).

D24 —*Opposition procedure (Art. 4)*

Article 4 of Regulation 556/89 provides for a quick clearance, or opposition, procedure. Under this, an agreement can be notified to the Commission and exemption (under TRa. 85(3)) arises automatically if no objection has been raised within the following six months. This procedure was first introduced into Community law in the Patent Exemption Regulation (No. 2349/84), and is likewise set out in Article 4 of that Regulation. It is understood that these opposition procedures have been little used.

D25 —*Other Articles in the Patent and Know-How Exemption Regulations*

Article 5 in each of these two Regulations is similarly worded, except for one very important distinction. This is that Article 5(1)(4) of the Know-How Regulation specifically states that this Regulation does *not* apply to the licensing of intellectual property, other than patents or trade marks. In particular, therefore, it does *not* apply to copyright and design rights, or to the licensing of software, except in circumstances which are explained in detail in this sub-paragraph (4).

Article 6 of the Know-How Exemption Regulation corresponds to Article 11 of the Patent Exemption Regulation and is worded in similar fashion. These Articles apply when the licensor is not the developer of the know-how or the patentee, but is authorised by the developer or the patentee to grant a licence or sub-licence. Some assignments are effectively exclusive licences in the sense that the assignor receives payment dependent upon the turnover attained by the assignee, and the Regulations apply to such assignments.

Article 7 of the Know-How Exemption Regulation corresponds to Article 9 of the Patent Exemption Regulation. The reference to arbitration awards in Article 7(1) arises out of drafts of the Patent Exemption Regulation which excluded from the scope of that Regulation awards made by arbitration unless these awards were communicated to the Commission. Its presence here now seems a historical accident because equally the Commission could object that effects incompatible with the conditions laid down in TRa. 85(3) apply from an award of a court. Article 7(2) would appear to envisage a situation whch might fall under TRa. 86 in that licensed products are not exposed to effective competition. Indeed, in *Tetra Pak's Agreement* (OJEC 4.10.88, L 272/27) the Commission would have used Article 9 of the Patent Exemption Regulation to withdraw exemption had not the exclusivity provision (which satisfied that Regulation) been voluntarily withdrawn, see further para. D20 *supra.*

Article 7(3) is important in that it states that any exclusive licence which extends to a period longer than five years, without a right of termination on the part of the licensor, is suspect.

Articles 8, 9 and 10 contain various transitional provisions. These are substantially the same as those in Articles 6, 7 and 8 of the Patent Exemption Regulation.

D26 *The Patent Licensing Exemption Regulation No. 2349/84*

As stated in para. D06 *supra*, this Patent Exemption Regulation has a similar construction to the later Know-How Regulation, with its Articles 4–9 and 11–13 being almost precise counterparts of Articles in the Know-How Exemption Regulation. In view of the adoption of this latter Regulation, the most important issue for consideration is which of the two Regulations is applicable in any particular instance when a combination of patents and know-how is being licensed. This problem is discussed in para. D28 *infra*.

As in the Know-How Regulation, Article 1 of Regulation No. 2349/84 defines the scope of the Block Exemption by setting out the types of clauses that may permissibly be present in a licence agreement which falls within the scope of this Regulation, and deals with the permissible restrictions on exclusivity and export bans and active and passive sales, as discussed in relation to the Know-How Regulation in para. D20 *supra*, but see para. D27 *infra*. Article 2 contains the "white list" which is very similar to the "white list" of the Know-How Regulation (discussed in para. D22 *supra*); and Article 3 contains a list of "black clauses" very similar to the "black list" of the Know-How Regulation (discussed in para. D23 *supra*). However, since Regulation No. 2349/84 is concerned with the licensing of patents, there are differences in detail of the language used. Because the scope of a patent licence can be defined by the life of the patent, there is no need to consider if the term of a permissible patent licence should be arbitrarily restricted for a number of years, as is the case with a licence which may be a pure know-how licence, see para. D20 *supra*.

—Export and import bans in patent licence agreements   **D27**

In view of the importance which may be attached to the permissibility of contractual bans on exports and imports, the *permissible* licensing practices set out in Article 1(1)–(6) of Regulation No. 2349/84 are summarised below:

The licensor (patentee) may grant an exclusive licence for a licensed territory, which may be a single country within the Common Market (Art. 1(1)(1));

The licensor may agree not to engage in active or passive sales in a territory licensed to the licensee (Art. 1(1)(2));

The licensee may agree not to engage in active or passive sales in any part of the Common Market which the patentee has reserved to himself (Art. 1(1)(3)) [For the meaning of "active" and "passive" sales, see para. D20, items (4) and (5) *supra*];

The licensee can be required not to manufacture or use the licensed product or process in countries within the Common Market which are licensed to other licensees (Art. 1(1)(4));

The licensee can be required not to pursue an active sales policy in any territory within the Common Market which is licensed to other licensees (Art. 1(1)(5)); and

The licensee can be required not to engage in any passive sales in any territory within the Common Market licensed to other licensees for a period not exceeding five years from the date when the product is first put on the market within the Common Market (Art. 1(1)(6)).

It must be emphasised that these restrictions are only possible so long as there are parallel patents in the countries concerned. Under the Patent Exemption Regulation, restrictions on the manufacture or sale of goods within any part of the Common Market, where (for whatever reason) a parallel patent is not in existence, may not be maintained. What similar restrictions may be proposed under the Know-How Exemption Regulation is discussed in para. D20 *supra*.

—Borderline between the Patent and Know-How Exemption Regulations   **D28**

One of the difficult issues to decide is the borderline between the Patent Exemption Regulation, which covers the combination of "necessary" patents, and know-how, and the later Know-How Regulation, which covers the combination of know-how and patents that are not "necessary". In deciding whether a particular licence agreement qualifies for a block exemption, the parties will first have to consider which of the two Regulations is applicable.

While Recital 9 of the Patent Exemption Regulation extends to mixed patent and know-how licences "insofar as the licensed patents are necessary for achieving the objects of the licensed technology and as long as at least one of the licensed patents remains in force", Recital 11 of the Know-How Exemption Regulation states that the provisions of the Patent Exemption Regulation are not applicable to agreements covered by the Know-How Regulation. Thus, a mixed know-how and patent licence cannot fall within the scope of the Patent Regulation when "the licensed patents are not necessary for the achievement of the objects of the licensed technology containing both patented and non-patented elements, which may be the case where such patents do not afford effective protection against the exploitation of this technology by third parties" (Regulation No. 556/89, Recital 2). This is purely a subjective test and in many, or most, cases it will be safer to assume that the licensed patents are not necessary in the mixed agreement so that, if an agreement is to take advantage of a Block Exemption Regulation, it will have to be the Know-How Exemption, rather than the Patent Exemption Regulation.

To qualify for exemption under the Know-How Exemption Regulation, the licensed know-how must be "secret, substantial and identified in any appropriate form", see para. D21 *supra*. There is a similar reference to secret know-how in the Patent Exemption Regulation, but the need for the know-how to be substantial is not present in that Regulation. It is clear from the decision in *Boussois and Interpane's Agreement* ([1988] 4 CMLR 124, *noted* [1988] FSR 215), discussed in para. D30 *infra*, that the Commission regards the Patent Exemption Regulation as only applying to situations where the know-how is not the essential or more important part of the agreement. The definition of "substantial" in the Know-How Regulation is thought to cover all but the most trivial know-how.

The need to identify the know-how is not referred to at all in the Patent Exemption Regulation, but is spelled out in some detail in the Know-How Regulation and different industries may find it easy or difficult to meet the requirements. Thus, if the parties justifiably take the view that the patents are "necessary", an agreement can be considered as exempted under the Patent Exemption Regulation, and there is then no need to identify the know-how in any particular way. However, if the patents are not "necessary", the Know-How Exemption Regulation applies and the know-how has to be identified in a particular manner.

Another type of mixed agreement which will not qualify for consideration under the Patent Exemption Regulation is one containing obligations which restrict competition in EEC countries where there is no patent protection. Thus, any mixed agreements where there are patents in only some of the licensed countries within the Common Market may only benefit from a block exemption under the Know-How Exemption Regulation, see Recital 2 thereof.

D29 *Commission decisions prior to 1984*

Prior to the preparation of the Patent Exemption Regulation No. 2349/84, there were a number of decisions of the E.C. Commission which set out its views on which clauses were or were not permissible in a patent licence agreement, either without offending against TRa. 85(1), or for which exemption could be granted under TRa. 85(3)). These decisions are now of limited value because of Regulation No. 2349/84, but the early decisions are worth studying as illustrating the development of the case law. Some of these are: *Raymond's Agreement* ([1972] CMLR D45; [1972] FSR 443); *Davidson Rubber's Agreement* ([1972] CMLR D52; [1972]

FSR 451); *Burroughs and Delplanque's Agreement* ([1972] CMLR D67; [1972] FSR 467); *Burroughs and Geha's Agreement* ([1972] CMLR D72; [1972] FSR 473); *Kabel and Luchaire's Agreement* ([1975] CMLR D40; [1976] FSR 18); and *Association des Ouvriers* v. *Beyrard* ([1976] 1 CMLR D14; [1976] FSR 181).

Later Commission decisions   **D30**

Some decisions of the E.C. Commission since 1984, which have dealt with permissible licensing practices, are discussed below but, because new decisions frequently appear, the Supplement hereto should be consulted for reference to later decisions which may show how the various Block Exemption Regulations have come to be interpreted in practice.

In *Boussois and Interpane's Agreement* ([1988] 4 CMLR 124, *noted* [1988] FSR 215) the Commission granted an individual exemption under TRa. 85(3) in respect of technology concerning the application of coatings to window glass for heat circulation. The package of non-patented technical knowledge referred to a production unit and to the coatings, whereas the patents concerned only one particular coating. The Commission decided that the Patent Exemption Regulation was not applicable because the licensed know-how related to a field that was far broader than the patents (which related only to one product) and patents did not exist throughout the Community. For Case Comment, see J. S. Venit ([1987] EIPR 164).

However, exemption under TRa. 85(3) was refused in *Velcro* v. *Aplix* ([1989] 4 CMLR 157) because: (a) exclusivity continued beyond the life of the basic patents; (b) the agreement was automatically extended by improvement patents; (c) there was an export ban against passive sales in the EEC territories reserved to the exclusive licensee; (d) a non-competition obligation existed between the parties; and (e) there was a requirement to pass title to patents on the licensee's improvements to the Licensor in other territories. These restrictions correspond, or are similar, to those set out in the "Black List", see para. D23 *supra*.

In *Jus-Rol and Rich Products' Agreement* ([1988] 4 CMLR 527, *noted* [1988] FSR 528) the Commission granted negative clearance (*i.e.* they found that the agreement did not fall within TRa. 85(1)) to an agreement relating to the licensing by *Rich Products* of its technology for the manufacture of frozen yeast dough products. The licensee was allowed to use the secret know-how, which was indicated to be substantial when the licensee agreed to pay for its use and which was apparently here identified as a body of written confidential non-patented information, for a period of ten years, but there was a right of termination by either party after five years. At the conclusion of the agreement, the licensee was not permitted to use the know-how for a period of ten years. It was clearly stated by the Commission that such a clause was not within TRa. 85(1) and that, if it were not possible for a licensor to require that a licensee should stop using the non-patented technical know-how, it would ultimately be harmful to the general transfer of technical knowledge. For Case Comment see [1989] EIPR 291.

In *DDD and Delta Chemie's Agreement* ([1989] 4 CMLR 535, *noted* [1989] FSR 52 and 497) an exclusive know-how licence was granted exemption under TRa. 85(3) with a prohibition on use of the licensor's know-how after the end of the agreement, but the licensee was permitted then to use the improvements thereto developed by itself provided that such would not involve use of the licensor's know-how. Also, while the licensee was required to collaborate in the prosecution of infringers, this provision is not to be taken as preventing the licensee from challenging the validity of the licensed right. Individual exemption was also granted in *Brown Boveri and NGK Insulators' Agreement* (OJEC 4.11.88, L 301/68) where, in a research and development agreement, one party undertook not to export into the EEC for ten years, the high risk of the project justifying the exemption.

In *Konica's Agreement* (OJEC 23.3.88, L 78/34) the Commission found objectionable (under TRa. 85) the conduct of *Konica* of Japan, and of some of its wholly-owned subsidiaries in Europe, on the basis that these subsidiaries did not receive instructions from Japan on the day-to-day running of their business. In other words, it is no longer safe to assume that any licensing practice as between a parent and its subsidiaries cannot be objected to under TRa. 85.

D31 *Compulsory licences*

In considering compulsory licensing of patents, it must now be recognised that there are two distinct sets of laws that may be applicable. A classic or well-established feature of many patent laws is that a compulsory licence may be granted because of abuse of monopoly as set forth in the Paris International Convention of 1883 (as amended). However, the anti-trust or restrictive trade practice law of a country (in this case the Common Market) may also mean that a compulsory licence may be granted by a source outside the patent law as such.

The grant of a compulsory licence on the ground of abuse of monopoly or for other reasons is a well-established feature of the Paris Convention. The principles involved are discussed in paras. 48.07–48.15, 50.03 and 50.04. However, case law from the ECJ may mean that a licence of right in certain circumstances is treated as a compulsory licence. Thus, in *Pharmon* v. *Hoechst (Case 19/84)* ([1985] 3 CMLR 775; [1986] FSR 108 (ECJ)), the ECJ considered the "exhaustion of rights" doctrine when a compulsory licence had been granted under section 41 [1949]. This is discussed in para. C15.

In *Allen & Hanburys* v. *Generics (Case 434/85)* ([1988] 1 CMLR 701; [1988] FSR 312 (ECJ)), discussed in paras. 46.28, C13 and C15, the effect of a licence compulsorily granted under a patent bearing a deemed "licence of right" endorsement was considered. It is an open point whether a patentee could assert, for example, his Dutch patent rights against the export of goods from the United Kingdom under a licence obtained as of "right" on the grounds that this was a compulsory licence, though it can be argued that any such licence does not result in the product being marketed by the licensee with the "explicit consent" of the patentee, as seems to be required for the doctrine of "exhaustion of rights" to apply, see para. C15. Also, in *Allen & Hanburys* v. *Generics (supra)*, the ECJ considered that the "licence of right" provisions in the British patent statutes, when they are applied automatically, are equivalent to provisions for the grant of compulsory licences, but there is no particular reason for the same position to obtain when the "licence of right" entry in the register has been imposed by the voluntary act of the patentee.

D32 *ECJ Decisions on contractual licensing*

There is little case law from the ECJ directed specifically to the allowability of contractual licensing conditions with respect to TRaa. 85 and 86. In *Nungesser* v. *E.C. Commission (Case 258/78)* ([1982] ECR 2015; [1983] 1 CMLR 278; [1983] FSR 309), also known as the *Maize Seed* case, *INRA*, a French official institute, had developed certain varieties of maize seed for which they held plant breeder's rights. An exclusive licence was granted in Germany to *Eisele*, and *INRA* undertook to ensure that its seeds were not exported to Germany, except via *Eisele*. *INRA* had other licensees in France who produced seeds, though it had no manufacturing capability itself. There have been a number of interpretations of the significance of the Court's decision in this case to contractual licensing. It is commonly held that the decision establishes that an open exclusive licence is outside the scope of TRa. 85(1). A licence is "open" if parallel importers are not prevented from importing into the territory where the exclusive licence has been granted and the same is true with respect to licensees from other territories. On this analysis, export restrictions may represent an infringement of TRa. 85(1). The *Maize Seed* case was decided by the Court in 1982 and the subsequent adoption by the Commission of the Block Exemption Regulations has meant that much of the debate on the effect of this decision is now only of academic interest.

In *Pronuptia* v. *Schillglais (Case 184/84)* ([1986] ECR 374; [1986] 1 CMLR 414, *noted* [1987] FSR 317 (ECJ)) the Court considered various clauses in a franchising agreement between a supplier of wedding dresses and accessories and its franchisees in certain parts of Germany and discussed the significance of TRa. 85(1) and (3) with respect to exclusivity agreements and export and import bans.

In *Erauw-Jacquery* v. *La Hesbignonne (Case 27/87)* ([1988] 4 CMLR 576, *noted* [1988] FSR 572) the Court approved a licence under plant breeder's rights which was limited to acts of propagation with a ban on selling or exporting the basic seeds, such bans being held to be necessary to protect the essential interests of the rights holder. This suggests a "rule of reason" approach to the grant of exclusive licences and to sales limitations on products produced under the licence, where the wording of the clauses does not otherwise comply with the wording of an appropriate Block Exemption Regulation.

Windsurfing International v. *E.C. Commission (Case 193/83)* ([1986] ECR 642; [1986] 3 CMLR 489; [1988] FSR 139 (ECJ)) was the first case considered by the ECJ with respect to the detailed clauses commonly found in a licence agreement. *Windsurfing* were the owners of EEC patents only in the United Kingdom (subsequently found invalid, see [1985] RPC 59) and Germany (where the Court found as a fact that the scope of the patent was restricted to a rig for a sailboard). At first instance, the Commission found (ignoring the British patent position, then *sub judice*) that the following licensing practices of *Windsurfing* were objectionable:

(1) Limitation of the licence to manufacture to a country where a patent existed, with the effect that royalties were to be paid even on products sold in parts of the EEC where no patent protection existed;

(2) The presence of provisions for terminating the licence if the licensee changed its manufacturing location;

(3) Requirements for a licensee's design to be approved, other than for objective reasons of quality control or safety factors based on the specific subject-matter of the patent;

(4) Provisions requiring marketing to be accompanied by a notice of the licence even when no patent or other right requiring a licence existed in the country of sale;

(5) Limitation of a licensee's power to supply the rig and the board separately;

(6) The requirement that the licensee should acknowledge the validity of the licensed trade mark;

(7) The placing of a notice that the product was marketed under licence on a part of the combination which was not the subject of the patent; and

(8) Charging a royalty based on the unpatented combination of the board and rig.

On the appeal the ECJ generally upheld the initial decision of the Commission with the exception that the court felt it was reasonable, for convenience, to base the royalty on the complete sailboard, rather than on the rig only, provided that it could be shown that the royalty based on the value of the rig alone was not excessive. For discussion of the basis of the fines imposed in this case, see para. C19.

RULES OF THE SUPREME COURT (Extracts)

(as amended up to S.I. 1989 No. 386)

E000.1   *Note.* This Appendix reprints those Rules of the Supreme Court, or parts thereof, which are of significance in relation to procedure before the Patents Court and on appeal therefrom to the Court of Appeal. Some other of the Rules likely to be helpful to patent agents are also included. However, no attempt is made in this work to deal in detail with practice and procedure before the High Court generally. For further information, the current version of *The Supreme Court Practice* ("The White Book") and its latest cumulative supplement should be consulted. That book contains extensive notes on practice under each of the Rules of Court. These Rules apply only to proceedings in the High Court [of Justice for England and Wales], but where there is no specific Patents Rule in point the Comptroller will follow these Rules of Court. While these Rules are generally applied in the High Court of Northern Ireland, the court in Scotland (and in the Isle of Man) has its own procedural rules. For those in Scotland, see para. 98.03.

    The Rules of the Supreme Court ("RSC") are made by Statutory Instrument and are divided into a number of detailed "Orders" ("Ord." or "O.") and these Orders are subdivided into rules ("r.") and sub-rules. However, for the origin of each Rule, and its amendments, the "White Book" should be consulted as references to these Statutory Instruments have been omitted from the present work. References in the RSC to "the Act" are to the Supreme Court Act 1981 (c. 54) (RSC Ord. 1, r. 4(1)).

    Ord. 104 is the special Order relating to practice before the Patents Court.

ORDER 2

Effect of Non-Compliance

Non-compliance with rules (O. 2, r. 1)

E002.1   **1.**—(1) Where, in beginning or purporting to begin any proceedings or at any stage in the course of or in connection with any proceedings, there has, by reason of any thing done or left undone, been a failure to comply with the requirements of these rules, whether in respect of time, place, manner, form or content or in any other respect, the failure shall be treated as an irregularity and shall not nullify the proceedings, any step taken in the proceedings, or any document, judgment or order therein.

    (2) Subject to paragraph (3) the Court may, on the ground that there has been such a failure as is mentioned in paragraph (1) and on such terms as to costs or otherwise as it thinks just, set aside either wholly or in part the pro-

ceedings in which the failure occurred, any step taken in those proceedings or any document, judgment or order therein or exercise its powers under these rules to allow such amendments (if any) to be made and to make such order (if any) dealing with the proceedings generally as it thinks fit.

(3) The Court shall not wholly set aside any proceedings or the writ or other originating process by which they were begun on the ground that the proceedings were required by any of these rules to be begun by an originating process other than the one employed.

Note. A breach of the Rules of the Supreme Court does not in itself result in termination of the proceedings. It is merely an irregularity which can be cured by the consent of the other party or parties, or by the leave of the court given on such conditions and award of costs as may be deemed appropriate. For extensions of time, see E003.1–E003.5.

ORDER 3

TIME

"Month" means calender month (O. 3, r. 1)

1.—Without prejudice to section 5 of the Interpretation Act 1978, in its application to these rules, the word "month", where it occurs in any judgment, order, direction or other document forming part of any proceedings in the Supreme Court, means a calender month unless the context otherwise requires.   **E003.1**

Reckoning periods of time (O. 3, r. 2)

2.—(1) Any period of time fixed by these rules or by any judgment, order or direction for doing any act shall be reckoned in accordance with the following provisions of this rule.   **E003.2**

(2) Where the act is required to be done within a specified period after or from a specified date, the period begins immediately after that date.

(3) Where the act is required to be done within or not less than a specified period before a specified date, the period ends immediately before that date.

(4) Where the act is required to be done a specified number of clear days before or after a specified date, at least that number of days must intervene between the day on which the act is done and that date.

(5) Where, apart from this paragraph, the period in question, being a period of seven days or less, would include a Saturday, Sunday or bank holiday, Christmas Day or Good Friday, that day shall be excluded.

In this paragraph "bank holiday" means a day which is, or is to be observed as, a bank holiday, or a holiday, under the Banking and Financial Dealings Act 1971, in England and Wales.

1105

Month of August excluded from time for service, etc., of pleadings (O. 3, r. 3)

E003.3   **3.**—Unless the Court otherwise directs, the month of August shall be excluded in reckoning any period prescribed by these rules or by any order or direction for serving, filing or amending any pleading.

Time expires on Sunday, etc. (O. 3, r. 4)

E003.4   **4.**—Where the time prescribed by these rules, or by any judgment, order or direction, for doing any act at an office of the Supreme Court expires on a Sunday or other day on which that office is closed, and by reason thereof that act cannot be done on that day, the act shall be in time if done on the next day on which that office is open.

Extension, etc., of time (O. 3, r. 5)

E003.5   **5.**—(1) The Court may, on such terms as it thinks just, by order extend or abridge the period within which a person is required or authorised by these rules, or by any judgment, order or direction, to do any act in any proceedings.

(2) The Court may extend any such period as is referred to in paragraph (1) although the application for extension is not made until after the expiration of that period.

(3) The period within which a person is required by these rules, or by any order or direction, to serve, file or amend any pleading or other document may be extended by consent (given in writing) without an order of the Court being made for that purpose.

(4) In this rule references to the Court shall be construed as including references to the Court of Appeal, a single judge of that Court and the registrar of civil appeals.

Note. An extension of time given by consent must be in writing (r. 5(3)).

ORDER 5

MODE OF BEGINNING CIVIL PROCEEDINGS IN HIGH COURT

Mode of beginning civil proceedings (O. 5, r. 1)

E005.1   **1.**—Subject to the provisions of any Act and of these rules, civil proceedings in the High Court may be begun by writ, originating summons, originating motion or petition.

Note. An action for patent infringement is commenced by writ, see Para. E005.2. An originating application to the court for revocation of a patent is brought by petition under Ord. 9.

Proceedings which must be begun by writ (O. 5, r. 2)

2.—Subject to any provision of an Act, or of these rules, by virtue of **E005.2** which any proceedings are expressely required to be begun otherwise than by writ, the following proceedings must, notwithstanding anything in rule 4, be begun by writ, that is to say, proceedings—

(*a*) in which a claim is made by the plaintiff for any relief or remedy for any tort, other than trespass to land;

(*b*) in which a claim made by the plaintiff is based on an allegation of fraud;

(*c*) . . .

(*d*) in which a claim is made by the plaintiff in respect of the infringement of a patent.

Note. An action for patent infringement falls generally under sub-rule (2)(*a*), and specifically under sub-rule (2)(d).

Proceedings to be begun by motion or petition (O. 5, r. 5)

5.—Proceedings may be begun by originating motion or petition if, but **E005.5** only if, by these rules or by or under any Act the proceedings in question are required or authorised to be so begun.

Note. Proceedings for revocation are to be brought by petition (O. 104, r. 4, for patents under the Act, and s.32(1) [1949] for "existing patents".

ORDER 6

WRITS OF SUMMONS: GENERAL PROVISIONS

Indorsement of claim (O. 6, r. 2)

2.—(1) Before a writ is issued it must be indorsed—

(*a*) with a statement of claim or, if the statement of claim is not indorsed on the writ, with a concise statement of the nature of the claim made or the relief or remedy required in the action begun thereby;

(*b*) . . .

(c) . . .
(d) . . .
(e) . . .
(2) . . .

Issue of writ (O. 6, r. 7)

E006.7   7.—(1) No writ which is to be served out of the jurisdiction shall be issued without the leave of the court unless it complies with the following conditions, that is to say—
    (a) each claim made by the writ is either—
       (i) one which by virtue of the Civil Jurisdiction and Judgments Act 1982 [c. 27] the Court has power to hear and determine, or
       (ii) one which by virtue of any other enactment the Court has power to hear and determine notwithstanding that the person against whom the claim is made is not within the jurisdiction of the Court or that the wrongful act, neglect or default giving rise to the claim did not take place within its jurisdiction;
       and
    (b) where a claim made by the writ is one which the Court has power to hear and determine by virtue of the Civil Jurisdiction and Judgments Act 1982, the writ is indorsed before it is issued with a statement that the Court has power under that Act to hear and determine the claim, and that no proceedings involving the same cause of action are pending between the parties in Scotland, Northern Ireland or another Convention territory.

(2) Except where otherwise expressly provided by these Rules, a writ may be issued out of:
    (a) the Central Office if it relates to proceedings intended to be conducted in the Queen's Bench Division; or
    (b) . . .
    (c) Chancery Chambers if it relates to proceedings intended to be conducted in the Chancery Division; or
    (d) a district registry.

(3) Issue of writ takes place upon its being sealed by an officer of the office out of which it is issued.

(4) The officer by whom a concurrent writ is sealed must mark it as a concurrent writ with an official stamp.

(5) No writ shall be sealed unless at the time of tender thereof for sealing the person tendering it leaves at the office at which it is tendered a copy thereof signed, where the plaintiff sues in person, by him or, where he does not so sue, by or on behalf of his solicitor.

(6) For the purpose of this rule, "Convention territory" means the territory or territories of any Contracting State, as defined by section 1(3) of

that Act, to which the Conventions defined in section 1(1) of that Act apply.

ORDER 9

PETITIONS: GENERAL PROVISIONS

Application (O. 9, r. 1)

1.—Rules 2 to 4 apply to petitions by which civil proceedings in the High   **E009.1**
Court are begun, subject, in the case of petitions of any particular class, to any special provisions relating to petitions of that class made by these Rules or by or under any Act.

Contents of petition (O. 9, r. 2)

2.—(1) Every petition must have printed or embossed by an officer of   **E009.2**
the Court at the head of the first page a replica of the Royal Arms and must include a concise statement of the nature of the claim made or the relief or remedy required in the proceedings begun thereby.

(2) Every petition must include at the end thereof a statement of the names of the persons, if any, required to be served therewith or, if no person is required to be served, a statement to that effect.

(3) Order 6, Rule 5, shall, with the necessary modifications, apply in relation to a petition as it applies in relation to a writ.

Presentation of petition (O. 9, r. 3)

3.—(1) A petition may be presented in one of the Chancery district   **E009.3**
registries.

(2) Subject to paragraph (1) a petition must be presented by leaving it at Chancery Chambers.

Fixing time for hearing petition (O. 9, r. 4)
4.—(1) A day and time for the hearing of a petition which is required to   **E009.4**
be heard shall be fixed—

(*a*) in the case of a petition presented in a District Registry, by the Registrar of that Registry, and

(*b*) in any other case, by the proper officer in Chancery Chambers.

(2) Unless the Court otherwise directs, a petition which is required to be served on any person must be served on him not less than seven days before the day fixed for the hearing of the petition.

ORDER 12

Acknowledgment of Service to Writ or Originating Summons

Mode of acknowledging service (O. 12, r. 1)

E012.1   **1.**—(1) Subject to paragraph (2) and to Order 80, rule 2, a defendant to an action begun by writ may (whether or not he is sued as a trustee or personal representative or in any other representative capacity) acknowledge service of the writ and defend the action by a solicitor or in person.

(2) The defendant to such an action who is a body corporate may acknowledge service of the writ and give notice of intention to defend the action either by a solicitor or by a person duly authorised to act on the defendant's behalf but, except as aforesaid or as expressly provided by any enactment, such a defendant may not take steps in the action otherwise than by a solicitor.

(3) Service of a writ may be acknowledged by properly completing an acknowledgment of services, as defined by rule 3, and handing it in at, or sending it by post to, the appropriate office, that is to say, if the writ was issued out of an office of the Supreme Court at the Royal Courts of Justice, that office, or if the writ was issued out of a district registry that registry.

(4) If two or more defendants to an action acknowledge service by the same solicitor and at the same time, only one acknowledgment of service need be completed and delivered for those defendants.

(5) The date on which service is acknowledged is the date on which the acknowledgment of service is received at the appropriate office.

Acknowledgment of service (O. 12, r. 3)

E012.3   **3.**—(1) An acknowledgment of service must be in Form No. 14 or 15 in Appendix A, whichever is appropriate, and, except as provided in rule 1(2) must be signed by the solicitor acting for the defendant specified in the acknowledgment or, if the defendant is acting in person, by that defendant.

(2) An acknowledgment of service must specify—

(*a*) in the case of a defendant acknowledging service in person, the address of his place of residence and, if his place of residence is not within the jurisdiction or if he has no place of residence, the address of a place within the jurisdiction at or to which documents for him may be delivered or sent, and

(*b*) in the case of a defendant acknowledging service by a solicitor, a business address (to which may be added a numbered box at a document exchange) of his solicitor's within the jurisdiction;

and where the defendant acknowledges service in person, the address within the jurisdiction specified under sub-paragraph (*a*) shall be his address for service, but otherwise his solicitor's business address shall be his address for service.

In relation to a body corporate the references in sub-paragraph (*a*) to the defendant's place of residence shall be construed as references to the defendant's registered or principal office.

(3) Where the defendant acknowledges service by a solicitor who is acting as agent for another solicitor having a place of business within the jurisdiction, the acknowledgment of service must state that the first-named solicitor so acts and must also state the name and address of that other solicitor.

(4) If an acknowledgment of service does not specify the defendant's address for service or the Court is satisfied that any address specified in the acknowledgment of service is not genuine, the Court may on application by the plaintiff set aside the acknowledgment or order the defendant to give an address or, as the case may be, a genuine address for service and may in any case direct that the acknowledgment shall nevertheless have effect for the purposes of Order 19, rule 1(5) and Order 65, rule 9.

Time limited for acknowledging service (O. 12, r. 5)

5.—References in these Rules to the time limited for acknowledging service are references—   **E012.5**

- (*a*) in the case of a writ served within the jurisdiction, to 14 days after service of the writ (including the day of service) or, where that time has been extended by or by virtue of these Rules, to that time as so extended; and
- (*b*) in the case of a writ, served out of the jurisdiction, to the time limited under Order 10, Rule 2(2) Order 11, Rule 1(3) or Order 11, Rule 4(4) or, where that time has been extended as aforesaid, to that time as so extended.

Late acknowledgment of service (O. 12, r. 6)

6.—(1) Except with the leave of the Court, a defendant may not give notice of intention to defend in an action after judgment has been obtained therein.   **E012.6**

(2) Except as provided by paragraph (1) nothing in these rules or any writ or order thereunder shall be construed as precluding a defendant from acknowledging service in an action after the time limited for so doing, but if a defendant acknowledges service after that time, he shall not, unless the Court otherwise orders, be entitled to serve a defence or do any other act later than if he had acknowledged service within that time.

Acknowledgment not to constitute waiver (O. 12, r. 7)

E012.7   7.—The acknowledgment by a defendant of service of a writ shall not be treated as a waiver by him of any irregularity in the writ or service thereof or in any order giving leave to serve the writ out of the jurisdiction or extending the validity of the writ for the purpose of service.

Acknowledgment of service to be treated as entry of appearance (O. 12, r. 10)

E012.10   10.—For the purpose of any enactment referring expressly or impliedly to the entry of appearance as a procedure provided by rules of court for responding to a writ or other process issuing out of the High Court, or of any rule of law, the acknowledgment of service of the writ or other process in accordance with these rules shall be treated as the entry of an appearance to it, and related expressions shall be construed accordingly.

ORDER 14

Summary Judgment

Application by plaintiff for summary judgment (O. 14, r. 1)

E014.1   1.—(1) Where in an action to which this rule applies a statement of claim has been served on a defendant and that defendant has given notice of intention to defend that action, the plaintiff may, on the ground that that defendant has no defence to a claim included in the writ, or to a particular part of such a claim, or has no defence to such a claim or part except as to the amount of any damages claimed, apply to the Court for judgment against that defendant.

(2) Subject to paragraph (3) this rule applies to every action begun by writ in the Queen's Bench Division (including Admiralty Court) or the Chancery Division other than—

[. . .]

(3) [. . .]

ORDER 15

Causes of Action, Counterclaims and Parties

Counterclaim against plaintiff (O. 15, r. 2)

E015.2   2.—(1) Subject to rule 5(2), a defendant in any action who alleges that he has any claim or is entitled to any relief or remedy against a plaintiff in the action in respect of any matter (whenever and however arising) may, instead of bringing a separate action, make a counterclaim in respect of that matter; and where he does so he must add the counterclaim to his defence.

(2) Rule 1 shall apply in relation to a counterclaim as if the counterclaim were a separate action and as if the person making the counterclaim were the plaintiff and the person against whom it is made a defendant.

(3) A counterclaim may be proceeded with notwithstanding that judgment is given for the plaintiff in the action or that the action is stayed, discontinued or dismissed.

(4) Where a defendant establishes a counterclaim against the claim of the plaintiff and there is a balance in favour of one of the parties, the Court may give judgment for the balance, so, however, that this provision shall not be taken as affecting the Court's discretion with respect to costs.

Declaratory judgment (O. 15, r. 16)

16.—No action or other proceeding shall be open to objection on the ground that a merely declaratory judgment or order is sought thereby, and the Court may make binding declarations of right whether or not any consequential relief is or could be claimed. **E015.16**

ORDER 18

PLEADINGS

Service of statement of claim (O. 18, r. 1)

1.—Unless the Court gives leave to the contrary or a statement of claim is indorsed on the writ, the plaintiff must serve a statement of claim on the defendant or, if there are two or more defendants, on each defendant, and must do so either when the writ is served on that defendant or at any time after service of the writ but before the expiration of 14 days after that defendant gives notice of intention to defend. **E018.1**

Service of defence (O. 18, r. 2)

2.—(1) Subject to paragraph (2), a defendant who gives notice of intention to defend an action must, unless the Court gives leave to the contrary, serve a defence on the plaintiff before the expiration of 14 days after the time limited for acknowledging service of the writ or after the statement of claim is served on him, whichever is the later. **E018.2**

(2) If a summons under Order 14, rule 1, or under Order 86, rule 1, is served on a defendant before he serves his defence, paragraph (1) shall not have effect in relation to him unless by the order made on the summons he

is given leave to defend the action and, in that case, shall have effect as if it required him to serve his defence within 14 days after the making of the order or within such other period as may be specified therein.

Service of reply and defence to counterclaim (O. 18, r. 3)

E018.3   **3.**—(1) A plaintiff on whom a defendant serves a defence must serve a reply on that defendant if it is needed for compliance with Rule 8; and if no reply is served, Rule 14(1) will apply.

(2) A plaintiff on whom a defendant serves a counterclaim must, if he intends to defend it, serve on that defendant a defence to counterclaim.

(3) Where a plaintiff serves both a reply and a defence to counterclaim on any defendant, he must include them in the same document.

(4) A reply to any defence must be served by the plaintiff before the expiration of 14 days after the service on him of that defence, and a defence to counterclaim must be served by the plaintiff before the expiration of 14 days after the service on him of the counterclaim to which it relates.

Pleadings subsequent to reply (O. 18, r. 4)

E018.4   **4.**—No pleading subsequent to a reply or a defence to counterclaim shall be served except with the leave of the Court.

Service of pleadings or amended pleadings in month of August (O. 18, r. 5)

E018.5   **5.**—Pleadings or amended pleadings shall not be served during the month of August except with the leave of the Court or with the consent all the parties to the action.

Pleadings: formal requirements (O. 18, r. 6)
E018.6   **6.**—(1) Every pleading in an action must bear on its face—
  (*a*) the year in which the writ in the action was issued and the letter and number of the action,
  (*b*) the title of the action,
  (*c*) the division of the High Court to which the action is assigned and the name of the judge (if any) to whom it is assigned,
  (*d*) the description of the pleading, and
  (*e*) the date on which it was served.

(2) Every pleading must, if necessary, be divided into paragraphs numbered consecutively, each allegation being so far as convenient contained in a separate paragraph.

(3) Dates, sums and other numbers must be expressed in a pleading in figures and not in words.

(4) Every pleading of a party must be indorsed—

(*a*) where the party sues or defends in person, with his name and address;

(*b*) in any other case, with the name or firm and business address of the solicitor by whom it was served and also (if the solicitor is the agent of another) the name or firm and business address of his principal.

(5) Every pleading of a party must be signed by counsel, if settled by him, and, if not, by the party's solicitor or by the party, if he sues or defends in person.

Facts, not evidence, to be pleaded (O. 18, r. 7)

7.—(1) Subject to the provisions of this rule, and rules 7A, 10, 11 and 12, every pleading must contain, and contain only, a statement in a summary form of the material facts on which the party pleading relies for his claim or defence, as the case may be, but not the evidence by which those facts are to be proved, and the statement must be as brief as the nature of the case admits.   **E018.7**

(2) Without prejudice to paragraph (1), the effect of any document or the purport of any conversation referred to in the pleading must, if material, be briefly stated, and the precise words of the document or conversation shall not be stated, except in so far as those words are themselves material.

(3) A party need not plead any fact if it is presumed by law to be true or the burden of disproving it lies on the other party, unless the other party has specifically denied it in his pleading.

(4) A statement that a thing has been done or that an event has occurred, being a thing or event the doing or occurrence of which, as the case may be, constitutes a condition precedent necessary for the case of a party is to be implied in his pleading.

Matters which must be specifically pleaded (O. 18, r. 8)

8.—(1) A party must in any pleading subsequent to a statement of claim plead specifically any matter, for example, performance, release, the expiry of the relevant period of limitation, fraud or any fact showing illegality—   **E018.8**

(*a*) which he alleges makes any claim or defence of the opposite party not maintainable; or

(*b*) which, if not specifically pleaded, might take the opposite party by surprise; or

(*c*) which raises issues of fact not arising out of the preceding pleading.

(2) . . .

(3) A claim for exemplary damages or for provisional damages must be

1115

specifically pleaded together with the facts on which the party pleading relies.

(4) A party must plead specifically any claim for interest under section 35A of the Act [Supreme Court Act 1981, c. 54] or otherwise.

Particulars of pleading (O. 18, r. 12)

E018.12   **12.**—(1) Subject to paragraph (2), every pleading must contain the necessary particulars of any claim, defence or other matter pleaded including, without prejudice to the generality of the foregoing words—

(*a*) particulars of any misrepresentation, fraud, breach of trust, wilful default or undue influence on which the party pleading relies; and

(*b*) where a party pleading alleges any condition of the mind of any person, whether any disorder or disability of mind or any malice, fraudulent intention or other condition of mind except knowledge, particulars of the facts on which the party relies.

(2) Where it is necessary to give particulars of debt, expenses or damages and those particulars exceed three folios, they must be set out in a separate document referred to in the pleading and the pleading must state whether the document has already been served and, if so, when, or is to be served with the pleading.

(3) The Court may order a party to serve on any other party particulars of any claim, defence of other matter stated in his pleading, or in any affidavit of his ordered to stand as a pleading, or a statement of the nature of the case on which he relies, and the order may be made on such terms as the Court thinks just.

(4) Where a party alleges as a fact that a person had knowledge or notice of some fact, matter or thing, then, without prejudice to the generality of paragraph (3), the Court may, on such terms as it thinks just, order that party to serve on any other party—

(*a*) where he alleges knowledge, particulars of the facts on which he relies, and

(*b*) where he alleges notice, particulars of the notice.

(5) An order under this rule shall not be made before service of the defence unless, in the opinion of the Court, the order is necessary or desirable to enable the defendant to plead or for some other special reason.

(6) Where the applicant for an order under this rule did not apply by letter for the particulars he requires, the Court may refuse to make the order unless of opinion that there were sufficient reasons for an application by letter not having been made.

(7) Where particulars are given pursuant to a request, or order of the Court, the request or order shall be incorporated with the particulars, each item of the particulars following immediately after the corresponding item of the request or order.

Admissions and denials (O. 18, r. 13)

13.—(1) Subject to paragraph (4), any allegation of fact made by a party in his pleading is seemed to be admitted by the opposite party unless it is traversed by that party in his pleading or a joinder of issue under Rule 14 operates as a denial of it.

(2) A traverse may be made either by a denial or by a statement of non-admission and either expressly or by necessary implication.

(3) Subject to paragraph (4), every allegation of fact made in a statement of claim or counterclaim which the party on whom it is served does not intend to admit must be specifically traversed by him in his defence or defence to counterclaim, as the case may be; and a general denial of such allegations, or a general statement of non-admission of them, is not a sufficient traverse of them.

(4) Any allegation that a party has suffered damage and any allegation as to the amount of damages is deemed to be traversed unless specifically admitted.

E018.13

Denial by joinder of issue (O. 18, r. 14)

14.—(1) If there is no reply to a defence, there is an implied joinder of issue on that defence.

(2) Subject to paragraph (3)—

(*a*) there is at the close of pleadings an implied joinder of issue on the pleading last served, and

(*b*) a party may in his pleading expressly join issue on the next preceding pleading.

(3) There can be no joinder of issue, implied or express, on a statement of claim or counterclaim.

(4) A joinder of issue operates as a denial of every material allegation of fact made in the pleading on which there is an implied or express joinder of issue unless, in the case of an express joinder of issue, any such allegation is excepted from the joinder and is stated to be admitted, in which case the express joinder of issue operates as a denial of every other such allegation.

E018.14

Statement of claim (O. 18, r. 15)

15.—(1) A statement of claim must state specifically the relief or remedy which the plaintiff claims; but costs need not be specifically claimed.

(2) A statement of claim must not contain any allegation or claim in respect of a cause of action unless that cause of action is mentioned in the writ or arises from facts which are the same as, or include or form part of, facts giving rise to a cause of action so mentioned; but, subject to that, a plaintiff may in his statement of claim alter, modify or extend any claim made by him in the indorsement of the writ without amending the indorsement.

E018.15

(3) Every statement of claim must bear on its face a statement of the date on which the writ in the action was issued.

Striking out pleadings and indorsements (O. 18, r. 19)

E018.19   **19.**—(1) The Court may at any stage of the proceedings order to be struck out or amended any pleading or the indorsement of any writ in the action, or anything in any pleading or in the indorsement, on the ground that—

    (*a*) it discloses no reasonable cause of action or defence, as the case may be; or

    (*b*) it is scandalous, frivolous or vexatious; or

    (*c*) it may prejudice, embarrass or delay the fair trial of the action, or

    (*d*) it is otherwise an abuse of the process of the court;

and may order the action to be stayed or dismissed or judgment to be entered accordingly, as the case may be.

    (2) No evidence shall be admissible on an application under paragraph (1)(*a*).

    (3) This rule shall, so far as applicable, apply to an originating summons and a petition as if the summons or petition, as the case may be, were a pleading.

Close of pleadings (O. 18, r. 20)

E018.20   **20.**—(1) The pleadings in an action are deemed to be closed—

    (*a*) at the expiration of 14 days after service of the reply or, if there is no reply but only a defence to counterclaim, after service of the defence to counterclaim, or

    (*b*) if neither a reply nor a defence to counterclaim is served, at the expiration of 14 days after service of the defence.

    (2) The pleadings in an action are deemed to be closed at the time provided by paragraph (1) notwithstanding that any request or order for particulars has been made but has not been complied with at that time.

ORDER 20

AMENDMENT

Amendment of judgment and orders (O. 20, r. 11)

E020.11   **11.**—Clerical mistakes in judgments or orders, or errors arising therein from any accidental slip or omission, may at any time be corrected by the Court on motion or summons without an appeal.

ORDER 23

SECURITY FOR COSTS

Security for costs of action, etc. (O. 23, r. 1)

1.—(1) Where, on the application of a defendant to an action or other   **E023.1**
proceeding in the High Court, it appears to the court—
  (*a*) that the plaintiff is ordinarily resident out of the jurisdiction, or
  (*b*) that the plaintiff (not being a plaintiff who is suing in a representa-
      tive capacity) is a nominal plaintiff who is suing for the benefit of
      some other person and that there is reason to believe that he will be
      unable to pay the costs of the defendant if ordered to do so, or
  (*c*) subject to paragraph (2) that the plaintiff's address is not stated in
      the writ or other originating process or is incorrectly stated therein,
      or
  (*d*) that the plaintiff has changed his address during the course of the
      proceedings with a view to evading the consequences of the litiga-
      tion,
then if, having regard to all the circumstances of the case, the court thinks
it just to do so, it may order the plaintiff to give such security for the
defendant's costs of the action or other proceeding as it thinks just.

(2) The court shall not require a plaintiff to give security by reason only
of paragraph (1)(*c*) if he satisfies the court that the failure to state his
address or the mis-statement thereof was made innocently and without
intention to deceive.

(3) The references in the foregoing paragraphs to a plaintiff and a
defendant shall be construed as references to the person (howsoever described on the record) who is in the position of plaintiff or defendant, as the
case may be, in the proceeding in question, including a proceeding on a
counterclaim.

Manner of giving security (O. 23, r. 2)

2.—Where an order is made requiring any party to give security for costs   **E023.2**
the security shall be given in such manner, at such time, and on such terms
(if any) as the Court may direct.

ORDER 24

DISCOVERY AND INSPECTION OF DOCUMENTS

Mutual discovery of documents (O. 24, r. 1)

1.—(1) After the close of pleadings in an action begun by writ there   **E024.1**
shall, subject to and in accordance with the provisions of this Order, be discovery by the parties to the action of the documents which are or have been

in their possession, custody or power relating to matters in question in the action.

(2) Nothing in this Order shall be taken as preventing the parties to an action agreeing to dispense with or limit the discovery of documents which they would otherwise be required to make to each other.

Discovery by parties without order (O. 24, r. 2)

E024.2   **2.**—(1) Subject to the provisions of this rule and of rule 4, the parties to an action between whom pleadings are closed must make discovery by exchanging lists of documents and, accordingly, each party must, within 14 days after the pleadings in the action are deemed to be closed as between him and any other party, make and serve on that other party a list of the documents which are or have been in his possession, custody or power relating to any matter in question between them in the action.

Without prejudice to any directions given by the Court under Order 16, rule 4, this paragraph shall not apply in third party proceedings, including proceedings under that Order involving fourth or subsequent parties.

(2) . . .

(3) . . .

(4) . . .

(5) On the application of any party required by this rule to make discovery of documents, the Court may—

    (*a*) order that the parties to the action or any of them shall make discovery under paragraph (1) of such documents or classes of documents only, or as to such only of the matters in question, as may be specified in the order, or

    (*b*) if satisfied that discovery by all or any of the parties is not necessary, or not necessary at the stage of the action, order that there shall be no discovery of documents by any or all of the parties either at all or at that stage;

and the Court shall make such an order if and so far as it is of opinion that discovery is not necessary either for disposing fairly of the action or for saving costs.

(6) An application for an order under paragraph (5) must be by summons, and the summons must be taken out before the expiration of the period within which by virtue of this rule discovery of documents in the action is required to be made.

(7) Any part to whom discovery of documents is required to be made under this rule may, at any time before the summons for directions in the action is taken out, serve on the party required to make such discovery a notice requiring him to make an affidavit verifying the list he is required to make under paragraph (1) and the party on whom such a notice is served must, within 14 days after service of the notice, make and file an affidavit in

compliance with the notice and serve a copy of the affidavit on the party by whom the notice was served.

Discovery to be ordered only if necessary (O. 24, r. 8)

8.—On the hearing of an application for an order under rule 3, 7 or 7A the Court, if satisfied that discovery is not necessary, or not necessary at that stage of the cause or matter, may dismiss or, as the case may be, adjourn the application and shall in any case refuse to make such an order if and so far as it is of opinion that discovery is not necessary either for disposing fairly of the cause or matter or for saving costs.

E024.8

Inspection of documents referred to in list (O. 24, r. 9)

9.—A party who has served a list of documents on any other party, whether in compliance with rule 2 or with an order under rule 3, must allow the other party to inspect the documents referred to in the list (other than any which he objects to produce) and to take copies thereof and, accordingly, he must when he serves the list on the other party also serve on him a notice stating a time within seven days after the service thereof at which the said documents may be inspected at a place specified in the notice.

E024.9

Inspection of documents referred to in pleadings and affidavits (O. 24, r. 10)

10.—(1) Any part to a cause or matter shall be entitled at any time to serve a notice on any other part in whose pleadings or affidavits reference is made to any document requiring him to produce that document for the inspection of the party giving the notice and to permit him to take copies thereof.

E024.10

(2) The party on whom a notice is served under paragraph (1) must within four days after service of the notice, serve on the party giving the notice a notice stating a time within seven days after the service thereof at which the documents, or such of them as he does not object to produce, may be inspected at a place specified in the notice, and stating which (if any) of the documents he objects to produce and on what grounds.

Order for production for inspection (O. 24, r. 11)

11.—(1) If a party who is required by rule 9 to serve such a notice as is therein mentioned or who is served with a notice under rule 10(1)—

E024.11

  (*a*) fails to serve a notice under rule 9 or, as the case may be, rule 10(2) or

  (*b*) objects to produce any document for inspection, or

  (*c*) offers inspection at a time or place such that, in the opinion of the

Court, it is unreasonable to offer inspection then or, as the case may be, there,

then, subject to rule 13(1) the Court may, on the application of the party entitled to inspection, make an order for production of the documents in question for inspection at such time and place, and in such manner, as it thinks fit.

(2) Without prejudice to paragraph (1) but subject to rule 13(1) the Court may, on the application of any party to a cause or matter, order any other party to permit the party applying to inspect any documents in the possession, custody or power of that other party relating to any matter in question in the cause of matter.

(3) An application for an order under paragraph (2) must be supported by an affidavit specifying or describing the documents of which inspection is sought and stating the belief of the deponent that they are in the possession, custody or power of the other party and that they relate to a matter in question in the cause of matter.

Provision of copies of documents (O. 24, r. 11A)

E024.11A   **11A.**—(1) Any party who is entitled to inspect any documents under any provision of this Order or any order made thereunder may at or before the time when inspection takes place serve on the party who is required to produce such documents for inspection a notice (which shall contain an undertaking to pay the reasonable charges) requiring him to supply a true copy of any such document as is capable of being copied by photographic or similar process.

(2) The party on whom such a notice is served must within seven days after receipt thereof supply the copy requested together with an account of the reasonable charges.

(3) Where a party fails to supply to another party a copy of any document under paragraph (2), the Court may, on the application of either party, make such order as to the supply of that document as it thinks fit.

Order for production to Court (O. 24, r. 12)

E024.12   **12.**—At any stage of the proceedings in any cause or matter the Court may, subject to rule 13(1) order any party to produce to the Court any document in his possession, custody or power relating to any matter in question in the cause or matter and the Court may deal with the document when produced in such manner as it thinks fit.

Production to be ordered only if necessary, etc. (O. 24, r. 13)

E024.13   **13.**—(1) No order for the production of any documents for inspection or to the Court or for the supply of a copy of any document shall be made under any of the foregoing rules unless the Court is of opinion that the order is necessary either for disposing fairly of the cause or matter or for saving costs.

(2) Where on an application under this Order for production of any document for inspection or to the Court or for the supply of a copy of any document privilege from such production or supply is claimed or objection is made to such production or supply on any other ground, the Court may inspect the document for the purpose of deciding whether the claim or objection is valid.

Use of documents (O. 24, r. 14A)

14A.—Any undertaking, whether express or implied, not to use a document for any purposes other than those of the proceedings in which it is disclosed shall cease to apply to such document after it has been read to or by the Court, or referred to, in open court, unless the Court for special reasons has otherwise ordered on the application of a party or of the person to whom the document belongs.

E024.14A

Document disclosure of which would be injurious to public interest: saving (O. 24, r. 15)

15.—The foregoing provisions of this Order shall be without prejudice to any rule of law which authorises or requires the withholding of any document on the ground that the disclosure of it would be injurious to the public interest.

E024.15

Failure to comply with requirement for discovery, etc. (O. 24, r. 16)

16.—(1) If any party who is required by any of the foregoing rules, or by any order made thereunder, to make discovery of documents or to produce any documents for the purpose of inspection or any other purpose or to supply copies thereof fails to comply with any provision of that rule or with that order, as the case may be, then, without prejudice, in the case of a failure to comply with any such provision, to rules 3(2) and 11(1) the Court may make such order as it thinks just including, in particular, an order that the action be dismissed or, as the case may be, an order that the defence be struck out and judgment be entered accordingly.

(2) If any party against whom an order for discovery or production of documents is made fails to comply with it, then, without prejudice to paragraph (1) he shall be liable to committal.

(3) Service on a party's solicitor of an order for discovery or production of documents made against that party shall be sufficient service to found an application for committal of the party disobeying the order, but the party may show in answer to the application that he had no notice or knowledge of the order.

(4) A solicitor on whom such an order made against his client is served

E024.16

and who fails without reasonable excuse to give notice thereof to his client shall be liable to committal.

ORDER 26

Interrogatories

Discovery by interrogatories (O. 26, r. 1)

E026.1   **1.**—(1) A party to any cause or matter may apply to the Court for an order—

    (*a*) giving him leave to serve on any other party interrogatories relating to any matter in question between the applicant and that other party in the cause or matter, and

    (*b*) requiring that other party to answer the interrogatories on affidavit within such period as may be specified in the order.

(2) A copy of the proposed interrogatories must be served with the summons, or the notice under Order 25, rule 7, by which the application for such leave is made.

(3) On the hearing of an application under this rule, the Court shall give leave as to such only of the interrogatories as it considers necessary either for disposing fairly of the cause or matter or for saving costs; and in deciding whether to give leave to the Court shall take into account any offer made by the party to be interrogated to give particulars or to make admissions or to produce documents relating to any matter in question.

(4) A proposed interrogatory which does not relate to such a matter as is mentioned in paragraph (1) shall be disallowed notwithstanding that it might be admissible in oral cross-examination of a witness.

ORDER 27

Admissions

Admission of case of other party (O. 27, r. 1)

E027.1   **1.**—Without prejudice to Order 18, rule 13, a party to a cause or matter may give notice, by his pleading or otherwise in writing, that he admits the truth of the whole or any part of the case of any other party.

Notice to admit (O. 27, r. 2)

E027.2   **2.**—(1) A party to a cause or matter may not later than 21 days after the cause or matter is set down for trial serve on any other party a notice requiring him to admit, for the purpose of that cause or matter only, such facts or such part of his case as may be specified in the notice.

(2) An admission made in compliance with a notice under this rule shall not be used against the party by whom it was made in any cause or matter other than the cause or matter for the purpose of which it was made or in favour of any person other than the person by whom the notice was given, and the Court may at any time allow a party to amend or withdraw an admission so made by him on such terms as may be just.

Judgment on admissions (O. 27, r. 3)

3.—Where admissions of fact or of part of a case are made by a party to a   **E027.3**
cause or matter either by his pleadings or otherwise, any other party to the cause or matter may apply to the Court for such judgment or order as upon those admissions he may be entitled to, without waiting for the determination of any other question between the parties and the Court may give such judgment or make such order, on the application as it thinks just.

An application for an order under this rule may be made by motions or summons.

Admission and production of documents specified in list of documents (O. 27, r. 4)

4.—(1) Subject to paragraph (2) and without prejudice to the right of a   **E027.4**
party to object to the admission in evidence of any document, a party on whom a list of documents is served in pursuance of any provision of Order 24 shall, unless the Court otherwise orders, be deemed to admit—
   (a) that any document described in the list as an original document is such a document and was printed, written, signed or executed as it purports respectively to have been, and
   (b) that any document described therein as a copy is a true copy.
This paragraph does not apply to a document the authenticity of which the party has denied in his pleading.

(2) If before the expiration of 21 days after inspection of the documents specified in a list of documents or after the time limited for inspection of those documents expires, whichever is the later, the party on whom the list is served serves on the party whose list it is a notice stating, in relation to any document specified therein, that he does not admit the authenticity of that document and requires it to be proved at the trial, he shall not be deemed to make any admission in relation to that document under paragraph (1).

(3) A party to a cause or matter by whom a list of documents is served on any other party in pursuance of any provision of Order 24 shall be deemed to have been served by that other party with a notice requiring him to produce at the trial of the cause or matter such of the documents specified in the list as are in his possession, custody or power.

1125

(4) The foregoing provisions of this rule apply in relation to an affidavit made in compliance with an order under Order 24, rule 7, as they apply in relation to a list of documents served in pursuance of any provision of that Order.

Notices to admit or produce documents (O. 27, r. 5)

E027.5   5.—(1) Except where rule 4(1) applies, a party to a cause or matter may within 21 days after the cause or matter is set down for trial serve on any other party a notice requiring him to admit the authenticity of the documents specified in the notice.

(2) If a party on whom a notice under paragraph (1) is served desires to challenge the authenticity of any document therein specified he must, within 21 days after service of the notice, serve on the party by whom it was given a notice stating that he does not admit the authenticity of the document and requires it to be proved at the trial.

(3) A party who fails to give a notice of non-admission in accordance with paragraph (2) in relation to any document shall be deemed to have admitted the authenticity of that document unless the Court otherwise orders.

(4) Except where rule 4(3) applies, a party to a cause or matter may serve on any other party a notice requiring him to produce the documents specified in the notice at the trial of the cause or matter.

ORDER 34

Setting Down for Trial Action Begun by Writ

Time for setting down action (O. 34, r. 2)

E034.2   2.—(1) Every order made in an action which provides for trial before a judge shall, whether the trial is to be with or without a jury and wherever the trial is to take place, fix a period within which the plaintiff is to set down the action for trial.

(2) Where the plaintiff does not, within the period fixed under paragraph (1) set the action down for trial, the defendant may set the action down for trial or may apply to the Court to dismiss the action for want of prosecution and, on the hearing of any such application, the Court may order the action to be dismissed accordingly or may make such order as it thinks just.

(3) . . .

ORDER 38

Evidence

1. General Rules

General rule: witnesses to be examined orally (O. 38, r. 1)

1.—Subject to the provisions of these rules and of the Civil Evidence Act **E038.1** 1968 and the Civil Evidence Act 1972, and any other enactment relating to evidence, any fact required to be proved at the trial of any action begun by writ by the evidence of witnesses shall be proved by the examination of the witnesses orally and in open court.

Evidence by affidavit (O. 38, r. 2)

2.—(1) The Court may, at or before the trial of an action begun by writ, **E038.2** order that the affidavit of any witness may be read at the trial if in the circumstances of the case it thinks it reasonable so to order.

(2) An order under paragraph (1) may be made on such terms as to the filing and giving of copies of the affidavits and as to the production of the deponents for cross-examination as the Court thinks fit but, subject to any such terms and to any subsequent order of the Court, the deponents shall not be subject to cross-examination and need not attend the trial for the purpose.

(3) In any cause or matter begun by originating summons, originating motion or petition, and on any application made by summons or motion, evidence may be given by affidavit unless in the case of any such cause, matter or application any provision of these rules otherwise provides or the Court otherwise directs, but the Court may, on the application of any party, order the attendance for cross-examination of the person making any such affidavit, and where, after such an order has been made, the person in question does not attend, his affidavit shall not be used as evidence without the leave of the Court.

Exchange of witnesses' statements (O. 38, r. 2A)

2A.—(1) [*Revoked*] **E038.2A**

(2) At any stage in any cause or matter, the Court may, if it thinks fit for the purpose of disposing fairly and expeditiously of the cause or matter and saving costs, direct any party to serve on the other parties, on such terms as the Court shall think just, written statements of the oral evidence which the party intends to lead on any issues of fact to be decided at the trial.

(3) Directions given under paragraph (2) may—

(*a*) make different provision with regard to different issues of fact or different witnesses;

(*b*) require any written statement served to be signed by the intended witness;

(*c*) require that statements be filed with the Court.

(4) Subject to paragraph (6), where the party serving a statement under paragraph (2) does not call the witness to whose evidence it relates no other party may put the statement in evidence at the trial.

(5) Subject to paragraph (6) and unless the Court otherwise orders, where the party serving the statement does call such a witness at the trial—

(*a*) the party may not without the consent of the other parties or the leave of the Court lead evidence from that witness the substance of which is not included in the statement served, except in relation to new matters which have arisen in the course of the trial;

(*b*) the Court may, on such terms as it thinks fit, direct that the statement served, or part of it, shall stand as the evidence in chief of the witness or part of such evidence;

(*c*) whether or not the statement or any part of it is referred to during the evidence in chief of the witness, any party may put the statement or any part of it in cross-examination of that witness.

(6) Where any statement served is one to which the Civil Evidence Acts 1968 and 1972 apply, paragraphs (4) and (5) shall take effect subject to the provisions of those Acts and Parts III and IV of this Order. The service of a statement pursuant to a direction given under paragraph (2) shall not, unless expressly so stated by the party serving the same, be treated as a notice under the said Acts.

(7) Where a party fails to comply with a direction given under paragraph (2) he shall not be entitled to adduce evidence to which such direction related without the leave of the Court.

(8) Nothing in this rule shall deprive any party of his right to treat any communication as privileged or make admissible evidence otherwise inadmissible.

ORDER 41

Affidavits

Form of Affidavit (O. 41, r. 1)

E041.1   **1.**—(1) Subject to paragraphs (2) and (3), every affidavit sworn in a cause or matter must be entitled in that cause or matter.

(2) Where a cause or matter is entitled in more than one matter, it shall be sufficient to state the first matter followed by the words "and other matters", and where a cause or matter is entitled in a matter or matters and between parties, that part of the title which consists of the matter or matters may be omitted.

(3) Where there are more plaintiffs than one, it shall be sufficient to state the full name of the first followed by the words "and others", and similar with respect to defendants.

(4) Every affidavit must be expressed in the first person and, unless the Court otherwise directs, must state the place of residence of the deponent and his occupation or, if he has none, his description, and if he is, or is employed by, a party to the cause or matter in which the affidavit is sworn, the affidavit must state that fact.

In the case of a deponent who is giving evidence in a professional, business or other occupational capacity the affidavit may, instead of stating the deponent's place of residence, state the address at which he works, the position he holds and the name of his firm or employer, if any.

(5) Every affidavit must be bound in book form and, whether or not both sides of the paper are used, the printed, written or typed sides of the paper must be numbered consecutively.

(6) Every affidavit must be divided into paragraphs numbered consecutively, each paragraph being as far as possible confined to a distinct portion of the subject.

(7) Dates, sums and other numbers must be expressed in an affidavit in figures and not in words.

(8) Every affidavit must be signed by the depondent and the jurat must be completed and signed by the person before whom it is sworn.

Contents of affidavit (O. 41, r. 5)

5.—(1) Subject to . . . paragraph (2) of this rule and to any order made **E041.5** under Order 38, rule 3, an affidavit may contain only such facts as the deponent is able of his own knowledge to prove.

(2) An affidavit sworn for the purpose of being used in interlocutory proceedings may contain statements of information or belief with the sources and grounds thereof.

Scandalous, etc., matter in affidavit (O. 41, r. 6)

6.—The Court may order to be struck out of any affidavit any matter **E041.6** which is scandalous, irrelevant or otherwise oppressive.

Alterations in affidavits (O. 41, r. 7)

7.—(1) An affidavit which has in the jurat or body thereof any interlinea- **E041.7** tion, erasure or other alteration shall not be filed or used in any proceeding without the leave of the Court unless the person before whom the affidavit was sworn has initialled the alteration and, in the case of an erasure, has rewritten in the margin of the affidavit any words or figures written on the erasure and has signed or initialled them.

(2) . . .

Affidavit not to be sworn before solicitor of party, etc. (O. 41, r. 8)

E041.8   **8.**—Without prejudice to section 1(3) of the Commissioners for Oaths Act, 1889, no affidavit shall be sufficient if sworn before the solicitor of the party on whose behalf the affidavit is to be used or before any partner or clerk of that solicitor.

Use of original affidavit or office copy (O. 41, r. 10)

E041.10   **10.**—(1) Subject to paragraph (2), an original affidavit may be used in proceedings in the Chancery Division with the leave of the Court, and in any other proceedings without such leave, notwithstanding that it has not been filed in accordance with rule 9.

(2) An original affidavit may not be used in any proceedings unless it has previously been stamped with the judicature fee stamp.

(3) Where an original affidavit is used then, unless the party whose affidavit it is undertakes to file it, he must immediately after it is used leave it with the proper officer in court or in chambers, as the case may be, and that officer shall send it to be filed.

(4) Where an affidavit has been filed, an office copy thereof may be used in any proceedings.

Document to be used in conjunction with affidavit to be exhibited to it (O. 41, r. 11)

E041.11   **11.**—(1) Any document to be used in conjunction with an affidavit must be exhibited, and not annexed, to the affidavit.

(2) Any exhibit to an affidavit must be identified by a certificate of the person before whom the affidavit is sworn.

The certificate must be entitled to the same manner as the affidavit and rule 1(1), (2) and (3) shall apply accordingly.

E041.11A   PRACTICE DIRECTION

A *"Note concerning the preparation of affidavits and exhibits"* was published in 1980 ([1980] FSR 118). Subsequently the following Practice Direction was issued (*Practice Direction (Evidence: Documents)*, [1983] 1 W.L.R. 922; [1983] 3 All E.R. 33) in much the same terms:—

This *Practice Direction* applies to the Court of Appeal and to all Divisions of the High Court. Any affidavit, exhibit or bundle of documents which does not comply with RSC, Ord. 41 and this direction may be rejected by the court or made the subject for an order for costs.

Affidavits

Marking

1. At the top right hand corner of the first page of every affidavit, and also on the back sheet, there must be written in clear permanent dark blue or black marking:

(i) the party on whose behalf it is filed;
(ii) the initials and surname of the deponent;
(iii) the number of the affidavit in relation to the deponent; and
(iv) the date when sworn. *For example*: 2nd Dft: E. W. Jones: 3rd: 24.7.82.

Binding

2. Affidavits must not be bound with thick plastic strips or anything else which would hamper filing.

Exhibits

Markings generally

3. Where space allows, the directions under para. 1 above apply to the first page of every exhibit.

Documents other than letters

4. (i) Clearly legible photographic copies of original documents may be exhibited instead of the originals provided the originals are made available for inspection by the other parties before the hearing and by the judge at the hearing.

(ii) Any document which the court is being asked to construe or enforce, or the trusts of which it is being asked to vary, should be separately exhibited, and should not be included in a bundle with other documents. Any such documents should bear the exhibit mark directly and not on a flysheet attached to it.

(iii) Court documents, such as . . . Orders, Affidavits or Pleadings, should never be exhibited. Office copies of such documents prove themselves.

(iv) Where a number of documents are contained in one exhibit, a front page must be attached, setting out a list of the documents, with dates, which the exhibit contains, and the bundle must be securely fastened. The traditional method of securing is by tape, with the knot sealed (under the modern practice) by means of wafers; but any means of securing the bundle (except by staples) is acceptable, provided that it does not interfere with the perusal of the documents and it cannot readily be undone.

(v) . . .

Letters

5. (i) Copies of individual letters should not be made separate exhibits, but they should be collected together and exhibited in a bundle or bundles. The letters must be arranged in correct sequence with the earliest at the top, and properly paged in accordance with para. 6 below. They must be firmly secured together in the manner indicated in para. 4 above.

(ii) When original letters, or original letters and copies of replies, are exhibited as one bundle the exhibit must have the front page attached, stating that the bundle consists of so many original letters and so many copies. As before, the letters and copies must be arranged in correct sequence and properly paged.

Paging of documentary exhibits

6. Any exhibit containing several pages must be paged consecutively at centre bottom.

Copies of documents generally

7. It is the responsibility of the solicitor by whom any affidavit is filed to ensure that every page of every exhibit is fully and easily legible. In many cases photocopies of documents, particularly of telex messages, are not. In all cases of difficulty, typed copies of the illegible document (paged with "a" numbers) should be included.

Exhibits bound up with affidavit

8. Exhibits must not be bound up with or otherwise attached to the affidavit itself.

Exhibits other than documents

9. The principles are as follows.

(i) The exhibit must be clearly marked with the exhibit mark in such a manner that there is no likelihood of the contents being separated; and

(ii) Where the exhibit itself consists of more than one item (*e.g.* a cassette in a plastic box), each and every separate part of the exhibit must similarly be separately marked with at least enough of the usual exhibit mark to ensure precise identification.

This is particularly important in cases where there are a number of similar exhibits which fall to be compared. Accordingly:

(*a*) The formal exhibit marking should, so far as practicable, be written on the article itself in an appropriate manner (*e.g.* many fabrics can be directly marked with an indelible pen), or, if this is not possible, on a separate slip which is securely attached to the article in such a manner that it is not easily removable. (N.B. Items attached by Sellotape or similar means are readily removable.) If the article is then enclosed in a container, the number of exhibits should appear on the outside of the container unless it is transparent and the number is readily visible.

Alternatively, the formal exhibit marking may be written on the container, or, if this is not possible, on a separate slip securely attached to the container. If this is done, then either:

    (i) the number of the exhibit and, if there is room, the short name and number of the case, the name of the deponent and the date of affidavit must be written on the exhibit itself and on each separate part thereof; or

    (ii) all these particulars must appear on a slip securely attached to the article itself and to each separate part thereof.

(*b*) If the article, or part of the article, is too small to be marked in accordance with the foregoing provisions, it must be enclosed in a sealed transparent container of such a nature that it could not be reconstituted once opened, and the relevant slip containing the exhibit mark must be inserted in such container so as to be plainly visible. An enlarged photograph or photographs showing the relevant characteristics of each such exhibit will usually be required to be separately exhibited.

Numbering

10. Where a deponent deposes to more than one affidavit to which there are exhibits in any one matter, the numbering of such exhibits should run consecutively throughout, and not begin again with each affidavit.

Reference to documents already forming part of an exhibit

11. Where a deponent wishes to refer to a document already exhibited to some other deponent's affidavit, he should not also exhibit it to his own affidavit.

Multiplicity of documents

12. Where, by the time of the hearing, exhibits or affidavits have become numerous, they should be put in a consolidated bundle, or file or files, and be paged consecutively throughout in the top right hand corner, affidavits and exhibits being in separate bundles of files.

Bundles of documents generally

13. The direction under 5, 6 and 7 above apply to all bundles of documents. Accordingly they must be:
  (i) firmly secured together;
  (ii) arranged in chronological order, beginning with the earliest;
  (iii) paged consecutively at centre bottom; and
  (iv) fully and easily legible.
14. Transcripts of judgments and evidence must not be bound up with any other documents, but must be kept separate.
15. In cases for trial where the parties will seek to place before the trial judge bundles of documents (apart from pleadings) comprising more than 100 pages, it is the responsibility of the solicitors for all parties to prepare and agree one single additional bundle containing the principal documents to which the parties will refer (including in particular the documents referred to in the pleadings) and to lodge such bundle with the court at least two working days before the date fixed for the hearing.

Affidavit taken in Commonwealth country admissible without proof of seal, etc. (O. 41, r. 12)

12.—A document purporting to have affixed or impressed thereon or subscribed thereto the seal or signature of a court, judge, notary public or person having authority to administer oaths in a part of the Commonwealth outside England and Wales in testimony of an affidavit being taken before it or him in that part shall be admitted in evidence without proof of the seal or signature being the seal or signature of that court, judge, notary public or person.

E041.12

ORDER 53

APPLICATIONS FOR JUDICIAL REVIEW

Cases appropriate for application for judicial review (O. 53, r. 1)

1.—(1) An application for—
  (*a*) an order of mandamus, prohibition or certiorari, or
  (*b*) an injunction under section 30 of the Act [Supreme Court Act 1981,

E053.1

c. 54] restraining a person from acting in any office in which he is not entitled to act,

shall be made by way of an application for judicial review in accordance with the provisions of this Order.

(2) An application for a declaration or an injunction (not being an injunction mentioned in paragraph (1)(*b*)) may be made by way of an application for judicial review, and on such an application the Court may grant the declaration or injunction claimed if it considers that, having regard to—

(*a*) the nature of the matters in respect of which relief may be granted by way of an order of mandamus, prohibition or certiorari,

(*b*) the nature of the persons and bodies against whom relief may be granted by way of such an order, and

(*c*) all the circumstances of the case,

it would be just and convenient for the declaration or injunction to be granted on an application for judicial review.

ORDER 59

APPEALS TO THE COURT OF APPEAL

Application of Order to appeals (O. 59, r. 1)

E059.1   1.—This Order applies, subject to the provisions of these Rules with respect to particular appeals, to every appeal to the Court of Appeal (including so far as it is applicable thereto, any appeal to that Court from an official referee, master or other officer of the Supreme Court or from any tribunal from which an appeal lies to that Court under or by virtue of any enactment) not being an appeal for which other provision is made by these Rules, and references to "the court below" apply to any court, tribunal or person from which such an appeal lies.

Interpretation (O. 59, r. 2A)

E059.2A   2A.—In this Order "a single judge" means a single judge of the Court of Appeal and "the registrar" means the registrar of civil appeals.

GENERAL PROVISIONS AS TO APPEALS

Notice of appeal (O. 59, r. 3)

E059.3   3.—(1) An appeal to the Court of Appeal shall be by way of rehearing and must be brought by motion and the notice of the motion is referred to in this Order as "notice of appeal".

(2) Notice of appeal may be given either in respect of the whole or in respect of any specified part of the judgment or order of the court below; and every such notice must specify the grounds of the appeal and the precise form of the order which the appellant proposes to ask the Court of Appeal to make.

(3) Except with the leave of the Court of Appeal, a single judge or registrar, the appellant shall not be entitled on the hearing of an appeal to rely on any grounds of appeal, or to apply for any relief, not specified in the notice of appeal.

(4) Every notice of appeal must specify the list of appeals in which the appellant proposes that the appeal shall be set down.

(5) A notice of appeal must be served on all parties to the proceedings in the court below who are directly affected by the appeal; and subject to rule 8, it shall not be necessary to serve the notice on parties not so affected.

(6) No notice of appeal shall be given by a respondent in a case to which rule 6(1) relates.

Note. Appeals from the Patents Court acting on appeal from the Comptroller are set down in the list entitled "Appeal Tribunals (Patent Tribunal Interlocutory List)" or that entitled "Appeal Tribunals (Patent Tribunal Final List)".

Time for appealing (O. 59, r. 4)

4.—(1) Except as otherwise provided by this Order, every notice of **E059.4** appeal must be served under rule 3(5) not later than four weeks after the date on which the judgment or order of the court below was sealed or otherwise perfected.

(2) In the case of an appeal from a decision in respect of which a certificate has been granted under section 12 of the Administration of Justice Act 1969 [c. 58] the period referred to in paragraph (1) shall be calculated from the end of the time during which, in accordance with section 13(5) of that Act, no appeal lies to the Court of Appeal.

(3) Where leave to appeal is granted by the Court of Appeal upon an application made within the time limit for serving notice of appeal under paragraph (1), a notice of appeal may, instead of being served within that time, be served within seven days after that date when leave was granted.

Setting down appeal (O. 59, r. 5)

5.—(1) Within 7 days after the later of (i) the date on which service of the notice of appeal was effected, or (ii) the date on which the judgment or order of the court below was sealed or otherwise perfected, the appellant must lodge with the registrar—

(*a*) a copy of the said judgment or order, and

(*b*) two copies of the notice of appeal, one of which shall be indorsed with the amount of the fee paid, and the other indorsed with a certificate of the date of service.

(2) Upon the said documents being left, the proper officer shall file one copy of the notice of appeal and cause the appeal to be set down in the proper list of appeals; and the appeal shall come on to be heard according to its order in that list unless the Court of Appeal or a single judge or the registrar otherwise orders.

(3) The proper list of appeals for the purpose of paragraph (2) shall be decided by the registrar, without prejudice, however, to any decision of the Court of Appeal on the question whether the judgment or order appealed against is interlocutory or final.

(4) Within four days after an appeal has been set down, the appellant must give notice to that effect to all parties on whom the notice of appeal was served, specifying the list in which the appeal is set down.

Respondent's notice (O. 59, r. 6)

E059.6   **6.**—(1) A respondent who, having been served with a notice of appeal desires—

    (*a*) to contend on the appeal that the decision of the court below should be varied, either in any event or in the event of the appeal being allowed in whole or in part, or

    (*b*) to contend that the decision of the court below should be affirmed on grounds other than those relied upon by that court, or

    (*c*) to contend by way of cross-appeal that the decision of the court below was wrong in whole or in part,

must give notice to that effect, specifying the grounds of his contention and, in a case to which paragraph (*a*) or (*c*) relates, the precise form of the order which he proposes to ask the Court to make.

(2) Except with the leave of the Court of Appeal or a single judge, or the registrar, a respondent shall not be entitled on the hearing of the appeal to apply for any relief not specified in a notice under paragraph (1) or to rely, in support of any contention, upon any ground which has not been specified in such a notice or relied upon by the court below.

(3) Any notice given by a respondent under this rule (in this Order referred to as a "respondent's notice") must be served on the appellant and on all parties to the proceedings in the court below who are directly affected by the contentions of the respondent, and must be served within 21 days after the service of the notice of appeal on the respondent.

(4) A party by whom a respondent's notice is given must, within 4 days after the later of (i) the date on which service of the respondent's notice was effected or (ii) the date on which he was notified under rule 5(4) that the appeal had been set down, lodge with the registrar two copies of the respondent's notice, one of which shall be indorsed with the amount of the fee paid, and the other indorsed with a certificate of the date of service of such respondent's notice.

Amendment of notice of appeal and respondent's notice (O. 59, r. 7)

7.—(1) A notice of appeal or respondent's notice may be amended—   E059.7

(*a*) by or with the leave of the Court of Appeal, a single judge or the registrar, at any time;

(*b*) without such leave, by supplementary notice served, before the date on which the appeal first appears in the List of Forthcoming Appeals referred to in r. 9(1) on each of the parties on whom the notice to be amended was served.

(2) A party by whom a supplementary notice is served under this rule must, within two days after service of the notice, furnish two copies of the notice to the registrar.

Directions of the Court as to service (O. 59, r. 8)

8.—(1) The Court of Appeal or a single judge or the registrar may in any   E059.8
case direct that a notice of appeal or respondent's notice be served on any party to the proceedings in the court below on whom it has not been served, or on any person not party to those proceedings.

(2) Where a direction is given under paragraph (1) the hearing of the appeal may be postponed or adjourned for such period and on such terms as may be just and such judgment may be given and such order made on appeal as might have been given or made if the persons served in pursuance of the direction had originally been parties.

Documents to be lodged by appellant (O. 59, r. 9)

9.—(1) Not less than 14 days after the appeal first appears in a list to be   E059.9
called "the List of Forthcoming Appeals" the appellant must cause to be lodged with the registrar the number of copies for which paragraph (2) provides of each of the following documents, namely—

(*a*) the notice of appeal;

(*b*) the respondent's notice;

(*c*) any supplementary notice served under rule 7;

(*d*) the judgment or order of the court below;

(*e*) the originating process by which the proceedings in the court below were begun, any interlocutory or other related process which is the subject of the appeal, the pleadings (including particulars) if any, . . . ;

(*f*) the transcript of the official shorthand note or record, if any, of the judge's reasons for giving the judgment or making the order of the court below or, in the absence of such a note or record, the judge's note of his reasons or, if the judge's note is not available, counsel's note of the judge's reasons approved wherever possible by the judge;

(g) such parts of the transcript of the official shorthand note or record, if any, of the evidence given in the court below as are relevant to any question at issue on the appeal or, in the absence of such a note or record, such parts of the judge's note of the evidence as are relevant to any such question.

(h) any list of exhibits made under Order 35, rule 11, or the schedule of evidence, as the case may be;

(i) such affidavits, exhibits, or parts of exhibits, as were as evidence in the court below and as are relevant to any question at issue on the appeal.

(2) Unless otherwise directed, the number of copies to be lodged in accordance with paragraph (1) is three copies except—

(a) where the appeal is to be heard by two judges in which case it is two copies; or

(b) . . .

(2A) When the transcripts, if any, referred to in items (f) and (g) in paragraph (1) have been bespoken by the appellant and paid for, the number of such transcripts required in accordance with paragraph (2) shall be sent by the official shorthand writer or transcriber direct to the registrar.

(3) At any time after an appeal has been set down in accordance with rule 5 the registrar may give such directions in relation to the documents to be produced at the appeal, and the manner in which they are to be presented, and as to other matters incidental to the conduct of the appeal, as appear best adapted to secure the just, expeditious and economical disposal of the appeal.

(4) The directions referred to in paragraph (3) may be given without a hearing provided always that the registrar may at any time issue a summons requiring the parties to an appeal to attend before him and any party to an appeal may apply at any time for an appointment before the registrar.

Practice Statement

E059.9A   An important Practice Statement was issued October 22, 1986 ([1986] 1 WLR 1318; [1986] 3 All ER 630), the relevant contents of which in relation to appeals on patent matters are:

Transcripts

All transcripts lodged (whether of evidence or of the judgment) must be originals. Photocopies are not permitted.

Core bundles

In cases where the appellant seeks to place before the Court bundles of documents comprising more than 100 pages, three copies of a core bundle containing the principal documents to which reference will be made must be lodged with the Court. In such circumstances, it will not usually be necessary to lodge multiple copies of the main bundle. It will be sufficient if a single set of the full trial documents is lodged so that the Court may refer to it if necessary.

Pagination and indexing

Bundles must be paginated clearly and there must be an index at the front of the bundle listing all the documents and giving the page references for each one. At present, many bundles are numbered merely by document. This is incorrect. Each page should be numbered individually and consecutively

Binding of bundles

All the documents (with the exception of the transcripts) must be bound together in some form (*e.g.* ring binder, plastic binder, or laced through holes in the top left-hand corner. Loose documents will not be accepted.

Legibility

All documents must be legible. In particular, care must be taken to ensure that the edges of pages are not cut off by the photocopying machine. If it proves impossible to produce adequate copies of individual documents, or if manuscript documents are illegible, typewritten copies of the relevant pages should also be interleaved at the appropriate place in the bundle.

Time limits

Time limits must be complied with and will be strictly enforced except where there are good grounds for granting an extension. The appellant's solicitor (or the appellant, if in person) should therefore set about preparing the bundles as soon as the notice of appeal has been lodged with the Civil Appeals Office (without waiting for the appeal to enter the list of Forthcoming Appeals); in that way, in most cases, the bundles should be ready to be lodged within the 14-day time limit prescribed by Order 59, rule 9. An extension of time is unlikely to be obtained where the failure to lodge the bundles, transcripts, notes of judgment or notes of evidence within the prescribed time limit is due to failure on the part of the appellant's solicitors (or the appellant, if in person) to start soon enough on the preparation of the bundles or the obtaining of the other documents.

Responsibility of the solicitor on the record

It seems likely that the work of documentation is often delegated to very junior members of the solicitor's staff, often without referring them to the relevant Rule and Practice Direction. Delegation is not, as such, objectionable, but (a) the member of staff must be instructed fully on what is required and be capable of ensuring that these requirements are met, and (b) the solicitor in charge of the case must personally satisfy himself that the documentation is in order before it is delivered to the Court. London Agents too have a responsibility. They are not just postmen. They should be prepared to answer any questions which may arise as to the sufficiency of the documentation.

Practice Notes of April 12, 1983 ([1983] 1 WLR 1055; [1983] 2 All ER 34) and of October 17, 1985 ([1985] 1 WLR 1156) and a more comprehensive *Practice Direction* (Court of Appeal: Presentation of Arguments) ([1989] 1 WLR 281; [1989] 1 All

ER 89) have stressed the importance of counsel providing the court in advance with skeleton arguments, and of counsel for the appellant preparing a written chronology of events relevant to the appeal as a separate document, preferably to be provided to the court with the skeleton argument, see para. 97.23.

General power of the Court (O. 59, r. 10)

E059.10   **10.**—(1) In relation to an appeal the Court of Appeal shall have all the powers and duties as to amendment and otherwise of the High Court including, without prejudice to the generality of the foregoing words, the powers of the Court under Order 36 to refer any question or issue of fact for trial before, or inquiry and report by, an official referee.

In relation to a reference made to an official referee, anything required or authorised under Order 36, rule 9, to be done by, to or before the Court shall be done by, to or before the Court of Appeal.

(2) The Court of Appeal shall have power to receive further evidence on questions of fact, either by oral examination in court, by affidavit, or by deposition taken before an examiner, but in the case of an appeal from a judgment after trial or hearing of any cause or matter on the merits, no such further evidence (other than evidence as to matters which have occurred after the date of the trial or hearing) shall be admitted except on special grounds.

(3) The Court of Appeal shall have power to draw inferences of fact and to give any judgment and make any order which ought to have been given or made, and to make such further or other order as the case may require.

(4) The powers of the Court of Appeal under the foregoing provisions of this rule may be exercised notwithstanding that no notice of appeal or respondent's notice has been given in respect of any particular part of the decision of the court below or by any particular party to the proceedings in that court, or that any ground for allowing the appeal or for affirming or varying the decision of that court is not specified in such a notice; and the Court of Appeal may make any order, on such terms as the Court thinks just, to ensure the determination on the merits of the real question in controversy between the parties.

(5) The Court of Appeal may, in special circumstances, order that such security shall be given for the costs of an appeal as may be just.

(6) The powers of the Court of Appeal in respect of an appeal shall not be restricted by reason of any interlocutory order from which there has been no appeal.

(7) Documents impounded by order of the Court of Appeal shall not be delivered out of the custody of that Court except in compliance with an order of that Court:

Provided that where a Law Officer or the Director of Public Prosecutions makes a written request in that behalf, documents so impounded shall be delivered into his custody.

(8) Documents impounded by order of the Court of Appeal, while in the

custody of that Court, shall not be inspected except by a person authorised to do so by an order of that Court.

(9) In any proceedings incidental to any cause or matter pending before the Court of Appeal, the powers conferred by this rule on the Court may be exercised by a single judge or the registrar.

Provided that the said powers of the Court of Appeal shall be exercisable only by that Court or a single judge in relation to

(a) the grant, variation, discharge or enforcement of an injunction, or an undertaking given in lieu of an injunction; and

(b) the grant or lifting of a stay of execution or proceedings.

Evidence on appeal (O. 59, r. 12)

12.—Where any question of fact is involved on an appeal, the evidence taken in the court below bearing on the question shall, subject to any direction of the Court of Appeal or a single judge or the registrar be brought before that Court as follows:

E059.12

(a) in the case of evidence taken by affidavit, by the production of a true copy of such affidavit;

(b) in the case of evidence given orally, by a copy of so much of the transcript of the official shorthand note as is relevant or by a copy of the judge's note, where he has intimated that in the event of an appeal his note will be sufficient, or by such other means as the Court of Appeal, or a single judge or the registrar, may direct.

Stay of execution, etc. (O. 59, r. 13)

13.—(1) Except so far as the court or the Court of Appeal or a single judge may otherwise direct—

E059.13

(a) an appeal shall not operate as a stay of execution or of proceedings under the decision of the court below;

(b) no intermediate act or proceeding shall be invalidated by an appeal.

(2) On an appeal from the High Court, interest for such time as execution has been delayed by the appeal shall be allowed unless the Court otherwise orders.

Applications to Court of Appeal (O. 59, r. 14)

14.—(1) Unless otherwise directed, every application to the Court of Appeal, a single judge or the registrar which is not made *ex parte* must be made by summons and such summons must be served on the party or parties affected at least 2 clear days before the day on which it is heard or in the case of an application which is made after the expiration of the time for appealing, at least 7 days before the day on which the summons is heard.

E059.14

(1A) In support of any application (whether made *ex parte* or *inter partes*) the applicant shall lodge with the registrar such documents as the Court of Appeal, a single judge or the registrar may direct, and rule 9(3) and (4) shall apply, with any necessary modifications, to applications as they apply to appeals.

(2) Unless otherwise directed, any application to the Court of Appeal for leave to appeal (other than an application made after the expiration of the time for appealing) must be made *ex parte* in the first instance; but unless the application is then dismissed or it appears to that Court that undue hardship would be caused by an adjournment, the Court shall adjourn the application and give directions for the service of notice thereof on the party or parties affected.

(3) Where an *ex parte* application has been refused by the Court below, an application for a similar purpose may be made to the Court of Appeal ex parte within 7 days after the date of refusal.

(4) Wherever under these rules an application may be made either to the court below or to the Court of Appeal, it shall not be made in the first instance to the Court of Appeal, except where there are special circumstances which make it impossible or impracticable to apply to the court below.

(5) . . .

(6) . . .

(7) An application, not being an application for leave to appeal, which may be heard by a single judge shall unless otherwise directed be heard in chambers.

(8) An application which may under the provisions of this Order be heard by the registrar shall be heard in chambers.

(9) The registrar may refer to a single judge any matter which he thinks should properly be decided by a single judge, and, following such reference, the judge may either dispose of the matter or refer it back to the registrar with such direction as the single judge thinks fit.

(10) A single judge may refer to the Court of Appeal any matter which he thinks should properly be decided by that Court, and following such reference, that Court may either dispose of the matter or refer it back to a single judge or the registrar, with such directions as that Court thinks fit.

(11) An appeal shall lie to a single judge from any determination made by the registrar and shall be brought by way of fresh application made within 10 days of the determination appealed against.

(12) An appeal shall lie to the Court of Appeal from any determination by a single judge, not being the determination of an application for leave to appeal, and shall be brought by way of fresh application made within 10 days of the determination appealed against.

Provided that an appeal shall not lie to the Court of Appeal without the leave of that Court in respect of a determination of the registrar which has been reviewed by a single judge.

Extension of time (O. 59, r. 15)

15.—(1) Without prejudice to the power of the Court of Appeal, a single judge or the registrar under Order 3, rule 5, to extend or abridge the time prescribed by any provision of this Order, the period for serving notice of appeal under rule 4 or for making application *ex parte* under rule 14(3) may be extended or abridged by the court below on application made before the expiration of that period.   **E059.15**

SPECIAL PROVISIONS AS TO PARTICULAR APPEALS

Appeal against order for revocation of patent (O. 59, r. 17)

17.—(1) The following provisions of this rule shall apply to any appeal to the Court of Appeal from an order for the revocation of a patent.   **E059.17**

(2) The notice of appeal must be served on the Comptroller-General of Patents, Designs and Trade Marks (in this rule referred to as "the Comptroller") as well as on the party or parties required to be served under rule 3.

(3) If, at any time before the appeal comes on for hearing, the respondent decides not to appear on the appeal or not to oppose it, he must forthwith serve notice of his decision on the Comptroller and the appellant, and any such notice served on the Comptroller must be accompanied by a copy of the petition or of the pleadings in the action and the affidavits filed therein.

(4) The Comptroller must, within 14 days after receiving notice of the respondent's decision, serve on the appellant a notice stating whether or not he intends to appear on the appeal.

(5) The Comptroller may appear and be heard in opposition to the appeal—

(*a*) in any case where he has given notice under paragraph (4) of his intention to appear, and

(*b*) in any other case (including, in particular, a case where the respondent withdraws his opposition to the appeal during the hearing) if the Court of Appeal so directs or allows.

(6) The Court of Appeal may make such orders for the postponement or adjournment of the hearing of the appeal as may appear to the Court necessary for the purpose of giving effect to the foregoing provisions of this rule.

Appeal from Patents Court on appeal from Comptroller (O. 59, r. 18)

18.—In the case of an appeal to the Court of Appeal from a decision of the Patents Court on an appeal from a decision of the Comptroller-General of Patents, Designs and Trade Marks the notice of appeal must be served   **E059.18**

on the Comptroller-General as well as on the party or parties required to be served under rule 3.

ORDER 62

Costs

PART II: ENTITLEMENT TO COSTS

General principles (O. 62, r. 3)

E062.3   **3.**—(1) This rule shall have effect subject only to the following provisions of this Order.

(2) No party to any proceedings shall be entitled to recover any of the costs of those proceedings from any other party to those proceedings except under an order of the Court.

(3) If the Court in the exercise of its discretion sees fit to make any order as to the costs of any proceedings, the Court shall order the costs to follow the event, except when it appears to the Court that in the circumstances of the case some other order should be made as to the whole or any part of the costs.

(4) The amount of his costs which any party shall be entitled to recover is the amount allowed after taxation on the standard basis where—

  (*a*) an order is made that the costs of one party to proceedings be paid by another party to those proceedings, or

  (*b*) an order is made for the payment of costs out of any fund (including the legal aid fund), or

  (*c*) no order for costs is required,

unless it appears to the Court to be appropriate to order costs to be taxed on the indemnity basis.

(5) Paragraph (3) does not apply to proceedings in the Family Division.

(6) Subject to rule 8, a term mentioned in the first column of the table below, when used in an order for costs, shall have the effect indicated in the second column of that table.

Term	*Effect*
"Costs"	(*a*) Where this order is made in interlocutory proceedings, the party in whose favour it is made shall be entitled to his costs in respect of those proceedings whatever the outcome of the cause or matter in which the proceedings arise, and
	(*b*) where this order is made at the conclusion of a cause or matter, the party in whose favour it is made shall be entitled to have his costs taxed forthwith;

Term	Effect
"Costs reserved"	(. . .) the party in whose favour an order for costs is made at the conclusion of the cause or matter in which the proceedings arise shall be entitled to his costs of the proceedings in respect of which this order is made unless the Court orders otherwise;
"Costs in any event"	This order has the same effect as an order for "costs" made in interlocutory proceedings;
"Costs here and below"	The party in whose favour this order is made shall be entitled not only to his costs in respect of the proceedings in which it is made but also to his costs of the same proceedings in any lower court, save that where such an order is made by the Court of Appeal on an appeal from a Divisional Court the party shall not be entitled by virtue of that order to any costs which he has incurred in any court below the Divisional Court;
"Costs in the cause" or "costs in application"	The party in whose favour an order for costs is made at the conclusion of the cause or matter in which the proceedings arise shall be entitled to his costs of the proceedings in respect of which such an order is made;
"Plaintiff's costs in the cause" or "Defendant's costs in the cause"	The plaintiff or defendant, as the case may be, shall be entitled to his costs of the proceedings in respect of which such an order is made if judgment is given in his favour in the cause or matter in which the proceedings arise, but he shall not be liable to pay the costs of any other party in respect of those proceedings if judgment is given in favour of any other party or parties in the cause or matter in question;
"Costs thrown away"	Where proceedings or any part of them have been ineffective or have been subsequently set aside, the party in whose favour this order is made shall be entitled to his costs of those proceedings or that part or that part of the proceedings in respect of which it is made.

PART III: TAXATION AND ASSESSMENT OF COSTS

Basis of taxation (O. 62, r. 12)

12.—(1) On a taxation of costs on the standard basis there shall be allowed a reasonable amount in respect of all costs reasonably incurred and any doubts which the taxing officer may have as to whether the costs are reasonably incurred or were reasonable in amount shall be resolved in favour of the paying party; and in these rules the term "the standard basis" in relation to the taxation of costs shall be construed accordingly.

(2) On a taxation on the indemnity basis all costs shall be allowed except

E062.12

1145

in so far as they are of an unreasonable amount or have been unreasonably incurred and any doubts which the taxing officer may have as to whether the costs were reasonably incurred or were reasonable in amount shall be resolved in favour of the receiving party; and in these rules the term "the indemnity basis" in relation to the taxation of costs shall be construed accordingly.

(3) Where the Court makes an order for costs without indicating the basis of taxation or an order that costs be taxed on any basis other than the standard basis or the indemnity basis, the costs shall be taxed on the standard basis.

Costs payable to a solicitor by his own client (O. 62, r. 15)

E062.15   **15.**—(1) This rule applies to every taxation of a solicitor's bill to his own client except a bill which is to be paid out of the legal aid fund under The Legal Aid Act 1974.

(2) On a taxation to which this rule applies costs shall be taxed on the indemnity basis but shall be presumed—

(a) to have been reasonably incurred if they were incurred with the express or implied approval of the client, and

(b) to have been reasonable in amount if their amount was expressly or impliedly approved by the client, and

(c) to have been unreasonably incurred if in the circumstances of the case they are of an unusual nature unless the solicitor satisfies the taxing officer that prior to their being incurred he informed his client that they might not be allowed on a taxation of costs inter partes.

(3) Taxations under this rule may be carried out only by a taxing master or a registrar.

APPENDIX 2

PART I

Amount of costs

E062A2.1   **1.**—(1) The amount of costs to be allowed shall (subject to rule 18 and to any order of the Court fixing the costs to be allowed) be in the discretion of the taxing officer.

(2) In exercising his discretion the taxing officer shall have regard to all the relevant circumstances, and in particular to—

(a) the complexity of the item or of the cause or matter in which it arises and the difficulty or novelty of the questions involved;

(b) the skill, specialised knowledge and responsibility required of, and the time and labour expended by, the solicitor or counsel;

(c) the number and importance of the documents (however brief) prepared or perused;

(d) the place and circumstances in which the business involved is transacted;

(e) the importance of the cause or matter to the client;

(f) where money or property is involved, its amount or value;

(g) any other fees and allowances payable to the solicitor or counsel in respect of other items in the same cause or matter, but only where work done in relation to those items has reduced the work which would otherwise have been necessary in relation to the item in question.

(3) The bill of costs shall consist of such items specified in Part II as may be appropriate, set out, except for item 4, in chronological order: each such item (other than an item relating only to time spent in travelling and waiting) may include an allowance for general care and conduct having regard to such of the circumstances referred to in paragraph (2) above as may be relevant to that item.

Fees to counsel

2.—(1) . . . no fee to counsel shall be allowed unless—   E062A2.2

(a) before taxation its amount has been agreed by the solicitor instructing counsel; and

(b) before the taxing officer issues his certificate a receipt for the fees signed by counsel is produced.

(2) Except in taxations under rules 14 and 15—

(a) no costs shall be allowed in respect of counsel attending before a master or registrar in chambers or of more counsel than one attending before a judge in chambers unless the master, registrar or judge, as the case may be, has certified the attendance as being proper in the circumstances of the case;

(b) a refresher fee, the amount of which shall be in the discretion of the taxing officer, shall be allowed to counsel either

    (i) for each period of five hours (or part thereof) after the first, during which a trial or hearing is proceeding, or

    (ii) at the discretion of the taxing officer, in respect of any day after the first day, on which the attendance of counsel at the place of trial was necessary.

Items to be authorised, certified, etc.

3.—(1) . . .   E062A2.3

(2) The costs of calling an expert witness with regard to any question as to which a court expert is appointed under Order 40, or a scientific adviser as appointed under Order 104, rule 11, shall not be allowed on a taxation

of costs on the standard basis, unless the Court at the trial has certified that the calling of the witness was reasonable.

(3) Where—

(*a*) an action or counterclaim for the infringement of a patent, or

(*b*) a petition for revocation of a patent under section 32 of the Patents Act 1949, or

(*c*) an application for revocation of a patent under section 72 of the Patents Act 1977, or

(*d*) a counterclaim for the revocation of a patent under section 61 of the Patents Act 1949, or

(*e*) a counterclaim in proceedings for the infringement of a patent under section 61 of the Patents Act 1977,

proceeds to trial, no costs shall be allowed to the parties serving any particulars of breaches or particulars of objection in respect of any issue raised in those particulars and relating to the patent except in so far as those issues or particulars have been certified by the Court to have been proven or to have been reasonable.

ORDER 63

OFFICES

Date of filing to be marked, etc. (O. 63, r. 3)

E063.3 3.—(1) Any document filed in the Central Office in any proceedings must be sealed with a seal showing the date on which the document was filed.

(2) Particulars of the time of delivery at the Central Office of any document for filing, the date of the document and the title of the cause or matter of which the document forms part of the record shall be entered in books kept in the Central Office for the purpose.

Right to inspect, etc. certain documents filed in Central Office (O. 63, r. 4)

E063.4 4.—(1) Any person shall, on payment of the prescribed fee, be entitled during office hours to search for, inspect and take a copy of any of the following documents filed in the Central Office, namely—

(*a*) the copy of any writ of summons or other originating process,

(*b*) any judgment or order given or made in court or the copy of any such judgment or order, and

(*c*) with the leave of the Court, which may be granted on an application made *ex parte*, any other document.

(2) Nothing in the foregoing provisions shall be taken as preventing any party to a cause or matter searching for, inspecting and taking or bespeak-

ing a copy of any affidavit or other document filed in the Central Office in that cause or matter or filed therein before the commencement of that cause or matter but made with a view to its commencement.

Date of filing and inspection of documents filed in other offices (O. 63, r. 4A)

4A.—Rules 3 and 4 shall apply in relation to documents filed in Chancery Chambers or . . .   **E063.4A**

Deposit of documents (O. 63, r. 5)

5.—Where the Court orders any documents to be lodged in court, they must, unless otherwise directed, be deposited in the Central Office.   **E063.5**

ORDER 64

Sittings, Vacations and Office Hours

Sittings of the Supreme Court (O. 64, r. 1)

1.—(1) The sittings of the Court of Appeal and of the High Court shall be four in every year, that is to say—   **E064.1**
- (a) the Michaelmas sittings which shall begin on October 1, and end on December 21;
- (b) the Hilary sittings which shall begin on January 11, and end on the Wednesday before Easter Sunday;
- (c) the Easter sittings which shall begin on the second Tuesday after Easter Sunday and end on the Friday before the spring holiday; and
- (d) the Trinity sittings which shall begin on the second Tuesday after the spring holiday and end on July 31.

(2) In this rule "spring holiday" means the bank holiday falling on the last Monday in May or any day appointed instead of that day under section 1(2) of the Banking and Financial Dealings Act 1971 [c. 80].

Supreme Court Offices: days on which open and office hours (O. 64, r. 7)

7.—(1) The offices of the Supreme Court shall be open on every day of the year except—   **E064.7**
- (a) Saturdays and Sundays,
- (b) Good Friday and the day after Easter Monday,
- (c) Christmas Eve or—
  - (i) if that day is a Saturday, then December 23,
  - (ii) if that day is a Sunday or Tuesday, then December 27,

(d) Christmas Day and, if that day is a Friday or Saturday, then December 28,

(e) Bank Holidays in England and Wales under the Banking and Financial Dealings Act 1971 [c. 80], and

(f) such other days as the Lord Chancellor, with the concurrence of the Lord Chief Justice, the Master of the Rolls and the President of the Family Division may direct.

(2) The hours during which any office of the Supreme Court shall be open to the public shall be such as the Lord Chancellor, with the concurrence of any other President of a Division concerned with the business performed in that office, may from time to time direct.

ORDER 65

Service of Documents

Ordinary service: how effected (O. 65, r. 5)

E065.5   **5.**—(1) Service of any document, not being a document which by virtue of any provision of these rules is required to be served personally or a document to which Order 10, rule 1, applies, may be effected—

(a) by leaving the document at the proper address of the person to be served; or

(b) by post, or

(c) where the proper address for service includes a numbered box at a document exchange, by leaving the document at that document exchange or at a document exchange which transmits documents every business day to that document exchange, or

(d) in such other manner as the Court may direct.

In this rule "document exchange" means any document exchange for the time being approved by the Lord Chancellor.

(2) For the purposes of this rule, and of section 7 of the Interpretation Act 1978 [c. 30], in its application to this rule, the proper address of any person on whom a document is to be served in accordance with this rule shall be an address for service of that person, but if at the time when service is effected that person has no address for service his proper address for the purposes aforesaid shall be—

(a) in any case, the business address of the solicitor (if any) who is acting for him in the proceedings in connection with which service of the document in question is to be effected, or

(b) in the case of an individual, his usual or last known address, or

(c) in the case of individuals who are suing or being sued in the name of a firm, the principal or last known place of business or the firm within the jurisdiction, or (*d*) in the case of a body corporate, the registered or principal office of the body.

(2A) Any such document which is left at a document exchange in compliance with paragraph (1)(*c*) shall, unless the contrary is proved, be deemed to have been served on the second business day following the day on which it is left.

(3) Nothing in this rule shall be taken as prohibiting the personal service of any document or as affecting any enactment which provides for the manner in which documents may be served on bodies corporate.

In this rule "business day" means any day other than a Saturday, a Sunday, Christmas Day, Good Friday or a bank holiday under the Banking and Financial Dealings Act 1971 [c. 80].

Note. Section 725 of the Companies Act 1985 (c. 6) in addition provides for service of a document on a company registered under the Companies Acts to be effected by sending it by post to the registered office of the company, service then being deemed to have been made the second working day after posting by first class mail and on the fourth working day after posting by second class mail.

ORDER 66

PAPER, PRINTING, NOTICES AND COPIES

Quality and size of paper (O. 66, r. 1)

1.—(1) Unless the nature of the document renders it impracticable, every document prepared by a party for use in the Supreme Court must be on A4 ISO paper of durable quality having a margin, not less than $1\frac{1}{2}$ inches wide, to be left blank on the left side of the face of the paper and on the right side of the reverse:

    (2) In these rules the expressions "A3," or "A4" and "A5" followed by the letters "ISO" mean respectively the size of paper so referred to in the specifications of the International Standards Organisation.

    E066.1

Regulations as to printing, etc. (O. 66, r. 2)

2.—(1) Except where these rules otherwise provide, every document prepared by a party for use in the Supreme Court must be produced by one of the following means, that is to say, printing, writing (which must be clear and legible) and typewriting otherwise than by means of a carbon, and may be produced partly by one of those means and partly by another or others of them.

    E066.2

    (2) For the purpose of these rules, a document shall be deemed to be printed if it is produced by type lithography or stencil duplicating.

    (3) Any type used in producing a document for use as aforesaid must be such as to give a clear and legible impression and must be not smaller than

11 point type for printing or elite type for type lithography, stencil duplicating or typewriting.

(4) Any document produced by a photographic or similar process giving a positive and permanent representation free from blemishes shall, to the extent that it contains a facsimile of any printed, written or typewritten matter, be treated for the purposes of these rules as if it were printed, written or typewritten, as the case may be.

(5) Any notice required by these rules may not be given orally except with the leave of the Court.

Copies of documents for other party (O. 66, r. 3)

E066.3   **3.**—(1) Where a document prepared by a party for use in the Supreme Court is printed the party by whom it was prepared must, on receiving a written request from any other party entitled to a copy of that document and on payment of the proper charges, supply him with such number of copies thereof, not exceeding 10, as may be specified in the request.

(2) Where a document prepared by a party for use in the Supreme Court is written or typewritten, the party by whom it was prepared must supply any other party entitled to a copy of it, not being a party on whom it has been served, with one copy of it and, where the document in question is an affidavit, of any document exhibited to it.

The copy must be ready for delivery within 48 hours after a written request for it, together with an undertaking to pay the proper charges, is received and must be supplied thereafter on payment of those charges.

Requirements as to copies (O. 66, r. 4)

E066.4   **4.**—(1) [*Revoked*]

(2) Before a copy of a document is supplied to a party under these rules, it must be indorsed with the name and address of the party or solicitor by whom it was supplied.

(3) The party by whom a copy is supplied under rule 3, or, if he sues or appears by a solicitor, his solicitor, shall be answerable for the copy being a true copy of the original or of an office copy, as the case may be.

ORDER 70

OBTAINING EVIDENCE FOR FOREIGN COURTS, ETC.

Interpretation and exercise of jurisdiction (O. 70, r. 1)

E070.1   **1.**—(1) In this order "the Act of 1975" means the Evidence (Proceedings in Other Jurisdictions) Act 1975 [c. 34] and expressions used in this Order which are used in that Act shall have the same meaning as in that Act.

(2) The power of the High Court to make an order under section 2 of the Act of 1975 may be exercised by a master of the Queen's Bench Division.

Application for order (O. 70, r. 2)

2.—(1) Subject to rule 3 an application for an order under the Act of 1975 must be made *ex parte* and must be supported by affidavit.   **E070.2**

(2) There shall be exhibited to the affidavit the request in pursuance of which the application is made, and if the request is not in the English language, a translation thereof in that language.

(3) Where on an application under section 1 of the Act of 1975 as applied by section 92 of the Patents Act 1977 an order is made for the examination of witnesses, the Court may allow an officer of the European Patent Office to attend the examination and examine the witnesses or request the Court or the examiner before whom the examination takes place to put specified questions to them.

ORDER 104

THE PATENTS ACTS 1949 TO 1961 AND 1977; THE REGISTERED DESIGNS ACTS 1949 TO 1971; THE DEFENCE CONTRACTS ACT 1958

Definitions (O. 104, r. 1)

1.—In this Order—   **E104.1**

"the 1949 Act" means the Patent Act 1949;

"the 1977 Act" means the Patents Act 1977;

"the Comptroller" means the Comptroller-General of Patents, Designs and Trade Marks;

"the Court", without prejudice to Order 1, rule 4(2) means the Patents Court;

"existing patent" means a patent mentioned in section 127(2)(*a*) or (*c*) of the 1977 Act;

"the journal" means the journal published pursuant to rules made under section 123(6) of the 1977 Act;

"1977 Act patent" means a patent under the 1977 Act;

"patent" means an existing patent or a 1977 Act patent.

Assignment of proceedings (O. 104, r. 2)

2.—(1) All proceedings in the High Court under the Patents Acts 1949 to 1961 and 1977, the Registered Designs Act 1949 to 1961 and the Defence Contracts Act 1958, and all proceedings for the determination of a question of the making of a declaration relating to a patent under the inherent   **E104.2**

jurisdiction of the High Court, shall be assigned to the Chancery Division and taken by the Court.

(2) Nothing in Order 4, rule 1, shall apply in relation to any proceedings mentioned in paragraph (1) but every writ, summons, petition, notice, pleading, affidavit or other document relating to such proceedings must be marked in the top left-hand corner with the words "Patents Court".

Application for leave to amend specification under section 30 of the 1949 Act or section 75 of the 1977 Act (O. 104, r. 3)

E104.3 3.—(1) A patentee or the proprietor of a patent intending to apply under section 30 of the 1949 Act, or under section 75 of the 1977 Act, for leave to amend his specification must give notice of his intention to the comptroller accompanied by a copy of an advertisement—

 (a) identifying the proceedings pending before the Court in which it is intended to apply for such leave;

 (b) giving particulars of the amendment sought;

 (c) stating the applicant's address for service within the United Kingdom, and

 (d) stating that any person intending to oppose the amendment who is not a party to the proceedings must within 28 days after the appearance of the advertisement give written notice to his intention to the applicant;

and the comptroller shall insert the advertisement once in the journal.

A person who gives notice in accordance with the advertisement shall be entitled to be heard on the application subject to any direction of the Court as to costs.

(2) As soon as may be after the expiration of 35 days from the appearance of the advertisement the applicant must make his application under the said section 30 or 75, as the case may be, by motion in the proceedings pending before the Court; and notice of the motion, together with a copy of the specification certified by the Comptroller and showing in coloured ink the amendment sought, must be served on the Comptroller, the parties to the proceedings and any person who has given notice of his intention to oppose the amendment.

(3) On the hearing of the motion the Court shall give such directions for the further conduct of the proceedings on the motion as it thinks necessary or expedient and, in particular, directions—

 (a) requiring the applicant and any part or person opposing the amendment sought to exchange statements of the grounds for allowing the amendment and of objections to the amendment;

 (b) determining whether the motion shall be heard with the other proceedings relating to the patent in question or separately and, if separately, fixing the date of hearing thereof;

 (c) as to the manner in which the evidence shall be given and, if the evidence is to be given by affidavit, fixing the times within which the affidavits must be filed.

(4) Where the Court allows a specification to be amended, the applicant must forthwith lodge with the comptroller an office copy of the order made by the Court and, if so required by the Court or Comptroller, leave at the Patent Office a new specification and drawings as amended, prepared in compliance with the 1949 or 1977 Act, whichever is applicable, and the rules made under those Acts respectively.

The Comptroller shall cause a copy of the order to be inserted at least once in the journal.

Note. O. 104, r. 3 is particularly discussed in para. 75.11.

Application for revocation of a patent (O. 104, r. 4)

4.—(1) An application under section 72 of the 1977 Act for the revo-   **E104.4**
cation of a patent shall be made by petition.

This paragraph does not apply to an application made in pending proceedings.

(2) The respondent to a petition under section 32 of the 1949 Act or section 72 of the 1977 Act must serve an answer on the petitioner within 21 days after service of the petition on him.

Note. The petition is issued by presenting it to Room 157, Royal Courts of Justice, an original and one copy being required. For "Petitions", see paras. E009.1–E009.4. For the procedure for presenting a petition to the court for revocation of a patent, see paras. 72.32 and 61.21–61.38.

Action for infringement (O. 104, r. 5)

5.—(1) Notwithstanding anything in Order 5, rule 4, proceedings in   **E104.5**
which a claim is made by the plaintiff in respect of the infringement of a patent shall be begun by writ.

(2) The plaintiff in such an action must serve with his statement of claim particulars of the infringement relied on, showing which of the claims in the specification of the patent are alleged to be infringed and giving at least one instance of each type of infringement alleged.

(3) If a defendant in such an action alleges, as a defence to the action, that at the time of the infringement there was in force a contract or licence relating to the patent made by or with the consent of the plaintiff and containing a condition or term void by virtue of section 44 of the 1977 Act, he must serve on the plaintiff particulars of the date of, and parties to, each such contract or licence and particulars of each condition or term.

Note. In the 1977 Act, "infringement" is defined in section 60, read in conjunction with section 125, and with a special provision for claims to chemical processes contained in section 100. The relief obtainable from an action for infringement is set out in section 61.

Objections to validity of patent (O. 104, r. 6)

E104.6   **6.**—(1) A person who presents a petition under section 32 of the 1949 Act or section 72 of the 1977 Act for the revocation of a patent must serve with his petition particulars of the objections to the validity of the patent on which he relies.

(1A) A party to an action concerning a patent who either challenges the validity of the patent or applies by counterclaim in the action for revocation of the patent must, notwithstanding Order 18, rule 2, serve his defence or counterclaim (as the case may be), together with particulars of the objections to the validity of the patent on which he relies, within 42 days after service upon him of the statement of claim.

(2) Particulars given pursuant to paragraph (1) or (1A) must state every ground on which the validity of the patent is challenged and must include such particulars as will clearly define every issue which it is intended to raise.

(3) If the grounds stated in the particulars of objections include want of novelty or want of any inventive step, the particulars must state the manner, time and place of every prior publication or user relied upon and, if prior user is alleged, must—

(*a*) specify the name of every person alleged to have made such user,

(*b*) state whether such user is alleged to have continued until the priority date of the claim in question or of the invention, as may be appropriate, and, if not, the earliest and latest date on which such user is alleged to have taken place.

(*c*) contain a description accompanied by drawings, if necessary, sufficient to identify such user, and

(*d*) if such user relates to machinery or apparatus, state whether the machinery or apparatus is in existence and where it can be inspected.

(4) If in the case of an existing patent—

(*a*) one of the grounds stated in the particulars of objections is that the invention, so far as claimed in any claim of the complete specification, is not useful, and

(*b*) it is intended, in connection with that ground, to rely on the fact that an example of the invention which is the subject of any such claim cannot be made to work, either at all or as described in the specification,

the particulars must state that fact and identify each such claim and must include particulars of each such example, specifying the respect in which it is alleged that it does not work or does not work as described.

(5) In any action or other proceedings relating to a patent in which the validity of the patent has been put in issue on the ground of obviousness a party who wishes to rely on the commercial success of the patent must state in his answer or in his pleadings the grounds upon which he so relies.

Amendment of particulars (O. 104, r. 7)

7.—Without prejudice to Order 20, rule 5, the Court may at any stage of **E104.7**
the proceedings allow a party to amend any particulars served by him
under the foregoing provisions of this Order on such terms as to costs or
otherwise as may be just.

Further particulars (O. 104, r. 8)

8.—The Court may at any stage of the proceedings order a party to serve **104.8**
on any other party further or better particulars of infringements or of
objections.

Application of rules 10 to 14 (O. 104, r. 9)

9.—Rules 10 to 14 of this Order apply to any action for infringement of a **E104.9**
patent (whether or not any other relief is claimed) and to any proceedings
by petition for the revocation of a patent.

Admissions (O. 104, r. 10)

10.—(1) Notwithstanding anything in Order 27, where a party desires **E104.10**
any other party to admit any facts, he shall, within 21 days after service of a
reply or answer or after the expiration of the period fixed for the service
thereof, serve on that other party a notice requiring him to admit for the
purpose of the action or proceedings the facts specified in the notice.

(2) A party upon whom a notice under paragraph (1) is served shall
within 21 days after service thereof serve upon the party making the
request a notice stating in respect of each fact specified in the notice
whether or not he admits it.

Note. For further RSC on "Admissions", see paras. E027.1–E027.5, and see
para. 61.34.

Discovery of documents (O. 104, r. 11)

11.—(1) Order 24, rules 1 and 2 shall apply in an action for infringement **E104.11**
of a patent except that the list of documents must be served by each party
within 21 days after service of the notice of admissions under rule 10(2), or
within 21 days after the close of pleadings.

(2) Order 24, rules 1 and 2 shall apply in proceedings for the revocation
of a patent as they apply to actions begun by writ except that the period
prescribed by rule 2(1) shall be that which is prescribed by paragraph (1) of
this rule.

Note. For further RSC on "Discovery", see paras. E024.1–E024.14A, and see paras. 61.28–61.31.

Experiments (O. 104, r. 12)

E104.12   12.—(1) Where a party desires to establish any fact by experimental proof he shall within 21 days after service of the lists of documents under rule 11 serve on the other party a notice stating the facts which he desires to establish and giving full particulars of the experiments proposed to establish them.

(2) A party upon whom a notice under paragraph (1) is served shall, within 21 days after service thereof, serve upon the other party a notice stating in respect of each fact whether or not he admits it.

(3) Where any fact which a party desires to establish by experimental proof is not admitted he may at the hearing of the summons for directions apply for directions in respect of such experiments.

Note. For discussion on "Experiments", see para. 61.35.

Experts (O. 104, r. 13)

E104.13   13.—Where a party intends to adduce oral expert evidence he shall not later than 14 days before the hearing of the summons for directions under rule 14 give notice to every other party and to the Court of the name of each expert he intends to call as a witness.

This rule is without prejudice to the power of the Court to restrict the number of expert witnesses.

Summons for directions (O. 104, r. 14)

E104.14   14.—(1) The plaintiff or petitioner must, within 21 days after the expiration of all the periods specified in rules 10 to 12, take out a summons for directions as to the place and mode of trial returnable before a judge of the Patents Court in not less than 21 days, accompanied by minutes of the order proposed, a copy of the specification of any patent in issue, copies of the pleadings and of any documents referred to therein and copies of all documents served under rules 10 and 12 and if the plaintiff or petitioner does not take out such a summons in accordance with this paragraph, the defendant or respondent, as the case may be, may do so.

(2) The judge hearing a summons under this rule may give such directions:

(*a*) for the service of further pleadings or particulars;

(*b*) for the further discovery of documents;

(*c*) for securing the making of further admissions;

(*d*) for the service of interrogatories and answers thereto;

(*e*) for the taking by affidavit of evidence relating to matters requiring expert knowledge, and for the filing of such affidavits and the service of copies thereof on the other parties;

(*f*) for the holding of a meeting of such experts as the judge may specify, for the purpose of producing a joint report on the state of the relevant art;

(*g*) for the exchanging of experts' reports, in respect of those matters on which they are not agreed;

(*h*) for the making of experiments, tests, inspections or reports;

(*i*) for the hearing, as a preliminary issue, of any question that may arise (including any questions as to the construction of the specification or other documents)

and otherwise as the judge thinks necessary or expedient for the purpose of defining and limiting the issues to be tried, restricting the number of witnesses to be called at the trial of any particular issue and otherwise securing that the case shall be disposed of, consistently with adequate hearing, in the most expeditious manner. Where the evidence is directed to be given by affidavit, the deponents must attend at the trial for cross-examination unless, with the concurrence of the Court, the parties otherwise agree.

(3) On the hearing of a summons under this rule the judge shall consider, if necessary of his own motion, whether:

(*a*) the parties' advisers should be required to meet for the purpose of agreeing which documents will be required at the trial and of paginating such documents;

(*b*) an independent scientific adviser should be appointed under rule 15 to assist the court.

(4) Part IV of Order 38 shall not apply to an action or proceedings to which this rule applies.

(5) No action or petition to which this rule applies shall be set down for trial unless and until a summons under this rule in the action or proceedings has been taken out and the directions given on the summons have been carried out or the time fixed by the judge for carrying them out has expired."

PRACTICE DIRECTION

E104.14A

A Practice Direction was issued ([1974] RPC 1) which set out a specimen Order for Directions for patent infringement actions. However, in 1986, the form of Ord. 104 was extensively revised, the changes including some new rules (now Ord. 104, rr. 9–14), replacing the former equivalent to Ord. 104, r. 14. Consequently, the original specimen Summons for Directions (reprinted below) now needs to be adapted to these new rules.

Specimen Form of Order on Summons for Directions in Action for Patent Infringement

In the High Court of Justice
Chancery Division
Patents Court

BETWEEN:		
	A.B.	*Plaintiffs*
	—and—	
	C.D.	*Defendants*

MINUTES OF ORDER UNDER RULES OF THE SUPREME COURT
ORDER 104, RULE 10 [now RULE 14]

UPON the Application of the Plaintiffs by Summons dated the ....
day of .... 19 ....
   AND UPON HEARING Counsel for the Plaintiffs and for the defendants
   AND UPON READING the pleadings in this action
   IT IS ORDERED that:—
   1. The official printers copies or legible facsimile copies of the specification of the [Letters] Patent in suit [and of the specifications of the [Letters] Patent cited in the Particulars of Objections together with legible facsimile copies of any other document cited therein] may be used at the trial without further proof thereof or of their contents.
   2. The Plaintiffs and the Defendants respectively do on or before the .... day of .... 19.......... make and serve on the other of them a list of the documents which are or have been in their possession custody or power relating to the matters in question in the Action [and Counterclaim] and on request file an affidavit verifying such list. If either party wishes to inspect such documents it shall give notice in writing that it wishes to do so and such inspection shall be allowed at all reasonable times upon reasonable notice.
   3. The Plaintiffs have leave to amend the writ by .... and that the service of the writ and the Defendants' appearance stand and that the costs of and occasioned by the amendment be the Defendants' in any event.
   4. The Plaintiffs have leave to amend the Statement of Claim [and Particulars of Infringements] as shown in red in the proposed amended Statement of Claim [and Particulars of Infringements] as signed by the solicitors for the parties and to reserve the amended Statement of Claim [and Particulars of Infringements] on or before the .... day of .... 19........, with leave to the defendants to re-serve an amended defence (if so advised) within .... days thereafter [and with leave to the Plaintiffs to re-serve an amended reply (if so advised) within .... days thereafter] and that the costs of and occasioned by the amendments be the Defendants' in any event.
   5. (a) The Defendants have leave to amend the Defence [and Counterclaim and Particulars of Objections] as shown in red in the proposed amended Defence [and Counterclaim and Particulars of Objections] as signed by the solicitors for the parties hereto and to re-serve the amended Defence [and Counterclaim and Particulars of Objections] on or before the .... day of ....
19......... [with leave to thePlaintiffs to re-serve an amended Reply [and Defence to Counterclaim] (if so advised) within .... days thereafter] and that the costs of and occasioned by the amendments be the Plaintiffs' in any event.
   (b) The Plaintiffs do, on or before the .... day of ....
19........ elect whether they will discontinue this action and withdraw their defence

to the counterclaim and consent to an order for the revocation of Letters Patent No. .... and if the Plaintiffs shall so elect and shall give notice thereof to the Defendants within the time aforesaid it is ordered that [Letters] Patent No. .... be revoked and that it be referred to the Taxing Master to tax the costs of the Defendants of this action up to and including the date of the delivery of the Particulars of Objections and the Counterclaim except in so far as the same have been increased by reason of the failure of the Defendants originally to deliver the Particulars of Objections in their amended form and to tax the costs of the Plaintiffs of this action subsequent to the date of the delivery of the Particulars of Objections to the date of this order and of the Counterclaim in so far as they have been increased by reason of the failure of the Defendants aforesaid AND it is ordered that the Taxing Master is to set off the said costs of the Defendants and of the Plaintiffs when so taxed as aforesaid and to certify to which of them the balance after such set-off is due AND it is ordered that such balance be paid by the party from whom to the party to whom the same shall be certified to be due.

6. The Plaintiffs do give security for the Defendants' costs in the sum of £....... [paying the said sum into court and giving notice of such payment in to the Defendants] [paying the said sum into an account at .... Bank of .... in the joint name of solicitors for the parties] [giving to the Defendants a bond securing the said sum] on or before the .... day of .... 19....... of this order and that in the meantime all further proceedings be stayed.

7. The Plaintiffs do serve on the Defendants on or before the .... day of .... 19....... the further and better Particulars of the Statement of Claim [and the Particulars of Infringements] specified in the Defendants' Request for further and better Particulars served on the .... day of .... 19.......

8. The Defendants do serve on the Plaintiffs on or before the .... day of .... 19....... the further and better Particulars of the Defence [and Counterclaim and the Particulars of Objections] specified in the Plaintiffs' Request for further and better Particulars of Objections] specified in the Plaintiffs' Request for further and better Particulars served the .... day of .... 19.......

9. The Plaintiffs do serve on the Defendants on or before the .... day of .... 19....... the further and better particulars of the Reply [and Defence to Counterclaim] specified in the Defendants' Request for further and better Particulars served the .... day of .... 19.......

10. The Plaintiffs do state in writing on or before the .... day of .... 19....... whether or not they make the admissions requested in the Defendants' Request for Admissions served the .... day of .... 19.......

11. The Defendants do state in writing on or before the .... day of .... 19....... whether or not they make the admissions requested in the Plaintiffs' Request for Admissions served the .... day of .... 19.......

12. (1) (a) If either party shall desire to rely at the trial of this Action [and counterclaim] upon any model apparatus drawing photograph or cinematograph film that party shall on or before the .... day of .... 19....... give notice thereof to the other; shall afford the other party an opportunity within .... days of the service of such notice of inspecting the same and shall, if so requested, furnish the other party with copies of any such drawing or photograph and a sufficient drawing photograph or other illustration of any model or apparatus.

(b) If either party shall wish to rely upon any experiment, that party shall, within the like period, give notice thereof to the other accompanied by full and precise details of the same and shall afford the other party an opportunity, if so requested, of inspecting a performance of such experiment. Any such inspection shall be requested within 14 days after delivery of the notice to which it relates and shall take place within .... days of the date of such request.

(2) If either party shall wish to rely upon any model apparatus drawing photograph cinematograph film or experiment in reply to any matter of which notice was given under sub-paragraph (1) of this paragraph, that party shall within ....
days after the last inspection to be made in pursuance of the said sub-paragraph (1) give to the other party a like notice, accompanied in the case of an experiment with like details, to that to be given under the said sub-paragraph (1); if so requested within 14 days of delivery of such notice shall afford like opportunities of inspection which shall take place within .... days of such request; and shall in like manner furnish copies of any drawing or photograph and illustration of any such model or apparatus.

(3) A party offering inspection under the foregoing provisions of this paragraph of the performance of any experiment shall (unless and to the extent that he shall have been given exemption by consent or by order of the Court) secure to the party inspecting the experiment an opportunity to obtain drawings or photographs or other sufficient illustrations or data as may be requested by that party of any apparatus on or in connection with which such experiment was performed and provide any samples as may be reasonably requested. A party making any such drawings or photographs or other illustrations shall within .... days after such inspection give notice to the other of any of them upon which he desires to rely at the trial and shall, if so requested, furnish copies thereof.

(4) No further or other model apparatus drawing photograph cinematograph film or experiment shall be relied upon in evidence by either party save with mutual consent or by leave of the Court.

13. Any of the times herein mentioned may be enlarged by mutual consent for a period not exceeding one month or otherwise by leave of the Court.

14. The trial of the proceedings shall be before an Assigned Judge alone in London.

15. Any party may set down this Action [and Counterclaim] for trial within 21 days after the expiry of all times provided for in this Order.

16. The costs of this application [save for those hereinbefore referred to] are to be costs in the Action.

17. The parties are to be at liberty on 2 days' notice to apply for further directions and generally.

Appointment of a scientific adviser (O. 104, r. 15)

E104.15   15.—(1) In any proceedings under the 1949 or 1977 Act the Court may at any time, and on or without the application of any party, appoint an independent scientific adviser to assist the Court, either—

(a) by sitting with the judge at the trial or hearing of the proceedings, or

(b) by inquiring and reporting on any question of fact or of opinion not involving a question of law or construction.

according as the Court may direct.

(2) The Court may nominate the scientific adviser and, where appropriate, settle any question or instructions to be submitted or given to him.

(3) Where the Court appoints a scientific adviser to inquire and report under paragraph (1)(b), Order 40, rules 2, 3, 4 and 6 shall apply in relation to his report as they apply in relation to a report made by a Court expert.

Note. For discussion on the appointment of a scientific adviser, see para. 96.25.

Restrictions on Admissions of Evidence (O. 104, r. 16)

16.—(1) Except with the leave of the judge hearing any action, or other   **E104.16**
proceeding relating to a patent, no evidence shall be admissible in proof of
any alleged infringement, or of any objection to the validity, of the patent,
if the infringement or objection was not raised in the particulars of
infringements or objections, as the case may be.

(2) In any action or other proceeding relating to a patent, evidence
which is not in accordance with a statement contained in particulars of
objections to the validity of the patent shall not be admissible in support of
such an objection unless the judge hearing the proceeding allows the evidence to be admitted.

(3) If any machinery or apparatus alleged to have been used before the
priority date mentioned in rule 6(3)(*b*) is in existence at the date of service
of the particulars of objections, no evidence of its user before that date
shall be admissible unless it is proved that the party relying on such user
offered, where the machinery or apparatus is in his possession, inspection
of it to the other parties to the proceedings or, where it is not, used all
reasonable endeavours to obtain inspection of it for those parties.

**Determination of question or application where comptroller declines to deal
with it (O. 104, r. 17)**

17. Where the comptroller—
(*a*) declines to deal with a question under section 8(7), 12(2), 37(8) or
61(5) of the 1977 Act;
(*b*) declines to deal with an application under section 40(5) of that Act,
or
(*c*) certifies under section 72(7)(*b*) of that Act that the question
whether a patent should be revoked is one which would more properly be determined by the court,
any person entitled to do so may, within 28 days after the comptroller's
decision, apply to the Court by originating summons to determine the
question or application.

**Application by employee for compensation under section 40 of the 1977 Act
(O. 104, r. 18)**

18.—(1) An application by an employee for compensation under section   **E104.18**
40(1) or (2) of the 1977 Act shall be made by originating summons issued
within the period which begins when the relevant patent is granted and
which expires one year after it has ceased to have effect:
Provided that, where a patent has ceased to have effect by reason of a
failure to pay any renewal fee within the period prescribed for the payment
thereof and an application for restoration is made to the comptroller under
section 28 of the said Act, the said period shall—

(*a*) if restoration is ordered, continue as if the patent had remained continuously in effect, or

(*b*) if restoration is refused, be treated as expiring one year after the patent ceased to have effect or six months after the refusal, whichever is the later.

(2) On the day fixed for the hearing of the originating summons under Order 28, rule 2, the Court shall, without prejudice to the generality of Order 28, rule 4, give directions as to the manner in which the evidence (including any accounts of expenditure and receipts relating to the claim) shall be given at the hearing of the summons and, if the evidence is to be given by affidavit, specify the period within which the affidavit must be filed.

(3) The Court shall also give directions as to the provision by the defendant to the plaintiff, or a person deputed by him for the purpose, of reasonable facilities for inspecting and taking extracts from the books of account by which the defendant proposes to verify the accounts mentioned in paragraph (2) or from which those accounts have been derived.

Appeals from the comptroller (O. 104, r. 19)

E104.19 **19.**—(1) An appeal to the Court from a decision of the comptroller in any case in which a right of appeal is given by the 1949 or 1977 Act must be brought by originating motion and the notice of motion is referred to in this rule as "notice of appeal".

(2) Notice of appeal shall be lodged with the proper officer—

(*a*) in the case of a decision on a matter of procedure, within 14 days after the date of the decision; and

(*b*) in any other case, within six weeks after the date of the decision.

(3) The comptroller may determine whether any decision is on a matter of procedure and any such determination shall itself be a decision on a matter of procedure.

(4) Notice of appeal may be given in respect of the whole or any specific part of the decision of the comptroller and must specify the grounds of the appeal and the relief which the appellant seeks.

(5) Except with the leave of the Court the appellant shall not be entitled on the hearing of the appeal to rely on any ground of appeal or to apply for any relief not specified in the notice of appeal.

(6) The appellant shall, within 5 days of lodging notice of appeal, serve a copy thereof on the comptroller and any other party to the proceedings before the comptroller.

(7) On receiving notice of appeal the comptroller shall forthwith transmit to the proper officer all the papers relating to the matter which is the subject of the appeal.

(8) Except by leave of the Court, no appeal shall be entertained unless notice of appeal has been given within the period specified in paragraph (2)

or within such further time as the comptroller may allow upon request made to him prior to the expiry of that period.

(9) A respondent who, not having appealed from the decision of the comptroller, desires to contend on the appeal that the decision should be varied, either in any event or in the event of the appeal being allowed in whole or part, must give notice to that effect, specifying the grounds of that contention and the relief which he seeks from the Court.

(10) A respondent who desires to contend on the appeal that the decision of the comptroller should be affirmed on grounds other than those set out in the decision must give notice to that effect, specifying the grounds of that contention.

(11) A respondent's notice shall be served on the comptroller and on the appellant and every other party to the proceedings before the comptroller within 14 days after receipt of notice of appeal by the respondent, or within such further time as the Court may direct.

(12) A party by whom a respondent's notice is given must, within 5 days after service of the notice on the appellant, furnish 2 copies of the notice to the proper officer.

(13) The proper officer shall give to the comptroller and to the appellant and every other party to the proceedings before the comptroller not less than 7 days' notice of the date appointed for the hearing of the appeal, unless the Court directs shorter notice to be given.

(14) An appeal shall be by way of rehearing and the evidence used on appeal shall be the same as that used before the comptroller and, except with the leave of the Court, no further evidence shall be given.

(15) [*Deleted*]

(16) Any notice given in proceedings under this rule may be signed by or served on any patent agent, or member of the Bar of England and Wales not in actual practice, who is acting for the person giving the notice or, as the case may be, the person on whom the notice is to be served, as if the patent agent or member of the Bar were a solicitor.

(17) [*Deleted*]

(18) Nothing in Order 42, rule 7 (except paragraph (1)), Order 55 (except rule 7(2) and (3) and (5) to (7) or Order 57 shall apply in relation to an appeal under this rule.

PRACTICE DIRECTION

E104.19A

The following direction has been issued as part of *Chancery Practice Direction No. 3 of 1978* ([1979] RPC 96):—

Notices of appeal and respondents' notices

2. (*a*) Appeals from the Comptroller must be brought by originating motion (Order 104, rule 19(1)). The originating motion (in the Rule called "notice of appeal") is issued by lodging copies in Chancery Chambers

(Room 157). If the Registrar of Patent Appeals and his deputy are not available, the copies may be lodged in the Chief Master's Secretariat (Room 169).

(*b*) Two copies of the originating motion (notice of appeal) will be required, one of which must be stamped with a £15 fee (Fee 8) and the other of which will be sealed and returned to the Appellant.

(*c*) A Respondent's notice under Order 104, rule 14(9) asking that the decision of the Comptroller be varied, must be stamped £10 (Fee 36).

By the direction of the Vice-Chancellor and with the concurrence of the Senior Judge of the Patents Court.

For the fee payable on a Notice of Appeal (and on a Respondent's Notice under r. 19(9) or (10)), see para. 97.12.

E104.19B   NOTICE OF APPEAL

A form for the Notice of Appeal under Ord. 104, rule 19 was issued in 1979 as a Practice Direction ([1979] RPC 56). This is reprinted below in the amended form now applicable.

Form of Notice of Appeal to Patents Court

In the High Court of Justice
Chancery Division
Patents Court

IN THE MATTER (*a*)
(*e.g.* of an Application by ....
                              and
        an Opposition by ....)

TAKE NOTICE that the HIGH COURT OF JUSTICE, CHANCERY DIVISION, PATENTS COURT, will be moved before a Judge of the Patents Court at a time to be set by the Patents Court not less than twenty-four days after service of this notice, or so soon thereafter as Counsel(*b*) can be heard, by Counsel(*b*) on behalf of(*c*) ....
....
by way of appeal from(*d*) ....
of the(*e*) ....
dated the .... day of .... 19 ....
whereby he(*f*) ....
....
The grounds of appeal are as follows:—(*g*)

I/WE ask the Patents Court to grant the relief set out below:—(*h*)

DATE ....
SIGNATURE .... (*i*)
ADDRESS ....
....

To .... (*j*)

NOTE:
Two copies of this Notice of Appeal must be lodged in Chancery Chambers (Room

157), Royal Court of Justice, London WC2A 2LL. It must be accompanied with the remittance for the prescribed fee. If the remittance is to be paid by cheque this should by made payable to H.M. Paymaster General and crossed. A copy of the notice must be sent to the Comptroller-General at the Patent Office, State House, 66–71 High Holborn, London WC1R 4TP and to any party entitled to appear before the Patents Court within the period prescribed by Order 104, Rule 19(6) of the Supreme Court Practice.

Fee £xx

(a) Here insert the nature of the application or proceedings, the name of the Patentee or Applicant, the number of the Patent or Application for Patent followed by the name of the Opponent (if any).
(b) or Solicitor or Patent Agent.
(c) Here insert name(s) and full address(es) of Appellant(s).
(d) Here insert "the decision" or "that part of the decision" as the case may be.
(e) Here insert "Comptroller General" or "Officer acting for the Comptroller General" as the case may be.
(f) Summarise the decision appealed against.
(g) Here set out the grounds of appeal.
(h) Here set out the relief which the Appellant seeks.
(i) To be signed by the Appellant personally or by his duly authorised representative.
(j) To be addressed to the other side and to their authorised representative.

Communication of information to the European Patent Office (O. 104, r. 20)

20.—(1) The Court may authorise the communication to the European Patent Office or the competent authority of any country which is a party to the European Patent Convention of any such information in the files of the court as the Court thinks fit.   **E104.20**

(2) Before complying with a request for the disclosure of information under paragraph (1) the Court shall afford to any party appearing to be affected by the request the opportunity of making representations, in writing or otherwise, on the question of whether the information should be disclosed.

Note. Communication of information to the EPO is governed by section 94 [1977].

Proceedings for determination of certain disputes (O. 104, r. 21)

21.—(1) The following proceedings must be begun by originating motion, that is to say—   **E104.21**
(a) proceedings for the determination of any dispute referred to the Court under—
    (i) section 48 of the 1949 Act or section 58 of the 1977 Act;
    (ii) . . . , or
    (iii) section 4 of the Defence Contracts Act 1958;
(b) any application under section 45(3) of the 1977 Act.
(2) There must be at least 10 clear days between the serving of notice of a

motion under this rule and the day named in the notice for hearing the motion.

(3) On the hearing of a motion under this rule the Court shall give such directions for the further conduct of the proceedings as it thinks necessary or expedient and, in particular, directions for the service of particulars and as to the manner in which the evidence shall be given and as to the date of the hearing.

Note. The Defence Contracts Act 1958 is reprinted at paras. B10–B17.

Application for rectification of register of patents or designs (O. 104, r. 22)

E104.22 **22.**—(1) An application to the Court for an order that the register of patents or the register of designs be rectified must be made by originating motion, except where it is made in a petition for the revocation of a patent or by way of counterclaim in proceedings for infringement or by originating summons in proceedings for an order under section 51 of the Trustee Act 1925 [15 & 16 Geo. 5, c. 19].

(2) Where the application relates to the register of patents, the applicant shall forthwith serve an office copy of the application on the comptroller, who shall be entitled to appear and to be heard on the application.

Note. Rectification of the register of patents is governed by section 34 [1977].

APPENDIX F

THE REGISTER OF PATENT AGENTS RULES

Note. At the time of going to press the Register of Patent Agents Rules 1978 (S.I. **F00**
1978 No. 1093, as amended by S.I. 1982 No. 1428) were still in force. However,
these are not reprinted here because they are shortly to be revoked as section 275
[1988] (reprinted at para. 102.05) is brought into force. A new set of such Rules will
then be made under section 275(1) and (2) [1988]. These will then be reprinted in
the Supplement hereto as paras. F01 *et seq*. The basis for these Rules is discussed in
para. 102.27.

APPENDIX G

EXAMINATION REGULATIONS FOR ENTRY TO THE REGISTER OF PATENT AGENTS

G00 *Note.* Entry to the Register of Patent Agent (for which see para. 102.27 and Appendix F) requires satisfaction of the conditions of the Examination Regulations made under the Register of Patent Agents Rules (for which see para. F00). The present Regulations are discussed in para. 102.30 where it is noted that, at the time of going to press, these are under review. When the new Regulations (which will be made under s.275 [1988], reprinted at para. 102.05, to conform with the new form of the Register of Patent Agents Rules) are issued, these will be reprinted in the Supplement hereto as paras. G01 *et seq.*

INDEX